Fodor's **up** CLOSE

FRANCE

the complete guide, thoroughly up-to-date

SAVVY TRAVELING: WHERE TO SPEND, HOW TO SAVE

packed with details that will make your trip

CULTURAL TIPS: ESSENTIAL LOCAL DO'S AND TABOOS

must-see sights, on and off the beaten path

INSIDER SECRETS: WHAT'S HIP AND WHAT TO SKIP

the buzz on restaurants, the lowdown on lodgings

FIND YOUR WAY WITH CLEAR AND EASY-TO-USE MAPS

FODOR'S TRAVEL PUBLICATIONS

NEW YORK • TORONTO • LONDON • SYDNEY • AUCKLAND

www.fodors.com

Second Edition

ISBN 0–679–00378–9

ISSN 1098–6227

FODOR'S UPCLOSE FRANCE

EDITOR: Donna Cornachio

Editorial Contributors: Ethan Gelber, Simon Hewitt, Nicola Keegan, Christopher Knowles, Alexander Lobrano, Sophie MacKenzie Smith, Christopher Mooney, Lauren Myers, Ian Phillips

Editorial Production: Stacey Kulig

Maps: David Lindroth Inc., Eureka Cartography, *cartographers*; Robert Blake, *map editor*

Design: Fabrizio La Rocca, *creative director*; Allison Saltzman, *cover and text design*; Jolie Novak, *photo editor*

Production/Manufacturing: Mike Costa

Cover Art: Owen Franken

SPECIAL SALES

CONTENTS

3. THE LOIRE VALLEY 106

4. BRITTANY 128

5. NORMANDY 164

6. CHAMPAGNE AND THE NORTH 192

7. ALSACE-LORRAINE AND FRANCHE-COMTÉ 211

8. BURGUNDY 236

9. GRENOBLE AND THE ALPS 267

10. LYON AND THE MASSIF CENTRAL 295

11. PROVENCE 316

12. THE RIVIERA 366

13. CORSICA 397

14. THE MIDI-PYRÉNÉES AND PAYS BASQUE 417

15. BORDEAUX AND THE AQUITAINE 455

16. THE ATLANTIC COAST 478

INDEX 501

TRAVELING
UPCLOSE

Take the train. Stay in a B&B. Try a hostel. Shop for a picnic. Have lunch on a hilltop park bench. Prowl the flea markets. Go to a festival. Commune with nature. Memorize the symphony of the streets. And if you want to experience the heart and soul of France, whatever you do, don't spend too much money.

The deep and rich experience of France that every true traveler yearns for is one of the things in life that money can't buy. In fact, if you have it, don't use it. Traveling lavishly is the surest way to turn yourself into a sideline traveler. Restaurants with white-glove service are great—sometimes—but they're usually not the best place to find the perfect pâté. Doormen at plush hotels have their place, but not when your look-alike room could be anywhere from Dusseldorf to Detroit. Better to stay in a more intimate place that truly gives you the atmosphere you traveled so far to experience. Don't just stand and watch—jump into the spirit of what's around you.

If you want to see France up close and savor the essence of the country and its people in all their charming, stylish, sometimes infuriatingly arrogant glory, this book is for you. We'll show you the local culture, the offbeat sights, the bars and cafés where tourists rarely tread, and the B&Bs and other hostelries where you'll meet fellow travelers—places where the locals would send their friends. And because you'll probably want to see the famous places if you haven't already been there, we give you tips on losing the crowds, plus the quirky and obscure facts you want as well as the basics everyone needs.

OUR GANG

Who are we? We're artists and poets, slackers and straight arrows, and travel writers and journalists, who in our less hedonistic moments report on local news and spin out an occasional opinion piece. What we share is a certain footloose spirit and a passion for La Belle France, which we celebrate in this guidebook. Shamelessly, we've revealed all of our favorite places and our deepest, darkest travel secrets, all so that you can learn from our past mistakes and experience the best part of France to the fullest. If you can't take your best friend on the road, or if your best friend is hopeless with directions, stick with us.

Ethan Gelber, stubbornly and eternally convinced that the saddle of his bicycle is always the best perch from which to travel and write regardless of the place and season, braved the chilly spring vineyarded byways of Burgundy, the microclimates of the Massif Central, and the sunny valleys of Lyon and Provence to update this book. Ethan has traveled and written extensively on his bike, particularly in the context of BikeAbout, a non-profit organization he founded that specializes in educational Internet adventures.

Simon Hewitt headed to Paris straight from studying French and art history at Oxford. It was a return to base: his grandmother was French, as are his wife and daughter. In 1996 he moved to Versailles to gain a different perspective on life in and around the French capital. When not contemplating the Sacre-Coeur's aesthetic fallout or the Sun King's bicep-flexing Baroque home, his thoughts often turn to cricket—he is captain of the French national team. He also writes regularly about antiques and the art market.

Nicola Keegan has spent the last ten years of her life musing on the strange and wonderful Parisian animal where cigarettes and coffee go hand-in-hand, eating during a movie is like dancing in church, and casually cutting your way through hordes of waiting people is an art form. She's learned that living with them is simple: love their food, love their beauty, and while you're at it, love their little French nastiness—just don't ever, ever let them cut in front of you in line.

Christopher Knowles, fluent French speaker and one-time resident of Paris, delighted in the opportunity to know better the cuisine of Corsica and Alsace, the summer slopes of the Alps, and the footpaths of Aquitaine. An expert in walks and hikes throughout Europe, he now sells walking holidays in Corsica and the French Pyrenees from his home in the Cotswolds in the west of England.

Alexander Lobrano has lived in Paris 14 years, after eating his way through Boston, New York, and London. He writes a weekly dining column for *Paris Time Out* and has reported on French food and restaurants for many British and American publications. In this guide, Alexander tells you where to splurge on a great French meal that won't leave you franc-less, find one of the finest falafels in Paris, or enjoy a simple but unforgettable picnic of bread and cheese.

Christopher Mooney came to Paris to study French philosophy, smoke Gitanes, and argue politics in late-night cafés. Nine years later he's still there, but his taste for Gallic thought and tobacco has given way to an unslakeable thirst for French wine. A born-again epicurean, he devotes his efforts to finding the best budget accommodations available in the French capital.

Ian Phillips, a native of Middlesbrough, England, originally moved from Britain to Paris by mistake. He had applied for a job in the Mediterranean, following his dream of sailing yachts on the Mediterranean, but ended up taking bateaux-mouches down the Seine in Paris instead. Still, he very swiftly found his way around the French capital—in his first three years in the city, he lived in 13 apartments. Finally he found his footing as a freelance journalist, writing on culture, fashion, and design for publications in Paris, London, and New York.

A SEND-OFF

Always call ahead. We knock ourselves out to check all the facts, but everything changes all the time, in ways that none of us can ever fully anticipate. Whenever you're making a special trip to a special place, as opposed to merely wandering, always call ahead. Trust us on this.

And then, if something doesn't go quite right, as inevitably happens with even the best-laid plans, stay cool. Missed your train? Stuck in the airport? Use the time to study the people. Strike up a conversation with a stranger. Study the newsstands or flip through the local press. Take a walk. Find the silver lining in the clouds, whatever it is. And do send us a postcard to tell us what went wrong and what went right. You can E-mail us at: editors@fodors.com (specify the name of the book on the subject line) or write the France editor at Fodor's upCLOSE, 201 East 50th Street, New York, NY 10022. We'll put your ideas to good use and let other travelers benefit from your experiences. In the mean time, bon voyage!

BASICS

If you've ever traveled with anyone before, you know that there are two types of people in the world—the planners and the nonplanners. Travel brings out the worst in both groups. Left to their own devices, the planners will have you goose-stepping from attraction to attraction on a cultural blitzkrieg, while the nonplanners will invariably miss the flight, the bus, and maybe even the point. This chapter offers you a middle ground; we hope it provides enough information to help you plan your trip to France without nailing you down. Keep flexible and remember that the most hair-pulling situations turn into the best travel stories back home.

AIR TRAVEL

AIRPORTS

The major gateway to France is Paris, which has two airports: **Orly** and **Charles de Gaulle.** Though there are international airports in other major cities in France, it is unusual to find a direct flight to anywhere but Paris. Air France (see Air Travel, **above**), however, has connecting flights to many other destinations in the country. For the most part, people fly into Orly or Charles de Gaulle, spend some time in Paris, and then take a train (see Train Travel, **below**) to their next destination in France. (See Chapter 2 for information on getting into Paris from the airports.) There is TGV service from Charles de Gaulle, but it only goes to a limited number of places and is difficult to coordinate with air travel; in general, if people do take it directly to the airport, they take it on their way back home. Rent a car at the airport (see Car Rental, **below**) only if you are planning to skip Paris and go directly to another destination; having a car in Paris can be a big nightmare.

AIRPORT INFORMATION • Charles de Gaulle (tel. 01/4862–2280).

BOOKING YOUR FLIGHT

When you book **look for nonstop flights** and **remember that "direct" flights stop at least once.** Try to avoid connecting flights, which require a change of plane.

CARRIERS

MAJOR AIRLINES • From the U.S.: Air France (tel. 800/237–2747) to Charles de Gaulle. **American** (tel. 800/433–7300) to Charles de Gaulle, Orly. **Continental** (tel. 800/231–0856) to Charles de Gaulle. **Delta** (tel. 800/241–4141) to Charles de Gaulle. **Northwest** (tel. 800/225–2525) to Charles de Gaulle. **TWA** (tel. 800/892–4141) to Charles de Gaulle. **United** (tel. 800/538–2929) to Charles de Gaulle. **US**

Airways (tel. 800/428–4322) to Charles de Gaulle. From Canada: **Air Canada** (tel. 800/361–8620 in Québec or 800/268–7240 in Ontario). **Canadian Airlines** (tel. 800/426–7000). From the United Kingdom: **Air France** (tel. 020/8742–6600). **British Airways** (tel. 0345/222111). **British Midland** (tel. 0345/554554). **Easyjet** (tel. 0990/292929) runs scheduled services to Nice from Luton. From Down Under: **Qantas** (tel. 02/957–0111). **Continental** (tel. 02/693–5266 in Sydney or 09/379–5682 in Auckland).

OFFICES IN FRANCE • **Air Canada** (tel. 01–44–50–20–20). **Air France** (tel. 08–02–80–28–02). **American Airlines** (tel. 01–69–32–73–07). **British Airways** (tel. 08–02–80–29–02). **Continental** (tel. 01–42–99–09–09). **Delta** (tel. 01–47–68–92–92). **Northwest** (tel. 01–42–66–90–00). **United** (tel. 08–01–72–72–72).

CHECK-IN & BOARDING

Assuming that not everyone with a ticket will show up, airlines routinely overbook planes. When that happens, airlines ask for volunteers to give up their seats. In return these volunteers usually get a certificate for a free flight and are rebooked on the next flight out. If there are not enough volunteers, the airline must choose who will be denied boarding. The first to get bumped are passengers who checked in late and those flying on discounted tickets, so **get to the gate and check in as early as possible,** especially during peak periods.

Always **bring a government-issued photo ID to the airport.** You may be asked to show it before you are allowed to check in.

CUTTING COSTS

The least-expensive airfares to France must usually be purchased in advance and are nonrefundable. It's smart to **call a number of airlines, and when you are quoted a good price, book it on the spot—** the same fare may not be available the next day. Always **check different routings** and look into using different airports. Travel agents, especially low-fare specialists (see Discounts & Deals, below), are helpful.

If you can't get a cheap flight into Paris, **look into other destinations.** Flying into Brussels is convenient; the train trip to Paris costs about 250F second class, takes about three hours, and the train station connects to the airport in Brussels. Amsterdam and Frankfurt are also good bets. One-way second-class train tickets cost around 390F and 550F respectively.

Consolidators are another good source. They buy tickets for scheduled international flights at reduced rates from the airlines, then sell them at prices that beat the best fare available directly from the airlines, usually without restrictions. Sometimes you can even get your money back if you need to return the ticket. Carefully read the fine print detailing penalties for changes and cancellations, and **confirm your consolidator reservation with the airline.**

When you **fly as a courier** you trade your checked-luggage space for a ticket deeply subsidized by a courier service. There are restrictions on when you can book and how long you can stay.

CONSOLIDATORS • **Cheap Tickets** (tel. 800/377–1000). **Up & Away Travel** (tel. 212/889–2345). **Discount Airline Ticket Service** (tel. 800/576–1600). **Unitravel** (tel. 800/325–2222). **World Travel Network** (tel. 800/409–6753).

DUTY-FREE SHOPPING

Duty-free shopping is no longer possible within the EU.

ENJOYING THE FLIGHT

For more legroom **request an emergency-aisle seat.** Don't sit in the row in front of the emergency aisle or in front of a bulkhead, where seats may not recline. If you have dietary concerns, **ask for special meals when booking.** These can be vegetarian, low-cholesterol, or kosher, for example. On long flights, try to maintain a normal routine, to help fight jet lag. At night **get some sleep.** By day **eat light meals, drink water** (not alcohol), and **move around the cabin** to stretch your legs.

FLYING TIMES

Flying time to Paris is 7½ hours from New York, 9 hours from Chicago, and 11 hours from Los Angeles. From the United Kingdom to Paris, flying time is about 1 hour.

HOW TO COMPLAIN

If your baggage goes astray or your flight goes awry, complain right away. Most carriers require that you **file a claim immediately.**

AIRLINE COMPLAINTS • U.S. Department of Transportation **Aviation Consumer Protection Division** (C-75, Room 4107, Washington, DC 20590, tel. 202/366–2220). **Federal Aviation Administration Consumer Hotline** (tel. 800/322–7873).

BIKE TRAVEL

French roads are well suited for bicycling. Michelin road maps distinguish major roads (marked in red) from minor ones (yellow) and local routes (white). You can rent a bike for about 60F to 120F a day (you'll generally need to give a deposit of 1,000F–2,000F on your credit card or leave your passport). Try rental agencies in towns or many train stations; for information about which train stations rent bikes, inquire at any station or call the main SNCF number (see Train Travel, below). A VTT (vélo tout terrain, or mountain bike) is generally more expensive than your average three-speed. Transporting your bicycle from one place to another isn't too difficult. On most local trains in France, you can bring your bicycle aboard for free. On others—generally those that cross regional or international borders—you have to register your bike as luggage (150F). The publication "Guide du Train et Vélo," available at large train stations, provides complete information on taking your bicycle on the train. For more specific information, see individual chapters.

BIKES IN FLIGHT

Most airlines accommodate bikes as luggage, provided they are dismantled and boxed. For bike boxes, often free at bike shops, you'll pay about $5 (at least $100 for bike bags) from airlines. International travelers can sometimes substitute a bike for a piece of checked luggage at no charge; otherwise, the cost is about $100. Domestic and Canadian airlines charge $25–$50.

INFORMATION • The **Fédération Française de Cyclotourisme** (8 rue Jean-Marie-Jégo, 13e, Paris, tel. 01–44–16–88–88) can provide you with more information about biking in France.

Ferry companies are working hard to compete with the Chunnel, and P&O Ferries occasionally offers round-trips for 100F. The catch is that you have to complete your trip within 48 hours—but how they force you to use the return portion of your ticket is unclear.

BOAT & FERRY TRAVEL

Lots of ferry and Hovercraft companies transport travelers and their cars across the Channel. With the arrival of the Channel Tunnel, **many ferry companies are slashing their prices.** Calais is becoming the Channel-crossing hub; only Hoverspeed still sends speedy Seacats between Boulogne and Folkestone (mid-April–September only). From Calais, Seafrance and P&O Ferries make the 1½-hour ferry trip to Dover all year long for approximately 100F–400F round-trip without a car or about 500F–1,500F with a car. Hoverspeed sends Hovercraft over in half the time and charges 90F–250F round-trip or up to 1,500F with a car.

Driving distances from the French ports to Paris are as follows: from Calais, 290 km (180 mi); from Boulogne, 243 km (151 mi); from Dieppe, 193 km (120 mi); from Dunkerque, 257 km (160 mi). The fastest routes to Paris from each port are via the N43, A26, and A1 from Calais and the Channel Tunnel; via the N1 from Boulogne; via the N15 from Le Havre; via the D915 and N1 from Dieppe; and via the A25 and A1 from Dunkerque.

BOAT & FERRY INFORMATION • **Hoverspeed** (tel. 08–00–90–17–77 in France; International Hoverport, Marine Parade, Dover CT17 9TG, 01304/865–000 in the U.K.). **P&O European Ferries** (tel. 01–44–51–00–51 in France; Channel House, Channel View Rd., Dover, Kent CT17 9TJ, 01304/863–000 in the U.K.). **Seafrance** (tel. 01–44–94–40–40 in France).

BUS TRAVEL

CLASSES

Slightly less expensive and significantly slower than the trains, **buses are generally used only to fill in the gaps left by the rail lines.** You buy tickets for short distances when boarding. For greater distances, buy the tickets in advance at the bus station. Buses are generally clean, comfortable, and punctual. You can also take a bus to over 1,500 European cities; **Eurolines** has service to London (7 hrs, 440F round-trip), Berlin (10 hrs, 880F round-trip), Barcelona (15 hrs, 1,000F round-trip), among other places.

BUS INFORMATION • Eurolines in Paris (28 av. du Général de Gaulle, tel. 08–36–69–52–52).

BUSINESS HOURS

The majority of stores (large and small), food shops (except for convenient minigroceries), and government offices close on Sunday.

BANKS & OFFICES

Banks are open weekdays roughly 9:30 AM–4:30 PM. Banks that stay open on Saturday close on Monday. Some small banks take a one-hour to 90-minute lunch break.

MUSEUMS & SIGHTS

Most **museums are closed one day a week** (usually Monday or Tuesday) and on national holidays (see Holidays, below). Normal opening times are from 9:30 AM to 5 or 6 PM, occasionally with a long lunch break between noon and 2; some museums stay open late one night a week.

SHOPS

Large stores stay open without a lunch break from 9 or 9:30 AM until 6 or 7 PM. Smaller shops often open an hour or so earlier and close a few hours later, sometimes with a lengthy lunch break in between.

CAMERAS & PHOTOGRAPHY

PHOTO HELP • Kodak Information Center (tel. 800/242–2424). *Kodak Guide to Shooting Great Travel Pictures,* available in bookstores or from Fodor's Travel Publications (tel. 800/533–6478; $16.50 plus $4 shipping).

EQUIPMENT PRECAUTIONS

Always **keep your film and tape out of the sun.** Carry an extra supply of batteries, and **be prepared to turn on your camera or camcorder** to prove to security personnel that the device is real. Always **ask for hand inspection of film,** which becomes clouded after successive exposures to airport X-ray machines, and **keep videotapes away from metal detectors.**

CAR RENTAL

Renting cars in France is expensive—about twice as much as in the United States. In addition, the price doesn't usually take into account the 20.6% VAT tax. Your best bet is to **make arrangements before you go.** Many agencies require that you be at least 23 years old and have a credit card in order to rent a car.

It is rare to find a car with automatic transmission in France, so **make sure you know how to drive a stick-shift** before you go. The cheapest cars are very small stick-shifts and go for around 300F per day or 1,000F–1,500F a week. Some agencies include mileage in the cost, while others may charge you extra once you reach a certain number of kilometers. Rates in Paris begin at $60 a day and $196 a week for an economy car with air-conditioning, a manual transmission, and unlimited mileage. This does not include tax on car rentals, which is 20.6%. Also, note that gas is very expensive (see Driving, below).

You won't need a car in the capital, so **wait to pick up your rental until the day you leave Paris.** Or take the train to your destination and pick up your rental there. Most major car-rental agencies have branches in major cities and large towns all over France. To save money, consider purchasing a rail/drive package (see Train Travel, below). You may also just want to have a car for a couple of days of back-road exploring (see Getting Around, below, for a discussion of various ways to travel around France).

LOCAL AGENCIES • In Paris: **Rent-A-Car** (79 rue de Bercy, 75012, tel. 01–43–45–98–99), which offers small Fiat Pandas or larger Rover 214s. **Locabest** (104 bd. Magenta, 75010, tel. 01–44–72–08–05). **ACAR** (99 bd. Auguste-Blanqui, 75013, tel. 01–45–88–28–38), with economy cars and Renault Espace minivans.

MAJOR AGENCIES • Alamo (tel. 800/522–9696; 020/8759–6200 in the U.K.). **Avis** (tel. 800/331–1084; 800/879–2847 in Canada; 02/9353–9000 in Australia; 09/525–1982 in New Zealand). **Budget** (tel. 800/527–0700; 0144/227–6266 in the U.K.). **Dollar** (tel. 800/800–6000; 020/8897–0811 in the U.K., where it is known as Eurodollar; 02/9223–1444 in Australia). **Hertz** (tel. 800/654–3001; 800/263–

0600 in Canada; 0990/90–60–90 in the U.K.; 02/9669–2444 in Australia; 03/358–6777 in New Zealand). **National InterRent** (tel. 800/227–3876; 0345/222525 in the U.K., where it is known as Europcar InterRent).

CUTTING COSTS

To get the best deal **book through a travel agent who will shop around.** Also **price local car-rental companies,** although the service and maintenance may not be as good as those of a major player. Remember to ask about required deposits, cancellation penalties, and drop-off charges if you're planning to pick up the car in one city and leave it in another. If you're traveling during a holiday period, also make sure that a confirmed reservation guarantees you a car.

Do **look into wholesalers,** companies that do not own fleets but rent in bulk from those that do and often offer better rates than traditional car-rental operations. Payment must be made before you leave home.

WHOLESALERS • Auto Europe (tel. 207/842–2000 or 800/223–5555, fax 800/235–6321). **Europe by Car** (tel. 212/581–3040 or 800/223–1516, fax 212/246–1458). **DER Travel Services** (9501 W. Devon Ave., Rosemont, IL 60018, tel. 800/782–2424, fax 800/282–7474 for information; 800/860–9944 for brochures). **Kemwel Holiday Autos** (tel. 914/825–3000 or 800/678–0678, fax 914/381–8847).

INSURANCE

When driving a rented car you are generally responsible for any damage to or loss of the vehicle. Before you rent see what coverage your personal auto-insurance policy and credit cards already provide.

Collision policies that car-rental companies sell for European rentals usually do not include stolen-vehicle coverage. Before you buy it, check your existing policies—you may already be covered.

REQUIREMENTS & RESTRICTIONS

In France, **visitors staying under 90 days may use their own driver's license.** An International Driver's Permit (IDP) is a good idea, however; it's available from the American Automobile Association ($10) or the Canadian Automobile Association, or, in the United Kingdom, from the Automobile Association or Royal Automobile Club. The IDP will cost you $10 and two passport-size photos. Nonmembers must pay cash. Some offices can issue an IDP on the spot in about 15 minutes, but be sure to call ahead; during the busy season IDPs can take a week or more. For information about rules of the road, see Car Travel, below.

SURCHARGES

Before you pick up a car in one city and leave it in another **ask about drop-off charges or one-way service fees,** which can be substantial. Note, too, that some rental agencies charge extra if you return the car before the time specified in your contract. To avoid a hefty refueling fee **fill the tank just before you turn in the car,** but be aware that gas stations near the rental outlet may overcharge.

CAR TRAVEL

Having a car gives you the ultimate travel freedom. Gas, however, is expensive in France (about 6F per liter). In France, **you may use your own driver's license,** but you must be able to prove you have third-party insurance. It might be a good idea to get an International Driver's Permit (IDP) before leaving home (see Car Rental, above).

For the fastest roads between two points, **look for roads marked A** for autoroutes. Most are toll roads. France's roads are classified into five types, numbered and prefixed A, N, D, C, or V. Roads marked A (Autoroutes) are expressways. There are excellent links between Paris and most French cities, but poor ones between the provinces (the principal exceptions being A26 from Calais to Reims, A62 between Bordeaux and Toulouse, and A9/A8 the length of the Mediterranean coast). It is often difficult to avoid Paris when crossing France—just **try to steer clear of the rush hours** (7–9:30 AM and 4:30–7:30 PM). A péage (toll) must be paid on most expressways: The rate varies but can be steep. The N (Route Nationale) roads—which are sometimes divided highways—and D (Route Départementale) roads are usually wide and fast, and driving along them can be a real pleasure. Don't be daunted by smaller (C and V) roads, either. The yellow regional Michelin maps—on sale throughout France—are invaluable.

AUTO CLUBS

IN AUSTRALIA • Australian Automobile Association (tel. 02/6247–7311).

IN CANADA • Canadian Automobile Association (CAA, tel. 613/247–0117).

IN NEW ZEALAND • **New Zealand Automobile Association** (tel. 09/377–4660).

IN THE U.K. • **Automobile Association** (AA, tel. 0990/500- -600). **Royal Automobile Club** (RAC, tel. 0990/722–722 for membership; 0345/121–345 for insurance).

IN THE U.S. • **American Automobile Association** (AAA, tel. 800/564–6222).

EMERGENCIES

If your car breaks down on an expressway, **go to a roadside emergency telephone** and call the breakdown service. If you have a breakdown anywhere else, find the nearest garage or contact the police (dial 17).

CONTACTS • **Automobile Club National (ACN)** (5 rue Auber, 75009 Paris, tel. 01–44–51–53–99, fax 01–49–24–93–99), the French motoring club, charges a small fee for towing and roadside breakdown service. If you're a AAA member, you can get reimbursed for ACN charges when you get home. For more information stop by your local AAA branch and ask for the pamphlet "Offices to Serve You Abroad." Or send a S.A.S.E. to the AAA's head office (1000 AAA Dr., Heathrow, FL 32746).

GASOLINE

When possible, **buy gas before you get on the expressway** to keep down costs and keep an eye on pump prices as you go. These vary enormously; anything from 5.80F to 6.80F per liter. The cheapest gas can be found at hypermarchés (very large supermarkets). It is possible to go for many miles in the country without passing a gas station—**don't let your tank get too low in rural areas.**

PARKING

Note that parking is a nightmare in Paris and often difficult in other large towns. Meters and ticket machines (pay and display) are common: Make sure you **have a supply of 1-, 2-, and 5-franc coins.** Deposit the right amount of money and you will receive a small receipt which you must display inside the front window of your car (the passenger side is best). If you are planning on spending some time in Paris with your car (although this is **not** a good idea), there are parking cards available for 100F in Tabacs which work like a credit card in the meters, thus avoiding the scramble for change. Parking is free during August only in certain residential areas indicated by a dense yellow circle on the meters. **If you do not see this circle, pay.** The dreaded parking police are efficient; fines are high, and towing is rapid. In smaller towns, parking may be permitted on one side of the street only—alternating every two weeks—so pay attention to signs.

ROAD MAPS

If you plan to drive through France, **get a yellow Michelin map,** for each region you'll be visiting. The maps are available from most bookshops and newsagents.

RULES OF THE ROAD

Remember while driving in France that you must **yield to drivers coming from the right.** Keep your eyes peeled for cars zipping out of impossibly small side streets. **Everyone must wear a seat belt (even in the back)** and children under 12 may not travel in the front seat. Speed limits are 130 kph (80 mph) on expressways, 110 kph (70 mph) on divided highways, 90 kph (55 mph) on other roads, 50 kph (30 mph) in towns. French drivers break these limits and police dish out hefty on-the-spot fines with equal abandon.

THE CHANNEL TUNNEL

Short of flying, the "Chunnel" is the fastest way to cross the English Channel: 35 minutes from Folkestone to Calais, 60 minutes from motorway to motorway, or 3 hours from London's Waterloo Station to Paris's Gare du Nord.

CAR TRANSPORT • **Le Shuttle** (tel. 0990/353–535 in the U.K.).

PASSENGER SERVICE • In the U.K.: **Eurostar** (tel. 0990/186–186), **InterCity Europe** (Victoria Station, London, tel. 0990/848–848 for credit-card bookings). In the U.S.: **BritRail Travel** (tel. 800/677–8585), **Rail Europe** (tel. 800/942–4866).

CHILDREN IN FRANCE

If you are renting a car don't forget to **arrange for a car seat** when you reserve.

FLYING

If your children are two or older **ask about children's airfares.** As a general rule, infants under two not occupying a seat fly at greatly reduced fares or even for free. When booking, **confirm carry-on allowances** if you're traveling with infants. In general, for babies charged 10% of the adult fare, you are allowed one carry-on bag and a collapsible stroller; if the flight is full the stroller may have to be checked or you may be limited to less.

Experts agree that it's a good idea to use safety seats aloft for children weighing less than 40 pounds. Airlines set their own policies: U.S. carriers usually require that the child be ticketed, even if he or she is young enough to ride free, since the seats must be strapped into regular seats. Do **check your airline's policy about using safety seats during takeoff and landing.** And since safety seats are not allowed just everywhere in the plane, get your seat assignments early.

When reserving, **request children's meals or a freestanding bassinet** if you need them. But note that bulkhead seats, where you must sit to use the bassinet, may lack an overhead bin or storage space on the floor.

LODGING

Most hotels in France allow children under a certain age to stay in their parents' room at no extra charge, but others charge for them as extra adults; be sure to **find out the cutoff age for children's discounts.**

CONSUMER PROTECTION

Whenever shopping or buying travel services in France, **pay with a major credit card** so you can cancel payment or get reimbursed if there's a problem. If you're doing business with a particular company for the first time, **contact your local Better Business Bureau and the attorney general's offices** in your state and the company's home state, as well. Have any complaints been filed? Finally, if you're buying a package or tour, always **consider travel insurance** that includes default coverage (see Insurance, below).

LOCAL BBBS • Council of Better Business Bureaus (4200 Wilson Blvd., Suite 800, Arlington, VA 22203, tel. 703/276–0100, fax 703/525–8277).

CUSTOMS & DUTIES

When shopping, **keep receipts** for all purchases. Upon reentering the country, **be ready to show customs officials what you've bought.** If you feel a duty is incorrect or object to the way your clearance was handled, note the inspector's badge number and ask to see a supervisor. If the problem isn't resolved, write to the appropriate authorities, beginning with the port director at your point of entry.

IN AUSTRALIA

Australia residents who are 18 or older may bring home $A400 worth of souvenirs and gifts (including jewelry), 250 cigarettes or 250 grams of tobacco, and 1,125 ml of alcohol (including wine, beer, and spirits). Residents under 18 may bring back $A200 worth of goods. Prohibited items include meat products. Seeds, plants, and fruits need to be declared upon arrival.

INFORMATION • Australian Customs Service (Regional Director, Box 8, Sydney, NSW 2001, tel. 02/9213–2000, fax 02/9213–4000).

IN CANADA

Canadian residents who have been out of Canada for at least 7 days may bring home C$500 worth of goods duty-free. If you've been away less than 7 days but more than 48 hours, the duty-free allowance drops to C$200; if your trip lasts 24–48 hours, the allowance is C$50. You may not pool allowances with family members. Goods claimed under the C$500 exemption may follow you by mail; those claimed under the lesser exemptions must accompany you. Alcohol and tobacco products may be included in the 7-day and 48-hour exemptions but not in the 24-hour exemption. If you meet the age requirements of the province or territory through which you reenter Canada, you may bring in, duty-free, 1.14 liters (40 imperial ounces) of wine or liquor or 24 12-ounce cans or bottles of beer or ale. If you are 16 or older you may bring in, duty-free, 200 cigarettes and 50 cigars. Check ahead of time with Revenue Canada or the Department of Agriculture for policies regarding meat products, seeds, plants, and fruits.

You may send an unlimited number of gifts worth up to C$60 each duty-free to Canada. Label the package UNSOLICITED GIFT—VALUE UNDER $60. Alcohol and tobacco are excluded.

INFORMATION • Revenue Canada (2265 St. Laurent Blvd. S, Ottawa, Ontario K1G 4K3, tel. 613/993–0534; 800/461–9999 in Canada).

IN FRANCE

Going through customs in Paris is usually pretty painless. The officials will check your passport but probably won't touch your luggage unless you look shady or their dogs have caught a whiff of something interesting in your bags.

If you're coming from outside the European Union, you may import duty free: (1) 200 cigarettes or 100 cigarillos or 50 cigars or 250 grams of tobacco (twice that if you live outside Europe); (2) 2 liters of wine and, in addition, (a) 1 liter of alcohol over 22% volume (most spirits) or (b) 2 liters of alcohol under 22% volume (fortified or sparkling wine) or (c) 2 more liters of table wine; (3) 50 milliliters of perfume and 250 milliliters of toilet water; (4) 200 grams of coffee, 100 grams of tea; and (5) other goods to the value of 300F (100F for those under 15).

If you're arriving from a European Union country, you may be required to declare all goods and prove that anything over the standard limit is for personal consumption. Since January 1993, however, there is no longer any limit or customs tariff imposed on goods carried within the EU.

Any amount of French or foreign currency may be brought into France, but foreign currencies converted into francs may be reconverted into a foreign currency only up to the equivalent of 5,000F.

IN NEW ZEALAND

Homeward-bound residents 17 or older may bring back $700 worth of souvenirs and gifts. Your duty-free allowance also includes 4.5 liters of wine or beer; one 1,125-ml bottle of spirits; and either 200 cigarettes, 250 grams of tobacco, 50 cigars, or a combination of the three up to 250 grams. Prohibited items include meat products, seeds, plants, and fruits.

INFORMATION • New Zealand Customs (Custom House, 50 Anzac Ave., Box 29, Auckland, New Zealand, tel. 09/359–6655, fax 09/359–6732).

IN THE U.K.

If you are a U.K. resident and your journey was wholly within the European Union (EU), you won't have to pass through customs when you return to the United Kingdom. If you plan to bring back large quantities of alcohol or tobacco, check EU limits beforehand. From countries outside the EU, you may bring home, duty-free, 200 cigarettes or 50 cigars; 1 liter of spirits or 2 liters of fortified or sparkling wine or liqueurs; 2 liters of still table wine; 60 ml of perfume; 250 ml of toilet water; plus £136 worth of other goods, including gifts and souvenirs. If returning from outside the EU, prohibited items include meat products, seeds, plants, and fruits.

INFORMATION • HM Customs and Excise (Dorset House, Stamford St., Bromley Kent BR1 1XX, tel. 020/7202–4227).

IN THE U.S.

U.S. residents who have been out of the country for at least 48 hours (and who have not used the $400 allowance or any part of it in the past 30 days) may bring home $400 worth of foreign goods duty-free.

U.S. residents 21 and older may bring back 1 liter of alcohol duty-free. In addition, regardless of your age, you are allowed 200 cigarettes and 100 non-Cuban cigars. Antiques, which the U.S. Customs Service defines as objects more than 100 years old, enter duty-free, as do original works of art done entirely by hand, including paintings, drawings, and sculptures.

You may also send packages home duty-free: up to $200 worth of goods for personal use, with a limit of one parcel per addressee per day (and no alcohol or tobacco products or perfume worth more than $5); label the package PERSONAL USE and attach a list of its contents and their retail value. Do not label the package UNSOLICITED GIFT or your duty-free exemption will drop to $100. Mailed items do not affect your duty-free allowance on your return.

INFORMATION • U.S. Customs Service (inquiries, 1300 Pennsylvania Ave. NW, Washington, DC 20229, tel. 202/927–6724; complaints, Office of Regulations and Rulings, 1300 Pennsylvania Ave. NW, Washington, DC 20229; registration of equipment, Registration Information, 1300 Pennsylvania Ave. NW, Washington, DC 20229, tel. 202/927–0540).

DINING

It's not by chance that France is known as one of the culinary capitals of the world; food is as important to French culture as the language. Supermarkets are plentiful and offer the best prices for your basics. Small **boucheries** (butcher shops) and **fromageries** (cheese shops) will sell you meats and cheeses by the slice and, although they are a bit more expensive, their quality is superior. **Charcuteries** or **traiteurs** are generally delis that have fresh salads and take-out stuff like quiche or lasagna sold by weight for pretty good prices. **Boulangeries** used to almost exclusively sell bread but, with fewer people having time for a hot lunch, they have since expanded their service to provide simple lunches to go such as sandwiches, salads, and quiche by the slice. (They also sell coffee to go with their warm croissants in the morning which you can have at small, makeshift counters.) **Pâtisseries** sell pastries almost exclusively. Beware of small corner stores that often charge twice as much as big chain stores like Casino, Franprix, Prisunic, Monoprix, and Leaderprice (where the very best bargains are to be had), though they're good in a late-night pinch, as they're often open later than other places.

It would be a crime, though, not to eat in a restaurant at least once in a while in France. Many restaurants offer a plat du jour (dish of the day), which includes meat, veggies, and pasta or potatoes, for around 50F. If you're hungry, **your best bet is to order a menu fixe or formule,** which usually includes two to three courses for 60F–150F, instead of ordering from the carte (menu). Try to **eat your big meal in the middle of the day, when prices are often reduced** by about a third. Restaurants operate in two shifts: Lunch is served from noon to 2:30 and dinner 7–10. Restaurants don't usually get full until around 8 or 8:30 PM. Eating out is usually an elaborate affair; a three-course meal is the norm. To avoid paying 15F for bottled water, which the waiter will inevitably try to serve, order simply a carafe d'eau (a carafe of tap water). Wine, which you may start to consider obligatory, starts around 60F a bottle, but you can get a pichet of 50 centiliters for as little as 30F.

Cafés, generally open all day and often late into the evening, usually serve croissants and other pastries and sometimes more substantial fare like baguette sandwiches with meat or cheese, salades, and the customary croque monsieur or madame (fried egg sandwiches with cheese or ham). Coffee (choose from café noir, an espresso, or café crème, with hot milk) and croissants or tartines (baguettes spread with butter) are the French version of breakfast. Brasseries serve up standard rather heavy meals like steak-frites (steak with french fries) or roast chicken for 50F or so. In major cities, McDonald's and Quick rear their ugly heads. Yet the best fast-food deal is the good old 25F donner-kebabs (gyros) that can be found in most large towns. Crepe stands also sell quick fixes for 12F–25F.

The restaurants we list are the cream of the crop in each price category.

RESERVATIONS & DRESS

Reservations are always a good idea: we mention them only when they're essential or are not accepted. Book as far ahead as you can, and reconfirm as soon as you arrive. We mention dress only when men are required to wear a jacket or a jacket and tie.

DISABILITIES & ACCESSIBILITY

Although the French government is doing much to ensure that public facilities provide for visitors with disabilities, it still has a long way to go. A number of monuments, hotels, and museums—especially those constructed within the past decade—are equipped with ramps, elevators, and special toilet facilities. Lists of regional hotels include a symbol to indicate which hotels have rooms that are accessible to people using wheelchairs. All places for those in wheelchairs are now in no-smoking first-class cars (for the price of a regular ticket). You need to **contact SNCF to request wheelchair assistance in advance** and for tickets; for more wheelchair access information, **contact the SNCF Accessibilité Service.** For a comprehensive list of the services offered by every train station in France, **ask for the _Guide du Voyageur à Mobilité Réduite,_** available free in all train stations. For an extensive guide that details all kinds of clear-cut, practical information on transportation, lodging, and tourist attractions accessible to travelers with disabilities, **request the government-published, excellent, booklet (in both French and English), _Paris for Everyone._** The booklet costs 60F and is available from tourist offices and from Paris's Comité National Français de Liaison pour la Réadaptation des Handicapés.

Unfortunately, most of Paris's métro lines are inaccessible to travelers with reduced mobility, with the exception of the new, fully automated line météor but, in general, the RER is slightly more accessible. For more details, **ask the Régie Autonome des Transports Parisiens (RATP) for its brochure on accessibility.**

Two bus lines are wheelchair accessible; all buses on line NE20 (Gare St. Lazare–Opéra, Bastille, Gare de Lyon) and NE19 (Montparnasse–Bastille).

Several companies that accommodate wheelchairs in their vans include **Renault Espace Taxis** (tel. 06–07–49–58–92 for reservations), **GIHP** (tel. 01–46–02–21–46), and **AIHROP** (tel. 01–40–24–34–76). A number of companies rent handicap-accessible cars, including **Hertz** (tel. 01–39–38–38–38). Note that although there are over 360 parking spaces reserved for drivers with disabilities in Paris, they are often used by other drivers. All parking in Paris is free provided you display a GIG sticker.

LOCAL RESOURCES • **Comité Nationale Français de Liaison pour la Réadaptation des Handicapés** (236 bis rue de Tolbiac, 75013 Paris, tel. 01–53–80–66–66). **RATP** (pl. de la Madeleine, 8e, tel. 01–43–46–14–14). **SNCF** (tel. 01–45–65–60–00). **SNCF Accessibilité Service** (toll-free in France, tel. 08–00–15–47–53) has more information on train access.

LODGING

Many French hotels are in buildings that are hundreds of years old and unsuited to guests with impaired mobility. When possible, **opt for newer accommodations,** which are more likely to have been designed with access in mind.

LOCAL RESOURCES • **Association des Paralysés de France** (17 blvd. Auguste-Blanqui, 13e, tel. 01–40–78–69–00) has a list of wheelchair-accessible hotels. **Handitour** (35 rue de la Goutte d'Or, 18e, tel. 01–42–51–68–09) a nonprofit organization, helps travelers with hotel reservations, transportation, and accessibility.

When discussing accessibility with an operator or reservations agent **ask hard questions.** Are there any stairs, inside or out? Are there grab bars next to the toilet and in the shower/tub? How wide is the doorway to the room? To the bathroom? For the most extensive facilities meeting the latest legal specifications **opt for newer accommodations.**

TRANSPORTATION

COMPLAINTS • **Disability Rights Section** (U.S. Department of Justice, Civil Rights Division, Box 66738, Washington, DC 20035-6738, tel. 202/514–0301; 800/514–0301; 202/514–0301 TTY; 800/514–0301 TTY, fax 202/307–1198) for general complaints. **Aviation Consumer Protection Division** (see Air Travel, above) for airline-related problems. **Civil Rights Office** (U.S. Department of Transportation, Departmental Office of Civil Rights, S-30, 400 7th St. SW, Room 10215, Washington, DC 20590, tel. 202/366–4648, fax 202/366–9371) for problems with surface transportation.

TRAVEL AGENCIES

In the United States, although the Americans with Disabilities Act requires that travel firms serve the needs of all travelers, some agencies specialize in working with people with disabilities.

TRAVELERS WITH MOBILITY PROBLEMS • **Access Adventures** (206 Chestnut Ridge Rd., Rochester, NY 14624, tel. 716/889–9096), run by a former physical-rehabilitation counselor. **Accessible Journeys** (35 W. Sellers Ave. Ridley Park, PA 19078, tel. 610/521–0339 or 800/846–4537, fax 610/521–6959). **Accessible Vans of the Rockies, Activity and Travel Agency** (2040 W. Hamilton Pl., Sheridan, CO 80110, tel. 303/806–5047 or 888/837–0065, fax 303/781–2329). **Accessible Vans of Hawaii, Activity and Travel Agency** (186 Mehani Circle, Kihei, HI 96753, tel. 808/879–5521 or 800/303–3750, fax 808/879–0649). **CareVacations** (5-5110 50th Ave., Leduc, Alberta T9E 6V4, tel. 780/986–6404 or 877/478–7827, fax 780/986–8332) has group tours and is especially helpful with cruise vacations. **Flying Wheels Travel** (143 W. Bridge St., Box 382, Owatonna, MN 55060, tel. 507/451–5005 or 800/535–6790, fax 507/451–1685). **Hinsdale Travel Service** (201 E. Ogden Ave., Suite 100, Hinsdale, IL 60521, tel. 630/325–1335, fax 630/325–1342).

TRAVELERS WITH DEVELOPMENTAL DISABILITIES • **Sprout** (893 Amsterdam Ave., New York, NY 10025, tel. 212/222–9575 or 888/222–9575, fax 212/222–9768).

DISCOUNTS & DEALS

Be a smart shopper and **compare all your options** before making decisions. A plane ticket bought with a promotional coupon from travel clubs, coupon books, and direct-mail offers may not be cheaper than the least expensive fare from a discount ticket agency. And always keep in mind that what you get is just as important as what you save.

DISCOUNT RESERVATIONS

To save money **look into discount-reservations services** with toll-free numbers, which use their buying power to get a better price on hotels, airline tickets, even car rentals. When booking a room, always **call the hotel's local toll-free number** (if one is available) rather than the central reservations number—you'll often get a better price. Always ask about special packages or corporate rates.

When shopping for the best deal on hotels and car rentals **look for guaranteed exchange rates,** which protect you against a falling dollar. With your rate locked in, you won't pay more, even if the price goes up in the local currency.

AIRLINE TICKETS • Tel. **800/FLY–4–LESS.** Tel. **800/FLY–ASAP.**

HOTEL ROOMS • **Hotel Reservations Network** (tel. 800/964–6835). **International Marketing & Travel Concepts** (tel. 800/790–4682). **Steigenberger Reservation Service** (tel. 800/223–5652). **Travel Interlink** (tel. 800/888–5898).

PACKAGE DEALS

Don't confuse packages and guided tours. When you buy a package, you travel on your own, just as though you had planned the trip yourself. Fly/drive packages, which combine airfare and car rental, are often a good deal. If you **buy a rail/drive pass** you may save on train tickets and car rentals. All Eurail- and Europass holders get a discount on Eurostar fares through the Channel Tunnel.

ELECTRICITY

To be able to use your U.S.-purchased electric-powered equipment, **bring a converter and adapter.** The electrical current in France is 220 volts, 50 cycles alternating current (AC); wall outlets take Continental-type plugs, with two round prongs. You can get by with just the adapter if you bring a dual-voltage appliance, available from travel gear catalogs. Don't use 110-volt outlets, marked FOR SHAVERS ONLY, for high-wattage appliances (like your hair dryer). Most laptop computers operate equally well on 110 and 220 volts and need only an adapter.

EMBASSIES

For information on embassies in Paris, see Chapter 2. Your embassy can help you if your passport has been stolen or lost, or if you need any other kind of international-level assistance.

EMERGENCIES

No matter what type of trouble you are having, **the best thing to do is yell for help** (au secours!) and attract as much attention as possible. In case you lose your French with your cool, here are a few phrases to keep you going: urgence (emergency), samu (ambulance), pompiers (firemen), poste de police (police station), médecin (doctor), médicament (medicine), and hôpital (hospital). If you are in Paris, there are a number of hot lines you can call if you or one of your companions is ill, but not all of them speak English (see Basics in Chapter 2). For nonemergency situations, **look in the phone directory for the number of the** commissariat or gendarmerie, both terms for the local police station; here you can report a theft or get the address of the local late-night pharmacies or pharmacist on call.

CONTACTS • **Police** (tel. 17). **Ambulance** (tel. 15). **Fire department** (tel. 18).

GAY & LESBIAN TRAVEL

The gay scene is happening in Paris, although it's fairly concentrated in one area, Le Marais. Lesbian spots are harder to find. Outside Paris, the gay scene is almost nonexistent, although a few cities and regions, particularly the Riviera, do have information centers and a bar or two. Fewer hate crimes are committed against gays in France than in the United States and the United Kingdom, but once you leave Paris, a less-than-warm welcome may await you in the more conservative provinces.

GAY- AND LESBIAN-FRIENDLY TRAVEL AGENCIES • **Different Roads Travel** (8383 Wilshire Blvd., Suite 902, Beverly Hills, CA 90211, tel. 323/651–5557 or 800/429–8747, fax 323/651–3678). **Kennedy Travel** (314 Jericho Turnpike, Floral Park, NY 11001, tel. 516/352–4888 or 800/237–7433, fax 516/354–8849). **Now Voyager** (4406 18th St., San Francisco, CA 94114, tel. 415/626–1169 or 800/

255–6951, fax 415/626–8626). **Skylink Travel and Tour** (1006 Mendocino Ave., Santa Rosa, CA 95401, tel. 707/546–9888 or 800/225–5759, fax 707/546–9891), serving lesbian travelers.

HEALTH

There are few serious health risks associated with travel in France, and no inoculations are needed to enter the country. If you get diarrhea, it's probably from upping your wine and rich food intake, not from a bacterial infection. Although tap water has such a high calcium content it sometimes looks like milk, it is drinkable, but it won't hurt you to know that eau non potable means nondrinkable water. In general, get plenty of rest, watch out for sun exposure, eat balanced meals—do we sound like your mother yet?

It's a good idea to **bring a basic first-aid kit** with bandages, antiseptic, cortisone cream, tweezers, a thermometer in a sturdy case, an antacid such as Alka-Seltzer, something for diarrhea (Pepto Bismol or Imodium), and, of course, aspirin. Learn the generic names of your favorite drugs if you insist on something familiar to stop your headache or unstuff your nose, and get your doctor to write a note with the generic name of your medicine in case of emergencies.

HOLIDAYS

Though only a small percentage of the population still treks to church on Sunday, the calendar reflects France's Catholic upbringing. If a holiday falls on a Tuesday or Thursday, many businesses font le pont (make the bridge) and close on that Monday or Friday, too. Note that on holidays in France, places really do close, so you should be stocked up with everything you might need. Here's a quick list of major holidays:

New Year's Day; Easter Monday (April 5, 2000); **Labor Day** (May 1); **World War II Armistice Day and Ascension Day** (May 8); **Pentecost Monday** (May 23, 2000); **Bastille Day** (July 14); **Assumption** (August 15); **All Saints' Day** (November 1); **World War I Armistice** (November 11); and **Christmas.**

INSURANCE

The most useful travel insurance plan is a comprehensive policy that includes coverage for trip cancellation and interruption, default, trip delay, and medical expenses (with a waiver for preexisting conditions).

Without insurance you will lose all or most of your money if you cancel your trip, regardless of the reason. Default insurance covers you if your tour operator, airline, or cruise line goes out of business. Trip-delay covers expenses that arise because of bad weather or mechanical delays. Study the fine print when comparing policies.

If you're traveling internationally, a key component of travel insurance is coverage for medical bills incurred if you get sick on the road. Such expenses are not generally covered by Medicare or private policies. U.K. residents can buy a travel-insurance policy valid for most vacations taken during the year in which it's purchased (but check preexisting-condition coverage). British and Australian citizens need extra medical coverage when traveling overseas.

Always **buy travel policies directly from the insurance company**; if you buy it from a cruise line, airline, or tour operator that goes out of business you probably will not be covered for the agency or operator's default, a major risk. Before you make any purchase **review your existing health and home-owner's policies** to find what they cover away from home.

TRAVEL INSURERS • In the U.S. **Access America** (6600 W. Broad St., Richmond, VA 23230, tel. 804/285–3300 or 800/284–8300), **Travel Guard International** (1145 Clark St., Stevens Point, WI 54481, tel. 715/345–0505 or 800/826–1300). In Canada **Voyager Insurance** (44 Peel Center Dr., Brampton, Ontario L6T 4M8, tel. 905/791–8700; 800/668–4342 in Canada).

INSURANCE INFORMATION • In the United Kingdom the **Association of British Insurers** (51–55 Gresham St., London EC2V 7HQ, tel. 020/7600–3333, fax 020/7696–8999). In Australia the **Insurance Council of Australia** (tel. 03/9614–1077, fax 03/9614–7924).

LANGUAGES FOR TRAVELERS

A phrase book and language-tape set can help get you started.

PHRASE BOOKS & LANGUAGE-TAPE SETS • *Fodor's French for Travelers* (tel. 800/733–3000 in the U.S.; 800/668–4247 in Canada; $7 for phrase book, $16.95 for audio set).

LODGING

APARTMENT & VILLA RENTALS

If you want a home base that's roomy enough for a family and comes with cooking facilities **consider a furnished rental.** These can save you money, especially if you're traveling with a group. Home-exchange directories sometimes list rentals as well as exchanges.

For groups of people staying in one place for more than a week, renting an apartment can be a good option. In summer, especially, it's pretty easy to find a place for 1,500F–3,000F per month; owners will often work out a weekly deal if they're desperate. France USA Contacts, a free magazine available around Paris (try Shakespeare & Company bookstore on the quay across from Notre-Dame), has apartment rental listings, as do CRIJ (Centre Régional Information Jeunesse) offices in larger cities.

INTERNATIONAL AGENTS • At Home Abroad (405 E. 56th St., Suite 6H, New York, NY 10022, tel. 212/421–9165, fax 212/752–1591). **Drawbridge to Europe** (5456 Adams Rd., Talent, OR 97540, tel. 541/512–8927 or 888/268–1148, fax 541/512–0978). **Europa-Let/Tropical Inn-Let** (92 N. Main St., Ashland, OR 97520, tel. 541/482–5806 or 800/462–4486, fax 541/482–0660). **Hometours International** (Box 11503, Knoxville, TN 37939, tel. 423/690- -8484 or 800/367–4668). **Interhome** (1990 N.E. 163rd St., Suite 110, N. Miami Beach, FL 33162, tel. 305/940–2299 or 800/882–6864, fax 305/940–2911). **Rental Directories International** (2044 Rittenhouse Sq., Philadelphia, PA 19103, tel. 215/985–4001, fax 215/985–0323). **Rent-a-Home International** (7200 34th Ave. NW, Seattle, WA 98117, tel. 206/789–9377 or 800/964–1891, fax 206/789–9379). **Vacation Home Rentals Worldwide** (235 Kensington Ave., Norwood, NJ 07648, tel. 201/767–9393 or 800/633–3284, fax 201/767–5510). **Villas and Apartments Abroad** (1270 Avenue of the Americas, 15th Floor, New York, NY 10020, tel. 212/759–1025 or 800/433–3020, fax 212/897–5039). **Villas International** (950 Northgate Dr., Suite 206, San Rafael, CA 94903, tel. 415/499–9490 or 800/221–2260, fax 415/499–9491). **Hideaways International** (767 Islington St., Portsmouth, NH 03801, tel. 603/430–4433 or 800/843–4433, fax 603/430–4444; membership $99).

B&BS

Chambres d'hôte (bed-and-breakfasts), popular in rural areas, can be relatively cheap, but don't expect to wake in a charming seaside cottage to a breakfast with homemade jam; the French version of the bed-and-breakfast is more often just a spare room that a local family rents out. Often table d'hôte dinners (meals cooked by and eaten with the owners) can be arranged for an extra, fairly nominal fee. Note that in bed-and-breakfasts, unlike hotels, it is more likely that the owners will only speak French. Staying in one may, however, give you more of an opportunity to meet French people. Check with the local tourist office for information about area bed-and-breakfasts or contact the French national bed-and-breakfast association, the Maison des Gîtes de France, below, for a list of places all over the country.

RESERVATION SERVICES • Maison des Gîtes de France (35 rue Godot-de-Mauroy, 75439 Paris, tel. 01–49–70–75–75).

CAMPING

If you're seeking peaceful seclusion among trees and streams, camping in much of France is not for you; generally you'll find yourself right next to a family-filled caravan in a shady parking lot on the outskirts of town. Unless you have some backwoods adventures in mind and plan to be far from the big cities in regions like the Alps or Brittany, it may not be worth schlepping your camping gear to France. Campgrounds usually charge anywhere from 30F to 100F per person depending on the facilities. Local tourist offices have lists of nearby campgrounds, all of which are marked by a little caravan sign.

CAMPING INFORMATION • Fédération Française de Camping et de Caravaning (78 rue de Rivoli, 75004 Paris, tel. 01–42–72–84–08) publishes a guide to France's campsites; they'll send it to you for 75 francs, plus shipping.

GITES D'ETAPE

Another cheap alternative, especially in rural areas (e.g., the Alps, the Vercors), is the gîte d'étape (rural hostel). Like hostels, gîtes usually feature dorm rooms and community showers and are occasionally housed in fantastic rustic buildings. Although they're often technically reserved for hikers, budget travelers can usually wheedle their way in. Some gîtes cost as little as 30F a night, others up to 60F. You can get a listing of gîtes d'etape in France in many bookstores (70F) or from the Féderation Nationale des Gîtes de France. If you're traveling in summer and early fall to popular areas (e.g., Provence and the Riviera), you're best off making reservations at least six months in advance.

GITES D'ETAPE INFORMATION • Fédération Nationale des Gîtes de France (59 rue St-Lazare, 75009 Paris, tel. 01–49–70–75–75) has a book of gîtes with prices, capacity, and photos of rentals all around France.

GITES RURAUX

If you're traveling with a family or a group of friends and would like to stay in one region of France (particularly rural areas), consider renting a gîtes ruraux—a very simple, furnished house. For information, contact the Fédération Nationale des Gîtes de France (see above), which lists gîtes ruraux for rent; request a catalog for the region that interests you (25F–80F) or order the annual nationwide guide (115F). The houses generally start at 3,000F and can accommodate 2–10 people. Make sure to make reservations at least six months in advance in summer for popular areas.

HOME EXCHANGES

If you would like to exchange your home for someone else's **join a home-exchange organization,** which will send you its updated listings of available exchanges for a year and will include your own listing in at least one of them. It's up to you to make specific arrangements.

EXCHANGE CLUBS • HomeLink International (Box 650, Key West, FL 33041, tel. 305/294–7766 or 800/638–3841, fax 305/294–1448; $93 per year). **Intervac U.S.** (Box 590504, San Francisco, CA 94159, tel. 800/756–4663, fax 415/435–7440; $83 for catalogs.

HOSTELS

No matter what your age you can **save on lodging costs by staying at hostels.** Although cheap hotel accommodations in France are easy to find, there's nothing like a hostel for meeting other travelers—something about sharing squeaky bunk beds and cold showers really seems to bring people together. Sometimes there isn't much economic reason for staying in a hostel, though, since they're often far out of town and you end up spending as much for transportation as you're saving by staying there.

In some 5,000 locations in more than 70 countries around the world, Hostelling International (HI), the umbrella group for a number of national youth-hostel associations, offers single-sex, dorm-style beds and, at many hostels, couples rooms and family accommodations. Membership in any HI national hostel association, open to travelers of all ages, allows you to stay in HI-affiliated hostels at member rates (one-year membership is about $25 for adults; hostels run about $10–$25 per night). Members also have priority if the hostel is full; they're eligible for discounts around the world, even on rail and bus travel in some countries.

Ask for the directory of hostels in Europe ($13.95). The French division of Hostelling International is **Fédération Unie des Auberges de Jeunesse (FUAJ);** your HI card is good at all FUAJ hostels. FUAJ puts out a great pamphlet showing the location of all the hostels with their addresses, phone numbers, and details like price and accessibility to hiking. Get the pamphlet at an HI office before you leave home, or ask for it at any French hostel. Most hostels run between 60F and 100F per night, and many include breakfast. Sheets are usually extra (about 16F) or you can bring your own.

ORGANIZATIONS • Australian Youth Hostel Association (10 Mallett St., Camperdown, NSW 2050, tel. 02/9565–1699, fax 02/9565–1325). **Hostelling International—American Youth Hostels** (733 15th St. NW, Suite 840, Washington, DC 20005, tel. 202/783–6161, fax 202/783–6171). **Hostelling International—Canada** (400–205 Catherine St., Ottawa, Ontario K2P 1C3, tel. 613/237–7884, fax 613/237–7868). **Youth Hostel Association of England and Wales** (Trevelyan House, 8 St. Stephen's Hill, St. Albans, Hertfordshire AL1 2DY, tel. 01727/855215 or 01727/845047, fax 01727/844126). **Youth Hostels Association of New Zealand** (Box 436, Christchurch, New Zealand, tel. 03/379–9970, fax 03/365–4476). Membership in the United States $25, in Canada C$26.75, in the United Kingdom £9.30, in Australia $44, in New Zealand $24.

HOTELS

Hotels in France are classified by the state in categories ranging from no stars to four stars. Approximate rates for stars are: One: 250F–350F, Two: 350F–500F, Three: 500F–800F, Four: 800+F (a room at the Ritz starts at 3,500F for example). A room with a douche (shower) is always cheaper than one with a baignoire (bath), but the cheapest rooms often only have a toilette (toilet), which means that you'll be sharing the communal down the hall, or a lavabo, which means just a sink and sometimes a bidet. The toilet and the shower are usually down the hall. Ask for le prix le plus bas (the lowest price) and you'll be shown to the rooms with the least plumbing. You'll save lots of money by doing without your own private bath, but expect to pay about 15F–25F for a shower down the hall. The number of rooms "with bath" are listed in all our reviews; this refers to rooms with a toilet plus a bath and/or shower, though not necessarily both. Prices must, by law, be posted at the hotel entrance, but they don't always match the price the proprietor asks. Hotel tax (séjour) usually runs 2F–7F per person per night and usually is not included in the posted price. Petit déjeuner (breakfast) is served in most places but costs about 20F–

50F, a high price for a piece of baguette and coffee; you're better off finding the nearest boulangerie or café. Many hotels will let you leave your luggage behind the desk if you want to go out for a day of exploring and are not planning to stay at the hotel again that night; it's worth asking. Keep in mind that hotels fill up quickly in summer, so it's a good idea to reserve ahead (even by a few months, if you can). All hotels listed have private bath unless otherwise noted.

UNIVERSITY & STUDENT HOUSING

As soon as students go home for the summer, many French schools rent out their rooms to travelers. To get a spot in one of these student dorms, contact the local **Centre Régional des Œuvres Universitaires (CROUS).** See the Where to Sleep section in individual cities for local CROUS telephone numbers.

MAIL & SHIPPING

Mail takes 5–7 days to make its way from France to the United States, about half that to reach Britain, and 10 days to two weeks to reach Australia. You can identify post offices by the yellow signs with blue letters that say LA POSTE; mailboxes are yellow, with one slot for letters heading for places within the region of France you're in, and one for autres destinations (everywhere else).

POSTAL RATES

Airmail letters and postcards to the United States and Canada cost 4.40F for 20 grams. Letters to the United Kingdom cost 3F. Postcards sent to most European countries cost 3F, 5.20F to Australia and New Zealand. Buy stamps in post offices or at one of Paris's ubiquitous tabacs (tobacco shops) and say "J'aimerais des timbres" (I'd like some stamps).

RECEIVING MAIL

American Express will hold mail gratis for cardholders, $2–$10 per piece for the rest of the world. Local post offices also hold mail that is marked POSTE RESTANTE. Have people address your letter with your last name first, in capital letters, and make sure they include the postal code.

MONEY MATTERS

It's hard to say how much money you need to travel in France. You may find it romantic sleeping in a run-down hotel with relatively few comforts or you might want cushy carpeting and your own bathtub. Assuming you fall somewhere in the middle, and are traveling with another person who you can share a room with, you can stay in France for about $50 a day (plus transportation expenses), more if you want to splurge, and still more if you spend an extended amount of time in Paris.

Although hostels are marginally the best deal if you're traveling alone, **two or more people traveling together are usually better off splitting a hotel room.** Expect to pay 140F–500F for a double, depending on what part of the country you are in (Paris and the Riviera are much more expensive the North and the Massif Central, for instance); singles are generally 40F less. Breakfast will cost you 20F–50F, if you eat in a hotel, and less if you go find the nearest boulangerie or café. Hostels cost anywhere from 50F to 170F per person, depending on what part of the country you are in, and campgrounds charge anywhere between 15F and 70F per person.

You can survive quite well on fresh produce, cheese, and bread bought at outdoor markets or grocery stores, but sitting down in a French restaurant for a multicourse meal at least once is a moral imperative. A three-course dinner will run you at least 70F, though **you can get a nice meal for less at lunchtime.**

Going out at night is where you can go broke fast. Cover charges for nightclubs range 70F–140F and usually include one drink. Drinks in clubs are outrageously expensive—about 80F each, and the price is no guarantee of quality. A beer in a bar costs 15F–50F, a glass of wine 15F–35F. Movies are pretty expensive (about 50F), but every theater has discount nights or matinees with tickets as low as 25F. Theater and concert tickets will run you 50F–500F, though you can often find free music, especially in summer.

Prices throughout this guide are given for adults. Substantially reduced fees are almost always available for children, students, and senior citizens. For information on taxes, see Taxes, below.

ATMS

Using **an ATM is often one of the best ways to get francs** at the excellent rates, especially in major cities and large towns (you won't find ATMs in most small towns). Keep in mind, however, that fees charged for ATM transactions may be higher abroad than at home but this might be about the same price as the commission charged on changing cash. Before leaving home, to increase your chances of happy encounters with cash machines in France, **make sure that your card has been programmed for ATM use there**—ATMs in France accept PINs of four digits only; if your PIN is longer, ask about changing it. If you know your PIN as a word, learn the numerical equivalent, since most France ATM keypads show numbers only. ATMs affiliated with the Cirrus, Plus, STAR, and Honor systems are now widely available in most major cities, but if you are planning on traveling extensively, ask your banker to provide a list of ATMs in the provinces. In Paris, Citibank Citicard users can go to Citibank on avenue des Champs–Elysées. All ATMs work around the clock.

You should also have your credit card programmed for ATM use (note that Discover is not usually accepted in France); a Visa or MasterCard can also be used to access cash through certain ATMs, although fees may be steep and the charge may begin to accrue interest immediately even if your monthly bills are paid up. Local bank cards don't always work overseas or may access only your checking account; **ask your bank about a MasterCard/Cirrus or Visa debit card,** which works like a bank card but can be used at any ATM displaying a MasterCard/Cirrus or Visa logo. These cards, too, may tap only your checking account; check with your bank about their policy.

ATM LOCATIONS • Cirrus (tel. 800/424–7787). A list of **Plus** locations is available at your local bank.

CREDIT CARDS

A major U.S. credit card (especially Visa, known in France as Carte Bleue) with accompanying personal identification number (PIN) is often the safest and most convenient way to pay for goods and services in major cities and large towns in France. Many **hotels, restaurants, and shops accept credit cards (though there is often a 100F–150F minimum), and you'll find ATMs** (see above) in most major cities and large towns.

CURRENCY

The units of currency in France are the franc and the centime (1 franc = 100 centimes). Bills come in denominations of 20, 50, 100, 200, and 500 francs. Coins are worth ½, 1, 2, 5, 10, and 20 francs and 5, 10, and 20 centimes. When you plan your budget, **allow for fluctuating exchange rates**; at press time, the exchange rate for the French franc was:

U.S.	Canada	Britain	Australia	New Zealand
$1 = 5.79F	C$1 = 4.52F	1 = 9.34F	AUS$1 = 4.55F	NZ$1 = 4.45F
¢ 1F = 17	1F = 22	1F = 11p	1F = 21	1F = 22

The French use two methods of listing prices that include centimes. While 5 francs is always 5F, a price of 4 francs and 70 centimes may be rendered either 4F70 or 4.70F.

CURRENCY EXCHANGE

Banks generally offer about the same rate of exchange as bureaux de change once you add in their commission.

Although ATM transaction fees may be higher abroad than at home, ATM rates are excellent because they are based on wholesale rates offered only by major banks. You won't do as well at exchange booths in airports or rail and bus stations, in hotels, in restaurants, or in stores. To avoid lines at airport exchange booths **get a bit of local currency before you leave home.**

EXCHANGE SERVICES • International Currency Express (tel. 888/842–0880 on East Coast; 888/278–6628 on West Coast). **Thomas Cook Currency Services** (tel. 800/287–7362 for telephone orders and retail locations in France).

TRAVELER'S CHECKS

Whether or not to buy traveler's checks depends on where you are headed. You should **take cash if your trip includes rural areas** and small towns, traveler's checks to cities. Although few merchants accept them in foreign currencies, you can exchange them for cash at many banks and almost all bureaux de change. If a thief makes off with your checks, they can usually be replaced within 24 hours. Always pay for your checks yourself—don't delegate—or there may be problems if you need a refund later on.

PACKING

You've heard it before and you'll hear it again: **Pack light.** The heaviness of your luggage is always directly proportional to how many days you've been carrying it around. Though it's important to pack pragmatically (comfortable, easy-to-clean clothes), you may feel uncomfortable if you're always dressing down, especially in Paris and other cities. In France the way you present yourself is important (some would argue too important); the French take pains to look good. Sure, they dress down and yes, they do wear sneakers, but it is definitely a studied kind of casual. You'll immediately stand out as a tourist in a complete outfit of T-shirt, shorts, and sneakers (with a camera and a hip pouch thrown in for good measure) but that should not stop you from being comfortable. The only real clothing rule to respect is **keep it simple.** It is a good idea to have at least one decent shirt you can wear every other day than a whole slew of old T-shirts. You can't go wrong with jeans, pants, or skirts with nice T-shirts and button-down shirts; expect to get a little more sophisticated at night in cities, a pair of khakis (for him) and a little black cotton dress (for her) would be perfect. It is best to think in terms of layers; a sweater for cool nights, a raincoat (the ones that fold up are great), and a large scarf you can use if it gets chilly in the evening or to cover your seat in the train or plane when you want to sleep. If you plan an extended stay, come prepared for all possible climates, and, whatever you do, bring comfortable walking shoes.

In your carry-on luggage **bring an extra pair of eyeglasses or contact lenses** and **enough of any medication you take** to last the entire trip. You may also want your doctor to write a spare prescription using the drug's generic name, since brand names may vary from country to country. Bring all the paraphernalia you need to conduct chemical warfare on your contact lenses if you wear them. In luggage to be checked, **never pack prescription drugs or valuables.** To avoid customs delays, carry medications in their original packaging. And don't forget to copy down and carry addresses of offices that handle refunds of lost traveler's checks.

The 50F bills have images from St-Exupéry's Little Prince on them, and the new rose-color 200F bills are graced with an intricate design of Paris's most famous monument and its illustrious creator, Gustav Eiffel.

CHECKING LUGGAGE

How many carry-on bags you can bring with you is up to the airline. Most allow two, but not always, so make sure that everything you carry aboard will fit under your seat, and get to the gate early. Note that if you have a seat at the back of the plane, you'll probably board first, while the overhead bins are still empty.

If you are flying internationally, note that baggage allowances may be determined not by piece but by weight—generally 88 pounds (40 kilograms) in first class, 66 pounds (30 kilograms) in business class, and 44 pounds (20 kilograms) in economy.

Airline liability for baggage is limited to $1,250 per person on flights within the United States. On international flights it amounts to $9.07 per pound or $20 per kilogram for checked baggage (roughly $640 per 70-pound bag) and $400 per passenger for unchecked baggage. You can buy additional coverage at check-in for about $10 per $1,000 of coverage, but it excludes a rather extensive list of items, shown on your airline ticket.

Before departure **itemize your bags' contents** and their worth, and label the bags with your name, address, and phone number. (If you use your home address, cover it so that potential thieves can't see it readily.) Inside each bag **pack a copy of your itinerary.** At check-in **make sure that each bag is correctly tagged** with the destination airport's three-letter code. If your bags arrive damaged or fail to arrive at all, file a written report with the airline before leaving the airport.

PASSPORTS & VISAS

When traveling internationally **carry a passport even if you don't need one** (it's always the best form of ID), and **make two photocopies of the data page** (one for someone at home and another for you, carried separately from your passport). If you lose your passport promptly call the nearest embassy or consulate and the local police.

ENTERING FRANCE
All U.S. citizens, even infants, need only a valid passport to enter France for stays of up to 90 days.

PASSPORT OFFICES
The best time to apply for a passport or to renew is during the fall and winter. Before any trip, check your passport's expiration date, and, if necessary, renew it as soon as possible.

AUSTRALIAN CITIZENS • Australian Passport Office (tel. 131–232).

CANADIAN CITIZENS • Passport Office (tel. 819/994–3500 or 800/567–6868).

NEW ZEALAND CITIZENS • New Zealand Passport Office (tel. 04/494–0700 for information on how to apply; 04/474–8000 or 0800/225–050 in New Zealand for information on applications already submitted).

U.K. CITIZENS • London Passport Office (tel. 0990/210410) for fees and documentation requirements and to request an emergency passport.

U.S. CITIZENS • National Passport Information Center (tel. 900/225–5674; calls are 35¢ per minute for automated service, $1.05 per minute for operator service).

SAFETY

Money belts may be dorky and bulky, but it's better to be embarrassed than broke. It's a good idea to **carry all cash, traveler's checks, credit cards, and your passport in your money belt or in some other inaccessible place**: front or inner pocket, or a bag that fits underneath your clothes. Keep a copy of your passport somewhere else. Waist packs are safe if you keep the pack part in front of your body. Keep your bag attached to you if you plan on napping on the train. And never leave your belongings unguarded, even if you're only planning to be gone for a minute.

WOMEN IN FRANCE

Although times are changing, the idea still exists that women traveling alone are fair game for lewd comments, leering looks, and the like. Harassment is usually verbal—always annoying, but not often violent. Dragueurs (men who persistently profess their undying love to hapless female passersby) tend to be very vocal, especially in large cities. But the threat they pose is no greater than in any big city back home.

There are precautions you can take to avoid some harassment. If someone keeps looking at you or starts talking to you, **do not try to lessen the blow by smiling at them.** Smiling to be pleasant is not something French people do. Look at French women, they have this serious, don't-mess-with-me face that they adapt for public life—borrow it. Dressing conservatively also helps, especially in certain areas. Walk with a deliberate step and don't be afraid to show your irritation. Avoiding eye contact and conversation with potential aggressors also helps. Finally, be aware of your surroundings and use your head; don't do things abroad that you wouldn't do at home. Hitchhiking alone, for example, is not a great idea, nor is walking back to your hotel at night along deserted streets. If you get into an uncomfortable situation, move into a public area and make your fear widely known.

RESOURCES • SOS Viol (tel. 08–00–05–95–95) is a national rape crisis hot line; they'll answer calls weekdays 10–6.

SENIOR-CITIZEN TRAVEL

To qualify for age-related discounts **mention your senior-citizen status up front** when booking hotel reservations (not when checking out) and before you're seated in restaurants (not when paying the bill). When renting a car ask about promotional car-rental discounts, which can be cheaper than senior-citizen rates.

EDUCATIONAL PROGRAMS • Elderhostel (75 Federal St., 3rd Floor, Boston, MA 02110, tel. 877/426–8056, fax 877/426–2166). **Interhostel** (University of New Hampshire, 6 Garrison Ave., Durham, NH 03824, tel. 603/862–1147 or 800/733–9753, fax 603/862–1113).

STUDENTS IN FRANCE

STUDENT IDS & SERVICES • Council on International Educational Exchange (CIEE, 205 E. 42nd St., 14th Floor, New York, NY 10017, tel. 212/822–2700 or 888/268–6245, fax 212/822–2699) for mail orders only, in the United States **STA Travel** (2871 Broadway, New York, NY, 10025, tel. 212/865–2700). **Travel Cuts** (187 College St., Toronto, Ontario M5T 1P7, tel. 416/979–2406 or 800/667–2887) in Canada.

STUDYING IN FRANCE

Studying in France is the perfect way to shake up your perception of the world, make international friends, and improve your language skills. You may choose to study through a U.S.-sponsored program, usually through an American university, or to enroll in a program sponsored by a French organization. Do your homework: programs vary greatly in expense, academic quality, exposure to language, amount of contact with locals, and living conditions. Working through your local university is the easiest way to find out about study-abroad programs in France. Most universities have staff members who distribute information on programs at European universities, and they might be able to put you in touch with program participants.

RESOURCES • American Institute for Foreign Study (102 Greenwich Ave., Greenwich, CT 06830, tel. 203/869–9090 or 800/727–2437, fax 203/869–9615). **American Council of International Studies (ACIS)** (19 Bay St., Boston, MA 02215, tel. 617/236–2051 or 800/888–2247). **Council on International Educational Exchange** (see Students in France, above). **Institute of International Education (IIE)** (809 U.N. Plaza, New York, NY 10017, tel. 212/984–5413). **World Learning** (Kipling Rd., Box 676, Brattleboro, VT 05302, tel. 802/257–7751 or 800/451–4465, fax 802/258–3248).

TAXES

VALUE-ADDED TAX (VAT)

Global Refund is a VAT refund service that makes getting your money back hassle-free. Global Refund services are offered in more than 130,000 shops worldwide. In participating stores, **ask for a Global Refund Cheque when making a purchase**—this cheque will clearly state the amount of your refund in local currency, with the service charge already incorporated (the service charge equals approximately 3%–4% of the purchase price of the item). Global Refund can also process other custom forms, though for a higher fee. When leaving the European Union, get your Global Refund Cheque and any customs forms stamped by the customs official. You can take them to the cash refund office at the airport, where your money will be refunded right there in cash, by check, or a refund to your credit card. Alternatively, you can mail your validated cheque to Global Refund, and your credit card account will automatically be credited within three billing cycles. Global Refund has a fax-back service further clarifying the process.

VAT REFUNDS • Global Refund (707 Summer St., Stamford, CT 06901, tel. 800/566–9828).

TELEPHONES

COUNTRY & AREA CODES

The country code for France is 33 and the country code for Monaco is 337. All phone numbers have a two-digit prefix determined by region: 01 for Paris and Ile-de-France; 02 for the northwest; 03 for the northeast; 04 for the southeast; and 05 for the southwest. When dialing a French number **from abroad, drop the initial 0 from the two-digit prefix.** But when calling **in France, dial the entire 10-digit number,** even if you are calling another region of the country. The country code is 1 for the United States and Canada, 61 for Australia, 64 for New Zealand, and 44 for the United Kingdom.

DIRECTORY & OPERATOR INFORMATION

Dial 12 to reach directory inquiries from any phone (though operators rarely speak English).

INTERNATIONAL CALLS

To call France from the United States, dial 011 (for all international calls), then dial 33 (the country code), and the number in France, minus any initial 0. To call France from the United Kingdom, dial 00–33, then dial the number in France minus any initial 0.

LONG-DISTANCE CALLS

To dial direct to another country, dial 00 + the country code (61 for Australia, 64 for New Zealand, 44 for the United Kingdom, and 1 for the United States and Canada) plus the area code and number. The cheapest time to call is between 10:30 PM and 6 AM (about 2.25F per minute to the States, 2.10F per minute to Britain). Middling rates apply 6–8 AM and 9:30–10:30 PM; rates are reduced all day Sunday and holidays. The cheapest way to make a long-distance call is to use the télécarte international, which costs 50F for 60 units or 100F for 120 units. Within France, you can call collect by dialing 12 for the operator and saying en PCV (on pay say vay), but they will add on a 44F service charge.

LONG-DISTANCE SERVICES

AT&T, MCI, and Sprint access codes make calling long distance relatively convenient, but you may find the local access number blocked in many hotel rooms. First ask the hotel operator to connect you. If the hotel operator balks, ask for an international operator, or dial the international operator yourself. One way to improve your odds of getting connected to your long-distance carrier is to travel with more than one company's calling card (a hotel may block Sprint, for example, but not MCI). If all else fails call from a pay phone.

ACCESS CODES • **AT&T** USADirect (tel. 0–800–99–00–11). **MCI** Call USA (tel. 0–800–99–00–19). **Sprint** Express (tel. 0–800–99–00–87).

MINITEL

The Minitel is a monitor/modem system that can dole out addresses and telephone numbers for all of France, receive electronic mail, conduct data searches, and even tell you the weather. You can **use them for free in any post office,** where Minitel terminals have for the most part replaced telephone books. Here's how it works: Press the button with a phone-receiver symbol on it and dial "11." When you hear the high-pitched tone, press CONNEXION/FIN. Database fields will then appear on the screen. Type in the nom (name), activité (subject), localité (city), or address relating to the information you're seeking. To advance a line press SUITE, to go back a line press RETOUR, to backspace press CORRECTION, and to begin a new search press ANNIHILATION. Press ENVOI to send your query; responses will then appear on the screen. To end your session, press CONNEXION/FIN.

PHONE CARDS

For local calls, buy the télécarte which costs 49F for 50 units or 97.5F for 120 units. The digital display on the phones in phone booths counts down your units while you're talking and tells you how many you have left when you hang up.

PUBLIC PHONES

Public phones can be found at post offices, train stations, cafés, and on the streets in large transparent phone booths. Prices for calls have dropped markedly since France Telecom lost its monopoly in 1998. Local calls cost about 70 centimes for three minutes. The few coin-operated phones left are located in cafés. **All other French phones accept the Télécarte,** a handy little card you can buy at tabacs, post offices, or métro stations.

TIPPING

At restaurants, cafés, and brasseries, **service is included,** and it's 100% normal not to leave a centime. If you love the service or you're in a more swanky establishment, then leave anywhere from 2F to 10F. Tip taxi drivers and hairdressers 10%; ushers who help opera- and theater-goers to their seats should get about 5F.

TOURS & PACKAGES

On a prepackaged tour or independent vacation everything is prearranged so you'll spend less time planning—and often get it all at a good price.

BOOKING WITH AN AGENT

Travel agents are excellent resources. But it's a good idea to collect brochures from several agencies because some agents' suggestions may be influenced by relationships with tour and package firms that reward them for volume sales. If you have a special interest **find an agent with expertise in that area;** ASTA (see Travel Agencies, below) has a database of specialists worldwide.

Make sure your travel agent knows the accommodations and other services of the place they're recommending. Ask about the hotel's location, room size, beds, and whether it has a pool, room service, or programs for children, if you care about these. Has your agent been there in person or sent others whom you can contact?

Do some homework on your own, too: Local tourism boards can provide information about lesser-known and small-niche operators, some of which may sell only direct.

BUYER BEWARE

Each year consumers are stranded or lose their money when tour operators—even large ones with excellent reputations—go out of business. So **check out the operator.** Ask several travel agents about its reputation, and try to **book with a company that has a consumer-protection program.** (Look for information in the company's brochure.) In the United States, members of the National Tour Association and United States Tour Operators Association are required to set aside funds to cover your payments and travel arrangements in case the company defaults. It's also a good idea to choose a company that participates in the American Society of Travel Agent's Tour Operator Program (TOP); ASTA will act as mediator in any disputes between you and your tour operator.

Remember that the more your package or tour includes the better you can predict the ultimate cost of your vacation. Make sure you know exactly what is covered, and **beware of hidden costs.** Are taxes, tips, and transfers included? Entertainment and excursions? These can add up.

TOUR-OPERATOR RECOMMENDATIONS • American Society of Travel Agents (see Travel Agencies, below). **National Tour Association** (NTA, 546 E. Main St., Lexington, KY 40508, tel. 606/226–4444 or 800/682–8886). **United States Tour Operators Association** (USTOA, 342 Madison Ave., Suite 1522, New York, NY 10173, tel. 212/599–6599 or 800/468–7862, fax 212/599–6744).

PACKAGES • The companies listed below offer vacation packages in a broad price range.

AIR/HOTEL • American Airlines Fly AAway Vacations (tel. 800/321–2121). **Continental Vacations** (tel. 800/634–5555). **Delta Dream Vacations** (tel. 800/872–7786). **DER Tours** (11933 Wilshire Blvd., Los Angeles, CA 90025, tel. 310/479–4140 or 800/937–1235). **4th Dimension Tours** (7101 S.W. 99th Ave., #105, Miami, FL 33173, tel. 305/279–0014 or 800/644–0438, fax 305/273–9777). **TWA Getaway Vacations** (tel. 800/438–2929). **United Vacations** (tel. 800/328–6877).

FLY/DRIVE • American Airlines Fly AAway Vacations (tel. 800/321–2121). **Delta Dream Vacations** (tel. 800/872–7786). **United Vacations** (tel. 800/328–6877). **Budget WorldClass Drive** (tel. 800/527–0700, 0800/181181 in the U.K.) for self-drive itineraries.

FROM THE U.K. • Contact **Cresta Holidays** (Tabley Ct., Victoria St., Altrincham, Cheshire WA14 1EZ, tel. 0161/926–9999) for hotel and apartment holidays. **Thomas Cook** (45 Berkeley St., London W1A 1EB, tel. 01733/335–530) offers fly-drive holidays that may include Disneyland Paris.

THEME TRIPS

Travel Contacts (Box 173, Camberley, GU15 1YE, England, tel. 011/44/1/27667–7217, fax 011/44/1/2766–3477) represents over 150 tour operators in Europe.

ADVENTURE • Adventure Center (1311 63rd St., #200, Emeryville, CA 94608, tel. 510/654–1879 or 800/227–8747, fax 510/654–4200). **Himalayan Travel** (110 Prospect St., Stamford, CT 06901, tel. 203/359–3711 or 800/225–2380, fax 203/359–3669). **Mountain Travel-Sobek** (6420 Fairmount Ave., El Cerrito, CA 94530, tel. 510/527–8100 or 800/227–2384, fax 510/525–7710).

ANTIQUES • Travel Keys Tours (Box 162266, Sacramento, CA 95816-2266, tel. 916/452–5200).

ART & ARCHITECTURE • Endless Beginnings Tours (12650 Sabre Springs Pkwy., Suite 207-105, San Diego, CA 92128, tel. 619/679–5374 or 800/822–7855, fax 619/679–5376). **Esplanade Tours** (581 Boylston St., Boston, MA 02116, tel. 617/266–7465 or 800/426–5492, fax 617/262–9829).

BALLOONING • Bonaventura Balloon Company (133 Wall Rd., Napa, CA 94558, tel. 707/944–2822 or 800/359–6272, fax 707/944–2220). **Buddy Bombard European Balloon Adventures** (855 Donald Ross Rd., Juno Beach, FL 33408, tel. 561/837–6610 or 800/862–8537, fax 561/837–6623).

BARGE/RIVER CRUISES • Alden Yacht Charters (1909 Alden Landing, Portsmouth, RI 02871, tel. 401/683–1782 or 800/662–2628, fax 401/683–3668). **Etoile De Champagne** (88 Broad St., Boston, MA 02110, tel. 800/280–1492, fax 617/426–4689). **European Waterways** (140 E. 56th St., Suite 4C, New York, NY 10022, tel. 212/688–9489 or 800/217–4447, fax 212/688–3778 or 800/296–4554). **Fenwick & Lang** (100 W. Harrison, South Tower, Suite, Seattle, WA 98119, tel. 206/216–2903 or 800/243–6244, fax 206/216–2973). **French Country Waterways** (Box 2195, Duxbury, MA 02331, tel. 617/934–2454 or 800/222–1236, fax 617/934–9048). **KD River Cruises of Europe** (2500 Westchester Ave., Purchase, NY 10577, tel. 914/696–3600 or 800/346–6525, fax 914/696–0833). **Kemwel's Premier Selections** (106 Calvert St., Harrison, NY 10528, tel. 914/835–5555 or 800/234–4000, fax 914/835–5449). **Le Boat** (10 S. Franklin Turnpike, Ramsey, NJ 07446, tel. 201/342–1838 or 800/922–0291).

BICYCLING • Backroads (801 Cedar St., Berkeley, CA 94710-1800, tel. 510/527–1555 or 800/462–2848, fax 510-527–1444). **Bridges Tours** (2855 Capital Dr., Eugene, OR 97403, tel. 541/484–1196, fax 541/687–9085). **Chateaux Bike Tours** (Box 5706, Denver, CO 80217, tel. 303/393–6910 or 800/678–2453, fax 303/393–6801). **Classic Adventures** (Box 153, Hamlin, NY 14464-0153, tel. 716/964–8488 or 800/777–8090, fax 716/964-7297). **Euro-Bike Tours** (Box 990, De Kalb, IL 60115, tel. 800/321–6060, fax 815/758–8851). **Europeds** (761 Lighthouse Ave., Monterey, CA 93940, tel. 800/321–9552, fax 408/655–4501). **Progressive Travels** (224 W. Galer Ave., Suite C, Seattle, WA 98119, tel. 206/285–

1987 or 800/245–2229, fax 206/285–1988). **Uniquely Europe** (2819 1st Ave., Suite 280, Seattle, WA 98121-1113, tel. 206/441–8682 or 800/426–3615, fax 206/441–8862).

CUSTOMIZED PACKAGES • Alekx Travel (519A S. Andrews Ave., Fort Lauderdale, FL 33301, tel. 954/462–6767, fax 954/462–8691). **Five Star Touring** (60 E. 42nd St., #612, New York, NY 10165, tel. 212/818–9140 or 800/792–7827, fax 212/818–9142). **The French Experience** (370 Lexington Ave., Suite 812, New York, NY 10017, tel. 212/986–1115).

FOOD & WINE • Annemarie Victory Organization (136 E. 64th St., New York, NY 10021, tel. 212/486–0353, fax 212/751–3149). **Cuisine International** (Box 25228, Dallas, TX 75225, tel. 214/373–1161 or fax 214/373–1162). **European Culinary Adventures** (5 Ledgewood Way, Suite 6, Peabody, MA 01960, tel. 508/535–5738 or 800/852–2625). **Le Cordon Bleu** (404 Airport Executive Park, Nanuet, NY 10954, tel. 800/457–2433).

HISTORY • Herodot Travel (775 E. Blithedale, Box 234, Mill Valley, CA 94941, tel./fax 415/381–4031).

HORSEBACK RIDING • Equitour FITS Equestrian (Box 807, Dubois, WY 82513, tel. 307/455–3363 or 800/545–0019, fax 307/455–2354).

HORTICULTURE • Expo Garden Tours (70 Great Oak, Redding, CT 06896, tel. 203/938–0410 or 800/448–2685, fax 203/938–0427).

LEARNING • Smithsonian Study Tours and Seminars (1100 Jefferson Dr. SW, Room 3045, MRC 702, Washington, DC 20560, tel. 202/357–4700, fax 202/633–9250).

MOTORCYCLE • Beach's Motorcycle Adventures (2763 W. River Pkwy., Grand Island, NY 14072-2053, tel. 716/773–4960, fax 716/773–5227).

MUSIC • Dailey-Thorp Travel (330 W. 58th St., #610, New York, NY 10019-1817, tel. 212/307–1555 or 800/998–4677, fax 212/974–1420).

NATURAL HISTORY • Questers (381 Park Ave. S, New York, NY 10016, tel. 212/251–0444 or 800/468–8668, fax 212/251–0890).

WALKING • Above the Clouds Trekking (Box 398, Worcester, MA 01602-0398, tel. 508/799–4499 or 800/233–4499, fax 508/797–4779). **Backroads** (see Bicycling, above). **Classic Adventures** (see Bicycling, above). **Country Walkers** (Box 180, Waterbury, VT 05676-0180, tel. 802/244–1387 or 800/464–9255, fax 802/244–5661). **Euro-Bike Tours** (Box 990, De Kalb, IL 60115, tel. 800/321–6060, fax 815/758–8851). **Mountain Travel-Sobek** (see Adventures, above). **Progressive Travels** (see Bicycling, above). **Uniquely Europe** (see Bicycling, above). **Wilderness Travel** (801 Allston Way, Berkeley, CA 94710, tel. 510/548–0420 or 800/368–2794, fax 510/548–0347).

TRAIN TRAVEL

Société Nationale de Chemins de Fer (SNCF) is France's railway system, and it's fast, extensive, and efficient. Be aware that trains fill fast on weekends and holidays, so purchase tickets well in advance at these times. Don't forget to validate your tickets (composter le billet) at the orange ticket punchers, usually at the entrance to the platforms (quais). If you board your train on the run and don't have time to punch it, look for a conductor (contrôleur) as soon as possible and get him to sign it. Otherwise, you're in for a nasty fine (amende). Bring food and drink with you on long trips, as the food sold on the train is very expensive and very bad.

CLASSES

All French trains have a first and second class. First class is 30%–50% more expensive, though the difference in comfort between the two is minimal, except on the lightning-fast TGV (Trains à Grande Vitesse, or Very Fast Trains) on which first class is really deluxe. First-class sleeping cars are very expensive, but second-class couchettes, bunks that come six to a compartment, cost only 100F more (check in advance to make sure that's what you're getting). When you're **going long distances, it's best to take the TGV.** Be sure to **make a seat reservation** (20F–80F), which is usually required, though SNCF now runs some **Train Verts,** which don't require a reservation and are less expensive. For information on the various passes available, see Rail Passes, below.

CUTTING COSTS

To save money **look into rail passes.** But be aware that if you don't plan to cover many miles, you may come out ahead by buying individual tickets.

If you plan to do a lot of train traveling, **compare costs for rail passes and individual tickets.** If you plan to cover a lot of ground in a short period, rail passes may be worth your while; they also spare you the time waiting in lines to buy tickets. To price costs for individual tickets of the rail trips you plan—**ask a travel agent or call Rail Europe** (in U.S. tel. 800/438–7245), **Railpass Express, or DER Tours.** If you're under 26 on your first day of travel, you're eligible for a youth pass, valid for second-class travel only (like Europass Youth, Eurail Youth Flexipass, or Eurail Youthpass). If you're over 26, you must buy one of the more expensive regular passes, valid for first-class travel, and it might cost you less to buy individual tickets, especially if your tastes and budget call for second-class travel. Be sure to **buy your rail pass before leaving the United States**; those available elsewhere cost more. All Eurail- and Europass holders get a discount on Eurostar fares through the Channel Tunnel (see Channel Tunnel, above). Finally, don't assume that your rail pass guarantees you a seat on every train—**seat reservations are required on some trains** (see above).

FRENCH RAIL PASSES • A France Railpass is valid within France only for three days of travel within a one-month period. First-class passes go for $185, second-class for $145; added days (up to six allowed) cost $30 each for either class. The France Railpass isn't available once you arrive (in fact, it can't even be used by residents or citizens of France), so be sure to pick one up before leaving home. Another good deal is the France Rail 'n Drive Pass; for only a bit more than the plain old train pass, you get three days of train travel and two days of Avis car rental within one month. A second-class pass goes for $219, and you can add car days for $39 each and rail days for $30 each (per person). You get unlimited mileage and can pick up and drop off the car anywhere in France at no extra charge (Avis has 520 agencies in France), so this might not be a bad deal for seeing out-of-the-way châteaux. Car-rental reservations must be made directly with Avis at least seven days in advance (tel. 800/331–1084 in the U.S.), and drivers must be age 24 or older. Neither the France Rail nor the France Rail 'n Drive pass is valid for travel in Corsica.

In France, there are also various train discounts available. If you purchase an individual ticket from SNCF in France and you're under 26, you will automatically get a 25% reduction (a valid ID, such as an ISIC card or your passport, is necessary). If you're under 26 and are going to be using the train quite a bit during your stay in France, **consider buying the Carte 12–25** (270F), which offers unlimited 50% reductions for one year (provided that there's space available at that price, otherwise you'll just get the standard 25% discount).

When traveling together, **two people (who don't have to be a couple) can save money with the "Prix Découverte à Deux."** Just say you're traveling together when you make a reservation or buy the tickets, and they'll give you a 25% discount during "périodes bleus" (blue periods; weekdays and not on or near any holidays). Note that you have to be with the person you said you would be traveling with (your names will be on the tickets).

There **are special fares if you're over age 60.** There are two options: The first, simply show a valid ID and you can get a 25% reduction on your ticket. The second, the **Carte Senior,** costs 285F and entitles an unlimited number of 50% reductions on trips within France and a 30% discount on trips outside of France for one year.

You can get discounts when you are traveling with a child under 12. There are special prices called the **Découverte Enfant Plus** which entitles anyone (maximum four adults) accompanying a child to a 25% reduction in fare. Simply show a justification of your child's age when you are buying the tickets. If you are planning to travel extensively throughout the year, invest in the **Carte Enfant Plus** which costs 350F and entitles four accompanying adults to a 50% reduction on the majority of all trains.

If you don't benefit from any of these reductions and you plan on traveling at least 200 km (124 mi) round-trip, **look into purchasing a Billet Découverte Séjour.** This ticket gives you a 25% reduction in fare, the only catch being that you have to stay over a Saturday. You can also get reductions if you reserve in advance.

If you don't want to purchase a rail pass, are under 26, and are planning on traveling long distances, **consider purchasing a Billet International de Jeunesse (International Youth Ticket),** usually known as a **BIJ** or **BIGE** ticket. Here's how it works: You can purchase a second-class ticket between two far-flung European cities at a 20%–30% savings and then make unlimited stops along the way for up to two months. BIJ tickets are available throughout Europe at budget travel agencies; try the European offices of STA and Council Travel (see Students in France, above).

EURAIL PASSES • The Eurailpass is valid for unlimited first-class train travel through 17 countries—Austria, Belgium, Denmark, Finland, France, Germany, Greece, Hungary, Italy, Luxembourg, the Netherlands, Norway, Portugal, the Republic of Ireland, Spain, Sweden, and Switzerland. It's available for periods of 15 days ($522), 21 days ($678), one month ($838), two months ($1,188), and three months ($1,468).

If you're under 26, the **Eurail Youthpass** is a much better deal. One or two months of unlimited second-class train travel costs $598 or $768, respectively. For 15 consecutive days of travel you pay $418.

A **Eurail Saverpass,** which costs a little less than a comparable Eurailpass, is intended for couples and small groups. A pass good for 15 days of first-class travel is $452, for 21 days $578, for one month $712. The pass requires that a minimum of two people each buy a Saverpass and travel together at all times. Between April 1 and September 30 there is a three-person minimum.

Unlike the Eurailpass and Eurail Youthpass, which are good for unlimited travel for a certain period of time, the **Eurail Flexipass** allows you to travel for 10 or 15 days within a two-month period. The Flexipass is valid in the same 17 countries as the Eurailpass and costs $616 for 10 days, $812 for 15 days. If you're under 26, the second-class **Eurail Youth Flexipass** is a better deal. Within a two-month period it entitles you to 10 ($438) or 15 ($588) days of travel.

For travel in France, Germany, Italy, Spain, and Switzerland, consider the **Europass** (first-class) or **Europass Youth** (second-class). All of the passes (5–15 days) are good for travel in any of the above-named countries. Associate countries (Austria, Hungary, Portugal, Greece, Holland, Belgium, and Luxembourg) can be incorporated into the pass package for additional fees. The basic five-day pass costs $316 (first-class) or $210 (second-class); the eight-day pass costs $442 (first-class) or $297 (second-class); and the 11-day pass costs $568 (first-class) or $384 (second-class). Additional days can be purchased for $42 each. In all cases the days of travel can be spread out over two calendar months. Call Rail Europe or ask a travel agent for the brochures "Europe On Track" or "Eurailpass and Europass" for details on adding extra travel days, buying a discounted pass for your companion, or expanding the reach of your pass.

Keep in mind that **the very first time you use any Eurail pass you must have it validated.** Before getting on the train, go to a ticket window and have the agent fill out the necessary forms—a painless but important procedure that could save you being asked to get off the train or being fined. Also, it's a good idea to **invest 10 bucks in Eurail's APass Protection Plan,** which must be arranged at the time of purchase. If you bought the protection plan and your pass mysteriously disappears, file a police report within 24 hours and keep the receipts for any train tickets you purchase. Then, upon your return home, send a copy of the report and receipts to Eurail. For your trouble you get a 100% refund on the unused portion of your stolen or lost pass.

INTERRAIL PASSES • European citizens and **anyone who has lived in the EU for at least six months can purchase an InterRail Pass,** valid for 15 days' travel in one zone (1,295F if you are less than 26 or 1,836F if you are 26 and older) or one month's travel in two or more zones (prices start at 1,700F). The passes work much like Eurail, except that you only get a 50% reduction on train travel in the country where it was purchased. Be prepared to prove EU citizenship or six months of continuous residency (rent receipts, pay slips, or electricity or telephone bills). In most cases you'll have to show your passport for proof of age and residency, but sometimes they'll accept a European university ID. To prove residency, old passport entry stamps may also do the trick, but be forewarned that each time passes are presented, the ticket controller has the option of looking at passports and confiscating illegitimate passes. InterRail can only be purchased in Europe at rail stations and some budget travel agencies; try the European branches of STA or Council Travel (see Students in France, above).

FARES & SCHEDULES

Train schedules for individual lines are available at all stations through which the line runs. Complete SNCF timetables are available at information counters in large stations. For information or to make reservations, call SNCF's main number from anywhere in France (there's a 2.23F per minute charge and they may keep you on the phone forever).

RESERVATIONS

For the most part, you can't make reservations by calling individual train stations; their numbers are only for station-related information. But you can go, in person, to any train station to make a reservation for train travel anywhere in the country.

CONTACTS • SNCF (tel. 08–36–35–35–35).

TRANSPORTATION AROUND FRANCE

You can get to just about anywhere in France by train. For long distances, it's better to take the lightning-fast TGVs (Trains à Grande Vitesse, or Very Fast Trains). You can then transfer to local SNCF train service to get to smaller towns and villages. If a train doesn't go to a place, there is often a bus to fill in the gap (see Bus Travel, above). If you really want to get out into the backroads—to explore some of the tiny hills above the Riviera or delve into the traditional lifestyles in remote areas of Brittany, for instance—renting a car or bicycle is a good idea (see Car Rental and Bicycling, above). Sometimes these more out-of-the-way areas are covered by bus companies, but service tends to be infrequent.

How do you figure out how to plan your trip? Say you are coming from Paris and want to see the small towns of Provence. You might take a TGV from Paris to Avignon or Aix-en-Provence and then transfer to local trains or rent a car there. Look into rail/drive packages, which can save you money on both (see Train Travel, above). Keep in mind that France is a large country and that you may not be able to see as much of it as you would like. One week would give you enough time to see Paris and one region nearby. Two weeks would allow you to see Paris and one, or maybe two, distant regions (e.g., the Riviera, Provence, or the Atlantic Coast). If you are planning on taking day trips from a destination and leaving your bags at the train station, note that most luggage storage lockers have been closed for security reasons and stations don't always have a luggage check.

TRAVEL AGENCIES

A good travel agent puts your needs first. Look for an agency that has been in business at least five years, emphasizes customer service, and has someone on staff who specializes in your destination. In addition **make sure the agency belongs to a professional trade organization.** The American Society of Travel Agents (ASTA), with 27,000 agents in some 170 countries, is the largest and most influential in the field. Operating under the motto "Integrity in Travel," it maintains and enforces a strict code of ethics and will step in to help mediate any agent-client disputes if necessary. ASTA also maintains a Web site that includes a directory of agents. (Note that if a travel agency is also acting as your tour operator, see Buyer Beware in Tours & Packages, above.)

DISCOUNT TRAVEL AGENCIES IN FRANCE

Several agencies in France sell discount plane tickets and other travel services for the cash-strapped voyager. Council Travel has a couple offices in Paris and Nice, as does STA (see Students in France, above). Nouvelles Frontières is the best place for discounted plane tickets all over France. Wasteels is the best-represented youth travel organization in France. For more information on specific agencies in major cities all over France, see Discount Travel Agencies in individual chapters.

LOCAL AGENT REFERRALS • American Society of Travel Agents (ASTA, tel. 800/965–2782 24-hr hot line, fax 703/684- -8319, www.astanet.com). **Association of British Travel Agents** (68–271 Newman St., London W1P 4AH, tel. 020/7637–2444, fax 020/7637–0713). **Association of Canadian Travel Agents** (1729 Bank St., Suite 201, Ottawa, Ontario K1V 7Z5, tel. 613/521–0474, fax 613/521–0805). **Australian Federation of Travel Agents** (Level 3, 309 Pitt St., Sydney 2000, tel. 02/9264–3299, fax 02/9264–1085). **Travel Agents' Association of New Zealand** (Box 1888, Wellington 10033, tel. 04/499–0104, fax 04/499–0786).

VISITOR INFORMATION

TOURIST INFORMATION • **Before you go on your trip, **you can get all kinds of information from the French Government Tourist Office or the Maison de la France. Agents for the French tourist office can answer questions about historic sites, art exhibitions, music festivals, transportation, restaurants, and lodging in the United States at tel. 410/286–8310. The Maison de France also has an office in Paris. Local tourist offices in France provide information about the destination; give out brochures (often in English) on lodging, transportation, sights, and upcoming events; dole out maps; reserve hotel rooms; and can point you in the right direction. See Visitor Information in individual chapters for more information.

**FRENCH GOVERNMENT TOURIST OFFICES • **U.S. Nationwide: (tel. 900/990–0040; costs 50¢ per minute). New York City: (444 Madison Ave., New York, NY 10022, tel. 212/838–7800). Chicago: (676 N. Michigan Ave., Chicago, IL 60611, tel. 312/751–7800). Beverly Hills: (9454 Wilshire Blvd., Beverly Hills, CA 90212, tel. 310/271–6665, fax 310/276–2835). Canada: (1981 Ave., McGill College, Suite 490, Montréal, Québec H3A 2W9, tel. 514/288–4264, fax 514/845–4868; 30 St. Patrick St., Suite 700, Toronto, Ontario M5T 3A3, tel. 416/491–7622, fax 416/979–7587). U.K.: 178 Piccadilly, London W1V 0AL, tel. 0891/244–123, fax 020/7493–6594). Calls cost 50p per minute peak rate or 45p per minute cheap rate. Australia: (BNP Building, 12th Floor, 12 Castlereagh St., Sydney, NSW 2000, tel. 02/

231–5244). **Maison de la France:** Canada (Montréal, tel. 514/288–4264; Toronto, tel. 416/593–4723). France (8 av. de l'Opéra Paris, tel. 01–42–96–70–00).

VOLUNTEERING

A variety of volunteer programs are available in Paris. CIEE (see Students in France, above) is a key player, running its own roster of projects and publishing a directory that lists other sponsor organizations, Volunteer! The Comprehensive Guide to Voluntary Service in the U.S. and Abroad ($12.95 plus $1.50 postage). Service Civil International (SCI), International Voluntary Service (IVS), and Volunteers for Peace (VFP) run two- and three-week short workcamps; VFP also publishes the International Workcamp Directory ($12). WorldTeach programs, run by Harvard University, require that you commit a year to teaching on subjects ranging from English and science to carpentry, forestry, or sports.

RESOURCES • SCI/IVS (5474 Walnut Level Rd., Crozet, VA 22932, tel. 804/823–1826). **VFP** (43 Tiffany Rd., Belmont, VT 05730, tel. 802/259–2759, fax 802/259–2922). **WorldTeach** (1 Eliot St., Cambridge, MA 02138–5705, tel. 617/495–5527, 800/483–2240, fax 617/495–1599).

U.S. GOVERNMENT ADVISORIES • U.S. Department of State (Overseas Citizens Services Office, Room 4811 N.S., 2201 C St. NW, Washington, DC 20520; tel. 202/647–5225 for interactive hot line; 301/946–4400 for computer bulletin board; fax 202/647–3000 for interactive hot line); enclose a self-addressed, stamped, business-size envelope.

WEB SITES

Do **check out the World Wide Web** when you're planning. You'll find everything from up-to-date weather forecasts to virtual tours of famous cities. Fodor's Web site, www.fodors.com, is a great place to start your on-line travels.

WHEN TO GO

Like many of its European neighbors, France is swamped with travelers in summer, especially after June 29, when all the European schools get out. In July and August you'll find many other travelers—Americans, Germans, Italians, Spanish . . . which can make things fun or overcrowded, depending on your perspective. During this time prices are higher and it's more difficult to find a space in hotels and hostels. To experience more temperate weather and less harried locals, travel during the late spring or early fall, if you can. Summer travel does have some advantages, however: more trains and buses, busier nightlife, and tons of festivals.

FORECASTS • Weather Channel Connection (tel. 900/932–8437), 95¢ per minute from a Touch-Tone phone.

FESTIVALS

France loves to fête. Most festivals are region- or town-specific and will be covered in the appropriate chapters, but a few of the biggies are mentioned here. Pay attention to when festivals occur in your travels; towns spring alive during this time, but lodging becomes especially tight.

Early spring ushers in **Carnival,** celebrated in towns throughout the country, most notably in Nice. Parades and general partying are enjoyed before Lent spoils the fun. May 1 is **May Day,** a celebration honoring workers worldwide. Trade unions organize marches, and street vendors sell lilies of the valley, a symbol of the labor movement. The **Cannes Film Festival** on the French Riviera also happens in late May, as does the **French Open Tennis Championship,** which brings the world's best players to Roland Garros Stadium in Paris. The **Fête de la Musique** explodes on June 21, the summer solstice, bringing live music to streets, cafés, and impromptu outdoor venues all over France. Do **not** miss the fireman's ball on the eve of July 13 (a prelude to the festivities of the following day) when all the pompiers (firemen) of Paris open the doors to their incredible caserns, or firehouses, hang multicolored lanterns, serve vats of ice-cold beer, and invite the world to come in and dance all night. By far the biggest French national holiday is **Bastille Day** on July 14, celebrating the storming of the state prison in 1789 that kicked off the Revolution. The **Tour de France,** the world's most famous bicycle race, wends its way through France in June and July, and it's a huge party when it ends up on the Champs-Elysées on the fourth Sunday in July. In towns all along the route, celebrations precede the Tour's arrival by a week or so. September and October see *vendanges* (grape harvests) begin, and local festivals pop up in towns throughout the wine regions.

CLIMATE

Average daily temps (in degrees Fahrenheit) stack up as follows:

	Jan. Feb.	Mar. Apr.	May June	July Aug.	Sept. Oct.	Nov. Dec.
THE ALPS	41	55	71	79	65	44
ALSACE-LORRAINE	40	54	70	74	63	42
BRITTANY	49	55	65	71	66	53
CORSICA	57	64	76	85	77	62
LOIRE VALLEY	45	57	71	78	66	47
PARIS	44	56	70	76	65	46
PYRÉNÉES	55	61	74	83	73	59
RIVIERA	56	61	72	82	73	61

WORKING IN FRANCE

There are over 3 million unemployed French people so working in France isn't easy to finagle. Obtaining the right to do it legally requires a lot of tenacity, especially for the nonstudent. France won't grant you a work permit unless you already have a French employer who can convince immigration officials that a native couldn't do the same job. However, **there are a few programs geared toward work exchanges between the two countries** which will help you obtain a long-term visa for work of a professional nature. Many native English speakers find work teaching their mother tongue to Francophones through one of the city's many private language schools. Each has its own guidelines and restrictions, and some (but not all) requiring a Teaching of English as a Foreign Language (TOEFL) certificate, which is obtainable after an expensive four-week training course. For addresses and phone numbers, **look in the Parisian Pages jaunes (Yellow Pages).**

The easiest way to arrange for work in Britain, France, Ireland, and Germany is through CIEE's Work Abroad Department (see Students in France, above), which enables U.S. citizens or permanent residents, 18 years or older, to work in Europe at a variety of jobs, for three to six months; you must have been a full-time student for the semester preceding your stay overseas and have a good working knowledge of French. Travel Cuts (see Students in France, above) has similar programs for Canadian students. CIEE publishes two excellent resources books with complete details on work/travel opportunities, including the valuable Work, Study, Travel Abroad: The Whole World Handbook and The High School Student's Guide to Study, Travel, and Adventure Abroad ($13.95 each, plus $3 first-class postage). The U.K.-based Vacation Work Press publishes the Directory of Overseas Summer Jobs ($14.95) and Susan Griffith's Work Your Way Around the World ($17.95). The first lists more than 45,000 jobs worldwide; the latter, though with fewer listings, makes a more interesting read. The Association for International Practical Training sponsors professional internships of 12 to 18 months in many foreign countries; you must be under 35 and seek a professional internship with a foreign company. The process moves more quickly if you find a potential employer before applying to the program, but be aware that it will still take several months before you're good to go.

RESOURCES • Association for International Practical Training (10400 Little Patuxent Pkwy., Suite 250, Columbia, MD 21044-3510, tel. 410/997-2200, fax 410/992-3924). In Paris, **France USA Contacts (FUSAC,** 26 rue Bernard, 14e, tel. 01–56–53–54–54) has job listings for native English speakers with French-language ability. **Vacation Work Press** (c/o Peterson's, 202 Carnegie Center, Princeton, NJ 05843, tel. 609/243–9111).

PARIS AND THE ILE-DE-FRANCE

UPDATED BY SIMON HEWITT, NICOLA KEEGAN, ALEXANDER LOBRANO,

CHRISTOPHER MOONEY, AND IAN PHILLIPS

To understand what Paris is all about, you need to understand the city's brooms. More than a decade ago, Paris decided to remake itself as the cleanest metropolis in the world. The city didn't want American-style urban renewal (this was tried unsuccessfully in the '60s and '70s), nor did it want to turn deteriorated neighborhoods into cutesy historical districts (that's Disney's domain). The idea was to keep Paris looking the same—only cleaner—so some bureaucrat decided to institute the regular sweeping of every street in Paris by hand. Of course, to do this they needed the perfect broom. After a painstaking search for the most efficient street-cleaning broom, a committee of urban undersecretaries settled on a traditional peasant model, like the ones made out of a bunch of twigs bound to a big stick. Of course, rather than use actual sticks and twigs, they came up with a durable plastic that could be cast in stick and twig molds. The plastic brooms look like their ancestors in almost every way—except for their fluorescent green color. Like the lime-green brooms used to sweep its streets, Paris is a strange concoction of tradition and high technology, of highly developed aesthetics and slightly screwy social conditions (observe the migrant workers pushing said peasant brooms).

Current president Jacques Chirac, then mayor of Paris, was the man responsible for this project. But it was his arch foe and predecessor, late president François Mitterrand, who saw through other major changes in the Parisian landscape. His Grands Travaux (literally Grand Projects, like the Louvre pyramid or the giant arch at La Défense) established him as one of the great builders in French history, alongside Louis XIV and Napoléon III. Even though the Grands Travaux were funded nationally, the biggest projects all happened in Paris. No coincidence: To many, Paris *is* France.

Paris is simultaneously a forum for politicians and self-appointed guardians of French tradition and a magnet for poets, philosophers, and social butterflies. When the government outlawed the commercial use of non-French (i.e., English) words in 1993, an odd coalition of merchants, academics, and journalists came together to protest—and the law was soon ruled unconstitutional. And, though keepers of the cultural flame try to preserve all that they hold dear, they can't keep modernity from encroaching on this city, one of the great urban centers of Europe. These contradictory forces explain how the frumpiest, run-down neighborhood bistro will swipe your credit card through a handheld computer, instantly debiting your account thousands of miles away.

Paris's tension between tradition and modernity, though, is not always apparent as you walk down the street. The city usually seems as carefully orchestrated as ever: Students spiff up to see and be seen, and

85-year-old matrons apply layers of makeup before venturing out to do the shopping. Even Paris's parks, last bastions of nature, are planned down to the last blade of grass. But when you see a sharp-suited businessman *en train de bavarder* (busy chatting) with an Algerian street sweeper leaning on his broom in front of an Internet café, you'll suddenly realize that Paris is a city of sometimes startling contradictions.

BASICS

AMERICAN EXPRESS

At any of Paris's two AmEx travel offices, cardholders can withdraw cash, pick up mail, buy traveler's checks in several currencies, and cash personal checks. The rue Scribe location is the most central and has several métro lines running by it. Have your mail addressed to: your name, c/o American Express Voyages France, 11 rue Scribe, 75009 Paris. The office holds mail for 30 days. Noncardholders can also receive mail (though it costs 5F for each pickup) and buy traveler's checks with French francs. Everyone can use the travel agencies and currency exchange offices. *11 rue Scribe, 9e, tel. 01–47–77–79–50. Métro: Opéra. Open weekdays 9–6:30, Sat. 9–5:30. Other locations: 38 av. de Wagram, 8e, tel. 01–42–27–58–80. Métro: Ternes; open weekdays 9–5:30.*

BUREAUX DE CHANGE

Before you even leave home, note the rate of exchange between your currency and the French franc. Next, change a small amount of money (200 francs will do) so that, upon arrival, you can bypass that exchange booth at the airport with its long line of grumpy travelers and its horrible rates.

For the best rate of exchange going, go directly to the Banque de France on the rue de Valois (2e) or to one of its branch offices (48 blvd. Raspail, 6e; 5 pl. de la Bastille, 4e; 31 rue Croix des Petits Champs, near pl. de la Victoire, 1e; or 1 pl. de Général-Catroux (17e). They close at 3:30 PM, but they are definitely worth the special effort. Other areas where changing money is good include the Opéra, the Palais Royal, the Champs-Élysées, and, on the Left Bank, rue Saint André des Arts. Places to avoid include boulevard St-Michel, the area around the Pompidou Center, airports, train stations, stores, and hotels.

In theory, the best way to change money is to use an ATM machine (*see* Money *in* Chapter 1). There are ATM machines on practically every street corner in Paris. Connections to the Cirrus, Visa, STAR, Plus, and Honor networks are now widely available, and instructions in all ATM machines are in both French and English. Just make sure that you have a four-digit PIN number that you won't forget because, in France, if you make three mistakes, the machine will eat your card and unless you are very, very lucky, people are **not** nice about giving it back (you'll have to trek back to the bank in the morning to pick it up).

For late-night currency exchange, you can use an automatic cash-exchange machine. To use exchange machines you need cash—and relatively crisp cash at that—and the exchange rate is not that great but, at 3 AM, who cares? Locations of 24-hour exchange machines include **Crédit du Nord** (24 blvd. Sébastopol, 1er, métro Châtelet–Les Halles); **CCF** (115 av. des Champs-Élysées, 8e, métro George V); and **BNP** (2 pl. de l'Opéra, 2e, métro Opéra).

DISCOUNT TRAVEL AGENCIES

The following agencies can get you cheaper rates than most commercial travel agencies, as well as student identification cards (ISICs): **Access Voyages**: *6 rue Pierre-Lescot, 1er, tel. 01–44–76–84–50. Métro: Rambuteau. Open weekdays 9–7, Sat. 10–6.* **Council Travel**: *1 pl. de l'Odéon, 6e, tel. 08–01–41–00–41. Métro: Odéon. Open weekdays 9:30–6:30, Sat. 10–5.* **CPS Voyages (STA)**: *20 rue des Carmes, 5e, tel. 01–43–25–00–76. Métro: Maubert-Mutualité. Open weekdays 9:45–6, Sat. noon–3.* **Forum Voyages**: *140 rue du Faubourg-St-Honoré, 8e, tel. 01–42–89–07–07. Métro: Champs-Élysées–Clemenceau. Open weekdays 9:30–7, Sat. 10–1 and 2–5.* **Nouvelles Frontières**: *Central office: 63 blvd. des Batignolles, 8e, tel. 08–03–33–33–33. Métro: Villiers. Open Mon.–Sat. 9–7 (Thurs. until 8:30).* **Usit Voyages**: *6 rue de Vaugirard, 6e, tel. 01–42–34–56–90. Métro: Odéon. Open weekdays 10–7, Sat. 1:30–5.*

Wasteels. This is the best-represented youth travel organization in town, with branches near most train stations. *113 blvd. St-Michel, 5e, tel. 08–03–88–70–03. RER: Luxembourg. Other location: 5 rue de la Banque, 2e, tel. 01–42–61–53–21. Métro: Bourse. Open weekdays 9–7.*

EMBASSIES

Australia. *4 rue Jean-Rey, 15e, tel. 01–40–59–33–00, 01–40–59–33–01 in emergencies. Métro: Bir-Hakeim. Open weekdays 9–6.* **Canada.** *35 av. Montaigne, 8e, tel. 01–44–43–29–00. Métro: Franklin D. Roosevelt. Open weekdays 9–5.* **Ireland.** *4 rue Rude, 16e, tel. 01–44–17–67–00. Métro: Charles-de-Gaulle—Étoile. Open weekdays 9:30–noon.* **New Zealand.** *7 ter rue Léonard-de-Vinci, 16e, tel. 01–45–00–24–11. Métro: Victor-Hugo. Open weekdays 9–1 and 2–5:30.* **United Kingdom.** *35 rue du Faubourg-St-Honoré, 8e, tel. 01–44–51–31–00. Métro: Madeleine. Open weekdays 9:30–1 and 2:30–6.* **United States.** *2 rue St-Florentin, 1er, tel. 01–43–12–22–22 or 01–43–12–46–71. Métro: Concorde. Open weekdays 9–4.*

ENGLISH-LANGUAGE BOOKS AND NEWSPAPERS

The **Free Voice,** a free monthly paper available at English-language bookstores, some restaurants, and the American Church (*see* Visitor Information, *below*), provides English-language commentary on Parisian life and lists upcoming events for the Anglophone community. **Time Out Paris** is a trendy magazine with listings for good restaurants, fun bars, and things to do with your kids. It is available free at tourist offices and English-language bookstores. English-language bookstores also carry the free **France USA Contacts,** better known as FUSAC, which has classified listings in English and French for apartment rentals, goods for sale, work exchange, et cetera. Most newsstands carry the **International Herald-Tribune,** as well as international versions of **Time, Newsweek, Vanity Fair,** and the **Wall Street Journal Europe.** Pariscope (3F) has a short English-language section with recommendations for concerts, theater, movies, museum expositions, and restaurant and bar picks. For more information on English-language bookstores in Paris, *see* Shopping, *below.*

LAUNDRY

Make your mother happy, and wash your jeans at a **Laverie Libre Service** (9 rue de Jouy, 4e; 212 rue St-Jacques, 5e; 28 rue des Trois-Frères, 18e; 2 rue du Lappe, 11e; 28 rue Beaubourg, 3e; 113 rue Monge, 5e; 27 rue Vieille-du-Temple, 4e).

LOST AND FOUND

Service des Objets Trouvés. The entire city shares one lost-and-found office, and this is it. They won't give information over the telephone; you have to trek over in person. *36 rue des Morillons, 15e, tel. 01–55–76–20–00. Métro: Convention. Open weekdays 8:30–5 (Tues. and Thurs. until 8).*

MAIL

You can identify post offices by the yellow signs with blue letters that say la poste. Mailboxes are yellow, with one slot for letters to Paris and one for autres destinations (everywhere else).

La Poste du Louvre. Paris's central post office is open 24 hours. At any time, day or night, the office has mail, telephone, telegram, Minitel (*see* Telephones *in* Chapter 1), photocopy, and poste restante services. During regular business hours (weekdays 8–7, Sat. 8–noon), you can also use the fax machines and exchange money. All post offices in Paris accept poste restante mail, but this is where your mail will end up if the sender fails to specify a branch. Have your mail addressed to: LAST NAME, first name, Poste Restante, 75001 Paris. Bring your passport with you to pick it up. *52 rue du Louvre, at rue Étienne-Marcel, 1er, tel. 01–40–28–20–00. Métro: Sentier.*

The **post office** on the Champs-Élysées has extended hours for mail, telegram, and telephone service. *71 av. des Champs-Élysées, 8e, tel. 01–44–13–66–00. Métro: Franklin D. Roosevelt. Open Mon.–Sat. 8 AM–10 PM, Sun. 10–8.*

MEDICAL AID

Hôpital Américain. The American Hospital, about a 45-minute trip outside Paris, operates a 24-hour emergency service and has a hot line with an English-speaking medical and dental service. If you're American and lucky enough to have Blue Cross/Blue Shield (carry your card with you), they should cover the cost at the time of your visit. Otherwise, you have to pay up front and hope to be reimbursed by your insurance company when you return to the States. EU citizens also have to pay first but can be reimbursed while still in France if they have form E-111, available at some of the bigger post offices. *63 blvd. Victor-Hugo, Neuilly-sur-Seine, tel. 01–46–41–25–25, English-speaking hot line tel. 01–47–47–70–15. Take métro to Pont de Neuilly, then follow blvd. du Château 15 mins.*

Hôpital Anglais. The English Hospital, also known as the Hôpital Britannique, in Levallois, about 45 minutes outside Paris, has 24-hour emergency service and two British doctors on duty. Here again, Americans have to pay up front and get reimbursed at home; EU citizens pay up front and can be reimbursed through form E-111. Note, however, that few staff members actually speak English. *3 rue Barbès, Levallois, tel. 01–46–39–22–22. Métro: Anatole-France.*

In a pinch, the American Embassy (tel. 01–43–12–22–22) has a list of English-speaking doctors. Hot lines to **doctors** (tel. 01–47–07–77–77), **dentists** (SOS Dentaire, tel. 01–43–37–51–00), a **suicide hot line** (tel. 01–45–39–40–00), and a **poison center** (Centre Anti-Poison, tel. 01–40–37–04–04) are available for emergencies, but there's no guarantee the staff will speak English. For **AIDS** information, call 0–800–36–66–36. Women who have been assaulted should call **SOS Femmes Battues** (14 rue Mendelssohn, 20e, tel. 01–43–48–20–40, métro Porte de Montreuil). There are no doctors on call at English-speaking **SOS Help** (tel. 01–47–23–80–80), but between 3 PM and 11 PM they'll help you with medical referrals. For drug-related issues, **Drogues Info Service** (tel. 0–800–23–13–13) is a free 24-hour hot line. The staff speaks some English.

PHARMACIES

Recognizable by their bright green neon crosses, pharmacies are a good place to go if you're having a small medical problem. By law, a pharmacist may administer first aid or recommend over-the-counter medication and, upon request, will also supply a list of physicians in the area. They also provide all sorts of useful health and beauty aids although at higher prices than the new discount parapharmacies that have sprung up throughout the city, which sell health and beauty aids and vitamins—but no medication. All pharmacies carry homeopathic medicines.

Regular pharmacy hours are about 9 AM to 7 or 8 PM, but **Pharmacie Dhéry** (84 av. des Champs-Élysées, 8e, tel. 01–45–62–02–41, métro George V) is open 24 hours. **Drugstore Publicis** (149 blvd. St-Germain, at rue de Rennes, 6e, tel. 01–42–22–92–50, métro St-Germain-des-Prés) is open daily until 2 AM. Three more pharmacies open until midnight are **Cariglioli** (10 blvd. Sépastopol, 4e, tel. 01–42–72–03–23, métro Châtelet); **La Nation** (13 pl. de la Nation, 11e, tel. 01–43–73–24–03, métro Nation); and **Caillaud** (6 blvd. des Capucines, 9e, tel. 01–42–65–88–29, métro Opéra). English-speaking pharmacies include **British & American Pharmacie** (1 rue Auber, 9e, tel. 01–47–42–49–40) and **Pharmacie Swann** (6 rue Castiglione, 1er, tel. 01–42–60–72–96).

VISITOR INFORMATION

Office de Tourisme de Paris. In spite of its airport lounge atmosphere and the hordes of lost travelers from around the planet, Paris's main tourist office is a good place to go to get information and, more importantly, your bearings when you arrive in the city. Just a few seconds' walk from the Arc de Triomphe on the Champs-Élysées; it has a lodging desk, a reasonable exchange counter, and a multitude of glossy brochures in English, which may give you a few interesting options for your stay. Do not be daunted by the coolness of the multilingual staff; they can give you lots of information on public transport and other practicalities, and can tell you about current cultural events, so **ask.** After all, that is what they are there for. The office sells *Télécartes* (phone cards), museum passes, and Paris Visite passes. Paris Visite passes are good for one, three, or five days of unlimited travel on métro, bus, and RER lines; if you plan to hop on the métro six or more times a day it *might* be worth it. If you're in a bind, they can find lodging for you, but only if you come down to the office in person. They run out of brochures pretty regularly during peak tourist season, but try to secure **"Les Marchés de Paris,"** which lists all the markets in Paris; **"Paris: A User's Guide,"** with all sorts of practical information in French and English; **"What's On in France,"** a guide to happenings in Paris and the provinces; and **"Time Out Paris,"** which highlights nightclubs and late-night restaurants. All are free. For 24-hour information in English on upcoming art exhibits and festivals, dial the cultural hot line at 08–36–68–31–12 (2.23F per minute). *127 av. des Champs-Élysées, 8e, tel. 01–49–52–53–54. Métro: Charles-de-Gaulle—Étoile. Open daily 9–8.*

Several branch offices also reserve rooms and dole out information on the city. The one at the **Eiffel Tower** (7e, tel. 01–45–51–22–15) is open May–September only, 11–6; the one in the **Gare de Lyon** (12e, tel. 01–43–43–33–24) is open year-round Monday–Saturday 8–8. Both have exchange booths with frightening rates.

The new **Espace du Tourisme de Paris et d'Ile-de-France,** conveniently located in the Carrousel du Louvre, is the only tourist office in Paris that you can call before you leave home to reserve a hotel room. (If your plans change, you are reimbursed 90%.) The friendly, multilingual staff deals mostly with one-to three-star hotels ("cheap and clean") and also sells tickets for museums and other tourist sites.

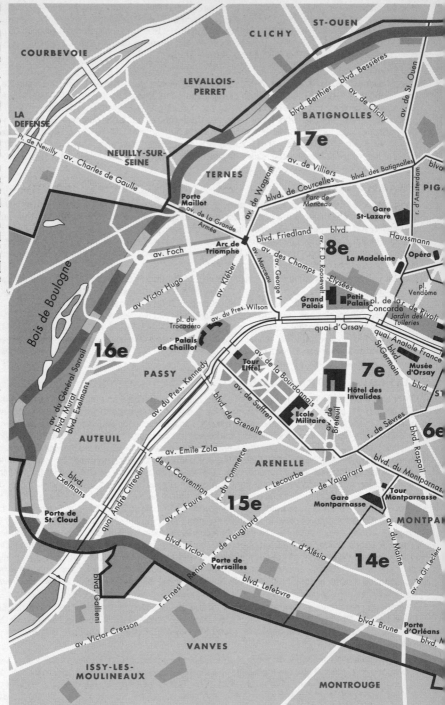

COURBEVOIE

CLICHY

ST-OUEN

LEVALLOIS-
PERRET

LA
DEFENSE

Pt. de Neuilly

av. Charles de Gaulle

NEUILLY-SUR-
SEINE

blvd. Berthier

blvd. Bessières

av. de Clichy

av. de St. Ouen

BATIGNOLLES

17e

av. de Villiers

blvd. des Batignolles

blvd.

PIGA

r. d'Amsterdam

TERNES

av. de Wagram

blvd. de Courcelles

Porte
Maillot

av. de la Grande
Armée

Parc de
Monceau

Gare
St-Lazare

Haussmann

av. Foch

Arc de
Triomphe

blvd. Friedland

blvd.

8e

La Madeleine

Opéra

av. des Champs

av. Kléber

av. Marceau

av. des Champs

av. George V

av. F.D. Roosevelt

-Elysées

pl.
Vendôme

Bois de Boulogne

av. Victor Hugo

Grand
Palais

Petit
Palais

pl. de la
Concorde

r. de Rivoli

Jardin des
Tuileries

pl. du
Trocadéro

av. du Pres. Wilson

quai d'Orsay

quai Anatole France

16e

Palais
de Chaillot

Tour
Eiffel

av. de la Bourdonnais

7e

Musée
d'Orsay

blvd.
St-Germain

S

PASSY

av. du Pres. Kennedy

av. de Suffren

Hôtel des
Invalides

av. du Général Sarrail

blvd. Murat

blvd. Exelmans

blvd. de Grenelle

av. de
Breteuil

r. de Sèvres

blvd. Raspail

6e

AUTEUIL

Ecole
Militaire

av. Emile Zola

r. de la Convention

r. du Commerce

r. Lecourbe

r. de Vaugirard

blvd. du Montparnas

blvd.
Exelmans

quai André Citroën

r. F. Faure

15e

Gare
Montparnasse

Tour
Montparnasse

Porte de
St. Cloud

av. du Maine

MONTPAR

blvd. Victor

r. de Vaugirard

r. d'Alésia

14e

av. du Gl. Leclerc

blvd. Galliéni

Porte de
Versailles

blvd. Lefebvre

blvd. Brune

Porte
d'Orléans

blvd. N

av. Victor Cresson

r. Ernest Renan

VANVES

blvd.

ISSY-LES-
MOULINEAUX

MONTROUGE

AUBERVILLIERS

A1

blvd. Ney

Porte
de la Chapelle

blvd. Macdonald

18e

MONTMARTRE

blvd. Ornano

r. de la Chapelle

blvd. Barbès

R. Riquet

r. Marx Dormoy

r. d'Aubervilliers

r. de Flandre

Canal de l'Ourcq

Parc de
la Villette

Sacré-
Cœur

av. Jean-Jaurès

blvd. de
Rochechouart

LE PRÉ-
ST-GERVAIS

de Clichy

LE

9e

r. La Fayette

blvd. de la   Chapelle

Gare
du Nord

r. du Faubourg
St-Martin

Gare de l'Est

blvd. de Magenta

Canal St-Martin

19e

Parc des
Buttes-Chaumont

blvd. de la
Villette

du Temple

BELLEVILLE

20e

blvd. de Belleville

10e

r. du Faubourg

blvd. de
Strasbourg

pl. de la
République

av. de la République

2e

r. de Turbigo

r. du Louvre

blvd. de Sébastopol

3e

r. Rambuteau

MARAIS

blvd. Beaumarchais

blvd. Richard Lenoir

11e

blvd. de Ménilmontant

av. Philippe Auguste

Cimetière du
Père-Lachaise

Palais
Royal

1er

r. de

Louvre

Centre
Pompidou

r. de Rivoli

Hôtel
de Ville

pl. des
Vosges

BASTILLE

blvd. Voltaire

NATION

Ile de la Cité

Notre
Dame

4e

pl. de la
Bastille

r. du

r. Rollin

Faubourg St-Antoine

pl. de la
Nation

Porte de
Vincennes

GERMAIN

St-Germain

Ile St-Louis

av. Ledru

cours de Vincennes

TOLBIAC

ardin du
xembourg

blvd. St-Michel

Sorbonne

r. Monge

Institut du
Monde Arabe

blvd. Diderot

Daumesnil

ASSE

Panthéon

5e

Jardin des
Plantes

Gare
de Lyon

12e

QUARTIER
LATIN

blvd.
St-Marcel

Gare
d'Austerlitz

blvd. de Bercy

BERCY

blvd. Arago

blvd. des Gobelins

blvd. de l'Hôpital

blvd. de la Gare

Bibliothèque
François Mitterrand

Parc
Zoologique

blvd. A. Blanqui

pl. d'Italie

13e TOLBIAC

Porte
de Bercy

Bois de
Vincennes

r. d'Alésia

av. de Choisy

av. d'Italie

av. d'Ivry

blvd. de Masséna

r. de Paris

Parc
ntsouris

ourdan

Cité
niversitaire

blvd. Kellerman

IVRY-SUR-SEINE

A6

GENTILLY

33

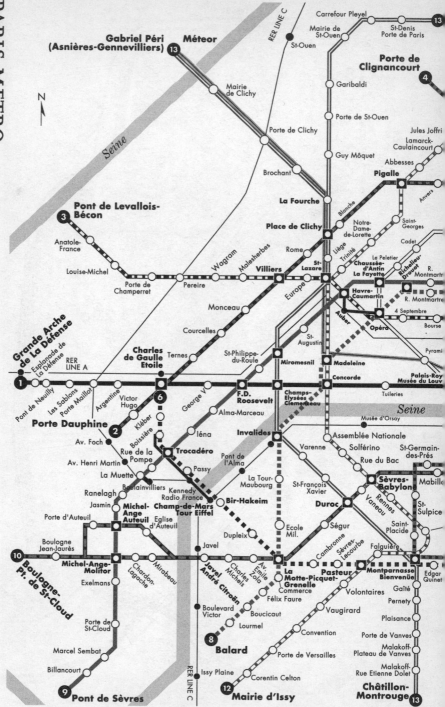

N

Seine

Gabriel Péri
(Asnières-Gennevilliers) ⑬ Méteor

RER LINE C

Carrefour Pleyel

Mairie de
St-Ouen

St-Denis
Porte de Paris ⑬

St-Ouen

Garibaldi

**Porte de
Clignancourt** ④

Porte de St-Ouen

Jules Joffri

Mairie
de Clichy

Guy Môquet

Lamarck-
Caulaincourt

Porte de Clichy

Abbesses

Brochant

Pigalle

Anvers

**Pont de Levallois-
Bécon** ③

La Fourche

Blanche

Saint-
Georges

Anatole-
France

Place de Clichy

Rome

Notre-
Dame-
de-Lorette

Liège

Cadet

Louise-Michel

Wagram

Malesherbes

Le Peletier

Porte de
Champerret

Pereire

Villiers

Trinité

St-
Lazare

**Chaussée-
d'Antin
La Fayette**

R.
Montmartr

**Richelieu-
Drouot**

Europe

R. Montmartre

Monceau

**Havre-
Caumartin**

4 Septembre

Courcelles

St-
Augustin

Auber

Opéra

Bourse

**Grande Arche
de La Défense** ①

St-Philippe-
du-Roule

Miromesnil

Pyrami

Esplanade de
La Défense

**Charles
de Gaulle
Etoile**

Ternes

Madeleine

**Palais-Roy
Musée du Louv**

RER
LINE A

Concorde

Pont de Neuilly

Les Sablons

Porte Maillot

Argentine

Victor
Hugo

George V

**F.D.
Roosevelt**

**Champs-
Elysées
Clemenceau**

Tuileries

⑥

Porte Dauphine

② Kléber

Alma-Marceau

Seine

Av. Foch

Boissière

Iéna

Musée d'Orsay

Rue de la
Pompe

Trocadéro

Pont de
l'Alma

Invalides

Assemblée Nationale

Av. Henri Martin

Passy

Varenne

Solférino

**St-Germain-
des-Prés**

La Muette

La Tour-
Maubourg

Rue du Bac

Ranelagh

Boulainvilliers

Kennedy
Radio France

Bir-Hakeim

St-François
Xavier

**Sèvres-
Babylone**

Mabille

Jasmin

**Michel-
Ange
Auteuil**

**Champ-de-Mars
Tour Eiffel**

Duroc

Rennes

St-
Sulpice

Porte d'Auteuil

Eglise
d'Auteuil

Dupleix

Ecole
Mil.

Ségur

Vaneau

Saint-
Placide

Boulogne
Jean-Jaurès

⑩

**Michel-Ange-
Molitor**

Javel

Cambronne

Sèvres-
Lecourbe

Falguière

Exelmans

Chardon-
Lagache

Mirabeau

**Javel
André Citroën**

Charles
Michels

Av.
Emile
Zola

**La
Motte-Picquet-
Grenelle**

Pasteur

**Montparnasse
Bienvenüe**

**Boulogne-
Pt. de St-Cloud**

Commerce

Volontaires

Edgar
Quinet

Porte de
St-Cloud

Boulevard
Victor

Félix Faure

Gaîté

Boucicaut

Vaugirard

Pernety

Marcel Sembat

Lourmel

Convention

Plaisance

Billancourt

⑧
Balard

Porte de Versailles

Porte de Vanves

Issy Plaine

Malakoff-
Plateau de Vanves

⑨ **Pont de Sèvres**

RER LINE C

⑫
Mairie d'Issy

Corentin Celton

Malakoff-
Rue Etienne Dolet

**Châtillon-
Montrouge** ⑬

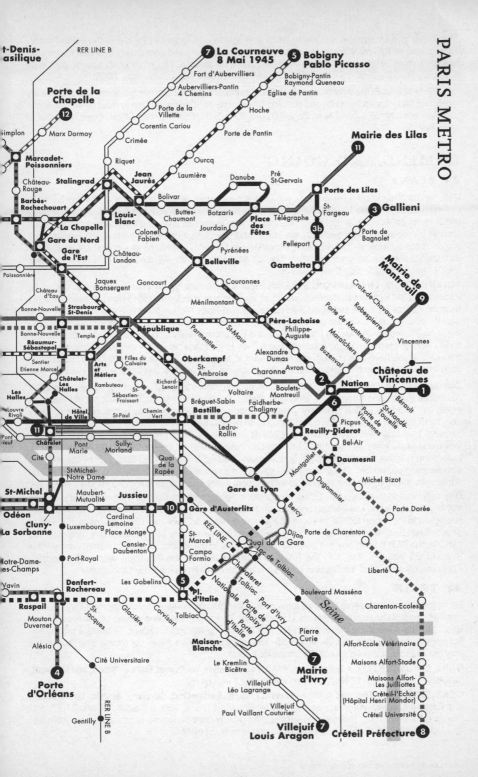

They'll also give information on reliable B&Bs and apartments to rent in Paris and the Ile-de-France. There is also an **RATP/SNCF** counter at the office that sells métro and train tickets by a staff that is a zillion times more helpful than those in the métro and train stations. *Le Carrousel du Louvre, 99 rue de Rivoli, 1e, tel. 01–44–50–19–98 . Métro: Louvre/Palais Royale.Open Tues.–Sun. 10–7.*

The utterly helpful **Église Américaine** (American Church) hosts concerts every Sunday at 6 and holiday meals and lists jobs, apartments, and contacts for expatriates. It's a great place to meet other Americans staying in the city. *65 quai d'Orsay, 7e, tel. 01–40–62–05–00. RER: Pont de l'Alma. Open Mon.–Sat. 9 AM–10 PM, Sun. 9–7.*

COMING AND GOING

BY PLANE

Paris's main airports are a fair distance outside town—**Charles de Gaulle** (known as **Roissy**) is 23 km (14 mi) northeast, **Orly** is 14 km (8½ mi) south—but transportation to both is extensive. If you plan to fly out of Paris, arrive at the airport a full two hours before departure time; you'll probably encounter long lines at the ticket counters and baggage check and complete indifference from airline employees if you're about to miss your flight. Both airports have currency exchange desks and 24-hour cash-exchange machines. *Airport information: Charles de Gaulle, tel. 01–48–62–22–80, 24 hrs a day. Orly, tel. 01–49–75–15–15, daily 6 AM–11:30 PM.*

TO AND FROM THE AIRPORTS • Both airports are served by **Air France buses** that depart for Paris every 12–15 minutes between 6 AM and 11 PM. The bus from Roissy (55F) stops on avenue Carnot near the Arc de Triomphe and at the Air France office at Porte Maillot; the one from Orly (45F) runs to the Hôtel des Invalides. The trip takes about 45 minutes from Roissy and 35 minutes from Orly, depending on traffic. Remember that in France, a bus will **not** automatically stop at designated stations unless hailed. Taking a **taxi** from the airport costs about 200F to get to the center of Paris from Roissy and 150F from Orly. If you have a lot of stuff, you might want to take the Air France bus or public transportation into Paris and then catch a cab to wherever you're staying, but note that it will cost you 6F extra per bag.

Charles de Gaulle/Roissy. Roissy has three terminals: aérogare 1, for all foreign flights; aérogare 2, for Air France flights; and aérogare T9, for charter flights. If you're trying to catch a plane out of Paris, your safest bet is to take **RER B** to **Roissy–Aéroport Charles de Gaulle.** This way you won't have to worry about traffic, which can delay the buses for up to an hour. A free *navette* (shuttle bus) runs between the Terminal 1 and the RER station; Terminal 2 has its own station. Tickets for the 40-minute ride cost 48F, and trains leave every 15 minutes. Trains start running at 5:30 AM toward the airport and at 6:30 AM toward town; either way they keep going until nearly midnight. The **ROISSYBUS,** run by the RATP, is also easy and convenient, though traffic can thwart the projected 45-minute ride time. It costs 45F, and it takes you straight from your terminal to métro Opéra every 15 minutes from 5:45 AM to 11 PM.

Orly. Orly has two terminals: Orly Ouest, for domestic flights, and Orly Sud, for international and charter flights. Make sure you know which one you want. **RER C** to Orly plus a free shuttle is cheap but slow, taking you to the airport for 30F in about 50 minutes between 5:30 AM and 10:30 PM; trains in the other direction run 5:30 AM–11:30 PM. Trains in either direction leave every 15 minutes. For a hefty 57F, you can take the **RER B** to Antony and grab the Orlyval shuttle to the airport. Journey time from central Paris is about 35 minutes. For 30F, the RATP-run **ORLYBUS** links the terminals with métro Denfert-Rochereau, just south of the Quartier Latin. Look for the emblem on the side of the shuttle.

BY TRAIN

Six major train stations serve Paris; all have cafés, newsstands, bureaux de change, and luggage storage—although most automatic lockers (15F–30F for 72 hours) have been sealed off for security reasons. All train stations are connected to the rest of Paris by the métro system. To make a reservation from anywhere in France, call 08–36–35–35–35 (note that there's a 2.23F per minute charge and that they are capable of leaving you on the phone for hours).

GARE D'AUSTERLITZ • Trains here serve the **Loire Valley, southwest France, Spain, and Portugal,** including Barcelona (9–12 hrs, 600F) and Madrid (13 hrs, 647F).

GARE DE L'EST • This station serves **eastern France, Switzerland, Germany, Austria, Luxembourg,** and **Eastern Europe,** with trains leaving daily for Frankfurt (6 hrs, 250F), Prague (14 hrs, 370F), and Vienna (13½ hrs, 510F). The station is smaller than nearby Gare du Nord and its services are more limited (open daily 7 AM–6:45 PM). The neighborhood is scary at night.

GARE DE LYON • Trains here go to the **south of France** (by TGV), **the Alps, Switzerland, Italy,** and **Greece.** Plenty of trains run to Lyon (2 hrs, 234F), Lausanne (4 hrs, 309F), Milan (6½ hrs, 312F), and Rome (13 hrs, 573F). There's a full range of services, including a bureau de change (open 7 AM–11 PM).

GARE MONTPARNASSE • Trains travel from here to **Brittany** and **western France** and the TGV to **southwestern France.** Daily trains run to Bordeaux (3 hrs, 255F), Rennes (2 hrs, 213F), and Biarritz (5½ hrs, 310F).

GARE DU NORD • Trains travel from here to **northern France** (Calais and Lille), and to **Belgium,** the **Netherlands, Scandinavia, Russia,** and **England** (Eurostar). Regular trains run to Amsterdam (5½ hrs, 223F), Copenhagen (14 hrs, 854F), and London (*see* Channel Tunnel, *in* Chapter 1). Showers cost 20F; soap and towels are extra. The neighborhood gets sketchy at night.

GARE ST-LAZARE • Trains serve **northwestern France,** and connect to the ferries to England.

BY BUS

Eurolines. Paris's lone bus company offers international service to more than 1,500 cities in Europe. If you take a bus into Paris, it will most likely drop you off at the Eurolines office close to métro Gallieni. Popular routes are to London (7 hrs, 440F), Barcelona (15 hrs, 1,000F), and Berlin (10 hrs, 880F). The company's international buses also arrive and depart from Avignon, Bordeaux, Lille, Lyon, Toulouse, and Tours. There are special rates for students and seniors. *28 av. du Général-de-Gaulle, Bagnolet, tel. 08– 36–69–52–52 (2.23F per min). Métro: Gallieni. Open daily 6–11.*

BY CAR

Expressways converge on the capital from every direction: A1 from the north (225 km/140 mi to Lille); A13 from Normandy (225 km/140 mi to Caen); A4 from the east (499 km/310 mi to Strasbourg); A10 from the southwest (579 km/360 mi to Bordeaux); and A7 from the Alps and Riviera (466 km/290 mi to Lyon). Each connects with the *périphérique* (the beltway), whose exits into the city are named, not numbered. Cars can be rented from agencies at both airports, as well as from **Avis** (60 rue de Ponthieu, 8e, tel. 08 00 51 52 53); **Budget** (160 rue Lafayette, 10e, 08–00–10–00–01); **Citer** (113 blvd. de Magenta, 13e, tel. 08–00–20–21–21); **Europcar** (Esplanade des Invalides, 7e, tel. 08–03–35–23–52); and **Hertz** (123 rue Jeanne-d'Arc, 13e, tel. 08–01–63–47–47).

GETTING AROUND

If you don't get anything else straight, at least learn the difference between the **Rive Gauche** (Left Bank) and the **Rive Droite** (Right Bank) before you step off the plane. The simplest directions will refer to these two sides of the Seine River. In the most stereotypical terms, the Rive Gauche is the artistic area; the Sorbonne and the Quartier Latin are here, along with other bustling neighborhoods full of young people. The Rive Droite is traditionally more elegant and commercial, though its less central areas are actually much cooler than the Left Bank (the Marais, the Bastille, and Belleville). It's home to ritzy shopping districts and the big-name sights like the Louvre and the Arc de Triomphe. Between the two banks you have the Ile de la Cité, where you'll find the Cathédrale du Notre-Dame and the smaller Ile St-Louis.

Once you have the Left and Right Banks figured out, move on to the **arrondissements,** or districts, numbered from 1 through 20. (For all addresses in this book, the arrondissement number is given, since it's the most common way to describe a location.) Arrondissements from 1 through 8 (*premier* to *huitième,* or 1e to 8e) are the most central and contain most of the big tourist attractions; from 9 through 20 (*neuvième* to *vingtième,* or 9e to 20e), they gradually spiral out toward the outskirts of the city.

Two million people somehow manage to cram themselves into the apartments, cafés, restaurants, bars, and streets of Paris. The long-running joke is that the streets—narrow, winding, labyrinthine, and vertiginous (except for urban planner Baron Haussman's 19th-century grand boulevards)—were paved according to the paths the cows wandered in more pastoral times. You *will* get lost—hell, most of the natives do, too. But that's part of the fun.

When you've had enough walking and you just want to *get there,* the city has an excellent public transportation system consisting of the métro (the subway system) and the municipal bus system, both operated by **RATP.** If you plan to stay in Paris for only a short time, stick to the métro; it's easier to use than the buses. To avoid getting lost on a regular basis, buy a *Plan de Paris par Arrondissement,* a booklet of detailed maps showing all métro stops and sights, as soon as you arrive. An index at the front alphabetically lists all streets and their arrondissements. It costs 35F–60F and is available at most bookstores.

RUES WITH A VIEW: SCENIC BUS RIDES

There are several bus lines that you can ride for a good, cheap tour of Paris, sans irritating commentary. Some routes are traveled by buses with small balconies at the rear, though the proximity to gusts of carbon monoxide is less than pleasant.

NO. 29: The interesting section of the route stretches from Gare St-Lazare, past the Opéra and Pompidou Center, and through the heart of the Marais, crossing place des Vosges before ending up at the Bastille. This is one of the few lines primarily running through small neighborhood streets, and it has an open back.

NO. 69: Get on at the Champ de Mars (the park right by the Eiffel Tower) and ride through parts of the Quartier Latin, across the bridge to the Right Bank near the Louvre, by the Hôtel de Ville (City Hall), and out to the Bastille area.

NO. 72: River lovers will appreciate this line. It follows the Seine from the Hôtel de Ville west past the Louvre, Trocadéro, and most of the big-name Right Bank sights. You also get good views of the Left Bank, including the Eiffel Tower.

You can also get less useful but free maps from the tourist offices (*see* Visitor Information, *above*). For information on all public transport, call 08–36–68–41–14 (in English) between 6 AM and 9 PM.

BY METRO AND RER

Except for the fact that it closes around 1 AM, the métro is the epitome of convenient public transportation. Fourteen métro lines and four main RER lines crisscross Paris and the suburbs, and you will almost never be more than a 10-minute walk from the nearest métro stop. Any station or tourist office can give you a free map of the whole system. Métro lines are marked in the station both by line number and by the names of the stops at the end of each line. Find the number of the line you want to take and the name of the terminus toward which you will be traveling, and follow the signs.

To transfer to a different line, look for orange signs saying CORRESPONDENCE and for the new line number and terminus you need. The blue-and-white signs that say SORTIE (exit) will lead you back above ground. You can identify métro stations by the illuminated yellow M signs, by the round red-and-white MÉTRO signs, or by the old, green, art nouveau arches bearing the full name, MÉTROPOLITAIN. The métro tends to be pretty safe at night, but bringing a companion is always a good idea.

The first métro of the day heads out at 5:30 AM, the last at 12:30 AM. The directional signs on the *quais* (platforms) indicate the times at which the first and last trains pass that station. Individual *billets* (tickets) cost 8F, but it's much more economical to buy a *carnet* (book of 10) for 52F. You can use one ticket each time you go underground for as many transfers as you like. For extended stays, consider getting a weekly or monthly pass, for which you need a photo. (Large métro stations usually have photo booths that cost 25F, and many film stores offer passport photos.) You can fill the card with a *coupon jaune* (weekly pass; 80F, valid Mon.–Sun.) or *carte orange* (monthly pass; 271F, valid from the 1st day of the month). You can buy these at any métro station or at any *tabac* (tobacco shop) with the sign "RATP" on the window. Whatever you use, **hang on to your ticket until you exit the métro** in case some uniformed French authority wants to see it, a particular danger toward the end of the month. If you don't have a ticket, the notoriously unpleasant "contrôleurs" (recognizable by their khaki-green uniforms and the fact that they always travel in packs) will give you a 250F fine that they will expect you pay on the spot.

Several métro stations also act as RER stations. The RER is a high-speed rail system that extends into the Parisian suburbs and is a fast way to travel between major points in the city. The four principal RER lines are also marked on the métro maps. You can use normal métro tickets on them within Zones 1 and

2, which will get you pretty much anywhere in Paris. To venture farther, into Zones 3–5—to Versailles, for example, or to the airports—you need to buy a separate, more expensive ticket.

Most of Paris's métro lines (like the bus system) are unfortunately inaccessible to travelers with disabilities with the exception of the new, fully automated line météor, but the RER is slightly more accessible. For more details, ask the **Régie Autonome des Transports Parisiens** (**RATP**) (pl. de la Madeleine, 8e, tel. 01–40–46–42–17, métro Madeleine) for its brochure on accessibility.

BY BUS

The buses are safe, and they have the distinct advantage of letting you see where you're going, how you're getting there, and anything interesting along the way. During rush hour they have the distinct disadvantage of getting you there very, very slowly.

In Paris, buses will **not** automatically stop at all stations; when you see the bus that you want, hail it. Métro tickets are accepted on the buses. In fact, even a *used* métro ticket will fly on most buses if you're subtle and don't mind a slight risk factor. If you're caught, though, you'll have to pay a 100F fine. Stamp your ticket in the machine at the front of the bus. If you have a Carte Orange don't *ever* stamp it, or it will become invalid—just flash it to the driver. When you want off, push the red request button and the ARRÊT DEMANDÉ sign will light up.

There are maps of the bus system at most bus stops; all 63 bus lines run Monday–Saturday 6:30 AM–8:30 PM, with limited service until 12:30 AM and all day on Sunday. A handy little service, the **Noctambus,** runs 18 lines every hour on the half hour between 1:30 AM and 5:30 AM; all lines start at métro Châtelet, leaving from just in front of the Hôtel de Ville (City Hall). Stops served by the Noctambus have a yellow-and-black owl symbol on them. Technically, a single ride gobbles up four tickets, though rarely does anyone pay all four; a monthly or weekly Carte Orange works on Noctambuses, too. For a map of the night-bus routes, ask for a "Grand Plan de Paris" at any métro station; the Noctambus lines are drawn in the corner. April 15–September, on Sunday and holidays from noon until 9, the RATP runs a bus line called the **Balabus,** which hits all major sights in the city and takes about an hour one-way. Buses start at the La Défense and the Gare de Lyon métro stations and stop at all bus stops with the sign BB-BALABUS. The full ride costs three tickets, though you can probably get away with stamping just one.

To figure out the zip code of any point in Paris, just tack the arrondissement number on to the digits 750. For example, for the fifth arrondissement, 5e, the five-digit zip code would be 75005—turning 5 into 05. One exception: For the 16e, it's 75016 or 75116.

BY TAXI

Even though there are approximately 15,000 taxis in Paris, finding one can be very frustrating, especially in summer. During peak times (7–10 AM and 4–7 PM), allow yourself 30 minutes to secure one—only taxis with lit signs are available. Your chances of picking up one are best at taxi stands, identifiable by a blue and white sign that says "Taxi" or "Tête de Station" or at major hotels. The meter starts running at 13F, and rates (ranging from 3.53F per kilometer in the daytime to 5.83F in the evening) are posted in both French and English on a decal on the passenger's left-side window. Two good companies are **Taxis Radio 7000** (tel. 01–42–70–00–42) and **Taxis Bleus** (tel. 01–49–36–10–10). If you order a taxi by phone, please note that the meter starts running when the driver takes the call. Your taxi driver may be able to speak a English word or two, but don't expect him or her to understand complicated directions; a map, finger, and half-coherent verb phrase ought to do the trick. Your best bet is to write down exactly where you want to go and hand it to the driver.

BY BIKE AND SCOOTER

If you feel brave enough to face Parisian drivers and bumpy cobblestones, you can zip around on a scooter or a bike. The most important thing to remember is that **drivers coming from the right have priority.** Paris is filled with tiny, dimly lit streets and Parisians drive **fast.** A good place to pick up a scooter is **Mondial Scooter** (14 rue St-Maur, 11e, tel. 01–43–48–65–80) or **Dynamic Sport** (149 rue Montmartre, 2e, tel. 01–42–33–61–82), if you're willing to part with 150F–300F per day and a deposit.
La Maison Roue Libre (RATP) rents bikes as well as helmets, anti-theft devices, and free baby seats upon request. It also organizes multilingual guided biking tours throughout Paris and the Ile-de-France. Bikes rent for 75F per day or 20F per hour; a three-hour guided discovery tour costs 165F. A photo ID and a 1,000F deposit are necessary. *95 bis rue Rambuteau, 1e, tel. 01–53–46–43–77. Métro: Châtelet–Les Halles. Open daily 9–7.*

Paris-Vélo rents bikes for 90F per day, 140F for 24 hours, 160F for two days and one night, and 500F per week. You have to provide a hefty 2,000F deposit, but they accept MasterCard and Visa. *2 rue du Fer-à-Moulin, 5e, tel. 01–43–37–59–22. Métro: Censier-Daubenton. Open Mon.–Sat. 10–12:30 and 2–7.*

BY BOAT

In summer, hordes of the **Bateaux-Mouches** (tel. 01–40–76–99–99) steal up and down the river, offering commentary in five languages and bouncing floodlights off the buildings at night. The lights show off the buildings to their best advantage, but they make people living along the river mad as hell. Dress warmly enough to ride on the upper deck, and you might avoid the crush below. Board the boat for a 48F, one-hour tour at the Pont de l'Alma. From April to September, a less touristy alternative is **Bat-O-Bus,** a small boat-bus that runs between Pont de la Bourdonnais at the Eiffel Tower and the Hôtel de Ville. There are five stations along the way, and you pay 12F per station, 60F for a day pass to the whole line. The boats begin running daily at 10 AM and leave about every 30 minutes until 9 PM.

WHERE TO SLEEP

Unless you're staying with friends (or planning to sleep on a train-station bench), a night in Paris will probably cost you more than in any other place in France. Nonetheless, soaking up the City of Light doesn't have to break the bank. It's possible to get a nice, if not large, immaculate double room for 500F or less. Expect to have to pay a minimum of 250F for a dead-simple, clean but perhaps slightly threadbare double with toilet and shower. If you don't mind sharing facilities, you can land equally spartan quarters with only a sink for about 200F. But for that price you may be better off staying in one of the nicer hostels. Unless otherwise stated, the hotels reviewed below accept credit cards.

HOTELS

Even with Paris's huge choice of hotels, you should always reserve well in advance, especially if you're determined to stay in a specific place (for more information, *see* Lodging *in* Chapter 1). If you're in Paris July–August or December–March—considered the city's low seasons—it's worth asking if lower rates are available.

Be prepared for a room that is considerably smaller than you're used to back home, and although air-conditioning has become de rigueur in middle- to higher-priced hotels, it is generally not a prerequisite for comfort (thankfully, it's not hot in Paris for long). Keep in mind, too, that the less you pay, the more likely it is that you will have to share bathroom facilities. If you're willing to pay 300F or more, you'll probably get a private bathroom. When booking a room in a rock-bottom budget hotel, don't assume that what is billed as a bathroom will necessarily contain a tub. Some rooms have toilets (what the French call *wc* or *cabinet de toilet*) or bidets only—with shower or bath facilities down the hall (and often at an extra charge). When you book, you need to specify if you require a private bathroom (*salle de bain privée*) with a tub (*baignoire*) or shower (*douche*). Hall showers (typically 5F–25F) are usually decent, but bring thongs just in case.

Almost all hotels in Paris charge extra for breakfast, starting at around 25F (the standard Continental breakfast of café au lait and baguette or croissant). Be sure to inform the desk staff if you don't plan to have breakfast at the hotel, so that they don't charge you for it. You're usually better off finding the nearest café or *boulangerie* (bakery).

ARC DE TRIOMPHE AND MONCEAU

The genteel, residential 16e and 17e arrondissements, extending out from the Étoile and the Parc Monceau, aren't packed with many budget finds. But staying here will put you within footsteps of the ultimate in Parisian elegance.

UNDER 350 • Belidor. On a tiny street off avenue des Ternes, the Belidor offers clean, simply furnished rooms at bargain prices. Singles start at 230F (sink only) and top out at 340F (private toilet and shower), while doubles run 260F–370F. The hotel's best features are the double-glazed windows and the breakfast, which is served free in a very funky, circa-1930 dining room. *5 rue Belidor, 75017, tel. 01–45–74–49–91, fax 01–45–72–54–22. Métro: Porte-Maillot. 20 rooms with toilet and bath, 27 with sink only.*

UNDER 450F • Palma. The friendly Couderc family runs this small, old-fashioned hotel between the Arc de Triomphe and Porte Maillot. Rooms have a cheery, if generic, feel; ask for one of the top-floor rooms for a view of the arch. Doubles with shower cost 410F. Five rooms have air-conditioning; all have satellite TV. *46 rue Brunel, 75017, tel. 01–45–74–74–51, fax 01–45–74–40–90. Métro: Argentine. 13 rooms with toilet and bath, 24 with toilet and shower.*

UNDER 500F • Hôtel des Deux Acacias. This fin-de-siècle hotel was modernized in the early '90s, though some of the belle epoque details remain. Singles with shower are 380F; doubles with shower are 450F. *28 rue de l'Arc de Triomphe, 75017, tel. 01–43–80–01–85, fax 01–40–53–94–62. Métro: Charles-de-Gaulle—Étoile. 31 rooms with toilet and bath.*

Keppler. Near the Champs-Élysées, this small hotel in a 19th-century building has airy rooms that are simply decorated with wood furniture and bright fabrics. Singles and doubles with toilet and shower go for 470F. There is a satellite TV. *12 rue Keppler, 75116, tel. 01–47–20–65–05, fax 01–47–23–02–29. Métro: George V. 31 rooms with toilet and bath, 18 with toilet and shower. Bar.*

BASTILLE

Spreading over the 11e and 12e arrondissements on the Right Bank, the Bastille is all about cool cafés, cheap restaurants, and more hip bars than you could visit in a lifetime. It's the only area in Paris still humming at 4 AM.

DIRT CHEAP • Hôtel de l'Europe. This small, professional outfit is popular with German tourists. It has roomy, clean, basic doubles; the cheapest (without shower) go for 185F. Ask for one with a balcony. *74 rue Sedaine, 75011, tel. 01–47–00–54–38, fax 01–47–00–75–31. Métro: Voltaire. 6 rooms with toilet and shower, 10 rooms with shower only, 6 rooms with sink only.*

Hôtel de la Herse d'Or. The "Golden Gateway," right off place de la Bastille, is popular with young travelers and backpackers. Rooms are basic and spotless; the ones off the street are infinitely quieter, but darker. A double without shower is 200F; rooms with shower or tub are more. Singles are 160F. *20 rue St-Antoine, 75004, tel. 01–48–87–84–09, fax 01–42–78–12–68. Métro: Bastille. 35 rooms, 20 with toilet and shower, 15 with sink only.*

UNDER 300F • Pax Hôtel. The Pax is no palace, which the 1970s-style lobby will clue you in to right away. But it is in a great location near the clubs and galleries and has meticulously maintained rooms with TV. Doubles with shower go for 290F; singles with sink only are 210F. *12 rue de Charonne, 75011, tel. 01–47–00–40–98, fax 01–43–38–57–81. Métro: Bastille. 37 rooms with toilet and shower, 10 with sink only.*

UNDER 350F • Jules-César. Open since 1930, this hotel has a rather glitzy marble lobby and, thankfully, more subdued rooms. Ask for one facing the street; they are larger and sunnier. For 345F you'll get a double (with bath or shower). *52 av. Ledru-Rollin, 75012, tel. 01–43–43–15–88, fax 01–43–43–53–60. Métro: Gare de Lyon, Ledru-Rollin. 4 rooms with toilet and bath, 44 with toilet and shower.*

Résidence Alhambra. You won't be in the midst of the Bastille nightlife at this hotel in a 19th-century building, but you will be within walking distance of the Marais and place de la République. Rooms are smallish, spartan, innocuously decorated in pastels, and have satellite TV. The least expensive doubles (with shower) run 320F. *13 rue de Malte, 75011, tel. 01–47–00–35–52, fax 01–43–57–98–75. Métro: Oberkampf. 10 rooms with bath, 48 with shower.*

BELLEVILLE AND PÈRE-LACHAISE

Young people, attracted to the cheaper prices around Belleville, in the northern part of the 20e arrondissement, have started to move to this immigrant-dominant neighborhood. A stay here can mean respite from the swarm of August tourists—and it's a must for Jim Morrison devotees who plan on spending days elbowing crowds at nearby Père-Lachaise.

UNDER 300F • Le Laumière. At this family-run hotel near the rambling Buttes-Chaumont park, request one of the rooms overlooking the pretty garden. Doubles range from 280F (with shower) to 360F (with tub). *4 rue Petit, 75019, tel. 01–42–06–10–77, fax 01–42–06–72–50. Métro: Laumière. 18 rooms with toilet and bath, 36 with toilet and shower.*

UNDER 350F • Garden Hôtel. This family-run hotel is on a pretty garden square 10 minutes from Père-Lachaise. Be prepared to try out your French, as the staff speaks little English. Rooms have private bathrooms and are spotless, if functionally decorated. Those with shower only are 300F. *1 rue du Général-Blaise, 75011, tel. 01–47–00–57–93, fax 01–47–00–45–29. Métro: St-Ambroise. 4 rooms with toilet and bath, 38 with toilet and shower.*

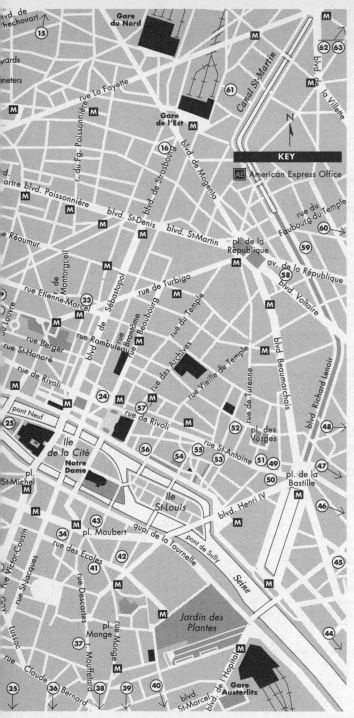

GARE DE L'EST

This part of Paris, surrounding the train station, isn't one of the city's most beautiful (or quietest) spots. But it's a convenient place to stay if you're on your way into or out of the city.

UNDER 250F • Terrage. The Terrage is a small hotel offering simply furnished rooms at modest prices. Doubles are 250F, singles 200F. *25 rue du Terrage, 75010, tel. 01–46–07–42–33, fax 01–46–07–46–72. Métro: Gare de l'Est. 25 rooms with toilet and shower.*

UNDER 300F • Hôtel de France. This modest, turn-of-the-century hotel is the biggest bargain near the Gare de l'Est. Don't expect frills: just a clean room with inoffensive pastel decor for 260F. *3 rue Jarry, 75010, tel. 01–45–23–50–00, fax 01–45–23–30–65. Métro: Gare de l'Est. 35 rooms with toilet and shower. In-room safes.*

LES HALLES

Lively and a bit more downscale than the rest of central Paris, Les Halles makes for a cheap but not necessarily quiet place to get some sleep. It's also steps from the Centre Pompidou and the Louvre. But steer clear of rue St-Denis, a sleazy (though fairly safe) pocket of prostitution and sex shops.

DIRT CHEAP • Hôtel des Boulevards. A short walk from Les Halles, this hotel has immaculate, basic rooms. The bargain option is the doubles for as little as 210F with a shower but no toilet. A toilet, shower, and TV will run you 295F. Breakfast is included in the deal. *10 rue de la Ville-Neuve, 75002, tel. 01–42–36–02–29, fax 01–42–36–15–39. Métro: Bonne-Nouvelle. 6 rooms with toilet and tub, 8 with toilet and shower, 4 with shower but no toilet.*

UNDER 250F • Andréa. You can get a relatively spacious double at this modest hotel, but insist on a room away from noisy rue de Rivoli. For the five smallish, bargain 250F singles (with sink only), be sure to book months in advance; the others are more expensive. *3 rue St-Bon, 75004, tel. 01–42–78–43–93, fax 01–44–61–28–36. Métro: Hôtel de Ville or Châtelet. 21 rooms with toilet and shower, 5 with sink only.*

Tiquetonne. If all you need is a simple, clean room on a quiet street near Les Halles, then this place is for you. If you're traveling solo, singles cost under 215F. Doubles (with private bathrooms) are 246F. *6 rue Tiquetonne, 75002, tel. 01–42–36–94–58, fax 01–42–36–02–94. Métro: Étienne Marcel. 35 rooms with toilet and shower, 12 with sink only.*

UNDER 400F • Sansonnet. This small hotel offers simple creature comforts and impeccable service. There's no elevator, but it's a small building. All rooms come with televisions and soundproof windows. Singles start at 270F, doubles at 360F. *48 rue de la Verrerie, 75004, tel. 01–48–87–96–14, fax 01–48–87–30–46. Métro: Hôtel de Ville. 21 rooms with toilet and shower, 5 with sink only.*

LOUVRE AND OPERA

You can't get any more central than this—smack in the historic heart of the city amid Paris's grandest monuments.

UNDER 250F • Hôtel Henri IV. Despite the bleak lobby and narrow, creaky hallway, the place, just steps from Notre-Dame, has rustic charm. Rooms with just a sink go for under 200F; the two with toilet and shower are 250F. Book well ahead. *25 pl. Dauphine, 75001, tel. 01–43–54–44–53. Métro: Pont Neuf. 2 rooms with shower, 20 with sink only. Cash only.*

UNDER 300 • Lille. Location, location, location: This is on a quiet little street just up from the Louvre, next to Palais Royal and around the corner from the St-Honoré shopping street. It ain't the Ritz, but the rooms are clean and quaint, with doubles starting at 240F (no shower). Nos. 1, 4, 7 and 10 are somewhat somber, but the other nine are just right. *8 rue du Pélican, 75001, tel. 01–42–33–33–42. Métro: Palais-Royal. 6 rooms with shower, 7 with sink and bidet only.*

UNDER 350F • Hôtel Haussmann. Near the grands magasins and right behind the Opéra, you'll find this clean, small, professionally run place. Mostly French people stay here, hence the slightly smoky rooms and ubiquitous mirrors. Book ahead: At this price (330F for a double), rooms go fast. *89 rue de Provence, 75009, tel. 01–48–74–24–57, fax 01–44–91–97–25. Métro: Havre-Caumartin. 32 rooms with toilet and bath.*

UNDER 400F • Hôtel des Arts. Geranium pots in the windows, a pretty pink facade, and Babar the talking parrot at the reception desk set this smooth-running establishment apart from the many other hotels in the neighborhood. All rooms have cable TV, hair dryers, and soundproof windows. Doubles start at 380F. *7 cité Bergère, 75009, tel. 01–42–46–73–30, fax 01–48–00–94–42. Métro: Rue Montmartre. 26 rooms with toilet and shower.*

UNDER 500F • Louvre Forum. The central location and the eager-to-please staff make this hotel a good place to stay, not to mention the clean, comfortable, well-equipped rooms (featuring satellite TV) starting at 425F (350F off-season). Breakfast is served in the vaulted cellar. *25 rue du Bouloi, 75001, tel. 01–42–36–54–19, fax 01–42–33–66–31. Métro: Louvre. 11 rooms with toilet and bath, 16 with toilet and shower. Bar.*

LE MARAIS

The Marais is Paris's answer to Greenwich Village, a Seine-side neighborhood sandwiched between Les Halles and the Bastille. It brims with Revolution-era architecture, fun shops, a clutch of kosher delis, an active gay community, and myriad wine bars and cafés.

UNDER 350F • Castex. This hotel in a Revolution-era building has rooms (320F to 360F) that are low on frills but squeaky clean, plus friendly owners. It's often booked months ahead, so reserve early. There's no elevator, and the only TV is on the ground floor. *5 rue Castex, 75004, tel. 01–42–72–31–52, fax 01–42–72–57–91. Métro: St-Paul. 4 rooms with toilet and bath, 23 with toilet and shower.*

Grand Hôtel Jeanne-d'Arc. At this recently renovated hotel you'll get a good-size, spotless, modern double with a bathroom, TV, telephone, and maybe even a couch for 310F and up. It's a good place for families, as there are rooms with extra single beds (an additional 75F) and the friendly, English-speaking manager will set up cribs or cots as needed. *3 rue de Jarente, 75004, tel. 01–48–87–62–11, fax 01–48–87–62–11. Métro: St-Paul. 36 rooms with toilet and shower.*

UNDER 450F • Hôtel du 7e Art. The theme of this hip Marais hotel is Hollywood from the '40s to the '60s. Rates start at 420F (but go as high as 670F), so ask for one of the cheaper rooms. It will be small and spartan, but clean, quiet, and equipped with cable TV. There's no elevator. *20 rue St-Paul, 75004, tel. 01–42–77–04–03, fax 01–42–77–69–10. Métro: St-Paul. 9 rooms with toilet and bath, 14 with toilet and shower. Bar, in-room safes.*

SPLURGE • Place des Vosges. An eclectic and loyal clientele swears by this small, historic hotel just off place des Vosges. Splurge on a top-floor room with a view (610F); the least expensive rooms (365F) are the size of walk-in closets. *12 rue de Biragues, 75004, tel. 01–42–72–60–46, fax 01–42–72–02–64. Métro: St-Paul. 11 rooms with toilet and bath, 5 with toilet and shower.*

MONTMARTRE

Perched on the northern edge of the city, Montmartre epitomizes Paris's bohemian alter ego. Most major attractions are just 10 minutes by métro, making it a good bet if you're budget-minded and into experiencing more than just the main sights.

UNDER 300F • Style. The style in question is Art Deco, from the wallpaper to the glass tulip lamps on the bedside tables. Doubles with bath or shower go for 287F. Ask for a room with a fireplace on the garden courtyard. *8 rue Ganneron, 75018, tel 01–45–22–37–59, fax 01–45–22–81–03. Métro: Place-de-Clichy/La Fourche. 70 rooms with toilet and shower, 10 with sink only.*

UNDER 400F • Grand Hôtel de Turin. Although it's on the seedy side of Montmartre near the Moulin Rouge, this hotel has clean, surprisingly spacious rooms with comfortable beds. Doubles go for 340F. *6 rue Victor-Massé, 75009, tel. 01–48–78–45–26, fax 01–42–80–61–50. Métro: Pigalle. 14 rooms with toilet and bath, 37 with toilet and shower.*

UNDER 450F • Regyn's Montmartre. Rooms here (starting at 430F) are smallish but comfortable. Each floor is dedicated to a Montmartre artist. Ask for a room on the top two floors for great views of the Eiffel Tower or the Sacré-Coeur. *18 pl. des Abbesses, 75018, tel. 01–42–54–45–21, fax 01–42–23–76–69. Métro: Abbesses. 14 rooms with toilet and bath, 8 with toilet and shower. In-room safes.*

Utrillo. For 440F you get fabulous views *and* a sauna at this hotel on a quiet side street. The Impressionist prints and marble-top breakfast tables in every room feel charmingly old-fashioned. Two rooms (Nos. 61 and 63) have views of the Eiffel Tower. *7 rue Aristide-Bruant, 75018, tel. 01–42–58–13–44, fax 01–42–23–93–88. Métro: Abbesses. 5 rooms with toilet and bath, 25 with toilet and shower.*

MONTPARNASSE

Montparnasse expands across the sprawling 14e arrondissement and nudges its way into neighboring Left Bank districts, including the Quartier Latin and St-Germain.

DIRT CHEAP • Hôtel de l'Espérance. Book well ahead for a 190F double at this "Hotel of Hope" on a small street. Rooms either look shabby or hopelessly romantic, depending on your disposition, but the proprietress is eager to please. *1 rue de Grancey, 75014, tel. 01–43–21–41–04, fax 01–43–22–06–02. Métro: Denfert-Rochereau. 4 rooms with shower, 13 with sink only.*

UNDER 350F • Beaunier. A friendly welcome, a flower-filled patio, satellite TV, and well-kept, if basic, rooms make this hotel a good choice. Doubles go for 330F. *31 rue Beaunier, 75014, tel. 01–45–39–36–45, fax 01–45–39–33–55. Métro: Porte d'Orléans. 19 rooms with toilet and bath.*

Broussais Bon Secours. This little hotel is ideal if you require little more than a clean room and a good bed. Doubles are 330F, with a special weekend rate of 195F per night. A communal refrigerator is available in the salon. *3 rue Ledion, 75014, tel. 01–40–44–48–90, fax 01–40–44–96–76. Métro: Plaisance. 25 rooms with toilet and shower.*

Parc Montsouris. This modest, recently renovated hotel in a 1930s villa (really more of a small house) is on a quiet street next to the Parc Montsouris. For 340F you'll get a small, tastefully done room with shower and satellite TV. *4 rue du Parc-Montsouris, 75014, tel. 01–45–89–09–72, fax 01–45–80–92–72. Métro: Montparnasse-Bienvenue. 28 rooms with toilet and bath, 7 with toilet and shower.*

NEAR THE EIFFEL TOWER

This is the Left Bank at its poshest. Stately apartment buildings line the wide, tree-lined avenues of the 7e arrondissement, often invisible to the hordes of tourists rushing to the Eiffel Tower and Les Invalides.

UNDER 350F • Family. This well-run hotel has clean rooms and an efficient staff. For 350F you'll get a spick-and-span, if basic, double equipped with a kitchenette—a great way to save a few francs by cooking at "home." *23 rue Fondary, 75015, 01–45–75–20–49, 01–45–77–70–73. Métro: Dupleix. 19 rooms with toilet and shower. Kitchenettes.*

UNDER 450F • Champ de Mars. Only a stone's throw from the rue Cler market and the Eiffel Tower, this little gem has comfortable rooms in cheery blue-and-yellow French country-house style. They're also equipped with satellite TV and CNN. Doubles with shower are 380F. *7 rue du Champ de Mars, 75007, tel. 01–45–51–52–30, fax 01–45–51–64–36. Métro: École Militaire. 19 rooms with toilet and bath, 6 with toilet and shower.*

Grand Hôtel Lévêque. On one of Paris's best market streets, this immaculate hotel has an eager-to-please staff, comfortable rooms, and satellite TV. Doubles are 420F. *29 rue Cler, 75007, tel. 01–47–05–49–15, fax 01–45–50–49–36. Métro: École Militaire. 45 rooms with toilet and shower, 5 with sink only. In-room safes.*

Nevers. In a cozy, 18th-century town house—on one of the city's ritziest streets—this hotel epitomizes unpretentious charm. Rooms are tiny, but they get lots of light and individual touches give them a homey atmosphere. Ask for No. 11, which has a terrace and a good view. Doubles are 470F. *83 rue du Bac, 75007, tel. 01–45–44–61–30, fax 01–42–22–29–47. Métro: Sèvres-Babylone. 11 rooms with toilet and bath.*

Tour Eiffel Dupleix. Ask for one of the rooms with a view of the Eiffel Tower at this comfortable hotel. All have modern bathrooms and cable TV. Doubles with shower are 460F, but in July and August they're 390F. *11 rue Juge, 75015, tel. 01–45–78–29–29, fax 01–45–78–60–00. Métro: Dupleix. 30 rooms with toilet and bath, 10 with toilet and shower. Laundry.*

PLACE D'ITALIE

The often overlooked 13e arrondissement has traditionally been a working-class district. Here you'll find Paris's Chinatown and the appealing Butte aux Cailles neighborhood, with its hilly cobblestone streets and old houses. The hub of this area is busy place d'Italie.

DIRT CHEAP • Coypel. Rooms at the Coypel are immaculate and basic in style, and have soundproof windows to block out the noise from the street below. Doubles with sink only can be had for under 160F; private bathrooms run 240F. *2 rue Coypel, 75013, tel. 01–43–31–18–08, fax 01–47–07–27–45. Métro: Place d'Italie. 30 rooms with toilet and shower, 9 with sink and bidet only.*

Tolbiac. This recently renovated hotel offers sun-filled, spacious rooms for under 250F and copious breakfasts for 25F. Ask for a room off the street, preferably 29, 39 or 49—they're the biggest and brightest. *122 rue de Tolbiac, 75013, tel. 01–44–24–25–54, fax 01–45–87–43–47. Métro: Tolbiac. 19 rooms with toilet and shower, 19 with sink only.*

QUARTIER LATIN

The Quartier Latin is one of the most heavily visited districts in the city, but it still delivers a very real, laid-back Paris experience.

DIRT CHEAP • Médicis. If you're looking for a Left Bank garret in which to hang your beret, and don't mind sharing a hall bathroom with other wanna-be bohemians, then this scruffy landmark is the place. Not much has changed here since Jim Morrison stayed in No. 4 some 30 years ago. Singles start at 80F, doubles at 170F. No reservations are accepted. *214 rue Saint-Jacques, 75005, tel. 01–56–24–02–82, fax 01–43–54–14–66. Métro: Luxembourg. 27 rooms with sink only.*

UNDER 250 • Port-Royal Hôtel. All spruced up after recent renovations, this simple, one-star hotel sports a pretty patio and cut-rate prices. Rooms on the street are soundproofed, but ask for one in back just the same. Singles start at 185F and doubles range 245F–365F. *8 blvd. Port-Royal, 75005, tel. 01–43–31–70–06, fax 01–43–31–33–67. Métro: Gobelins. 20 rooms with toilet and shower, 26 with sink only.*

UNDER 350F • Marignan. A friendly French-American couple owns this modest hotel with functionally decorated rooms. Doubles with shared facilities are 320F; with a private bathroom they're 350F. *13 rue du Sommerard, 75005, tel. 01–43–54–63–81. Métro: Maubert-Mutualité. 10 rooms with toilet and shower, 20 with sink only. Laundry.*

UNDER 450F • Cluny-Sorbonne. Overlooking the Sorbonne, this hotel has neoclassic furnishings and old-fashioned glass lamp shades. The staff is friendly and the feel of the place is relaxed. Doubles start at 430F. *8 rue Victor-Cousin, 75005, tel. 01–43–54–66–66, fax 01–43–29–68–07. Métro: Luxembourg. 12 rooms with toilet and bath, 12 with toilet and shower.*

SPLURGE • Familia. Rooms start at 380F, then climb to above 450F for a walk-out balcony on the second or fifth floor (well worth the price). Or ask for a room with a sepia fresco depicting a celebrated Paris monument; others are furnished with Louis XV–style furnishings. *11 rue des Écoles, 75005, tel. 01–43–54–55–27, fax 01–43–29–61–77. Métro: Cardinal-Lemoine. 14 rooms with toilet and bath, 16 with toilet and shower.*

Grandes Écoles. Rooms here cost 510F, but it's worth splurging to feel like you're staying at a country cottage. Louis-Philippe–style furnishings, lace bedspreads, and the absence of TV all add to the rustic ambience. *75 rue du Cardinal-Lemoine, 75005, tel. 01–43–26–79–23, fax 01–43–25–28–15. Métro: Cardinal-Lemoine. 45 rooms with toilet and bath, 6 with toilet and shower.*

ST-GERMAIN-DES-PRÉS

This Left Bank district bordering the Seine cradles the oldest church in Paris (Église St-Germain) and has some of the most captivating and romantic streets in the city.

UNDER 400F • Hôtel du Globe. At this tiny hotel, very French floral fabrics, wood beams, and, if you're lucky, a canopy bed give it a rustic feel. Though the cheapest rooms (390F) are very small, they make you feel like you're in your own little garret. Reserve at least two weeks ahead. *15 rue des Quatre-Vents, 75006, tel. 01–46–33–62–69. Métro: Mabillon. 6 rooms with toilet and bath, 9 with toilet and shower. Closed Aug.*

Petit Trianon. Overlooking the lively rue de Buci market, this little hotel has sunny rooms with old-style upholsteries and a better quality of furnishings than you normally get for this price. The least expensive doubles (with toilet and shower) are 300F (though they go up to 700F) and the least expensive singles are 170F. But be forewarned: Prices vacillate according to season, so always get confirmation in writing. *2 rue de l'Ancienne-Comédie, 75006, tel. 01–43–54–94–64. Métro: Odéon. 12 rooms with toilet and shower, 1 with sink only.*

UNDER 450F • Acacias St-Germain. If you book early enough, you can snag one of the least expensive rooms (doubles start at 400F but go up as high as 700F). Everything is done up in *style anglais* (English style), with sturdy pine furniture and summery upholstery. Ask about weekend discounts. *151 bis rue de Rennes, 75006, tel. 01–45–48–97–38, fax 01–45–44–63–57. Métro: St-Placide. 33 rooms and 4 apartments with bath, 8 rooms with shower. In-room safes, laundry.*

HOSTELS AND FOYERS

At 100F–170F a night for a bed in a clean room with free showers and breakfast, Paris's many hostels and foyers are not only a bargain but they're placed in some of the city's prime locations. Furthermore, they're great places to meet people, find travel companions, get tips, and hear about other travelers' adventures (or misadventures). And if you're traveling solo—and sick of being stiffed for a double rate by hotels—this is definitely the cheapest way to go, regardless of your age. Note that hostels and foyers often have fairly strict rules regarding curfews, late-night carousing, and alcohol intake, but be prepared for the occasional rowdy group making your night a sleepless hell.

In summer, you should reserve *in writing* a month in advance. You'll probably have to provide a credit card number or fork over a deposit for the first night, so don't forget to get written confirmation in case of a mix-up. Because hostels book up quickly in summer, it's a good idea to check in as early as 7 AM. Unless otherwise noted, assume that hostels take MasterCard and Visa.

HI HOSTELS

All three HI hostels are run by the Fédération Unie des Auberges de Jeunesse (FUAJ), the French branch of Hostelling International. For 130F, you'll nab a bed, sheets, shower, and breakfast. Best of all, there's no curfew, which is a rare thing among Paris's hostels. Most rooms are single-sex, although if it's really crowded they'll put you wherever they can. To reserve a space ahead of time at the Cité des Sciences or d'Artagnan hostel, call the HI-AYH office in Washington, D.C. (tel. 202/783–6161) and give them your credit card number; they'll charge you for the price of a night's stay plus a $6 booking fee. The third HI hostel is at 84 boulevard Jules-Ferry and doesn't take reservations. Show up before 10 AM to secure a spot. Be sure to note the afternoon lockout hours (noon–3 PM). First you'll need a hostel card, which you can buy for 100F at any of four FUAJ offices. **FUAJ Beaubourg:** *9 rue Brantôme, 75003, tel. 01–48–04–70–40, métro Châtelet.* **FUAJ Ile de France:** *9 rue Notre-Dame-de-Lorette, 75009, tel. 01–42–85–55–40, métro Notre-Dame de Lorette.* **FUAJ République:** *4 blvd. Jules-Ferry, 75011, tel. 01–43–57–02–60, métro République.* **FUAJ Centre National:** *27 rue Pajol, 75018, tel. 01–44–89–87–27, métro La Chapelle.*

Auberge de Jeunesse d'Artagnan. This clean, enormous hostel is only steps away from Père-Lachaise. It gets loud and packed in summer. A bed in a three- or four-bed dorm room costs 110F (including sheets and breakfast); beds in double rooms go for 121F (130F with private shower). Three meals are served daily (menus for 28F–50F) at the very social bar and cafeteria. *80 rue Vitruve, 75020, tel. 01–43–61–08–75, fax 01–40–32–34–55. Métro: Porte de Bagnolet. 411 beds. Reception open 8 AM–midnight. Lockout noon–3. Laundry.*

Auberge de Jeunesse Cité des Sciences. Although technically in the suburbs, this hostel is well served by the ever-efficient métro, so you can be smack in the center of Paris in less than 20 minutes. A mellow staff welcomes you to standard three- to six-bed dorm rooms. Though the rooms close every day noon–3 PM, the reception desk and a small common room stay open 24 hours. Beds cost 110F per night. *24 rue des Sept-Arpents, 93000 rue du Pré-St-Gervais, tel. 01–48–43–24–11, fax 01–48–43–26–82. Métro: Hoche. 128 beds. Reception open 24 hrs. Lockout noon–3 PM. Laundry.*

Auberge de Jeunesse Jules-Ferry. Come early and be ready to socialize. This hostel is extremely popular with friendly and rowdy backpackers. It's also well located, overlooking a canal of the Seine and close to place de la République and the Bastille. Bed and breakfast in a dorm runs 115F (120F per person for the few doubles). Cheap food and groceries are close by, as are clubs and cafés. *8 blvd. Jules-Ferry, 75011, tel. 01–43–57–55–60, fax 01–40–21–79–92. Métro: République. 100 beds. Reception open 24 hrs. Lockout 10–2.*

PRIVATE HOSTELS

Aloha Hostel. This welcoming place has rooms that sleep two to six. Supermarkets, laundromats, and La Tour Eiffel are all nearby—you'll feel particularly safe in the midst of the hubbub if you're traveling alone. The friendly, English-speaking staff will usually let the one-week maximum stay slide during the school year. You'll pay 127F (107F off-season) per person for a double, 107F (97F off-season) for a dorm bed. Guests have kitchen access until 11 PM. *1 rue Borromée, 75015, tel. 01–42–73–03–03, fax 01–42–73–14–14. Métro: Volontaires. 140 beds. Reception open 8 AM–2 AM. Curfew 1:30 AM, lockout 11–5. Kitchen.*

Le Village. Though a tad pricier than the competition, this brand-new 26-room hostel is a notch above the rest—it has beautiful rooms for two to six people, with wood-beamed ceilings and spectacular views of the nearby Sacré-Coeur (especially stunning from the sixth floor). Breakfast is included in the price (247F for a double), and the café-bar and terrace stay open until 2 AM. *20 rue d'Orsel, 75018, tel. 01–42–64–22–02, fax 01–42–64–22–04. Métro: Abbesses. 26 rooms with toilet and shower. Kitchen. Internet access.*

Young and Happy Youth Hostel. Among the cafés, shops, and restaurants of rue Mouffetard in the Latin Quarter, this hostel is no stranger to young American and Japanese travelers. A double costs 247F, while a bed in one of the dorm rooms (three to six beds) costs 107F. The rooms are clean and a simple breakfast is included. Sheets rent for 15F, towels 5F. Phone reservations with Visa or MasterCard are accepted; otherwise try to show up before 11 AM. *80 rue Mouffetard, 75005, tel. 01–45–35–09–53. Métro: Monge. 75 beds. Curfew 2 AM, lockout 11–5.*

BVJ FOYERS

Both of these two foyers for travelers aged 16–35 are in great locations. The immaculate rooms hold up to 10 people. For 120F, you'll get a bed, breakfast, sheets, and a shower, plus access to the kitchen, 10F lockers, and a 24-hour reception desk. Unfortunately, you can't make reservations, so show up early in the morning. If one branch is booked, the staff will call the other for you. Singles cost 10F more in the Quartier Latin. The Louvre location has a restaurant, where guests at any of the four foyers can eat for 55F. There's also a shuttle service to Orly (59F) and Charles de Gaulle (69F), which you can reserve at the desk. **BVJ de Paris/Louvre:** 20 rue J.-J. Rousseau, 75001, tel. 01–42–36–88–18, fax 01–42–33–82–10, métro Palais-Royal. **BVJ de Paris/Quartier Latin:** 44 rue des Bernardins, 75005, tel. 01–43–29–34–80, fax 01–42–33–40–53, métro Maubert-Mutualité.

MIJE FOYERS

In a trio of medieval palaces and 18th-century Marais town houses, Maisons Internationales des Jeunes Étudiants (MIJE) foyers are more comfortable than many budget hotels. The catch is that you must be between the ages of 18 and 30. The 130F rate includes a bed, sheets, breakfast, showers, and free luggage storage. Doubles with private bath cost 158F. (For those over 30, rates are 206F for a single and 158F per person for a double.) MIJE foyers don't accept reservations, so show up between 7 and 8:30 AM for one of the 450 beds. There's a seven-night maximum and a 1 AM curfew. A restaurant in the Fourcy location serves meals to visitors (menus are 42F to 52F). The lockout is between noon and 3 PM. **Hôtel le Fauconnier:** 11 rue de Fauconnier, 75004, tel 01–42–74–23–45, fax 01–42–74–08–93, métro St-Paul. **Hôtel le Fourcy:** 6 rue de Fourcy, 75004, tel. 01–42–74–23–45, fax 01–42–74–08–93, métro St-Paul. **Hôtel Maubuisson:** 12 rue des Barres, 75004, tel. 01–42–74–23–45, fax 01–42–74–08–93, métro St-Paul or Hôtel de Ville.

Auberge Internationale des Jeunes. If you enjoy going out at night, this is the place for you. An impeccable, modern hostel right next to place de la Bastille and 10 minutes from the Gare de Lyon, it is popular with young, international backpackers. The friendly (albeit hectic) management accepts reservations. Rooms for two to six people rent for 81F–91F per person, breakfast included. 10 rue Trousseau, 75011, tel. 01–47–00–62–00, fax 01–47–00–33–16. Métro: Bastille or Ledru-Rollin. 240 beds. Reception 24 hrs. Lockout 10 AM–3 PM. Laundry.

Maison des Etudiants. This fabulous house with a flower-filled courtyard has beds in a double for 140F and singles for 160F. There's a four-night minimum stay and breakfast is included. The maison accepts students year-round and tourists of all ages in summer. 18 rue J.-J. Rousseau, 75001, tel. 01–45–08–02–10, fax. 01–40–28–11–43 . Métro: Palais Royal. 50 beds.

FOOD

Experiencing the French appreciation for fine food is much more than selecting a restaurant with "Chez" in the title, forking out a three-digit sum in francs, and knowing the best vintages of vin rouge (red wine) and vin blanc (white wine). Whether you buy baguettes at the boulangerie (bread shop), pastries at the pâtisserie (pastry shop), or the cheeses at the fromagerie (cheese shop), you'll soon discover that your francs will go much further at the markets than at Paris's restaurants.

It is imperative, however, that you indulge in at least one slightly drunken, drawn-out meal and treat it as religiously as the French do. The best deals at restaurants are usually the prix-fixe (fixed-price) menus, which might include an entrée (appetizer), a plat (main course), and dessert for 60F and up. Some restaurants serve a filling plat du jour (daily special), which includes meat, vegetables, and pasta or potatoes for as little as 45F. The commonly seen words service compris mean that tip is included in the prices. You can leave an extra 2F–5F pourboire (tip) for an extrafriendly server.

The French start their day with a petit déjeuner (breakfast) that usually consists of coffee and bread or croissants. Lunch, or déjeuner, is normally served noon–2 and dîner (dinner) 7–10 or 11. Assume that most places take credit cards and are open for lunch and dinner, unless otherwise noted.

A VEGETARIAN IN PARIS

Though French food is very meat-based, Paris does have a number of restaurants that serve vegetarian meals. AQUARIUS: 54 rue Ste-Croix-de-la-Bretonnerie, 4e, tel. 01–48–87–48–71, métro Hôtel de Ville. COUNTRY LIFE: 6 rue Daunou, 2e, tel. 01–42–97–48–51, métro Opéra. LE JARDIN DES PATES: 4 rue Lacépède, 5e, tel. 01–43–31–50–71, métro Monge. LA PETITE LÉGUME: 36 rue des Boulangers, 5e, tel. 01–40–46–06–85, métro Cardinal-Lemoine. SURMA: 5 rue Daubenton, 5e, tel. 01–45–35–68–60, métro Censier-Daubenton.

RESTAURANTS

BASTILLE

It's only fitting that a great nighttime area would have a great selection of restaurants. Take-out joints of all stripes serve cheap falafel and sandwiches along **rue de la Roquette;** on the rue's first block off place de la Bastille, homesick Americans take comfort in the thick pizza at **Slice.** Otherwise, you'll find plenty of cafés open late and many opportunities for quality meals. As you get farther away from place de la Bastille toward **place de la République** and along **boulevard Voltaire,** prices drop and ethnic eateries pop up more often.

UNDER 50F • Le Bistrot du Peintre. This popular café and bar serves food until midnight. The standard French cuisine includes a great *soupe à l'oignon* (onion soup; 34F) and the city's best *salade au chèvre chaud* (warm goat-cheese salad; 38F). *116 av. Ledru-Rollin, 11e, tel. 01–47–00–34–39. Métro: Ledru-Rollin.*

UNDER 75F • Café Moderne. Despite the name, it seems more like an old Paris bistro, with wooden tables, mirrored bar, and *sympathique* atmosphere. The house specialty is couscous—mounds of it—complete with raisin and pimiento garnish (50F–60F). *19 rue Keller, 11e, tel. 01–47–00–53–62. Métro: Bastille. Closed Sun.*

Crêpes-Show. A cadaverous-looking mannequin beckons you into Crêpes-Show, though horror-flick gore is not what they serve here. The 42F lunch menu gets you a salad, a main-course crepe (like cheese and mushroom), and a dessert crepe; the 63F dinner menu includes all of the above plus wine. *51 rue de Lappe, 11e, tel. 01–47–00–36–46. Métro: Bastille. Cash only.*

La Plancha. If you don't get carried away with the sangria and choose judiciously, you can make a pleasant meal out of the really good tapas, slices of potato omelet, fresh tuna, and grilled squid for about 80F at this very friendly and popular little bodega not far from the Bastille. It's tiny, so come early if you want to land a bar stool, or drop by late for a light snack and a drink after a movie; they stay open until 2 AM. *34 rue Keller, 11e, tel. 01–48–05–20–30. Métro: Ledru-Rollin. Cash only. Closed Sun., Mon.*

Le Temps des Cerises. This tiny lunch-only restaurant has been around since 1900. The words to the restaurant's namesake revolutionary song, "The Cherry Season," are written on the walls. Get here by noon to rub elbows with locals over a hearty 68F menu of traditional French home cooking or one of the many meat and salad specials. The bar is open until 8 PM. *31 rue de la Cerisaie, 4e, tel. 01–42–72–08–63. Métro: Sully-Morland or Bastille. Closed weekends and Aug. No dinner.*

UNDER 100F • Chez Paul. A modest sign welcomes you to the Bastille's best splurge. The grilled salmon (80F), rabbit with goat-cheese sauce (75F), and escargots (40F) are delectable; spring for a bottle of wine (100F) and whip out that credit card. The place is crowded with locals, so make reservations. *13 rue de Charonne, by rue de Lappe, 11e, tel. 01–47–00–34–57. Métro: Ledru-Rollin.*

BELLEVILLE

Belleville's African, Asian, and Eastern European restaurants are a refreshing alternative to standard Parisian cuisine. On **rue de Belleville, rue des Pyrénées,** and the streets stretching south from them you'll find some of the most varied and affordable dining in town, often in the front room of the owner's home. Sephardic Jews have kosher shops here; try the **Maison du Zabayon** (122 blvd. de Belleville, 20e, tel. 01–47–97–16–70), a kosher bakery with good nougat and pastries (8F–10F).

UNDER 50F • Restaurant Lao Siam. Laotian and Thai specialties fill the vast menu of this humble institution, which focuses on basics like chicken with bamboo shoots (40F) and sautéed rice with spicy Thai sauce (42F). *49 rue de Belleville, 19e, tel. 01–40–40–09–68. Métro: Belleville. Cash only.*

UNDER 75F • Modas. This small, artsy *crêperie* (crepe restaurant) on rue de Ménilmontant has as much personality as Gabriel, its owner—which means it's colorful, chaotic, and eccentric. Come and enjoy the rotating art exhibits along with Belleville regulars munching on a broad selection of crepes (under 30F) and grilled meats (50F–60F). *110 rue de Ménilmontant, 20e, tel. 01–40–33–69–58. Cash only. Closed Mon.*

UNDER 100F • La Boulangerie. In case you didn't know, the real trendy folks in Paris have moved on to Ménilmontant, a neighborhood that straddles the 11e and 20e arrondissements, and this is a great area to check out lively, inexpensive bars and restaurants like this one. Owned by the same family that runs the hip but friendly Lou Pascalou bar across the street, this attractive, welcoming bistro offers a really good feed for really low prices; the lunch menus (also served at dinner until 8:30 PM) run 45F, 59F, or 65F, while a three-course dinner goes for 78F. It's fun to hang out here, too, since it attracts an interesting and easygoing mixed crowd, and the food's excellent, with dishes like tuna tartare, shepherd's pie made with preserved duck, roast chicken, red mullet on a bed of fresh spinach, and excellent desserts including fruit crumbles and a rhubarb mille-feuille. *15 rue des Panoyaux, 20e, tel. 01–43–58–45–45. Métro: Père-Lachaise.*

Feast your eyes on the fine displays at the world-famous Fauchon (26 pl. de la Madeleine, 8e, tel. 01–47–42–60–11, métro Madeleine) and Hédiard (21 pl. de la Madeleine, 8e, tel. 01–42–66–44–36, métro Madeleine) food shops.

Chez Justine. Chez Justine serves up traditional southern French cooking in a rustic log-cabin decor. The 72F lunch menu (53F without dessert and wine) and 88F dinner menu come with an all-you-can-eat appetizer buffet, a meat dish, dessert, and wine. Salads are 40F. *96 rue Oberkampf, 11e, tel. 01–43–57–44–03. Métro: St-Maur. Closed Sun. and Aug. No lunch Sat.*

CHAMPS-ELYSEES

It's one of Paris's best-known boulevards, but the area around it is the worst neighborhood in which to seek out a decent meal for under 200F. Restaurants here serve mostly traditional French fare for the ultrachic and ultrasleek. Hunt around **rue La Boétie** and **rue de Ponthieu** for your most reasonable options.

UNDER 100F • Chicago Pizza Pie Factory. Happy-hour drinks (Mon.–Sat. 6–8) are 50% off at this deep-dish pizza–sports bar institution. In addition to pizzas—84F for a two-person cheese pizza, 200F for the four-person everything-on-it—you can order all sorts of big salads (20F–55F), garlic bread (21F), and good ol' California wine. The factory is open late daily—until 1AM. *5 rue de Berri, 8e, tel. 01–45–62–50–23. Métro: George V.*

GARE DE L'EST AND GARE DU NORD

A jazzy, post–World War II expatriate crowd infused new life into this inconspicuously cool neighborhood that spreads southwest of the two stations. Happily, the spirit of the 1940s has been quietly maintained in a few restaurants near **place St-Georges,** as well as in the hidden jazz joints sprinkled around the area. With a large Jewish population, this area is also good for cheap kosher meals, and you'll find good falafel around **rue de Montyon.**

UNDER 50F • Restaurant Chartier. The old revolving door here whirls you into a turn-of-the-century dining hall agleam with brass and mahogany. Main dishes include grilled steak with fries (46F) and grilled mackerel (36F). The 80F menu, which includes dessert and wine, is the best way to sample everything. *7 rue du Faubourg-Montmartre, 9e, tel. 01–47–70–86–29. Métro: Rue Montmartre.*

A FULL LOAD
OF COURSES

You'll hear mixed reviews of the university cafeteria-style restaurants, but dig this: You can get a three-course meal for about 15F. If you've been gnawing on bread and Brie for a week, this is nirvana. They're supposed to ask to see a student ID card (if you don't have one, the price gets jacked up 10F), but they often don't. Tickets come in sets of 10; if you only want one meal it'll cost 30F (just buy a ticket off a nice French student for the 15F deal). Lunch hours hover around 11:30–2; dinner is served 6:30–10. The "Resto-U" at 115 boulevard St-Michel (RER Luxembourg) doles out all-you-can-eat couscous or lentils with meat, vegetables, salad, and bread.

For a complete list of university restaurants, stop by CROUS (39 av. Georges-Bernanos, 5e, tel. 01–40–51–37–17, RER Port-Royal). Otherwise, try one of the following: 39 av. Georges-Bernanos, 5e, RER Port-Royal; 10 rue Jean-Calvin, 5e, métro Censier-Daubenton; 3 rue Mabillon, 6e, métro Mabillon; 45 blvd. Diderot, 12e, métro Gare de Lyon; 156 rue de Vaugirard, 15e, métro Pasteur; av. de Pologne, 16e, métro Porte Dauphine.

UNDER 100F • Chez Casimir. Friendly service, a low-key decor, bare wood tables, and a very good and inexpensive chalkboard menu (95F), plus a wine list with a starting price of 65F, have made this annex of chef Thierry Breton's excellent, adjacent Chez Michel a big hit. The crowd has a certain hip chic, too—this is the type of place where you might fall into conversation with a web-site designer and a painter at a neighboring table. The menu changes daily but runs to hearty, flavorful dishes like cream of lentil soup and roast lamb and white beans. *6 rue de Belzunce, 10e, tel. 01–48–78–28–80. Metro: Gare du Nord. Closed weekends.*

Haynes. In 1947 Leroy "Roughhouse" Haynes decided that the French could use a little soul in their diet, in the form of chicken gumbo, fried chicken, T-bone steaks, and barbecue ribs (60F–90F). When there isn't live piano music, Leroy gets out his great collection of jazz and blues. *3 rue Clauzel, 9e, tel. 01–48–78–40–63. Métro: St-Georges. Closed Sun., Mon.*

IN AND AROUND PLACE D'ITALIE

Even to people who know Paris well, the 13e arrondissement on the Left Bank often remains a mystery. Several things are bringing this very pleasant part of the city into the spotlight again (it was often in the news in the '60s when the Butte aux Cailles district was popular with hippies), including the new Bibliothèque Nationale de France on the banks of the Seine and the multiscreen movie complex at place d'Italie. Beyond these attractions, you can visit the Gobelins tapestry works and do as the Parisians do and check out the latest in good, cheap eats in the area's booming Chinatown.

UNDER 100F • La Chine Massena. With a wonderfully overwrought decor that includes what looks like a whole catalog's worth of restaurant supply company Asiana, plus four monitors showing the very latest in Hong Kong music videos, this is a fun place to come hungry with friends. Not only is the Chinese-Vietnamese-Thai food good and moderately priced, but the setting itself has a lot of entertainment value and on weekends there are variety shows followed by Asian disco that come as part of your meal. Steamed dumplings and lacquered duck are specialties, but for best value come at noon for the 52F, 78F, and 88F lunch menus; otherwise, a three-course meal without wine or beer runs about 100F. *Centre Commercial Massena, 13 pl. de Venetie, 13e, tel. 01–45–83–98–88. Métro: Porte de Choisy.*

Keryado. Though a bit off the beaten track, this friendly fish house is worth the trawl for really good food at easygoing prices. The set-price dinner menu at 110F (59F at lunch) is a chance to throw your nets without pulling in a big bill, and though the offer varies according to the catch of the day, a crab terrine in cucumber sauce is a typical starter, followed by fresh cod with mixed vegetables. And if you want to splurge on one of the most legendary of all French maritime dishes, this place is well known for it bouillabaisse, the hearty fish soup from Marseilles, here served in two courses: first soup, and then fish. *32 rue Regnault, 13e, tel. 01–45–83–87–58. Métro: Porte d'Ivry. Closed Sun.*

SPLURGE • L'Avant-Gout. With his excellent contemporary bistro cooking at very reasonable prices, young chef Christophe Beaufort is pulling hungry crowds to this small, noisy restaurant on a quiet street not far from place d'Italie. Service is laid-back in keeping with the Buttes aux Cailles neighborhood, which was popular with French hippies. The set-price menu—65F at lunch, including wine and coffee, and 145F at dinner—changes daily but runs to dishes like artichoke salad and tomato stuffed with oxtail and served with tiny cheese-filled ravioli. There are great desserts, too, and a very moderately priced wine list. *26 rue Bobillot, 13e, tel. 01–53–80–24–00. Métro: Place d'Italie. Closed Sun., Mon.*

LES HALLES AND BEAUBOURG

Les Halles has the distinction of having the worst crepe stands in town, and plenty of places around here will happily take your francs for a plate of muck. The solution: On sunny days stroll through the daily market on **rue Montorgueil** and picnic in the park next to the Église St-Eustache. At least many restaurants stay open until the wee hours, including **Pizza Pino** (open daily 11 AM–5 AM) on place des Innocents.

UNDER 50F • Dame Tartine. Squeeze in with the yuppies at this restaurant–cum–art gallery next to the Centre Georges-Pompidou on place Igor-Stravinsky. The specialty is the *tartines* (hot or cold open-faced sandwiches); try the *poulet aux amandes* (chicken with almonds; 35F). Add an inspiring glass of Bordeaux (15F) and ponder the works by local artists. *2 rue Brisemiche, 3e, tel. 01–42–77–32–22. Métro: Rambuteau or Châtelet–Les Halles. Cash only.*

Fish and Fun. Don't let the name put you off—this well-intentioned rapid eats (as opposed to fast food) place offers a tasty, healthy feed in reasonably attractive surroundings for irresistibly low prices—it's hard to spend more than 50F for a meal here. With a catch of the day that changes but regularly features swordfish and salmon, you choose how you want your fish prepared—steamed or grilled—and it's served with a side of steamed carrot puree, mashed potatoes or vegetables, plus a choice of different sauces. *55 blvd. de Sébastopol, 1st, tel. 01–42–21–10–10. Métro: Les Halles. Cash only. Closed Sun.*

Jip's. This boisterous Afro-Cuban café-restaurant blares reggae and salsa from a corner of Les Halles. The friendly dreadlocked clientele comes for dishes such as *pescado en salsa* (fish with fresh salsa; 45F) or *manioc en frite* (fried manioc; 28F). *41 rue St-Denis, 1er, tel. 01–42–33–00–11. Métro: Châtelet–Les Halles. Cash only.*

UNDER 75F • Au Petit Ramoneur. Sit outside at this family-run restaurant steps from the sex shops of Les Halles. The 72F menu has choices like fried potatoes and sausage and tripe cooked in Calvados, plus half a liter of wine or beer. At lunch the place is packed with regulars. *74 rue St-Denis, 1er, tel. 01–42–36–39–24. Métro: Les Halles or Étienne Marcel. Cash only. Closed end of Aug.*

UNDER 100F • Entre Ciel et Terre. This happy, crunchy place with wood and stone walls focuses on healthy meals of fruits and vegetables. The three-course vegetarian menu runs 92F, or try a tasty meal-size special like vegetable lasagna (58F) with a 16F glass of organic grape juice. *5 rue Hérold, 1er, tel. 01–45–08–49–84. Métro: Les Halles or Louvre-Rivoli. Closed weekends.*

LOUVRE TO OPÉRA

The names "Louvre" and "Opéra" should clue you in to the fact that most of this neighborhood is likely to be out of your range. On the up side, when you *do* sit yourself down for a bite here, it usually means you'll be served in true Parisian style. Workers from ritzy neighborhood shops find refuge on **rue du Faubourg-St-Honoré**, which has some good lunch deals. For Japanese restaurants and stores, check out **rue Ste-Anne** and, across avenue de l'Opéra, **rue St-Roch.** Some of the best sushi in town is served at **Foujita** (41 rue St-Roch, 1er, tel. 01–42–61–42–93), where a sushi sampler costs 100F.

UNDER 75F • Country Life. For health nuts, this may be the best deal in town: 65F gets you unlimited access to the quality pickings of both a hot and a cold vegetarian buffet (dessert and drinks are extra). The health-food store in front has a wide selection of dried fruits, nuts, organic vegetables, and soy products. *6 rue Daunou, 2e, tel. 01–42–97–48–51. Métro: Opéra. Closed Sat.*

BISTROS A VINS

Bistros à vins *(wine bistros), a quintessentially Parisian institution, are earthy places that are all about wine—sold by the bottle or by the glass—although you can also order food from a limited menu.*

LE BARON ROUGE. *Refreshingly mellow, the "Red Baron" has enough cheap wine to keep its youthful crowd happy. Wine starts at 6F; a plate of smoked duck is 18F. About twice a week there's live rock or blues. 1 rue Théophile-Roussel, near pl. d'Aligre, 12e, tel. 01–43–43–14–32. Métro: Ledru-Rollin. Closed Mon.*

LE BOUCHON DU MARAIS. *For a relatively quiet meal at this bistro, grab a table downstairs. For something boisterous, reserve ahead for a table "à l'étage" (on the second floor). Wine by the glass is 30F–40F; 70F gets you a glass of wine, a main dish, and dessert. You can eat here past midnight. 15 rue François-Miron, 4e, tel. 01–48–87–44–13. Métro: St-Paul. Closed Sun.*

JACQUES MÉLAC. *Jolly Jacques has the largest moustache in Paris and grows his own grapevine up the outside wall. His choice of wines is immense, with the fruity Lirac from his family vineyard in the Rhône Valley starting at around 70F. You can also have omelets (20F–50F) and plates of meats and cheese (20F–60F). 42 rue Léon-Frot, 11e, tel. 01–43–70–59–27. Métro: Charonne. Closed weekends and Aug.*

LE MOULIN À VINS. *The atmosphere and the crowd at this popular wine bar recall postwar Paris as depicted by photographers like Doisneau and Boubat. Danielle, the welcoming owner, once worked in a bank but has never looked back since she traded in her calculator for a corkscrew. A fascinating mix of locals come for excellent cheese trays (60F), salads (50F), and delicious dishes like rabbit in mustard sauce (75F) or quiche Lorraine (60F). Wines by the glass run 14F–25F. 6 rue Burq, 18e, tel. 01–42–52–81–27. Métro: Abbesses. Closed Mon., Sun. No lunch Tues., Fri., or Sat.*

LE GAVROCHE. *"Tout le monde bascule!" is shouted as everyone pounds a glass of the house Beaujolais at this neighborhood bistro. A loyal group of middle-age locals comes for the 70F menu of Provençal specialties. Or splurge on some foie gras for 75F. 19 rue St-Marc, 2e, tel. 01–42–96–89–70. Métro: Richelieu-Drouot. Closed Sun.*

LE MARAIS

A variety of kosher restaurants, delis, and bakeries indicate the strong presence of the Marais's Jewish community. For falafel, look no further than the stands on **rue des Rosiers.** The Marais's other main contingent, the hip gay crowd, means you'll also find more expensive, artsy, trendy joints; try the gay-owned restaurants, cafés, and bars on **rue Ste-Croix-de-la-Bretonnerie** and **rue Vieille-du-Temple.**

UNDER 25F • L'As du Fallafel. The best falafel in town comes out of this cramped hole-in-the-wall, once mentioned by Lenny Kravitz in a *Rolling Stone* interview. A falafel costs 23F, but shell out an extra 5F for the deluxe with grilled eggplant, hummus, tahini, and hot sauce. *34 rue des Rosiers, 4e, tel. 01–48–87–63–60. Métro: St-Paul. Cash only. Closed Sat.*

UNDER 50F • Sacha et Florence Finkelsztajn. Walk through the brightly colored mosaic doorway and enter a world of Eastern European and Russian snacks and specialties. Small *pirojki* (pastries filled with fish, meat, or vegetables) cost 10F (20F for a large, almost meal-size version). Even heftier sandwiches are 30F–40F. *Sacha: 27 rue des Rosiers, 4e, tel. 01–42–72–78–91. Métro: St-Paul. Closed July. Florence: 24 rue des Ecouffes, 4e, tel. 01–48–87–92–85. Métro: St-Paul. Cash only. Closed Tues., Wed., and Aug.*

UNDER 75F • Chez Marianne. Marianne's place serves excellent Middle Eastern and Central European specialties. The sampler platter lets you try four items for 55F, five for 65F, or six for 75F. If you aren't into waiting, make reservations, grab something from the deli, or order the 25F Israeli-style falafel (with beets and cabbage) from the window outside. *2 rue des Hospitalières-St-Gervais, 4e, tel. 01–42–72–18–86. Métro: St-Paul.*

UNDER 100F • Baracane. First-rate southwestern French food is served at this pleasant, easygoing restaurant. If you watch the price of wine, you'll be able to eat for less than 100F a head at lunch, especially if you order the 54F or 82F lunch menus. The 135F dinner menu may stretch your budget a bit, but it includes wine and coffee. *38 rue des Tournelles, 4e, tel. 01–42–71–43–33. Métro: Bastille. Closed Sun.*

> *Looking for great take-out sandwiches, salads, snacks, and even cheesecake in the heart of town? Head for Marks & Spencer, the British department store at 88 rue de Rivoli, 4e, tel. 01–44–61–08–00, métro Hôtel de Ville.*

MONTMARTRE

The first rule of eating in Montmartre is: Don't buy a thing near the Sacré-Coeur and place du Tertre, where you're sure to be overcharged. Instead, try going behind the church to **rue Lamarck** and **rue Caulaincourt** for relatively cheap French fare. Better yet, head down the stairs toward **rue Muller,** where the food is less expensive. For the most authentic African cuisine, go east to the area between **rue de la Goutte-d'Or** and **rue Doudeauville.**

UNDER 50F • La Pignatta. This Italian pizzeria and deli sells fresh pastas and *panini* (grilled sandwiches with mozzarella, basil, and tomato; 18F) to go, so-so pizzas for 32F, and some non-Italian items like hummus and tabbouleh (70F per kilo). *89 rue des Martyrs, 18e, tel. 01–42–55–82–05. Métro: Pigalle. Cash only.*

Rayons de Santé. The menu here is entirely vegetarian, featuring 20F–30F appetizers like vegetable pâté and artichoke mousse. Main courses (35F–45F) include spicy couscous with vegetables and soy sausage or vegetarian goulash. Mornings, come for an omelet (30F) and then check out the mini health-food store in front. *8 pl. Charles-Dullin, 18e, tel. 01–42–59–64–81. Métro: Abbesses. Cash only. Closed Sat. No dinner Fri.*

UNDER 75F • Le Fouta Toro. Some of the Senegalese dishes at this friendly, little hole in the wall are terrific—try the *mafé au poulet* (chicken in peanut sauce) for 54F—and some only so-so (the fish dishes). *3 rue du Nord, 18e, tel. 01–42–55–42–73. Métro: Marcadet-Poissonniers. Closed Tues.*

UNDER 100F • Au Refuge des Fondus. Decisions are kept to a minimum here; the waiter simply asks "*viande ou fromage?*" (meat or cheese?) and "*rouge ou blanc?*" (red or white wine?), then sets you up with an aperitif, appetizers, fondue, dessert, and wine. Not bad for 89F. You'll probably feel pretty stupid drinking wine out of a baby bottle (no joke), but you'll also have a hell of a good time. Reservations are advised. *17 rue des Trois-Frères, 18e, tel. 01–42–55–22–65. Métro: Abbesses.*

La Bouche du Roi. The "Mouth of the King" blends West African cuisine with traditional French cooking. Weekday nights often feature live music; Friday nights an African *conteuse* (storyteller) weaves her tales. A 57F lunch menu (82F at dinner) includes specialties like *maffé* (beef in seasoned peanut sauce) and *tale tale* (fried bananas). *4 rue Lamarck, 18e, tel. 01–42–62–55–41. Métro: Abbesses or Château-Rouge. Closed Wed.*

MONTPARNASSE

Boulevard du Montparnasse marks the stark line between upscale St-Germain-des-Prés and lower-key Montparnasse. As a result, meals range from cheap and filling to expensive and froufrou. If your budget is tight, you can always get a good crepe around **rue d'Odessa** or **rue Daguerre.**

UNDER 75F • Chez Papa. Rowdy waitresses serve southwestern French food at this crowded place. Mongo salads packed with potatoes, egg, ham, cheese, and tomato are known as *boyardes* and cost a piddling 35F. Escargots "Papa" (49F) come piping hot in a bright orange pot. Set menus go for 52F until 1 AM. *6 rue Gassendi, 14e, tel. 01–43–22–41–19. Métro: Denfert-Rochereau. Other location: 206 rue Lafayette, 10e, tel. 01–42–09–53–87. Métro: Louis-Blanc.*

Mustang Café. This is the most popular of the many Tex-Mex café-bars in Montparnasse. It's open continuously 9 AM–5 AM, and it's dark, loud, and cramped all night. Taco salads run 50F, quesadillas 40F, enchiladas 59F, and Dos Equis 30F. Weekdays 4–7 margaritas and cocktails are half price. *84 blvd. du Montparnasse, 14e, tel. 01–43–35–36–12. Métro: Montparnasse.*

UNDER 100F • Aux Artistes. This restaurant is as artsy as its name suggests: It's covered in paint and posters from top to bottom. Your 76F lets you choose from 29 appetizers, 35 main dishes, and several cheeses or simple desserts. Get a bottle of house wine (33F) to top it all off. *63 rue Falguière, 15e, tel. 01–43–22–05–39. Métro: Pasteur. Closed Sun. No lunch Sat.*

NEAR THE EIFFEL TOWER

The restaurants in this area cater primarily to diplomats and politicians, stray groups of tourists, and a small handful of solemn locals. In other words, you won't be eating many meals here. **Rue de Babylone,** which attracts the shopping crowd, is a promising walk for a good lunch.

UNDER 100F • Chez l'Ami Jean. One good bet in the area is this Basque restaurant that dishes up pâté *de campagne* (country-style pâté; 25F), *truite meunière* (trout rolled in flour and sautéed in butter; 55F), and Basque chicken (with tomatoes and red peppers; also 55F). Equally tempting desserts run 25F–40F. *27 rue Malar, 7e, tel. 01–47–05–86–89. Métro: La Tour–Maubourg. Closed Sun.*

SPLURGE • Au Bon Accueil. As soon as you hit town, make reservations at this bustling little bistro, just a few steps from the Eiffel Tower. Join the well-heeled crowd dining on the 135F lunch menu (155F at dinner)—a deal for such great food. You'll get to sample skillfully cooked dishes like veal fillet in a lemon-caper sauce and pot-au-feu. *14 rue de Monttessuy, 7e, tel. 01–47–05–46–11. Métro: École Militaire. Closed Sun.*

QUARTIER LATIN

Competition is high among French, Greek, and Tunisian joints on **rue de la Huchette.** For more upscale dining, check out the area behind **square René-Viviani.** Try **rue Mouffetard** for a 13F crepe at one of the stands; you'll also find many French, Greek, and Mexican places serving full meals for 50F–70F.

UNDER 50F • Al Dar. The deli side of this otherwise expensive Lebanese restaurant serves delicious sandwiches (24F) and small plates (30F) of falafel and spicy chicken sausage. *8–10 rue Frédéric-Sauton, 5e, tel. 01–43–25–17–15. Métro: Maubert-Mutualité.*

Cousin Cousine. This spacious, airy crêperie picks up on the French fetish for old flicks, with *galettes* (buckwheat pancakes) named L'Ange Bleu (Blue Angel; walnuts, blue cheese, crème fraîche; 36F) and Mad Max (ground beef, cheese, ratatouille; 42F). A *bolée* (bowl) of cider starts at 15F. *36 rue Mouffetard, 5e, tel. 01–47–07–73–83. Métro: Monge. Cash only under 150F.*

UNDER 75F • Le Boute Grill. Some Maghrebian expats feel this Tunisian restaurant serves the best couscous in Paris. The servings are enormous and come with a choice of—count 'em—14 kinds of meat. A huge three-course menu is 72F. *12 rue Boutebrie, 5e, tel. 01–43–54–03–30. Métro: Cluny–La Sorbonne. Cash only. Closed Sun.*

Au Jardin des Pâtes. The "Garden of Pasta" serves freshly made, organic-grain pastas (45F–75F) lavished with toppings such as mixed vegetables with ginger and tofu and smoked duck sauce with cream and nutmeg. *4 rue Lacépède, 5e, tel. 01–43–31–50–71. Métro: Monge. Closed Mon.*

SPLURGE • Chantairelle. The young team who runs this place hails from south-central Auvergne, and they've created an ambience that makes you feel like you're there. The big portions of delicious hearty food—stuffed cabbage (65F) and *potée* (pork and potatoes)—will fill you up. *17 rue Laplace, 5e, tel. 01–46–33–18–59. Métro: Maubert-Mutualité. Closed Mon.*

ST-GERMAIN-DES-PRES

Beyond the chichi galleries and boutiques of St-Germain are plenty of substantial dining options, although the classic French fare here often falls flat. **Rue Monsieur-le-Prince** is one of the best restaurant streets in the city, featuring Asian spots with three-course menus for as little as 50F. **Rue des Canettes** and the surrounding small streets are best for crepes and other fast eats.

UNDER 50F • Cosi. At this fancy sandwich shop you can have an array of ingredients—including chèvre, salmon, mozzarella, tomatoes, and curried chicken—on fresh focaccia bread for 30F–50F. Add to this a glass of wine (20F), a changing selection of opera music, and voilà: French deli. *54 rue de Seine, 6e, tel. 01–46–33–35–36. Métro: Odéon. Cash only.*

UNDER 75F • Le Coffee Parisien. This popular spot, frequented by St-Germain's young leisure class, serves brunch all day at the diner-style counter or at tables. We're talking *real* brunch, like eggs Benedict (70F), pancakes (50F), and eggs Florentine (70F). *4 rue Princess, 6e, tel. 01–43–54–18–18. Métro: Mabillon or St-Germain-des-Prés.*

UNDER 100F • Le Petit Mabillon. In a section of St-Germain where restaurants are prohibitively expensive, this friendly Italian spot puts them all to shame with a delicious, filling three-course menu (77F). In good weather, sit outside. Pastas are made fresh daily and cost 55F à la carte. *6 rue Mabillon, 6e, tel. 01–43–54–08–41. Métro: Mabillon. Closed Mon. No dinner Sun.*

Village Bulgare. Tucked into a quiet street near the Pont Neuf, this restaurant was started by a Bulgarian dancer and his wife, who used to cook for homesick dance-troupe members. Sample Bulgarian specialties like *kebabtcheta* (a grilled meat roll; 52F) and *banitza* (a pastry filled with cheese; 35F); the three-course menu costs 85F. *8 rue de Nevers, 6e, tel. 01–43–25–08–75. Métro: Pont-Neuf. Cash only. No lunch Mon. or dinner Sun.*

If you're wandering around and need to find a bathroom, try one of the city's ubiquitous cafés. Proprietors are required by law to let anyone use their bathroom, whether they're a patron or not. Some require payment (a few francs, usually).

CAFES

Along with wine, cigarettes, and the three-course meal, the café remains one of the basic necessities of life in Paris. Avoid the ones in tourist areas: The more modest establishments (look for nonchalant locals) will give you a cheaper cup of coffee and a feeling of what real French café life is like. Cafés are required to post a *tarif des consommations* (price list) for drinks taken *au comptoir* (at the counter), *en salle* (at a table), or *à la terrasse* (outside). Below we give the seated indoor prices. If you just need a cup of coffee, have it at the counter and save a lot of money.

Amnésia Café. The music's just loud enough to keep conversations private at this dimly lit gay café with big, soft, comfy chairs. Huge salad plates run 45F–65F. Coffee is 10F. *42 rue Vieille-du-Temple, 4e, tel. 01–42–72–16–94. Métro: St-Paul.*

Au Soleil de la Butte. A local crowd hangs out on the covered terrace sipping coffee (11F) and beer (11F–16F). *32 rue Muller, 18e, tel. 01–46–06–18–24. Métro: Château-Rouge.*

Café Beaubourg. Despite the Beaubourg's intimidatingly slick exterior, the waiters are actually *friendly* here. Tackle a large salad (50F), but beware of the expensive coffee (15F, 18F after 7 PM). *100 rue St-Martin, 4e, tel. 01–48–87–63–96. Métro: Rambuteau.*

Café de l'Industrie. Every twentysomething in town flocks to these large, smoky rooms where funky art hangs from the red walls. Hang out until 2 AM with French night owls schmoozing at the bar. Beers are 16F. *16 rue St-Sabin, 11e, tel. 01–47–00–13–53. Métro: Bastille or Bréguet-Sabin. Closed Sat.*

Café Marly. This café's stunning view, name-dropping clientele, and snooty reputation might justify 16F for a coffee or 35F for a chocolate tart—once. The extralong hours (until 2 AM) are a bonus. *Cour Napoléon, 1er, tel. 01–49–26–06–60. Métro: Palais Royal–Musée du Louvre.*

Café au Petit Suisse. With private booths and an indoor balcony, the Petit Suisse draws you onto its sunny terrace without being flashy or touristy. Coffee is 11F, café crème 18F, and cold drinks 19F. *9 rue Corneille, at rue Vaugirard, 6e, no phone. Métro: Odéon. RER: Luxembourg. Closed weekends.*

Le Fumoir. This new café-restaurant has passed over the curve of red-hot chic to become a permanent and useful address. Its location just across from the Louvre helps, but ultimately what makes it work is that the fashionable folks—press attachés with portable phones, sulky tatooed model-artists, and so on, actually like this place, with its decor variously inspired by Vienna, Edward Hopper, and Scandinavia. The food's expensive and indifferent, so come play for the price of a coffee or a glass of wine (14F). *Place du Louvre, 6 rue de l'Amiral-Coligny, 1er, tel. 01–42–92–00–24. Métro: Louvre.*

La Palette. This old, muted café amidst rue de Seine's galleries lets you sip a café crème (12F) or wine (20F) and contemplate the splotched and signed palettes of local artists on the walls. On balmy evenings, sit outside under the cherry trees. *43 rue de Seine, 6e, tel. 01–43–26–68–15. Métro: Mabillon. Closed Sun.*

Pause-Café. This Bastille café has an outdoor terrace overlooking the rue de Charonne, loaded with art galleries and music stores. Coffee is a reasonable 8F, the succulent salmon quiche 42F. *41 rue de Charonne, 11e, tel. 01–48–06–80–33. Métro: Bastille or Ledru-Rollin.*

MARKETS AND SPECIALTY SHOPS

As well as a number of open-air markets, Paris hosts a whole medley of specialty shops and late-hour markets. **Monoprix** and **Prisunic** both house low-priced supermarkets; Monoprix is all over and usually open until 8 or 9; the Prisunic just off the Champs-Élysées (109 rue de La Boétie, 8e, tel. 01–42–25–10–27) is open Monday–Saturday until midnight. On most side streets, especially in budget lodging areas, look for *alimentations générales*—small grocery stores that offer standard snack items at steep prices. They're generally open until 9 or 10 PM.

A lifesaver for anyone on a budget, **Ed l'Épicier** is the cheapest supermarket in Paris. Although it's an outlet whose selection varies, you can always find the basics for way less than anywhere else. Bring your own grocery bags. *84 rue Notre-Dame-des-Champs, 6e, métro Notre-Dame-des-Champs. Other locations: 80 rue de Rivoli, 4e, métro Hôtel de Ville; 123 rue de Charonne, 11e, métro Bastille.*

OPEN-AIR MARKETS

There's no better way to experience the "real" Paris than by joining the haggling, pushing, pointing, and hawking that take place at Paris's 84 open-air markets. Don't be intimidated; not much French is needed—shopping in markets just requires a little body language. Unless you see a sign saying LIBRE SERVICE (self-service), the grocer chooses your items for you. You can, however, object to anything she chooses or point to the items you prefer.

The cheapest market is on **place d'Aligre** (12e; open Mon.–Sat. 8–1 and 3–7, Sun. 8–1). Here you'll find fresh fruit, vegetables, cheese, pastries, coffee, clothing, flowers, and cooking utensils. The market at **place Monge** (5e; open Wed., Thurs., and Sun. 7 AM–1:30 PM) is also cheap. Paris's biggest outdoor market is held on **boulevard de Reuilly** between rue de Charenton and place Félix-Éboué (12e; open Tues. and Fri. 7 AM–1:30 PM). For organic food, try the **Marché Biologique** (6e; open Sun. 7 AM–1:30 PM), on boulevard Raspail between rue du Cherche-Midi and rue de Rennes.

One of the most enjoyable market streets is **rue Montorgueil,** with a smattering of restaurants and bars clustered around. The market that wins hands down for visual and olfactory delight is the flower market on Ile de la Cité's **place Louis-Lépine** (Mon.–Sat. 8 AM–7:30 PM). There's a great **Chinese market** near Paris's Chinese district in the 13e arrondissement; take the métro to **Porte de Choisy** and you can't miss it. If you're still not satisfied, try the south end of **rue Mouffetard** (5e), **rue de Buci** (6e) near St-Germain, **rue Cler** (7e), **rue Daguerre** (14e) in Montparnasse, and **rue Lepic** in Montmartre (18e), all with huge arrays of produce, cheeses, meats, breads, candies, and flowers.

EXPLORING PARIS

Proudly bearing the scars of an illustrious 2,000-year history, and serving today as home to some 2 million people, Paris could take you multiple lifetimes to explore from top to bottom—and that's not counting the Louvre. The métro system is extremely efficient and will aid you in see-and-flee sightseeing. However, the bus—or even better, your feet—will give you a better feel for the city. You might even consider a ride on the scenic **Bateaux-Mouches** (Pont de l'Alma, tel. 01–42–25–96–10, 8e, métro Alma-Marceau), which, although extremely touristy, do take you past some quintessentially Parisian sights.

MAJOR ATTRACTIONS

ARC DE TRIOMPHE

The Arc de Triomphe remains the largest triumphal arch in the world. The sculpture surrounding it includes François Rude's famous *La Marseillaise,* depicting the uprising of 1792. Climb the 164-ft arch for one of the best views of Paris, highlighting the city's unmistakable design. The arch marks the intersection of the 8e, 16e, and 17e arrondissements; radiating out from the arch are 12 avenues. Gaze along the precise lines to La Défense, down the Champs-Élysées to place de la Concorde, and on to the Louvre. *Pl. Charles-de-Gaulle—Étoile, tel. 01–55–37–73–77. Métro: Charles-de-Gaulle—Étoile. Admission 35F. Open Apr.–Sept., daily 9:30 AM–11 PM; Oct.–Mar., daily 10 AM–10:30 PM.*

BASILIQUE DU SACRE-COEUR

This horrific white concoction was dreamt up by overzealous Catholics to "expiate the sins" of the citizens participating in the Paris Commune of 1871, massacred by government troops that same year. Designed by Paul Abadie and built between 1875 and 1914, the Sacré-Coeur met with criticism even during construction, but today it is the most popular postcard subject in Paris. The Romanesque-Byzantine structure looks white because the stone (taken from Château-Landon, 96 km/60 mi south of Paris) secretes calcite when wet; the more it rains, the more the Sacré-Coeur gleams. The interior is hardly awe-inspiring, though the red-toned stained glass can give off a fiery glow in the evening. The 15F admission fee to the 367-ft **bell tower** will give you a magnificent view of the city, but you can get almost the same view for free from the front of the basilica. *35 rue du Chevalier-de-la-Barre, tel. 01–53–41–89–00. Métro: Anvers. Basilica open daily 6:45 AM–11 PM. Tower open daily 9–7 (until 6 off-season).*

CATHEDRALE DE NOTRE-DAME

For centuries Notre-Dame (built between 1163 and 1361) has watched Paris go through all sorts of phases, riding out periods of neglect and hostility like a patient parent, emerging as one of the best-known houses of worship in the world. The richly sculpted portals depict (from left to right) the Virgin (to whom the cathedral is dedicated), the Last Judgment, and St. Anne, Mary's mother. Above is a row of statues depicting 28 kings of Judah and Israel, all of whom lost their heads during the Revolution, when the cathedral became the Temple of Reason. Once all the fuss had died down, the great architect Viollet-le-Duc rolled up his sleeves and took on serious restoration, including replacing the kings' heads.

The interior of Notre-Dame is vast and echoing, but before the Revolution, rich tapestries and paintings adorned the interior, diminishing the tomblike aura it has today. Even the stained-glass windows have changed: In the 18th century, the originals were removed to let in more light. The gray windows that replaced them were then replaced this century by abstract patterns created with medieval colors and techniques. Luckily, three spectacular rose windows were left intact.

Throughout the centuries, kings, lords, generals, and other churches have everything from statues to war banners. Notice the statues flanking the altar: They represent Louis XIII, who, after years of trying unsuccessfully for a child, promised to repay the Virgin if she would grant him a son; and Louis XIV, who carried out his father's vow with these gifts to the cathedral. Climb the cathedral's **towers** (around to the left as you face the building) for a gape at tons of bells and eerie gargoyles and a terrific view of Paris. *Pl. du Parvis Notre-Dame, 4e, tel. 01–44–32–16–70. Métro: Cité. Open daily 8–7. Towers: tel. 01–43–29–50–40. Admission 32F. Open Apr.–Sept., daily 9:30–7:30; Oct.–Mar., daily 10–5.*

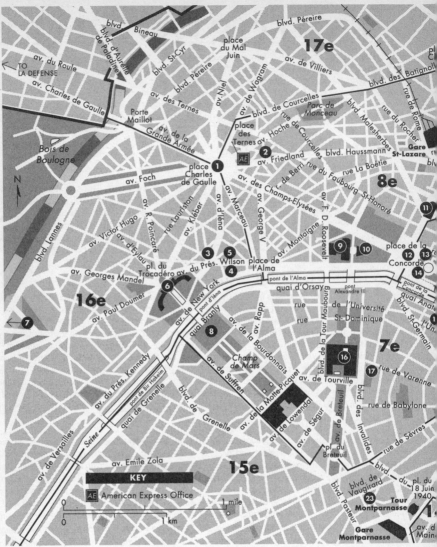

KEY

AE American Express Office

PEI DAY

Late president François Mitterrand declared that the remaking of the Louvre was to be the central element of his Grands Travaux (Grand Projects), which makes it, according to the French, the most important building project in the world. Mitterrand, who always participated in choosing architects for Parisian projects, offered the commission to I. M. Pei, a New York–based Chinese-American architect who made his reputation designing modernist mega-structures. The French were not pleased with the selection, the cost, or the proposal—namely, the relocation of all central services to an excavated Cour Napoléon, which would then be topped by a glass pyramid. Pei explained that by moving the ticket windows and stores underground, the Louvre could have a single entrance capable of handling the massive crowds. He also argued that his stark design would contrast with the older parts of the Louvre rather than mimic them. Pei's proposal was pushed through, and in 1988 the Pyramide was inaugurated to a chorus of mixed reviews. The public and critics eventually warmed up to the new entrance, and when it came time to decide on an architect for the 2.7-billion-franc ($500 million) phase-two renovations, Pei was again chosen.

CENTRE GEORGES-POMPIDOU AND MUSEE NATIONAL D'ART MODERNE

Along with the Louvre and the Musée d'Orsay (*see below*), the Musée National d'Art Moderne, housed within the Centre Georges-Pompidou, completes the chronological triumvirate of national museums. Also known as Beaubourg, the center brings a circuslike multitude of fire-eaters, tourists, and carica-turists to its plaza and fountains out front. Inside, a museum, a library, a theater, and a cinema act as the "laboratory" envisioned when the center was first conceived in the early 1970s. What wasn't envi-sioned was that the center would be so popular that it would need renovating a mere quarter-century after being built; the complex has been undergoing restoration for more than two years and is expected to be fully revamped by January 2000.

There are two breeds of art exhibits here: those that cost money and those that don't. The free ones are scattered throughout the temporary galleries on the ground floor and in the library halls; these are usu-ally related to the blockbuster temporary exhibit housed in the Grande Galerie. For everything else, you need to pay the cashier on the first floor, who will issue you a ticket that you pop into a machine, métro-style, at the entrance to the galleries. The information desks have a bimonthly program of events printed in English, as well as a full listing of gallery events, prices, and the wheres and whens of guided tours in your mother tongue. *Pl. Georges-Pompidou, 4e, tel. 01–44–78–12–33. Métro: Rambuteau. Admission details unavailable at press time.*

In 1977, after six years of demolition and construction, the riot of steel crossbraces and snaky escala-tors designed by Italy's Renzo Piano and Gianfranco Franchini and Britain's Richard Rodger was inau-gurated before an astonished city—the Pompidou Center looks like someone turned the building inside out and then went to town on it with a box of crayons. The exposed pipes in bright primary colors (green for water, blue for air, yellow for electricity, red for communications) may be the most memorable part of the building, but it is with the interior structure that the architects were truly innovative. To eliminate the need for columns to hold the building up, steel beams were cross-strutted and hinged over its length and width, connecting to the exterior skeleton. Water fills the large steel tubes, stabilizing the outward push made on the structure from the pressure of the floors. This never-before-tried system was supposed to give the center an unheard-of flexibility—walls could be taken down or put up anywhere at will allowing the building to change shape to accommodate different exhibitions and displays.

Although the building itself became a working model for architecture classes everywhere, its two major tenants, the museum and the **Centre des Créations Industriel (CCI)**, soon defined the center's role in Parisian life. The CCI, the interactive part of the center, is composed of two parts: the **Bibliothèque Publique d'Information (BPI)**, or the Public Library of Information, and the **Institut de Recherche et Coordination de l'Acoustique et de la Musique (IRCAM)**, or Sound and Music Research Institute (*see* Opera, Classical Music, and Dance, *below*).

THE COLLECTION • The Pompidou's permanent collection picks up around 1905, where the Orsay leaves off. Encompassing more than 40,000 works, it is the largest single gathering of modern art in the world. The historical part starts off with Matisse, then takes off through the cubists, futurists, surrealists, Bauhaus, European abstractionists, abstract expressionists, pop artists, and minimalists.

Because the museum got into the collecting business rather late in comparison to New York's Museum of Modern Art or Guggenheim Museum, there aren't as many postcard-famous works here as you'd expect. Of course, there are some stunners: **Alexander Calder's** (1898–1976) *Josephine Baker* was one of the sculptor's earliest and most graceful versions of the mobile—a form he made famous. Also here is **Marcel Duchamp's** (1887–1968) *Valise*, a collection of miniature reproductions of his most famous Dada sculptures and drawings conveniently displayed in their own ironic carrying case. One of the last works by the piously abstract **Piet Mondrian** (1872–1944), *New York*, marks one of the few breaks with the style of the *Compositions* he had been painting for the previous 25 years. Also here is *Out of the Deep*, **Jackson Pollock's** (1912–56) attempt a year before his death to return to the abstraction of his earlier drip paintings, though alcoholism and fame were suffocating his career.

Fans of the band Dead Can Dance should search out the grave of François Raspail to see the enigmatic statue used for the cover of "Within the Realm of a Dying Sun."

CIMETIERE DU PERE-LACHAISE

The world's most celebrated necropolis, Père-Lachaise is the final stop for more illustrious people than you could meet in a lifetime. The former farm of Louis XIV's confessor, Father Lachaise, has since been transformed into *the* minicity of death and remembrance. Plots in the 118-acre cemetery are prime real estate, and now only the outrageously wealthy can afford to be laid to rest with the famous. Despite hordes of Jim Morrison fans joining the eternal party raging in Division 6, a serene Gothic aura pervades the place. Though the famous names deserve a visit, it's just as fun to wander aimlessly amid the disorderly array of decaying tombstones.

The oldest residents at Père-Lachaise are the celebrated lovers **Abélard** (1079–1142) and **Héloïse** (1101–64). But let's face it, most young travelers are tromping out here to see **James Douglas Morrison** (1943–71). A gendarme is now posted to keep crowds from mussing up nearby graves; Jim's grave site is periodically cleaned of spray-painted messages left by well-intentioned devotees. If you're a Doors fan, check out the virtual shrine dedicated to Jim Morrison at the Czech restaurant (17 rue Beautreillis, 4e, métro Sully-Morland) across the street from where he once lived. You can even sit in the same wicker chair where the Lizard King once slammed whiskey shots.

Even in death, there are those who are greater among equals. Here they include precocious composer **Georges Bizet** (1838–75), dancer **Isadora Duncan** (1878–1927), musician **Frédéric Chopin** (1810–49), city planner **Baron Haussmann** (1809–91); writers **Colette** (1873–1954), **Honoré de Balzac** (1799–1850), **Oscar Wilde** (1854–1900), **Marcel Proust** (1871–1922), **Gertrude Stein** (1874–1946), and (in the same grave) **Alice B. Toklas** (1877–1967), and 1967 Nobel Prize winner **Miguel Angel Asturias** (1899–1974); poet and critic **Guillaume Apollinaire** (1880–1918); playwrights **Jean-Baptiste Molière** (1622–73) and **Pierre-Augustin Beaumarchais** (1732–99); painters **Théodore Géricault** (1791–1824), **Jean-Auguste Ingres** (1780–1867), **Eugène Delacroix** (1798–1863), **Louis David** (1748–1825), **Amedeo Modigliani** (1884–1920), **Camille Pissarro** (1830–1903), **Georges Seurat** (1859–91), and **Max Ernst** (1891–1976); illustrator **Honoré Daumier** (1808–79); and singer **Edith Piaf** (1915–63). In the southeastern corner of the cemetery is the **Mur des Fédérés** (Commundards' Wall), a memorial to the brutal killing of 147 Communards in 1871 who were shot by a firing squad at this very spot. Nearby are equally humbling memorials to World War II concentration camp victims and Resistance workers. All of these graves (and oh-so-many more) are located on free photocopied maps occasionally available at the cemetery office. Or you can buy a detailed map (10F) from surrounding florists. *Blvd. de Ménilmontant or av. du Père-Lachaise, 20e, tel. 01–43–70–70–33. Métro: Père-Lachaise or Gambetta. Open daily 8 AM–6 PM.*

HOTEL DES INVALIDES

The Hôtel des Invalides was commissioned by Louis XIV to house soldiers wounded during his many military campaigns. The **Musée de l'Armée** has mildly interesting displays of armor, weapons, maps, plus 18th-century scale models of fortified French towns and models of soldiers in war garb. Admission to the museum also buys a visit to Napoléon's tomb, housed in the **Église du Dôme.** Here he lies ensconced in five coffins, one inside the next. *Esplanade des Invalides, 7e, tel. 01–44–42–37–67. Métro: Latour-Maubourg or Varenne. RER: Invalides. Admission (valid for 2 days) 38F, 28F on Sun. Open Apr.–Sept., daily 10–5:45; Oct.–Mar., daily 10–4:45.*

INSTITUT DU MONDE ARABE

More than a museum, this is a mega-multimedia cultural center. Built with funds from the French and most Arab governments, the institute is attempting to become a "cultural bridge" between Europe and the Arab world. In addition to its huge library and audiovisual center, the institute has two exhibition spaces: The **permanent collection** is a combination of the institute's and some of the Louvre's Arab artifacts, with works dating from the pre-Islamic era to the present. The traveling exhibitions are usually blockbuster events, well publicized by a large banner on the facade facing rue des Fossés-St-Bernard. A café and a restaurant reside on the ninth floor, though the former makes you pay dearly for the splendid view of the Seine and Notre-Dame, and the latter serves surprisingly bland food. *1 rue des Fossés-St-Bernard, 5e, tel. 01–40–51–38–38. Métro: Jussieu or Cardinal-Lemoine. Admission 40F. Open Tues.–Sun. 10–6.*

MUSEE DU LOUVRE

One of the grandest and most stunning museums in the world, and certainly one of the most visited, the Louvre houses an overwhelmingly comprehensive collection of art and artifacts from just about all cultures and regions, from ancient times up to the 19th century. Join the crowds flocking to the "Mona Lisa," taking a photo, and leaving. Or, better yet, take some time to bask in the grandeur for a while. *Entrances from pl. du Carrousel, pl. du Palais-Royal, or Cour Napoléon, 1er, tel. 01–40–20–51–51. Métro: Palais Royal–Musée du Louvre. Admission 45F, 26F daily after 3 PM and all day Sun. Open Wed. 9 AM–9:45 PM, Thurs.–Mon. 9–6 (Richelieu open Mon. until 9:45 PM); galleries empty 30 mins before closing. Cafés and stores in Carrousel du Louvre open daily 9 AM–9:45 PM.*

To get into the Louvre, you may have to wait in two long lines: one outside the Pyramid and another downstairs at the ticket booths. Unless you come during the midday tourist rush, the first line shouldn't be a problem. The second usually is. Your ticket will get you into any and all of the wings as many times as you like during one day.

Before you skip down the escalator and turn into the first wing you see, remember that the Louvre is *enormous.* In the bookstore you can buy a pamphlet called **"Guide for the Visitor in a Hurry"** (20F), which directs you to the biggies with room numbers and illustrations; the **"Visitor's Guide"** (60F), which ups the number of covered works but cuts the directions; and the weighty **"Louvre: The Collections"** (130F), which is too cumbersome to be a good visitor's guide and too incomplete to be a true catalog. Finally, you've got the cool cellular phone–style recorded tours (30F)—they're worth the investment.

RICHELIEU WING • The Richelieu wing contains all eras of French sculpture, ancient Mesopotamian, Iranian, and Islamic artifacts on the below-ground and ground floor; pre-17th-century French objets d'art and the apartments of Napoléon III on the first floor; and Dutch, German, and early French painting on the second floor. The most stunning part of this wing are the two sculpture courtyards, the **Cour Marly** and **Cour Paget,** which both contain 17th-, 18th-, and 19th-century French academic sculpture. Also in this wing is the Oriental Antiquities collection, including one of the oldest statues known to humanity, a 6th-millennium BC neolithic figure. Here you'll also find the Louvre's best cup of coffee at **Café Richelieu,** where a 10F drink gets you a terrace view overlooking the Pyramid in Cour Napoléon. The top floor has a hall devoted to an epic series of canvases by **Peter Paul Rubens** (1577–1640) charting the glorious history of Maria de' Medici.

SULLY WING • The entrance into the Sully wing from the Pyramid is the coolest—you get to walk around and through the foundations and moat of the castle built by Philippe-Auguste in the 12th century and expanded by Charles V in the 14th. This wing contains the medieval Louvre below ground, and ancient Iranian, near Eastern, Egyptian, and Greek artifacts on the ground floor. The northern galleries of the first floor continue with the **objets d'art** collection started in the Richelieu wing, picking up at the 17th century and continuing through the Revolution to the Restoration. Running alongside the **Egyptian galleries** to the south are works from the early period of the **Greek collection**—a smattering of coins, pottery, and other everyday objects from the 7th to 3rd centuries BC. On the second floor, Sully picks up French painting where the Richelieu wing leaves off, somewhere around the 16th century.

DENON WING • The Denon wing contains Germanic and 11th- to 15th-century Italian sculptures below ground; 16th- to 19th-century Italian sculptures and Greek, Etruscan, and Roman artifacts on the ground floor; Italian paintings and drawings, large-scale 19th-century French paintings, and the crown jewels on the first floor; and temporary exhibits on the second floor. In this wing is one of the most recognizable works of art in the world: the armless 2nd-century BC *Venus de Milo*. This is also where you can find the Most Famous Painting in the World, **Leonardo da Vinci's** "Mona Lisa" (*La Gioconda*), smirking eternally behind layers of bulletproof glass. The grandest rooms of the Denon wing display the epic-scale French paintings of the 19th century, including the 1806 *Coronation of Emperor Napoléon* by **Louis David** (1748–1825) and the 1819 *Raft of the Medusa* by **Théodore Géricault** (1791–1863). You might recognize Delacroix's *Liberty* from the pocket-size version on the back of the old 100F note.

SPECIAL EXHIBITS AND EVENTS • Temporary photography shows, exhibits of new acquisitions and donations, and events honoring individual painters usually take place in either the Hall Napoléon, the basement galleries of the Richelieu and Sully wings, the second-floor galleries of the Denon wing, or the showrooms of the Carrousel du Louvre. Your Louvre ticket may give you free access, or you may have to shell out another 28F, depending on the exhibit. Lectures and films take place in the **Louvre Auditorium** on topics such as archaeology, architecture, and art criticism (25F–50F); the films showcase everything from silent works to the history of art in Paris (25F–100F). Occasionally, chamber music concerts

The Grande Pyramide is not the quickest way into the Louvre. Try the staircase alongside the Arc du Carrousel (called the Porte Jaujard), or enter through the métro stop Palais Royal–Musée du Louvre—both put you inside the underground mall.

happen in the auditorium as well (130F). A smattering of films, lectures, concerts, and exhibits are included in what's called **Les Midis du Louvre**; these noontime events cost 30F–50F. For a recorded message announcing the week's agenda, call 01–40–20–52–99; if you'd rather talk to a human being, call 01–40–20–51–86 between 9 AM and 7 PM.

MUSEE D'ORSAY

The Musée d'Orsay has a spectacular collection, encompassing art produced between 1848 (where the Louvre drops off) and about 1908 (where the Pompidou picks up). Of course, most of the work of any worth created during this time, at least according to Parisians, was French, and most was painted by the Impressionists, working from the 1870s to the turn of the century. The Orsay is not just an Impressionism museum, though; much more was happening during this period than bluish hues and soft brush strokes. This artistically tumultuous time saw the rise and fall of literary salons and the creation of the concept of the avant-garde. If you're itching to see a van Gogh, Monet, Toulouse-Lautrec, or Renoir, this is the place. *1 rue de la Légion-d'Honneur, 7e, tel. 01–40–48–48–84. Métro: Solférino. RER: Musée d'Orsay. Admission 40F; separate admission for temporary exhibits. Open Tues.–Sat. 10–6 (Thurs. until 9:45), Sun. 9–6; in summer, Mon.–Sun. from 9 AM.*

The Gare d'Orsay was built in 1898 to handle the onslaught of trains expected for the 1900 World's Fair. The platforms of the station were soon too short for modern trains, and the building was abandoned in the 1960s. There were a few tenants now and then—the city auction-house moved in for a while, and Orson Welles shot scenes from *The Trial* here—but it wasn't until 1986 that the station reopened as a museum. The interior of this former train station may overwhelm you with its weighty postmodern architecture, sculptures, and hordes of people furiously milling around. Take a deep breath before diving into it all. The museum shop sells the **"Guide for Visitors in a Hurry"** (20F), an efficient if abbreviated outline of the most important works of the collection, and **"Guide to the Orsay"** (110F), a more comprehensive look at the collection with better pictures.

GROUND FLOOR • This floor contains groundbreaking 19th-century paintings, including works by the sensualist **Jean-Auguste Ingres** (1780–1867), the Romantic **Delacroix,** and subtle landscapist **Camille Corot** (1796–1875). Perhaps the most famous painting on this floor is *Olympia* (1863) by

Edouard Manet (1832–83). When it was unveiled at the Salon des Refusés, it drew scathing remarks: The image of a nude, youngish courtesan with unfinished hands—they were described as monkey paws—stretched out next to a black cat beside a bouquet of flowers *sketched* in paint was far too much. All but two reviews of the painting were negative. Next door is **Claude Monet's** (1840–1926) pre-1870 work. Between the banks of galleries running along the Seine side of the Orsay is a large, open room containing the Realist works of **Gustave Courbet** (1819–77), considered by current scholars to be the first modernist. (For more Courbet, check out the **Petit Palais** *in* Art Museums, *below*.) And trailing up along the staircase in the northeast corner of the museum is a montage of Parisian facades, starting with the Restoration and moving chronologically through the July Monarchy, Second Republic, Second Empire, and Third Republic.

MIDDLE FLOOR • Covered here are early 20th-century sculptures, including works by **Auguste Rodin** (1840–1917) and **Camille Claudel** (1864–1903). (Rodin and Claudel enthusiasts should also check out the Musée Rodin; *see* Museums, *below*.) The galleries on either sides of the battlements are filled with architecture and furniture design from the turn of the century. Across the terrace are rooms dedicated to non-French designers of the same period, including the American architect **Frank Lloyd Wright** (1867–1959) and the Scot **Charles Rennie Mackintosh** (1868–1928), an early modernist.

UPPER FLOOR • Entering the first gallery from the northeastern stairs or elevator, you'll find the Impressionist works. The Impressionists challenged the status quo with their detailed theories about the effects of light, movement, and color, finding a slew of new subjects to paint with the advent of huge, modern boulevards, cafés, and department stores in late 19th-century Paris. On this floor is Manet's controversial *Déjeuner sur l'Herbe*. The subject, naked ladies and clothed men in a bucolic setting, wasn't new to the French public in 1863; everybody was familiar with similar scenes from the Italian Renaissance and French Baroque paintings hanging in the Louvre. But there was something about the modern dress of the men, the discarded clothes of the women, and the way two of the figures look at the viewer with a slightly confrontational gaze that upset the critics.

This floor also contains the famous portrait of the mother of **James McNeill Whistler** (1834–1903), embodying all the spartan puritanism associated with the rural United States of the late 19th century, and works by **Claude Monet** and **Auguste Renoir** (1841–1919). Another gallery is devoted to **Paul Cézanne** (1839–95), who challenged the salons of Paris by ignoring them and playing with color and spatial relationships. Around the corner, past the Café des Hauteurs, is a room filled with the work of **Vincent van Gogh** (1854–90), who spent his most productive years in France. Next, you have the work of **Le Douanier Rousseau** (1844–1910), whose naive and flattened touch delineated fairy tale–like jungle scenes complete with exotic animals hidden in the dense underbrush. Farther along are works by **Georges Seurat** (1859–91), whose use of dots of color became known as pointillism.

At the end of the hallway are early works by **Henri Matisse** (1869–1954), whose 1904 *Luxe, Calme, et Volupté* helped him earn the label fauvist, an uncomplimentary term coined by the critics, who thought his bright colors were *comme un fauve* (like a wild beast). For another big batch of Impressionists and Postimpressionists in a smaller setting, make time for the Musée de l'Orangerie and the Musée Marmottan (for both, *see* Museums, *below*).

PLACE DE LA CONCORDE

In no other spot in Paris can you turn 360 degrees and see so many monuments. Place de la Concorde is a Kodak dream come true, provided you aren't flattened by the hundreds of cars that tear through it. It was at this spot that Louis XVI lost his head (literally), as did Marie-Antoinette and hundreds of others during the French Revolution. The place is flanked on the northern side by the **Hôtel de la Marine** and the ritzy **Hôtel Crillon,** with the **Église de la Madeleine** (*see* Houses of Worship, *below*) rising up between them. To the west you can stare right up the Champs-Élysées to the Arc de Triomphe and, on unusually clear days, to La Défense and its huge, futuristic office towers. On the eastern side is the Jardin des Tuileries, leading to the Louvre. To the south you have the fancy **Pont de la Concorde,** leading to the colonnaded facade of the **Assemblée Nationale** (house of representatives). Smack-dab in the middle of the square, looking not so very French, is the **Obélisque de Luxor,** packed off to King Louis-Philippe from Thebes by Egyptian leader Mohammed Ali in 1831. The hieroglyphics, which run 75 ft high, tell the tales of Ramses II; the more modern tale of how they got the 230-ton monument from Egypt to Paris is engraved on the bottom (a special ship equipped with cranes and pulleys was built to carry it). *8e and 1er. Métro: Concorde.*

SAINTE-CHAPELLE

Sainte-Chapelle is a sublime Gothic chapel with wall-to-wall stained glass. Ascending to the upper chapel is like climbing into a jewelry box: Brilliantly colored windows fill the interior with light—you get the exhilarating feeling that the building has walls of glass. Be sure to try and go on a sunny day, or when the sun is setting. The less-grand lower chapel, once reserved for the king's servants, is paved with the faceless, worn tombstones of clerics and forgotten knights.

In the middle of the 13th century, Louis IX ordered the building of Sainte-Chapelle. The elegant result was completely unlike massive contemporaries Chartres (see Ile-de-France, below) and Notre-Dame (see above); rather than impressing with scale, Sainte-Chapelle turns its efforts toward piously luxuriant details. Louis's influence is everywhere in the cathedral; he even had his own private entryway to the chapel so he wouldn't have to mingle with the less worthy. Inside Palais de Justice, 4 blvd. du Palais, 1er, tel. 01–53–73–78–51. Métro: Cité. Admission 32F, joint ticket with La Conciergerie (see below) 50F. Open daily 9:30–6:30 (10–5 off-season).

TOUR EIFFEL

It's funny to think that a construction so abhorred by the French public upon its conception could become the monument most closely associated with the country. In 1885, the city held a contest to design a 1,000-ft tower for the 1889 World Exposition: Gustave Eiffel won. It was slated for the junkyard even as it was being built, but somewhere along the way people realized it might actually have a practical use or two—deciphering German radio codes during World War I, hosting a forest of TV and radio antennae, or acting as a launching pad for 350 airborne suicides.

If you want to pop into a museum just before closing, keep in mind that ticket offices close 15–45 minutes before the posted closing time of the galleries.

The close-up view of the Eiffel Tower is considerably more striking than the view from across town. When you venture a glance down from the top, remember that this was the world's tallest building until New York's Chrysler Building took over that title in 1930. Nowadays, it's simply a source of wonder for legions of visitors, especially at night when it's entirely, and subtly, lit up. The hour-long lines to ascend in summer are decidedly less wonderful; to avoid them, try visiting early in the morning or late at night. The best view, though, is on a clear day an hour before sunset, when visibility from the top extends nearly 90 km (54 mi). To save money, walk up to the second level and take the elevator from there to the top. Champ de Mars, 7e, tel. 01–44–11–23–23. Métro: Bir-Hakeim. RER: Champ de Mars. Admission (elevator) 21F to 1st level, 43F to 2nd level, 60F to top. Admission (stairs) 15F to 2nd level. Open daily 9:30 AM–11 PM (until midnight July–Aug.).

Just across the Pont d'Iéna bridge from the Eiffel Tower is the **Trocadéro** plaza, home to gardens, spectacular fountains, and the Palais de Chaillot museum complex. The view of the Eiffel Tower from here is unsurpassed, especially when the fountains shoot up and frame it. During the day and into the evening in summer, performers, vendors, skateboarders, and tourists all gather around the plaza and do their thing. Some even visit the museums.

MUSEUMS

In addition to the big museums covered above, Paris has many smaller spaces that may fit your various tastes and moods. Like everything else in Paris, though, most of these museums are not cheap, but you may qualify for a discount. Youths and students can get discounts, though these vary from place to place—sometimes they are given to those 25 and under or sometimes to students only. Other discounts are available to the elderly and children; in national museums, visitors in wheelchairs and their attendants also receive reduced rates. In addition, some sights have reduced admission one day of the week or after 3 PM. Bring many forms of ID and hope for the best.

The association InterMusée spends a large sum of money advertising its **Carte Musées et Monuments** (Museums and Monuments Pass), valid for entry to most of Paris's museums. The pass—valid for either one day (70F), three days (140F), or five days (200F) and sold at participating museums and most major métro stations—is only a deal if you both (a) don't qualify for any discount admissions and (b) have the stamina of a marathon runner. Keep in mind that after 3 PM at the Louvre you only have to pay 26F for 6,000 years of art.

ART MUSEUMS

ESPACE MONTMARTRE—DALÍ • This museum has more than 300 works by the self-proclaimed master of surrealism, **Salvador Dalí** (1904–89), but it isn't quite as exciting as the Dalí museum in Spain. Nonetheless, the dark, sunken chambers of Espace Montmartre still contain an impressive display of the artist's dream landscapes, psychedelic sculptures, and ink etchings. But be warned: Most of the works are lithographs and castings produced in the winter of the artist's life, when a sick and senile Dalí was signing his name to works by his students. *11 rue Poulbot, 18e, tel. 01–42–64–40–10. Métro: Anvers or Abbesses. Admission 35F. Open July–Aug., daily 10–7; Sept.–June, daily 10–6.*

FONDATION CARTIER • The Fondation Cartier has a reputation as one of the corporate world's greatest patrons of contemporary art; its new exhibition space highlights its commitment. Designed by Jean Nouvel, the building is one of Paris's most stunning, a mélange of vast glass panes, complicated steel structures, and exposed mechanical work. Upstairs the watch-and-jewelry empire executives are hard at work in the Cartier headquarters, and in the basement and ground floor are galleries. The best way to experience both the art and Nouvel's building is to come on Thursday nights when the series **"Les Soirées Nomades"** (Evenings of the Nomad) offers dance, performance art, or live music around and about the art. *261 blvd. Raspail, 14e, tel. 01–42–18–56–50. Métro: Denfert-Rochereau. Admission 30F; "Les Soirées Nomades" included in admission. Open Tues.–Sun. noon–8 (Thurs. until 10).*

GRAND PALAIS AND PETIT PALAIS • Intended as temporary additions to the Parisian landscape for the 1900 Exposition Universelle, these domed extravaganzas dodged the wrecking ball to become full-time tourist attractions. The **Grand Palais** became a salon space and the site of ballooning exhibitions, at which well-heeled ladies and gentlemen would gather under the glass-domed ceilings, heads tilted toward the puffed-up names of Michelin and Goodyear, and marvel at the future of travel. In more recent years, big-time art exhibitions have been filling the modest halls of the building's wings, although, unfortunately, its landmark glass-and-iron main hall is closed for renovation until at least 2002. *3 av. du Général-Eisenhower, 8e, tel. 01–44–13–17–17. Métro: Champs-Élysées–Clemenceau. Admission 25F–45F, depending on exhibit. Open Thurs.–Mon. 10–8, Wed. 10–10.*

The **Petit Palais,** across the street, displays works in rich, vaulted halls that are grander than those of the Grand Palais. In addition to temporary exhibits, there's a permanent collection featuring 17th-century Flemish works and particularly strong coverage of 19th-century French painters—Courbet's risqué 1866 *Le Sommeil,* of two naked women napping together, is especially popular—and a handful of Impressionist-era works. There are also large cases of turn-of-the-century jewelry, including many art nouveau pieces. *Av. Winston-Churchill, 8e, tel. 01–42–65–12–73. Métro: Champs-Élysées–Clemenceau. Admission 27F; temporary exhibits about 25F–45F extra. Open Tues.–Sun. 10–5:40.*

JEU DE PAUME • Named for the indoor tennis court that once stood in the royal Jardin des Tuileries (see *Parks and Gardens,* below*),* the Jeu de Paume held much of the national Impressionist collection until the Musée d'Orsay (see *Major Attractions,* above*)* opened in 1986. The building stood neglected for five years until renovation created one of Paris's most inviting exhibition spaces. Exhibits feature modern and contemporary masters, and the **cinema** shows related documentaries (free with gallery admission). There's a small café and a bookstore with a strong collection of art criticism and catalogs. *1 pl. de la Concorde, 1er, tel. 01–42–60–69–69. Métro: Concorde. Admission 38F. Open Tues. noon–9:30, Wed.–Fri. noon–7, weekends 10–7.*

MUSÉE D'ART MODERNE DE LA VILLE DE PARIS • Even though it was founded at the turn of the century, the City of Paris's Modern Art Museum has had a difficult time convincing the world that there is another major venue for modern art in Paris besides the Centre Georges-Pompidou (*see* Major Attractions, *above*): Many of the 30,000 works forming the permanent collection were donated by artists such as Henri Matisse and Robert Motherwell, but there is still a dearth of high-profile pieces. The museum focuses on the contemporary works of more controversial artists and also hosts temporary exhibits and occasional concerts. On the way to the top floor it is impossible not to notice **Raoul Dufy**'s (1877–1953) *Fée Electricité,* in which 720 square yards of bright colors fervently depict the harnessing of electricity by humanity. Off the terrace on the ground floor is a bookstore that stocks a diverse selection of art books in English and French. *11 av. du Président-Wilson, 16e, tel. 01–47–23–61–27. Métro: Iéna. Admission: permanent collection 30F; temporary exhibitions 30F–40F. Open Tues.–Fri. 10–5:30, weekends 10–6:45.*

MUSÉE DES ARTS DÉCORATIFS • You may finally realize just how big the Louvre is when you consider that this major collection of decorative arts occupies only part of one of its wings. Spread confusingly over the museum's four floors are chairs, vases, sword cases, and other necessities of life from the Middle Ages down to the present. The art nouveau era is best represented. A sluggish restoration program, causing parts of the collection to be off limits, was scheduled for completion sometime in 1999. *107 rue de Rivoli, 1er, tel. 01–44–55–57–50. Métro: Palais-Royal. Admission 35F. Open Tues.– Sun. 11–6.*

MUSÉE MARMOTTAN–CLAUDE MONET • This is the perfect museum if you're a fan of Impressionism but don't feel up to the mighty Musée d'Orsay (*see* Major Attractions, *above*). A couple of years ago this museum tacked "Claude Monet" on to its official name—and justly so, as it has a wonderful collection of the artist's works. Pictures by fellow Impressionists, illuminated medieval manuscripts, and gilded Napoleonic furniture fill out the rest of this fine mansion. Among such well-known Monet works as the series *Cathédrale à Rouen* and *Parlement à Londres*, you'll find *Impressions: Soleil Levant* (1873), now recognized as the first Impressionist painting. Some of the rooms make you feel as if you're at an actual salon, with comfy couches and grand windows overlooking the Jardin de Ranelagh on one side, the hotel's private yard on the other. *2 rue Louis-Boilly, 16e, tel. 01–42–24–07–02. Métro: La Muette. Admission 40F. Open Tues.–Sun. 10–5:30.*

MUSÉE NATIONAL DU MOYEN-AGE • The National Museum of the Middle Ages, formerly known as the Musée de Cluny, is built upon the remains of some Roman baths. Featured are medieval stained glass, furniture, jewelry, carvings, music manuscripts, and some exquisite tapestries. One of the finest tapestry series—found half eaten by rats before being brought here—is *The Lady and the Unicorn*, comprising six panels in which a refined lady demonstrates the five senses to a unicorn. The museum also displays a set of sculpted heads of the kings of Judea that once looked out from the facade of the Cathédrale de Notre-Dame (*see* Major Attractions, *above*); thought to have been lost during the Revolution, they were rediscovered in a bank vault in 1977. *6 pl. Paul-Painlevé, 5e, tel. 01–53–73–78–00. Métro: Cluny–La Sorbonne. Admission 30F, 20F Sun. Open Wed.–Mon. 9:15–5:45.*

MUSÉE DE L'ORANGERIE • This small but rewarding collection of Impressionist and Postimpressionist paintings sits peacefully near the Jardin des Tuileries. Like the Musée Marmottan (*see* Major Attractions, *above*), this museum is especially nice if you're in the mood for turn-of-the-century art but can't deal with the enormity of the Musée d'Orsay. Below generous rooms of Renoirs and thorough displays of Cézanne, Manet, and Modigliani lies the museum's most popular room: a magical, watery oval space lined with Monet's huge water-lily paintings. Inspired by Monet's home at Giverny (*see* Ile-de-France, *below*), the *Nymphéas* are perhaps the best known of his "series" works—repeated studies of the effects of different lighting upon the same subject. *Pl. de la Concorde, 1er, tel. 01–42–97–48–16. Métro: Concorde. Admission 30F, 20F Sun. Open Wed.–Mon. 9:45–5.*

MUSÉE PICASSO • Because Spaniard Pablo Picasso's family couldn't come up with enough cash to settle the taxes on his estate, they donated a large number of his works to the French government instead. The government then created a museum for them, in the beautiful 17th-century Hôtel Salé in the heart of the Marais district. The Musée Picasso is one of the most popular museums in Paris, largely because the place is so pleasant: a tailored garden out back; a stately driveway out front; a covered sculpture garden in between; and art all over the basement, the attic, and the two stories of the mansion. *5 rue de Thorigny, 3e, tel. 01–42–71–25–21. Métro: Chemin Vert or St-Paul. Admission 30F, 20F Wed. Open Apr.–Sept., Wed.–Mon. 9:30–6; Oct.–Mar., Wed.–Mon., 9–5:30.*

MUSÉE RODIN • The Musée Rodin is possibly the most beautiful museum in all of Paris. The undisputed master of 19th-century French sculpture left his house, the early 18th-century Hôtel Biron, and all the works in it to the state when he died. The mansion, with the second-largest garden in the neighborhood (after the prime minister's), is as much a part of the museum as the art. In addition to the gardens (which are only 5F if you don't care about the museum) and the pavilion exhibiting temporary shows, you can see Rodin's personal collection of Impressionist and Postimpressionist paintings. The Rodin museum also allows some space to works by **Camille Claudel** (1864–1943). Rodin's mistress, Claudel was a remarkable sculptor in her own right. *77 rue de Varenne, 7e, tel. 01–44–18–61–10. Métro: Varenne. Admission 28F, 18F Sun. Open Tues.–Sun. 9:30–5:45 (9:30–4:45 Oct.–Mar.).*

FRENCH HISTORY AND CULTURE

LA CONCIERGERIE • This complex of towers and halls served as the royal palace until 1358, when a young Charles V sought to place a safe distance between himself and his potentially revolutionary masses by building the Louvre across the Seine. Since the 14th century, the Conciergerie (named for the title of the official who administered the castle) has served as a tribunal hall and prison, but its most macabre period came in the 18th century, when the Revolutionary court mercilessly issued death proclamations—2,780 to be exact—from its halls. Much of the nobility passed through these cells, but the most famous resident was Marie-Antoinette, who spent her final days here before being hauled off in a garbage cart to be guillotined. The court disbanded after the execution of Robespierre, who became

TURKISH DELIGHTS

For a decadent experience, spend an afternoon at the "hammam" (39 rue Geoffroy-St-Hilaire, 5e, tel. 01–43–31–38–20), the Turkish baths in La Mosquée. Lie around naked in one of the steam rooms or in the bathing area, listening to Arabic music and drinking mint tea (10F). To maximize your pleasure, bring something to slather all over your body, a sponge, and some water so you don't get dehydrated. Women are admitted Monday and Wednesday–Saturday, men on Tuesday and Sunday. Admission is 85F and towel rental is 12F. The baths are open Wednesday–Monday 10–9 and Tuesday 2–9.

the victim of the Terror he had himself initiated. Now the Conciergerie is merely the basement of the Palais de Justice, which also houses Sainte-Chapelle (*see* Major Attractions, *above*). *1 quai de l'Horloge, 1er, tel. 01–53–73–78–50. Métro: Cité. Admission 32F, 50F joint ticket with Sainte-Chapelle. Open Apr.–Sept., daily 9:30–6:30; Oct.–Mar., daily 10–5.*

MAISON DE VICTOR HUGO • The former home of France's literary hero has become a two-story museum in his honor, though it displays none of the manuscripts for which he was so adored. What is interesting here is the re-created rooms on the second floor (where Hugo's apartment was) and the artwork on the first, including some Gothic-horror watercolors by Hugo and illustrations for his writings by other painters, including Bayard's rendition of Cosette from *Les Misérables* (now a famous T-shirt). *6 pl. des Vosges, 4e, tel. 01–42–72–10–16. Métro: St-Paul. Admission 27F. Open Tues.–Sun. 10–5:45.*

MUSÉE CARNAVALET • It takes two hôtels particuliers in the Marais—the Carnavalet and Le Peletier de St-Fargeau—to house this worthwhile collection paying homage to Parisian history. Basically, the Carnavalet (through which you enter) covers ancient Paris through the reign of Louis XVI, and the Peletier covers the Revolution through the 20th century. In the courtyard off rue de Sévigné stands the last remaining bronze statue of a Louis: Louis XIV, whose representation by Antoine Coysevox was saved from Revolutionary meltdown only by oversight. Other treasures include Jean-Jacques Rousseau's inkwell and blackened blotting sponge; keys to the Bastille; and a copy of Napoléon I's death mask. Most entertaining, however, are the re-created rooms, particularly Marcel Proust's bedroom. *23 rue de Sévigné, 3e, tel. 01–42–72–21–13. Métro: St-Paul. Admission 27F. Open Tues.–Sun. 10–5:40.*

MUSÉE DE LA MODE ET DU COSTUME • In the 1920s, Paris decided it needed a fashion museum, and after a couple of trial runs at World Expos, this is where it wound up. The temporary exhibits, usually centering on fashionable aspects of Paris's past, feature hundreds of items of clothing and accessories. *10 av. Pierre-1er-de-Serbie, 16e, tel. 01–47–20–85–23. Métro: Iéna. Admission 40F. Open Tues.–Sun. 10–5:40.*

MUSÉE DE MONTMARTRE • This space houses a fascinating but small collection of photos and changing exhibits on life in Montmartre, including displays about famous former inhabitants, drawings by Toulouse-Lautrec, and minor works by Modigliani, Utrillo, and others. *12 rue Cortot, 18e, tel. 01–46–06–61–11. Métro: Lamarck-Caulaincourt. Admission 25F. Open Tues.–Sun. 11–6.*

MUSÉE DES MONUMENTS FRANÇAIS • Architects will appreciate this collection—at press time, scheduled for reopening in 1999 after being damaged by fire in 1997—which displays models of all of Paris's great monuments in one small space. Hundreds of reproductions of portals, statues, and other pieces represent all the blockbuster structures in France from Chartres to Mont-St-Michel. *1 pl. du Trocadéro, 16e, tel. 01–44–05–39–05. Métro: Trocadéro. Admission 25F. Open Wed.–Mon. 10–6.*

MUSÉE DE LA POSTE • This is a whole museum dedicated to stamps and the history of written communication, including the balloon used to get mail out of Paris during the 1870 Prussian siege. Ongoing renovation at press time should have been completed during 1999, with the museum staying open in the meantime for exhibitions on the ground floor. *34 blvd. de Vaugirard, 15e, tel. 01–42–79–23–45. Métro: Montparnasse-Bienvenue. Admission 30F. Open Mon.–Sat. 10–6.*

MUSÉE DU JUDAÏSME • It took a 20-year, $35 million restoration scheme to transform the 17th-century Hôtel St-Aignan—whose clifflike courtyard ringed by giant pilasters is one of the most awesome sights in the Marais—into a museum of Jewish art and history, opened in 1998. Jews settled in the Rhone Valley in the 1st century BC, and there is record of a synagogue in Paris in 582, but Jews were not granted French citizenship until 1791. The carefully lit exhibits, including silverware, costumes, and furniture, are flanked by lengthy explanatory English texts. Highlights include an artful array of 13th-century tombstones excavated in Paris; wooden models of destroyed East European synagogues; a roomful of early Chagalls; and Christian Boltanski's stark tribute to Holocaust victims, with wall plaques naming the inhabitants of the Hôtel St-Aignan in 1939, and canvas hangings listing the personal details of the 13 Jews among them who died in concentration camps. *71 rue du Temple, 3e, tel. 01–53–01–86–53. Métro: Rambuteau. Admission 40F. Open Sun.–Fri. 11–6.*

PAVILLON DE L'ARSENAL • Home to the Centre d'Urbanisme et d'Architecture de la Ville de Paris, this spacious late-19th-century arsenal is devoted entirely to documenting and exploring the buildings of Paris. Dominating the ground floor is the **Grande Modèle,** a 432-square-ft model of Paris, complete with interactive computer screens. Temporary exhibits take up the ground floor and upper loft. The **library** has architecture periodicals and 70,000 photographs of Paris. *21 blvd. Morland, 4e, tel. 01–42–76–33–97. Métro: Sully-Morland. Admission free. Open Tues.–Sat. 10:30–6:30, Sun. 11–7.*

NATURAL HISTORY

GRANDE GALERIE DE L'ÉVOLUTION • Part of the Musée National d'Histoire Naturelle (Natural History Museum complex), this 19th-century Hall of Evolution, tastefully renovated at the start of the 1990s, is popular with children and

The Musée de l'Homme's prize piece is Descartes's skull, the answer to the mind-body problem preserved forever in a little glass case.

includes a grand parade of stuffed bears, tigers, elephants, and giraffes. Admire the remnants of extinct species, and sit yourself down in the comfortable leather chairs in front of TV screens documenting the fascinating art of taxidermy. Thursday nights the museum hosts a debate, lecture, or film on some aspect of natural history, included in the admission price. *Jardin des Plantes, 36 rue Geoffroy-St-Hilaire, 5e, tel. 01–40–79–30–00. Métro: Censier-Daubenton. Admission 40F. Open Wed.–Mon. 10–6 (Thurs. until 10).*

MUSÉE DE L'HOMME • Visiting this anthropology museum in the Palais de Chaillot is like taking a trip around the world and through about 3 million years of history. Permanent exhibits show clothing, musical instruments, and other artifacts of the major cultures of the world (African, Asian, Middle Eastern, European, Native North and South American, indigenous Australian, South Pacific, Arctic). Excellent temporary exhibits highlight topics such as prehistoric funeral rites. *17 pl. du Trocadéro, 16e, tel. 01–44–05–72–72. Métro: Trocadéro. Admission 30F. Open Wed.–Mon. 9:45–5:15.*

PHOTOGRAPHY

CENTRE NATIONAL DE LA PHOTOGRAPHIE • Photographs previously housed in the Palais de Tokyo have been relocated to the ground floor of the sprawling Hôtel Salomon de Rothschild, home of the Centre National de la Photographie. Big-name shows featuring a single genre or artist dominate the main gallery, though peripheral rooms may display works from the permanent collection. *11 rue Berryer, 8e, tel. 01–53–76–12–32. Métro: George V. Admission 30F. Open Wed.–Mon. noon–7. Closed Aug.*

MAISON EUROPÉENNE DE LA PHOTOGRAPHIE • This modern, three-story photographic center in the Marais has a frequently changing program of exhibitions by European and American postwar photographers. *5 rue de Fourcy, 4e, tel. 01–44–78–75–00. Métro: St-Paul. Admission 23F. Open Wed.–Sun. 11–8.*

MISSION DU PATRIMOINE PHOTOGRAPHIQUE • Set up by the Ministry of Culture, this small photography gallery, with continually changing exhibits, specializes in avant-garde and contemporary work. Housed in a corner of one of the Marais's grandest mansions, the Hôtel de Sully, the gallery overlooks a beautiful courtyard leading into place des Vosges. *62 rue St-Antoine, 4e, tel. 01–42–74–47–75. Métro: St-Paul. Admission 25F. Open Tues.–Sun. 10–6:30.*

SCIENCE AND TECHNOLOGY

CITE DES SCIENCES ET DE L'INDUSTRIE • This museum of science and industry is a mammoth orgy of everything industrial and scientific, inviting you to play with, test out, or simply marvel at its many exhibits. Give yourself at least half a day to see everything. The structure is indeed the size of a small city—it's three times the size of the Pompidou—and was built in 1986 on land that once housed

Paris's slaughterhouses. Now the area is all glass and stainless steel, crisscrossed by bridges and suspended walkways. The permanent exhibit is dedicated to scientific exploration, with explanations in English, French, German, Spanish, and Italian. Hands-on experiments include futuristic musical instruments, environmental manipulation, a simulated space voyage, and cutting-edge photography. The second-floor **planetarium** is well worth a stop. The magnificent steel sphere in front of the exhibit building is the **Géode cinema** (tel. 01–40–05–12–12), with the largest projection screen in existence; tickets for films (usually nature flicks) are sold separately for 57F. The Cité backs up to the equally playful **Parc de La Villette** (*see* Parks and Gardens, *below*). *Parc de La Villette, 30 av. Corentin-Cariou, 19e, tel. 01–40–05–70–00. Métro: Porte de La Villette. Admission 50F. Open Tues.–Sun. 10–6.*

PALAIS DE LA DÉCOUVERTE • The worst thing about this museum, in a back wing of the Grand Palais (*see above*), is the preponderance of grammar-school student groups. The best thing is its quality displays on all branches of science, from the solar system to the human brain. The exhibits are informative and eye-catching. **Planetarium** shows cost an extra 13F. *Av. Franklin-D.-Roosevelt, 8e, tel. 01–40–74–81–73. Admission 27F. Open Tues.–Sat. 9:30–6, Sun. 10–7.*

WORLD HISTORY AND CULTURE

MUSÉE DES ARTS D'AFRIQUE ET D'OCÉANIE • The excellent collection on display here is divided by region and well explained, *if* you read French. The ground floor houses displays on **South Pacific cultures** and temporary exhibits. The first floor turns to **central African cultures,** looking at great kingdoms in the Congo and Benin. The top floor is dedicated to the heavily colonized countries of the **Maghreb** (Algeria, Tunisia, and Morocco). Finally, in the basement lurk crocodiles of the Nile, in a ditch that curators have tried their hardest to transform into a natural habitat. The calm **aquarium** surrounding the crocs is home to a second ditch (filled with turtles) and beautiful sea creatures. *293 av. Daumesnil, 12e, tel. 01–44–74–84–80. Métro: Porte Dorée. Admission 30F. Open Wed.–Mon. 10–5:30.*

MUSÉE GUIMET • Much of the enormous collection of religious and secular artwork from China, Japan, India, Indochina, Indonesia, and central Asia, spanning more than 3,000 years, has sadly been hidden from view since 1996, when momentous renovations began; the museum was expected to reopen in early spring 2000. Some of the finest pieces have been on exhibit at the museum **annex** (19 av. d'Iéna), which majors in Buddha images from China and Japan. *6 pl. d'Iéna, 16e, tel. 01–45–05–00–98. Métro: Iéna. Admission details unknown at press time.*

HOUSES OF WORSHIP

CATHEDRALE DE ST-DENIS

The first major Gothic building built anywhere in the world, the Cathedral of St-Denis, also known as the Basilique de St-Denis, sits in the square of an industrial suburb to the north of Paris. Built in the 12th and 13th centuries, St-Denis—with loads of stained glass, high-pointed arches, and a rose window with the signs of the zodiac—set the style for the next four centuries of French cathedrals. The real excitement of a trip to the cathedral involves the distinguished (though dead) company you will keep. The 32F admission to the **choir, ambulatory,** and **crypt** allows you access to 15 centuries of French royalty, including peeks at their mismatched bones and a delightful cabinet of embalmed hearts—including one former pumper encased in a glass bulb. It seems like everyone is here, including Catherine de' Medici (depicted in one statue conspicuously young, dead, and naked), Marie-Antoinette (gently grazing her right nipple for all eternity), and Louis XIV. While checking out the corpses, note the foundations of previous crypts; the site has been used as a necropolis since Roman times. *Tel. 01–48–09–83–54. Métro: St-Denis–Basilique, north of 18e. Admission to choir, ambulatory, crypt 32F. Crypt open summer, Mon.–Sat. 10–7, Sun. noon–7; winter, Mon.–Sat. 10, Sun. noon–5. Sun. mass at 7:30, 8:30, and 10 AM.*

EGLISE DE LA MADELEINE

When the Église de la Madeleine finally opened its huge bronze doors in 1842, it instantly became one of the largest French neoclassical buildings ever built. The church stands alone in the center of a busy thoroughfare as a proudly inflated, though unfaithful, version of the classic Greek temple. The loose interpretation was intentional: The overproportioned porticoes, the interior barrel vaults–cum–domes, and the opulent versions of the Ionic and Corinthian orders were meant to be Parisian one-upping of anything Athens had to offer. Nowadays the opulent interior witnesses lots of concerts (many expensive, with the occasional afternoon freebie), as well as daily masses. A world away from the scale and politics of the church proper is the **crypt** (admission free), in whose intimate chapel weekday masses (7:30 and 8 AM) are held. The crypt is accessible from either the nave of the church or the northwest side of place de la Madeleine. *Pl. de la Madeleine, 8e, tel. 01–42–65–52–17. Métro: Madeleine. Open daily 8–7. Sun. mass at 8, 9, 10 (choral mass), and 11 AM, 12:30, and 6 PM.*

EGLISE ST-ETIENNE DU MONT

Tucked away behind the grandiose Panthéon, the church of St-Étienne, begun in the 13th century, is home to the remains of St. Geneviève, the patron saint of Paris. Inside, Gothic arches blend into the nave's columns without capitals, and a double-spiral staircase ascends the only remaining rood screen (a screen that separates the nave and the chancel) in Paris. Recent restorations have left the place clean and luminous—it's one of Paris's best churches to visit. Behind the altar are plaques marking the remains of Ste. Geneviève, Pascal, Racine, and Marat. *1 rue St-Étienne-du-Mont, 5e, tel. 01–43–54–11–79. Métro: Cardinal-Lemoine. Sun. mass at 9 and 11 AM and 6:45 PM.*

EGLISE ST-EUSTACHE

Right next door to the modern shopping structure at Les Halles, the Église St-Eustache presents a ponderous reminder that the Right Bank wasn't always all glitz and neon: The site was once the city's main marketplace, which Emile Zola dubbed "the belly of Paris." The main structure was built over nearly 100 years (1537–1632) and fuses Gothic and Renaissance in a schizophrenic stylistic mishmash, but the bland 18th-century facade is a letdown. Look for the painting *The Departure of the Fruits and Vegetables from the Heart of Paris* (1968), Raymond Mason's animated and very unchurchlike interpretation of the closing of Les Halles marketplace. *Pl. René-Cassin, 1er, tel. 01–42–36–31–05. Métro: Les Halles. Open summer, daily 8:30–8; winter, daily 8:30–7. Sun. mass at 8:30, 9:30, and 11 AM and 6 PM.*

The remains of Nobel Prize–winning scientist Marie Curie were moved into the Panthéon on April 19, 1995, making her the first woman to earn a berth among France's great dead citizens solely on merit.

EGLISE ST-GERMAIN-DES-PRES

The oldest church in Paris, St-Germain-des-Prés traces its roots to the 6th century, when then-archbishop Germanus (now known as St. Germain) built an altar to St. Symphorien on land left to the Benedictine monks by Childebert I. Though most of the present church dates from the 12th and 13th centuries, the purported remains of the original altar still stand near the entrance. Some of the remains of René Descartes (his heart) have found peace in the seventh chapel. The nave walls are covered in 19th-century frescoes by Hippolyte Flandrin. *Pl. St-Germain-des-Prés, 6e, tel. 01–43–25–41–71. Métro: St-Germain-des-Prés. Sun. mass at 9, 10, and 11:15 AM and 5 (in Spanish) and 7 PM.*

EGLISE ST-SEVERIN

This ivy-covered Gothic isle of calm amid the craziness of the St-Michel area dates from the 11th century, though most of what you see comes from 16th-century construction efforts and 18th- and 19th-century renovations. The double aisle of the ambulatory has a subterranean feel, with the ribbing of the vaults looking more as if it were holding up the earth than soaring toward the heavens. The church is at its best at night, when the only lighting comes from the base of the columns and from behind the altar. Daylight, however, is necessary to fully appreciate the stained-glass windows (1966–70) depicting the Seven Facets of the Sacrament. *Corner of rue St-Jacques and rue St-Séverin, 5e, tel. 01–43–25–96–63. Métro: St-Michel. Sun. mass at 10, noon, and 6.*

EGLISE ST-SULPICE

Glowering down on a vast, tranquil square just off bustling boulevard St-Germain, St-Sulpice is an unusual departure from most Parisian churches: The double-story loggia with freestanding columns was the first example of French neoclassicism on a monumental scale. The facade was designed in 1736 (after most of the church had already been built) by painter Jean-Nicolas Servandoni, who conceived the scheme with little regard for stodgy architectural tradition. Pity he never managed to finish the towers. Check out the huge Delacroix frescoes in the first chapel on the right. Free organ concerts are often held here. *Pl. St-Sulpice, 6e, tel. 01–46–33–21–78. Métro: St-Sulpice. Sun. mass at 7, 9, 10:15, noon, and 6:45. Half-hour organ concerts Sun. 11:30–noon; call for other concerts.*

LA MOSQUEE

Behind the Jardin des Plantes (*see* Parks and Gardens, *below*), the city's main mosque is the hub of the Parisian Muslim community. Built in the 1920s as a memorial to North African Muslims who died fight-

LA REVOLUTION

In the late 18th century, the French aristocracy was frantically trying to hold on to its privileges, the middle class was frustrated by its lack of power, and the peasants were ticked off about being taxed into oblivion. It all finally exploded with the French Revolution. The bourgeois members of the government kicked things off on June 17, 1789, by proclaiming themselves a new legislative body called the National Assembly and vowing to write a new constitution.

On July 14, Parisians of every political stripe joined the fray, storming the Bastille in search of arms for the citizen militia. In September 1791, the National Assembly adopted a constitution, all but shutting King Louis XVI out of all political proceedings. Unfortunately for him, that wasn't enough for the radical antimonarchists, called the Jacobins, who eventually gained control. They tried and executed the king in January 1793 at place de la Révolution (place de la Concorde).

Throughout the year, the newly appointed Committee of Public Safety beheaded thousands of "enemies of the Revolution." In 1794 Jacobin leader Maximilien Robespierre lost his own head. The Directory of Five then took over until Napoléon Bonaparte worked his way up to become "Emperor of the French."

ing for France in World War I, its modest white walls enclose colorful, intricately tiled courtyards, which surround the prayer room, *hammam* (baths), and an equally opulent tearoom, all designed in the tradition of North African secular architecture. Upstairs from the peaceful public gardens are institutes devoted to the study of Islam and Arab cultures. Admission to the whole complex is 15F, but you can wander around the garden for free.

Since the prayer room is used throughout the day (daily prayer times are posted inside), you should be aware of some basic customs before entering. Cover all skin above the elbow and above the calf and remove your shoes. The carved wooden altar indicates the direction of Mecca; if you sit, point your feet away. Non-Muslims are never allowed in during daily calls to prayer; at other times, depending on the orthodoxy of the person nearest the door, women and non-Muslims may be asked to view the prayer room only from the courtyard. *Pl. du Puits-de-l'Ermite, 5e, tel. 01–36–68–70–05. Métro: Monge. Open for tours Sat.–Thurs. 10–noon and 2–6.*

DEAD FOLK

Paris's cemeteries are not just the eternal hangout of generations of famous dead folk; they also have tree-lined cobblestone paths, well-tended flowers, and ample benches where we mortals can sit and contemplate the sands of time.

Although Père-Lachaise, Montmartre, and Montparnasse take center stage, there are several other haunting burial grounds where the famed remain a little more incognito. The intimate, high-walled **Cimetière de Passy** (2 rue du Commandant-Schloesing, near pl. du Trocadéro, 16e, métro Trocadéro) is particularly inviting; it's also the everlasting home of French Impressionist **Edouard Manet** (1832–83) and modern music pioneers **Gabriel Fauré** (1845–1924) and **Claude Debussy** (1862–1918). *Hrs for all city cemeteries: mid-Mar.–early Nov., weekdays 8–6, Sat. 8:30–6, Sun. 9–6; early Nov.–mid-Mar., weekdays 8–5:30, Sat. 8:30–5:30, Sun. 9–5:30.*

For a more offbeat funerary excursion, head northwest to the **Cimetière des Chiens** (Dog Cemetery), along the Seine near the Gabriel-Péri métro station. On the second-highest point in all of Paris you'll find the **Cimetière de Belleville** (40 rue du Télégraphe, 20e, métro Télégraphe), with no famous folks but a fabulous view.

LES CATACOMBES

"Arrête! C'est ici l'Empire de la Mort" ("Stop! This is the Empire of Death"). This message scrawled at the entrance of the catacombs was enough to convince German troops in World War II to beat it. They never guessed that Resistance fighters used the creepy tunnels as a base. This dire warning now welcomes you after a winding descent through dark, clammy passages to Paris's principal ossuary and most disturbing collection of human remains. The legions of bones dumped here are separated not by owner but by type—witness the piles of skulls, rows of tibias, and stacks of spinal disks. There are also some bizarre attempts at bone art, like skulls arranged in the shape of hearts. It's all very nightmarish and unsavory and makes you feel quite . . . mortal. Be prepared to walk long distances when you come here—the tunnels stretch for miles, and the only light comes from the flashlight you bring. *1 pl. Denfert-Rochereau, 14e, tel. 01–43–22–47–63. Métro: Denfert-Rochereau. Admission 27F. Open Tues.–Fri. 2–4, weekends 9–11 and 2–4.*

CIMETIERE DE MONTMARTRE

Despite being crammed underneath a traffic bridge and next to a busy road, the Montmartre cemetery still manages to be a beautiful resting place, with big leafy trees, crumbling stones, and prowling cats. Smaller but similar to the Cimetière du Père-Lachaise (*see* Major Attractions, *above*), it has the advantage of not being mobbed by Jim Morrison fans. Though the neighborhood was once home to a lively art scene, today the dead artists draw more attention than the breathing ones. Residents here include director **François Truffaut** (1932–84), painters **Edgar Degas** (1834–1917) and **Jean-Honoré Fragonard** (1732–1806), writers **Stendhal** (1783–1842) and **Alexandre Dumas** *fils* (son; 1824–95), composer **Hector Berlioz** (1803–69) and **Jacques Offenbach** (1819–80), Russian ballet dancer **Vaslav Nijinski** (1890–1950), physicist **Jean-Bernard Foucault** (1819–68), and German poet **Heinrich Heine** (1797–1856). There's a lavish Art Nouveau tomb near the entrance in honor of novelist **Émile Zola** (1840–1902), but his remains were moved to the Panthéon in 1908. *20 av. Rachel, 18e. Métro: Blanche or Place de Clichy.*

CIMETIERE DU MONTPARNASSE

A leafy canopy hides the modern buildings looming above this peaceful cemetery with flat, orderly rows and few tourists. Denizens include angst-ridden existentialist **Jean-Paul Sartre** (1905–80), who is buried with longtime companion and fellow troubled writer **Simone de Beauvoir** (1908–86). **Charles Baudelaire** (1821–67) is memorialized here in a striking sculpture, though the poet actually reclines nearby in a tomb with other members of his family. Company for these resting greats includes author **Guy de Maupassant** (1850–93), theater-of-the-absurd guru **Eugène Ionesco** (1912–94), singer-songwriter **Serge Gainsbourg** (1929–91), composer **Camille Saint-Saëns** (1835–1921), American photographer **Man Ray** (1890–1976), and **Alfred Dreyfus** (1859–1935), the Jewish army captain falsely convicted of spying for the Germans. *3 blvd. Edgar-Quinet, 14e. Métro: Edgar-Quinet.*

PANTHEON

The Panthéon alternated as a church and a nondenominational burial ground until the funeral procession of Victor Hugo came rolling up from the Arc de Triomphe into the crypt, making it an official tomb for French VIPs. **Victor Hugo** (1802–85), the prolific author and chronicler of his generation, wasn't the first resident of the Panthéon, though; he was joining philosopher **Jean-Jacques Rousseau** (1712–78) and Rousseau's philosophical opposite, **Voltaire** (1694–1778). Writer **Émile Zola** (1840–1902) was a populist intellectual and a supporter of labor movements. His brave condemnation of anti-Semitism during the Dreyfus affair brought out as many supporters as protesters to his funeral. **Louis Braille** (1809–52) was considered worthy of a spot in the Panthéon, too—100 years after his death. His all-important hands remain at his parish churchyard. Blind, Braille taught himself to read through feeling embossed Roman letters, eventually devising the system of raised dots we know today. You can admire some colossal frescoes by Puvis de Chavannes, and a model of the giant pendulum hung here in 1851 by Léon Foucault to prove his theories about the earth's rotation. *Pl. du Panthéon, 5e, tel. 01–44–32–18–00. Métro: Cardinal-Lemoine. RER: Luxembourg. Admission 32F. Open Apr.–Sept., daily 9:30–6:30; Mar.–Oct., daily 10–6:15.*

PARKS AND GARDENS

If you need a rest from Paris's bustling streets and just want a place to sit down without having to order a cup of coffee, more than 350 green spots come to the rescue. Two sprawling *bois* (woods) on the western and eastern edges of the city can make you feel like you've escaped Paris altogether. Parks are either *à l'anglaise*, which means they're naturally overgrown in the style of English gardens, or *style français*, which means everything's planted in maddeningly neat, symmetrical rows. In most parks, you can stroll along paths and read on benches, and in only a very few can you sit on the grass—read the signs first or the *gendarmes* will not hesitate to lecture (and pursue) you. Some exceptions to the rule include the user-friendly grass in Bois de Boulogne, Bois de Vincennes, Parc des Buttes-Chaumont, and Parc de La Villette. Most parks open at dawn and are locked at dusk.

BOIS DE BOULOGNE

The Bois de Boulogne is such a convenient and pleasant place to go to get away from the urbanity of Paris that only the Eiffel Tower has more annual visitors. You are allowed to sit on (most of) the lawns, climb the trees, and do all those other park-type things you never thought you'd miss until you visited the Jardin du Luxembourg (*see below*). Boating on **Lac Inférieur** is an integral part of many a Parisian Sunday; you can rent a boat here for 45F per hour (200F deposit). Or take the ferry to the lake's islands, well worth the 7F round-trip ticket. A café serves expensive snacks and 17F cafés; you may want to bring a picnic. Other attractions include the **Jardin d'Acclimatation,** a hands-on kiddie park-zoo-playground at the north end of the park, and the incredible flower collection of the **Parc de Bagatelle.**

The park is huge and can be difficult to get around. The métro stops at the perimeter, and buses (like Bus 52 or 241 from Porte d'Auteuil or Bus 244 from Porte Maillot) cross the Bois. You can also rent bikes (20F per half hour, 30F per hour) from the stand northwest of Lac Inférieur. Though families and nice folks frequent the Bois during the day, a sleazier element dominates it at night: The Bois has always been the city's prostitution center, and it's estimated that more than 5 million francs (about $1 million) changes hands here every night. *16e. Métro: Porte Maillot, Porte Dauphine, or Porte d'Auteuil. RER: Avenue Foch.*

BOIS DE VINCENNES

Southeast of the city is another huge, relatively unmanicured, wooded area. You can rent a rowboat on either of two major lakes, **Lac des Minimes** or **Lac Daumesnil.** Also near Lac Daumesnil are the Musée des Arts d'Afrique et d'Océanie (*see* Museums, *above*), a zoo, and a Buddhist center, including a Tibetan Buddhist temple where you can meditate on weekends at 5 PM (Métro: Porte Dorée). *12e. Métro: Château de Vincennes, Porte Dorée, Porte de Charenton, or Liberté. RER: Fontenay-sous-Bois.*

JARDIN DU LUXEMBOURG

The Jardin du Luxembourg possesses all that is unique and befuddling about Parisian parks: swarms of pigeons, cookie-cutter trees, ironed-and-pressed dirt walkways, and perfect lawns meant for admiring, not touching. But the tree- and bench-lined paths offer a necessary reprieve from the incessant bustle of the Quartier Latin. The park's northern boundary is dominated by the **Palais du Luxembourg,** which is surrounded by a handful of well-armed guards; they are protecting the senators who have been deliberating in the palace since 1958. (They're handy for giving directions since they've got nothing better to do.) One of the park's great attractions is the **Théâtre des Marionnettes,** where, on Sunday morning and on Wednesday and Sunday afternoon, you can catch one of the classic *guignols* (marionette shows) for 32F. *6e. RER: Luxembourg.*

JARDIN DU PALAIS ROYAL

This garden is the picture of Parisian romance, with lines of trees, a dramatic central fountain, and benches for snuggling couples. The southern end of the park, however, receives the most attention—and controversy. In truly Parisian style, artist Daniel Buren decided in 1986 to clash the traditional with the ultramodern. His black and white columns rise up from water flowing beneath the courtyard, accompanied by fountains of rotating silver balls. At night, airport runway lights glow green and red and blue lights illuminate the columns. *1er. Métro: Palais-Royal. Open Apr.–May, daily 7 AM–10 PM; June–Aug., daily 7 AM–11 PM; Sept., daily 7 AM–9:30 PM; Oct.–Mar., daily 7 AM–8:30 PM.*

JARDIN DES PLANTES

In 1626, Louis XIII intended for this park to become "The King's Garden of Medicinal Herbs." Today, the Jardin des Plantes is the city's official botanical garden and houses more than 10,000 varieties of plants (all tidily arranged in little rows and labeled, of course), a zoo, hothouses, museums with huge collections of rocks and insects, stuffed animals at the **Grand Galerie de l'Évolution** (*see* Museums, *above*), and lots of students attending the nearby École Normale Supérieure. With the Gare d'Austerlitz along its southeastern edge, the park is a great discovery if you have a long wait for your train. *5e. Métro: Jussieu, Monge, or Gare d'Austerlitz. Admission to museums 15F–40F.*

JARDIN DES TUILERIES

A stroll around this stately (albeit dusty) onetime royal garden is like a mini monument tour: You'll see the Louvre, place de la Concorde, the Musée d'Orsay, the Eiffel Tower, and the Seine. In one direction you can see straight down the Champs-Élysées all the way to the Arc de Triomphe; in the other, you see a long, orderly expanse of garden between you and the Louvre. Besides small lawns you can't sit on and a thriving pickup scene for gay men along the Seine, the Tuileries offer statues aplenty, led by a series of women sculpted by **Aristide Maillol** (1861–1944), as well as a place to rest your weary feet after the trek down the Champs-Élysées. The park is a part of the big Louvre renovations, meaning it's been tidied up and replanted, with lots more flowers and designer hedges shooting off at odd angles. If the summer heat makes you delirious, take refuge in one of the two art museums at the west end: the **Orangerie** and the **Jeu de Paume** (*see* Museums, *above*). *1er. Métro: Tuileries or Concorde. Open summer, daily 8–9; winter, daily 8–7.*

PARC DES BUTTES-CHAUMONT

This park wins the prize for most dramatic transformation: It's been a quarry for plaster of paris, a garbage dump, slaughterhouse, and refuse pile for dead horses. A treatise on the merits of simulated nature, Buttes-Chaumont now hosts steep lawns, a mountain made of cement and rock, and a waterway and grotto. The park has gorgeous views of the city below, ducks to feed, and, just so you don't feel like you've completely escaped civilization, a small neoclassical temple at the top of the hill. *Bordered by rues de Crimée, Manin, and Botzaris, 19e. Métro: Buttes-Chaumont or Botzaris.*

Paris has not one but TWO tiny models of the Statue of Liberty (a likeness of sculptor Frédéric Bartholdi's mom): one hidden in the bushes at the Jardin du Luxembourg, the other on the allée des Cygnes (15e, Métro: Bir-Hakeim).

PARC MONTSOURIS AND CITE UNIVERSITAIRE

This hilly park (its name means "mouse mountain") is filled with sloping fields, clusters of stately trees, and a pond. But abandoned railway tracks and active RER lines cross the park, and traffic speeds around its perimeter, reminding you that you aren't in paradise yet. Across boulevard Jourdan from the park is the Cité Universitaire, a campus-style collection of residences built by foreign countries to house their nationals while they study at Parisian universities. The Cité is a nice complement to the Parc Montsouris, as you can run around, throw a Frisbee, or climb a tree without being pestered by park police. *14e. RER: Cité Universitaire.*

PARC DE LA VILLETTE

What was Paris's largest complex of slaughterhouses and stockyards is now a nice big green park with tons of high-tech buildings and toys to run around in and play with. The cattle that were once driven through this neighborhood on their way to becoming *bifteck* departed in the mid-1970s; you can check out photos documenting the good old days at the **Maison de La Villette** (tel. 01–40–03–75–10; closed Mon.). The largest park this side of the Bois de Boulogne, it's also the city's most fun. There are things like Claes Oldenberg's oversize *Buried Bicycle* to ogle, a monstrous dragon slide, catwalks, and no fewer than 11 special theme gardens, including the meditative **Jardin des Bambous** (Bamboo Garden), the steamy **Jardin des Brouillards** (Fog Garden), the **Jardin des Miroirs** (Mirror Garden), and the **Jardin des Frayeurs Enfantines** (Scary Children's Garden).

The park is bordered by the Canal St-Denis to the west and is split by the Canal de l'Ourcq through the middle; the **information folly** (211 av. Jean-Jaurès, tel. 01–40–03–75–03), near the confluence of the canals, dispenses maps and general park information. To the north of the canal de l'Ourcq is the **Cité des Sciences et de l'Industrie** museum and the nearby Géode (*see* Museums, *above*), and the semi-buried *Argonaute,* a 1950s nuclear submarine. To the south of the Canal de l'Ourcq is the slaughterhouse turned concert venue Grande Halle, which hosts jazz festivals and other big events, and the **Théâtre Paris-Villette** (tel. 01–42–02–02–68). Nearby is the state-of-the-art Cité de la Musique, which contains an assortment of theaters and recital rooms, including the **Conservatoire National Supérieur**

de Musique et de Danse (*see* Opera, Classical Music, and Dance, *below*). In addition, there's a high-tech museum of musical instruments. *19e. Métro: Porte de La Villette or Porte de Pantin.*

NEIGHBORHOODS

The following neighborhoods are in alphabetical order. If you'd rather tackle things geographically, the neighborhoods on the Right Bank are the Bastille, Belleville, Bercy, the Champs-Élysées, La Défense, Gare de l'Est/Gare du Nord, Les Halles and Beaubourg, Louvre to Opéra, the Marais, and Montmartre. On the Left Bank you'll find Montparnasse, the Quartier Latin, St-Germain-des-Prés, and Tolbiac. In the heart of the city are the Seine's two islands: the Ile de la Cité and the smaller Ile St-Louis.

BASTILLE

The only storming of the Bastille that you'll see today is that of Opéra-goers lining up for seats at the **Opéra Bastille** (*see* Opera, Classical Music, and Dance, *below*) and hip Parisians out on the town. **Place de la Bastille** is a big traffic nightmare, but it has witnessed more than speeding Renaults: A fortress—famed as a prison—once stood here, and quite a ruckus occurred on July 14, 1789. That was more than 200 years ago. Over the last 10 years, the area around the former prison has undergone a revolution of a different sort: gentrification. Galleries, shops, theaters, cafés, restaurants, and bars now occupy formerly decrepit buildings and alleys, bringing an artsy crowd to mingle with blue-collar locals. Especially good streets for exploration are **rue de la Roquette** and **rue de Charonne,** which lead you into areas largely inhabited by African and Arab Parisians. Myriad small streets between the two, such as **rue Keller** and **rue des Taillandiers,** hide cool art galleries and funky clothing and music shops.

Nocturnal activities are the Bastille's specialty. Parisians from the farthest corners of the city make the trip to hit their favorites among the amazing variety of bars here. **Rue de Lappe** and **rue de la Roquette** are packed with bars, restaurants, and the self-consciously hip. Try **rue de Charonne** to discover places with funkier crowds.

BELLEVILLE

Belleville is one of Paris's most unique and quickly changing neighborhoods. Victim to the city's urban renewal frenzy, the area's historic buildings are being replaced with ugly modern structures. Although not the most aesthetically pleasing area of Paris, Belleville does have charm; relaxed groups of men while away the hours chatting on street corners and doorsteps. It's an approachable, friendly quartier—though women traveling alone might find it a little *too* friendly. One refreshing change taking place in Belleville is the recent influx of artists, musicians, and young people who can afford to stay in this relatively undiscovered part of town. The arrival of waves of immigrants in the 20th century, most fleeing persecution in their homelands, has contributed to Belleville's international esprit: Polish, Russian, German, and Sephardic Jews; Armenians; Greeks; Spanish Republicans; Africans; Eastern Europeans; Chinese . . . all have brought their specialties to shops, markets, and restaurants throughout the district.

BERCY-TOLBIAC

The Bercy-Tolbiac neighborhood in east Paris is testimony to the French genius for urban renewal. Tucked away on the far Right Bank of the Seine, the Bercy district was for decades filled with crumbling wine warehouses. Now sports and money set the tone, with the mighty glass walls of the **Ministère des Finances** (Finance Ministry) facing off against the odd, grass-covered slopes of the pyramid-shape **Palais Omnisports** stadium. Leading east is the ultimate designer garden, and across it is American architect Frank Gehry's witty, postmodern **American Center.**

Towering directly across the Seine are the four, glass, L-shape towers of Dominique Perrault's **Bibliothèque François-Mitterrand** (11 quai François-Mauriac, 13e, tel. 01–53–79–59–59, métro Bibliothèque), open Tuesday–Saturday 10–7, Sunday noon–7, the new national library opened in 1996 and named for the late bookworm president who masterminded the project. With 11 million volumes, it surpasses the Library of Congress as the largest library in the world. The library, with its lavish, airy interior that is open to visitors, anchors the Tolbiac district. The area's most salient feature is still the myriad train tracks heading into Gare d'Austerlitz. But these are being covered as new housing sprouts up all around. The neighborhood was linked to central by a new métro line (No. 14) in 1998.

CHAMPS-ELYSEES

What was once an aristocratic pleasure park is now a commercialized tourist trap living off its reputation. Although there's a certain thrill about strutting down the world's most famous street in the shadow of the Arc de Triomphe, the abundance of characterless, overpriced shops and restaurant chains (and the lack of actual Parisians) makes the experience less than exciting. The city's attempt at bringing back splendor has included widening the white-granite sidewalks and planting lots of trees, but it still feels like the world's grandest outdoor shopping mall: Lots of French kids and tourists

Grab some wine and the one you love; then head out over the Seine on the pedestrian Pont des Arts, where musicians, artists, and other folks flock to watch the sun go down behind the Eiffel Tower.

cruise around, scoping each other out. The only exclusive thing left in the area is the private nightclubs and the haute-couture shops on the surrounding streets, particularly **avenue Montaigne.**

LA DEFENSE

With sleek modern buildings and urban art, La Défense is Paris's version of Futureland. About 2 km (1 mi) outside Paris proper, La Défense does not exactly fit the traditional idea of a "neighborhood." The 35,000 residents who live in the high-rise housing projects are easily eclipsed by the 110,000 people who work in the complex of business towers and shops. La Défense is designed to continue the longest urban axis in the world, from the Louvre westward to the **Grande Arche de La Défense,** an enormous arch that hides an office building within its walls. The Grande Arche, along with La Défense's first building, the concrete, curvaceous **CNIT** (Centre National des Industries et des Techniques), draws thousands of tourists daily. The **esplanade,** the wide concrete promenade extending along the axis, is lined with big-name art, including a sculpture by Joan Miró that sparked furious controversy over its bizarre shape; Yaacov Agam's *Waterfall,* a fountain powered by 50 computer-controlled jets; and Takis's neat-o fountain filled with traffic signal–like lights. Though it may not jibe with your sense of aesthetics, La Défense is too enormous, popular, and spectacular to ignore. Visit the information center by the Grande Arche to pick up a map outlining all the sculptures and architectural details, including information about the history of La Défense. *Métro: Grande Arche de La Défense; RER: La Défense. Admission to arch 40F. Open daily 10–7.*

GARE DE L'EST AND GARE DU NORD

Tourists breeze through this quartier on their way from the center up to Montmartre; those who stop get a more satisfying taste of Paris than you could soak up from 38 portrait sittings on place du Tertre. This is a working neighborhood filled with people who shop at functional stores and eat at reasonably priced restaurants. Many of Paris's old *passages* (covered walkways) are here, but unlike the spruced-up ones in the center, these passages are old and crumbling, housing Indian restaurants or used-book vendors. The area right around the train stations can get a little sleazy, but if you head south toward **rue du Château-d'Eau** or east toward **quai de Valmy,** you'll be rewarded with a down-to-earth look at Paris.

Come to the 9e and 10e arrondissements to ramble, hit some of Paris's hottest clubs, and eat. A large Jewish population sustains kosher restaurants and bakeries, especially in the area above métro Grands-Boulevards, and Indian and Eastern European joints crowd the 10e. Head to **rue d'Enghien** for a great marketplace. Unfortunately, it isn't a good idea to come here alone at night, particularly if you're female or if you don't know exactly where you're going; it's one of Paris's worst areas for theft.

LES HALLES AND BEAUBOURG

The site of Paris's 19th-century marketplace, Les Halles (especially the northern part) has evolved into one of Paris's most popular spots; a city project to redo the streets has proved to be successful, and nifty cafés surround **rue Montorgueil,** lined with food markets and restaurants. In the other direction, to the south of the Forum, you have the **Fontaine des Innocents,** for ages the site of a market-side common-trench cemetery, which was emptied into the Catacombes (*see* Dead Folk, *above*) after the overabundance of bodies pushed themselves above street level and the smell became unbearable. Now the public square here is filled day and night with Rasta bongo players, hair weavers, and truckloads of tourists.

Farther south are small streets filled with jazz clubs and trendy shops until you hit **place du Châtelet** and its facing theaters. The square takes its name from a notoriously harsh prison that sat on the present site of Théâtre du Châtelet until its destruction in the 19th century. That random tower just off the square is the **Tour St-Jacques,** built as an addition to a church that was torn down during the Revolution. The tower has since served as Pasteur's lab for experiments on gravity, as a quarry, and currently as a meteorological observatory.

A couple blocks northeast from Châtelet is the best-known landmark of the neighborhood: the **Centre Georges-Pompidou** (*see* Major Attractions, *above*). Around the corner at **place Igor-Stravinsky** is a wild and fanciful fountain by Jean Tinguely and Niki de Saint-Phalle. A pair of big red lips, a rotund woman, a treble clef, and other wacky sculptures turn and gurgle in the spitting streams of water, a stark contrast to the sternly Gothic **Église St-Merri** nearby.

ILE DE LA CITE

Beyond its appeal as the city's ancient heart, the Ile de la Cité is home to two of the finest Gothic buildings anywhere: **Sainte-Chapelle** and **Notre-Dame** (*see* Major Attractions, *above*). The **Crypte Archéologique** (tel. 01–43–29–83–51), on place du Parvis in front of the cathedral, became a museum after ruins were discovered in 1965 while building an underground parking structure here. Among the excavated details are parts of the 3rd-century wall of Lutetia; a Merovingian cathedral (Notre-Dame's predecessor) from AD 600; and bits of Roman and medieval houses. Diagrams, pictures, and photographs go along with the ruins and detail the history of the isle. Admission to the crypt is 32F and it's open daily 9:30–6 summer; 10–4:30 winter.

For the most tranquil moment you are likely to have on the Ile de la Cité, head to the **square du Vert-Galant** at the island's western tip for a view out over the Seine, or picnic on shady **place Dauphine.** The small garden behind Notre-Dame is another peaceful spot, where you can gaze at flying buttresses. From the back of Notre-Dame head across the street and down the steep granite stairs to the **Mémorial de la Déportation,** a striking tribute to the 200,000 French sent to death camps by the Vichy government during World War II. Inside, 200,000 crystals memorialize the victims, and the walls are lined with moving quotations by famous French writers, poets, and philosophers, etched in angular, blood-red letters. It's worth bringing a dictionary to translate the passionate sentiments.

ILE ST-LOUIS

If it weren't sitting directly behind Notre-Dame, attached by a bridge, you might not think of going to Ile St-Louis. But it is, and there is an entire street of restaurants and shops waits you. Actually, the **rue St-Louis-en-l'Ile** may be the most charming tourist street in Paris, and as a result, plenty of locals join visitors here on warm days and clear evenings. You'll find many of them standing in line at the island's best-known attraction: **Berthillon** (31 rue St-Louis-en-l'Ile, 4e, tel. 01–43–54–31–61), hands down Paris's most famous ice creamery. As you wander around the Ile St-Louis, keep an eye out for the building plaques describing who lived where when, and why it's important. The **Hôtel de Lauzun** at 17 quai d'Anjou was one of Baudelaire's haunts. An especially somber reminder adorns 19 quai de Bourbon: "Here lived Camille Claudel, sculptor, from 1899 to 1913. Then ended her brave career as an artist and began her long night of internment." Claudel's family committed her to an insane asylum where she was forbidden to practice her art. Some of her works are displayed in the Musée Rodin (*see* Museums, *above*).

LOUVRE TO OPERA

Yeah, it's terribly expensive, snobbish, and packed with tourists. But any neighborhood that has the centers of the Western art, theater, and music worlds all within a 15-minute walk can't be all bad. The **Louvre** (*see* Major Attractions, *above*) is the biggie here, displaying thousands of works in what was originally a royal palace. Just a block above it is the **Comédie Française** (*see* Theater, *below*), tacked on to another royal residence, the **Palais Royal** (*see* Parks and Gardens, *above*), and pointing the way up **avenue de l'Opéra.** At the end of this promenade is, of course, the **Opéra Garnier** (*see* Opera, Classical Music, and Dance, *below*).

If you don't come to this district to pose with the pretentious or shop in the nearby grands magasins, you'll probably come for practical reasons—it's home to all of the major airlines, travel agencies, and tourist bureaus. Off avenue de l'Opéra, however, you'll find the famous restaurants, age-old bistros, and upscale shops that form the opulent heart of the quarter. Lately, a sizable Japanese population has moved in, bringing restaurants, bookstores, and specialty shops with them. North of the **Jardin du Palais Royal** is **rue des Petits-Champs,** whose bounty of iron-and-glass passages makes it one of the neighborhood's best spots for roaming. The street ends in the intimate **place des Victoires**; its matching facades were designed in 1685 by Versailles architect Hardouin-Mansart. Louis XIV was so pleased with the results that he had Hardouin-Mansart do another, **place Vendôme,** on the other side of avenue de l'Opéra. Snobbish and self-important, place Vendôme is also unarguably gorgeous; property laws have kept away cafés and other such banal establishments, leaving the plaza stately and refined, the perfect home for the Ritz and Cartier (Chopin lived and died at No. 12).

West of the Louvre and Opéra is the decadent **Église de la Madeleine** (*see* Houses of Worship, *above*); the surrounding area is where rich French do their shopping. **Place de la Madeleine** is home to a great flower market Tuesday–Sunday. To stroll among the well-heeled of Paris, head to its version of Rodeo Drive, **rue du Faubourg-St-Honoré,** where ridiculously expensive clothes grace the windows of ridiculously expensive boutiques. While you're in the area, stop in and tell the president what you think of his country—the **Palais de l'Élysée** on place Beauvau has been the official residence of the head of state since 1873.

Next to the Église Madeleine you'll find the most beautiful pay toilets in all of Paris—a stunning display of art deco and porcelain. The cost for this luxury is a mere 2F.

LE MARAIS

The Marais covers the 3e and 4e arrondissements, and though its narrow streets get crowded in summer, this is one of Paris's best neighborhoods for eating, drinking, singing, walking, and just hanging out. The last 20 years have seen the transformation of the Marais into the trendy, artsy neighborhood that it is today, with a good mix of artists' studios and working-class folk. Jewish immigrants from North Africa have brought new life to the quarter, and you'll discover a hodgepodge of falafel stands, kosher butchers, and bookstores with tomes in Hebrew, Arabic, and French. The **Jewish quarter,** centered on rue des Rosiers and rue des Écouffes, adds to the Marais's bustling, sometimes bizarre character: Hasidic Jews with beards and yarmulkes emerge from the kosher stores, passing young men in tight shirts heading to gay bars. Though interior visits are discouraged (most effectively by the locked gate), at least walk past the **1913 synagogue** (10 rue Pavée, 4e) designed by art nouveau great Hector Guimard. The **Mémorial du Martyr Juif Inconnu** (Memorial of the Unknown Jewish Martyr) and the **Centre de Documentation Juive Contemporaine** (17 rue Geoffroy-l'Asnier, 4e, tel. 01–42–77–44–72) share the same building. The memorial houses temporary art and history expositions, as well as the ashes of concentration camp victims; the center is a great resource for Jewish studies.

Rue Ste-Croix-de-la-Bretonnerie and **rue Vieille-du-Temple** form the center of gay life in Paris, with bars, bookstores, cultural information, and all the accessories needed for a night out at Le Queen (*see* Dance Clubs, *below*). **Rue des Francs-Bourgeois** is another great street, full of sleek cafés and homey restaurants, and just north of it are a couple of the city's best museums, the **Musée Picasso** and **Musée Carnavalet** (*see* Museums, *above*).

And at the end of rue des Francs-Bourgeois is the gorgeously elegant **place des Vosges.** The stately arcades under the surrounding mansions harbor the open gardens of the **Hôtel de Sully** and the **Maison de Victor Hugo** (*see* Museums, *above*). Try to come on a weekend afternoon, when sporadic free classical music concerts add to the already royal atmosphere. Between the Seine and rue de Rivoli lies the calmer part of the Marais, packed with beautiful old hôtels particuliers and green patches. Look for the tiny garden behind the **Hôtel de Sens,** a mansion transformed into the Bibliothèque Forney, an art-history library. Wander along **rue St-Paul** for cool shops and antiques.

MONTMARTRE

Rising above the city on the highest hill in Paris is Montmartre, site of the **Basilique du Sacré-Coeur** (*see* Major Attractions, *above*) and home to a once-thriving artistic community. Even now, after many of the artists have headed for cheaper areas and tour buses deliver hordes to its minuscule streets, Montmartre remains first and foremost a village where a special breed of Parisian lives and drinks. A trip through the streets of this neighborhood affords you glimpses of gardens, small cafés filled with locals, and perhaps the sound of a practicing violinist. For details on the history and illustrious personalities of Montmartre, visit the **Musée de Montmartre** (*see* Museums, *above*), where Renoir once had his studio. Today, the aggressive third-rate painters clustered around place du Tertre, one of the most tourist-attacked spots in the entire city, are the only reminders of Montmartre's artistic heritage. Real artists live behind the hill, often in million-dollar homes on **avenue Junot** or the picturesque **villa Léandre** just off it. To the east, on **rue des Saules,** is the last remaining vineyard in Paris, producing 125 gallons of wine per year. Nearby, off place des Quatre-Frères-Casadesus, is a small park where old men gather every day to play *pétanque* (a kind of ball game).

In eastern Montmartre, demarcated by rue Doudeauville to the north and boulevard de la Chapelle to the south, is the **Goutte d'Or** (Drop of Gold), named after the white wine the vineyards here used to produce. A bastion of the Algerian independence party (the FLN) during the Algerian-French war, the area has absorbed constant waves of immigrants, most recently from the Antilles and Africa. Today, Muslim markets sit next to African textile manufacturers, wholesale grocers, and old horse butchers in this multiethnic working-class quarter. The neighborhood gets most festive on Sunday; streets are often blocked off for daylong street markets, and most shops stay open late.

MONTPARNASSE

The name Montparnasse is burdened with images of all kinds of brilliant expatriates doing silly drunken things in the years surrounding World War I. Acting as an intellectual counterweight to all of the artistry going on up in Montmartre, a quartet of cafés on the corner of **boulevard du Montparnasse** and **boulevard Raspail**—La Coupole, Le Dôme, Le Sélect, and La Rotonde—became the center for American writers who lived, lolled, loved, and left if the service displeased them. The four cafés are still here, though only Le Sélect still has a stylish crowd. The rest of the neighborhood, on the surface anyway, looks like the same mixture of old buildings, manicured parks, and out-of-place new buildings that you see in the rest of Paris. The huge commercial center finished in 1973 detracts substantially from the neighborhood's charm, as does the **Tour Montparnasse,** the second-tallest structure (at 690 ft) in the city; you can take an elevator up the tower to the rooftop bar, for an overpriced drink and a spectacular view.

Stretching out from the tower and the Gare Montparnasse train station are several uninspired commercial and residential developments, as well as a few more adventurous buildings. Ricardo Bofil's semi-circular **Amphithéâtre** housing complex, with its whimsical postmodernist quotations of classical detail, is the most famous. The glass-cubed **Fondation Cartier** (*see* Museums, *above*), a center for contemporary art, and the Montparnasse train station with its giant glass facade and designer garden above the tracks, are other outstanding examples. On a more historical note, just north of the tower, **place du 18 juin 1940** commemorates the speech Charles de Gaulle gave in exile in London urging the French to resist the German invaders. The huge student population in Montparnasse, having fled the expensive 5e and 6e arrondissements, ushers in the latest developments in nightlife along boulevard du Montparnasse and tucked into offshoots of **avenue du Maine.** Other sights worth seeing are the **Parc Montsouris and Cité Universitaire** (*see* Parks and Gardens, *above*), as well as the **Cimetière du Montparnasse** and the **catacombs,** which you can slither into at place Denfert-Rochereau (*see* Dead Folk, *above*).

QUARTIER LATIN

The center of French intellectual life for more than 700 years, the Quartier Latin has drawn the metaphysically restless, the politically discontent, the artistically inspired, and their wanna-bes to the neighborhood's universities, cafés, garrets, and alleys. The presence of several institutions of higher learning such as the **Sorbonne** keeps the quarter youthful, creative, and relatively liberal. Cafés, bookstores, bars, and cheap restaurants proliferate, and even the presence of millions of tourists doesn't break the mood (though it can seriously dampen it in summer). Down toward the Seine, the confusing maze of streets surrounding **rue de la Huchette** is the ultimate experience in crowd tolerance, though you might find some good crepes or street music there. Just to the west, **place St-Michel** and its fountain act as a meeting-pickup spot for tourists year-round. Pretty **place de la Contrescarpe,** and tumbling **rue Mouffetard** leading off it, is lively day and night, when students from the nearby Grandes Écoles congregate here.

A good place to get lost is in the labyrinthine streets between place Maubert and the Seine; these streets manage to retain their medieval feel despite the presence of fast-food shops and expensive residences (Mitterrand's private home was at 22 rue de Bièvre). The **square René-Viviani,** just east of the Huchette madness, is a pleasant little park with the oldest tree in Paris, sprouted in 1601. **Shakespeare & Com-**

pany, a bookstore that's a handy refuge for Anglophones, is next door (*see* Shopping, *below*). The area around the Sorbonne and behind the **Panthéon** (*see* Dead Folk, *above*) merits serious exploration as well. **Rue de la Montagne-Ste-Geneviève,** winding between the Panthéon and place Maubert, is one of the oldest streets in Paris, with a number of buildings dating from the Middle Ages. Don't forget to check out the bibliophilic *bouquinistes* (booksellers) along the Seine.

ST-GERMAIN-DES-PRES

The venerable tower of **St-Germain-des-Prés** (*see* Houses of Worship, *above*), the oldest church in Paris, anchors a neighborhood of bookstores, art galleries, designer boutiques, and cafés where Picasso, Camus, Sartre, and de Beauvoir spent their days and nights. The cynical and the nostalgic bemoan that the area has relinquished its spirit to the hands of the mainstream, the upscale, and the comfortable—and it's true that in summer you'll encounter many tourists in the shops and cafés. But wander off the traffic-clogged boulevard St-Germain and you'll find winding streets, ancient facades, and hidden courtyards that defy the onrush of modernity.

A short walking tour: Start at Église St-Germain, where monks who set up camp here infused the area with its initial intellectual flair, bringing international art and culture to the city. Rousseau and Voltaire, unable to get support elsewhere, were published in the St-Germain abbey. Literati have continued to haunt the neighborhood, particularly the tables of **Les Deux Magots** and **Le Flore,** two overpriced neighboring cafés on boulevard St-Germain. Deux Magots was the favorite of Verlaine and Mallarmé, Le Flore of Jean-Paul and Simone, Camus, and Picasso. From the Église St-Germain, take rue Bonaparte toward the river and you'll soon reach the once-great **École Nationale Supérieure des Beaux-Arts** (National Fine Arts School). Take a detour to your right down **rue Visconti**: At No. 17 a young Balzac founded an unsuccessful press. On the other side of the Beaux-Arts school, singer and national idol Serge Gainsbourg had his Parisian digs at 5 bis rue Verneuil (today well covered with spray paint) until his death in 1991. Turn right at the river and walk past the **Institut de France** (at the corner of quai de Conti and Pont des Arts), the seat of the Académie Française, which Richelieu created in 1635 in an attempt to supervise the activities of Parisian intellectuals. The Académie is still around, defending the French language from foreign invaders—its latest stroke of brilliance was to *outlaw* the commercial use of non-French (read: English) words in France, though this was soon declared unconstitutional as violating freedom of expression.

Walking along the Seine toward the Louvre, you pass **rue des Grands-Augustins,** where at No. 5–7 Picasso enjoyed his last—and most luxurious—Parisian home from 1936 to 1955. Turn away from the river again on rue Dauphine, veering left at the fork a few blocks up, and you'll hit the **cour de Rohan,** where Dr. Joseph-Ignace Guillotin invented an execution device he described as a "puff of air on the neck" of the victim. Farther ahead, near Odéon, a statue of Danton marks where this great revolutionary once lived (Haussmann had his way with the actual building). Great streets branch south off place Henri-Mondor, including the tiny **rue de l'École-de-Médecine,** where Sarah Bernhardt was born at No. 5. To the west lies **rue Monsieur-le-Prince**; No. 14 was at various times home to American writer Richard Wright (from 1948 to 1959) and composer Camille Saint-Saëns (from 1877 to 1889). Head west a few blocks to **rue de Tournon,** whose 18th-century hôtels particuliers have housed too many celebrities to mention, among them Casanova (No. 27) and Balzac (No. 2). If you roam St-Germain with your eyes tilted upward, you'll find plenty of commemorative plaques to keep you busy.

Don't miss **rue St-André-des-Arts,** a pedestrian street roughly between place St-Michel and carrefour de Buci, lined with crêperies, postcard shops, and a good experimental cinema. The nearby **cour du Commerce-St-André** (an alley between rue St-André-des-Arts and boulevard St-Germain) was opened in 1776 and saw all sorts of revolutionary activity, including the printing of Marat's *L'Ami du Peuple* at No. 8, the beheading of subversives at No. 9, and the daily life of Danton at No. 20.

SHOPPING

Paris may be one of the world's most expensive cities, but a shopping spree here needn't leave you franc-less. It's possible to find shops where you can get a good deal on items from Kookaï T-shirts to Hermès scarves. Window-shopping—what the French call *lécher les vitrines* (literally, licking the windows)—is also fun, and you won't have to part with one centime. But the truth is, shopping here can be contagious, and if you don't buy something—a book, shoes, lingerie (this is Paris)—you're missing out on a truly Parisian experience. Be aware, however, that the French have not yet cottoned to the idea of service, and shop assistants can be shockingly rude. Most stores in Paris stay open until 6 or 7 PM and close on Sunday, and many take a lunch break sometime between noon and 2 PM.

Le Marais (4e) has scores of interesting gift and clothing shops—and they're open on Sunday, which is unusual for Paris. Good streets for browsing include **rue des Francs-Bourgeois, rue Ste-Croix-de-la-Bretonnerie,** and **rue Vieille-du-Temple. Rue des Rosiers** and **rue Pavée** are known for their kosher delis and Jewish-interest bookstores. Around **Les Halles** (1er) most of the pedestrian streets are lined with fast-food joints, jeans outlets, and souvenir stands, though rue du Jour is the exception. In the middle of the action is the **Forum des Halles** (métro Châtelet), a multilevel underground shopping mall. Under the Louvre you'll find **Le Carrousel du Louvre** (1er, 99 rue de Rivoli, métro Palais-Royal), a fancy mall containing over 30 big-name stores. Though you may want to walk up the **Champs-Élysées** (8e), it isn't great for shopping, with its overpriced, glitzy malls and nondescript car showrooms, fast-food chains, and cinemas. Instead, go window-shopping along **avenue Montaigne** and **rue du Faubourg-St-Honoré,** where fashion's big names—Chanel and Dior to Hermès and Valentino—have boutiques.

Shops in the **Quartier Latin** (5e) cater to the local student population, so you'll find many stores selling cheap clothes at cheap prices. Although **boulevard St-Michel** is schlocky and crowded, the smaller streets around **place Maubert** are lined with tiny music stores and good-to-browse bookstores. **Rue Mouffetard** is better for wandering than shopping, especially if you head all the way downhill to the open-air produce market at the bottom. Around **St-Germain-des-Prés** (6e), you'll find one-of-a-kind shops and big-name designer boutiques. Some of the best shopping streets are **boulevard St-Germain, rue de Grenelle, rue des Saints-Pères,** and the **streets off place St-Sulpice.** Need proof that bargains do exist in Paris? Head south to **Montparnasse** (14e) and **rue d'Alésia** (métro Alésia), where there are a bunch of boutiques stocks—outlets where designer clothes are sold at a big discount. Leave the charmless commercial center in the Tour Montparnasse to those who don't know any better.

DEPARTMENT STORES

Les grands magasins offer one-stop convenience and a good overview of Parisian style, but they're generally more expensive than their American counterparts. Most department stores are open Monday–Saturday from about 9:30 AM to 7 PM: **Au Bon Marché** (22 rue de Sèvres, 7e, tel. 01–44–39–80–00, métro Sèvres-Babylone); **Au Printemps** (64 blvd. Haussmann, 9e, tel. 01–42–82–50–00, métro Havre-Caumartin, Opéra, or Auber); **Galeries Lafayette** (40 blvd. Haussmann, 9e, tel. 01–42–82–34–56, métro Chaussée d'Antin, Opéra, or Havre-Caumartin); **Marks & Spencer** (35 blvd. Haussmann, 9e, tel. 01–47–42–42–91, métro Havre-Caumartin, Auber, or Opéra; 88 rue de Rivoli, 4e, tel. 01–44–61–08–00, métro Hôtel de Ville); and **La Samaritaine** (19 rue de la Monnaie, 1er, tel. 01–40–41–20–20, métro Pont-Neuf or Châtelet).

FLEA MARKETS

Le Marché aux Puces St-Ouen (18e, métro Porte de Clignancourt), on Paris's northern boundary, still attracts crowds on weekends and Monday, even though its prices aren't as low as they used to be. There are some vintage clothes and some cheap junk, as well as excellent finds in the bins of old prints and vintage advertisements. Go for the fun of haggling and never, ever pay the asking price. **Le Marché aux Puces Montreuil** (20e, métro Porte de Montreuil) is smaller and funkier than St-Ouen. Asian and African trinkets abound but, above all, this market is best for secondhand and vintage clothing. It's open all weekend but is less crowded on Monday mornings.

SPECIALTY SHOPS

BOOKSTORES

Bookstores of all shapes and subjects are spread throughout Paris, but those specializing in art, literature, economics, politics, language, and gastronomy are most abundant on the Left Bank. The best places to look are on **boulevard St-Michel, place de la Sorbonne,** and all of those little streets tucked in between. Gibert Joseph, Presses Universitaires, and the FNAC (Forum des Halles, 1er, tel. 01–40–41–40–00, métro Les Halles) in Les Halles are also good places to try. Finally, be sure to check out the *bouquinistes* (booksellers) along the Seine, particularly between **boulevard du Palais** and the **Pont au Double,** for inexpensive secondhand books, prints, and old postcards.

Paris has several English-language bookstores, including **Brentano's** (37 av. de l'Opéra, 2e, tel. 01–42–61–52–50, métro Opéra); and **W. H. Smith** (248 rue de Rivoli, 1er, tel. 01–44–78–88–99, métro Concorde). English-language books are generally not one of France's bargains since they can cost twice as much as at home. At **Shakespeare & Company** (37 rue de la Bûcherie, 5e, no phone, métro St-Michel), you can find new and used books, often at bargain prices. **Tea & Tattered Pages** (24 rue Mayet, 6e, tel. 01–40–65–94–35, métro Duroc) is best of all for cheap, secondhand paperbacks, plus new books (publishers' overstock) at low prices.

CLOTHING AND ACCESSORIES

DISCOUNT DESIGNER • A one-stop mecca for 40%–50% reductions on well-known labels in the boutiques stocks is **rue d'Alésia** (14e, métro Alésia). Some of the best are **Cacharel Stock** (No. 114), **Majestic by Chevignon** (No. 12), **Régina Rubens Stock** (No. 88), and **SR Store** (No. 64), where Sonia Rykiel prices are sliced 50%.

Anna Lowe (104 rue du Faubourg St-Honoré, 8e, tel. 01–42–66–11–32, métro Miromesnil) and **Annexe des Créateurs** (19 rue Godot de Mauroy, 8e, tel. 01–42–65–46–40, métro Madeleine) are both treasure troves of classic designer names for women at a substantial discount. **Le Mouton à Cinq Pattes** (15 rue Vieille-du-Temple, 4e, tel. 01–42–71–86–30, métro Hôtel de Ville) sells clothes from last year's collections at a huge discount. **Stock Kookaï** (82 rue Réaumur, 2e, tel. 01–45–08–93–69, métro Réaumur-Sébastopol) gives deep savings on end-of-series items in the Kookaï line.

PERFUME AND MAKEUP • Parisian women swear by the two beloved French dimestores, **Monoprix** and **Prisunic,** for inexpensive, good-quality cosmetics. (The Prisunic branch at 109 rue de la Boétie, 8e, métro Franklin D. Roosevelt is the best-stocked.) Also, come here if you run out of toothpaste, shampoo, batteries, pantyhose, or other inexpensive essentials. **Catherine** (5 rue Castiglione, 1er, tel. 01–42–61–02–89, métro Concorde) typically gives reductions of 30% off retail designer perfume prices. **Les Halles Montmartre** (85 rue Montmartre, 2e, tel. 01–42–33–11–13, métro Bourse) routinely discounts its wide range of perfumes and cosmetics by 30%–40%. **Sephora** (70 av. des Champs-Élysées, 8e, tel. 01–53–93–22–50, métro Franklin D. Roosevelt; 1 rue Pierre Lescot, 1er, tel. 01–40–13–72–25, métro Les Halles), the leading chain of perfume and cosmetic stores in France, sells its own makeup label as well as all the big brands.

Key lingo: "soldes" or "promotion" (sale); "dégriffe" or "stock" (discounted designer labels); "braderie" or "fin de série" (clearance); "occasions," "fripes," "dépôts-ventes," "troc," or "brocante" (secondhand); "nouveautés" (new arrivals).

RESALE AND VINTAGE CLOTHING • Resale shops sell barely worn designer wear, and vintage stores sell your usual Hawaiian shirts and leather jackets. **Réciproque** (88, 89, 92, 95, 101, and 123 rue de la Pompe, 16e, tel. 01–47–04–30–28, métro Rue de la Pompe) is Paris's largest and most exclusive swap shop. **Didier Ludot** (23 galerie Montpensier, 1er, tel. 01–42–96–06–56, métro Palais-Royal) sells secondhand accessories in impeccable condition by Hermès and Chanel. **Guerrisold** (17 bis blvd. Rochechouart, 9e, tel. 01–42–80–66–18, métro Barbès-Rochechouart) is a bargain thrift shop popular with Parisian club kids and fashion fiends. Around Les Halles you'll find fun and trashy used clothes; try **rue St-Martin, rue St-Merri, rue de la Grande-Truanderie,** and **rue St-Denis.**

SHOES • Go to **rue de Rivoli** (1er), **boulevard St-Michel** (5e), **avenue du Général-Leclerc** (14e), and **rue Grégoire de Tours** (6e) to find inexpensive shoe chains like André and Ormond. In addition, the **Forum des Halles** (1er) houses about a dozen shoe shops selling cheap footwear. **Mi-Prix** (27 blvd. Victor, 15e, tel. 01–48–28–42–48, métro Porte-de-Versailles) is an unruly jumble of end-of-series designer footwear priced at up to 60% below retail. **Beaubourg 59** (59 rue Beaubourg, 3e, tel. 01–42–78–40–25, métro Rambuteau) offers samples and the former collections of two stylish labels, Charles Kammer and Colisée by Sacha, at less than half the normal price. **Shoe Bizz** (42 rue du Dragon, 6e, tel. 01–45–44–91–70, métro St-Germain-des-Prés; 25 rue Beaubourg, 3e, tel. 01–42–74–72–40, métro Rambuteau) zeroes in on the season's hottest shoe styles and replicates them at 30% cheaper than you'll find elsewhere in the city.

TRENDSETTERS • **Colette** (213 rue Saint-Honoré, 1er, tel. 01–55–35–33–90, métro Tuileries) is Paris's last word in everything stylish, where you'll find the hippest objects in design, the most cutting-edge fashions, and the trendiest books and magazines. **L'Épicerie** (30 rue du Temple, 3e, tel. 01–42–78–12–39, métro Hôtel de Ville) is a cross between a boutique and an art gallery, selling its own clothing label, as well as one-off designs by hip young international designers. **Raw Essentials** (46 rue Étienne-Marcel, 2e, tel. 01–42–21–44–33, métro Louvre) specializes in raw denim and stocks jeans in labels like G-Star and Evisu. **Le Shop** (3 rue d'Argout, 2e, tel. 01–40–26–21–45, métro Sentier), an emporium housing 20 hip designers, is the address for fans of street wear and techno.

GIFTS AND HOUSEWARES

Rue de Paradis is lined with discount china and crystal showrooms. **La Tisanière** (No. 21) sells china seconds, while **Baccarat Crystal** (No. 30 bis) has an in-house museum. **Christian Liaigre** (42 rue du Bac, 7e, tel. 01–53–63–33–66, métro Rue du Bac) is currently the world's top interior designer. Though you probably won't be able to afford any of his sleek, minimalist furniture, that shouldn't stop you from admiring it. **Compagnie Française de l'Orient et de la Chine** (163 blvd. St-Germain, 6e, tel. 01–45–48–00–18, métro St-Germain-des-Prés) imports ceramics and furniture from China and Mongolia. **Diptyque** (34 blvd. St-Germain, 5e, tel. 01–43–26–45–27, métro Maubert-Mutualité) sells the best scented candles in Paris (Karl Lagerfeld is a fan), while **La Chaise Longue** (20 rue des Francs-Bourgeois, 3e, tel. 01–42–78–40–25, métro St-Paul) stocks wonderful and wacky objects for the kitchen and bathroom. **Nature et Découvertes** (Carrousel du Louvre, 1er, tel. 01–47–03–47–43, métro Palais-Royal) is a good place to pick up presents. There are children's toys, as well as a range of objects linked to nature—telescopes, aromatherapy diffusers, even miniature Zen gardens.

AFTER DARK

Whether you're a jazz fiend or a dance freak, a patron of the arts or a lounge lizard seeking refuge in a smoky bar, Paris's streets provide all sorts of destinations for nocturnal activities. From rich, sprawling opera houses to low-key bars, dance floors in 17th-century caves, or just a lazy walk around a light-splintered Seine—Paris nightlife is there for you.

There is plenty of free music in Paris. **Église St-Merri** (78 rue St-Martin, 4e, tel. 01–42–71–93–93, métro Châtelet) has free classical concerts Saturday at 9 PM and Sunday at 4 PM. **L'Église Américaine** (65 quai d'Orsay, 7e, tel. 01–40–62–05–00, métro Invalides) has choral and organ music Sunday at 6 PM; and the **Conservatoire National Supérieur de Musique** (209 av. Jean-Jaurès, 19e, tel. 01–40–40–46–47, métro Porte de Pantin) has student concerts practically every day at 12:30 PM and 7 PM. The **École Normale de Musique** (78 rue Cardinet, 17e, tel. 01–47–63–85–72, métro Courcelles) has student concerts Tuesday and Thursday at 12:30 PM. Other venues worth checking for free concerts include the **Maison de Radio France** (*see* Opera, Classical Music, and Dance, *below*). In summer, **place des Vosges, place Ste-Catherine,** and the **front of the Centre Pompidou** are all home to impromptu performances of guitar, jazz, and accordion music. From the beginning of May to the end of September, the **Parc Floral de Paris** (Esplanade du Château de Vincennes, 12e, tel. 01–43–43–92–95, métro Château de Vincennes) organizes free jazz concerts at 4 PM on Saturday and free classical concerts at 4 PM on Sunday.

For events information, consult the ubiquitous advertisement boards or buy a copy of the entertainment weeklies, *Pariscope* (3F) or *L'Officiel des Spectales* (2F), which come out every Wednesday, at your local newsstand. *Pariscope* has a small section in English. For more alternative events, check out the selective listings in the hip monthly *Nova Magazine* (10F), also available at most newsstands. Another source of information is the Paris Tourist Office's 24-hour hot line in English (tel. 08–36–68–31–12; www.paris.touristoffice.com).

Gay life in Paris has its geographic base in the Marais, though it's not the raging scene that American urban dwellers might be used to. Lesbian life is less visible. Try contacting the **Maison des Femmes** (163 rue de Charenton, 12e, tel. 01–43–43–41–13), a feminist-lesbian resource center and cafeteria, or the **Centre Gai et Lesbien** (3 rue Keller, 11e, tel. 01–43–57–21–47) for information on events. The free monthly magazines *Illico, CQFG, Out,* and *Double Face,* found in gay bars and cafés, have calendars of gay events.

BARS

Most Parisian bars (at least the ones that aren't open as cafés earlier in the day) open around 6 PM and close at 2 AM, even on weekends. Also note that cafés, bars, and *boîtes* (dance clubs) in Paris tend to mutate over the course of an evening—something that was a restaurant at lunch could become a bar at

8 PM and then a dance club until sunrise. Law requires that prices be posted, and in most bars you will find two different tariffs—*au comptoir* (standing at the bar—it's cheaper) and *en salle* (sitting at a table). In many places, prices go up a few francs after 10 PM. In general, expect to pay 15F–30F for a half pint of draft beer, referred to as *une pression, une demi-pression,* or simply *une demi.*

Amnésia. This is the most mixed of all the gay bars in the Marais. Day and night, a cool crowd sinks into deep armchairs, surrounded by plants, mosaic tiles, and ceiling fans. Beers cost 16F–22F. Prices go up 5F after 10 PM. *42 rue Vieille-du-Temple, 4e, tel. 01–42–72–16–94. Métro: Hôtel de Ville.*

La Belle Hortense. This is a cross between a bar and a bookstore, where you'll find intellectual types sitting at the counter sipping wine (16F–45F a glass) and flicking through the latest novel. There are readings on Wednesday at around 7:30 PM and literary debates at 10 AM on Sunday. *31 rue Vieille-du-Temple, 4e, tel. 01–48–04–71–60. Métro: St-Paul.*

La Chaise au Plafond. A heterosexual haven in the gay Marais, this bar has a nice old Parisian feel to it. Beer is 17F and excellent wine by the glass is 20F. You can also get a light meal. Don't leave without checking out the futuristic metal toilets downstairs. *10 rue du Trésor, 4e, tel. 01–42–76–03–22. Métro: St-Paul.*

Chesterfield Café. This lively spot is particularly popular with Americans. There are rock and blues concerts at 11 PM (Keanu Reeves played here when he came to Paris with his group Dogstar) and gospel singers from 2 to 5 on Sunday afternoons. Happy hour is 4–8 PM on weekdays. *124 rue de la Boétie, 8e, tel. 01–42–25–18–06. Métro: Franklin D. Roosevelt.*

Le Central (33 rue Vieille-du-Temple), Cox's (15 rue des Archives), and Le Quetzal (10 rue de la Verrerie) are the prime gay pickup joints in the Marais (4e, métro Hôtel de Ville).

Chez Georges. This upstairs bar has been serving glasses of red wine, pastis, and beer (20F–30F) to older men in work clothes for the past 60-odd years. Don't be intimidated if the place looks packed—there's always room to squeeze in somewhere. *11 rue des Canettes, 6e, tel. 01–43–26–79–15. Métro: Mabillon.*

Chez Prune. This lively, young bar overlooks one of the footbridges of the picturesque Canal Saint-Martin. Its terrace is the perfect place to while away a summer evening. A demi costs as little as 12F and light meals of cheese or cold meats are also served. *36 rue Beaurepaire, 10e, tel. 01–42–41–30–47. Métro: République.*

Connolly's Corner. Come to this friendly Irish bar near rue Mouffetard to play darts and have a demi (19F) or a pint of Guinness (38F). Don't wear a tie or it will be snipped off and stuck on the wall (though you will be compensated with a free pint). Pints are only 28F during happy hour Monday–Friday 4–8 PM, and there's traditional Irish music on Monday at 8 PM. *12 rue Mirbel, 5e, tel. 01–43–31–94–22. Métro: Place Monge.*

Les Couleurs. This laid-back bar has a great atmosphere. Sit underneath the palm-tree mural and sip Cuban milk shakes (32F) or mango and tamarind juice (12F). Every Saturday (10 PM–4 AM) join the crowds for tango, or come earlier on Saturday or Sunday (6 PM–10 PM) for a jazz or world music concert. *117 rue St-Maur, 11e, tel. 01–43–57–95–61. Métro: St-Maur or Parmentier.*

La Fabrique. One of a number of lively spots along rue du Faubourg Saint-Antoine, this bar-cum-restaurant brews its own beer (check out the huge copper vats by the entrance). A 30cl glass costs 26F and during happy hour (7–8 PM) you get two drinks for the price of one. At 9 PM a DJ hits the turntable. *53 rue du Faubourg Saint-Antoine, 11e, tel. 01–43–07–67–07. Métro: Bastille.*

Le Frog & Rosbif. This English pub has everything you could want from a "local" hangout. Beers are brewed on premises and sold at 22F for a half pint or 35F a pint (25F a pint during happy hour 6–7 PM weekdays). You can also watch rugby and soccer matches on the giant-screen TV or come to the jazz brunch on Sunday (noon–4 PM). *116 rue St-Denis, 2e, tel. 01–42–36–34–73. Métro: Étienne Marcel.*

Lou Pascalou. This low-key neighborhood joint has pool tables indoors and melancholy youth on the terrace. Cheap (11F) beers and the requisite jazz background music make this a good place to catch a glimpse of old Belleville life. *14 rue des Panoyaux, 20e, tel. 01–46–36–78–10. Métro: Ménilmontant.*

L'Open Café. With its sunny yellow walls, this café is one of the most relaxed and convivial gay spots in the Marais. In summer, it is so popular that the crowd of beautiful boys spills out onto the street. *17 rue des Archives, 4e, tel. 01–42–72–26–18. Métro: Hôtel de Ville.*

Le Sancerre. A nightly gathering of jovial Montmartrois fills up this neighborhood bar; during the day, young artist types sun themselves outside and roll their eyes at the passing tourists. The 11F pression goes up to 18F after 10 PM. *35 rue des Abbesses, 18e, tel. 01–42–58–08–20. Métro: Abbesses.*

Les Scandaleuses. This bar has quickly established itself as one of the hippest lesbian hangouts in Paris. Men are also allowed in (in small numbers) as long as they are accompanied by a number of "scandalous women." A beer will set you back 20F. During happy hour (6–8 PM), you get two for the price of one. *8 rue des Écouffes, 4e, tel. 01–48–87–39–26. Métro: St-Paul.*

La Tartine. This is a place for those who like to step back in time to the Paris of years gone by. There is cheap wine (from 9F a glass), *tartines* (large open-face sandwiches), and a tatty, almost seedy turn-of-the-century decor that has earned antihero status among the cognoscenti. *24 rue de Rivoli, 4e, tel. 01–42–72–76–85. Métro: St-Paul.*

Le What's Up. This is one of those hip Parisian places, a hybrid bar-cum-nightclub. The design is decidedly modern, the clientele trendy, and the music (from 10:30 PM) a mixture of house and garage. On Friday and Saturday, there is a 50F cover (which includes one drink). *15 rue Daval, 11e, tel. 01–48–05–88–33. Métro: Bastille.*

CABARET

Cabaret in Paris is not what it once was. Today the more famous cabarets, such as **Le Moulin Rouge** (82 blvd. Clichy, 18e, tel. 01–53–09–82–82, métro Blanche) and **Le Lido** (116 bis av. des Champs-Élysées, 8e, tel. 01–40–76–56–10, métro George V), cater almost exclusively to foreign businessmen and Japanese tourists, and the world-famous **Folies-Bergères** (32 rue Richer, 9e, tel. 01–44–79–98–98, métro Cadet) no longer holds cabaret at all. **Au Pied de la Butte** (62 blvd. Rochechouart, 18e, tel. 01–46–06–02–86, métro Anvers), however, is everything you ever hoped for from a Paris cabaret, including glittery, flashy numbers mixed with Edith Piaf favorites. The 210F cover includes one drink. **Au Lapin Agile** (22 rue des Saules, 18e, tel. 01–46–06–85–87, métro Lamarck-Caulaincourt; closed Mon.) has been around since 1860. Today, it's still serving up classic French oldies with solo pianists, singers and other musicians, who rotate from 9 PM to 2 AM. Entrance with one drink is 130F. At **Madame Arthur** (75 bis rue des Martyrs, 18e, tel. 01–42–54–40–21, métro Pigalle), boys will be girls. The wacky, burlesque show starts at 10:30 PM and features male artists who imitate famous French female vocalists. The entrance fee is 165F and includes the first drink. Additional drinks are a rather steep 95F.

DANCE CLUBS

Les Bains. This former Turkish bath has been Paris's hottest nightspot for the past 15 years. Stars and models regularly have private parties here, and new owners are once again attracting a younger, trendier crowd. Cover is 100F. The door policy is extremely strict, so do yourself up. *7 rue du Bourg-l'Abbé, 3e, tel. 01–48–87–01–80. Métro: Étienne Marcel. Closed Mon.*

Le Balajo. The granddaddy of Paris's discos keeps 'em coming back, decade after decade, with the same hyper-kitschy decor and rock, salsa, and mainstream disco. *9 rue de Lappe, 11e, tel. 01–47–00–07–87. Métro: Bastille. Closed Mon. and Tues.*

Le Bus Palladium. "Le Bus" was the hottest nightspot in Paris during the '60s. A fashionable but relaxed crowd now comes once again to dance to rock, funk, and disco. Cover is free for women on Tuesday and for everyone on Wednesday. At other times, admission is 100F (with a drink). *6 rue Fontaine, 9e, tel. 01–53–21–07–33. Métro: Pigalle. Closed Mon.*

L'Élysée Montmartre. The Élysée Montmartre holds extremely popular *bals* (balls) every other Saturday. The music runs the gamut of hits from the '40s to the '80s and there is a live 10-piece orchestra. Cakes and sweets are given out free. Cover is 90F. On alternate Saturday, it also hosts the hottest club night of the moment, "Scream," which attracts a mainly gay crowd. *72 blvd. Rochechouart, 18e, tel. 01–55–07–06–00. Métro: Pigalle.*

Les Folies Pigalle. This small, red-hot club is situated in a former erotic cabaret and plays techno and hip-hop for a crowd crammed onto the two-level dance floor. On Friday and Saturday (8:30 PM—11:30 PM), there are male strip shows for women only, while on Sunday, there are men-only gay tea dances (5–11 PM). There are also "afters" 6 AM–midday on Saturday and Sunday for those who just can't drag themselves to bed. Admission is free on Wednesday and Sunday, 100F on other days, and 150F for shows. *11 pl. Pigalle, 9e, tel. 01–48–78–25–26. Métro: Pigalle.*

Keur Samba. The richer, more stylish, and more African you look, the better your chances of gaining entry into this supersleek club near the Champs-Élysées. The music ranges from reggae to African soukous to American hip-hop. Dress up and bring generous funds for the 120F entrance and first drink; the next will cost you 100F. *79 rue la Boétie, 8e, tel. 01–43–59–03–10. Métro: St-Philippe du Roule.*

Le Pulp! This is one of the few lesbian nightclubs in town and certainly the most popular. There are regular theme nights (Wednesday–Saturday) such as "Housewife" and "One Night Stand." The music is a mix of disco and house. *25 blvd. Poissonnière, 2e, tel. 01–40–26–01–93. Métro: Grands Boulevards.*

Le Queen. This high-profile, super-cool gay nightclub usually admits women if they're accompanied by a man. Thursday are strictly men-only. Everyone gyrates to house music on the vast dance floor (Monday is '70s night), and the whole scene is outrageous and definitely very image-conscious. The cover is free during the week (except on Monday, when it's 50F) and 100F on the weekend. *102 av. des Champs-Élysées, 8e, tel. 01–53–89–08–90. Métro: George V.*

Rex Club. The Rex's decor is about as '70s as it gets, with a roller-rink dance floor and mirrored backdrop. The club now devotes itself almost exclusively to techno (Friday) and house music (Saturday). The cover varies from 50F to 80F. Beer is always 30F. *5 blvd. Poissonnière, 2e, tel. 01–42–36–83–98. Métro: Bonne-Nouvelle. Closed Sun.–Wed.*

LIVE MUSIC

On June 21, France comes alive with free music in celebration of the summer solstice. During this Fête de la Musique, Paris's churches, clubs, parks, and squares fill with musicians and onlookers.

Most jazz clubs are in Les Halles or St-Germain. You can usually stay all night for the price of a drink, a 50F–100F drink, that is. For cheaper shows, keep an eye on some of the museums and cultural centers around town (the Institut du Monde Arabe, for example); they occasionally host free or almost-free concerts. The free monthly *Paris Boum-Boum* (available at boulangeries) has a section on world-music happenings around town. For most thrash and punk shows, look to the Pigalle area. The **Élysée Montmartre** (*see* Dance Clubs, *above*) is one of the better venues for alternative bands. The legendary **Thétre de l'Olympia** (22 rue Caumartin, 9e, tel. 01–47–42–25–49, métro Opéra, Havre-Caumartin) is the temple of *la chanson française* (French songs) and plays host to older French stars and middle-of-the-road international stars. Top international rock and pop acts like Céline Dion, Bruce Springsteen, and Mariah Carey generally perform at either **Palais Omnisports Paris Bercy** (8 blvd. Bercy, 12e, tel. 01–44–68–44–68, métro Bercy) or **Le Zénith** (211 blvd. Jean-Jaurès, 19e, no phone, métro Porte de La Villette). Megaconcerts by the likes of French rocker Johnny Hallyday or the Rolling Stones occasionally take place at either **Le Parc des Princes** or **Le Stade de France** in St-Denis. You can reserve tickets in advance at **Virgin Megastore** (tel. 08–03–02–30–24) or FNAC (tel. 01–49–87–50–50). For information on future concerts, check out the boards at FNAC or keep an eye on the billboards in the métro.

Au Duc des Lombards. Quality European blues and jazz acts regularly fill up this Les Halles club for 10 PM shows. Admission varies between 50F and 100F and beers only cost 28F (12F before 10 PM). *42 rue des Lombards, 1er, tel. 01–42–33–22–88. Métro: Châtelet.*

Le Baiser Salé. This bar's small, potentially hot upstairs room is the perfect venue for small, potentially hot jazz ensembles. Shows are at 8 PM and 10:30 PM every night; cover charges are 40F–90F. Beers cost about 25F (30F after 10 PM). *58 rue des Lombards, 1er, tel. 01–42–33–37–71. Métro: Châtelet.*

Le Caveau de la Huchette. This classic *caveau* (underground club) has been serving up swing and Dixieland to hepcats since the 1950s. Entrance is 60F, 75F on weekends, and 55F for students on weekdays. *5 rue de la Huchette, 5e, tel. 01–43–26–65–05. Métro: St-Michel.*

La Cigale. This old-style theater turned concert hall is just the right size for a good mosh pit. A small bar in the basement keeps you fueled with 25F beers. Tickets run 80F–200F. *120 blvd. Rochechouart, 18e, tel. 01–49–25–89–99. Métro: Pigalle.*

Gibus. Dark, smoky, and a little intimidating, the Gibus is now a temple to techno and house music, with special trans-goa evenings on Wednesday. A live band usually kicks off the evening before a DJ takes over at the turntable. Cover is 100F with a drink. Beers are 50F. *18 rue Faubourg-du-Temple, 11e, tel. 01–47–00–78–88. Métro: République. Closed Mon.*

La Java. In the past, both Edith Piaf and Maurice Chevalier made their names here. Nowadays, it's devoted to Latin music, and Paris's best salsa and samba bands frequently animate the place. Cover with a drink is 80F on Thursday and 100F on Friday and Saturday. *105 rue Faubourg-du-Temple, 10e, tel. 01–42–02–20–52. Métro: Belleville. Closed Mon., Tues.*

New Morning. This is Paris's big-time jazz club. Greats such as Archie Shepp, Dizzy Gillespie, and Miles Davis have sweated on its stage at one time or another. Entrance to the dark, 600-seat club is 110F–130F. Drinks are 30F. *7–9 rue des Petites-Écuries, 10e, tel. 01–45–23–51–41. Métro: Château d'Eau.*

Le Petit Journal. This is one of Paris's most legendary jazz spots. Nowadays, there are two venues, specializing in Dixieland and New Orleans jazz. Concerts start at 9 PM and the cover charge ranges from 110F to 120F (30F for students). *71 blvd. St-Michel, 5e, tel. 01–43–26–28—59, métro Cluny–La Sorbonne/RER: Luxembourg; 13 rue du Commandant-Mouchotte, 14e, tel. 01–43–21–56—70, métro: Montparnasse-Bienvenüe. Closed Sun.*

FILM

On any given night, the range of films screening in Paris is phenomenal. You'll find all kinds of classics and independent at the small cinemas, which are mostly congregated in and around the Quartier Latin. Two of the bigger, flashier cinemas in the city are **Gaumont Grand Écran** (30 pl. d'Italie, 13e, tel. 01–45–80–77–00, métro Place d'Italie) and **Max Linder Panorama** (24 blvd. Poissonnière, 9e, tel. 01–48–24–88–88, métro Rue Montmartre), both of which have immense screens and seat hundreds of people. The Champs-Élysées is also a good spot to cruise for new screenings.

Almost all foreign films are played in the *version originale* (original language) with French subtitles, marked "v.o." in listings; the abbreviation "v.f." (*version française*) means a foreign film is dubbed in French. Both of Paris's entertainment weeklies, *L'Officiel des Spectacles* and *Pariscope,* have comprehensive film listings that include prices, which normally run 35F–55F. Different theaters also offer price breaks on morning screenings and on certain days of the week, most often Monday. In February, cinemas in the city organize **18 Heures/18F** during which you pay only 18F for 6 PM shows. At the end of June, during the three-day **Fête du Cinéma,** theaters across Paris let you see all the movies you want for 10F after you pay for the first film. In August, the city of Paris subsidizes the festival **Août au Ciné** (August at the Movies), during which all those under 25 pay only 25F a film. Throughout July and August, classics and more recent, popular movies are shown outdoors on the huge screen at La Villette; admission is free. Take along a blanket and picnic, or rent a chair for 30F.

Cinémathèque Française. This world-famous cinephile heaven has different classic French and international films showing Wednesday–Sunday. Film schedules often pay homage to a certain filmmaker. Tickets are 28F and 30F. *Palais de Chaillot at Trocadéro, 16e, tel. 01–55–73–16–80. Métro: Trocadéro. Other location: 42 blvd. Bonne-Nouvelle, 10e, tel. 01–40–22–09–79. Métro: Bonne-Nouvelle.*

L'Entrepôt. This all-in-one cinema, café, bar, restaurant, and bookstore is a must for film lovers. Tickets cost 42F (32F for students and for everyone on Monday). *7 rue Francis-de-Pressensé, 14e, tel. 01–45–43–41–63. Métro: Pernety.*

Le Forum de l'Image. Though hard-core moviegoers may scoff at the idea of videotapes, the Vidéothèque is one of Paris's most important resources for moving images. A full day of audiovisual stimulation costs just 30F. It's open Tuesday–Sunday 1–9 PM (until 10 PM on Thursday). *2 Grande Galerie, Forum des Halles, 1er, tel. 01–44–76–62–00. Métro: Les Halles. Closed Mon.*

Le Grand Rex. The grandest of Paris's cinemas, this movie palace should not be confused with the other smaller Rexes that don't have the painted ceiling, the cloud machine, or the same capacity (2,750 seats). Seats are 45F–48F. *1 blvd. Poissonnière, 2e, tel. 01–42–36–83–93. Métro: Bonne-Nouvelle.*

Le Lucernaire. This multimedia supercenter has two stages, three cinemas, occasional concerts, art expositions, a restaurant, and a café. Tickets are 42F, and 32F on Monday and Wednesday. *53 rue Notre-Dame-des-Champs, 6e, tel. 01–45–44–57–34. Métro: Notre-Dame-des-Champs.*

OPERA, CLASSICAL MUSIC, AND DANCE

The performing arts scene in Paris is overwhelming, with two of the world's greatest opera houses, more than 150 theaters, and a daily dose of at least a dozen classical concerts. Scan *Pariscope* or *L'Officiel des Spectacles* each week for listings, and look for the words *entrée gratuite* or *entrée libre* ("freebie," in other words). The posters and notices pasted on the walls of métro stations are also good ways to keep up with the calendar.

Tickets to major performances are not impossible to get if you use a little foresight. At most venues, the box office starts selling tickets two weeks before a performance (a limited number are available one month in advance if you charge by phone); most are open Monday–Saturday 11 AM–6 or 7 PM. Last-minute, day-of-performance tickets are often available for students ages 25 and under, and sometimes to others. Depending on the show, you should arrive 15–90 minutes early to try for any leftover tickets; sometimes excellent seats can be had for as little as 10% of the original price. Of course, you can always get tickets by phone from **FNAC** (tel. 01–49–87–50–50) or **Virgin Megastore** (tel. 08–03–02–30–24), though you'll pay a service charge and availability may be limited.

Centre Georges Pompidou–IRCAM. One of the four divisions within the Centre Georges-Pompidou (*see* Major Attractions, *above*), IRCAM takes care of the "gestural" arts. Performances at the institute's multipurpose hall, under place Igor-Stravinsky, include contemporary music, computer-generated videos, dance, drama, lectures, philosophy seminars, and debates. Tickets are sold at the counter on the ground floor. *31 rue St-Merri, on pl. Igor-Stravinsky, 4e, tel. 01–44–78–12–33. Métro: Rambuteau. Open weekdays 9:30–6:30.*

Cité de la Musique. Architect Christian de Portzamparc's postmodern building at La Villette houses two concert halls and the excellent **Musée de la Musique** (Music Museum), displaying 900 instruments dating from 2500 BC to the present. Concerts vary from individual recitals and world music to special creations mixing music with dance and circus. *221 av. Jean-Jaurès, 19e, tel. 01–44–84–44–84 (reservations). Métro: Porte de Pantin.*

Conservatoire National Supérieur de Musique et de Danse. Since its founding in 1784, the Conservatoire has featured concerts by its budding students. Most are free and aren't planned far in advance—stop by and check the information desk for flyers and schedules. *209 av. Jean-Jaurès, 19e, tel. 01–40–40–46–47. Métro: Porte de Pantin.*

Maison de Radio France. The government's broadcasting center until the privatization of the airwaves, this vast complex is now home to countless radio and TV stations. In addition to studios and a small museum (tours in French are 18F), the complex includes the smallish, modern Salle Olivier Messiaen, home to the **Orchestre National de France,** which also performs regularly at larger venues. Seats are available one month before a show, or turn your radio dial to 91.7 or 92.1 (France Musique) to hear the concert for free. *116 av. du Président Kennedy, 16e, tel. 01–42–30–15–16. Métro: Renelagh. RER: Maison de Radio France.*

Opéra Bastille. Designed by Uruguayan-born, Canadian architect Carlos Ott and inaugurated on July 14, 1989, to commemorate the bicentennial of the French Revolution, the Bastille received resoundingly negative criticism and was unflatteringly compared to a sports arena. This has not stopped people from enthusiastically filing in to experience the "perfect" acoustics and clear sight lines available to all 2,700 of the Opéra Bastille's democratically designed seats (45F–650F for operas). Just before a performance, you can try to get 60F rush tickets. *120 rue de Lyon, 12e, tel. 01–44–73–13–99 (information) or 01–44–73–13–00 (reservations). Métro: Bastille.*

Opéra Comique. It stages a dozen operas and concerts each season in a more intimate setting than other major theaters. Performances cost 50F–500F, with 50F rush tickets available 15 minutes before curtain time to students. *5 rue Favart, 2e, tel. 01–42–44–45–46. Métro: Richelieu-Drouot.*

Opéra Garnier. The Opéra Garnier is rich, velvety, and gaudy, with an extraordinary number of gilt statuettes and a ceiling repainted by Marc Chagall in 1964. Spring for the 30F visitor's fee and you can climb the ornate stairway and check out the plush auditorium and small museum. Call or stop by to reserve seats (30F–650F); for the 30F–60F cheapie seats, you must come in person. *8 rue Scribe, 9e, tel. 08–36–69–78–68 (reservations) or 01–40–01–22–63 (information on visits). Métro: Opéra. Open daily 10–4:30 for visits; 11–6:30 (box office).*

Sainte-Chapelle. The intimate size and utter exquisiteness of Sainte-Chapelle (*see* Major Attractions, *above*) justify the cost and hassle of getting a ticket. Seats range from 100F to 150F, and the concerts often sell out early. *4 blvd. du Palais, 1er, tel. 01–42–05–25–23. Métro: Cité.*

Salle Gaveau. This high-quality concert venue named after the famous French piano makers has an Old World atmosphere. The program features chamber music, piano, and singing recitals by international stars and young prizewinners. Seats go from 85F to 500F. *45 rue La Boétie, 8e, tel. 01–49–53–05–07. Métro: Miromesnil.*

Salle Pleyel. This is the main stomping ground of the Orchestre de Paris. The Pleyel also sees some dance and jazz, with regular stops by the Golden Gate Quartet. *252 rue du Faubourg-St-Honoré, 8e, tel. 01–45–61–53–00. Métro: Ternes.*

Théâtre des Champs-Élysées. This large, fancy musical theater stages a bit of everything—operatic soloists, ballets, orchestras, marionette shows, and jazz. Tickets run 40F–750F. *15 av. Montaigne, 8e, tel. 01–49–52–50–50. Métro: Franklin D. Roosevelt.*

Théâtre Musical de Paris. Better known as the Théâtre du Châtelet, this theater is ideally located on du Châtelet by the Seine. Tickets cost 50F and up. The theater also features its "Midis Musicaux" (Musical Noons) series, with concerts in the foyer on Monday, Wednesday, and Friday starting at 12:45; seats cost 50F. Its "Dimanches Musicaux" (Musical Sundays) start at 11 and cost 120F. *1 pl. du Châtelet, 1er, tel. 01–40–28–28–40. Métro: Châtelet.*

Théâtre de la Ville. The fraternal twin of the Thétâtre Musical de Paris across the square, the Théâtre de la Ville stages contemporary dance and music in its starkly renovated theater. Most shows cost 95F–140F. The box office opens at 11 AM. *2 pl. du Châtelet, 4e, tel. 01–42–74–22–77. Métro: Châtelet.*

THEATER

The Parisian theatrical scene goes back to 17th-century French playwrights like Corneille, Racine, and Molière. If this nearly 400-year-old tradition intimidates you a bit, note that Paris has also been a center for great 20th-century experimental theater; Antonin Artaud, Samuel Beckett, and Jean-Paul Sartre all staged works here in the 1930s, '40s, and '50s. For listings, check *Pariscope* and *L'Officiel des Spectacles.* Note that the kiosks at the **Gare Montparnasse** (pl. Raoul Dautry, 15e, métro Montparnasse-Bienvenüe) and **La Madeleine** (15 pl. de la Madeleine, 8e, métro Madeleine) sell tickets for same-day performances at up to half the original price. Both are open Tuesday–Saturday 12:30–8 and Sunday 12:30–4. Remember that many of the best performances are actually in the Parisian suburbs at theaters like the **MC93** in Bobigny (1 blvd. Lénine, tel. 01–41–60–72–72) and the **Théâtre des Amandiers** in Nanterre (7 av. Pablo Picasso, tel. 01–46–14–70–00).

Les Bouffes du Nord. Founded by famed British theater man Peter Brook, this out-of-the-ordinary theater is beautifully decrepit, lending an otherworldly feel to any performance. Tickets are cheap: 70F–130F. *37 bis blvd. de la Chapelle, 10e, tel. 01–46–07–34–50. Métro: La Chapelle.*

Chaillot. Founded by Jean Vilar in post–World War II Paris as part of the movement to revive live theater, France's first *théâtre national* (national theater) stages highly regarded theatrical and musical productions in its two halls under the terrace of the Trocadéro. Tickets run 120F–160F; discounted 80F rush tickets for students are available on the day of the performance. The box office is open Monday–Saturday 11–7, Sunday 11–5. *1 pl. du Trocadéro, 16e, tel. 01–53–65–30–00. Métro: Trocadéro.*

Comédie-Française–Salle Richelieu. The Comédie-Française has a reputation as a bastion of traditionalism; the fact that the lobby holds the chair in which Molière collapsed and died after a performance in 1673 only reinforces this aura. Tickets run 30F–190F, with 65F tickets available 45 minutes before curtain time to students under 27 and those under 25. Matinée performances on July 14 are free. *2 rue de Richelieu, 1er, tel. 01–44–58–15–15. Métro: Palais Royal–Musée du Louvre.*

Odéon Théâtre de l'Europe. For several decades, the Odéon has made pan-European theater its primary focus. Tickets run 30F–170F, with rush tickets for just 20F available 90 minutes before curtain time. If you're a student or under 26, and are a regular theatergoer, consider buying the Carte Complice Jeune for 100F. It gives you 25% off all seats. The basement holds the experimental **Petit Odéon,** where all seats are 30F. *1 pl. Paul-Claudel, 6e, tel. 01–44–41–36–36. Métro: Odéon.*

Théâtre de la Huchette. It was at La Huchette that Eugène Ionesco founded and developed a theatrical and philosophical style that came to be known as Theater of the Absurd. Tickets are generally 100F. The box office is open Monday–Saturday 5–9 PM. *23 rue de la Huchette, 5e, tel. 01–43–26–38–99. Métro: St-Michel.*

Théâtre Mogador. One of the largest and most sumptuous theaters in Paris, this is the place for musicals and other popular productions. *25 rue Mogador, 9e, tel. 01–53–32–32–00. Métro: Trinité.*

ENGLISH-LANGUAGE THEATER

If you aren't quite ready to brave the French language, keep an eye out for Paris-based English-language troupes such as **Dear Conjunction** and the **On Stage Theater Company.** Larger troupes like the Royal Shakespeare Company also occasionally pass through town.

Théâtre de Nesle. Although not exclusively English-language, this theater frequently hosts the On Stage Theater Company, who put on plays by the likes of Harold Pinter and Bertolt Brecht. Tickets run 80F–90F. *8 rue de Nesle, 6e, tel. 01–46–34–61–04. Métro: Odéon.*

ILE-DE-FRANCE

With its rural pace, peaceful villages, and stately châteaux, the Ile-de-France is an ideal getaway. It's easy to spend a morning in a Paris museum and an afternoon walking through the Forest of Fontainebleau, gawking at the cathedral at Chartres, or biking in Compiègne. At the other end of the spectrum are the region's hard-core tourist sites: the palace at Versailles, the controversial Disneyland Paris, and Parc Astérix, all of which have their share of outrageous prices and heavy crowds.

Although not actually an *île* (island), the Ile-de-France is cordoned off from the rest of the country by three rivers: the Seine, Marne, and Oise. These and a large number of brooks and streams have long stood to defend the area and keep it lush, two factors that once attracted royalty keen to flee the masses in the city. Forests stocked with easily catchable animals were also a big draw for regal hunters.

Summer weekends, Parisians flock to the forests and small towns of the Ile-de-France, while tourists make their way to its châteaux and palaces, driving prices for food and lodging turret-high. The only way to eat without plunking down serious cash is to picnic; luckily, this is one of the best ways to enjoy the countryside, and markets are plentiful. As a general rule, towns make their *fermeture hebdomadaire* (weekly closing) on Tuesday, so museums and markets may be closed—call ahead if in doubt.

VERSAILLES

Louis XIII originally built the château in Versailles as a rustic hunting lodge in 1631, but when Louis "Sun King" XIV converted it from a weekend retreat to the headquarters of his government, he didn't cut any corners. Architect Louis Le Vau restored and added to the original lodge, while Charles Le Brun handled the interior decoration. Jules Hardouin-Mansart later remodeled the whole thing, expanding on Le Vau's improvements. They began in 1661 and spent the next 50 years designing everything his royal acquisitiveness could want, including a throne room dedicated to Apollo, the king's mythological hero. Jacques-Ange Gabriel later added an opera house so Louis XV could be entertained at home without troubling himself to mingle with the common folk. Reconstruction efforts aimed at bringing the entire estate back to how it looked when the Sun King lived here will continue for the next couple of decades; billboards provide updates on what's currently being worked on.

Picture France's overdressed nobility promenading through the gardens plotting dangerous liaisons, perhaps fawning over the king and queen in the dazzling **Galerie des Glaces** (Hall of Mirrors). Imagine Louis XVI and Marie-Antoinette entertaining in the **Grands Appartements,** decorated with sumptuous marble, gilded bronzes, and ceiling paintings of mythological figures. Now imagine the day in 1789 when a revolutionary mob marched the 24 km (15 mi) from Paris to Versailles to protest the bread shortage, only to find the queen munching cake. It's no wonder these revolutionaries forced the royals to leave Versailles and set up camp at the Tuileries palace in Paris, so they could keep an eye on them.

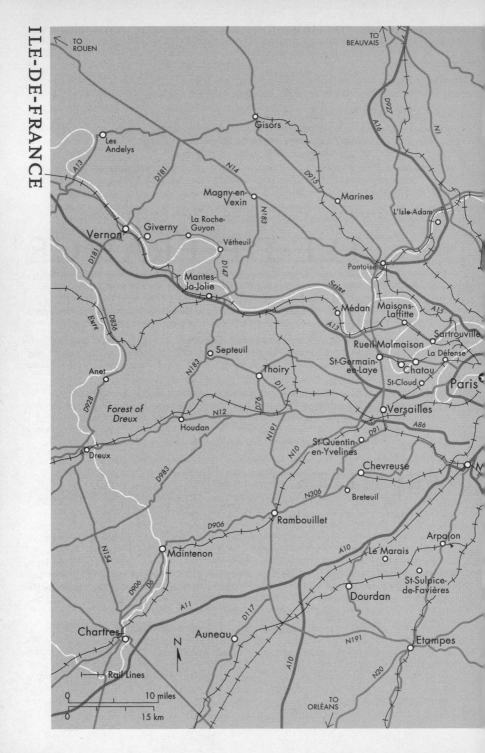

ILE-DE-FRANCE

TO
ROUEN

TO
BEAUVAIS

Gisors

Les
Andelys

Magny-en-
Vexin

Marines

L'Isle-Adam

Vernon

Giverny

La Roche-
Guyon

Vétheuil

Mantes-
la-Jolie

Pontoise

Seine

Médan

Maisons-
Laffitte

Rueil-Malmaison

Sartrouville

La Défense

Septeuil

Eure

Anet

Thoiry

St-Germain-
en-Laye

Chatou

St-Cloud

Paris

Forest of
Dreux

Versailles

Houdan

Dreux

St-Quentin-
en-Yvelines

Chevreuse

Breteuil

Rambouillet

Arpajon

Le Marais

St-Sulpice-
de-Favières

Maintenon

Dourdan

Chartres

N

Auneau

Etampes

Rail Lines

0   10 miles

0   15 km

TO
ORLÉANS

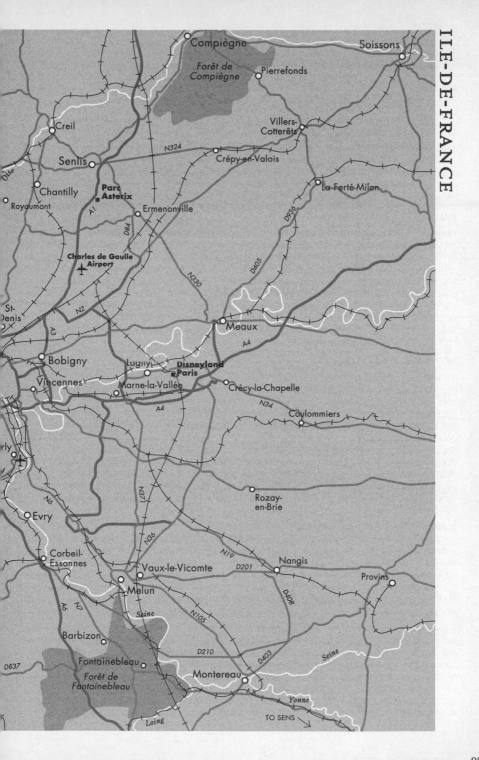

BASICS

There are three **Office de Tourisme** locations in Versailles. The branch (tel. 01–39–53–31–63) opposite the Gare Rive Gauche train station in Les Manèges, a shopping mall, is closed on Monday. The main office (7 rue des Réservoirs, tel. 01–39–50–36–22), just north of the château, is closed on Sunday. May–September, a third, constantly crowded office sets up Tuesday–Sunday at the château's main gate. All three locations have loads of brochures and helpful English-speaking employees, and all are open until around 6 PM.

COMING AND GOING

The cheapest way to reach Versailles from Paris is via the **yellow RER Line C** to Versailles–Rive Gauche (30–40 mins, 15F). Otherwise, trains from Paris's Gare Montparnasse stop at Gare des Chantiers (rue des États-Généraux) south of the château, and trains from Paris's Gare St-Lazare and La Défense arrive at the Gare Rive Droite behind place du Marché Notre-Dame, northeast of the palace. All three stations are within walking distance of the château.

FOOD

Picnicking is the cheapest and easiest way to eat here. If you don't bring your own food, try the sandwich shop **Class Croûte,** in the Les Manèges shopping mall just across from the Gare Rive Gauche. The decent sandwiches cost 18F–30F. There's a **Monoprix** market on avenue du Général-de-Gaulle, five minutes to your right as you exit the Gare Rive Gauche. If you're not hot on the picnic idea, try one of the small restaurants on **place du Marché-Notre-Dame** (about three blocks northeast of the château entrance), or one of the brasseries on **avenue de Paris,** the main street that runs smack-dab into the château's gates. The farther you get from the château, the better luck you'll have finding something that isn't priced for tourists with a capital T. If you have time, walk five blocks southeast of the château to the St-Louis district (beyond the cathedral) and stand in line with the locals for a freshly made sandwich (15F–20F) at **Traiteur Philippe Joly** (62 rue d'Anjou, tel. 01–39–50–28–46).

WORTH SEEING

It's hard to tell which is larger at Versailles—the tremendous château that housed Louis XIV and 20,000 of his courtiers or the crowd of 20,000 visitors standing in front of it. You may be able to avoid the 1½-hour wait for a tour if you arrive here at 9 AM sharp, when the château opens. The hard part is figuring out where you're supposed to go once you arrive: There are different lines depending on tour, physical ability, and group status. Frequent guided tours in English visit the private royal apartments. More detailed hour-long tours explore the opera house or Marie-Antoinette's private parlors. The opera house is especially interesting because the architect, wanting the acoustics of a violin, built the hall entirely of wood and then had it all painted to resemble marble. You can go through a few rooms, including the Hall of Mirrors, without a tour—by means of yet another line, of course. To figure out the system, pick up a brochure at the information tent at the gates of the château, or consult the information desk at the ticket center. *Tel. 01–30–84–76–18. Admission 45F. Tours 25F–50F. Open Tues.–Sun. 9–6:30 (Oct.–Apr. until 5:30).*

If you don't feel like hassling with crowds and lines, or if you don't have any money left but still want to say that you've been to Versailles, check out the free **gardens** in back. This is where you'll find Versailles's hundreds of famous fountains. By the way, if you're wondering why the fountains don't work, they do—but you'll have to come on a summer Sunday and shell out 28F to see them in action. Or, lose the tourists huddled around the fountains and discover 250 acres of gardens a little farther away from the château. Tourist brochures request that you not picnic on the lawns, but they don't say anything about the grottoes, groves, and grassy areas scattered throughout the woods. Chances are good that you won't run into a gendarme if you stay away from the main attractions. *Gardens open daily 7–sunset.*

A guide written by Louis XIV himself, *Manière de montrer les jardins de Versailles* (How to Show the Versailles Gardens), is being consulted as the gardens are returned to their Sun King days. Landscape architect André Le Nôtre's gardens are brimming with walkways, pools, viewpoints, woods, velvet lawns, a **colonnade** of 24 marble columns, an **orangery,** and tons of statuary. Perhaps most impressive are sculpture groupings emerging from two pools: the **Bassin de Neptune** (Fountain of Neptune) sea god with dragons and cherubs and the **Bassin d'Apollo** (Fountain of Apollo) sun god in his chariot emerging amid sea monsters to bring light to the world. Beyond the Fountain of Apollo is the **Grand Canal,** which Louis XIV equipped with brightly colored gondolas. A boat ride costs about 25F.

COMPIEGNE

It's possible to do Compiègne itself in an afternoon, but you'll have to move fast to see the château, the forest, and nearby Pierrefonds all in one swoop. You may be tempted to stay a little longer than you expect—biking the Oise Valley is a welcome change from fighting métro crowds.

You may want to focus as much attention on Compiègne's surrounding forest as you do on the town itself, and rightly so. It's nice for hiking, and the tourist office can give you information about free guided walking tours run by Compiègne AVF Accueil on the weekends. If you don't have a lot of time, the real way to go is to rent a bike (see Outdoor Activities, below), which will get you to the **Clarière de l'Armistice** and to **Pierrefonds** (see Near Compiègne, below) without dealing with infrequent buses. It's a straight shot to Pierrefonds, but once you enter the maze of trails, you'll get lost if you don't have a map—pick up a free one when you rent a bike, or buy the 15F *Circuits Pédestres* (*Walking Tours*) booklet at the tourist office. Note that all trail markers have a red dash in the direction of Compiègne. Once you enter the forest, you're truly spoiled—it's flat, easy riding with gorgeous, varying scenery.

BASICS

The bustling **Office de Tourisme** next to the Gothic Hôtel de Ville has brochures on Compiègne, the forest, and the castle at Pierrefonds. *Pl. de l'Hôtel-de-Ville, tel. 03–44–40–01–00. Open Mon.–Sat. 9:30–12:15 and 1:45–6:15, Sun. 9:30–12:30 and 2:30–5; Nov.–Easter, closed Sun.*

The Château of Chantilly had an excellent reputation for fine cuisine in the 17th century and today remains the eponym for fresh whipped cream. Anything you order "à la chantilly" will come with a dollop of the stuff.

COMING AND GOING

Trains leave nearly every hour (some requiring a change at Creil) from Paris's Gare du Nord for the 69F, 40- to 75-minute trip to Compiègne. The train and bus station is a 10-minute walk across the river from the center of town. Take the bridge to the right of the station and continue straight on rue Solférino through to place de l'Hôtel-de-Ville. On the other side of the square, rue Solférino becomes rue Magenta. Head off left for the palace, and right for the cobblestone pedestrian zone. City Buses 1, 2, and 5 are free and run from the station into the center of town (except on Sunday).

WHERE TO SLEEP

Cheap options are rare, and all are a good deal less charming than the hostel at Pierrefonds (see Near Compiègne, below). Two of the best are the **Hôtel du Lion d'Or** (4 rue Général-Leclerc, tel. 03–44–23–32–17, fax 03–44–86–06–23), with small singles for 120F and doubles for 150F; and the **Hôtel St-Antoine** (17 rue de Paris, tel. 03–44–23–22–27), with doubles for 95F–140F.

FOOD

Brasseries abound around place de l'Hôtel-de-Ville and in the pedestrian area, but they're not cheap. Try **Le Songeons** (40 rue de Solférino, tel. 03–44–40–23–98), one block down toward the river from the center, for a decent 50F plat du jour. **Pizzeria Stromboli** (2 rue des Lombards, in passage de la Potène, tel. 03–44–40–06–21), closed Sunday, is a local favorite, a fact that comes in handy when you're trying to find it. You may have to wait a while to be seated, but the crispy-crusted pizzas and pungent pastas (38F–50F) are worth it. For picnic packers, the open-air **Marché Place-du-Change** behind the pedestrian zone, open until 12:30 PM on Wednesday and Saturday, will ready you for the road. **Djerba** (9 cours Guynemer, tel. 03–44–40–01–36), open daily 8–8, has everything from trail mix to fresh Sicilian olives, homemade couscous, fruit, and vegetables. **Monoprix**, at 35 rue Solferino, has the cheapest bulk grocery supplies.

WORTH SEEING

Compiègne is a mix of ramshackle, half-timber houses and modern stucco buildings that went up after World War I flattened parts of the town. In fact, the armistice ending the war was signed in a railway car just 6 km (4 mi) away from the then wiped-out town. If you rent a bike (see Outdoor Activities, below), you can visit the railcar in a memorial park called the **Clairière de l'Armistice** (tel. 03–44–85–14–18) and pay 10F to look through the windows at memorabilia of the event. (No buses come here, and it's closed Tuesday.)

The following are quirks unique to Mickey's European pied-à-terre. Wine is served in the park (they changed their no-alcohol policy in 1993). Tombstone inscriptions at Phantom Manor read: "Jasper Jones, loyal manservant, kept the master happy; Anna Jones, faithful chambermaid, kept the master happier." No Mickey walking around—he was too mobbed by kiddies, so he stays in one spot, and you have to line up to see him. Cast members look like they need a cigarette. If you so much as think about sitting on the lawn, "happy" Disney characters lose the grin and use the whistle.

Louis XV built the **Palais de Compiègne** in the 18th century. It's a grand estate like Fontainebleau, not a Sleeping Beauty–type structure. It lost its original furniture during the Revolution, but Napoléon decked out the whole shebang in marble, gold, and silk, and the stylishly restored interior is a monument to the tasteful bombast of his "Empire" style. You can see everything during a one-hour guided visit, although you won't get much out of it if you don't speak French. The colorful English **garden** and wide expanse of grass and trees make one of the nicest hangout spots in France, and it's free—the gate is right off place du Château. Admission to the châteaus also gets you into two museums. At the **Musée de la Voiture** (Car Museum) in the north wing, follow the tour guide to get the lowdown on some of France's four-wheel pioneers. Old-fashioned bicycles sneak their way in, too. The ho-hum **Musée du Second Empire** is a mishmash of furniture, clothes, and art set up in stark rooms. *Tel. 03–44–38–47–00. Admission 35F, 23F Sun. Open Wed.–Mon. 9:15–5:30 (Oct.–Mar. until 3:45).*

AFTER DARK

Au Bureau (6 rue Jean-Legendre, tel. 03–44–40–10–11) makes a good starting point for an evening out. In booths surrounded by English pub paraphernalia, you can enjoy a 46F pizza as you down your first cold one from a choice of more than 100 beers from 20-odd countries. For a cozier, more youthful scene, go to **Sweet Home Pub** (49 rue St-Corneille at the corner with rue d'Austerlitz), where things get wild later in the evening as more and more 25F brews are consumed.

OUTDOOR ACTIVITIES

Endless trails—paved, unpaved, and downright sloshy—wind through shady groves of birch, oak, and French broom in the **Forêt de Compiègne.** There are only a couple of steep trails, but you'll have plenty of opportunities for exploration and discovery. The man at **Picardie Forêt Verte** (4 rue de la Gare, tel. 03–44–90–05–05) is terrific, but you need to call the day before you want a bike; he'll have it waiting for you at the station. Tell him what you want to explore and how steep a ride you want, and he'll give you a map with your own personalized route. His office is just to your right as you exit the train station, but he is seldom there; you have better luck on weekends and holidays when you can find him at the Carrefour Royal by the campground. All of this pampering has a price, of course—120F per day.

NEAR COMPIEGNE

PIERREFONDS

Tucked away in the Forêt de Compiègne, the 12th-century **Château de Pierrefonds** has round towers with pointy tops, cannon notches in the walls, a moat—everything a proper château should have. Between the château and a lake, half-timber houses and teardrop spires rise out of Pierrefond's cute village; the interior of the château is decorated with medieval memorabilia. *Tel. 03–44–42–72–72. Admission 32F. Open May–Aug., daily 10–6; Sept.–Apr., daily 10–noon and 2–5.*

COMING AND GOING • Getting here from Compiègne is a beautiful and easy bike ride—a flat 14 km (8½ mi) through lush green forest—and the initial view of the château as you round the final curve is worth the effort. Buses from Compiègne run three times daily (fewer on Sunday, none on holidays) from the station and charge 14F; if you get stranded in Pierrefonds, the taxi will cost a whopping 180F.

WHERE TO SLEEP AND EAT • The **Château de Jonval** (2 rue Séverine, tel. 03–44–42–80–97), also known as the *Maison Familiale de Vacances Cité Joyeuse,* has been converted into a hostel with rooms for two to eight people. Ever wondered what it would be like to open the window of your own castle bedroom and gaze across a tiny valley at a majestic medieval château glistening in the morning light? Here's your chance to find out. For 70F (plus a 30F membership fee per room), you get a simple bed and breakfast, but the superb setting makes it worthwhile. Cheap picnics are difficult to come by, so stock up in Compiègne. One option is Pierrefonds's **Crêperie Ouradon** (8 rue du Beaudon, tel. 03–44–42–86–62), where the oversize, delicious galettes (25F–40F) put any crepe you get in Paris to shame.

FONTAINEBLEAU

If you love the sight of a richly decorated château but can't handle Versailles's crowds, head for Fontainebleau, a quick 65 km (40 mi) south of Paris. Elaborate, garish, and even occasionally beautiful, Fontainebleau's palace dates back further than Versailles. If its regimented gardens seem too uptight, forage in the thick forest nearby (*see* Outdoor Activities, *below*).

The last weekend in May, Compiègne hosts the Foire aux Fromages et aux Vins, a big wine-and-cheese fair complete with wandering minstrels and Frenchmen determined to consume more than 58,000 bottles of wine and 17,000 pieces of cheese.

BASICS

If you're only interested in Fontainebleau's château, you can pick up everything you need at the main entrance. If the forest is calling, however, the **Office de Tourisme** has some crucial items, including a very detailed forest map (35F) and the schedules of irregular local buses. *4 rue Royale, tel. 01–60–74–99–99. Open weekdays 9:30–12:30 and 2–6:30, Sat. 9:30–6:30, Sun. 10–12:30 and 3–5:30; Oct.–Apr., closed Sun.*

COMING AND GOING

Trains leave every hour from Paris's Gare de Lyon and cost 47F for the 40-minute trip. The 3-km (2-mi) walk from the train station in Avon to the château takes about 30 uninteresting minutes along avenue Franklin Roosevelt, unless you stop to rent a bike (*see* Biking, *below*). Or take **Bus A/B** (every 15 mins) from the station until you see the château. During high season, when the bus is crowded, many people slip on without a ticket; honest types buy the 9F ticket on board.

FOOD

At **Au Délice Impérial** (1 rue Grande, tel. 01–64–22–20–70), near the tourist office, large salads set you back only 40F. A few doors over, **La Taverne Alsacienne** (23 rue Grande, tel. 01–64–22–20–85) serves a 62F three-course menu of French specialties. For general groceries, there's a **Prisunic** a few blocks from the center toward Avon at 58 rue Grande.

WORTH SEEING

Chateau de Fontainebleau. In 1528 King François I had license to kill just about anything he wanted, so no one complained when he commissioned this upscale hunting lodge—*way* upscale. The château has been used as both a hunting lodge and an official residence for nearly eight centuries by more than 30 sovereigns. Each king who lived here left his mark—a tower here, a staircase there—with additions that reflect the style of his period. Because of these hundreds of years of architectural influences, Napoléon I called Fontainebleau "La Maison des Siècles" (The Home of Centuries).

The **gardens** of Fontainebleau, like the château, reflect a mix of styles. Designed in part by Versailles's landscape architect extraordinaire, Le Nôtre, they don't quite achieve the same magnificence. Yet the nice thing about these gardens (and Fontainebleau in general) is that there aren't as many tourists roaming around. Locals fish for salmon and carp in the Grand Canal and walk their dogs along Le Prairie, the grassy expanse on the edge of the sculptured gardens.

One 35F ticket lets you into the **Grands Appartements** and the **Salles Renaissance,** the fully furnished living quarters of François I, Napoléon III, and all the royalty in between. The same ticket admits you to the **Musée Napoléon** (15 rooms filled with arms, guns, hats, uniforms, and other relics of Napoléon's life) and the **Musée Chinois,** which holds the Empress Eugénie's private collection of Chinese knick-knacks. An extra 16F gives you access to the kings' private rooms, the **Petits Appartements.** If you really have your heart set on seeing these smaller rooms, call ahead (tel. 01–60–71–50–70) to find out if tours are running that day. In addition, there are regular free concerts on the castle's organ in the **Chapelle de la Trinité;** call 01–64–22–68–43 for information. *Admission 35F, plus 16F for Petits Appartements. Open June–Oct., Wed.–Mon. 9:30–5; Nov.–May, Wed.–Mon. 9:30–12:30 and 2–5.*

OUTDOOR ACTIVITIES

The château's gardens back right onto 42,000 acres of the **Forêt de Fontainebleau,** one of the biggest forests in France. If you want to play in the woods, don't come on a Monday, however, when most of the rental-equipment facilities are closed. The tourist office sells a 35F top guide called *Guide des Sentiers de Promenade dans le Massif Forestier de Fontainebleau,* which covers paths throughout the forest. For a good view of the whole beech-, birch-, and pine-covered expanse, head up to the **Tour Denecourt,** about 5 km (3 mi) northeast of the château.

BIKING • The trails here are a dream—endless and totally unrestricted. The tourist office has trail maps and guides, but you can easily explore the former hunting grounds on your own. **À la Petite Reine** (32 rue des Sablons, tel. 01–60–74–57–57) rents mountain bikes for 80F per weekday, 100F per weekend day with a 2,000F or credit-card deposit. Most of the steeper trails are west of town, but ask the bike-store people to point out the best places.

CLIMBING • Rock clusters and small gorges abound, but getting the gear and then both the gear and yourself to them is tricky. **Top Loisirs** (10 passage Ronsier, tel. 01–60–74–08–50) rents gear in town but doesn't open until 10 AM, and if you're relying on buses to get here, the day will be over before you touch rock. Your best bet is to rent in Paris, then arrive in town early enough to stop at the tourist office to book one of the many guides.

DISNEYLAND PARIS

It's controversial, expensive, and fun. No matter how you feel about the Americanization of Europe, though, it can be tempting to blow a month's pay on the spotless grounds, good rides, and long lines that characterize this meticulously conceived fantasy world. The park has the best attractions of the American Disney parks rolled into one condensed version. **Star Tours, Captain Eo, Big Thunder Railroad, It's a Small World, Peter Pan** . . . they're all here, and more state-of-the-art than ever. Newer stuff includes **Indiana Jones and the Temple of Doom,** with Disney's first-ever roller coaster loop, and the $120 million **Space Mountain,** the scariest Disney ride. Although Adventureland's **Middle Eastern Grand Bazaar** and Fantasyland's **Alsatian Village** give the park a bit of *faux* international flair, it's definitely more "Disneyland" than "Paris."

Though Disneyland Paris will never be a travel bargain, you can save money by timing your visit carefully. Rates do not simply rise with the temperature; they fluctuate with school and national holidays, weekends, and season. During most of June, for example, entrance costs 195F, but during February and March (ski season) it jumps back up to 250F. Call ahead to verify prices for specific dates—going a day later could make a big difference. Lines within the park are usually ridiculous on weekends, but apparently everyone rushes to get here first thing in the morning, then poops out by early afternoon. *Tel. 01–60–30–60–30. Take RER Line A to Marne-la-Vallée–Chessy (39F). Admission 160F–570F depending on number of days and time of year. Open daily 10–6 (until 9–11 in summer).*

WHERE TO SLEEP

The least expensive hotels within the resort, the **Hotel Santa Fe** and **Hotel Cheyenne,** have rooms for up to four people for 300F–650F, and April–September the **Davy Crockett Ranch** has cabins for up to six people starting from 475F. Hotel-park admission packages can make a night here slightly more attractive. For reservations, call 01–60–30–60–30 (call 407/W–DISNEY from the United States; 01701–753–2900 from the United Kingdom).

FOOD

Your best bet may be to just smuggle food into the park, but a few restaurants inside actually have menus that won't break the bank, including the **Café Hyperion** (inside Videopolis in Discoveryland), with a menu from 40F; the **Pizzeria Bella Notte** (Fantasyland), with a menu from 50F; and the **Cowboy Cookout Barbeque** (Frontierland), also with a menu from 40F.

ELSEWHERE NEAR PARIS

PARC ASTERIX

All French kids know comic-book hero Astérix and his loyal, larger sidekick, Obélix. In the year 50 BC, these stubby Gauls beat up invading (and usually pretty idiotic) Romans trying to attack their village in Brittany. A swig of magic potion makes Astérix invincible in battle, and menhir-toting Obélix fell into a vat of the stuff as a child and was permanently fortified. Most of the attractions are glorified versions of carnival rides, spinning and twirling you around until your lunch makes an encore appearance. There are some fun ones, though, like the ultraloopy **Goudurix** roller coaster and **Grand Splatch,** which will get you soaked. Be warned that some attractions close on weekdays, and the park is often empty—call ahead. *Tel. 03–44–62–34–34. Admission 160F. Open mid-Apr.–mid-Oct., daily 10–6.*

COMING AND GOING • From Paris, take **RER Line B3** to the Charles de Gaulle/Roissy terminus (48F), where you can catch a special 15F shuttle (20 mins) that runs to the park (9:30–1:30) and back (4:30–park closing) every half hour. Food, of course, is exorbitantly expensive. If you don't want to sneak in a picnic, you might decide to skip lunch.

PROVINS

If you've never seen a fortified medieval town, visiting Provins is a must. Built mostly in the 12th and 13th centuries, the **ville haute** (upper town) is entirely surrounded by stone walls and has all kinds of medieval stuff to explore. See the tower where they used to keep criminals; an enormous church with imposing wooden doors and a big, black dome; an executioner's house; subterranean passages running under the whole town; tiny, flowered, cobblestone streets; and, of more recent origin, a beer garden where locals come to hear live music. From the train station, walk across the bridge, through the commercial center, and up the hill, following the signs that say ITINÉRAIRE PIÉTON (pedestrian route).

The ramparts and medieval building are courtesy of the Count of Champagne, who brought money, people, and ideas to Provins in the early 13th century, turning it into a major commercial center. People came to buy, sell, and trade their goods, paying taxes to the count, who, in turn, offered them protection. Apparently the system worked; the count made enough money to build the town and the convent in the neighboring forest. Everything was running smoothly until river transportation became all the rage in Europe, and Provins found itself high and dry. Eight centuries later, without its superpower status, it's merely a great day trip from Paris. Hit Provins in late May or early June and you'll find the Fête Médiévale, when the whole town dresses up, acts like characters from the Middle Ages, and eats a lot of junk food. Entrance is 30F, free if you happen to have a medieval costume.

BASICS • The 70-minute train ride from Paris's Gare de l'Est will set you back 61F. Trains aren't exactly frequent: If you don't fancy the one at 7:41 AM, you'll have to wait until noon. The first afternoon train, at 1:42 PM, won't leave you much time to do Provins justice. If you miss the last train back to Paris—at 8 PM—the local nightlife isn't exactly kicking, but cheap, hostel-like rooms (60F–90F) are provided by **Claude Lebel** (3 pl. Honoré-de-Balzac, tel. 01–64–00–02–27). For a bit more luxury, check out the beautifully converted farmhouse at **La Ferme du Châtel** (5 rue de la Chapelle-St-Jean, tel. 01–64–00–10–73), where fancy doubles go for 260F. As for food, it's all overpriced meals in the walled village, but there's a fine 60F weekday lunch menu at **La Boudinière** (17 rue Hugues-le-Grand) in the low town, and a **Monoprix** market on your walk from the train station, where you can stock up.

3 THE LOIRE VALLEY

UPDATED BY SIMON HEWITT

I f Brittany is stubbornly independent and Paris arrogantly cosmopolitan, then the Loire Valley is, quite simply, French. The vineyards, orchards, gentle climate, and château-littered, poppy-covered hillsides do wonders for the French temperament—Parisians should be required to spend at least a week a year here.

The châteaux of the Loire Valley are full of aristocratic dirty laundry. A scared, insecure, and still crownless Charles VII hid from the English in the fortresses of Loches and Chinon; Charles VIII worked his men overtime to complete the splendiferous Amboise; and François I used the Renaissance extravagance of Chambord to hunt, feast, and cheat on his spouse. The women of the valley are equally impressive (and more fondly remembered): Joan of Arc lifted the siege of Orléans; six remarkable women took their turns presiding over Chenonceau; and Catherine de' Medici made an appearance at nearly every château in the valley while concealing all manner of poisons? jewels? lovers? in the secret panels at Blois.

The châteaux are worthwhile and impressive, but if you race around you'll miss the subtleties of the region. Builders, boring into hillsides to extract stones for the Renaissance châteaux demanded by trendy dukes and counts, left in their wake three Loire Valley sights: *caves champignonnières* (mushroom cellars), where more than 60% of France's edible fungi grow on the walls; *caves de vin* (wine cellars), where the constant 14°C temperature ages wines to perfection; and *maisons troglodytiques* (troglodyte houses), dwellings scooped out of cliffs or rock. In the smaller towns, the population consists mostly of older folks who proudly practice trades like carpentry, masonry, or basket making. The younger generation has fled the valley most likely because many of these trades are no longer profitable. As a result, the nightlife of the region (apart from in the student-dominated Tours) moves at a measured pace—people are more likely to be seen chatting away in a café or restaurant than sweating on a dance floor.

BASICS

VISITOR INFORMATION

The Loire Valley sees hundreds of thousands of visitors each year—and it's ready for them. All but the tiniest château towns have tourist offices, though some are only open in summer. The **Comité Départemental de Tourisme de l'Indre-et-Loire** distributes detailed information for all of the Loire Valley. *9 rue Buffon, Tours, tel. 02–47–31–42–60. Open Mon.–Sat. 9–noon and 2–6.*

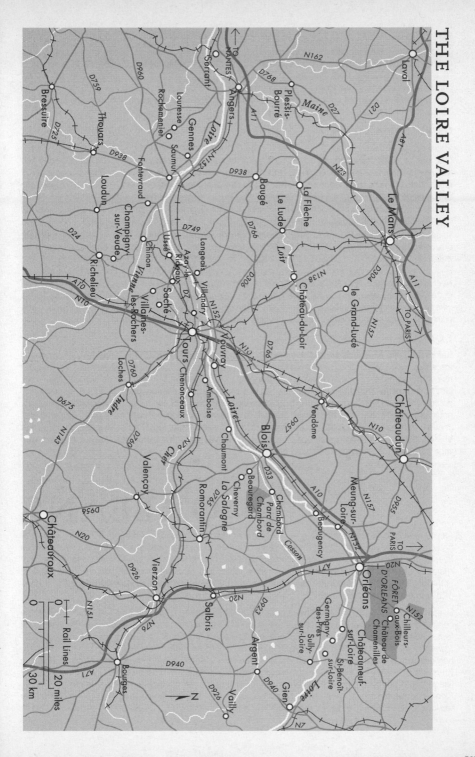

COMING AND GOING

Orléans (111F), the first stop on a downstream tour, is only a 65-minute train ride from Paris. Angers (243F), all the way at the other end, is just 90 minutes from the capital by TGV (243F), or a couple of hours along the valley from Orléans by regional train. Tours (211F), the biggest base for visiting châteaux, is served by TGV from Paris in just over an hour. For specific schedules and prices of trains that come to the Loire and circulate within the region, call **SNCF**'s national number (tel. 08–36–35–35–35), but be brief because they charge 2F per minute.

GETTING AROUND

The shortage of train and bus lines within the region means that even though it's *possible* to reach the châteaux by public transport, it's extremely difficult for anyone with limited time. If you find a train or bus that heads out to a château at 6 AM and returns to town at 5 PM, consider yourself lucky. Two free SNCF guides help out: The thick, comprehensive "Guide Régional des Transports" and the more specific "Les Châteaux de la Loire en Train," which also indicates which trains you can take your bike on for free. Both include SNCF-subsidized bus services to villages not served by train. It's annoying that both guides are only available at big stations like Tours or Angers.

To see lots of châteaux in limited time without your own wheels, you might have to settle for a **private bus company** out of Tours or Blois. Although they force you to visit the châteaux according to their stop-watch and are not cheap (usually 130F–200F), they sometimes include excellent guided visits and English commentary you wouldn't get on your own. Three or four people can make **renting a car** (*see* Near Tours, *below*) a deal, and you can't beat creating your own itinerary. But the best transport method in the valley is by **bike**: The countryside is flat, the châteaux are accessible, and you can usually take a bike with you on trains and buses. Rent them in the cities to avoid the high prices of small towns. If you plan to do some serious biking, buy the detailed yellow regional map *Michelin 64*.

FOOD

Before the Loire River was controlled by dams, the river would flood to 3 km (2 mi) in width, irrigating the entire valley. When the river slinked back to the confines of its banks, inventive cooks made good use of the abundant fruits and vegetables bursting from the fertile soil. Specialties like *rillettes*—cold, fatty potted meat—may make you queasy, but freshwater fish like salmon, carp, and pike elegantly prepared with *asperges* (asparagus), *champignons* (mushrooms), or *pommes de terre nouvelles* (new potatoes) grown in the Loire and served steeped in butter and shallots are worth a splurge. Regional goat cheese, particularly the *crottin de Chavignol* (crottin means "little turd"), is strong and flavorful. For dessert, there's *tarte tatin* (apple upside-down cake served with crème fraîche). Wash it all down with wine from Saumur, Vouvray, Chinon, or Touraine.

ORLEANS

As you walk outside the train station in Orléans, you might find yourself wishing that Joan of Arc never bothered to obey God and lift the English siege. Had she been less obedient, the English might still be keeping the Orléanais in . . . and ugly modern buildings out. Whereas the *vieille ville* (old town), around rue de Bourgogne, is attractive, with cobblestone streets and renovated wooden-beam houses, the rest of the city has suffered from industrial development. It takes the arrival of the **jazz festival** the first week of July to really spice things up.

Despite the city's lackluster neighborhoods, Orléans's inexpensive lodging and restaurants make it a comfy base for exploring the châteaux, villages, and forests nearby. It's also a pilgrimage site of sorts for fans of Jeanne d'Arc, known to English speakers as Joan of Arc and to Orléans locals as *la pucelle d'Orléans* (the maiden of Orléans). In AD 1429, in the midst of the Hundred Years' War, the 18-year-old shepherdess from Lorraine arrived in Orléans, rallied the troops, and helped liberate the city from the English (thus setting France on the path toward victory). Much of Orléans is consecrated to Joan's memory; her likeness and her name are everywhere, from a Center for Joan of Arc Studies to a Jeanne d'Arc Dry Cleaners down the block. Joan aside, there's no particular attraction or scene to keep you in Orléans for too long, other than a few decent museums and a big cathedral.

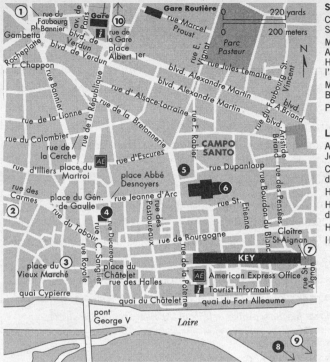

Sights ●
Cathédrale
Ste-Croix, **6**

Musée
Archéologique et
Historique de
l'Orléanais, **4**

Musée des
Beaux-Arts, **5**

Parc Floral, **8**

Lodging ○
Auberge de
Jeunesse, **2**

Camping Municipal
d'Olivet, **9**

Hôtel Coligny, **10**

Hôtel L'Etoile
d'Or, **3**

Hôtel Jackotel, **7**

Hôtel de Paris, **1**

BASICS

AMERICAN EXPRESS

The office cashes traveler's checks at good rates. For free 24-hour refund assistance, dial 0–800–90–86–00. *19 av. des Droits-de-l'Homme, tel. 02–38–22–15–45. Open weekdays 9–12:30 and 1:45–6.*

LAUNDRY

Lav'45 is close to the train station. Washing costs 16F–22F, drying 2F, and soap 2F. *137 rue du Faubourg-Bannier, tel. 02–38–88–23–84.*

MAIL

The **post office** changes money for good rates and handles phone and fax services. The postal code is 45000. *Pl. du Général-de-Gaulle, tel. 02–38–77–35–35. Open weekdays 8–7, Sat. 8–noon.*

MEDICAL AID

Many doctors speak English at Orléans's main hospital, **Centre Hôpitalier Régional d'Orléans** (1 rue de la Porte-Madeleine, tel. 02–38–51–44–44). If you speak French, the **SOS** line (tel. 02–38–54–44–44) has emergency medical information.

VISITOR INFORMATION

It's hard to miss the '70s horror that is the **tourist office** as you walk out of the train station. The staff speaks English, has plenty of brochures and maps, and reserves a hotel room for 7F (plus half the room rate up front). *Pl. Albert-Ier, tel. 02–38–24–05–05. Open Oct.–Mar., Mon.–Sat. 9–6:30, Sun. 10–noon; Apr.–Sept., Mon.–Sat. 9–7, Sun. 9:30–12:30 and 3–6:30.*

The **Centre Régional d'Information Jeunesse** sells cheap train tickets and vacation deals to those under 26. *5 blvd. de Verdun, tel. 02–38–78–91–80. Open Mon. and Thurs. 1–6, Tues., Wed., and Fri. 10–noon and 1–6.*

A DUKE'S HOME IS HIS CASTLE

Dukes and counts began building châteaux in the 11th century, when they needed to watch over the king's lands (vulnerable to river invasions) and to protect themselves from each other. Sparse, cold, and uninviting châteaux in those days were drafty stone structures lined with wall-size tapestries for insulation. Objects you'll often see are the massive high-back chairs that prevented the user from being stabbed in the back during dinner, and the "crédence," a table on which the meal was checked for poison by an official taster.

Fortifications continued to come in handy during the Hundred Years' War. When the war was over, Charles VIII, and his successors, Louis XII and François I, went to Italy, looking for someone else to fight, and came back with the Renaissance (François I literally brought home Leonardo da Vinci). The Valois line of kings, who ruled from the early 14th to the late 16th century, built outrageous homes on the riverbanks, using a chalky, local stone called tuffeau (tufa), whose softness and whiteness made it ideal for the sculpted details of the new architectural style.

COMING AND GOING

Orléans is just 65 minutes from Paris's Gare d'Austerlitz (111F), as you go toward Blois (35–45 mins, 52F) and eventually Tours (70–95 mins, 88F). Orléans's **train station** (pl. Albert-Ier, tel. 02–38–79–91–89), only four blocks from the center of town, is connected to local and regional bus services (*see* Near Orléans, *below*) and the tourist office. Note that some trains depart from the station at Les Aubrais, rather than from Orléans; to reach Les Aubrais (a 10-minute ride), get to the Orléans station at least 30 minutes early and catch the free *navette* (shuttle).

You'll probably use **SEMTAO** (the city bus system) only for trips into Orléans's suburbs; distances in town are short. Tickets from the driver cost 8F and are good for an hour. Buses run every few minutes and stop running around 8:30 PM, and many lines don't run on Sundays and holidays. Better yet, you might choose to rent a bike to explore the flat, pretty land. Rentals are difficult to find, but **Kit Loisirs** in Olivet (1720 rue Marcel-Belot, tel. 02–38–63–44–34), a suburb of Orléans, rents bikes for 60F per day and *VTTs* (mountain bikes) for 100F. They accept credit cards and require a passport deposit.

GETTING AROUND

The center of Orléans is flat, and easy to navigate on foot; you can get a good introduction to the city by following the marked pedestrian circuit of the old town, which is described in a leaflet "D'un point à l'autre" (From One Point to Another), available at the main tourist office (*see* Visitor Information, *above*). City buses converge at the **gare routière,** or bus station (2 rue Marcel-Proust, tel. 02–38–53–94–75). You can rent bicycles at the Ile Charlemagne leisure base—3 km (2 mi) south of the city center (tel. 02–38–65–62–99)—which may be reached by buses that depart hourly from place du Martroi.

WHERE TO SLEEP

Budget accommodations are all over the place in Orléans; try **rue Bannier** (off rue Cappon, southwest of the train station) for a decent selection. **Hôtel Coligny** (80 rue de la Gare, north of the train station, tel. 02–38–53–61–60), the cheapest place in town after the youth hostel, has modern doubles with showers for 140F. Otherwise, the tourist office distributes a free list of hotels and their prices.

UNDER 175F • Hôtel L'Étoile d'Or. The hotel and connecting bar-restaurant are a little musty, slightly run-down, and old-fashioned. But the crowd here seems to enjoy it, and the place is usually full. Singles and doubles run 160F with bath, 100F without—but beware, there are no hallway showers. *25 pl. du Vieux-Marché, tel. 02–38–53–49–20. 15 rooms, 3 with bath. Cash only.*

Hôtel Jackotel. The two-star Jackotel gives you a choice between smart double rooms with bath (290F) and smaller rooms in the *bâtiment annexe,* a restored adjacent building in old Orléans, where you'll have a clean, comfy, 170F double with the works—shower, bathroom, telephone, and TV. Most rooms overlook a quiet courtyard, and some have beautifully refurbished old-style decor. *18 cloître St-Aignan, tel. 02–38–54–48–48. 20 rooms, all with shower.*

Hôtel de Paris. The French proprietor's fluent New Yorkese is almost as much of a draw as the bright and clean rooms, bike storage, and low prices. This hotel is popular, so make reservations. Simple doubles go for 145F, 15F more if the room has a shower. An extra bed costs 40F. Showers are 10F. The restaurant below serves breakfast (25F) and lunch (40F). *29 rue du Faubourg-Bannier, tel. 02–38–53–39–58. 13 rooms, 6 with bath.*

HOSTEL • Auberge de Jeunesse. Five minutes from the train station by bus (20 minutes by foot), this hostel has excellent amenities—courtyard, TV, and kitchen. You can rent bikes from the charming couple for 60F a day, and they'll hand over the entrance key if you have a good reason to break the 10:30 curfew. Sheets run 17F and breakfast 19F. They require an HI card but will sell you one for 100F. *14 rue du Faubourg-Madeleine, tel. 02–38–62–45–75. By bus: Bus B (direction: Paul Bert), get off at Beaumont. On foot: Turn right on blvd. de Verdun (it becomes blvd. Rocheplatte past pl. Gambetta), right on rue du Faubourg-Madeleine. 50 beds. Reception open daily 5:30 PM–10:30 PM. Lockout 9.30–5.30. Cash only. Closed Dec.–Jan.*

> *Orléans feels like Paris during the day, when everybody's hustling to and from work, and like a small town at night, when it rolls up the sidewalks.*

CAMPING • Camping Municipal d'Olivet. On a gorgeous wooded site by the little Loiret River, south of the city, this campground has hot showers, laundry facilities, and a small store. The rates are 14F per person, 9F per car, and 10F per tent. The gates close to cars 10 PM–7 AM, but pedestrians can enter whenever they want. *Rue du Pont-Bouchet, tel. 02–38–63–53–94. Take Bus S to Aumône stop. 40 sites. Closed mid-Oct.–Mar.*

FOOD

Orléans's main dining area is the lively, pedestrian **rue de Bourgogne,** where traditional French cooking rubs elbows with African, Middle Eastern, and Asian cuisines. The restaurants here are cheaper than the overpriced joints around place du Martroi and rue Royale, and much prettier than the bland, cheap restaurants around the train station. If you must be near the train station, **Packman** (3 rue de la République, tel. 02–38–62–11–67), a peculiar fast-food–bakery combination, serves two croissants and coffee for only 9F, and **La Nouvelle Orléans** (5 rue de la Cerche, tel. 02–38–54–82–82), a French-Mexican jazz-loving spot, has fajitas for 55F. Grocery stores are everywhere: **Carrefour** (3 rue St-Yves, tel. 02–38–24–21–00), the shopping mall by the train station, is the cheapest, but the outdoor markets scattered about town every day except Monday have fresher-looking produce.

UNDER 50F • Crêperie Bretonne. In the pedestrian section of rue de Bourgogne, this restaurant has a 46F *menu d'ouvrier* (worker's menu), with a salad, a ham and cheese galette, a dessert crepe, and an excellent glass of hard cider. For dinner, the *patatas fermière* (45F), a huge potato covered with sour cream, ham, cheese, and walnuts, and the *assiette nordique* (smoked salmon salad; 45F) are delicious excuses to sit on the terrace and people-watch. Vegetarians: They'll make dishes without meat upon request. *244 rue de Bourgogne, tel. 02–38–62–24–62. Cash only. No dinner Wed., no lunch Sun.*

UNDER 75F • La Brasserie. As the stork emblem above the door suggests, this bustling restaurant—halfway between the train station and old town—specializes in hearty dishes from Alsace, with choucroute and sausage leading the way. Menus start at 68F and there is a wide choice of salads for 45F–50F. Service runs through midnight. *rue Gourville, tel. 02–38–62–51–42.*

UNDER 100F • Les Fagots. This friendly, down-to-earth eatery, in the heart of the old town near the Loire, has a lunch menu at 65F; evening menus start at 85F. Charcoal-grilled meat cuts are the chef's forte, as you'll gather from the jumbo-size fireplace that dominates the restaurant. Old posters and a quirky collection of coffeepots complete the nostalgic decor. *32 rue du Poirier, tel. 02–38–62–22–79. Next to the temple off rue de Bourgogne. Cash only. Closed Sun. and Mon.*

WORTH SEEING

Housed in the historic **Hôtel Cabu** (pl. Abbé-Desnoyers, tel. 02–38–79–25–60), the **Musée Archéologique et Historique de l'Orléanais** has some spectacular Gallo-Roman bronzes but not much else. Admission is 15F. The **Musée des Beaux-Arts** (1 rue Ferdinand-Rabier, tel. 02–38–79–21–55) has a few Rodins and Gauguins, Velásquez's *L'Apôtre St-Thomas,* and images of Mademoiselle Joan in many different shapes and sizes. Admission is 20F. Both museums are open Tuesday–Sunday 11–6.

CATHEDRALE STE-CROIX

This magnificent cathedral stands on a site that has hosted religious rituals for thousands of years. Digs have turned up remains of churches from the 4th, 8th, and 12th centuries. Most importantly to the Orléanais, Joan of Arc prayed here for the lifting of the siege by the English; don't miss the stunning stained-glass windows telling her life story. The cathedral has been under restoration since World War II, when it took a few bombs in one of its towers. It's worth the 30F to tour the *hauteurs* (heights), accessible every afternoon in summer and on Saturdays in spring. *Pl. Ste-Croix, tel. 02–38–77–87–50. Open daily 9–noon and 2–6; mass Sun. 10:30 AM.*

PARC FLORAL

This enormous garden changes with the season—tulips in April, irises and roses in May, and chrysanthemums in November. The source of the Loiret River is here, and you'll find swans and ducks gliding past. *Tel. 02–38–49–30–00. Take Bus S to Parc Floral stop and make 1st left. Admission 20F. Open Apr.–mid-Nov., daily 9–6 (June–Aug. until 8); mid-Nov.–Mar., daily 2–4.*

AFTER DARK

Orléans doesn't exactly hop at night, unless you count the high-school kids cruising around. Oddly enough, most of the action takes place near the train station. Try **Le Grand Café** (1 blvd. de Verdun, tel. 02–38–53–11–23), which plays '80s music and sells small pitchers of wine for 12F, or **Au Bureau** (3 blvd. de Verdun, tel. 02–38–81–14–15) with two-for-one drinks weekdays 7–8 PM. The retro and macho **Le Rive Droite** (31 blvd. Rocheplatte, tel. 02–38–54–01–25) has free Brazilian music nightly in the summer and a complimentary drink for women; it opens at 10:30 PM and are closed on Monday. **Paxton's Head** (264 rue de Bourgogne, tel. 02–38–81–23–29), near the Loire, has a wide choice of English, German, and Belgian beers and hosts live jazz Thursday–Saturday; it's open until 3 AM.

NEAR ORLEANS

From Orléans's **gare routière** (2 rue Marcel-Proust, tel. 02–38–53–94–75), **Rapides du Val de Loire** runs buses (known as *autocars*) in the early morning, at noon, and in the late afternoon that will drop you off in St-Benoît (38F) or Sully (45F). A good plan is to take the early bus to one town, walk along the Loire to the other, and take the evening bus back to Orléans from there. If you want to see more than two towns, inquire at the bus station in Orléans about the complex schedule that has you leaving Orléans at 6:45 AM and returning at 7:15 PM for about 80F. If you're up for a workout, bike the 80-km (50-mi) round-trip from Orléans to St-Benoît and Sully. Just stick to the river and you'll find them easily.

BEAUGENCY

Beaugency, 30 km (19 mi) downriver from Orléans, is one of those villages not yet ransacked by tourism—which means you can experience its history without being bombarded by postcard racks and tacky shops. Inhabitants look almost surprised to see visitors—a rarity in this valley. You can easily wander through this tiny town on your own—white plaques near all the monuments give background information in English and French. The major attraction here is the **Château Dunois** (2 pl. Dunois, tel. 02–38–44–55–23). Though it's not much to look at from the outside, it houses the **Musée Régional de l'Orléanais,** with thematic rooms displaying local crafts—jewelry, costumes, furniture, embroidery, and a great selection of toys. The mandatory, French-only guided tour (22F) is offered Wednesday–Monday hourly in the morning and then again after 2 PM. Check out the nearby 12th-century **Église Notre-Dame** (rue de l'Abbaye), notable for both its Romanesque architecture and the fact that France's first feminist, Eleanor of Aquitaine, had her marriage to Louis VII annulled here in 1152. Also, the park next to **Tavers Gate** (the only gate still remaining from the medieval wall) has a magnificent view of the valley and the many-times-rebuilt **Vieux Pont** (Old Bridge).

BASICS • The cheery ladies at the **tourist office** will give you free maps and information about the area. *3 pl. du Docteur-Hyvernaud, tel. 02–38–44–54–42. Open Mon.–Sat. 9:30–12:30 and 2:30–6:30, Sun. 10–noon.*

COMING AND GOING • Trains run to Beaugency from Orléans (25 mins, 29F) several times a day. You can store your bags behind the counter. To take advantage of the pretty surroundings, rent a bike for 60F a day (50F for multiple days) at **Duvallet** (30 rue du Chat-qui-Dort, next to pl. du Martroi, tel. 02–38–44–52–72). Call ahead in summer.

WHERE TO SLEEP AND EAT • To stay right in town, try the beautiful **Hôtel des Vieux-Fossés** (4 rue des Vieux-Fossés, tel. 02–38–44–51–65); rooms with bath are 140F–150F, and rooms without are 100F (free showers down the hall). The 104-bed **Auberge de Jeunesse** (152 rte. de Châteaudun, tel. 02–38–44–61–31, fax 02–38–44–14–73), 2½ km (1½ mi) from the station, has a large kitchen, an outdoor courtyard, and a comfortable lounge area. The motto here is "*liberté*," which means you can sleep as late as you want, and there's no curfew or lockout. Cost is 51F per night, with an extra 17F for sheets, 19F for breakfast, and 50F for lunch or dinner. The manager will also let campers set up a tent outside with access to all amenities for 25F, and he rents out bikes for 50F a day.

Beaugency isn't overflowing with cheap restaurants, but the **Crêperie de la Tour** (26 rue de la Cordonnerie, tel. 02–38–44–83–93) will whip up béchamel-mushroom galettes for under 40F. For classy French cooking, try **Le P'tit Bateau** (54 rue du Pont, tel. 02–38–44–56–38), where dishes like *poulet rôti aux pommes de terre nouvelles* (roasted chicken with new potatoes) come for under 60F.

ST-BENOIT

If you venture 35 km (22 mi) upriver from Orléans, you hit the **Abbaye St-Benoît** (pl. de l'Abbaye, tel. 02–38–35–72–43). The basilica holds the crypt of St. Benedict, whose disciples have been living in austere simplicity for centuries. In the chapel, note a small plaque with the name Max Jacob on it. This surrealist painter took brief refuge in the crypt before being transferred to a concentration camp in 1944, where he died the same year. French-speaking guides lead two visits through the basilica daily.

SULLY-SUR-LOIRE

Keep on 5 more km (3 mi) up the Loire from St-Benoît to the moated château at **Sully-sur-Loire,** best known for its wood interiors and trompe l'oeil paintings. The guided visit in French is mandatory, but ask for the English-language booklet, translated with unintended hilarity word-for-word from the French. *Chemin de la Salle Verte, tel. 02–38–36–36–86. Admission 27F. Open June–Aug., daily 10–6; Sept.–Nov., Jan., and Mar., daily 10–noon and 2–5.*

On weekends in June and July, this little town gains worldwide attention for its **international music festival** (tel. 02–38–36–23–70).

BLOIS

The architecturally jumbled château of Blois (pronounced Blwah) is well worth a visit. In the early years of the Renaissance, Blois was the unofficial capital of France and home to Louis XII. Things went downhill after that and Blois was pretty boring until Jack Lang, Mitterrand's former Minister of Culture and now the mayor of Blois, pulled this staid, wealthy town out of its conservative coma. Unfortunately, the taxes to finance the modern renovations have made Blois an expensive place to stay.

BASICS

LAUNDRY

Votre Laverie, near the Hôtel du Bellay, is your best bet. *6 rue des Minimes, tel. 02–54–78–18–38.*

THE CUCKOLD COUNT
OF CHEVERNY

The construction of the Château de Cheverny was ordered by Henri, second count of Cheverny, whose young wife carried on an affair with her page while the count was away. King Henri IV, on a visit to the Chevernys' manor house, walked in on the couple. Always a joker, the king later made the cuckold sign to the couple and assembled courtiers. A mirror reflected the king's gesture back to the count, who realized he was the cuckold. He soon had the page executed and then appeared in his wife's bedroom with a vial of poison. The countess gulped it all down, and the count then rebuilt his château.

MAIL

The main **post office** has the best exchange rates and handles phone and fax services. The postal code is 41000. *2 rue Gallois, off pl. Victor-Hugo opposite the château, tel. 02–54–57–17–17. Open Mon. 8:30–7, Tues.–Fri. 8–7, Sat. 8–noon.*

VISITOR INFORMATION

Blois's **tourist office** is in the pavilion where Anne de Bretagne and Louis XII prayed for a male heir. You'll find an English-speaking staff that can help you with transportation to châteaux and lodging in the city. *3 av. du Dr-Jean-Laigret, tel. 02–54–90–41–41. Open June–mid-Sept., Mon.–Sat. 9–7, Sun. 10–7; mid-Sept.–May, Mon.–Sat. 9–noon and 2–6.*

COMING AND GOING

About 15 trains a day stop at the Blois **train station** (pl. de la Gare, tel. 02–54–55–31–00) on the way from Orléans (35–45 mins, 52F) and Tours (30–40 mins, 51F); the 1½-hour trip from Paris via Orléans costs 123F. The station is a 10-minute walk from place Victor-Hugo and the *centre ville* (town center).

GETTING AROUND

The centre ville isn't all that big, but the winding medieval streets, sometimes connected by haphazard flights of steps, make the town easy to get lost in, especially since the tourist-office map is poorly drawn. The commercial center is around **place Louis-XII, rue Port-Côte,** and **rue Denis-Papin.** You probably won't need the local bus service unless you're going to the suburbs. Tickets, good for one hour, cost 6F. Pick up a schedule at the tourist office or at **Point Bus** (2 pl. Victor-Hugo, under the château, tel. 02–54–78–15–66). For bike rental, **Cycles Leblond** (44 levée des Tuileries, tel. 02–54–74–30–13), open daily 9–9, has 10-speeds for 35F–50F a day plus a passport deposit.

WHERE TO SLEEP

UNDER 200F • Hôtel du Bellay. This hotel has kept select vintage oddities—low ceilings and old-fashioned bathtubs—in modern rooms with long beds, direct phones, and CNN. Everyone seems to know about the place, so reserve early. Doubles start at 150F without showers, 160F with. *12 rue des Minimes, tel. 02–54–78–23–62. From train station, take av. Jean Laigret, left on rue Gallois after the church, left on rue du Bourg-Neuf, left on rue des Minimes. 12 rooms, 8 with bath.*

Hôtel St-Jacques. Literally five seconds from the station, this cheery place is run by a friendly couple. Make reservations early for the 115F attic rooms or the triples (205F) with shower. The hotel serves a huge breakfast. Showers are 25F. *7 rue Ducoux, to the right as you exit the station, tel. 02–54–78–04–15. 33 rooms, 10 with bath, 14 with shower.*

HOSTEL • Auberge de Jeunesse. This rustic spot has good kitchen facilities and a setting among rose-bushes and old farmhouses. The downside is that the hostel is 5 km (3 mi) outside Blois (don't miss the last bus out at 7:30 PM). Beds are 41F. An HI card is required. *18 rue de l'Hôtel-Pasquier, tel. 02–54–78–27–21. From pl. Valin (corner rue du Commerce and quai de la Saussaye), take Bus 4 to Église stop. 48 beds. Reception open 6 PM–10:30 PM. Checkout 10 AM. Flexible 10:30 PM curfew. Lockout 10–6. Cash only. Closed mid-Nov.–Feb.*

FOOD

Don't get caught at the tourist traps immediately around the château. Instead, head one block closer to the river to rue St-Lubin; here you'll find **Les Banquettes Rouges** (16 rue des Trois-Marchands, tel. 02–54–78–74–92), a regional restaurant serving a seasonal 89F lunchtime menu, and **Pizzarella** (15 rue des Trois Marchands, tel. 02–54–78–05–07), with an eclectic array of pizzas (35F–45F) and a large list of desserts. **L'Estaminet** (25 rue de St-Lubin, tel. 02–54–74–37–45) serves good drinks at outdoor tables. There's a **Timy** supermarket (tel. 02–54–78–40–33) at 29 avenue du Président-Wilson.

UNDER 50F • La Jeune France. Despite its self-proclaimed status as a snack bar, this place serves huge, delicious salads. An unheard-of 40F gets you an *océane* (seafood salad with clams). The casual outdoor seating is just down from place Victor-Hugo. *62 rue Denis-Papin, tel. 02–54–78–07–44.*

UNDER 100F • La Garbure. Come to this small haven for the 80F *garbure*, an old duck and vegetable soup recipe from Périgord, France, to which the chef has added his own regional touch. Forget ordering an appetizer; the bowl is huge. *13 rue Robert-Houdin, tel. 02–54–74–32–89. Cash only.*

> *Most of the châteaux in northern France were built during the Hundred Years' War (1337–1453), which actually spanned 116 years.*

WORTH SEEING

After visiting the château (*see below*), you might as well walk the two extra blocks to see the **Cathédrale St-Louis** (tel. 02–54–78–17–90) at the bottom of rue Fosses du Château. Its fifth reconstruction has left it as it is today—not exactly Notre-Dame but worth a glance. Mass is held Monday–Saturday at 7:45 AM, Sunday at 9:30.

CHATEAU DE BLOIS

Sightseeing in Blois is pretty much limited to its patchwork château, which covers every major style from Gothic to 17th-century classicism. Group tours in French or English are given upon request. For the self-guided experience, start your visit in the interior courtyard and compare the 13th-century medieval hall with Louis XII's late-Gothic entrance wing, François I's Renaissance stairway, and Gaston d'Orléans's unfinished classical wing. François I, the son-in-law and cousin of Louis XII, began his additions to the château in 1515. The dramatic **staircase** and the **François I wing** are adorned with his salamander logo, chosen because the amphibian was believed to spit forth the fires of good and put out the fires of evil—hence the king's Latin motto, NUTRISCO ET EXTINGO (I NOURISH AND I EXTINGUISH).

The **Salle Gaston d'Orléans** is what the rest of the château would have looked like if Gaston had had his way. In 1635, he brought in his personal architect to launch a major classical "restoration" of the château, which basically involved demolishing the whole thing and starting again from scratch. Luckily, he dropped dead and the sculptors stopped work immediately. On the château's third floor, Blois reached its bloodiest heights. Here Henri III ordered the assassination of the duke of Guise, a popular Catholic rival who came to the château to raise a revolt against the king. The duke was summoned to Henri's chambers and ambushed in a narrow hallway by six guards armed with daggers. *6 pl. du Château, tel. 02–54–78–06–62. Admission 35F. Open Oct.–mid-Mar., daily 9–12:30 and 2–5:30; mid-Mar.–Sept., daily 9–6:30; July–Aug., daily 9–8.*

NEAR BLOIS

If château hopping is your thing, head to the château-studded area surrounding Blois. The châteaux at **Chambord** and **Cheverny** are accessible year-round via regular bus routes (around 40F round-trip); **Chaumont,** however, is only accessible by train during the off-season, which means you'll sometimes be dropped off 4–5 km (2½–3 mi) from your destination and will need to hoof the rest. **Transports du Loir et Cher** (TLC, 2 pl. Victor Hugo, tel. 02–54–78–15–66) is the only bus company with château trips out of Blois. It starts running the circuit the second week in June; the ride costs about 110F to see three châteaux (entrance fees not included).

If you can't stand the thought of a bus-tour château experience, fear not: The area around Blois is flat, and rental bikes are cheap (see Coming and Going *in* Blois, *above*). To plot the best route, pick up the free pamphlet "Effeuillez Blois" from Blois's tourist office, which includes lots of maps, though the text is in French only. You won't be able to stay in most château towns unless you swipe some antique furniture during a tour to pay for your room. Restaurants are no cheaper.

CHATEAU DE CHEVERNY

Perhaps best remembered as Capitaine Haddock's mansion in the Tintin comic books, the château grounds include a hunting reserve, an orangery where the "Mona Lisa" and other art treasures were hidden during World War II, a kennel of 70 hounds, and a trophy room of 2,000 antlers. The château's interior, however, is warm, luxurious, and homey; it feels lived in despite the priceless Delft vases, Gobelin tapestries, and Persian embroideries. You can also take a ride on the tethered hot-air balloon in the park (80F). *Tel. 02–54–79–96–29. Admission 34F. Open June–mid-Sept., daily 9:15–6:45; mid-Sept.–May, daily 9:30–noon and 2:15–5.*

CHATEAU DE CHAUMONT

At last—a château on the train lines. Chaumont is a 10-minute train ride downriver from Blois (get off at Onzain station). The château is a steep 2-km (1-mi) trek from the station. Follow the signs.

Well defended from attack, surrounded by acres of prime hunting ground, and enjoying great panoramas of the Loire, Chaumont should have made any 16th-century courtier an ideal home. But for most of its inhabitants, it has been second best. The counts of Amboise built the château at the end of the 15th century after Louis XI evicted them from Amboise; Henri II's mistress, Diane de Poitiers, who was given Chaumont after being kicked out of Chenonceau by the queen, spitefully refused to live here more than a few days; and author Madame de Staël, in exile from the capital by order of Napoléon, said she would take the gutter behind her Paris home over the Loire River any day.

Notice the dry moat—water couldn't be pumped all the way up the hill to fill it, but it's deep enough to make attackers flounder against the smooth, round walls of the château's foundation. You have to pay to see Chaumont's famous working stables (free with entrance to the château), with porcelain troughs and electric lights that were installed even before the château got power. The horses will take you on a tour of the grounds for 90F an hour. *Tel. 02–54–20–98–03. Admission 32F. Open mid-Mar.–Sept., daily 9:30–6:30; Oct.–mid-Mar., daily 10–5.*

CHATEAU DE CHAMBORD

The immensity and luxury of Chambord, the largest château in the Loire Valley and a one-hour bike ride upriver from Blois, are a constant reminder of how far one man will go to indulge his tastes. And to think this was just a hunting lodge—all 440 rooms, 365 fireplaces, and 5,500 acres of it. François I started work on Chambord in 1519 and never took a break, even when he was so broke he couldn't ransom his sons out of Spain and had begun confiscating and melting down his subjects' silverware. The king even wanted to divert the Loire, more than 5 km (3 mi) away, to pass in front of the château, but he settled for the smaller and closer River Cosson.

The 5F brochure available at the entrance does little to help you navigate the massive château, but try to find the **terrace** upstairs, where hundreds of chimneys form a veritable city skyline. The double-helix **staircase,** which many believe was designed by Leonardo da Vinci, is the highlight of the château. Two people can go up and down the opposite stairs while keeping in sight of each other but never meeting. Check out the second floor's **Musée de la Chasse et de la Nature** (Hunting and Nature Museum) if you want to see a bunch of dead animals in grotesque poses.

Chambord's park, a hunting reserve full of deer and wild boar, is a great place for biking. You can rent one for 80F (plus passport deposit) at the **tourist office** (tel. 02–54–20–34–86) on place St-Michel. The 45F equestrian show, "Le Cheval Roi" (The Noble Horse), happens daily May–September at 11:45 AM and 4 PM. You can also watch animals feed at **observatories** in the park outside the château. *Tel. 02–54–50–40–28. Admission 40F. Open Mar.–Sept., daily 9:30–6:30; Oct.–Feb., daily 9:30–5:15.*

TOURS

If you're looking for action in the Loire Valley, here it is: Tours is the region's largest and most commercial city whose greatest asset is energy—the cobblestone streets in the pedestrian-only vieille ville crackle with cafés, bars, and restaurants. Students make up a quarter of the city's population and give it a lively, hard-edged night scene. Because this is studentsville, you'll have no problem finding an inexpensive bed or meal here, and transport from Tours is fast and efficient.

Though much of Tours was destroyed during World War II (it was bombed by both German *and* Allied forces), some pretty buildings do remain, notably the **train station,** built by the same architect who did the Gare d'Orsay in Paris, and the **Hôtel de Ville** (Town Hall) near place Jean-Jaurès. At the Hôtel de Ville, notice the two reclining figures near the clock that symbolize Tours as the city between two rivers—the woman represents the Loire, and the man stands for the Cher.

BASICS

BUREAU DE CHANGE

Next to place Jean-Meunier, the **Banque de France** changes money for excellent rates. *2 rue Chanoineau, tel. 02–47–60–24–00. Open Mon.–Sat. 8:45–noon and 1–3:30.*

LAUNDRY

Close to the train station, you'll find **Lavomatique** (23 pl. Michelet, tel. 02–47–64–91–84), where you can do your wash for 10F and dry for 5F.

MAIL AND PHONES

The main **post office** has international phone and fax services and holds poste restante for 15 days. It also changes money at decent rates and cashes American Express traveler's checks. Tours's postal code is 37000. *1 blvd. Béranger, tel. 02–47–60–34–20. Open weekdays 8–7, Sat. 8–noon.*

MEDICAL AID

Next to the botanical gardens, **l'Hôpital Bretonneau** (2 blvd. Tonnellé, tel. 02–47–47–47–47) handles medical emergencies night and day.

VISITOR INFORMATION

The staff at the enormous tourist office across from the train station aren't that helpful; it's up to you to weed through the brochures they hand out. If you're into museums, the 50F **Carte de Visite** will get you into almost everything. *78 rue Bernard-Palissy, tel. 02–47–70–37–37. Open May–Sept., Mon.–Sat. 8:30–6:30, Sun. 10–12:30 and 3–6; Oct.–Apr., Mon.–Sat. 9–12:30 and 1:30–6, Sun. 10–1.*

COMING AND GOING

From **place Jean-Jaurès,** a few blocks to the left of the **train station** (pl. du Général-Leclerc, tel. 08–36–35–35–35), extend the two main commercial streets that link Tours's two rivers: **Rue Nationale** leads to the Loire and most of Tours's restaurants, hotels, and monuments, and **avenue de Grammont** crosses the Cher toward the youth hostel and residential neighborhoods. Trains to Tours run frequently from Paris (65 mins, 211F), Orléans (70–95 mins, 88F), Bordeaux (2½ hrs, 221F), and Nantes (1¾ hrs, 149F). For information on how to get to nearby châteaux, *see* Near Tours, *below.*

GETTING AROUND

Tours is a moderately sized and very flat city, easily manageable on foot. Should you opt for public transportation, tickets on **Fil Bleu** (Galerie Jean-Jaurès, tel. 02–47–66–70–70), the city bus service, cost 7F (five for 30F) and are good for an hour. Most buses pass by place Jean-Jaurès and run until 8 PM. For a **taxi,** hail one at the train station or call **Taxis Radio** (tel. 02–47–20–30–40). If you decide to bike it, **Amster Cycles** (5 rue du Rempart, tel. 02–47–61–22–23) rents mountain bikes during the summer for

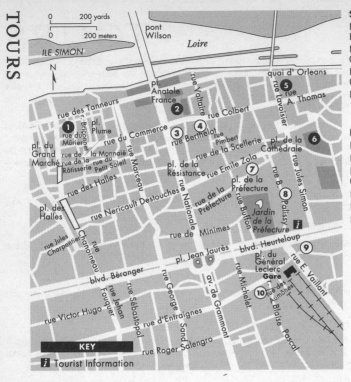

| 0 | 200 yards |
| 0 | 200 meters |

Sights ●

Musée des
Beaux-Arts, **6**

Musée du
Compagnonnage, **2**

Musée du
Gemmail, **1**

Musée Grévin, **5**

Lodging ○

Le Foyer, **8**

Hôtel Berthelot, **3**

Hôtel des
Capucines, **10**

Hôtel Voltaire, **4**

Mon Hôtel, **7**

Le Val de Loire, **9**

KEY

i Tourist Information

70F per day with a passport deposit. For car rental information—not a bad idea if you're going to do the châteaux—*see* Near Tours, *below*.

WHERE TO SLEEP

If you're tired and want to find a quick place to sleep in a pinch, **Hôtel des Capucines** (6 rue Blaise-Pascal, tel. 02–47–05–20–41) and **Le Val de Loire** (33 blvd. Heurteloup, tel. 02–47–05–37–86) both have decent doubles in the 150F–200F range. You take your chances staying in the dubious dives around the train station, which start as low as 60F per night.

UNDER 150F • Hôtel Voltaire. Except for the 140F tab, the doubles with a balcony and a shower make you feel like you're spending the night at your mom's. The hotel also stores luggage and bikes for free. There's a TV room, and showers cost 10F. *13 rue Voltaire, tel. 02–47–05–77–51. 10 rooms, 9 with shower.*

Mon Hôtel. Quiet rooms with thick down quilts make this hotel a bargain at 125F–150F for doubles with shower. The chatty Madame Jacquet has been running this hotel for 20 years, and her file cabinet is well stocked with information on Tours. Showers are 15F. *40 rue de la Préfecture, tel. 02–47–05–67–53. 9 rooms, 5 with bath. Cash only.*

UNDER 175F • Hôtel Berthelot. The owner has just remodeled this centrally located, inexpensive gem. Doubles without shower are 110F, and for 160F you get an immaculate room with a garden view, balcony, and shower. Reception is open 24 hours. *8 rue Berthelot, tel. 02–47–05–71–95. 10 rooms, 8 with shower.*

HOSTEL

Le Foyer. The central location off place de la Gare and big, comfy double rooms (68F per person) make this a great option. Le Foyer is often full in July and August, and you can't reserve ahead, so arrive early. Even without a room, the 15F membership card will give you cafeteria privileges with three-course lunch and dinner meals (40F). Breakfast costs 10F. *16 rue Bernard-Palissy, tel. 02–47–60–51–51. 100 beds. Reception open Mon.–Sat. 9–7. Checkout 10 AM. Cash only.*

FOOD

In the pedestrian quarter around **place Plumereau** (place Plume to locals), on streets such as rue de la Rôtisserie, rue Briçonnet, and rue du Commerce, most restaurants have outdoor seating and all are great for people-watching. Since they're all competing for your business, low prices abound—witness the family-run **Il Cappuccino** (14 rue du Grand-Marché, tel. 02–47–20–87–51), with pizzas and pastas for 35F–45F. For a picnic, try **Aux Produits du Terroir** (24 rue du Petit-Soleil, tel. 02–47–05–99–81) for pâtés or ham; then head to **Au Vieux Four** (7 pl. des Petites-Boucheries, tel. 02–47–66–62–33), near the cathedral, for the best bread in town, made from organic grains and a wood-fire oven. If you're really pinching pennies, don't forget the **outdoor market** Wednesday and Saturday at place de la Victoire. There's also an **ATAC** supermarket (tel. 02–47–05–29–51) just outside the train station at 5 place du Général-Leclerc.

UNDER 50F • Palais de Laido. The enormous Chinese, Vietnamese, and Thai selections provide enough variety to satisfy everyone's tastes. Huge menus start at 40F (lunch) and 50F (dinner). *12 rue de la Rôtisserie, tel. 02–47–20–85–16.*

Le Steven. This restaurant is in the center of it all, and the young staff will serve you large salads (30F–40F) and delicious crepes starting at 12F. Try the conspicuously unkosher salad chèvre *chaude*—warm goat cheese on an immense crouton with bits of ham (39F). *102 rue du Commerce, tel. 02–47–64–72–68. No lunch Mon.*

UNDER 75F • Le Quatre Saisons. This restaurant is also a culinary academy, and you might end up eating someone's final exam—salmon terrine or steak with crispy shallots. Chances are you'll pass the student with flying colors. The seasonal ingredients in the 60F lunch and dinner menu are grown in the region and arrive on your plate after a brief but magical delay in the hands of chef André Loviton and his apprentices. *18 pl. de la Résistance, tel. 02–47–20–52–91. Closed weekends.*

If the natives of Tours are known for one thing, it's their perfect French. Paris may be the capital, but in the eyes of the Tourangeaux, Parisians are the ones with the accent.

SPLURGE • Les Tuffeaux. You'll find this dining spot—one of the city's best—between the city cathedral and the Loire. Dishes may include fennel-flavored salmon, pigeon with endive and walnut dressing, or oysters with egg sauce seasoned with Roquefort. Lunchtime menus are 110F and 135F, and the 200F evening menu (wine included) is worth the splurge. *19 rue Lavoisier, tel. 02–47–47–19–89. Closed Sun. No lunch Mon.*

WORTH SEEING

Tours hosts some amazing museums, but that doesn't mean you have to be cooped up inside all day. Take a stroll down **rue Nationale** and do some window-shopping; or enjoy yourself at one of the cafés that cover the promenade of the tree-lined **boulevard Béranger**. Don't miss the flower market, the largest in western France, on this boulevard every Wednesday and Saturday. Even if you find wax museums unbearably tacky, you might enjoy the **Historial de la Touraine** (25 quai d'Orléans, tel. 02–47–61–02–95), which has scenes from important events in the region's history. Entry costs 35F. It's open mid-June–mid-September, daily 9–6:30; April–mid-June and mid-September–mid-November, daily 9–noon and 2–6; mid-November–March, daily 2–5:30. Remember that all the following museums close for lunch (usually noon–2).

MUSEE DES BEAUX-ARTS

Located in a gorgeous palace that used to be the archbishop's residence, the Musée des Beaux-Arts holds a few goodies: two panels by Mantegna, minor works by Impressionists Degas and Monet, and a tiny Rembrandt you can hardly see behind a heavy pane of glass. *18 pl. François-Sicard, tel. 02–47–05–68–73. Admission 30F. Open daily 9–12:45 and 2–6.*

MUSEE DU COMPAGNONNAGE

"Man thinks because he has hands" is the motto of the Compagnonnage, an organization that nurtures the idea that perfecting one's trade means perfecting one's soul. The masterpieces in the Trade Guild

Museum are graduation works of artisans who acquire the status of *compagnon.* Check out the château done in pink frosting that a Japanese compagnon spent 1,000 hours sculpting. *8 rue Nationale, tel. 02–47–61–07–93. Admission 25F. Open mid-Sept.–mid-June, Wed.–Mon. 9–noon and 2–5; mid-June–mid-Sept., daily 9–6.*

MUSEE DU GEMMAIL

This museum features artworks made from layers of broken colored glass lit from behind, a modern style developed in Tours. A gorgeous **hôtel particulier** (mansion) houses most of the works, but don't forget to descend into the 12th-century chapel below, where you'll find an inventive arrangement of religious pieces. *7 rue du Mûrier, tel. 02–47–61–01–19. Admission 30F. Open Apr.–Oct., daily 10–noon and 2–6:30; Nov.–Mar., weekends 10–noon and 2–6:15.*

CHEAP THRILLS

Le circuit des vignobles (Wine Road) is a great place to take your rented bike and do a little *dégustation* (tasting); this winery route meanders all the way up to the **Grange de Meslay** (tel. 02–47–29–19–29), a 45-minute bike ride out of town. The 13th-century fortified *grange,* or barn, is only open on weekends during the winter, but the adjacent pond is a great place to picnic. For dessert, walk across the N10 road to the **Jardins de Meslay,** where you can eat all the seasonal fruit you want while you pick a basket or two to purchase. To get to the Grange, hug the N152 (it runs along the Loire) for about 6 km (4 mi); then hang a left at the ugly tourist office just sitting by itself on the right side of the road. You should see CIR-CUITS DES VIGNOBLES signs right away; follow them until you get to the Grange.

AFTER DARK

Place Plumereau and its surrounding streets are bursting with bars and nightclubs; the bars get going around 10 PM, the clubs around midnight. **Louis XIV** (37 rue Briçonnet, tel. 02–47–05–77–17) has tables of young people spilling out into place Plume and a piano bar for older folks upstairs. Next door, **L'Excalibur** (35 rue Briçonnet, tel. 02–47–64–76–78), the city's most popular disco, plays music videos in a 12th-century setting. The 30F cover (40F weekends) includes one drink. Just south of place Plume, **Le Paradis Vert** (9 rue Michelet, tel. 02–47–64–78–50) has 30 kinds of beer, 50 kinds of whiskey, and every bar game imaginable. For information on gay and straight clubs hosted in venues around town, contact **La Maison des Homosexualités de Touraine** (tel. 02–47–20–55–30).

NEAR TOURS

Welcome to the Land of the Big-Name Châteaux. In summer, the region around Tours teems with tourists, so get to the châteaux near opening or closing hours for the smallest crowds. Inexpensive accommodations around here are scarce. Unless you like camping and staying in youth hostels, stick to Tours as a home base and branch out to the châteaux from here. The free guide "Visites et Découvertes," found at the Tours tourist office, has information on all the nearby sites.

Many of the following châteaux can be reached via regular SNCF trains out of Tours. The free schedule "Les Châteaux de la Loire en Train" gives all the details but doesn't come out until summer. A word to the wise: Examine closely the "Notes" included in this brochure. Some of the trains and *autocars* (buses) listed run only once a week, some not on August 15 (a national holiday) or Sunday.

Les Circuits Châteaux de la Loire (tel. 02–47–05–46–09) has a booth in the train station open Monday–Saturday 8–11 AM and 3:30–7 PM, Sunday 8–11 AM. Even if you *hate* bus tours, give this one a try. For 180F you get a half-day trip that takes you to two nearby châteaux and the winery of Vouvray. **Touraine Évasion** (tel. 02–47–63–25–64) runs half-day (140F) and full-day (200F) excursions in a minibus; the entrance fees are not included, but you'll see three to four châteaux.

Three people renting a car can often beat bus prices and make their own schedule to boot. **Calypso** (6 rue George-Sand, tel. 02–47–61–12–28) rents cars starting at 250F a day (650F for five days), insurance included. The catch is that you must have $900 available credit on your credit card for the deposit, and you must reserve early because it's the cheapest rental company in town.

AMBOISE

The legions of tourist buses make the otherwise pleasant Renaissance town of Amboise a carbon monoxide nightmare. The locals only emerge in late afternoon when the tourists have moved on. In the off-season you might find it charming, but in the summer Amboise is tacky and annoying. So why come? The château, although small, is beautiful in its simplicity. (Mick Jagger liked the area well enough to pick up his own little château nearby.) You might not always get what you want, but you just might find you get what you need from the overworked staff of the **tourist office** (tel. 02–47–57–01–37) on quai Général-de-Gaulle (from the train station, make a right as you cross the Vieux Pont). They'll bend over backward to find you a room in this packed little town.

COMING AND GOING • From Amboise, trains run often to Blois (20 mins, 34F) and Tours (18 mins, 28F), and you can dump your bags in the station for 10F. From Amboise's station, the town is across the Loire (the island in the middle of the river is the less-than-exciting Ile d'Or). Follow the signs across two bridges to the centre ville and place Richelieu. To explore other regions, **Cycles Richard** (2 rue de Nazelles, tel. 02–47–57–01–79), just before the first bridge, rents bikes Monday–Saturday for 50F–80F with a passport deposit.

WHERE TO SLEEP AND EAT • Amboise is not a cheap place to sleep, which makes the **Centre Charles Peguy/Auberge de Jeunesse** (Ile d'Or, tel. 02–47–57–06–36, fax 02–47–23–15–80) all the more precious: Rooms overlooking the river and château cost a mere 51F, and they accept credit cards. After the first bridge (which lands you on the Ile d'Or), make an immediate right; the hostel is at the back of the cluster of buildings. The reception is open daily 3 PM–9 PM; lockout starts at 9 AM. The **Hôtel La Pergola** (33 bis av. de Tours, tel. 02–47–57–24–79) has 24 rooms starting at 195F; make sure to reserve ahead in the summer. If you're willing to splurge, book a room at **Le Blason** (11 pl. Richelieu, tel. 02–47–23–22–41), a small hotel built around an old courtyard near the château. Rooms come in various shapes and sizes and cost 270F–300F with bath; room 229 has exposed beams and a vaulted ceiling. The hotel is closed in January.

Food is no cheaper than lodging: Your best bet is to find a bakery or snack shop on rue Nationale (one block up from the river). **Au Cours des Halles** (62 rue Nationale, tel. 02–47–57–04–77) has expensive but delicious produce, and **Pâtisserie Bigot** (pl. Michel-Debré, tel. 02–47–57–04–46) specializes in Amboisienne pastries and serves pizzas, quiches, and sandwiches for under 30F.

WORTH SEEING • The **Château d'Amboise** sits on a cliff high above town. The spectacular **Tour des Minimes** drops down the side of the cliff, enclosing a massive circular ramp designed to lead horses and carriages up, and is one of the château's few remaining structures. In fact, when first built in the 15th century, the château was five times bigger than it is today. It fell into disrepair after the Revolution, and under Napoléon the owner knocked down most of it and sold the stones to pay for what remained. For a while, Amboise was the favorite spot of Charles VIII, until he banged his head on a low door here and died. The château was practically abandoned by royalty after the 1560 Conspiracy of Amboise, when a group of armed Huguenots marched to the château, demanded the right to practice their religion, and were executed. You can see where François II and his wife, Mary Stuart, came out on the balcony to see the hanging bodies. You can also visit a couple of royal apartments and the chapel where Leonardo da Vinci's bones are supposedly buried. *Tel. 02–47–57–00–98. Admission 39F. Open June–Sept., daily 9–6:30; Oct.–May, daily 9–noon and 2–5:30.*

After falling into ill repute in Italy, Leonardo da Vinci accepted François I's invitation and spent the last three years of his life at the **Clos Lucé.** Now a shrine to his memory, this mansion is decorated with his drawings and maxims. Downstairs, you can see constructions of da Vinci's designs: everything from war machines to the predecessors of the parachute and automobile. The garden in the back of the mansion is a great place for a picnic. *2 rue Clos-Lucé, just up road from château, tel. 02–47–57–62–88. Admission 39F. Open July–Aug., daily 9–7; Sept.–June, daily 9–6.*

CHATEAU DE CHENONCEAU

The graceful facade, the string of delicate, sunlit galleries overlooking the water, and the airy apartments have given Chenonceau a reputation as the prettiest château in the Loire. Known as the Château of the Ladies (the design was entirely overseen by women), this beautiful monument has an undeniable feminine touch. The first lady of Chenonceau was Catherine Briçonnet, a tax collector's wife who had the main body of the château built between 1513 and 1521. Henri II's mistress, Diane de Poitiers, picked up the slack, ordering gardens and a bridge across the Cher river for easy access to her hunting grounds. Henri's wife, Catherine de Médicis, kicked Diane out and ordered her *own* gardens (both versions have survived) and tacked galleries on to the bridge.

In 1589 the château passed to Henri III's widow, Louise de Lorraine, after his assassination by a crazed monk. In mourning until the day she died, Louise did her second-floor room in black and gray and decorated it with shovels, skulls, and thorns. Chenonceau escaped destruction during the Revolution—some say because the then-owner, Madame Dupin, was in good with the townsfolk. The château also made it through both world wars undamaged. The bridge galleries served as a field hospital during World War I and, since it was just about the only border bridge not to get bombed, as an escape point for the French Resistance during World War II. *Tel. 02–47–23–90–07. Admission 45F (château), 10F (museum). Open mid-Mar.–mid-Sept., daily 9–7; mid-Sept.–mid-Mar., daily 9–4:30.*

COMING AND GOING • From Tours's gare routière (pl. du Général-Leclerc, tel. 02–47–05–30–49), **Fil Vert** has a 10 AM bus to Chenonceaux village (30 mins, 38F), leaving you 1½ hours to visit the château before catching the 12:30 bus (or the 4:40 in summer) to Amboise (15F). Trains also go to Chenonceaux (35 mins, 32F). The château is a well-marked kilometer (½ mi) from the station.

CHINON

Chinon, next to the River Vienne, is not the easiest place to reach. But with its proximity to other towns (*see* Ussé, *below*) and its youth hostel, campground, and reasonable places to eat, you might find it the most enticing château village around. Despite the ominous fortress towering over the medieval streets, Chinon is essentially a tranquil little village that invites walks along the river and sips of its wine at one of the terraced cafés.

The first weekend in August brings the famous **Marché Médiéval** (tel. 02–47–93–17–85 for information), a medieval-Renaissance fair celebrating Chinon's native son, Rabelais, and the arts, crafts, and music of an era long extinct. For 50F (10F if you can whip up a costume), you will enjoy regional food, wine, and dance and have free run of the château and town museums. If you can stick around for another two weeks, the **Marché à l'Ancienne,** a free wine-tasting extravaganza punctuated with musical and theatrical performances, will give you yet another excuse to sponge up some French grape. Pick up the latest schedules at Chinon's **tourist office** (pl. Hofheim, tel. 02–47–93–17–85); it's open mid-June–mid-September, Monday–Saturday 9–12:15 and 2–9, Sunday 10–12:30.

COMING AND GOING • SNCF trains (45 mins, 46F) and buses (65–80 mins, 46F) leave for Chinon from Tours's train station at least three times a day. From Chinon's train station, make a left, follow the quay to the Rabelais statue, and head to your right for the city center.

WHERE TO SLEEP AND EAT • The only cheap hotel in town is **Hôtel du Point du Jour** (102 quai Jeanne-d'Arc, tel. 02–47–93–07–20), where doubles go for 170F (with showers) and 125F (without). **Hôtel de France** (47 pl. du Général-de-Gaulle, tel. 02–47–93–33–91), one of the town's oldest lodgings, is housed in a 16th-century building off the main square and has views of the hilltop fortress. Its pretty courtyard is lined with fruit trees; the 30 rooms are comfortable (340F–390F) with private baths, but be sure to ask for one of the more recently refurbished ones. The **Auberge de Jeunesse/Maison des Jeunes** (60 rue Descartes, tel. 02–47–93–10–48, fax 02–47–98–44–98), a combination hostel and youth center along the riverside park, is a 5-minute walk from the train station and 10 minutes from town. Beds cost 48F, sheets 17F; the reception is open daily 6 PM–10:30 PM. The **Camping Municipal** (quai Danton, tel. 02–47–93–08–35) is a clean, woodsy site across the bridge just to the left of the Rabelais statue in Chinon. Your 38F covers two adults and a tent (48F with car).

Chinon's restaurants cluster on rue Voltaire and rue Rabelais (which run parallel to the river). Two affordable dining spots are **La Bonne France** (4 pl. Victoire-de-Verdun, tel. 02–47–98–41–41) and **La Grappa** (50 rue Haute-St-Maurice, tel. 02–47–93–19–29), which serve large lunch menus for under 60F. For dinner, you're probably better off going to **Super U** (rue de la Digue St-Jacques). Place Jeanne-d'Arc and place Général-de-Gaulle both host Thursday-morning markets; the latter location also has a market on Sunday mornings.

WORTH SEEING • Don't miss the **Musée Animé du Vin et de la Tonnellerie** (Animated Wine and Cooperage Museum), where robots give a 20-minute lesson in English and French on wine and barrel making, as they repeat Rabelais's famed words: "Drink always and never die." A free glass of Chinon red is an integral part of the visit. *12 rue Voltaire, tel. 02–47–93–25–63. Admission 22F.*

Once a favorite home of English kings, the **Château de Chinon,** an old and crumbling shell of a fortress looming high above the town, is now a reminder of Joan of Arc's trip here in 1429 to meet the dauphin, Charles. Suspicious of the whole Joan of Arc thing, Charles dressed as a courtier and put an impersonator on his throne, but Joan picked him out from the crowd with hardly a blink. Still unconvinced, he sent her to the theologians in Poitiers for a spiritual sounding out and virginity check. She passed. *Tel. 02–47–93–13–45. Climb steps behind pl. Général-de-Gaulle. Admission 28F. Open mid-Mar.–Sept., daily 9–5; Oct.–mid-Mar., daily 9–noon and 2–5.*

USSE

If you have a car, it's a cinch to get here. If you don't, the best way is to rent a bike for 50F a day from Chinon (*see above*), 14 km (9 mi) to the south and enjoy the hilly but beautiful ride to the romantic château of Ussé. Follow La Route de Tours near the Chinon château; then turn left at the roundabout to Huismes (D16) and follow the signs to Ussé.

The **Château d'Ussé** is the kind you imagined when you read fairy tales as a kid (perhaps because Charles Perrault based his version of the Sleeping Beauty tale on Ussé and its setting). The dwindled forest of today may have lost its enchantment, but the château, with its well-kept interior, still provides a pretty picture. You can also ascend the tower, where life-size dolls tell the story of Aurora and that nasty witch who cursed her. *Tel. 02–47–95–54–05. Admission 60F. Open mid-Mar.–Sept., daily 9–noon and 2–5; mid-Feb.–mid-Mar. and Oct.–mid-Nov., daily 9–noon and 2–6.*

LOCHES

Loches is the first place Joan of Arc tried to see Charles VII and persuade him to reclaim the French throne from the Brits. Her visit was refused, but she might have caught a glimpse of Chuck and thus have been able to see through his disguise in Chinon (*see* Worth Seeing *in* Chinon, *above*).

The Loches **château,** a heavily fortified medieval edifice, peers down a hill at the village it protected during Norman and British invasions. The dungeon, the *logis royal* (dwelling), and the *porte royale* (the keep or the inner fortified tower) make up the three wings of the fortress. The guided tour (in French) of the logis royal and the dungeon gives the lowdown on the ancestry and history of its occupants.

The newer part of the **logis royal** is dominated by images of Charles VII's rapturously beautiful lover, Agnès Sorel, the first mistress of a king to have children bearing his name. Paintings of her in the château show one breast popping out of her dress, a symbol of maternity, and all the hair plucked off her forehead. When you pass the bust of Charles VII, rub his nose for 20 years of good luck—the tour guide–created superstition has polished the monarch's honker to a shiny gold.

Unaccompanied, you can climb the **Tour Ronde** for great views and see prisoners' graffiti in the subterranean prison, but the guided tour will take you to the torture room and the cell of Ludovico Sforza, duke of Milan, who covered the walls with frescoes during his seven years in the slammer (1501–08). The duke held out until the end of his sentence but died the day of his release at the top of the stairway that leads out of his cell. *Tel. 02–47–59–01–32. Admission to château 31F. Open Feb.–June and Sept.–Nov., Thurs.–Tues. 9–noon and 2–5; July–Aug., daily 9–6.*

The **porte royale** was built by the counts of Anjou as defense against their nosy neighbors, the counts of Blois. It was only once taken in battle, by Richard the Lionheart of England. When Philippe-Auguste took it back in 1205, Loches became a state prison, a function it served up until World War II when it held German and French collaborators. The keep's **Musée du Terroir** has a weapon-bedecked prison cell and a remodeled 19th-century Tourangeais interior. *Tel. 02–47–59–05–45. Admission 20F. Open Apr.–Sept., daily 10–7; Oct.–Mar., Wed.–Mon. 1:30–5.*

COMING AND GOING • Up to six times daily, SNCF autocars make the trip (50 mins, 44F) from Tours down the Indre River. They let you off in front of Loches's **tourist office** (tel. 02–47–91–82–82) on place de la Marne, across the bridge from the château.

WHERE TO SLEEP AND EAT • Hôtel de France (6 rue Picoys, tel. 02–47–59–00–32), a former post house near the citadel, has a flower-strewn courtyard and functional rooms (including cable TV) priced from 285F with shower to 360F with bath. The restaurant has 85F and 120F menus. It's closed January. For 55F, two campers can pitch a tent at the three-star **Camping de la Citadelle** (tel. 02–47–59–05–91), a 10-minute walk from the bus stop on rue Quintefol (turn left on route de Châteauroux). Bargain food is scarce in Loches, but **La Cordelière** (31 Grande Rue, tel. 02–47–59–21–33) will feed you two appetizers, a plat du jour, cheese, dessert, and wine for around 50F. The **George Sand** (39 rue Quintefol, tel. 02–47–59–39–74) has a beautiful terrace above the part of the Indre River that was used as a public pool in the old days. Their cheapest menu will run you 100F, but you might want to pay 20F for a *kir* (white wine with cassis) and enjoy the view.

ANGERS

Although the expression "*douceur angevine*" (Angevine sweetness) conjures up everything from peaceful rivers and sunflowered hills to rich liqueurs and chocolates, this hardly describes the large, modern city of Angers. But not all is lost: Despite its skyscrapers and industrial complexes, the western gateway to the Loire Valley is worth a day's exploration, if only for its handful of intriguing museums, its medieval fortress, and its good restaurants.

BASICS

The **tourist office,** next to the château, changes money at decent rates, makes hotel reservations, and provides a free brochure, "A Walk Through History," which guides you through three different walks of the city. *1 pl. du Président-Kennedy, tel. 02–41–23–51–11. Open June–Sept., Mon.–Sat. 9–7, Sun. 10–1 and 2–6; Oct.–May, Mon. 11–6:30, Tues.–Sat. 9:30–6:30, Sun. 10–1.*

The main **post office** (1 rue Franklin-Roosevelt, tel. 02–41–20–81–81) is behind place du Ralliement; another is next to the train station. Both handle phone services, but only the Ralliement office has fax services and exchanges currency. In a pinch, the **Centre Hospitalier Universitaire** (4 rue Larrey, tel. 02–41–35–36–37), next to the river, has a few English-speaking doctors.

COMING AND GOING

Trains from Tours (1 hr, 100F) and Nantes (45 mins, 71F–81F) stop in Angers several times a day. You can also get here on the TGV from Paris (1½ hrs, 243F). To reach the city center from the **train station** (pl. de la Gare, tel. 02–41–86–41–28), take rue de la Gare and veer right at place de la Visitation.

GETTING AROUND

Most everything of interest in Angers is within walking distance of the château, which is hemmed in by the Maine River in the centre ville. Getting around town is easy on foot, but to go outside you'll need the city bus system, **COTRA**; buy your 6F ticket from the driver if there's no machine by the stop. Most buses stop running around 8 PM, with reduced night service until 1 AM. If you're camping or staying at the hostel, you have to catch the last bus out by 12:30 AM.

WHERE TO SLEEP

You should have no problem finding a room in Angers year-round, though it's wise to reserve ahead in summer. If you want to stick near the station, **La Coupe d'Or** (5 rue de la Gare, tel. 02–41–88–45–02) has doubles for 130F, 160F with shower and TV.

UNDER 150F • Hôtel du Centre. This cozy hotel is above a lively (and somewhat noisy) brasserie and is right smack in the center of Angers. The rooms are clean and have a view of the pedestrian street below, but the walls are pretty thin (sometimes affording you intimate knowledge of the famed French sexual prowess). The showerless 110F single on the top floor is hot in the summer, but much nicer doubles go for 130F. Add another 35F for your own shower. *12 rue St-Laud, tel. 02–41–87–45–07. From station, take rue de la Gare 1 block, veer right at pl. de la Visitation, cross blvd. du Roi René to rue des Lices, left onto rue Plantagenêt, right on rue St-Laud. 15 rooms, 7 with shower.*

UNDER 200F • Hôtel des Lices. The hospitable managers of this hotel, between the station and centre ville, put you at ease in bright, clean rooms, the cheapest of which (112F for showerless singles and doubles) are at the top of steep, skinny stairways—your reward is a great sunset view over the rooftops. Singles and doubles with showers and fewer stairs cost 165F. Showers are 10F. *25 rue des Lices, tel. 02–41–87–44–10. From station, take rue de la Gare 1 block, veer right at pl. de la Visitation, and cross blvd. du Roi René to rue des Lices. 13 rooms, 6 with bath. Cash only.*

SPLURGE • Hôtel d'Anjou. This hotel has been in business since 1846 and is now run by Best Western. It has spacious rooms with high ceilings, double doors, double glazed windows, and modern bathrooms complete with terry bathrobes. Room prices start at 380F. *1 blvd. du Maréchal-Foch, tel. 02–41–88–24–82, fax 02–41–87–22-21. 19 rooms with bath or shower. Closed Jan.*

HOSTEL

Centre d'Hébergement/Auberge de Jeunesse. Right on the Lac de Maine you'll find a hostel with quad rooms for 81F per person, breakfast included. Lunch or dinner is an additional 42F. Their four-star campground (tel. 02–41–73–05–03) charges 63F (77F in the summer) for two people and a tent. Take advantage of the lake by visiting the *centre nautique,* which rents Windsurfers, small sailboats, and kayaks. *49 av. du Lac de Maine, tel. 02–41–48–17–58, fax 02–41–22–32–11. Take Bus 6 across bridge to Camping stop. 120 beds. Reception open 8–6.*

FOOD

Angers's pedestrian *quartier,* around place du Ralliement in the center of town, is chock-full of restaurants, pizzerias, crêperies, and cafés. If you're looking for steak, *moules-frites* (mussels and french fries), or tapas, try the **Café du Jour** (13 rue Bodinier, tel. 02–41–86–80–70). For cheap eats, your best bet is **Les Halles** (rue Plantagenêt), an indoor market where roasted chicken, carrot or cucumber salads, and fresh fruit are sold at fair prices. On Saturday, there's an even better **outdoor market** on boulevard Foch (just behind the Chapelle St-Martin).

UNDER 75F • La Crémaillère. This old, wooden-beamed Breton restaurant has a 60F dinner menu consisting of a salmon galette, a dessert crepe, and a glass of cider. A similar 45F menu is served at lunch. *30 rue Bressigny, 4 blocks behind cathedral, tel. 02–41–87–77–12.*

La Ferme. This tip-top restaurant lives up to its name (The Farm) in every way, with country decor, hunting weapons, and stuffed victims on the wall. Meals are enormous, featuring specialties like the fabulous *magret de canard* (duck breast; 68F) or the *poulet au pot* (chicken in a pot; 58F); there is a 72F menu weekdays. *2 pl. Freppel, near cathedral, tel. 02–41–87–09–90. Closed Wed. No dinner Sun.*

> *If your wine etiquette bothers a snobbish wine merchant, remind him that in the 1890s most of the French vines were ravaged by phylloxera and that the wine he is now serving probably comes from an American vine imported to strengthen the sickly Euro stock.*

Le Petit Mâchon. As an entrée to the huge three-course, 70F menu, the adventurous can try the delicious *andouillettes* (pork tripe), but other entrées like lasagna or roasted pork will appeal to all tastes. The meal is so decadent it almost demands an after-dinner cigarette (not included). *43 rue Bressigny, 5 blocks behind cathedral, tel. 02–41–86–01–13. Cash only.*

WORTH SEEING

Don't miss the magnificent **Cathédrale St-Maurice** (pl. Freppel), with its phenomenal Baroque altar and stained glass. A few other churches are also worth a peek if you're in the neighborhood: **Église de la Trinité** is across the Pont de Verdun on the south bank, two blocks down rue Beaurepaire; and **Église St-Serge** (av. Marie-Talet) is near the Jardin des Plantes. Next to the cathedral, the medieval **Maison d'Adam** has devilish carved figurines climbing along its wooden beams.

CHATEAU D'ANGERS

No, you're not going crazy from looking at too many châteaux; this one *is* flip-flopped. The forbidding black walls are made of *ardoise,* a strong slate usually saved for Loire château rooftops, and the towers are topped with the white tufa stone usually used for château walls. The building was thrown together in 10 short years during the 13th century to defend the gateway to the Loire against pesky English attackers. With a guide, you can take the French-only tour of the **logis royal,** which shelters some fine 14th- to 17th-century tapestries. But that's just a warm-up for the stunning *Tenture de l'Apocalypse,* housed next door in a 20th-century addition. The oldest preserved tapestry in the world, this 328-ft wool- and gold-thread masterpiece depicts scenes from the Book of Revelation. Commissioned by Louis I, duke of Anjou, and completed between 1375 and 1380, the tapestry is remarkable because the back side, which would normally be covered with knots and loose threads, looks just like the front. It's incredible that 18th-century church officials tried to sell the tapestry because it muffled their singing voices. No one wanted it, so they hacked it to bits, sold off some pieces as rugs, used others as horse blankets, and used the rest to protect the floor when their church walls were being redone. In 1848, a very patient member of the church put the whole thing back together with only 10 pieces missing. Right next to the château, the friendly staff at **La Maison du Vin** (5 pl. Kennedy, tel. 02–41–88–81–13), open Tuesday–

Sunday, serves free samples of last year's jury-selected Anjou wines and hands out an informative guide to wineries and wines of the region. *Pl. du Président-Kennedy, tel. 02–41–87–43–47. Admission 35F. Open June–mid-Sept., daily 9–7; mid-Sept.–May, daily 10–5.*

MUSEE DAVID D'ANGERS

The main room has dramatic sculptures of Molière plays and scenes from American history, as well as a huge, corpulent sculpture of the pirate Jean Bart (the original scared ships off the port of Dunkerque). The upstairs gallery has busts of romantic writers like Balzac, Victor Hugo, and Goethe. The works are all given a new dimension of beauty, thanks to the sunbeams that pass through the glass ceiling of the 11th-century abbey. *33 rue Toussaint, tel. 02–41–87–21–03. Admission 10F. Open mid-June–mid-Sept., daily 9:30–1 and 2–9; mid-Sept.–mid-June, Tues.–Sun. 10–noon and 2–6.*

MUSEE JEAN LURCAT

Jean Lurçat, a moderately successful painter, visited the *Tenture de l'Apocalypse* (*see* Château d'Angers, *above*) in 1938 and was so struck by it that he became a weaver. Now his own tapestry—the bright, almost garish *Le Chant du Monde* (The Song of the World)—is housed in the dark, 12th-century St-Jean hospital. Your 20F ticket also lets you into the adjacent **Tapisserie Contemporaine** museum, displaying the latest trends in the tapestry art scene. *4 blvd. Arago, on the north side of the river, tel. 02–41–24–18–45. Admission 20F. Open mid-June–mid-Sept., daily 9–6:30; mid-Sept.–mid-June, Tues.–Sun. 10–noon and 2–4.*

NEAR ANGERS

SAUMUR

Saumur is a quintessential bourgeois French town, with elegantly dressed citizens, an upscale shopping district, and a famous equestrian school. It retains a refined dignity extending all the way to its château, converted into three well-kept museums. Saumur is also known for its wines, mushroom and wine caves, and troglodyte dwellings (*see* Village Troglodytique de Rochemenier, *below*). The **tourist office** can direct you through the city. *Pl. de la Bilange, tel. 02–41–40–20–60. Open June–Aug., Mon.–Sat. 9:15–7, Sun. 3:30–6:30; Sept.–May, Mon.–Sat. 9:15–12:30 and 2–6.*

COMING AND GOING • Saumur is 20 minutes by train from Angers (42F) and 40 minutes from Tours (56F). From Chinon, take the bus (Monday–Saturday only) to Port-Boulet (15F) and hop a train to Saumur (19F). From the station, make a right and take the bridge across the Loire and the Offard Island in the middle of the river (a 15-minute walk).

WHERE TO SLEEP AND EAT • Hotel pickings are slim and expensive. **Hôtel de Bretagne** (55 rue St-Nicolas, tel. 02–41–51–26–38), in the center of town, offers clean doubles for 150F (without shower) and 175F (with). The hostel selection is more appealing. **Le Foyer des Jeunes Travailleurs** (3 rue Fourrier, tel. 02–41–51–05–53), at the bottom of the château, has 80F rooms with bath, including sheets and breakfast. The only catch is the 50F membership fee. The renovated **Auberge de Jeunesse** (blvd. Verden, left as you reach the island, tel. 02–41–40–30–00, fax 02–41–67–37–81) has eight-bed rooms for 80F, two-bed rooms for 105F, and individual rooms for 125F (call to reserve). Sheets and breakfast are included, lockout is 10–5, and there is no curfew. If you have a tent, the hostel charges 45F for sites plus 25F per person (prices are a bit cheaper in winter).

There are decent—but overpriced—cafés, crêperies, and pizzerias on the side streets behind **quai Carnot,** which is bustling during the day and absolutely dead at night. Get stuffed with a great crepe (from 11F) or omelet at the **Crêperie St-Pierre** (2 rue Haute-St-Pierre, tel. 02–41–51–31–98). The 15th-century wood-beamed **Auberge St-Pierre** (pl. St-Pierre, tel. 02–41–51–26–25)—on the sloping church square in the heart of the old town—serves French staples (steak frites, salads), with menus priced 50F–80F. For bulk groceries, there's a **Marché U** store on rue du Clois-Coutard and a Saturday-morning **market** on place St-Pierre.

WORTH SEEING • Saumur is known for its white wines, and the **Maison du Vin** is the place to plan your tastings. The staff will direct you to local cellars with dégustations, explain the various Saumur wines, and let you sip a whole slew of the region's best. Best of all, the tastings and info are free. *25 rue Beaurepaire, tel. 02–41–51–16–40. Open Mon.–Sat. 9–12:30 and 2–6:30.*

Built in 1360 by Louis I of Anjou, the **Château de Saumur** became a Protestant stronghold in the 16th century and was expanded to include a religious academy and 12 publishing houses. But when the

Edict of Nantes was revoked in 1685 and anti-Protestant violence picked up, both town and château suffered. The château became a prison, where the original sadist, the Marquis de Sade himself, was held for 15 days. In 1906 the city shelled out 2,500F to buy and restore the decrepit structure. Don't forget to descend into the *cachots* (dungeons) and the *salle souterraine* (underground vault), where a fascinating slide show depicting the château's history is projected onto three stone walls. The château also contains three museums (toys, decorative arts, and a harness collection), all included in the admission fee. To reach the château, take the walkway behind place St-Pierre. *Tel. 02–41–40–24–40. Admission 38F. Open Oct.–May, Wed.–Mon. 9:30–noon and 2–6; June–Sept., daily 9–6:30; night visits July–Aug., Wed. and Sat. 8:30–10:30.*

VILLAGE TROGLODYTIQUE DE ROCHEMENIER

This sight is a great day trip from Angers (*see above*). Some caves in the Loire Valley are just transmogrified rock quarries, but this troglodyte village was carved out by farmers who felt that digging into solid rock was easier than building the usual huts and cottages. The French peasants who created this village made wine and walnut oil for a meager profit and sustained themselves by farming and shepherding. Newcomers to the village scooped out a personal sleeping nook in the communal sleeping room, a much warmer option than sleeping exposed on the dry, cold limestone floor. As you take the excellent guided tour, you'll see that Rooms 18 and 19 have been renovated into a modern dwelling still inhabited by one of the tour guides. *14 rue du Musée, Rochemenier, tel. 02–41–59–18–15. From bus station in Angers: Louresse bus (6 buses daily, 30F) toward Doué la Fontaine and walk about 1 km (½ mi) from the Louresse bus stop. Admission 22F. Open Apr.–Nov., daily 9:30–7:30.*

BRITTANY

UPDATED BY SIMON HEWITT

T he turbulent Atlantic Ocean gnaws at the peninsula of Brittany, creating a seascape of wave-battered crags, isolated coves, and an island-swathed coastline. Ports and beaches are rhythmically flushed by strong tides, while a late-afternoon sun, known to the Bretons as *l'heure dorée (literally, "the golden hour")*, gilds the green, blue, gray, and pink shades of the land, sea, and granite houses. The soul of Brittany is pierced by only a few visitors, but those who straggle through the region often find themselves seduced into unexpectedly long stays.

Fleeing from the Anglo-Saxon invasions on the British Isles, the Bretons settled the Armorican peninsula in the 4th century BC, dubbing it "Little Britain." After centuries of squabbling between English and French aristocracies, its "French" nationality wasn't settled until 1491, when France adopted the region in the form of a dowry from Anne de Bretagne, Duchess of Brittany, to Charles VIII, King of France. The Bretons were expected to welcome the change with open arms, and, if not, with broken limbs. From then on the relationship between the French and the Bretons has been a troubled one, whether in the form of nationwide stereotypes (the French stereotype the Bretons as stubborn and somewhat backward) or Breton nationalism (Breton activist groups have been known to blow up French relics). Recently, though, the relationship has thawed, and Parisians now flock to summer homes in the Breton countryside. Today, the French government even sponsors the Breton Diwan *schools, which teach the once-outlawed Breton as a first language.*

Today, Nantes, the working-class heart of Brittany, pumps the economy of the region and provides a daily swig of Breton life, while Rennes, the student-fueled mind of Brittany, gives way to poets and painters, bringing a refreshing breeze to the historical heaviness of the region. The Côtes d'Armor has some startlingly beautiful granite coastline. But skip the rest of Brittany if you're on a furious Eurail fly through; it takes time to take in a medieval town like Dinan or enjoy an invigorating swim in the brisk waters of the isle of Ouessant.

BASICS

COMING AND GOING

The **TGV Atlantique** travels faster than a speeding bullet from Paris to Rennes (2¼ hrs, 283F) and through to Brest (4½ hrs, 370F). A dozen or so TGVs link Paris to Nantes daily (2¼ hrs, 291F). Normal trains make all these connections but usually take longer and cost the same. To plan your travel, pick up the *Guide TGV Atlantique* in any station.

GETTING AROUND

BY BUS • A confusing patchwork of bus companies covers the area. SNCF usually runs buses when its trains don't go the distance; the train station and tourist office always have information on local routes. Though slow, buses are cheap, less crowded, and allow you to see a lot more than you would on a train. They tend to be reliable and work in tandem with the SNCF when you have to transfer from train to bus. Service is often limited or nonexistent on Sunday.

BY TRAIN • To travel by train from the northern coast to the southern coast, you'll have to make a huge loop, either through Brest to the west or Rennes to the east. The free *Guide Régional des Transports*, available in any tourist office, helps with planning, but be sure to double-check everything with the train station before making plans; the guide is sometimes *very* wrong.

BY BIKE • Biking is the ideal way to see Brittany, with its astounding natural beauty and generally flat terrain. Larger tourist offices sometimes stock bikers' guides and can point you to bike rental places nearby. Many train stations and youth hostels also rent; ask about one-way rentals. *VTTs* (mountain bikes) are usually 80F–90F a day, regular bikes 40F–70F.

ON FOOT • An exhaustive web of footpaths winds all across Brittany: Sentiers de Grande Randonnée, abbreviated to GRs, sometimes stretch hundreds of kilometers. The **Sentier Douanier** (Customs Path), also known as the **Sentier Côtier** (Coastal Path), rings the coastline and some of the islands. One amazing 360-km (225-mi) stretch follows a canal from Nantes to Brest. The friendly folks at Rennes's **Maison de la Randonnée** (9 rue des Portes-Mordelaises, tel. 02–99–67–42–20) have maps on short and long-distance hikes and sell the comprehensive book *Sentier des Douaniers en Bretagne*.

The three most important festivals in Brittany, all meant for dancing and drinking and other Celtic activities, are the Festival des Tombées de la Nuit in Rennes; the Festival de Cornouaille in Quimper; and the Festival Interceltique in Lorient.

WHERE TO SLEEP

Lodging is rarely a problem in Brittany. Many hotels allow you to stay two weekend nights for the price of one. To take advantage of this offer, you must reserve a week in advance and confirm by either mail or fax. Pick up the brochure *Bon Weekend en Villes* at any tourist office for a list of participating hotels throughout France. When there's no youth hostel nearby, look for one of Brittany's 18 *gîtes d'étape* (rural hostels), which usually cost about 48F per night. Similar to youth hostels, gîtes almost always have a common room and complete kitchen facilities. Another option is a **chambre d'hôte**—basically the French equivalent of a bed-and-breakfast, except you usually have to pay extra for the breakfast. Camping is the cheapest and most flexible way to go, and farmers will usually let you throw a tent down on their land; just ask at the house.

FOOD

Breton cooking, true to the region's character, shuns the finicky haute cuisine of Paris in favor of simpler dishes. Brittany's most exported food is the *galette*, a thin buckwheat pancake. Crepes are flimsier galettes, made of wheat flour and filled with sugar, butter, jam, or chocolate. Several specialties testify to Brittany's passion for seafood: *cotriade*, a distinctive fish soup with potatoes, onions, garlic, and butter; *coquilles St-Jacques* (scallops); and *langoustines*, which are something between a large shrimp and a lobster. *Kouign* are delectable sugar cakes made from yeast dough, while *kouign-amann* are the same thing with butter or cream. A *far breton* is a warm or cold flanlike dessert made with prunes.

RENNES

One Christmas day in 1720, a drunken carpenter started a fire in his studio that ended up taking down most of Rennes's medieval quarter. Gray granite and tufa buildings gradually replaced many of the original colorful, wood-beamed houses that lined the twisting streets, creating a chessboardlike configuration of squares; the city's austerity surely must have appealed to the Czech writer Milan Kundera, who taught here from 1975 to 1979. Since the 1980s, the city has brightened, thanks to the construction of

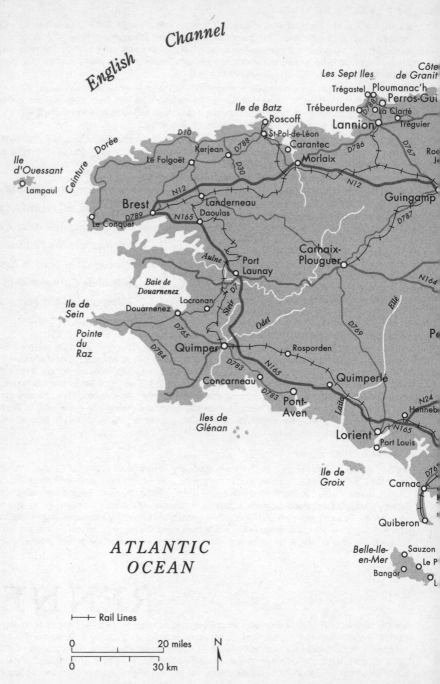

English Channel

Les Sept Iles
Côte de Granit
Trégastel Ploumanac'h
Perros-Gui
Trébeurden La Clarté
Ile de Batz
Roscoff
St-Pol-de-Léon
Lannion
Tréguier
Carantec
Roc
Je
Ceinture Dorée
D10
Kerjean
D788
Morlaix
D786
Le Folgoët
D30
N12
N12
Ile d'Ouessant
Guingamp
Lampaul
Brest
Landerneau
D789
Le Conquet
N165
Daoulas
D787
Aulne
Port Launay
Carhaix-Plouguer
N164
Baie de Douarnenez
Locronan
Steir
Elle
Ile de Sein
Douarnenez
Odet
D765
D769
Pe
Pointe du Raz
D784
Quimper
Rosporden
D783
N165
Quimperlé
Concarneau
D783
Pont-Aven
Laita
N24
Henneb
N165
Lorient
Port Louis
Iles de Glénan
Ile de Groix
D76
Carnac

ATLANTIC OCEAN

Quiberon

Belle-Ile-en-Mer
Sauzon
Le P
Bangor
L

Rail Lines

0   20 miles
0   30 km
N

Ile de
Bréhat

Golfe de
St-Malo

Paimpol

D786

Pontrieux

Coutances

Granville

D973

Avranches

Côte
d'Emeraude

St-Malo

Cancale

Mont-
St-Michel

Dinard

Dol-de-
Bretagne

D98

St-Brieuc

D266

N176

D265

Dinan

N137

La Bourbansais

Combourg

Nançon

D20

Fougères

D700

Rance

D27

Tinténiac

N12

Couesnon

D178

Loudéac

N164

Montmuran

D798

St-Méen-
le-Grand

Caradeuc

N137

Vitré

ivy

Paimpont

Rennes

Vilaine

N168

Josselin

FORÊT DE
PAIMPONT

N24

Oust

Plélan-le-Grand

D177

N137

D178

Elven

Rochefort-
en-Terre

Vilaine

D178

Auray

D28

Vannes

Redon

Châteaubriant

N165

Ile aux
Moines

Ile d'Arz

D20

D114

té-
Mer

Muzillac

N171

D178

Golfe du
Morhiban

Missillac

St-Lyphard

D51

aria

La Baule

Savenay

A11

Le Croisic

N165

Loire

St-Nazaire

Nantes

D751

Pornic

Ste-Pazanne

more modern edifices. On boulevard de la Tour d'Auvergne, note the **cité judiciaire,** the postmodern mirrored administration of justice, and the razor-edged **Crédit Mutuel de Bretagne.**

The capital of Brittany, Rennes is one of the liveliest cities in the region. While the student rhythm (some 40,000 of them) churns through the city September–June, the festival Les Tombées de la Nuit (see Festivals, below), the first week of July, brings a happy delirium to the streets. Although summer seems to happen elsewhere for most *Rennais,* it's still a pleasant time to wander the city's cafés and bookstores.

BASICS

BUREAUX DE CHANGE

Change money during the day, because Rennes has no late-night exchange places. One of the few places open Saturday (8:30–12:30 and 1:30–4) is the **Banque de Bretagne** (2 rue Motte-Fablet, east of pl. Ste-Anne, tel. 02–99–38–81–66), which has acceptable rates.

LAUNDRY

Lav' Club is close to the station and many hotels. A wash is 18F, soap is 2F, and five minutes of dryer time costs 5F. *59 rue Duhamel, no phone. Open daily 8 AM–10 PM.*

MAIL

The **post office** has poste restante service, sends faxes, and changes money and traveler's checks at fair rates. The postal code is 35000. *Pl. de la République, tel. 02–99–78–43–35. Open weekdays 8:30–5:30, Sat. 9–noon.*

MEDICAL AID

For 24-hour medical aid, call the English-speaking staff of **SOS Médecins** (2 pl. de Bretagne, tel. 02–99–67–30–30). The local paper *Ouest-France* lists late-night pharmacies, or call 02–99–79–11–11.

VISITOR INFORMATION

The reception at the **Office de Tourisme** is downright cold. You have to harangue the hostess to get information on sights, the bus system, sports, and festivals. They have little information on the surrounding area, and a pretty poor map of Rennes. *11 rue St-Yves, tel. 02–99–67–11–11. From station: walk down av. Jean-Janvier, turn left after quai Émile-Zola. Open Tues.–Sat. 9–6, Mon. 1–6.*

For tons of information on things to do in Rennes and Brittany, mosey on over to the **Centre Information Jeunesse Bretagne.** If you read French, browse through the dark blue binders directly behind the receptionist for ideas on regional walking, sailing, windsurfing, biking, and skiing. *6 cours des Alliés (in Maison du Champ de Mars, next to bus station), tel. 02–99–31–47–48. Open Sept.–June, weekdays 10–6, Sat. 10–noon and 2–6; July–Aug., weekdays 1–6.*

COMING AND GOING

BY TRAIN

The **Gare SNCF** (pl. de la Gare, tel. 02–99–36–35–35–35 for reservations) is about a 20-minute walk from the heart of the city. Trains leave for Paris (2¼ hrs, 283F), Nantes (2 hrs, 132F), St-Malo (55 mins, 69F), and Bordeaux (6 hrs, 306F). The upper level houses a small shopping complex.

BY BUS

The **gare routière,** or bus station (16 pl. de la Gare, tel. 02–99–30–87–80), is next to the train station, but it's not a safe place to hang out. Buses go to Nantes (2 hrs, 96F), St-Malo (2 hrs, 55F), Dinan (1 hr, 48F), Mont-St-Michel (85 mins, 61F), Fougères (1 hr, 47F), and the Forêt de Paimpont (1 hr, 16F).

GETTING AROUND

The Vilaine's channeled waters flow westward through the center of Rennes. North of the Vilaine River, which unfairly means Ugly River, middle-aged houses jut from neoclassic structures, while south of the Vilaine is modern Rennes. Major north–south roads south of the canal are **boulevard de la Tour d'Auvergne** and **avenue Jean-Janvier.** To get to the center of town from the station, take avenue Jean-Janvier, turn left on quai Châteaubriand, and take a right on rue d'Orléans to place de la Mairie. North of the canal is place Ste-Anne, where rue St-Malo (north), rue St-Melaine (east), and rue St-Michel (south) meet up.

The city bus system, **STAR,** will deliver you to almost any destination. Buy single tickets for 6F from the bus driver or *carnets* (books) of 10 tickets for 46F from the information stand (tel. 02–99–79–37–37) next to the post office on place de la République. Most bus lines stop running around 8 PM.

The easiest way to reach Vitré, Fougère, the Forêt de Paimpont, and even the nearby cities of Dinan and St-Malo is by car. **ADA** (49 av. Aristide-Briand, tel. 02–98–27–22-22) has the cheapest car-rental rates; 250F a day gets you a small Fiat Punto and 100 km (62 mi) of mobility (1,400F for a week with 1,000 km/620 mi mobility).

WHERE TO SLEEP

Although Rennes can be crowded in summer, especially during the festival Les Tombées de la Nuit, the lodging situation is hardly ever dire. Many cheap hotels cluster around the train station.

UNDER 150F • Hôtel d'Angleterre. Though it's been around since 1910, the hotel has since been modernized and attracts regular guests each year. Do they return for the firm mattresses, comfortable rooms, or for Gypsy, the toe-licking poodle? The energetic proprietress keeps the old apartment building very tidy. Doubles with shower are 155F, 130F without. Showers cost 15F. *19 rue du Maréchal-Joffre, tel. 02–99–79–38–61, fax 02–99–79–43–85. From station, walk down av. Jean-Janvier, left on blvd. de la Liberté, right on rue du Maréchal-Joffre. 30 rooms, 17 with bath. Closed Sun. afternoon.*

UNDER 175F • Hôtels Maréchal Joffre. This prim hotel has soundproof rooms. The one single is 120F and a few doubles go for 140F; the rest of the rooms have showers and start at 175F. *6 rue du Maréchal-Joffre, tel. 02–99–79–37–74. 22 rooms, 10 with bath.*

Hôtel Tour d'Auvergne. The reception area is up the stairs of an apartment building. The nice owner rents out older, compact rooms with ornate ceilings; most of them come with   balcony overlooking the busy street below. Doubles are 180F with shower, 155F without. Showers cost 15F. *20 blvd. de la Tour-d'Auvergne, tel. 02–99–30–84–16. From station, take blvd. Beaumont, right on rue d'Isly, left on rue le Plélo, then right on blvd. de la Tour-d'Auvergne. 12 rooms, 7 with bath.*

UNDER 200F • Hôtel de Léon. Off of Rennes's busy streets in a quiet residential area down from the Quai Richemont, the rooms here have tacky pink wallpaper and '70s-style dressers, but they are very clean, with comfy spring mattresses. Those on the top floor can be a bit hot during the summer but have a great view over Rennes's rooftops. Doubles without shower are 130F (190F with bath). Showers cost 18F. *15 rue de Léon, tel. 02–99–30–55–28, fax 02–99–36–59–11. 11 rooms, 3 with bath.*

UNDER 250F • Garden Hôtel. This isn't a budget hotel, but it does participate in the buy-one-night-get-one-night-free Bon-Weekend-en-Villes program (*see* Where to Sleep *in* Brittany's Basics, *above*). The Garden has rooms named after flowers—the color of each room corresponds to its respective bloom. Some rooms look onto the patio where you can have breakfast. Singles without shower start at 175F; doubles with shower are 250F (320F with bath). *3 rue Duhamel, tel. 02–99–65–45–66, fax 02–99–65–02–62. From station, rue Duhamel is to the right of av. Jean-Janvier. 24 rooms, 20 with bath.*

HOSTEL

Auberge de Jeunesse. This mediocre hostel a half-hour walk from the station (but only 10 minutes from the bars) features lumpy beds, high-pressure showers, and washing machines (20F). Beds are 80F in triples, 90F in doubles, and 130F in a single, breakfast and sheets included. Lockers are 10F. *10–12 canal St-Martin, tel. 02–99–33–22–33. From station, take Bus 1 to pl. de la Mairie and Bus 18 to Coëtlogon on weekends, otherwise take Bus 20 directly to Coëtlogon; from there follow the signs. Or from pl. Ste-Anne, take rue St-Malo and turn right after bridge. 90 beds. Reception open 7 AM–11 PM. No curfew or lockout. Laundry.*

CAMPING

Camping des Gayeulles. Although tents get little space and no privacy at this uninspiring spot, the campground is right next to the verdant Parc des Bois and has phones and showers. You pay 12F for a tent plus 13F per person. *Rue du Professeur-Maurice-Audin, tel. 02–99–36–91–22. Take any bus to mairie (town hall), transfer to Bus 3 to Gayeulles, and walk 10 mins. Closed Oct.–Mar.*

FOOD

Restaurants cooking up food from all corners of the globe are everywhere, particularly around place Ste-Anne. For Vietnamese treats, **Le Ky-Khoi** (8 quai Émile-Zola, tel. 02–99–79–61–73) serves take-out cold shrimp roll (8F) or *nem,* fried crab rolls (4F), as well as spicy pineapple chicken and a drink for 35F. For kebabs, try **L'Ile aux Brochettes** (33 rue St-Mélaine, tel. 02–99–87–50–25). A large **market** sets up on Saturday mornings at place des Lices, and there's a **Stoc** supermarket at 20 rue d'Isly, just west of the train station. A great spot for those of you with a late appetite and not much money is the **Épicerie de Nuit** (11 rue de l'Hôtel-Dieu, tel. 02–99–38–48–77), a market open 6 PM–1 AM.

UNDER 50F • La Bolée. This tiny place on a popular street serves a 32F lunch and dinner menu with mineral water, a cheese-and-ham galette, a dessert crepe, and coffee. *40 rue St-Mélaine, tel. 02–99–38–81–87. Cash only. Closed 1st 3 wks in Aug.*

Crêperie Ar Billig. Bas-relief wall carvings and woodwork set this crêperie apart. The warm, courteous staff serve galettes of various persuasions (11F–38F) and enticing crepes (11F–34F) to a vivacious clientele. *10 rue d'Argentré, just below main tourist office, tel. 02–99–79–53–89. Closed Sun.*

UNDER 75F • Angkor. Don't be put off by the somewhat somber dining room, because the Cambodian 60F, three-course menu is satisfying. The nem appetizers—crunchy crab-filled rolls accompanied with lettuce and mint leaves—are tasty, and the pork, chicken, and beef entrées are prepared with delicate spices. A similar dinner menu runs for 76F. *36 rue St-Mélaine, tel. 02–99–38–74–77.*

Le Cosmo. At this kitschy spot, the imaginative menu changes every month with a new plate focusing on a particular cuisine. The *assiette des Balkans* (Balkan plate; 59F) has dolmas, hummus, *pasturma* (dried Turkish meat), and the possibility of the Balkan liquor *Raki* for an additional 15F. A similar Scandinavian plate (64F) has herring, smoked salmon, smoked mackerel, and an iced vodka for an extra 20F. *14 rue St-Malo, tel. 02–99–79–57–27.*

WORTH SEEING

JARDIN DU THABOR

Full of twisting paths, grottoes, tree-lined alleys, and manicured lawns, this park cajoles you away from Rennes's mean streets with the promise of picnics, promenades, and naps (on the benches, that is—lounging on the tempting grass is frowned upon). Enter through the geometric lawn beside the church of **Notre-Dame-en-St-Mélaine,** at the eastern end of rue St-Mélaine. *Open daily 7:15 AM–9:30 PM.*

PLACE DE LA MAIRIE

Built in 1734 after the fire, the **Hôtel de Ville** (Town Hall) looks like a magnificent bird that has no hope of ever flying. The empty pocket at the center of the facade used to have a statue of a woman (Brittany) kneeling in front of a man (France) but was pulverized shortly after World War I by a Breton extremist organization. Right in front is the **Grand Théâtre**; if the earth moved suddenly, the two buildings would fit nicely together like puzzle pieces. Just to the north, on place du Palais, is more recent evidence of Breton extremism: angry fishermen, demanding state subsidies, set fire to the majestic 17th-century **Parlement de Bretagne** in 1994, and the onetime regional parliament—widely considered the architectural showpiece of Rennes—is gradually being restored to its original majesty.

QUARTIER MEDIEVAL

A handful of medieval streets that survived the 1720 fire are all that remain of this once immense medieval fortress city. The best-preserved streets are between place Ste-Anne, rue des Portes Mordelaises, and quai Duguay Trouin. Especially remarkable is **rue Psalette,** skirting the **Cathédrale St-Pierre.** You have to look twice to make sure you're really facing a cathedral; the unimpressive edifice should probably be demoted to a simple church. However, you can get a good view of St-Pierre through the **Porte Mordelaise,** the entrance to the old, rampart-enclosed city that the dukes of Brittany would ceremonially cross on the way to the cathedral before being crowned.

FESTIVALS

One bright spot in the otherwise slow summer months is the gigantic **Les Tombées de la Nuit** ("Nightfalls"), a seven-day romp of music, dance, and street theater the first week in July. Musical and theatrical performances fill every concert hall in the city, and the streets overflow with endless entertainment.

The majority of performances are free; others cost 25F–80F. The tourist office can give you the complete schedule of times and places. Make lodging reservations weeks in advance, and when you do, ask about getting two consecutive nights for the price of one; many hotels make this offer to festival goers.

AFTER DARK

Get *L'Echo des Bistros* at the tourist office for a schedule of theater and music events organized by Rennes's bars and cafés. A **Nabuchodonosor** (12 rue Hoche, tel. 02–99–27–07–58) is a 15-liter bottle of wine, but in this case, it's the name of a terrific wine bar adorned with postcard collages; a glass of wine goes for 12F–30F. Rue de la Soif (Street of Thirst) is fuzzily defined as running from **rue St-Michel** to **rue St-Malo.** One thing is certain, however, the bars on both streets are packed until 1 AM. On rue St-Malo, the owners of **McCartan's** (31 rue St-Malo, tel. 02–99–38–66–06) are musicians and have Irish folk music playing every night on the stage of the cellar. The younger crowd can get pretty rowdy late at night. For something a little mellower, walk down to place de Bretagne, where you'll find an older crowd enjoying a glass of 17F Brouilly wine and listening to jazz at the **Elsa Popping** (19 rue Poullain Duparc, tel. 02–99–78–31–71). Movies in Rennes are hugely popular, and the **Arvor** cinema (29 rue d'Antrain, tel. 02–99–38–72–40) shows classic French and subtitled foreign films.

NEAR RENNES

FORET DE PAIMPONT

The wood needed by kings for the building of huge war frigates has reduced the immense legendary forest of Brocéliande, which used to cover all of central Brittany, to a 70-square-km (27-square-mi) Forêt de Paimpont. The change in name indicates the waning of the mythological spirit of the place, although some parts are still humid and shady enough to remind one of the legends imported by the Bretons: King Arthur and the knights of the Round Table searched for the Holy Grail here. Today, a mysterious and impenetrable sect of Druids can still be found performing magical religious ceremonies in the forest. Four times a year, during the spring equinox (March 23), the summer solstice (June 22), the autumn equinox (September 21), and the winter solstice (December 23), the Druids open their ceremonies to the public. Arthurian folklore aside, the moss-covered stones and glens are great for hiking, biking, and exploring—though the sights in the forest are not easy to find.

BASICS

The **Syndicat d'Initiative** in Paimpont has guided tours of the whole forest in the summer on Thursday and Saturday. The guide covers the eastern part of the forest in the morning (18F) and the western part in the afternoon (30F). If you're going to explore the forest by yourself, you should invest in the somewhat-detailed map (15F), or the very-detailed *VTT en Brocéliande* (35F), which clearly indicates mountain-bike trails and routes. *5 esplanade Brocéliande (at the foot of the abbey), tel. 02–99–07–84–23. Open Oct.–May, Wed.–Sun. 10–noon and 2–5; June–Sept., daily 9:30–12:30 and 1:30–6:30.*

COMING AND GOING

Eight **buses** run daily from the gare routière in Rennes to Plélan-le-Grand (1 hr, 20F), on the eastern edge of the forest. Six of those buses continue on to Paimpont, another 6 km (4 mi) northwest, smack-dab in the middle of the forest. The last bus leaves Paimpont at 5 PM; another leaves from Plélan at 6:30 PM. No buses run on Sunday. Once you get here, there is no public transportation.

GETTING AROUND

Hiking **trails** start directly from Paimpont, but to see any of the sights, you'll have to be on wheels. Drivers often pick up hitchhikers, but most roads only see a handful of cars per hour. On a **bicycle,** you can ride right up to most of the sights, or park just a short walk away. Rent VTTs at the bar **Le Brécilien** (tel. 02–99–07–81–13) in Paimpont for 90F a day, 60F a half day, and a passport deposit. Otherwise, some hotels and gîtes d'étape (*see* Where to Sleep, *below*) also rent out bicycles.

WHERE TO SLEEP

Plélan-le-Grand and Paimpont are both tiny villages with little to do and few places to eat or sleep. You're better off staying in a bed-and-breakfast, or a gîtes d'étape inside the forest around Paimpont. Otherwise, in Plélan, the dubious **Hôtel des Bruyères** (10 rue Brocéliande, tel. 02–99–06–81–38) has three doubles with shower (200F) and three with bath (260F). It also rents two mountain bikes for 80F per day and has a three-course menu (65F). Paimpont's **Camping Municipal** (tel. 02–99–07–89–16), just outside the village along the D773 (rte. de Gaël), has sites for 13F plus 15F a person.

A couple of miles south of Paimpont, in Le Canné, Annie and Robert Morvan oversee three **chambres d'hôte** (La Corne de Cerf, tel. 02–99–07–84–19) with distinct color schemes: the yellow Amaryllis (290F), the blue Emeraldine (300F), and the green attic Olivine (310F). Staying here is a splurge, but the artist couple (she does tapestries, he teaches painting) have renovated their beautiful house with brightly painted antique furniture. At the **Ferme de Trudeau** (tel. 02–99–07–81–40), you can get the farm experience in three different ways: The gîte d'étape has 30 beds, each for 48F, in a spartan atmosphere; the seven-room chambre d'hôte (240F—3,000F) is simple yet clean and comfortable; lastly, there is camping à la ferme (June–September), where you can pitch your tent in a field for 45F (for two). In summer, the farm also does **auberge à la ferme**, a dinner (90F) cooked in an outside wood-fire oven. From Paimpont, take the D38 and make a left on the D40. There are two other gîtes d'étape near Paimpont for the same price—48F. **Plélan-les-Forges** (tel. 02–99–06–81–59) is 4 km (2½ mi) south of Paimpont, and **Beauvais** (tel. 02–99–07–82–52) is 6 km (4 mi) to the west and closest to the majority of sights.

HOSTEL • The only **Auberge de Jeunesse** (tel. 02–97–22–76–75), in the forest at Choucan, is a stiff 12 km (7 mi) from Plélan-le-Grand and 6 km (4 mi) from Paimpont. The bus will drop you at Paimpont, so either bike from there or break in your hiking boots. Head north on D773, and look for the sign after Paimpont. Follow the road toward Concoret, and look for the hostel sign right around Isaugovët. It's open May–September and charges 46F a night with an HI card.

FOOD

You won't find much to eat around here. You're best off stocking up on supplies at the big **Comod Supermarché** (30 av. de la Libération, tel. 02–99–06–88–95), just across from the Office de Tourisme in Plélan-le-Grand. There's also a **market** here on Sunday mornings in front of the mairie.

OUTDOOR ACTIVITIES

Most of the good trails cluster around the forest's western border near Tréhorenteuc and La Folle Pensée, where you'll also find the gorgeous **Val Sans Retour** (Valley of No Return). King Arthur's sister, Morgan, kept her lovers prisoner here until Sir Lancelot, the bravest knight of King Arthur's court, broke the charm. The southern loop, a 10-km (6-mi) diversion off the main trail, will take you past the "Giant's Tomb," a conglomeration of stones dating from the Bronze Age, and the "House of Viviane," a few erected stones dating from 2500 BC. Both are on the way to the picturesque 15th-century **Château de Trécesson,** unfortunately closed to the public. On the opposite side of the forest, northeast of Paimpont, you can visit the **Fontaine de Jouvence** (Fountain of Youth)—though it only works if you go before sunrise seven days in a row; the **Château de Comper** (open Wednesday–Monday), where Viviane lifted up Lancelot from the lake; and **Merlin's tomb,** where he remains after having been duped by Viviane and made hers forever, at the very northeast tip. All these sights can be seen by bike in one afternoon.

VITRE

The **Château de Vitré** was one of the more successful fortifications during the Hundred Years' War; its plunging walls and massive towers never succumbed to repeated English attacks. The interior hardly compares to its magnificent exterior, but it's worth the admission to see the natural history museum, which displays stuffed frogs in crazy getups: playing pool, on crutches, in swim trunks—the French *do* have a sense of humor. *Tel. 02–99–96–76–51. Admission 20F. Open Apr.–Sept., daily 10–12:30 and 2–5:30; Oct.–Mar., Sat.–Mon. 2–5:30, Wed.–Fri. 10–noon and 2–5:30.*

Even more interesting than the castle is the small medieval walled town that spreads out from its gates. The town is the best preserved in all of Brittany and utterly beguiling.

BASICS

To reach the **Office de Tourisme** (pl. St-Yves, tel. 02–99–75–04–46), head left from the station—it's 330 ft ahead. From here, continue on and make a right at place St-Yves; wonderful winding streets will lead you to the château (veer left).

COMING AND GOING

Several trains traveling between Paris and Rennes stop daily in Vitré. The trip from Rennes takes 30 minutes and costs 39F. Both **SNCF** and **TIV** (tel. 02–99–26–11–11) run a couple of daily buses between Vitré and Fougères (35 mins, 36F) but only one round-trip on Sunday. Rent bikes in Vitré at **Gigquel** (4 blvd. Châteaubriand, tel. 02–99–74–43–40), which charges 70F a day with a passport deposit.

WHERE TO SLEEP AND EAT

Great prices, a chummy owner, and several rooms with a view of the château make **Le Grillon** (14 rue du Bourg-aux-Moines, tel. 02–99–74–57–84) the best hotel for the money. Singles run 110F, doubles 140F with hall showers; the hotel is closed Sunday. If that doesn't work out, the **Foyer des Jeunes Travailleurs** (13 rue Pasteur, tel. 02–99–74–61–73), next door to the Musée St-Nicolas, has perhaps one of the only centrally located gîtes d'étape in Brittany. A dorm bed here costs 50F per night.

Of course you'll find the usual collection of crêperies and pizzerias within the walled town, but for one simple, meaty meal, follow local families to **Le Viaduc** (44 rue de Brest, tel. 02–99–75–03–22) for the four-course (plus wine and coffee) 55F menu; it's only open weekdays at lunch. A **market** graces rue de la Poterie on Saturday mornings, and an even bigger one fills up the area on Monday from place Notre-Dame to place de la République.

FOUGERES

> *Genealogical trivia: Jack Kerouac was a descendant of the dukes of Brittany.*

At first glance, you wonder who the dunce was that built Fougères's enormous 12-tower **château** at the bottom of the valley rather than on top of a hill. But if you put on a pair of medieval glasses, you'll notice that the castle's ramparts are surrounded by a part of the Nançon River, which acts as a natural moat. Water back then was a good soldier repellent, and it wasn't until the discovery of gunpowder that the assailants got the upper hand. Even after all of the invasions, the castle is still in beautiful shape. It can be visited alone or with a tour guide (an English one in the summer). *Tel. 02–99–99–79–59. Admission 23F. Open mid-June–Sept., daily 9–7; Oct.–mid-June, daily 10–noon and 2–5.*

BASICS

To reach the **Office de Tourisme** from the bus station, go up boulevard Jean-Jaurès and curve right on rue de Verdun to place Aristide-Briand. They'll give you maps with walking tours of the fascinating medieval quarter and *ville haute* (upper town). *1 pl. Aristide-Briand, tel. 02–99–94–12–20. Open Sept.–June, Mon.–Sat. 9:30–12:30 and 2–6, Sun. 10–noon and 2–4; July–Aug., daily 9–7.*

COMING AND GOING

No trains go to Fougères, but buses make the one-hour trip from Rennes hourly (47F). Buses also run to Vitré (35 mins, 36F) and Mont-St-Michel (1 hr, 65F). Call the **gare routière** (pl. de la Gare, tel. 02–99–99–08–77) for information (open 11–12:30 and 4–6:30). Within Fougères, those great streets will make you sweat for their incredible views, thanks to all the steep hills and stairs. Still, this small town is best done on foot, which is a good thing, because there's no public transportation. To reach the château, make a right from the tourist office and go down the pretty rue de la Pinterie.

WHERE TO SLEEP AND EAT

Affordable beds in Fougères have been hard to come by ever since the youth hostel closed in 1991. The idiosyncratic couple at **Hôtel de Bretagne** (7 pl. de la République, tel. 02–99–99–31–68), directly across the street from the bus station, rents out oddly decorated doubles for 150F with shower and 115F without. They fill up quickly, so you might want to try **Hôtel de Flaubert** (1 rue Gustave-Flaubert, tel. 02–99–99–00–43), a few blocks in the opposite direction from the bus station; doubles with showers are 140F (110F without).

Stock up on picnic supplies at the **Shopi** supermarket **(9 rue Porte Roger, tel. 02–99–94–01–32) next door to the tourist office, or try pizza and pasta (36F–59F) at Pizzeria Lorenzo** (4 rue de la Pinterie, tel. 02–99–99–21–29). The weekly **market** takes place Saturday mornings in the historic district.

COTES D'ARMOR

The Côtes d'Armor, the long stretch of Brittany's northern coast, recounts a dramatic struggle between sea and granite shore. The coastline is loosely divided into two parts: the **Côte d'Emeraude** (Emerald Coast), stretching westward from Cancale, where cliffs are punctuated by golden, curving beaches and chin-high forests of ferns; and the peaceful **Côte de Granit Rose** (Pink Granite Coast), including the stupefying Perros-Guirec, where Brittany's granite glows an otherworldly pink. Although this area is truly remarkable, things aren't cheap and transportation can be problematic, so always plan in advance.

ST-MALO

Fed up by the large amounts of money the Breton dukes Jean IV and Jean V extorted in the 15th century and, later, unwilling to participate in France's Catholic-Huguenot religious wars of the 16th century, the people of St-Malo declared "Ni Français, ni Breton, Malouin suis" ("Neither French nor Breton, Malouin I am"). They tossed French and Breton authority to the wind in order to exist as their own independent city-state for four years. Until Henry IV renounced Protestantism, the city's wars and treaties were signed in the Malouin name. The feisty Malouin *corsaires* (king's pirates), like Robert Surcouf (1773–1827), became more tolerant of authority after receiving the royal blessing to pillage merchant ships of countries warring with France—especially British ships coming back from India. After the king pocketed a percentage of the profits, the corsaires still had enough left over to build the beautiful mansions you'll find next to the **porte de Dinan.**

Detached in spirit from the continent, Malouins continued to behave like islanders and fished cod all the way into Canadian waters. But recent restrictions on territorial fishing have forced them to shift their enterprising eyes towards the shores. It's paid off because, like Mont-St-Michel, St-Malo is packed. With its long stretch of gorgeous beach and famous *intra muros* (a fortified medieval town on a peninsula), St-Malo now prospers from the swarms of early morning tour buses that terrorize the streets.

BASICS

Next door to the gare routière, the **Office de Tourisme** (esplanade St-Vincent, tel. 02–99–56–64–48) gives out detailed maps and information on bus and ferry schedules. It's open April–September daily; October–March, Monday–Saturday. The tourist office's small booth outside the train station is only open mid-June–August.

COMING AND GOING

The **train station** (sq. Jean-Coquelin, tel. 08–36–35–35–35–35) is a 15-minute walk from the walled town—walk straight up avenue Louis-Martin. Trains connect St-Malo to Dol (15 mins, 25F) and Rennes (55 mins, 69F), where you can transfer to Paris. Trains also go to Dinan via Dol (65 mins, 72F), but the bus is cheaper and faster. **TIV** (tel. 02–99–40–83–33) runs buses to Rennes (1¾ hrs, 56F), Dinard (40 mins, 20F), and Cancale (30 mins, 21F). **CAT** (tel. 02–96–39–21–05) makes the trip to Dinan (35 mins, 34F), and **Les Courriers Bretons** (tel. 02–99–56–79–09) makes the 1¼-hour journey to Mont-St-Michel for 52F. Buses leave from the gare routière, immediately outside the intra muros. You can also take a day trip down to Dinan (120F; 90F one-way) and Dinard (30F; 20F one-way) on a ferry with **Emeraude Lines** (tel. 02–99–40–48–40).

GETTING AROUND

The intra muros is pretty small, but the rest of the city isn't. You may want to use **St-Malo Bus** (esplanade St-Vincent, tel. 02–99–56–06–06) to get to the hostel and around town; tickets are 7F. To pick up some oysters in the nearby town of Cancale or to take a day trip to the Mont-St-Michel, you may wish to save yourself transportation hassle and rent a car; **ADA** (15 av. Pasteur, tel. 02–99–56–06–15) rents small cars for 369F a day (400 km/250 mi free). For a smaller perimeter, **Cycles Diazo** (47 quai Duguay-Trouin, tel. 02–99–40–31–63) rents discounted bikes for 55F and VTTs for 85F (show them this guide and you'll get a discount; the company requires a passport deposit).

WHERE TO SLEEP

Most rooms within the intra muros are way out of budget range, and come July and August, establishments all over town start their summer let's-milk-tourists-for-all-they're-worth rates; prices increase about 20F a room. You'll find most of the budget hotels clustered around the train station on busy **boulevard de la République.** They're all pretty similar, unfortunately, with bars downstairs and dreary settings, but most rooms are decent. Cheapest option intra muros is **Hôtel Cap à l'Ouest** (2 rue St-Benoist, tel. 02–99–40–87–03), near the Plage de Bon-Secours, with 11 pretty basic rooms running 150F–260F. Facing the plage Rochebonne (3 km/2 mi from the station), the **Hôtel les Charmettes** (64 blvd. Hébert, tel. 02–99–56–07–31, fax 02–99–56–85–96) is in a pleasant residential area among pricey mansions. The main hotel, at the end of a short pathway, has some doubles with bath and a gorgeous view of the ocean for 240F (320F in summer). A similar annex has cheaper doubles with showers in the hall for 180 year-round. From the station, head toward Courtoisville and follow the THERMES MARINS signs; the hotel is 130 yards northeast of the Thermes. Reserve ahead for both in summer.

HOSTEL • Auberge de Jeunesse. This institutional hostel feels like a palace when you enter, but watch out for the showers—they randomly shoot out three-second blasts of boiling water. The hostel itself is two blocks from the beach and a great place to meet French travelers. With the obligatory HI card, you get a bed for 68F, breakfast included. Sheets are 17F; lunch and dinner, served weekdays only, are both 50F. *37 av. du Révérend-Père-Umbricht, tel. 02–99–40–29–80. From station, Bus 5 to Auberge de Jeunesse stop. From intra muros, Bus 1 or 5. By foot, turn right out of train station onto rue Jean Jaurès, left on av. St-Pierre, right on av. du Révérend-Père-Umbricht. 300 beds. Reception open 9 AM–10 PM. No curfew, lockout 10–5. Kitchen, laundry.*

CAMPING • Camping de la Cité d'Aleth, close to the city, overlooks the bay and is the most attractive of St-Malo's five campgrounds. Prices are 30F per site and 22F per person. *St-Servan peninsula, south of intra muros, tel. 02–99–81–60–91.*

Unlike other towns flattened by World War II bombs, St-Malo was rebuilt with extreme care. Architects numbered all the jumbled stones and, like a big jigsaw puzzle, reconstructed the original intra muros houses according to old pictures.

FOOD

Most intra muros restaurants are touristy, except for a few unusual ones slightly off the beaten track (get a map). The facade of **L'Art Caddy** (7 rue des Petits-Degrès, tel. 02–99–40–82–78) warns "Danger—Crocodiles. No swimming." It is, however, the alligators that get the bum rap here; they're served on your plate "émincé style" (i.e., in thin slices; 89F). For a less adventurous meal, **Le Teddy Bear** (Gare Maritime de la Bourse, tel. 02–99–56–03–80) serves *gambas* (giant prawns) Indiana style (69F) or steak tartare (65F) to patrons, who are surrounded by teddy bear decorations as they dine. Intra or extra muros, any *poissonnerie* (fishmonger) sells the famous Cancale oysters. A dozen costs around 30F. Stock up on groceries at the **Intermarché** supermarket near the train station.

WORTH SEEING

The **Musée d'Histoire de St-Malo** in the château has an interesting collection of Malouin coffers, paintings, sculptures, and cannons. There is a beautiful Celtic tapestry on the second floor, but you'll find the most interesting part of the museum by climbing the spiral staircase up the watchtower to the highest point in the city. Here you'll have a great panoramic view of St-Malo, the Fort National, and l'Ile Grande; the Breton duke Jean V built it in the 15th century to keep watch over the turbulent Malouins. *Tel. 02–99–40–71–57. Admission 27F. Open Tues.–Sun. 10–noon and 2–6*

Definitely take a walk out to the **Fort National,** one of many island fortresses built around St-Malo in the late 17th century. Here, Surcouf supposedly killed off 12 Prussian officers, sparing one to serve as a witness to his prowess. The fort was also used as an execution site—the condemned would say their last prayers in front of the large cross before they were burned to a crisp. Tours (written explanations are given in English) are offered for 20F at low tide—which is the only time you can get here. Likewise for the northward **Ile du Grand Bé,** a fortress island just off the intra muros, where Romantic writer Châteaubriand's tomb was miraculously spared by Allied bombings during World War II. Before you leave the intra muros, take a peek inside the **Cathédrale St-Vincent,** where a gorgeous rose light illuminates the curved nave. You'll also see the tomb of Jacques Cartier.

OUTDOOR ACTIVITIES

Centre de Voile (plage de Bon Secours, west of the intra muros, tel. 02–99–40–11–45) rents kayaks for 90F a half day; a small catamaran is 395F and a dinghy 220F–295F for the same time period. All activities require a 1,000F deposit. Across the Rance River, the expensive resort town of **Dinard** has beautiful beaches; call **Emeraude Lines** (tel. 02–99–40–48–40) for information on the short ferry ride here

(30F round-trip). The same company will also take you to **Ile de Cézembre** (50F round-trip), a tiny island with 50 beaches, reputed to get more sunlight than anywhere else in the area. A strenuous 30-km (19-mi) trail, the **GR34,** follows the coastline east of St-Malo around the scenic Pointe du Grouin to **Cancale,** famous for its oysters.

DINAN

During the frequent wars that devastated other cities throughout the Middle Ages, the merchants who ruled Dinan got rich selling goods to whichever camp had the upper hand, well aware that loyalty to any side, be it the French, the English, or the Bretons, would eventually lead to the destruction of their homes. The strategy worked; today, Dinan has one of the biggest preserved medieval towns in Brittany. Seven-hundred-year-old ramparts tower on steep hillsides that slope down to the Rance River. The friendly people, good restaurants, and amazing youth hostel make it all the more appealing. If you're lucky enough to be in Dinan the first weekend in September, the town wears itself out for three days with the **Fête des Remparts,** when you can watch chivalric duels and townsfolk cavort in medieval getups and listen to musicians. It's all free, but happens only every even-numbered year (every odd-numbered year, the festival is in Dinan's sister city, Quebec). Call 02–96–87–94–94 for information.

BASICS

Signs will direct you to the **Office de Tourisme,** in the center of the walled town. To help it stay open all year long, the office sells a *guide touristique* (15F) that has a mediocre map but a great historic overview of Dinan. *6 rue de l'Horloge, tel. 02–96–39–75–40. Open mid-June–mid-Sept., Mon.–Sat. 9–7, Sun. 10–12:30 and 3–5:30; mid-Sept.–mid-June, Mon.–Sat. 8:30–12:30 and 2–6.*

COMING AND GOING

If you come to Dinan by train, you'll arrive in the art deco **train station** (pl. du 11-Novembre-1918, tel. 08–36–35–35–35). The old walled town sits above and to the west of the Rance River; to get here from the train station, angle left across place du 11-Novembre-1918 onto rue Carnot and continue east.

Trains leave frequently for Rennes via Dol (45 mins, 72F), St-Malo via Dol (50 mins, 47F), St-Brieuc (55 mins, 56F), Dol (25 mins, 29F), and other major towns in Brittany. **CAT** buses (tel. 02–96–39–21–05) leave from the train station for St-Malo (1 hr, 31F), Dinard (45 mins, 23F), and Plancoët (20 mins, 23F). **TAE** buses (tel. 02–99–50–64–17) also connect Dinan to Rennes (1¼ hrs, 46F) several times a day. No buses run on Sunday. For a chic and sleek ride, **Emeraude Lines** (tel. 02–99–40–48–40) runs one boat a day to Dinard and St-Malo for 90F (120F round-trip). The tourist office has timetables.

WHERE TO SLEEP

Dinan is a popular town in summer, so reserve a room at least two weeks in advance. The friendly couple that runs the **Hôtel de l'Océan** (9 pl. du 11-Novembre-1918, tel. 02–96–39–21–51) rents out 14 comfortable, well-kept rooms that have firm mattresses for a change; it's across the street from the train station. Doubles go for 150F with shower (120F with hall shower). For a more central location, **Hôtel du Théâtre** (2 rue Ste-Claire, tel. 02–96–39–06–91) has low prices and a friendly owner that runs one of those old-men-only bars downstairs. The lone single goes for 95F without shower, and doubles are 110F (170F with shower).

The **Logis du Jerzual** is a three-story chambres d'hôte in the lower half of the Jerzual artisan street. The common areas lead to large, ornate guest rooms with slanted skylights, trinkets, baubles, and Persian rugs. Don't miss a walk to the highest point in the garden, for a breathtaking view of the Rance River, the town of Dinan, and the port. Rooms run 280F–380F, with one small single for 150F. An extra bed is 70F. *25 rue du Petit-Fort, tel. 02–96–85–46–54, fax 02–96–39–46–94. 5 rooms with shower. Cash only.*

HOSTEL • Auberge de Jeunesse. The châteaulike mansion—a 30-minute walk from the center of town—sits at the bottom of a forested valley. The majority of rooms with six and eight beds attract a younger, rowdy crowd in summer, but there are a few rooms with two and four beds in a quieter part of the house for couples or groups of friends. A bed costs 48F, and a cot in the tent outside is 26F; an HI card is required. The rooms are locked 11 AM–5 PM, and the reception closes noon–3, but the dining room and kitchen stay open and serve large 50F lunches and dinners. *Moulin de Méen, Vallée de la Fontaine des Eaux, tel. 02–96–39–10–83, fax 02–96–39–10–62. From station, turn left onto rue Clos du Hêtre, left across tracks, and follow signs to hostel. No curfew. Cash only.*

CAMPING • Camping Municipal. If you don't have the energy to make it to the sites at the youth hostel, this campground 15 minutes from the station is on a busy street. It's pleasant enough, though, and you'll pay just 38F for two people and a tent. *103 rue Châteaubriand, tel. 02–96–39–11–96. Follow signs from pl. Duclos in centre ville. Reception open 8–1 and 2–8. Closed Oct.–May.*

FOOD

Many of Dinan's restaurants and good crêperies line rue du Petit Fort, from the Porte du Jerzual down to the riverbank. Try the cozy **Les Jardins du Jerzual** (15 rue du Petit Fort, tel. 02–96–85–28–75), with crepes for 15F–45F. Just a short way down the footpath, you'll find **La Lumachelle** (80 rue du Petit Fort, tel. 02–96–39–38–13), a relaxed local hangout with romantic nooks next to a fireplace. The pizzas (40F–50F) are cooked inside a wooden oven, and the salmon pasta (48F) is filling. A large **market** animates place du Champ and place Duguesclin Thursday mornings until noon, and you'll find a **Monoprix** supermarket (7 pl. du Marchix) just below place Duclos.

UNDER 75F • Chez Flochon. This provincial French restaurant has a warm, homey atmosphere, thanks to its charming owner. The specialty here is fondue. Beer or cider fondue is around 60F, and you can get chocolate fondue for dessert. They also serve a great 49F menu that includes a hearty salad, a galette du jour, a dessert crepe, and a glass of cider. *24 rue du Jerzual, tel. 02–96–87–91–57. Cash only under 100F. Closed Sun. and Mon., and Dec.–Mar.*

UNDER 100F • Le Jacobin. In this elegant restaurant with hardwood floors and brick walls you'll find a three-course menu (80F) that's more for the delicate palate than the strong appetite. It includes such dishes as oysters, fish in a light cream sauce, and lamb. The atmosphere is a bit formal, complete with a maître d' who cleans the table between each course. *11 rue Haute-Voie, tel. 02–96–39–25–66.*

The Fort National and Ile du Grand Bé are only accessible at low tide. Don't laugh at the tourist hordes who got stuck on the island because they crossed when the tide was rising—it might just happen to you.

WORTH SEEING

Dinan is a fun place to walk around and marvel at the medieval buildings, especially those near place des Cordeliers. Medieval rue du Jerzual houses the studios of the city's numerous artisans. A sinning crusader promised to build a church in Dinan if he returned from Jerusalem alive, and the **Basilique St-Sauveur** is the result. The church reflects 600 years' worth of conflicting styles, and the original sections show strong Byzantine and Arabic influences, evidence of the knight's distant crusades. Off to one side, a stone slab holds the heart of Bertrand du Guesclin, the 14th-century soldier who drove the English out of France. Behind the basilica is the **Jardin Anglais** (English Garden), with a fine view of the valley.

The **Château de la Duchesse Anne** was originally built in the 16th century as a defense against foreign armies (and occasionally Dinan's rebellious townsfolk). The château now houses the local museum, complete with a weaver's workshop and artifacts from the city's past. The entrance fee also lets you into the **Tour de Coëtquen,** where fascinating sculpted tombs are on display three floors below. *Tel. 02–96–39–45–20. Admission 25F. Open June–Sept., daily 10–5:30; Oct.–May, daily 10–noon and 2–5:30.*

During the Middle Ages, the intersection of rue de l'Horloge and rue de l'Apport was the crossroads of the St-Malo–Rennes and Paris–Brest roads, the two biggest trading roads in Brittany. Lacking stoplights, the town built the **Tour de l'Horloge** (Clock Tower) to keep an eye on the surrounding countryside. On a clear day, you might just be able to see all the way to Mont-St-Michel from the tower. *Rue de l'Horloge. Admission 10F. Open Apr.–June, daily 2–6; July–Sept., daily 10–7.*

AFTER DARK

At night, steer yourself toward the center of town, which is crammed with small bars. **Le Bistrot d'En-Bas** (20 rue Haute-Voie, tel. 02–96–85–44–00) serves 12F beers and stays open until 2 AM. Those in the know come here for cheap food (sandwiches are 18F–26F); the young, spunky crowd; and great Breton, French, or rock music. For something quieter, try **La Truye Qui File** (14 rue de la Cordonnerie, tel. 02–98–39–72–29), where the owner plays his guitar and sings French songs. Beers are 12F–16F.

SHOPPING

At the top of **rue du Jerzual,** you'll find a renowned artisan community. Around 20 artisans work along this cobblestone street, which winds all the way down to the port. Inside the skewed wood-beamed medieval houses, you'll find glassblowers, wood sculptors and carvers, pottery makers, jewelry makers, and even a baker that sells his delicious *Kouin-Amende* (a puff pastry made with lots of butter and sugar) by the pound.

Plancoët, 13 km (8 mi) from Dinan (*see* Coming and Going, *above*), is known for its excellent mineral water devoid of any nitrates but also for its famous *maroquineries* (shops). The maroquinerie **Renouard** (rue Connétable-de-Clisson, tel. 02–96–84–21–42) and **Swann** (pl. Châteaubriand, tel. 02–96–84–13–66) both sell high-quality handcrafted goods.

PAIMPOL

Paimpol once teemed with fishing schooners. The saturation of cultivated lands in Brittany drove people to the sea, and Paimpol was a prime spot for the cod-fishing enterprise that flourished here in the mid-19th century. In his famous novel, *Pêcheurs d'Islande,* Pierre Loti romanticized the brave Paimpolais, who left for six months during the winter to fish the capricious waters of Iceland. The book painted such a mystical portrait of the widows and their husbands who never returned that tourists acquainted with the book are often disappointed to find that the old marina has turned into somewhat of a ghost port. Today, all of Paimpol's charm lies not in the town itself but on the peninsula north of it. If you walk along the **circuit pédestre** (pedestrian way), you'll discover a magnificent violet-color granite coast, the **Croix des Veuves** (Widows' Cross) next to Pors-Even where the wives of the Paimpolais fishermen prayed for their husbands' safe return, and the Pointe de l'Arcouest, the embarkation point for the boat to the pink-color granite **Ile de Bréhat** (38F round-trip). Between l'Arcouest and Paimpol, along the D789, you'll find **Ploubazlanec**'s fishermen cemetery, a moving testimony to the 2,000 men who died for Paimpol's prosperity.

The **Abbaye de Beauport** is a 30-minute walk south of centre ville along the coast. Founded in 1202 by Count Alain de Goëlo, this is the oldest abbey on France's Atlantic coast. An English-language brochure guides you through the gorgeous ruins of the roofless church, the living quarters, and the gardens where the monks used to grow hemp. The abbey is complemented by twisting vines and colorful roses, plus a wonderful view of the calm waters just beyond. *Chemin de l'Abbaye, tel. 02–96–55–18–58. Admission 20F. Open daily 10–noon and 2–5, slightly later in summer.*

There are several beaches east of the port, the biggest and most popular being **Plage de la Tossen**; just beyond it is **Pointe de Guilben,** a beautiful lookout spot.

BASICS

The **Office de Tourisme** (pl. de la République, tel. 02–96–20–83–16) has loads of information on Paimpol, but carrying around their glossy, poster-size map of town may make you feel like an idiot. To get to the office from the train station, take rue du 18-Juin until it ends and turn left; signs will guide you from here. It's open Monday–Saturday 9–7:30. A **post office** across from the station exchanges money.

COMING AND GOING

From Paimpol, trains go to Guingamp (45 mins, 36F), and CAT buses (tel. 02–96–68–31–20) go to St-Brieuc (1½ hrs, 42F); both towns are on the Paris–Brest TGV line. You can keep your bags behind the counter for a day or two. The centre ville is a block down from the station; to get to the port, follow the main street to your right for three or four blocks. To bike around the area, **Cycles du Vieux Clocher** (pl. de Verdun, tel. 02–96–20–83–58) rents bicycles for 60F with a passport deposit.

WHERE TO SLEEP

A 15-minute walk from the train station is a grassy park area northwest of town—host to a youth hostel, a gîte d'étape, and a campground. In an old mansion, the 90-bed **Auberge de Jeunesse** (Château de Kerraoul, tel. 02–96–20–83–60, fax 02–96–20–96–46) has comfortable doubles and quadruples, some with a view of the ocean. The friendly owner is also a sea kayak instructor and may be able to organize a trip to l'Ile de Bréhat for around 100F. A bunk costs 48F per night, breakfast is 19F, and sheets are 17F. There is no curfew or lockout. If you just can't make the walk, the clean and bright **Hôtel Berthelot** (rue du Port, tel. 02–96–20–88–66) has doubles (160F) and quads (230F).

FOOD

You'll find plenty of crêperies and brasseries near the port, many with outdoor seating. The small dining room at the **Restaurant du Port** (17 quai Morand, tel. 02–96–20–82–76) is more cramped than cozy; the "Paon" menu (98F), however, includes excellent seafood in various cream sauces. The first course of fresh oysters goes down well with a 55F bottle of Muscadet. A similar dinner menu costs 110F at **La Vieille Tour** (13 rue de l'Église, tel. 02–96–20–83–18); the atmosphere is somewhat formal and the food delicately prepared. For groceries, the town **market** takes place Tuesday mornings in all the central squares. If you miss it, there's a huge, cheap **Intermarché** across the street from the train station.

NEAR PAIMPOL

CHATEAU DE LA ROCHE-JAGU

The gîte d'étape here (48F a night) is within the gates of the château grounds, adjacent to the château—which means that when the château closes down, you've got the grounds, valley, and river below to explore. To get here, you must either ride a bike from Paimpol, 12 km (7 mi) to the north, or take a train to Pontrieux from Guingamp (25 mins, 22F) or from Paimpol (18 mins, 19F), and then walk the remaining 5 km (3 mi). Either way, it's a pleasant, mostly flat journey. Bring some groceries along, though, because your only other dining option is the restaurant (tel. 02–96–95–16–08) next to the gîte, and its 69F, three-course menu is only available for weekday lunch.

Rebuilt in the 14th century, the château is what the French call a *maison forte,* a cross between a lord's manor and a fortress. The fortress side above the Trieux River has 10-ft-thick walls, as opposed to the 3½-ft-thick walls of the entrance of the manor. Every bedroom in the château has an adjoining bathroom—an oddity in the 14th century—and almost every room has a fireplace, including small ones in the bathrooms. All these details were rarely implemented by men of the time when designing their châteaux, so it appears the design of this particular mansion was influenced by one of the women of the house. The third and fourth floors have jaw-dropping panoramic views of the Trieux River. *Tel. 02–96–95–62–35 (château information and gîte reservations) or 02–96–95–14–03 (Pontrieux tourist office). Admission 35F. Open Sept.–June, daily 10:30–12:30 and 2–6; July–Aug., daily 10–7.*

The merchant marines school in Paimpol was closed down in 1996 because, the rumor goes, Jacques Chirac frowned upon the mayor's socialist ties to writer André Malraux.

PERROS-GUIREC

Oddly enough, 90% of the postcard and tourist brochure photos of Perros are actually of the nearby commune of **Ploumanac'h** (*see below*). *Ploum (as the locals call it) is not only a great tourist bait, it's also the best place on the Côtes d'Armor to see the astonishing pink granite boulders. Once visitors are lured to Perros, however, the two beaches are sure to seduce even the palest of sunbathers.* **Trestraou,** *the bigger and more famous of the pair, is a typical French resort lined with a grassy area, a boardwalk, and tons of shops and restaurants;* **Trestrignel,** *the more secluded and beautiful sister to the east, is the ideal spot to plant a parasol and read a good book. In summer, Perros is crammed, but in June and September, room prices are reasonable, and this heaven is all yours.*

BASICS

The **Office de Tourisme** has information on sailboarding, sailing, scuba diving, and nightclubs, and it sells useful maps of streets and scenic paths. *21 pl. de la Mairie, tel. 02–96–23–21–15. Open daily (hrs vary); Sept.–May, closed Sun.*

COMING AND GOING

To get to Perros-Guirec you have to go through Lannion, a town 8 km (5 mi) inland and served by **train.** The trains run from Lannion to Plouaret-Trégor about eight times per day (17 mins, 19F). Plouaret-Trégor is then on the main Paris–Brest train line. **CAT** (tel. 02–96–46–76–70) runs five buses a day from Lannion to Perros-Guirec (25 mins, 16F)—you can stop at the port, centre ville, or the beach at Trestraou—and to neighboring Ploumanac'h (35 mins, 18F). From Lannion, buses also go to Tréguier (30 mins, 30F), Trébeurden (30 mins, 20F), and Pleumeur-Bodou (30 mins, 20F). You can rent a bike (55F all day until midnight) at the Lannion railway station or from the hostel in Trébeurden (*see below*) for 50F per day. Otherwise, you'll be doing a lot of walking as there's no public transportation in Perros-Guirec. The plage de Trestrignel is toward the tip of Perros-Guirec's peninsula; its main beach, the plage de Trestraou, is on the western edge. The centre ville is above and between the two.

WHERE TO SLEEP

Finding inexpensive lodging can be difficult and requires some planning. **Hôtel Les Violettes** (19 rue du Calvaire, tel. 02–96–23–21–33) in the centre ville has two buildings: The main one has the reception desk and an uninteresting restaurant, while the annex (25 rue du Maréchal-Foch) has some rooms with great views of the Trestraou beach. Doubles are 140F–190F depending on the plumbing. If you're ready to splurge (and this is the time to do it), stay at the **Hôtel Le Gulf** (26 rue des Sept-Iles, tel. 02–96–23–21–86), which hangs off a cliff over the water near Trestraou. Simple doubles go for 180F; hard-to-get triples and quadruples with shower are 290F. The hotel is closed November 15–March. Prices at both hotels increase about 20F in summer. For names of chambres d'hôte in the area, contact the tourist office.

HOSTELS • To stay in the gîte d'étape **Ferme de Kerangloff** (tel. 02–96–23–28–67) in nearby Barnabanec, call for directions (they speak English)—it's at least a half-hour walk from town. A bunk bed in a common room is 48F, and breakfast is 20F. Better yet, stay in one of the welcoming youth hostels. In Lannion, 12 km (7 mi) south of Perros-Guirec, the **Auberge de Jeunesse** (6 rue du 73e-Territorial, tel. 02–96–37–91–28) is just a minute's walk from the train station and has no curfew or lockout. A bed in a quadruple with its own toilet and shower is 52F, breakfast included; sheets are 22F. The Scandinavian-design **Auberge de Jeunesse** in Trébeurden (tel. 02–96–23–52–22), 10 km (6 mi) southwest of Perros-Guirec, charges 48F for a bed, 19F for breakfast. The sheets are 17F and dinner 50F.

FOOD

The crêperies or pizzerias that line the beach at Trestraou capitalize on their outdoor seating and really milk the tourists. **La Pizzeria** (plage de Trestraou, tel. 02–96–23–15–23) is cheaper than most; it serves pizzas with salad for around 45F. If you're more into beer-guzzling than sun-worshiping, head over to **Le Dinghy** (19 bis rue Anatole-Le Braz, tel. 02–96–23–05–85), a jazzy port-side joint, where the 12F *demis* (half pints) are served with sausage slices. Still hungry? Then drop by **Intermarché** (10 rue Lejeune) or the **Comod** supermarket (2 blvd. Aristide-Briand) to pick up some groceries.

Crêperie Hamon. François and Marie Kissillour, the jovial owners, make sure that the highest-quality ingredients appear on your plate, from the local sarazin wheat of the galettes to the Calvados used to flambé the crepe. Start with a plain galette (10F) to savor the quality of the batter, and then try the Pompidou (28F), an egg, ham, and cheese galette, supposedly the ex-president's favorite. You must make a reservation, and arrive on time (7 PM; there's an extra 9:30 PM sitting during the summer). *36 rue de la Salle, tel. 02–96–23–28–82. From the Port de Plaisance, take rue Anatole, make a left on rue La Salle. Cash only. Closed Mon. (also Fri. off-season).*

WORTH SEEING

A footpath, the **Sentier des Douaniers,** starts up at the west end of Trestraou beach; from there it's a two-hour walk through fern forests and past cliffs and pink granite boulders to the beach at Ploumanac'h (*see below*). There aren't many sights in town, but the weatherworn 12th-century **church** (place de l'Eglise) has squat columns sporting fantastic Celtic-Breton figures.

In Pleumeur-Bodou, the **Musée des Télécommunications** (Telecommunications Museum) has a sound-and-light show inside the Radome, a huge, inflated cloth dome; the show deals with France's early successes in satellite communications. In 1962, a satellite dish in the museum received the first television transmission between France and the United States. An English version shows Tuesday and Thursday, July to August. *Pleumeur-Bodou, tel. 02–96–46–63–64. Admission 40F. Open May–Sept., daily 10–6; call for off-season times.*

NEAR PERROS-GUIREC

PLOUMANAC'H AND TREGASTEL

These communities were sardonically called Plomazout and Trégasoil in 1967 after the channel currents swept the disemboweled Liberian Torré-Canyon tanker's fuel all over the pink granite coast. It took three years to clean up the rocks and the birds of the marée noire *(black tide). Today, for a good reason, the locals are* really *proud of their rocks (houses, benches, and curbs are made from rose granite) and their birds—a 96F, 2½-hour boat ride leaves from Trégastel and circles the uninhabited* **Sept-Iles,** *where fou de Bassan (a kind of goose), cormorants, and even seals live in peace and quiet.*

On Ploum's pleasant beach, **Plage de la Bastille,** you'll find the **Oratoire de St-Guirec,** a rose-granite chapel lodged in the sand with other rocks. Notice the statue of St. Guirec's broken nose. In the past, young girls would stick pins in the saint's nose and, if they stuck, a promise of marriage was to arrive in the coming year. Facing the beach is the **Château de Costaeres.** It was built at the end of the 19th century by a Polish engineer, Bruno Abakanowicz, but made famous after his friend Henryk Sienkiewicz, wrote *Quo Vadis* there. While Ploumanac'h is more family-oriented, Trégastel's **Plage de Coz-Porz** attracts a more youthful crowd. For those of you who find the sea water in these parts just too cold, Trégastel also has the **Forum,** an indoor heated seawater pool. Admission is 50F.

For an amazing view of granite boulders, walk the 4 km (2½ mi) Sentier des Douaniers from Perros-Guirec to Ploumanac'h (*see* Worth Seeing *in* Perros-Guirec, *above*). As you hike along the coast, notice how the wind and waves have chiseled surrealist sculptures out of the pink granite—a human skull, a tipped bottle, and Napoléon's hat inside M. Eiffel's property. There's also the **château du diable** (the devil's castle) and the **skuewel** (chair in Breton), two impressive masses of granite boulders. Past the carrefour de Ploumanac'h, **Vallée des Troueros** (between Ploum and Trégastel), the narrow valley that extends toward Lannion, has a granite quarry. Wear strong boots.

If you can't bear to leave, the **Hôtel de l'Europe** (158 rue St-Guirec, tel. 02–96–91–40–76) has 18 modernized rooms from 205F to 335F. **West Camping** (carrefour de Ploumanac'h, tel. 02–96–91–43–82), open April–September, charges 20F per person, 16F per site. A cluster of crêperies and restaurants serve cheap meals near the beach.

Crepes are eaten from the triangular tail up to save the most flavorful buttery part for last. Folklore, however, permits older folks to eat the best part first in case some awful tragedy prevents them from enjoying "la part de Dieu."

LA CLARTE

High above Perros, Ploumanac'h, and Trégastel, at an equal distance from and with a great view of all three, La Clarté is the perfect hub to drop your bags. The vine-covered **La Bonne Auberge** (pl. de la Chapelle, tel. 02–96–91–46–05, fax 02–96–91–62–88) has small rooms, three with views of the sea. June through August, rooms are rented out only as *demi-pension* (a room plus breakfast and lunch or dinner) and doubles cost between 190F and 215F. The simple, unpretentious restaurant serves a meat dish for lunch and a fish dish for dinner, and the bar has a fireplace with cozy sofas.

Besides the view, you'll find the little **chapelle Notre Dame de la Clarté** (pl. de la Chapelle) built with the local pink granite; on its grounds are the 14 stations of the cross painted by Maurice Denis (Pont-Aven school). Rumor has it that the chapel was built by a 16th-century sea captain who promised God that he would erect it if he survived a treacherous storm. During the pardon of la Clartée (August 15), a bishop preaches an outdoor mass for the Virgin Mary. The congregation leaves from the chapel to the *tertre* (knoll), which has a great view of Ploum, the Sept-Iles, and Trégastel. You'll see girls in traditional Breton Trégor costumes carrying the chapel's statue of the Virgin Mary.

LE FINISTERE

Literally meaning "the end of the earth," Finistère encompasses Brittany's westernmost point. Ties to ancient Celtic culture are strong here in Basse Bretagne (Lower Brittany); elders speak Breton, and Irish pubs replace French cafés. Best yet, the farther west you go, the friendlier the people are. From cheery, riverside villages like Pont-Aven to the bustling port towns of Roscoff and Concarneau to the secluded islands of Batz and Ouessant, this region has it all. Brest and Morlaix have good nightspots, and most of the region's hostels are excellent and inexpensive.

MORLAIX

With their town built at the end of an estuary to guard against yet another British invasion, defensive locals here used to bark "*S'ils te mordent, mords-les*" (if they bite, bite back) to anyone approaching from land or sea. At that time, you might have thought of Morlaix as Brittany's watchful Doberman. But today, with its intimate boutiques, flower-lined windowsills, and pretty homes, Morlaix looks more like a poodle that has crossed the line between "cute" and "too cute." Its saving graces are its down-to-earth locals and the large number of good-natured pubs. Every Wednesday night mid-July–mid-August, the free musical and theatrical festival, **Les Arts dans la Rue,** takes place in the center of town. Morlaix's distinctive houses cluster around rue Ange-de-Guernisac, Grande Rue, and rue du Mur. Most ornate is the **Maison de la Duchesse Anne** (33 rue du Mur), open April–September.

BASICS

The very welcoming **Office de Tourisme,** in a pavilion on place des Otages, sells the "Circuit de Venelle" walking itineraries of Morlaix (5F) and gives out free street maps. *Pl. des Otages, tel. 02–98–62–14–94. Open Mon.–Sat. 9–7, Sun. 9–noon (Mon.–Sat. 9–noon and 2–6 off-season).*

COMING AND GOING

The **TGV** from Paris (4 hrs, 356F) blasts through Morlaix eight times a day. Regular **trains** also run to Brest (35 mins, 54F), to Quimper via Landerneau (2 hrs, 98F), and to Roscoff (28 mins, 30F). **Les Cars du Kreisker** (2 rue Albert-de-Mun, tel. 02–98–69–00–93) sends three buses a day to Roscoff (1 hr, 31F). They leave from the Gare SNCF at the viaduct.

GETTING AROUND

Long, narrow Morlaix snuggles down at the bottom of a valley. A viaduct spans the two central, adjacent squares–parking lots, place Cornic and place des Otages. Slightly to the southeast lie the town hall and, continuing in a straight line, the historic town streets and place des Halles. Once you walk down the hill from the station, you won't have any problem getting around on foot. To avoid the 1-km (½-mi) climb back up, however, you might want to take the bus. Most **TIM** buses (6F) pass the information booth (tel. 02–98–88–82–82) on place Cornic and the corner of rue Gambetta and rue Carnot every half hour, though none run on Sunday.

WHERE TO SLEEP

Good, cheap hotels are rare. The **Hôtel Saint-Mélaine** (77 rue Ange-de-Guernisac, tel. 02–98–88–08–79), in front of the viaduct, has clean doubles for 150F, triples for 170F, all with hall showers. The pristine **Hôtel-Restaurant des Halles** (23 rue du Mur, tel. 02–98–88–03–86) has 14 rooms, each one with a phone and TV—a total luxury, considering that doubles are only 130F (165F with shower).

HOSTEL • Auberge de Jeunesse. It's not too far from the train station (a 20-minute walk), and it's clean and simple. The helpful owner rents beds in quintuples for 48F, sheets for 17F (HI card required). Breakfast is 19F, and large dinners run 50F (but are only served if more than 10 people show up). *3 rte. de Paris, tel. 02–98–88–13–63. From station, follow CENTRE VILLE signs down rue Gambetta, continue on rue Carnot, right on rue d'Aiguillon (rte. de Paris veers off to left). 57 beds. Reception open daily 8 AM–11 AM and 6 PM–11 PM (until midnight in summer). Curfew 11 PM. Kitchen.*

FOOD

On rue Ange de Guernisac, **Le Pizzaïolo** (No. 31, tel. 02–98–88–46–42) and **La Dolce Vita** (No. 3, tel. 02–98–63–37–67) serve pizzas and pasta in a casual atmosphere for 30F–50F. On the other side of place de Viarmes, **Crêperie Ar Bilig** (6 rue au Fil, tel. 02–98–88–50–51), closed Monday, has good 15F–30F galettes and crepes, but the best deal is the 46F menu with two galettes and a dessert crepe. There's a **market** all day Saturday in the centre ville, and a **Monoprix** on rue d'Aiguillon; tote your groceries up the pedestrian alleys along rue du Mur to the picnic-friendly park, **Square du Château.**

NEAR MORLAIX

CARANTEC

Carantec, which means "love" in Breton, has one of Brittany's most popular postcard subjects: the **Château du Taureau,** a gorgeous, barren castle-island in the middle of the Baie de Morlaix. At low tide, you can take the walkway to the **Ile Callot** to visit the island's breathtaking beaches and the château (guided tours available July–August). Carantec's **Office de Tourisme** (4 rue Pasteur, tel. 02–98–67–00–43) has a schedule of the tides. **Les Cars du Kreisker** (tel. 02–98–69–00–93) makes the 15-km (9-mi) run from Morlaix to Carantec several times a day for 20F; the bus leaves from the train station in Morlaix. There are not a lot of businesses in Carantec, but you'll find the essentials—a market, bakery, bank, and crêperie—all close to the church where the bus drops you off.

BREST

Brest—the seat of the Royal Navy for four centuries—can be summed up in one word: gray. The Germans hid an important submarine base here during World War II, until the Allied bombers, trying their hand at a famous Breton recipe, flattened it (and the city) like a crepe in 1944. In his hurry to rebuild the city, a sloppy architect destroyed the few remaining original fortifications and rebuilt the new concrete city high above the old port. After the Soviet collapse, the French navy moved most of its fleet to Toulon in the Mediterranean. Brest's port of war, once the largest in France, has now been reduced to a small fleet of nuclear submarines with the French intelligence headquarters supposedly lurking underneath the **château**. The arsenal (which can be visited only with the possession of a French passport) completed its last warship, the *Charles de Gaulle*, in 1999, and is now being seriously downsized.

To offset the working population exodus, the city administration has given Brest a face-lift. The new university has added more than 25,000 students to the city's population. Lovers of nautical history can walk all the way down to the **Port de Commerce** and the **Port de Plaisance** to see the old, reconstructed ships docked next to the transatlantic racing beasts of renowned sailors Olivier de Kersauson and Florence Artaud. You can still enjoy the unusually friendly Brestois and the **Jeudi du Port**, a free outdoor concert at the Port de Commerce (every Thursday in summer).

In 1686 three princes of Siam (now Cambodia) came to Brest on a diplomatic visit to see Louis XIV. Dressed in gold and silver, they made such an impression on the Brestois that the town's main street, la rue de Siam, was named after them.

BASICS

The **Office de Tourisme** has a good map of Brest, as well as a brochure of 25 walks outside the city. Ask about a boat ride on the 1945 schooner *Notre Dame de Rumengol*; it costs around 75F for a sail around Brest's harbor. *8 av. Georges-Clemenceau, tel. 02–98–44–24–96. Turn right on street facing train station. Open Mon.–Sat. 10–12:30 and 2–6 (July–Aug., also open Sun. 10–noon and 2–6).*

The **post office** has fax services and changes money at good rates. *Rue de Siam, off pl. du Général-Leclerc, tel. 02–98–46–51–07. Open weekdays 8:30–5.30, Sat. 9–noon.*

COMING AND GOING

TGV trains reach Brest from Paris in 4½ hours several times a day (370F). Trains also connect Brest to Morlaix (35 mins, 54F), St-Brieuc (80 mins, 120F), Rennes (2¼ hrs, 173F), and Quimper (1¼ hrs, 82F). The **train station** is on place du 19ème R.I. From the **gare routière** (tel. 02–98–44–46–73), right across from the train station, a bewildering arrangement of private bus companies serve Roscoff (1½ hrs, 46F), Quimper (1¼ hrs, 81F), the Crozon peninsula (1¼ hrs, 54F), and a host of other regional destinations. From the Port de Commerce, the Penn ar Bed **ferry company** (tel. 02–98–80–24–68) runs daily ferries to the islands of Molène (2 hrs, 162F round-trip) and Ouessant (2½ hrs, 182F round-trip). Reservations are recommended. **Vedettes Armoricaines** (tel. 02–98–44–44–04) gives daily tours of Brest's harbor (1½ hrs, 80F) and ferries people to Le Fret on the Crozon peninsula.

GETTING AROUND

To get from the train station to the central place de la Liberté, turn right up avenue Georges-Clemenceau. The city bus system is **Bibus** (tel. 02–98–80–30–30), and most bus lines radiate out from place de la Liberté, where you can pick up schedules and buy tickets (6F) at the information booth. The *lignes du soir* (evening lines) run until 11 PM.

WHERE TO SLEEP

Lodging is cheap, easy to find, and generally uninspiring.

UNDER 150F • Hôtel Bar du Musée. The rooms are a little frayed at this local hangout, but there's plenty of space. An extremely friendly couple runs the place. Singles are 110F, doubles 130F, and triples 190F. Showers are free. *1 rue du Couëdic, tel. 02–98–44–70–20. Follow rue de Siam downhill, turn left on rue du Couëdic. 12 rooms, none with bath. Closed 1st 2 wks of Aug.*

Hôtel Saint-Louis. Close to the Halles St-Louis (the fresh food market), good restaurants, and bars, this simple hotel has clean rooms with firm beds and small windows. Doubles start at 130F (160F with shower). *6 rue d'Algésiras, tel. 02–98–44–23–91. From station, take av. Georges-Clemenceau, left at pl. de la République, right on rue Algésiras. 20 rooms, some with bath.*

HOSTEL • Auberge de Jeunesse. In the middle of a huge garden a block away from the beach, this Bauhaus-style hostel has good showers, a TV, a Ping-Pong table, a bar, a billiards table, and even heaters. Try to get a bed in the cozier cottage next to the hostel; the doubles or quadruples there are the same price as in the main building (68F). Factor in a bus ticket, since the hostel is 4 km (2½ mi) from Brest's center. An HI card is required. Lunch or dinner goes for 50F; sheets are 17F. There's no curfew. *5 rue de Kerbriant, Port de Plaisance du Moulin Blanc, tel. 02–98–41–90–41, fax 02–98–41–82–66. From train station, Bus 7 (direction: Port de Plaisance) to end, turn uphill, and follow signs. 130 beds. Reception open weekdays 9–10 and 5–8, weekends 6–8 PM. Kitchen, laundry.*

CAMPING • Of Brest's two campgrounds, the unremarkable **Camping du Goulet** (Ste-Anne du Portzic, tel. 02–98–45–86–84) charges 20F per site plus 18F per person. To get here from the center of town, take Bus 7 to the Cruguel stop, walk up the hill behind you, and follow the signs. It's about a 1½-km (1-mi) walk. Or try the **Camping de St-Marc** (45 rue de Kérampéré, tel. 02–98–02–30–64), near the Moulin Blanc beach. Open all year, it costs 8F per person and 10F per site. Bus 3 will take you in the right direction.

FOOD

Cheap food is easy to come by in Brest; head up rue Jean-Jaurès and you'll be bombarded with options. If you want to do the full crepe thing (with a galette, cider, and dessert crepe), swing by **Crêperie Les Goélettes** (9 rue de la Porte, tel. 02–98–45–08–27), closed Monday, in the Recouvrance quarter. The 49F lunch menu gets you three delicious crepes, a cider, and coffee. You'll find lots of little restaurants at the bottom of rue de Siam, almost all of which have outdoor seating. A daily outdoor **market** appears on place St-Louis 8 AM–1 PM in Les Halles. There's also a **Monoprix** supermarket (49 rue de Siam).

UNDER 75F • La Scala. This spot has 15 varieties of carpaccio (thin slices of raw beef marinated in olive oil), and a 69F meal lets you select two with a plate of fries or a salad—the peppered, caper, and mozzarella versions are delicious. Pizzas start at 45F. *30 rue d'Algésiras, tel. 02–98–43–11–43.*

UNDER 100F • La Taverne du Maître Kanter. You can pick a fish or shellfish for your pot from the Maître's aquarium, except for Caroline, the huge spring lobster who has been in the aquarium since the restaurant opened. The specialty here, however, is *choucroute de la mer* (seafood sauerkraut; 95F), which combines the German and Alsacian sauerkraut with the local Breton seafood—langoustine, haddock, salmon, pollack. *15 av. Georges-Clemenceau, tel. 02–98–80–25–73.*

Le Vieux Gréement. It looks like an old wooden boat with a bar in the cockpit and a restaurant down the hatch. The service is very friendly and the fish entrées are tremendous. Try the *tournedos de lotte,* a monkfish wearing a bacon strip and bathing in cream sauce (92F). *2 rue Fautras, tel. 02–98–43–20–48. From pl. de la Liberté, take rue de Siam, right on rue de Lyon, and left on rue Fautras.*

WORTH SEEING

One of the few structures to survive the war, the restored **Château de Brest** (rue de Siam, tel. 02–98–22–12–39) now houses the unspectacular **Musée de la Marine,** where you can see remnants of Brest's maritime past. Admission is 29F; it's open Monday and Wednesday–Sunday 10–noon and 2–6. The **Tour Tanguy** (sq. Pierre-Péron, tel. 02–98–45–05–31) was built in the 14th century as a bastion to either protect or block relations between Brest's left bank and right bank. Pre–World War II models of the city, on the top floor of the tower, show the beautiful medieval *ruelles* (small streets) and a neighborhood bursting with life around the tower before the Allied bombings changed all that. Admission is free; it's open daily 10–noon and 2–7.

The crab-shape **Océanopolis** (Port de Plaisance, tel. 02–98–34–40–40), modeled on the Monterey Bay Aquarium in California, has good exhibits and films for an hour's worth of distraction. Admission is 50F; it's open June–August, daily 9:30–6; September–May, daily 9:30–5. Take Bus 7 (direction: Port de Plaisance) to the Océanopolis stop.

AFTER DARK

Brest has its fair share of Irish pubs. Next to the quartier St-Martin, where you can always find a bevy of cafés and bars, the **Dubliners** (28 rue Mathieu-Donnart, tel. 02–98–80–20–99), an Irish-Breton whiskey spot, has a winter college-crowd and Irish sailors in the summer. This pub is small, smoky, and very Irish—from the bar maids down to the music. The local Coreff beer costs 25F a pint. If you prefer your bars with a little more oxygen, try the larger **Tara Inn** (tel. 02–98–80–36–07) at the Port de Commerce. You'll find live Breton and Irish music during the weekends (some during the week in the summer), and a Caffrey's, a lighter-color Bass-like beer, costs 25F.

Arizona Café (228 rue Jean-Jaurès, tel. 02–98–46–52–67) is one of the only clubs in town open after 1 AM. Despite the live music, from reggae to rock, there's no cover, and beers are only 11F during the day, 22F at night. **Les Fauvettes** (27 rue du Conseil, tel. 02–98–44–46–47) has a collection of 600 beers from all over the world (12F–30F), plus a huge selection of whiskey (about 25F a glass). While you're experimenting with flavors, amuse yourself at the pool tables or pinball machines.

SHOPPING

The Port of Commerce has several stores devoted to the Celtic tradition. The **Comptoir Irlandais** (32 quai de la Douane, tel. 02–98–43–15–15) sells all sorts of Irish ware from sweaters and scarves in lamb's wool and Shetland to good old Irish whiskey. Farther down the street, the famous St-James sweaters (Breton navy sweaters with the British label) are sold at **Comptoir du Marin** (12 quai Douane, tel. 02–98–44–62–77).

ILE D'OUESSANT

The Ile d'Ouessant is only 20 km (12 mi) from the mainland, yet at the complete caprice of the sea. Around the lobster-claw-shape island, a strong current called the Fromveur and an unforgiving ocean floor continue to disembowel tankers, fishing boats, and recreational sailboats, while violent storms sometimes leave island residents stranded, with no access to supplies. Most visitors make Ouessant a day trip, but it's worth staying the night so you can enjoy the place in relative solitude. The irregular coastline has an austere, unadulterated beauty best captured by the morning light. At night, you can let yourself fall asleep to the sounds of the wailing sea.

Your time here is best spent hiking around the island and admiring its craggy coast, compact farmhouses, and thousands of sheep. Ouessantins raise sheep called *pré-salé* (salted meadow), so-called because of the sea-salted grass they graze. You can taste the difference in a *ragout de mouton,* a Ouessant specialty. Take a trip out to the far western point for a view of wave-torn boulders, abandoned outposts, and occasional glimpses of the island's seals and rare birds.

COMING AND GOING

Penn ar Bed (tel. 02–98–80–24–68 or 02–98–48–80–13 on Ouessant) charges 182F for a round-trip ticket from Brest. Ferries leave on this 2½-hour jaunt daily from the dock in Brest at 8:30 AM and leave from the island at 5 PM (7 PM on Sunday and in summer).

GETTING AROUND

Lampaul, the town at the island's center, is 45 minutes from the port on foot; the western end of the island is 45 minutes farther. Lampaul is easy to get around on foot, but to see the whole island, you must either take a minibus tour (60F) or rent a mountain bike (50F–80F per day), available at three identical places at the dock: **Malgorn, OuessanCycles,** and **Savina.** Before you rent a bike, though, know that the coastal trails are open to pedestrians only; find out which trails are open to bikes when you rent. The public bus runs between towns for 10F. At the entrance to town, the **Office du Tourisme** (pl. de l'Église, tel. 02–98–48–85–83) has the same maps as those available at the ferry-ticket counter in Brest.

WHERE TO SLEEP

Since the ferry only gives you six hours on the island if you're on a day trip, consider staying overnight. The hotels in Lampaul are cheap and, in summer, crowded. **Hôtel de la Duchesse Anne** (tel. 02–98–48–80–25) has rooms for 130F–160F, without shower, and the **Hôtel Roc'h Ar Mor** (tel. 02–98–48–80–19), closed January–February, has showerless doubles for 145F (160F for an ocean view). Both are centrally located in Lampaul and easy to find; just ask around if you don't see them. The **Camping Municipal** (tel. 02–98–48–84–65), open April–September, has a pleasant view and temperamental showers. A site is 10F plus 15F per person (36F if you're using one of their pre-pitched tents).

FOOD

The **Crêperie du Stang** (tel. 02–98–48–80–94), at the entrance to Lampaul, is one of the best in Brittany. Crepes and galettes are around 30F each, and their filling specialty, *galette de pomme de terre* (potato crepe), costs 36F. It's open noon–1:30 and 7–8:30. The grocery in Lampaul charges slightly steeper prices than you'll find in Brest.

OUEMAN'S LIB

On the Ile d'Ouessant you can still glimpse Brittany's traditional coastal matriarchy. Up until the mid-20th century, the Ouessantin men would, from the age of 11, hire themselves out as ship hands for voyages of two or more years. Often they would not return, and at one point three-quarters of the island's Ouessantines were widows, forced to eke out a living for themselves and their children. Today, the mayor and the police chief are women, and women traditionally work the land and even make the marriage proposals.

QUIMPER

Inhabitants of what is simultaneously a pricey tourist town and the administrative capital of the Finistère, the Quimperois are sure of one thing: They're smarter, better, and more bourgeois than the working-class Brestois. While this may or may not be true, it's certain that their hometown is prettier than concrete-bound Brest. Quimper has all the amenities of the standard Breton tourist town—a medieval town center, a soaring cathedral, and a pleasant river—and despite the busy streets that spear through centre ville, the place is eminently manageable. But let's face it: There's not much to do here, and since the hostel is a bit shabby, the high hotel prices make other Breton towns more appealing.

BASICS

The helpful staff at the **Office de Tourisme** provides free maps, makes hotel reservations for 2F, and gives tours of Quimper (30F). *7 rue de la Déesse, tel. 02–98–53–04–05. From station, turn right on av. de la Gare, follow Odet River, and look for pavilion behind the parking lot on left. Open July–Aug., Mon.–Sat. 8:30–8 (mid-June–mid-Sept., also open Sun. 9:30–12:30 and 3–6); mid-Sept.–mid-June, weekdays 9–noon and 1:30–6.*

The **post office** has poste restante and fax services; it also exchanges money. The postal code is 29000. *37 blvd. de Kerguelen, tel. 02–98–64–28–50. Open weekdays 8:30–5:30, Sat. 9–noon.*

COMING AND GOING

From the **train station** (av. de la Gare), trains leave for Lorient (40 mins, 62F), Brest (1¼ hrs, 82F), Nantes (2¾ hrs, 186F), and Paris (4½ hrs, 376F by TGV). **CAT** runs buses to Brest (1¼ hrs, 81F). **Transports Caoudal** goes to Concarneau (40 mins, 40F round-trip) and then to Pont-Aven (1 hr, 53F round-trip). Both bus companies leave from the **gare routière** (2 pl. Louis-Armand, tel. 02–98–90–88–89), next to the train station.

GETTING AROUND

The Odet River curves through Quimper; to the north lies most of the town, and to the south the odd-looking Mont Frugy pokes out. The town isn't tiny, but you shouldn't have any problem getting around on foot. **Lennez** (13 rue Aristide-Briand, tel. 02–98–90–14–81) rents regular bikes (60F a day) and mountain bikes (90F) with a passport deposit. Plan on making reservations at least a week in advance in July and August. For day trips to Pont-Aven or Concarneau, **ADA** (2 bis av. de la Gare, tel. 02–98–52–25–25) rents cars starting at 279F with 100 km (60 mi) of mobility.

WHERE TO SLEEP

Hotels are expensive in Quimper, and for the Festival de Cornouaille (*see* Festivals, *below*) in late July, rooms are booked months in advance. Unless one of them has your name on it, plan to stay elsewhere. During the summer, the city of Quimper collects an extra 2F a night per person, so don't be surprised by the extra sum tacked on to your total.

UNDER 200F • Le Celtic. The lobby sets the tone for the rest of the hotel: a bit old, but with lots of character. The spunky owners rent sunny and spotless doubles for 120F, 160F with your own shower.

Showers are free. *13 rue de Douarnenez, tel. 02–98–55–59–35. Turn right from station and follow river, then right at rue Amiral-Ronarc'h (which becomes rue de Douarnenez). 40 rooms, 11 with bath.*

Hôtel de l'Ouest. The nice Breton proprietress rents out cheerful pink- and blue-color rooms. A spiral staircase branches off into trompe l'oeil doors, which lead to small, well-lit singles (110F). The larger doubles (160F without shower; 195F with) rest behind low doorways and small corridors. In summer, reserve early because many foreign travelers flock here. *63 rue Le Déan, south of the station, tel. 02– 98–90–28–35. 14 rooms, 7 with bath.*

Hôtel Pascal. Clean but drab rooms await you at this unassuming lodging just across the street from the train station. The chipper owner also runs the adjoining restaurant. Singles are 185F, doubles 210F; both have shower. *17 av. de la Gare, tel. 02–98–90–00–81. 20 rooms, 17 with bath.*

HOSTEL • Auberge de Jeunesse. The 8- and 14-bed rooms (48F) are cramped and fill up in summer with a younger crowd that doesn't seem to mind the disheveled state. For more privacy, ask either for the two singles (56F) or for a student room (80F) in the annex. Breakfast costs 19F. *6 av. des Oiseaux, tel. 02–98–64–97–97, fax 02–98–55–38–37. From station, take Bus 1 toward pl. de Pehars to the Chaptal stop. 54 beds. Reception open 8–noon and 4–9, checkout 10 AM. No curfew. Cash only.*

CAMPING • You can set up tents in the **Camping Municipal** (tel. 02–98–55–61–09) in the forested area directly behind the youth hostel (*see* Hostel, *above*). It costs 16F per site plus 5F per tent. For a pricier but prettier stay, try **Camping L'Orangerie de Lanniron** (Château de Lanniron, tel. 02–98–90–62– 02), 2 km (1 mi) outside town. It runs 27F per person plus 48F per site.

FOOD

For daily Breton specialties, try the fancy **Grand Café de Bretagne** (18 rue du Parc, tel. 02–98–95–00– 13). They occasionally serve a heavy but delicious *kig ha farz* (79F), a rye-wheat-based Breton stew with pork. Near the cathedral, **Le Saint-Co** (20 rue du Frout, tel. 02–98–95–11–47) is a local hangout that serves a lot of red meat and a little seafood. Sample the 65F lunch and dinner menu. **Le Flamboyant** (32 quai Odet, tel. 02–98–52–94–95) has a large selection of appetizers plus *acras du morue* (fried cod dumplings; 38F) and the famous *boudins créoles* (spicy blood sausages; 29F). **Gandhi** (13 blvd. Amiral-de-Kerguélen, tel. 02–98–64–29–50) serves a copious Indian spread. For 59F, you get nan (bread), an entrée, a curry dish, and coffee. The **Pâtisserie Boule de Neige** (12 rue des Boucheries, tel. 02–98– 95–88–22) is nationally recognized as one of the best pastry shops in France. A permanent covered market, **Les Halles,** is bordered by rue St-François and rue Astor. There's also a **Monoprix** at 1 rue René-Madec.

WORTH SEEING

The vast 13th- to 15th-century **Cathédrale St-Corentin** (pl. St-Corentin) is the most impressive of its kind in Brittany. The mysteriously curved nave and beautiful stained-glass windows create a meditative aura. Across the street from the cathedral, the **Musée des Beaux-Arts** (40 pl. St-Corentin, tel. 02–98– 95–45–20) includes a fascinating series of paintings depicting traditional life in Breton villages; the 25F entrance fee will also get you into the special exhibits that pass through town. The museum is open September–June, Wednesday–Monday 10–noon and 2–6; July–August, daily 9–7.

FESTIVALS

The **Festival de Cornouaille,** a weeklong bash held between the third and fourth Sunday in July, attracts musicians and dancers from all over Europe. Although some of the action takes place indoors (with tickets costing 25F–100F), much of it happens in the streets. **Label Nocturne,** nighttime *théâtre en plein air* (outdoor theater), happens every year preceding the **Fête de la Musique** on June 21. It's usually in one of the central squares, and it doesn't cost a dime. If you don't make it to Quimper for a festival, settle for Breton music and dance performances in the park alongside St-Corentin at 9 PM on Thursday June–September; tickets are only 25F.

SHOPPING

Quimper is famous for its hand-painted faience (earthenware). The techniques were brought to Quimper by Normands in the 17th century, but the Quimperois customized them by painting typical local Breton scenes on the pottery. In 1984 American importers took over the **Faïenceries de Quimper HB Henriot** operation just southwest of the town center in Locmaria (17 rue Haute, tel. 02–98–90–09–36) and kept the pottery tradition while adding a few tourist gimmicks—it's hard to resist buying at least one bowl (45F) that has your name on it.

FESTIVAL INTERCELTIQUE IN LORIENT

The humdrum town of Lorient, which lost everything to fires and bombs during World War II, compensates for its lack of tourist attractions with a great 10-day party beginning the first week of August, during which 5,000 performers and 250,000 revelers come from all over Europe for a Celtic celebration. Call 02–97–21–24–29 or Lorient's Office de Tourisme (tel. 02–97–21–07–84) for the schedules of performances and information on tickets (30F–120F). Lorient's youth hostel (41 rue Victor-Schoelcher, tel. 02–97–37–11–65) is 3 km (2 mi) out of town.

NEAR QUIMPER

CONCARNEAU

Hordes of summertime tourists come to Concarneau to see the **Ville Close** (island fortress) and transform it into one big, tacky souvenir stand. They're missing the point: Concarneau's true character lies in its fishing industry, the epitome of Breton maritime life. Begin your education on Concarneau's fishing industry at the fantastic **Musée de la Pêche** (3 rue Vauban, tel. 02–98–97–10–20), a striking museum on boats and fishing techniques; the 30F admission fee includes access to two trawlers. It's open July–August, daily 9:30–7:30; September–June, Tuesday–Sunday 10–noon and 2–6. Next, watch the unloading of fish that takes place on the docks behind the big warehouse on quai Carnot, Sunday–Wednesday midnight–6 AM. Catch 40 winks and then return for the morning *criée* (fish auction), Monday–Thursday 7–9 AM. For an idea of what happens next, take the tour of the family-run **Conserveries Courtin** (3 rue du Moros, tel. 02–98–97–01–80), where fish soup, lobster bisque, and other goodies are prepared and canned by hand. Tours cost 8F and run Tuesday–Thursday 9–noon.

BASICS • The harried staff at the **Office de Tourisme,** conveniently located right next to the bridge to the ville close, has free maps. *Quai d'Aiguillon, tel. 02–98–97–01–44. Open July–Aug., Mon.–Sat. 9–8, Sun. 9–1 and 5–8; May, June, and Sept., Mon.–Sat. 9–12:30 and 1:45–7, Sun. 10–noon; Oct.–Apr., Mon.–Sat. 9–noon and 2–6.*

COMING AND GOING • No trains arrive in Concarneau, so you'll probably have to come by bus or by rental car (*see* Getting Around, *in* Quimper, *above*). Buses run almost every hour until 7 PM from Quimper (40 mins, 25F) and Pont-Aven (30 mins, 20F); call 02–98–90–88–89 for details. You'll be dropped off at the port, with the ville close directly in front of you; just beyond it is place Jean-Jaurès.

WHERE TO SLEEP • The cheapest hotel in town is **Hôtel Renaissance** (56 av. de la Gare, tel. 02–98–97–04–23), in the opposite direction of the ville close, with decent showerless rooms starting at 140F for your own shower). The **Auberge de Jeunesse** (pl. de la Croix, tel. 02–98–97–03–47, fax 02–98–50–87–57) has rooms for 48F, breakfast 19F, sheets 17F. To get here from the port, just walk straight beyond the ville close; as the road curves, the hostel will be on your left.

FOOD • Follow the sailors to restaurants along quai Carnot, alongside the port, where prices are low and servings generous. At **L'Escale** (19 quai Carnot, tel. 02–98–97–03–31), a three-course seafood meal costs 51F. Keep in mind that most restaurants here cater to the life of the sea voyager: They open before sunrise and are closed Sunday. There's a large **market** at place Jean-Jaurès Monday and Friday mornings, as well as a daily covered market at the same square. There's a **Stoc** supermarket near the post office at 17 quai Carnot.

PONT-AVEN

The lovely village sits astride the Aven River, descending from the Montagnes Noires to the sea and turning the town's windmills along the way; it's also surrounded by one of Brittany's most beautiful stretches of countryside. The introduction of the railroad in the 19th century put travel to Brittany in vogue, and it was here that Gauguin and other like-minded artists founded the famous Pont-Aven school. Inspired by the vibrant colors and beautiful vistas to be found here, they created *synthétisme,* a painting style characterized by broad patches of pure color and strong symbolism, in revolt against the dominant impressionist school in Paris. Today, Pont-Aven seems content to rest on its laurels. Although it is labeled a *cité des artistes,* the galleries that line its streets display paintings that lack the unifying theme and common creative energy of Gauguin's era.

Works of Pont-Aven's luminaries are displayed in the modern **Musée des Beaux-Arts** in the center of the village. The first Pont-Aven painters were American students who came here in the 1850s. The only one to gain recognition, Charles Fromuth, has some paintings on display. Though Gauguin's works are surprisingly absent, except for a few of his early zincographs, the exhibit "*Hommage à Gauguin*" is an interesting sketch of his life using various photos and quotations by those who knew him. The museum shows a good film in French paying homage to Gauguin and those under his tutelage: Maurice Denis, Émile Bernard, Émile Jordan, and Paul Sérusier. *Pl. de l'Hôtel-de-Ville, tel. 02–98–06–14–43. Admission 25F. Open Sept.–June, daily 10–12:30 and 2–6; July–Aug., daily 9:30–7:30.*

One glance at the nearby forest will make you realize why artists continue to come here. You can even visit Gauguin's inspiration for his painting "The Yellow Christ"—a wooden crucifix inside the secluded **Chapelle de Trémalo** just outside the **Bois d'Amour** woods; from the tourist office, go left and walk along the river for five minutes.

BASICS • The **Office de Tourisme** has 3F French and English brochures that provide a good history of Pont-Aven, and three walking itineraries. *5 pl. de l'Hôtel-de-Ville, tel. 02–98–06–04–70. Open 9:30–6 (hrs vary); closed Oct.–early-Nov. and Sun. Nov.–Mar.*

COMING AND GOING • **Buses** make the 20-km (12½-mi) run from Quimper (1¼ hrs, 32F) and Concarneau (30 mins, 20F) several times a day. The last buses leave early in the evening, and service is limited on Sunday.

WHERE TO SLEEP • There is never a shortage of tourists in this famous village, so it doesn't have much in the way of budget travel; the hotels range 250F–900F. Try **Les Mimosas** (22 rue du Square-Botrel, tel. 02–98–06–00–30), where prices range 295F–360F. Rooms at the less-welcoming **Les Ajoncs d'Or** (tel. 02–98–06–02–06), next to the tourist office, start at 290F. However, your best bargains can be found at the charming chambres d'hôte run by the friendly inhabitants of this town—check at the tourist office for a list of locations. At **Camping Le Spinnaker** (tel. 02–98–06–01–77), in the woods just outside Pont-Aven, sites are 29F plus 27F per person.

FOOD • The crêperies and pizzerias that surround **place de l'Hôtel-de-Ville** cater to the lazy visitor, just emerging from the tourist office. Instead, walk the few paces to **Le Moulin du Grand Poulguin** (2 quai Théodore-Botrel, tel. 02–98–06–02–67), which is just as touristy but at least provides the truly delightful experience of eating your crepe (10F–40F) on a terrace directly on the flowing waters of the Aven River in view of the footbridge. For a spot of tea with your meal, the crêperie–tea salon **Chez Candide** (8 rue des Abbés-Tanguy, no phone) serves cups for 16F and crepes for 10F–30F in a cozy, studylike atmosphere. Those of you with a sweet tooth can just fill up on the buttery Traou Mad cookies at the **Biscuiterie** (10 pl. Gauguin, tel. 02–98–06–01–94); they're baked with the local wheat of the last running windmill in Pont-Aven. There's also a **market** Tuesday mornings at place de l'Hôtel-de-Ville (the quai Botrel in the summer), just down the street from the museum.

LE MORBIHAN

From Lorient to Nantes, Brittany's breathtakingly beautiful Morbihan coast is a popular vacation spot for Europeans in the know yet somehow manages to retain its culture, history, character, and friendliness. So while everyone else heads for the Riviera, enjoy Brittany's best-kept secret: Here you'll find coastline with sand, not rock; crystal-clear water; and beaches that are free, not private. Nothing beats a long bike ride along the craggy coast in Quiberon or on Belle-Ile, with an occasional stop along the way to take in the gorgeous swaths of sand. Although the twisting streets and tottering medieval houses in port towns like Vannes and Auray are often the traditional crowd-pullers in this area, and beaches like La Baule and Carnac turn into sunny resort towns in July and August, be warned: The rest of the year you're risking cold, wind, and rain. But regardless of the temperature, Brittany's southern coast—a gulf forming an almost complete circle enclosing 40 inhabited islands—is sure to astound.

QUIBERON

The *presqu'île de Quiberon* (Quiberon peninsula) is a 15-km (9-mi) stretch of rough coastal cliffs and resort-town beaches joined to the mainland by a hair's breadth of sand. Though in many ways similar to other crowded and pricey beach towns, Quiberon also draws outdoorsy types, who bike along the spectacular coast and stay at one of the 15 campgrounds or the rustic youth hostel. With one of the most magnificent stretches of beach in all of France, Quiberon's **Côte Sauvage** becomes more spectacular near the northern point at Port Blanc; it's most picturesque near the private **Château Turpaul,** just west of Port Maria. An 18-km (11-mi) footpath follows the Côte Sauvage, while bikers can ride alongside it on boulevard de la Côte Sauvage. A word to the wise: Swimming is absolutely prohibited on this part of the peninsula, and they mean it. Every year the ferocious undertow throws some risk-takers against the rocks. Swim your heart out on the other side of the peninsula where beaches—the **Grande Plage** being the most popular—ring the coast like pearls.

BASICS

The **Office du Tourisme** has information on lodging, campsites, ferries, walking trails, and rentals of anything from Windsurfers and kayaks to airplanes. *14 rue de Verdun, tel. 02–97–50–07–84. Open Sept.–June, Mon.–Sat. 9–12:30 and 2–6:30; July–Aug., Mon.–Sat. 9–8, Sun. 10–noon and 5–8.*

COMING AND GOING

Trains only make it to Quiberon July–September, and the station opens up June 15 to give information and take reservations (tel. 08–36–35–35–35). The only town serviced by train from Quiberon is Auray (40 mins, 37F). Otherwise, **Cariane Atlantique** (tel. 02–97–47–29–64) buses run to Vannes (1¾ hrs, 52F); along with **Transports Le Bayon** (tel. 02–97–24–26–20), they also run several buses daily from Carnac (25 mins, 22F) and Auray (30 mins, 37F). Buses stop at the train station and the ferry dock at Port Maria. Service is limited in winter and on Sunday.

GETTING AROUND

In Quiberon, **Cycl'omar** (47 pl. Hoche, tel. 02–97–50–26–00) rents bikes by the day or half day. The daily price depends on the model, as well as variations on the bicycle theme: scooters (219F), regular bikes (50F), tandem bikes (130F), and pedal-powered carts (198F for three people). ISIC holders get a 10% discount. An 800F–3,500F deposit on a Visa card is required for all rentals.

WHERE TO SLEEP

Hotels in Quiberon don't come cheap, with the exception, perhaps, of the **Hôtel Au Bon Accueil** (6 quai de Houat, tel. 02–97–50–07–92). The friendly owner has simple doubles for 150F, 190F with shower. It's closed December–January. But make reservations because in July and August everything—including the campsites—is packed.

HOSTEL • Auberge de Jeunesse. This hostel has only 30 beds plus another 20 tents out back, so it's imperative that you make reservations in summer. The highly social manager, Benoît, will happily give you travel tips between organizing barbecues and making you a wonderful breakfast (cereal, juice, bread, and coffee). The kitchen is equipped with pots and dishes. Beds go for 48F, tent spaces for 38F; if you bring your own tent, make that 27F per person. Breakfast costs 19F, sheets 17F. An HI card is required to stay here. *45 rue du Roch-Priol, tel. 02–97–50–15–54. From station, turn left at Crédit Agricole, left in front of church onto rue du Port Haliguen, continue to small intersection, right on blvd. Anatole-France, left on rue du Roch-Priol. 30 beds. Reception open 8–noon and 6–8 (until 9:30 July–Aug.). Kitchen. Cash only. Closed Oct.–Apr.*

CAMPING • Of the many campgrounds, **Camping du Goviro** (blvd. du Goviro, tel. 02–97–50–13–54) is the closest to Quiberon and the only one open year-round. Unfortunately, it's often full in summer. They charge 7F per site, plus 12F per person and 7F per car; showers are 8F. **Camping du Bois d'Amour** (rue St-Clément, tel. 02–97–50–13–52) is open April–October with sites for 68F (shower included), plus 35F per person.

FOOD

Most of Quiberon's restaurants post a nearly identical 50F menu of mussels, fries, and beer. Should this be too rich for your blood, there's always **Armor Express** (tel. 02–97–30–42–26), across from the station, which serves a fishy main dish for 45F, or **Grilloramix** (51 rue de Port-Maria, tel. 02–97–30–52–

87), for grilled fish and meat menus for around 55F. A huge **market** sets up Saturday morning at place Hoche, and the **Comod** supermarket (2 rue de Verdun) will feed you in a pinch.

NEAR QUIBERON

CARNAC

Many people leave Carnac's fields of megaliths in disappointment. If you're not terribly into archaeology, they just look like a bunch of stones surrounded by an equal number of tourists. But if you surprise them in the morning or late in the evening—when all their mysterious power can concentrate itself solely on you—they *are* fairly impressive. Once you've done your sightseeing for the day, oil your body and plop down with the few thousand other travelers who populate Carnac's five beaches. **Cariane Atlantique** (tel. 02–97–47–29–64) runs buses from the town (Carnac-Ville) to the beaches (Carnac-Plage) around nine times daily for 10F, but the schedule is erratic. You might save time making the easy 15-minute walk. The entire town is a quick 25-minute bus ride (22F) from Quiberon.

The largest **menhirs** (single upright stones) in Carnac top 13 ft, but most are much more modest. The majority stand in long rows called *alignements,* and those at Le Ménec and Kermario—about a 15-minute walk north of town—are the most impressive. Unfortunately, all the stones are now fenced off to protect them. You can still get a good look from the viewing platforms, such as the Archeoscope at the west end of route des Alignements. Most of the *dolmens* (two menhirs supporting a slab) lie a half-hour walk farther north. The **Musée de la Préhistoire** presents a detailed introduction to humanity's prehistory; ask for the English explanation. *10 pl. de la Chapelle, tel. 02–97–52–22–04. Admission 30F. Open Sept.–June, Wed.–Mon. 10–noon and 2–5; July–Aug., daily 10–6.*

Turn left out of the museum at place de la Chapelle, and take rue du Tumulus up to the **Tumulus St-Michel,** a burial mound of the chief of an ancient hierarchical society. He was buried with jewelry, servants, and his favorite pets. *Admission 8F. Open Easter–Sept., daily 10–noon and 2–5.*

BASICS • Pick up useful maps of the region at the **Office de Tourisme,** near the beaches in Carnac-Plage. Or, check out the **tourist office** in Carnac-Ville. *Carnac-Plage: 74 av. des Druides, tel. 02–97–52–13–52; open weekdays 9:30–5(hrs vary); Apr.–mid-June, Sept., and Oct., closed Mon. Carnac-Ville: pl. de l'Église, tel. 02–97–52–13–52, near menhirs; open Apr.–Sept., daily 9–6; Sept.–June, closed Sun.*

WHERE TO SLEEP • Hotel prices are astronomical, but if you're set on staying here, **La Frégate** (14 allée des Alignements, tel. 02–97–52–97–90) is probably your best bet April–September; its cheapest doubles start at 180F. The secluded and woodsy **Camping de Rosnual** (chemin de Rosnual, tel. 02–97–52–14–57), open Easter–October, charges 32F per site plus 18F per person and 12F per car. Best of all, it lies right next to some awesome ancient stones.

FOOD • For some of the best crepes in all of Brittany, swing by the long-established, family-run **Crêperie Chez Marie** (3 pl. de l'Église, tel. 02–97–52–07–93), which serves galettes and crepes (10F–50F) in a tavernlike environment. Carnac's **market** takes place in front of the museum Wednesday and Sunday.

BELLE-ILE-EN-MER

A visit to Belle-Ile can only be hedonistic. With no history to master and no native cultures to appreciate, you'll have to spend your time enjoying the diversity of the sandy white beaches, the wild coast, and the flat, occasionally forested interior. Restaurants and hotels tend to cater to upper-class weekenders from the mainland, but there's a great youth hostel, tons of camping, and plenty of supermarkets.

BASICS

The **Office de Tourisme,** next to the dock in the town of Le Palais, sells maps and the informative *Guide Touristique* in French only. The staff can help you find a place to stay—help you'll desperately need if you arrive without reservations. *Quai Bonnelle, tel. 02–97–31–81–93. Open mid-Sept.–Mar., Mon.–Sat. 9–12:30 and 2–6; Apr.–mid-Sept., Mon.–Sat. 9–6:30, Sun. 9:30–1.*

COMING AND GOING

The **Compagnie Morbihannaise et Nantaise de Navigation** (tel. 02–97–31–80–01) runs several daily ferries (hourly July–August) from Quiberon's Gare Maritime to Belle-Ile's Le Palais (40 mins, 105F round-trip). Mid-April to mid-September, they also run a few ferries from Quiberon to the town of Sauzon

(25 mins) for the same price. And July and August only, ferries make the 1½-hour run to Sauzon from Lorient for 105F. Reservations are recommended in summer.

GETTING AROUND

Belle-Ile's biggest town is the tourist-inundated **Le Palais,** in the center of the landward side. Farther northwest lies the smaller harbor town of **Sauzon.** If you're not up for the 6-km (4-mi) walk from Le Palais to Sauzon, **Les Cars Verts** (with information desks in both maritime stations) runs several buses a day between the ports for 14F. It also arranges car rental on the island and charge 355F a day for an old 2CV (you must have had your license for at least two years). For reservations and information, call 02–97–31–81–88. Otherwise, Belle-Ile has a reputation for easy hitchhiking, and several places rent bikes for around 50F per day (80F–100F for mountain bikes); try **Reversade** (14 rue de l'Église, Le Palais, tel. 02–97–31–84–19). To add a little carbon monoxide to the island, rent a scooter at **Au Bonheur des Dames** (quai Jacques-Leblanc, Le Palais, tel. 02–97–31–80–52) for 200F a day.

WHERE TO SLEEP

The cheapest hotels on the island start at 175F a night; ask the tourist office for a list. If you're stuck, the tourist office also has a list of locals who rent out rooms.

HOSTEL • Auberge de Jeunesse. This hostel puts grungy backpackers under a spell with its fully equipped kitchen, tropical bar, grassy volleyball court, and immaculate rooms. Bunk beds in doubles cost 48F, sheets 17F, breakfast 19F; other meals are 50F. There's no lockout or curfew. If you're staying more than one night, reserve in advance. *Haute-Boulogne, tel. 02–97–31–81–33. From Le Palais dock, follow signs to La Citadelle parking lot, then take tiny road at opposite end of museum and watch for* AUBERGE *signs. 94 beds. Reception open 8–noon and 6–8. Kitchen. Cash only. Closed Oct.*

CAMPING • Eleven inexpensive campgrounds dot the island, though most are on the northern coast. Hedge-sheltered **Les Glacis** (tel. 02–97–31–41–76), along the route to the youth hostel, is far from pretty but is closest to the Le Palais port. Its reception is open Monday–Saturday 9–11 and 4:30–6, Sunday 9–11:30. A site is 25F plus 16F per person; it's closed October–mid-April. Other sites mostly cluster around Sauzon. Closest to a beach is **Camping des Grands Sables** (tel. 02–97–31–84–46), where sites are 9F plus 15F per person. It's closed September–June.

FOOD

A handful of crêperies populate Le Palais and Sauzon. In Le Palais, **La Chaloupe** (8 av. Carnot, tel. 02–97–31–88–27) and the regional **Traou Mad Crêperie** (rue Williaumez, tel. 02–97–31–84–84) are pleasant; in Sauzon, **Crêperie des Embruns** (quai Joseph-Nadon, tel. 02–97–31–64–78) is also good. Both have crepes for 16F–40F. There's a small, daily **market** and small supermarkets in Le Palais's place de République; Kervilahouen (near the southern coast) also has a supermarket.

WORTH SEEING

Northwest of Sauzon, the craggy **Pointe des Poulains** overlooks the stormy bay; you'll also find two beaches here, one relatively secluded, the other great for swimming. Two kilometers (1 mi) southeast of the point are a few menhirs, cutely named Jean et Jeanne (characters from a locally concocted love story). The gorgeous **Plage de Donnant** to the west, with fine sand and gentle waves, will blow you away. A grotto lurks at **Pointe du Talut,** and the coast from there to **Locmaria** shelters several more protected beaches. Just north of Locmaria, the 2-km (1-mi) **Grands Sables** beach attracts swimmers, surfers, sneaky snorkels, and sand sloths.

Vauban, the celebrated 17th-century military architect, left fortifications all over Belle-Ile, the most prominent being the starfish-shape **Citadelle**; it'll be the first thing you see when you reach Le Palais. You can explore the innumerable chambers and tunnels of this massive fort and later stumble through an exhaustive exhibit on Belle-Ile. *Near port, tel. 02–97–31–84–17. Admission 30F. Open Apr.–Oct., daily 9:30–6, Nov.–Mar., daily 9:30–noon and 2–5.*

OUTDOOR ACTIVITIES

An 80-km (50-mi) footpath winds all the way around the island's coast, past tortured cliffs and hidden sandy coves. Hiking the entire path would require about five days. Less committed hikers should look through their *Guide Touristique,* which proposes several 1½- to 2½-hour walks. More practical is taking a bike along the oceanside roads. You can cover the whole island in a day if you're *hyper sportif.* Rent scuba gear from **Atmos'air** in Le Palais (1 rte. de Bangor, tel. 02–97–31–55–55). Expect to pay 140F a day for a wet suit and mask; air tanks cost another 160F for two dives.

VANNES

At the northern edge of the Golfe du Morbihan, Vannes serves as the most popular launching point for the gulf's spectacular islands. **Ile-aux-Moines,** otherwise known as "the pearl of the gulf," and **Ile d'Arz** are the best known of these tiny but popular islands. Though it draws tourists in droves to its wonderful vieille ville (old town), Vannes remains relatively untainted. There are a few museums and an aquarium here—as well as fascinating ramparts left from the ancient château and wall that once encircled the town—but the true appeal of Vannes is walking through the winding pedestrian streets, shopping at the lively outdoor market, or sipping coffee outdoors near the sedate harbor.

BASICS

The **Office de Tourisme** changes money in summer for a stiff 5% commission. *1 rue Thiers, tel. 02–97–47–24–34. From station, take av. Victor-Hugo, turn right on rue Joseph-Le Brix, left on rue Thiers. Open July–Aug., Mon.–Sat. 9–7, Sun. 10–1 and 3–7; Sept.–June, Mon.–Sat. 9–noon and 2–6.*

The **post office** (pl. de la République) changes money at excellent rates and provides poste restante service; it's open weekdays 8:30–5, Saturday 9–noon.

Laverie Primus (5 av. Victor-Hugo) and **Laverie Libre Service** (8 rue du 116e-R.I.) both charge 20F per wash, 2F per five minutes of dryer time.

COMING AND GOING

Trains speed their way from Vannes to Nantes (1½ hrs, 120F via Redon), Rennes (65 mins, 108F), Quimper (1¼ hrs, 93F), and Paris via Rennes (3½ hrs, 324F by TGV) almost every hour. The Vannes train station has an information desk (tel. 02–97–42–50–50).

TIM, a cooperative representing 12 different bus companies, occupies the **gare routière** (pl. de la Gare, tel. 02–97–01–22–10). It offers 20% student discounts, so don't forget to show your ID when you board. The two most useful bus companies are **Cariane Atlantique** (4 rue du 116e-R.I., tel. 02–97–47–29–64) at the intersection of boulevard de la Paix and rue Victor-Hugo; and **Transports Le Bayon** in Auray (4 rue du Cimetière, tel. 02–97–24–26–20). Both run buses to Auray (50 mins, 21F), Quiberon (2 hrs, 52F), and Nantes (3 hrs, 96F).

Boats to the Ile-aux-Moines leave Port-Blanc, 14 km (9 mi) southwest of Vannes, every 30 minutes 7 AM–8 PM (20F round-trip); call 02–97–26–31–45 for details. To get to Port-Blanc from Vannes, you must rely on Cariane Atlantique (*see above*). Boats to the neighboring Ile d'Arz leave from Vannes's Port-Conleau just about every hour (30F round-trip); call **Le Didroux** (tel. 02–97–66–92–06) for details. For guided tours of the gulf, **Compagnie des Iles** (tel. 02–97–46–18–19) and **NAVIX** (tel. 02–97–46–60–00) both run boats from Vannes harbor; tours start at 70F.

WHERE TO SLEEP

If you like to be at the heart of the action, you'll find 14 small but impeccable rooms in the waterfront **Marina Hôtel** (4 pl. Gambetta, tel. 02–97–47–22–81), but you won't find Room 13—the Bretons are very superstitious. The rooms facing the port have a great view only tainted by the hustle and bustle of the lively bars below, which go on until 1:30 AM. The doubles at of the hotel are less noisy and the same price (180F–300F). An even quieter option is the **Hôtel Le Bretagne** (36 rue du Mené, tel. 02–97–47–20–21), where half of the rooms have views of the ramparts. The bright and comfortable doubles with shower are 170F–180F, and the one small room without shower goes for 120F.

HOSTELS • Foyer des Jeunes Travailleuses. In spite of its name, the hostel accepts male guests. It's located in a beautiful old stone building in the center of town. For 75F (85F if you're over 25), you'll get a clean, single room. The atmosphere is mellow, and the curfew is a relatively generous 1 AM. Breakfast is 12F, sheets 25F. *14 av. Victor-Hugo, tel. 02–97–54–33–13. 75 beds. Curfew 1 AM. Cash only.*

Foyer Mixte des Jeunes Travailleurs. Farther from town, but a lot more fun, is this ultramodern hostel. You'll find a bar, a Ping-Pong table, and cooking facilities on every floor. A single room with sheets and a tiny balcony is 95F regardless of your age; breakfast is included. There's no curfew, and they don't kick you out until 2 PM the next day. *2 rue Paul-Signac, tel. 02–97–63–47–36. From bridge, take Bus 1 (direction: 3 Rois) to unmarked Bonard stop. From station, make immediate right, then right on av. Président Wilson, left on av. Edgar-Degas to rue Paul Signac (15 mins). 95 rooms. Reception open weekdays 9–1 and 2–10, weekend afternoons only, checkout 2 PM. Lockout 8 PM. Kitchen, laundry. Cash only.*

CAMPING • The nearest campground is the **Camping de Conleau** (tel. 02–97–63–13–88), closed October–March, a site situated 3 km (2 mi) south of Vannes with a view of the sea. It's 45F for a tent and car, plus 20F per person. To avoid the hour-long walk, take Bus 5 from the station (direction: Limur) to République; then transfer to Bus 2 (direction: Conleau) and get off at the "Camping" stop.

FOOD

Ignore the all-flash, no-substance *menus rapides* of the port eateries and cross the Porte St-Vincent to **Le Sinagot** (5 rue St-Vincent, tel. 02–97–54–19–17), an unpretentious restaurant where the reception is all smiles and the menu of the day (68F) has quality seafood. A typical menu starts with a fish soup or herring salad followed by grilled salmon with *oseille* (sorrel). Buy your groceries at the **Monoprix** supermarket on place Joseph-Le Brix, unless you're here on Wednesday and Saturday mornings, when the outdoor **market** is an event in itself. Extending from place de la République to place Lucien-Laroche is a wide variety of things to buy: paella, fresh vegetables, flowers, used books, and kitchen appliances, all sold among street performers and musicians.

UNDER 50F • **Cave St-Gwénhaël.** Excellent crepes (12F–36F) are served in this half-timbered historical house (it contains an 18th-century Curiosity Fountain) across from the cathedral. The dark wheat of the galettes is produced locally in the moulin du Pavillon in the Côte d'Armor. You must try the Chouchen aperitif (14F), a honey liqueur that once made people raving mad because of the untreated bee's poison. *23 rue St-Gwénhaël, tel. 02–97–47–47–94. Cash only. Closed Sun.*

UNDER 75F • **La Paëlla.** Hidden away on a small side street, this simple restaurant serves sizable quantities of its title dish; a small serving of paella is 48F, a larger serving 60F; the copious prawn, fish, and shellfish version runs 75F. Meals are served in the comfy, unpretentious dining room or out on the terrace. *7 rue Brizeux, off rue du Mené, no phone. Closed Sun. and Mon.*

WORTH SEEING

Many of Vannes's tourist spots are concentrated in the vieille ville, hemmed in by rue Thiers on the west and a long stretch of ramparts, towers, and gates to the east and south. The **ramparts** crumble prettily under ivy blankets, and each gateway has a character all its own. Vannes's favorite church is **Cathédrale St-Pierre,** a boxy structure with enough interesting details on the facade and inside to amuse for a while. *22 rue des Chanoines. Open June 22–Sept. 12, daily 10:30–12:30 and 1:30–5:30. Mass weekdays 9 AM and 6:30 PM, Sat. 6:30 PM, Sun. 9:30 AM, 11 AM, and 6 PM.*

The Cohue, a spacious passageway facing the cathedral, was designed as a 13th-century marketplace and courthouse. The area now houses the **Musée de la Cohue,** with a fine Delacroix canvas, some good Breton portraits, and displays on the history of the region. *15 pl. St-Pierre, tel. 02–97–47–35–86. Admission 25F. Open June–Sept., daily 10–noon and 2–6; Oct.–May, Mon. and Wed.–Sat. 10–noon and 2–6.*

If you head down to the **Parc du Golfe,** a 15-minute walk from the center of town, the **Aquarium de Vannes** on rue Daniel-Gilard (tel. 02–97–40–67–40) is actually worth the hefty 50F admission. The museum itself is shaped like a huge shellfish, and it contains many ocean critters in tanks that resemble their natural habitats. *Open June–Aug., daily 9–7; Sept.–May, daily 9–noon and 1:30–6:30.*

FESTIVALS

Over the first week of July, Vannes puts on the **Fêtes Historiques** (tel. 02–97–42–71–20), featuring all sorts of medieval madness. Musicians, fire-eaters, and storytellers provide free entertainment, capped by a 60F *Souper Royale* (Royal Supper) on the last night. At the end of July, jazz musicians from around the world converge on Vannes for the four-day **Festival de Jazz** (tel. 02–97–47–24–34); impromptu street performances are free, but tickets for big names cost 110F–160F.

AFTER DARK

Celtic sympathies here are evident in the startling number of pubs. One example is the **Swansea** (3 rue du Four, tel. 02–97–42–74–92), which features 12F beer, darts, and a young crowd. On summer nights, you'll find both young and old at the cafés by the port; the stone walls of **L'Océan** (4 pl. Gambetta, tel. 02–97–47–22–81) keep the bar nice and cool during the day, perfect for savoring the beer of the month (13F). Vannes takes its jazz seriously with several good jazz clubs throughout town, but a favorite hangout is **Le Contretemps** (22 rue Hoche, tel. 02–97–42–40–11). While the musical influence is mainly American, the joint retains a distinctly French flavor.

NANTES

The novelist Stendhal once remarked of 19th-century Nantes, "I hadn't taken 20 steps before I recognized a great city." Since then, the inland port town sliced in half by the Loire, with industrial cranes on one side and aristocratic châteaux along the northern Erdre River, has been trying hard to live up to its reputation. Modernization has put some obstacles in the way; the river that flowed around the wealthy Ile Feydeau has been filled in and replaced with a rushing torrent of traffic that cuts through the heart of the city. Still, Nantes is more than the sum of its traffic jams: Its 15th-century **château** (*see* Worth Seeing, *below*) is in relatively good shape; the **Bouffay** quarter has great Halloween, Mardi Gras, and other spontaneous festivities (Les Années Trente finds everyone decked in wonderful 1930s costumes); and there are a few fine museums. You'll also find countless gardens and flower-bedecked plazas, often hemmed in by sex shops and panhandlers. The Loire River flows along the southern edge of the vieille ville, making Nantes officially part of the Loire region; historically, though, it belongs to Brittany. In town you'll see many references to Anne de Bretagne—the last independent ruler of Brittany—who married the region away to French kings Charles VIII and then Louis XII.

Although the traffic grates and temperatures can be broiling in the summer, Nantes's attractions make up for its weaknesses. It's on the way to the beaches and cliffs of Brittany's Morbihan coast, and the bustling student nightlife in this city of 250,000 is a friendlier and cheaper alternative to the elite scene in Paris and other large cities. The first week in July, things liven up with international musical performances (starting at 30F) during the **Festival International d'Été** (tel. 02–40–08–01–00).

BASICS

BUREAU DE CHANGE

Monday–Saturday, go to **Au Change Graslin,** on place Graslin in the vieille ville. *17 rue Jean-Jacques Rousseau, tel. 02–40–69–24–64. Open weekdays 9–12:30 and 2–6, Sat. 10–noon and 2–4:45.*

LAUNDRY

Laverie Libre Service has two locations: right across from place du Commerce and near the cathedral. You can wash a load for 20F–30F; soap is 2F, and the dryers are 2F for five minutes. *3 allée Duguay-Trouin and 56 rue du Maréchal-Joffre. Both open daily 7 AM–8:30 PM.*

MAIL

Send your mail or faxes from the central post office, right next to that unmistakable skyscraper, the Tour Bretagne. The clerks here can help you with international phone calls and give you the best exchange rates in town. The postal code for Nantes is 44000. *Pl. Bretagne, tel. 02–40–12–60–00. Open weekdays 8:30–5:30, Sat. 9–noon.*

MEDICAL AID

For 24-hour medical assistance, call **SAMU** (tel. 02–40–08–37–77). The **Pharmacie Nantaise du Pilori** (1 pl. du Pilori, tel. 02–40–47–48–35) is open until 9 PM. For pharmacies with later hours, call the police station (tel. 02–40–37–21–21).

VISITOR INFORMATION

Harried but helpful receptionists at the **Office de Tourisme** have an exhaustive brochure on Nantes and a serviceable map. An office upstairs makes reservations for *gîtes ruraux,* houses in the countryside you can rent by the week. They also give two-hour walking tours of the city (in English, upon request) for 35F. *Pl. du Commerce, tel. 02–40–20–60–00. Open Mon.–Sat. 9–7.*

COMING AND GOING

BY TRAIN

Nantes's **train station** (27 blvd. Stalingrad) is across the street from the Jardin des Plantes and a 10-minute walk from the vieille ville. Several times a day, trains leave for Paris (2¼ hrs, 291F by TGV),

Sights ●

Cathédrale
St-Pierre, **1**

Château des Ducs
de Bretagne, **6**

Jardin des
Plantes, **4**

Musée des
Beaux-Arts, **2**

Musée d'Histoire
Naturelle, **7**

Musée Jules Verne
and Planetarium, **11**

Lodging ○

Auberge de
Jeunesse
"La Manu", **3**

Camping du Petit
Port, **12**

Hôtel
de l'Océan, **10**

Hôtel St-Daniel, **9**

Hôtel St-Patrick, **8**

Hôtel Surcouf, **5**

Rennes (1¾ hrs, 132F), Bordeaux (4 hrs, 237F), and Angers (45 mins, 81F by TGV). The station has an exchange booth and phones that take coins as well as télécartes, but no bathrooms.

BY BUS

No buses connect Nantes to Paris, but **Cariane Atlantique Otages** (5 allée Duquesne, tel. 02–40–20–46–99), off cours des 50-Otages, runs four daily buses from Nantes to Rennes (2 hrs, 98F), as well as to other nearby towns.

GETTING AROUND

Think of Nantes as a semicircle snuggled up against the north bank of the Loire. One long highway runs roughly parallel to the riverbank. Its name changes constantly, but east–west along the center of the city it goes by cours Franklin-Roosevelt, cours John-Kennedy, and boulevard de Stalingrad. To make things more confusing, these grand boulevards are often divided up into smaller sections, called *allées*. The train station is just south of boulevard de Stalingrad near rue Henri-IV. All the major sights and most of the cheap lodgings are clustered within the vieille ville (usually called centre ville on maps). If you're really in a hurry, call **Allô Taxis** (tel. 02–40–69–22–22).

BY TRAM AND BUS

Nantes's public transport system, **TAN** (tel. 02–51–81–77–00), consists of trams and buses. The idiot-proof tram has two lines, one running east–west along the big boulevard, the other running north–south along cours des 50-Otages. The ticket stand at the Commerce tram stop has free maps of the bus and tram systems. One ticket, good for an hour on both tram and bus, is 8F; 5 tickets are 32F; 10 are 58F. If you plan to move around a lot, consider the 21F *ticket journalier* (one-day pass). And don't forget to stamp (*composter*) your ticket when you get on.

WHERE TO SLEEP

Nantes has lots of cheap hotels around the centre ville and a few student residences just outside town.

UNDER 175F • Hôtel de l'Océan. The burgundy, green, and brown decor is a strain on the eyes, but when the lights go out it's the firm, cozy mattresses that count. Comfortable doubles with showers (150F on the street side, 160F on the courtyard side) will send you off into dreamland. *11 rue du Maréchal-de Lattre-de Tassigny, tel. 02–40–69–73–51. From station, Tram 1 to Médiatèques stop. 24 rooms, all with shower.*

Hôtel St-Daniel. The '50s French decor is not to everyone's liking, but the St-Daniel more than makes up for it in comfort. It may be the best hotel in Nantes for your money. The rooms are large, the beds are firm, the lighting is worthy of a theater stage, and the very clean bathrooms all come equipped with a wall blow-dryer. Doubles with shower are 170F. Three rooms are really basic (read: they don't even have a private WC). Parking costs 25F, and television 20F. *4 rue du Bouffay, tel. 02–40–47–41–25, fax 02–51–72–03–99. From station, Tram 1 to Bouffay, or turn left on blvd. de Stalingrad to pl. du Bouffay (rue du Bouffay is in NW corner). 19 rooms, 15 with shower. Closed Sun. afternoon.*

Hôtel St-Patrick. Next to the Église St-Nicolas, this modest hotel, run by a friendly owner, has large rooms with balconies and high ceilings. The simple furniture is a bit tacky, but the location of the hotel couldn't be more central. Doubles with showers are 140F–160F (120F without). Reception is on the third floor. *7 rue St-Nicolas, next to pl. Royale, tel. 02–40–48–48–80. 25 rooms, 16 with shower.*

UNDER 200F • Hôtel Surcouf. The Surcouf is tastefully decorated and the quiet street lies a stone's throw from the château and cathedral. Doubles are 125F (with an 12F shower down the hall), 170F (with shower), and 190F (with bath). Register at their hotel across the street (No. 38). *41 rue Richebourg, tel. 02–40–74–17–25. From station, turn left on blvd. de Stalingrad, right on rue Henri-IV, right on rue Richebourg. 38 rooms, 13 with bath.*

Gilles de Rais accompanied Joan of Arc on her military campaigns; after her death, he was charged with devil worship and the murder and sodomy of 144 children. He was excommunicated, hanged, and burned next to where the château is now.

HOSTEL

Auberge de Jeunesse "La Manu." During the school year, this building goes by the name Cité Universitaire Internationale "La Manu" (tel. 02–40–74–61–86) and accepts travelers with hostel cards (when there's space) for 70F. In summer, it becomes the city's youth hostel. Modern and antiseptic, La Manu is a 15-minute walk from the train station and 30 minutes from most sights. Singles are 100F, and doubles and quadruples go for 87F; both require an HI card. *2 pl. de la Manu, tel. 02–40–29–29–20; call after 10 AM. From train station, turn right on blvd. de Stalingrad, left on rue de Manille; or Tram 1 to Manu stop. 165 beds. Reception closes at 10 PM. Lockout 10–5. Cash only. Closed Sat.*

CAMPING

Camping du Petit-Port. A 45-minute walk from the station, this campground is a sight for city-weary eyes, featuring pleasant spots right on the edge of a forest, as well as hot water and showers. A site is 28F plus 20F per person. *21 blvd. du Petit-Port, tel. 02–40–74–47–94. From pl. Commerce, Tram 2 to Morrhonnière stop.*

FOOD

Thanks to a wholesome mix of students and working folk, a good gamut of restaurants has flourished in Nantes. You can choose from the bow-tied waiters of the 1895 brasserie **La Cigale** (4 pl. Graslin, tel. 02–51–84–94–94), who serve a fancy 75F three-course menu until 12:30 AM, to **La Ciboulette** (9 rue St-Pierre, tel. 02–40–47–88–71), which serves a copious 45F lunch menu (cheese and dessert included), a four-course, 75F dinner, which starts with a *kir pétillant*, and 10F glasses of wine, as you sit elbow to elbow with a local Nantais crowd. Otherwise, a stroll though the Bouffay quarter should spark your appetite, especially when the weather is nice and diners are served on the outdoor terraces. Shop for groceries at the small place du Bouffay **market** (as the Nantais have done since the 16th century), open Tuesday–Sunday 8–1. For something meatier, try the supermarket in the basement of the Nouvelles Galeries building on rue du Moulin, or the barely cheaper **Monoprix** (2 rue du Calvaire).

UNDER 50F • Chez L'Huître. Jean-Luc, the young owner, sells (as you might guess) oysters of various persuasions. Try the *panaché* (68F), for a dozen oysters from all over the Atlantic Coast: Prat-arcoum, Marenne, Morbihan, and Vendée. Otherwise *l'apéri-huîtres,* a half dozen oysters served with a glass of Muscadet (29F), works as a great cocktail before lunch or dinner. One word of warning: During Mardi Gras, Jean-Luc dresses like a butcher and only sells meat products. *5 rue des Petites-Écuries, tel. 02–51–82–02–02. Closed Sun.*

La Crêperie du Bouffay. This is a crêperie that understands what a crepe should be: cheap, filling, and delicious. The 39F menu gets you a plain galette, a ham and cheese galette, and a dessert crepe with jam to stuff you silly. *15 rue des Petites-Écuries, tel. 02–40–89–10–14.*

La Crêperie Jaune. For 30 years, the woman who runs the place has been making the famous Pavais Nantais (45F), a huge crepe made of ingredients she won't reveal. *1 rue des Échevins (in the Bouffay quarter), tel. 02–40–47–15–71. Closed Sun.*

UNDER 100F • Le Guinguois. This traditional restaurant serves wholesome French food (the kind that sticks to your ribs) amid the constant buzz of the talkative Nantais post-yuppie set. The lunch menus start at 65F; try the wonderful onion tart and great fish entrées. If you're willing to splurge, order a homemade foie gras appetizer (82F). *3 bis rue Santeuil, tel. 02–40–73–36–49. Closed Sun., Mon., and 3 wks in Aug.*

Le Petit Bacchus. The black-and-white erotic pictures in the dining room are a foreplay to the delicious 59F, three-course lunch menu (85F at dinner)—an appetizer, a *suggestion du jour* like fish with fennel, and dessert, all delicately prepared. *5 rue Beauregard, tel. 02–40–47–50–46. Closed Sun.*

WORTH SEEING

Except for the Musée Jules Verne and nearby planetarium (*see below*), most sights in Nantes are no more than a 10-minute walk from each other. The cheapest way to see Nantes's museums is with the 32F **Carte d'acces à 4 musées** (four-museum access card), which actually admits you to six museums: the Musée des Beaux-Arts (*see below*), the Musée Jules Verne, the ho-hum **Musée d'Histoire Naturelle** (Museum of Natural History, 12 rue Voltaire, tel. 02–40–99–26–20), and three museums in the Château des Ducs de Bretagne (*see below*). If you're really hard up, visit the museums on Sunday, when they're free. Then you can plop down on a bench (the temptingly thick carpet of grass is forbidden) in the beautiful 18-acre **Jardin des Plantes** (open daily 8–8), across from the train station.

CHATEAU DES DUCS DE BRETAGNE

Not an ornate pleasure palace like the Loire Valley châteaux, this 15th-century, heavily fortified castle was built by the dukes of Brittany to emphasize their independence from French sovereigns. Today, the alignment of French flags on top of the ramparts is perhaps a reminder of the failed ambition of the poor Breton *ducs*; it was, after all, in this château that Anne de Bretagne married the French king Louis XII, permanently linking Brittany to France. The 20F guided tour of the castle is dull and offered in French only (except July–August), but on the tour you'll have access to several rooms barred to the nonpaying throngs. The castle's **Musée des Arts Populaires** (Museum of Popular Arts) contains Breton artifacts from the 17th century. *Entrance on rue des États, tel. 02–40–41–56–56. Admission 20F. Château and museum open Sept.–June, Wed.–Mon. 10–noon and 2–6; July–Aug., daily 10–7.*

CATHEDRALE ST-PIERRE

Yet another cathedral that took 400 years to build, this one, started in 1434, has suffered its share of abuse. It had its windows blown out by a gunpowder explosion in 1800, was bombed by the Allies in 1944, and had its roof burned off in 1972. Despite all the ruckus, the renovated interior is stunning (the stained glass is best in the morning). *Pl. St-Pierre. Open daily 8:30–7. Mass Sat. at 7 PM, Sun. at 9 AM.*

MUSEE DES BEAUX-ARTS

Located in a spacious, bright building, the Museum of Fine Arts displays everything from medieval to modern art—Monet, Kandinsky, Metzinger, and Chagall, to drop a few names. Be sure to check out the huge Rubens in the men's bathroom. *10 rue Georges-Clemenceau, tel. 02–40–41–65–65. Admission 20F. Open Wed.–Thurs., Sat., and Mon. 10–6, Fri. 10–9, Sun. 11–6.*

MUSEE JULES VERNE AND PLANETARIUM

Way off to the southwest of the centre ville along the route of Bus 21, the Musée Jules Verne is heavy on pictures and light on actual facts about Verne, who spent his life in Nantes. The nearby planetarium has astronomy shows weekdays at 10:30, 2:15, and 3:45, Sunday at 3 and 4:30. *Museum: 3 rue de l'Hermitage, tel. 02–40–69–72–52. Admission 10F. Planetarium: 8 rue des Acadiens, tel. 02–40–73–99–23. Admission 25F.*

VIEILLE VILLE

The Old Town contains several dozen medieval buildings—these days housing restaurants and bars—that lie scattered north of cours Franklin-Roosevelt, roughly between the château and place Graslin. Mingled with these medieval remnants are buildings from Nantes's rich 18th-century past, especially around place Graslin and rue Crébillon; don't miss the ornate **Passage Pommeraye** off rue Crébillon. The 18th-century houses only get taller and more intricate on the **Ile Feydeau,** just south of cours Franklin-Roosevelt, where wealthy slave and sugar-beet traders built houses that now tilt on the Ile's uncertain terrain. Even though it's no longer truly an island, the Ile retains its special character and is more dignified than the surrounding city.

AFTER DARK

The tourist office has a useful brochure called *Nantes: Des Jours et Des Nuits,* a monthly theater and music schedule. **Au Puits d'Argent** (5 rue Santeuil, tel. 02–40–69–36–89), or "bar des amoureux" as students call it, is also a favorite spot for reporters of the nearby *Presse Océan.* Just off rue Crébillon, this bar-café has a wishing-well and an owner who looks like Elton John. Cram yourself into one of the many nooks and miniature grottoes, sit down on the cowhide seats, and place your beer (15F) near an antique sewing machine. A mellow crowd fills the dark corners of the **Le Tie-Break** (1 rue des Petites-Écuries, tel. 02–40–47–77–00), with live jazz Monday–Saturday and no cover. If you want to dance, fork over 60F–80F to **L'Évasion** (3 rue de l'Emery, tel. 02–40–47–99–84); it draws a mixed-age crowd. The **American Dance Café** (10 pl. de la Bourse, tel. 02–40–08–06–45), hosts regular theme nights. Come sip beer amid Jimmy Dean cutouts and pinball machines daily until 5 AM.

NORMANDY

UPDATED BY SIMON HEWITT

I f you're in search of peaceful nooks and crannies, you'll find them in the region's cliff-lined coast, apple orchards, and green countryside—places where a crowd is a Norman farmer and a couple of cows. Normandy's medieval city of Rouen and the popular seaside resorts along the Côte Fleurie swarm with tourists in the summer. You can also try your luck at the casinos of Cabourg or Trouville or attempt to beat the galloping tides at Mont-St-Michel in a breakneck race.

Descendants of the Vikings, the Normans have merged pretty seamlessly with the rest of the French. Maybe they felt guilty after terrorizing and pillaging the country, or maybe they realized that the weather in Normandy was much warmer than in Scandinavia—either way, the Normans are free of the nationalistic struggles that characterize the Bretons, the Basques, and the Corsicans. Not that Normandy hasn't seen its share of fights. William the Bastard, duke of Normandy, got restless in 1066, invaded England, and captured the English crown from King Harold in the Battle of Hastings. The Brits may still call him a bastard, but in France they changed his name to William the Conqueror. Ironically enough, the first town liberated by the British during the D-day invasion was the town of Bayeux, where William's conquest of England is immortalized on the eponymous tapestry.

The region is perhaps best remembered for its role during World War II. Because of the strategic value of its numerous ports, the Germans seized Normandy and built what seemed like an impenetrable Atlantic Wall. After a disastrous invasion at Dieppe in 1942, the Allies gave up on capturing port towns and focused on the cliffs and uneven terrain around Arromanches. On June 6, 1944, Allied planes bombed Normandy (killing Germans and civilians alike) to allow thousands of troops to storm the beaches. The 2½-month Battle of Normandy that followed ended the war, but it turned most of the region into rubble. Although some villages like Honfleur managed to escape unmarred, other towns, like Le Havre, have never fully recovered.

BASICS

GETTING AROUND

The **SNCF** is not your best transportation friend in Normandy; you're best off with a car, your feet, or a bike. Trains connect all the major towns, but they often require inconvenient, time-consuming transfers—train times may vary depending on how long you have to wait for a connection. In Haute-Normandie (Upper Normandy), many routes require a transfer at Rouen. In Basse-Normandie (Lower Normandy), trains are more direct, but you may have to transfer at Caen or Lison. The handy *Guides Régional des Transports*—one for Basse-Normandie and one for Haute-Normandie—are available in train stations or tourist offices and list hours and routes for regional trains, buses, and ferries. Public transportation runs less frequently on weekends and rarely on Sunday.

BY BUS • Four main bus systems cover the towns not served by trains. **CNA** (Compagnie Normande Autobus; tel. 02–35–52–92–29) runs around Upper Normandy from Rouen to the towns along the Côte d'Albâtre, including Le Havre. **Autos-Cars Gris** (tel. 02–35–28–19–88) runs buses from Fécamp to Le Havre, stopping in Etretat along the way. **Bus Verts du Calvados** (tel. 02–31–44–77–44) covers the coast from Honfleur to Caen and Bayeux, as well as the special D-day Circuit 44. Bus Verts has the **Carte Liberté,** which allows you seven consecutive days of unlimited travel on its lines (except on express buses and to Le Havre) for 190F. **STN** buses (tel. 02–33–77–44–88) travel through the Cotentin Peninsula.

BY CAR • **Hertz** is the cheapest chain, with offices in Caen (34 pl. de la Gare, tel. 02–31–84–64–50), Le Havre (1 av. du Général-Archinard, tel. 02–35–19–01–19), and Rouen (130 rue Jeanne-d'Arc, tel. 02–35–70–70–71). They charge 350F–400F for the first day for the smallest car, and you must be 21.

BY FERRY • **Brittany Ferries** (tel. 02–31–36–36–00) sends ferries from Ouistreham, just outside Caen, to Portsmouth, England (6 hrs, 280F), and from Cherbourg to Poole (4¼ hrs, 260F). **P&O European Ferries** (tel. 08–03–01–30–13) run from Le Havre to Portsmouth (5½ hrs, 270F). **Irish Ferries** (tel. 02–33–23–44–44) run from Cherbourg to Rosslare in Ireland (17 hrs, 420F–600F). **Hoverspeed** (tel. 08–00–90–17–77) sends catamarans from Dieppe to Newhaven in summer (2 hrs, 270F). Make sure to call for exact times and prices; they vary greatly according to the season, and there are cheap deals for three- and five-day returns.

FOOD

Normandy is known for its food—especially rich, creamy, carnivorous dishes like salt-meadow lamb, pork in cider, and duck. From the ubiquitous cows of Normandy come Camembert, Livarot, and Pont l'Évêque cheeses, all named after towns in the region; any dish *à la Normande* is served with a cream sauce. Luckily, the Normans have a solution for all this heavy eating: the fiery Calvados brandy. It can be made from pears as well as from apples. Simply take a swig between courses to burn a *trou normand* (Norman hole) in your stomach and make room for more food. In coastal towns, there is no escaping seafood, especially mussels, shrimp, and fish stew. *Galettes* (buckwheat crepes stuffed with vegetables, cheese, or meat) are the bread and butter, so to speak, of budget travelers in Normandy.

ROUEN

Once the capital of the duchy of Normandy, Rouen overflows with monuments, medieval streets, and churches. It's also a busy industrial port city of about a half-million people. Writers Pierre Corneille and Gustave Flaubert lived here (in different centuries, of course), and Claude Monet took a liking to the Cathédrale de Notre-Dame and did a series of paintings of it in various kinds of light. Jeanne d'Arc once posed the question, "Oh Rouen, art thou then my final resting place?" It was. Held captive in the still-standing Tour Jeanne d'Arc at the age of 19, she was condemned as a heretic and then burned at the stake on May 30, 1431. A cross now marks the spot in the center of place du Vieux-Marché.

Rouen's recent history is even more somber. Heavy bombing by the Germans destroyed countless lives and buildings, and anything that escaped obliteration by the Germans still had to endure Allied raids. However, parts of the medieval town survived (even though the Germans set fire to the whole thing), and the restored half-timbered houses and rebuilt cathedral make Rouen less morose than its history would imply. The city is big enough that you can escape all the kitschy cafés, souvenir shops, and miniature sightseeing trains. There's plenty of affordable lodging and dining, as well as an energetic bar scene.

Baie de la Seine

Cherbourg
N13
Valognes
Cotentin
D2
Pointe du Hoc
UTAH OMAHA GOLD JUNO SWORD
Arromanches
D514
Colleville-sur-Mer
Longues-sur-Mer
D516
La Haye-du-Puits
D903
Isigny-sur-Mer
Passage de la Déroute
Peninsula
Lison
Bayeux
N13
Benouville
Îles Chausey
D900
St-Lô
D572
Caen
Coutances
D972
N174
N175
D212
Orne
Laize
Entrée de la Déroute
D971
D999
Ferrière-Harang
D577
Thury-Harcourt
D562
Villedieu-les-Poêles
Clécy
Pont d'Ouilly
Granville
N175
Vire
Conde-sur-Noireau
D973
Rabodanges
Cancale
Putanges-Pont-Ecrépin
Mont-St-Michel
Avranches
D19
Dol-de-Bretagne
N175
Domfront
Bagnoles-de-l'Orne
Pontorson
N176
D916
D155
Antrain
D998
D177
D23
N176
Combourg
Pré-en-P
D795
Fougères
N12
Mayenne
D35

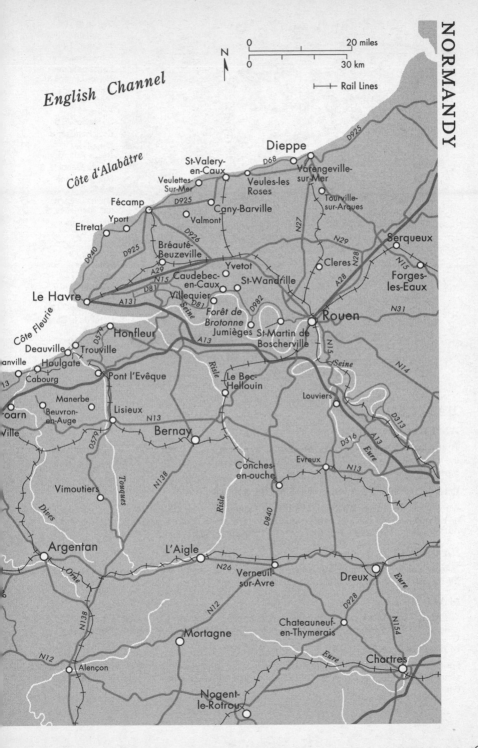

English Channel

Côte d'Alabâtre

0   20 miles
0   30 km

⊢—+— Rail Lines

N

Dieppe

D925

St-Valery-en-Caux

Veulettes-Sur-Mer

Veules-les-Roses

Varengeville-sur-Mer

D68

Fécamp

D925

Cany-Barville

Tourville-sur-Arques

Yport

Valmont

Etretat

D926

N27

N29

Serqueux

D940

D925

Bréauté-Beuzeville

A29

N15

Yvetot

Cleres

N28

Forges-les-Eaux

N13

Caudebec-en-Caux

St-Wandrille

A28

Le Havre

D81

Villequier

D81

Seine

Forêt de Brotonne

D982

Rouen

N31

A131

St-Martin de Boscherville

Côte Fleurie

D579

Honfleur

Jumièges

A13

N15

Seine

N14

Deauville

Trouville

Risle

Le Bec-Hellouin

Louviers

anville

Houlgate

Pont l'Evêque

D213

13

Cabourg

Manerbe

Lisieux

oarn

Beuvron-en-Auge

N13

Ville

D579

Bernay

Conches-en-ouche

Evreux

D316

A13

Eure

N13

Vimoutiers

Touques

N138

Risle

D840

Dives

Argentan

L'Aigle

Verneuil-sur-Avre

Dreux

Eure

N26

Orne

N12

Chateauneuf-en-Thymerais

D028

N154

N138

Mortagne

Eure

N12

Alençon

Chartres

Nogent-le-Rotrou

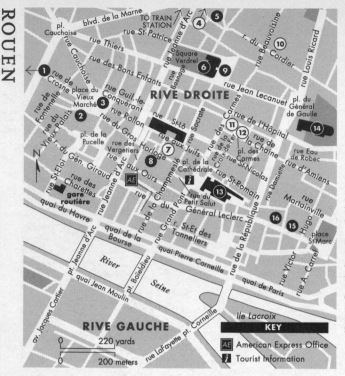

Sights ●
Abbatiale
St-Ouen, **14**
Aître St-Maclou, **15**
Cathédrale de
Notre-Dame, **13**
Eglise Jeanne
d'Arc, **3**
Eglise
St-Maclou, **16**
Gros Horloge, **8**
Musée des
Beaux-Arts, **6**
Musée Flaubert, **1**
Musée Jeanne
d'Arc, **2**
Musée le Secq
des Tournelles, **9**
Tour Jeanne
d'Arc, **5**

Lodging ○
Hôtel des
Arcades, **11**
Hôtel Bristol, **7**
Hôtel
des Carmes, **12**
Hôtel de la Gare, **4**
Hôtel du
Sphynx, **10**

KEY
AE American Express Office
i Tourist Information

BASICS

AMERICAN EXPRESS

The office changes money, holds mail, and takes care of lost or stolen cards. There is also an office in the tourist office open July–September. *1–3 pl. Jacques-Le Lieur, tel. 02–32–08–19–20. Open weekdays 8:45–noon and 1:30–6.*

DISCOUNT TRAVEL AGENCIES

Across from the station, **Wasteels** (111 bis rue Jeanne-d'Arc, tel. 02–35–71–06–77) has special rates on car rentals (592F gets you a small Renault for three days). **Forum Voyages** (72 rue Jeanne-d'Arc, tel. 02–35–98–32–59) deals mostly with organized tours but also has good airfare deals.

LAUNDRY

Take your dirty duds to **Lavomatic,** where a wash costs 20F, a spin in the dryer 10F. *56 rue Cauchoise, tel. 02–35–70–57–58.*

MAIL

The **central post office** holds poste restante, changes money, and sells traveler's checks. The postal code is 76000. *45 rue Jeanne-d'Arc, tel. 02–35–08–73–73. Open weekdays 8–7, Sat. 8–noon.*

MEDICAL AID

For information on late-night pharmacies, check in the local paper, *Paris-Normandie,* or call **Pharmaciens de Garde** (tel. 02–32–81–25–00) after 7 PM. For 24-hour medical assistance, call **SOS Médecins** (tel. 02–35–03–03–30).

VISITOR INFORMATION

The English-speaking staff at the beautiful **Office de Tourisme,** facing the cathedral, dispenses free maps and brochures on Rouen and books rooms for 15F. *25 pl. de la Cathédrale, tel. 02–32–08–32–40. Open May–Sept., Mon.–Sat. 9–7, Sun. 9:30–12:30 and 2:30–6; Oct.–Apr., Mon.–Sat. 9–6:30, Sun. 10–1.*

The **Centre Information Jeunesse** has information on everything from AIDS to sports, travel, and upcoming musical events. If you don't speak French, this won't be too helpful; if you do, it's invaluable. *84 rue Beauvoisine, tel. 02–35–98–38–75. Open weekdays 10:30–6:30.*

COMING AND GOING

BY TRAIN

Open 24 hours a day, the **gare SNCF** is at the northern end of rue Jeanne-d'Arc, a 12-minute walk from the center of town. Trains travel to Paris's Gare St-Lazare (65 mins, 123F), Caen (2 hrs, 114F), Le Havre (45 mins, 91F), and Dieppe (45 mins, 75F). *Pl. Bernard-Tissot, tel. 08–36–35–35–35). Information office open Mon.–Sat. 8–7.*

BY BUS

Compagnie Normande d'Autobus (CNA) runs several buses a day from Rouen to Dieppe (2 hrs, 68F) and Le Havre (3 hrs, 85F), but the train is faster. CNA is best used for areas not served by train, like the Route des Abbayes. Buses leave from the **gare routière** (bus station) just north of the Seine. *25 rue des Charrettes, tel. 02–35–52–92–29. Information office open weekdays 8–6:30, Sat. 8–11:30.*

GETTING AROUND

Like Paris, Rouen is divided by the Seine. The Rive Droite (Right Bank) is where everything happens; the Rive Gauche (Left Bank) is mostly an industrial and residential area. Three main streets run roughly north–south to the river from the Rive Droite: **Rue Jeanne-d'Arc** passes by the train station; rue Beauvoisine turns into the bustling **rue des Carmes**; and **rue de la République** runs by the Hôtel de Ville and Église St-Ouen. **Rue du Gros Horloge** runs east–west between place du Vieux Marché and the Cathédrale de Notre-Dame, intersecting rue Jeanne-d'Arc. Rouen's *vieille ville* (old town) is fairly compact, and many of the pint-size streets are for pedestrians only. In a pinch, call **Radio-Taxis** (67 rue Jean-Lecanuet, tel. 02–35–88–50–50) any time of day or night.

BY BUS AND METRO

Rouen's **métrobus** system allows you to use one ticket, good for an hour, on both the métro and the city bus system. Single tickets cost 7.50F; a ticket worth 10 trips is 56F. Buy tickets on the platform and validate them inside the métro car. If you speak French, **Allô Le Bus** (tel. 02–35–52–52–52) can explain how to get around. Anglophones might have an easier time at the information booth in the train station, or at the office (open Monday–Saturday 7–7) next to the gare routière; get maps at the tourist office.

BY BIKE

Rouen Cycles rents 10-speeds for 75F a day and 100F for the weekend. *VTTs* (mountain bikes) are 125F a day and 200F for the weekend. Both require a 2,000F deposit. Call ahead if you want a bike on a summer weekend. *45 rue St-Éloi, tel. 02–35–71–34–30. Open Tues.–Sat. 8:30–noon and 2:30–7.*

WHERE TO SLEEP

Except for at the youth hostel, prices on the Rive Gauche are no cheaper than on the Rive Droite, so you might as well stay in the middle of the action. The **Hôtel des Arcades** (52 rue des Carmes, tel. 02–35–70–10–30) is in a great location with doubles for 160F (210F with shower).

UNDER 125F • Hôtel du Sphynx. This convenient hotel is about 10 minutes from the station. The attractive and incredibly spacious rooms have, if you're lucky, a view of the courtyard. Singles and doubles both go for 100F–110F; a third bed is 60F extra. Showers cost 10F. *130 rue Beauvoisine, tel. 02–35–71–35–86. 14 rooms, none with bath. Cash only.*

UNDER 175F • Hôtel de la Gare. Though next to the train station, this hotel is still fairly quiet. The owner provides discounts for longer stays. Doubles with firm mattresses are 140F, 180F with shower. *3 bis rue Maladrerie, tel. 02–35–71–57–90. 16 rooms.*

UNDER 250F • Hôtel Bristol. This venerable, timber-framed mansion, opposite the medieval law courts, has nine modernized rooms with bath or shower, starting at 220F. *45 rue aux Juifs, tel. 02–35–71–54–21. 9 rooms.*

Hôtel des Carmes. On a lively square midway between the cathedral and the Abbatiale St-Ouen, this cheerful hotel has brightly painted rooms (all with TV) starting at 210F for a double with shower, 250F with bath. *33 pl. des Carmes, tel. 02–35–71–92–31. 18 rooms.*

FOOD

Place St-Marc hosts an open-air **market** all day Tuesday, Friday, and Saturday, and until 1 PM on Sunday. There's also one at place du Vieux-Marché Wednesday–Saturday and on Sunday morning. There's always the **Monoprix** supermarket (73 rue du Gros-Horloge, tel. 02–35–70–25–39) or **Flunch** (60 rue des Carmes, tel. 02–35–71–81–81), which serves quick sandwiches and snacks.

UNDER 50F • Natural. Just off place de la Cathédrale, this vegetarian health-food store opens up its restaurant for lunch. The menu changes daily, but there's usually a wholesome plate of vegetables and grains for around 40F. *Tartes* (quichelike things) with salad run 43F. Service is leisurely and the atmosphere relaxed. *3 rue du Petit-Salut, tel. 02–35–98–15–74. Closed Sun. and Mon. No dinner.*

UNDER 75F • Brasserie Paul. The service is a bit cold, but the good food served until 11 PM on a terrace facing the cathedral makes up for the waiters' attitude. For 60F you get creamy ray with capers or a slightly sweet steak tartare; wash it all down with a bottle of Duboeuf (50F)—red like the raw beef. *1 pl. de la Cathédrale, tel. 02–35–71–86–07.*

Le P'tit Bec. This place just south of the Abbatiale St-Ouen looks like a cross between a bistro and a candy store. The menu is heavy on the beef and cheese. The 73F three-course menu is served with gratin, made with veggies or potatoes topped with cheese and baked in the oven. *182 rue Eau de Robec, tel. 02–35–07–63–33. Closed Sun. No dinner Mon.–Thurs. or Sun.*

UNDER 100F • Au Temps des Cerises. The name means "at the time of the cherries," but this restaurant has nothing to do with cherries and everything to do with cheese. Filling dishes such as veal with Camembert are 63F, and creamy cheese fondues for two are 72F–86F per person. Lunch menus are 60F, dinner menus 90F. The young crowd sometimes forms a line out the door. *4–6 rue Basnage, off rue Jean-Lecanuet, tel. 02–35–89–98–00. Closed Sun.*

WORTH SEEING

It's practically impossible to see every one of Rouen's museums and churches in less than a week, and you should also leave yourself time to walk through the medieval streets. **Rue St-Romain,** north of the cathedral, and **rue Damiette,** near Église St-Maclou, have well-preserved half-timbered houses, several of which contain interesting antiques shops. The most important sights lie close together between **place du Vieux-Marché** and **St-Maclou** and can be covered on a walking tour of the old town; a potential route is marked on the tourist office's free map of the city. Most museums and churches are closed Tuesday.

ABBATIALE ST-OUEN

This church is all that remains of an ancient abbey founded by Benedictine monks back in the Carolingian era. Even if you think you've seen enough of Gothic churches, check this one out—it's particularly magnificent. Because the church is no longer in use, the interior is almost completely empty, making it seem even more spacious. A little stream runs through the abbey grounds, which have been converted into a picnic-perfect grassy park. *Pl. du Général-de-Gaulle. Open Jan. 16–Mar. 14 and Nov. 1–Dec. 14, Wed. and weekends 10–12:30 and 2–4:30; Mar. 15–Oct. 31, Wed.–Mon. 10–12:30 and 2–6.*

ALL ABOUT JEANNE D'ARC

Mementos of the heroic woman—often very tacky—are all over the city. The three following honest-to-goodness sights, though only marginally less tacky, at least provide a brief history review. First, there's the **Tour Jeanne d'Arc** (rue du Donjon, tel. 02–35–98–16–21), where Joan was tortured (and where a few hundred years later French Resistance fighters were tortured by the Gestapo). You can visit the gruesome tower, as well as its small museum, Monday and Wednesday–Sunday 10–noon and 2–5; admission is 10F. The architectural logic behind the odd **Église Jeanne d'Arc** (pl. du Vieux-Marché, tel. 02–35–88–02–70), completed in 1979, is highly unclear. The roof's shape was designed to evoke the flames of Joan's funeral pyre, yet to actually see it this way requires phenomenal imagination. Outside, a cross marks the spot where Joan went up in smoke. Finally, directly across the street and hidden amidst the tourist shops is the **Musée Jeanne d'Arc** (29 pl. du Vieux-Marché, tel. 02–35–88–02–70). Here, housed in a 15th-century crypt, Joan's entire story will be recounted to you, *very* slowly, via wax figures and a lame audio commentary translated into four languages. Admission is 25F. The museum is open May–August, daily 10–6:30; September–April, daily 10–noon and 2–6:30.

CATHÉDRALE DE NOTRE-DAME

The Cathédrale de Notre-Dame was built and rebuilt between the 12th and 16th centuries. The simple, Romanesque **Tour St-Romain** on the left dates from 1145; the **Tour du Beurre** (Butter Tower) on the right was built in the 15th century in a Flamboyant Gothic style, with intricate tracery. The cast-iron steeple, the tallest in France, was added in the 19th century. In the courtyard to the left is the **Portail des Libraires** (Booksellers' Portal), illustrating scenes from the Resurrection; the dead struggle to open their coffins below, while God straightens out the hierarchy of saints and sinners above. The cathedral caught fire twice during the war; Hitler ordered his troops to rescue it the first time, and the *Rouennais* saved it from Allied bombs the second time. *Pl. de la Cathédrale. Admission free, guided tours 15F. Open daily 8–7 (until 6 on Sun.). Mass Tues.–Fri. at 10 AM, Sun. at 8 AM, 9 AM, 10:15 AM, and noon.*

ÉGLISE AND ÂITRE ST-MACLOU

The **Église St-Maclou** (pl. Barthélémy) is relatively plain but has beautifully carved wooden doors from 1552 and a magnificent altar. Classical concerts are performed here during summer; tickets start at around 40F (call 02–35–70–84–90 for more information). The fountain on the side of the church features peeing angels—a heavenly urinal of sorts. And behind the church is the **Aître St-Maclou** (186 rue Martainville), a 16th-century half-timbered building that originally served as a charnel house.

Rouen commemorates Joan of Arc during a festival thrown from late May to the beginning of July, with fireworks, concerts, medieval fairs, and outdoor theater.

GROS HORLOGE

Ninety-nine percent of the postcards sold in Rouen feature this 14th-century gilded clock, so why not peer up at the real thing? The tower is on rue du Gros-Horloge, so overrun by tourists and shops it's tough to see the early Renaissance houses that drew tourists here in the first place.

MUSÉE DES BEAUX-ARTS

This beautiful museum, situated in a pleasant park, takes you through six decades of fine art. One room is dedicated solely to a piece by Géricault, which only takes form when a mirrored cylinder is placed upon it. You can also see a Delacroix self-portrait; a small gallery devoted to Impressionists, with works by Monet and Renoir; and a large number of paintings by Jacques-Émile Blanche. *Square Verdel, tel. 02–35–71–28–40, 02–35–52–00–62 for guided tours. Admission 20F. Open Wed.–Mon. 10–6.*

OTHER MUSEUMS

The **Musée Flaubert et de l'Histoire de la Médécine** (Hôtel-Dieu, 51 rue de Lécat, tel. 02–35–15–59–95) marks Flaubert's birthplace and houses the novelist's papers and belongings; it also contains freaky medical equipment that belonged to his father. It's open Tuesday–Saturday 10–noon and 2–6; admission is free. Finally, there's the **Musée Le Secq des Tournelles** (2 rue Jacques-Villon, tel. 02–35–71–28–40), where intricate wrought-iron objects such as keys, coffeemakers, and weapons are on display in a Gothic church. It's open Wednesday–Monday 10–1 and 2–6, and admission is 15F.

AFTER DARK

Things don't really get going until 10 or 11. **Le Big Ben Pub** (30 rue des Vergetiers, tel. 02–35–88–44–50), closed Sunday, is a low-key bar with a terrace below the Gros Horloge; they have whiskey- (Adelscott) and apple- (Grimbergen) flavored beers for 17F. A bit cheesy, but packed day and night, **Café Leffe** (36 pl. des Carmes, tel. 02–35–71–93–30) dominates the medieval quarter with its outdoor tables that spill across the square. The Belgian Leffe, a sweetish lager, costs 16F. For a more authentically local pub, try the **Taverne St-Amand** (11 rue St-Amand, tel. 02–35–88–51–34), in an old half-timbered house with an outdoor terrace. It has a huge list of Belgian, Irish, and German beers on tap for 20F–35F a pint. Friendly waiters serve expensive wines by the glass (16F and up) at **Le Petit Zinc** (20 pl. du Vieux-Marché, tel. 02–35–89–39–69). The only gay bar in town is **Le Kox** (138 rue Beauvoisine, tel. 02–35–07–71–97); it has beers starting at 20F.

NEAR ROUEN

ROUTE DES ABBAYES

From Rouen to Le Havre, the Seine River winds back and forth through forests and green countryside along the **Route des Abbayes,** a passage that includes six abbeys, two priories, three châteaux, and six museums. To help you, the tourist offices in Rouen and Le Havre have the free guide, *Abbayes, Châteaux, Musées,* which details points of interest along the route. Although most people choose to come by car or bike so they can penetrate the forest and see lots of small towns, it's feasible to take the bus to the more popular spots. Listed below are some of the route's highlights, all of which are served by CNA buses. There are fewer buses on Saturday, and only three run on Sunday.

COMING AND GOING

CNA runs two different bus routes here: One goes from Rouen to Caudebec-en-Caux (often referred to as Caudebec), the other from Caudebec to Le Havre. Take the bus from Rouen to St-Martin de Boscherville (30 mins, 25F), then on to Jumièges (30 mins, 29F), St-Wandrille (20 mins, 18F), Caudebec-en-Caux (5 mins, 9F), and Villequier (5 mins, 9F). You can continue on to Le Havre (1½ hrs, 57F). If you're going back to Rouen (52F), you have to return through Caudebec-en-Caux. There are about 11 buses on weekdays, but only three hit Jumièges, so you have to plan accordingly. For more information, call the bus station in Rouen (*see* Coming and Going, *above*) or in Le Havre (tel. 02–35–26–67–23).

Since bus fares add up quickly, consider renting a car. You can also rent good mountain bikes for 80F a day (60F per half day) from the tourist office in Caudebec (*see below*).

WHERE TO SLEEP AND EAT

Hotel prices in most small towns are outrageous, but campgrounds are plentiful. For information, call the **Maison du Parc** (tel. 02–35–37–23–16), or stop by the tourist office in Caudebec. Nearby is the campground **Barre-Y-Va** (rte. de Villequier, tel. 02–35–96–26–38); sites are 11F plus 14F per person and 10F for a car; it's closed October–March. There is one youth hostel at **Yvetot** (4 rue de la Brique-terie, tel. 02–35–95–37–01), north of Caudebec; it has only eight beds (42F; 63F without an HI card). At the same location there's a campground; it's closed November–March. Food prices are exorbitant here; bring a picnic or fall prey to overpriced restaurants. There's a **market** in Caudebec on Saturday morning; Yvetot has one Wednesday and Saturday mornings.

EXPLORING THE ROUTE DES ABBAYES

ST-MARTIN DE BOSCHERVILLE • One of the first towns you reach on your trip along the Seine is St-Martin de Boscherville, home to the **Abbaye St-Georges.** Although the abbey was founded in 1050 by William the (future) Conqueror's grand chamberlain, the existing buildings date from the 12th century, when the abbey was rebuilt by Benedictine monks. The simple, serene Romanesque church survives with its two towers and pyramidal lantern tower intact. Peep into the chapter house next door to see fine carved statues and columns. *1 pl. de l'Abbaye, tel. 02–35–32–10–82. Admission 25F. Open Apr.–Sept., daily 9–noon and 2–7; Oct.–Mar., Thurs.–Tues. 9–noon and 2:30–5.*

ABBAYE DE JUMIÈGES • Farther down the road are the remains of the Abbaye de Jumièges, one of the most influential centers of religion and learning in the Middle Ages. Founded in 654, it was destroyed in the 9th century by Viking invaders and rebuilt around 925 under the reign of Guillaume Longue Epée (William Long Sword). In the 19th century, a merchant bought the land and began to tear down the buildings to sell the stones; the abbey has since been partially restored. The Jumièges ruins are perhaps the most impressive of the Seine group, with wild grass creeping into the roofless buildings. *Tel. 02–35–37–24–02. Admission 32F. Open Nov.–Mar., daily 9:30–1 and 2:30–5:30; Apr.–mid-June and mid-Sept.–Oct., daily 9:30–12:30 and 2:30–5:30; mid-June–mid-Sept., daily 9–7.*

ST-WANDRILLE • Originally founded in the 8th century, the abbey in the small town of St-Wandrille has some remaining 13th- and 14th-century church ruins. More interesting are the 13th- and 15th-century cloisters, which you can see during the guided tour led by a monk. The order continues to worship here, singing Gregorian chants during worship services that are open to the public. *Tel. 02–35–96–23–11. Admission 25F, guided tours 10F extra. Tours Mon.–Sat. at 3 and 4, Sun. at 11:30, 3, and 4. Mass Mon.–Sat. at 9:30 AM, Sun. at 10 AM.*

CAUDEBEC-EN-CAUX • Caudebec-en-Caux, halfway between Rouen and Le Havre, is a peaceful resort town on the Seine that still draws plenty of visitors. Make sure to visit the 15th-century **Église Notre-Dame,** which Henri IV called the most beautiful church in his kingdom; a perfect opportunity to take a long look is during the free organ concerts held in July and August at 4 PM on Sunday. For information, stop by the **tourist office** (Quai Guilbaud, 76490 Caudebec-en-Caux, tel. 02–35–96–20–65).

VILLEQUIER • Sure, there's a château in Villequier, but visit the **Musée Victor Hugo,** the writer's lovely mansion, which houses photographs and sketches by Hugo. It was in this town that Hugo's daughter and son-in-law drowned in a boating accident, an event that devastated the writer. *Tel. 02–35–56–78–31. Admission 20F. Open Wed.–Mon. 10–12:30 and 2–5 (until 6:30 May–Sept.).*

COTE D'ALBATRE

The scenic Côte d'Albâtre (Alabaster Coast) is named for the white cliffs that stretch between Dieppe and Le Havre. In the 19th century, these bathing resorts attracted writers and artists like Maupassant, Proust, Monet, and Braque. Perhaps they were inspired by the scenery—the small coastal towns of Dieppe, Fécamp, and Etretat have châteaux, distilleries, and unusual rock formations—but they probably didn't spend much time sunbathing in their Speedos; the coast is known for its *galets*—large pebbles that cover the beaches.

Enjoy festivals? Dieppe's got quite a variety, from the International Dog Expo (mid-July) to the Kite Flying Festival (mid-September) to the Herring Fair (mid-November).

DIEPPE

Although Dieppe was a simple fishing and trading port for centuries, its huge chalk cliffs and pebbly beaches couldn't remain unexploited forever. The town is known as the first seaside resort to be discovered by the British, and it seems none of them ever left. Each summer the place fills with weekenders who have come to sunbathe on the beach, shop on the lively Grande Rue, or have a go at the card tables in the casino. To enjoy Dieppe's hidden charm, wake up early, watch the countless fishermen unload their morning's catch in the dense fog at the port, and get a glimpse of what Dieppe used to be like. Besides having one of the few remaining hostels on Normandy's coast, Dieppe's hotels and restaurants are reasonable. July and August are the town's busiest months, but unlike other coastal towns, it doesn't shut down too much in the winter.

BASICS

The **Office de Tourisme** at the port has a lot of information but makes you beg for it. Cut to the chase and ask for the free English brochure "A Taste of Dieppe"—it tells you everything you need to know. *Quai du Carénage, tel. 02–35–84–11–77. Open Apr.–Sept., Mon.–Sat. 9–1 and 2–8, Sun. 10–1 and 3–6; Oct.–Mar., Mon.–Sat. 9–noon and 2–6.*

COMING AND GOING

No matter where you're coming from, you'll have to go though Rouen to catch a train to Dieppe. The **train station** (blvd. Clemenceau, tel. 08–36–35–35–35) runs 10 daily trains to Rouen (45 mins, 75F), Paris via Rouen (2¼ hrs, 145F), and Le Havre via Rouen or Malaunay (2½ hrs, 95F). The station is open daily 5:30 AM–9:30 PM. The **bus station** (tel. 02–35–84–21–97) next to the train depot sends one bus a day to Rouen (1½ hrs, 68F) and three daily to Fécamp (2½ hrs, 73F) via St-Valéry. **Hoverspeed** (tel. 08–00–90–17–77) makes at least two round-trips to Newhaven daily in summer from the *gare maritime* (harbor); its catamaran takes two hours and costs 270F.

GETTING AROUND

Dieppe is bordered to the east by the port and quai Duquesne, to the north by the beach and the parallel boulevards Maréchal-Foch and de Verdun. **Grande Rue** is two blocks below boulevard de Verdun and turns into quai Henri-IV, lining the north side of the port. To reach town from the station, walk straight on quai Duquesne. You can reach the main sights in town on foot, but buses can save you an uphill haul to the hostel. The **Société des Transports Urbains Dieppois** (tel. 02–35–84–49–49) distributes bus schedules at 1 place Ventabren, off quai Duquesne. Tickets cost 6F (38F for 10). Buses run until 8 PM.

WHERE TO SLEEP

Dieppe has lots of little bar-hotels, but many either rent only by the week or are full of Parisians with reservations; be sure to book ahead in July and August. If the hotels below are filled, try **La Pêcherie** (3 rue du Mortier-d'Or, tel. 02–35–82–04–62), closed Monday, near Église St-Jacques, which has basic doubles for 120F (200F with full bath and TV). To camp, take Bus 2 to the Vasarelery stop (direction: Val Druel) to the well-equipped **Camping Vitamin** (chemin des Vertus, tel. 02–35–82–11–11), open year-round. Facilities include nice showers, a washer and dryer, and a swimming pool. Sites cost 44F plus 22F per person.

UNDER 175F • L'Entracte. This bar-hotel only has six rooms, but where else in the world will 95F get you such a fine sea view? For two beds with a view, you'll pay 120F. Doubles with a shower are 155F. Unfortunately, there's no common shower for the showerless. *39 rue du Commandant-Fayolle, 1 block behind casino, tel. 02–35–84–26–45. 6 rooms, 3 with bath. Cash only.*

UNDER 200F • Hôtel de la Jetée. Run by a very cheerful couple who seem to like foreign travelers, the Jetée is as good as it gets in Dieppe. The rooms are clean and attractive, and some have large windows with sea views. Singles and doubles cost 140F, and 195F with a shower; triples and quads are 250F. *5 rue de l'Asile-Thomas, tel. 02–35–84–89–98. From quai Henri-IV, left on rue de la Rade, right on rue de l'Asile-Thomas. 10 rooms, 5 with bath.*

HOSTEL • Auberge de Jeunesse. The youth hostel is inconveniently located atop a hill southwest of town in St-Aubin. Its clean and sometimes unisex dorm rooms, however, are still the cheapest in town: 68F a night, breakfast included. There is no curfew and no meals, but the kitchen, barbecue, and supermarket near the bus stop make up for it. Sheets are 17F. An HI card is required. *48 rue Louis-Fromager, quartier Janval, tel. 02–35–84–85–73. From bottom of rue Gambetta, take Bus 2 (direction: Val Druel) to Château Michel. On foot (30 mins), turn left out of train station, follow blvd. Clemenceau to end, turn right, walk uphill on rue Gambetta (pass circular intersection), right on rue Dablon. 45 beds. Reception open 8 AM–10 AM and 5 PM–7:30 PM. Lockout 10–5 Kitchen. Cash only.*

FOOD

On the port, **Le Festival** (11 quai Henri-IV, tel. 02–35–40–24–29), a typical brasserie with yellow and green palm-tree decor, serves a small but delicious *assiette de fruits de mer* (seafood plate; 50F) with oysters, clams, sea snails, and more. On the beach, **Club House** (tel. 02–35–84–59–22), open May–September, has a large variety of mussels and fries starting at 50F.

UNDER 75F • Ankara. The talkative owner serves a large assortment of vegetarian dishes, like roasted eggplant or dolmas, for around 30F–45F. Turkish pizzas cost 45F; yogurt brochettes (shish kebabs with yogurt sauce) are 65F. *18 rue de la Rade, tel. 02–35–84–58–33. Closed Wed.*

Les Tourelles. Here's a comfortable place for decent seafood and traditional Norman cuisine. You can eat inside with locals or, when the weather permits, outside on the terrace. Specialties like *matelotte dieppoise* (fish stew; 62F) and lemon sole cooked in butter (42F) are superb. Lunch and dinner menus start at 59F. *43 rue du Commandant-Fayolle, 1 block south of blvd. de Verdun, tel. 02–35–84–15–88. Closed Oct.–June. No dinner Tues. or Wed.*

WORTH SEEING

Although the town was largely rebuilt after World War II, it still has some historic neighborhoods with old houses and narrow streets, especially around the **Église St-Jacques** (rue St-Jacques). The church itself is an elegant, mossy 14th-century building with ornate Renaissance carvings. Sun worshipers now cover the long stretch of sand and the huge grassy area just in front of it. This beach is where Canadian and other Allied troops attempted a landing on August 19, 1942, and failed miserably. Only 2,500 of the original force of 6,000 made it back to Britain. The failed raid convinced the Allies that seizing a single harbor to open the way for an invasion of France was impossible. The **Canadian Cemetery**, south of town in Hautot-sur-Mer, has 944 gravestones, many inscribed with poems honoring the soldiers. Take Bus 6 from the bus station (direction: Carrefour du Vallon) to the rue des Canadiens stop.

Overlooking the town from cliffs to the northwest, a 15th-century **château** has a flattering perspective of the beach, making it seem much calmer than it really is. You also get a view of the city and its rooftops. Up close, the château itself is disappointing; reconstructed with tinted glass and red brick, it doesn't really evoke that 15th-century mood. The **museum** inside, however, has a worthwhile collection of paintings, maps, and 17th-century African ivory carvings. With your ticket, they'll give you a "passport" good for a discount at some museums in Honfleur, Le Havre, and Rouen. *Chemin de la Citadelle, tel. 02–35–84–19–76. Admission 15F. Open June–Sept., daily 9–6; Oct.–May, Tues.–Sun. 10–noon and 2–5.*

AFTER DARK

A number of English pubs dominate the scene, especially behind the beach on rue Gustave-Roland and rue de l'Épée. Try the **Scottish Pub** (12 rue St-Jacques, tel. 02–35–84–13–16), which is dim, smoky, and alluring; it advertises "100 Bières et Whiskies" on the sign outside. More upbeat is the disco **Djin's Club** (3 blvd. de Verdun, tel. 02–35–82–33–60), in the ugly **casino** near the beach; the cover is 50F, with one drink included. To get in the game room, you have to exchange 100F into gambling tokens. If you're in a mellower mood, a few of the cafés near the port are pleasant and stay open late, like **Tout Va Bien** (3 quai Henri-IV, tel. 02–35–84–12–67), at the corner of quai Duquesne and quai Henri-IV.

FECAMP

The home of the sharp, sweet Benedictine liqueur, the town's easy atmosphere, friendly locals, and reasonable restaurants and hotels (for a seaside resort, that is) make it a great place to visit while seeing neighboring villages. In addition to its active port, chalky cliffs, and rocky beaches, the town has its share of sights, including the 19th-century **Benedictine palace and distillery** (*see* Worth Seeing, *below*).

BASICS

The **Maison de Tourisme,** across the street from the Benedictine palace, has a helpful staff that will load you up with maps, brochures, and as much advice as you can handle. In July and August, an annex (tel. 02–35–29–16–34), open daily 11–1 and 3–8, opens near the port on quai de la Vicomté. *113 rue Alexandre le Grand, tel. 02–35–28–51–01. Open July–Aug., weekdays 10–6; Sept.–June, Mon.–Sat. 9–12:15 and 1:45–6.*

COMING AND GOING

Several trains run daily to Le Havre (50 mins, 62F), Rouen (65–75 mins, 88F), and Paris (2¼ hrs, 166F) from the **train station** (blvd. de la République, tel. 08–36–35–35–35) in the *centre ville* (town center) behind avenue Gambetta. All trains require a transfer at Bréauté-Beuzeville.

Autos-Cars Gris runs frequent buses to Le Havre via both Goderville (1¼ hrs, 44F) and Etretat (1½ hrs, 44F). Pick up schedules at their office (8 av. Gambetta, tel. 02–35–27–04–25), which is also where the bus stops. **CNA** (tel. 02–35–84–21–97) also runs buses to Dieppe (1½ hrs, 72F).

GETTING AROUND

The town center is bordered to the west by the beach and boulevard Albert-Ier, which runs parallel to the water. The town is small enough to get around on foot, but to visit outside areas, rent a bike for 50F a day at **Folio Cycles** (2 av. Gambetta, tel. 02–35–28–45–09); VTTs are 85F with a passport deposit.

WHERE TO SLEEP

Most inexpensive hotels lie around place St-Étienne, one block south of avenue Gambetta. You'll feel right at home at the **Hôtel-Restaurant Martin** (18 pl. St-Étienne, tel. 02–35–28–23–82); the accommodating owners have clean, comfortable singles and doubles for 130F (150F with shower). The popular restaurant downstairs has a 65F menu. The only catch is that there are only seven rooms and the hotel is closed Sunday night, all day Monday, the first two weeks in March, and the first two weeks in September. Just next door is **Hôtel du Commerce** (28 pl. Bigot, tel. 02–35–28–19–28), with 28 nicely decorated rooms that start at 190F. Groups should ask for the 280F or 450F suites, designed to luxuriously accommodate three or five people. The **Hôtel Moderne** (3 av. Gambetta, tel. 02–35–28–04–04) is one of the cheapest places in town, with rooms at 150F (200F with shower).

CAMPING • Camping de Reneville. Above the cliffs on the south side of town is this campsite with gorgeous views for 40F a night for two people, a tent, and a car. To get here, follow the winding uphill street between rue de la Plage and rue d'Yport. *Tel. 02–35–28–20–97. Reception open daily 7–noon and 2–8. Closed Jan.–Feb.*

FOOD

There's no avoiding seafood in this town. Look along the quay for relatively inexpensive brasseries, or try the **Brasserie des Halles** (3 pl. Bellet, tel. 02–35–28–62–03), a casual place serving fish soup (20F), salads and sandwiches (12F–33F), and full menus (48F–60F). The atmosphere is low-key, but **Le Vicomté** (4 rue du Président-Coty, tel. 02–35–28–47–63) has an excellent 87F menu, featuring meals such as a huge artichoke with Roquefort cheese, a fish or meat dish, and dessert or cheese. There's a **market** all day Saturday in the centre ville, and there are supermarkets at place Bellet.

WORTH SEEING

In 1863 entrepreneur Alexander the Great (no relation to *the* Alexander the Great) rediscovered a 16th-century monk's liqueur recipe, and he proceeded to build a distillery and a gaudy neo-Baroque, neo-Renaissance mansion, known as the **Benedictine palace and distillery.** Even if the building is tasteless, the famous drink they make here isn't; it goes down very strong and sharp. The entrance fee lets you visit the distillery, with a tasting thrown in. *110 rue Alexandre-le-Grand, tel. 02–35–10–26–10. Admission 29F. Open Mar. 16–May 15 and Sept. 2–Nov. 11, daily 10–noon and 2–5; May 16–Sept. 1, daily 9:30–6; Jan. 2–Mar. 15 and Nov. 12–Dec. 30, daily tours only at 10:30 AM and 3:30 PM.*

The same architect who designed the Benedictine palace was also responsible for the **Abbatiale de la Trinité** (pl. Général-Leclerc), and you can tell. However, the Byzantine design in such an immense and bright church passes as unwontedly beautiful.

OUTDOOR ACTIVITIES

The coastline here is beautiful, but the beaches aren't so great; the largest one is just beyond the port. For a view of the town from the water, take a 45-minute **boat ride** (50F) with a local fisherman. In July and August, boats run every day; otherwise, call to set up a trip. If you don't speak French, the tourist office will happily make arrangements for you. For more information on boat tours, contact **Tourisme et Loisirs** (15 rue Vicomté, tel. 02–35–28–99–53). A traditional maritime festival, **Fête de la Mer,** perks up the first weekend in July with food booths and performers.

NEAR FECAMP

YPORT

Why come here? Because Yport isn't swamped by tourists, and it still has a few coastal fishing boats called *caïques* along a beautiful old port. The town has the GR21, a walking and biking trail that makes for pleasant day trips from Fécamp or Etretat. And finally, it has cheap lodging, good seafood, and a pebbled beach where you can swim at high tide or rummage for shellfish at low tide. Fishing tip: Try the west for small gray shrimp and the east for mussels.

BASICS • Autos-Cars Gris (tel. 02–35–27–04–25) arrive from Fécamp (15 mins, 14F) and Etretat (25 mins, 18F) six times a day on weekdays, and a couple of times a day on weekends. The **Office de Tourisme** (pl. J.P.-Laurens, tel. 02–35–29–77–31) has good, free maps of the GR21 trails.

WHERE TO SLEEP AND EAT • La Sirène (7 blvd. Alexandre-Dumont, tel. 02–35–27–31–87) has rooms with shower overlooking the beach at 200F, as well as a seafood restaurant with menus from 75F. **Le Petit Navire** (26 rue Emmanuel-Foy, tel. 02–35–27–65–97) has dorm beds for 51F a night, and 162F doubles (213F triples). The old house, next to the port, is in need of a paint job, but the owners are nice, the rooms are colorful, and there's a primitive camping stove at your disposal. If camping is more your style, hike up rue Hottière to **Le Rivage** (tel. 02–35–27–33–78). Some tent sites (18F per site plus 21F per person) are shaded and have a magnificent view of the cliffs and Fécamp. For food, Yport has a Wednesday morning **market** and a small **grocery store** (73 rue Emmanuel-Foy, tel. 02–35–27–30–67).

ETRETAT

The plunging chalk cliffs of Etretat, 17 km (10 mi) west of Fécamp, are so gorgeous and strange that they seem surreal at first. (The crowds of camera-toting tourists, however, will bring you back to reality in a jiffy.) The town of Etretat lost its soul long ago, but if you head straight for the cliffs in early morning or late evening, you'll see what drew artists like Monet, Boudin, and Maupassant here. When you come, wear good shoes and bring lots of film—you'll be just as inspired by this natural beauty as old Claude was. Ascension Day (the Thursday 40 days after Easter) brings the **Benediction of the Sea,** when a priest blesses the ocean, followed by a fair with music, food, and dancing.

BASICS

Autos-Cars Gris (tel. 02–35–27–04–25 in Fécamp, tel. 02–35–26–67–23 in Le Havre) runs several buses a day from Fécamp (35 mins, 27F) and Le Havre (1 hr, 36F). They'll drop you in front of the **Office de Tourisme** (pl. Maurice-Guillard, tel. 02–35–27–05–21). It's open June–September, daily 9—6; October–May, Monday and Wednesday–Sunday 10–noon and 2–5. From here, you can explore Etretat by walking straight down rue Monge to place Victor-Hugo (Falaise d'Aval is on your left, Falaise d'Almont on your right).

WHERE TO SLEEP

Hotel prices are exorbitant, so you'd better make Etretat a day trip from Fécamp or Le Havre. If you must stay the night, just south of the tourist office looms **Hôtel New-Windsor** (9 av. George-V, tel. 02–35–27–07–27); the cheapest double is 200F. If you're going to spend that much, you might as well go all out and stay at the gorgeous, historic **Hôtel La Résidence** (4 blvd. René-Coty, tel. 02–35–27–02–87), with rooms for 275F–390F. The mansion is run by a young owner who keeps things lively, and you can eat the 35F breakfast in bed.

From June 21 to July 14, during Festivagues in Le Havre, free concerts are held all over town.

FOOD

For a few hundred francs you can eat at a restaurant with a view of the cliffs; for under 75F you get a view of a parking lot at **Le Gavroche** (pl. Général-de-Gaulle, tel. 02–35–10–00–49). A salad and grilled sardine menu costs 65F and delicious fish platters are 45F–55F. At 45 rue Notre-Dame, on the corner with rue Abbé-Cochet, is **Crêperie de Lann-Bihoué** (tel. 02–35–27–04–65), with simple butter and sugar crepes for 15F and a salmon crepe with cream sauce for 45F.

WORTH SEEING

To the south is the **Falaise d'Aval** (Downhill Cliff); just beyond it is the **Aiguille,** a needle-shape rock formation jutting almost 330 ft into the air. The walk takes you to one amazing cliff after another; it takes 1½ hours to do the whole circuit. At low tide, you can walk through the many caves here, but caution is advised. The schedule of tides is posted near the stairway and also at the tourist office (*see above*).

To the north towers the **Falaise d'Almont** (Uphill Cliff). Halfway up is a small **aquarium** (tel. 02–35–29–80–59) carved into the cliffs. It's open Easter–June and September, Wednesday and weekends 2–5; July–August, daily 10–noon and 2–6; admission is 13F. At the peak is a small chapel (closed to the public) and the **Musée Nungesser et Coli** (tel. 02–35–27–07–47), a less-than-thrilling museum dedicated to two pilots who died in 1927 trying to cross the Atlantic. The latter is open May–mid-June, weekends 2–6; mid-June–mid-September, daily 2–6; admission is 6F. In this direction there is also a stairway that leads down to a calmer and prettier beach than the main one bordering town.

LE HAVRE

Le Havre has never been pretty. If you've read Sartre's *The Age of Reason* recently, you should have an idea of what it's like. In the book, Roquentin flips out after a hearty sandwich of existential angst and a hillside view of Bouville (Mudville), a fictional town inspired by Le Havre. Drop a few thousand tons of World War II bombs on this image; hand over the hurried reconstruction to Auguste Perret, who needs to house tens of thousands of homeless; and you have the hideous beauty of modern Le Havre.

From the centre ville, you can see the ocean through the **Porte de l'Océan**; from the nearby **rue de Paris** you can see the large port. The 350-ft tower of Perret's **Église St-Joseph** (blvd. François-Ier) powers into the sky like a fat rocket. The interior has sci-fi magnificence, its 250-ft octagonal lantern filled almost to the top with abstract stained glass that hurls colored light at the bare concrete walls.

BASICS

You get the feeling you're bothering the staff of the **Office de Tourisme,** which is inside the Hôtel de Ville (Town Hall); you'll have to excuse them, but they're not used to tourists. To get here, turn left out of the train station and walk 10 minutes down boulevard de Strasbourg. *186 blvd. Clemenceau, tel. 02–32–*

74–04–04. Open May–Sept., Mon.–Sat. 9–7, Sun. 10–12:30 and 2:30–6; Oct.–Apr., Mon.–Sat. 8:45–12:15 and 1:30–6:30, Sun. 10–1.

Le Havre has the only **American Express** office in Normandy outside Rouen. *57 quai George-V, tel. 02–35–19–05–93. Open weekdays 8:45–noon and 1:30–6.*

COMING AND GOING

BY TRAIN • Trains run to Rouen (45 mins, 91F), Dieppe (2½ hrs, 95F), and Paris's Gare St-Lazare (2 hrs, 168F). Trains also arrive from Fécamp (50 mins, 62F), with a transfer in Bréauté-Beuzeville, but it's an impractical way to get here (you're better off taking the bus). To reach the centre ville from the main **train station** (cours de la République, tel. 08–36–35–35–35), follow the long boulevard de Strasbourg (which leads to place de l'Hôtel de Ville).

BY BUS • The seedy bus station is across from the train station. **CNA** buses (tel. 02–35–26–67–23) run along the Seine and the Route des Abbayes (*see* Near Rouen, *above*) toward Rouen. Use them to reach the small towns between Le Havre and Rouen but not Rouen itself (the train is three times faster and costs the same). **Bus Verts** (tel. 02–31–44–77–44) goes twice daily to Caen (1½–2½ hrs, 122F), Deauville (1 hr, 59F), and Honfleur (30 mins, 43F). **Autos-Cars Gris** runs to Fécamp via Etretat (1½ hrs, 45F) or via Goderville (1¼ hrs, 45F). *Blvd. de Strasbourg, tel. 02–35–26–67–23. Information office open weekdays 7:45–1:30 and 2:15–6.*

BY FERRY • **Irish Ferries** (Gare Maritime, tel. 02–33–23–44–44) has a complicated schedule of ferries to Rosslare and Cork, Ireland, but redeems itself by accepting Eurail passes. Good thing, since the 21-hour passage costs 400F–650F. **P&O European** ferries (Terminal de la Citadelle, off av. Lucien-Corbeaux, tel. 02–35–19–78–78) depart for Portsmouth three times daily for 190F (360F round-trip); call and ask about special deals. Their offices are open weekdays 9–6, Saturday 9–1. A **shuttle service** takes you from the train station to the ferry port once a day (around 2 PM) for 8F.

GETTING AROUND

Boulevard Strasbourg and rue Jules-Lecesne are the two big streets running across town to the Hôtel de Ville. From here, **Espace Oscar Niemeyer** is directly south two blocks and leads to the popular St-François quarter. The area around the train station is a little sketchy; if you're feeling paranoid, buy tickets (7F50 or 48F for 10) and a map of the local **Bus-Océane** (115 rue Jules-Lecesne, tel. 02–35–19–75–75) system; there are information booths outside both the train station and the Hôtel de Ville. **Loca-Détente** (77 rue Irène Joliot Curie, tel. 02–35–46–48–84) rents VTTs for 75F a day with a 400F deposit. Hours and the yearly closing (usually between October and November) vary, so call ahead to reserve a bike.

WHERE TO SLEEP

UNDER 150F • **Séjour Fleuri.** The Fleuri is characterless, but the couple who run it certainly aren't, and they have a great Siamese cat. The rooms, though simple, are comfortable and clean. Singles and doubles are 105F–135F, 145F with shower. *71 rue Émile-Zola, tel. 02–35–41–33–81. From espace Niemeyer, follow rue de Paris to rue É mile-Zola. 29 rooms, 7 with bath.*

UNDER 200F • **Astoria.** Local charm isn't a characteristic of Le Havre lodging establishments, and this hotel just opposite the train station is no exception. But if you want a practical, friendly, well-equipped stopping place, try it. Rooms range from 160F to 395F for four. *13 cours de la République, tel. 02–35–25–00–03, fax 02–35–26–48–34. 37 rooms with bath or shower. Restaurant.*

CAMPING • **Camping de la Forêt de Montgeon.** Two kilometers (1 mi) from Le Havre's center, this campsite is in the middle of a forest, with hot showers and nearby stores. One or two people with a tent and a car pay 61F for one night; discounts are given for longer stays. *Tel. 02–35–46–52–39. Bus 7 or 11 to Porte de la Forêt. Gates close at 11 PM. Closed Sept.–May.*

FOOD

Fast-food joints cluster around the train station and place de l'Hôtel de Ville. The **supermarket** in the Nouvelles Galeries (138 rue Victor-Hugo) is the stop for picnic packers. **Le Flores** (106 rue Victor-Hugo, tel. 02–35–41–72–74) has huge gourmet salads (49F–59F) but like many restaurants in Le Havre is closed for dinner. Cheap huts line the beach April to mid-October and serve everything from Moroccan plates to seafood; **Chez Polo** (tel. 02–35–42–69–89) serves mussels in a cream or white wine sauce for 33F; and **Tutti Frutti** (tel. 02–35–21–40–59) has comfortable reclining beach chairs facing the beach and the pedestrian boardwalk. Here you can enjoy Brazilian music and fruity drinks (19F).

UNDER 75F • **Le Crocus.** At noon, this unpretentious place fills with boisterous French workers taking lunch breaks. The 57F menu includes an appetizer, a hearty fish or meat special, cheese or salad, dessert, and wine or cider. Friday and Saturday nights, when the menu costs 72F, the owner throws theater or music soirées (30F). *67 rue Jules Tellier, tel. 02–35–53–25–96. From station, turn right on cours de la République, left on rue Jules-Tellier. Closed Sun.*

WORTH SEEING

The **Musée André-Malraux,** the city art museum, is an innovative glass-and-metal structure from the 1960s, ringed by a moat. The spacious, airy design floods the interior with natural light, and there's an extensive collection of works by two of Le Havre's most famous artistic sons: the coastscapist Eugène Boudin, a forerunner of the Impressionists; and the colorful Raoul Dufy. The museum reopened in 1999 after a two-year restoration program. *Chaussée John-Kennedy, tel. 02–35–42–33–97. Admission 25F. Open Wed.–Mon. 11–6.*

On Espace Oscar Niemeyer, the huge white building that resembles a squashed nuclear reactor is the **Maison de la Culture du Havre** (tel. 02–35–19–10–10), where various theatrical productions are staged September–June. Tickets start around 50F; the information desk is open weekdays 1:30–6:30. The entire center closes in August. And if you're feeling city-weary, the **Forêt de Montgeon** and the **Parc de Rouelles** sit right on the edge of town, seducing hikers and picnickers alike. From the Hôtel de Ville, take Bus 11 to the Porte de la Forêt stop to reach the forest; or take Bus 1 to the Parc de Rouelles stop.

AFTER DARK

Le Havre is not only ugly, it's also boring. For dancing, **L'Alexia** (26 rue Georges-Heuillard, tel. 02–35–21–28–70) draws a young crowd. **Cinéma l'Eden** (tel. 02–35–19–10–40), in the cultural center on espace Oscar Niemeyer, plays films in their original language. Prices are 40F but they're closed July–August. Whatever you do at night, single women should be careful—Le Havre has a higher-than-average number of sleazier-than-average men.

Driving through the countryside, you'll see signs in front of farms that say "Calvados!" Many Norman families make their own brew and welcome the public to come in and try it.

CÔTE FLEURIE

Between a rolling valley and a plush forest lies the Côte Fleurie (Flowered Coast), a string of resort towns that now serve as a playground for city dwellers from Paris and London. Although all the towns here resemble each other (with grand hotels, casinos on the beach, and long boardwalks), each has something unique to offer; the port town of **Honfleur** is in a league of its own. The Côte Fleurie is beautiful but can also be hard on the pocket—you might want to make day trips here from Caen or stay at a *chambre d'hôte* (bed-and-breakfast)—they usually begin at 150F for one person, 180F for two.

HONFLEUR

Honfleur is the most interesting of the Côte Fleurie's little seaside towns; accordingly, tourist crowds and hotel prices are outrageous. Unscathed by World War II, much of the city's Renaissance architecture remains intact, especially around the 17th-century **Vieux Bassin** harbor. Here, two-story stone houses with low, sloping roofs and taller buildings with wooden facades crouch precariously over the water. Stop at **place St-Catherine,** with its wood-shingled **clock tower** and the 15th- to 16th-century **Église Ste-Catherine,** itself made entirely of wood. The church features two unusual naves shaped like boat hulls. **Le Calypso** (tel. 02–31–89–32–25) has half-hour (40F) or two-hour (80F) boat tours of the harbor.

This alluring town has served as a haven for artists; nearby at the St-Siméon Farm, Eugène Boudin (1824–98) started a colony of artists who would greatly influence the development of Impressionist painting. In addition to the many art galleries scattered around town, you can visit Honfleur's **Musée Eugène Boudin** (pl. Erik-Satie, tel. 02–31–89–54–00). Admission is 25F. It's open April–September, Monday and Wednesday–Sunday 10–noon and 2–6; October–December and March, Monday and Wednesday–Sunday 2–6.

BASICS

The **Office de Tourisme,** behind the Hôtel de Ville near the old port, has information on art exhibits and concerts and a brochure on local chambres d'hôte (which range between 150F and 250F for two people) and will reserve them for 10F. *9 rue de la Ville, tel. 02–31–89–23–30. From pl. Albert Sorel, walk down rue de la République, right on rue Montpensier, left on rue de la Ville. Open July–Aug., Mon.–Sat. 9–7:30, Sun. 10–4; Sept.–June, Mon.–Sat. 9–noon and 2–5:30 (10–4 on Sun.).*

COMING AND GOING

Bus Verts (tel. 02–31–89–28–41) travels here frequently during the summer from Caen (1–2 hrs, 69F–88F) and from Le Havre (30 mins, 43F). Get off at the Albert Sorel stop and walk straight down rue de la République toward the town center. The only bike rental in town is at the **Otelinn** hotel (62 cours Albert-Manuel, tel. 02–31–89–41–77), which charges a steep 100F a day with a 1,200F deposit.

WHERE TO SLEEP

By far the cheapest hotel in town, **Hôtel-Restaurant Hamelin** (16 pl. Hamelin, tel. 02–31–89–16–25), just west of the harbor, has four doubles for 150F–230F and a three-person room for 300F, all with bath, but the owner is a bit pushy about the "optional" 32F breakfast. Camp at the centrally located **Le Phare** (pl. Jeanne-de-Vienne, at west end of blvd. Charles-V, tel. 02–31–89–10–26). Sites cost 35F plus 26F per person; the reception desk is open 9–noon and 2–7:30. It's closed October–March.

FOOD

La Cotriade (7 rue de la Ville, tel. 02–31–89–02–41) serves a plate of sea snails with mayo followed by two crepes for 65F. **Les Bagues d'Argent** (30 rue de l'Homme de Bois, tel. 02–31–89–27–97), off place Ste-Catherine, serves up a four-course menu (92F) in a cozy, atmospheric old house. For take-out, **La Bonne Idée** (22 rue de la Ville, tel. 02–31–89–55–56) has a variety of fresh-cut sandwiches 18F–30F. The Saturday-morning **market** around the harbor is lively and fun, and there's a **Champion** supermarket at 46 rue de la République.

DEAUVILLE AND TROUVILLE

Twin towns on the beach, divided only by the Touques River, Deauville and Trouville compete for the title of Most Extravagant Norman Town. Called the 21st arrondissement of Paris, the towns sport boulevards of expensive boutiques and a contingent of well-dressed, poodle-promenading ladies. The beaches in both cities are similar stretches of sand—though you might not be able to see them through the thick crust of striped umbrellas. When you're tired of the beach, head up to the **casinos,** where you have to pay 70F at night to get into the game room (the pool and slots rooms are free). The one in Deauville (tel. 02–31–98–66–66) is totally decked out with marble staircases and elegant chandeliers; the one in Trouville, dubbed the **Louisiane Follies** (pl. Maréchal-Foch, tel. 02–31–87–75–00), has been recently revamped; there are garish theme areas like the Bluesy Bar and Bourbon Street.

Deauville hosts an **American Cinema Festival** in early September; one-day tickets run around 200F weekdays, 300F weekends. Both towns have a **tourist office** that distributes glossy brochures and maps. The Deauville office (pl. de la Mairie, tel. 02–31–14–40–00) is open Monday–Saturday 9–12:30 and 2–7, Sunday 11–4. The Trouville office (32 quai Fernand-Moureaux, tel. 02–31–14–60–70) is open Monday–Saturday 9:30–12:30 and 2–7, Sunday 10–12:30.

COMING AND GOING

Day tripping from Honfleur or Caen is the best way to visit these posh resorts; the two towns are so busy catering to the jet set that they don't have many affordable hotels or restaurants. The **train station** is in Deauville near the Pont des Belges, which connects the two towns. In summer, trains run to Caen (55 mins, 65F via Lisieux), Paris (2 hrs, 165F), Rouen (2 hrs, 105F via Lisieux), and Cabourg (35 mins, 26F). **Bus Verts** (tel. 02–31–88–95–36) has service from Caen (1¼ hrs, 53F), Honfleur (35 mins, 22F), Cabourg (35 mins, 27F), and Le Havre (1 hr, 59F). You'll be dropped at the train station in Deauville or in the town center at Trouville (get off at the "Église" stop and walk downhill; the beach and casino are on your right, the tourist office on your left).

HOULGATE AND CABOURG

Less pretentious than their neighbors to the east, these two towns, separated by the Dives estuary, sport a relaxed and friendly atmosphere—you can actually walk into the stores here without attracting snobby looks. Cabourg is distinguished by its association with Marcel Proust, who immortalized the town under the pseudonym Balbec in his novel *A l'Ombre des Jeunes Filles en Fleurs* (literally, "In the Shadow of Blossoming Girls"). What's funny is that Cabourg is proud of Proust, even though he often slammed the town in his writings: He describes in endless detail the silly, pretentious characters staying in the **Grand Hôtel** (promenade Marcel-Proust, tel. 02–31–91–01–79) and the townspeople peeping through the windows to watch them. You can still visit this elegant, 19th-century hotel (and even stay in it if you've got 900F to spare).

The beautiful hotels and villas along Cabourg's boardwalk (promenade Marcel-Proust) have unfortunately been marred by the arrival of ugly condos since Marcel's time. The promenade starts to have some character around 6 PM, when the crowds leave, and you can enjoy the sunset at **Le Bar des Dives** in front of the Grand Hôtel. The mansions along Houlgate's promenade are free of these modern ugly ducklings and the beach here is more isolated at night. In either town, there's not much to do but lie on the beaches or try your luck at the casinos; the one in Houlgate is small, modest, and packed with young people. In Cabourg, the **Office de Tourisme** (tel. 02–31–91–01–09) is right across from the Grand Hôtel and hands out maps and bus schedules. It's open Easter–September, daily 9–noon and 2–6; October–Easter, Monday and Wednesday–Sunday 2–5. The office in Houlgate (10 blvd. des Belges, tel. 02–31–24–34–79) is open July–August, daily 9–7; September–June, daily 9–noon and 2–5.

> Norman people are reluctant to speak openly about World War II and other painful matters. They're likely to hem and haw; the rest of France jokes that the typical Norman response to a question is "Peut-être que oui, peut-être que non" (maybe yes, maybe no).

COMING AND GOING

The Dives-Cabourg **train station** (pl. Tréfouel, tel. 08–36–35–35–35) is south of town across the Dives River; trains run to Houlgate (6 mins, 8F), Deauville (35 mins, 26F), and Paris (2½ hrs, 176F via Deauville) regularly in summer, but only on weekends in winter. **Bus Verts** (tel. 02–31–44–77–44 in Caen or 02–31–88–95–36 in Deauville) runs several buses a day to Cabourg from Caen (45 mins, 32F), Deauville (30 mins, 27F), and Honfleur (1¼ hrs, 44F). You can rent bikes in Cabourg at **Cycles Raleigh** (3 av. du Président-Poincaré, tel. 02–31–91–85–98) for 80F a day with a passport deposit.

WHERE TO SLEEP

You're better off sleeping in Houlgate than Cabourg: Both **Hôtel 1900** (17 rue des Bains, tel. 02–31–28–77–77) and **Hôtel de la Plage** (99 rue des Bains, tel. 02–31–28–70–60) are well situated, with clean rooms. The former has rooms with shower starting at 250F, with bath at 350F. At the latter, rooms begin at 180F with shower. In Cabourg, **Camping de la Plage** (59 rue Henri-Dobert, tel. 02–31–28–73–07) has tennis courts, a restaurant, and a killer location by the sea; sites are 35F per person and 63F per tent; it's closed December–March. Houlgate's slightly cheaper **Camping de la Vallée** (tel. 02–31–24–40–69) charges 30F per person and 40F per site.

FOOD

Crêperies, pizzerias, and fast-food places line avenue de la Mer in Cabourg. **Au Petit Cannibale** (56 av. de la Mer, tel. 02–31–91–17–01) serves a good 78F menu that changes seasonally—expect sea snails or fried squid as appetizers and meat or fish for the main dish. In Houlgate, lively rue des Bains, running parallel to the beach, is lined with cafés and restaurants, most serving seafood. The Hôtel 1900 (*see above*) has an excellent menu for around 100F. For something more casual, try Houlgate's **Le Globe** (44 rue des Bains, tel. 02–31–28–74–50)—mussels and french fries are a staple here. On Thursday there's an outdoor **market** in downtown Houlgate; there's also a covered, permanent market at place du Marché, on the main street. In Cabourg, the outdoor **market** takes place Wednesday and Sunday morning year-round (daily during July–August) off avenue du Commandant Berteaux-Levillain.

CAEN

Caen, about 15 km (9 mi) south of the Orne River, was founded in the 11th century by William the Conqueror and built on top of an ancient Gallo-Roman settlement. In 1944 Caen was reduced to a mass of rubble by artillery and bombing as Allied troops descended on the town to recapture it from the Germans. Luckily, two magnificent abbeys survived the war, revealing hints of Caen's elegant and provincial past. The city also has several interesting museums, including an exceptional one that thoroughly examines the two world wars, inspiring an understanding of the value of peace.

BASICS

The **Office de Tourisme,** across from the church, has tons of information on the city, including ferry and bus schedules. It has a currency exchange and books hotels in Caen free of charge. The office can also provide schedules of the horse races, which run May–June and September–November in Caen, and July–August in Cabourg and Deauville. *Pl. St-Pierre, tel. 02–31–27–14–14. Open May–Sept., Mon.–Sat. 9–7, Sun. 10–noon and 3–6; Oct.–Apr., Mon.–Sat. 9–12:30 and 2–6, Sun. 10–noon.*

The **post office** changes money at fair rates and handles poste restante; the postal code is 14000. There's also a smaller office outside the train station on rue de la gare. *Pl. Gambetta, next to préfecture, tel. 02–31–39–35–78. Open weekdays 8–7, Sat. 8–noon.*

Lavomatique (129 rue St-Jean, tel. 02–31–50–20–05) charges 20F for its washers, 5F for dryers.

For medical emergency, contact **SOS Médecins Calvados** (81 rue d'Auge, tel. 02–31–34–31–31).

COMING AND GOING

BY TRAIN

The **train station** (pl. de la Gare, tel. 08–36–35–35–35), south of town, sends trains to Paris (1¾ hrs, 174F), Rouen (2 hrs, 114F), Cherbourg (70 mins, 118F), and Bayeux (15 mins, 31F). The station is open Monday–Saturday 5:30 AM–9 PM, Sunday 6 AM–10 PM. The information office is open Monday–Saturday 7:30 AM–9 PM.

BY BUS

From the **Bus Verts** depot (tel. 02–31–44–77–53), next to the train station, buses leave for Le Havre (1½–2½ hrs, 122F), Honfleur (1 hr, 69F), Deauville (1¼ hrs, 53F), and Cabourg (45 mins, 32F). The **Carte Liberté** (*see* Chapter Basics, *above*) is good for free travel on Caen city buses. Bus Verts also sponsors **Circuit 44,** a series of routes leaving from Caen and Bayeux to explore D-day sites; an all-day pass costs 95F. Buses leave from the gare routière next to the train station or from place Courtonne.

BY FERRY

Brittany Ferries (tel. 02–31–36–36–00) makes the six-hour journey to Portsmouth, England, three times a day from Ouistreham's **gare maritime,** a 25-minute bus ride (20F) from Caen. Mid-July–August, you'll pay 320F; April–June and September–October, tickets are 280F. And though you'll freeze nameless parts of your body off, the journey November–March runs only 180F.

GETTING AROUND

Caen's centre ville is easily explored on foot. At the north end of town is the château, and to the east is the Abbaye aux Dames. Across town to the west are the Abbaye aux Hommes and the Hôtel de Ville. The train station is southeast of town, just across the Orne River. To get from the station to the centre ville, head down rue de la Gare, which becomes avenue du 6-Juin.

To maneuver around, you might want to hop on **CTAC,** Caen's city **bus system,** which has an office on 11 boulevard Maréchal-Leclerc (tel. 02–31–15–55–55) and an information booth near the train station. Get tickets from the driver—one trip costs 6F10, a 10-pack 52F, an all-day pass 16F. Buses stop running around 10:30 PM. **Abeilles Taxis** (52 pl. de la Gare, tel. 02–31–52–17–89) are available 24 hours a day; they charge 3.50F per 1 km (½ mi) plus a 13F surcharge.

WHERE TO SLEEP

This city is a gold mine of budget hotels. If the places below are full, go down avenue du 6-Juin and look for budget hotels around place de la Résistance. **Hôtel Bernières** (50 rue de Bernières, tel. 02–31–86–01–26) has a great location between the station and centre ville, and it's open 24 hours—a rarity in France. Doubles run 140F, 160F with toilet, 220F with shower. The **Central Hôtel** (23 pl. Jean-Letellier, tel. 02–31–86–18–52) is impersonal but lives up to its name; it's in the center of town and near the château. Doubles are 180F, triples 210F, both with shower.

UNDER 125F • Hôtel Auto-Bar. The no-frills rooms are clean, the management is friendly, and the hotel is conveniently near the town center. Singles cost 90F, doubles start at 115F, and showers are free. *40 rue de Bras, 1 block south of rue St-Pierre, tel. 02–31–86–12–48. 12 rooms, none with bath.*

UNDER 175F • Hôtel de la Paix. The rooms here are clean and colorfully decorated. Showerless doubles are 170F; another 30F gets a shower. There is even one spartan 95F single. If you need an aspirin or a needle and thread, don't hesitate to ask: Friendly service is what distinguishes this place from others. *14 rue Neuve St-Jean, tel. 02–31–86–18–99. From station, head down rue de la Gare (which becomes av. du 6-Juin), right on rue Neuve St-Jean. 19 rooms, 16 with bath, 3 with toilet.*

HOSTEL

Auberge de Jeunesse/Foyer des Jeunes Travailleurs. It may be far from town, but the bus stop is close, the rooms with showers and kitchenettes are pretty nice, and the guy in charge is from North Carolina—so you can drop the French. Beds cost 61F, breakfast 19F. An HI card is required. *68 rue Eustache Restout, tel. 02–31–52–19–96. From station, Bus 5 or 17 to Lycée Fresnel stop. 58 beds. Reception open daily 7 AM–10 AM and 5 PM–10 PM. Cash only. Closed Oct.–May.*

CAMPING

Camping Municipal. Uncrowded, covered with trees, and only 2 km (1 mi) southwest of the city, Municipal is Caen's best. Sites are 10F plus 18F a person and 10F a car, hot showers included. Buy groceries in town, though, or be prepared to eat leaves and berries. *Rte. de Louvigny, tel. 02–31–73–60–92. From centre ville, take Bus 13 (direction: Louvigny) to Camping stop. Closed Oct.–Apr.*

FOOD

Cafés and brasseries catering to a young crowd cluster around place Courtonne, and the south part of rue Vaugueux is lined with small restaurants, most offering outdoor seating on this pedestrian-only street. **Le Bouchon du Vaugueux** (12 rue de Graindorge, tel. 02–31–44–26–26) has an interesting *salade pleine forme* (literally, an "in shape" salad; 48F) with oranges, avocado, and apples. There are outdoor **markets** on place Courtonne on Sunday and place St-Sauveur on Friday; or stop by the **Monoprix** supermarket at 45 boulevard du Maréchal-Leclerc.

UNDER 75F • La Petite Auberge. The traditional Norman food is first-rate, and the 70F menu served on a sunny terrace includes an appetizer, daily special, and dessert. Try anything that comes in their delicate cream sauce. *17 rue des Équipes d'Urgence, off rue St-Jean by pl. de la Résistance, tel. 02–31–86–43–30. Closed Mon. No dinner Sun.*

UNDER 100F • Caen-Grill. If you don't mind abandoning French culture and choosing quantity over quality, welcome to this all-you-can-eat buffet. The salad and dessert bar is 60F, or you can get the salad buffet and an entrée for 75F. *17 pl. de la République, off rue de Strasbourg, tel. 02–31–85–23–64.*

WORTH SEEING

Most of Caen's sights, except for the memorial museum, can be reached on foot. While trudging about, take a look inside the **Église St-Pierre** (pl. St-Pierre), which has a late Gothic choir carved in incredible detail; on 52–54 rue St-Pierre, two 16th-century half-timber houses have fascinating wood carvings.

ABBAYE AUX DAMES

When Mathilda of Flanders blew her chance to get into heaven by marrying her cousin, William the Conqueror, she founded this abbey to atone for her sins. The Abbaye aux Dames is less ornate than William's Men's Abbey (*see below*), but it's still a fine example of Romanesque architecture. The recently restored abbey church, **Église de la Trinité,** is gorgeous in its simplicity. The oldest part of the church is the not-quite-underground **crypt;** the sunlight bounces off the 16 columns. Free guided tours are given in French (and in English, if there's enough demand) daily at 2:30 and 4. *Off blvd. de la République, tel. 02–31–06–98–98. Church open daily except during services.*

ABBAYE AUX HOMMES

Like his wife (and cousin) Mathilda, William the Conqueror suffered from severe salvation anxiety, and thus commissioned the construction of a "Men's Abbey." The nave and towers remain from the original 11th-century abbey church, **Église St-Étienne,** a mixture of Gothic and Romanesque styles. The elegant monastic buildings attached to the church were built in the 18th century, converted into a high school by Napoléon, and became the town hall in 1965. *Pl. Louis-Guillouard, tel. 02–31–30–42–01. Abbey tours (10F) daily at 9:30, 11, 2:30, and 4. Church open daily 8:15–noon and 2–7:30.*

CHÂTEAU

The spacious grounds of William the Conqueror's château (enter on north side by the Porte de Ville) consist of the Église St-Georges (which holds regular expositions), sculpted gardens, a café, and two museums. Only real museum hounds will want to visit the **Musée de Normandie** (tel. 02–31–86–06–24), a regional archaeology and ethnology museum with Viking artifacts. Admission is 10F and free on Wednesday. The more interesting **Musée des Beaux-Arts** (tel. 02–31–85–28–63) has a large collection of 17th-century Italian and French works, plus paintings by Rubens, Boucher, and van der Weyden. Admission is 20F. Both museums are closed Tuesday.

MÉMORIAL: UN MUSÉE POUR LA PAIX

Normandy's war museums are legion, but its one *peace* museum is special. Beginning at the end of World War I, the museum outlines the events, economics, and sentiments that developed into the Second World War. Exhibits focus not only on past failures to keep peace but also on hopes for peace in the future; one gallery is dedicated to winners of the Nobel Peace Prize. All displays are translated into English, and you can buy a guide for 29F. Give yourself two hours to walk around the museum and an hour to see the three films that close the tour—they're excellent. *Esplanade Eisenhower, tel. 02–31–06–06–44. Bus 17 to Mémorial stop. Admission 72F. Open daily 9–9 (Sept.–May until 7).*

NEAR CAEN

This section of France's coast is fascinating for those interested in exploring the history and remnants of "the longest day." Museums, cemeteries, and memorials run up and down the coast, and since the 50th anniversary of D day back in 1994, museums have been spiffed up, road signs are idiot-proof, and public transport to the main D-day sites is easier than ever. Bayeux is the best place to base yourself for excursions to the D-day sites.

BAYEUX

Most famous for its 11th-century tapestry depicting William the Conqueror's invasion of England, Bayeux made history almost 900 years later as one of the first towns to be liberated during the D-day invasion. Because Bayeux had nothing strategically useful like factories or a military base, it was never bombed by either side, and the beautiful cathedral and houses of the old town remained intact. Nowadays, the cheery citizens of this peaceful town welcome visitors and thrive off the money they bring in. With some worthwhile museums, a great hostel, and reasonable restaurants, Bayeux is a great place to set up camp before exploring the D-day beaches and memorials 10–20 km (6–12 mi) away. The first weekend in July, the little town goes wild with the **Fêtes Médiévales,** two full days of craziness in the streets outside the cathedral, all free to the public.

BASICS

Bayeux's **Office de Tourisme** has information on the town and the D-day beaches and arranges rooms. During the summer, the American Express desk inside changes money and traveler's checks commission-free. Otherwise, the office will exchange currency for a fee when banks are closed. *Pont St-Jean, tel. 02–31–92–16–26. Open Sept.–June, Mon.–Sat. 9–noon and 2–6; July–Aug., Mon.–Sat. 9–6, Sun. 9:30–noon and 2:30–6.*

Money From Home In Minutes.

If you're stuck for cash on your travels, don't panic. Millions of people trust Western Union to transfer money in minutes to 165 countries and over 50,000 locations worldwide. Our record of safety and reliability is second to none. For more information, call Western Union: USA 1-800-325-6000, Canada 1-800-235-0000. Wherever you are, you're never far from home.

www.westernunion.com

The fastest way to send money worldwide.

COMING AND GOING

Trains run to Caen (15 mins, 31F), Cherbourg (50 mins, 100F), and Paris (2 hrs, 188F) from Bayeux's **train station** (pl. de la Gare, tel. 02–31–92–80–50). A few trains a day also make it to Pontorson (2 hrs, 104F), a 10-minute bus ride from Mont-St-Michel (*see* Cotentin Peninsula, *below*). To reach the centre ville from the station, head straight onto rue de Crémel and turn right on rue St-Jean (about a 10-minute walk). **Bus Verts** (tel. 02–31–92–02–92) has buses to Caen (50 mins, 38F) and Arromanches (30 mins, 16F).

WHERE TO SLEEP

UNDER 175F • Hôtel de la Gare. The rooms here are small and dingy, but generally comfortable; it's also right across from the station. The owners' son, Jean-Marc, leads tours to the D-day beaches and knows all the inside stories, especially about the Resistance. Singles cost 95F, doubles 110F, 175F with shower. *26 pl. de la Gare, tel. 02–31–92–10–70. 20 rooms. Closed Feb.*

UNDER 300F • Argouges. This 18th-century mansion is an oasis of calm in the town center. Most of the simply furnished rooms have wood beams and TVs; the quieter ones overlook a garden. The least expensive rooms with shower start at 280F; those with bath cost up to 440F. *21 rue St-Patrice, tel. 02–31–92–88–86. 25 rooms with bath.*

HOSTEL • Auberge de Jeunesse/Family Home. A comfy dorm bed in this 17th-century house near the centre ville goes for 90F (100F without an HI card), but check out the rooms to avoid those with the quicksand mattresses. A single with private bath costs 160F, a "grand comfort" room with its own shower is 115F per person. A huge breakfast is included in all prices. At night, there's a delicious five-course feast (65F), including wine. *39 rue Général-de-Dais, tel. 02–31–92–15–22. Follow signs from station (15 mins). 30 beds. Check-in 5 PM–7:30 PM, checkout 8 AM–10 AM. Curfew 11 PM.*

CAMPING • Camping Municipal charges 15F per person and 19F per site. The facilities are good: hot showers, a snack shop, volleyball court, and TV lounge. There's a huge Champion supermarket across the street, so snacks are no problem. *Blvd. d'Eindhoven, tel. 02–31–92–08–43. From station, go straight on rue de Crémel, left on rue St-Jean, right on rue Foch, left on av. Georges-Clemenceau, right on av. de la Vallée, right on blvd. d'Eindhoven. Closed mid-Nov.–mid-Mar.*

FOOD

Several inexpensive crêperies surround the cathedral; brasseries and pizzerias are on rue St-Jean. The **Bar des 12 Apôtres** (17 rue St-Jean, tel. 02–31–92–34–30) is a popular brasserie that serves soups, sandwiches, and *croque-monsieurs* (toasted ham and cheese sandwiches) for 20F and Calvados for 23F. **Le Printanier** (pl. aux Pommes, tel. 02–31–92–03–01) has a typical 75F Norman menu; the daily appetizer and entrées are good, but the light desserts—like apple soufflé and chocolate and coffee charlotte—are exceptional. The town **market** is on Saturday mornings at place St-Patrice and Wednesday on rue St-Jean.

UNDER 75F • La Table du Terroir. On the allée de l'Orangerie, connected to the butcher shop on rue St-Jean, this modest gastro-cabana has a jovial staff and friendly atmosphere. The 57F three-course menu is heavy on the meat, and for dessert the good butcher makes a divine *teurgoul,* a caramelized rice-and-milk Bayeux specialty. *42 rue St-Jean, tel. 02–31–92–05–53.*

UNDER 100F • Amaryllis. This small restaurant, 1 km (½ mi) from the cathedral, offers a three-course 75F menu with a half-dozen choices per course, perhaps including oysters, fillet of sole in a cidery sauce, and pastries for dessert. *32 rue St-Patrice, tel. 02–31–22–47–94. Closed Mon. and Jan.*

WORTH SEEING

Maximize your sightseeing with the 37F ticket that admits you to three museums, including the Bayeux Tapestry. It's available at all the museums.

BAYEUX TAPESTRY • This tapestry, one of the world's largest, is actually a linen embroidery that stretches an amazing 230 ft yet is only 1½ ft high. It narrates William the Conqueror's trials and victory over his cousin Harold, culminating in the Battle of Hastings on October 14, 1066. The tapestry features 58 amusing, hand-embroidered scenes, including gory battles and the hand of God reaching down from the sky to meddle in human activities and help Will out. Centre Guillaume-le-Conquérant, 13 bis rue de Nesmond, tel. 02–31–92–05–48. Admission 39F. Open mid-Mar.–Apr. and Sept.–mid-Oct., daily 9–6:30; mid-Oct.–mid-Mar., daily 9:30–12:30 and 2–6; May–Aug., daily 9–7.

CATHÉDRALE NOTRE-DAME • Bayeux's magnificent Gothic cathedral was begun in the 11th century and is lit up by beautiful stained glass, some of which dates from the 13th century. Don't miss the angels that decorate the pillars of the underground Romanesque crypt. *Rue du Bienvenu. Open July–mid-Sept., daily 9–7; mid-Sept.–June, daily 10–12:30 and 2–6.*

MUSÉE BARON GÉRARD • The Baron Gérard had a rich collection of paintings and incredibly fine lace, as well as porcelain from Bayeux and Rouen. Don't overlook David's *Le Philosophe,* who meditates eternally on his finger, and Boucher's *La Cage,* a playful seduction scene between a shepherd and shepherdess. *Pl. de la Liberté, tel. 02–31–92–14–21. Admission 39F (joint ticket with Tapestry Museum). Open June–mid-Sept., daily 9–7; mid-Sept.–May, daily 10–12:30 and 2–6.*

MUSÉE MEMORIAL DE LA BATAILLE DE NORMANDIE • If you're interested in the history of D day, this memorial has a massive collection of military equipment, news clippings, photographs, and uniformed mannequins. The British Cemetery is across the street. *Blvd. Fabian-Ware, tel. 02–31–92–93–41. Admission 32F. Open May–mid-Sept., daily 9–6:30; mid-Sept.–Apr., daily 10–noon and 2–6.*

D-DAY BEACHES

Operation Overlord was the code name for the planned invasion of France by the Allies. Given the strength and experience of the German army in France, the task was a daunting one. The invasion took more than a year to plan and included several deceptive schemes designed to make the Germans believe the invasion would take place around Calais to the north. Hitler and his army never dreamed that the Allies would be crazy enough to attempt an invasion through the hedge-ridden *bocage* (copse) country in the first place, and on D day, Hitler's elite were busy defending Calais and the coast of Belgium. The Führer himself slept through the landings, and the German commander, Field Marshal Erwin Rommel, was in Germany for his wife's birthday.

Originally set for June 5, the invasion was initially called off due to bad weather. Although the skies weren't much better the next day, General Dwight D. Eisenhower gave the word, and in the predawn darkness of June 6, 1944, thousands of paratroopers of the U.S. 82nd and 101st and British 6th airborne divisions dropped from the sky along an 80-km (50-mi) stretch of coast west of Cabourg. Their mission was to blow up river crossings, sever enemy communications, and distract the Germans so they would be unable to attack the seaborne assault troops due to land between 6 AM and 7:30 AM.

The seaborne troops landed on five beaches, designated as Omaha and Utah (American) and Sword, Gold, and Juno (British and Canadian). Omaha Beach was a disaster. Not only was it defended by the only solid German division on the coast, but 27 of the Allied tanks were launched too far out to sea and immediately went under. Struggling through heavy surf with no cover and facing a constant barrage of machine-gun fire, 2,000 soldiers were dead or wounded in only two short hours. Fortunately, losses were comparatively light on the other four beaches. Within eight days the Allies secured their position on the coast and penetrated as far as Bayeux. Reinforcement and supplies came from artificial ports maintained off the coast. Within three weeks, after heavy fighting, American forces finally took Cherbourg from the Germans. Having gained control of one of Normandy's major ports, the Allied troops could now receive a steady stream of supplies. Following a major tank battle at Falaise, Allied forces flooded through France, and by late August Paris was liberated.

GETTING AROUND

From July to August, **Bus Verts** (tel. 02–31–44–77–44), closed Sunday, with an office directly across from the train station in Bayeux, has a special D-day route called **Circuit 44.** For 90F, you can see as many D-day sites as you can squeeze into one day. They propose certain routes (for example, Pointe du Hoc, Colleville-sur-Mer, Longues-sur-Mer, and Arromanches), but the timing is essentially up to you. Buses depart from the train station in Bayeux and from Caen. During October–Easter, Circuit 44 shuts down and regular lines continue (infrequently) to Arromanches, Colleville-sur-Mer, and Pointe du Hoc, and eastward to the British cemetery at Hermanville on Sword Beach. You shouldn't pay more than 30F to get from any one point to the next. If you want to bike, the area is flat but dangerous: There are no bike paths, and the roads that connect the major sights are very narrow. Still, the youth hostel in Bayeux (*see above*) rents bikes for 60F a day if you want to risk it.

GUIDED TOURS • If you prefer a guided tour or are coming in the off-season (October–Easter) two tour companies run out of Bayeux. **Normandy Tours** (tel. 02–31–92–10–70), which carries up to eight people in its minivan, leaves from Bayeux's Hôtel de la Gare (*see* Where to Sleep, *above*). The guides are walking encyclopedias of local war lore and may be flexible about visiting beaches or cemeteries of particular interest to you. The half-day tours are available all year in English and in French for about 100F per person. Admission to the Arromanches museum is included. Reserve ahead and he'll pick you up from your hotel. **Bus Fly** (tel. 02–31–22–00–08) also has half-day tours in English and French for 160F, admission to Arromanches's museum included. During June–mid-September, the company makes regular stops at Bayeux's hostel or will pick you up at your hotel. Reservations are required.

WHERE TO SLEEP AND EAT

Unless you're a real World War II buff, you'll probably only want to come for a day. Most of the tours leave from and return to Bayeux anyway. If you plan to spend the night, ask the Bayeux tourist office for lists of campgrounds or chambres d'hôte.

The **Hôtel de la Marine** (quai du Canada, tel. 02–31–22–34–19) in Arromanches has great rooms, some with a view of the ocean, but doubles go for a stiff 200F (380F with bath). It's closed November–February. **Camping Arromanches** on avenue de Verdun (tel. 02–31–22–36–78) is located right above town near the beach. It charges 15F per person, 12F per site, and 12F per car. Munch on the standard crepes and pizza at the restaurants lining the main street leading to the Musée du Débarquement's entrance, or get picnic supplies at the small **market** next to the tourist office.

EXPLORING THE D-DAY BEACHES

GOLD BEACH • Arromanches, a town on Gold Beach 10 km (6 mi) northeast of Bayeux, is the largest city along the D-day strip and a good place to start exploring the surrounding area. Here the Allies erected Port Winston, and its remains still lie on the beach. Built in England, this prefab port was tugged over to the Normandy coast for the D-day invasion (by bringing their own ports with them, the Allies were able to outsmart the Nazis, who at the time controlled all coastal outlets through which the Allies might unload supplies and reinforcements). The **Musée du Débarquement,** overlooking the ocean, provides a detailed account of the construction of Port Winston, as well as the usual collection of Allied invasion paraphernalia like uniforms, military equipment, and news footage. Make sure to ask to see the slide show–diorama that reenacts the seizure of the Normandy beaches. The visit concludes with a short film. Both presentations are in French and English. Don't miss the **Arromanches 360°** (tel. 02–31–22–30–30), a circular movie theater just uphill from the museum that shows a 20-minute film entitled *The Price of Freedom*. Pl. du 6-Juin, tel. 02–31–22–34–31. Admission 35F, movie theater 20F. Open May–mid-Sept., daily 9–7; mid-Sept. Dec. and Feb–May, daily 9:30–12:30 and 1:30–5.

OMAHA BEACH • If you're interested in seeing some of the last remnants of Hitler's Atlantic Wall—essentially 4,500 km (3,000 mi) of batteries, shelters, and bunkers designed to ward off a coastal invasion—stop by **Longues-sur-Mer,** just west of Arromanches, before you reach Omaha Beach. Farther west, at **Colleville-sur-Mer,** overlooking Omaha Beach, you can walk through the somber 172-acre **American Cemetery,** covered with endless rows of white crosses and Stars of David, marking the graves of the almost 10,000 men buried here (only 40% of the original number—14,000 others were sent back to be buried in the States). A statue of *The Spirit of the American Youth* adorns the memorial at the east end of the cemetery. Most of the 4,649 American casualties on D day occurred on Omaha Beach. The German fighting force, probably the best there was, was assisted in its defense by the terrain—look down the cliffs to the beach and you'll see why. The cemetery is open May–September, daily 8—6; October–April, daily 9–5.

UTAH BEACH • On the morning of D day, 225 American Rangers under Lieutenant Colonel James Rudder scaled the sheer 100-ft cliffs of **Pointe Du Hoc,** 13 km (8 mi) west of Omaha Beach, to destroy the German artillery that covered both Utah and Omaha beaches. Only half made it to the top and roughly a third were left when they were finally picked up two days later, after a brutal counterattack by the Germans. A granite memorial pillar now stands on top of a concrete bunker, but the site otherwise remains as the Rangers left it—look down through the barbed wire at the jutting cliffs the troops ascended and see the huge craters left by exploded shells.

THE COTENTIN PENINSULA

If you were to visit only the Cotentin Peninsula's southernmost point, Mont-St-Michel, you would see one of the most impressive, jaw-dropping sights in France. However, you would come away believing that the peninsula is something that it's not: overrun with tourists and too expensive for budget travelers. Although Mont-St-Michel is far and away the most famous attraction in the area, there are other photogenic coastal towns worth attention, even if (and perhaps because) they're neglected by most travelers.

GRANVILLE

Thrust out on the edge of the peninsula and generally unexceptional, Granville has an attractive vieille ville and a few ho-hum museums. Its centre ville, the newer part of town that includes a rather ugly port, wears its beach atmosphere just fine. The weathered, 15th-century **Église Notre-Dame** sits perched up on the hill at the end of rue Notre-Dame. Nearby, the **Musée du Vieux Granville** (2 rue Lecarpentier, tel. 02–33–50–44–10) exhibits local historical artifacts and art. On rainy days, you could stand on the empty streets soaked to the bone, or you could spend a few minutes checking out the museum's so-so collection, occasionally spiced up by a temporary exhibit. Admission is 10F. It's open April–September, Wednesday–Monday 9–noon and 2–6; October–March, Wednesday and weekends 2–6. A bit more gripping is Granville's **Aquarium du Roc/La Féerie des Coquillages** (blvd. Vaufleury, tel. 02–33–50–19–83). It's open daily 9:30–noon and 2–6 and charges 40F to check out its ship models, dried blowfish, shells, and live local and tropical specimens.

BASICS

To reach the **tourist office,** turn right out of the train station on avenue Maréchal-Leclerc. The post office two doors up will exchange money for you. *4 cours Jonville, tel. 02–33–91–30–03. Open Sept.–June, Mon.–Sat. 9–12:30 and 2–7; July–Aug., Mon.–Sat. 9–7:30, Sun. 10:30–12:30 and 3–6:30.*

COMING AND GOING

Though hilly, Granville is small and easy to get around. The **train station** (pl. Pierre-Sémard, tel. 08–36–35–35—35) is between avenue de la Gare and avenue Maréchal-Leclerc on a hill above the centre ville. From here you can reach Paris (3½ hrs, 215F), Cherbourg (2¼ hrs, 116F via Lison), and Caen (2 hrs, 126F via Folligny). The STN office at **Tourisme Verney** (cours Jonville, tel. 02–33–50–77–89) is right across from the tourist office. Buses hit Avranches (1 hr, 32F) and, in July and August, make the two-hour journey directly to Mont-St-Michel (76F round-trip). One bus a day leaves Granville around 9:30 AM and then leaves Mont-St-Michel around 4:30. All buses leave from the train station.

WHERE TO SLEEP

Same old story—reserve in advance in July and August. The **Hôtel Terminus** (5 pl. Pierre-Sémard, tel. 02–33–50–02–05), across from the station, has clean, quiet singles (150F) and doubles (185F with shower), all with toilet and TV. **La Falaise** (7 rue Jules-Michelet, tel. 02–33–50–03–60), above the casino on a quiet street, has singles for 105F–115F; add 20F for a second person. The one room with a shower goes for 130F. It's closed December and January.

HOSTEL • Auberge de Jeunesse. The hostel at the port shares a building and a great view with the town's sailing center. Most rooms have balconies overlooking the beach; all rooms have full bathrooms. Four-bed rooms cost 58F per person, doubles and triples are 78F per person, and single rooms are 99F. There's no curfew. Be sure you have an HI card—they're rabid about it. *Blvd. des Amiraux, tel. 02–33–50–18–95. From station, go to tourist office in centre ville and follow CENTRE NAUTIQUE signs to left. 160 beds. Reception open Apr.–Sept., daily 8 AM–3 AM; Oct.–Mar., Mon.–Sat. 9 AM–11 PM. Check-in 5 PM–7:30 PM, checkout 7:30 AM–10 AM. Cash only. Closed 1 wk at Christmas.*

FOOD

L'Orient Express (93 rue des Juifs, tel. 02–33–50–18–47) is a popular restaurant with decent pasta dishes (25F–50F) and salads (30F–48F). It's open until midnight but closed Monday and during lunch on Tuesday. **L'Échauguette** (24 rue St-Jean, tel. 02–33–50–51–87) is a traditional crêperie in the vieille ville, with stone walls and a huge fireplace; crepes go for 12F–40F. On Saturday and Sunday mornings, do the market thing at place de Gaulle, outside the tourist office. Stock up at **Monoprix** (32 rue Lecampion, at the corner with rue Poirier).

WORTH SEEING

Did you know that Christian Dior lives in a pink house? Well, he does, and you can take your very own photo of it from among the lush sculpted gardens of the **Jardin Christian Dior**; the garden swimming pool was designed by the fashion god himself. The great views of the coastline are simply an added bonus. As if Granville needed another **musée,** Dior's house hosts temporary exhibitions during the summer. *Rue Estouteville, tel. 02–33–61–48–21 for information and hrs.*

After a day sleepwalking though Granville's museums, you'll have a heightened appreciation for the small but pretty **casino** (tel. 02–33–50–00–79) on the beach behind place Maréchal-Foch. It opens at 11 AM, but the real games don't get serious until much later.

OUTDOOR ACTIVITIES

Beaches definitely aren't breathtaking here, but people seem to flock to them anyway, especially to **Plage du Plat Gousset** on the peninsula's north side. Try to go at high tide—low tide sucks this place dry. There's also a swimming "pool" amidst the rocks if you don't feel like walking to the ocean. You could also explore the **Iles Chausey** islands northwest of Granville; they're famous for granite (used to build much of Paris and Mont-St-Michel). **Emeraude Lines** (tel. 02–33–50–16–36) runs several boats daily for 92F round-trip, but reserve ahead in the summer.

MONT-ST-MICHEL

Acting as a homing signal to every traveler in France, Mont-St-Michel's genuine beauty makes a lasting impact only when appreciated at the right moment—namely, *not* on summer afternoons. This 264-ft mound of rock, topped by a delicate abbey, looms a few hundred yards off the coast in dramatic contrast to the sandy bay and flat grasslands that surround it. The racing tides are part of Mont-St-Michel's beauty; they roll in almost to the edge of the man-made, 2-km (1-mi) causeway that links the island to the mainland. The alarming speed of the water's advance and retreat has become such a danger that there are plans to forbid cars and only use well-timed buses to get people to the rock. But for now, the Mont is yours

For centuries both Normandy and Brittany bickered over Mont-St-Michel, which lies on the border between the two regions. Even today some postcards with pictures of the Mont read Brittany, others Normandy.

to discover any way you want to. Do everything you can to visit off-season or at the least crowded times—morning and sunset (a sunset here is fairly dramatic). It makes all the difference.

Legend has it that in AD 708, the Archangel Michael appeared in a dream to Archbishop Aubert of Avranches and commanded him to build an abbey on the island. From then until the 16th century, a succession of Romanesque and Gothic buildings were built, resulting in the jumbled buildings that now stand on the rock.

All year long, the hour-long guided tour (in English and French) takes you through the impressive Romanesque and Gothic abbey and the abbey church, as well as the **Merveille,** a 13th-century, three-story collection of rooms and passageways, built around and on top of the monastery. This will cost you 40F. Another tour, which includes the delicate **Escalier de Dentelle** (Lace Staircase) and **pre-Roman church,** is longer and costs 60F. Invest in at least one tour while you're here—some of them get you on top of or into things you can't see alone. Best of all, visit June–September for the "Imaginaires," when the abbey is bathed in soft light and music. Nearly the entire abbey is at your disposal during the Imaginaire, crowd-free. The Imaginaires are held Monday–Saturday 10 PM–1 AM; in September, they're 9 PM–midnight. *Tel. 02–33–60–14–14. Abbey open May–Sept., daily 9:30–noon and 1:30–6; Oct.–April, daily 9:30–4:30. Sun. mass at 12:15.*

BASICS

The **tourist office** is on the left, behind the first gate as you enter town. It has information on the various festivals and concerts in the area and sells books and posters. If you've come by car, pick up a tide table while you're here or check the board outside for the tide schedules; if you don't move your car in time, you may drive home in a submarine. *Corps de Garde des Bourgeois, blvd. de l'Avancée, tel. 02–33–60–14–30. Open July–Aug., daily 9–7; Sept.–June, Mon.–Sat. 9–noon and 2–6.*

COMING AND GOING

STN buses (tel. 02–33–77–44–88) run from Pontorson (*see below*), 10 minutes away. The buses take you directly to the Porte du Roi main gate for 14F (22F round-trip). **Les Courriers Bretons** (tel. 02–99–56–20–44) runs a daily service to the Mont from Rennes train station (1¾ hrs, 61F).

GETTING AROUND

You approach the Mont's maze of chambers and Gothic and Romanesque spires via a single winding street, usually seething with human activity. You'd never suspect that only 120 people live on the island when you find yourself stuck in swarms of people on the **Grande Rue.** Lined with overpriced restaurants, hotels, and shops selling awful souvenir pottery and miniature replicas of the Mont, the Grande Rue still retains some historical character and beauty, as do the ramparts and various look-out points at the top of the street. The **Maison de la Baie** (tel. 02–33–70–86–46) leads worthwhile 35F walking tours across the mud of the bay to the Mont at low tide. Don't wander off by yourself, though—people get caught by surprise and drown . . . and there is quicksand everywhere.

WHERE TO SLEEP

Finding a cheap hotel on the island during July and August is a nightmare. Your best bet is to sleep in a nearby town like Pontorson or Avranches (*see below*), or simply make the Mont a day trip from St-Malo or Rennes (*see* Chapter 4).

Hôtel Du Guesclin. One of the few places on the Grande Rue where you won't be completely swindled, this hotel has simple but clean doubles for 200F–380F. Make sure you book a month in advance. *Grande Rue, tel. 02–33–60–14–10. 22 rooms, all with shower. Closed Nov.–Easter.*

Hôtel St-Aubert. Two kilometers (1 mi) from the Mont at the beginning of the causeway, this modern hotel is comfortable and efficiently run. Even better, it has a swimming pool and garden in back. Singles and doubles are 150F–350F. The restaurant has a 75F dinner menu (55F for lunch) and breakfast for 30F. *Rte. du Mont, Beauvoir, tel. 02–33–60–08–74. 27 rooms, all with bath.*

CAMPING • The nearest campground, **Camping du Mont** (tel. 02–33–60–09–33), is 2 km (1 mi) away, but it's often crowded in summer. It costs 15F per person, 11F per tent, and 13F per car; it's closed mid-November–mid-February. Four kilometers (2½ mi) away in Beauvoir (on the Pontorson–Mont-St-Michel bus line) is **Camping du Gué de Beauvoir** (tel. 02–33–60–09–23), charging 10F per site plus 14F per person; it's closed October–March.

FOOD

Food prices are extravagant on the Mont; you could end up paying 120F for a *mère poulard* (a hearty omelet). Granted, it's beaten to a funky rhythm and cooked over a wooden fire, but it's still just eggs and butter. There is really no point in eating inside the restaurants that line the causeway of the Grande Rue—most don't have a view, are crammed with tourists, and have mediocre 55F–75F menus. Instead, pack a picnic and walk up the *promenade des remparts,* where the view will spice up the blandest sandwich. If you absolutely need to eat in a restaurant, **Le Saint-Michel** (Grand Rue, tel. 02–33–60–14–37) is as near as you'll get to honest bistro cuisine, with the cheapest menu at 79F.

NEAR MONT-ST-MICHEL

AVRANCHES

You'll save money and your sanity by staying in Avranches, which is just 22 km (14 mi) east of Mont-St-Michel. The **Foyer des Jeunes Travailleurs** (15 rue du Jardin des Plantes, tel. 02–33–58–06–54) rents out vacant rooms with private showers for 100F a night, breakfast included. **Hôtel de Normandie** (2 blvd. Léon Jozeau-Marigné, tel. 02–33–58–01–33) has pleasant singles for 150F, doubles for 180F; free showers are down the hall.

If you're here in July or August, check out the 8th- to 15th-century illuminated manuscripts, made by monks from the Mont, at the town hall, the **Mairie d'Avranches** (pl. Littré, tel. 02–33–89–29–40); admission is 20F. The **tourist office** (tel. 02–33–58–00–22) is next to the town hall at 2 rue Général-de-Gaulle; it is open daily 9–noon and 2–6:30, and 9–noon and 2–7 July–August. The **STN bus station** (tel. 02–33–58–03–07) is in the same building and runs one bus a day to and from Mont-St-Michel in July and August. The one-hour trip costs 24F (46F round-trip) and leaves at 10:45 AM, returning at 5:40 PM. Trains travel from the Avranches **train station** (pl. de la Gare, tel. 02–33–58–00–77) several times daily to Granville (30 mins, 54F via Folligny), Rennes (70 mins, 81F), Caen (2 hrs, 109F), and Cherbourg (2½ hrs, 118F via Lison).

PONTORSON

This town is basically used and abused by people who want to see Mont-St-Michel and need a cheap place to stay. Pontorson is 9 km (5½ mi) south of the popular tourist sight. Don't get stuck here—there's basically nothing to do except buy postcards of the Mont. What got you here in the first place is the **Auberge de Jeunesse** (21 blvd. Patton, tel. 02–33–60–18–65), housed in a small farmhouse 10 minutes from the train station. The place has a good atmosphere but is pretty spartan—no sheets, no breakfast. At least they have a kitchen. Dorm bunk beds are 41F. You can also try **Hôtel de l'Arrivée** (14 rue du Docteur Tizon, tel. 02–33–60–01–57), right across the street from the train station. Clean, decent singles or doubles go for 90F, 155F with shower. Near the hostel and a small canal is the treeless **Camping Municipal** (chemin des Soupirs, off rue Patton, tel. 02–33–68–11–59), charging 12F per person and 12F per site.

BASICS • For information on chambres d'hôte, stop by the **Syndicat d'Initiative** (pl. de l'Église, tel. 02–33–60–20–65), closed for lunch and Sunday, as well as Monday off-season. Trains make it to Pontorson from Rennes (55 mins, 68F), St-Malo via Dol (40 mins, 42F), Caen (2¼ hrs, 120F), and Paris via Caen (4 hrs, 252F). **STN** buses (tel. 02–33–50–08–99) leave for Mont-St-Michel from the train station (pl. de la Gare, tel. 02–33–60–00–35) in Pontorson all day long in summer (22F round-trip); the rest of the year, they leave in the morning and evening on weekdays, in the afternoon on weekends. The last bus out of Mont-St-Michel takes off in the early evening. If you want to stay for the night show, either bum a ride (most people you see on the Mont are living or staying inland) or plunk down 120F for a **taxi** (tel. 02–33–48–24–09 or 02–33–60–33–23).

CHAMPAGNE AND THE NORTH

UPDATED BY CHRISTOPHER KNOWLES

A history of bickering monarchies, two world wars, and encroaching industrial gloom have left their marks on Champagne and the North. This area was once an important center of trade and scholarship, the site of stately bourgeois residences and beautiful abbeys. Yet from pre-Roman times to the end of World War II in 1945, some of Europe's bloodiest wars have been fought on the windswept land of the North. The effects of World War I still linger in the trenches dug near the cemeteries at Arras. Some of what remains is still remarkable, however. Both Lille and Arras have striking examples of Flemish brick architecture, and the vast Cathédrale Nôtre-Dame of Amiens is a Gothic masterpiece. All this architectural extravagance is grafted onto lazy fields full of the North's trademark cows, scenery that lends itself to the austere medieval majesty of these towns rising up out of the rolling green plains. And the war cemeteries near Arras—dizzying rows of crosses stretching out toward infinity—are a somber reason to visit the area.

An altogether different, more uplifting landscape tumbles about Reims and Epernay, perhaps because its inhabitants treat themselves to a regular infusion of the local champagne. Each year, millions of bottles of bubbly mature in hundreds of miles of chalk tunnels carved under the towns' streets. Although you may not be able to afford a bottle, you just might be able to land yourself a complimentary glass of champagne at the end of a tour—just the thing to take the sting out of bad war memories.

BASICS

Most cities have a well-stocked, well-informed tourist office. But if that's not enough for you, the regional tourist office in Châlons-en-Champagne, **Comité Régional du Tourisme de Champagne-Ardenne,** has maps and brochures aplenty. Buses stop here on the way to Troyes, Epernay, and Reims. *15 av. du Maréchal-Leclerc, tel. 03–26–21–85–80, fax 03–26–21–85–90.*

COMING AND GOING

Sadly, getting around the North is not that easy without a car. Train lines tend to radiate from Paris, and you sometimes need to return to Paris to change lines. Regional buses aren't much cheaper than the trains, and they stop in every town. Ferries can scoot you from Boulogne and Calais to England and Ireland; their prices (from 160F) have been lowered to compete with high-speed Eurostar trains zipping to London from Paris (3 hrs, 645F), Lille (2 hrs, 615F), and Calais (1 hr 40 mins, 490F). Information on schedules, bus stops and stations can be obtained from the **Conseil Régional** (tel. 03–26–70–31—61).

REIMS

Reims has been the center of champagne production for more than two centuries, stocking the cellars of its many conquerors—Napoléon, Czar Nicholas I, the Duke of Wellington, and the present-day crowds of case-toting bubblyphiles. Yet long before a drink put it on the map, Reims was renowned for its cathedral, which was the coronation ground of almost all the kings of France, from Clovis I, the king of the Franks, up to Charles X in 1825.

More recent historical events have treated the city less kindly: The destruction of World War II left only 16 buildings intact by the time American forces arrived to liberate the city (Eisenhower later accepted the formal German surrender here on May 7, 1945). The champagne industry today remains relatively unscathed, however, and tunnels under the city serve as the damp and moldy berth for Mumm, Taittinger, Pommery, and Veuve-Clicquot. Above ground, Reims resembles any other provincial capital, replete with manicured flower beds, parks, and the compulsory Joan of Arc statue.

BASICS

BUREAUX DE CHANGE

Place Drouet-d'Erlon has a few banks, as well as a bureau de change. The best rates are at **Banque de France** (1 pl. de l'Hôtel de Ville, tel. 03–26–89–52–52) or **Banque Nationale de Paris** (101 rue Gambetta and 167 av. de Laon, tel. 03–26–77–33–90). **Crédit Agricole** (25 rue Libergier, tel. 03–26–53–30–00) operates a 24-hour automatic change machine with mediocre rates.

DISCOUNT TRAVEL AGENCIES

For cheap train tickets and other travel services, try **Voyages Wasteel** (22 rue Libergier, tel. 03–26–85–79–79) or **Forum Voyages** (14 cours Jean-Baptiste-Langlet, tel. 03–26–47–54–22).

LAUNDRY

Rid your clothes of those foul odors at the *laverie* (laundromat) at 129 rue de Vesle. Other locations are 2 bis avenue Georges Hodin, 162 avenue Jean-Jaurès, and 288 avenue de Laon. A wash costs 20F, and 6F gets you 15 minutes of dryer time.

MAIL

The main post office has poste restante service (postal code 51100) and a bureau de change. *Rue Olivier-Métra, at pl. du Boulingrin, tel. 03–26–50–58–01. Open weekdays 8–7, Sat. 8:30–noon.*

MEDICAL AID

To treat champagne-cork accidents call the **Hôpital Régional** (tel. 03–26–78–78–78). For urgent cases call **SAMU** (tel. 03–26–06–07–08) or dial 15 (toll-free) from any pay phone.

VISITOR INFORMATION

Tourists swamp the frenetic staff of the **Office de Tourisme** and often take most of the good maps. Luckily, Reims has installed funky illuminated city maps that double as map dispensers (2F)—one such device is on boulevard Joffre, to the left of the train station. Their exchange desk has unimpressive rates but no commission, and they can make reservations for you in a *chambre d'hôte* (bed-and-breakfast). *2 rue Guillaume-de-Machault, next to cathedral, tel. 03–26–77–45–25, fax 03–26–77–45–27. Open Easter–June and Sept., Mon.–Sat. 9–7:30, Sun. 9:30–6:30; July–Aug., Mon.–Sat. 9–8, Sun. 9:30–7; Oct.–Easter, Mon.–Sat. 9–6:30, Sun. 9:30–5:30.*

COMING AND GOING

Bordered by the train station to the northwest and the Canal de l'Aisne to the southwest, the *centre ville* (town center) contains most of Reims's tourist attractions. **Transports Urbains de Reims** (6 rue Chanzy, tel. 03–26–88–25–38) runs the checkered city buses; most stop in front of the train station. Bus drivers sell single tickets for 5F; the vending machine in the train station sells a *carnet* (book) of 10 for 32F. **Taxis de Reims** (tel. 03–26–47–05–05) answers its phone around the clock.

BY TRAIN

The **train station,** across from the parc Driant-Estienne, is a 10-minute walk from the center of town. Trains run from here to Paris's Gare de l'Est (90 mins, 118F), Épernay (20 mins, 52F), Châlons-en-Champagne (40 mins, 70F), and Dijon (4 hrs, 206F). *Blvd. Joffre, tel. 03–26–65–17–07. Open daily 5:30 AM–11:30 PM.*

BY BUS

STDM Trans-Champagne (tel. 03–26–65–17–07) runs two or three daily buses to Troyes (2¼ hrs, 103F) by way of Châlons-en-Champagne (1 hr, 40F); the buses stop at place du Forum and in front of the train station. **RTA** (tel. 03–23–50–68–50) sends one bus per day to Laon (2 hrs, 43F) from rue St-Symphorien at rue Eugène-Desteuque, one block behind the cathedral.

WHERE TO SLEEP

UNDER 150F • Hôtel Linguet. The Linguet has a small garden and stained-glass windows in a quiet location just minutes from the cathedral. The sunny rooms are a steal: Singles, available in summer only, are 95F; showers are 15F. Doubles with bath are 135F. *14 rue Linguet, tel. 03–26–47–31–89. 13 rooms, some with bath. Cash only. Closed 3rd wk of Aug.*

UNDER 200F • Au Bon Accueil. "The Good Welcome" has large clean rooms near the train station and budget restaurants. Singles are 85F, and doubles start at 105F; showers cost 10F. Doubles with shower are 190F. *31 rue de Thillois, tel. 03–26–88–55–74. 9 rooms, some with bath.*

Hôtel St-André. The easygoing owner rents out bright, floral rooms at great prices. One single goes for 89F; doubles without bath run 105F–122F; and doubles with bath, phone, and TV run 189F–199F. It's a 20-minute walk from the station, or you can take Bus B from the center to the Église St-André, just across the street from the hotel. If no one is at the reception desk, ask at the bar downstairs. *46 av. Jean-Jaurès, tel. 03–26–47–24–16. 20 rooms, some with bath. Cash only.*

Hôtel Thillois. Despite the well-tattooed dude running the evening reception, this hotel's lacy curtains and flowery bedspreads suggest the work of the more matronly owner visible during the day. Every room has a sink and TV, with singles starting at 115F and doubles at 135F, 185F with shower. Get the door code before you hit Reims's bars at night—you're a block away from place Drouet d'Erlon, center of the city's nightlife. *17 rue de Thillois, tel. 03–26–40–65–65. 19 rooms, 13 with shower.*

HOSTEL

Auberge de Jeunesse/Centre International de Séjour. Twenty minutes from the station, this modern, antiseptic hostel lacks the usual rowdy hostel atmosphere. Singles are 82F, doubles and triples 65F per person. Breakfast is 10F. Even if you do have a reservation, arrive early because they don't always hold them. There's no curfew or daytime lockout, and the surrounding parks are great places to kick back and relax. An HI card is required. *Esplanade André-Malraux (near Parc Leo-Lagrange), tel. 03–26–40–52–60, fax 03–26–87–35–70. From train station, Bus K (direction: Bezannes) to Colin. 73 beds. Reception open 7 AM–11 PM. Check-in 5 PM–8 PM, checkout 7 AM–10 AM. Cash only.*

FOOD

Reims claims to have more restaurant and hotel stars than any other French town. Though this is bad news for the budget traveler, everything from outrageously expensive restaurants to low-cost sandwich joints speckles **place Drouet-d'Erlon.** Near the canal, **Stalingrad** (pl. Stalingrad, tel. 03–26–40–30–70) serves standard brasserie meals for 56F in its upstairs restaurant. A large **market** fills up the pavilion on place du Boulingrin Wednesday and Saturday mornings.

UNDER 75F • Fleur de Mai. Slightly more popular than its neighboring Asian restaurants, the Fleur de Mai serves decent Chinese and Vietnamese specialties. The 55F weekday lunch comes with a chicken salad, mushroom pork or pineapple beef, rice, and a "dessert biscuit"; a similar dinner menu goes for 70F. *112 rue de Vesle, tel. 03–26–40–52–32.*

L'Os et l'Arête. This rustic little restaurant around the corner from the hostel serves 55F three-course lunch menus on pink tablecloths—pizzas and yummy salads both hover between 30F and 56F. In summer, eat outside on the patio. *15 rue du Colonel Fabien, tel. 03–26–04–63–12. Closed Mon.*

UNDER 100F • Le Chamois. This small, romantic nook serves your choice of beef or chicken cooked up on a volcanic rock, plus cheese or dessert—all for 75F. At least two people have to order this meal, so bring your significant other. Le Chamois also serves fondues, raclettes, and huge 45F lunch salads. *45 rue des Capucins, off rue de Vesle, tel. 03–26–88–69–75. Closed Wed. No lunch Sun.*

Table en Périgord. This pleasant, low-key restaurant specializes in two particularly rich French dishes: a two-course menu of either pâté de foie gras with a walnut salad (75F) or *magret de canard* (duck breast cooked in its own fat) with an entrée (80F). *47 pl. Drouet d'Erlon, tel. 03–26–47–73–74. Closed Sun.*

WORTH SEEING

Most sights cluster around the cathedral, but the Basilique St-Rémi and most of the champagne houses lie closer to place des Droits de l'Homme, a half-hour walk or a short ride away on Bus A. If you only have one day in Reims, concentrate your efforts in the centre ville.

BASILIQUE ST-RÉMI

This sober church rises above peaceful lawns, modestly displaying its Gothic curves and bright stained-glass windows. St-Rémi, the bishop of Reims between 459 and 533 and the city's namesake, snoozes in a tomb behind the altar. After the destruction of World War II, the Basilique was not reopened for worship until 1958. *53 rue St-Rémi, tel. 03–26–85–31–20. From train station, Bus A (direction: Maison Blanche). Admission free. Open Wed.–Mon. 10–noon and 2–6.*

Some champagne tunnels are so moldy that penicillin grows freely on the walls—workers rub their cuts on it.

CATHÉDRALE NOTRE-DAME

Thirty-four French kings and eight queens were crowned under the ethereal heights of this cathedral (including all 11 Louis, seven Charleses, six Philippes, two Henris, and one François, plus a guest appearance from Joan of Arc), but you wouldn't know it by the more fanciful ˀeatures of its exterior—giggling angels, stern saints, and a grinning bovine creature. The elegant Gothic edifice dates from the 13th century; the fiery rose window was done in the 16th century; and Marc Chagall's colorful stained-glass windows depicting biblical scenes are 20th-century touches. Guided tours, in French only, include a promenade around the parapet; they leave every 30 minutes 10–11:30 (except Sunday) and 2–5:30. On Saturday nights June–August, a free son-et-lumière (sound and light) show illuminates the cathedral's facade. *Pl. du Cardinal Luçon. Tours 15F. Open daily 7:30–7:30.*

Many of the cathedral's deteriorating statues have been replaced; the originals stand next door in the **Palais du Tau** (tel. 03–26–47–81–79), a T-shape (thus the name) 15th-century archbishop's palace that houses the cathedral's treasures. The giant saints and gargoyles are even more entertaining at close range. The museum also includes a magnificent series of tapestries. *2 pl. du Cardinal-Luçon, tel. 03–26–47–74–39. Admission 32F. Open July–Aug., daily 9:30–6:30; mid-Mar.–June and Sept.–mid-Nov., daily 9:30–12:30 and 2–6; mid-Nov.–mid-Mar., daily 10–noon and 2–5 (weekends until 6).*

CHAMPAGNE HOUSES

Not only is the region's chalky soil ideal for nourishing champagne grapes, but chalk tunnels, often excavated as quarries by the Romans, also maintain the 11°C (52°F) temperature perfect for champagne production. Most of the champagne houses give informative tours of their *caves* (cellars). The quality of the tours is inconsistent, ranging from hilarious to despairingly tedious, though a glass of champagne at the end makes even the mediocre ones worth it. In general, tours take place weekdays 9–noon and 2–5 and last around an hour, and you should reserve in advance. The tourist office posts a list of the day's tours and can give you maps with all the houses marked. Most tours have English-speaking guides, especially if you reserve in advance, and cost 20F.

Mumm (34 rue du Champ-de-Mars, tel. 03–26–49–59–70, fax 03–26–49–59–01) is the closest champagne house to the centre ville, a 10-minute walk north from the cathedral. Other caves cluster just southeast of the center. Make reservations in advance for **Veuve-Clicquot Ponsardin** (1 pl. des Droits de l'Homme, tel. 03–26–89–54–41). The introductory film here isn't the blatant attempt at audiovisual hypnosis that it is at other houses. **Pommery** (5 pl. du Général-Gouraud, tel. 03–26–61–62–56, fax 03–26–61–62–96) gives a tour of its ancient Roman chalk pits and tunnels, where the widow Pommery had friezes sculpted for the viewing pleasure of her workers. **Taittinger** (9 pl. St-Nicaise, tel. 03–26–85–45–33, fax 03–26–85–84–05), set on the remains of the 13th-century St-Nicaise abbey, has some of the best tunnels.

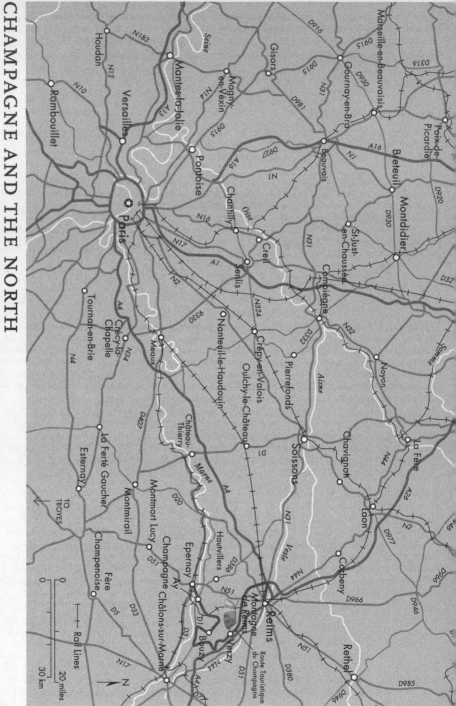

Rail Lines

0
20 miles
30 km

N

TO
TROYES

Route Touristique
du Champagne

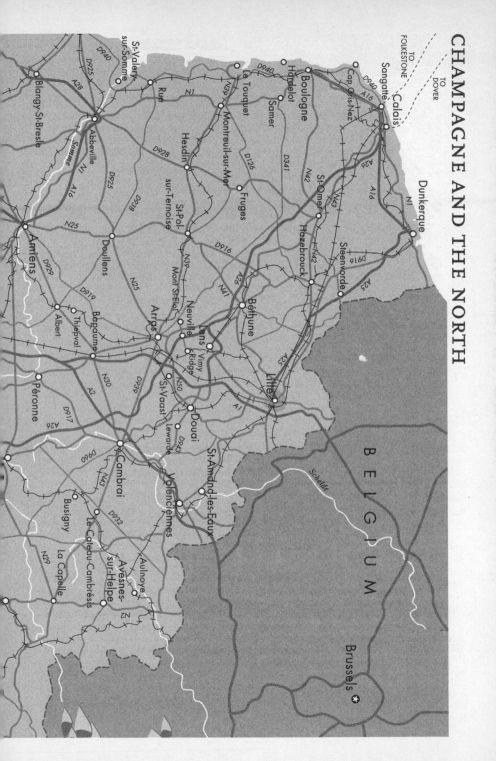

TO
FOLKESTONE

TO
DOVER

Sangatte
Calais

Cap Gris-Nez

Dunkerque

Wissant

Boulogne

Hardelot

Samer

Le Touquet

Montreuil-sur-Mer

Hesdin

St-Omer

Hazebrouck

Steenvoorde

Fruges

St-Pol-
sur-Ternoise

Mont St-Éloi

Béthune

Lille

Neuville

Arras

Lens

Vimy
Ridge

Doullens

Bapaume

St-Vaast

Douai

Lewarde

St-Amand-les-Eaux

Valenciennes

Amiens

Albert

Thiepval

Péronne

Cambrai

Busigny

Le Cateau-Cambrésis

Avesnes-
sur-Helpe

Aulnoye

La Capelle

St-Valery-
sur-Somme

Rue

Abbeville

Blangy-St-Bresle

Somme

B E L G I U M

Schelde

Brussels

197

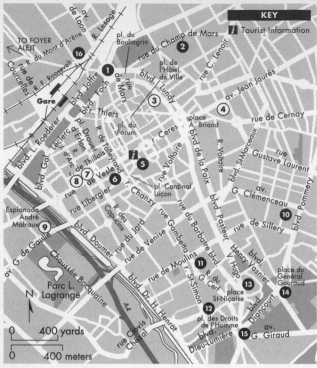

REIMS

KEY

i Tourist Information

Sights ●

Basilique/Musée
St-Rémi, **12**

Cathédrale
Notre-Dame, **5**

Centre Historique
de l'Automobile
Française, **10**

Mumm, **2**

Musée de l'Ancien
Collège des
Jésuites, **11**

Musée de la
Reddition, **16**

Musée des
Beaux-Arts, **6**

Pommery, **14**

Porte de Mars, **1**

Taittinger, **13**

Veuve-Clicquot
Ponsardin, **15**

Lodging ○

Auberge de
Jeunesse, **9**

Au Bon Acceuil, **8**

Hôtel Linguet, **3**

Hôtel St-André, **4**

Hôtel Thillois, **7**

MUSEUMS

A 15F ticket, available at any of the participating museums, gives you access to all of Reims's museums except the Musée Hôtel le Vergeur (a medieval town house with a collection of Dürer engravings) and the Centre Historique de l'Automobile Française (*see below*). Otherwise, individual tickets are 10F each. Most of the city's museums close on Tuesday, except for the Musée St-Rémi and the car museum, which are open daily.

The **Musée des Beaux-Arts** (8 rue Chanzy, tel. 03–26–47–28–44) has a small but stimulating collection, including an entire room of Corot; a few works by van Gogh, Matisse, Delacroix, and Pissarro; and David's copy of his own masterpiece, *La Mort de Marat*. The **Musée de la Reddition** (12 rue Franklin-Roosevelt, tel. 03–26–47–84–19) preserves Eisenhower's World War II headquarters, site of the German surrender on May 7, 1945. Close by stands the **Musée de l'Ancien Collège des Jésuites** (1 pl. Museux, tel. 03–26–85–51–50), a 17th-century college featuring several richly decorated rooms, a gorgeous Baroque library, and subterranean tunnels. For those longing for the ambience of car showrooms, rows and rows of sleek cars adorn the **Centre Historique de l'Automobile Française** (84 av. Georges-Clemenceau, tel. 03–26–82–83–84); admission is 30F. The **Musée St-Rémi** (rue Simon, tel. 03–26–85–23–36), housed in the magnificent abbey next door to the Basilique St-Rémi, is the city's archaeological and historical museum.

AFTER DARK

The recently renovated **place Drouet d'Erlon** is the place to be after nightfall. The young staff at the tourist office can point out the latest "in" disco. At **Le Boss** (17 rue Lesage, tel. 03–26–88–33–83) you can dance all night, with no cover for women until 1 AM. You can also play snooker upstairs for 50F an hour at **César's Club** or sip 55F cocktails and soak up the Mafia-esque atmosphere. From the train station, head to avenue de Laon and take the first right onto rue Lesage. **Le Croque-Notes** (24 rue Ernest Renan, tel. 03–26–88–41–28) has live jazz most nights at 10.

NEAR REIMS

The tourist office in Reims stocks reams of information on the region. For the car- or cycle-blessed, it suggests the **Route du Champagne,** a long circuit involving frequent stops and *dégustations* (tastings) at local champagne houses. Signs in Reims point you in the right direction, and after 75 km (47 mi) of rolling through vineyards and tiny villages like **Verzy** and **Ay** you'll arrive in **Epernay.** The brochure *La Route Touristique du Champagne* (available free in English at the tourist office) is invaluable.

EPERNAY

Although Reims loudly proclaims itself to be the last word in champagne production, Epernay is really the center of the bubbly drink's spirit. It was here in 1741 that the first full-blown champagne house, Moët (now Moët et Chandon), took the lifetime passion of Dom Pérignon and turned it into an industry. Above ground, 19th-century houses cover the city, but most visitors head directly for the underground chalk tunnels. Most champagne houses have tours and tastings for 20F, though smaller ones usually require reservations. **Moët et Chandon** (20 av. de Champagne, tel. 03–26–51–20–20), makers of the prestigious Dom Pérignon champagne, give large and frequent English-language tours. The tours at **De Castellane** (57 rue de Verdun, tel. 03–26–51–19–19) are refreshingly unpretentious. There is, thankfully, no film, and admission (20F, 35F with butterfly garden) includes entry to a champagne museum and a water tower, plus a glass of champagne. You can enter their **Jardin de Papillons Vivants** (Garden of Live Butterflies) for 22F mid-May–mid-September. **Mercier** (70 av. de Champagne, tel. 03–26–51–22–23) conducts annoyingly glitzy tours of its tunnels from laser-guided trains.

BASICS • The helpful **Office de Tourisme** has a list and map of all of Epernay's champagne houses and information on the region. It also has discount cards for the discotheque **Tap-Too** (5 rue du Pré-Dimanche, tel. 03–26–55–64–01), a flashy local nightspot. *7 av. de Champagne, behind Hôtel de Ville, tel. 03–26–55–33–00. Open Easter–mid-Oct., Mon.–Sat. 9:30–12:30 and 1:30–7, Sun. 11–4; mid-Oct.–Easter, Mon.–Sat. 9:30–12:30 and 1:30–5:30.*

COMING AND GOING • Trains leave for Reims (20 mins, 52F), Châlons-en-Champagne (15 mins, 51F), and Paris (70 mins, 109F) from Epernay's **train station** (tel. 03–26–88–50–50), about a five-minute walk north of the central place de la République. **STDM Trans-Champagne** (tel. 03–26–65–17–07) runs two buses weekdays to Châlons-en-Champagne (1 hr, 33F) from the train station's parking lot on boulevard de la Motte.

WHERE TO SLEEP • Rooms are scarce in Epernay, so call way ahead of time. The best deal is the **Foyer des Jeunes Travailleurs** (2 rue Pupin, tel. 03–26–51–62–51, fax 03–26–54–15–60), with cozy singles and doubles for 72F per person and bargain 16F breakfasts. Another good deal is the **Hôtel St-Pierre** (1 rue Jeanne-d'Arc, tel. 03–26–54–40–80), closed Sunday afternoon, an old bourgeois residence whose 15 well-kept singles and doubles (11 rooms with shower, 125F–200F) should cost twice as much as they do. It's a 20-minute walk north of town to Epernay's riverfront **campground** (allée de Cumières, tel. 03–26–55–32–14), where for 18F a site and 14F per person you can battle caravans; it's closed November–March.

FOOD • Scale the flight of stairs to **Le Kilimandjaro** (15 pl. de la République, tel. 03–26–51–61–60), where 20F–50F buys you hefty salads and crepes. The **Auberge d'Epernay** (30 rue du Dr-Verron, tel. 03–26–51–94–67) dishes out three-course Chinese, Vietnamese, and Thai meals for 59F, 73F on weekends. **La Terrasse** (5–7 quai de la Marne, tel. 03–26–55–26–05) cooks up fine French cuisine, with 60F two-course "express lunches" and four-course dinner menus from 90F. Across from the train station, **Le Chapon Fin** (2 pl. Mendés-France, tel. 03–26–55–40–03) has an excellent traditional three-course meal for 65F or a four-course menu for 160F. (If you're so full you can't walk afterward, basic 120F–160F doubles await you upstairs.) Your best bet if you're almost broke is the great **market** at Halle St-Thibault (Wednesday and Saturday mornings) or place Auban-Moët (Sunday morning).

TROYES

Though Troyes falls geographically within Champagne, its strongly medieval atmosphere reflects little of the flamboyant 19th-century spirit of Reims or Epernay. The half-timbered houses in the **Vauluisant** and **St-Jean** districts have been maintained with care, creating a central core of pleasantly rambling narrow

THE RIDDLER KNOWS

Dom Pérignon, a blind 17th-century Benedictine monk, was reputedly the first to discover the secret of bubbly. Today, champagne production is not all that different from the way the Dom did it 300 years ago. Chardonnay, Pinot Noir, and sometimes Pinot Meunier grapes ferment separately and are then mixed into each house's distinctive blend and bottled. Left upside down in chilly underground tunnels, the heavy-walled bottles are frequently turned by "riddlers," people who spend three years learning exactly how to turn bottles in order to nudge the sediment down into the neck. After turning, the bottle necks are quickly frozen, the caps are taken off, and the frozen sediment shoots out. A small quantity of liqueur is then added, and the corks are tied down for good with wire. It takes about three years of fermentation to produce the proper level of fizz, alcohol, and taste. Only wine from Champagne can legally be called champagne; otherwise it's sparkling wine.

walks. Oodles of churches, several fine museums, and low hotel and food costs add to the appeal of the town. Troyes is also the center of France's knitwear industry.

BASICS

On the right of the square in front of the station, the **Office de Tourisme** dispenses information on Troyes and the surrounding region, including *Sorties,* a list of music and theater events. You can change money here when the banks are closed. Individual guided tours can be arranged July to mid-September. *16 blvd. Carnot, tel. 03–25–82–62–70, fax 03–25–73–06–81. Open Mon.–Sat. 9–12:30 and 2–6:30; June–Aug., also open Sun. 10–noon and 2–5. Other location: rue Mignard (opposite Église St-Jean), tel. 03–25–73–36–88; open daily 10–noon and 2–5.*

COMING AND GOING

The tourist literature is quick to tell you that Troyes's old town resembles a champagne cork; the Seine flows around what would be the top half and the train station is at the bottom. Though large for a cork, Troyes is small for a town; everything is accessible by foot. **Le Bus** (tel. 03–25–70–49–00), the city bus service, stops in front of the tourist office; buy tickets from the driver (7F per ticket or three for 16F).

BY TRAIN

Troyes is 1½ hours and 135F from Paris. About nine trains a day run between the two, which is a good thing since you have to go through Paris to get almost anywhere from Troyes. The same number of trains head daily the other way to Chaumont (50 mins, 84F), where you can change for Dijon (3 hrs, 167F from Troyes). Troyes's **train station** (Cours de la Gare, tel. 03–25–70–41–27) is open 4:30 AM–9 PM.

BY BUS

To traverse Champagne without passing through Paris you must board an **STDM Trans-Champagne** bus (tel. 03–26–65–17–07). Buses go to Reims (2¼ hrs, 103F) by way of Châlons-en-Champagne (1¼ hrs, 72F). The bus stop is on your left as you exit the train station.

WHERE TO SLEEP

UNDER 150F • Les Comtes de Champagne. This old brick-and-timber building is in the heart of the old town. Breakfast is served in the elegant, wood-beamed dining salon or the ivy-trellised courtyard. Clean and well-groomed singles or doubles run 120F–270F. *54–56 rue de la Monnaie, tel. 03–25–73–11–70, fax 03–25–73–06–02. From station, turn right to roundabout, left on rue Colonel Driant (which becomes rue de la Monnaie). 29 rooms, some with bath.*

Hôtel Butat. This two-star hotel has immaculate rooms, artfully decorated with flower prints. Two singles cost 120F each and doubles are 140F (170F with bath); hall showers are free. Count on lugging your luggage up, up, and up. *50 rue de Turenne, tel. 03–25–73–77–39. Turn right out of train station, left on rue H. Truelle, right on rue de Turenne. 24 rooms, 13 with bath.*

HOSTEL

Auberge de Jeunesse. This overstaffed hostel lies 7 km (4½ mi) from Troyes on the edge of a modest wood. Unfortunately, delinquent school kids sometimes fill the place. Beds cost 48F, or you can camp on the lawn for 25F. The cafeteria has a single 48F ticket good for both lunch and dinner; you can also cook in their kitchen. Sheets cost 16F. On school days September–June, take Bus 6 to the end and then Bus 24 to the hostel. *Chemin Ste-Scholastique, Rosières, tel. 03–25–82–00–65, fax 03–25–72–93–78. From tourist office, take Bus 6 to end of line, turn right at water tower onto rue Pasteur, walk for 30 mins, turn left on rue Jules Ferry, hoof it another 10 mins, then left on chemin Ste-Scholastique. 100 beds. Reception open 8 AM–10 PM. Curfew 11 PM. Cash only.*

CAMPING

Camping Municipal, a half-hour walk away from town, charges 16F per person and 16F per site . *7 rue Roger Salen, tel. 03–25–81–02–64. Follow rue Voltaire onto the RN60 or take Bus 1 from the tourist office. Closed mid-Oct.–Mar.*

FOOD

Reasonable restaurants freckle Troyes's old town; a short stroll usually turns up a gaggle of 50F–60F menus, and the outdoor tables of a half-dozen crêperies and pizzerias clog the pedestrian streets around Église St-Jean. **Grill St-Jean** (21 rue Champeaux, tel. 03–25–73–52–26) is open daily and has well-presented, filling Italian and traditional menus for 66F, with several main dishes under 30F. The **Marché Couvert** near Église St-Rémi has local produce; upstairs is the supermarket **Prisunic** (75 rue Émile Zola, tel. 03–25–68–67–07).

UNDER 75F • Le Bouchon Champenois. Hidden in a courtyard off rue des Quinze-Vingts, Le Bouchon serves traditional food a cut way above the slightly cheaper surrounding joints. The four-course 70F menu, including whipped avocados, duck, and banana flambé, is well worth the investment. *1 cour du Mortier d'Or, between ruelle des Chats and rue des Quinze-Vingts, tel. 03–25–73–69–24. Closed Mon. No dinner Sun.*

Soleil de l'Inde. Tucked in old Troyes, this is an Indian experience in the midst of a medieval time capsule, with sitar music and incense wafting through the air. The 59F menu (not served Saturday night) includes nan bread, chicken tandoori or *pallack penhir* (spinach dish with yogurt), and dessert. A four-course vegetarian meal is 80F. *33 rue de la Cité, down street from cathedral, tel. 03–25–80–75–71.*

WORTH SEEING

The 16th-century timber and brick houses, cantilevered out over the pedestrian streets, are the best reason to visit the city. These structures fill two of Troyes's districts: The more active centers on the Église St-Jean and the other, a bit more run-down, on the Hôtel Vauluisant. The somber churches pick up in the evenings from mid-June to mid-September every Thursday–Saturday evening when they host **son-et-lumière shows**; check the tourist office for performance times and prices.

CHURCHES

Flamboyant flames lick the outlandish facade of the **Cathédrale St-Pierre et St-Paul** (pl. St-Pierre), but the nave is classic Gothic. Infinitely more breathtaking is one of France's most intricate *jubés* (a rood screen of lacy stonework), which spans the plain nave of the 12th-century **Église Ste-Madeleine** (rue de la Madeleine). Under the riot of marble frills, the carver's body is buried with an epitaph that translates as HE WAITS FOR THE JUDGMENT WITH NO FEAR OF BEING CRUSHED. The **Église St-Pantaléon** (rue de Vauluisant) bursts with 16th-century sculpture. The three churches are open daily 9–noon and 2–6, except St-Pantaléon, which is open only in July–August.

MUSEUMS

Four of Troyes's museums have conveniently banded together; one 60F ticket gets you into all city-run museums (an individual museum ticket costs 30F) and all are free on Wednesday. The truly first-class **Musée d'Art Moderne** (pl. St-Pierre, tel. 03–25–76–26–80) displays works by all the modern masters, including Degas, Vuillard, Maillol, and Braque, along with an extensive collection of works by Fauvist artist André Derain (1880–1954). The nearby **Musée des Beaux-Arts et d'Archéologie** (1 rue Chrétien-de-Troyes, tel. 03–25–76–21–68) presents, in the rambling old **Abbaye St-Loup,** the skeletons of various critters; flowery 16th- and 17th-century paintings; and chipped remnants of Troyes's renowned 16th-century sculpture. You can find more 16th-century sculpture in the **Hôtel de Vauluisant** (4 rue de Vauluisant, tel. 03–25–73–05–85). Or check out the beautiful **Pharmacie-Musée** (quai des Comtes-de-Champagne, tel. 03–25–80–98–97). The Musée d'Art Moderne is open Wednesday–Monday 11–6; the other three museums are open Wednesday–Monday 10–noon and 2–6.

OUTDOOR ACTIVITIES

PARC DE LA FORET D'ORIENT

Just east of Troyes, the multipurpose Parc de la Forêt d'Orient balances "real" nature with three large artificial lakes and hiking trails. Twice a day (in the morning and afternoon), a **Courriers de l'Aube** bus (tel. 03–25–73–59–89) leaves from near Troyes's train station for various points near the lakes (1 hr, 33F). The **park center** (tel. 03–25–41–35–57), at the Maison du Parc bus stop, doles out information.

Hundreds of hiking trails wind through the forest around the lakes and lead south through the Seine valley past champagne vineyards and cider houses. For most trails you need to bring a tent, though you can always crash in one of four *gîtes d'étape* (rural hostels; around 40F per person) in **Loge-aux-Chèvres, Amance, Unienville,** and **Lusigny-sur-Barse.** For information about these hostels, consult **Gîtes de France** (tel. 03–25–73–00–11) in Troyes. For information on hiking, contact the **Comité Régional de la Randonnée Pédestre** in Troyes (2 blvd. Carnot, tel. 03–25–74–98–94). October–February is hunting season for all things antlered, so unless you want to go down with the deer, wear bright colors and sing loudly.

THE NORTH

Despite the torrent of tourists that pours through the port towns of Calais and Boulogne, the North remains one of the least-visited regions in France. Historically known as the country's breadbasket and coal pit, the region has suffered economically due to competition from cheaper coal producers and the government's focus on nuclear energy. World War I trenches and shells plowed up the countryside, sowing endless fields of gravestones and war monuments: The cemeteries north of Arras are a particularly moving example. While many towns lost their historic centers to World War II bombs, **Lille** and **Arras** are speckled with 17th-century Flemish architecture. **Laon's** *haute ville* preserves its religious roots in honey-color stone, while **Amiens** has the largest cathedral in France.

The North features a number of gastronomic idiosyncrasies. *Potjevleesch* (pronounced potsch-flesh) is made of nothing but veal, rabbit, and lard, and *hochepot,* also a vegetarian's nightmare, is a beef, mutton, pork, and veal stew. *Waterzooï* is a chicken casserole, and *lapin aux pruneaux* is rabbit cooked with prunes. Mussels bathe in myriad sauces, and *genièvre,* a juniper-berry liqueur, washes everything down. Monks rule the cheese scene. They invented the soft and strong *maroilles,* from which the *vieux Lille* is derived, and Trappist monks still make the milder *Mont des Cats* in their mountain abbey.

LILLE

During the 17th century, Lille was a thriving center of commerce and culture and one of the richest cities ruled by the powerful dukes of Burgundy. Today the richness has faded, and few tourists bother with a town that seems most often talked about in the past tense. That said, the thick brick buildings, rain-sodden stones, wooden beams jutting out here and there, and sunken walkways are all photogenic reminders of Lille's 17th-century Flemish heritage. For a taste of the past, check out **vieux Lille** (the old town); the more modern pedestrian streets center on **rue de Béthune**. Because tourists are so scarce, the Lillois are remarkably welcoming for such a large town.

BASICS

Housed in the remains of a 15th-century ducal palace (look for the huge war memorial *Aux Lillois),* the **Office de Tourisme** has handy indexed maps of town, and *Sortir,* a guide to Lille goings-on. It also runs a bureau de change, but beware the high charges and poor rate of exchange. *Pl. Rihour, tel. 03–20–30–81–00. From train station, walk along rue Faidherbe, turn left on rue des Manneliers toward pl. Rihour. Open Mon.–Sat. 9–7, Sun. 10–noon and 2–5.*

The main **post office** has all the usual services (postal code 59000). *8 pl. de la République, tel. 03–20–12–74–94. Open weekdays 8–7, Sat. 8–noon.*

For emergencies you can get the **police** at tel. 03–20–62–47–47, and the **central hospital** at tel. 03–20–44–59–62 (or dial 17).

COMING AND GOING

Lille is the regional rail hub. From here trains head to Paris (1 hr, 203F by TGV); Calais (65 mins, 90F; 35 mins, 107F by TGV); Brussels (75 mins, 113F); and Amsterdam (4 hrs, 250F). The **Lille-Flandres** train station (pl. de la Gare, tel. 03–20–87–30–00) is centrally located; the **Lille-Europe** station (tel. 03–20–55–57–16) is a long block away on rue Le Corbusier and serves TGV trains.

GETTING AROUND

Even with a map, Lille's spiderweb of streets can be confusing; without a map, you may never be seen again. The narrow streets of vieux Lille spread north from place de Gaulle, also referred to simply as the **Grand' Place;** the broader boulevards of the pedestrian zone stretch in the opposite direction. You'll rarely need the two-line métro system.

WHERE TO SLEEP

Hotels (many of which are right by the station) are either cheap and unpleasant or overpriced.

UNDER 175F • Hôtel des Voyageurs. An agreeable proprietress and her burly dog watch over this hotel across from the station. The rooms have been restored, although the beds are some of France's lumpiest. Singles cost 130F, small doubles 150F, showers 10F (170F for both shower and toilet). There's a 1 AM curfew. Reservations are recommended. *10 pl. de la Gare, at rue du Priez, tel. 03–20–06–43–14. 33 rooms, most with shower.*

UNDER 250F • Le Brueghel. In the heart of the pedestrian district near Lille-Flandres train station, this large redbrick hotel, extensively renovated in 1996 and tastefully decorated with art deco furniture, will give you a warm welcome. Room prices range from 180F with sink, up to 470F for a room with bath. *5 parvis St-Maurice, tel. 03–20–06–06–69, fax 03–20–63–25–27. 75 rooms with bath or shower.*

HOSTEL • The Auberge de Jeunesse de Lille has 150 spanking new beds for 65F per person per night—reserve in advance for doubles. *12 rue Malpart, tel. 03–20–57–08–94, fax 03–20–63–98–93. 150 beds.*

FOOD

Lille has a swarm of top-notch restaurants, many serving Flemish specialties. Unfortunately, prices are as *haute* as the cuisine. A handful of places on rue de Béthune specialize in versions of *moules marinières* (mussels cooked in white wine and onions). **Aux Moules** (34 rue de Béthune, tel. 03–20–57–12–46) has dishes for 45F–55F, as well as Flemish potjevleesch (55F). **La Tarterie de la Voute** (4 rue des Débris St-Étienne, tel. 03–20–42–12–16), north of the Grand' Place, serves up large salads (36F–40F), tarts (32F), and *gratins* (cheese-topped dishes; 45F). Farther north, **La Pâte Brisée** (63 rue de la Monnaie, tel. 03–20–74–29–00) is a local favorite with two-course (69F) and three-course (82F) menus and plenty of inexpensive tarts and quiches available for take-out. Arab restaurants cluster north of the city center: **Les Saveurs du Liban** (155 rue Nationale, tel. 03–20–63–98–99; closed Sun.) has 44F–49F weekday lunch menus with hummus, tabbouleh, falafel, or *kefta* (spicy meatballs) and 59F–83F menus in the evening; sandwiches (15F–20F to go) are also worth the trek. Lille has a host of **markets,** including one Tuesday–Sunday on place de la Nouvelle-Aventure.

WORTH SEEING

Lille is rich in 17th-century Flemish architecture, a blend of redbrick walls and fanciful stone decorations. The best places to ogle this style are the Grand' Place and vieux Lille. The **Vieille Bourse,** originally the nexus of a stock exchange catering to the 24 identical buildings around the Grand' Place, was built to rival the commercial exchanges in Holland. Inside there are plaques dedicated to Pasteur, Pascal, Dumas, Monge, Gay Lussac, and all of those other street names you couldn't place in Paris. From Tuesday through Sunday there's a market with stalls of flowers and books.

Built by Vauban, the 17th-century brick **citadel** at the end of boulevard de la Liberté is still used by the French military. The citadel can only be visited as part of a 35F tour put on by the tourist office April–October on Sunday at 3 or 3:30, but the park that circles the ramparts is always open.

Lille's renowned **Musée des Beaux-Arts** is the largest art museum in France outside Paris. It houses a noteworthy collection of Dutch and Flemish paintings, works by the Impressionists, as well as dramatic canvases by El Greco, Tintoretto, Paolo Veronese, and Goya. *Pl. de la République, tel: 03–20–06–78–00. Admission 30F. Open Mon. 2–6, Fri. noon–8, Wed.–Thurs. and weekends noon–6.*

The **Musée de l'Hospice Comtesse,** in the old town, has a fine collection of Flemish furniture, art, and tiles. *32 rue de la Monnaie, tel. 03–20–49–50–90. Admission 15F, 5F Wed. and Sat. afternoons. Open Wed.–Mon. 10–12:30 and 2–6.*

AFTER DARK

Nightlife is one of the best reasons to stop in Lille. Vieux Lille houses a phalanx of great bars, and the universities and open borders provide an international crowd. The weekly magazine *Sortir* is available free from the tourist office and gives information on what's hot in Lille. The brooding **Le Balatum** (13 rue de la Barre, tel. 03–20–57–41–81) is a great introduction with frequent live bands; beers start at 13F and at lunch you can get a good sandwich for 20F. **Le B.J.** (55 rue Basse, tel. 03–20–06–61–31), on the eastern continuation of rue de la Barre, is another good choice. Around the corner, the tiny **Kremlin** (51 rue Jean-Jacques-Rousseau, tel. 03–20–51–85–79) has a predictable specialty: dozens of vodka varieties, most at 20F. **Le Bateau Ivre** (41 rue Lepelletier, tel. 03–20–55–40–33) is yuppie heaven and is hard to squeeze into on weekend nights. **L'Observatoire Café** (30 pl. Philippe-Lebon, tel. 03–20–54–66–69) fills its haphazardly designed space with one of the liveliest crowds around.

AMIENS

If you think that all of the North is industrial and war-scarred, you haven't been to Amiens—a medieval town that's grown into a lively modern city of shady parks and wide streets. The **Quartier St-Leu,** the canal district behind the Cathédrale Notre-Dame (*see* Worth Seeing *below*), has given Amiens the title the "Little Venice of the North." It can get touristy but is generally a pleasant place to ponder old-fashioned streets and the waterside activity.

BASICS

The **Office de Tourisme** has an extra outpost in front of the cathedral (summer only) and another in the train station (weekdays only). *Main office: 12 rue du Chapeau de Violettes, tel. 03–22–91–79–28. From train station, head north on rue de Noyon, right on rue Victor Hugo, left on rue Cormont, continue past cathedral (look for belfry), right on rue du Chapeau de Violettes. Open Mon.–Sat. 9–12:30 and 1:30–6 (until 7 in summer).*

COMING AND GOING

Trains travel from Amiens to Paris (75 mins, 116F), Calais (1¾ hrs, 118F), and Lille (1¾ hrs, 93F) from the **train station** (pl. Alphonse-Fiquet, tel. 08–36–35–35–35), about six blocks east of the town center and the Hôtel de Ville. **Courriers Automobiles Picards** (tel. 03–22–91–46–82), based in the mall just outside the train station, runs buses to Arras (2 hrs, 48F).

WHERE TO SLEEP

The **Hôtel du Cirque** (24 blvd. Jules-Verne, tel. 03–22–89–35–79) has budget-friendly prices and eight respectable doubles (90F, 110F with shower). It's a pleasant, 10-minute walk from the train station and just by the town center. The **Hôtel de Normandie** (1 bis rue Lamartine, tel. 03–22–91–74–99) has bare, neutral singles from 135F and doubles from 150F, just a block away from the train station. The rooms at the **Hôtel le Prieuré** (17 rue Porion, tel. 03–22–92–27–67, fax 03–22–92–46–16), located near the cathedral, are a good splurge, starting at 260F for a double with bath. Also try the restaurant for good regional cooking; set meals start at 110F.

FOOD ·

For those seeking green pastures, the popular **Saladin** (4 rue des Chaudronniers, tel. 03–22–92–05–15) dishes out Frisbee-size salads, most for 50F–60F. Near the train station and a leap up in quality is **Le T'chiot Zinc** (18 rue de Noyon, tel. 03–22–91–43–79), where locals fill the tables for afternoon tea or old-fashioned, 65F two-course menus; a three-course traditional French menu with wine is a worthwhile 89F. **Les Marissons** (68 rue des Marissons, tel. 03–22–92–96–96) showcases imaginative regional fare such as rabbit with mint and goat cheese; it has menus priced at 110F and 135F.

WORTH SEEING

The 13th-century **Cathédrale Notre-Dame** is a Gothic hulk of architectural harmony and the largest cathedral in France. There are no pews to clutter the nave, so the labyrinth pattern of the floor tiles is exposed. Monks used to walk the labyrinth clockwise-in and counterclockwise-out as a form of meditation. The cathedral's treasury includes ornate church valuables and half of John the Baptist's skull. *Pl. Notre-Dame, tel. 03–22–80–03–41. Open 8–noon and 2–6.*

Some of the best views of the cathedral's colossal spire are from the south across the **Hortillonages,** an erstwhile swamp transformed into hundreds of fertile garden plots. You can visit the plots, farmed continually since the Roman occupation, on foot via the **chemin de Halage** (towpath) that follows the River Somme through the middle. From April through October you can tour the Hortillonages more extensively by boat (30F); make arrangements through the tourist office.

AFTER DARK

Cinéma le Régent (36 rue de Noyon, tel. 03–22–91–61–23) shows some great artsy and offbeat French and American films. A huge pool hall, **Le Caveau Cadillac** (44 rue de l'Amiral-Courbet, tel. 03–22–80–86–15), hovers unsuspected near the cathedral, with beers from 15F. The canal-side bars along quai Bélu—most notably **La Lune des Pirates** (17 quai Bélu, tel. 03–22–97–88–47)—are rowdy till the wee hours, charging up to 32F for mixed drinks and all that watery ambience. Nearby place du Don has the snug, noisy **Riverside Café** (pl. du Don, tel. 03–22–92–50–30) and **Vents et Marées** (48 rue du Don, tel. 03–22–97–37–78); beers here hover around 20F.

BOULOGNE

A hop, skip, and hydroplane from the south coast of England, Boulogne, like Calais, suffers from an overload of British day-trippers who come to buy cheap French liquor. Unlike Calais, the town's fine walled vieille ville, high above the port, is actually worth a stop for its curvy, steep roads and heavy stone ramparts. For a dizzying panorama of the whole area, wheeze your way up the 13th-century **belfry** (pl. de la Résistance), open weekdays 8–5:30; access is free through the Hôtel de Ville. Next to the belfry and underneath the 19th-century **Cathédrale Notre-Dame** (parvis Notre-Dame), an extensive crypt holds fragments of a 3rd-century Roman temple, among other treasures; the church is open Tuesday–Sunday 9–5. The **Château Musée** (rue de Bernet, tel. 03–21–80–00–80), closed Tuesday, tickles all manner of fancies with its eclectic collection of Egyptian bric-a-brac, Greek vases, Alaskan fishing gear, medieval doodads, and the Largest Hat Ever Worn by Napoléon. Admission is 20F. The moat around the château is worth the free promenade. The museum is open Monday and Wednesday–Sunday 10–5; October–April, Monday and Wednesday–Sunday 11–4.

BASICS

The **Office de Tourisme** adeptly dispenses information about the town. A kiosk at the western gate of the ramparts, open Easter–September, shares the work. *Quai de la Poste, tel. 03–21–31–68–38. From Gare Boulogne-Ville, go right on blvd. Voltaire, left on blvd. Daunou to blvd. de Postes. From Gare Mar-*

itime, cross train tracks to pont Marguet (office is on right). Open July–Aug., daily 9–8; Sept.–June, Mon.–Sat. 9–12:30 and 1:30–7, Sun. 10–1 and 2–5.

COMING AND GOING

BY TRAIN • Boulogne has two train stations: the **Gare Maritime** (03–21–30–27–26) on quai Thurot near the ferry terminal, with service to Paris timed to coincide with ferry arrivals; and the **Gare Boulogne-Ville** (blvd. Voltaire, tel. 03–21–80–48–44), a good walk from the center of town. Trains from the latter head to Calais (40 mins, 42F) and through Amiens to Paris (3 hrs, 179F).

BY BUS • **Cariane Littoral** (tel. 03–21–34–74–40) runs several buses Monday–Saturday from boulevard Daunou at rue Belvalette to Calais (1 hr, 27F). Be prompt, because they don't wait. To get around town take the **TCRB** buses; their main station is on place de France across from the tourist office.

BY FERRY • The ferry terminal lies across the river from central Boulogne. To get here from the tourist office, cross the bridge and veer right. In deference to Calais, regular ferry service from Boulogne to England no longer exists, though **Hoverspeed** (tel. 03–21–30–27–26) still sends sleek Seacats from Boulogne to Folkestone February–Christmas for 200F, 40F extra for bikes.

WHERE TO SLEEP

Cheap places to spend a night in Boulogne include the **Hôtel Hamiot** (1 rue Faidherbe, tel. 03–21–31–44–20), where 20 singles and doubles (120F–210F) with shower rest above a popular dockside bar and restaurant. **Hôtel Sleeping** (18 blvd. Daunou, tel. 03–21–80–62–79) has comfy singles (108F) and doubles (164F) with shower. The **Auberge de Jeunesse** (pl. Rouget-de-Lisle, tel. 03–21–80–14–50, fax 03–21–80–45–62), across from the Boulogne Ville train station, is your best budget bet—80F includes breakfast and sheets, and an HI card gets you a bed in a triple with its own bathroom and crucial alarm-clock radio, plus breakfast.

FOOD

Boulogne is France's foremost fishing port, so it's worth sampling at least one seafood meal here; try the friendly **Le Doyen** (11 rue du Doyen, tel. 03–21–30–13–08), near place Dalton, where the 90F menu changes according to the day's catch. **Place Dalton** and the surrounding streets harbor some semi-interesting bistros, one of the liveliest of which is **Chez Jules** (pl. Dalton, tel. 03–21–31–54–12), where generous pizzas run 40F–55F. Place Dalton also hosts a Wednesday and Saturday **market.** Other days, a giant **PG Supermarché** lurks in the mall by square Michelet, where you can stock up on groceries. Up the hill, the vieille ville is home to plenty of touristed, overpriced restaurants and still more British pubs, excluding **Le Provençal** (107 rue Porte Gayole, tel. 03–21–80–49–03), which, despite its name, specializes in couscous (49F if ordered to go) and other Middle Eastern specialties for around 65F.

CALAIS

The opening of the Channel Tunnel, which helps connect Paris to London in three hours, has done little to change Calais's status as the stomping ground for millions of British visitors. Calais is a relatively charmless place to spend more than a few hours; it's best used as a convenient base to reach Dover or visit the Channel beaches. Still, an ascetic landscape of rugged, grass-combed hills plunging into the sea can make the coastline a decent place to relax and contemplate the forces of nature.

BASICS

The **Office de Tourisme** has a great brochure on the history and sights of Calais, maps, and bus schedules. *12 blvd. Clemenceau, tel. 03–21–96–62–40, fax 03–21–96–01–92. From train station, go left on rue Royale past the park (office is on right). Open July–Aug., Mon.–Sat. 9–7:30, Sun. 10–1 and 4:30–7:30; Sept.–June, Mon.–Sat. 9–7, Sun. 10–1.*

COMING AND GOING

BY TRAIN • Calais has two stations: **Calais-Ville** (blvd. Jacquard, tel. 08–36–35–35–35), close to the Hôtel de Ville, and the **Calais-Fréthun** (tel. 08–36–35–35–35), near the entry to the Channel Tunnel, used for high-speed trains. Destinations include Paris (1½ hrs, 274F by TGV), Lille (35 mins, 107F by TGV), and Boulogne (40 mins, 42F). Calais's municipal Opale Bus 7 connects the Gare Calais Ville and the docks. **Cariane Littoral** buses (tel. 03–21–34–74–40) also stop in front of the Gare Central on their way to Boulogne (1 hr, 26F).

BY CHANNEL TUNNEL • The much-touted Chunnel opened in 1994, zipping millions of cheery, smiling folk under the English Channel between Calais and London in less than an hour for a smooth 470F. Discounts apply by reserving more than eight days in advance or traveling Monday–Thursday. If you head back within five days, the one-way ticket price covers both trips. Contact **Le Shuttle** for information about car transport and **Eurostar** for that about people transport (*see* Channel Tunnel *in* Chapter 1).

BY FERRY • Despite the Chunnel's novelty, good old-fashioned ferries are still the more reasonable option, especially if you want to suck in some of that sea air and get a look at the white Dover cliffs before landing on English soil. Two ferry companies link Calais with Dover, namely **Sealink** (Car-Ferry Terminal, tel. 03–21–46–80–00) and **P&O Ferries** (Car-Ferry Terminal, tel. 03–21–46–04–40). The crossings take 1¼ hours; bicycles are free. Sealink costs 190F and P&O 200F (per person or for five-day returns). **Hoverspeed** (Hoverport, tel. 03–21–46–14–14) Hovercrafts cost 200F and slice across the Channel in half the time. All prices quoted here will get you a return ride to Calais, too, provided you catch it within five days of your original departure. Free shuttle buses run between the ferry and Hovercraft terminals and the train station near the center of each town.

WHERE TO SLEEP

Hotels fill up quickly here, so reserve ahead. **Au Brazza** (149 blvd. Gambetta, tel. 03–21–34–33–11) has drab singles (100F) and doubles (130F) with caved-in mattresses, but there's often space and showers are free. A definite step up, **Hôtel du Littoral** (71 rue Aristide Briand, tel. 03–21–34–47–28) has nice doubles (120F, 150F with shower), but they're almost always taken during the summer. The cheery **HI hostel** (av. du Maréchal-de-Lattre-de-Tassigny, tel. 03–21–34–70–20, fax 03–21–96–87–80) is a 15-minute walk from the Calais Ville station and town center; if you're tired, catch Bus 3, which stops at the train station. The cheap brasserie, bar, and cafeteria here have reasonable hours, and the small library, TV room, and pool table will make rainy days more enjoyable. An HI card gets you a bed and breakfast for 77F (87F without card) per night; sheets are an extra 16F.

FOOD

Au Coq d'Or (31 pl. des Armes, tel. 03–21–34–79–05) has 59F and 75F multicourse menus on lacy tablecloths in a tapestried brasserie every day except Wednesday. Across the square, **Crêperie la Bigoudène** (22 rue de la Paix, tel. 03–21–96–29–32) has 38F–70F menus with cider and 30 crepes to choose from 24F a go. Duck into **SAM American Grill** (41 rue de la Mer, tel. 03–21–96–16–65) for a surreal experience of French Tex-Mex. Burger plates are 39F, chili con carne 44F. By the beach, try **L'Imprévu** (26 rue des Thermes, tel. 03–21–96–01–26), which has 54F and 80F menus and specializes in mussels and scallops. Place Crèvecur hosts a **market** on Thursday and Saturday mornings.

ARRAS

Over the centuries, Arras's central squares hosted magnificent markets; the sale of cloths, rich tapestries, and wagons of wheat made Arras one of the North's richest towns. During World War II, bombings flattened the city, and the remaining evidence of the mercantile work ethic lies in the completely rebuilt 17th- and 18th-century Flemish-inspired houses. If you don't come on a market day, the empty cobbled squares will seem more like ghostly reminders of a once powerful trading economy—sit down at one of the many cafés sheltered in the vaulted arcades and contemplate the rise and fall of bartered fortunes.

BASICS

The **Office de Tourisme,** housed in the Hôtel de Ville, provides information on Arras and the surrounding area. *Pl. des Héros, tel. 03–21–51–26–95, fax 03–21–71–07–34. Open daily until 6 PM, until 5 or so in winter, with lengthy lunch breaks.*

COMING AND GOING

Trains rattle the rails from here to Lille (40 mins, 71F), Amiens (50 mins, 57F), and Paris (50 mins, 130F by TGV). The **train station** (pl. Maréchal-Foch, tel. 08–36–35–35–35), on the southeast edge of town, is a 10-minute walk from the center. **Colvert** buses (tel. 03–21–22–62–62) run to Lille (1¾ hrs, 28F) from the bus station (a short walk to your left upon exiting the train station) six times a day, Monday–Saturday.

THE BURGHERS OF CALAIS

The group of patina-coated bronze figures called the "Burghers of Calais," in front of Calais's Hôtel de Ville, is one of Rodin's finest works. The sculpture commemorates six city elders who, in 1347, offered their lives to King Edward III of England in return for sparing the city. Edward's wife intervened on the burghers' behalf; both they and the town were saved. In the late 1800s, Calais commissioned Rodin to immortalize the burghers' act. Instead of depicting stately leaders bravely facing death, Rodin sculpted an asymmetrical group of anguished old men weighed down by chains.

WHERE TO SLEEP

Try to make it out of town before nightfall. If you get stuck here, the best deal in town (if you have an HI card) is a 63F bed (22F sheet rental) at the centrally located **HI hostel** (59 Grand' Place, tel. 03–21–22–70–02, fax 03–21–07–46–15), which brims with rambunctious Canadian youths in the summer; you should probably reserve a day in advance. Unfortunately, it closes in December and January, in which case you can try the tolerable rooms at convenient **Hôtel le Passe-Temps** (pl. du Maréchal-Foch, next to train station, tel. 03–21–71–58–38), with singles for 130F and doubles for 180F, and a brasserie serving a basic 59F three-course menu downstairs. **Café-Hôtel du Beffroi** (28 pl. de la Vacquerie, tel. 03–21–23–13–78) has several decent rooms at 170F right behind the Hôtel de Ville; the bar downstairs serves respectable brasserie-type meals with 40F plats du jour.

FOOD

Bar food and pizzas form the basis of available noshes; the 30F–40F pies are comparable at almost all the joints around the three central squares. **Chez Annie** (14 rue Paul-Doumer, tel. 03–21–23–13–51) serves generous 41F, 55F, and 65F lunch-only menus of inventive regional dishes in a subdued, slightly chintzy interior. The only pub where you might get a decent brasserie meal is at **La Taverne de l'Écu** (18 rue Wacquez-Glassow, tel. 03–21–51–42–05); Welsh specialties are 42F–48F, and they have several dinner-size salads under 50F. The supermarket **Monoprix** is at 30 rue Gambetta. The **markets** that fill all three squares on Saturday mornings date from AD 828; edibles are sold on place de la Vacquerie.

WORTH SEEING

The restoration effort has created some worthwhile sights, notably the Flamboyant Gothic **belfry** (admission 14F) and the neighboring **Hôtel de Ville** on place des Héros. Several of the Hôtel de Ville's rich chambers are open to the public, and entrance to the belfry includes a short film on the history of Arras in French, English, or German. Deep beneath the building are the **boves,** an extensive labyrinth of chilly chalk tunnels that have been used since the 10th century as a quarry, a secret place of cult worship, wine cellars, and a hospital for World War I English soldiers. The **tourist office,** housed in the Hôtel de Ville, leads 35-minute guided tours of the boves for 35F.

Nearby loom the cavernous **Cathédrale St-Vaast** and the **Musée des Beaux-Arts,** housed in the Benedictine abbey connected to the cathedral. The museum displays a modest collection of 17th-century Flemish paintings, including Brueghel the Younger's copy of his father's *The Census-Taking of Bethlehem*. *Rue Albert Ier de Belgique, tel. 03–21–71–26–43. Admission 15F. Open Apr.–Sept., Mon. and Wed.–Sat. 10–noon and 2–6, Sun. 10–noon and 3–6; Oct.–Mar., Mon. and Wed.–Fri. 10–noon and 2–5, Sat. 10–noon and 2–6, Sun. 10–noon and 3–6.*

NEAR ARRAS

WAR CEMETERIES

Under a patchwork of brick houses, splintering old barns, and fields that stretch to infinity lies the burial ground of millions of French, English, Canadian, and German soldiers—somehow brought together under the weight of time and the delicate fibers of a zillion forgiving lawns. Life has managed to continue peacefully in this rural region north of Arras, but not without a few scars. Occasionally you'll come across pits and ditches obviously not dug by erosion—craters and trenches where soldiers shivered and died 80 years ago. The war cemeteries are the best reason to visit Arras.

Neuville-St-Vaast has a handful of cemeteries on its outskirts; from the bus stop, follow the signs for 15 minutes to **La Targette,** a peaceful hillside where 6,000 French soldiers from both wars rest next to a smaller British cemetery. From the intersection, it's another well-marked 10-minute walk to the **Deutscher Soldatenfriedhof** (German Military Cemetery), where each stark iron cross marks four of the 45,000 German soldiers buried here.

From Neuville-St-Vaast, signs mark the 45-minute walk to **Vimy Ridge,** scene of a surprising Canadian victory during World War I. At the hilltop clearing, enthusiastic young Canadians give free tours of the preserved trenches and tunnels. A slightly jubilant tone marks their descriptions of what was one of the few clear Allied successes of the war. Farther on, the towering Vimy Memorial expresses Canada's grief for its 65,000 World War I dead.

COMING AND GOING • Getting to the war memorials can be a pain, but it's well worth the trip. Trains run to Vimy from Arras (12 mins, 15F), but Vimy Ridge is a 45-minute walk from the station. **Colvert** (tel. 03–21–22–62–62) sends Bus 33 from Arras to Neuville-St-Vaast (25 mins, 10F). Buses leave once a day in the early afternoon. Either way, you should definitely check the bus schedules at Arras's **gare routière**; from the train station, go left on rue du Dr-Brassard to avenue du Général-Leclerc.

LAON

Lofty Laon was once the site of two abbeys and so many churches it was called the *montagne couronnée* (crowned mountain). Since then this hilltop town has been shorn of all but three. Even so, twisting streets crisscross fortified Laon, every turn revealing some crumbling sandstone house, mossy gate, or vertiginous view across the plains below.

The Gothic **Cathédrale Notre-Dame** (pl. du Parvis, tel. 03–23–20–26–54) is a gorgeous work of modest but harmonious proportions. An unusual degree of artistry graces the exterior, including a deeply recessed facade, imaginative gargoyles, and no fewer than five towers decorated with statues of the oxen that appeared miraculously to help with construction. Inside the north transept, a head of Christ painted on wood has been classified by the church as a "mandylion," an artifact not made by the hand of man. The church is open daily 8–noon and 2–6.

BASICS

The **Office de Tourisme** in the restored Hôtel Dieu shares place du Parvis with the Cathédrale Notre-Dame. *Pl. du Parvis, tel. 03–23–20–28–62, fax 03–23–20–68–11. Open July–Sept., Mon.–Sat. 9–7, Sun. 10–7; Oct.–June, Mon.–Sat. 9–12:30 and 2–6:30, Sun. 11–1 and 2–5.*

COMING AND GOING

The **train station** (pl. des Droits-de-l'Homme, tel. 03–23–79–10–79) lies at the foot of Laon's plateau. Trains leave from here for Paris (1¾ hrs, 89F), Reims (35 mins, 49F), and Amiens (1½ hrs, 85F). To get from the station to the *haute ville* (upper town), either climb the 427 steps to the tourist office or take the wheelchair-accessible **POMA 2000,** a 12-seat Tonka toy–like cable car. Catch the POMA from its terminus to the left of the train station. Rides cost 6F (8F round-trip), take about 10 minutes, and are offered Monday–Saturday 7 AM–8 PM (also on Sunday afternoons June–August).

WHERE TO SLEEP

The only cheap hotel in the haute ville, the **Hôtel de la Paix** (52 rue St-Jean, tel. 03–23–23–21–95) rents six acceptable 95F singles and six 140F doubles, five with bath. Behind the cathedral, the very friendly **Foyer des Jeunes Travailleurs** (20 rue du Cloître, tel. 03–23–20–27–64) usually has space in

August but is otherwise often full; the Office de Tourisme will make reservations for you. A mere 65F gets a spot in rooms of one to three, with bathrooms as bad as you'd expect for this price.

In the basse ville (lower town), close to the station, the **Hôtel Welcome** (2 av. Carnot, tel. 03–23–23–06–11) greets you with a somewhat alarming toothpaste-green interior, but there are comfortable beds in the bright 120F–150F doubles, and showers are free. The **Hôtel Carnot** (16 av. Carnot, tel. 03–23–23–02–08, fax 03–23–23–71–67) has 21 attractive rooms above a boisterous bar. Singles are 135F, doubles 145F (220F with bath). The tiny campground **Camping Lachenai** (38 rue Jean-Pierre-Timbaud, tel. 03–23–20–25–56) is a 25-minute walk east of town (from the station, turn right on blvd. Pierre Brossolette and follow signs); a site is 8F plus 14F per person. It's closed November–mid-April.

FOOD

The restaurant on the ground floor of the Hôtel de la Paix (*see* Where to Sleep, *above*) has 56F three-course menus and *pichets* (small pitchers) of wine for 14F. **La Crêperie** (23 rue St-Jean, tel. 03–23–23–05–53) serves unusual crepe permutations, many under 30F, until midnight. Touristy **Les Arcades** (pl. de l'Hôtel de Ville, tel. 03–23–23–26–81) tortures you with horrible plastic chairs but lets you make your own salad (41F) or pizza (45F). Just around the corner, **Monoprix** (2 rue du Bourg) has groceries. A **market** is held on Thursday mornings at place Victor-Hugo, a five-minute walk from the train station along boulevard Gras Brancourt.

ALSACE-LORRAINE AND FRANCHE-COMTE

UPPDATED BY CHRISTOPHER KNOWLES

U ntil France won the Thirty Years' War in 1648 (inasmuch as it was won by anyone), there was no such place as Alsace-Lorraine. The Alsace region, between the Rhine and Vosges mountains, was a loose collection of feudal towns that were more or less controlled by the Hapsburgs. On the other side of the Vosges, Lorraine was a patchwork of villages bandied about from one duke to another while peasants attended to daily tasks. Metz stood by itself as an independent city-state with power, importance, and influence that have since been lost. Then Germany tried to get control of the area, France got miffed and snatched it back, and by the end of the 17th century Alsace and Lorraine were thrown together, ever after to be linked as Alsace-Lorraine. The area has changed hands between France and Germany about once per century for the past 350 years; Germany keeps annexing Alsace-Lorraine and the loyal French citizens vote, fight, or flee—anything to snuggle back up to France. At least, that's what the French will tell you. In reality, German influence is everywhere: Half-timbered houses line the streets, people speak with a German lilt, and potatoes, sauerkraut, and fruity white wines dominate the culinary scene. If you're yearning for a folksy, not-so-French experience without crossing political borders, this is a good destination.

Museums here pay homage to both French and German artistic movements; the art nouveau works in the Musée de l'École de Nancy are especially impressive. A strong sense of history also permeates the region; battle sites like Verdun are carefully maintained as a reminder of past atrocities. The cosmopolitan city of Strasbourg, capital of Alsace and home to the University of Strasbourg, supports both a French and German working population, as well as the European Parliament, all in the shadow of one of France's most impressive cathedrals. It also has a vibrant nightlife. Lodging, food, and culture are pretty affordable, and sights like the renowned Route du Vin, which winds its way south of Strasbourg through small towns and wineries, attract loads of travelers every year.

Of course, you can always leave history, gastronomy, and culture behind for the meadows, forests, and rocky gorges that carve out the land extending south from Alsace into the Franche-Comté. An unassuming region between Burgundy and Switzerland, the Franche-Comté roughly covers the French part of the low but rugged Jura Mountains.

BASICS

The best places to get information are at local tourist offices; well-stocked ones are in Strasbourg, Nancy, Metz, and Besançon. For pre-trip research, rely on the **Comité Régional du Tourisme de l'Al-**

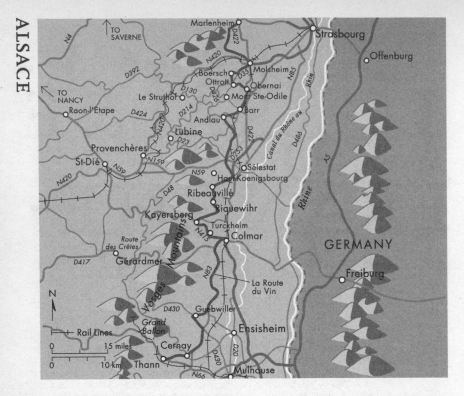

ALSACE

sace, which carries general information on all of Alsace. *6 av. de la Marseillaise, BP 219, F-67005 Strasbourg Cedex, tel. 03–88–25–01–66, fax 03–88–52–17–06. Open weekdays 8:30–12:30 and 2–6.*

For research on Lorraine, contact the **Comité Regional du Tourisme de Lorraine.** *1 pl. Gabriel Hocquard, BP 81004, 57036 Metz Cedex 1, tel. 03–87–37–02–16, fax 03–87–37–02–19. Open weekdays 8:30–12:30 and 2–6.*

GETTING AROUND

Trains are a cinch in Alsace, but in Lorraine you need to take the bus to get from Verdun to the battle-grounds. In the Franche-Comté, you'll need a lot of time to really see the region well. To find out which towns are on the rail lines, pick up the "Guide Régional des Transports," a free train and bus guide, at stations and *tabacs* (shops that sell cigarettes, candies, postcards, and stamps). Be flexible if you want to use buses; schedules change frequently. Biking and hiking are also good ways to see this region; Saverne, Colmar, and Dole are good starting points.

FOOD

Alsatians swear their food is the best in France, and if you like heavy, rich, filling meals, you may agree. This is a budget traveler's dream: You can fill up on a hearty *plat principal* (main dish) and have extra to spend on dry, fruity Alsatian wines and local beers like Fischer and Kronenbourg. Dishes are laced with cream and are influenced by northern Europe's love of hearty, potato-and-sausage dishes. The tourist staple (Alsatians only eat it in winter) is *choucroute garni alsacienne,* a huge serving of sauerkraut topped with mounds of meat and sausage. Other regional favorites include *baeckoffe,* a baked dish of pork, beef, and lamb with potatoes and onions, and *tarte flambée,* a thin-crusted pizzalike thing, topped with everything from fresh cream and cheese to mushrooms, bacon, and spiced apples. Quiche lorraine (quiche with cheese and ham or bacon) is popular and is often the most affordable thing on the menu. A popular dessert around here is *kougelhopf,* a buttery upside-down cake commonly served with kirsch, a liqueur made from cherries.

OUTDOOR ACTIVITIES

Don't pass up the opportunity to hike or bike somewhere in the Vosges or Jura mountains. Though they hardly qualify as adventure destinations, they are a fine escape from city-related stress. For details, *see* Near Strasbourg, *and* the Franche-Comté, *below.*

STRASBOURG

Strasbourg is one of the most happening French cities outside Paris; if you visit only one city in Alsace-Lorraine, this should be it. The capital of Alsace, Strasbourg has often changed hands between the French and Germans in the last 350 years. This back-and-forth has left a mark on the city—German half-timbered houses and geranium-filled flower boxes clash with a very French café scene. The charming little streets were once canals that connected Strasbourg to the Ill and Rhine rivers.

The University of Strasbourg—attended by Pasteur, Goethe, and Napoléon, to name a few—means that the city has plenty of students (around 40,000) and bars. Parliamentary activities (in 1949, Strasbourg was chosen to host the European Parliament) bring an international grown-up crowd to the Palais de l'Europe (*see* Worth Seeing, *below*) for two weeks each month. Strasbourg's real attractions, however, are the villagelike atmosphere of La Petite France, the looming presence of the Cathédrale de Notre-Dame, the rich museums, and bars and *winstubs* (wine pubs).

BASICS

AMERICAN EXPRESS

The AmEx office has some of the best exchange rates in town and doesn't charge commission. *19 rue des Francs-Bourgeois, tel. 03–88–21–96–59. Open weekdays 8:45–noon and 1:30–6.*

CONSULATES

Canada: Rue Ried, 67610 La Wantzenau, tel. 03–88–96–65–02. **United States**: 15 av. d'Alsace, tel. 03–88–35–31–04 for information or 03–88–35–38–20 for cultural services.

LAUNDRY

At the **Salon Lavoir,** near the train station, you can wash and dry a load for 20F–25F. *12 blvd. Lyon, tel. 03–88–75–58–12. Open daily 9–8.*

MAIL

The **main post office** has telephone, telegram, and poste restante services, as well as a fair exchange rate. Smaller branches next to the train station (pl. de la Gare) and the cathedral (pl. de la Cathédrale) have the same services and hold similar hours. The postal code is 67000. *5 av. de la Marseillaise, tel. 03–88–52–31–00. Open weekdays 8–7, Sat. 8–noon.*

VISITOR INFORMATION

The main **Office de Tourisme** has brochures on the city and surrounding region and makes hotel reservations; many of the same services are available at the **train station branch** (2nd level, tel. 03–88–32–51–49). The main office also gives tours (adults 38F, students 20F) of the city June–September every day at 10:30 AM and 8:30 PM; in April, May, and October at 2:30. Tours are in French, German, and English. *17 pl. de la Cathédrale, tel. 03–88–52–28–28. Open June–Sept., daily 9–7; Oct.–Easter, Mon.–Sat. 9–6, Sun. 9–12:30 and 1:30–5.*

COMING AND GOING

BY TRAIN

Trains speed from the **train station** (20 pl. de la Gare) daily to Lyon (5 hrs, 272F), Frankfurt (2½ hrs, 236F), and Paris's Gare de l'Est (4 hrs, 285F) by way of Nancy (1½ hrs, 128F). If the anti-terrorist security measures known as "Opération Vigipirate" have been canceled, you can store luggage in small,

STRASBOURG

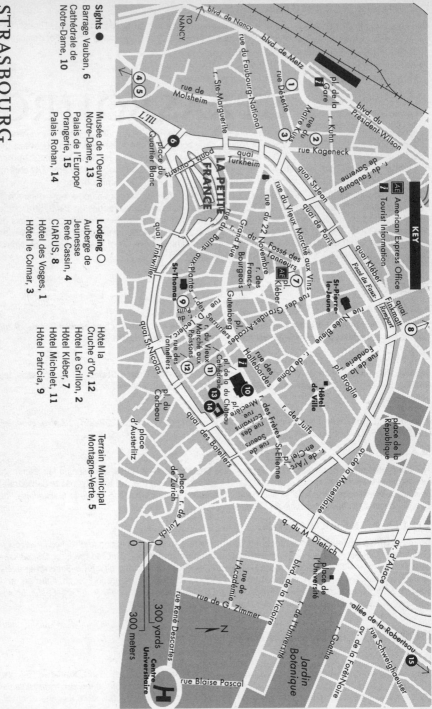

medium, or large lockers for 15F–30F per 72 hours. The consignment desk (tel. 03–88–75–41–63) will hang on to bags for 30F a day, bicycles for 35F a day. The station's public toilets (2F) and showers (10F) are open 24 hours.

BY PLANE

Strasbourg's **airport** (rte. de Strasbourg, Entzheim, tel. 03–88–64–67–67) is 15 km (9 mi) southwest of the center. **Air France** (reservations tel. 0802–802–802) flies direct to Paris (880F one-way), Lille, Lyon, Marseille, and Nice. The airport shuttle bus **Navette Routière** (25F one-way, 45F return) leaves from the center every half hour. It stops at the regular city bus stop at place de la Gare and place de l'Homme de Fer before making the 15-minute trek to the airport.

GETTING AROUND

Strasbourg's center is an eye-shape island created by the Ill River and canals that connect it to the Rhine. The Cathédrale de Notre-Dame lies at the east end of the island, and La Petite France lies at the west end, about ⅓ km (¼ mi) away. Narrow pedestrian streets lined with shops and restaurants connect the two, so that the whole island is just one mesh of Alsatian fare. If you feel lost, look for the cathedral tower and navigate from there.

The train station is across the river from the center (about 1⅓ km/¾ mi from the cathedral), in the far west corner of the city. Strasbourg's administrative and university district is northeast of the center between the Palais de l'Europe and place de la République. This is a big town, but the center is easily explored on foot. If you need a **taxi** call 03–88–36–13–13.

BY BUS

Most of the 15 efficient lines of **Compagnie des Transports Strasbourgeois** (tel. 03–88–77–70–11) leave from the train station, travel down rue du Vieux Marché aux Vins, and part ways at place de la République. Tickets (7F) are good for one hour and can also be used on Strasbourg's sleek tram that travels from the train station to place de l'Homme de Fer and out to the burbs. Both run 4 AM–midnight.

BY BIKE

The bike-friendly streets prove that people here are serious about cycling. Green signs mark bike routes, which are laid out along paved (not cobblestone) streets. Though you don't need one for getting around the center, a bike is handy (and fun) for going to places off the island, like the Palais de l'Europe and the Kronenbourg brewery. Rent bikes south of the station at **Vélocation St-Aurélie** (1 blvd. de Metz, tel. 03–88–52–01–01) for a mere 30F a day (20F a half day). They also store bikes for 5F per bike per day. You can take bikes on the tram (except for weekdays 7–9 AM) for free.

WHERE TO SLEEP

Strasbourg doesn't have a lot of double rooms for less than 200F, but those it does have are very respectable and close to (if not in the middle of) Strasbourg's action. If you're traveling by train, you can't find a more convenient place than **Hôtel des Vosges** (3 pl. de la Gare, tel. 03–88–32–17–23), and it's not as expensive as it looks: Singles and doubles start at 185F without bath. Generally, though, you get more for your money in the attractive city center. The hostels here are not a particularly good deal; they charge high prices for standard accommodations, and they are often invaded by tour groups. All require an HI card. Reservations are a must for most places.

UNDER 175F • Hôtel le Colmar. Smiling management and spiffy, carpeted rooms welcome you to this hotel between the station and the city center. Rooms on the street get a lot of racket from the cafés and food stands nearby, but it's a safe neighborhood. Singles with shower runs 172F, doubles 192F. One room overlooking an alley costs 115F; otherwise, singles without showers are also available at less cost. *1 rue du Maire Kuss, tel. 03–88–32–16–89. 17 rooms, 5 with shower. Cash only.*

Hôtel Michelet. Budget travelers swamp this hotel around the corner from the cathedral and near the museums. The alarm clock and phone in your slightly dingy room have earned the hotel one tiny star. The owners are as nice as and speak with thick Alsatian accents. Singles cost between 140F and 205F, and doubles start at 165F and go up to 250F (with bath). Showers cost 12F. The best deal, though, is for three people: An extra bed costs just 25F. Breakfast is served in your room. *48 rue du Vieux Marché aux Poissons, tel. 03–88–32–47–38. 15 rooms, 8 with bath.*

A TIPPLER'S GUIDE TO ALSATIAN WINES

Just because Alsatian vintners use German grapes, don't expect their wines to taste like their counterparts across the Rhine. German vintners aim for sweetness, creating wines that are best appreciated as an aperitif. Alsatian vintners, on the other hand, eschew sweetness in favor of strength, and their wines go wonderfully with knock-down, drag-out meals. The main wines you need to know about are Gewürztraminer, Riesling, Muscat, Pinot Gris, and Sylvaner, all white wines. The only red wine produced in the region is the light and delicious Pinot Noir.

Hôtel Patricia. These comfortable rooms on a tiny, winding street near La Petite France are a great deal: Singles cost 145F–210F, doubles 170F–260F (with private bath). Showers are 12F. The hip young staff cuts out at 8 PM and usually won't wait for late arrivals. *1a rue du Puits, tel. 03–88–32–14–60. 20 rooms, 6 with bath.*

UNDER 250F • Hôtel Le Grillon. Fresh carpet, new wood furniture, and handwoven bedspreads give this place a warm but modern feel. The friendly staff and good location—halfway between the station and city center—make it hard to beat. Singles are 170F–280F and doubles are 220F–330F (with bath). *2 rue Thiergarten, off rue du Maire Kuss, tel. 03–88–32–71–88, fax 03–88–32–22—01. 35 rooms, 28 with bath.*

Hôtel Kléber. Here you'll be a tram ride away from the train station on Strasbourg's highly social place Kléber. It's no steal, but the rooms are nice and you can eat at the cafeteria next door to make up for the difference. Singles go for 180F, doubles for 260F–395F. *29 pl. Kléber, tel. 03–88–32–09–53, fax 03–88–32–50–41. 31 rooms, 27 with bath.*

SPLURGE • Hôtel la Cruche d'Or. If you like cleanliness and modernity, this is a worthwhile splurge. The rooms sit over one of Strasbourg's liveliest side streets, which are full of restaurants. Singles cost 170F, small doubles with a modern bathroom and TV 290F–310F. An extra bed costs 60F. *6 rue des Tonneliers, tel. 03–88–32–11–23. 12 rooms, all with bath. Closed early Aug. and 2 wks in Feb.*

HOSTELS • Auberge de Jeunesse René Cassin. This lively place in the Montagne-Vert suburb 2 km (1 mi) southwest of the train station is Strasbourg's best deal for Auberge de Jeunesse members of all ages. The nearby park overlooking a canal is a favorite for picnicking and sunbathing. Singles are 149F, rooms that sleep two to four go for 99F a head, and a bed in a room of six costs 69F, breakfast included. The restaurant serves a good lunch or dinner for 49F and will even fix it to go. Camping under the trees behind the hostel costs 42F, including breakfast. Sheets are 17F. *9 rue de l'Auberge de Jeunesse, off rte. de Schirmeck, tel. 03–88–30–26–46, fax 03–88–30–35–16. From train station, Bus 3 or 23 to Auberge de Jeunesse stop. 286 beds. Reception open daily 7 AM–11 PM. Curfew 1 AM Apr.–Oct., 11 PM Nov.–Mar. Cash only. Closed Jan.*

CIARUS (Centre International d'Accueil et de Rencontre Unioniste de Strasbourg). This large university dorm is the best (and only) hostel Strasbourg has to offer within walking distance of the city center. The doubles go for 118F a night, singles are 185F, and dorm beds in three- to eight-person rooms are 86F–96F. Prices include breakfast, and all rooms have their own bathroom and shower. There's no age limit; families are welcome and baby beds provided. If you're calling ahead, they only accept over-the-phone reservations weekdays 9–noon and 2–5 (Tuesday 2–5 only). *7 rue Finkmatt, tel. 03–88–15–27–88, fax 03–88–23–17–37. From train station, Bus 10 to pl. du Faubourg-de-Pierre; or walk left out of station along blvd. du Président Wilson, right onto blvd. du Président Poincaré, right on rue Finkmatt. 199 beds. Reception open 24 hrs. Curfew 1 AM.*

CAMPING • Terrain Municipal Montagne-Verte. Caravans infest this shady plot of grass on the river's edge. Hot showers, a grocery store, a restaurant, a bar, and a laundry make it more attractive. One person with a tent pays 26F; each extra person pays 20F. Reserve ahead in July and August. *2 rue Robert Forrer, near René Cassin hostel (see above), tel. 03–88–30–25–46. From train station, take Bus 3, 13, or 23. Curfew 10 PM. Closed Nov.–Mar.*

FOOD

Strasbourg restaurateurs are so excited about Alsace's rich gastronomic traditions that they forget it's possible to get sick of sauerkraut. Luckily, minority groups have imported regional specialties of their own: Donner-kebab stands, concentrated on Grande Rue and rue du Maire Kuss, serve sandwiches (20F) and full Middle Eastern meals (45F) well into the night. Young locals tend to frequent the restaurants and bars in the winding streets behind the cathedral; eat here and you can roll straight into the best bars. The **Bar du 7e Art** (18 rue du 22-Novembre, tel. 03–88–23–13–15) has a fine breakfast of coffee, bread, butter, and jam. For groceries, try the morning **outdoor markets** on place Broglie and quai Turkheim (Wednesday and Friday), boulevard de la Marne (Tuesday and Saturday), and rue de Zurich (Wednesday). For bulk supplies, there's a great **ATAC** supermarket (rue des Grands Arcades), right off place Kléber. There are also small markets on rue du Maire Kuss and rue du 22-Novembre.

UNDER 50F • À la Tête de Lard. Robust and lively Alsatian owners serve delicious food on a little side street in the *centre ville* (town center). Crowds of young locals gather for good tartes flambées and salads with cold cuts. *3 rue Hannong, tel. 03–88–32–13–56. Closed Sun. No lunch Sat.*

Le Roi et Son Fou. An elegant little bistro around the corner from the cathedral, this is the perfect place for coffee or drinks and a light meal, like *tarte à l'oignon* (onion tart) with salad or one of the hot daily specials. Too bad it's closed for dinner. Sit outside on the serene terrace, or inside, where you can listen to jazz or classical music, read the *International Herald-Tribune* (provided), and gaze at vintage photographs. *37 rue du Vieil-Hôpital, off rue Mercière, tel. 03–88–23–22–22. Closed Tues. No dinner.*

UNDER 75F • Flam's. The cooks here only do salads and tartes flambées. Other than the daily special, the toppings are the same as everywhere else. Still, if you want to make a meal of a tarte flambée, this is the place to do it. *29 rue des Frères, behind cathedral, tel. 03–88–36–36–90; also 1 rue de l'Épine, near rue de la D. Leclerc, tel. 03–88–75–77–44.*

Pfifferbrieder. This tiny, warm winstub tacked on to a building near the cathedral looks so cute it's almost too much—but the locals love it and often outnumber the tourists. In winter it's one of the best places to sip *glühwein* (warm, spiced red wine), at 15F for a small pitcher. They serve hearty traditional meals year-round, including a tasty tarte à l'oignon. *9 pl. du Marché aux Cochons de Lait, south of cathedral via rue du Maroquin, tel. 03–88–32–15–43. Closed Sun.*

Restaurant du Petit Pêcheur. The Pêcheur, just off the central island, offers the same Alsatian cuisine served across the bridge at expensive waterside restaurants but for about half the price. In nice weather, eat outside overlooking the river. *3 pl. du Courbeau, tel. 03–88–36–11–49. Closed Wed. and several days in Jan. and June.*

WORTH SEEING

This town is serious about its museums, most of which are conveniently close to the Notre-Dame Cathedral. The tourist office sells a "Strasbourg Pass" (50F), valid for three days, which pays for itself if (1) you're not a student under 25 and (2) you want to visit several museums, the astronomical clock, and take a guided city tour or boat trip. Sunday is a good sightseeing day, since most shops are closed anyway and the museums stay open through lunch.

CATHEDRALE DE NOTRE-DAME

The "pink angel of Strasbourg" thrusts her perfectly Gothic spire dramatically skyward. Built atop a Roman temple dedicated to Mercury, the first church here was a 6th-century chapel dedicated to the Virgin Mary. As Strasbourg gained status as a trade center and crossroads, the cathedral expanded with it to become a point of reference and economic center for Alsace. The spire—one of Europe's highest, at 471 ft—was supposed to have a twin, but when construction began, the builders realized that the marshy ground beneath the cathedral couldn't handle it. After surviving many battles over the centuries, the exterior statuettes were replaced several decades ago; the originals are in the Musée de l'Oeuvre Notre-Dame (*see below*) next door. The interior displays splendid 13th-century stained-glass windows and an *horloge astronomique* (astronomical clock), built in 1547. The clock only opens for a 12:30 show

(5F), when the apostles walk past a likeness of Christ as a rooster crows three times. *Pl. de la Cathédrale. Admission free. Open Mon.–Sat. 7–11:30 and 12:40–7, Sun. 12:45–6.*

MUSEUMS

The **Palais Rohan,** one of a number of mansions built in Strasbourg in the 1700s, today houses three quality museums. The **Musée Archéologique** focuses on finds within Alsace ranging from Neolithic artifacts (600,000 BC) to glass, armor, and sculpture from Strasbourg's Roman days as Argentorate. The text accompanying the exhibits is translated into English. The **Musée des Arts Décoratifs** includes re-created apartments of the prince-bishops who once lived here, as well as decorative pieces and ceramics—dinnerware, animals, false plates of food—by Paul and Charles-François Hannong. Finally, the **Musée des Beaux-Arts** has an excellent collection of mostly northern-European pieces, as well as works by Giotto, Corot, Botticelli, and Goya. *2 pl. du Château, tel. 03–88–52–50–00. Admission to 1 museum 20F, to all museums 40F. Open Wed.–Mon. 10–noon and 1:30–6, Sun. 10–5.*

When it became clear that pollution was damaging the Cathédrale de Notre-Dame's exterior, curators undertook a major restoration, strengthening the walls and replacing statuettes. Many original pieces found their way to the **Musée de l'Oeuvre Notre-Dame,** housed in a 14th-century hostelry and *boulangerie* (bakery). The rich collection includes all types of religious art from the past 700 years—stained-glass windows, ornate wood furniture, and jewelry that looks like it came from *Elle* magazine. *3 pl. du Château, tel. 03–52–50–00. Admission 20F. Open Tues.–Sat. 10–noon and 1:30–6, Sun. 10–5.*

Across from the Ponts Couverts (literally, "the covered bridges," even though they aren't covered anymore), the **Barrage Vauban** (Vauban Dam) has statues from the cathedral that are waiting to be restored and put in the Musée de l'Oeuvre (*see above*). There are some great ones here—a lion with a halo holding a Bible, and several cross-eyed saints. The terrace up top (take the stairs at the place du Quartier Blanc entrance) gives you a rooftop view of La Petite France. It's free and open daily 9–8.

PALAIS DE L'EUROPE

Next to a gorgeous tree-lined neighborhood north of place de la République, the seat of the European Parliament is an example of modern European design, not the "palace" its name suggests. The flags, guards, and luxury automobiles outside are an indication of the heavy-duty business that goes on inside; it mostly deals with human rights issues and cultural affairs. If you're at all interested in politics, you can arrange a free weekday visit (in English or French) of the **congressional halls** by calling 03–88–41–20–29. Otherwise, head over to the adjacent **Orangerie,** a vast expanse of formal gardens, fountains, and flowers. *Av. de l'Europe. Bus 23 to Palais de l'Europe. Open daily 9–4:30.*

CHEAP THRILLS

Kronenbourg has free tours of its principal brewery just outside town. Reservations are required, but if you show up and the next group isn't filled, you can go along. The hour-long tour culminates in a half-hour tasting session where you can try two beers and eat as many pretzels as you like. *68 rte. d'Oberhausbergen, tel. 03–88–27–41–58. From pl. Kléber, Bus 7 to rue Jacob or Tram A to St-Florent, and follow rte. d'Oberhausbergen. Tours weekdays at 9, 10, 2, and 3.*

FESTIVALS

The June **Festival de Musique de Strasbourg** is more than 50 years old and usually honors the works of selected classical composers. Big concerts are held at the Palais de la Musique et des Congrès, but small happenings take place in spots such as the cathedral and Palais Rohan. Call 03–88–32–43–10 for information; tickets start at 100F. In July, the **Festival de Jazz** is run much like the Festival de Musique but trades Mozart for Marsalis. Call 03–88–37–17–79 for information.

AFTER DARK

BARS

Some Strasbourg bars have live music, some just a jukebox; some have a Latin jazz scene, others serious hip-hop dance competitions; some close promptly at 2 AM, others stay open until dawn. One thing that stays pretty much the same is price; most bars are cover free, but expect to pay 20F–25F for a beer and up to 50F for mixed drinks. **Place du Marché Gayot,** a small plaza between the cathedral and place St-Étienne, is a cheery square with several good bars, among them **Le Perroquet Bleu** (13 rue des

Soeurs, tel. 03–88–24–22–00), with expensive specialty drinks that are worth the splurge, and **Le Saxo** (8 rue des Frères, tel. 03–88–24–10–96), which plays Louis Armstrong tunes. **Bar de l'Abattoir** (1 quai Charles Altorffer, at the south end of quai St-Jean, tel. 03–88–32–28–12) is as chic as it gets this side of Paris, and as cheap as it gets in Strasbourg—beer is 16F, cocktails 20F. Come mingle with the well-dressed thirtysomething crowd while acid jazz and dim lights do their thing.

MUSIC AND DANCING

Rock, blues, jazz, reggae, rap, and square dancing all find their way into the live music scene and discos of Strasbourg. A 100F cover is typical at a disco and includes one drink. During the academic year, **Le Bistro Piano Bar** (30 rue Tonneliers, tel. 03–88–23–02–71) has free jazz concerts Thursday–Sunday and jam sessions Wednesday nights. A few doors down, the **Best of Music** (25 rue des Tonneliers, tel. 03–88–32–61–50) is a subterranean disco that blasts blues and acid jazz every night but Monday and serves highballs for 40F and up. **Café des Anges** (42 rue Krutenau, tel. 03–88–37–12–67) is a popular live music joint that showcases local reggae, funk, and country groups.

NEAR STRASBOURG

COLMAR

Sitting in the foothills of the southern Vosges Mountains 71 km (44 mi) south of Strasbourg, Colmar has preserved intact its magical *vieille ville* (old town), with candy-color, half-timbered houses hanging over the cobbled streets in a charmingly ramshackle way. Canals run through town, creating **La Petite Venise,** a picturesque "Little Venice" with houses and flowers right along the banks. All this attracts hordes of German daytrippers with pulled-up socks and cash to spend, so everything is pricey except the central, inexpensive youth hostel. Even if Colmar is not ideal for budget travelers, the eclectic **Musée d'Unterlinden** (*see below*) and the town's sunny charm are reason enough for a day trip.

The illustrator Waltz Hansi, popular at the turn of the century, created the ubiquitous wide-eyed waifs in Alsatian folk costume that adorn souvenir mugs, dish towels, coasters, and ash trays on sale around the region; his original work was less clichéd.

BASICS

The **Office de Tourisme** has excellent information and a plethora of maps of Colmar and the surrounding area. *4 rue des Unterlinden, across from Musée d'Unterlinden, tel. 03–89–20–68–92. Open Apr.–June and Sept.–Dec., Mon.–Sat. 9–6, Sun. 10–2; July–Aug., Mon.–Sat. 9–7, Sun. 9:30–2; Jan.–Mar., 9–noon and 2–6, Sun. 10–2.*

COMING AND GOING

Colmar is on the main rail line between Strasbourg (40 mins, 57F), Dijon (3½ hrs, 194F), and Basel, Switzerland (45 mins, 62F). All of the centre ville and La Petite Venise are manageable on foot—if you don't mind walking a bit. The **train station** (rue de la Gare) is in the far southwestern corner of town; from here, walk 15 minutes down avenue de la République for the tourist office, pedestrian shopping areas, and museums. Otherwise, take Bus 1, 2, 3, 4, or 5 from the station to the tourist office. The buses are operated by **Trace** (4a rue des Unterlinden, tel. 03–89–20–80–80). You can buy a one-way ticket from the driver for 5.30F or a book of 10 tickets at tabacs for 41F.

The cheapest place to rent bikes is right across the street from the hostel. **La Cyclothèque** (31 rte. d'Ingersheim, tel. 03–89–79–14–18) charges 90F a day for a mountain bike.

WHERE TO SLEEP

Colmar's hotels are close to the center, but they book up fast in summer. Walk straight out of the station, hang a left on avenue de la République, to **La Chaumière** (74 av. de la République, tel. 03–89–41–08–99), with a bar downstairs and rooms with showers for 180F–240F, single or double. **Hôtel Primo 99** (5 rue des Ancêtres, tel. 03–89–24–22–24) is two blocks from the tourist office via rue du Rempart. Its modern, spotless singles (149F, 299F with shower) and doubles (199F, 319F with shower) are a good deal. Also in the middle of town, and also above a bar (this one has billiards and darts), **À La Ville de Nancy** (48 rue Vauban, tel. 03–89–41–23–14) charges 160F for singles without toilet, 240F–260F with,

LA ROUTE DU VIN

The "Wine Road" stretches 170 km (100 mi) between Thann and Marlenheim and is easily accessible from Strasbourg or Colmar. Many of the towns and villages have designated "vineyard trails" winding between towns (a bicycle will help you cover a lot of territory). Riquewihr, Hunawihr, and Ribeauvillé—accessible by bus from Colmar (40 mins, 16F)—are connected by an especially picturesque route. Stop at any DÉGUSTATION sign for a free tasting. Before heading off, stock up on maps and information at the Maison des Vins d'Alsace in Colmar (12 av. de la Foire aux Vins, tel. 03–89–20–16–20) and pick up the brochure "The Alsace Wine Route" at any tourist office.

and 295F for doubles, all with shower or bath and all spotless and cute as a button. Make a right onto rue des Unterlinden off avenue de la République, then a left onto rue Vauban.

HOSTEL • A 10-minute walk from the center (25 mins from the station), the **Auberge de Jeunesse Mittelhart** (2 rue Pasteur, tel. 03–89–80–57–39) charges 68F for a bed in a room of six. There's no age limit; families are welcome. You get showers and breakfast, and there's a midnight curfew. To get here from the station, take Bus 4 to Pont Rouge; on foot, from the tourist office head away from the center on rue des Unterlinden (it becomes route d'Ingersheim) to rue Pasteur and go right.

FOOD

Restaurants here serve Alsatian fare for a few francs less than you might expect. Across from the tourist office, on place d'Unterlinden, **Monoprix** (tel. 03–89–41–48–65) has groceries and an upstairs cafeteria where you can get steak and fries (29F) and a salad bar (9F) with a view of the museum. For cheap quiche lorraine (33F) or rhubarb pie (15F) served in a floral-papered tearoom or at outside tables, stop at **Au Croissant Doré** (28 rue des Marchands, tel. 03–89–23–70–81), right next to the Musée Bartholdi (*see below*). **Maison Rouge** (9 rue des Écoles, tel. 03–89–23–53–22), across the street from the Collège Victor Hugo, is a nice splurge with a three-course menu for 75F and a four-course weekday lunch for 60F; their *assiette de crudités* (salad plate; 42F) is a vegetarian's dream. **Le Petit Gourmand** (9 quai de la Poissonnerie, tel. 03–89–41–09–32) offers excellent *tartiflette* (cheese, bacon, potato, and mushroom casserole) and charcuterie for 65F. **Le Bec Fin** (54 Grande Rue, tel. 03–89–41–73–76) has hot homemade *pâté en croûte* (in a crust) served with salad (59F). Quiche lorraine with veggies costs 38F.

WORTH SEEING

The **Musée d'Unterlinden** (1 rue des Unterlinden, tel. 03–80–20–15–50), once a Dominican convent, houses a large collection of Roman carvings, full suits of armor, wine presses, a Dubuffet sculpture, and a 17th-century locksmith's chest with a closing mechanism made of 47 moving levers. The famous **Retable d'Issenheim** (Issenheim altarpiece), the museum's most prized possession, was designed in 1512 by painter Mathias Grünewald. Admission is 30F. The museum is open April–October, daily 9–6; November–March, Wednesday–Monday 9–noon and 2–5. The **Musée Bartholdi** (30 rue des Marchands, tel. 03–89–41–90–60) is dedicated to Auguste Bartholdi, the man who designed the Statue of Liberty; come here to see where his lesser-known pieces are hiding. The museum costs 20F; it's open March–December, Wednesday–Monday 10–noon and 2–6.

AFTER DARK

Bar le Gaulois (6 pl. de la Cathédrale, tel. 03–89–41–09–11) has a bunch of beers on tap and live music on weekends. For quiet conversation alfresco, share a pitcher of Riesling on the broad terrace outside **Au Kolfhus** (2 pl. de l'Ancienne-Douane, tel. 03–89–23–04–90).

THE VOSGES

The Vosges Mountains reach their high point at 4,272 ft—they might be considered "hills" else-where—and run north–south from Wissembourg to Belfort, separating Alsace from Lorraine. They're rather tame compared to the Alps or the Pyrénées—think Smokies or Ozarks—but they're easily accessible from Strasbourg or Colmar and perfect for weekend warriors or train-weary travelers. The range is split into two regional national parks: **Parc des Vosges du Nord** (in the north) and **Parc des Ballons des Vosges.** If you're serious about getting into the woods, hit the Ballons, where glacial lakes crown the range's highest peaks. For easy promenades to medieval ruins, stick to the Vosges du Nord.

BASICS • You can get decent information about where to go and what to see from the tourist offices in Strasbourg and Colmar. For maps of the trails (*see below*), contact **Club Vosgien** (16 rue Ste-Hélène, tel. 03–88–32–57–96) in Strasbourg; or ask for a "Carte de Randonnées des Vosges" from tabacs and bib-liothèques in any Vosges town.

OUTDOOR ACTIVITIES • There are seven *circuits* (hikes), from 5 to 10 days long, that cover the entire range. For a general overview of them, ask for the booklet entitled "Les Grandes Traversées des Vosges" (free) at tourist offices in Strasbourg, Colmar, or Sav-erne. You can pick up food along the way, and stay at various hostels and hotels, so you only have to carry the basics. Each trail has its own emblem (a red X, blue square, green circle, etc.) posted on trees (light posts when the trail enters a town) for the length of the route. Just pick a symbol you like and fol-low it.

At Colmar's public baths, housed in a 19th-century building next to the tourist office, you can shower (15F), swim (18F), or take a sauna (59F). It's open Tuesday–Saturday 9–noon and 2–6.

SAVERNE

Once an outpost along an east–west trade route through the Vosges, Saverne is an easy day trip from Strasbourg and a great place to base yourself if you want to spend a few days in the mountains. The Rohan family, bish-ops of Strasbourg, lived here during the 17th century and left behind a remarkable palace—called the "ancient Versailles"—which now houses the **Musée des Saverne** (pl. Général-de-Gaulle, tel. 03–88–91–06–28) and a good **hostel.** The well-stocked **Office de Tourisme** (tel. 03–88–91–80–47) is in one of the guard houses out front.

Across place Général-de-Gaulle, the city's spacious center, is **quai de l'Écluse,** where a large board shows marked routes (with times and distances) through the mountains. The locals' favorite one-hour hike is to Haut-Barr, an 18th-century château carved from pink stone. The hike itself is mediocre, but the view from the top is awesome.

COMING AND GOING • Trains between Strasbourg (40 mins, 42F) and Nancy (1½ hrs, 101F) stop in Saverne about six times per day each direction. To get to town from the station, walk straight down rue de la Gare to Grande Rue (the main thoroughfare) and turn left.

WHERE TO SLEEP • Saverne's **Auberge de Jeunesse** (Palais des Rohan, tel. 03–88–91–14–84) is on the third floor of the south wing of the Rohan palace, a quiet location with stunning views. It charges 63F for a bed in a room of six, 83F for a single or double, breakfast included. Auberge members of all ages are welcome. Reception is open 8–10 AM and 5–10 PM, with lockout and a 10 PM curfew. Saverne doesn't have any inexpensive hotels. You can try the prosaic **Hôtel National** (2 Grand'rue, tel. 03–88–91–14–54), which has doubles without bath from 210F (360F with) and cheap menus (50F–85F) in its restaurant.

FOOD • The best place to eat is **Taverne Katz** (80 Grand Rue, tel. 03–88–71–16–56), a brewery built in 1605. The sausage and sauerkraut (55F) and the salmon in Gewürztraminer sauce (90F) are both worth every centime. For cheaper eats, head up rue Poincarré from place Charles-de-Gaulle and go left on rue des Frères to **S'Zawermer Stuebel** (4 rue des Frères, tel. 03–88–71–29–95), where 39F gets you a three-course meal; a glass of wine starts at 6F. There's a well-stocked **Co-op** market (116 Grand'rue, tel. 03–88–91–17–57).

LORRAINE

Misunderstood and usually ignored by travelers, Lorraine has been passed back and forth between the Germans and the French, but unlike Alsace, Lorraine retains a distinctly French flavor. (Quiche, after all, is the quintessential French food.) Joan of Arc, Frenchwoman par excellence, was born here, and she helped kick the English out of France way back when. The Maginot Line was supposed to have the same effect on the Germans during World War II, but all it did was give the region a false sense of security; the Nazis plowed right through the line of fortification and decimated the region. Until the burst of nationalism during the French Revolution, the four departments of Lorraine functioned quite separately, each revolving around its capital—Metz, Verdun, Nancy, and Epinal. Things are less fragmented nowadays, and you need only explore a few places to get a feel for Lorraine. Nancy and Metz are both good exploration bases, with train connections, university-driven nightlife, and good hostels. Go to Metz in the summer to swim in the *plan d'eau* (man-made lake) and Nancy in the winter for the lively café scene.

BASICS

Nancy, Metz, and Verdun all have well-equipped tourist offices. The **Comité Régional de Lorraine** (pl. Gabriel-Hocquard, F-57036 Metz Cedex 01, tel. 03–87–37–02–16) has information on camping, lodging, and sightseeing for the whole area.

COMING AND GOING

There are approximately 12 trains daily to and from Paris to both Nancy (230F one-way) and Metz (245F one-way). Once in Nancy or Metz, you'll need **Les Rapides de Lorraine** (tel. 03–83–32–34–20) buses to get you where you want to go.

FOOD

More resistant to German influence than Alsace, Lorraine has a few regional specialties, including quiche lorraine, made with cheese and ham or bacon. Metz is known for its honey, Nancy for macaroons and bergamot candy (a yellow hard candy flavored with bergamot liqueur from Morocco), and Verdun for candy-covered almonds called *dragées*. Mirabelle plums are found throughout the region in everything from tarts to eau-de-vie (brandy).

NANCY

Due west of Strasbourg on the other side of the Vosges Mountains, Nancy enjoyed a noble period as the home to the powerful dukes of Lorraine—rivals of the dukes of Burgundy and frequent spouses of the Hapsburgs. The last duke of Lorraine, Stanislas of Poland, ordered the creation of neoclassic **place Stanislas,** one of the few breathtaking sites of Nancy, and its undisputed hub. The rest of Nancy's architecture and ambience is fairly urban, though art nouveau buildings and the aqua-shuttered vieille ville perk things up. When the northern part of Lorraine fell into Germany's clutches at the end of World War II, Nancy became a frontier town and the stronghold of French culture. The artists who took refuge from the Germans here gave birth to art nouveau and the **École de Nancy** (picture those fancy green Paris métro archways). Enthusiasts should ask the tourist office for the free English-language pamphlet that points out 22 of the more important architectural landmarks.

BASICS

LAUNDRY • You can wash and dry (about 30F per load) at **Lavomatique** on rue de l'Armée Patton at rue Raymond-Poincaré, near the train station.

MAIL • The best place to change traveler's checks is at the central **post office.** Fax, poste restante, and phone services are also available. Nancy's postal code is 54000. *8 rue Pierre Fourier, tel. 03–83–39–27–17. Behind Hôtel de Ville and pl. Stanislas. Open Mon.–Sat. 8–7.*

VISITOR INFORMATION • The **Office de Tourisme** will give you a useful map and *Spectacles à Nancy,* a free monthly publication devoted to goings-on around town. *14 pl. Stanislas, tel. 03–83–35–22–41. Open Mon.–Sat. 9–7, Sun. 10–1.*

The **Centre Information Jeunesse Lorraine** (20 quai Claude le Lorrain, tel. 03–83–37–04–46) sells youth hostel cards and has information on hostels, outdoor activities, and student-oriented travel deals.

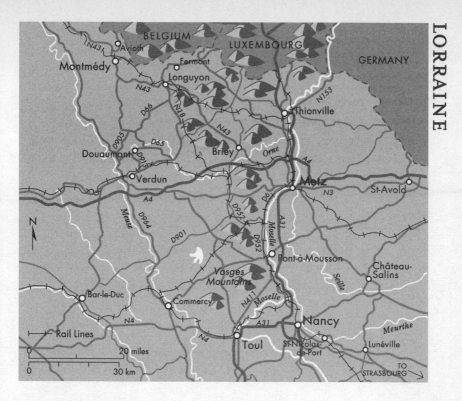

COMING AND GOING

More than a dozen trains a day leave Paris's Gare de l'Est for Nancy (3 hrs, 223F), and as many leave Nancy for Strasbourg (1½ hrs, 128F). The **train station** (3 pl. Thiers, tel. 03–83–22–15–15), a 15-minute walk down rue Stanislas from the town center, is open 24 hours. The regional lines of **Les Rapides de Lorraine** (52 blvd. Austrasie, tel. 03–83–32–34–20) arrive at and depart from the parking area on rue St-Georges near the cathedral and cover ground in all directions from Nancy.

GETTING AROUND

Nancy is fairly spread out, but the central area is manageable on foot. There are good maps posted at all bus stops and in the train station. **Allô Bus** (tel. 03–83–35–54–54) runs buses all over the city and to the suburbs, most of them making their way along rue St-Jean at one point or another. A ticket from the driver will run you 7F, and a 10-ride pass is available at tabacs and newspaper kiosks for 50F. Pick up schedules and maps from Window 22 at the train station. A 24-hour **taxi** stand operates right next to the train station; to order a taxi, call 03–83–37–65–37.

WHERE TO SLEEP

There are plenty of two-star hotels (with rooms for around 200F) between the train station and place Stanislas—a good, central location. In a more residential area but still near the station is **Hôtel le Jean Jaurès** (14 blvd. Jean-Jaurès, tel. 03–83–27–74–14), a homey hotel that feels like an old mansion and offers doubles (190F without bath, 230F with bath). Each July and August, one of Nancy's university residence halls opens to travelers, charging about 60F a night for a single. Individual rooms, scattered through available dorms, are available year-round. To reserve, call **CROUS** (75 rue de Laxou, tel. 03–83–91–88–00). The **Groupe des Étudiants Catholiques** (35 cours Léopold, tel. 03–83–32–30–87, fax 03–83–30–60–76) has rooms with a sink for 80F a day, breakfast included, with showers and toilets in the hall. The university refectory is close by. Reservations are essential. It's closed in August.

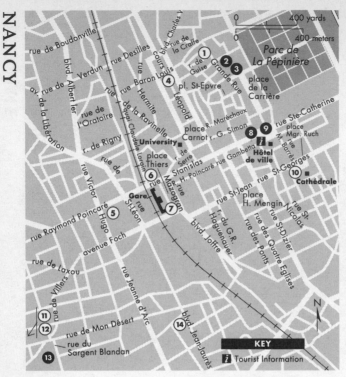

Sights ●
Musée de l'Ecole de Nancy, **13**
Musée des Arts et Traditions Populaires, **2**
Musée des Beaux-Arts, **8**
Musée Historique Lorrain, **3**
Place Stanislas, **9**

Lodging ○
Auberge de Jeunesse/Château de Remicourt, **11**
Camping Brabois, **12**
Groupe des Étudiants Catholiques, **4**
Hôtel Akena, **5**
Hôtel de Guise, **1**
Hôtel de la Poste, **10**
Hôtel Foch, **7**
Hôtel le Jean Jaurès, **14**
Hôtel-Restaurant Piroux, **6**

UNDER 150F • Hôtel de Guise. This former residence of a countess hides in a peaceful part of the vieille ville, just off bustling Grande Rue, and north of place Stanislas. The grand staircase and long, oddly mirrored halls can get spooky, but the whole setup is clean and will do. Singles start at 115F, doubles at 125F (200F with shower). *18 rue de Guise, tel. 03–83–32–24–68. 45 rooms, 30 with bath. Closed 2nd wk of Aug. and last 2 wks of Dec.*

UNDER 175F • Hôtel Foch. Down a short alleyway around the corner from the south side of the train station, this hotel has well-worn but clean rooms with TVs. Singles and doubles are 170F without shower (showers 20F), 190F with shower. *8 av. Foch, tel. 03–83–32–88–50. 40 rooms, 33 with bath.*

Hôtel-Restaurant Piroux. Across from the train station, this small hotel has a comfortable lobby and serves sumptuous traditional dishes in its adjacent restaurant. The owners are gracious and as welcoming as the aromas steaming from the kitchen. Singles are 130F, doubles 160F–200F. Lunch and dinner are 72F each. Reserve ahead in summer. *12 rue Raymond-Poincaré, tel. 03–83–32–01–10. 22 rooms, 16 with bath. Closed Dec. 25–Jan. 1.*

UNDER 200F • Hôtel Akena. Built in 1995 with prefab everything, this McDonald's of hotels is sparkling clean—some would say sterile. The rooms are small and sparse, but each one has a bathroom, phone, and TV (with cable and a remote control). Its quiet yet central location (1,000 ft from the train station) and 175F price tag (for one, two, or three people) make it a good deal. *41 rue Raymond-Poincaré, tel. 03–83–28–02–13. 58 rooms, all with bath.*

Hôtel de la Poste. The most striking thing about this hotel is that it looks like it's part of the cathedral. Inside it's just as impressive and the staff looks after your every need. The cathedral bells aren't too loud—but bring earplugs if you're a light sleeper. Singles are 105F, doubles 165–220F. *56 pl. Mgr. Ruch, tel. 03–83–32–11–52, fax 03–83–37–58–74. 44 rooms, all with bath.*

HOSTEL • Auberge de Jeunesse/Château de Remicourt. This hostel, in a château in the suburb Villers-Lès-Nancy, is surrounded by the Parc Remicourt, an ultragreen spot where people play soccer and Frisbee. It's a bit isolated, being 4 km (2½ mi) southwest of the town center, but buses make it easy to reach. Children and grown-ups are welcome (no age limit) and parking is available. There's no lockout or curfew (the last bus from town is at midnight, though). Beds are 70F per night, breakfast included. *149 rue de Vandoeuvre, Villers, tel. 03–83–27–73–67. From center or station, take Bus 26 to St-Fiacre stop, walk down hill, turn right on rue de la Grange aux Moines, and follow signs; after 8 PM, take Bus 4 (direction: Brabois) to Brasch and follow rue de Vandoeuvre past the botanical garden. 60 beds. Reception open 5:30 PM–10:30 PM. Kitchen. Closed Dec. 25–Jan. 1.*

CAMPING • On the border of Forêt de la Haye, **Camping Brabois** is about as green as it gets so close to a big city. Families swarm all over the place in August, but it's serene the rest of the year. Between June and September, sites cost 15F plus 16F per tent; October–May, sites go for 13F and 6F per tent. From the station, take Bus 26 or 46 to Cottages, about 5 km (3 mi) southwest of town. *N74, in Villers-Lès-Nancy, tel. 03–83–27–18–28.*

FOOD

Rue des Maréchaux, north of place Stanislas, is the pedestrian restaurant street par excellence; browse through the posted menus for a comfortable price. **Grande Rue** is an even better place for a meal. Pick up groceries at the central **Prisunic** (20 rue St-Georges, tel. 03–83–32–87–34) or the huge covered **market** that's held Tuesday–Saturday at place Henri Mengin. The best place for a sandwich is off lively place St-Epvre at **Made in France** (1 rue St-Epvre, no phone).

UNDER 50F • Au Petit Bourgeois. Off by itself in a narrow alley at the end of Grande Rue, this place attracts friendly locals and dishes out remarkably good, cheap food. There are salads, skewers of chicken or lamb served with vegetables, and a plat du jour day or night. *17 rue le Petit Bourgeois, tel. 03–83–30–02–13. Cash only.*

La Gavotte. An exceptionally friendly atmosphere and good deals on gourmet crepes make this the crêperie to try if you've been holding out. Options range from the simple buttered crepe at 13F to the smoked duck with mushrooms and bird liver at 45F. *47 Grande Rue, tel. 03–83–37–65–64. Cash only. Closed Sun.*

UNDER 75F • Excelsior. Built in the early 1900s by several of Nancy's art nouveau artists, this large brasserie is an essential stop for coffee or drinks. If you can afford a full meal (65F for lunch, 200F for dinner), you'll find professional service and excellent food. Otherwise come for the quiche lorraine or the *faim de nuit* (night hunger) menu, served past midnight, which includes three courses and wine. *50 rue Henri Poincaré, tel. 03–83–35–24–57. Cash only.*

Pizzeria le Rimini. This centrally located restaurant draws a young, friendly crowd with its long list of pizzas and salads and its cheap menu (which includes salad, spaghetti carbonara or lasagna, and dessert). There's outdoor seating in back and jazz music inside. *21 rue Héré, off pl. Stanislas, tel. 03–83–35–59–67. Cash only.*

SPLURGE • Au P'tit Cuny. From the Musée des Arts et Traditions Populaires (*see* Worth Seeing, *below*), cross the street to sink your teeth into authentic Lorraine cuisine in the form of *tête de veau* (veal head), or tangy veal *tourte* (pie) for 100F–150F with wine. *97–99 Grande Rue, tel. 03–83–32–85–94. Closed Sun., Mon.*

WORTH SEEING

Most sights revolve around **place Stanislas,** the magnificent neoclassical square built in the 18th century at the command of Stanislas Leszczynski, who, as former king of Poland, found Nancy a bit too rustic for his royal taste. To gain favor with his son-in-law (and the king of France) Louis XV, he built the square "in honor of the king" and put a statue of Louis smack-dab in the center. Louis's statue was made into cannons during the Revolution, leaving room for the one that's there now, of Stanislas.

MUSÉE DE L'ÉCOLE DE NANCY • The only museum in France dedicated solely to art nouveau houses re-created rooms and original works by local art nouveau stars like Gallé, Daum, Muller, and Walter. Gallé (1846–1904) was the engine that drove the whole art nouveau movement. He called upon artists to resist the imperialism of Paris, follow examples in nature (not those in Greece or Rome), use a variety of techniques and materials, and make things accessible to the common people. The house has furniture, art, glassware, and even a grand piano in the flowing art nouveau style; it was constructed for Eugène Corbin, a famous patron of the movement. *36 rue du Sergent-Blandon, tel. 03–83–40–14–86. Admission 20F. Open Wed.–Mon. 10–noon and 2–5 (Apr.–Sept. until 6).*

MUSÉE DES BEAUX-ARTS • The spacious building housing the Museum of Fine Arts on place Stanislas would be a great place to walk through even without all the art; add a massive collection of works by many renowned artists and you have a don't-miss sight. The Collection Galilée, comprising works displayed in Paris between 1919 and 1930, dominates; look for pieces by Bonnard, Dufy, Matisse, Modigliani, Utrillo, Picasso, and many others. You'll also find Caravaggios and 17th-century Dutch, Flemish, and French paintings. Delacroix's *La Bataille de Nancy* (1833) is one of the museum's prized possessions; the artist himself modestly called it "one of my least-weak works." The museum devotes a wing to sculpture and modern pieces by Duchamp-Villon and Zadkine. *3 pl. Stanislas, tel. 03–83–85–30–72. Admission 20F, free Wed. Open Wed.–Sun. 10:30–6, Mon. 2–6.*

MUSÉE HISTORIQUE LORRAIN/MUSÉE DES ARTS ET TRADITIONS POPULAIRES • The former palace of the duke of Lorraine and its adjacent Franciscan chapel make impressive settings for equally impressive museums. The first, the Museum of Lorraine History, holds Lorraine's most comprehensive and well-displayed collection of artifacts—from Roman glass to Callot's copper etching plates to Stanislas's microscope collection—while the second, the Museum of Lorraine Folklife, displays Lorraine's various folk art styles in furniture, clothing, and architecture. *64–66 Grande Rue, tel. 03–83–32–18–74. Admission to each museum 20F. Open Wed.–Mon. 10–noon and 2–6.*

PARC DE LA PÉPINIÈRE • Formerly the gardens of the Ducal Palace, the Parc de la Pépinière (Tree Nursery) has a rose garden, a zoo, carnival rides, playgrounds, picnic spots, jogging paths, and continuous games of *boules* (lawn bowling). Come on a Sunday and you might luck into a free concert. Nancy goes crazy over jazz, and in October this park hosts a festival to prove it. *Pl. Stanislas. Open daily 6 AM–8 PM, longer hrs in summer.*

CHEAP THRILLS

Nancy has some nifty art nouveau–influenced architecture—head down any side street and check out doorways, doors, and windows decorated with tile, stained glass, and ornate iron grilles. The **Pôle Universitaire Européen de Nancy-Metz** has an American library stocked full of novels, masterpieces, science and language books, language dictionaries, and travel guides, plus the latest copies of the *International Herald-Tribune* and various magazines. *34 cours Léopold, tel. 03–83–17–67–38. Open Sept.–mid-July, Mon.–Thurs. noon–6, Fri. noon–5.*

AFTER DARK

More than 45,000 university students and a healthy yuppie-bohemian population keep the vieille ville and Stanislas neighborhoods hopping after sundown. Grab a sidewalk seat at one of the cafés on the square and pay the cost of a drink for a night's worth of entertainment—**Jean Lamour** (7 pl. Stanislas, tel. 03–83–32–53–53) is especially popular. Join university students at the **Café Noir** (6 rue Guerrier de Dumast, off rue de Serre, tel. 03–83–30–44–11) for darts, billiards, and Alsatian beer among Russian Revolution decor. The **Be Happy Bar** (23 rue Gustave Simon, tel. 03–83–35–56–41) has the largest selection of beers in Nancy, while **Le Mezcalito,** next to La Gavotte (*see* Food, *above*), serves up exotic cocktails. For music, try the **Blue Note** (3 rue des Michottes, between rue Stanislas and pl. Carnot, tel. 03–83–30–31–18), a cover-free jazz club with five beers on tap, or **Batchi Bar** (3 rue St-Epvre, tel. 03–83–35–45–38), where techno rules and gays and lesbians flirt unabashedly.

METZ

With its abundance of water, parks, and narrow pedestrian streets built of *pierre de jaumont,* a dark yellow stone that comes from local hillsides, Metz claims to be the most beautiful city in Lorraine. It's definitely one of the oldest: A Roman outpost since 300 BC, Metz was the wealthiest independent city-state in France during the Middle Ages. Layers of history are visible in its architecture—keep your eyes peeled for Gothic windows cemented into walls finished in 17th-century detail.

The giant **Cathédrale St-Étienne** (tel. 03–87–75–54–61), the third highest in France, was built between the 13th and 16th centuries; it has the largest surface area of stained glass in the world, including some amazing pieces (in the left transept) by Marc Chagall. The cathedral's entrance, built in the 18th century to match the arcaded buildings of place d'Armes, is decked with symbolic ornamentation that rivals Notre-Dame's in Paris. The cathedral is open daily 9–5. Metz's other highlights are the 22 km (13 mi) of pathways that run along the Moselle River and its tributaries. Take a dunk in the plan d'eau, rent a pedal boat (25F per half hour) from one of the stands along the quay, or watch a game of boules in the Esplanade. Off its south side is **St-Pierre-aux-Nonnains,** a 16th-century church enclosed in 4th-century Gallo-Roman walls. The church is open April–October, Wednesday–Sunday 2—5, and November–March, weekends 2–5.

BASICS

Facing the cathedral, Metz's friendly **Office de Tourisme** has maps, a free hotel guide, good advice, and a cool place to sit down. For 50F you can catch an exhaustive two-hour tour (daily at 3 PM in summer, Mon.–Sat. in winter) or rent a headset and go at your own pace; both are available in English. *Spectacles à Metz*, a monthly events magazine, is available free here and at cafés and cinemas. *Pl. d'Armes, tel. 03–87–55–53–76. Open July–Aug., Mon.–Sat. 9–9, Sun. 10–1 and 2–5; Sept.–June, Mon.–Sat. 9–7, Sun. 10–1 and 3–5.*

COMING AND GOING

Frequent trains run between Metz's **train station** (pl. du Général-de-Gaulle, tel. 03–87–38–87–48) and Nancy (30 mins, 50F) and Paris's Gare de l'Est (3 hrs, 223F). For about the same price, **Les Courriers Mosellans** (tel. 03–87–34–60–06) and **Les Rapides de Lorraine** (tel. 03–83–32–34–20) buses connect Metz with Nancy and other major cities. The **bus station** is on place Coislin.

GETTING AROUND

To reach the center and tourist office, turn right out of the train station and then left up rue des Augustins; after crossing straight through a couple of squares, go left again on rue En Fournirue, which leads right to place d'Armes. Although you'll rarely need it, Metz has a remarkably user-friendly **Minibus system,** whose stops are marked by cartoonlike BUS signs. Rides are 4F. To reach place d'Armes, just take Minibus B across the street from the train station and ask the driver to drop you off in front of the tourist office.

During one Occupation period, the Germans built Metz's clunky neo-Roman train station and Protestant church (pl. Comédie, across the canal from the cathedral) from dark gray stone, claiming that the local "pierre de jaumont" looked too French.

WHERE TO SLEEP

Across the street from the train station, **Hôtel le Globe** (3 pl. du Général-de-Gaulle, tel. 03–87–56–02–06) has renovated singles and doubles from 200F; all have private bathrooms. The kind, timid management of the central **Hôtel Lafayette** (24 rue des Clercs, tel. 03–87–75–21–09) rents tattered but clean doubles from 140F with a sink (175F with bath). **Hôtel Moderne** (1 rue Lafayette, tel. 03–87–66–57–33) has neat and, as the name suggests, modern rooms for 240F. **Hôtel du Centre** (14 rue Dupont-des-Loges, tel. 03–87–36–06–93) is in the middle of the pedestrian zone but stays reasonably quiet. A room for one or two with shower, TV, and phone costs 220F. Campers should head to the green and peaceful **Metz Plage** (tel. 03–87–32–05–58), on the banks of the Moselle near the Auberge de Jeunesse. One person with a tent pays 21F.

HOSTELS • Right off place Jeanne d'Arc, at the southern end of rue Jeanne d'Arc, the large, impersonal **Foyer Carrefour** (6 rue Marchant, tel. 03–87–75–07–26) rents out singles for 79F, breakfast and showers included. Sheets are 25F. Cheaper, quieter, and more aesthetically pleasing lodging is at the riverside **Auberge de Jeunesse** (1 allée de Metz Plage, tel. 03–87–30–44–02), where 85F gets you a bed, breakfast, and a variety of room formats. Adults and children are welcome, with some family rooms available. All rooms have been renovated, and the staff makes your life easy—from changing money at good rates and lending bikes to guests for free to serving a filling 41F dinner. From the station or center, take Bus 3 or 11 to Pontiffroy. If you're walking (it's about 10 minutes from the cathedral, 30 minutes from the station), take rue des Bénédictins to the end, and then go right around the bend.

FOOD

Metz is a good place to sample Moselle wines and the Côte de Toul gris (rosé)—and anything made with the mirabelle, small yellow plums that make especially good tarts, jam, and eau-de-vie. The pedestrian area, particularly around place St-Jacques, has the widest range of menus and prices. For crepes, head to **St-Malo Crêperie Glacier** (14 rue des Clercs, tel. 03–87–74–56–85), which serves an affordable ham, cheese, and tomato galette. A favorite local restaurant is **Jean d'Apremont** (10 rue Taison, tel. 03–87–36–72–02), one block off place d'Armes via rue En Fournirue, always bustling and serving up specialties of the Savoie and Dauphine regions. For good, cheap menus with potatoes au gratin and home-made tarts, try **Le Dauphiné** (8 rue du Chanoine-Collin, tel. 03–87–36–03–04), between place d'Armes and the labyrinthine Musée d'Art et d'Histoire. In the golden shadow of the cathedral, **La Baraka** (25 pl. Chambre, tel. 03–87–36–33–92) has congenial hosts who serve heaping plates of couscous with vegetables, chicken, or skewers of lamb. For a friendly welcome and really good food, such as lamb served with roast potatoes and cream cheese with herbs, go to **Restaurant Le Breg Much** (51 rue Mazelle, tel. 03–87–74–39–79), with set meals between 58F (lunch) and 115F (dinner). It's closed Sunday dinner and Monday.

AFTER DARK

Most nightlife happens on place Jeanne d'Arc and place St-Jacques, where you are welcome to BYOB. If you must have a waiter, a beer will run you about 16F in a café. A good compromise is the **Bar St-Jacques** (10 pl. St-Jacques, tel. 03–87–75–08–20), which has terrible service but only charges 11F for a beer. For dancing, try the ever-popular **Tiff Club** (24 rue Coëtlosquet, tel. 03–87–75–23–32). In summer, the city puts on concerts in place St-Étienne (check the tourist office for schedules). If you have the chance (and an extra 80F), check out a concert in the 3,000-seat **L'Arsenal** (av. Ney, tel. 03–87–39–92–00) at the south end of the Esplanade.

VERDUN

If you have a penchant for World War I history, make a trip to Verdun—though infrequent (and expensive) transport might deter you unless you're absolutely committed. The Battle of Verdun, launched in 1916 over possession of a few hilltops, lasted 18 months and saw more than 700,000 killed, marking the beginning of a bloody stalemate between German and French forces. Two years later, the arrival of 450,000 American troops under the command of General Pershing helped defeat the Germans. The Treaty of Versailles was signed later that year, ending the war in France but leaving nine villages wiped off the map and a countryside too full of mines to ever be built on or cultivated again. Though the cemeteries and memorials lie in the battle area 9 km (5½ mi) north of town, one powerful testimony stands in Verdun's relatively untouched medieval center: the **World Center for Peace,** opened in 1995. The poignant exhibits deal mostly with destruction and recuperation. *Pl. Monseigneur Ginisty, tel. 03–29–86–55–00, fax 03–29–86–15–14. Admission 25F. Open Feb.–mid-June and mid-Sept.–mid-Nov., Wed.–Mon. 10–1 and 2–6; mid-June–mid-Sept., daily 10–1 and 2–6.*

To visit the battlegrounds, you must rent a car or a bike, or take the guided bus tour offered by the Verdun **Office de Tourisme.** *Pl. de la Nation, tel. 03–29–86–14–18. Tours cost 145F with commentary in English and are given May–mid-Sept., daily at 2.*

In the bomb-pitted forests that have overgrown the disputed hills, you'll find the **Ossuaire de Douaumont,** a towering art deco ossuary holding the bones of 130,000 unidentified soldiers; the defensive works of the **Fort de Vaux,** marking the farthest advance of German troops; the heartrending foundations of the school, town hall, and houses of the destroyed village of **Fleury**; and the **Tranchée des Baïonnettes** (Trench of Bayonets), where an entire French regiment was buried alive, still standing, by the astonishing force of German bombardment (the bayonets that once were visible above ground gave the place its name). The **American Cemetery of Romagne** contains the bodies of 14,192 killed in the war, six of whom were female nurses; the **Mémorial de Verdun** contains panoramas, weapons, and the pathetic artwork of trench-bound soldiers, including art nouveau vases hammered from artillery shells. *Mémorial: Fleury-devant-Fouaumont, tel. 03–29–84–35–34. Admission 20F. Open mid-Apr.–mid-Sept., daily 9–6; mid-Sept.–mid-Dec. and mid-Jan.–mid-Apr., 9–noon and 2–5:30.*

COMING AND GOING

It's easiest to reach Verdun by bus from Nancy. **Les Rapides de Lorraine** sends four buses a day (only one on Sunday) from Nancy's cathedral on a beautiful, if meandering, three-hour ride (91F) through the countryside. **Les Rapides de la Meuse** (tel. 03–29–86–02–71) has six buses a day going from Verdun to Nancy. Only one or two trains a day travel between Verdun and Nancy (1 hr, 87F), Paris (3½ hrs, 197F), and Metz (1½ hrs, 120F).

WHERE TO SLEEP

The **Hôtel St-Paul** (12 pl. St-Paul, tel. 03–29–86–02–16) is a convenient, safe, and comfortable 31-room hotel with a good restaurant, set meals for 90F–180F, and rooms from 165F without bath to 260F with bath. Right in the shadow of the porte Chaussée bridge on the banks of the Meuse River is the **Hôtel de la Porte Chaussée** (porte Chaussée, tel. 03–29–86–00–78), a 17-room hotel with doubles starting at 150F (180F with shower). All toilets are down the hall.

FOOD

Cheap eateries and grocery stores flank **rue Chaussée.** More expensive outdoor cafés lie along the river on **quai de Londres,** a better spot for a beer than for a meal. Your best bet, though, may be **Restaurant le Baltard** in Hôtel St-Paul (*see* Where to Sleep, *above*), with a meal-size Alsatian salad (lettuce smothered with cold cuts) and fresh, local fish.

FRANCHE-COMTÉ

Bordered by Alsace to the north, Switzerland to the east, and Burgundy to the west, the Franche-Comté is a hilly, forest-gorge region known for the rivers Le Doubs and La Loue, cross-country ski trails, and Comté cheese. The Jura Mountains here have good hiking and cross-country skiing, but if serious hiking is on your agenda, these "mountains" will soon feel like molehills; if leisurely hikes punctuated with historic sites and places to have a beer are your thing, these mountains fit the bill.

Vauban, Louis XIV's favorite engineer, had his hands all over this region, as the massive citadels of Belfort and Besançon attest to. During World War II, the French Resistance used the Jura's network of caves and grottoes (carved by the rivers) to fight against Vichy's regime, which had set up a deportation camp in Dole. Some of the region's forests are still recovering from the fighting that took place here; trees are small and suspiciously orderly.

Monumental Besançon, the capital of the Franche-Comté, is the region's must-see attraction. Other cities are smaller and less attractive than Besançon—good as excursion bases, but that's about it. If you have plenty of time and energy, consider doing the region completely by bike so you can get to the tiny towns that form the heart of the Franche-Comté. The whole area perks up in late June and early July, during **Jazz Franche-Comté,** when musicians plug into local theaters, clubs, bars, parks, and public squares and often perform for free.

BASICS

The **Comité Régional de Tourisme de Franche-Comté** (9 rue de Pontarlier, Besançon, tel. 03–81–83–50–47) is a rich source of regional information. Plan ahead for your Jura trip by stopping in at **Maison de la Franche-Comté** (2 blvd. de la Madeleine, 9e, Paris 75009, tel. 01–42–66–26–28). More local regional offices are set up in each of the Franche-Comté's four départements: **Doubs** (4 ter Faubourg Rivotte, Besançon, tel. 03–81–82–80–77); **Jura** (Maison du Tourisme, pl. du 11 Novembre, Lons-le-Saunier, tel. 03–84–24–65–01); **Haute-Saône** (Maison du Tourisme, rue des Bains Vesoul, tel. 03–84–75–43–66); and the **Territoire de Belfort** (2 bis rue Clémenceau, tel. 03–84–55–90–90, fax 03–84–55–90–99).

COMING AND GOING

Though the Franche-Comté's hubs are well served by train, visiting the smaller and infinitely more attractive villages requires the assistance of a good mountain bike, sturdy hiking boots, or **Monts-Jura Buses** (4 rue Berthelot, tel. 03–81–63–44–44 in Besançon), which will get you almost anywhere you want—getting there *when* you want is another problem entirely. The SNCF has some buses that pick up where the train line ends; rail passes are valid on these. Pick up a regional timetable (good for trains and buses) at the train station in Belfort, Besançon, or Dole.

FOOD

Comté cheese (very similar to Swiss Gruyère) is the Franche-Comté's proud offering to the culinary world, and local fondues are delicious and hearty. A salad or *assiette comtoise* (Comté plate) usually has Comté cheese, Morteau sausage, potatoes, lettuce, and hard-boiled eggs. The local wines here are Côte du Jura Blanc and Arbois, both of which taste very earthy compared to the fruity whites of Alsace and drier ones of Burgundy. Near Dole, hard nougat candy made with almonds or hazelnuts is a favorite, as is chocolate flavored with lemon and orange.

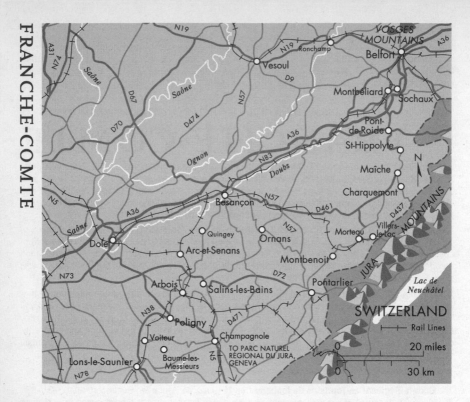

OUTDOOR ACTIVITIES

With its limited transportation, the Franche-Comté is better suited for long-distance adventures than short day hikes. The GR5 and GR9 (which together connect Holland to the Mediterranean) overlap in the Jura as the GR59 and GR559. The trails make several loops—or *boucles* (buckles)—good for overnight or three- to four-day hikes. Since you can eat and sleep in hotels along the way, all you need are good shoes, a map, and a day pack. Pick up the brochure "Randonner dans le Jura" from a tourist office (*see* Basics, *above*), decide which trail interests you, then do your serious research: Tourist offices tend to be more helpful when you have a specific question. The **Comité Départemental de Tourisme du Jura** (8 rue Louis Rousseau, tel. 03–84–87–08–88, fax 03–84–24–88–70) in Lons-le-Saunier (50 km/31 mi from Dole) is infinitely helpful. There is also a guide (again, at the tourist office) called "Tous les Circuits VTT du Jura," a good starting point for mountain bikers.

Winter sports are best in the Franche-Comté's southernmost département, the Jura, which also boasts the two highest peaks in the region, **Mont d'Or** at 4,799 ft and **Crêt de la Neige** at 5,635 ft. Both peaks make for good, very accessible hikes. Mont d'Or is near the town of **Pontarlier,** accessible by train from Besançon; Crêt de la Neige is near **St-Claude,** accessible by train (and bus) from Dole. The GR59 runs across both of them.

BESANÇON

The train ride south into Besançon is astonishingly beautiful, swishing through green fields and forests along the Doubs River. The ride, though, is only a preview of Besançon, the greenest city in France. The topography here is remarkable: Four steep hills of about the same height protect the centre ville, which is almost entirely encircled by the Doubs. An impressive citadel stands guard from one hill, while three annex fortifications garnish the others. Besançon's attractive centre ville reflects its varied past: Within a few blocks you can see the Roman *porte noire* (black gate), Renaissance Granvelle Palace, and Spanish-influenced Cathédrale St-Jean. Finally, Besançon's large student population gives it a hip café scene and a good ethnic mix. You'll find reasonably priced lodging and plenty of affordable restaurants.

BASICS

The **Office de Tourisme** has tons of brochures and maps; look for it across the Doubs near the Pont de la République. *2 pl. de la 1ère Armée Française, tel. 03–81–80–92–55. Open Apr.–mid-June, Mon. 10– 7, Tues.–Sat. 9–7, Sun. 10–noon and 3–5; mid-June–Sept., Mon. 10–7, Tues.–Sat. 9–7; Oct.–Mar., Mon. 10–6, Tues.–Sat. 9–6.*

The main **post office** (4 rue Demangel, tel. 03–81–80–20–30) changes money at good rates and is where poste restante mail winds up (the postal code is 25000); it is open Monday–Friday 8:15–5:15. The **PTT annex** (23 rue Proudhon, off sq. St-Amour, tel. 03–81–65–55–82) in the center of town is more convenient; it is open Monday–Friday 8–7, Saturday 8–noon.

COMING AND GOING

Besançon's **train station** (av. de la Paix, tel. 03–81–35–35–35) is at the northern end of the city; walk downhill and across the Doubs (about 15 minutes) or take any bus to reach the center of town. One daily TGV arrives from Paris (2½ hrs, 250F); more frequent direct trains arrive from Strasbourg (3 hrs, 178F), Dijon (1 hr, 82F), Lyon (3 hrs, 161F), and—along a beautiful rural route— from Belfort (1 hr, 97F).

Bus service to the surrounding area is limited, but you'll have to use it anyway to reach small towns in the mountains. The centrally located **Autogare** (9 rue Proudhon, tel. 03–81–21– 22–00) posts schedules. The **Centre Information Jeunesse** (27 rue de la République, tel. 03–81–21–16–16) runs an *auto-stop* (hitchhiking) service; check its bulletin board for drivers headed in your direction.

A bottle of sharp Savagnin, a pink slab of air-dried ham, a patty of silky Vacherin Mont d'Or melted over potatoes: You don't need pink linens to dine on this primal mountain food, just a hiker's appetite, whetted by exploring the forested Jura gorges.

GETTING AROUND

The Doubs River makes a horseshoe bend around Besançon's centre ville; everything worth seeing is within or just outside this boundary. The cathedral and the Vauban citadel lie at the horseshoe's southern opening, while the Musée des Beaux-Arts sits at the top. If you don't have the oomph or the hours it would take to walk around town, hop on a **CTB bus.** A ticket costs 6F, payable to the driver. You can also buy tickets and get a schedule and route map at the **Espace Bus** office (4 pl. du 8 Septembre, off Grande Rue, tel. 03–81–48–12–12), open Monday–Saturday 9– 12:30 and 1–7. There are two **taxi** stations (tel. 03–81–80–17–76), one in front of the Palais de Justice and the other at the train station. **Cycles Robert** (rte. de Vesoul, next to supermarket Carrefour, tel. 03– 81–53–64–68), near the train station, rents VTTs by the half day (65F), full day (90F), and weekend (175F) with a 2,000F deposit.

WHERE TO SLEEP

Hotels in town are economical if you're traveling with someone, and pricier places often have one or two cheap rooms. Start a search around place de la Révolution; exit from the train station onto avenue du Maréchal Foch, turn left on quai de Strasbourg, and cross the river at Pont de Battant. If you must stay next to the train station, far from most of the action, the only affordable option is **Hôtel Florel** (6 rue de la Viotte, tel. 03–81–80–41–08, fax 03–81–50–44–40), with 24 singles and doubles priced from 140F without bath, 260F with bath. From July through September, **CROUS** (av. de l'Observatoire, tel. 03–81– 48–46–46) arranges stays in university housing (about 60F per person per night) in the Cité Universi- taire, northwest of town; from the station take Bus 8 to Campus, at the end of the line.

UNDER 175F • Hôtel du Commerce. This place on the southern edge of the center often has rooms when other hotels are full. You enter through an attached restaurant, which serves inexpensive, unspec- tacular meals. The rooms themselves are adequate and cheap: Singles are 110F (155F with bath), dou- bles 160F (205F with bath). *8 pl. de Lattre de Tassigny, tel. 03–81–81–37–11. 7 rooms, 2 with bath.*

Hôtel-Restaurant du Levant. If you can manage to distract one of the family members from the busy restaurant downstairs, you can get a single for 98F or a double for 130F–180F. The rooms are a bit dusty but all have a view either of the river or the mountains. Showers cost 12F. *9 rue des Boucheries, off pl. de la Révolution, tel. 03–81–81–07–88. 12 rooms, 7 with bath.*

UNDER 200F • Hôtel Gambetta. The terrific location two blocks from place de la Révolution doesn't prevent Gambetta from being calm and quiet. The rooms are comfy and well tended and run 190F and up with bath for one or two people. A couple of extremely popular singles without bath go for 135F; you can also rent a room for a day (10–6) for 135F. Be sure to ask for the door code if you plan to stay out past 11 PM. *13 rue Gambetta, tel. 03–81–82–02–33. 27 rooms, most with bath.*

UNDER 250F • Hôtel Regina. A warm welcome, comfortable rooms, and the central location make this one of the best options in town. Plus, all the rooms are protected from street noise by the flowery courtyard. A few rooms with bath cost 194F for one or two people; the rest cost 200F for one person, up to 265F for two. Rooms have phone and TVs. *91 Grande Rue, tel. 03–81–81–50–22, fax 03–81–81–60–20. 21 rooms, all with bath.*

HOSTELS • Besançon has a handful of hostel-type accommodations; the best is the **Centre International de Séjour** (19 rue Martin du Gard, tel. 03–81–50–07–54), northwest of the center and near the university. A room to yourself costs 94F; a room for two costs 60F a person, showers and sheets included. There's no age limit. Take Bus 8 from the station to l'Intermarché. The **Foyer des Jeunes Filles** (18 rue de la Cassotte, tel. 03–81–80–90–01), just five minutes east of the train station, has a beautiful garden, pleasant lounge, and a single or double is yours for 80F per person but is only available to women (aged 16–26 years); shower and breakfast are included. Sheets cost 15F.

CAMPING • Camping de Chalezeule. This classy campground north of town borders the Doubs River; the setup includes a pool and free showers. A site costs 20F plus 11F per person. Call to reserve ahead. *Rte. de Belfort, tel. 03–81–88–04–26. Bus 1 to end of line and walk 2 km (1 mi) north. 113 sites. Closed Oct.–Mar.*

FOOD

Good, cheap restaurants lurk around the university (south of the center) and the Palais de Justice. Rue Battant (between the station and the center) is a good street for kebabs and boulangeries. Tuesday and Friday mornings and all day Saturday there's a huge **outdoor market** on place de la Révolution; **covered markets** set up Tuesday–Saturday on place de la Révolution and Tuesday–Friday on rue Goudimel. For groceries, hit **Monoprix** (10 Grande Rue, tel. 03–81–65–36–36). If you'd rather have someone else make you a mammoth sandwich, look for **La Fringale** (40 Grande Rue, tel. 03–81–81–07–86) between the Hôtel de Ville and the Doubs; the restaurant's name means "fit of hunger."

UNDER 75F • Au Petit Polonais. A veritable institution in Besançon, the Polonais has been serving up traditional French fare in a coffee-shop setting for more than 100 years. At lunch and dinner, locals cram in for the 58F three-course menu, which could include pork chops and penne with tomato cream sauce. *81 rue des Granges, tel. 03–81–81–23–67. Closed Sun. No dinner Sat.*

Bistrot du Jura. In an intimate, corner-bar setting of checkered tiles and bentwood, you can sample regional specialties like clams in cider vinegar, herring with steamed potatoes, omelets with morelle mushrooms, or andouillette in Jura wine—a fine selection of which is served by the glass. *35 rue Charles-Nodier, tel. 03–81–82–03–48.*

Quignon Comtois. The dreadful setting—a former shop window cozied up with mail-order decor—is more than offset by earthy, delicious Franche-Comté cooking, served to loyal crowds of young locals. There's simple fried carp, *morteau* (local sausage), rich ham gratin with mushrooms, mouthwatering Vacherin melted over salad and roasted potatoes, and Swiss-style *röesties* (hash browns). Sample from a good list of open Jura wines. *10 rue G. Courbet, tel. 03–81–83–36–13. Closed Sun. No lunch Sat.*

WORTH SEEING

Besançon's acropolis in Gallo-Roman times, Vauban's **Citadelle de Vauban** gets its name from Louis XIV's engineer-architect who masterminded the thing. A walk around its ramparts is worth the admission, but since you paid you might as well check out the museums now housed inside: The **Musée Comtois** has provincial arts, including a vast waffle-iron display; the **Musée d'Histoire Naturelle** is a predictable yawner; and the **Musée de la Résistance et de la Déportation** (the unquestionable highlight) will impress even those who have studied the Holocaust in depth. *Rue des Fusillés de la Résistance, tel. 03–81–65–07–44. Admission (includes all museums) 45F–50F. Open Apr.–Sept., daily 9:15–6:15; Oct.–Mar., daily 9:45–4:45.*

Downhill from the citadel, in the ornate 18th-century **Cathédrale St-Jean,** is Besançon's huge **Horloge Astronomique** (Astronomical Clock). This one was assembled in the 19th century with more than 30,000 moving parts and gives you up-to-the-minute details on the tide at Mont-St-Michel. *Rue de la*

Convention, tel. 03–81–81–12–76. Admission to Horloge Astronomique 14F. Open Wed.–Mon. 10–noon and 3–6; Oct.–Apr. closed Wed.

Modernized by Louis Miquel, a student of Le Corbusier, the **Musée de Beaux-Arts et d'Archéologie** (Museum of Fine Arts and Archaeology) has Egyptian sarcophagi, ornate belt buckles that once secured Marovian warriors' pants, and Gallo-Roman mosaics found here in Besançon. The museum is perfect on a rainy day: It's right in the town center. *1 pl. de la Révolution, tel. 03–81–81–44–47. Admission 21F, free Sun. and Wed. Open Wed.–Mon. 9:30–noon and 2–6.*

FESTIVALS

Besançon's tourist office (*see* Basics, *above*) is festival central: It's got a list of upcoming and current events and sells tickets. In early July, **Jazz Franche-Comté** bebops in Besançon with all kinds of free performances at the Théâtre Municipal, Café du Théâtre, Foyer Mixte des Jeunes Travailleurs, and public squares. The **Festival International de Musique de Besançon,** during the first two weeks of September, has paid respects to classical music for half a century and includes some free events.

AFTER DARK

Start on rue de la Madeleine, cross Pont de Battant, veer right on rue Pasteur and left on rue Mégevand, and you've pretty much done the circuit of the city's nightlife. Near the Palais de Justice and on a street which is, by Besançon standards, packed with bars (it has three) is a wood-paneled, smoky place known as **Blackhawks** (21 rue Pasteur, tel. 03–81–81–23–41), serving *pressions* (half-pints of draft beer; 12F) and the only Guinness in town (15F). **Bar de l'Étoile** (2 Grande Rue, tel. 03–81–81–18–36) and **Brasserie de la Fontaine** (4 rue des Boucheries, tel. 03–81–81–29–09) are hip university cafés during the day and busy smoky bars at night. Both are right off place de la Révolution. **Le Privé** (1 rue Antide-Janvier, off Pont de Battant, tel. 03–81–81–48–57) is a gay disco and the best place in town to dance until sunrise.

BELFORT

Belfort is a mellow little town watched over by an impressive, red stone lion. Auguste Bartholdi (of Statue of Liberty fame) sculpted the lion into the hillside to commemorate the heroic defense of the city during the 1870–71 siege. Today, you can climb to the lion's **terrace** and look out over the town and surrounding countryside of wooded foothills. Admission is 3F; it's open daily 8–6:45. Within the **château** that the lion guards are two worthwhile museums (tel. 03–84–54–25–52). The **Musée Militaire** has uniforms, weapons, and Colonel Denfert Rochereau's pocket journal, which he kept during the Thirty Years' War. The surprisingly rich **Musée des Beaux-Arts** has a good contemporary collection that includes a photo sequence of Picasso by Anders Villers. Admission to both museums is 11F and both are open daily 10–7. The château is part of the 9-km (5½-mi) fortification that surrounds Belfort—an insurance policy Louis XIV took out when he borrowed the city from Austria in 1648. You can walk "Les Hauts de Belfort" in a couple of hours, taking in good views of the walls and passing by Belfort's man-made lake. Ask for the map-guide at the tourist office, or hang a left when you exit the lion's terrace and follow the signs marked with yellow rectangles.

Down the hill looms Belfort's vieille ville. From its place d'Armes, a small **tourist train** (30F) departs every hour, giving some historical background on the city and saving your legs from the hike up to the fortress. Place d'Armes is also where the **Festival International de Musique Universitaire** takes place during the first weekend in June. You can hear everything from jazz to rock to traditional Greek music. During the first weekend of July, Belfort hosts the **Eurokéenes,** a three-day modern rock extravaganza. Tickets run 160F–190F a night. For information, call 03–84–22–46–58.

BASICS

The **Office de Tourisme** has maps of the city and nearby hiking routes, information on Belfort's festivals, and comfy chairs. A smaller branch with similar information is in the château; it's open Tuesday–Sunday 10–7. *Passage de France, tel. 03–84–28–12–23. From station, exit left, follow road as it curves to right, and take first left in pedestrian zone. Open Mon.–Sat. 9:30–6:30.*

COMING AND GOING

Belfort's **train station** (av. Wilson, tel. 08–36–35–35–35) is less than five minutes from the pedestrian zone. Several trains a day run from Paris (4 hrs, 296F) to Belfort on their way to Basel, Switzerland.

Trains also run regularly to Besançon (1 hr, 97F) and Strasbourg (1½ hrs, 133F). In town, walking is much simpler than figuring out the buses, though the tourist office and the **bus office** (pl. Corbis) have schedules if you're so inclined.

WHERE TO SLEEP

The plethora of budget places in the center means you shouldn't have to resort to the seedy joints around the station. The quiet **Hôtel de Turenne** (1 rue de Turenne, tel. 03–84–21–43–60) near the river has comfortable singles and doubles starting at 130F without bath. In the pedestrian zone, the warm, convenient **Nouvel Hôtel** (56 Faubourg de France, tel. 03–84–28–28–78) is the best deal for quiet, decent singles and doubles at 120F without bath, 300F with bath. Rustic **Hôtel St-Christophe** (pl. d'Armes, tel. 03–84–28–02–14), perhaps the best-located hotel in town, is a worthy splurge, even though the management is a bit rude; doubles with bath start at 245F. The lunch-only restaurant downstairs is equally good, with three-course menus from 58F.

HOSTEL • A cheaper option for *jeunes* of all ages is the marginally clean, well-run **Foyer des Jeunes Travailleurs,** 10 minutes from the station. Exit left, take the underground passage, and go straight past the campground. Here 70F gets you a bed (in a single or double room), shower, sheets, 24-hour access to your room, and young French neighbors. Breakfast is an extra 14F. *6 rue de Madrid, tel. 03–84–21– 39–16. 160 beds.*

CAMPING • A 10-minute walk from the station is **Camping Municipal des Promenades d'Essert,** where you'll pay 6F per tent plus 6F per person to sleep in a fenced-in, grassy, tree-shaded area. *Av. Leclerc, tel. 03–84–21–03–30. Exit left from the station, take the underground passage at the first light, keep to your right, and walk straight up rue Parisot. Closed Oct.–Apr.*

FOOD

There are a host of kebab stands and cheap sandwich shops across from the station. Near the tourist office, atmosphere-free **Tutti Frutti** (passage de France, tel. 03–84–21–83–66) has plats du jour, crepes, and sundaes until 1 AM if enough people are ordering. At the opposite end of the spectrum are the excellent meals at **Hôtel St-Christophe** (*see* Where to Sleep, *above*). In picturesque little place de la Fontaine, between place d'Armes and the château, is **Le Brasero** (pl. de la Fontaine, tel. 03–84–22–91– 76), where you can get spaghetti carbonara or a good vegetarian pizza served by nice young Italians. Finally, for sandwiches and drinks with an appealing crowd, swing by the **Café du Théâtre** (pl. Clovis, behind Théâtre de Belfort, tel. 03–84–28–37–37). Stock up on basics at the elegant old **Marché Frery,** on rue Frery, between the tourist office and the château.

NEAR BELFORT

RONCHAMP

Smack-dab in the middle of a beautiful valley, Ronchamp is home to the chapel **Notre-Dame du Haut,** designed by Le Corbusier in the early 1950s. Architecture buffs and busloads of retirees flock here to see the awesome concrete structure with its Mondrianesque stained-glass windows, curvilinear walls, winged roof, and minimalist interior. The chapel is situated on the top of a hill overlooking Ronchamp and the Jura Mountains; it's a 1½-km (1-mi) hike up a steep hill. Only a few painfully timed trains (6:16 AM or 5:08 PM) travel the 20 km (12 mi) between Belfort and Ronchamp (24F), making it necessary to spend the day there. If you must spend the night, **À La Pomme d'Or** (34 rue Le Corbusier, tel. 03–84– 20–62–12, fax 03–84–63–59–45) rents spacious singles and doubles with bath for 195F–230F.

DOLE

Dole is worth a visit, if only to check out its colorful markets (*see* Food, *below*) and flower-lined canals. Architecture fans will enjoy the Renaissance courtyards and staircases that seem to lurk behind every corner. Of course, the big attraction in town is the **Maison Natale de Louis Pasteur,** where the inventor of pasteurization was born. If you're interested in science—the museum has some of Pasteur's original notebooks—or the work of the Pasteur Institute, which discovered the AIDS virus, pay the fee to check it out. *43 rue Pasteur, tel. 03–84–72–20–61. Admission 20F. Open Apr.–June and Sept.–Oct., Mon. and Wed.–Sat. 10–noon and 2–6; July–Aug., Mon. and Wed.–Sat. 10–6, Sun. 10–5.*

As capital of the Franche-Comté, Dole has seen its fair share of wars, including heavy action in World War II when Vichy set up a deportation camp just outside town. But those days are long gone, and today "capital" just translates to "transportation hub." You must pass through Dole to get to the more picturesque villages in the Jura Mountains about 60 km (38 mi) east. Stop by the well-stocked, if slightly uninformed, **tourist office** for maps and books on hiking, biking, and skiing in the area. *6 pl. Grévy, tel. 03–84–72–11–22. Open Sept.–June, weekdays 9–12:30 and 2–6:30, Sat. 9–noon and 2–6; July–Aug., Mon.–Sat. 9–12:30 and 1:30–7.*

COMING AND GOING

Dole's **train station** (pl. de la Gare, tel. 08–36–35–35–35) is small but has an Avis car rental and piles of regional bus and train schedules. Trains arrive regularly from Strasbourg (3½ hrs, 210F) via Besançon (20 mins, 54F), and from Paris by TGV (2 hrs, 288F). A map of the city—which lies three long blocks to the south—and the region is posted outside. **Buses** to Lons-le-Saunier stop directly in front of the station. Dole is decidedly walkable—venture 10 minutes from the center and you're in a horse pasture.

WHERE TO SLEEP

Hôtel Moderne (27 pl. de la Gare, tel. 03–84–72–27–04), right across from the station, has a smoky bar downstairs, and surprisingly comfortable rooms for 80F (120F with toilet and bath), single or double. If you're under 26, the best place to stay in Dole is at the grand old **Foyer Accueil Dolois** (8 rue Charles-Sauria, tel. 03–84–82–15–21, fax 03–84–82–25–81), where 84F gets you a single dorm-type room, sheets, shower, and breakfast, with no lockout or curfew. Doubles cost 168F. The filling meals served in the cafeteria downstairs cost 44F for guests, 52F for nonguests. The **Auberge de Jeunesse Le St-Jean** (pl. Jean-XX111 South-West, tel. 03–84–82–36–74, fax 03–84–79–17–69), just behind the Church of Saint Jean, has 70 beds and costs 64F for a single room and 40F for a meal.

You'll share green space next to the Doubs and Dole's municipal stadium at **Camping du Pasquier** (18 chemin Thévenot, tel. 03–84–72–02–61), closed November–mid-March, with plenty of caravans; from the town center, walk downhill to the Doubs, cross either bridge, and head to the left (there are plenty of signs). Two people pay 63F for a site; there's a grocery, snack bar, and washing facilities.

FOOD

A couple of grocery stores in the center and the **market**—where you can find anything from apricots to fresh crab to underwear—across from the town basilica will help you put together a picnic. The market is open Tuesday, Thursday, and Saturday mornings and Friday afternoons. For a sit-down meal, **La Demi Lune** (39 rue Pasteur, tel. 03–84–72–82–82), next to the Pasteur museum, has fondue, crepes, and a cheap menu that includes a salad bar and ice cream; sit down on the terrace overlooking the canal where Pasteur's father tanned leather. At the sophisticated **Les Templiers** (35 Grande Rue, tel. 03–84–82–78–78) imaginative three-course menus start at 90F and are served in a luxurious setting under the ribbed vaults of a 13th-century chapel.

OUTDOOR ACTIVITIES

The terrain surrounding Dole is pretty tame; you can try an easy hike on a tranquil trail along the Doubs River that starts 2 km (1 mi) southeast of town. For a nice afternoon jaunt, head up to **Notre-Dame de Mont Roland,** where a neo-Gothic church houses a statue of the Blessed Virgin found on the site in 1946, after the area had been decimated by war. The fields surrounding the church are prime picnic material. To reach the church, head right out of the station, over the bridge that crosses the railroad tracks, and veer right onto rue Claude Lombard; when you hit boulevard de London, go left.

BURGUNDY

UPDATED BY ETHAN GELBER

Burgundy's landscape is curvaceous, swelling with the fertility that gives rise to its world-renowned wine. Speckled unevenly with hills, canals, forests, vineyards, and the occasional cow clinging to 30-degree inclines, this region attracts more ramblers than city slickers. Train access is limited, so it takes a little maneuvering (or a car or bike) to land yourself in one of the medieval villages scattered across the region—Sens, Vézelay, Tournus, and Tonnerre. But the warm hospitality and the fairy-tale countryside merit the effort. If the taste of mustard—combined with calm, safe, and marginally exciting city life—is what you're seeking, head to Dijon. A medium-size city, Dijon is a fine place to set up camp before plunging south to sip your way through the famous vineyards along what is known as the Côte d'Or (Gold Slope). Or, travel west to hike your way through the immense Parc Naturel Régional du Morvan (Morvan Regional Park).

Surprisingly, this sedate region once had a very big influence over the rest of France and Western Europe. The duchy of Burgundy was particularly powerful between 1364 and 1477, under Philippe *le Hardi* (the Daring), Jean *sans Peur* (the Fearless), Philippe *le Bon* (the Good), and Charles *le Téméraire* (the Foolhardy), collectively known as the Great Dukes of the West. The dukes controlled a huge chunk of France along the Rhine River, as well as parts of present-day Belgium and the Netherlands. They also retained a high level of independence from the kings of France, siding with the English during the Hundred Years' War and even delivering up Jeanne d'Arc to be tried and condemned by the bishop of Beauvais in 1430. After Charles the Foolhardy was defeated in battle and eaten by wolves, the French crown got the upper hand, and Burgundy gradually lost its autonomy.

BASICS

Local tourist offices can provide you with heaps of information, though each of Burgundy's four *départements* (administrative regions) has an additional information-dispensing headquarters. The one for the **Côte d'Or** is in Dijon (14 rue de la Préfecture, tel. 03–80–63–66–00); the one for the **Saône et Loire** is in Mâcon (389 av. Maréchal de Lattre de Tassigny, tel. 03–85–21–02–20); the one for the **Nièvre** is in Nevers (3 rue du Sort, tel. 03–86–36–39–80); and the one for the **Yonne** is in Auxerre (1–2 quai de la République, tel. 03–86–72–92–00, fax 03–86–72–92–09, E-mail cdt-89@tourisme-yonne.com). Burgundy's **regional tourist office** is in Dijon (12 blvd. de Brosses, tel. 03–80–50–90–00, fax 03–80–30–59–45). At any of these offices, ask for the free, informative series of brochures on wine, food, art, and Romanesque architecture.

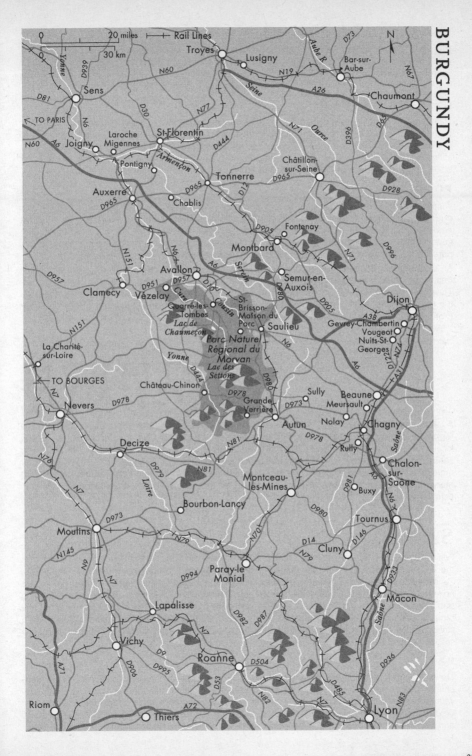

0 20 miles ├─┼─┤ Rail Lines

0 30 km

N

Yonne
D926
D81
Sens
TO PARIS
N6
A6
N60
Joigny
Laroche
Migennes
Pontigny
D30
Armençon
St-Florentin
D444
Auxerre
D965
Chablis
D965
Clamecy
N151
D957
D951 D957
Avallon
Vézelay
Cure
Quarré-les-
Tombes
Lac de
Chaumeçon
Yonne
La Charité-
sur-Loire
N151
TO BOURGES
N7
Château-Chinon
D444
Nevers
D978
Decize
N76
N7
D979
Loire
Moulins
D973
N145
N9
N7
Bourbon-Lancy
Lapalisse
A71
Vichy
D906
D9
D995
Riom
N7
Thiers
A72
N82
Troyes
N60
Lusigny
Seine
N19
N77
Tonnerre
D965
D12
D905
Montbard
A6
Serein
D957 D10
St-Brisson-
Maison du
Parc
Saulieu
Parc Naturel
Régional du
Morvan
Lac des
Settons
D978
Grande
Verrière
Sully
D973
N81
Autun
D978
Rully
N81
Montceau-
les-Mines
D980
N70
Paray-le-
Monial
D994
D982 D987
N7
Roanne
D53
D504
Aube R.
D73
Bar-sur-
Aube
N19
A26
Chaumont
N67
N71
Ource
D396
D63
Châtillon-
sur-Seine
D965
D928
Fontenay
N71
D996
Semur-en-
Auxois
D980
D905
Dijon
A38
Gevrey-Chambertin
Vougeot
Nuits-St-
Georges
D122
N74
A31
Beaune
Meursault
Nolay
Chagny
Saône
Chalon-
sur-Saône
A6
N6
D981
Buxy
D980
Tournus
D14
D146
Cluny
N79
D933
Mâcon
Saône
D485
D936
Lyon
N83

WHEN TO GO

Burgundy is at its best from late spring to harvest time in late October. This is when the fields are full of wheat, the grapevines are colorful, the hills are covered with flowers, and the *caves* (wine cellars) are open for business. Many establishments close down for a week or two in August, and for a month or more in winter.

GETTING AROUND

Trains run regularly between the bigger towns in Burgundy (Sens, Auxerre, Avallon, Dijon, and Bourges), but much less frequently, if at all, to the smaller ones (Autun, Vézelay, Saulieu, Beaune, and Chalon-sur-Saône). The free *Guide Régional des Transports,* available at train stations, shows rail lines, schedules, and the few SNCF bus connections. Plenty of private bus companies cover the region. Ticket prices range from 30F to 50F. Ask for information about bus service at the local tourist offices.

FOOD AND WINE

Welcome to the land of Appéllation d'Origine Contrôlée (AOC), an organization that slaps its mark onto quality products according to sacred rules of food and wine cultivation. In Burgundy, this means that the *poulet de Bresse* (Bress chicken), *boeuf bourguignon* (beef stew with vegetables, braised in red Burgundy wine), *coq au vin* (chicken stewed in red wine), or *escargots* (snails) you ordered came from a pure lineage and were raised on natural ingredients before landing on your dinner table.

All four Burgundy départements produce wine; the Yonne and Nièvre offer mostly dry, brisk white wine (made from the Chablis region's Chardonnay grapes) and fruity whites from Pouilly's Sauvignon grapes. The Côte d'Or and Saône et Loire make Chardonnay whites and great reds from Pinot Noir grapes. Get the free brochure "Touring the Wine Presses and Vineyards of Burgundy," and the *Guide des Caves* (25F), available at tourist offices.

NORTHERN BURGUNDY

A trail of medieval cities snakes its way down the Yonne River, leading inexorably toward the rich wine regions of Burgundy around Auxerre. The pace here can be slow, but it's a perfect region for buying local wine and picnicking your way through towns. **Sens** has preserved vestiges of its intricate, 16th-century wood architecture, and the lofty Basilique Ste-Madeleine in **Vézelay** is a sculptural feast. A far more modernized **Bourges** hums in the distance to the west, and the vast **Parc Naturel Régional du Morvan** occupies an expansive wilderness barely contained within the nine cities that act as its entry points.

SENS

For centuries, Sens was an admired central hub. First under the Gauls, then the Romans, and finally as the seat of a powerful archbishopric that controlled the religious practices of Paris and six other cities, Sens drew to it the glitterati of many centuries, including kings, queens, and popes. Today, the town is no longer so important, but it does still have an appeal. Visiting the Cathédrale St-Étienne (whose flying buttresses predate those at Chartres), or strolling along the medieval streets and passageways where the ramparts once stood, makes for a pleasant afternoon. On Monday, the cathedral square is crowded with stalls, and the colorful covered **market** throbs with people buying fresh produce. On Friday morning a smaller market takes place.

BASICS

The friendly staff of the **tourist office** will book you a hotel room and provide you with informative pamphlets. The currency-exchange desk is open on Sunday and bank holidays in July and August. *Pl. Jean Jaurès, tel. 03–86–65–19–49, fax 03–86–64–24–18. From train station, cross bridges into town, turn left on quai J. Moulin, and right on blvd. Maupeou to pl. Jean-Jaurès. Open July–Aug., Mon.–Sat. 9–12:30 and 2–7:30, Sun. 10–12:30 and 2–5:30; Sept.–June, weekdays 9–noon and 1:30–6:15 (5:15 on Sat.).*

COMING AND GOING

The **train station** (tel. 03–86–64–20–54) is west of town across the Yonne River. Trains zip daily to Paris (1½ hrs, 88F), Dijon (2 hrs, 138F), and Auxerre (1 hr, 56F). By car, you can reach Sens from Paris via highways N6 and A5; it's 112 km (70 mi) southeast of the capital. Sens is a town split down the middle by rue de la République; the cathedral is in the center of it all. To reach the *centre ville* (town center) from the station, cross the river to the pedestrian Grande Rue, which intersects rue de la République. **Buses** 1 and 2 (both 8F) take you to the center from the station, but they don't run on Sunday. There is a **taxi** stand at the train station (tel. 03–86–65–16–99).

WHERE TO SLEEP

Sens has a few budget hotels, but be sure to call ahead on weekends. Right in front of the train station is the newly renovated **Hôtel de la Gare** (3–5 av. de la Gare, tel. 03–86–64–08–08, fax 03–86–95–40–54). The best deal in town, it offers doubles for 110F–150F and solid prix-fixe meals for 55F–90F. Closer to the centre ville, don't let a slightly shabby exterior stop you from enjoying the **Hôtel Esplanade** (2 blvd. du Mail, tel. 03–86–83–14–70, fax 03–86–83–14–71). Just a few steps from the tourist office, it has simple double rooms for 146F–236F and a bar downstairs. **Hôtel Virginia** (3 km/2 mi from town on rte. N60 to Troyes, tel. 03–86–64–66–66, fax 03–86–65–75–11) has small, cheery rooms ranging from 210F to 260F. The reception is closed on Sunday evenings September–May; and the hotel is closed late December–early January. *Dormez bien* (sleep well) at **Hôtel le Brennus** (21 rue des Trois Croissants, tel. 03–86–64–04–40, fax 03–86–65–44–10) in the centre ville. Comfortable doubles are 250F–280F. Four kilometers (2½ mi) from Sens, the **Chambre d'Hôtes Chez Lafolie** (3 rue des Champs Rouge, direction Courtois from Sens; tel. 03–86–97–00–33) has cheery singles (180F–200F) and doubles (220F–240F). Dinner with the hosts is 85F; reservations are strongly recommended.

FOOD

For a quick meal, grab a galette or a crepe (20F–50F) at **Au P'tit Creux** right around the corner from the cathedral (rue de Brennus, tel. 03–86–64–99–29), closed Tuesday night and Wednesday. A traditional French meal can be had at the **Restaurant de la Cathédrale** (13 pl. de la Cathédrale, tel. 03–86–65–17–79), closed Tuesday, for 90F. For *bon rapport qualité-prix* (good-value) dining in a lovely garden setting, **Croix Blanche** (9 rue Victor Guichard, tel. 03–86–64–00–02, fax 03–86–65–29–19), closed Friday night and Saturday, a five-minute walk from the cathedral, has prix-fixe menus of 78F–180F, including salmon with sorrel. On a midday walk to or from the train station, you might want to join the lunchtime business set at **Le Soleil Levant** (52 rue Émile Zola, tel. 03–86–65–71–82) for a fish meal for only 67F. A **Casino** supermarket, open Monday–Saturday until 7:30 PM, is on the Grande Rue.

WORTH SEEING

Sens's most prominent monument is the **Cathédrale St-Étienne.** Begun around 1130, it is commonly considered to be the prototype of the great Gothic cathedrals. The 12th- to 14th-century portals and stained-glass windows, the intricate carvings of the Salazar altar, the choir gates, and the grand organ merit a look. Apropos the organ, if you want to catch those pipes a-tooting, July–September, every Sunday between 4 and 5 PM, there is a free concert in the cathedral.

Attached to St-Étienne are the **Museums of Sens,** including the 13th-century **Palais Synodal,** topped with a colorful tiled roof typical of Burgundy and built over a warren of well-preserved prison cells and passageways; the **Trésor de la Cathédrale,** the cathedral treasures, among the richest in Europe, including 16th-century tapestries and the hat Napoléon wore at Waterloo; and the former **Archbishops' Palace,** which houses, among other things, a marvelous collection of Gallo-Roman statues. Admission to the museums is 20F. *Pl. de la Cathédrale, tel. 03–86–64–46–22. Open June–Sept., Wed.–Mon. 10–noon and 2–6; Oct.–May, Wed. and weekends 10–noon and 2–6, Mon. and Thurs.–Fri. 2–6.*

Sens is proud of its few remaining historic 16th-century houses. Unfortunately, you can't go inside most of them, but they're worth a look. Some intricate wood detailing graces the exterior of the **Ancien Musée Jean-Cousin** (rue Jossey) and the **Maisons d'Abraham and du Pilier** (corner of rue de la République and rue Jean Cousin). The amusing, turn-of-the-century **Hôtel de Ville** (Town Hall; 100 rue de la République, tel. 03–86–65–67–23) resembles a giant whipped-cream wedding cake, and the main cathedral's eclipsed 12th-century grandmother, the **Église St-Maurice** (quai de l'Yonne), sits humbly along the banks of the Yonne River.

Another point of pride for Sens is its four-leaf ranking as a *ville fleurie,* or floral city. This finds full botanical expression in the excellently manicured city parks (the **moulin à tan** and the **square Jean-Cousin**)

NAY, I KNOW NOT THE NAVE FROM THE NARTHEX

Consider these architectural terms before passing through the next portal (front door):

CHANCEL: The space around the altar that's off-limits to everyone but the clergy. It's usually at the east end of the church and is often blocked off by a rail.

CHOIR: The section of the church set off to seat the choir. It's either in the chancel or in a loft in another part of the church.

CLERESTORY: The upper part of the church walls, typically lined with windows (often the stained-glass variety) to bathe the nave with light.

CRYPT: An underground chamber usually used as a burial site and often found directly below a church's nave.

NARTHEX: A hall or small room leading from the main entrance to the nave.

NAVE: The main section of the church that stretches from the chancel to the narthex. This is where worshipers sit during services.

TRANSEPT: The part of the church that extends outward at a right angle from the main body, creating a cruciform (cross-shape) plan.

TYMPANUM: A recessed triangular or semicircular space above the portal, often decorated with sculpture.

and municipal greenhouses, as well as during the **Fête de la Saint-Fiacre,** named after the patron saint of gardeners. For the latter, on the second Sunday in September, everything and everyone are festooned with flowers as entertainment fills the streets. If you can't make it then, definitely try to be in town for the **National Dance Festival** (end of June to early July).

AUXERRE

The **Cathédrale St-Étienne** looms above a confusing maze of medieval streets that collide and spill down hilly, high-walled passageways before tumbling into the waters of the Yonne River—a strange stage, it would seem, for the cheers emanating from the soccer fans who rove around the place during matches at the giant stadium. That said, Auxerre has been the site of many unexpected events since it grew up at the spot where the Roman Agrippian Way, linking the Mediterranean to the North Sea, crossed the Yonne, which provided a navigable waterway to Paris and the Atlantic. Take some time to explore the neighboring cities and the immense Parc Naturel Régional du Morvan (*see below*). Don't expect to see too much late-night activity—the city tends to fall asleep early, except during the annual **Couleurs de l'Été,** Colors of Summer, beginning in June with the one-week **Jazz Festival** and finishing in September with the one-week **Piano Festival.** It is also a series of autumn wine events that take place throughout the region.

BASICS

The main **post office** takes care of currency exchange, poste restante, and everything else a good post office should. The postal code is 89000. *Pl. Charles Surugue, tel. 03–86–48–57–21. Open weekdays 8– 7, Sat. 8–noon.*

The staff at the **tourist office** is energetic and able, and happy to provide you with free town maps and brochures. It will also book you a room for 15F and, on Sunday and bank holidays only, exchange currency. *1–2 quai de la République, near cathedral, tel. 03–86–52–06–19, fax 03–86–51–23–27. Open mid-June–mid-Sept., Mon.–Sat. 9–1 and 2–7, Sun. 9:30–1 and 3–6:30; mid-Sept.–mid-June, Mon.– Sat. 9–12:30 and 2–6:30, Sun. 10–1.*

COMING AND GOING

The **train station** (rue Paul Doumer) is east of the Yonne River and sends daily trains to Paris (2½ hrs, 121F), Dijon (2 hrs, 123F), Sens (1 hr, 56F), and Tonnerre (40 mins, 53F). To reach the centre ville, turn left from the station onto rue Paul Doumer, right on rue Jules Ferry (which becomes rue Gambetta), and cross Paul Bert bridge.

The **bus station** (rue des Migraines, tel. 03–86–46–90–66) is northwest of the centre ville. Infrequent SNCF buses make the trip to Vézelay, but you are better off consulting schedules and leaving from the train station. **Les Rapides de Bourgogne** (3 rue des Fontenottes, tel. 03–86–94–95–00, fax 03–86–46– 49–14) has sporadic buses to Chablis (20 mins, 26F), Tonnerre (1 hr, 42F), and the impressive Cistercian abbey at Pontigny (20 mins, 25F); these buses transport schoolchildren, so the schedule varies according to school vacations. This makes them often less-than-convenient. However, if you don't have access to a car, these buses are the only public transportation option available. To get to the bus station from the tourist office, walk north along the riverbank, turn left on boulevard de la Chainette, and continue along rue des Migraines at the roundabout. **J. P. Bruno** minivans and taxis (tel. 03–86–54–45–56) will take up to six people to Pontigny, Chablis, Tonnerre, or Vézelay for 160F per hour.

GETTING AROUND

Get a map from the tourist office because the layout of the town is confusing. The main part of the old town is west of the Yonne River and ripples out from place des Cordeliers. Rue de Paris will get you there from the north, rue du Temple from the south, and rue d'Egleny from the east. You can walk with no problem, or rent a bike Monday–Saturday from **Oskwarek** (22 rue de Preuilly, tel. 03–86–52–71–19), a 15-minute walk southwest of the center, for 160F per day with a passport deposit. A few bikes might also be available through the tourist office April–October. **Taxis** can also be had on place Charles Surugue (tel. 03–86–52–30–51) and at the train station (tel. 03–86–46–91–61).

WHERE TO SLEEP

Centrally located **Hôtel de la Renommée** (27 rue d'Egleny, off pl. Charles Lepère, tel. 03–86–52–03– 53, fax 03–86–51–47–83) has simple doubles (115F–165F) off a quiet courtyard. Reception is closed Sunday night (which means you can't check in on that night) and the hotel is closed the last three weeks of August. Smack-dab in the middle of the action is the **Hôtel du Commerce** (5 rue René-Schaeffer, tel. 03–86–52–03–16, fax 03–86–52–42–37), with doubles for 200F–255F, and **Hôtel de la Poste** (9 rue d'Orbandelle, off pl. des Cordeliers, tel. 03–86–52–12–02, fax 03–86–51–68–61) at 195F–395F for a double. Picturesque, vine-covered **Hôtel Normandie** (41 blvd. Vauban, tel. 03–86–52–57–80, fax 03– 86–51–54–33) occupies a grand-looking building a short walk from the cathedral. Singles (250F–290F) and doubles (290F–370F) are very clean and have private bathrooms, but it is the amenities, including hair dryers, sauna, gym, and bar, that you are paying for. The **Parc des Maréchaux** (6 av. Foch, tel. 03– 86–51–43–77, fax 03–86–51–31–72) is a tasteful retreat a stroll from the center with 25 well-appointed rooms (doubles run 430F–510F). Otherwise, for a true quiet adventure into truffle-speckled countryside, head for **Domaine de Montpierreux** (in Venoy, on the D965 route to Chablis, tel. 03–86–40–20– 91, fax 03–86–40–28–00), 10 km (6 mi) from Auxerre. The delightful doubles in this 19th-century manor house run 280F–340F including breakfast. Cash only.

HOSTELS • The best deals in town are the hostels. The coed **Foyer des Jeunes Travailleuses** (16 blvd. Vaulabelle, tel. 03–86–52–45–38) is close to the center of town and charges 77F for a bed and breakfast and 38F–43F for a cafeteria dinner. Half of the rooms have a magnificent view of the cathedral. From the station, take pont Paul Bert across the river and turn left onto quai de la République. The road curves to the right and becomes boulevard Vaulabelle; the foyer is on the left. The same organization also has another coed **Foyer des Jeunes Travailleurs** (16 av. de la Résistance, tel. 03–86–46–95–11) for the same rates and no dinner cafeteria, but it's farther from the center. From the train station, cross the train tracks to rue St-Gervais and continue along avenue de la Résistance.

CAMPING • Camping Municipal (8 rte. de Vaux, tel. 03–86–52–11–15) costs 15F per person plus 13F per tent. The well-kept, grassy campground in front of the soccer stadium is open April–September; to reach it from the station, cross pont Paul Bert and turn left onto quai de la République, right onto boulevard Vaulabelle, and left again onto rue de Preuilly.

FOOD

Auxerre has a fair number of reasonably priced restaurants but not many true bargains. The best is **Le Quai** (4 pl. Saint Nicolas, tel. 03–86–51–66–67). On a lovely Yonne-side square, this welcoming bar-brasserie-restaurant offers pizzas (35F–50F), good menus (59F–125F), and a full bar. Other reasonable options are **Le Carré du Temple** (25 rue du Temple, tel. 03–86–52–31–62), closed Sunday and Monday nights, with a *plat du jour* for 56F and menus from 98F, and **Le Toon's** (82 rue de Paris, tel. 03–86–51–32–71), where good salads and pizzas are named after *bande dessinée* (comic strip) characters; it closes Saturday at noon and Sunday. Meals run 40F–100F. Traditional Burgundian cuisine is the specialty at the **Hôtel-Restaurant du Commerce** (5 rue René-Schaeffer, tel. 03–86–52–03–16), which has menus starting at 85F. **La Taverne de Maître Kanter** (11 pl. Charles Lepère, tel. 03–86–52–16–21) serves hearty, three-course meals for 56F at lunch and has a full dinner menu. Centre ville **markets** centered on place de l'Arquebuse sell fresh produce Tuesday and Friday mornings. There is the also the **Casino** supermarket at 120 rue de Paris, open daily.

If food for you consists of a half-pint, the big-windowed **Bar du Marché** (2 pl. des Cordeliers, tel. 03–86–52–08–42) serves a subtly sweet, 15F Belgian variety on a busy patio. Wine lovers should contact the tourist office about the summer Thursday guided wine tastings at the **Maison du Vignoble Auxerrois,** Auxerrois Regional Wine Center (14 route de Champs, Saint-Bris-le-Vineux, tel. 03–86–53–66–76), open Monday–Saturday 9–noon and 2–6.

WORTH SEEING

On Tuesday, all the museums of Auxerre are closed. When open, though, students pay a reduced price. Otherwise, consider stopping by the tourist office and buying the "Découverte d'Auxerre" pass (26F) for all of the sights at any of the museums.

The 13th- to 16th-century **Cathédrale St-Étienne** has a Flamboyant Gothic facade with slightly damaged (but still interesting) portal carvings depicting Bible stories. Inside, the beautiful stained-glass medallions around the choir date from the 13th century. For 10F each, or 15F for both, you can see 12th- to 13th-century manuscripts and enamels in the **treasury,** as well as a rare fresco of Christ on horseback in the 11th-century medieval **crypt.** There are free summer organ recitals every Sunday at 5 PM, and sound-and-light shows every night June–August at 10 PM and in September at 9:30 PM. *Pl. St-Étienne. Except for public holidays, open in season Mon.–Sat. 9–noon and 2–6, Sun. 2–6.*

A bit farther north, via a number of venerable streets lined with 16th-century half-timber houses, sprawls the almost intact monastic complex of the **Abbaye St-Germain,** originally founded more than a thousand years ago. It has Carolingian crypts with 9th-century frescoes, a medieval Romanesque tower standing far apart from its church, and several later buildings now housing the so-so **Musée d'Histoire de la Ville,** City History Museum. Also check out the abbey's beautiful **Musée St-Germain,** with exhibits of prehistoric, Gallo-Roman, modern, and contemporary art. Price of admission includes a tour of the crypts and entry to both museums. *Pl. St-Germain, tel. 03–86–51–09–74. Admission 20F. Open June–Sept., Wed.–Mon. 10–6:30; Oct.–May, Wed.–Mon. 10–noon and 2–5.*

Other attractions include the **Musée Leblanc-Duvernoy** (rue d'Egleny, tel. 03–86–51–09–74), admission 12F, open Wednesday–Monday 2–6, with its collection of porcelains, paintings, and tapestries; the 15th-century **Tour de l'Horloge** (Clock Tower), with, get this, a sun-hand and a moon-hand; and the free **Musée d'Histoire Naturelle** (Natural History Museum; blvd. Vauban, tel. 03–86–72–96–40), open July–August, weekdays 10–6, weekends 2–6, and September–June, weekdays 10–noon and 2–6, weekends 2–6.

VEZELAY

A pilgrimage destination for centuries, Vézelay is accustomed to accommodating a ridiculous number of tourists, considering its small size. But then again, the history of this little burg has for a long time been connected to Cluny (*see below*), Siantiago di Compostella (in Spain), the Crusades, and some of

Christianty's great saints. Exploring involves merely climbing and descending the central cobblestone walkway, **rue St-Pierre** and **St-Étienne.** At the hilltop, the spectacular basilica and the panoramic view of the Parc Naturel Régional du Morvan's rolling, green landscape will be your long-anticipated rewards. If you plan to be here around July 22, make advance reservations: Religious pilgrims descend en masse for festivities in honor of the Virgin Mary.

BASICS

The staff at the tourist office near the basilica is helpful but busy. They provide free maps and have lists of local accommodations including *chambres d'hôte* (bed-and-breakfasts), as well as book rooms for 10F. *13 rue St-Pierre, tel. 03–86–33–23–69, fax 03–86–33–34–00. Open daily 10–1 and 2–6 (closed Thurs. Nov.–mid-June.*

COMING AND GOING

Vézelay is 51 km (32 mi) south of Auxerre on D957 and 13 km (8 mi) southwest of Avallon. For seasonal bus information pertaining to Vézelay, contact the tourist office here or in Avallon. From Auxerre, you can take the train (45 mins, 40F) only as far as Sermizelles (from Avallon it's 15 minutes and 17F), which leaves you 10 km (6 mi) from Vézelay. You can take a taxi from there, although if you have checked departure times, you are better off taking an SNCF bus directly from Auxerre or Avallon. Otherwise, the nearest taxi is in Domecy-sur-Cure, but it calls itself **Vézelay Taxi** anyway (tel. 03–86–32–31–88). **Garage Gauché** (tel. 03–86–33–30–17), along the road toward Avallon, has a few mountain bikes for rent for 120F per day with a 1,000F deposit. A short distance away, in Saint-Père on the road to Quarré-les-Tombes, **Grands Espaces** (tel. 03–86–40–69–98 or 03–86–33–38–38, fax 03–86–34–52–28), on rue Gravier, has a larger stock at the same rate.

WHERE TO SLEEP

Treat yourself to a night in the abbey's 12th-century hostelry, where Louis XII and the Count of Nevers numbered among its guests: **Cabalus** (rue St-Pierre, tel. 03–86–33–20–66, fax 03–86–33–38–03, www.rent-a-holiday.com/info/cabalus), a stone's throw from the tourist office, retains its rustic character while providing modern amenities (doubles run 180F–320F). Most of the other *chambres d'hôte,* like the **Atelier van den Bossche** (80 rue St-Pierre, tel. 03–86–33–32–16), run by some friendly sculptors and entered through their gallery, are also on rue St-Pierre. Definitely make reservations June–August. The **Centre Ste-Madeleine** (rue St-Pierre, tel. 03–86–33–22–14), a hostel run by Franciscan sisters, charges a reasonable 50F–110F per person (bring your own sheets) for beds in small rooms and dorms. You can use the kitchen. The **Hôtel du Cheval Blanc** (pl. du Champ-de-Foire, tel. 03–86–33–22–12, fax 03–86–33–34–29) has reasonable rates, at 100F–250F for a double. The relatively posh **Auberge de Jeunesse** (rte. de l'Étang, tel./fax 03–86–33–24–18), 1 km (½ mi) from town, has four- and six-bedrooms and dorms at 46F–56F per person. Camping in back costs 18F per person, plus 5F–10F per tent. Be warned: These prices do not include breakfast. The kitchen is being remodeled and may not be available. Four kilometers (2½ mi) downhill from the basilica, riverside campsites are 30F for two adults at the St-Père-sous-Vézelay **Municipal Campground** (tel. 03–86–33–36–58 or 03–86–33–26–62, fax 03–86–33–34–56), open mid-April–September.

FOOD

The father-and-son-owned crêperie **L'Auberge de la Coquille** (81 rue St-Pierre, tel. 03–86–33–35–57) serves a delicious ham-and-mushroom crepe (40F) and three-course meat or fish menus (45F–110F) in a lovely 12th-century setting; November–January it's open weekends only. **La Fortune du Pot** (pl. du Champ-de-Foire, tel. 03–86–33–32–56), closed Saturday night–Sunday, serves a 65F menu with steak or pork tripe. Right off place du Basilique, **La Terrasse** (tel. 03–86–33–25–50) has solid menus for 45F and 58F. Pick up picnic items at the **Casino** supermarket (rue St-Étienne), near the bottom of the hill; it's closed Monday, Wednesday, and Sunday afternoons. You can purchase a bottle of Vézelay Chardonnay '96 or '97 (42F–43F) from **Guyard** (tel. 03–86–33–33–29), an 11th-century wine cave on rue St-Étienne.

WORTH SEEING

Tourists and sinners have been making the pilgrimage to Vézelay since the 12th century, when it was the departure point for the Second and Third Crusades. The **Basilique Ste-Madeleine** is a feast of sculptural details—complete with biblical scenes, Christ figures, and a tongue-flailing demon bearing a strange resemblance to Jim Morrison in concert. The tympanum above the central portal dates from around 1125 and features a huge Christ surrounded by the apostles, zodiac signs, and scenes of the evangelists' mission to convert all the races of the world. In July and August, you can request a free tour of the basilica at the tourist office (*see* Basics, *above*) and attend concerts in the church (Tuesday and Friday nights only). The cathedral is open from dawn to dusk daily. Next door to the basilica, the small **Musée de l'Oeuvre** houses sculptures borrowed from the church. It's open July–September, Wednesday–Monday 10–noon and 3–7; admission is 10F. The small **park** behind the basilica is a great spot for a picnic or a game of boules with the locals. It also has one of the best views of the Parc Naturel Régional du Morvan, an expansive stretch of fields and valleys.

AVALLON

Avallon's church and *vieille ville* (old town) may pale in comparison to those of Vézelay, but Avallon has its charms and makes a better base for visiting the Parc Naturel Régional du Morvan to the south. And though meandering through town may not be terribly thrilling, walking or cycling *around* Avallon is—especially southwest along the town's ramparts, where there are terrific views of the surrounding forests and fields. For a longer excursion, follow the signs down the **route de Lormes,** which winds along the eastern side of town toward Quarré-les-Tombes.

BASICS

The **tourist office,** in a 15th-century town house beside the clock tower, has plenty of information on Avallon, as well as on activities in the Parc Naturel Régional du Morvan. *4 rue Bocquillot, tel. 03–86–34–14–19, fax 03–86–34–28–29. Open Mon.–Sat. 9:30–noon and 2–6.*

COMING AND GOING

Avallon is 16 km (10 mi) east of Vézelay via route D957 and 53 km (33 mi) southeast of Auxerre via routes D957 and N6. Buses and trains run unpredictably through the region to Tonnerre, Autun, Auxerre, and Vézelay; ask the tourist office for current schedules. The **train station** (tel. 03–86–34–01–01) north of town sends several trains a day to Auxerre (1 hr, 50F), Paris (3–4 hrs, 149F), and Sermizelles-Vézelay (15 mins, 17F). To reach the vieille ville from the station, head down avenue du Président Doumer through the tree-lined promenade des Capucins; turn right onto place Vauban and left onto Grande Rue Aristide Briand. Continue straight and pass under the clock tower. The **SNCF** runs buses from Avallon to Vézelay (22F) a few times a day July and August, and much less frequently off-season. For mountain bikes, try **Tout Vélo** (26 rue de Paris, tel. 03–86–34–28–11), where a day's rental is 100F (70F per half day) plus a passport deposit. Avallon has a wealth of taxis; **Taxi Station** (tel. 03–86–34–11–49) is right on place Vauban.

WHERE TO SLEEP

When it comes to hotels next to the train station, the **Hôtel du Parc** (3 pl. de la Gare, tel. 03–86–34–17–00, fax 03–86–34–28–48) is an anomaly; it has cheap, clean, comfortable singles and doubles 115F–210F. Be warned that there is no floor shower, so it's a sponge bath you get if you don't want to pay for better. The cheapest double with amenities is 130F. The **Hôtel des Capucins** (6 av. Président Doumer, tel. 03–86–34–06–52, fax 03–86–34–58–47) has doubles for 190F–290F and a marvelous restaurant (menus range 85F–260F). On the other side of town, directly below the vieille ville, to the south, on a gentle spot within earshot of the gurgling Cousin River, the **Hôtel du Rocher** (11 rue des Isles Labaume, tel. 03–86–34–19–03) is another bargain with doubles for 100F–150F. Closer into town, Philippe and Sonia Amand run the warm and familial **Auberge du Cheval Blanc** (55 rue de Lyon, tel. 03–86–34–55–07). With doubles running 150F–210F and a bustling local-filled restaurant downstairs (traditional menus starting at 68F), this place smacks of charm. It's worth asking for the slightly more expensive rooms away from the street. For a splurge, try the **Moulin des Ruats** (Vallée du Cousin, 4 km/2½ mi southwest of Avallon, tel. 03–86–34–97–00, fax 03–86–31–65–47). Once an old flour mill, this inn has many rooms (380F–680F) with balconies that overlook the Cousin River. The extensive menu in the adjoining restaurant features traditional Burgundian specialties (155F–235F).

HOSTEL • Foyer des Jeunes Travailleurs. This hotel has beds for 80F a night. Is it worth the 30-minute walk from the train station? The clean rooms and billiards table make up for the industrial setting. *10 av. Victor Hugo, tel. 03–86–34–01–88. From station, head left down av. du Président Doumer, turn right on rte. de Paris toward Vézelay, left on av. de Pépinster (before the Casino supermarket), and left on av. Victor Hugo. Reception open 8 AM—8 PM. 150 beds. Laundry.*

CAMPING • Camping Sous Roche. This pretty site between river and forest is a 2-km (1-mi) trek southeast of town along the route des Lormes and the Cousin River. For 18F per person plus 13F per tent, you'll get a site and a good view of Avallon's fortifications. *Rte. des Lormes, tel. 03–86–34–10–39. 24 sites. Closed mid-Oct.–mid-Mar.*

FOOD

The **Bistro des Quat' Pattes** (35 rue de Paris, tel. 03–86–34–30–67) serves real Burgundian dishes, such as savory grilled lamb, at great prices (menus starting at 75F). Otherwise, the very popular **Restaurant la Tour** (84 Grande Rue A. Briand, near clock tower, tel. 03–86–34–24–84) serves the usual crepes (25F–40F) and pizzas (38F–55F). In winter, it's closed Sunday lunch and Monday. For the pizzeria with the greatest variety in town at no more than 50F a pop, try **Le Capella** (13 rue de Paris, tel. 03–86–34–59–64). One of Avallon's best restaurants, the **Relais des Gourmets** (47 rue de Paris, tel. 03–86–34–18–90), has an 85F prix-fixe menu that will let you taste some of Burgundy's best in a refined atmosphere. If you're up for some sustenance after hours, Avallon doesn't have much to offer. Try **Le Rock's Club** (13 bis rue de l'Hôpital, tel. 03–86–34–30–61) Tuesday–Sunday (Thursday–Sunday in winter) after 10 PM. The **Casino** supermarket (rte. de Paris, tel. 03–86–34–12–08), open Monday–Saturday 8:30–7:30, and the weekly Saturday **market** are for the do-it-yourselfers. During **Gastronomy Weekend** (early October), the best restaurants in town show off their favorite menus at unusually low prices (150F–350F). Be sure to try some of the local specialties made from cold cuts and mushrooms from the Morvan, the *treuffe* (local potato), regional cheeses, and, of course, the meats—charolais beef, spring lamb, and farm chicken.

WORTH SEEING

Avallon's medieval center is full of history. The best way to see it all is to take a 90-minute stroll with a free pamphlet from the tourist office. That said, Avallon's main draw is the cavernous **Collégiale St-Lazare** (rue Bocquillot, south of the bell tower), a church built in the 12th century. In the 17th century the original north clock tower collapsed, destroying the left portal. Only two portals remain, decorated with sculpted angels, musicians, and zodiac signs. It's open daily 8:45–6. Name that sculptor: The Statue of Vauban in the center of town was sculpted by the same artist who designed the Statue of Liberty (answer: Bartholdi). Take a tour of the evolution of artisanal materials at the **Maison des Traditions Agricoles & Artisanales** (66 rue de Lyon, tel. 03–86–34–53–50); it welcomes visitors May–September, 10–noon and 2–6, or call for visits during the off-season. At the **Musée des Costumes** (rue Belgrand, tel. 03–86–34–19–95) traditional 18th-century clothes are on display. Admission is 25F, including a one-hour guided tour. It's open May–October 10:30–12:30 and 1:30–5:30.

A little bit off the beaten path (in more ways than one) is the **Presidential Cars Museum** (in Château Monjalin, 7 km/4½ mi east of Avallon, tel. 03–86–34–46–42, fax 03–86–31–66–83), where you'll find the cars of Kennedy, Brezhnev, and even a Popemobile; admission is 30F for visits every day 9–7 in July and August, and April–October on weekends 9–7 or by arrangement. Another adventure is a trip by car or bike into the **Parc Naturel Régional du Morvan** (*see below*). Take D944 out of Avallon and turn left on D10 to **Quarré-les-Tombes,** so called because of the empty Merovingian stone tombs today arrayed eerily around the church but about which very little is known. The **Rocher de la Pérouse**, 8 km (5 mi) south of Quarré-les-Tombes, is a mighty outcrop worth scrambling up for a view of the Morvan and the Cure Valley.

BOURGES

For centuries Bourges was the capital of the quiet, rural region of Berry, once a duchy like Burgundy, yet weaker and more loyal to the French crown. In fact, this town is attached to Burgundy only physically, as it bears little resemblance to other towns in the region. The preserved old part of town retains its medieval cathedral and streets. **Rue Mirabeau** and **rue Coursalon,** pedestrian streets full of timber-frame houses, are particularly nice places to stroll and shop. Thanks to the Institut Universitaire de Technologie (IUT) there is some youthful life. Groups like U2 have been known to appear at the city's **Experimental Music Festival,** called Synthèse and held in early June.

BASICS

The simplest of free city maps is available at the **tourist office.** In July and August, ask them about the four free museums and the troupes that animate the streets with theater, mime, and music. *21 rue Victor Hugo, tel. 02–48–23–02–60, fax 02–48–23–02–69. From station, take av. H. Laudier to av. J. Jau-*

rès, then, at pl. Planchat bear left on rue Commerce, which becomes rue Moyenne, to rue Victor Hugo. Open May–Sept., Mon.–Sat. 9–7:30 (7 PM May and June), Sun. 10–7; Oct.–Apr., Mon.–Sat. 9–6, Sun. 10–12:30.

COMING AND GOING

The **train station** is north of the center and serves Nevers (50 mins, 59F) and Paris (2½ hrs, 193F). From here, avenue H. Laudier leads downtown. The large center of Bourges demands at least a map and possibly some bus use; for information and day passes (15F), stop at the **bus office** (cours Avaricum, tel. 02–48–50–82–83). Otherwise, tickets cost 8F, payable to the driver.

WHERE TO SLEEP

Au Rendez-vous des Amis (6 av. Marx-Dormoy, tel. 02–48–70–81–80) has 20 modest rooms (130F–180F for the 8 rooms with shower) near the train station. Directly in front of the station, the **Hôtel la Bécasse** (2 pl. du Général Leclerc, tel. 02–48–24–20–87, fax 02–48–69–00–67) is characterless but affordable (160F–200F per room) and very convenient to the weary arriving late. In town, the plain, but definitely not characterless **Hôtel-Brasserie Central** (6 rue Docteur-Témoin, just off rue Moyenne, tel. 02–48–24–10–25) has a few rooms for 100F–160F. More upscale is the nearby **Hôtel d'Angleterre** (1 pl. des Quatres-Piliers, tel. 02–48–24–68–51, fax 02–48–65–21–41), which has singles (385F) and doubles (440F) with all the modern conveniences. The hotel's restaurant has menus starting at 91F. At the **Centre International de Séjour** (17 rue Félix Chédin, tel. 02–48–70–25–59, fax 02–48–69–01–21), a short walk from behind the train station, a dorm bed is 98F with breakfast. The **Auberge de Jeunesse** (22 rue Henri Sellier, tel. 02–48–24–58–09, fax 02–48–65–51–46) has beds for 67F a night, breakfast included (48F without); from the train station, take Bus 1, 2, or 12 to Condé. It closes mid-December–early January, and an HI card is required.

FOOD

You won't have any problems feeding yourself in Bourges: There are reasonably priced restaurants all over town, especially on **rue Moyenne.** To get here, follow avenue Jean Jaurès to rue du Commerce, which veers left and becomes rue Moyenne. **Le St-Alban** (32 rue Moyenne, tel. 02–48–65–89–75) specializes in food from the Auvergne region; menus start at 65F at lunch but are more expensive (115F–135F) in the evening. The Chinese restaurant next door, **Tan Hong Phueh** (34 rue Moyenne, tel. 02–48–69–00–83), has a deli, as well as three-course menus (38F–55F). There's an open-air **market** with fresh goodies every Saturday morning at Halle au Blé, Sunday morning on place St-Bonnet, and Wednesday morning at the Chancellerie.

WORTH SEEING

The Gothic **Cathédrale St-Étienne,** next to the tourist office on the northern edge of Archevêché Park, was built during the 13th century and is the fifth-largest cathedral in France. The five interior aisles match the fantastically carved portals, and the surviving 13th-century stained-glass windows depict the lives of the saints. The tour of the enormous crypt is unfortunately only in French, but it's worth the 28F investment even if you don't understand the language.

The **Palais Jacques Coeur** (rue Jacques Coeur, tel. 02–48–24–06–87) was built in the 15th century by a successful local merchant who had nabbed a job as a treasurer for Charles VII. Although there's not much left in the interior, the Gothic building itself is beautiful, from the carving- and fresco-lined walls to the sculpture-covered facade. Visits are by guided tour, in French only, and cost 32F. Tours are given daily 9–noon and 2–7 and at various other times depending on the season.

AFTER DARK

Especially around place Gordaine, the centre ville is packed with cafés, bars, and clubs, many of them lively from early afternoon into the night. The artsy and popular **Beau Bar** (rue des Beaux-Arts, off rue Moyenne at rue Coursarlon, tel. 02–48–24–40–49) has a youthful crowd and charges 13F for a *pression* (draft beer), 14F if you want to drink it outside. **Birdland** (4 av. Jean Jaurès, tel. 02–48–70–66–77) has a more casual atmosphere and jazz grooves and specializes in beer and whiskey at prices ranging 15F–30F. Shows at **La Soupe aux Choux** (pl. Gordaine, tel. 02–48–65–43–66), a lively café-theater putting on low-budget productions in a more casual environment, normally run 70F or so, with music for less. You can grab a bite to eat at the restaurant downstairs before the show: crepes for the pocketwatcher or 100F for a full meal. Unfortunately, it isn't as active in summer.

PARC NATUREL
RÉGIONAL DU MORVAN

The Parc Naturel Régional du Morvan stretches across a 3,500-square-km (1,290-square-mi) expanse of Burgundy, swallowing rich ecological communities, lush forests, six major lakes, and a good number of hikers and bikers brawny enough to attempt its 2,000 km (1,200 mi) worth of *Grandes Randonnées* (GRs, or big trails). By car (take the A6 to RN6) it could take a day to explore the roads twining around all the park's streams, forests, lakes, dilapidated farms, and forgotten villages; by bike or foot it could take a lifetime.

The park has the advantage of being one of the least known and least populated regions of France. Oddly enough, more foreigners seem to purchase residences here than the French. Little towns pepper the huge forests, and you can almost imagine Obélix and Astérix chasing boar through the woods. In **Château-Chinon** to the south, you'll find the **Musée du Septennat** (6 rue du Château, tel. 03–86–85–19–23), the Seven Years' Museum (for the length of the French presidency), which flaunts all the presents François Mitterrand received during his term. Entrance is 27F, and the museum is open February–mid-April and October–December, Wednesday–Monday 10–noon and 2–6; mid-April–June and September, Wednesday–Monday 10–1 and 2–6; and July–August every day 10–1 and 2–7. The **Fontaine Niki de St-Phale,** also in Château-Chinon, is worth a quick peek. At the foot of Mont Beuvray in the south is the incredible **Musée Bibracte de Civilisation Celtique** (tel. 03–85–86–52–35, fax 03–85–82–58–00), a huge, modern warehouse with videos, artifacts, and models of the early Celtic Gauls, les Edouens, open daily 10–6. Admission is 35F and it's closed Tuesday and mid-November–mid-March. The guided tour of the museum in French (or in English with a week's notice), given by local archaeologists, is worth the 50F.

Local and regional tourist offices have maps of specific trails (40F and up) and simple postcard-style ones (5F), along with information on the region's ecology and artisans working in the area. There are several main points of entry into the park. Avallon and Vézelay (*see above*) give access to the open prairies of the northern region; Saulieu and Arnay-le-Duc to the east and Chatillon-en-Bazois to the west are planted in the park's watery and foresty midriff; and Autun, Luzy, and St-Honoré-les-Bains cradle the *petite montagne* (little mountain) region of the south. The lakes are ideal for swimming, windsurfing, boating, and camping.

BASICS

The main information center for the park is the **Maison du Parc** (tel. 03–86–78–79–00, fax 03–86–78–74–22) in St-Brisson about 15 km (10 mi) west of Saulieu and 35 km (22 mi) southeast of both Vézelay and Avallon. It's open April–mid-November, daily 10:15—6, and mid-November–March, weekdays 8:45–12:15 and 1:45–5:30. The tourist office in **Saulieu** (24 rue d'Argentine, tel. 03–80–64–00–21, fax 03–80–64–21–96) has bicycle maps (40F), topographical trail maps (46F), and postcard-size walking maps (5F). The office in **Autun** (3 av. Charles-de-Gaulle, tel. 03–85–86–30–00, fax 03–85–86–10–17), straight up the hill from the train station on the left before the main square, has similar information.

COMING AND GOING

Trains and SNCF buses travel from Avallon to Saulieu (50 mins, 41F) and to Autun (2 hrs, 71F). From Saulieu, **Cars Taboureau** (tel. 03–86–78–71–90 or 03–86–78–75–02) will take you to Montsauche-les-Settons, close to the Lac des Settons.

GETTING AROUND

Unfortunately, no buses go directly to the center of the park, and walking to the Maison du Parc from Saulieu can take up a full day. If you're not a hike-a-holic, we strongly suggest you rent a car or bike. Many *mairies* (town halls), tourist offices, and campgrounds rent bikes. In Autun, **Cycles Tacnet** (1 rue de l'Arquebuse, tel. 03–85–86–37–83), above the center of town, charges 110F for a day and 600F for a week with a passport deposit; it's closed Sunday. Prices are better at Saulieu's **Camping le Perron** (tel. 03–80–64–16–19, fax 03–80–64–19–81), which rents bikes for 80F per day (500F for a week) with a 500F deposit. Of course, you could also take a taxi. In Autun, try **Taxi Alvarez** (tel. 03–85–52–15–33) and in Saulieu there's **Christian Rose** (tel. 03–80–64–27–51). For more bike rental and taxi options, *see* Coming and Going *in* Avallon and Vézelay, *above*.

WHERE TO SLEEP

The cheapest lodgings in the park are the *gîtes d'étape* (rural hostels equipped with mattresses, bathrooms, and stoves; 30F–220F per person, but mostly around 40F–60F); it's up to you to catch a wild boar and skewer it. Many have the possibility of *demi-pension*, meaning they will do the cooking if you choose. Otherwise, you can stay in a hotel in one of the bordering towns, or rest your tired dogs in one of the park's many campgrounds.

The gîte d'étape **Moulin du Pliéjus** (tel. 03–85–82–58–37) is a beautiful stone farm inside the park, toward la Grande Verrière from Autun. A bed costs 63F per night, and you can either do the cooking or let the friendly owner whip up a healthy meal for 65F, although you do the dishes. Breakfast costs 25F, and a picnic lunch is 30F. It's open March–November. A couple of miles away from Saulieu is the **Base de Loisirs des Settons** (tel. 03–86–84–51–98, fax 03–86–84–56–70), where you can get a bed (52F–58F per night 1 week minimum stay in July and August) in a comfortable dorm room for six and enjoy what the lake has to offer mid-March–October. Reserve in advance.

OUTDOOR ACTIVITIES

Hiking and biking are popular activities in the park, but the latest craze is *l'escalade granitique* (rock climbing); ask tourist offices about guides and equipment. If you'd rather get really, really wet, go river rafting (180F) on the *eaux-vives* (rapids) with Lac de Chaumeçon's **Base Nautique Activital Plainefas** (tel. 03–86–22–61–35). Most lakes in the park are open to swimmers, pedalboaters, anglers, and windsurfers; rent the *pédalos* (pedalboats) and fishing boats from the **Centre Nautique de Pannecière** through the Ouroux-en-Morvan tourist office (tel. 03–86–78–20–11) or *planches à voile* (Windsurfers) through the **Base Nautique de Branlasses** (tel. 03–86–84–51–98).

SAULIEU

Saulieu has been attracting pilgrims since the 2nd-century martyred St. Andoche and St. Thyrse left behind relics. It was also on an important trade route and welcomed fairs and markets. Today, it has lost much of its importance, relying for tourist revenue on the proximity of the Parc Naturel Régional du Morvan, the reputation of the sculptor François Pompon (a contemporary of Rodin), and the dowdy 12th-century Basilique St-Andoche. Still, give the city a stroll. And, if you can, try to make it for the **Festival de Musique Cajun** (early August) or the **Fête du Charolais** (second-to-last week in August), the latter being when the huge charolais steer are honored . . . and then eaten.

BASICS

The small, compact centre ville is located to the west of the *route nationale* 6, which, in town, is called rue Courtépée, rue d'Argentine, and rue Grillot. The well-stocked and useful **tourist office** has more information than you need to know about Saulieu, as well as on the Parc Naturel Régional du Morvan. Ask in particular about local gîtes d'étape. *24 rue d'Argentine, tel. 03–80–64–00–21, fax 03–80–64–21–96. From the station, walk straight up av. de la Gare. Open Sept.–June, Mon.–Sat. 9:30–noon and 2–6, Sun. (Oct.–Apr.) 10–noon; July–Aug., Mon.–Sat. 9:30–7, Sun. 10–noon and 2–5.*

COMING AND GOING

The **train station** (tel. 03–80–64–19–31) does not see a lot of traffic, so if you are trying to get to Avallon (1 hr, 41F) or Autun (1 hr, 43F), consult at the tourist office or check the schedule at the station. For buses into the park, try **Cars Taboureau** (tel. 03–86–78–71–90 or 03–86–78–75–02), which runs to Montsauche-les-Settons (near Lac des Settons) via Moux-en-Morvan. **Camping le Perron** (tel. 03–80–64–16–19, fax 03–80–64–19–81) rents bikes for 80F per day (500F for a week) with a 500F deposit. For taxis, give **Christian Rose** (9 rue du Marché, tel. 03–80–64–27–51) a call.

WHERE TO SLEEP AND EAT

Above the **Maison du Pays** there is an in-town gîte d'étape that has 47F beds (55F in winter) in rooms that hold two to six people, and a kitchen; contact the tourist office for details and obligatory reservations. The hotels are almost all located along N6. The least expensive option is the basic **Hôtel aux Poids Lourds** ("Mac Truck" Hotel, 12 rue Courtépée, tel. 03–80–64–19–83) at the northern edge of town, with charmless rooms for 85F–115F, basic meals for 59F, and the kind of clients you can expect from the hotel's name; it is closed on weekends. Farther south, there is the pleasant **Hôtel du Lion d'Or** (5 rue Courtépée, tel. 03–80–64–16–33, fax 03–80–64–14–64). Each of the six sunny rooms costs 185F, with

In case you want to see the world.

At American Express, we're here to make your journey a smooth one. So we have over 1,700 travel service locations in over 130 countries ready to help. What else would you expect from the world's largest travel agency?

do more   AMERICAN EXPRESS

Travel

Call 1 800 AXP-3429 or visit
www.americanexpress.com/travel

In case you want to be welcomed there.

We're here to see that you're always welcomed at establishments everywhere. That's why millions of people carry the American Express® Card – for peace of mind, confidence, and security, around the world or just around the corner.

do more AMERICAN EXPRESS

Cards

In case you're running low.

We're here to help with more than 190,000 Express Cash locations around the world. In order to enroll, just call American Express at 1 800 CASH-NOW before you start your vacation.

do more

And in case you'd rather be safe than sorry.

We're here with American Express® Travelers Cheques. They're the safe way to carry money on your vacation, because if they're ever lost or stolen you can get a refund, practically anywhere or anytime. To find the nearest place to buy Travelers Cheques, call 1 800 495-1153. Another way we help you do more.

do more AMERICAN EXPRESS

Travelers Cheques

dinner menus running 96F–250F. It's closed Sunday evening and Monday. Farther along, the elegant **Hôtel de la Borne Impériale** (tel. 03 80 64–19–76, fax 03–80–64–30–63) is a study in taste. Views from the rooms (215F–300F) facing away from the main street take in a lovely garden and dinner patio. The menus (95F at lunch and 120F–205F for dinner) are full of regional specialties, including braised *jambon du Morvan* (smoked ham). It's closed on Tuesday night and Wednesday. For meat lovers, **La Renaissance** (5 rue Grillot, tel. 03–80–64–08–72) has an impressive grill and a reasonable selection (78F–175F) à la carte. The **campground** (tel. 03–80–64–16–19, fax 03–80–64–19–81) at Le Perron in Saulieu charges 20F per tent, 13F per person, and is near a lake, pool, and tennis courts; it is open April–mid-October. The **campground** (tel. 03–80–64–13–67) at St-Martin-de-la-Mer, near Chamboux Lake, is open May–September and charges 14F per person.

WORTH SEEING

The 12th-century **Basilique St-Andoche** merits more than just a glance. Although this Cluny-inspired Romanesque construction has suffered quite at bit, it still maintains its grace. Keep an eye out for the 50-plus renowned sculpted capitals and a copy of Charlemagne's 6th-century gospel book. The **Musée François Pompon** (next to the basilica, tel. 03–80–64–19–51, admission 20F) contains not only work by the celebrated eponymous animal sculptor but sacred art and ancient artifacts as well. It is open all year round, Wednesday–Saturday and Monday 10–12:30 and 2–6 (5:30 in winter), and Sunday 10:30–noon and 2–5. Two of Pompon's sculptures can also be found in the city: the Bull on place Pompon (near the tourist office), and the Condor over his actual tomb, near the cathedral.

AUTUN

It's unfortunate that people don't often think of Autun when creating their Burgundian itineraries. Founded by the Roman Emperor Augustus as Augustodunum, Autun was once the second city of Burgundy. With a wealth of ancient monumental architecture, a busy sports facility, an active tourist board, close proximity to the Parc Naturel Régional du Morvan, and affordable food and lodging, today's Autun is worth the couple of days it would take to fully appreciate its 2,000 years of history.

Two dates to keep in mind: In July every night for two weeks, melody fills the air when Autun plays host to the classical music festival **Musique en Morvan**; on Friday and Saturday nights in August, **Augustodunum** comes to life. Unique in France, Augustodunum draws 600 people to the ancient Roman theater where they bring Celtic and Gallo-Roman times to life. It's goofy, but for 80F you can enjoy gladiators, chariot races, Roman Legionnaires, and more. Check for details at the tourist office (*see below*).

BASICS

The large and info-filled **tourist office** is matched in its usefulness only by the bright staff. There are gobs of free information about the city and surrounding area, as well as photographs, postcards, and posters for a reasonable price. *2 av. Charles-de-Gaulle, tel. 03–85–86–80–38, fax 03–85–86–80–49. From the train station, walk uphill on av. Charles-de-Gaulle; it's on the left a block before the main pl. du Champ de Mars. Open Sept.–June, weekdays 9–noon and 2–6 (5 on Sat.); July–Aug., daily 9–7 (10–6 on Sun.).*

COMING AND GOING

Autun's **train station** (tel. 03–85–52–73–65) is on avenue de la République at the western edge of town, not far from the Arroux River. With moderately frequent service (sometimes by SNCF bus), you are within easy reach of Auxerre (2 hrs, 71F), Saulieu (1 hr, 43F), and Dijon (2–3 hrs, 94F). Autun is a good hub for buses to the southern reaches of the Parc du Morvan. Consult the tourist office for destinations and time schedules.

Autun is a medium-size and hilly city with well-dispersed attractions. While distances are rarely huge, moving around on foot can take some time. **Cycles Tacnet** (1 rue de l'Arquebuse, tel. 03–85–86–37–83), above the center of town, charges 110F for a day's bike rental and 600F for a week with a passport deposit; it's closed Sunday. If your hamstrings can't hack it anymore, try **Taxi Alvarez** (tel. 03–85–52–15–33).

WHERE TO SLEEP

Right in front of the train station, there are two similar side-by-side options. The **Hôtel du Commerce** (20 av. de la République, tel. 03–85–52–17–90, fax 03–85–52–37–63) has doubles running 145F–250F, and those at the **Hôtel de France** (18 av. de la République, tel. 03–85–52–14–00, fax 03–85–86–14–52) go for 140F–220F. Farther afield, the five-room **Bar-Hôtel François 1er** (14 rue Mazagran, tel. 03–85–86–10–11) fills up fast at 110F–150F per room. Call ahead. Otherwise, the popular, friendly, and very central **Hôtel Le Grand Café** (19 bis rue de Lattre-de-Tassigny, tel. 03–85–52–27–66) has sunny if sometimes noisy doubles for 200F–285F. **Chambre d'Hôte Andriot** (tel. 03–85–52–22–99), a bed-and-breakfast on a farm in Monthelon, 5 km (3 mi) from Autun on N41, has three rooms (220F for two people, 185F for one) with private bath. The breakfasts alone have made it so popular that you need to reserve in advance. **Camping Municipal de la Porte d'Arroux** (tel. 03–85–52–10–82) is about 3 km (2 mi) from the train station. It's open mid-March–October and costs 13F per site and 14F per person (15F in July and August).

FOOD

In the lower city, the only real treat other than hotel restaurants is **Le Chateaubriand** (14 rue Jeannin, tel. 03–85–52–21–58) with prix-fixe menus at 72F–210F; it is closed Sunday night and Monday. Otherwise, in the upper city, there is a fine collection of reasonable choices clustered around the cathedral. For French fare, try the **Croustine** (28 rue des Cordiers, tel. 03–85–52–70–60) with dishes running 60F–100F; it's closed Sunday. Rue des Bancs has two solid international food options: **Le Petit Banc** (4 rue des Bancs, tel. 03–85–52–64–32) has a yummy paella, and **La Trattoria** (2 rue des Bancs, 03–85–86–10–73) will serve up a full Italian repast for 58F–78F. For something novel and a little dose of America away from home, go to the **Bowling du Lac** (route de Chalon, next to the McDonald's out by the lake, tel. 03–85–86–90–25); 55F–60F will get you a *plat du jour,* a drink, and a game. The **Casino** supermarket on rue St-Saulge is open Tuesday–Saturday 7:30–12:30 and 3–7:30, Sunday 8–noon and 4–7. The city **markets** are held on Wednesday and Friday on place du Champ de Mars. Try some of the delicious local honey.

WORTH SEEING

Some of the Gallo-Roman remains are quite awesome, open all year round (free of charge), and beautifully lit at night. The much-touted **Théâtre Romain** (facing the plan d'eau du Vallon on the northeastern edge of the city) is unfortunately no longer majestic. Little remains of what was once—in the 1st century BC—the largest of the Roman theaters. In contrast, the remains of the **Janus Temple** (400 yards beyond the Arroux River just minutes northwest of town) are quite striking. Eighty feet high, this structure was once part of a much larger sanctuary. Both the **Port d'Arroux** (on the Arroux northwest of town) and the **Port St-André** (north of the center at the end of rue de la Croix-Blanche) date from the 1st century BC as do the extensive city **remparts.** The far side of the Port d'Arroux is by far the best-conserved façade.

The **Cathédrale St-Lazare** dominates the upper part of the medieval city. Originally completed in the 12th century, this Romanesque structure was built to house the remains of St. Lazarus. The Last Judgment tympanum over the main portal is considered a masterpiece.

A great way to see these open-air monuments is to join tourist-office-organized *visites spectacles nocturnes, tours a vélo gourmand,* and *visites guidées à thème.* Costing between 30F and 70F, these tours—by night, by bike, or by theme, respectively—are worth ever centime. Ask at the tourist information office for specifics.

The best of Autun's museums is the **Musée Rolin,** one of the richest in Burgundy. Named after Nicolas Rolin, a native Autunois who made a mighty mark in Burgundy (*see* Beaune, *below*), the museum contains exhibits—from Gallo-Roman artifacts and art to 19th-century painting—as expressive as the 15th-century palace in which they are presented. *3 rue des Bancs, tel. 03–85–52–09–76, fax 03–85–52–47–41. Admission 20F. Open Oct.–Mar., Wed.–Sat. 10–noon and 2–4, Sun. 10–noon and 2:30–5; Apr.–Sept., Wed.–Mon. 9:30–noon and 1:30–6.*

If you're a book lover, the 18th-century **Bibliothèque Municipale** in the Mairie, or City Hall, has more than 60,000 volumes and a unique collection of medieval manuscripts, some from before the 12th century. This helps explain the popularity of the mid-April **Fête du Livre de Pays** (Country Book Festival). *In the Mairie, behind the tourist office, tel. 03–85–86–80–35. Admission free. Open Mon.–Sat. 10–6.*

For the vine inspired, the free **Mini Musée de la Vigne et du Vin** run by the Cellier de Jean-Patrice Laly has a nice introduction to everything you need to know about wine. For a small price, you may also taste wines in the adjoining cellar. *14 rue de la Grange-Vertu, tel. 03–85–52–24–83. Open Mon.–Sat. 9–noon and 2–7.*

AFTER DARK

There is a healthy nightlife here much in contrast to the surrounding cities of the Morvan. The epicenter is place du Champ de Mars. Bars-brasseries like **Le Central** (34 pl. du Champ de Mars, tel. 03–85–52–23–64), **Le Commerce** (27 pl. du Champ de Mars), and the café of the **Hôtel Le Grand Café** (19 bis rue de Lattre-de-Tassigny) attract a young crowd. The nearby **Irish Pub** (5 rue Mazagran, tel. 03–85–52–73–90) has a ready pint of stout (28F) for the thirsty. **Le Lutrin** (1 pl. du Terreau, tel. 03–85–86–59–05), looking up at the cathedral, is a fine place for a warm eve's pause.

DIJON

Dijon is a mix of historical monuments, art, gastronomy, gardens, and university students. For centuries an insignificant Roman colony called Divio, Dijon was a comparatively late bloomer. The city became the capital of the duchy of Burgundy in the 11th century and acquired most of its important architecture and art treasures during the 14th and 15th centuries under the four Burgundian dukes of the west. Today, the city's churches, the ducal palace, and one of the finest art museums in France are impressive evidence of the dukes' generous patronage.

Like any major hub, Dijon has an array of department stores and ritzy shops along the city's main drag, **rue de la Liberté.** Dijon mustard is the biggest tourist scam here—watch out for those 150F, small ceramic pots—*without* the mustard. Since Dijon is a medium-size city, it is easy to get around on foot. There are many good restaurants, and the vineyards to the south are only a short trip away.

BASICS

BUREAUX DE CHANGE

The tourist office exchanges currency for a 5% commission. Otherwise, the post office has an ATM machine (which also takes major credit cards) and changes American Express traveler's checks. There are also plenty of banks that exchange money, usually for a commission.

INTERNET ACCESS

In the center of Dijon, **Station Internet** in the bus station is your best bet for reading your E-mail or surfing the Web. Rates are 40F (or 36F with proof of student status) an hour paid to the nearest minute. *Gare Routière, tel./fax 03–80–42–89–84. Open weekdays 11—8, Sat. noon–5.*

LAUNDRY

There are laundromats near the center at 8 rue Bannelier (tel. 06–80–02–85–49), open daily 7 AM–8:30 PM; 28 and 55 rue Berbisey (same hours); as well as near the train station at 36 and 42 rue Guillaume Tell, open daily 6 AM–9 PM. The facility at number 42 is for dry cleaning only (60F per load). In general, a wash costs 17F–22F, drying is 5F for 14 minutes, and soap is 2F per *dose*.

MAIL

The main **post office** changes money (AmEx checks only) and holds poste restante; the postal code is 21000. *Pl. Grangier, tel. 03–80–50–61–11. Open weekdays 8–7, Sat. 8–noon.*

For regular postal business, there is also a branch bureau. *3 pl. de la Liberté, in front of the Palais des Ducs. Open Mon. 1–6, Tues.–Fri. 9–6, Sat. 9–noon.*

MEDICAL AID

The **Hôpital Général** (3 rue du Faubourg Raines, off rue de L'Hôpital, tel. 03–80–29–30–31), at the southwest corner of the centre ville, is open 24 hours. The address of the late-night pharmacy is printed daily in the local paper *Bien Public.*

VISITOR INFORMATION

There are two **tourist offices,** the larger and much friendlier one at place Darcy, not far from the train station, the other on rue des Forges, in the middle of town. Both have excellent city and environs maps for 30F. They also change money and book hotels for 15F. Inquire about tours of the wine region and

DIJON

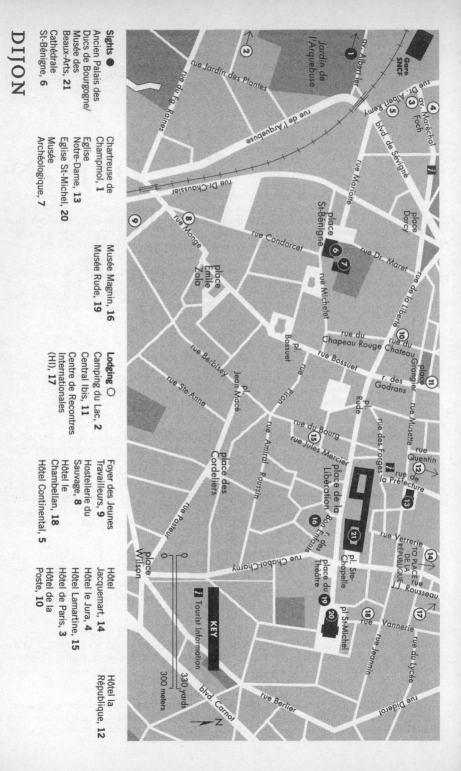

Sights ●

Ancien Palais des Ducs de Bourgogne/
Musée des Beaux-Arts, **21**
Cathédrale St-Bénigne, **6**
Chartreuse de Champmol, **1**
Église Notre-Dame, **13**
Église St-Michel, **20**
Musée Archéologique, **7**
Musée Magnin, **16**
Musée Rude, **19**

Lodging ○

Camping du Lac, **2**
Central Ibis, **11**
Centre de Recontres
Internationales
(HI), **17**
Foyer des Jeunes
Travailleurs, **9**
Hostellerie du
Sauvage, **8**
Hôtel le
Chambellan, **18**
Hôtel Continental, **5**
Hôtel
Jacquemart, **14**
Hôtel le Jura, **4**
Hôtel Lamartine, **15**
Hôtel de Paris, **3**
Hôtel de la
Poste, **10**
Hôtel la
République, **12**

KEY

i Tourist Information

330 yards
300 meters

N

walking tours of the city. *Pl. Darcy, from train station take av. Foch 1 block. Open mid-Oct.–Apr., daily 9–1 and 2–7; May–mid-Oct., daily 9–9. For the office at 34 rue des Forges, continue down rue de la Liberté to pl. Rude and then bear left onto the pedestrian rue des Forges. Open mid-Oct.–Apr., weekdays 10—6; May–mid-Oct., Mon.–Sat. 10–6. Tel. for both is 03–80–44–11–44.*

COMING AND GOING

Dijon is linked by expressway A6 via A38 to Paris, 311 km (193 mi) away; to Lyon by A6 via A31, 190 km (117 mi); and to Strasbourg by A36, 300 km (186 mi). The centre ville is easy to get around by foot. Most museums and churches are on streets branching off **rue de la Liberté. Place de la République** roughly forms the northern boundary of the centre ville. **Travel'Bike** (2 av. Poincaré, tel. 03–80–72–31–00) rents bikes for 80F a day with a 1,000F or passport deposit. If you need a taxi, try **Taxi Radio Dijon** (tel. 03–80–41–41–12).

BY TRAIN

The **train station** is on the western edge of the centre ville at the end of avenue Foch. Trains zoom many times a day to Paris (3 hrs and 189F on a regular train, or 1½ hrs and 217F–267F by TGV), to Lyon (2 hrs, 132F), to Strasbourg (3 hrs, 202F), and to many smaller cities throughout Burgundy. *Av. Foch, tel. 03–80–40–10–00. Ticket office open 24 hrs, information office open weekdays 9–7, Sat. 9–6.*

BY BUS

The **TRANSCO** bus station (rue des Perrières, tel. 03–80–42–11–00), adjacent to the train station, is open weekdays 7:30–6:30, Saturday 7:30–12:30. Frequent buses follow the wine route to Chalon-sur-Saône (70F), stopping in Beaune (40F) and towns along the way. Fares are comparable to the train.

WHERE TO SLEEP

The centre ville is the place to stay; it's safe and full of reasonable hotels, though reservations are a good idea in summer. The train station is open 24 hours and the hotels nearby accommodate arrivals around the clock.

UNDER 150F • Hôtel le Chambellan. On one of Dijon's quieter streets, this well-kept place has rooms that are a shade nicer than those in your average budget hotel. The floral wallpaper and the views of the courtyard would almost be cloyingly charming if it weren't for some funky touches. There are six 120F doubles with free hall showers, though the rest of the rooms are 220F–270F and have private toilets and showers. All have TVs. An extra bed is 30F. *92 rue Vannerie, tel. 03–80–67–12–67, fax 03–80–38–00–39. 23 rooms, 17 with bath.*

UNDER 250F • Hôtel de Paris. This hotel, between the tourist office and the train station, has simple doubles (160F–290F), of which there are only three at 160F and 22 at 250F. You can dance till 4 AM in the disco, the **Rio** (60F Thursday–Saturday, 50F Sunday) on the first floor, and then easily drag your tired self up three floors to your room. From up there, you shouldn't hear the sound of music. *9–11 av. Foch, tel. 03–80–43–41–88, fax 03–80–43–36–10. 40 rooms, most with bath.*

Hôtel du Jacquemart. With airy doubles at 170F–350F, this charming hotel just north of the center is as smart as its balconied facade suggests. The nine rooms at 170F are with neither shower nor toilet, although there are a few rooms at 180F with a shower only. *32 rue Verrière, tel. 03–80–60–09–60, fax 03–80–60–09–69. 32 rooms, 23 with shower or bath.*

Hôtel Lamartine. Hidden on a narrow side street in about as central a location as you could imagine (less than five minutes from both place de la Libération and place Rude), this hotel is one of Dijon's best bargains. It is, however, small, and fills quickly. Medium-size doubles go from 165F–215F. *12 rue Jules Mercier, tel. 03–80–30–37–47, fax 03–80–30–03–43. 7 rooms, all with shower or bath.*

UNDER 300F • Hostellerie du Sauvage. Near the train station in a pretty 15th-century stone house, you'll find doubles that run 230F–310F. The fanciest room, for up to five, is 510F. The restaurant **Le Sauvage** (tel. 03–80–41–17–33), closed Saturday at noon and Sunday, serves delicious grilled steaks and Burgundian cuisine. Prix-fixe menus start at 80F. *64 rue Monge, tel. 03–80–41–31–21, fax 03–80–42–06–07. 21 rooms, all with shower or bath. Restaurant, bar.*

Hôtel Continental. Within a late-night stagger of the train station, this modern hotel is a surprising bargain given what it provides. Modern and soundproofed, small doubles are 265F; there's an indoor pool

FLIGHT CRU

If Burgundy looks sublime from the ground, have you ever wondered what it looks like from the air? Wonder no longer: Put a little wind beneath . . . your wine-soaked wings.

A 30-minute plane ride over the vineyards of Burgundy runs 250F per person (for up to three people) through the Aéroclub Beaunois (tel. 03–80–22–21–93). The Aérodrome de Saulieu–Liernais (tel. 03–80–64–30–32) will overfly the Morvan. Cosmos' Centre de Formation Pilote at the Aérodrome Dijon–Darois (tel. 03–80–35–68–00, fax 03–80–35–68–01, www.cosmos.fr) has information about ultralight flights as well. And for the easygoing drifters at heart, the France Montgolfière Balloon Company (tel. 01–47–00–66–44, fax 01–47–00–66–55, www.franceballoons.com) can float you for hours over the châteaux of the Morvan region (and other areas throughout France) for 1,500F per person.

and Jacuzzi (the sauna is 50F per person). The attached restaurant has cheap all-you-can-eat lunch and dinner buffets too. *7–9 rue Albert Rémy, tel. 03–80–53–10–10, fax 03–80–53–10–38, www.continental-hotel.com. 80 rooms, all with shower or bath. Restaurant.*

Hôtel de la Poste. On a central pedestrian drag just a block from rue de la Liberté, this somewhat kitschy, brightly colored hotel offers doubles for 195F–370F. The attractive tourist-trap **Grand Café** on the ground floor has affordable menus (98F–125F), but you should make a bolder selection in this gastronomically well-endowed city. *5 rue du Château, tel. 03–80–30–51–64, fax 03–80–30–77–44. 55 rooms, all with shower or bath. Restaurant.*

Hôtel la République. The 15-minute walk from the train station to this comfortable hotel also puts you at the northern doorstep of the centre ville. Quiet singles run 195F–280F and doubles are 215F–300F. From the station, take avenue Foch to place Darcy. Follow boulevard des Brosses eight blocks to rue du Nord. *3 rue du Nord, tel. 03–80–73–36–76, fax 03–80–72–46–04. 21 rooms, most with bath.*

UNDER 400F • Central Ibis. This central, old, established hotel (now part of a national chain) offers comfort in excess of price. Doubles run 370F–405F. *3 pl. Grangier, tel. 03–80–30–44–00, fax 03–80–30–77–12. 90 rooms, most with bath.*

SPLURGE • Hôtel le Jura. One block from the train station, this modern hotel has an outdoor courtyard and amenities such as air-conditioning, hair dryers, and extra-firm beds. Singles (360F) and doubles (400F) in pastel colors are spacious and, on the courtyard side, are also sunny and quiet. *14 av. Foch, tel. 03–80–41–61–12, fax 03–80–41–51–13. 79 rooms. Air-conditioning.*

HOSTELS

Centre de Rencontres Internationales (HI). A big room with three beds and a shower and toilet costs 144F (130F with shower only); otherwise, an HI card and 72F–76F gets you a clean dorm bed in a room for four, and breakfast (without an HI card is an extra 8F per night). The cafeteria serves breakfast for 20F, as well as other mediocre meals. *1 blvd. Champollion, tel. 03–80–72–95–20, fax 03–80–70–00–61. Until 8:30 PM, Bus 6 stops at the train station every 15 mins. Transfer to Bus 5 at the pl. de la République. After 8:30 PM, take Bus A, which stops at the station every 30 mins, and runs directly to the hostel. The hostel is at stop Epirey. 265 beds. Laundry.*

Foyer des Jeunes Travailleurs. This foyer, as well as the Foyer des Jeunes Travailleuses next to it, rents out rooms to men or women. The Travailleurs has singles with private showers and toilets for 120F; the Travailleuses (9 rue Aubriot, tel. 03–80–41–19–56), with 150 beds, is not quite as nice, and singles run 105F. Both include breakfast. Space is particularly tight September–May, so call ahead. *4 rue des Ponts* des Tanneries, tel. 03–80–43–00–87, fax 03–80–42–03–31. From station, walk right along rue de l'Arquebuse past pl. 1er Mai; foyer is near hospital. 250 beds. Reception open 9–8.

CAMPING

Camping du Lac. This mediocre spot a half-hour walk west of town has its fair share of city and car noise, but it is beside the pleasant Ouche River and the green banks of Lake Kir. Sites are 12F, plus 14F per person and 8F per car parked on the site. 3 blvd. Chanoine Kir, tel. 03–80–43–54–72. From station, take Bus 12 or 18. By foot, head under overpass and right along av. Albert 1er to end, then turn left. 121 sites. Closed mid-Oct.–Mar.

FOOD

Finding a good restaurant is no problem in Dijon and it's worth spending the extra few francs to try the excellent local cuisine. Restaurants on **rue Berbisey** are good bets, as well as around place **de la République,** and on **rue Jeannin.** Try place **Émile Zola** and the nearby **rue Monge** for Portuguese and Chinese food. **Avenue Foch** and **place Darcy** have pizzerias and crêperies. **Markets** take place on Tuesday, Friday, and Saturday mornings throughout the quartier Notre-Dame (Les Halles). A large **Casino** supermarket (12 blvd. Clemenceau, tel. 03–80–73–30–68), open Monday–Saturday until 9 PM, is north of place de la République.

On December 7, 1513, 30,000 Swiss and German soldiers came knocking impolitely at Dijon's gates. Far outnumbered, the Burgundians sent negotiators with a generous supply of wine. The soldiers drank, reconsidered, and retreated cheerfully.

UNDER 50F • L'Entresol. This sunny, quiet vegetarian restaurant, behind a health food store, has prix-fixe *envies du jour* for 39F–72F, or vegetables and soups for 25F–35F and main courses like fish and vegetable ravioli for 37F–45F. The all-you-can-eat vegetarian buffet is 55F. 29 rue Musette, tel. 03–80–30–15–10. Closed Sun. No dinner.

Le Petit Kouni. Convenient, tasty, and just a touch greasy, this Lebanese takeout is three blocks from the train station, with 15F–40F appetizers like tabbouleh, and sandwiches and grilled dishes for 20F–40F. The filling Tunisian sandwich consists of bowl-shape bread filled with tuna, eggs, olives, jalapeños, tomatoes, potatoes, and lettuce. 3 blvd. de Sévigné, tel. 03–80–30–81–63. Closed Sun.

For other cheap options, remember that the lunch menus and *plats du jour* of most restaurants are usually more reasonable than what is available for dinner. In a number of places, they roll in for just under 50F. Check out: the **Brasserie du Théâtre** (1 bis pl. du Théâtre, tel. 03–80–67–13–59), closed Tuesday night, also for its huge salads; **Triskell** (31 rue Verrière, tel. 03–80–30–65–84), closed Saturday noon, Sunday, and Monday noon, also for its excellent crepes; and the Italian **Restaurant Simpatico** (30 rue Berbisey, tel. 03–80–30–53–33), closed Saturday noon, Sunday, and Monday noon.

UNDER 75F • L'Bout d'la Rue. "End of the road" is the name of this restaurant on a quiet street in the center of town. The cozy atmosphere lures locals every night of the week. The menu specializing in mussels also has salads and meat dishes (50F–70F). 52 rue Verrerie, tel. 03–80–71–37–92. Closed Sun. and Mon. noon.

La Cabane à Saumon. Eclectic '50s music has almost everyone tapping a foot while savoring the restaurant's perfectly cooked salmon dishes (60F–80F). Choose from salmon cooked an array of ways, and you'll also get an appetizer, a fat oven-roasted potato, dessert, and coffee. The decor is like a funky warm chalet, all the way down to the waiter's alpine boots. 44 rue des Godrans, tel. 03–80–30–85–87. Closed Sun.

Le Dôme. A local and tourist favorite, this high-ceilinged single room with an old-fashioned brasserie feel packs crowds in by the droves, sitting and standing. The popular 69F lunch menu changes daily but always satisfies, as does the 72F dinner option. Call ahead to reserve, or elbow your way to the bar with the rest. 16 bis rue Quentin, tel. 03–80–30–58–92. Closed Sun.

Le Germinal. If you've been trying to work up the nerve to eat frogs' legs, here's your chance: This popular restaurant on lively place Zola specializes in them. Variations include legs with a simple garlic and parsley sauce (48F), or with baby lobsters in the deliciously juicy Méli-Mélo (62F). If you listen closely you'll hear little froggy croaks in the background (no kidding). A half-bottle of Côte de Beaune costs 48F. 44 rue Monge, tel. 03–80–44–97–16. Closed Mon.

Restaurant Mayne Rose. Located in the Hôtel Continental, this buffet-based affair caters to all cares. By far the best deals are the all-you-can-eat appetizer service (48F at lunch, 58F in the evening) and appetizer-plus-dessert service (58F at lunch, 69F in the evening). The full menu also has prix-fixe options beginning at 70F. *7–9 rue Albert Rémy, tel. 03–80–53–10–10.*

UNDER 100F • Au Moulin à Vent. Looking out at the fountain in the center of town, this restaurant is almost a culinary institution. Sure, it's packed with tourists, especially during the summer, but that's because it's so good. Try the classic *boeuf bourguignon* or the more unusual *poêlée d'escargots au basilic* (skillet-fried snails with basil). Dinner menus start at 75F. *8 pl. François Rude, tel. 03–80–30–81–43. Closed Sun. evenings and Mon.*

Le Saint Germain. As soon as you step through the mirrored door, you know you are in for something more than you expected. Hidden on a side street not far from place de la République, this plush, comfortable place serves up a feast of Burgundian specialties to fit any palette. Prix-fixe menus are 87F–187F will make the excellent coq au vin crow in every plate. *10 rue du Nord, tel.03–80–73–56–01. Closed Sat. noon and Wed.*

Les Moules Zola. For mussel lovers who can't squeeze into L'Bout d'la Rue, this bigger and glitzier sister establishment is the place. Mussels and only mussels—prepared a half dozen ways—are served. The large windows overlook the square and the ambience is jovial. The lunch menu at 60F is the cheapest option; the à la carte dinner menu starts at 80F. Reservations are a good idea. *3 pl. Émile Zola, tel. 03–80–58–93–26. Closed Mon.*

UNDER 125F • Hostellerie de l'Étoile. In a surprisingly bright and airy room tucked under the heavy stone arches of a centuries-old former postal relay point, the Colombo family treats you and your food like gold. Try the unrivalled *oeuf en meurette* (poached eggs served in a red wine sauce) or any of the fish or poultry. And indulge in one of the best wine lists around. Menus start at 103F. Reservations are highly recommended. *1 rue Marceau or 5 av. Garibaldi, just north of pl. de la République, tel. 03–80–73–20–72. Closed Sun. evenings and Mon.*

SPLURGE • Côte Saint-Jean. For something cozy, romantic, and gastronomically refined, head here (request the downstairs dining room). Revel in the duck and fish on menus starting at 140F. Reservations are essential. *13 rue Monge, tel. 03–80–50–11–77. Closed Sat. noon and Tues.*

WORTH SEEING

Dijon is a fun city to explore—it has the liveliness of a capital city without being too large and crowded, as well as impressive art and architecture. You might consider any of a number of tours organized by the tourist office. For 35F and lasting approximately 1½ hours, it runs (in French) at 3 PM on Saturday October–June and daily July–September, as well as (in French and German) at 10:15 AM daily June–October. There is a nightly tour (in English and French) during the summer at 10 PM. Otherwise, for the self-motivated, there's the "Clés de la Ville-Dijon" (the Key of the City-Dijon), a pass (45F) that gets you a self-guided audio tour (in English) and entrance to all the major museums in town. It is available at the tourist offices. On Sunday, some of the museums are free for everyone (for students they're free all the time). If you're craving some greenery, the **Jardin de l'Arquebuse** (Botanical Garden) is a pretty spot south of the train station on avenue Albert 1er. In the other direction, **place Darcy,** next to the tourist office, is a peaceful place to regroup with your new maps and brochures. Don't miss Saulieu sculptor Pompon's famous polar bear, a copy of which is in the Musée d'Orsay in Paris.

ANCIEN PALAIS DES DUCS DE BOURGOGNE

Abandoned after Charles the Foolhardy's regrettable end as wolf fodder, the Ducal Palace was revamped in the 17th century with the help of Versailles architect Jules Hardouin-Mansart. The west wing now houses the Hôtel de Ville (Town Hall), and the east wing holds the collection of the **Musée des Beaux-Arts,** one of the most important such collections in France. Don't miss the collection of cubist art on the third floor, particularly the works of Picasso and Braque. The spectacular *salle des gardes* (guard room) contains the richly decorated tombs of Philippe *le Hardi* (the Daring), Jean *sans Peur* (the Fearless), and Jean's missus, Marguerite de Ba-vière. In a wing west of the museum, the **Salon Apollon** frequently hosts free expositions. *Pl. de la Libération, tel. 03–80–74–52–70. Admission 18F. Open Wed.–Mon. 10–6.*

MUSEE ARCHEOLOGIQUE

Dijon's archaeology collection, set up in the former 11th-century abbey of St-Bénigne, is much more exciting than the usual crumbling stones dimly suggestive of statues. The rare wood and stone sculptures, and the pottery, are in excellent condition, as are the eye-catching bronze and gold jewelry and dishes. Unfortunately, explanations and tours are exclusively in French. *5 rue Docteur Maret, tel. 03–80–30–88–54. Admission 12F. Open June–Sept., Wed.–Mon. 9:30–6; Oct.–Mar., Wed.–Mon. 9–noon and 2–6.*

MUSEE MAGNIN

Housed in the elegant 17th-century Hôtel Lantin, this museum displays paintings from the 17th to 19th centuries. Though you won't find many by big-name artists, it's still a fine collection. *4 rue des Bons-Enfants, tel. 03–80–67–11–10. Admission 16F. Open June–Sept., Tues.–Sun. 10–6; Oct.–May, Tues.–Sun. 10–noon and 2–6.*

MUSEE RUDE

The sculptor François Rude is a native son of Dijon, though he is best known for his relief *Departure of the Volunteers,* better known as *La Marseillaise,* which adorns the Arc de Triomphe in Paris. Dijon has thoughtfully devoted a cloister of a deconsecrated church to a dozen or so of Rude's celebrated works. Included is a full-scale plaster cast of *La Marseillaise. 8 rue Vaillant, tel. 03–80–66–87–95. Admission free. Open June–Oct., Wed.–Mon. 10–noon and 2–5:45.*

OTHER MUSEUMS

Depending on how much time you have and what you find inspiring, there are other places on the list of cool museums. The **Musée d'Art Sacré** (15 rue Ste-Anne, tel. 03–80–44–12–69), admission 9F, is open year-round, Wednesday–Monday 9–noon and 2–6, and houses religious art and objects. In the same 17th-century complex is the **Musée de la Vie Bourguignonne Perrin de Puycousin** (tel. 03–80–44–12–69), admission 12F, open year-round, Wednesday–Monday 9–noon and 2–6, with rooms that bring to life Burgundian traditions. The **Muséum d'Histoire Naturelle** (1 av. Albert 1er, Jardin de l'Arquebuse, tel. 03–80–76–82–76), admission 12F, open year-round except mornings on Tuesday, Saturday, and Sunday, 9–noon and 2–6, has a good collection of geographical, zoological, and ethnographic exhibits.

CHURCHES

Three churches in town are worth seeing. The 13th- to 14th-century **Cathédrale St-Bénigne** (pl. St-Bénigne) presents an austere facade and a colorful roof pattern; a 300-ft 19th-century spire lightens the effect. Get a look at the early 11th-century circular crypt (5F) and the pitiful attempts at character carvings on top of the columns. Construction of the **Église St-Michel** (pl. St-Michel) began at the end of the 15th century and included a Renaissance facade and towers. The choir inside has some fine 18th-century woodcarvings. The Gothic **Église Notre-Dame** (pl. Notre-Dame), just north of the Ducal Palace, houses a rare 11th-century statue of the *Vierge Noire* (Black Virgin) and a tapestry commemorating Dijon's 1944 liberation from German occupation. It also has the most gargoyle-studded facade you may ever see.

CHEAP THRILLS

If you're in town at 3 PM on a Wednesday or Saturday during the low season (any day but Sunday mid-June–mid-September), call to arrange a 15F tour in English or French of the **Musée de la Moutarde** (Mustard Museum; 48 quai Nicolas Rolin, tel. 03–80–44–11–44) at the Amora mustard factory.

Stop by the specialty beer store **Le Diable Rouge** (2 rue Neuve Dauphine, off rue du Bourg, tel. 03–80–30–09–79), admire the selection, and see what their ear to the ground has picked up.

FESTIVALS

Throughout the summer, Dijon hosts a series of festivals, starting in June with the classical concerts of **L'Été Musical.** From mid-June to early-August, **L'Estivade** features music and plays throughout the city. In late August and early September, during the **Fête de la Vigne et Folkloriades** (International Folk Festival and Wine Festivities), there are parades, dancing in the streets, and wine tastings. In the first week of November, the **Foire Internationale et Gastronomique** features Burgundian and French food and wine (read: free samples).

SHOPPING

If you're continuing on to Beaune (*see below*) or traveling along the Wine Route, buy wine there, where you can first have a tour and tasting in the cellars. Otherwise, at **Nicot** (48 rue J. J. Rousseau, tel. 03–

80–73–29–88) you can pick up a bottle or two directly from the vineyards at discount prices. Dijon's **Maille (Grey Poupon)** mustard shop (32 rue de la Liberté, tel. 03–80–30–41–02), established in 1777, still sells that popular condiment in painted ceramic pots at outrageous prices. For a loaf of Dijon's traditional *pain d'épices* (spiced bread), stop by **Mulot et Petitjean** (13 pl. Bossuet, tel. 03–80–30–07–10). Some cheese to go with your bread? There's no place like the **Crèmerie Porcheret** (18 rue Bannelier, tel. 03–80–30–21–05). If chocolate is more your speed, try a *dijonnaise* (pink praline) from **Au Parrain Généreux** (21 rue du Bourg, tel. 03–80–30–38–88).

AFTER DARK

BARS

Dijon's nightlife is low-key, which makes you feel welcome to join in the festivities, but most bars close Sunday night and all of August. **Le Cappuccino** (132 rue Berbisey, tel. 03–80–41–06–35) is a cheerful, casual place owned by an Italian family who will serve you a beer any time of day. At night, it fills up with a cool local crowd sometimes to hear live music; a simple pression costs 10F, but the 50F *flambée* (beer topped with flaming liquor) seems to please all pyro-enthusiasts. Also on rue Berbisey are numerous other watering holes, including **Café de l'Univers** (47 rue Berbisey, tel. 03–80–30–98–29) and **Crocodile** (88 rue Berbisey, tel. 03–80–50–10–50). Nearby **place Émile Zola** is packed with the tables of (relatively—1 AM) late-night restaurants and cafés. Farther north, **Café au Carillon** (2 rue Mariotte, at pl. St-Bénigne. tel. 03–80–30–63–71), open every night, is popular with a young crowd.

MUSIC AND DANCING

A young crowd comes to **l'Atmosphère** (7 rue Audra, tel. 03–80–30–52–03), a café north of place Darcy, to dance to house music and play pool. Trendy **Le Cintra** (13 av. Foch, tel. 03–80–43–65–89) has a piano-karaoke bar upstairs, and a small and crowded discotheque downstairs. Entrance is the price of a drink: 30F and up. **Le Messire** (3 rue Jules-Mercier, tel 03–80–30–16–40) attracts a primarily twentysomething crowd with mixed drinks (30F) and German beers (30F a bottle). It is open until 2 AM. Place de la République is a center of after-hours activity; head to the **Rhumerie (La Jamai**que) (14 pl. de la République, tel. 03–80–73–52–19) for live music, beer, and mixed drinks in a cabanalike environment.

SOUTHERN BURGUNDY

Southern Burgundy's geographical landscape and vineyards are its history, inextricably linked to the religious and political forces that have shaped the social landscape and culture. As a function of the richness of the soil, the kinds of grapes used, the climate, and the knowledge brought to the wine-making process, the wines of this stretch of land have made and unmade fortunes and careers. Towns have arisen and fallen, and along with them great families and related political figures, all under the influence of both the quality and quantity of wine production. Beaune, Chalon-sur-Saône, and Mâcon have become what they are today thanks to the local elixir.

The Côte d'Or, or Gold Slope, as the region is known, is an oenophile's nirvana. Burgundy's most famous vineyards branch out the rolling, rich countryside, which extends from Dijon southward all the way to Mâcon. Basically, there are four great vineyard-covered côtes (slopes or hillsides) in southern Burgundy. The northernmost, the Côte de Nuits, often called the "Champs-Élysées of Burgundy," is the land of the unparalleled Grand Cru reds from the Pinot Noir grape. The Côte de Beaune, just to the south, is known for both full-bodied reds and some of the best dry whites in the world. Even farther south, the Côte Chalonnaise, while not as famous, produces bottle after bottle no less rich than its northern vineyard-kin of the same Chardonnay grape. Finally, the Côte Mâconnaise, the largest of the four côtes, brings its own quality whites to the market.

Throughout the countryside redolent with the distinct mildew unique to wine cellars, in the small sparsely populated towns with big wine names, you can partake in wine tastings. Just look for signs saying DÉGUSTATIONS (tastings).

In addition to the wine producers, there are, of course, the wine experts united in special wine guilds. The most important of these is the much-heralded international **Confrérie des Chevaliers du Tastevin.** This fabled Brotherhood of the Knights of Winetasting has its headquarters and banquet center in the Renaissance **Château du Clos de Vougeot** (tel. 03-80-62-86-09, fax 03-80-62-82-75), residence of the abbots of Cîteaux since the 12th century, in the little town of Vougeot near Gilly-les-Cîteaux. Seize the 20F opportunity to see a film about the Confrérie, an ancient *cave,* huge grape presses, and more. It's open October–March, Sunday–Friday 9–11:30 and 2–5:30, Saturday 9–5; April–September, Sunday–Friday 9–6:30, Saturday 9–5.

The best way to visit the area is by car, though the adventurous might opt to tour along the colorful banks of the Saône or, even better, the dramatic vineyard-lined "Route des Grands Crus" (D122) by bicycle. Most of the towns served by train are rather dull, but most have at least one bike-rental shop where you can pick up a *VTT* (mountain bike) for around 70F–100F a day with a minimum 1,000F deposit (inquire at tourist offices). The landscape, patchwork-quilted by grapevines, is glorious and easy to cover on two wheels. TRANSCO buses (*see* Dijon, *above*) also stop in most of these towns on their way toward Mâcon. Pick up schedules at the Dijon tourist office or the TRANSCO office next to the Dijon train station.

If you like excavated remains of the original 1st-century BC Edouens who inhabited the area, pop by the **Chantiers de Fouilles des Bolards** in Nuits-St-Georges. It's free and open May–October, Wednesday and Sunday 2–6. Most of the artifacts have been moved to the 13F-entrance **museum** (12 rue Camille Rodier, tel./fax 03-80-61-13-10), open April–November, Wednesday–Monday 10–noon and 2–6. Back in Chenôve, not far from Dijon, the **Pressoirs des Ducs de Bourgogne** (rue Roger Salengro, tel. 03-80-52-52-30) exhibit two huge wooden-screw grape presses from the 15th century that can create 20 tons of pressure and turn out 23,000 liters of grape juice a day. They were used until 1926. It's free and open mid-June–September, daily 2–7; call ahead at other times of the year.

South of Beaune, don't skip the **Château de La Rochepot** (tel. 03-80-21-17-37), a private residence perched on a hill, complete with drawbridge, all for 32F. It's open April–June and September–October, Wednesday–Monday 10–11:30 and 2–5:30 (4:30 in October); July and August, Wednesday–Monday 10–noon and 2–6. Five kilometers (3 mi) away, in the half-timber town of Nolay, is one of the oldest **Halles** in France. A 14th-century oak frame that shows its age, it is still used for markets today.

BASICS

Just about every little town has a tourist office or *syndicat d'initiative.* You can count on a wealth of information about the local area, the region, its principal cities, and an overdose of pamphlets about wine. More importantly, if you find yourself in need of a place to eat or sleep, ask at these offices. Most of these villages have restaurants at all price levels, as well as a variety of sleeping accommodations. One of the better ones is the **tourist office of Nuits-St-Georges** (rue Sonoys, tel. 03-80-61-22-47, fax 03-80-61-30-98). It's open mid-September–mid-June, Monday–Saturday 9–noon and 2–6; mid-June–mid-September, Monday–Saturday 10–noon and 2–7, Sunday 9–noon.

BEAUNE

There are two reasons to go to Beaune: to buy wine and to see the **Hôtel Dieu,** which worms its way into just about every Burgundy brochure, showing off its colorfully patterned roof tiles and medieval courtyard. It's easy to get both your cultural and your viticultural fill wandering through the crowded streets of the vieille ville—almost every block contains a minor masterpiece of architectural craftsmanship and a cave with free tastings; the tourist office also has a listing of caves. Expect to do a significant amount of elbowing, however—Beaune is one of Burgundy's star attractions. In July, Beaune celebrates its annual **International Festival of Baroque Music.** Beaune's famous wine festival–auction, **Les Trois Glorieuses,** is held on the third Sunday in November at Les Hospices de Beaune, a former hospital whose origins date from 1443.

BASICS

The swamped but able **tourist office** hands out maps and brochures on Beaune and the wine country, makes hotel reservations (10% of the hotel bill is paid up front at the tourist office) and for no commission changes money when banks are closed. *Pl. de la Halle–1 rue de l'Hôtel-Dieu, tel. 03-80-26-21-30, fax 03-80-26-21-39. From train station, follow av. du 8 Septembre (which becomes rue du Château), walk through pl. Monge and pl. au Beurre to rue Carnot, turn left on rue Monge to pl. de la*

QUAFFING WINE
FROM COTE TO COTE

Throughout the villages of the different côtes, wine tastings abound. Some we've imbibed at include Caveau Napoléon (12 rue Noisot, tel. 03–80–52–45–48) in Fixin, which specializes in the Côte de Nuits-Villages and a Fixin Premier Cru. It's open weekends 10–noon and 2–6; on weekdays, call for an appointment or ring the bell across the way at 9 rue Noisot. Only 2 km (1 mi) south is Gevrey-Chambertin, where you can sample one of 10 wines—including the unusual Crémant de Bourgogne sparkling white—at Caveau du Chapître (1 rue de Paris, tel. 03–80–51–82–82), open Monday 3–7 and Tuesday–Saturday 10–1 and 3–7. Still a couple of miles farther south in the celebrated village of Vougeot, you will come upon the Grand Cave (R.N. 74, tel. 03–80–62–87–13). Open daily 9–7, it offers a trip through the cellars of the old castle of Vougeot as well a chance to try a drop of wine from the barrels of the nearby "clos" (vineyard). Just down the road in the town of Gilly-les-Cîteaux, visit the Maison l'Héritier (rue des Clos Prieurs, tel. 03–80–62–86–58), one of the most distinguished wine houses in the Côte de Nuits, and try the refreshing Aligoté or the Clos de Vougeot Grand Cru. It's open weekdays (except in August) 8–noon and 2–4.

Halle. Open Apr.–Sept., Mon.–Sat. 9–8 (Apr.–mid-June, Mon.–Thurs. 9–7), Sun. 9–7 (9–6 Apr.–mid-June); Oct.–mid-Nov., daily 9–6 (9–7 PM Fri. and Sat.); mid-Nov.–Mar., daily 9–6.

COMING AND GOING

The **train station** (av. du 8 Septembre, tel. 03–80–22–13–13) is a 10-minute walk from town and serves Dijon (20 mins, 37F), Chalon-sur-Saône (20 mins, 31F), and Lyon (2 hrs, 113F) daily. Route **A31** connects Beaune to Dijon, 45 km (28 mi) north; route **N74** is the slower, more-scenic route of the two, but if it's scenery you want, **D122** is the Route des Grands Crus, which meanders through every wine town and village and the thick of the grape-growing fields. This latter road is ideal for cyclists who can pick up a steed at **Bourgogne Randonnées** (7 av. du 8 Septembre, tel. 03–80–22–06–03) for 20F an hour or 90F a day.

WHERE TO SLEEP

Crowds and high prices dominate Beaune's hotel and restaurant scene. Reserve ahead or make a day trip here from Dijon, Chalon-sur-Saône, or one of the nearby wine towns. The **Hôtel Foch** (24 blvd. Foch, tel. 03–80–24–05–65, fax 03–80–24–75–59) on a quiet stretch of the ring road at the northern edge of the city has just nine simple rooms for 160F–200F and a rustic-feeling bar downstairs. **Hôtel Rousseau** (11 pl. Madeleine, tel. 03–80–22–13–59) has 12 old-fashioned rooms and a calm, cool garden on the southeast edge of the town center; singles start at 130F, doubles at 175F. Rates include breakfast, but a shower is an extra 20F. About five minutes north of the city on the route de Dijon (RN74) are two small hotels with extremely hospitable hosts. The **Hôtel Alésia** (4 av. des Sablières, tel. 03–80–22–63–27, fax 03–80–22–45–46) has 15 rooms for 195F–330F, all with bath or shower. The **Hôtel Au Raisin de Bourgogne** (164 rte. De Dijon, tel. 03–80–24–69–48, fax 03–80–24–99–77) has a plush wine bar retreat in addition to its 11 rooms (two without shower) for 175F–290F. Just north of Beaune, **Camping les Cent Vignes** (10 rue Auguste Dubois, tel. 03–80–22–03–91) is mediocre, packed in summer, and closed November to mid-March. Each person pays 16F plus 23F per tent. From place Monge, take rue Lorraine out of town and follow the arrow left for 1 km (½ mi).

FOOD

For traditional local dishes such as escargots (30F per half-dozen) and *jambon persillé* (a ham dish with parsley; 50F), try **Restaurant Grilladine** (17 rue Maufoux, tel. 03–80–22–22–36), closed Monday, which also has menus for 72F and 99F. The family-run **Café l'Hallebarde** (24 bis rue d'Alsace, tel. 03–80–22–07–68), closed Sunday evening and Monday, has a wood-beam ceiling, tile floors, and rustic-looking bar and tables. In summer enjoy a drink on the shady courtyard terrace. Seasonal menus (70F–120F) feature Burgundian classics.

Caveau des Arches (10 blvd. Perpreuil, tel. 03–80–22–10–37), closed Sunday and Monday, a sophisticated 15th-century wine cellar–cum–dining room, has four-course menus (92F–149F) featuring Burgundian specialties. The 1930s-style **Le Gourmandin** (8 pl. Carnot, tel. 03–80–24–07–88), closed Tuesday and Wednesday noon, serves beef bourguignon, duck pie, and other regional fare, accompanied by local wines on the 90F–150F menus. If you are skimping so you can buy a special bottle of wine instead, there are always the **Casino** markets on rue Monge and rue Carnot near the tourist office; they're open Monday–Saturday. Beaune's **markets** are on place de la Halle every Wednesday and Saturday morning.

WORTH SEEING

After visiting the Marché aux Vins (*see below*), head over to **Musée du Vin de Bourgogne** (rue d'Enfer, tel. 03–80–22–08–19), open 9:30–6 daily, in the Hôtel des Ducs, to learn more about wine. The Burgundy Wine Museum traces the history of wine making in excruciating detail with wine presses, bottles, silver taster cups, and an Aubusson tapestry entitled "Wine, source of life and conqueror of death." Check out the wooden statue of the Virgin and a merry Child holding a cluster of grapes in the first room. Your 25F ticket includes entry to all the municipal museums. The **Musée des Beaux-Arts** (rue de l'Hôtel de Ville, tel. 03–80–24–56–92), open April–October, daily 2–6, has a tiny collection of Gallo-Roman and Flemish art, as well as a good 18th-century map of the town. At the same address and especially fascinating, the **Musée Étienne-Jules Marey** (tel. 03–80–24–56–92; same open hrs as above) presents the history and work of Étienne-Jules Marey, the inventor of chronophotography, a precursor to the moving picture. The 12th-century church **Collégiale Notre-Dame** (just off av. de la République) contains five tapestries narrating the life of the Virgin, as well as 15th-century frescoes of the resurrection of Lazarus. They're viewable April–mid-November, Sunday afternoon–Saturday; for open hours, call the tourist office (*see* Basics, *above*).

Chancellor and tax collector Nicolas Rolin, hoping to get a ticket to heaven, founded the hospital **Hôtel-Dieu** with his wife, Guigone de Solins, in 1443. Its attractions include the Salle des Pôvres, with hospital beds parked back-to-back, a pharmacy and kitchen, and many works of art. Especially notable is Rogier van der Weyden's (1399–1464) polyptych *The Last Judgment,* a divine example of *art primitif,* a style popular right before the Renaissance. The intense colors and mind-tripping imagery were meant to scare the illiterate patients into religious submission. Notice the touch of misogyny; more women are going to hell than to heaven, while Christ, the judge, remains completely unmoved. For 40F there is a relaxing English sound-and-light show in the courtyard April–November after 10 PM (check for specific times). *Rue de l'Hôtel-Dieu, tel. 03–80–24–45–00. Admission 32F. Open Apr.–mid-Nov., daily 9–6:30; mid-Nov.–Mar., daily 9–11:30 and 2–5:30.*

The best deal for wine is at the **Marché aux Vins,** housed in a 13th- to 15th-century former church, where 50F (which includes the price of the cup you get to keep, known as a *tastevin*) sets you loose in low-lit musty tunnels filled to the brim with bottles of 18 of the best Burgundian wines. People also dillydally upstairs where the really good stuff is kept, notably a Corton *grand cru* (world-renowned, high-quality wine). Although food is officially prohibited, many visitors smuggle in a pocketful of crackers. There is cheaper tasting to be had in town, but nothing on this scale. *Rue Nicolas-Rolin, across from Hôtel-Dieu, tel. 03–80–25–08–20. Open daily 9:30–noon and 2–6.*

Just because the Marché aux Vins has the most open bottles doesn't mean it's the only ticket in town. The tourist office has a list of registered caves and what they offer, but you can do nearly as well on your own, wandering the streets and checking out every place with a DÉGUSTATION sign. The following are a few friendly joints. For 20F, you can try the Beaune-Grèves Premier Cru and five other *appellations* in the 13th-century former cloister, which now houses the **Caves Réunies du Couvent des Cordeliers** (6 rue de l'Hôtel-Dieu, tel. 03–80–24–53–79), open April–September, daily 9:30–7 (closed for lunch in the winter). The **Caves Patriarche** (7 rue du Collège, tel. 03–80–24–53–78) are the largest in Burgundy, and the extensive tour, complete with the opportunity to taste 13 crus, is well worth the 50F. It's open daily 9:30–11:30 and 2–5:30. It isn't for nothing that 150,000 people a year have visited the wine cellars of **Reine Pédauque** (Porte St-Nicolas, tel. 03–80–22–23–11). A trip through the labyrinth storage areas, as well as the commented sipping of four wines, runs 30F (and includes the glass). Just outside town, the cave of **Albert Ponnelle** (38 Faubourg St-Nicolas, on the road to Nuits-St-Georges, tel. 03–80–22–00–05) has one of the best assortments of Beaune wines, including a Beaune Premier Cru. It's open weekdays 8–noon and 2–6 and weekends (summers only) 9–7.

Finally, if you are fan of the kir (crème de cassis mixed with white wine) and need some ingredients, head over to **Védrenne** (28 rue Carnot, tel. 03–80–22–16–30), the cream of the crèmes.

CHALON-SUR-SAÔNE

Neglected and tourist-hungry, Chalon-sur-Saône has a hard time trying to prove it's more than a pit stop, and the Mac trucks that look committed to flattening it don't help. With a little patience, however, you might find it a pleasant enough base for exploring the **Côte Chalonnaise,** which produces five grand crus: Mercurey, Montagny, Bouzeron, Givry, and Rully. The best time to pedal around is mid-July to mid-August, when local farms hold a festival-like open house, offering wine, cheese, and fruit. The town, birthplace of photography, has a **museum of photography,** some photogenic pedestrian streets, old houses, and a **rose garden** (across the Saône River from the centre ville) that is one of the largest and most beautiful in Europe. Chalon also boasts three magical annual festivals: **Carnaval** hits town in full fest for two weeks starting at the end of February and takes over with full New Orleans–style parades and masked balls; the early summer Pentecost weekend **Festival de Montgolfière** brings hundreds and hundreds of hot air ballooners from all over Europe to the Côte Chalonnaise for a colorful rally in the skies; the end of July sees thousands of artists from around the world gather for one extended weekend at the **Chalon Dans la Rue.**

BASICS

The **tourist office** has maps and brochures of the region, including a detailed map (5F) of the Côte Chalonnaise. The friendly people behind the desk are happy to recommend day trips to neighboring villages, make hotel reservations (15F), and change money (for a hefty 50F commission) when banks are closed. There is some information also available at www.chalon-saone.cci.fr. *Sq. Chabas–Blvd. de la République, tel. 03–85–48–37–97, fax 03–85–48–63–55. From train station, walk down av. Jean-Jaurès to the start of blvd. de la République. Open July–Aug., Mon.–Sat. 9–12:30 and 1:30–7:30, Sun. 10:30–12:30 and 3–6; Sept.–June, Mon.–Sat. 9–12:30 and 1:30–6:30, Sun. 10–noon.*

COMING AND GOING

Chalon-sur-Saône is 69 km (43 mi) south of Dijon via toll route A6. The **train station** (pl. de la Gare) is in the southwestern part of town. To reach the centre ville from the station, take avenue Jean-Jaurès to boulevard de la République. Trains run daily to Dijon (45 mins, 58F), Tournus (15 mins, 27F), and

Mâcon (45 mins, 52F). **SNCF** (tel. 03–85–44–61–45) and other bus companies based in the station right next door have connections to Cluny (1½ hrs, 46F). **Autocars Girardot** has seven-seat vans that do excursions all over Burgundy by reservation (tel. 03–85–45–85–85, fax 03–85–45–85–74). **Europe Vélos** (12 rue Michelet, tel. 03–85–48–14–81) rents bikes for 80F per day or 150F for a three-day weekend including Monday (plus a 1,000F cash-only deposit). It is closed on Monday.

INTERNET ACCESS

Desperately need to read your E-mail? Check out **Undernet Café** (8 rue des Poulets, tel. 03–85–48–74–88). With both Macs and PCs, this mix of a new market with an old-fashioned bar feel is a winner. You pay 20F for the first 30 minutes (minimum) or 35F for one hour and then in 15-minute blocks after that (or 150F for one month's unlimited access). It's open Monday–Saturday 9 AM–1 AM, Sunday 11 AM–1 AM.

WHERE TO SLEEP

The **Hôtel Au Saint Pierre** (10 pl. de l'Hôtel de Ville, tel. 03–85–48–44–92) is far and away the best deal in town in this couldn't-be-more-central location. All 20 rooms go for 110F–160F. **Hôtel le Kiosque** (10 rue des Jacobines, tel. 03–85–48–12–24, fax 03–85–46–47–80) has 28 comfortable doubles for 155F to 170F. The same owners manage the nearby, upscale **Hôtel Clarine** (35 pl. de Beaune, tel. 03–85–48–70–43, fax 03–85–48–71–18) with doubles running 265F–295F and an automatic key distribution machine for very late arrivals. The **Hôtel Aux Vendanges de Bourgogne** (21 rue du Général-Leclerc, tel. 03–85–48–01–90) has old-world rooms (150F–240F) upstairs from an almost art-deco-y *crêperie Bretonne.* The nearby **Hôtel Central** (19 pl. de Beaune, tel. 03–85–48–35–00, fax 03–85–93–10–20) is a definite step up in quality (doubles are 200F–220F) and has a very amiable staff. If it's late and you're ready for a splurge, the **Hôtel St-Georges** (32 av. Jean-Jaurès, tel. 03–85–48–27–05, fax 03–85–93–23–88) is close to the train station and the town center. Its modern, spacious rooms (380F–470F) are above the cozy **restaurant** where you can indulge in dishes like foie gras with truffles and roast pigeon (110F–180F). **Camping de la Butte** (17 rue Julien Leneveu, tel./fax 03–85–48–38–86), east of the Saône, is a large, grassy tract by the river; it charges 22F per site, plus 17F per person, and is open year-round.

HOSTEL • The withered-looking **Auberge de Jeunesse** is sandwiched between an ugly velodrome and the pleasant Saône River. A dorm bed costs 47F; breakfast is an extra 19F, and sheets are 20F. The reception is closed on Monday evenings mid-September–mid-March. *Rue d'Amsterdam, tel./fax 03–85–46–62–77. From train station, take av. Jean-Jaurès (which becomes blvd. de la République), turn right on rue du Général-Leclerc to the river, left on quai des Messageries; rue d'Amsterdam is on your right. 82 beds. Reception 7 AM–10 AM and 6:30 PM–10:30 PM. Kitchen. Closed mid-Dec.–mid-Jan. and Mon. nights mid-Sept.–mid-Mar.*

The new **Foyer des Jeunes Travailleurs** is a long walk or short bus ride from the train station (Bus 1 or 6 to the Monnot stop) and not cheap (117F per person including breakfast). That said, the cafeteria serves good cheap dinners for 41F. *18 av. Pierre Nugues, tel. 03–85–46–44–90, fax 03–85–41–42–75. From the station follow the flow of traffic down av. Jean-Jaurès (which becomes blvd. de la République) through pl. de Beaune and then out rue de Belfort into av. Monnot; at the traffic circle, rue Pierre Nugues is on the right, as is the Foyer. Reception Mon.–Sat. 8–6:30 and Sat. 9–11:30 AM.*

FOOD

Chalon's food scene is nothing to brag about, but in the centre ville you can at least find cheap meals. The best places to look are on place St-Vincent and on rue de Strasbourg on the Ile-St-Laurent just across the bridge to the south of the old town. The **Café du Verre Galant** (8 pl. St-Vincent, tel. 03–85–93–09–87) has some of the best meals in town. A huge menu with entrées like baked veal (66F), salad, dessert, and a glass of wine keeps the Galant packed—call for a reservation. It's closed Sunday, Monday, and the month of October. At **Le Cupidon** (57–59 rue de Strasbourg, tel. 03–85–48–08–18). The large southern terrace makes its good 75F menu sparkle just that much more. **Le P'tit Bouchon** (9 pl. St-Laurent, tel. 03–85–93–33–76) always draws a crowd with its traditional Burgundian fare at 85F for three services. It is closed Saturday noon and Monday. Elsewhere in the city, the **Crêperie le Rétro** (21 rue du Général-Leclerc, tel. 03–85–48–01–90), closed Sunday, serves crepes and galettes (18F–45F). **Le Petit Comptoir d'à Côté** (32 av. Jean-Jaurès, tel. 03–85–93–44–26) has a 60F buffet that will appease both vegetarians and carnivores. Just down the street from the train station is a large **Casino** supermarket open Monday–Saturday 8:30–8. There's also the big **Prisunic** on place Général de Gaulle; it's open Monday–Saturday 8:30–7:30. **Market** days are Friday morning (food) on place St-Vincent, all day (clothes) on place de Beaune, and Sunday morning (food and regional products) on place St-Vincent.

WORTH SEEING

The **Musée Nicéphore Nièpce** (28 quai des Messageries, tel. 03–85–48–41–98), honoring the Chalonnais who invented photography, is worth the 14F entrance fee. It has exhibits of contemporary photography, the history of photography, and cameras, including the first one ever created. Opening hours are September–June, Wednesday–Monday 9:30–11:30 and 2:30–5:30, and July–August, Wednesday–Monday, 10–6. The **Cathédrale St-Vincent** (pl. St-Vincent), three blocks from the Saône River and a few blocks upriver from the Nièpce Museum, has intricately sculpted stonework in the choir and several wooden statues. The cathedral looks out over lovely place St-Vincent in the heart of old half-timbered Chalon. On selected Thursday in July and August, there is a nighttime guided tour through the area for 50F. Reserve at the tourist office. The **Musée Denon** (pl. de l'Hôtel de Ville, tel. 03–85–90–50–50) in the centre ville has an impressive collection of art, from Gallo-Roman bronzes to 19th-century paintings and furniture. Entrance is 12F; it is open year-round, Wednesday–Sunday 9:30–noon and 2–5:30. Finally, don't miss the **Roseraie** (rose garden) in the **Parc de Loisirs St-Nicolas.** With 600 varieties and more than 26,000 actual plants, this garden is a floral paradise.

CLUNY

The **Abbaye de Cluny** was founded in AD 909 and reached its peak in the 12th century, when more than 10,000 Cluniac monks followed its orders in hundreds of affiliated "daughter abbeys" throughout Europe. The tiny town that formed around it still has some old houses, but the abbey is the reason to come here. The basilica, a symbol of the order's wealth and power, was built between 1088 and 1130 and was the world's largest church before St. Peter's was built in Rome. Sadly, little remains other than magnificent ruins. In the 14th century, Cluny began to lose its importance, and at the end of the 16th century, during the Wars of Religion between the Protestants and Catholics, it was ransacked and pillaged. By the 18th century, the abbey was nothing more than a rich merchant's stone quarry.

BASICS

The **tourist office** has maps and brochures and makes hotel reservations. It also changes money when the banks are closed. *6 rue Mercière, tel. 03–85–59–05–34, fax 03–85–59–06–95. From the VILLE bus stop, take rue de Paris with the Abbaye on your right, then go left on pl. du Commerce (which becomes rue Lamartine); tourist office is ahead on the left. Open Oct.–June, Mon.–Sat., 10–12:30 and 2:30–7 (until 6 Nov.–Mar.); July–Sept., daily 10–7.*

COMING AND GOING

SNCF buses arrive six times a day from Mâcon (45 mins, 25F) and five times daily from Chalon-sur-Saône (1½ hrs, 46F). Trains from Dijon will take you as far as Chalon-sur-Saône (45 mins, 58F). Once you're at Cluny, bikes can be rented from **Association "Le Pont"** (Camping Saint Vital, tel. 03–85–59–08–34) for 10F an hour, 40F a day, or 60F a weekend (plus 200F deposit). It's open mid-May–October, Monday, Wednesday, Friday, and Saturday 9–noon and 2–6 (7 on Wednesday and Saturday) and Tuesday and Thursday 1–6.

WHERE TO SLEEP

The **Hôtel du Commerce** (8 pl. du Commerce, tel. 03–85–59–03–09, fax 03–85–59–00–87) has attentive management and 17 comfortable rooms, with singles going for 110F and doubles for 140F without shower and 200F with. Farther up the same street, the **Restaurant-Pension Candy** (38 rue du Merle, tel./fax 03–85–59–29–63) has 10 small rooms (150F–250F) hidden above a quaint restaurant. The **Hôtel de l'Abbaye** (av. Charles-de-Gaulle, tel. 03–85–59–11–14, fax 03–85–59–09–76), a simple hotel-restaurant on the outskirts of town (a five-minute walk), has nice doubles for 190F–320F but is closed Sunday night, Monday, and mid-January–mid-February. The **Hostellerie du Potin Gourmand** (4 pl. du Champ de Foire, west of town just off rue d'Avril, tel. 03–85–59–02–06, fax 03–85–59–22–58) has three rooms that run 250F–350F. It is closed Sunday night and Monday. A budget traveler's haven is **Cluny Séjour** (rue Porte de Paris, right next to the bus stop, tel. 03–85–59–08–83, fax 03–85–59–26–27). Its 71 beds in 23 rooms go for 76F a night including breakfast. Reserve in advance. For camping, **St-Vital** (rte. Azé, Les Griottons, tel. 03–85–59–08–34) costs 17F per person plus 10F per site and is open May–

September. It is about 1 km (½ mi) outside town; cross the Grosne River on the main drag (rue de la Levée by the river) and watch for the campground on your right. The views toward town are wonderful, especially in the evening, despite the din of the superfast train tracks behind it.

FOOD

For such a small and out-of-the-way place, Cluny has a good collection of traditional Burgundian meals. The **Café du Centre** (4 rue Municipale, behind the tourist office, tel. 03–85–59–10–65) is a classic one-room brasserie with a fine assortment of daily specials, usually meat, for 50F–60F. The nearby **Brasserie du Nord** (pl. de l'Abbaye, tel. 03–85–59–09–96) has a little of everything (for around 100F) including a gorgeous view of the Abbaye from the upstairs dining area. On the main drag, the broad terrace area of **La Nation** (21 rue Lamartine, tel. 03–85–59–04–45), closed Sunday, offers dinner menus for 68F–110F. **La Renaissance** (47 rue Mercière, tel. 03–85–59–01–58), closed Monday evening, is a casual, small-town, family-style restaurant at the center of town. For beef-eaters craving a real steak, stop by the **Auberge du Cheval Blanc** (1 rue Porte de Mâcon, tel. 03–85–59–01–13), closed Friday evening and Saturday. Classic dishes, like a true *pavé charolais* (thick cut of the famous local steer), in an authentic old-fashioned setting will tame the carnivore within. Finally, dessert lovers shouldn't miss **Au Péché Mignon** (rue Lamartine, tel. 03–85–59–11–21) for Cluny's best ice cream, pastries, and even chocolate-dipped orange slices. There is an **ATAC** supermarket five minutes south of the center on avenue Charles-de-Gaulle; it is open Tuesday–Saturday 8:45–12:15 and 2:30–7:15 and on Sunday mornings. Saturday the weekly market comes to Cluny.

WORTH SEEING

Visitors from all over the world come to see this once-impressive monument and often leave grumbling, in various languages, "Is this all that's left?" But what remains is interesting, and the guided tours give an idea of the enormous size of the original layout. The price of admission gets you into the **Abbaye** as well as the **Musée Ochier d'Art et d'Archéologie de Cluny,** housed in the 15th-century abbey palace, with fragments from the church's central portal. *Tours leave from Musée Ochier, tel. 03–85–59–23–97 (Abbaye tel. 03–85–59–12–79). Admission 32F. Open July–Sept., daily 9–7; shorter hrs off-season.*

For the "neigh"-sayers, well worth a trot is the **Haras National** (tel. 03–85–59–85–00). Created by Napoléon 1er, it is where 70 or so magnificent stallions are luxuriously stabled. The Haras can be visited for free year-round 9–7.

MACON

At the southern end of Burgundy, only 72 km (47 mi) north of Lyon, Mâcon already starts to display the accent of the *midi* (southern France). Perhaps it's the warmer climate that puts smiles on people's faces. Lacking the historical weight of surrounding towns, this colorful city bubbles with cafés, shops, and restaurants. Mâcon is also the capital of the Saône et Loire département and serves as a good transportation hub if you plan to explore the Mâconnais and Beaujolais wine regions.

BASICS

The new **tourist office** is chock-full of pamphlets about Mâcon and the surrounding cities of the département. The engaging staff will reserve a room for 15F, offer detailed maps of the city, and provide decent information on the Mâconnais wine country. From the train station, head straight down rue Gambetta and turn left on rue Carnot. *1 pl. St-Pierre, tel. 03–85–21–07–07, fax 03–85–40–96–00. Open June–Sept., Mon.–Sat. 10–7, Sun. 2–6; Oct.–May, Mon.–Sat. 10–6.*

For **Internet access,** go to the **Bar Victor Hugo,** where for 60F per minute, you can get at all the cyber info and E-mail you crave. *37 rue Victor Hugo, tel./fax 03–85–39–29–15. Open daily until 1 AM.*

COMING AND GOING

The **train station** (pl. de la Gare) is in the southwest corner of town, on a line that runs from Mâcon through Tournus (20 mins, 34F) and Chalon-sur-Saône (30 mins, 52F), to Dijon (1 hr, 87F). The Saône River forms the eastern boundary of the small centre ville. **La Navette Speciale** (2 rue de l'Épée, tel. 03–85–38–49–52) has vans that shuttle tourists on special-request excursions for a pretty penny; rates depend on how far you go and whether you hire a tour guide.

WHERE TO SLEEP AND EAT

The **Hôtel Escatel** (4 rue de la Liberté, tel. 03–85–29–02–50, fax 03–85–34–19–97) has 72 rooms, starting at 100F for a single and 140F for a double; there is also a pool. The classy restaurant in the hotel serves Burgundian specialties and menus from 52F. Closer into town, and not far from the tourist office, **Le Relais Fleuri** (26–28 rue des Minimes, tel./fax 03–85–38–36–02) has 21 simple rooms for 110F–200F, only four of which have showers. Straight up the hill, the lovely half-timbered **Hôtel-Restaurant Le Charollais** (71 rue Rambuteau, tel. 03–85–38–36–23) has a few rooms for 110F–155F. The comfortable restaurant has three menus (73F, 120F, and 185F) specializing in regional specialties. Both hotel and restaurant are closed on Sunday evening, Monday, and in June. Around the corner you can also find **Le Concorde** (73 rue Lacretelle, tel. 03–85–34–21–47, fax 03–85–29–21–79). Doubles run 120F–185F in this very clean and quiet family-run establishment. Closer to the train station is **La Boiserie** (56–58 rue Victor Hugo, tel. 03–85–38–00–90). The reception is in the bar downstairs, as are the breakfast (28F), dinner if you give prior warning (menu is 49F), and a lot of local character. The nine rooms upstairs are 165F–215F.

Other choices by the waterfront include the **Hôtel Beaujolais** (86–88 pl. de la République, tel. 03–85–38–42–06, fax 03–85–38–78–02), which faces the Pont de St-Laurent. Front rooms run 180F–245F for doubles. **Camping Mâcon** (rte. Nationale 6, tel. 03–85–38–16–22, fax 03–85–39–39–18) is next to an industrial zone and packed with German tourists, but 8F per site and an extra 18F per person will get you a cheap patch of grass. From the tourist office, follow the banks of the river north and continue along quai Maréchal de Lattre de Tassigny, which becomes avenue du Général de Gaulle; the campground is on the right.

Along the waterfront, the **quai Lamartine** has a run of theme restaurants and bars, all of which will gladly serve a dinner menu for 50F–100F, or a *plat du jour* or pizza for 50F, and a cocktail for 25F–40F. For something a little more local, try **Le Charolais** (71 rue Rambuteau, tel. 03–85–38–36–23), closed Sunday evening and Monday, where a taste of Burgundy's gastronomy will run you 73F–185F. Farther north along the river the restaurant of the **Maison Mâconnaise des Vins** (484 av. Maréchal de Lattre de Tassigny, tel. 03–85–38–62–51) serves appetizers (20F–35F), main dishes with a heaping side of sauerkraut (40F–65F), and desserts (15F–20F).

WORTH SEEING

While in town, check out the **Musée des Ursulines** (5 rue des Ursulines, off pl. de la Baille, tel. 03–85–39–90–38), which has collections of prehistoric and Gallo-Roman art, regional art, and paintings from Le Brun to Monet, Corot, and more contemporary artists. If you're a fan of French poet and politician Alphonse de Lamartine, the **Musée Lamartine**, also called the Hôtel Sénecé (41 rue Sigorgne, tel. 03–85–39–30–38), tells the story of his life. Admission to either museum is 15F or 20F for both; both are open Wednesday–Monday 10–noon and 2–6 (afternoons only on Sunday). During the third week in May, Mâcon hosts the **Foire Nationale des Vins de France,** a weeklong extravaganza of wine tastings and expositions. During the summer **L'Été Frappé** rules the town with free musical events on all occasions. This period is begun in June with the **Festival des Conteurs,** devoted entirely to storytelling.

GRENOBLE AND THE ALPS

UPDATED BY CHRISTOPHER KNOWLES

O ne of the world's most important mountain ranges, revered by mountaineers, skiers, and tourists, the Alps should not be left out of any French itinerary. Studded with tiny, unfrequented towns and surging from one billowy mountaintop to another, the Alps manage to overrun the borders of eight European countries in a gallant sweep from the tip of the Riviera to Germany in the north, Austria to the northeast, and Italy and Slovenia to the east. This area can be a little difficult to explore, but any difficulties you encounter traveling in the Alps will be immediately forgotten when you experience their overwhelming beauty. Chamonix, at the foot of Mont Blanc (Europe's highest peak, at 15,863 ft), has one of Europe's most impressive examples of glaciers and peaks that you can easily reach by train.

The possibilities for exploring the Alps are endless, from hiking in September to skiing in July to sipping hot wine in the sauna of a chalet in December. Although Grenoble serves as a good springboard for getting to the Alps, cities like Annecy, Bourg-St-Maurice, and Chamonix, which is actually already in the Alps, will work just as well. The lesser-known Vercors mountains, southwest of the Alps, are little explored and well worth the trip from Grenoble or Valence (*see* Chapter 10) if limestone caves and gorges, hairy cliff-hanger roads, or the history of the World War II resistance interests you. If not, you can always take advantage of the year-round skiing in Tignes, whisk yourself to the lofty slopes of the Val d'Isère, or explore the wild habitat of France's oldest park, the Parc National de la Vanoise.

GRENOBLE

Grenoble, the capital of the Dauphiné (Lower Alps) region, sits at the confluence of the Isère and Drac rivers and lies nestled within three *massifs* (mountain ranges): La Chartreuse, Le Vercors, and Belledonne. This cosmopolitan city gets a great deal of its energy from its large, international student population; its university hosts a number of foreign (mostly British and American) as well as French students. The major nuclear research station perched on the banks of the Drac and the Hewlett-Packard aircraft company headquarters also contribute a diverse business class to the population.

Native Grenoblois, known for their down-home friendliness, consider themselves mountain people. The ancient village of **St-Hugues,** once a separate community and now lined with antiques shops and art

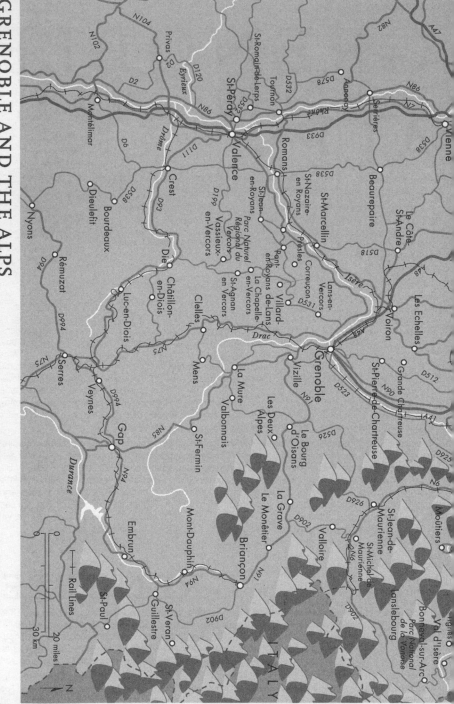

GRENOBLE AND THE ALPS

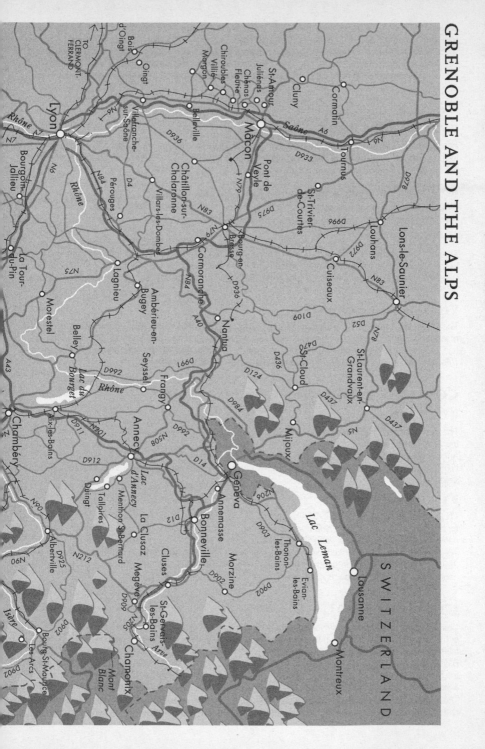

galleries, has an active arts scene. Across the river, the heart of Grenoble pulsates around its *vieille ville* (old town), once enclosed by a Roman wall and now a collection of small squares—place de Gordes, place St-André, and place aux Herbes. The squares are filled with open markets in the morning and beer-drinking students in the evening. The 19th-century writer and music critic Stendhal remains the town's most celebrated citizen, although people are generally surprised if you know who he is.

BASICS

BUREAU DE CHANGE

The **Comptoir Grenoblois de Change** has slightly better rates than the banks or post office, and it's close to the tourist office. The owner closes up tight 12:30–2 and all day Sunday. *5 rue Philis de la Charce, tel. 04–76–51–33–76.*

LAUNDRY

At **Lavomatique,** washes cost 12F, and dryers 10F for 10 minutes. *14 rue Thiers, tel. 04–76–46–37–58. Open daily 7 AM–10 PM.*

MAIL

There's a post office just outside the train station (*see* Coming and Going, *below*) on your right and next to the tourist office. The **central post office** is near the Parc Paul Mistral and tram stop Hôtel de Ville (Line A). It handles poste restante (postal code 38000) and changes money. *7 blvd. Maréchal-Lyautey, tel. 04–76–43–51–39. Open weekdays 8:15–6:45, Sat. 8–noon.*

VISITOR INFORMATION

The **Office de Tourisme** in the center of town gives out Grenoble maps and brochures, makes hotel reservations, sells tickets to local events, and leads daily guided tours of the city (45F). The office also has an in-house SNCF and VFD (the regional bus company) information booth. *14 rue de la République, tel. 04–76–42–41–41. Open Mon.–Sat. 9–12:30 and 1:30–7.*

COMING AND GOING

BY TRAIN

The very busy **train station** (pl. de la Gare, tel. 08–36–35–35–35), on the western edge of town, serves the Alps and sends frequent trains to Paris (3 hrs, 370F by TGV), Bourg-St-Maurice (2 hrs, 129F), Annecy (2½ hrs, 87F), Chambéry (1 hr, 55F), Chamonix (4 hrs, 172F), Lyon (1¼ hrs, 94F), and Nice (10 hrs, 310F). The station is open all night, with an ATM machine that takes Visa, Plus, and Cirrus cards.

BY BUS

The **gare routière** (tel. 04–76–87–90–31), or bus station, right next to the train station, is the central hub for the three bus lines that serve Grenoble. **Intercars** (tel. 04–76–46–19–77) serves international destinations like Barcelona (9 hrs, 289F) and London (15 hrs, 550F). **VFD** (square Docteur-Martin, tel. 04–76–47–77–77) has regular service to Annecy (2 hrs, 93F), Geneva (3 hrs, 143F), and Nice (7 hrs, 299F). The VFD information booth in the station is open weekdays 7:20 AM–6:30 PM and Saturday 8–noon and 2–5; the other booths close an hour earlier and usually during lunch.

GETTING AROUND

Grenoble's layout is maddening; your only hope lies in the big, illuminated maps posted throughout town or the free map of Grenoble from the tourist office or TAG office outside the train station. Use the mountains for orientation: The sheer Vercors plateau is behind the train station; the Chartreux, topped by the Bastille and *téléphérique* (cable car), are on the other side of the Isère River; and the distant peaks of the Belledonne are behind the park. Sights, hotels, restaurants, and nightspots are all within the boundaries of these landmarks.

The heart of Grenoble forms a crescent around a bend of the Isère, with the train station at the western end and the university all the way at the eastern tip. As it fans out from the river toward the south, the

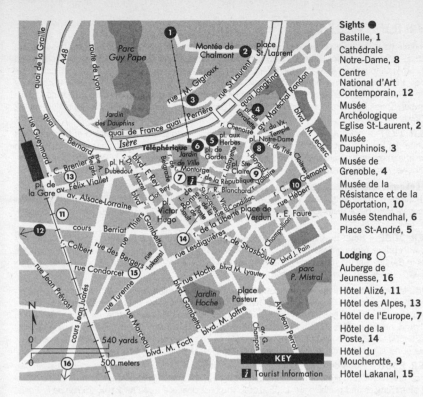

Sights ●

Bastille, **1**

Cathédrale
Notre-Dame, **8**

Centre
National d'Art
Contemporain, **12**

Musée
Archéologique
Eglise St-Laurent, **2**

Musée
Dauphinois, **3**

Musée de
Grenoble, **4**

Musée de la
Résistance et de la
Déportation, **10**

Musée Stendhal, **6**

Place St-André, **5**

Lodging ○

Auberge de
Jeunesse, **16**

Hôtel Alizé, **11**

Hôtel des Alpes, **13**

Hôtel de l'Europe, **7**

Hôtel de la
Poste, **14**

Hôtel du
Moucherotte, **9**

Hôtel Lakanal, **15**

---

crescent seems to develop a more modern flavor. **Place Victor Hugo,** with its flowers, fountains, and cafés, is the hub of the city, though most sights and nightlife are near the Isère in **place St-André, place de Gordes,** and **place Notre-Dame; avenue Alsace-Lorraine,** a major pedestrian street lined with modern shops, cuts right through it. Taxis line up in front of the train station and on place Victor Hugo, or call 04–76–54–42–54.

BY BUS

The 21 efficient bus lines of Grenoble's **Transports de l'Agglomération Grenobloise** (TAG; tel. 04–76–20–66–66) cover every corner of the city. Place Victor Hugo is the central point from which to catch most buses. Tickets cost 8F onboard or 53F for a book of 10 at any TAG office (there's one outside the train station). Tickets are valid for an hour and can be used for the tram. A 23F ticket available from the automatic dispensers around town is good for one day of unlimited travel on the bus and tram. Buses usually run 6 AM–10 PM, but hours vary from line to line and are often cut short in summer.

BY TRAM

TAG also runs a tram system with roughly the same hours. Both Lines A and B run parallel to each other from the train station along avenue Alsace-Lorraine to the tourist office, where Line B splits northeast toward the Isère and the university (Line A continues south toward Parc Mistral). The blue-and-silver trams come every three minutes or so and take the same tickets as the bus.

BY BIKE

Being one of the flattest cities in France makes Grenoble perfect for biking, and bike lanes run alongside most main streets. The **Mistral Shop** (13 pl. Ste-Claire, tel. 04–76–51–11–50), across from the tourist office, rents mountain bikes from 120F per day, and **Borel Sports** (42 av. Alsace-Lorraine, tel. 04–76–46–47–46) charges 90F for regular bikes.

WHERE TO SLEEP

Most hotels near the train station have jacked-up prices; cheaper lodging can be found between the train station and place Victor Hugo. It's easy to find a room in summer (July–September), but you should call ahead in October and May. If all rooms haven't been taken by monthly residents, women can try **Le Foyer de l'Étudiante** (4 rue Ste-Ursule, tel. 04–76–42–00–84), an 85-room dorm with a kitchen, TV room, and laundry facilities; singles are 95F, doubles 145F. Men *and* women can stay mid-June to mid-September. Space in a dormitory room with multiple beds may be granted for 70F, sheets included. Ask about lower weekly rates.

UNDER 175F • Hôtel Alizé. Top to bottom, floor to ceiling, this hotel is decorated entirely in black and white. Its location just south of the station as you exit to the right makes it especially popular, so reserve ahead or show up around 10 AM. Singles go for 120F, doubles begin at 160F, and all rooms have a TV. Showers are free. *1 rue A. Courbet, tel. 04–76–43–12–91. 35 rooms, some with bath.*

Hôtel Lakanal. The rooms here are some of the shabbiest, but 120F–160F will get you a double in a quiet hotel next to markets, bars, and cheap sandwich stands. Showers are 15F. It's also just a five-minute walk from place Victor Hugo. *26 rue des Bergers, tel. 04–76–46–03–42. 27 rooms, 4 with bath. Cash only.*

UNDER 200F • Hôtel de L'Europe. In the center of Grenoble this warm and comfortable hotel has rooms with prices ranging from 150F for a double with a sink to 260F for one with bath. Although the hotel is in the heart of the café and bar district, the rooms are all soundproofed. *22 pl. Grenette, tel./fax 04–76–46–16–94. 46 rooms, 30 with bath.*

Hôtel du Moucherotte. The animated older gentleman who runs this pleasant 18th-century apartment-cum-hotel is very *chauvin* (jingoistic) about Grenoble and will tell you all you need to know about its history and pop culture. The hotel itself is in the artsy-antiquey area close to nightlife, cafés, and both tram lines. Large, bright doubles with shower are 194F. A warning: There are no hall showers. *1 rue Auguste-Gaché, tel. 04–76–54–61–40, fax 04–76–44–62–52. From station, tram Line B to pl. Ste-Claire and look for blue HÔTEL sign between cathedral and covered market. 19 rooms, 9 with bath.*

UNDER 250F • Hôtel de la Poste. High ceilings, antique furniture, free showers, good mattresses, and a central location make this the best deal in town. From the station, take either tram to the Félix-Poulat stop. Singles and doubles are 120F–160F; the best deal is a quad for 210F. *25 rue de la Poste, tel. 04–76–46–67–25. 8 rooms, 2 with bath.*

SPLURGE • Hôtel des Alpes. This modest hotel escapes being average thanks to its reasonably comfortable rooms with Skai armchairs and attractive wallpaper, calm ambience (windows overlooking the street are double-glazed), and, above all, handy location midway between the station and downtown. Doubles average 230F–290F. *45 av. Félix-Viallet, tel. 04–76–87–00–71, fax 04–76–56–95–45. 67 rooms with bath.*

HOSTEL

Auberge de Jeunesse. A 12-minute ride south of town, this well-equipped hostel is a good place to meet fellow travelers en route to the mountains. It might end up a cozier encounter than you planned, though, in light of the shoeboxlike dorm rooms crammed with four to six bunk beds (68F with breakfast). The management tries to make up for it with a bar, Ping-Pong table, soccer field, TV room, and self-service restaurant. The 11 PM curfew is actually cut short by the last bus from town at 9 PM. HI membership is required; there's no age limit. *18 av. du Grésivaudan, Echirolles, tel. 04–76–09–33–52. From center, Bus 1 or 8 to Quinzaine. 120 beds. Reception open 7:30–11. Laundry. Cash only.*

FOOD

Grenoble's culinary specialty is anything that has to do with *noix* (walnuts), from cakes and candies to wine and sauces. Especially good is the *salade campagnarde* (country salad) with goat cheese, walnuts, croutons, and sometimes bacon. *Sassenage,* a blue cheese named after the Grenoble suburb, is the region's favorite cheese.

The small streets between place Notre-Dame and place St-André are filled with hole-in-the-wall restaurants that serve anything from Indian to Moroccan food; there are also stands that serve sandwiches and *donner-kebabs* (unleavened bread filled with slices of lamb and salad) for under 25F. For picnic supplies, hit **Prisunic** (22 rue Lafayette, tel. 04–76–54–33–64), across from the tourist office. Grenoble's large **covered market,** also across from the tourist office, is open 8–noon Tuesday–Sunday. The **Marché**

aux Fruits ice cream stand on rue D. Raoult, just off place de Gordes, carries more than 20 flavors of homemade ice cream.

UNDER 75F • Le Valgo. Specialties of the Hautes-Alpes (Upper Alps) are served here family-style, outdoors or on calico-covered tables inside. The *ravioles* (potatoes, eggs, and herbs baked into long batons) come in big bowls. The *oreilles d'ânes* ("donkeys' ears," or ravioles stuffed with spinach in a delicate cream sauce) are well worth the 45F. *2 rue St-Hugues, off pl. Notre-Dame, tel. 04–76–51–38–85. Closed Sun. and Mon. No dinner Tues. or Wed.*

La Belle Étoile. Popular with large groups, this Tunisian place serves couscous for 35F–55F. Red-check tablecloths and wooden beams give the place an atmosphere that outdoes the cheap prices. Appetizers include *briks* (similar to crepes) filled with beef and cheese, ham and egg, or tuna and tomato; and a generous tabbouleh salad. *2 rue de Lionne, off quai Jongkind near pont St-Laurent, tel. 04–76–51–00–40.*

Le Petit Creux. On the neon-lit strip on the north bank of the Isère, this pizzeria is the place that most locals recommend. The owner, from Naples, strongly believes that olive oil and garlic are the keys to good health. Sit outside overlooking the river or inside among crowded wooden tables and eat gooey pizzas (43F–55F), tangy *spaghetti all'arrabbiata* (literally, angry spaghetti; 33F), or a generous *salade caprese* (31F), with tomatoes, basil, and fresh mozzarella. *6 quai Perrière, tel. 04–76–87–51–81.*

UNDER 75F • Chez la Mère Ticket. This two-story, family-run restaurant hosts a crowd of regulars who order classic entrées like *côtelette du porc* (pork chops), *gigot d'agneau* (leg of lamb), and escargots. The three-course dinner menu is filling, but if you're really hungry, order the regional dish *gratin dauphinois* (potatoes with cream, cheese, and garlic) as an appetizer. *13 rue J-J Rousseau, between pl. Grenette and pl. Ste-Claire, tel. 04–76–44–45–40. Cash only. Closed Sun. No lunch Mon.*

UNDER 100F • Caffè Forte. A high-ceilinged space in an old building with stone archways is the atmospheric setting of this classy joint. Traditional fare, like the *ravioles du Royans* in cream sauce and lamb skewers in a spicy peanut sauce, is served with flair. You can always just dawdle over some wine and have one of their stunning desserts—like marquis chocolate with Chartreux cream. *4 pl. Lavalette, tel. 04–76–03–25–30.*

Gallo-Roman fortifications built around 293 AD enclosed the original city of Grenoble, Gratinopolis, an area of about 22 acres. Most of the walls were destroyed in the 16th century, but you can thank them for the layout of Grenoble's streets.

La Hotte du Père Joël. Several wine-included menus (lentils, pigs' feet, and Beaujolais for 85F, for example) make this intimate, old-fashioned spot less than a splurge—and it's next door to the cathedral in the old town. *8 bis rue du Vieux-Temple, tel. 04–76–42–04–00. Cash only.*

CAFES

Place Notre-Dame and **place St-André** are filled with Grenoble's most bustling cafés. Most places serve lunch noon–2, so if you just want to hang out, head to a nearby bar. High ceilings, a dark green interior, and lots of shady trees make **Brasserie les Archers** (2 rue Dr. Bailly, tel. 04–76–46–27–76) a sumptuous retreat. The giant 15F café crème is worth its weight in caffeine. The upscale **Café de la Table Ronde** (pl. St-André, tel. 04–76–44–51–41) is supposedly the second-oldest café in France, established in 1739. Stendhal used to come here for coffee.

WORTH SEEING

Most of the major sights lie between the tourist office and the Isère and can be explored in one full day on foot or by tram. Museum admission runs around 15F–20F, and all the city's museums close on Tuesday. The streets east of the tourist office, off place Notre-Dame, merit some perusing, with their art galleries, boutiques, and antique bookstores. The **Centre National d'Art Contemporain** (155 cours Berriat, tel. 04–76–21–95–84), behind the train station, is well worth the out-of-the-way trip for anyone interested in modern art and innovative, warehouse architecture. The tourist office distributes a "Stendhal Itinerary" that directs you to the writer's birthplace, which now houses a roomful of memorabilia grandly called the **Musée de la Résistance et de la Déportation** (14 rue Hébert, tel. 04–76–42–38–53). Move on to the **Maison Stendhal** (20 Grande Rue), Stendhal's grandfather's home and the place where he spent the "happiest days of his life"; to the **Musée Stendhal** (1 rue Hector-Berlioz, tel. 04–76–42–02–62), which has copies of original manuscripts; and finally to the **Jardin de Ville,** where you-know-who

MONK-EYING AROUND WITH 110-PROOF LIQUEUR

The formula for the green, 110-proof liqueur Chartreuse is a secret, entrusted to three monks at the Chartreuse Distillery (10 blvd. Edgar Kofler, tel. 04–76–05–81–77), 20 minutes by bus north of Grenoble in Voiron. The liqueur was originally presented to the monastery in 1605 as a health elixir by Marshall d'Estrées and is known to use a combination of plants and herbs. You can visit the distillery and its museum at the original site of the monastery, founded by St. Bruno in 1084. Tours (in French) and tastings are free, but count on spending 40F for the round-trip fare on Bus 715.

met his first love. Admission is free along the whole itinerary, but the sites have different hours, so check at the tourist office before heading out.

THE BASTILLE

Grenoble's most obvious sight, this maze of walls and stairways at the foot of the Chartreuse mountains was constructed at the beginning of the 19th century to replace a decaying hillside fortress. The city has filled in some of the stone spaces with a café and souvenir shop, but the uncontested attraction is the view; you can see Mont Blanc on a clear day. Three different paths lead down to the city (the prettiest one is through the Jardin Dauphinoise), and various hiking trails start from behind the restaurant (*see* Outdoor Activities, *below*). The scenic journey up to the top of the Bastille via the bubble-shape **téléphérique** is worth the trip just for the ride. This aerial tramway runs April–October daily 10 AM–midnight, with reduced hours on Sunday and November–March. Buy the one-way 20F ticket to ride up, the 33F round-trip deal, or forget both and make the whole journey on foot.

CATHEDRALE NOTRE-DAME

Despite its 12th-century exterior, the 19th-century interior of this cathedral is somewhat bland. But don't miss the adjoining bishop's house, which has been transformed into a museum on the history of the city of Grenoble; one of its high points is the recently discovered 4th-century baptistery. *Pl. Notre-Dame. Admission prices and hrs available through tourist office.*

MUSEE ARCHEOLOGIQUE EGLISE ST-LAURENT

Walking into this church-cum-museum promises to be a strange experience: There's no floor. Instead, you walk out onto suspended metal grates that let you see what's below: a 6th-century crypt and 4th-century cemetery that were built upon until the 18th century. *Pl. St-Laurent, tel. 04–76–85–19–20. Admission 15F, free Wed. afternoon. Open Wed.–Mon. 9–noon and 2–6.*

MUSEE DAUPHINOIS

Housed in the 17th-century Ursuline convent of Ste-Marie-d'en-Haut, at the foot of the Bastille hill on the north bank of the Isère, this museum uses excellent lighting, audiovisual aids, and interactive displays to recount the history of skiing (with much attention given to women's progress in the sport) and the life of early Alpine settlers. Check out the rough-hewn tools and "primitive" equipment used to explore the Alps in the olden times before going up with your Gore-Tex. *30 rue Maurice Gignoux, tel. 04–76–85–19–00. Admission 20F, free Wed. afternoon. Open Wed.–Mon. 10–6 (until 7 May–Oct.).*

MUSEE DE GRENOBLE

This slick museum, designed by two local architects, carries some worthy pieces by Matisse, de la Tour, Delacroix, and Picasso, as well as a smattering of contemporary paintings and sculptures. *5 pl. de*

Lavalette, on the Isère east of the téléphérique, tel. 04–76–63–44–44. Admission 25F. Open Wed. 11–10, Thurs.–Mon. 11–7.

PLACE ST-ANDRE

This medieval square, now filled with umbrella-shaded tables, is graced by the **Palais de Justice** on one side and the **Église St-André** on the other. The church was here first, built entirely of brick in the 13th century, and is a good example of regional craftsmanship. The Palais de Justice was built in three stages: The tall, skinny middle portion with Gothic decoration was first; the Renaissance branch to the right was second; and, finally, the section on the left was built in the 18th century with both Renaissance and Gothic influences.

FESTIVALS

During the second week of June, environmentalists turn out to demonstrate the latest earth-friendly modes of transportation and architecture during **Les Journées de l'Environnement,** an event designed to promote ecological awareness. The **Festival du Théâtre Européen** comes into town one month later, bringing everything from staged plays to street performers. Regular tickets run 120F–190F. In July, the **Festival du Film de Court Métrage en Plein Air** attracts European artists and plain old film fans for frequent free, short *séances* (showings) projected onto the sides of buildings around town.

AFTER DARK

Before the sun sets, get a free copy of *Le Petit Bulletin* (available at movie theaters, bars, and the tourist office), which lists (in French) the week's movies, concerts, and general goings-on. Approaching jam-packed place St-André on a warm summer night is akin to approaching a waterfall—the roar is tremendous. This *place,* along with nearby place aux Herbes and place de Gordes, is Grenoble's after-dark pulse.

Grenoble's nightlife revolves around its crowded cafés; just be aware that their prices go up after 10 PM. The sports bar **Le Couche Tard** (1 rue Palais, off pl. St-André, tel. 04–76–44–18–79) charges 10F for a *sérieux* (literally "serious," which in this case means a pint) Monday and Wednesday 8–10 PM. Around the corner, **Le Saxo** (5 pl. d'Agier, tel. 04–76–51–06–01) serves cocktails from 25F and plays music on its large terrace; people usually dance when it gets crowded. The ornate candelabra and American junkyard remnants that adorn **Cybernet Café** (3 rue Bayard, off pl. Notre-Dame, tel. 04–76–51–73–18) merit a glance, even if you can't afford the 25F per half hour Internet hook-up. Drinks are 15F–20F. For dancing, **L'Entre-Pôt** (8 rue Auguste Gemin, tel. 04–76–48–21–48) gets rock and funk groups that really put people in motion. If you're into jazz, head for **La Soupe aux Choux** (7 rte. de Lyon, tel. 04–76–87–05–67), which attracts a mellow crowd of all ages.

OUTDOOR ACTIVITIES

HIKING

Info-Montagnes/Cimes (14 rue de la République, tel. 04–76–42–45–90) is quite possibly France's best resource for hike-a-holics. It has folders full of maps that describe hikes from Grenoble, the Vercors, Chartreuse, and Belledonne massifs (all of which provide day-hike options), as well as guides and maps (50F–150F) for the Alps. Tell the staff what you're looking for—a leisurely afternoon jaunt, nice views, or whatever—and they'll give you a few hikes to choose from. It's up to you to find out which bus gets you to the trailhead, stock up on water, and check your chocolate reserves.

Two popular half-day hikes are to **Lac Archard** and to **Lac Robert.** They both require taking Bus 601 from the gare routière toward Chamrousse (56F), a winter ski station in the Chartreux, and hiking up an easy, scenic incline for about two hours. From Grenoble there are endless possibilities from atop the téléphérique: Head down to the left, past the toilets, through the gate, and then up the road to the Restaurant du Père-Gas; from here, the GR9 makes a very steep ascent to the Col de Vence, and the *Vierge Noire* (Black Virgin) trail undulates through the woods to an old chapel.

SKIING

Cars VFD (tel. 04–76–47–77–77), the local bus company (*see* Coming and Going, *above*), has a 155F package that includes round-trip transportation, lift ticket, and (if you want) a half-day ski lesson in

Chamrousse (about 1½ hours by bus). The same deal for Les Deux Alpes, a bigger and more challenging resort (2 hours away), is 210F. Rent ski equipment at **Borel Sports** (42 av. Alsace Lorraine, tel. 04–76–46–47–46), two blocks from the station, for 65F a day; prices drop if you rent three or more days, but it's closed on Sunday.

THE VERCORS

The Parc Naturel Régional du Vercors region southwest of Grenoble is dominated by a huge limestone plateau crowned with verdant meadows and austere cliffs and peaks. The plateau drops off sharply on the west side, revealing a series of magnificent stratified valleys furrowed with deep gorges. At the southern end of the plateau, near the small hub of La Chapelle-en-Vercors, a huge natural reserve protects the Tétras-Lyre (the magnificent Black Grouse, with lyre-shape tail) and wild tulip from cars, dogs, and campfires.

The geology alone of this region is enough to draw you here. Billions of years ago, a shallow sea covered the region, and the tiny critters living in it contributed their skeletons to the immense limestone plateau that remains. Receding water left behind fissures, tunnels, and minerals, notably calcium, which created otherworldly stalactite and stalagmite formations in the region's renowned, 5-million-year-old caves. The **Grotte de la Draye Blanche** (in Vassieux-en-Vercors) and **Grottes de Choranche** (near St-Jean-en-Royans) are both excellent examples of these subterranean chambers.

The hiking trails GR9, GR92, GR93, and GR95 all run through the reserve, although you can also get around by hitching from larger towns. Although Grenoble, Lans-en-Vercors, and Villard-de-Lans are all part of the northern Isère département, La Chapelle and all the towns south of it are part of the larger Drôme region. Isère buses serve Isère destinations and Drôme buses serve the Drôme, making traveling between the two practically impossible. From Grenoble and the Alps, buses go to **Lans-en-Vercors**; from the west they go to **St-Jean-en-Royans** and **La-Chapelle-en-Vercors.** All towns have tourist information, food, and lodging options.

Hikers come to the Vercors for the views; others take to activities like *spéléologie* (spelunking), mountain biking, cross-country skiing, or rock climbing. You can contact a sports company to go on a week excursion for 2,100F. Call **Maison de l'Aventure** (tel. 04–75–48–22–38) in La Chapelle for information. Hikers should definitely check out the *Grande Traversée du Vercors* (GTV), a 150-km (93-mi) trail that goes from Lente to Méaudre and passes through La-Chapelle-en-Vercors; in winter you can do the whole thing on cross-country skis.

LANS-EN-VERCORS

This bustling sport center is alive year-round with people hiking, biking, and skiing for about half what they'd pay to do the same in the Alps. It's the best option for anyone heading out from Grenoble. Of course, the scenery is not the same—here the mountains are smaller, the gorges narrower, and the cliffs more sheer—but the towns are friendlier and you're likely to meet as many French people as Germans or Scandinavians. The stone church and calm town square give the town a pleasant air. Poised at the foot of Le Moucherotte peak, Lans is served by several daily buses from Grenoble (1 hr, 43F). The **tourist office** in the center of town has maps and a list of accommodations. *Tel. 04–76–95–42–62, fax 04–76–95–49–70. Open daily 9–noon and 2–6:30.*

WHERE TO SLEEP

You can stay overnight in Lans cheaply, thanks to bed-and-breakfast rooms (100F–200F); numerous *gîtes d'étape* (rural hostels), with half-pension deals for 160F–200F; and the nearby **Camping le Peuil** (tel. 04–76–95–47–02), a meadow overtaken by mobile homes 1 km (⅔ mi) southeast of town. They charge 65F per tent plus 20F per person, with showers included. If you must spend money on a hotel, **Le Val Fleuri** (rte. D531, tel. 04–76–95–41–09) is centrally located and has nice rooms for 168F–310F with bath or shower, but it's only open mid-June–mid-September.

HOSTEL • The gîte **Inouk** (tel. 04–76–95–42–47, fax 04–76–95–66–57), 1 km (⅔ mi) from the center, is the best deal in town (92F for three- and four-bed rooms, including breakfast). Private hotel-style doubles with full bathrooms cost 240F. The owner, Joëlle, also cooks a delicious dinner for an additional 80F. From December through March, the Inouk runs weeklong cross-country ski tours from 2,490F (equipment, lessons, accommodations, and meals included). From May through September, it arranges horseback rides and has great hiking information. Call or fax to reserve a spot, especially December–February and July–August.

FOOD

The best meals to be had in Lans are the home-cooked ones at **Inouk** (*see* Where to Sleep, *above*), only available if you stay there. **L'Escalade** (Les Arcades, tel. 04–76–95–65–50), about halfway through town on your right, will serve you a big ole "American breakfast" with juice, cereal, toast, and yogurt for 39F and is (thankfully) open on Sunday. **Bar St-Michel** (tel. 04–76–95–40–20), across from the tourist office, brews a huge coffee and serves draft beer until 10 PM (earlier if there are no customers). The *pâtisserie* (pastry shop) next door has a tempting array of sweet treats.

OUTDOOR ACTIVITIES

Joëlle at Inouk (*see* Where to Sleep, *above*) has lived in Lans for more than 15 years and knows the Vercors like the back of her hand. She speaks terrific English— ask for suggestions on outdoor activities if the scenery hasn't inspired you to discover your own. Maréchal Sports (*see below*) can hook you up with a caving guide if you want to pay 160F to get really dirty crawling through the nearby plateau orifices.

If you're into roughing it, the lush green hillsides are yours for the taking; just be discreet or ask the owner of the nearest residence. Signs saying INTERDIT DE PASSAGE and PASSAGE PRIVÉE mean it's a no-no to enter or camp.

HIKING • You can buy maps with clearly marked hiking trails from the tourist office. For a challenging half-day trip, head south from Lans to the hamlets of **Bouilly** and **Les Françons**; pick up the trail that branches to the right of the road as you hit the outskirts of Les Françons.

MOUNTAIN BIKING • Lans is an ideal place to push your biking limits—the hairy hills and high altitude dare you with steep, bumpy rides; logging trails and back roads have scenic journeys for those not so cardiovascularly inclined. The friendly, English-speaking staff at **Maréchal Sports** (tel. 04–76–95–41–46), on the central square in Lans, rents out mountain bike and helmet for 95F per day (with an ID as a deposit) and has topo maps of nearby trails. Nearby, **Archard Sports** (D531, tel. 04–76–95–40–72) rents and sells bikes, skis, and equipment at comparable prices.

SKIING • In winter, Lans is first and foremost a ski center, and though downhill skiing in the Vercors isn't exactly steep and deep, it's definitely cheap. **Stade de Niege** (tel. 04–76–95–43–04) has decent skiing December–April; depending on snow conditions, the 70F lift ticket could be a steal. **Les Allières** (tel. 04–76–95–90–90) is a cross-country ski center with a gîte on top. Lans has a network of marked ski trails open to all; pick up a map at one of the tourist offices in Lans-en-Vercors, Villard-de-Lans, or Corrençon. Rent equipment at Maréchal Sports (*see above*) for 44F–200F per day.

ST-JEAN-EN-ROYANS

Set at the foot of Combe-Laval, a massive rock outcropping, St-Jean-en-Royans, 1½ hours from Valence by bus (65F), is immersed in beautiful and very typical Vercors scenery. It's also close to some of the area's most spectacular sights (*see* Pont-en-Royans, *below*). From the town center, the **Chemin des Chartreux** follows a 9-km (5½-mi) loop to neighboring St-Laurent-en-Royans, past farms and artisans that specialize in regional products like honey, walnut liqueur, goat cheese, and hand-carved wooden bowls. The route is marked with yellow and green stripes on poles and trees, but you should pick up a free map from St-Jean-en-Royan's **Office de Tourisme** in the center of town (Pavillion du Tourisme, tel. 04–75–48–61–39, fax 04–75–47–54–44), open daily 9–noon and 2–6:30. The farms are usually open daily 9–noon and 2–6, though some close Sunday afternoon.

COMING AND GOING

Three **RVD buses** (tel. 04–75–40–16–60) pass through St-Jean-en-Royans en route from Valence (1½ hrs, 62F) to La-Chapelle-en-Vercors (40 mins, 20F). The same number go to Pont-en-Royans (20 mins, 12F). Buses stop in front of the tourist office.

WHERE TO SLEEP AND EAT

Right in the town center is the **Maison des Royans,** a *refuge* (shelter) that sleeps 18 people in two rooms for 30F a night, with a shower and well-equipped kitchen. Reservations aren't usually necessary, but it's good to call the morning you plan to arrive. Arrangements are made through the **Municipal Campground** (tel. 04–75–47–74–60); the campground itself, 1 km (⅔ mi) west of the town center along La Lyonne (the small river that passes through town), has grassy, hedged-in spots for 15F per person. Tent-toters will be in good company here (though still the minority). **Le Castel Fleuri** (pl. du Champ de Mars, tel. 04–75–47–58–01) has 12 slick, spare rooms (180F–230F; 9 with bath) and a rather grand modern restaurant with a good 87F menu; you'll feel most relaxed on the shady terrace. **L'Hermitage** (rte. Rochechinard, tel. 04–75–47–57–87), on the fringe of town (walk downhill two blocks from the tourist office toward the river), serves winter meals of grilled meats and potatoes baked in a wood-burning oven; in summer, there are outdoor barbecue specialties. There's a **Casino** market (rue Jean-Jaurès) one block from the tourist office and a large **Intermarché** (rue de l'Industrie) west of the town center (it is well marked from the tourist office).

NEAR ST-JEAN-EN-ROYANS

PONT-EN-ROYANS

The sight of Pont-en-Royans's houses suspended over the Bourne River is worth the 9-km (5½-mi) walk or 13F bus trip from St-Jean-en-Royans. The river itself is prime swimming and sunbathing territory, and the several bars that overlook the whole scene will encourage you to while away an afternoon over a beer or coffee. If you're looking for an inspirational spot to write postcards, this is it.

Another 9 km (5½ mi) from town in the direction of La-Chapelle-en-Vercors or Villard-de-Lans, the river has carved the incredible **Gorges de la Bourne,** a stretch of sheer 400-ft walls at the bottom of which flows a stretch of the swift, blue-green river. A road that winds downward through the gorges, some 200 ft above the river, leads to the **Grottes de Choranche.** This cave, with millions of pencil-thin, 25-ft-long tubular stalactites, should not be missed. The opening to the cave is actually *behind* a waterfall; enough light splinters through the water so as to reflect the stalactites in the lake that stretches over 2 km (1¼ mi) back into the cave. There is no public transportation to the cave, but there's only one road between Pont-en-Royans and Villard-de-Lans or La Chapelle-en-Vercors, so if you catch a ride in this direction you'll automatically pass the turnoff. It's a 2-km (1¼-mi) uphill walk to the entrance and ticket booth, where there's also a bar and café. *Tel. 04–76–36–09–88. Admission 40F. Open daily Nov.–Mar., daily 10–5; Apr.–June and Sept.–Oct., daily 9:30–6; July–Aug., daily 9–6:30.*

LA CHAPELLE-EN-VERCORS

This little town is the hub of the southern Vercors. As in most other Alpine towns, life here revolves around cross-country skiing in winter and hiking, horseback riding, mountain biking, or caving in summer. The town itself consists of little more than a boulangerie, a church, a couple of bars and restaurants, and some souvenir shops jammed with everything from hiking equipment to the nougat that's a regional specialty. But three campgrounds, two adventure-oriented hostels, a nearby cave, and a helpful tourist office make La Chapelle a logical base for exploring the more remote corners of this spectacularly elevated valley.

BASICS

The **Office de Tourisme** on the central square has maps and lodging-dining lists. The staff sells 10F hiking maps that mark nearby trails; more extensive topographic maps cost 58F. *Pl. du Marché, tel. 04–75–48–22–54. Open daily 9–noon and 2–6:30.*

COMING AND GOING

Two **RVD buses** (tel. 04–75–40–16–60) leave daily from Valence, passing through St-Jean-en-Royans and several other mountain villages on the way to La Chapelle (2 hrs, 70F). From Grenoble, take a **Trans-Isère** bus to Villard-de-Lans (1½ hrs, 42F), but you'll need a car to go south to La Chapelle.

WHERE TO SLEEP

If you want to stay in town, the 48-bed **Maison de l'Aventure** (av. des Bruyères, tel. 04–75–48–22–38) has clean, four-bed dorm rooms with breakfast and a three-course dinner for 165F a night. You can have lunch for another 40F. The house sits 2 km (1 mi) northeast of the town center behind the **Municipal Campground**; from the tourist office, head uphill and follow the signs. The **Hôtel du Nord** (av. de Provence, tel. 04–75–48–22–13) is a fantastic little hotel with double rooms with shower starting at 145F. The restaurant is also a find, offering good home cooking and regional specialties, including nougat; set meals are from 70F. If you want to do nature in style, the renovated **Hôtel des Sports** (av. des Grands Goulets, tel. 04–75–48–20–39) will put you a safe distance away from all those insects for 145F–250F per night; it's closed in December. Outside La Chapelle, within an 18-km (11-mi) radius, several gîtes have rooms and half-board (160F–210F) for individuals and groups; pick up a list at the tourist office.

CAMPING • The **Municipal Campground** has 150 sites with hot showers and incredible scenery at 15F per person and 12F per tent. The owner also rents out two small mobile homes in summer for 80F plus 16F per person. Otherwise, head 2 km (1 mi) south on N158 toward **Grottes de la Draye Blanche**; when you see a peach-color sign on your left saying VENTE À LA FERME and CAMPING, you've arrived at the Royannies's sheep field and their 17th-century farmhouse, named **La Cime du Mas.** Madame Royannies charges 12F per person for campsites and 60F for caravans. Call 04–75–48–21–81 to reserve, and bring some food unless you really like goat cheese and eggs (the only things for sale here at the farm).

FOOD

Prices in local markets are high, and restaurants don't serve much more than your basic cheap sandwiches, salads, and croques-monsieurs (toasted ham and-cheese sandwiches), so plan on some meals in hotels or gîtes. Abundant *alimentation générale* (general food) stores carry regional specialties like St-Marcellin cheese, cured ham, and local honey and fruits. A big **market** sets up in front of the tourist office on Thursday and Saturday mornings. **La Miraillonne** (pl. de la Fontaine, tel. 04–75–48–21–22), 4 km (2½ mi) away in St-Agnan, is a good lunch or dinner spot serving regional specialties (mountain cheese salads, ravioles), big steaks, and a 45F plat du jour.

The roofs of some Vercors dwellings are designed so that their terraces break up falling snow into smaller clumps, thereby merely covering, and not burying, innocent passersby.

OUTDOOR ACTIVITIES

Entre Ciel et Terre (tel. 04–75–48–25–91), part of the Maison de l'Aventure (*see* Where to Sleep, *above*), organizes trips of any duration for any number of people doing just about any activity. Day trips cost 80F–300F; longer adventures (three days to a week) that take you to remote corners of the Vercors are 250F–1,500F, including meals, lodging, and equipment. **TVS Voyages** (tel. 04–75–48–21–14) rents mountain bikes for 50F per hour or 110F per day with a credit-card deposit; it also gives daily accompanied tours. **Foyer de Ski de Fond** (tel. 04–75–48–22–75), 7 km (4 mi) southwest of La Chapelle at Col de Carri, rents cross-country ski equipment (100F per day) and arranges lodging. **Phillip Smith** (tel. 04–75–48–11–24), an English guide based in St-Agnan-en-Vercors, runs beginning and advanced mountain-bike and cross-country ski tours for about 100F per day or, with minibus transport, lodging, and food, about 250F per day.

There are six well-marked trails of various lengths and difficulty that leave from the tourist office. For longer journeys, the **Grande Traversée du Vercors** (GTV)—a 150-km (93-mi) trail from Lente to Méaudre—and the **GR91** are worth investigating. The GTV runs right through town, and the GR91 can be picked up 3 km (2 mi) east of La Chapelle. A topographic map from the tourist office and water are indispensable for either one, though food and lodging can be found at gîtes along the way (marked by small green and yellow signs). Head south for a couple of hours on the GR91 to reach the crest of the Vercors, which has great views over the southern end of the area, including a view of **Mont Aiguille,** a strange limestone formation resembling a giant thumb.

VASSIEUX-EN-VERCORS

A 10-km (6-mi) walk or hitch south of La Chapelle on the winding N185, Vassieux became an important center for the French Resistance in World War II as the headquarters for Vercors military operations. The town was completely demolished by a German air assault in August 1944. It has been rebuilt (with little regard for aesthetic concerns), but the memorabilia and graphic photographs in the **Musée de la Résistance** (tel. 04–75–48–26–00), on the hill behind the church, are vivid reminders of what happened here less than 60 years ago. Anyone interested in World War II history should definitely make a pilgrimage here. Entrance is free; the museum is open daily October—mid-November and mid-December–March 10–5 and April–September 10–6, and is closed mid-November–mid-December. The **Nécropole de la Résistance,** 1 km (⅗ mi) outside town on the road to La Chapelle, supplements the museum with gravestones and a film in French about the Resistance. The walk through pastures is pleasant, giving you time to reflect on what went on in this now-peaceful valley. Admission is free; it's open May–September, daily 10–12:30 and 1:30–6. In mid-June, the **Fête de la Forêt** comes to Vassieux, bringing Robin Hood–like games, food, folk dancing, and local crafts. Call 04–74–48–22–21 for information.

Spelunkers should not miss the 5-million-year-old **Grotte de la Draye Blanche,** 4 km (2½ mi) north of Vassieux on the road to La Chapelle. Platforms and stairways traverse the underground caves and allow views of stalagmites, stalactites, cascades, and columns of calcite that grow only a minuscule amount per century. Several years ago, geologists were digging a tunnel to facilitate visits and came across a pile of ancient animal bones: the remains of deer, wolves, and bison that fell into a natural crevice. Grenoble's natural history museum is presently excavating the site. The oldest animals discovered so far are 18,000 years old, and even older skeletons are lodged, experts hope, in the lower layers. The only way to cover the ground from Vassieux to the caves is on foot or by hitching. *Tel. 04–75–48–24–96. Admission 26F. Open Apr.–Sept., daily 9–6:30; Feb.–Mar., daily 10–4.*

OUTDOOR ACTIVITIES

Vassieux is an excellent starting point for hikers. An easy one-hour hike northeast takes you to the tiny hamlet of **Le Château**; a longer hike east out of town leads up the Côte Belle or through the Forêt de la Trompe. For a one- to two-day hike, head south from Vassieux where you can pick up the GR95, which crosses GR93 after 4 km (2½ mi); go up a grueling path to **Col de Rousset** (4,511 ft) and onto the plateau to hit the GR91 and GR9, which head north through some of the most remote and beautiful areas of the Vercors reserve. Bring lots of water and a warm sleeping bag—snow on the 3,000-ft plateau in July is not unheard of. Camping for one night is allowed in the reserve. Pick up the 10F *Sentiers du Vercors,* a guide and map, in La Chapelle or Lans-en-Vercors for precise routes.

THE ALPS

Words can't describe the awesome beauty that millions of years of geologic activity have left behind. Massive domes, knife-blade ridges, and granite fingers pointing toward an unadulterated blue sky are sure to make anyone gape in wonder and reverence. Rolling green meadows, wildflower mosaics, and brilliant gurgling streams bring you back to reality long enough to thank whatever power or deity you believe in for making such landscapes possible.

The French Alps are part of a chain that stretches across eight countries, culminating in Mont Blanc, Europe's highest peak (15,863 ft) on the French-Italian border. Home to more than 10 Winter Olympic Games cities (Albertville, Chamonix, and Val d'Isère, to name a few), the Alps have long attracted tourists. This is frustrating for real tree-huggers but helpful for anyone searching out Alpine experience without making a serious outdoors commitment. A user-friendly train and bus system makes getting around easy if expensive; if you want to see traditional chalets surrounded only by cows and greenery, you'll have to escape major recreation hubs and visit the small villages in between (most have at least one hotel or gîte and restaurant). Two long-distance hiking trails—the Grande Randonnée (GR5) and Grand Traversée des Alps—and the protected **Parc National de la Valoise** make it easy to leave civilization behind. Otherwise, **Chamonix** provides knock-your-socks-off mountain scenery, **Annecy** has a quaint old town and stunning lake, and **Bourg-St-Maurice** makes a good base for exploring a cross section of Alpine activity.

BASICS

VISITOR INFORMATION

All towns listed have their own tourist offices (open roughly 8:30–6) and are your best bet for town-specific information. If you want to do some pre-trip research, you can get excellent information about the Parc National de la Vanoise in Chambery (135 rue du Docteur Julliand, B.P. 705, 73007, tel. 04–79–62–30–54, fax 04–79–96–37–18), and information about the Parc Régional du Vercors in Lans-en-Vercors (Parc Naturel Régional du Vercors, Chemin des Fusillés, 38250 Lans-en-Vercors, tel. 04–76–94–38–26, fax 04–76–94–38–39). The **Maison Alpes-Dauphiné** (2 pl. André Malraux, 1er, tel. 01–42–96–08–43, fax 01–42–96–07–02) in Paris handles a wide range of queries. Youth hostels are also an excellent source of information in this region, especially for outdoor activities. Hit the hostel at its most animated hours in the morning (8–10) or evening (5–8).

ORIENTATION PROGRAMS

Plenty of organizations have weeklong *stages* (programs) that include food, lodging, equipment, instruction, and transportation for 2,500F in one or more activities like skiing, windsurfing, paragliding, and rafting. Check the **Fédération Unie des Auberges de Jeunesse (FUAJ)** guide, available at any HI hostel, for stages affiliated with various hostels. The hostels in Tignes and Bourg-St-Maurice are popular spots for this; a few gîtes in the Vercors, mostly out of La-Chapelle-en-Vercors and Lans-en-Vercors, have similar programs. Other organizations in Paris are the **Union des Centres de Plein Air** (62 rue de la Glacière, 13e, tel. 01–43–36–05–20); **Chalets Internationaux de Haute Montagne** (15 rue Guy-Lussac, 5e, tel. 01–43–25–70–90), which specializes in mountain climbing; and **OCCAJ Voyages Vacances** (95 rue d'Amsterdam, 8e, tel. 01–45–26–21–21), which takes you skiing at the five biggest ski stations in the Alps: Chamonix, Les Menuires, Les Coches, Les Arcs, and Val-Thorens.

WHEN TO GO

You can technically ski year-round in the Alps, although the best skiing is January–March. Hiking is best in summer or fall, depending on how much snow you'd like to see. Visitors swamp the towns in July and August. Come in June or September and you'll have the towns and trails all to yourself, though there won't be much in the way of nightlife. Lots of weary locals take a break when high season is over, leaving many hotels and restaurants closed October–November and May–June. January is the coldest and least-touristed month and brings discounts on lodging, meals, and lift tickets; the same goes for December 15–25.

WHAT TO PACK

A couple of essentials should accompany every Alps goer (although you don't need these for Grenoble): (1) sturdy shoes with closed toes; (2) a raincoat or windbreaker; (3) lip balm and sunscreen; (4) a pack for day hikes and picnics; (5) polarized sunglasses; (6) at least one piece of woolen, polypropylene, or otherwise warm clothing for layering, as even in July it can drop to 0°C (32°F) on some peaks; (7) a swimsuit for lake dips and/or saunas.

You can usually rent skis, boots, and poles (80F–150F), rock-climbing equipment (60F), and backpacks (20F) in most mountain towns. Though food is often expensive, you'll usually find sportswear and equipment at very competitive prices. Three reliable chains that appear in most mountain hubs are **Sport 2000, Technicien Sport,** and **Intersport.**

COMING AND GOING

Unless you have a car, **trains** are the most efficient way to get from town to town in the Alps. The three major stations, from north to south, are **Annecy** (tel. 04–50–66–50–50), **Chambéry** (tel. 04–79–75–67–95), and **Grenoble** (tel. 04–76–47–50–50). All lie on the same line, with smaller lines branching east to Bourg-St-Maurice, Tignes, and Chamonix and south to Briançon and Gap (near Ecrins National Park). Most small towns have train stations. **Regional buses** are always ready to whisk you from the train off to higher elevations in small or large towns. Train stations and tourist offices are the best places to find local bus schedules.

WHERE TO SLEEP

Hotels in this popular vacation area are expensive in high seasons (usually around the Christmas holidays, January–Easter, and July–August), and they're especially crowded during school vacations. Consider half-board options, weeklong price reductions, and spring or fall travel to keep costs down.

HOSTELS

Hostels are abundant in the Alps, but many of them operate on a half-board or weekly organized-vacation basis, in which case rates end up averaging about 100F per night. In many major ski stations

SKIING BY NUMBERS IN THE ALPS

Skiing can be a costly pastime, but if you're committed to the sport, the Alps are unbeatable, with verticals up to 9,240 ft and seemingly endless networks of pistes (runs), most above the tree line. The resorts in Tignes and Les Arcs have year-round skiing, although skiers seeking the true Alpine experience will head straight for the better-known resorts in Chamonix, Bourg-St-Maurice, and the Val d'Isère.

Big resorts tend to congregate in one valley—Tignes, Val d'Isère, and Les Arcs are one example—making it possible to stay in one place for a week and never cross your own tracks. The ideal situation is to gather a few friends together and rent an apartment for a week; four people can get a two-room place with kitchen, fireplace, and washer-dryer for about 2,800F per week; contact the local tourist office for rental information. A stay of five or more days can get you discounts on lift tickets (700F versus 180F per day) and lodging. Equipment is also cheaper (320F versus 80F per day); just be sure to rent from the town closest to the resort to get the cheapest prices. For shorter ski stints, Grenoble has one-day packages (155F–210F) to Chamrousse and Les Deux Alpes (see Outdoor Activities in Grenoble, above).

(Chamonix, Aix-les-Bains, Tignes), the hostels lie far from the town center, so call to discern exactly where they are and how often buses run before you set out on foot with a 2-ton backpack.

GITES D'ETAPE AND COLLECTIVES

The gîtes d'étape, indicated by green and yellow signs all over the Alps, are often refurbished chalets or old houses. They have mattresses, showers, and kitchen facilities for 60F–200F per night. You might be required to buy meals, which at these rural hostels are usually a good deal. *Gîtes ruraux* are houses in the country or woods that three to eight people can rent for about 800F–1,600F per week. *Collectives* come under the same listings as gîtes in tourist offices and also offer hostel-like accommodations, but during the winter they favor guests staying at least a week who'll pay for a full-pension deal. For a list of gîte addresses and phone numbers, pick up a free "Randonnée Info" pamphlet at Grenoble's tourist office (14 rue de la République, tel. 04–76–42–45–90). For a full France list, write, visit, or call the **Maison des Gîtes de France** (35 rue Godot de Mauroy, 9e, 75009 Paris, tel. 01–49–70–75–75).

CAMPING

As you'd expect, Alpine campgrounds are usually in amazing settings. But don't forget—it gets very, very cold at night; pack accordingly. Some campgrounds are caravan-free, but even the tents-only atmosphere gets a little too close in summer. Prices run 15F–20F per tent plus 10F–15F per person, including hot showers. Most gîtes and many hostels will let you pitch a tent outside and use their shower for 10F.

REFUGES

Along the marked hiking routes traversing France, the Alps, and national or regional parks, you can get a dorm bed for under 50F a night at refuges. These are ideal if you want to do an overnight hike but don't have camping gear. The tourist office at your point of departure will have a list of the refuges along the route you want to take, or you can look on a map for house-shape icons. A "guarded" refuge means that someone is there taking care of the place and you need to reserve (even in the off-season, to be polite); you might have to buy a meal or two per day. An "unguarded" refuge can be anything from an abandoned shack to a fully equipped bunkhouse. Refuges on major hiking routes have a one-night limit.

FOOD

Every regional specialty here involves cheese, cheese, and more cheese, eaten raw, layered with potatoes and cream in *gratin,* melted with wine and herbs for fondue, or melted by the fire and eaten with potatoes, ham, and cornichons for the regional specialty, raclette. If you're a true aficionado, head into a *fromagerie* (cheese store) and pick up some nutty Beaufort (in the Swiss cheese family), mild Tomme, or St-Marcellin, all made on local farms.

OUTDOOR ACTIVITIES

BIKING

Vélo tout terrain, or "VTT," the French word for a mountain bike, is now a favorite summer toy in the Alps, where you can pedal over hills and through woods on trails that are used for cross-country skiing in winter. Just look for the little yellow bicycle sign pointing you toward the *VTT Circuit* (mountain-biking trail), or ask at any local bike shop, where bikes go for 80F–120F per day, for a map of the local routes. Helmets and water bottles are usually included in rental prices.

HIKING

The Alps, Vercors, and even Grenoble have well-marked trails and circuits for every level of *randonneur* (hiker). Routes are usually marked by colored stripes (painted on rocks, trees, and poles), which correspond to a route marked on a map (available from a local tourist office). Excellent resources are

Marie Paradis was the first woman to reach Mont Blanc's summit in 1809, though her companions carried her most of the way. Henriette d'Angerville is the first woman to have actually climbed the mountain unassisted, in 1838.

Info-Montagnes (14 rue de la République, tel. 04–76–42–45–00) in Grenoble, **Maison de la Montagne** (190 pl. de l'Église, tel. 04–50–53–00–88) in Chamonix, or, for pre-trip research, the **Fédération Française de Randonnée Pédestre** in Paris (8 av. Marceau, 8e, tel. 01–47–23–62–32). Two major routes, the **Grande Randonnée (GR),** which winds its way through France, and the **Grande Traversée des Alpes (GTA)** guide you from town to town and to refuges along the way. Some of the routes, like the Tour du Mont Blanc or the Tour de la Vanoise, can take up to nine days and require a guide to lead the way—or careful planning and experience. Small sections of these routes make good day trips or overnighters.

CHAMONIX

Sometimes it is hard to believe that people live in the Chamonix valley, where the ice that crumbles down from two glacial peaks overlooking the area comes within 1 km (⅗ mi) of the town itself. The largest city of nine other communities in the valley, Chamonix was little more than a quiet mountain village until a group of Englishmen "discovered" the spot in 1741 and sang its praises far and wide. In 1760, when Horace de Saussure offered a reward for the first Mont Blanc ascent, the town became forever tied to mountaineering (two local men, Jacques Balmat and Dr. Michel Gabriel Paccard, finally reached the summit in 1786). Nowadays the valley's complex transportation infrastructure takes people up to peaks like the **Aiguille du Midi** (7,616 ft) and past freeway-size glaciers like **La Mer de Glace** (literally, "the sea of ice") via téléphériques, *télécabines* (gondolas), *télésièges* (chairlifts), and narrow-rail cars. The required train ride from St-Gervais-Les-Bains to Chamonix is in itself an incredible trip, up the steepest railway in Europe.

Chamonix still manages to provide a few affordable lodgings and some convivial nocturnal fare, despite the tourist glitz and resort hotels hounding the area. As with other Alpine towns, skiers, hikers, mountain bikers, and climbers just might be overwhelmed by the infinite possibilities here. Chamonix has some of the longest ski runs in Europe, with verticals ranging from 2,970 to 9,240 ft.

BASICS

From the train station, walk straight down avenue Michel Croz to the **Office de Tourisme de Chamonix Mont-Blanc** (85 pl. du Triangle de l'Amité, tel. 04–50–53–00–24, fax 04–50–53–58–90); it's open June–September, daily 8:30–7:30, and October–May, daily 8:30–12:30 and 2–6. There is also the **Office de Tourisme d'Argentière** (24 rte. du village, tel. 04–50–54–02–14). The staff in both gives out free maps, reserves rooms, gives trail-condition reports, and sells the excellent *Carte des Sentiers de Montagne en Eté* (25F) map for summer hiking. The **Maison de la Montagne** (190 pl. de l'Église, tel. 04–50–53–00–88), across the street, is the hub for hikers and climbers. The staff will discuss your route, let you photocopy any of their maps and guidebooks for 2F per page, sell topographic maps, and provide the latest weather reports: three bulletins daily are posted in front of the Maison de la Montagne and the tourist office. The office is open daily 8–noon and 2–6. Mountain guides and ski instructors can be booked from the **Compagnie des Guides de Chamonix** (office in the Maison de la Montagne, tel. 04–50–53–00–88). The main post office is at 89 place Balmat (tel. 04–50–53–15–50).

COMING AND GOING

Chamonix's **train station** (pl. de la Gare, tel. 04–50–53–00–44), three blocks up from the central place de l'Église, serves Grenoble (4 hrs, 161F), Geneva (3½ hrs, 112F), and Annecy (2½ hrs, 103F). Once you're in Chamonix, transportation is easy on foot or by local buses (7F) (Mont-Blanc Bus; tel. 04–50–53–05–55) that make the loop through the nine communities of the Chamonix valley. The biggest are Les Bossons, Les Praz, Argentière, Le Tour, and Chamonix–Mont Blanc; the smaller ones are Vallorcine, Montroc, Les Houches, and Servoz. Bus hours change seasonally and are posted in the train station, tourist office, and at bus stops.

WHERE TO SLEEP

Chamonix is chock-full of affordable hotels, but the best place to stay is outside town away from the tourist throngs. For those seeking seclusion or adventure, the 15-minute, 7F bus ride to Argentière is well worth it to stay in a 50F dorm-style room in **Chalet Refuge La Boerne** (Tré-lé-Champs, tel. 04–50–54–05–14), a secluded, refurbished farm.

UNDER 225F • El Paso Hôtel. Run by an outgoing Australian, El Paso has wood-lined rooms and splashes of ocher paint on the walls. Singles start at 150F, doubles at 200F (20F more with bath). La Cantina bar downstairs rages until 2 AM and serves surprisingly good Mexican food (60F–100F) at night. Showers are free. *37 impasse des Rhododendrons, tel. 04–50–53–64–20. From station, take av. Michel Croz to rue Joseph Vallot, turn right, then left at the 2nd street. 22 rooms, 18 with bath.*

UNDER 275F • Au Relais des Gaillands. This reliable lodging has cozy, wood-trimmed rooms; some have a balcony. Doubles with bath start at 250F; the half-board plan includes regional specialties. *964 rte. des Gaillands, tel. 04–50–53–13–58, fax 04–50–55–85—06. 21 rooms with bath.*

HOSTELS • Auberge de Jeunesse. Two kilometers (1 mi) south of town in the small community of Les Pélerins at the foot of Bossons glacier, this busy hostel has a terrific view of the mountains from its spacious common area, patio, fireplace, and bar. There's no age limit. You may share your four-bed room with a hard-core hiker, a mother of three, or Eurail backpacker, but chances are he or she won't be from France. Rates are 76F per person, including hot showers and a big breakfast; a private double with shower costs 9F more. Sheets rent for 19F. *127 montée Jacques Balmat, tel. 04–50–53–14–52. 120 beds. No curfew or lockout. Laundry.*

Le Vagabond. This renovated gîte is an easy stumble from town, with its own bar and late-night snack spot. Bright, six-bed dormlike rooms are 65F per person. *365 av. Ravanel-le-Rouge, tel. 04–50–53–15–43. From train station, walk up av. Michel Croz, left on pl. Balmat (it becomes rue du Dr-Paccard, which then becomes av. Ravanel-le-Rouge). 38 beds. Cash only.*

CAMPING • Campgrounds near Chamonix are plentiful, but in July and August they tend to fill up with post- and pre-trip mountain folk. Large **Les Rosières** (121 clos des Rosières, tel. 04–50–53–10–42) charges 24F per person, 22F per tent; you'll pay a little more July–August. It's closed mid-October–mid-December. From the train station, follow the Arve River north past the Centre Sportif; clos de Rosières is on the right.

The campgrounds **Les Arolles** (281 chemin du Cry, tel. 04–50–53–14–30), **L'Ile des Barrats** (tel. 04–50–53–51–44), and **Les Moliasses** (tel. 04–50–53–16–81) are all near one another in Les Pélerins. Les Moliasses has a market-pizzeria on sight, plus large terraced spots, but it's right near the highway. From the Chamonix train station, head south and look for signs. All charge 22F–25F per person and 16F–25F per tent; they're closed November–April.

FOOD

Little rue des Moulins (off av. Michel Croz) is a good spot for nontraditional Savoyard cuisine and has a lively after-dark scene. **Le Bumblebee** (65 rue des Moulins, tel. 04–50–53–50–03) is owned by a young English-French couple that makes spiced curries and Jamaican chicken with rice and salad (and pours generous pints of Murphy's Irish stout). Most bars and restaurants in Chamonix seem to have "authentic" fondue, or raclette, for 70F–100F per person; **Le Fer à Cheval** (pl. du Poilu, tel. 04–50–53–13–22), housed in a decrepit old train station, is one local favorite that has traditional meals for 40F–70F and a great bar. The self-service **Le Grillandain** (corner of av. du Mont-Blanc and rue Joseph Vallot, tel. 04–50–55–89–90) has better-than-cafeteria food at cafeteria prices and good people-watching from sidewalk tables. **Le Chaudron** (79 rue des Moulins, tel. 04–50–53–40–34) serves *tartiflette* (cheese, bacon, potato, and mushroom casserole) and other Savoie treats in a die-hard romantic setting of old wood and stone. The **Maison Carrier** (rte. du Bouchet, tel. 04–5053–00–03), located in a renovated Savoyard farmhouse, has great atmosphere and is great value for money with fixed daily menus from 145F; it serves local dishes including fondue. Reservations are strongly recommended.

There's a **Petit Casino** (200 av. Michel Croz) market a block away from the train station, and the **Super U** (rue Joseph Vallot, off pl. Balmat, tel. 04–50–53–12–50) market is often very busy.

WORTH SEEING

Aiguille du Midi is a 12,619-ft granite peak topped with a needlelike observation tower from where you can see the massif du Mont Blanc from end to end. The tram costs 74F (62F one-way) to get to the plan d'Aiguille; another 158F via téléphérique gets you to the tower. (You can also make the two-hour hike to plan d'Aiguille from Les Pélerins.) You're sure to feel your body doing funky things to adjust to the pressure change. For another 49F you can continue by téléphérique across the Vallée Blanche ice field into Italy. If you make it up here before 9 AM, you'll see the mountains in their full glory before the cloud cover sets in and the mid-day crowds take over.

In July, Chamonix's Musical Weeks of Mont Blanc combine rough mountain energy and refined classical music for one of the most glorious festivals in France.

The **Mer de Glace** glacier can be seen up close and personal via the *train du Montenvers* (tel. 04–50–53–12–54), a mountain train that leaves from behind the SNCF train station (exit right and cross over the bridge). You can take the train May–June and September, daily 8:30–5:30; July and August, daily 8–6; October—April, daily 10–4. It costs 49F to go up the glacier (65F round-trip), and the hike back down is an easy two-hour ramble. From the top of the train you can mount yet another transportation device—a mini-téléphérique that suspends you over the glacier for five minutes (10F)—or visit a somewhat less awesome ice cave (15F). The tourist office has a list of seasonal prices and the ever-changing hours for all lifts in the valley.

The very good **Musée Alpin** documents early ascents on Mont Blanc and the development of Chamonix's tourism and has handmade skis, Alpine furniture, tools, and a room of massive, mystical paintings by Gabriel Loppé, a local artist who climbed and painted glacial landscapes in the 1880s. *Av. Michel Croz, near rue Whymper, tel. 04–50–53–25–93. Admission 20F. Open Dec.–May, daily 3–7; June–mid-Oct., daily 2–7.*

AFTER DARK

There is no way you can avoid the Anglophones in Chamonix, so you might as well join 'em. In the center of town, the pedestrian streets rue des Moulins and rue du Dr-Paccard, near place Balmat, are lined with cafés and bars where people relax and swap mountain stories. A favorite is the **Mill Street Bar** (123 rue des Moulins, tel. 04–50–55–80–92), a Brit hangout with outside tables. On the other side of avenue du Mont-Blanc is a hole-in-the-wall bar called **Avalon** (79 galerie Alpine, tel. 04–50–53–56–61), whose rough-and-ready crowd waits outside for the 5 PM opening and usually stays until the 8 AM closing. This is a good place to meet hard-core ski-bike-climb-do-it-again types. For late-night munchies, **Belouga** (56 av. Ravanel-le-Rouge, tel. 04–50–53–68–60) serves what might just be the best sandwiches in town until 4 AM.

OUTDOOR ACTIVITIES

BIKING • The owner of **Chamonix Mountain Bike** (138 rue des Moulins, tel. 04–50–53–54–76) brought the first mountain bike and the first snowboard to Chamonix Valley. Now his English-speaking, very hip staff rents bikes for 100F per day, snowboards and boots for 99F per day, and gives helpful trail suggestions. Before you head out, pick up a free copy of *Itinéraires Autorisés aux Vélos Tout Terrain* at the tourist office (*see above*) or bike shop.

HIKING • Mont Blanc and the surrounding mountains are mighty high; don't head up to the *haute montagne* (stuff above 6,600 ft) at any time of year without the proper gear and experience. Guides are highly recommended if you don't want to run into a glacier. July to early September, the **Compagnie des Guides** (in Maison de la Montagne, *see above*; tel. 04–50–58–00–88) gives daily guided hikes for 100F. On the second floor of the same building, the **Office de Haute Montagne** (tel. 04–50–53–22–08), open June–September 8:30–12:30 and 2:30–6:30, has maps and books you can photocopy for 2F per sheet and experienced local climbers to talk to.

An easy half-day hike leads northeast of town along the Arveyron stream past Les Gaudenays to the hamlet of Le Lavancher. If you're itching to get a bit higher, wait until the snow line has retreated in July for safer viewing and hiking conditions. Or, walk or take the train 9 km (6 mi) east from Chamonix to Vallorcine, where a Barberine tram will put you up at a good 6,600 ft on the edge of Lac d'Emosson in Switzerland. The Lac du Vieux Emosson, another 990 ft up, is accessible only if the snow isn't too deep. The entire trip from Chamonix to the lake takes about four hours.

The most popular day hike from near Chamonix is a three-hour hike up to Lac Blanc from Les Praz (a quick bus ride from Chamonix) or a 10-minute, 42F trip via the Les Praz–La Flégère téléphérique. The glacial deposits in the lake make it look bright turquoise, and from its banks you get a magnificent view of Mont Blanc. More involved but less crowded is the six-hour hike up to **Lac Cornu** and **Lacs Noirs,** near the top of Le Brévent téléphérique (44F). The téléphérique leaves from behind the church near the tourist office in Chamonix. From either above-mentioned téléphérique, you can take an easy stroll with stunning Mont Blanc views along the **Grand Balcon Sud** and hike up or down the mountain if you choose.

RAFTING • The biggest white-water river in the Alps is the Dora. Those bored with hurtling down the river in a raft have at least a few options: Hydroglissing requires that you hurl yourself down white-water rapids with nothing more than a glorified kickboard between you and foam, and canyoning involves swimming, rappelling, and climbing your way down a river that runs through a narrow canyon. **Hydroglisse** (Centre Sportif, promenade du Fori, tel. 04–50–53–55–70) has Dora trips for 470F–640F, beginner hydroglisse runs for 210F, and canyoning excursions for 350F. It provides equipment, instruction (ask for an English-speaking guide), and transportation.

SKIING • As expected, skiing doesn't come cheap here. Chamonix's runs don't connect, so you have to go from one lift to another by bus; you then have to pay separately each time you get on a lift (43F–55F) unless you buy the one-day 220F Chamski pass, which gives access to all of them plus free bus rides. To ski the granddaddy of runs—the 19-km (12-mi) trip down the Mer de Glace from the Aiguille du Midi, you need to hire a guide; the Compagnie des Guides (*see* Hiking, *above*) runs a half-day trip for 410F.

ANNECY

Everything about Annecy—from its overpriced restaurants to the paddleboat vendors that try to outcharm each other for your business—says "touristville." But its flower-lined canals and stunning lake still make it a good place to dawdle awhile. Lac d'Annecy, one of the few lakes in the Alps where you can swim for any length of time without turning blue, has windsurfing and kayaking opportunities as well as excellent scenery for those who prefer hanging out on the grassy beach or in Annecy's massive lakeside garden. Summer brings a very international, bacchanalian crowd; illuminated shows on the lake; and concerts in the courtyard of Annecy's château (built to house the dukes of Savoie when they were exiled from Geneva during the Reformation). From mid-September to July you'll pretty much have the place to yourself, which makes it more charming by day but a bit lonely at night. There *are* two constants in this extremely seasonal town: the funky, asymmetrical, added-on, squished-in buildings of its vieille ville and the sheer limestone cliffs and jagged peaks behind the lake.

BASICS

The high-tech **Office de Tourisme** keeps all of its brochures behind the counter, so be sure to ask for a free *plan de la ville* (city map). The staff also leads daily two-hour guided tours (32F) and provides free maps of the area. *Centre Bonlieu, 1 rue Jean-Jaurès, tel. 04–50–45–00–33, fax 04–50–51–87–20. From train station, walk 3 long blocks down rue Sommeiller. Open July–Aug., daily 9–6:30; Sept.–June, Mon.–Sat. 9–noon and 1:45–6:30, Sun. 3–6.*

The main **post office** is conveniently located three blocks in front of the train station. It handles poste restante (postal code 74000) and standard postal needs. *4 rue des Glières, tel. 04–50–33–67–00. Open weekdays 8–7, Sat. 8–noon.*

COMING AND GOING

Trains run regularly from Annecy's centrally located, subterranean **train station** (pl. de la Gare, tel. 08–36–35–35–35) to Chamonix (2½ hrs, 105F), Chambéry (50 mins, 48F), Grenoble (2½ hrs, 89F), Lyon (3½ hrs, 115F), Paris (5½ hrs, 377F on the TGV), and Geneva, Switzerland (2 hrs, 133F).

All buses leave Annecy from the **gare routière** right next to the train station. **Autocars Frossard** (tel. 04–50–45–73–90) sends buses to Geneva (2 hrs, 50F) and Chambéry (1 hr, 48F), and **Voyages Crolard** (tel. 04–50–45–08–12) will take you down the east side of Lac d'Annecy as far as Talloires (45 mins, 14F) and down the west side as far as St-Jorioz (9 daily; 30 mins, 12F). **Autocars Francony** (tel. 04–50–45–02–43) serves Chambéry and Chamonix twice daily Monday–Saturday.

GETTING AROUND

From mid-June to early September, the small, green-topped **Ligne des Vacances** Bus 91 travels to the train station, campground, youth hostel, and Hôtel de Ville 9 AM–7 PM. **SIBRA** (tel. 04–50–51–70–33) Bus 1 runs year-round from the train station (direction: Paradis or Marquisats) to near the youth hostel; buy a 7F ticket from the driver. To reach the vieille ville from the train station, head straight onto rue de la Poste and turn left on rue Royale, which takes you through the new part of Annecy; hang a right when you get to the lake.

WHERE TO SLEEP

As long as you reserve ahead in summer you can find well-situated, affordable accommodations. Otherwise, dingy budget hotels are clustered in an ugly industrial section near the train station. If need be, try the **Hôtel les Terraces** (15 rue Louis Chaumontal, tel. 04–50–57–08–98), right behind the station, where beautiful modern singles and doubles go for 160F (180F with shower). Take a left out of the station, another left at the end of the block, and another left two blocks later.

Though you might be intimidated by the presence of the very fine (and very expensive) seafood restaurant in **Le Belvédère** (7 chemin du Belvédère, tel. 04–50–45–04–90), most rooms in the intimate garden hotel command spectacular lake views for less than the price of dinner. Its eight rooms (WC down the hall) cost 190F–240F; wear your clean socks for the 35F breakfast. The hotel is open mid-May–September. A worthy splurge are the antique-style rooms of the **Hôtel de Savoie** (1 pl. St-François, tel. 04–50–45–15–45), in an 18th-century building adjoining a church, smack in the heart of the vieille ville. Doubles are 200F (280F with bath) overlooking the courtyard, or 350F for a room with bath looking out at quai Perrière. From the station, take rue de la Poste toward the vieille ville, and then follow the canal upstream along rue Jean-Jacques Rousseau.

HOSTEL • The super-duper **Auberge de Jeunesse** (opened in 1995) has lots of beds, a bar, and a game room. It's far from the train station, but getting here is half the fun (in summer, take Bus 91 from the train station straight to the hostel for 7F). Once here, it's a 5-minute walk downhill to the lake, about 10 minutes to the vieille ville, and 2 minutes to hiking trails. A card-key gives access to your room and the front door, thus eliminating the need for a curfew. A clean dorm room with breakfast is 70F. Sheets are 17F, and lunch and dinner are around 45F each. *Rte. de Semnoz, tel. 04–50–45–33–19, fax 04–50–52–77–52. 117 beds. Cash only.*

CAMPING • Annecy's mild climate and pleasant lake make it an excellent place to pitch a tent. The terraced **Camping le Belvédère** (8 rte. du Semnoz, tel. 04–50–45–48–30) is next to the youth hostel on the road to Semnoz. It's packed nylon-to-nylon in July and August, but spaces are large, and its well-stocked market and proximity to town (five minutes by foot) make up for the crowds. The rates are 26F per person, 23F per tent. The campgrounds are closed mid-October–mid-December. If you head down the east side of the lake by bus or bike, you'll run into more than 20 campgrounds. Among them, the small **Camping l'Universe** (impasse de la Tuilerie, St-Jorioz, tel. 04–50–68–98–25) charges only 12F per person plus 15F per tent for a plot five minutes from the lake; from rue Tuilloire, follow the signs from the bus stop. It's closed October–mid-May.

FOOD

You'll find fondue, raclette, and *pierrade* (where you cook your own meat over a little stove on the table) in almost every restaurant in the vieille ville and sandwich stands and pizza joints, for those who want something cheaper. The bargain **Buck John Grill** (1 passage des Clercs, off Faubourg-Ste-Claire, tel. 04–50–51–87–68), in the heart of the vieille ville, has steaks on its two-course (59F) and three-course (67F) menus. **Le Petit Zinc** (11 rue du Pont-Morens, tel. 04–50–51–12–93), a cozy, beamed, vieille ville bistro (the oldest in town), serves Savoie specialties like melted cheese croquettes on salad, *diots* (sausage cooked with onions and white wine), and *frikacoffe,* a pork fricassee with onion- and red-wine sauce. There's a **Supermarché** on rue de Glières, two blocks from the station and across the street from the post office.

WORTH SEEING

The **Château d'Annecy** (pl. du Château, tel. 04–50–33–87–30) houses an observatory (with a nice aquarium and underwater archaeology display) and a regional art display with beautiful 16th-century wooden sculpture and folksy, hand-hewn furniture from higher Alpine towns. Admission is 30F; it's open October–May, Wednesday–Monday 10–noon and 2–6, and June–September, daily 10–6. Down below in the vieille ville is the **Palais de l'Isle** (tel. 04–50–33–87–30), a 12th-century fortress turned prison that now houses a decent "History of Annecy" exhibit. Hours are the same as for the château; admission is 20F.

Annecy's biggest attraction is the **lake.** Swim from the beach south of the vieille ville along quai Bayreuth, rent a paddleboat (about 40F per half hour) from one of the many stands along quai Napoléon III, or go for a tour of the lake by boats (57F per person per hour), which leave from Pont de la Halle (where the vieille ville meets the water).

AFTER DARK

Try **Le Munich** (Quai Perrière, tel. 04–50–45–02–11), which serves 130 beers, 13 of them on draft. In the vieille ville, **Au Roi Arthur** (14 rue Perrière, tel. 04–50–51–27–06), with six good tap beers for 15F–20F, has a raucous happy hour weekdays 7:30–9 PM. For a touch of sophistication, head for the bar at the **casino** (32 av. d'Albigny, tel. 04–50–09–30–00). The drinks are a bit overpriced, but the view of the lake is good, and there's no cover if you're over 18 and want to play the slots. Do yourself a favor and wear something more than sandals and shorts. At the other extreme, the **Comedy Café** (passage des Sorbiers, off 13 rue Royale, tel. 04–50–52–82–83) is a glittery, '80s-ish, campy gay bar-café-theater replete with pool table, disco ball, dim lights, and Saturday-night drag shows.

OUTDOOR ACTIVITIES

BIKING • Leisure bikers should try the flat trail stretching along the lake just south of Annecy to Duingt. Great mountain-bike trails lace the Forêt Communale. Rent clunky 10-speeds at the train station for 55F per day (with a 1,000F deposit) or mountain bikes (70F per half day, 100F per day) from **Sports Passion** (3 av. du Parmelan, tel. 04–50–51–46–28) or **Loca Sports** (37 av. de Loverchy, tel. 04–50–45–44–33). Both are closed Monday.

HIKING • Annecy's hiking trails through the Forêt Communale have plenty of shade but very few glimpses of the lake. A good trail map is posted across from the entrance of Camping Le Belvédère (*see* Where to Sleep, *above*), where several well-marked routes begin. For a nice day hike, take the **Perimètre trail** (marked with a blue stripe on the trees) to where it joins the GR96 (marked with a red and yellow stripe) and continue two hours up to the summit of Mont Semnoz. From here you can see everything from Mont Blanc to Grenoble on a clear day. The *Traversée du Lac Annecy* makes a full loop around the lake and takes about five days to complete. The **Maison de la Presse,** next to the tourist office and open daily 8–7, has good maps.

WATER SPORTS • In summer, **SRVA** (31 rue des Marquisats, on the lake south of the vieille ville, tel. 04–50–45–48–39) rents Windsurfers for 150F for two hours, provided you leave a deposit and promise you know what you're doing. You can also rent a 15-ft, three-person Hobie Cat for 250F for two hours. Even cheaper is renting a battered canoe or kayak (35F an hour, 140F a day) from **CKCA** (Canoe and Kayak Club of Annecy, tel. 04–50–45–03–98), right next door to SRVA.

CHAMBERY

Ruled by the counts and dukes of the Savoie, Sicilian kings, and Sardinia from the 11th to 18th centuries, Chambéry was once crowned the capital of the Savoie for its strategic location in the narrow Jurian Valley, one of the few access routes to the Alps. Although Chambéry today still has some flair—primarily exhibited in its university, jazz clubs, and cafés—little evokes its past, except for maybe Les Charmettes, the country house of writer-philosopher (and exhibitionist, you'll discover, if you read his *Confessions*) Jean-Jacques Rousseau, who was born here. During July–September, you can arrange to visit Les Charmettes during a "Soirée Rousseau," with costumed guides and musicians recalling the writer's life and work. Call 04–79–33–42–47 for prices and information. The town's most important sight, the **Château des Ducs de Savoie** (pl. du Château), can be visited by taking a tour, which is given July and August from 2:30 to 5:30 on the half hour, May, June, and September at 2:30. Cost is 25F. The building otherwise acts as an office for the Préfecture and the Conseil Général.

BASICS

The **Maison de Tourisme** has free maps, brochures, and train schedules. The **Association Départementale de Tourisme de la Savoie** (tel. 04–79–85–12–45) on the second floor of the same building can answer specific questions about towns or activities in the Savoie. *24 blvd. de la Colonne, tel. 04–79–33–42–47. From train station, turn left on rue Sommeiller; at big intersection, blvd. de la Colonne is on left. Open Mon.–Sat. 9–noon and 2–6.*

Chambéry's main post office is two blocks from the train station. The postal code is 73000. *Pl. Paul Vidal, tel. 04–79–96–69–15. Open weekdays 8 AM–7 PM, Sat. 8–noon.*

COMING AND GOING

From Chambéry's **train station** (pl. de la Gare, tel. 04–79–75–67–99), there's regular service to Annecy (50 mins, 48F), Chamonix (3½ hrs, 167F), Grenoble (1 hr, 55F), and Lyon (1½ hrs, 86F). For Paris, you must pass through Annecy; catch a regular train (4 hrs, 310F) or, September–June, the TGV (3 hrs, 359F). To reach the center, veer left as you exit the station and follow rue Sommeiller for two blocks. Buses leave from the **gare routière** (tel. 04–79–69–11–88) right outside the train station, which sells tickets for **VFD** buses (tel. 04–79–69–28–78) to Grenoble (1½ hrs, 65F).

GETTING AROUND

There's a big, colorful map posted in front of the train station. Getting around Chambéry on foot is easy: The commercial district is bounded by the railroad station, Parc Savoiroux, the Malraux arts complex, the Château des Ducs du Savoie, and the Jardin du Verney. The main pedestrian shopping avenues are **place St-Léger** and **rue Croix d'Or,** with the arcaded rue de Boigne bisecting the former and running from an elephant-ringed statue at one end to the château at the other.

WHERE TO SLEEP

Chambéry's few budget hotels are near the château—a good deal for sightseers, a bum deal for the quick-stop train crew. Across the street from the train station is the renovated (that means phones, bathrooms, and TVs in the rooms) **Hôtel Le Revard** (41 av. de la Boisse, tel. 04–79–62–04–64). Singles start at 150F, doubles at 195F.

UNDER 125F • Bar-Hôtel du Château. It's hard not to like the couple that runs this hotel-bar–tattoo parlor. The cheerful husband offers everyone tattoos while the wife puffs on cigarettes, pouring drinks. The rooms are (surprisingly) well kept, clean, and cheap: Singles are 85F, doubles 120F. Even better, it's near the château and a few good bars, and not too far from the train station. Showers are free. *37 rue Jean-Pierre Veyrat, tel. 04–79–69–48–78. From station, cross blvd. du Musée and walk 3 long blocks until you see HOTEL sign on left. 16 rooms, 2 with bath. Cash only.*

UNDER 300F • Art Hôtel. This quiet, très moderne lodging, not far from the train station, has big rooms for 210F–280F and a 35F breakfast buffet. *154 rue Sommeiller, tel. 04–79–62–37–26. Step out of the train station and turn left. 36 rooms with bath.*

FOOD

Sandwich shops, pizzerias, and markets line the pedestrian streets. The big straw chairs on the terrace of **Café de l'Horloge** (107 pl. St-Léger, tel. 04–79–33–39–26) are a great place to kick back and get a drink to accompany a sandwich you've bought somewhere else. **La Chaumière** (14 rue Denfert-

Rochereau, tel. 04–79–33–16–26) serves standard French dishes, including home-canned foie gras, and a good 75F menu. **Le Poterne** (3 pl. Marché, off rue Trésorie, tel. 04–79–99–23–70) has great Savoie specialties served in its woodsy dining room or on its shaded terrace; cheese or meat fondues are 55F for lunch, 60F–75F for dinner. **Les Trois Voûtes** (110 rue de la Croix-d'Or, tel. 04–79–33–38–56) has fondue and two inexpensive menus in a spacious, lively setting. For groceries, check out the **Express** (1 pl. de la Gare), one block left of the train station.

BOURG-ST-MAURICE

In winter, this normally quiet town transforms into a bustling Haute-Savoie ski station at the base of the **Les Arcs** triple ski resort—referred to by their meter elevations as Arc 1600, Arc 1800, and Arc 2000. In summer, it's Grand Central for hikers, mountain bikers, summer skiers, paragliders, white-water rafters, and the world-championship canoeists and kayakers who come every July for the European finals. Bourg-St-Maurice rests on a valley floor at an elevation of 2,673 ft, at the foot of peaks that rise up to more than 9,900 ft—and they just go straight up. Bourg-St-Maurice itself retains a community feeling that a lot of its chic ski-resort neighbors have lost; you'll still find cows heading up the mountains to feast on the summer wildflowers that give the local Beaufort cheese its sweetness. Near the *base de rafting* (rafting center), 1 km (½ mi) west of town, you can visit artisanal workshops and watch people make cheese, carve wood, and spin wool. There are plenty of hiking options from Bourg-St-Maurice, although the real thrillers start from the top of the funicular at Les Arcs; it costs 32F one-way for the ascent (with shuttle connection) to Arc 1800 and on to Arc 2000. A round-trip funicular ride plus the three connections it takes to reach the 10,585-ft **Aiguille Rouge Summit** costs 75F. If you've got the cash, the visual pleasures are worth it.

BASICS

The **Office de Tourisme,** across from the train and bus station, is the hub of Bourg's activities. The office organizes free day hikes and mountain excursions and sells a map (38F) that lists most hikes in the Bourg–Val d'Isère–Tignes area. The free pamphlet "Les Arcs–Bourg-St-Maurice" shows the terrain covered by the funicular and should be enough to get you back to town. Mountain guides are here 6–7 every night during July and August to answer questions. *Pl. de la Gare, tel. 04–79–07–12–57, fax 04–79–07–45–96. Open Mon.–Sat. 9–noon and 2–7, Sun. 9–noon.*

Next door to the tourist office is the **Bureau Parc National La Valoise** (tel. 04–79–07–02–70). Maps and books that cover the trails, geology, and flora and fauna of the park are available June–September. The helpful staff make gîte and refuge reservations.

COMING AND GOING

The TGV runs a direct service from Paris's Gare de Lyon to Bourg-St-Maurice departing every Friday, Saturday and Sunday. There is a direct Eurostar service from London to Bourg-St-Maurice (8 hrs). Contact SNCF (08–36–35–35–35) for fare information. The modern **train station** has a bureau de change with decent rates. Most trains are met by the buses of **Auto Cars Martin** (tel. 04–79–07–04–49), which runs buses to Val d'Isère (1 hr, 63F) and Tignes (50 mins, 63F); the ticket booths are in the train station. Taxis can be booked by calling 04–79–07–03–94. There is a free bus service around the valley linking d'Hautville-Gondon, Seez, and Bourg-St-Maurice/funicular. Inter-resort shuttle buses are free and run frequently during the ski season.

WHERE TO SLEEP

The two-star **Hôtel Béguin** (Village des Deux Têtes, tel. 04–79–07–02–92, fax 04–79–07–72–6), closed May–November, has good-size, modern, two-, three-, and four-person rooms with stunning views for 240F–300F with bath. To get here, hop on the funicular next to the station and cruise on up to Arc 1600. If you're just passing through and don't have the time to go searching for a spot, the **Hôtel Valée de l'Arc** (49 Grande Rue, tel. 04–79–07–04–12, fax 04–79–07–75–59) has comfy rooms and homemade breakfasts. A single room costs 160F; doubles range from 200F to 280F. **Hôtel Arolla** (192 av. du Centenaire, between Grande Rue and av. Maréchal Leclerc, tel. 04–79–07–01–78, fax 04–79–07–37–72) has doubles starting at 170F with bath, and you can capitalize on Monsieur Benoît's mountain-guide experience over breakfast.

HOSTELS • The **Auberge de Jeunesse "La Verdache,"** 5 km (3 mi) from town in the neighboring community of Seez, is a hostel that organizes rafting, canoeing, and mountain-bike excursions. That means that the six-bed dorms and 12-cot tents are packed with outdoorsy types from all over Europe. There's no lockout or curfew. It costs 120F per night (98F for a cot), including breakfast, a hearty dinner, and showers. If you *really* just want a bed and breakfast, they'll usually knock the price down to 70F. An HI card is required. To get here, hop a bus to Tignes or Val d'Isère for 15F and ask the driver to drop you off at the auberge. *Seez, tel. 04–79–41–01–93. 68 beds. Reception open 9–noon and 2–5.*

The **Gîte de Vulmix** is a nice, old country house that rents out six-bed rooms (120F per person) and will feed you dinner for a steep 100F. It's 3 km (2 mi) up from Bourg toward Le Villaret; the owners will usually offer to pick you up at the station. Otherwise, from the tourist office, head south along avenue Maréchal Leclerc, turn right on rue de la Météo, and cross the bridge; the gîte is on your right. *Tel. 04–79–07–62–50.*

CAMPING • The official campground is **Le Versoyen** (tel. 04–79–07–03–45), ½ km (¼ mi) northeast of town off avenue du Stade, with 200 sites, tennis courts, and a 24F per person price tag. The **municipal campground,** 1 km (½ mi) west of town near the rafting center, charges 12F per tent for push-button showers and meager toilets.

FOOD

Aside from casual spots on Grande Rue, restaurants generally charge elevated prices for their high-elevation cuisine. It's worth your while to take a break from bread and cheese one night and head to **Casa Quintino** (102 Grande Rue, tel. 04–79–07–04–11), where they dress their fresh pasta with tomato and basil or tangy Gorgonzola cheese; be sure to have a delicious green salad and some Italian red wine. Decent pizza or regional specialties like raclette (both versions of potatoes, melted cheese, and diced ham) are 40F–60F January–March and July–September at **Le Grenier des 5 Lacs Pizzeria** (45 av. de l'Arc en Ciel, tel. 04–79–07–37–10), in the small restaurant row to the right of the train station. **Crêperie La Petite Fringale** (205 av. du Maréchal Leclerc, tel. 04–79–07–31–49) serves a tasty assortment of crepes and salads for 45F–70F.

OUTDOOR ACTIVITIES

BIKING • From Arc 1600 and Arc 1800 there are numerous steep, well-marked VTT trails, including rough-and-tumble ones that just go *down*; you can spend the whole day going down (then up by funicular) with a 95F all-day pass. **Sport 2000** (42 av. Général Leclerc, tel. 04–79–07–55–14) and **Inter-Sport** (18 Grande Rue, tel. 04–79–07–04–64) both rent VTTs for 75F per half day or 100F per day with a helmet. Prices fall if you rent more than three days.

HIKING • The tourist office sells an excellent 30F topographic guide. Without it, know that well-marked hikes start at all three Arc elevations; if you'd rather spend energy than money to go uphill, begin walking from the small chapel across the river from town (at the base of Les Arcs). Final altitudes and approximate lengths of hikes are listed on the signs. From Les Arcs 2000 you can do a half-day hike of **Les 5 Lacs** (The Five Lakes); the hike takes you to a crystal-clear, black-bottom lake. A popular day hike is to the **Petit Col St-Bernard** from La Rosière (take an Autocars Martin bus to the trailhead; 35 mins, 20F), a route used by the Romans to cross the Alps.

SKIING • The three levels of Les Arcs are connected to Tignes and Val d'Isère by frequent *navettes,* or shuttles. Together they constitute the largest ski resort in the world—you could ski all day, every day, for a solid week and not cross the same run twice. Prices are as varied as the terrain, starting at 100F for a one-day, one-resort pass, and going up to 1,500F for a weeklong, all-resort ticket. Usually the best bet is to get a demi-pension deal in a hotel or gîte that includes lift-ticket options. The Auberge de Jeunesse (*see* Where to Sleep, *above*) in Seez has a one-week package, including all food, lodging, transportation, and equipment for 2,500F per person.

WATER AND AIR • Downstream from Bourg-St-Maurice, the Isère bubbles and swirls through a 24-km (15-mi) stretch of water that is world famous with canoeists and kayakers. If you know your stuff, rent kayak equipment (85F per day) from the canoe-kayak club (tel. 04–79–07–33–20) at the base of rafting, 1 km (⅔ mi) west of town. Otherwise, sign up with **Arc Aventures** (tel. 04–79–41–55–40 or 04–79–07–43–79), which has an office in the centre ville and at Arc 1800 (Les Tournavelles), as well as a monopoly on rafting, kayaking, canoeing, and paragliding in the area. Prices start at 140F for a 12-km (7-mi) raft trip down the Isère, although the half-day 275F "Isère intégral" paddle is a better deal.

NEAR BOURG-ST-MAURICE

If you think you've really *seen* the Alps from Bourg-St-Maurice, think again. As soon as you round the first bend on the road to Tignes and Val d'Isère, the peaks you were gazing at (with your jaw on the ground) will seem dainty in comparison to the scenery surging ahead of you. The two towns are only 4 km (2½ mi) apart and ideal if all you want to do is hike, bike, ski, or sit and swoon by the mountains. Pin-drop quiet during the day, the bars and restaurants bubble during the night with tales of mountain adventures exchanged over 25F beers and 80F meals. It's peaceful October–December and April–June, but lodging, food, and nightlife options are extremely limited.

TIGNES

A commercial developer's resort built from scratch with parking-garage aesthetics, Tignes has five separate communities distributed among three elevation levels that have all sorts of activities. Four of these communities are connected by free, frequent shuttles: **Le Val Claret, Le Lac,** and **Le Lavachet,** all within 2 km (1 mi) of each other, are perfect for hitting the slopes in winter or summer, windsurfing, biking, or playing tennis by day and chilling out in a bar by night; **Tignes-les-Boisses,** 5 km (3 mi) from the trio, is for people who want to kick back, do some hiking and milder skiing, and maybe have a beer at the local pub **La Cordée** (tel. 04–79–06–40–26). Tignes-les-Boisses sits over a huge dam, at the bottom of which is **Tignes-les-Brévières,** where families come in the summer to camp in the caravan-free **L'Escapade** (tel. 04–79–06–41–27) and cruise around the river and lakeshore by foot or by bike. A massive glacier makes year-round skiing possible at the first three towns, but only when the funicular is running, 7:15 AM–2:30 PM. Summer ski passes run 163F per day; multiday passes are a bit cheaper. About 10 shuttles a day run between four of the Tignes communities, which means you can get a taste of the resort activity of Tignes-le-Lac and its neighbors while staying in the more affordable and peaceful Tignes-les-Boisses.

Tignes is also one of the doors to the **Parc National de la Vanoise.** Just past the Tignes-les-Boisses youth hostel (*see* Where to Sleep and Eat, *below*), where all the cars are parked by the side of the road, is a trailhead with hikes that go into the Vanoise, including a trail to the **Refuge la Martin,** where you can crash for 60F after a three- to five-hour hike.

BASICS • The main **Office de Tourisme** in the valley is in **Tignes-le Lac** (Le Palafour, tel. 04–79–40–04–40). It can help you out with schedules for sporting activities and transportation options. It's open June 15–August and December 15–April. Hotel reservations in the area may be made through **Tignes Organisation** (tel. 04–79–40–03–03) at Val Claret.

COMING AND GOING • **Auto Cars Martin** (tel. 04–79–06–30–75) makes two trips daily from the Bourg-St-Maurice train station; the 40-minute trek upward is 50F. Your best bet is to buy the cheapest ticket to Tignes-les-Boisses (48F) and take the free shuttle from here to the other Tignes communities. To pass through Les Brévières, which isn't normally serviced by bus, just ask the bus driver when you get on, and he'll swing by for you.

WHERE TO SLEEP AND EAT • The **Auberge de Jeunesse "Les Clarines"** in Tignes-les-Boisses (tel. 04–79–06–35–07) is run by a superfriendly staff, and each big, clean room has its own bathroom. Four-bed rooms run 65F a head, with 20F for sheets and 40F for an excellent dinner (you help set the table). There's no lockout or curfew—in summer the hostel is about the most lively place around anyway. You can pretty much show up anytime 8 AM–10 PM, but it's best to call first in case the staff is heading to the hills for the day. A free shuttle operates between Tignes and Les Boisses (5 km/3 mi between the two) at least twice a day. If you really must stay elsewhere, **Le Lavachey** (tel. 04–79–06–31–43) has basic doubles with TVs for 220F (300F with bath). Your best food bet is the **supermarket** around the corner from the tourist office in Le Lac.

VAL D'ISERE

This big-time ski station stretches for 1½ km (1 mi) along the Isère River between peaks that rise 6,600 ft above the town center. It's much more compact than Tignes, with stone and wood buildings that live up to the "Alpine chalet" image. Over the past several years, Val d'Isère has shucked its chic, upper-crust image in favor of becoming the snowboarding capital of the Alps—almost two-thirds of the schussing done here is on boards rather than skis. In summer, its attraction lies in its proximity to hiking and biking trails and the skiable glacier at the **Col d'Iserau.** Its campground is also one of the prettiest around, and about the only affordable place to stay. Other food and lodging options, however, remain high. In winter, stay at the Auberge de Jeunesse in Tignes (*see above*) and just ski or take a free shuttle over.

BASICS • The **tourist office,** a wooden building halfway through town on your left (going away from Bourg-St-Maurice), has a *guide pratique* in English that lists prices of places to stay, eat, and rent equipment. Its *Balades et Sentiers* map (45F) is great for anyone spending several days here; otherwise, the staff will make suggestions for day or half-day hikes. The in-house **Parc National de la Vanoise desk** has all the information you need for the park, which can be reached on foot from Val d'Isère. Mountain guides are on hand every night 6–7:30 (Saturday to 8) to answer specific questions. In winter, you'll find free trail maps here and in most hotels, cafés, and public offices. *Tel. 04–79–06–06–60. Open daily 8:30–7:30.*

There are loads of bureaux de change up here, but none give better rates than the **post office,** across from the tourist office, which also has an ATM machine.

COMING AND GOING • **Autocars Martin** (tel. 04–79–06–00–42) makes the 30-minute, 63F trip from Bourg-St-Maurice four times daily. Once you're in Val d'Isère, a free shuttle bus loops around the tourist office, campground, and summer ski station every 20 minutes 9 AM–8 PM. From December through March, hours are expanded to 8:30 AM–midnight and the buses stop at most hotels and all ski lifts.

WHERE TO SLEEP • If possible, come for a week and rent an apartment or chalet through **Val Location** (B.P. 228, tel. 04–79–06–06–60), part of the tourist office. The average price for a four-person cabin for one week is 2,800F in winter, 1,900F in summer. Reserve about a month in advance in winter; in summer you need only call 48 hours in advance.

The owner of the Seez (near Bourg-St-Maurice) and Tignes-les-Boisses hostels has cost-saving weeklong packages that include full room and board, training, and equipment for rafting, skiing, snowboarding, kayaking, or mountain biking.

Blanche Neige (tel. 04–79–06–04–02), on the main street at the far end of town, is one of the few bed-and-breakfasts around. Comfortable rooms with killer views, TVs, and bathrooms are 280F in summer, 400F in winter. The small, centrally located **Relais du Ski** (tel. 04–79–06–02–06), next to the Super U on the main street in the middle of town, has a half-pension deal for 285F per person from December to April, 225F May to September; doubles are 410F (260F May–September), including breakfast. Rooms are a bit run down, but they all have baths. One of the cheapest places in town is also an English-style pub. The **Moris Pub** (tel. 04–79–06–22–11) has a few rooms at 150F per person, including breakfast.

Camping doesn't get much better than at **Les Richardes** (tel. 04–79–06–26–60), at the far end of town toward Col d'Iserau, where 32F gets two people and a tent a spot of grass, hot showers, easy access to town (on foot or the free shuttle), and hiking trails. It gets crowded July–August.

FOOD • The **Super U** markets dotting the main street (the one at the far end of town is open daily 8–8) have good prices, wine sections, and cheese and meat cut to order. **Bananas** (tel. 04–79–06–04–23), next to the central lift ticket office and tennis courts, is a great local hangout where you can drink beers on the deck while watching people swish down the hill. There are Tex-Mex specialties and burgers for the homesick. For a serious dinner with Alpine ambience, try **La Vieille Maison** (tel. 04–79–06–11–76), a 300-year-old dark-wood chalet in the *vieux village* "La Daille." Rib-sticking mountain specialties (79F–98F) include veal with crème fraîche and walnuts, as well as fondue and raclette.

OUTDOOR ACTIVITIES • Nifty yellow panels mark the beginnings and crossroads of the many **hiking trails** that depart from Val d'Isère. The trail number (at the top of the panel) corresponds to the *Balades et Sentiers* map available from the tourist office; times to get to various destinations and points of interest are also indicated.

One favorite half-day hike is the very steep, 2½-hour ascent to the Col d'Iseran, where you can drink a coffee with the hordes who have come in their air-conditioned vehicles. Console yourself with the knowledge that only you enjoyed the view of the surrounding peaks and wildflowers on the way up. A bit less traveled is the one-hour route to Lac de l'Ouilette in the Parc à Moutons. Both of these hikes start from the GR5 trailhead just above the campground.

L'Espace Killy (named after world-champion skier Jean Claude Killy) encompasses Val d'Isère and Tignes, with more than 100 lifts and endless skiing possibilities. The ski season is roughly November–April. A one-day ticket costs 219F, half day (12:30–4:30) is 148F. If you get a multiday pass (545F for three days, 1,115F for a week), you can use it for one day at Les Arcs (*see* Bourg-St-Maurice, *above*) and nearby La Plagne. For information, call central reservations at 04–79–06–34–66. The tram **Le Fornet** (a stop on the free shuttle route) will take you to the top of the lift if you want to ski July–mid-August for 125F (100F for a half day). It's awfully slushy at the top, but great for sun worshipers.

PARC NATIONAL DE LA VANOISE

Created in 1963 to protect the Alpine ibex, France's oldest national park sits between Bourg-St-Maurice, Val d'Isère, Modane (in Italy), and Moûtiers. Glacial activity created its breathtaking landscape of meadows that cushion sharp granite cliffs, whose peaks are always encased by ice and snow. Winter blankets the meadows with more snow, attracting snow campers and back-country skiers, while June lets the wildflowers bloom free as groundhogs, ibex, and hikers cruise the hills. You really need to get *into* the park to appreciate its savage beauty, either on a long day hike from **Pralongnan-la-Vanoise,** the park's real hub and a popular rock-climbing spot, or on a multiday excursion from Tignes, Val d'Isère, or Les Arcs (above Bourg-St-Maurice).

BASICS • Each of these towns has a **Parc National de la Vanoise information bureau** next to or in its main tourist office. The staff will let you look at or buy the 69F *Vanoise Massif et Parc National* map, suggest hiking itineraries, and make reservations in gîtes and refuges (*see* Where to Sleep, *below*). If you're planning a trip, write or call the park's head office (135 rue Docteur Julliand, B.P. 705, 73007 Chambéry Cedex, tel. 04–79–62–30–54) and ask for free copies of *l'Estive,* the park's seasonal information publication, and its English-language *Presentation* pamphlet.

COMING AND GOING • By train and bus, head to Pralognan-la-Vanoise: Three buses per day go from Moûtiers (on the Chambéry–Bourg-St-Maurice train line) to Pralognan (1 hr, 63F) and back. Hitchhiking back down from Pralognan is quite easy, since there's only one road. You can also spend three to five hours hiking into the park from Tignes or the Val d'Isère; it's another three hours to a refuge.

WHERE TO SLEEP AND EAT • There are 64 gîtes throughout the park, under both private and park ownership. Most require reservations June–September through the park's central reservations office (tel. 04–79–08–71–49). Breakfast and bed in four- to eight-bed rooms runs 68F–105F per person. Hearty breakfasts and dinners (55F) are often served family-style in very charming, very Alpine dining rooms. Not all refuges serve food, so be sure to check if you're not planning on bringing your own. You can also camp for free next to most gîtes and refuges, but nowhere else in the park.

In Pralognan, **La Chèvrerie** (av. Chasseforêt, tel. 04–79–08–73–93), behind the church on the hill above town, and **La Maison du Randonner** (tel. 04–79–08–71–54), in the municipal campground, have nice dorm accommodations for 70F and 52F, respectively. A good half-pension gîte in the middle of town is **Le Petit Mont Blanc** (tel. 04–79–08–72–73), one block up from the tourist office; 170F gets you a spotless four-bed room and a great four-course meal. Or opt for a large, modern room (200F–280F) with French doors and a balcony at **Hôtel Le Parisien** (rue des Grands Près, tel. 04–79–08–72–31, fax 04–79–08–76–26), one block up from the church; it has a restaurant and good ski packages. The **Camping Municipal la Chamois** (tel. 04–79–08 –71–54) has large, grassy spaces; modern bathrooms with push-button showers; and stunning scenery for 11F per tent, 14F per person. Its neighbor, **Camping Isertau** (tel. 04–79–08–75–24), charges 24F per tent, 24F per person for slightly larger spaces.

LYON AND THE MASSIF CENTRAL

UPDATED BY ETHAN GELBER

Central France has some of the country's most spectacular settings and the added bonus of passing mostly unnoticed by the hordes of summertime tourists speeding their way to the overcrowded Mediterranean shores. The Massif Central's amazing volcano formations are the ideal backdrops to hiking, biking, hang gliding, and rafting—with none of the crowds that plague the more famous Alps. At the other extreme is Lyon, a big city just a hop, skip, and a jump from the Massif Central and the vineyards of the Beaujolais. Though most towns in this region have about one *boulangerie* (bakery), Lyon has top-notch restaurants, an active nightlife, and, *mais oui*, plenty of smog.

The Massif Central is everything that Lyon isn't: This provincial and sparsely populated region has low prices, few crowds, and pastoral landscapes. But what sets the Massif Central apart from the rest of France is its topography: Birthplace of the Dordogne, Loire, and Lot rivers, this volcanic plateau is scattered with dormant cone-shape craters, lakes, and "plugs" (enormous granite outcroppings). Many of the houses are built of the dark, volcanic stone, making the landscape that much more dramatic. It does, however, require some effort to travel here. Trains and buses often don't venture to mountain villages, so it's best to have your own wheels or be willing to embark on extended backpacking trips.

LYON

Lyon's history stretches back to 43 BC, when the invading Romans found its position at the confluence of the Rhône and Saône rivers an ideal site for the future capital of Roman Gaul, Lugdunum. During the Renaissance, Lyon became a center of silkworm cultivation, evidence of which is still visible in the Croix-Rousse and Vieux-Lyon districts, where a maze of *traboules* (covered passageways) protected the precious silk as it was carried from place to place.

Including the surrounding suburbs, Lyon's population exceeds 2 million, making it the second-largest city in France, after Paris. Lyon continues to prosper from industry, particularly metallurgy and chemical production—although the wealth is not shared among all. Lyon, like most modern cities, suffers from urban sprawl and smog, not to mention hot, humid summers. But attractions of the Presqu'île and Vieux-Lyon (Old Lyon) combined with an entertaining nightlife make the city worth your time.

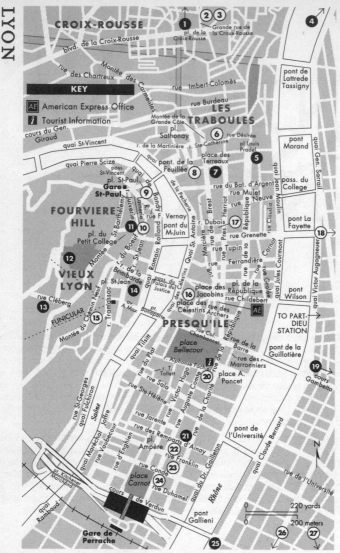

LYON

CROIX-ROUSSE

pl. de la
Croix-Rousse

Grande rue de
la Croix-Rousse

blvd. de la Croix-Rousse

Montée des Carmélites

rue des Chartreux

rue Imbert-Colomès

rue Burdeau

LES
TRABOULES

KEY

AE American Express Office

i Tourist Information

Montée de la
Grande Côte

rue Désirée

cours du Gén.
Giraud

quai St-Vincent

pl.
Sathonay

r. de la Martinière

place des
Terreaux

pl Louis
Pradel

quai Pierre Scize

pass.
St-Vincent

pl. St-Paul

pont de la
Feuillée

pont
Morand

Gare
St-Paul

rue du Bat. d'Argent

rue Mulet

rue Neuve

pass. du
College

FOURVIERE
HILL

pont du
M-Juin

r. Dubois

rue Grenette

pont La
Fayette

pl. du
Petit College

rue Tupin

VIEUX
LYON

Ferrandière

place des
Jacobins

pl. de la
République

pont
Wilson

FUNICULAR

place des
Célestins

rue des
Archers

TO PART-
DIEU
STATION

PRESQU'ILE

pont de la
Guillotière

place
Bellecour

rue des
Marronniers

place A.
Poncet

cours
Gambetta

rue Victor Hugo

pont de
l'Université

pl.
Ampère

rue des Remparts d'Ainay

rue Franklin

place
Carnot

rue Duhamel

cours de Verdun

rue de l'Université

Gare de
Perrache

pont
Gallieni

220 yards
200 meters

Sights ●

B. Fourvière, **12**
C. St-Jean, **14**
Centre de la
Résistance et de la
Déportation, **25**
H. de Gadagne, **11**
Institut Lumière, **19**
M. d'Art
Contemporain/Parc
de la Tête d'Or, **4**
M. des
Beaux-Arts, **7**
M. des Canuts, **1**
M. Historique des
Tissus, **21**
Opéra de Lyon, **5**
Théâtres and Musée
Gallo-Romains, **13**

Lodging ○

A. de Jeunesse-
Vénissieux, **27**
A. de Jeunesse-
Vieux Lyon, **15**
Celtic Hôtel, **9**
H. d'Ainay, **22**
H. Bayard, **20**
H. de Bretagne, **17**
H. de la Croix-
Rousse, **2**
H. du Dauphiné, **24**
H. de France et
Quatre Nations, **6**
H. de Paris, **8**
H. Au Patio
Morand, **18**
H. de la Poste, **3**
H. Le Terminus
St-Paul, **10**
H. du Théâtre, **16**
H. Vichy, **23**
Résidence Benjamin
Delessert, **26**

BASICS

BUREAUX DE CHANGE

As usual, the best place to cash traveler's checks is at the main post office (*see* Mail, *below*). Banks, which give good rates but take a hunk of commission, are near place des Terreaux on rue du Président Edouard Herriot. There are two **AOC** bureaux de change in the city: across place Bellecour from the tourist office at 20 rue Gasparin (open Monday–Saturday 9:30–6:30, Sunday 10–5), and near the Opéra at 3 rue de la République (open weekdays 9–6). You can find ATM machines outside most post offices.

ENGLISH-LANGUAGE BOOKSTORES

There are two excellent choices, both on place Bellecou. **Decitre's**, at No. 29, has the best collection of current English-language best-sellers, as well as classics and dictionaries; it is open Monday–Saturday

10–7. Flammarion, at No. 19, has a good selection of guidebooks, maps, and coffee-table books; it's open Monday–Saturday 9:30–7.

INTERNET ACCESS

In Vieux-Lyon, check out the wood décor of **Le Cyber** (50 montée du Gourguillon, tel. 04–78–36–60–09). It costs 1F per minute of online time. On the quai St-Antoine at the northern end of the Presqu'île, there is the **Connectik Café** (19 quai St-Antoine, tel. 04–72–77–98–85, fax 04–72–40–04–95). Lyon's leading cyber-spot since 1995, it has connections using debited time cards: A 10-minute card costs 20F, an hour costs 75F, and a five-hour card runs 250F. It is open daily 10–8 (1 AM on Friday and Saturday). Just north of place des Terreaux is the strange and futuristic bar-Internet café **Le Chantier** (18–20 rue Ste-Catherine, tel. 04–78–39–05–56, fax 04–78–28–56–66). Internet connections cost 25F per half hour or 35F per hour. It is open every night from 5 PM until 3 AM year-round.

LAUNDRY

Lavadou's central locations and long hours (7:30 AM–8:30 PM) are a godsend for travelers. Branches are at 19 rue Ste-Hélène, off rue Victor Hugo near the Gare de Perrache, and at 226 rue Paul Bert, near the Gare de la Part-Dieu. A wash costs 16F, drying 2F for five minutes, and 2F–4F for a little box of soap. There is another laundromat in Vieux-Lyon at 12 rue des Laineries. It's open daily 7 AM–9 PM. Washes cost 20F–45F, dryers 2F for five minutes.

MAIL

At the **main post office,** a less-than-efficient staff sends telegrams and faxes, changes traveler's checks at pretty good rates, and holds poste restante. Lyon's postal code is 690 followed by the two-digit *arrondissement* (district) number; in other words, the 2e district is 69002. *Pl. Antonin Poncet, off pl. Bellecour. Open weekdays 8–7, Sat. 8–noon.*

MEDICAL AID

The staff at the centrally located **Hôtel-Dieu** (1 pl. de l'Hôpital, tel. 04–72–41–30–00) is bilingual. **SOS Médecin** (tel. 04–78–83–51–51) answers questions in English and gives out names of doctors on duty around the clock. The **Pharmacie Defaux Berthet** (on the corner of rues Victor Hugo and Ste-Hélène, tel. 04–78–37–81–31) is open 24 hours Monday–Saturday and all night Sunday starting at 7 PM.

VISITOR INFORMATION

The new, central **tourist office,** called the Pavillon du Tourisme, is on place Bellecour, hidden among the flower vendors, beside the métro exit. The helpful staff has free maps, will make hotel reservations, and can give you the lowdown on any special events in town. The in-house SNCF booth has train schedules and sells rail tickets. Helpful Lyon Web sites are www.mairie-lyon.fr and www.lyon-city.org. *Tel. 04–72–77–69–69, fax 04–78–42–04–32. Open mid-Sept.–mid-June, Mon.–Sat. 10–7, Sun. 10–6; mid-June–mid-Sept., Mon.–Sat. 10–8, Sun. 10–6.*

For the weekly nitty-gritty on movies, clubs, bars, and restaurants, starting on Wednesday pick up a *Lyon Poche* (7F) at any *tabac* (tobacco shop). The free but extremely hard-to-get student-written *Guide du Petit Paumé* comes out in fall and has the most comprehensive listing; ask your hotel for a copy.

COMING AND GOING

BY TRAIN

Three train stations make Lyon a major transportation hub, and many a traveler has an awful story about waiting for hours in a giant train traffic jam. The Gare de la Part-Dieu has the most international departures and is the departure point for the TGV north to Paris and south to Marseille. Most trains leaving from the Gare de Perrache also stop at the Gare de la Part-Dieu. The neighborhoods around Gare de la Part-Dieu and Gare de Perrache both can seem rough at night, but the *centre ville* (city center) and Vieux-Lyon are more upscale and the Croix-Rousse is largely residential. It is best to schedule your arrivals and departures during daytime hours if possible.

GARE DE LA PART-DIEU • Across the Rhône from the Presqu'île, this modern complex is Lyon's main station, serving Paris daily (2 hrs, 304F–384F by TGV), Nice (5–6 hrs, 319F by TGV), Geneva (2 hrs, 118F), and most major destinations in Italy (350F–500F). Frequent trains also run to nearby towns like Grenoble, St-Étienne, Valence, and Vienne. Luggage storage costs 30F per day. Inside, the **SOS**

Voyageurs office (tel. 04–72–34–12–16) books accommodations and has information on Lyon. To get to the Gare de Perrache, on the other side of town, you can usually stay on the train as it continues for 10 minutes to the station. Otherwise, the easiest way to get between the centre ville or Vieux-Lyon and this station is via Bus 28 (8F). A third option is to take métro line B (8F) to Charpennes and transfer to line A, direction Perrache; the Bellecour stop—also on this line—is right across from the tourist office. The station's Thomas Cook office exchanges money at lousy rates; the AmEx ATM is much better, if you have their card. The gigantic shopping mall across the street is a good place to wait for your train and find cheaper alternatives to rip-off station food.

GARE DE PERRACHE • This station serves many of the same regions and cities as the Gare de la Part-Dieu, but it's more central and closer to budget hotels and restaurants. This space-age-gone-too-far (architecturally speaking) complex houses Lyon's main bus station, an **SOS Voyageurs** office (tel. 04–78–37–03–31), closed Saturday; a Thomas Cook exchange bureau; a rooftop garden; and a modern art gallery.

GARE ST-PAUL • More fashion than function, this tiled station runs hourly trains to smaller cities such as Brignais, Lozanne, and Lamure for 25F–50F and also houses a post office. On place St-Paul, at the base of Fourvière in Vieux-Lyon, it's surrounded by outdoor cafés and is worth a peek if you're in the neighborhood.

BY PLANE

The modern **Aéroport International de Lyon Satolas** (tel. 04–72–22–72–21) is 30 km (19 mi) east of town and serviced by most major European airlines. **Air Inter** (tel. 04–72–11–56–56) has direct flights to Paris and other major hubs. To reach town from the airport, hop on a **Satobus** (tel. 04–72–22–71–27), which travels to and from the Gare de Perrache and the Gare de la Part-Dieu (49F) every 20 minutes daily 6 AM–11 PM from the airport and 5 AM–9 PM from town.

BY CAR

If you decide to rent a car, beware the traffic: Lyon is a major transportation hub. Travelers from all over the country pass through the city via the toll routes A6 and A7. From Lyon, the rolling hills of Burgundy and the Beaujolais region are accessible via toll route A6 heading north. The volcanic landscapes between Clermont-Ferrand (155 km/96 mi west) and Le Puy-en-Velay (140 km/87 mi southwest) are accessible via toll route A7. Geneva is 150 km (93 mi) northeast via toll route A42. Most major U.S. car-rental agencies have offices in downtown Lyon, including **Avis** (8 rte. de Vienne, 04–78–58–33–44) and **Budget** (201 av. Berthelot, 04–78–72–46–09).

GETTING AROUND

East to west the town goes like this: the modern business district around the Gare de la Part-Dieu, the Rhône, the Presqu'île, the Saône, Vieux-Lyon, and Fourvière Hill. Most sights are in Vieux-Lyon at the foot of Fourvière Hill (crowned by the basilica) and on the Presqu'île between place des Terreaux (in the north) and place Carnot (where the Gare de Perrache is). Place Bellecour, in the center of the Presqu'île, is Lyon's tourist hub. You can cover most of Lyon on foot, navigating north–south along the *quais* (walkways along the rivers) and east–west across the bridges. Lyon has nine arrondissements: The first and second are on the Presqu'île, the third is east of the Rhône, the fourth is north of place des Terreaux on the Presqu'île (encompassing the Croix-Rousse), and the fifth is Vieux-Lyon.

BY BUS

Lyon's **TCL buses** are the most efficient form of travel in town. Métro and bus tickets are interchangeable; drivers also sell the 8F tickets, and you're supposed to put your ticket in the orange stamper every time you board a bus. Pick up a map of the 99 bus lines at the TCL office across from the Gare de la Part-Dieu or on the ground floor of the Gare de Perrache. For bus information, call 04–78–71–70–00.

BY METRO

Four métro lines crisscross the city, hitting most major squares, streets, and stations. Automatic dispensers in each station spit out 8F tickets and—a better bargain—booklets of 10 (68F); for unlimited same-day travel, buy the 24F *ticket liberté*. It's an honor system: There are no turnstiles to bar the way, only stamping machines, which you are supposed to run your ticket through. If you get caught without a ticket you could get slammed with a very hefty fine. Métro trains run 5 AM–midnight.

BY TAXI

Cabs here just flat-out ignore you if you try to hail them. Call the dispatch center and one will usually arrive within minutes. Most in-town trips cost 50F–75F, but you can sometimes get a deal. **Allô Taxi** (tel. 04–78–28–23–23) and **Taxi Radio Lyon** (tel. 04–72–10–86–86) run cabs 24 hours a day.

BY BICYCLE

Using a bike in Lyon is not as suicidal as it might sound. There are more than enough pedestrian streets in Presqu'île for two wheels to be perfectly reasonable. There is even a Rhône-side bike path (east side of the river) that makes travel a snap, unless you are heading into the hills of the Croix-Rousse or the Fourvière. To rent, call **Holiday Bikes** (8 quai Lassagne, tel. 04–72–07–06–77, fax 04–72–98–89–56, www.r-plus.com/holibike, métro Croix-Paquet). Bikes cost 60F–90F a day or 300F–500F a week with a 1,000F–1,500F deposit. Holiday Bikes also rents inline skates, electric and regular scooters, and mopeds.

WHERE TO SLEEP

There are a number of hotels near the Gare de Perrache, within walking distance of sights and nightlife. As you go farther away from the station, the neighborhoods get nicer and quieter. Generally, hotels fill up with business travelers on weeknights, making it easier to find weekend accommodations. In either case, call a week ahead or get ready to do some footwork.

UNDER 200F • Hôtel de la Poste. Probably the best budget hotel in Lyon, the rooms here are small but exceptionally well maintained, the reception is well informed and friendly, and it is close to food, entertainment, and mass transportation. Singles start at 100F and doubles at 140F. There are rooms with showers for 180F–190F, triples for 165F–250F, and extra beds for 40F. *1 rue Victor Fort, tel./fax 04–78–28–62–67. Métro: Croix-Rousse. 20 rooms, 10 with showers.*

Hôtel Vichy. This immaculate hotel five blocks from the Gare de Perrache is not luxurious, but it covers all the basics. Small singles run 140F–165F; doubles with sink and bidet are 150F–160F (the hall shower is 20F) or 180F–220F with shower; triples and quadruples with two double beds are a steal at 230F–260F. *60 bis rue de la Charité, east of pl. Carnot, tel. 04–78–37–42–58, fax 04–72–41–76–31. Métro: Ampère. 14 rooms, 8 with bath. Breakfast room.*

UNDER 250F • Celtic Hôtel. The Celtic has two addresses, both of which will lead you to the same place: a big building overlooking place St-Paul but entered from rue François Vernay. Singles are 135F–195F, doubles 160F–260F, and most have a private balcony. Ask for one on the upper floors for a picture-perfect view of Vieux–Lyon. Use of the well-kept hall showers costs 25F. *10 rue François Vernay and 5 pl. St-Paul, tel. 04–78–28–01–12, fax 04–78–28–01–34. Métro: Vieux Lyon. 39 rooms, 32 with shower.*

Hôtel d'Ainay. Two blocks north of place Carnot, this is the kind of hotel you wish were waiting for you after every long train ride. The basic rooms are basic but clean. Bonuses are the laundry nearby and the market a few doors down. Singles go for 139F–225F, doubles 175F–235F. The least expensive double rooms have toilets only. *14 rue des Remparts d'Ainay, off rue Victor Hugo, tel. 04–78–42–43–42, fax 04–72–77–51–90. Métro: Ampère. 21 rooms, 11 with bath.*

Hôtel de Bretagne. Above a bar, this little hotel is one of the best deals in Lyon. The rooms on the street have big French doors but aren't very quiet; the fifth-floor rooms are 10F less, to compensate for the long climb. Singles are 190F–200F, doubles 230F–285F. *10 rue Dubois, tel. 04–78–37–79–33, fax 04–72–77–99–92. Métro: Cordeliers. 30 rooms, all with shower.*

Hôtel du Dauphiné. A nice couple keeps this cozy hotel squeaky clean. The street-side singles (135F) are small and noisy, but doubles (240F) and triples or quads (300F) are spacious, quiet, and equipped with shower (or bath) and TV. *3 rue Duhamel, tel. 04–78–37–24–19, fax 04–78–92–81–52. Métro: Perrache. 31 rooms, all with bath.*

Hôtel du Théâtre. On a quiet side street in the theater district, this small hotel is tastefully decorated with theater posters and props. The students who manage the place will be happy to tell you about current dance performances, concerts, and plays. Singles run 180F–310F, doubles 290F–350F, and extra beds 50F. *10 rue de Savoie, near pl. des Célestins, tel. 04–78–42–33–32, fax 04–72–40–00–61. Métro: Bellecour. 21 rooms, all with shower.*

Hôtel Le Terminus Saint Paul. Right across the street from the Celtic Hôtel (*see above*), this recently renovated place shares a lot of its business with its neighbor. Singles are 170F–325F and doubles

200F–345F. There is a laundry right next door. *6 rue des Laineries, tel. 04–78–28–13–29, fax 04–72–00–97–27. Métro: Vieux-Lyon. 20 rooms, most with shower.*

UNDER 300F • Hôtel Bayard. If you are going to spend money on a hotel in Lyon, this is the place to do it. Singles go for 240F–360F, doubles for 260F–400F, all with shower. Three people can get a room for 360F. The rooms are stylishly decorated and furnished with antiques; try to get the one overlooking the inner courtyard. Reservations are essential. *23 pl. Bellecour, tel. 04–78–37–39–64, fax 04–72–40–95–51. Métro: Bellecour. 15 rooms, all with shower.*

Hôtel de la Croix-Rousse. This relaxed, family-run hotel is just off place de la Croix-Rousse, in a hip, residential part of town. Many rooms open onto a quiet inner courtyard; the uppermost floors have terrific views of the centre ville. The friendly desk staff are also a plus. *157 blvd. de la Croix-Rousse, tel. 04–78–28–29–85, fax 04–78–27–00–26. Métro: Croix-Rousse. 34 rooms, all with bath.*

Hôtel de France et Quatre Nations. Tidy rooms overlooking an interior garden are a safe haven from the rumble of the city. Singles are 150F–250F, while doubles go for 190F–310F (210F with a shower). There are triples (290F–360F) and quadruples (350F–390F) too. *9 rue Ste-Catherine, tel. 04–78–28–11–01, fax 04–78–28–05–34. Métro: Hôtel de Ville. 30 rooms, 23 with bath or shower.*

UNDER 350F • Hôtel Au Patio Morand. This quiet hotel is in a residential area, a 10-minute taxi ride from both main train stations. The rooms are not large, but they are cheery and comfortable. Ask for one that opens out onto the pretty inner courtyard where breakfast is served or that overlooks the street; the rest don't have the benefit of much light. Singles go for 250F–320F and doubles run 270F–340F. *99 rue de Créqui, tel. 04–78–52–62–62, fax 04–78–24–87–88, www.hotel-morand.fr. Métro: Foch. 32 rooms, all with shower or bath.*

Hôtel de Paris. Just south of place des Terreaux, this place is a good option. In the thick of things but aware of the need for calm, it offers simple rooms and a quiet common area for 250F–350F a double. *16 rue de la Platière, tel. 04–78–28–00–95, fax 04–78–39–57–64. Métro: Cordeliers. 30 rooms, most with shower.*

HOSTELS

Auberge de Jeunesse–Vieux Lyon. Lyon's gorgeous new auberge is perched above (and only a few minutes' walk from) the heart of Vieux-Lyon on the sunny (city) side of Fourvière Hill. At 71F a bed (including breakfast, plus 17F for sheets), you have access to a garden, a sun-soaked patio, indoor lounges, a bar, a bike shed, laundry facilities, a kitchen, Internet terminals, and luggage lockers. The closest métro stop is the funicular station Minimes, from which it is a short walk downhill to the hostel. Otherwise it's an uphill lug from métro Vieux-Lyon (St-Jean). *41–45 montée du Chemin Neuf, tel. 04–78–15–05–50, fax 04–78–15–05–51. From métro Vieux-Lyon, walk north on rue Tramassac to first left uphill on montée du Chemin Neuf; hostel is on left. From métro Minimes, head from pl. des Minimes downhill on montée du Chemin Neuf. 180 beds. Reception is open 7–noon and 2 PM–1 AM.*

Auberge de Jeunesse–Vénissieux. Clean and efficiently run, this hostel has large rooms with comfortable 51F beds (plus 17F for sheets), hot showers, a big, sunny common area, a TV room, Internet access, a rooftop deck and patio, and a bar with 12F beers. Breakfast is 17F. Ask for Rooms 12–28 to avoid noise from the bar and kitchen. *51 rue Roger Salengro, Vénissieux, tel. 04–78–76–39–23, fax 04–78–77–51–11. From Part-Dieu, take Bus 36 to Vivani-Joliot-Curie, walk left under PARIS/MARSEILLE freeway sign; hostel is on right. 120 beds. Reception open 7–11 AM and 5:30–11 PM. Kitchen, laundry.*

Résidence Benjamin Delessert. It's removed from all the action, but this residence has clean singles with desk, sink, telephone, and plenty of closet space for 90F per night (shower included) July–September. You also have access to a pool, weight room, and library. Reservations aren't usually necessary, but the staff are more friendly if you call to tell them you're coming. *145 av. Jean Jaurès, tel. 04–78–61–41–41, fax 04–78–61–40–24. Métro: Jean Macé. From métro stop, walk 10 mins south on av. Jean Jaurès. 200 rooms.*

CAMPING

There are two campgrounds in the suburbs, but don't bother with these unless you enjoy sleeping next to droves of mobile homes. A better option is 10 km (6 mi) north of Lyon in Dardilly at **Camping International de Lyon** (tel. 04–78–35–64–55). It charges 17F per adult and 35F per tent and has a pool and game room. To get there, take Bus 89 from beside métro Gare de Vaise; allow for 30–45 minutes from the centre ville for the entire trip.

FOOD

Dining is Lyon's most popular pastime, and the city has more multistar restaurants than anywhere, except Paris, of course. Regional, gastronomic goodies like *andouillette* (tripe sausage), *quenelles* (sausage-shape dumplings made with flour, eggs, and fish or veal), and *salade lyonnaise* (salad with bacon, croutons, and a poached egg on top) are all served with giant carafes of red wine from the nearby Beaujolais region. **Rue Mercière** (running north–south between place d'Albon and place des Jacobins), **rue St-Jean** (in Vieux-Lyon), and **rue des Marronniers** (near places Bellecour and Antonin Poncet) are streets full of small *bouchons* (small bistros endemic to Lyon, with homey wooden benches, zinc counters, and paper tablecloths).

If you're not into traditional Lyonnais fare, you can find anything from Turkish to Brazilian food on the side streets around **place des Terreaux,** as well as stands that sell *donner-kebabs* (lettuce, spicy lamb, and yogurt sauce in a pita) all over the place. At the morning **market** along quai St-Antoine (on the east bank of the Saône), elbow your way to fresh meat, produce, and cheese every day except Monday. If you can find a table on the crowded terrace, enjoy heavenly homemade ice cream at **René Nardone's** (3 pl. Ennemond Fousseret, just past 26 quai de Bondy, tel. 04–78–28–29–09); it's closed December–March.

UNDER 75F • All Sports Café. In a sprawling characterless building by the banks of the Saône and a short walk from the Gare de Perrache, this place is the mecca for the city's sports fans. On days when the local soccer team is playing or there is an important international match, every spot of floor sees stamping feet. Reserve long in advance for this kind of occasion or get there really early for a bar stool. Giant salads (48F–69F), hamburgers (59F–73F), plats du jour (52F) and much more fill out a well-rounded menu. You can even get pitchers of beer (79F–89F) until 3 AM Thursday–Saturday. *12 quai Maréchal Joffre, tel. 04–78–38–48–38. Métro: Perrache.*

During World War II, scores of skilled Lyonnais workers were deported to Germany to boost the Nazi war machine. The anger inspired by this act turned Lyon into an early center of the French Resistance.

Brasserie La Belle Époque. Come here for one of 30 different kinds of beer, heaping bowls of *moules* (mussels) served with home fries (55F–69F), and salad (55F), or the three-course menu that might include fresh salmon and *salade lyonnaise* (69F–99F). Jazz trios usually play on weekends, turning the terrace into a lively bar scene after 11 PM. *4 rue du Palais de Justice, off rue St-Jean in Vieux-Lyon, tel. 04–78–42–54–43.*

UNDER 100F • Brasserie Le Caveau. Traditional *cuisine lyonnaise* graces the tables of this classic brasserie with a wide and airy terrace. Two menus for under 100F (86F and 98F) and impeccable service will leave you content to enjoy the air of the traffic-free place Antonin Poncet. *3 pl. Antonin Poncet, tel. 04–78–37–35–04. Métro: Bellecour. Closed Mon. and Feb.*

Brunet. Come here to try good, traditional Lyonnais fare; besides the mandatory andouillette sausage and tripe, there is usually excellent roast pork on the 99F menu and a full list of chef's recommendations (60F–140F) from fresh salmon and beef fillet with cream and forest mushrooms to steaming pot-au-feu. *23 rue Claudia, tel. 04–78–37–44–31. Métro: Cordeliers. Closed Sun., Mon., and first 3 wks of Aug.*

Mister Higgins. Who would have thought that an Englishman could open a restaurant in the French capital of gastronomy and succeed? But he has—in a bright spot in the Croix-Rousse district. At his restaurant you can have delicious salads (50F–70F), mouthwatering entrées such as salmon in a light curry sauce (70F), a French-style fish-and-chips menu (72F–83F), and desserts to charm any sweet tooth. On Sunday, come for the big brunch (95F) from 10:30 to 2; reserve in advance as it's very popular. *16 rue Dumenge, tel. 04–78–30–10–20. Take the métro to the Croix-Rousse stop, cross pl. de la Croix-Rousse to rue du Mail, and follow it to rue Dumenge. Closed Mon. No lunch Tues.–Sat., no dinner Sun.*

Le Pâtisson. One of Lyon's few vegetarian restaurants, Le Pâtisson uses only organically grown produce and grains. At lunch you can get a heaping plate of vegetables, legumes, and a grain, and a dessert for 65F. At dinner the price goes up to 90F, with some tofu specialties thrown in. *17 rue Port-du-Temple, off pl. Jacobins, tel. 04–72–41–81–71. Métro: Bellecour or Cordeliers. Cash only. Closed weekends.*

UNDER 125F • Brasserie Rôtisserie Le Nord. A creation of world-famous Lyon-based chef Paul Bocuse, this restaurant is one of three throughout the city that bring haute cuisine to the height of a normal table. Get an appetizer, house-special *broche* (skewer with roasted meat), and main dish for 115F. Waiters in traditional black vests and ankle-length aprons complete the picture. *18 rue Neuve, tel. 04–72–10–69–69. Métro: Cordeliers or Hôtel de Ville.*

UNDER 150F • La Mère Jean. This bouchon, in business since 1923, dishes up quenelles, andouillette in mustard sauce, and other traditional Lyonnais fare. The cozy dining area twinkles with brass and is usually jam-packed. The 69F lunch menu is a good deal; various dinner menus go for 81F–149F. Reservations are essential. *5 rue des Marronniers, tel. 04–78–37–81–27. Métro: Bellecour. Closed weekends.*

Restaurant de Fourvière. Your eye will be distracted even if you are with the people you love the most. The panoramic view of the city from the wide-windowed dining room is breathtaking, especially at night. The restaurant is located in the hilltop compound that includes the Basilique Notre-Dame de Fourvière and can be reached after a gentle stroll through the gardens below. The lunch menu of 70F is more expensive and elaborate at dinner (110F–145F). *9 pl. de Fourvière, tel. 04–78–25–21–15. Métro-Funiculaire: Fourvière. Closed Tues.*

WORTH SEEING

Get a feel for Lyon by walking along the banks of the Saône and the Rhône, sipping coffee on place des Terreaux, and window-shopping on rue de la République. The Saône flows through Burgundy and the Beaujolais, irrigating some of France's most renowned vineyards, before it gets to Lyon. On the west side of the river is the medieval St-Jean quarter and, on the east side, the 18th- and 19th-century pastel-painted facades of the Presqu'île.

The Rhône has a totally different feel. This broad, gray river rushes through Lyon on its descent from the Alps toward Marseille. In winter it brings biting winds, but in summer it's a pleasure to ride a bike or take a long walk along its banks lined with late 19th–and early 20th–century apartment buildings. On the centre ville side of the Rhône the new **Opéra de Lyon** (1 pl. de la Comédie, tel. 04–72–00–45–00) stylishly mixes classic and contemporary style: When the building was renovated in the 1980s, its 19th-century facade was preserved, but 20th-century elements—broad, glass ceilings, and a metallic, black interior—were integrated into the design. Performances of classic operas are also often given a modern flair here in Lyon. The old **Gare des Brotteaux** (pl. Jules Ferry, Métro Brotteaux), now an art auction house, is also worth a peek. Be sure to go for a stroll in the Parc de la Tête d'Or and take note of the mansions lining Boulevard des Belges (*see* Cheap Thrills, *below*).

The tourist office leads guided tours (in English and French) of the city for 50F, starting from the Bureau des Guides (av. Adolphe Max) in Vieux-Lyon for the tour of the Old Town and its *traboules,* and at the exit of the métro station on place de la Croix-Rousse. The **traboules,** or covered passageways originally built to protect silk from the elements as weavers carried it around the city, look like entrances to ancient apartment buildings. Many are just run-down alleys with roofs, but others pass through beautiful Renaissance courtyards. The classiest traboules lie along rue St-Jean and rue Juiverie in Vieux-Lyon. The **Maison des Canuts** (10 rue d'Ivry, tel. 04–78–28–62–04, fax 04–78–28–16–93) has demonstrations of traditional silk weaving and a good video (ask them to play the English version) that covers silk cultivation from the worm to the wearing. From the Croix-Rousse métro, walk two blocks north, through place de la Croix-Rousse. It's open Monday–Saturday 8:30–noon and 2–6:30; admission is 20F. The city's other museums also cover a wide range of topics from Lyon history to filmmaking. If you plan to go to more than three museums in a day, buy the 40F museum pass.

CENTRE DE LA RESISTANCE ET DE LA DEPORTATION

Possibly the best of its kind in France, this museum does an excellent job chronicling a difficult period in French history: the Vichy regime, the Resistance, and the deportation of Jews. Housed in the former Gestapo headquarters of Lyon, the museum has original photographs and books listing the names of the deported. Definitely get the English-language headsets (free) for a self-guided tour. *14 av. Berthelot, just over Pont Gallieni, tel. 04–78–72–23–11 or 04–72–73–33–54, fax 04–72–73–32–98. Métro: Jean Macé or buses 11, 26, 32 and 39 pass by it. Admission 25F. Open Wed.–Sun. 9–5:30.*

FOURVIERE HILL

The sinister-looking Roman Catholic **basilique** sitting on top of Fourvière Hill is young by French standards (built between 1872 and 1896), but what it lacks in age it makes up for in ornate detail. Look closely at the base of the walls and doorways: That's red marble, not wood. And note that the basilica appears, self-congratulatingly, in most of the rich mosaics that cover the walls. The church is open daily 9–noon and 2–6. The hike up to the church, along the tree-lined *chemin du rosaire* (path of the rosary), has plenty of views and picnic spots. More direct (and less tiring) is the 7F50 funicular ride from place

St-Jean (at the bottom of the hill in Vieux-Lyon). South of the basilica via rue Roger Radisson are **théâtres Gallo-Romains**—the oldest Roman theaters in France, built in 15 BC by Emperor Augustus (a.k.a. Octavian). The **Musée de la Civilisation Gallo-Romaine** (17 rue Cléberg, tel. 04–72–38–81–90, fax 04–72–38–77–42), overlooking the theaters, winds through Lugdunum's history; the huge archaeological collection includes mosaics, pottery, money, and jewelry. It's open Wednesday–Sunday 9:30–noon and 2–6; admission is 20F.

INSTITUT LUMIERE

The Lumière brothers essentially invented motion pictures when they made *Leaving the Lumière Factories* in 1895. This museum in their former home includes loads of projection inventions, old stereoscopes, and some of the first animated cartoons. October through June, alternative, art, and classic films are shown on-site Tuesday–Sunday at 7 and 9 PM. The National Foundation of Photography is also housed here and has changing exhibitions in the art deco–art nouveau main parlor. *25 rue du Premier-Film, tel. 04–78–78–18–95, fax 04–78–01–36–62. Métro: Frères Lumières. Admission 25F, film entry prices 25F–29F. Museum open Tues.–Sun. 2–7.*

MUSEE D'ART CONTEMPORAIN

This modern museum, open only during special exhibitions, is on the west edge of the Parc de la Tête d'Or. Its construction of glass, light wood, stone, and metal usually perfectly complements the works inside: the likes of Dubuffet, Nikki de St-Phalle, and a bunch of local artists. If you don't like the erotic, exotic, or industrial, you'll find solace in landscapes and lunarscapes that border on the metaphysical. *Cité International, 81 quai Charles de Gaulle, tel. 04–72–69–17–17, fax 04–72–69–17–00. Take either Bus 47 or 4 (from métro Massena or Foch) to the end of the line. Admission 25F. Open Wed.–Sun. noon–7.*

In 1600, Henri IV came to Lyon to meet his Italian fiancée, Marie de Médicis. He took one look at her, gave her the okay, and they were married immediately in the Cathédrale St-Jean.

MUSEE DES BEAUX-ARTS

This museum houses France's largest collection of art after the Louvre, in a 16th-century abbey. Besides an extensive display of romanticism, neoclassicism, and impressionism, one whole wing is dedicated to Lyonnais painters of the 18th and 19th centuries. The collection of Egyptian artifacts dates from 500 BC and is almost worth its own museum. Even if you don't go inside, check out the Rodin sculptures in the inner courtyard (free). *Palais St-Pierre, 20 pl. des Terreaux, tel. 04–72–10–17–40, fax 04–72–28–12–45. Métro: Hôtel de Ville. Admission 25F. Open Wed.–Sun. 10:30–6.*

MUSEE HISTORIQUE DES TISSUS

This museum focuses on Lyon's former monopoly of the silk world. Next door (and on the same admission ticket), the **Musée des Arts Décoratifs,** admission 28F, open 10–noon and 2–5:30, illustrates the development of Lyonnais decorative arts. *34 rue de la Charité, tel. 04–78–38–42–00, fax 04–72–40–25–12. Métro: Ampère. Admission 28F. Open Tues.–Sun. 10–5:30.*

VIEUX-LYON

The **Cathédrale St-Jean** (pl. St-Jean) may look odd, but it has a good excuse: Construction began in 1180, stopped in 1268 because of violent religious struggles, and never picked up again. The site dates from around AD 300, when the first building in this neighborhood was constructed on this plot. Inside, check out the astrological clock and the gorgeous stained-glass windows.

Of the two museums inside the 16th-century **Hôtel de Gadagne** (pl. du Petit College, tel. 04–78–42–03–61), the **Musée Historique de Lyon** and the **Musée de la Marionette,** the latter is by far the most impressive. This museum has an incredible marionette collection, including the original Guignol, Gaufron, and Madelon (France's version of Punch and Judy), as well as puppets from England, Java, Cambodia, and Czechoslovakia. There are some Roman columns and city keys in the "historic" part, but they definitely take the backseat. It's open Wednesday–Monday 10:45–6; admission is 25F.

CHEAP THRILLS

The best way to recuperate from a heavy dose of rich French cuisine is to take a walk in the **Parc de la Tête d'Or** (bordered by quai Charles de Gaulle, blvd. des Belges, and blvd. de Stalingrad; bus line 47

GAY AND LESBIAN LYON

Bar des Traboules (86 Grande Rue de la Croix-Rousse, tel. 04–78–29–20–09) is a leather kind of place. Le Village (8 rue St-Georges, in Vieux-Lyon, tel. 04–78–42–02–19) is a women-only bar; Friday and Saturday are about dancing. L'Échequier (38 rue de l'Arbre Sec, tel. 04–78–29–18–19), just east of place des Terreaux, is the best gay club, complete with stage shows, special events, and dancing until dawn. Slightly lower key is La Ruche (22 rue Gentil, tel. 04–78–39–03–82), with a 1930s-style armchair bar on the first floor.

ends here), which has more than 265 acres for running, strolling, picnicking, and sunning. There are also rowboats, pedal boats, a miniature golf course, bicycle carts, a rose garden, botanical gardens, and a zoo. **Les Berges du Rhône,** a bike and running path, follows the banks of the Rhône for several miles, starting just across avenue de Grande-Bretagne from the park's main, southwest gate.

FESTIVALS

Every July, the **Nuits Symphoniques** festival features one classical composer's music performed by orchestras from around the world. In early fall Lyon puts on the **Biennale de la Danse** in even years and the **Biennale d'Art Contemporain** in odd years, although in the year 2000, both will be held simultaneously (tel. 04–78–30–50–66 for information on both). Late September brings a **Chamber Music Festival** that attracts musicians from all over Europe. On the 8th of December, Lyon is the place to be: Lyonnais celebrate the **Fête de la Lumière** (Festival of Light) by lighting candles in their windows and going to candlelit concerts in churches and a big son-et-lumiere show in Vieux-Lyon. In November and December, the musical **Festival du Musique du Vieux-Lyon** (tel. 04–78–42–39–04 for information) takes place with a program of classical music concerts in churches and music halls throughout the city.

SHOPPING

Lyon is a shopper's paradise. For chic clothing try the stores on **rue du Président Edouard-Herriot** and **rue de la République** in the center of town. Lyon is still the nation's silk and textiles capital and as a result all big-name designers have shops here. For antiques, wander down **rue Auguste Comte** (from place Bellecour to the Gare de Perrache), which is littered with antiques shops and art galleries. Look for Lyonnais puppets on Vieux-Lyon's **place du Change.** For chocolates in pretty boxes to take home to friends, try **Bernachon** (42 cours Franklin Roosevelt).

AFTER DARK

Lyon's nightlife is not for the "early to bed, early to rise" crowd. Many bars and clubs get going around 11 PM and don't stop until the roosters start to crow. Clubs and drinks aren't exactly cheap, but you have to live it up sometimes. One serious drawback: Public transportation stops at midnight. Be prepared to walk home or take a cab for a hefty fare. Although it's happening during the day, place Bellecour, and everything south of it, is completely dead after dark. The "alternative" scene, complete with blue lights and leather, is centered on **place des Terreaux,** in rues Ste-Catherine and Désirée, and north on the way up the Croix-Rousse hill. Most of the discos along **quai Romain Rolland** in Vieux-Lyon won't let you in if they don't like the way you look, but if they do it's often for free. Try **L'Alibi** (13 quai Romain Rolland, tel. 04–78–42–04–66), which has a laser show to go along with the music. Vieux-Lyon and **place St-Paul** are popular late-night café hangouts. For a sampling of local slapstick café-théâtre—funny, low-budget productions in a casual setting (though hard to follow for non-French speakers)—head to **Espace Gerson** (1 pl. Gerson, tel. 04–78–27–96–99) or **Café-Théâtre de l'Accessoir** (26 rue de l'Annonciade, tel.

04–78–27–84–84). Check the weekly *Lyon-Poche,* published on Wednesday and sold at newsstands (7F), for cultural events and goings-on.

BARS

La Mi-Graine (11 pl. St-Paul, tel. 04–78–27–73–88) serves just as much coffee (7F) as it does beer (14F–25F). Here you will find drunken French folks singing songs by Cyndi Lauper and the Commodores. **L'Antidote** (108 rue St-Georges, in Vieux-Lyon, tel. 04–78–37–54–94) is a real Irish bar, complete with wood paneling, a dartboard, and Guinness (32F). The **Albion Public House** (tel. 04–78–28–33–00), the **Barrel House** (tel. 04–78–29–20–40), and the **Shamrock** at 12, 13, and 15 rue Ste-Catherine (just north of place des Terreaux) are watering holes for displaced English and Irish youth. Computer jocks can head into cyberspace at **Le Chantier** (18–20 rue Ste-Catherine, tel. 04–78–39–05–06) while their friends listen to jazz and nibble on tapas. The **Smoking Dog** (16 rue Lainerie, between pl. St-Paul and pl. du Change in Vieux-Lyon, tel. 04–78–28–38–27) is Lyon's version of Cheers, with friendly regulars, an undemanding atmosphere, and pitchers of beer (30F).

CINEMAS

CNP Terreaux (40 rue du Président Edouard-Herriot, off pl. des Terreaux) has Saturday midnight showings (44F) of American greats like *Easy Rider* and *The Big Lebowski.* The small **CNP Odéon** (6 rue Grôlée) and **CNP Bellecour** (12 rue de la Barre, off north side of pl. Bellecour) both show lots of nonmainstream Anglophone films with French subtitles—look for the marking "v.o." (*version originale*). For all the CNP theaters, call 08–36–68–69–33 for a recording of what's playing. **Cinéma Opéra** (6 rue Joseph Serlin, tel. 04–78–28–80–08) is home to some great "v.o." film festivals. The cheapest ticket (39F, instead of the normal 44F) is at **Cinemas Ambience** (12 rue de la République, near pl. des Terreaux, tel. 08–36–68–20–15), which plays American classics like *Some Like It Hot* and *The Wizard of Oz.* The **Institut Lumière** (*see above*) shows a variety of eclectic films in original languages.

MUSIC AND DANCING

Le Hot Club (26 rue Lanterne, between pl. des Terreaux and the Saône, tel. 04–78–39–54–74) celebrated its 50th birthday in 1999 and has swing, big band, and Django Reinhardt–inspired musicians. An all-ages Americans-style concert and dance hall is the **Eden Rock Café** (68 rue Mercière, tel. 04–78–38–28–18), which has weekend shows covering rock, blues, funk, country, and more. For a romantic, subdued setting, stop in the intimate **Le Cintra** (43 rue de la Bourse, tel. 04–78–42–54–08). For jump-up-and-dance-a-jig Irish music, 12F cider, and Guinness on tap (24F), head to the **Tudor Rose Public House** (9 quai de Bondy, tel. 04–78–28–80–82) any night but Sunday and Monday.

NEAR LYON

LE BEAUJOLAIS

How much does it cost to have the whole Beaujolais wine region at your feet? About 35F for the northbound train from Lyon to Villefranche-sur-Saône and another 100F for a bike rental. Or you can go the easy route and rent a car at the Lyon train stations. Either way, Villefranche is 30 km (19 mi) due north. By car, take the meandering N6 or speedy A6. Small villages, usually consisting of a church, a bar, and a boulangerie, pop up here and there out of the rolling, vine-covered hillsides. Country roads connecting the towns are uncrowded, and the hills are very doable by bike. There are also buses from Villefranche that take you to the region's little villages, which you can easily tour on foot. Belleville and Villefranche, both on the Saône River, are the largest towns in the region and lie along the Lyon–Dijon train line, making them good bases from which to explore the many *vignobles* (vineyards) in the 40-km (25-mi) north–south stretch of the Beaujolais. Lyon's tourist office has a decent map of the Beaujolais; better is the "Vignobles de Beaujolais" map, available (free) at the tourist offices in Belleville and Villefranche and at most wineries with DÉGUSTATION (wine tasting) signs out front.

Beaujolais wine is made exclusively from the *gamay noir à jus blanc* grape. The region's 10 best wines—Brouilly, Côte-de-Brouilly, Chénas, Chiroubles, Fleurie, Julienas, Morgon, St-Amour, Moulin-à-Vent, and Régine—are all labeled "Grands Crus," a more complex version of the otherwise light, fruity Beaujolais. Although the region's wines get better with age, many Beaujolais wines are drunk nearly fresh off the vine; every third Thursday in November marks the arrival of the **Beaujolais Nouveau**, a bacchanalian

DRINK FOR FREE

Wine tasting is the key. Just walk into a cellar, tell them you want a "dégustation," and walk out with a wealth of knowledge (and a little buzz) all for the price of one bottle. The Beaujolais has hundreds of "caves" (cellars where wine is made, stored, and sold), from big-time tourist operations to mom-and-pop stops. Make sure the ones you pick have DÉGUSTATION *signs out front. Signs that say* VENTE EN DIRECT *(sold directly from the property) and* VENTE AU DÉTAIL *(sold by the bottle) are also good indicators. Most towns have a cooperative "caveau" (wine cellar), where you can pay a few francs to taste all the wine you want.*

festival that also showcases regional cuisine. Another regional festival, the **Fête de la Musique et des Cultures,** celebrating music and world cultures from mid-June to the end of July, is held all over the Beaujolais countryside.

The northern section of the Beaujolais, near Belleville, is where the Grands Crus come from, so it's the best place to go for tastings. Literally hundreds of vineyards are in this concentrated area, giving you the chance to taste 10 different appellations of wine ranging from the light Fleurie to the coarser Morgon. Twenty kilometers (12 mi) farther south, near Villefranche, the concentration of vineyards gives way to medieval villages built of *pierres dorées,* soft, golden-color stones quarried from the local hillsides. For more information about Beaujolais and its cities, check out www.beaujolais.net.

VILLEFRANCHE-SUR-SAONE

Villefranche is the largest town in the region, making it a good base for biking around the area. The town itself really has only one sight: the 13th-century church, **Notre-Dame des Marais** (49 rue Roland, off rue de la Gare, tel. 04–74–60–05–17). Also check out **rue Nationale,** lined with photogenic, authentic examples of Renaissance architecture, courtyards, and alleyways. From the train station, walk up rue de la Gare and you'll hit most of the hotels, restaurants, bars, and, eventually, the **tourist office** (290 rue de Thizy, tel. 04–74–68–05–18), open Monday–Saturday 9–noon and 1:30–6.

COMING AND GOING • Trains run frequently from Lyon (20 mins, 32F) to Villefranche's **train station** (pl. de la Gare). Probably the easiest way to get to the vineyards is by car, but biking is another alternative. Although getting to the vineyards by bike is not easy from Villefranche, this is the place to rent one and then take a train to a small town, bike around for the day, and come back. (Most local trains have a bike car you can take your bike on for free, but check to be sure.) Rent a mountain bike for 100F at **V.T.T. Villefranche** (152 rue des Jardiniers, off rue Stalingrad, tel. 04–74–65–38–57), with a 1,200F deposit or a Visa or MasterCard.

WHERE TO SLEEP AND EAT • In the center of town, simple **Le Moulin au Vent** (81 rue d'Anse, tel. 04–74–68–36–13) has singles and doubles with shower for 140F. If you'd rather camp on the banks of the Saône, **Camping Municipal** (rte. de Riottier, tel. 04–74–65–33–48) charges 43F for two people and a tent. To get here from the train station, take route de Riottier (it starts right behind the station) for about 1½ km (1 mi) to the water; it's closed mid-October–April. **Brasserie du Rhône** on place Carnot has a 59F three-course menu and, on Sunday nights, live music. **L'Épicerie** (55 rue Thizy, tel. 04–74–62–04–04) is a piano jazz bar that serves relatively inexpensive Lyonnais dishes for 45F–75F, at dinner only. Otherwise, stock up on groceries at **La Vie Claire** (119 rue d'Anse, tel. 04–74–68–03–52).

BELLEVILLE

Belleville is not at all *belle* and hardly a *ville*: This wine town turned auto stop merely serves as a base from which to explore the Grand Crus region; within 10 km (6 mi) are towns home to some of the most celebrated wines in the world. The major paths into the vineyards (and the tastings) begin behind the train station. The **Office de Tourisme** (105 rue de la République, tel. 04–74–66–44–67, fax 04–74–06–43–56) has information on all these paths. The idea is to rent a bike in Villefranche or Lyon, catch a train to Belleville, head to the tourist office, choose a trail that looks interesting, and hit the road.

BASICS • Belleville is served by train from Lyon (50 mins, 46F) and by bus from Villefranche (20 mins, 25F). The train station is at the west end of rue Maréchal (which becomes rue de la République). If you must stay here overnight, the **Hôtel La Route des Vins** (1 pl. de la Gare, tel. 04–74–66–34–68), right across the street from the station, has showerless singles and doubles at 155F (270F–330F with bath).

VIENNE

If you do nothing but climb up to théâtre Romain and look out over the red-tile roofs of the Rhône Valley, you'll be happy you made the 20-minute trip to Vienne from Lyon. Vienne is a historian's Candyland, and every street seems to take you to yet another ancient church, another stoic Roman ruin, and another postcard-perfect view of crumbling walls and sloped roofs.

BASICS

The **tourist office** has the very useful *Guide Touristique* to Vienne, with a map and a list of good hotels. Summer-only guided tours (40F) of the city leave from the tourist office Monday–Saturday at 10 or 3 and Sunday at 4 from the ancient theater. *Cours Brillier, tel. 04–74–53–80–30, fax 04–74–53–80–31. Open June–Sept., daily 9–1 and 2–7; Oct.–May, Mon.–Sat. 8:30–noon and 2–6, Sun. 10–noon.*

COMING AND GOING

Trains from Lyon make the 20-minute run to Vienne's centrally located **station** (pl. Pierre Sémard) eight times daily for 34F. Step out of the station onto place Pierre Sémard, take a look at the posted map, and strike out on foot.

WHERE TO SLEEP

Of the few good, small hotels in Vienne, **Pile ou Face** (35 cours Brillier, tel. 04–74–85–05–84), just a few blocks down from the station, is the most reasonable and the most convenient. Small rooms over a local bar-restaurant (specializing in paella) run 180F–200F for a single and 200F–300F for a double. Also close by is the **Hôtel de la Poste** (47 cours Romestang, tel. 04–74–85–02–04, fax 04–74–85–16–17). A doting staff has trouble keeping this big place spotless, but the rooms are more than adequate. Doubles run 275F–330F (with two small showerless rooms at 200F). Otherwise, the **Central** (3 rue de l'Archevêché, tel. 04–74–85–18–38, fax 04–74–31–96–33), which is in the old town and close to the cathedral, has medium-size doubles starting at 295F.

HOSTEL • **Auberge de Jeunesse.** This small hostel, on the Rhône two blocks south of the tourist office, has dorm beds in rooms of eight for 65F and in rooms of three or four for 84F; the two doubles go for 92F per person (breakfast included). Sheets are 17F. Reception is only open evenings, mid-September–mid-May 5 PM–8 PM, mid-May–mid-September 6–9. But once you check in and get your key, you can come and go as you please. *11 quai Riondet, tel. 04–74–53–21–97, fax 04–74–31–98–93. From tourist office, walk 2 blocks south along the Rhône. 55 beds.*

FOOD

Loads of sandwich stops and boulangeries line pedestrian **rue Marchande** and **rue Boson.** For more elegant fare, head down rue de la Table-Ronde to **L'Estancot** (4 rue de la Table-Ronde, tel. 04–74–85–12–09), for *paillasson* (shredded potatoes) and *crique* (the same, mixed with egg and parsley) topped with vegetables (51F), beef, and tomatoes (55F), spinach and chicken (70F), or snails and mushrooms (76F). It's closed Wednesday dinner and Sunday. Just opposite the cathedral, **Le Bec Fin** (7 pl. St-Maurice, tel. 04–74–85–76–72) is the place for an elegant, formal evening (a jacket is required) of French fare. Four-course menus range 130F–300F. It's closed Sunday dinner and Monday.

WORTH SEEING

Vienne's landmark attraction, **théâtre Romain,** was built during the 1st century into the lush hillside overlooking the Rhône. This outdoor amphitheater holds 8,000 people and is the largest of its kind in France. Concerts are held year-round, and the acoustics are great. On your way up to the theater, via rue Joseph-Brenier and rue Jacquier, be sure to have a look at the **Temple d'Auguste et de Livre,** a mini-acropolis built in 10 BC. Above the theater, via rue Pipet, the terrace of **Église St-André-le-Haut** gives an awesome view of Vienne's rooftops and monuments, the Rhône, and surrounding hills.

Across the Rhône, an entire Roman village, **St-Romain-en-Gal,** has been excavated. You can get a good view of the excavation's temple, baths, and roads from an observation deck (free) atop the new **Musée Archéologique,** the space-age-looking building on the Rhône across from place St-Louis. For a look at the goodies they've uncovered at the site, pay 30F and head inside. The museum is open Tuesday–Sunday 9:30–6:30. Vienne's other sites are in the town center, conveniently mapped out as a tourist route by the tourist office. If you want to visit more than two, buy the *carte circulaire* (29F), which gives access to all of them; otherwise each one is 11F.

Near the tourist office, the **Église St-Pierre** (pl. St-Pierre) is a 5th-century abbey that now acts as a warehouse for sculptures, friezes, and mosaics from around Vienne. The **Cathédral St-Maurice** (rue Boson) is important architecturally because it has a Romanesque infrastructure, a Gothic interior, and cubist stained-glass windows. Four blocks west, along rue de Bourgogne, the **Cloître St-Andre-le-Bas,** once a powerful abbey, was built in the 6th century and now houses temporary modern art exhibits; ask at the front desk to see its adjacent church, decorated with spirals, zigzags, and intricate floral patterns. The **Musée des Beaux-Arts** (pl. de Miremont) has cool stuff in it—Roman dinnerware made of pure silver, a mummified head, 3rd-century coins—but looks like a fifth-grade science classroom.

FESTIVALS

During the first two weeks in July, **Jazz à Vienne** musicians like Wynton Marsalis breeze into town. Tickets to the main concert (held in théâtre Romain) sell for 160F—worth the price for jazz fans—but smaller concerts are held outdoors in the courtyard of the Hôtel de Ville and Jardin de Cybelle for free. For ticket information, call the tourist office. Vienne is also host to a two-week national **Festival d'Humour** at the end of March. If you can follow French humor, this is the place to be; tickets run 60F–100F.

VALENCE

If it weren't an hour and a half south of Lyon and a gateway to the Vercors mountains (*see* Chapter 9), nobody would stop in this sluggish capital of the Drôme region for longer than the hour it takes to admire the dramatic 12th-century cliff-top ruins. The city's steady but faint pulse comes from its university, founded in 1452, and its position as "the big city" for surrounding farm communities. If you do pass through, though, it's worth getting off the bus or train long enough to check out the **Musée de Valence** (4 pl. des Ormeaux, tel. 04–75–79–20–80, fax 04–75–79–20–84), which has a large modern art collection and one of only eight Roman mosaics dedicated to Hercules. It's open Monday–Tuesday and Thursday–Friday 2–6, Wednesday and weekends 9–noon and 2–6; admission is 15F. The adjacent **Cathédral St-Apollinaire** (pl. des Ormeaux), begun in the 11th century, has a Romanesque bell tower made of stone from the hill that the cliff-top ruins sit on. **Parc Jouvet,** only two blocks from the train station, is a good-size spread of "feet-on" grassy areas and sculptured gardens. The multilingual staff at the new **tourist office** in the train station is very knowledgeable and happy to load you up with pamphlets about the Rhône, the Drôme, and Valence itself. *Parvis de la gare, 04–75–44–90–40, fax 04–75–44–90–41. Open Sept.–May, Tues.–Sat. 9–12:30 and 2–6:30, Mon. 2–6:30; June–Aug. Mon.–Sat. 9–7, Sun. 9–noon.*

COMING AND GOING

The **train station** (pl. Leclerc), on the border of the *vieille ville* (old town) two blocks inland from Parc Jouvet, sends regular trains to Lyon (1½ hrs, 82F), Grenoble (1½ hrs, 77F), and Avignon (1 hr, 94F). The consignment desk holds bags for 30F per 24 hours. The main **bus station** (tel. 04–75–81–23–25), just outside the train station, runs **Rapides Bleus** buses to Lyon (2 hrs, 77F) and Grenoble (2½ hrs, 58F). For Vercors-bound travelers, **RVD** buses (tel. 04–75–40–16–60) leave for La Chapelle and Vassieux; the two-hour treks cost about 50F.

GETTING AROUND

Valence is definitely walkable. There is a good map posted outside the train station, and there are others at most squares in the vieille ville. Boulevard Général-de-Gaulle, boulevard Bancel, and boulevard Maurice-Clerc all form one wide, tree-lined stretch that wraps around the old town from the park up to place Leclerc. Avenue Victor Hugo cuts across the boulevard at place de la République and intersects the pedestrian streets of the vieille ville. **Ets Valla** (29 rue Faventines, tel. 04–75–43–34–32) rents mountain bikes (100F, with 1,200F deposit or credit card) and three-speed clunkers (50F, with a deposit) every day except Sunday and Monday. It can also point you in the direction of some great day trips along the Rhône, like the artisan hamlets of Cliouselat and Mirmonde and the winery towns of St-Péray and Cornas. The shop closes for a week in mid-August.

WHERE TO SLEEP

You have plenty to choose from along avenue Pierre Sémard, which runs from the station toward avenue Victor Hugo. A short walk away is the somewhat frumpy **Hôtel d'Angleterre** (11 av. Félix Faure, tel. 04–75–43–00–35, fax 04–75–43–75–17), with plain single or double rooms for 120F–180F (rooms with showers start at 160F). **Hôtel de l'Europe** (15 av. Félix Faure, tel. 04–75–43–02–16, fax 04–75–43–61–75), has doubles without shower starting at 215F (with a shower they run 260F). The quads (with two double beds) are a great deal at 350F.

HOSTEL • L'Épervière Auberge de Jeunesse. If you don't mind the pleasant 3-km (2-mi) walk through Parc Jouvet, over the highway, and down the road to your left, this hostel complex—complete with miniature golf, a swimming pool, and cafeteria—charges 45F–60F for dorm spaces (varying according to the number of beds per room) and 78F for two people and a tent. With a hostel card everything is 5F less. Breakfasts cost 28F, dinner specials 20F–42F, and sheets 13F. If you're tired, you can take CTAV Bus 1 toward Algoud, get out at the Valensolles stop, and walk 10 minutes north to the hostel. During July and August, the bus also stops directly in front of the hostel. The last bus out runs at 8:12 PM. *Chemin de l'Épervière, tel. 04–75–42–32–00, fax 04–75–56–20–67.*

FOOD

The cafés on **place Belat** and **place des Clercs** (behind the cathedral) are popular hangouts for young people at lunch- and dinnertime. The terraced cafés on tree-filled **place de la Pierre** are more charming, more gourmet, and more expensive. **One Two Tea** (37 Grande Rue, tel. 04–75–55–96–31) is one of the few reasonably priced restaurants–*salons de thé* (tea shops) in the pedestrian shopping district: A pot of Earl Grey and a scone runs 32F, and ravioli with mushrooms and cream sauce is 45F. **Le Coq Au Vin** (6 rue de l'Hôtel de Ville, tel. 04–75–43–14–87) has a filling 75F menu of traditional Lyonnais food. The same can be had at **L'Oliveraie** (20 rue Jean Louis Barrault, tel. 04–75–78–00–33), closed Sunday, where 85F will get you a classic taste of Provence. For groceries, stock up at the **Casino** supermarket on Grande Rue, Monday–Saturday 8–8.

THE MASSIF CENTRAL

Almost all of France's major rivers (including the Loire, Dordogne, and Lot) radiate from the Massif Central, a volcanic plateau at the geographic heart of the country. Roughly demarcated by Burgundy, the Rhône River, Languedoc-Roussillon, and the Dordogne River valley, the Massif Central is an isolated and insular region. It claims as its own the famous warrior Vercingétorix, who led the Gallic revolt against the Romans in the 1st century BC and is immortalized in *Astérix* comic books.

Few tourists ever venture up to the region's volcanic peaks, making the Massif Central a great alternative to the Alps for outdoor adventurers. Train rides through the region reveal lush, rolling hills and sweeping volcanic rock formations. Since there's more oxygen here than in the Alps—the highest peak measures in at 6,561 ft here, compared to a maximum height of more than 9,842 ft in the Alps—biking and mountain climbing are exceedingly popular. Don't miss the **Parc Naturel Régional des Volcans,** the largest regional park in the country. **Mont-Dore** and **Clermont-Ferrand** are great bases from which to explore, while **Le Puy-en-Velay** is the region's former religious hub. The cheeses produced in the Auvergne include the dry, nutty **Cantal**; soft, pungent **St-Nectaire**; and the oh-so-strong **Bleu d'Auvergne.** In summer, boulangeries turn *myrtilles* (blueberries) into pies, cakes, and tarts.

CLERMONT-FERRAND

Unlike most other French towns, with their well-preserved medieval streets, Clermont-Ferrand is marked by a curious mix of stark 1960s architecture, shopping malls, and automotive stores with the stone and half-timbered structures of the past. Luckily for the town's developing tourist industry, Clermont-Ferrand is conveniently close to the volcanoes of the **Parc Naturel Régional des Volcans** (*see below*). As a transfer point to the rest of the Auvergne region or the mountains, Clermont-Ferrand is ideal, especially since food and lodging are cheap. Plus, ever since the brothers Edouard and André

Michelin completed a Paris to Clermont-Ferrand race in the first car with air-filled tires, the Michelin Man (his official name is Bibendum) has been a father to the citizens of Clermont-Ferrand. Bibendum basically built the town, providing schools, housing, and health centers to Michelin's employees.

Clermont-Ferrand is also the regional center for festivals. In early February, the **Festival National et International du Court Métrage** brings the makers of short films to the "Cannes of Shorts." For more information call 04–73–91–65–73 or fax 04–73–92–11–93. The **Festival International d'Arts Vidéo et Nouvelles Technologies** in March brings video and high-tech artists together for displays and round tables. For three days in mid-June, hundreds of people don medieval costumes and turn the city into a bouncing treasure from the past. The **Fêtes Médiévales de Dauphin d'Auvergne** is a romp of parades, staged combat, markets, balls, and shows. For heavy thinkers, the **Pascalines** of the end of June is a public attempt to bring philosophy to the people through cultural activities. Finally, three music festivals—the **Festival Européen des Musiques Rares** (early July), **Rock au Max Festival** (mid-July), and the **Concours International de Chant** (early October)—make Clermont-Ferrand the place to go to for music in the streets.

BASICS

The helpful **tourist office** just outside the train station has enough information to launch your stay in town or an adventure into the regional park. For city info, ask for the excellent *Guide d'Étudiant,* made by and for young people. If you feel the need to tote more brochures or are interested in guided tours, visit the **main office** on place de la Victoire in the shadows of the basilica, a 20-minute walk from the train station: Take avenue Charras, cross place Delille to rue du Port, and turn left onto and up rue Marcombes, which ends at the basilica. Also at this office can be found an in-house **SNCF desk** (tel. 04–73–90–33–04), open weekdays 10–5:30, Saturday 9–noon and 2–5:30, and the **Espace Massif Central** (tel. 04–73–42–60–00, fax 04–73–42–60–09 for information about the Massif Central. *At train station: tel. 04–73–91–87–89. Open June–Sept., Mon.–Sat. 9:15–11:30 and 12:15–5; Oct.–May, weekdays 9:15–11:30 and 12:15–5. Main tourist office: pl. de la Victoire, tel. 04–73–98–65–00, fax 04–73–90–04–11. Open June–Sept., daily 8:30–7; Oct.–May, weekdays 8:45–6:30, Sat. 9–noon and 2–6, Sun. 9–1.*

For more information on activities in the Parc des Volcans or to make hostel reservations, visit the **FUAJ** office (tel. 04–73–92–26–39), open weekdays 1–6, in the Auberge de Jeunesse (*see below*).

INTERNET ACCESS

If you are researching your trip on the Web, or you just want to send an I'm-OK E-mail to mom and dad at home, the **Internet Café** (34 rue Ballainvilliers, tel. 04–73–92–42–80) has computers available for 25F a half hour or 40F an hour.

COMING AND GOING

Trains run regularly to Bordeaux (6 hrs, 227F), Limoges (5 hrs, 142F), Lyon (3 hrs, 136F), St-Étienne (2 hrs, 106F), and Paris (3½ hrs, 235F). The **train station** (32 av. de l'Union Soviétique) is on the east edge of town, near the budget hotels. Interurban and international buses leave from their own **bus station** (blvd. François Mitterand, tel. 73–93–13–61) and also pass by the train station. By car, Lyon is 180 km (110 mi) east via A72, and if you detour to St-Étienne, it's closer to 220 km (136 mi).

In summer (July–September) special tour buses do day trips (70F–320F) into the Parc des Volcans, including stops at Puy-de-Dôme, the Mont-Dore, and the Massif du Sancy. For information, contact either of the tourist offices or **Voyages Maisonneuve** (24 rue Georges Clemenceau, tel. 04–73–93–16–72, fax 04–73–30–86–02). It's open weekdays 8:30–noon and 2–6:30, Saturday 8:30–noon.

GETTING AROUND

Clermont-Ferrand is big enough that it takes too long to walk from place to place but small enough that you feel cheated paying the driver 7F for a local bus ticket. Local buses run daily until about 9 PM, with a few running (marked BDN for *bus de nuit*) as late as 11 PM. If you need them, cabs for local and long-distance trips can be called 24 hours a day at **Taxi Radio Clermontois** (tel. 04–73–19–53–53) and **Taxi 63** (tel. 04–73–31–53–15).

WHERE TO SLEEP

For a warm welcome and a good night's sleep the **Hôtel de Zurich** (65 av. de l'Union Soviétique, tel. 04–73–91–97–98) has rooms without shower or toilet for 90F–140F; those with go from 150F to 200F. **Hôtel Ravel** (8 rue de Maringues, tel. 04–73–91–51–33, fax 04–73–92–28–48) offers cheerful, modern rooms with bath for 150F–220F. If these hotels are both full, there are other cheap but acceptable alternatives on rue Charras. In the heart of the city itself, tucked in right behind the tourist office, is the **Hôtel Blaise Pascal** (6 rue Massillon, tel. 04–73–91–31–82). Well kept and with an amazing terrace overlooking the city, this gem has 31 rooms for 85F–170F, only three of which have a shower. At the modern, very comfortable **Dav'Hôtel** (10 rue des Minimes, tel. 04–73–93–31–49, fax 04–73–34–38–16) doubles with bath run 280F–290F (or 10F less without). The quiet, terraced **Hôtel Foch** (22 rue Maréchal Foch, tel 04–73–93–48–40, fax 04–73–35–47–41) has 19 doubles for 155F–205F (singles are 10F less for the same rooms), most with showers. Hall showers cost 20F.

HOSTELS • Auberge de Jeunesse. Across from the station, this hostel has dorm facilities, a full-function kitchen, stand-up toilets, and push-button showers. Bed and breakfast cost 67F (sheets 17F). *55 av. de l'Union Soviétique, tel. 04–73–92–26–39, fax 04–73–92–99–96. Reception open 7:30 AM–9:30 AM and 5 PM–11 PM, curfew 11 PM. Kitchen. Cash only. Closed Nov.–Mar.*

Corum St-Jean. This hostel for those 25 and under only is closer to the action. It has no curfew, a big patio, a decent cafeteria (meals are 43F), and a bar. Carpeted singles, doubles, and triples with shower and toilets go for 90F per person (80F with HI card), sheets and breakfast included. From the station, take Bus 2 or 4 to the Gaillard stop or walk 20 minutes. *17 rue Gaulthier-de-Biauzat, tel. 04–73–31–57–00, fax 04–73–31–59–99. 157 beds. Reception open weekdays 9 AM–7 PM.*

FOOD

You can eat well and cheaply in Clermont-Ferrand. Head down **rue St-Dominique** from **rue des Minimes** and place de Jaude, or down **rue de la Boucherie** from place St-Pierre, and you'll find Spanish, Portuguese, Moroccan, Indian, Turkish, and Vietnamese food options for way under 80F. **La Crémaillère** (61 av. de l'Union Soviétique, tel. 04–73–90–89–25), closed Saturday dinner and Sunday, has three-course menus of classic French cuisine for 50F, 75F, and 85F, plus single-course daily specials for 37F. **Crêperie le 1513** (2 rue des Chaussetiers, tel. 04–73–92–37–46) offers a variety of lunch and dinner crepes (35F–56F), a limited all-you-can-eat buffet (39F), and other fare. A young crowd goes to **Pizzeria Tino** (40 pl. de Jaude, tel. 04–73–35–18–15), where 36F–46F gets you a flavorful pizza. For a picnic, go to the **market** on place St-Pierre, open Monday–Saturday until 7:30 PM, for local goodies. Otherwise, there is an **Eco Service** market on avenue Charras (near the train station) open Monday–Saturday 8:30–7:30, Sunday 9–noon.

WORTH SEEING

The 13th-century **Cathédrale Notre-Dame** (pl. de la Victoire) epitomizes Gothic architecture, with peaked arches and intricate spires made out of unusual dark stone from the nearby Volvic Mountains. For 12F you can climb 261 steps to the cathedral tower, where you are rewarded with a great view of Puy-de-Dome. Be sure to walk around the outside, too: Behind the cathedral is a baffling contemporary mural, and behind and to the north is a host of narrow pedestrian streets with 18th-century-style lamps. The **Maison des Architectes** (34 rue des Gras), a block from the cathedral, was built in 1578 and gets its name from the many restorations it has undergone. The building now houses the free **Musée du Ranquet** (tel. 04–73–37–38–63), where you can see intricately carved wooden furniture, the first "calculator," and shoes that used to be worn by the Auvergnois. It's open Tuesday—Sunday 10–6. The best view of the house is from petite rue St-Pierre, off rue des Gras.

Notre-Dame-du-Port (rue Notre-Dame-du-Port, off rue du Port from pl. Delille), a stunning 12th-century Romanesque basilica, features comical sculptured columns that typify Romanesque sculpture; check out the parody of Adam and Eve behind the main alter. The black virgin in the crypt was found in the walls of the church during an 18th-century restoration. The decorated lid she is guarding sits atop a Celtic well from the pre-Christian days of water worship. Just south of the old town is the unique **Musée du Tapis d'Art** (45 rue Ballainvilliers, tel. 04–73–90–57–48), devoted to the history of rugs and the cultures that make them. Admission is 23F (10F more for a highly informative guided tour). The museum is open Tuesday–Sunday 10–6.

An unfortunate distance from the centre ville, in Montferrand, is the extensive **Musée des Beaux-Arts** (pl. Louis Deteix, tel. 04–73–23–08–49). More than a thousand pieces trace the history of art from the Middle Ages to the present. It costs 23F and is open Tuesday–Sunday 10–6. Also worth a stop are the freaky **Fontaines Pétrifiantes** (rue St-George, tel. 04–73–37–15–58), at the bottom of rue Gaultier-de-Biauzat, where you can check out animals that have been stuffed and then put under dripping water from local springs to form an ivorylike crust of calcium deposits. Admission is 18F; it is open daily 9–noon and 2–6 (9–7:30 in July and August).

The **Michelin complex** is east of the train station, but the huge factory is not visitor friendly. A better bet is the promotional store, where you can find out everything you ever wanted to know about *pneus* (tires), and see cool art nouveau posters. *43 rue Montlosier, off pl. Delille, tel. 04–73–32–22–01. Open Mon.–Tues. 10:30–5, Wed.–Sat. 10:30–6.*

SHOPPING

The commercial center is off place de Jaude. Shops line cobblestone rue des Gras and old-style vendors surround the modern market on place St-Pierre. For Auvergne cheeses stop at the odiferous **Le Buron** (24 rue de la Boucherie, tel. 04–73–31–46–60). **Produits de la Ferme** (4 pl. St-Pierre, tel. 04–73–37–79–07) sells regional specialties including honey and *tripoux d'Auvergne* (lamb intestine).

PARC NATUREL REGIONAL DES VOLCANS

Stretching 150 km (90 mi) from north to south, the Regional National Volcano Park contains 80 or so dormant volcanoes, with all kinds of craters, dikes, domes, prismatic lava flows, caldera cones, and basaltic plateaus. They are (relatively) young, the most recent only 6,000 to 8,000 years old, which explains why their shapes are so well preserved. The Monts Dômes just west of Clermont are your classic cone-shape volcanoes. The best known is **Puy-de-Dôme** (*see below*). The granite peak of Puy-de-Sancy, the highest point in the Massif Central, stands 6,188 ft tall above the mellow town of **Le Mont-Dore.** On the lower slopes of Cantal are meadows, famous for their wildflowers and butterflies.

There is no public transportation to the region because of the area's "regional park" standing (though plenty of cars and private buses ensure that the area is not traffic free). You need to organize your own transportation to the park, either by renting a car or joining an organized tour of the region (for information on tours contact the tourist office in Clermont-Ferrand; *see above*). Many miles of trails go through the park, past little villages with *gîtes d'étape* (rural hostels), where you can stay overnight. Five GRs in particular cross the park: GR4, 30, 41, 400, and 441. You can also rent a mountain bike and go crazy for a few days. In the winter the region is snowbound, and cross-country skiing is the transportation mode of choice. The Parc des Volcans's central **tourist office** (Centre d'Information du Parc des Volcans) in Montlosier (tel. 04–73–65–64–00, fax 04–73–65–66–78), open April–October, Tuesday–Sunday 10–12:30 and 1:30–6 (7 PM in July and August), 20 km (12 mi) southwest of Clermont-Ferrand, can give you the scoop on the park as a whole; tourist offices in Clermont-Ferrand, Le Mont-Dore, and Le-Puy-en-Velay (*see below*) have area-specific information. Good topo maps are available at tabacs and bookstores all around the region.

PUY-DE-DOME

The most famous *puy* (peak) of all is also the most convenient, ideal for the day-trip crowd based out of Clermont-Ferrand, 12 km (7 mi) to the north. The Puy-de-Dôme is one hell of a climb at 4,800 ft—just ask the Tour de France riders who consider it one of the most challenging stages of the race. Needless to say, it has an incredible view of the surrounding volcanoes and craters. At the summit you'll find the remains of a vast temple dedicated to Mercury, some displays about the region's natural history, as well as the requisite restaurant-bar and gift shop.

To reach the summit, take Bus 14 from the train station or place de Jaude in Clermont-Ferrand to **Royat** (20 mins, 6.50F). From here walk 6 km (4 mi) along the road toward **Col de Ceyssat** until you come to the *sentier des muletiers* (path of the mule keepers), a wide, rocky switchback trail leading up to the top. If you're not up for the hike, **Voyages Maisonneuve** (*see* Clermont-Ferrand, Coming and Going, *above*) runs a bus from Clermont-Ferrand's train station to the top a couple of times a week, July–September (72F). Since two-thirds of the Puy-de-Dôme hike is on a paved road (which sees a good bit of traffic), anyone searching for hard-core nature is out of luck. Luckily, once you're at the top, there are trails in every direction—one two-hour hike takes you to Puy-de-Dôme, a cone-shape crater just south of Puy-de-Dôme. The **salle d'exposition** (exhibition hall) in Royat has good hiking maps, as do tourist offices in Clermont-Ferrand (*see above*).

LE MONT-DORE

At the head of the Chaudefour Valley, Le Mont-Dore stretches out along the Dordogne River. This spa town turned sports resort is surrounded by sheer cliffs and granite peaks that are not so high, but are very rugged and green and even sport an occasional waterfall. Le Mont-Dore makes a good base for a week of summer hiking: Lodging is cheap, nightlife exists, and well-marked trails radiate from the town center. There's even a funicular and a téléphérique to do half the work for you. In winter, trade your bike for a pair of skis and hit the mostly intermediate slopes (though not without calling ahead to make sure there is snow). Avoid coming in October or November, when the whole town shuts down.

BASICS • The **tourist office** has topo guides, maps, and a small biking trail guide, as well as all the overnight information you'll need for gîtes along the GRs. Daily half-day guided hikes and tours (55F) leave from in front of the office; get a schedule and tickets inside. In winter call for ski information. If there's no snow the town is probably closed down; if there's a lot you'll need reservations. *Av. de la Libération, tel. 04–73–65–20–21, fax 04–73–65–36–03. Open Mon.–Sat. 9–12:30 and 2–6:30, Sun. 10–noon.*

The post office here does not change money, so try to get cash before you come. In dire straits, one of the banks or big hotels will probably cash traveler's checks for a ridiculous fee. There are also the ubiquitous ATMs.

COMING AND GOING • From Clermont-Ferrand, catch one of four daily trains (1½ hours, 56F) to Laqueille; then buy your second ticket on one of the waiting buses (1½ hrs, 62F) that go up to Le Mont-Dore. You could take a train directly to Le Mont-Dore (65F), but the buses are more frequent. Either way, you get dropped off at the **train station** (av. Michel Bertrand); in the afternoon (2–6 PM) a bus makes a loop between the train station, tourist office, and Sancy (where the hostel and téléphérique are) for 12F a ride.

At night, it's standing-room-only at the packed Juanita Banana (39 blvd. Trudaine, off pl. Delille, Clermont-Ferrand, tel. 04–73–92–38–28), where salsa, reggae, and funk keep the place moving.

WHERE TO SLEEP • On a quiet street behind the *thermes* (medicinal baths), **Hôtel le Progrès** (5 rue Marie-Thérèse, tel./fax 04–73–65–05–96) has homey rooms for 100F–200F and a cozy restaurant with a good 70F menu. **La Closerie de Manou** (tel. 04–73–65–26–81, fax 04–73–81–11–72), a *chambre d'hôte* (bed-and-breakfast) 3 km (2 mi) out of town on D996, has cheery, tranquil rooms for 340F. One of the campgrounds in town is **Les Crouzets** (av. les Crouzets, tel./fax 04–73–65–21–60), open year-round; it's across the river from the station and costs 14F for a site and 15F for each person. The **Auberge de Jeunesse** (rte. du Sancy, tel. 04–73–65–03–53, fax 04–73–65–26–39) is a steep 4 km (2½ mi) from town, at the base of the Sancy ski area (you can take the free shuttle from the tourist office). Beds are 51F, 70F with breakfast, and 120F with breakfast and a four-course dinner (only when there are enough interested people around to make this possible).

FOOD • Being an outdoor vacation town, Le Mont Dore has many places to eat, but not many that are fancy. For basics, there's an **Eco**, a **Petit Casino,** and a **covered market** (open daily 8:30–noon and 1–7; morning only on Sunday), as well as the Friday-morning weekly market on place de la République. If sitting near a warm fire, smelling melting Bleu d'Auvergne cheese, will ease your hiking pains, you need a tasty wood-stove pizza (45F–65F) from **Pizza Le Tremplin** (3 av. Foch, tel. 04–73–65–25–90). **La Farinade** (15 pl. Charles-de-Gaulle, tel. 04–73–65–02–63), open 11 AM–midnight, has 40 different beers and crepes for 15F–40F. If you're extremely ravenous, **Le Boeuf dans l'Assiette** (9 av. Michel-Bertrand, tel. 04–73–65–01–23) serves simple, good fare; for 175F two people get a three-course menu and a bottle of wine.

OUTDOOR ACTIVITIES • There are plenty of good trails right from town; ask at the tourist office for a "Randonnée à Pied" guide (35F for the map, or 45F for the map and guide). Two favorites are to the *grande cascade* (big waterfall) and to the *sommet du capucin* (the top of a sheer volcanic plug that watches over the town); both are hour-long hikes, one-way. For more rugged and wide-open trails, take Sancy's **téléphérique** (tel. 04–73–65–02–23), open daily 9–5:30, to the top of Puy-de-Sancy, from where a volcanic plateau extends north to the Monts-Dôme and south to Monts-du-Cantal. The ride is 31F one-way, 36F round-trip. Downtown, rent bikes for 90F–200F at **Bessac Sports** (3 rue du Maréchal-Juin, tel. 04–73–65–02–25), open daily 9–noon and 2–6. Across from the hostel, **Le Roc** (rte. du Sancy, tel. 04–73–65–00–28) rents bikes for 120F a day or 70F a half day. In winter, both also rent snowboards (80F–140F), downhill skis (75F–130F), and cross-country skis (65F). The **Club Hippique** (rte. du Sancy, tel. 04–73–65–03–82) will let you take a horse out for a two-hour canter at 170F, or 500F for the whole day.

LACE MAKING
IN LE PUY

Since the reign of Louis XIV, women in the Velay region have made lace. Now that machines do the work more cheaply, village squares are no longer full of women deftly manipulating "fuseaux" (spindles). But Le Puy is still home to the Centre d'Enseignement de la Dentelle au Fuseau, a lace-making school (three years of eight hours' practice daily) with craftswomen who demonstrate techniques and a small lace display. Admission is 12F. Go to 38–40 rue Raphaël, tel. 04–71–02–01–68, fax 04–71–02–92–56. It is open mid-September–mid-June, weekdays 10–noon and 2–5:30; mid-June–mid-September, Monday–Saturday 9–noon and 1:30–5:30.

LE PUY-EN-VELAY

Southeast of Clermont-Ferrand in the département of the Haute-Loire, Le Puy-en-Velay is a stunning sight, built up on volcanic peaks that stick out of the fertile valley like pyramids. On top of these are the major sights, the not-so-subtle beacons of power and religion that made Le Puy into a major pilgrimage destination—even Charlemagne came to visit. To this day, Le Puy-en-Velay is one of the four principal departure points for the pilgrimage routes to Santiago di Compostella in Spain. The unusual Cathédrale Notre-Dame sits squarely between the adjoining Romanesque cloister and 11th-century baptistery on top of the steep streets of the medieval *haute ville* (upper town).

The steep, cobbled streets of the medieval town are great for visiting, but the rest of Le Puy is rather provincial. If the shabby buildings aren't under restoration, then they usually house an overpriced boutique selling the tacky remains of the town's once-great *dentelle* (lace) tradition. If you get sick of climbing up to churches with hordes of tourists, you can always take off, leaving the architecture buffs at the cathedral, and hike up into the surrounding hills. Le Puy-en-Velay shuts down from Saturday evening through Monday afternoon. Try not to arrive during this time; not much is open.

BASICS

The **tourist office** is in the theater, in the middle of town. It has maps and brochures (ask specifically for the *Guide Pratique,* which describes three walking circuits throughout the city) can help find lodging. From May–October it also sells a 45F ticket that gets you into the city's four principal sights. There is a **smaller office** open mid-June–mid-September at 23 rue des Tables (04–71–05–99–02). *Pl. du Breuil, tel. 04–71—09–38–41, fax 04–71–05–22–62. Open Oct.–Mar., Mon.–Sat. 8:30–noon and 1:30–6:15, Sun. 10–noon; Apr.–Sept., daily 8:30–noon and 1:30–6:15 (8:30–7:30 July and Aug.).*

COMING AND GOING

The **train station** (pl. Maréchal Leclerc) is a five-minute walk from place du Breuil and even closer to the cheap sleeps. There are connections (sometimes you'll need an SNCF bus connection) to Lyon (3 hrs, 107F), Clermont-Ferrand (2 hrs, 107F), and St-Étienne (1½ hrs, 71F). Buses into the region theoretically leave from the **gare routière** (pl. Maréchal Leclerc, tel. 04–71–09–25–60) by the train station, but the service is extremely erratic; check for specific routes and schedules. The station is closed Saturday, Sunday, and daily 12:30–2. If you need a **taxi,** call for service from place du Breuil (04–71–09–33–68) or from the train station (04–71–09–21–10).

WHERE TO SLEEP

Budget lodging is limited in Le Puy, so you should definitely reserve if you're coming on any festival days (*see below*). **Hôtel Le Régional** (36 blvd. Maréchal Fayolle, tel. 04–71–09–37–74) is on a main street and has small but clean 160F–250F doubles with shower and 120F without. **Hôtel le Dyke** (37 blvd.

Fayolle, tel. 04–71–09–05–30, fax 04–71–02–58–66), near the centre ville, has comfortable doubles with bath for 230F–250F.

HOSTEL • Auberge de Jeunesse. Up a very steep hill, this hostel has beds in a clean, sterile environment for 41F. Sheets are 21F, breakfast 11F. The kitchen is always available unless groups have reserved it. The only bummer is the strictly enforced curfew. *9 rue Jules Vallès, tel. 04–71–05–52–40, fax 04–71–05–61–24. 72 beds. Reception open 8–noon and 1:30–11, registration 1:30–10, curfew 11:30 PM. Closed weekends Oct.–Mar.*

CAMPING • Camping Bouthezard. Down by the Borne River under St-Michel d'Aiguilhe, this great spot is only 1½ km (1 mi) from the tourist office. Sites cost 22F, plus 10F per person. Be prepared for cold nights. *Chemin de Bouthezard, off av. d'Aiguilhe, tel. 04–71–09–55–09, fax 04–71–04–07–60. 80 sites. Closed mid-Oct.–Easter.*

FOOD

A **Casino** supermarket, open Monday–Saturday 8:30–8, and a bunch of pizzerias line boulevard Maréchal Fayolle, but more exciting cheap grub isn't easy to find. On Saturday mornings pick up some local cheeses (such as *le Velay*) at the **market** on place du Plot. Near the cathedral, **Le Nom de la Rose** (48 rue Raphaël, tel. 04–71–05–90–04), closed Monday dinner and Tuesday, serves a loose interpretation of Mexican food; the 55F menu includes a salad and a dessert. Even when things elsewhere are dead, you can always find some life at **Le Majestic** (8 blvd. Maréchal Fayolle, tel. 04–71–09–06–30), where you can drink a *verveine de Velay,* a local green liquor, after eating from a generous 48F menu.

WORTH SEEING

CATHÉDRALE AND CLOÎTRE NOTRE-DAME • Begun in the early 5th century by Bishop Scutarius on the site of a Gallo-Roman temple, the cathedral was enlarged all the way until the end of the 12th century as the pilgrim crowd continued to grow. Somehow it has managed to incorporate the various influences successfully. Check out the crazy Byzantine facade along with the amazing view of the old town and mountains. Inside, note the Black Madonna on the high altar, a copy of the original model, which was burned by overzealous revolutionaries in 1794. The origin of the first statue—perhaps a figure of Isis transformed into a Madonna, perhaps a statue carved by an Arab craftsman in Le Puy—remains a mystery. The **cloister** (admission 25F) to the left of the cathedral has strange stone carvings. *Cathedral open daily 9:30–noon and 2–7. Cloister open Apr.—June, daily 9:30–12:30 and 2–6; July–Sept., daily 9:30–6:30; Oct.–Mar., daily 9:30–noon and 2–4:30.*

ROCHER CORNEILLE AND STATUE NOTRE-DAME DE FRANCE • If you exit the cathedral through the **King's Door** (to the left) as did Charlemagne and 13 other kings on pilgrimage, you'll see the path that leads up to the huge, red statue of Madonna with Child. The Bishop of Le Puy in 1855 optimistically asked to be given the cannons that Napoléon III would capture when he beat the Russians in the Crimea. France won, the cannons were melted down, and the statue was blessed in 1860. The view from the base of the 75-ft statue is great—beyond all the red roofs you can see the castle of Polignac in the distance. It's hard to imagine how this 835-ton statue got to the top of this impossibly high peak. *Admission 20F. Open mid-Mar.–Sept. 9–7 (6 PM mid-Mar.–Apr.; 7:30 PM July and Aug.); Oct.–mid-Mar., 10–5.*

ST-MICHEL D'AIGUILHE • This 10th-century chapel, perched on what was once the vent of an old volcano, also has an amazing view that's worth the climb. Notice the white, black, and red tiles on the facade, which reflects a blending of Romanesque and Islamic traditions. Lightning destroyed the original bell tower in 1245; the current tower dates from the 19th century. Come early to beat the backup along the winding staircase. *Admission 13F. Open mid-June–mid-Sept., daily 9–7; mid-Sept.–mid-June, daily 10–noon and 2–5 (with slight changes according to the season); closed mornings mid-Dec.–mid-Mar.*

FESTIVALS

For two weeks in mid-July, there are back-to-back festivals: **Festival de Musique Vocales–Les Musicales du Puy-en-Velay** and **Festival International de Folklore du Puy-en-Velay.** On August 15, the Assumption Day, the Black Virgin is paraded through town among thousands of visitors who have made the pilgrimage here. The evening before, a torch-lit procession goes up to the cathedral. During the second week of September, the whole town dresses up in Renaissance garb and celebrates the **Fête Renaissance du Roi de l'Oiseau.**

PROVENCE

UPDATED BY ETHAN GELBER

What you may remember best about Provence is the light. The sunlight here is vibrant, bathing the vineyards, olive groves, and fields full of lavender and sunflowers with an intensity that captivated the likes of Picasso, Cézanne, and van Gogh. But Provence's appeal extends beyond the beauty of its light, climate, and fertile lands. Over the centuries Provence, bordering the Mediterranean and flanked by the Alps and the Rhône River, has attracted a variety of visitors, including Romans, Greeks, Celts, Ligurians, Teutons, and Franks. All left behind a rich historical and cultural legacy. Today locals still follow the traditions passed on by their ancestors, celebrating them in the region's many festivals. Refreshingly friendly and laid back, the people here have sun-worn skin and a song in their voices. Check out Peter Mayle's *A Year in Provence* for a witty characterization of the Provençaux.

Provence is also a center for culinary delights, specializing in dishes with garlic, olive oil, and seafood. In addition, you can see some of the best-preserved Roman monuments in the world in lively Arles, Spanish-influenced Nîmes, and smaller towns like Orange and Vaison-la-Romaine. The city of Avignon is dominated by a more recent influence from Rome—the grandiose Papal Palace built in the 14th century, following the Great Schism. Marseille, in contrast, makes no pretense of being picturesque and instead greets you with the seedy, lively spirit of a port city. Not far away, Aix-en-Provence indulges in bourgeois luxury. Return to reality in Montpellier, where the huge student population provides a vibrant and budget-friendly atmosphere.

Better yet, escape to a *chambre d'hôte* (bed-and-breakfast) tucked away in the beautiful wine country between Avignon and Vaison-la-Romaine. Life here moves at a slower pace and biking is the best mode of transportation. Follow the rich landscape of the Route des Vignobles (Vineyard Route) through the region; the regional tourist office can give you information. Or, pack your tent and take a breathtaking hike up Mont Ste-Victoire, Mont Ventoux, or the white-cliffed Calanques.

FOOD

The staples of Provençal cuisine are olive oil, garlic, tomatoes, and seafood. These are the essential ingredients of classic dishes such as ratatouille, *soupe au pistou* (a tomato-based, minestrone-like soup with a garlic and basil sauce), aioli (a garlic- and lemon-based mayonnaise), and bouillabaisse, a fish and shellfish soup that requires lengthy preparation and is served with much fanfare (*see more at* Marseille, *below*). The deliciously light Côte du Rhône wine makes a perfect accompaniment.

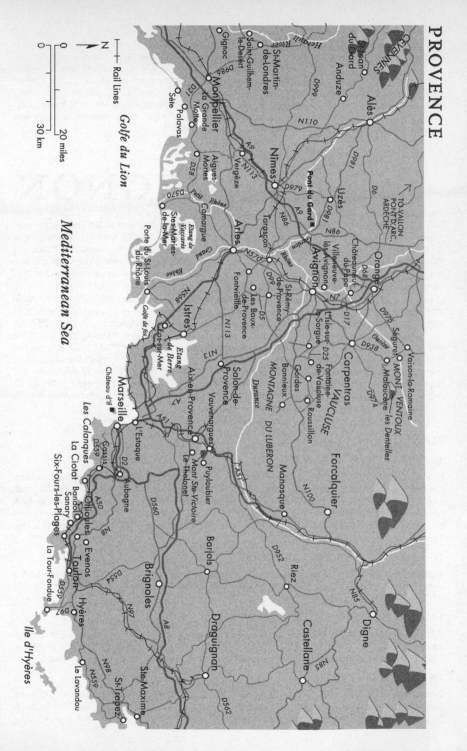

PROVENCE

Rail Lines

Golfe du Lion

Mediterranean Sea

Ile d'Hyères

N

0
20 miles
0
30 km

CEVENNES
St-Jean-du-Gard
Anduze
Alès
St-Martin-de-Londres
St-Guilhem-le-Desert
Gignac
Montpellier
La Grande Motte
Sète
Palavas
Aigues-Mortes
Vergèze
Nîmes
Ste-Maries-de-la-Mer
Stes-Maries-de-la-Mer
Aigues-Mortes
Porte du St-Louis du Rhône
Rhône
Petit Camargue
Grand Camargue
Etang de Vaccarès
Arles
Tarascon
Pont du Gard
Uzès
TO VALLON PONT-D'ARC, ARDÈCHE
Châteauneuf-du-Pape
Villeneuve-les-Avignon
Avignon
Orange
Séguret
Vaison-la-Romaine
MONT VENTOUX
Malaucène-les-Dentelles
St-Rémy-de-Provence
Les Baux-de-Provence
Fontvieille
L'Isle-sur-la-Sorgue
Fontaine-de-Vaucluse
Carpentras
VAUCLUSE
Bonnieux
Gordes
Roussillon
MONTAGNE DU LUBERON
Forcalquier
Digne
Istres
Fos-sur-Mer
Golfe de Fos
Etang de Berre
Salon-de-Provence
Vauvenargues
Aix-en-Provence
Manosque
Riez
Castellane
Marseille
Château d'If
L'Estaque
Les Calanques
La Ciotat
Cassis
Aubagne
Puyloubier
Mont Ste-Victoire
Le Tholonet
Barjols
Draguignan
Ollioules
Evenos
Bandol
Sanary
Six-Fours-les-Plages
Toulon
Brignoles
La Tour-Fondue
Hyères
Le Lavandou
Ste-Maxime
St-Tropez

317

OUTDOOR ACTIVITIES

The varied terrain and mild climate of Provence make it an ideal region for hiking, bicycling, mountain climbing, and swimming. A number of Grandes Randonnées (known as GRs), France's well-mapped-out hiking paths, wind their way through Provence. It's probably best to avoid colder, windier December–March as well as hot and touristy July–August. Particularly good places to explore are the river-studded Cévennes mountains, the Hérault Valley, Mont Ventoux, and Mont Ste-Victoire. Horseback riding is the best way to see the Camargue. You can go snorkeling along the shores of the Mediterranean, especially in Cassis, the Calanques, and Iles d'Hyères. Tourist offices have hiking maps, and *Topoguides,* found in any bookstore, are useful for serious hikers.

AVIGNON

Nestled in the fertile Rhône River valley, Avignon has a colorful history and a rich culture dating from its period as the capital of Christendom. In 1309, due to violence in Italy and a little enticement from French King Phillip the Fair, French-born pope Clement V shifted the papacy from Rome to Avignon in what became known as the Babylonian Captivity. Over the next 40 years, the magnificent **Palais des Papes** (Papal Palace) was created. It served as the official papal residence until 1377, when the seventh Avignon pope, Gregory XI, returned to Rome. The following year, new popes were elected in both Rome and Avignon, creating a schism in the Catholic Church that lasted nearly four decades.

During the Avignon Papacy, the arts flourished in this city as artists attached themselves to the papal entourage, forming a partnership that later became the Avignonnais school of art. Avignon celebrates its cultural legacy in July and August, when the world-famous **Festival d'Avignon** and **Festival Off** bring opera, ballet, theater, dance performances, and music to every street. Unfortunately, this time of the year is the most expensive. This may also be the case for much of the year 2000, since Avignon has been selected as one of the "European Cities of Culture for the Year 2000." Contact the tourist office (*see below*) or the **Avignon Mission 2000** (9 rue Rempart de l'Oulle, tel. 04–90–86–17–65, fax 04–90–86–92–49), for more information. The rest of the time, the city is calmer and a bit cheaper, although it's more urban than you'd expect and a little sketchy for the lone female traveler at night. Nevertheless, it's a good base for exploring the surrounding Vaucluse region.

BASICS

BUREAUX DE CHANGE

Change your money at either **Banque de France** (pl. de l'Horloge, tel. 04–90–80–43—00), open Monday–Saturday 10–6, or **Lyonnaise de Banque** (13 rue de la République, tel. 04–90–27—75–00), open weekdays 8:15–noon and 1:30–5, near the train station (just head north on cours Jean-Jaurès). Both have decent rates, and the latter has an ATM with Cirrus access. Stay away from Banque Chaix, the first bank you see on cours Jean-Jaurès. There is also a **Mondiale Exchange** office nearby (34 rue de la Balance, tel. 04–90–80–81–60).

DISCOUNT TRAVEL AGENCIES

Frantour (tel. 04–90–27–25–50), next to the train station, primarily sells discounted train tickets to students, but it also functions as a regular travel agency. **Nouvelles Frontières** (14 rue Carnot, tel. 04–90–82–31–32) specializes in charter flights.

ENGLISH-LANGUAGE BOOKSTORE

If you are in need of a new paperback to accompany you on your travels, **Shakespeare** (155 rue Carreterie, tel. 04–90–27–38–50), at the northeast corner of town, stocks a good collection of classics in English, as well as scones and brownies to remind you of home. It is closed Sunday and Monday.

INTERNET ACCESS

Cyberdrome brings the cyberworld to Avignon—E-mail and Web access, games, training, and more. Connection time costs 50F an hour or 400F for 10 hours. *68 rue Guillaume Puy, tel. 04–90–16–05–15, fax 04–90–16–05–14, www.cyberdrome.fr. Open daily 7 AM–1 AM.*

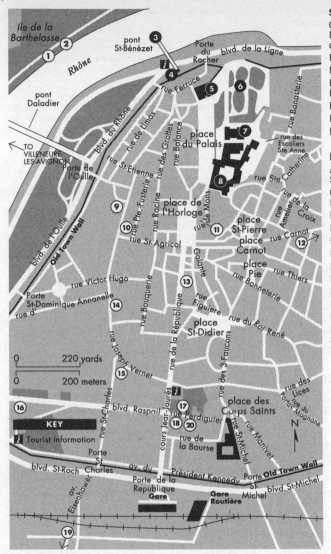

Sights ●
Cathédrale
Notre-Dame
des Doms, **7**
Musée Calvet, **14**
Musée en Images, **4**
Palais des
Papes, **8**
Petit Palais, **5**
Pont St-Bénézet, **3**
Rocher des Doms, **6**

Lodging ○
Avignon
Squash Club, **12**
Camping
Bagatelle, **2**
Foyer Bagatelle, **1**
Hôtel Angleterre, **16**
Hôtel Central, **13**
Hôtel Colbert, **18**
Hôtel Innova, **15**
Hôtel Mignon, **9**
Hôtel de Mons, **11**
Hôtel du Parc, **17**
Hôtel Provençal, **10**
Hôtel Le
Splendid, **20**
Hôtel St-Roch, **19**

LAUNDRY

Near the station, you can wash and dry for about 35F at **Laverie La Fontaine** (66 pl. des Corps Saints, at rue Perdiguier, tel. 04–90–27–16–85). It's open daily 7 AM–8 PM. You can even make photocopies for 1F on the self-service machine. If all the machines are full, a few minutes' walk east is **Lav'matic** (27 rue du Portail Magnanen), with washes for 18F, dryers for 4F; it's open daily 7 AM–7:30 PM. There are other branches at 9 rue du Chapeau Rouge and 113 avenue St-Ruf.

MAIL

At the main **post office** it seems as if you have to wait forever and the employees are having a bad day— every day. Nonetheless, you can cash traveler's checks at reasonable rates. *Av. du Président Kennedy,* *at cours Jean-Jaurès, tel. 04–90–27–54–00. Open weekdays 8–7, Sat. 8–noon. Branch office on pl. Pie, open same hrs as main post office.*

MEDICAL AID

Avignon's main hospital is the **Hôpital de la Durmance Henri Duffaut** (305 rue Raoul Follereau, tel. 04–90–80–33–33). The tourist office has a list of English-speaking doctors.

VISITOR INFORMATION

The multilingual staff at the main **tourist office** will happily load you down with shiny brochures and information on upcoming events and hiking and skiing in the area. *41 cours Jean-Jaurès, tel. 04–90–82–65–11, fax 04–90–82–95–03. Open Apr.–Sept., weekdays 9–1 and 2–6, weekends 9–1 and 2–5 (longer hrs during the festival); Oct.–Mar., closed Sun.*

COMING AND GOING

BY TRAIN

The busy **Gare d'Avignon** (blvd. St-Roch, porte de la République) is across the street from the main entrance to the walled city and has car-rental agents, hotel information, and a restaurant. From Avignon, trains go all over France, including Arles (20 mins, 35F), Nîmes (30 mins, 46F), Marseille (1 hr, 91F), Aix-en-Provence (1½ hrs, 112F), Toulouse (4 hrs, 203F), Bordeaux (6½ hrs, 310F), and Paris (3½ hrs by TGV, 362F–426F).

BY BUS

The **bus station** is right by the train station. Buses will take you to almost any nearby town, including Châteauneuf-du-Pape (30 mins, 19F), Carpentras (45 mins, 21F), and Fontaine-de-Vaucluse (50 mins, 30F). The information office is closed weekends, but buses still run on a limited schedule, and you can get more information at the tourist office. Buy your ticket on board. *5 av. Monclar, tel. 04–90–82–07–35. Open weekdays 8–noon and 1:30–6, Sat. 9–noon.*

GETTING AROUND

Avignon has two different scenes: One is where the tourists are, and the other is where they are not. "They" congregate all along the linear strip of **cours Jean-Jaurès,** which becomes rue de la République and leads to place de l'Horloge. Place de l'Horloge, in turn, leads to **place du Palais,** the site of almost all of Avignon's historical attractions. To see Avignonnais leading their daily lives, turn off these tourist paths and get lost among the cobblestone streets. You could rent a bike or a moped, but the streets are very narrow and sometimes the cars are fast and reckless. The best place for rentals in July and August is **Transhumance Voyage** (tel. 04–90–95–57–81) with bikes going for 60F–100F (plus a credit card deposit of 1,000F–2,000F). Year-round, **Aymard–Cycles Peugeot** (80 rue Guillaume Puy, tel./fax 04–90–86–32–49) rents bikes for 60F a day plus 1,500F deposit. **Taxi Radio Avignonnais** is available from place Pie by calling 04–90–82–20–20.

WHERE TO SLEEP

Finding a place to sleep in Avignon shouldn't be a problem—unless you arrive in July or August, or during the festival, when reservations are a must and even the cheapest room prices skyrocket. Most of the inexpensive hotels are bunched on **rue Perdiguier** and **rue Joseph Vernet.** The former intersects the main drag, cours Jean-Jaurès (which turns into rue de la République), not far from the Porte de la République and the train station; the latter is parallel to place de l'Horloge a few streets to the west. Most hotels serve breakfast for 25F–35F and will store your luggage for a day (which is important since the station no longer does).

UNDER 200F • Hôtel Innova. This clean and comfortable hotel is on an elegant street near the Musée Carnet. Basic singles are 140F and doubles run 150F–200F. It may not be the Ritz, but they do leave little candies by the bed. *100 rue Joseph Vernet, tel. 04–90–82–54–10, fax 04–90–82–52–39. 11 rooms, 8 with bath.*

UNDER 250F • Hôtel Central. Right off the main drag and overlooking a quiet interior courtyard, this hotel is about as central as it gets. Simple doubles are 170F–230F (100F more during the festival). *31–33 rue de la République, tel. 04–90–86–07–81, fax 04–90–27–99–54. 27 rooms, 19 with shower.*

Hôtel du Parc. This popular, central hotel is surprisingly cheap and a bit nicer than similarly priced hotels in the area. The rooms are sunny, clean, and relatively modern. Singles start at 145F, doubles at 165F (185F–230F with shower). Showers are an extra 5F. *18 rue Agricol Perdiguier, just off cours Jean-Jaurès, tel. 04–90–82–71–55, fax 04–90–85–64–86. 14 rooms, 7 with bath.*

Hôtel Provençal. If you can't bear to be more than a few streets from the action but still want the relative calm of a side neighborhood, this hotel is for you. The 190F–240F price tag for a double is more than fair. *13 rue Joseph Vernet, tel. 04–90–85–25–24, fax 04–90–82–75–81. 11 rooms, all with shower.*

Hôtel Le Splendid. Not quite as "splendid" as its neighbors, this hotel is an excellent alternative when there are few vacancies. The rooms are small but clean, and the management is charming. It's 180F–230F for a double. *17 rue Agricol Perdiguier, tel. 04–90–86–14–46, fax 04–90–85–38–55. 17 rooms, all with shower.*

UNDER 300F • Hôtel Angleterre. The Angleterre is snazzier than most of the hotels in this price range, with lots of modern furniture and big bathrooms. Singles and doubles start at 190F (210F–380F with shower); hall showers are 15F. *29 blvd. Raspail, tel. 04–90–86–34–31, fax 04–90–86–86–74. From train station, take rue Jean-Jaurès to blvd. Raspail and turn left. 40 rooms, 37 with bath. Closed late Dec.–early Jan.*

Hôtel Colbert. This very reasonably priced hotel is just 50 yards from the tourist office. Rooms are small and basic but air-conditioned. Doubles go for 200F–280F. *7 rue Agricol Perdiguier, tel. 04–90–86–20–20, fax 04–90–85–97–00. 15 rooms, all with shower. Air-conditioning.*

Hôtel Mignon. In the same street as the Hôtel Provençal (*see above*) and similar in all ways but price and exterior gloss, the Mignon is frequently booked out weeks in advance. Call ahead for double rooms at 220F–300F. *12 rue Joseph Vernet, tel. 04–90–82–17–30, fax 04–90–85–78–46. 16 rooms, 15 with shower.*

Hôtel de Mons. Right off place de l'Horloge, this simple hotel is in a 13th-century chapel that was once a part of the Palais des Papes (it's still connected). Spend a night here and you'll get to sleep where Napoléon I's chaplain, Étienne Martin Morel de Mons, stayed 1821–30. Doubles run 240F–280F. *5 rue de Mons, tel. 04–90–82–57–16, fax 04–90–85–19–15. 11 rooms with shower or tub.*

UNDER 350 • Hôtel St-Roch. Although it's in a dingy neighborhood, this gracious hotel has a friendly owner and is only a five-minute walk from Avignon's walls. Some rooms have garden patios, living rooms, and antique furniture. Doubles start at 280F. *9 rue Paul Mérindol, tel. 04–90–16–50–00, fax 04–90–82–78–30. From train station, go west along ramparts to porte St-Roch, then take av. Eisenhower to rue Paul Mérindol. 26 rooms, all with shower or bath.*

HOSTEL AND CAMPING • Avignon Squash Club. Beyond the walls, on the northeastern edge of town and right in front of the Université Sainte-Marthe, this hostel–sports facility is very popular. A jovial reception, clean rooms, and good location ensure that this will remain the case. Dorm beds are 58F a night, and a few rooms have beds (with sheets) for 88F–110F. Breakfast is 18F and sheet rental (only for dorm beds) is 16F. Prices go down during the festival, but good luck getting a bed. *32 blvd. Limbert, tel. 04–90–85–27–78, fax 04–90–82–90–84. From the station, walk right along the walls. 26–58 beds depending on the season. Reception open 8–11 AM and 5–11 PM. No credit cards.*

Foyer and Camping Bagatelle. People of all ages from all over the world stay in this huge year-round hostel on Ile de la Barthelasse, a 15-minute walk from the center of town. The complex includes an incredible view of town, two cafeterias, a pricey supermarket, a small store, a public swimming pool next door, and a campground (238 sites plus full access to hostel facilities—all for 45F–50F per site for two people). The place is noisy 8 AM–11 PM; then "quiet time" begins. In the hostel, single-sex rooms have two to six beds (60F a pop) and sheets are provided. Breakfast is available for 20F and luggage can be stored. *Ile de la Barthelasse, tel. 04–90–86–30–39, fax 04–90–27–16–23. From main post office, take Bus 10 to island. 180 beds. Laundry.*

FOOD

It isn't hard to eat well in Avignon if you're willing to search beyond the tourist traps in front of the Papal Palace. Avignon has many ethnic restaurants that serve good meals at fair prices. But if you're concerned most with getting food in your stomach fast, head for **rue de la République,** with dozens of stands selling sandwiches and crepes. **Rue des Lices** and **rue des Teinturiers,** which extend from rue Bonneterie, are dotted with tiny restaurants, bars, and bistros. You can buy produce at the large **indoor market** on place Pie, Tuesday–Sunday mornings, or weekend mornings at the **outdoor market** by porte St-Michel, outside the ramparts near the train station.

UNDER 50F • Tapalocas. You can't beat the 12F tapas at this small place with a big mural of Spanish dancers. Make a fiesta of it: Try them all with a pitcher of the house sangria (59F) while you listen to the nightly live music. *10 rue Galante, south of pl. de l'Horloge, tel. 04–90–82–56–84.*

UNDER 75F • Les Apprentis de la Bonneterie. Chef Christian prepares his dishes with a perfection often reserved for four-star restaurants. Given the quality of food, the prices are unbeatable. You can dine inside under the Picasso reproductions, or outside in the breeze. On Thursday, dinner is followed by poetry readings. The 75F menu, which changes daily, may include a vegetable terrine, or *lapin à la moutarde* (rabbit with mustard sauce). *28 rue de la Bonneterie, tel. 04–90–27–37–97.*

La Maison du Traiteur. Main dishes cost 40F–50F and a 65F prix fixe of dishes selected from the full menu is available 11–6:30. There are also sandwiches and snack foods. *25 pl. des Corps Saints, off rue Perdiguier, tel. 04–90–85–58–70.*

La Table de Patrick and **La Petite Anglaise.** Head over to these Provençal restaurants where chef Patrick and his brother Alain insist on everyone being well fed and happy. At both places there is always a 50F–60F menu, sometimes including an all-you-can-eat crudité (salad) bar, a plat du jour, and dessert. Patrick prepares only what's fresh at the market and will substitute a vegetarian dish if requested. La Petite Anglaise also serves as an English-style *salon de thé* during the afternoon. *La Table de Patrick: 22 rue du Chapeau Rouge, off rue Carnot. La Petite Anglaise: 25 rue de la Croix. Tel. for both 04–90–86–10–46. Both closed Sun. Sept.–June.*

Tarasque. Come for tea and stay for dinner. The prix-fixe menu for 50F is good all day, as are the grilled meats (50F–70F) and salads (35F–50F). *18 rue des Teinturiers, tel. 04–90–14–98–44. Cash only.*

UNDER 100F • L'Épicerie. Next to the Église St-Pierre, this colorful, intimate restaurant serves cuisine à la Provençale (such as polenta topped with olives and tuna or saltimbocca with eggplant) for 60F–100F. *10 pl. St-Pierre, tel. 04–90–82–74–22. No lunch Sun.*

La Tache d'Encre. Avignon's actors and dancers frequent this cozy joint. With creative dishes (60F–90F) like pineapple on basmati rice and ginger pork on its menu, and jazz or theater performances on weekends, it's the perfect artsy haunt. *22 rue des Teinturiers, tel. 04–90–85–81–03. Closed Mon. No dinner Tues., no lunch Sun.*

UNDER 150F • Grand Café. The setting is dramatic: spread over a terrace and in an airy room at the foot of the Rocher des Doms. And the food—from cake and coffee during the day to full menus at lunch (85F) and dinner (140F)—is excellent. *La Manutention, cours Maria Casares, 4 rue des Escaliers Ste-Anne, tel. 04–90–86–86–77. Closed Mon.*

CAFES

Avignon's many cafés are always packed. The more expensive ones are on **place de l'Horloge,** where you pay for the central location. Look for more low-key (and cheaper) cafés on **place Pie, place St-Didier,** at the north end of **rue des 3-Faucons,** and on **place des Corps Saints** (at the south end of rue des 3-Faucons). **Les Faits Libres** (14 rue Limas, tel 04–90–27–39–05) is a French *salon de thé* (tearoom) serving confectionaried delights starting at 25F. A more English tearoom is **Simple Simon** (26 rue Petite Fusterie, tel. 04–90–86–62–70); it's closed Sunday, Monday, and evenings.

WORTH SEEING

Everything worth seeing (except the Pont St-Bénézet) is confined within the city walls. Most sights cluster around place **du Palais,** with signs pointing the way. If you want to be paraded around Avignon, a small train makes a tour of the city's prime spots for 35F. It departs from the main tourist office every 35 minutes April–October. If you plan on visiting more than one attraction, make sure you ask about the *AVIGNON PASS'ion.* You pay full fare for the first entry or activity and receive a card entitling you to half-price access to everything else. You'll need at least a full day to see the town.

MUSEE CALVET

One of France's best collections of Greek antiquities and modern art this side of Paris is housed in this 18th-century mansion. On display are works by Avignonnais Joseph Vernet, as well as greats like Manet, Utrillo, and Modigliani. There are also salons decorated in elegant Louis-XV style. *65 rue Joseph Vernet, tel. 04–90–86–33–84. Admission 30F. Open Wed.–Mon. 10–1 and 2–6.*

PALAIS DES PAPES

Avignon's character is best defined by the colossal Papal Palace, where nine Avignon popes held court. Notice how the portraits of the holy ones are surprisingly similar; the artist used the same model for every portrait. Also note the two different architectural styles. The severe **Palais Vieux** (Old Palace) was built between 1334 and 1342 by Pope Bénédict XII, a member of the Cistercian order, which frowned on frivolity. The more decorative **Palais Nouveau** (New Palace), built the following decade, is courtesy of the more artsy Pope Clement VI. The **Grand Court** (Great Court), where you'll enter, forms a link between the two. A tour of the palace's austere interior takes you through the pope's bedroom, with its surprisingly ornate decor, his chapel, the treasury, and banquet hall. Unfortunately, fire and time have done away with the original lavish palace decorations. In the **Chapelle St-Jean** and the **Chapelle St-Martial** look for the frescoes and artist Matteo Giovanetti's extravagant use of blue paint, made from the gemstone lapis lazuli. During the Revolution, the palace was used to house prisoners and soldiers, who chipped off pieces of the frescoes to sell to tourists. In summer, the Palais hosts excellent art exhibits, which, in the past, have included the likes of Botero, Rodin, and Picasso. *Pl. du Palais, tel. 04–90–27–50–00. Admission 45F. Open Apr.–Oct., daily 9–7 (until 8 mid-Aug.–Sept.); Nov.–Mar., daily 9:30–5:45. English-language tours daily at 11 AM and 2:30 PM (additional times in summer).*

Gay bars are hard to come by in these parts, which makes l'Esclave (12 rue de Limas, tel. 04–90–85–14–91) a real find. It's open 10 PM–5 AM and charges a 50F cover (including one drink).

PETIT PALAIS

Built in the 14th century, the Little Palace used to be a residence for cardinals and archbishops. Now a museum, it houses an outstanding collection of Italian paintings (works by Botticelli and Carpaccio among them) and Avignonnais art from the Middle Ages and the Renaissance. *Pl. du Palais, tel. 04–90–86–44–58. Admission 30F, free Sun. off-season. Open Wed.–Mon. 9:30–noon and 2–6.*

PONT ST-BENEZET

This famed bridge was the first to span the Rhône at Avignon. According to legend, a shepherd boy named Bénézet built it in the 12th century, acting on orders from heaven. Today it looks anything but heaven-sent—only four of the original 22 arches remain. Flooded innumerable times by the river, it was rebuilt time and time again until the 17th century, when everyone finally gave up. For a fee, you, too, can dance "Sur le pont d'Avignon," just like in the famous song. *Rue Ferruce, tel. 04–90–85–60–16. Admission 17F for bridge only, 53F for bridge and museum. Open Apr.–Sept., daily 9–7; Oct.–Mar., daily 9:30–5:30.*

ROCHER DES DOMS

From the entrance to the Pont d'Avignon, walk along the ramparts to a spiral staircase leading to Doms Rock, a park on a bluff above town. The fenced lake looks pretty fake, but you get great views of the bridge and Villeneuve-les-Avignon across the river. Check out the sundial on which your own body creates the shadow. Just down from the park is the **Cathédrale Notre-Dame des Doms,** a 12th-century structure with an immense 19th-century statue of the Virgin Mary rising above it. Inside the ornate church are the tombs of Popes Benoît XII and John XXII. *Park open until sunset.*

FESTIVALS

The town is at its best—and its most crowded—in July and August during the **Festival d'Avignon,** which brings together a variety of music, dance, and theater groups from around the world. Tickets go on sale in mid-June and cost 120F–180F. Contact the office (Bureau du Festival d'Avignon, 8 bis rue de Mons, tel. 04–90–27–66–50) as early as March to get a program. The **Festival Off** is similar to the Festival d'Avignon and takes place at the same time but features more amateur performances and more free concerts. Tickets cost 70F–80F; it's a little cheaper if you attend three or more shows. Contact the Avignon Public Office in Paris (tel. 01–48–05–01–19) for information.

AFTER DARK

Pick up the free bimonthly publication *Rendez-vous* at the main tourist office for an overview of all the cultural goings-on. October–June, the **Opéra d'Avignon** (pl. de l'Horloge, tel. 04–90–82–42–42 for information, 04–90–82–23–44 for tickets) hosts ballets, plays, operas, and other classical music performances. Many of these events are free or inexpensive; inquire at the tourist office. **Utopia Cinemas** (5 rue Figuière and 4 rue des Escaliers Ste-Anne, tel. 04–90–82–65–36) shows classic and cult films in their original version (i.e., American films are in English, not dubbed in French). Tickets cost 40F.

The **AJMI Jazz Club** at the Théâtre du Chêne Noir (8 bis rue Ste-Catherine, tel. 04–90–86–08–61) organizes jazz shows; call for current listings. **Le Blues** (25 rue Carnot, tel. 04–90–85–79–71) is a popular piano bar, which often has live music and karaoke and is open late; cocktails cost 50F. **Pub Z** (58 rue Bonneterie, tel. 04–90–85–42–84) is an art-deco-style café for the label-conscious. For a taste of the American Midwest—a big bar, pool tables, and heavy wood furniture in a hangar-size structure—try **Bokao's Café** (9 bis quai St-Lazare, tel. 04–90–82–47–95).

NEAR AVIGNON

Avignon is an ideal base for exploring the surrounding Vaucluse region, which stretches from the Rhône valley eastward to the Alpine foothills, and from Avignon north to **Orange** and **Vaison-la-Romaine**. Nearby towns, mostly small and quiet, make excellent day trips and are good places to hike, bike, and mountain climb. If it's wine you're after, bike, bus, or drive to **Châteauneuf-du-Pape** or the small villages around Vaison-la-Romaine. Between sips of wine, visit the Roman ruins and the psychiatric home where van Gogh stayed in **St-Rémy**.

VILLENEUVE-LES-AVIGNON

Villeneuve has a treasure trove of historical sites and fewer tourists than Avignon. It gained importance during the Avignon papacy, when it served as a summer residence for cardinals living in Avignon. It was also a heavily fortified stronghold for the French kings, who competed for power with the popes in Avignon. Take Bus 11 (10 mins, 6F), which leaves every half hour from the post office in Avignon and drops you off at place Charles David, right by the **tourist office** (1 pl. Charles David, tel. 04–90–25–61–33, fax 04–90–25–91–55); it's open September–June, Monday–Saturday 8:45–12:30 and 2:30–6, until 6:30 and also on Sunday in July and August. It's a 15-minute walk from Ile de la Barthelasse: Walk across pont Daladier and turn right on avenue Gabriel Péri; then follow the signs. If you are planning on visiting a number if attractions here, keep in mind that the AVIGNON PASS'ion (*see* Avignon, *above*) is also valid for all the sights here.

WHERE TO SLEEP AND EAT

Hotels and restaurants are less plentiful here than in Avignon, but they're also less crowded. **Hôtel Beauséjour** (61 av. Gabriel Péri, tel. 04–90–25–20–56) has rooms starting at 145F (180F–250F with shower). Overlooking the Rhône, the **Foyer YMCA** (7 bis chemin de la Justice, tel. 04–90–25–46–20, fax 04–90–25–30–64) costs 84F–175F per person, depending on the number of beds per room (1–3), and includes breakfast. You can find homemade pasta and pizza for 40F–80F at **La Mamma (Mama Lucia)** (pl. Victor Basch, tel. 04–90–25–00–71). **La Calèche** (35 rue de la République, tel. 04–0–25–02–54), closed Sunday and Thursday dinner, specializes in thick steaks (*onglet*) in a pepper sauce. Menu prices are 59F–98F. If you prefer light food, **L'Automate** (50 rue de la République, tel. 04–90–25–68–71), closed Thursday dinner and Sunday dinner, fires up excellent crepes and galettes.

WORTH SEEING

At the **Chartreuse du Val de Bénédiction** (rue de la République, tel. 04–90–15–24–24), open October–March daily 9:30–5:30, and April–September daily 9:30–6:30, you can get a sense of the lonely and reflective life monks lived. A magnificent 14th-century charterhouse, it is now an important cultural center hosting art exhibits, concerts, and other events. The building is a maze of corridors and chambers, including a chapel, bedrooms, and cloisters. Admission is 32F. On a hill overlooking the Chartreuse are the twin towers and colossal gateway of **Fort St-André** (tel. 04–90–25–45–35). Admission is 25F and it's open October–March, daily 10–noon and 2–5, and April–September, daily 10–12:30 and 2–6. The fort was built by John the Good and Charles VII in the 14th century to protect the Benedictine abbey and town of St-André. The remains of the town and abbey stand in silent grandeur. The **Musée Municipal Pierre de Luxembourg** (rue de la République, tel. 04–90–27–49–66) displays mostly religious paintings dating from the 14th and 15th centuries. Admission is 20F; it's open October–January, Tuesday–Sunday 10–noon and 2–5, and March–September, daily (except Monday March–mid-June) 10–12:30 and 3–7. Walk to **Tour Philippe le Bel** (rue Montée de la Tour, tel. 04–90–27–49–68) for great views of Avignon. Philippe the Fair had the tower built in the 13th century after agreeing to make Villeneuve a French possession. It served as a gateway to the kingdom. Admission is 10F and it's open the same hours as the Musée Luxembourg.

FONTAINE-DE-VAUCLUSE

The natural beauty of Fontaine-de-Vaucluse is so spectacular that you might almost forget it's a tourist mecca. The star attraction of this small village, 50 minutes east of Avignon by bus (30F), is a spring, believed to be the source of the emerald-green Sorgue River. But the village also has a surprisingly impressive collection of historical odds and ends. The **tourist office** (chemin de la Fontaine, tel. 04–90–20–32–22, fax 04–90–20–21–37) has lots of town information and is open year-round Monday–Saturday 10–7.

WHERE TO SLEEP

There is not a wealth of affordable in-town hotels here. Your best bargain bet is the **Hôtel du Château** (quartier Petite Place, tel. 04–90–20–31–54, fax 04–90–20–28–02), which has five small rooms at 195F, none with a private shower, and a very popular family-style restaurant. Otherwise, you should head over to the **Hôtel du Parc** (rue des Bourgades, tel. 04–90–20–31–57, fax 04–90–20–27–03), where there are 12 rooms, all with amenities, at 280F. Here too you can dine in a lovely garden restaurant. The **Auberge de Jeunesse** (chemin de la Vignasse, tel. 04–90–20–31–65) is a 10-minute walk from town. For a bed and breakfast, you'll pay 67F (with a HI card, 19F more without). The hostel also rents bikes for 80F. From town, cross the bridge and follow route de Cavaillon until it hits the *route touristique de Gordes* (Gordes's tourist route); turn left and follow the AUBERGE DE JEUNESSE signs. Reception is open 5:30 PM–10 PM and the hostel 8 AM–10 AM and 5–11 PM, when curfew begins. Nearby, **Le Camping Municipal** (rte. de Cavaillon, tel. 04–90–20–32–38), ½ km (¼ mi) from town, charges 14F a person and 13F per campsite. From town, cross the bridge and follow route de Cavaillon 1 km (½ mi).

FOOD

There are far too many *frite* (french fry) stands and very few other options for cheap food here. Since there are only a couple of pricey grocery stores in town, you might want to stock up on food before coming so you can enjoy a picnic under a shady tree. Or splurge in one of the cafés on chemin de la Fontaine right next to the Sorgue River. Of these, perhaps the most impressive is the **Restaurant Philip Jardin de Petrarch** (tel. 04–90–20–31–81), closed October–March, right at the base of the waterfall. **Lou Fanau** (tel. 04–90–20–31–90) specializes in regional dishes; in early spring France's famous black truffles are the delicacy. Tuesday is **market** day on place de l'Église.

WORTH SEEING

The **fontaine** is at the foot of steep cliffs, a 10-minute walk from the center of the village. Numerous attempts have been made to identify the source of the spring, but the mysterious pool defies modern technology. The most intelligent theory is that it's fed by an underground stream supplied with rainwater from the Vaucluse Plateau. In March and April, the fountain gushes with runoff from the melting snow, but from late spring through summer it's usually still.

Le Monde Souterrain (chemin de la Fontaine, tel. 04–90–20–34–13) houses a collection of stalagmites, stalactites, and other limestone drippings and man-made lakes and frescoes. You can only see the place by guided tour, given every 40 minutes in French. There's a skimpy written English translation, but if you have seen caves before and you don't speak French, it may not be worth the 30F admission. It's closed Monday.

The ruins of the Bishop of Cavaillon's 14th-century **château** teeter on a hill above the village. Climb the stairs to the right of the entrance to **Musée Petrarque** (tel. 04–90–20–37–20, admission 20F) to reach the ruins and an outstanding rooftop view. Italian poet Francesco Petrarch (1304–74) was a big fan of

VICHY FRANCE AND THE UNDERGROUND

While southern France bowed under the rule of the Vichy government in 1943, a few brave individuals resisted the occupation. Under the direction of Jean Moulin, these people created MUR (Mouvement Unifié de la Résistance) to fight the Nazi occupation. Members formed "maquis," secret armies that circulated underground newspapers, collected and hid arms for Allied soldiers, and infiltrated enemy camps. Hiking in the Mont Ventoux area (or nearby Mont Ste-Victoire), you're certain to stumble upon the remains of stone farmhouses where they hid weapons and held secret meetings.

the village and lived in the house where the museum is for 16 years. Take a walk through the 14th-century **moulin à papier** (paper mill; chemin de la Fontaine, tel. 04–90–20–34–14), no admission charge, where the river forces heavy wooden mallets down to create a watery paper pulp. The French Resistance had an active base in Fontaine (*see* box, *above*), and the **Musée de l'Histoire et de la Résistance** (tel. 04–90–20–24–00) documents French life under German occupation and acknowledges the role the Vichy regime played in the Holocaust. Most of the exhibit materials are in French, so don't dish out the 20F if it's all Greek to you. Ever wonder where the Pope's elegant crystal place settings are made? Believe it or not: here. The **Cristallerie des Papes** (tel. 04–90–20–32–52), operational since the temporary move to Avignon, is still in this little village. The four huge glassblowing furnaces can be visited for free year-round.

OUTDOOR ACTIVITIES

Kayak Vert (tel. 04–90–20–35–44) and **Canoe Evasion** (tel. 04–90–38–26–22) rent single and double kayaks and canoes for 100F–150F for the 8-km (5-mi), 2½-hour ride down the Sorgue; it also organizes guided trips. Exploring the region is well worth the 80F you'll pay to rent a bike (*see* Where to Sleep, *above*); a spectacular, challenging ride takes you 15 km (9 mi) away to **Gordes**; ask for a map and directions. Caution: Hiking during July and August is strongly discouraged. The historically poor rainfall and high summer temperatures in the area make it unusually prone to the risks of fire.

CHATEAUNEUF-DU-PAPE

This small hillside town, just a half-hour bus ride (19F) from Avignon, lends its name to some of the world's most renowned wines. The pebbly soil here is particularly suited to the growth of vines: The small stones act like a wool sweater, retaining the heat of the sun's rays and keeping the vines warm and cozy during the night. The 36 vineyards produce more than 13 million bottles of very expensive (mostly red) wine each year, and the relaxed tempo of life here centers on its production.

You can taste wines for free in *caves de dégustation* (wine-tasting cellars) on nearly every street, but you may have to endure haughty looks from streetwise merchants who know you're not going to shell out 150F and cram a bottle into your backpack. Etiquette dictates that you leave a few francs' tip if you've been slurping down glass after glass. Get a free map of the caves from the **tourist office** (pl. du Portail, tel. 04–90–83–71–08). It's open October–March, Monday–Saturday 9–12:30 and 2–6, and April–September, daily 9–7.

The **Musée des Vieux Outils de Vignerons** (av. Pierre de Luxembourg, tel. 04–90–83–70–07) uses a video to show you cellars and vineyards instead of bothering to take you around the real McCoy. However, it does have free wine tastings and an English-speaking staff. Take the five-minute walk up to the ruins of a **château** once used by the Avignon popes as a summer residence (1316–77). When we say ruins, we mean it—only two walls remain; the rest were ravaged by Baron des Adrets in 1562, then by the Germans in 1945. At the top is an amazing view of the vineyards.

WHERE TO SLEEP

Spending the night in Châteauneuf is ridiculously expensive, and the sneaky devils have set up the September–June bus schedules so you can't go and come back in one day. But in July and August, take your wine and get back on the bus. If you're stranded, the cheapest hotel is **La Garbure** (3 rue Joseph du Cots, tel. 04–90–83–75–08) at 340F for a good-size double, including breakfast and dinner. You can get a list of bed-and-breakfast places from the tourist office, but these run about the same price.

FOOD

The town doesn't have many restaurants either; bring a picnic or buy groceries at the store next to the tourist office. One good spot for lunch or dinner is **La Mule du Pape** (2 rue de la République, tel. 04–90–83–79–22), where the 65F, 78F, or 110F menu will allow you to dine heartily on the regional fare and local wines. Or splurge for a beautiful view and pricier food (150F menu) at **La Mère Germaine** (rue Commandant Lemaître, tel. 04–90–83–54–37). The restaurants on **rue Joseph Ducos** are better and cheaper than the rip-offs on place du Portail.

ST-REMY-DE-PROVENCE

Forty minutes from Avignon by bus (29F), St-Rémy sits at the base of the Alpilles, a range of mountains on the east side of the Rhône that run south toward Les Baux. A small town, it has outstanding Roman ruins, excellent hiking terrain, and legendary status as "home" to van Gogh when he was confined to its psychiatric institution. Find out more about van Gogh and about the many festivities that take place in St-Rémy at the **tourist office** (pl. Jean-Jaurès, tel. 04–90–92–05–22, fax 04–90–92–05–22). It's open October–May, Monday–Saturday 9–noon and 2–6, and June–September, Monday–Saturday 9–noon and 2–7, Sunday 9–noon.

WHERE TO SLEEP

In town, the best deal is the **Hôtel Ville Verte** (pl. de la République, tel. 04–90–92–06–14, fax 04–90–92–56–54), a 17th-century building, which has a pool and terrace; rooms run 195F–270F. Otherwise, across the street, try the **Cheval Blanc** (6 av. Fauconnet, tel. 04–90–92–09–28, fax 04–90–92–69–05) with fewer bonuses but welcome service: 220F–300F for a double. If you want to linger in St-Rémy and hike, you can camp at **Camping Pegomas** (av. Jean Moulin, tel. 04–90–92–01–21, fax 04–90–92–56–17), with more than 100 sites. It's a 10-minute walk from town and costs 75F–89F for two and a tent.

FOOD

Try **Le Café des Arts** (30 blvd. Victor Hugo, tel. 04–90–92–08–50), the oldest restaurant in town, where classic French cuisine runs 110F–150F. But the characters at the bar are worth any price. You can also spend the night here; doubles run 285F–350F. There are a number of small, moderately priced restaurants lining rue Carnot and its extension, avenue de la Libération, of which **La Source** (13 av. de la Libération, tel. 04–90–92–44–71) seems to be a local favorite.

WORTH SEEING

One kilometer (½ mi) south of the center of town are two prominent Roman remains, planted off the road as if stuck in a time warp. The **Arc Municipal,** a triumphal arch, marks the point where the Roman road from Arles, Via Domitia, entered the ancient city of Glanum. Nearby, the **Mausolée** (Mausoleum) has statues of Emperor Augustus's adopted sons, Caius and Lucius Caesar. Across the street from the monuments are the remains of **Glanum.** The city of Glanum developed under Hellenistic influence in the 3rd and 2nd centuries BC, only to be revamped by the Romans and later destroyed by Germanic tribes in the 3rd century AD. Amazingly, some architecture survived the warfare, and you can visit the remains of baths and houses. Most of the artifacts from the ruins are currently stored in the **Musée Archéologique** (Hôtel de Stade, rue du Parage, tel. 04–90–92–64–04); it's open April–September, Tuesday–Sunday 10–noon and 2–6, October–March, Tuesday–Sunday 10–noon and 2–5. *Av. Vincent van Gogh, tel. 04–90–92–23–79. Admission to Glanum and the museum 36F (Glanum only 32F, museum only 15F). Open Apr.–Sept., daily 9–7; Oct.–Mar., daily 9–noon and 2–5.*

Down the street to the east of the excavations is the former monastery of **St-Paul-de-Mausolée,** now a private hospital with a Romanesque church and cloister. You can visit the cloister for free, but not the mental hospital where van Gogh was confined in 1889 and 1890. Van Gogh fans will recognize much of the landscape; he did more than 150 canvases and 100 drawings during his year in the hospital. Pick up a free map at the tourist office if you want to follow in the steps of the painter; the orchards and fields where he painted are clearly marked. There are also guided tours; ask at the tourist office. If you're not just a fan but a fanatic, go to the **Maison d'Amandiers** to admire van Gogh's stone toilet, which rests in the garden. *Hôtel de Lubières, pl. Favier, tel. 04–90–92–02–28. Admission free. Open Mon.–Sat. with erratic hrs, so call ahead.*

Van Gogh wasn't the only character in St-Rémy who may have been one slice short of a loaf. Nostradamus (1503–66), the astrologer who wrote more than 600 obscure verses that supposedly predict major world events, was born here. Unfortunately, St-Rémy doesn't have all that much information on this psychic character, though one small room in the **Musée des Alpilles** is dedicated to him. The rest of the museum covers local arts and traditions. *Pl. Favier, tel. 04–90–92–68–24. Admission 16F. Open Nov.–Dec., daily 10–noon and 2–5; Apr.–Oct., daily 10–noon and 2–6 (7 in July and Aug.).*

Four yearly events worth noting all involve animals. The **Fête de la Transhumance,** on the morning of Whit Monday, sees several thousand local ewes, rams, goats, donkeys, and more shepherded through the center of town on the annual migration to higher pastures. On August 15, during the **Carreto Ramado,** an enormous cart loaded with local produce is pulled through town by 50 cart horses on a 330-ft long harness. Finally, the **Feria,** or bullfight (no bulls are killed here) follows the carreto ramado. The **Fêtes de St-Rémy,** last 10 days starting on the third or fourth Sunday in September, also has bullfights.

ORANGE

Orange, cradled in northern Provence in the land of Côte du Rhone vineyards, really isn't very big—but when compared to the sleepy wine villages that surround it, it's a thriving metropolis. In many ways, Orange captures the essence of the region: The Provençal accent here is quite thick, and savory food and wine can be had . . . for a price. Come to see its two Roman monuments, the **Théâtre Antique** and the **Arc de Triomphe,** spectacular vestiges of history that seem transported from a different world. The people who live here haven't sold out to tourism and continue going about their daily lives amid the narrow, cobbled streets of the *centre ville* (city center). You can probably see everything in an afternoon.

BASICS

The main **tourist office** has a friendly, English-speaking staff who provide free maps, brochures, and a full hotel and restaurant list. The exchange rate is lousy and there's a hefty commission on traveler's checks and cash exchanges. *5 cours Aristide Briand, tel. 04–90–34–70–88, fax 04–90–34–99–62. Open Apr.–Sept., Mon.–Sat. 9–7, Sun. 10–6; Oct.–Mar., Mon.–Sat. 9–1 and 3–6.*

For better exchange rates, try **Société Générale,** on rue de la République. There is also a second seasonal tourist office (pl. des Frères Mounet), across from the entrance to the Théâtre Antique (*see below*). It's open April–September, Monday–Saturday 10–1 and 2—7, and July–August, Sunday 10–1 and 2–7.

If your unanswered E-mail is piling up, sweep over to the **Cyber Station** where you pay 1F per minute for Internet access, 25F per half hour, and 45F per hour. *2 cours Aristide Briand, tel. 04–90–34–27–27. Open Mon., Wed., and Thurs. 9:30 AM–11 PM, Tues. 9:30–7, Fri.–Sat. 9:30 AM–1 AM.*

COMING AND GOING

The center of the city is a 15-minute walk from the **train station** (av. Frédéric Mistral, tel. 04–90–11–88–00): Head up the avenue onto rue de la République and then follow the signs to the centre ville. Trains run to Avignon (30 mins, 29F), Nîmes (1 hr, 64F), and Marseille (1½ hr, 108F). Orange also has TGV service to Paris (3½ hrs, 370F–434F); buy your ticket in advance and be sure to make reservations. The **bus station** (cours Pourtoules, tel. 04–90–34–15–59), on the eastern edge of the centre ville, has direct service to Avignon (45 mins, 29F), Vaison-la-Romaine (45 mins, 26F), and Marseille (3 hrs, 105F). Orange itself is small enough that you don't really need anything but your feet for getting around. That said, if you want to hit some of the surrounding countryside, bikes can be rented from **M.T.S. 84** (571 blvd. Edouard Daladier, tel. 04–90–34–94–92) for 120F a day plus a deposit. It's open Tuesday–Saturday 9–noon and 4–8, Monday 4–8.

WHERE TO SLEEP

UNDER 150F • Le Milan. There are only eight small rooms in the space above the local downstairs bar, but, as the cheapest digs in town (136F–146F per room), they are more than acceptable. *22 rue Caristie, tel. 04–90–34–13–31. 8 rooms, all with shower.*

UNDER 175F • Villages Hotel. It's completely sterile and pedestrian, but it's also cheap and spotlessly clean. A mere 155F will get you a room for one to three people. There's 24-hour check-in. *Chemin de Queyradel, tel. 04–90–11–03–66, fax 04–90–11–03–83. 70 rooms, all with shower.*

UNDER 200F • Arcotel. This pleasant space with decent rooms overlooking a lively central town square offers one single for 110F and doubles are 150F–310F. *8 pl. aux Herbes, tel. 04–90–34–09–23, fax 04–90–51–61–12. 19 rooms, most with shower.*

CAMPING

Camping le Jonquier (rue Alexis Carrel, tel. 04–90–34–19–83), open mid-March–October, has a pool, miniature golf, and bungalows. The campground is a 15- to 20-minute walk from the Arc and charges 64F for one person, 96F for two. From the train station, follow avenue Frédéric Mistral to rue de la République bus stop and take Bus 1 to the Arc de Triomphe. Then walk east, turn left on rue des Phocéens, right on rue des Étudiants, and left on rue Limousin.

FOOD

Many pricey restaurants serve typical Provençal meals for 90F and up, although you'll find cheaper sandwich shops and *crêperies* (crepe stands) around the Théâtre Antique. On rue St-Martin, there are several excellent bakeries, as well as fresh fruit and veggies at **Le Petit Marché.** Food and clothes are sold every Thursday morning at the **general market** on cours Aristide Briand. After a generous lunch, if all you want to do is hang out in a café and soak up the sun, head over to the **Brasserie du Théâtre** (tel. 04–90–34–12–39), right in front of the Roman theater (*see* Worth Seeing, *below*).

UNDER 75F • La Grotte. This Italian eatery is aptly named, with tables nestled snugly in a carved-out room. The 70F menu includes salad, pizza, and dessert, or you can try tagliatelli with smoked salmon for 45F. *10 montée des Princes, tel. 04–90–34–70–98. No lunch Sat.*

UNDER 100F • Le Bouchon. Lunches at le Bouchon, around the side of the theater (*see* Worth Seeing, *below*), are a family affair. The terrace is often packed on warm days and the waiters are a blur of activity. Lunch runs 60F–90F. *3 cours Pourtoules, tel. 04–90–51–85–24. No dinner Sun.–Fri.*

La Sangria. One of the cheaper French restaurants in town, La Sangria occupies a great spot on place de la République. When the weather is nice, savor a 60F–100F meal under shady trees, or take it inside and upstairs. The house specialty is paella *Catalane* (75F), a rice and seafood dish. *3 pl. de la République, tel. 04–90–34–31–96. Closed Sun., and last 2 wks in Oct. No dinner Tues.*

Sitting Bull–Chez Daniel. The young local crowd can't get enough of this place. And with good reason. Pizzas are big (30F–60F), the dinner menu is copious (90F), and there are seafood platters to match every appetite. The narrow pedestrian street echoes until late. *Rue Segond Weber, tel. 04–90–34–63–48. Closed Wed. No dinner Tues.*

WORTH SEEING

ARC DE TRIOMPHE

On the northern side of town, on avenue de l'Arc de Triomphe, the magnificent Arc de Triomphe was built in the 1st century AD on the ancient Via Agrippa, the road that used to link Lyon with Arles. It commemorates Julius Caesar's triumph over the Gauls, a fact of which the Romans were inordinately proud. The monument is composed of three archways and is decorated with images of warfare, particularly naval warfare, as symbolized by a ship's prow (honoring Caesar's naval victories). The 70-ft-tall central arch is the third-highest Roman arch still standing.

MUSEE MUNICIPAL

Across the street from the Théâtre Antique, the Town Museum has a collection of seemingly random odds and ends. On the ground floor, note the tablets that recorded land registry and administrative subdivisions during Roman times, as well as objects excavated in the vicinity. Another section of the museum is dedicated to the history of noble Orange families and the local tradition of making printed fabrics. An admission ticket from the Théâtre Antique gets you into this museum. *Rue Madeleine-Roch, tel. 04–90–51–18–24. Open Apr.–Sept., daily 9–7; Oct.–Mar., Mon.–Sat. 9:30–noon and 1:30–5:30.*

THEATRE ANTIQUE

Orange's Roman theater is 100 yards long and 40 yards high, with a seating capacity of 9,000. The back wall of the stage dominates the town—King Louis XIV called it the finest wall in his kingdom, and it's the only one of its kind still standing in its entirety. The theater is surrounded by the crumbling ruins of a temple and ongoing excavations of what is thought to have been a Roman gymnasium. If you want to avoid the admission fee, simply make the five-minute climb up the steps of the St-Eutrope hillside to the statue of the Virgin Mary. From here you get a free view of the stage (including an impressive statue of Caesar), as well as an excellent rooftop view of Orange. Also atop **Colline St-Eutrope** are the ruins of the château of Orange's princes, razed by Louis XIV when he annexed the principality of Orange for France. *Pl. des Frères Mounet, tel. 04–90–51–17–60. Admission 30F, admission to Musée Municipal (see above) included. Open Oct.–Mar., daily 9–noon and 1:30–5; Apr.–Sept., daily 9–6:30.*

FESTIVALS

Like so many other towns in Provence, Orange loves a good party, and every summer it holds three biggies in the Théâtre Antique. The most famous is **Les Chorégies,** a 130-year-old festival in July, during which symphonies, operas, and choral concerts are performed. Tickets aren't cheap and often sell out early; your best bet is to fight for a view atop St-Eutrope. If you're determined to make it to a show, call the ticket office (tel. 04–90–34–24–24) in January for a brochure, which includes an order form. Operas cost 40F–900F and symphonies are 20F–200F. **Les Nuits du Théâtre Antique** kicks off in mid-June and provides a wide variety of music through August. It is possible to get same-day tickets (15F–30F). At the end of May, Orange hosts the **Festival de la Bande-Dessinée** (Comic-Strip Festival).

NEAR ORANGE

VAISON-LA-ROMAINE

On the banks of the Ouvèze River amid vast vineyards, Vaison-la-Romaine is a jumble of architectural styles and neighborhoods that reflect the town's Gallo-Roman past. The Roman ruins are the main draw.

BASICS

The **tourist office** has a bureau de change, but you'll get better rates across the street at the post office. The staff speaks English and is very friendly, probably in hopes of lessening the blow that you have to pay for tourist brochures. Ask for the "Randonnées en Ppays Voconces avec Cimes et Sentiers" (35F), which describes eight excellent hikes and 60 bike routes with detailed maps. You can taste and buy wine at the classy **Maison du Vin** (Wine House) adjacent to the tourist office, but you must buy to taste. *Pl. du Chanoine Sautel, tel. 04–90–36–02–11, fax 04–90–28–76–04. From bus stop, follow av. Victor Hugo, pass pl. Monfort, turn right on Grande Rue. Open July–Aug., daily 9–12:30 and 2–6:45; Sept.–June, daily 9–noon and 2–5:45.*

COMING AND GOING

Les Cars Lieutaud buses (tel. 04–90–36–05–22) from Avignon (1¾ hrs, 39F), Orange (45 mins, 26F), and Séguret (15 mins, 11F) arrive in Vaison-la-Romaine on avenue des Choralies, near its intersection with either avenue Victor Hugo or avenue Général de Gaulle. You can easily get around town on foot. If you want to rent a bicycle to explore the countryside, try **Peugeot** (17 av. Jules Ferry, tel. 04–90–36–03–29) or **Mag 2 Roues** (cours Taulignan, tel. 04–90–28–80–46). VTTs (*vélo tout terrain,* or mountain bikes) run about 80F per day at Peugeot and 100F at Mag 2; both require a piece of ID as a deposit.

WHERE TO SLEEP

With an outstanding panoramic view of the Ventoux, **À Coeur Joie** (av. César Geoffray, tel. 04–90–36–00–78, fax 04–90–36–09–89) is the cheapest option in town if you can convince the charming hosts to let you pay for a bed only. In spotless rooms it has dorm-style bunks that are 85F for space in a triple, 180F for a single. Otherwise, campsites at **Le Carpe Diem** (rte. de St-Marcellin, tel. 04–90–36–02–02) cost 30F–49F plus 21F–25F per person (depending on the season); it's closed November–March. The most reasonable hotel in town is the rustic **Théâtre Romain** (av. Général de Gaulle, tel. 04–90–28–71–98, fax 04–90–36–20–71) with rooms at 155F–260F.

FOOD

Vaison-la-Romaine is a city that caters to tourists, and the restaurant prices reflect just that. You'll find most restaurants and cafés on **cours Taulignan, place Montfort,** and **Grande Rue.** Take advantage of the **Super U,** a huge grocery store at the end of avenue Victor Hugo near the bus stop. A general **market** selling food and clothing takes place Tuesday and Saturday mornings on major streets in town. Just off place Monfort, **L'Oursinade** (10 av. Victor Hugo, tel. 04–90–36–27–24) serves good pizzas (45F–50F) and pasta dishes (45F). It's closed Wednesday. **Auberge de la Bartavelle** (12 pl. Sus-Auze, tel. 04–90–36–02–16) is a gourmet's delight, with menus starting at 100F and rising steeply from there. Splurge on southwestern specialties like lamb with pine nuts, or the delectable foie gras with truffles. It's closed Monday.

WORTH SEEING

On either side of avenue Général de Gaulle, the two major excavation sites, **Fouilles de Puymin** and **Fouilles de la Villasse,** are as much a testimony to the accomplishments of 20th-century archaeology as they are examples of Roman architecture. The floors and walls of houses, villas, a basilica, and a theater have been unearthed, and the Roman street plan is partly discernible. If you love Roman history, or if piles of stones intrigue you, you'll take a shine to this place. You can see most of the sites without paying, but there are daily tours of the sites in English that are interesting and make the entrance fee worthwhile. Also included is admission to the **Musée Theo Desplans,** where you'll find mosaics and various other statues and pieces found in a Roman home. The origins of the **Cathédrale Notre Dame de Nazareth** date from the 1st century when the Gallo-Roman foundations were laid. Over the centuries contemporary architects left their imprint. Nonetheless, the mostly Roman-style cathedral achieves an elegant and unified appearance that blends the marks of many centuries. *Av. Jules Ferry. Admission 45F, ticket good for guided tours of all sights; valid 5 days. Excavation sites and cathedral open Nov.–Feb., daily 10–noon and 2–4:30; Mar.–May and Oct., daily 10–12:30 and 2–6; June–Sept., daily 9–6. Museum and cloister open and close 30 mins later than excavation site.*

Cross the Ouvèze via the **pont Romain** (Roman bridge), five minutes away on foot, to reach the enchanting *haute ville* (upper town), built during the Middle Ages. The bridge is still in good shape (and still in use) after 18 centuries. Dominated by the ruins of a medieval château, the haute ville is full of fountains and steep, twisting alleyways.

FESTIVALS

In July, Vaison-la-Romaine celebrates with an opera, choral, theater, and ballet festival. Most shows are held in the Roman theater, and buying tickets the day of the performance is quite possible. During **Les Journées Gourmandes,** a festival of Provençal food that's usually held the first week in November, you can taste local specialties. For 12 days prior to this, there is also a **Festival des Soupes,** during which there are contests (and free tastings) throughout the city. The tourist office has a list of the month's events, or call 04–90–28–74–74 for festival information.

MONT VENTOUX

Twenty kilometers (12 mi) east of Vaison-la-Romaine looms the 6,234-ft Mont Ventoux, dominating the Vaucluse region and marking the northern boundary of Provence. *Vent* means "wind," and there's plenty of it here. Icy winds whip around the peak, sometimes reaching 250 kph (155 mph). Throughout history, the lonely mountain has been plagued with an ungodly reputation due to the destructive winds. Attempts at saving its soul are evidenced by the chapels lining its slopes. Whether it's possessed by the devil or not, outdoor enthusiasts shouldn't hesitate to take advantage of its challenges. In July it's a cyclist's dream (or nightmare) during the Tour de France, and in winter you can swoop down the slopes at the two ski resorts.

COMING AND GOING

Route D974 goes all the way to the top. If you don't have a car, the only other way up is to take a bus to one of the nearby towns and then hitchhike or walk. **Cars Comtadins** buses (tel. 04–90–67–20–25) go from Vaison-la-Romaine to Carpentras (45 mins, 22F) about four times a day; from here you can continue to Malaucène (10 mins, 17F) or Bédoin (40 mins, 19F), the best towns for setting up base.

WHERE TO SLEEP

Two kilometers (1 mi) from the bus stop in Malaucène is a **gîte d'étape** (la Boissière, rte. de Souzette, tel. 04–90–65–25–33) with dorm beds (70F) and access to a pool (20F). Dinner including wine is an extra 100F. Bédoin has several campsites: The closest to town is **Domaine Naturiste** (tel. 04–90–65–60–18), which charges 143F for two people and a tent. The Vaison-la-Romaine tourist office will indicate the site on a map.

OUTDOOR ACTIVITIES

Mont Ventoux was the sight of the first recorded attempt at *l'escalade (mountain climbing)*, when Italian poet-philosopher Petrarch grunted his way up in AD 1336. Although people had obviously climbed mountains before, this was the first "do it because it's there" feat. Inquire at the gîte d'étape for the best places to try it. Hiking maps (10F–25F) are available at almost any tabac (tobacco shop) or at the **tourist offices,** open 9–noon daily, in Bédoin (espace Marie-Louis Gravier, pl. du Marché, tel. 04–90–65–63–95, fax 04–90–12–81–55) and Malaucène (pl. de la Mairie, tel. 04–90–65–22–59, fax 04–90–65–22–59). Town-to-town treks are also a great way to explore the area; one of the most beautiful trails is from Malaucène to Séguret.

ARLES

Sitting on the banks of the Rhône River, Arles is both a vibrant example of Provençal culture and the gateway to the Camargue, a wild and marshy region that extends south to the Mediterranean. West of Marseille and south of Avignon, Arles once outshone Marseille as the major port of the area before sea gave way to sand. The first inhabitants of Arles were Greek, but the Romans colonized the city in 46 BC and left a greater mark. Arles competes with Nîmes for the title "Rome of France" with a magnificent Roman theater and *arènes* (amphitheater). The numerous sights are all affordable, and although the centre ville is filled with touristy spots, Arles can accommodate budget travelers. The small *vieille ville* (old town) is speckled with residential pockets where time seems to have stood still since 1888, the year Vincent van Gogh immortalized the city in his paintings.

BASICS

BUREAUX DE CHANGE

BNP (10 pl. de la République, tel. 04–90–96–22–27), close to the St-Trophime cloister, has good rates and charges no commission. It's open Monday–Saturday 9–11:30 and 1:30–4. The ATMs accept both Cirrus and Plus cards. **Banque de France** (35 ter rue Dr. Fanton) is also a good bet.

MAIL

The main **post office** has a bureau de change and personnel of varying levels of friendliness. The postal code is 13200. *5 blvd. des Lices, tel. 04–90–18–41–00. Open weekdays 8:30–7, Sat. 8:30–noon.*

VISITOR INFORMATION

The **tourist office,** with a small annex in the train station (tel. 04–90–49–36–90; open Oct.–Mar., Mon.–Sat. 9–1 and 1:30–5, and Apr.–Sept., Mon.–Sat. 9–1 and 2–6), hands out an extensive free brochure and map covering Arles and makes hotel reservations for a 5F fee. The exchange rates here, however, are awful. Get a copy of "Farandole," the monthly guide to activities in Provence towns, as well as the booklet *Arles and van Gogh,* which outlines a walking tour of the scenes that he painted. *Esplanade Charles de Gaulle, tel. 04–90–18–41–20, fax 04–90–18–41–29. Open Oct.–Mar., Mon.–Sat. 9–6, Sun. 10–noon; Apr.–Sept., Mon.–Sat. 9–7, Sun. 9–1.*

COMING AND GOING

Beyond the attraction-filled vieille ville lies urban sprawl of little interest. All you need to get around the vieille ville is your feet. Nevertheless, bicycles are for rent at **Europbike** (newspaper kiosque "Le

Provençal," esplanade Charles de Gaulle, tel. 04–90–96–44–20) for 70F a day and a 700F deposit. Opening hours are Monday–Saturday 8–6 (7 PM in summer).

BY TRAIN

The **train station** (av. Paulin Talabot) serves all regions of France, with frequent trains to Avignon (20 mins, 35F), Nîmes (30 mins, 41F), Marseille (45 mins, 70F), and Paris (4 hrs, 374F–439F by TGV). Inside the station there's a tourist-office annex. To reach town, walk two minutes south on avenue Talabot until you hit place Lamartine; you'll be facing the north edge of the vieille ville.

BY BUS

The **gare routière** (bus station; av. Paulin Talabot, tel. 04–90–49–38–01) is in front of the train station. On weekdays, five buses go daily to Aix-en-Provence (2 hrs, 68F) and Marseille (2½ hrs, 87F); only two make the run on weekends. Others travel daily to Stes-Maries-de-la-Mer (30 mins, 37F), Avignon (45 min, 40F), and Nîmes (1 hr, 34F).

WHERE TO SLEEP

Many well-maintained hotels in the vieille ville offer singles and doubles for 100F–200F. If you arrive late at night, the following hotels are near the train and bus stations on place Lamartine:
Hôtel de France et de la Gare (1–3 pl. Lamartine, tel. 04–90–96–01–24, fax 04–90–96–90–87) has rooms for 165F–220F;
Hôtel Terminus et van Gogh (5 pl. Lamartine, tel./fax 04–90–96–12–32) has singles and doubles for 150F–220F.

Every three years locals in Arles elect a "Queen of Arles," chosen not for her looks but for her knowledge of Provençal customs and dialect.

UNDER 150F • Le Gallia. The prices at this small, clean, and centrally located hotel can't be beat. Spacious and comfortable singles and doubles with shower run 125F–150F. *22 rue l'Hôtel de Ville, tel. 04–90–96–00–63. 9 rooms, all with bath. Closed end-Oct.–mid-Nov.*

Hôtel Rhodania. In an odd side street at the foot of the Pont de Trinquetaille, this clean and colorful hotel is a meeting place for young people from around the world. It's a true bargain, except when you end up in a slightly cramped room with bunk beds. Rooms run 110F–185F. *1 rue du Pont, tel./fax 04–90–96–08–14. 10 rooms, 4 with bath.*

UNDER 200F • Hôtel Gauguin. The rooms (180F–220F) are clean and accommodating and do what they are meant to: provide you with a comfortable place to sleep. The hotel is in a lovely and bustling neighborhood square north of the amphitheater. *5 pl. Voltaire, tel. 04–90–96–14–35, fax 04–90–18–98–87. 18 rooms, all with shower.*

Le Mirador. This is probably one of the best mid-range centre ville hotels, with rooms 190F–260F. Street-side rooms can be noisy but are well lit. *3 rue Voltaire, tel. 04–90–96–28–05, fax 04–90–96–59–89. 15 rooms, all with shower or bath.*

UNDER 300F • Hôtel Calendal. If you long for luxury, it's worth spending the extra francs to stay at this secluded hotel, one block south of the Arènes. Pristine doubles (290F and up) decorated in Provençal fashion come with all the amenities (including air-conditioning—a big plus in summer); some have views of the garden courtyard and the Arènes; and others sleep up to four. *22 pl. du Dr. Pomme, tel. 04–90–96–11–89, fax 04–90–96–05–84. 27 rooms, all with bath. Restaurant, air-conditioning.*

Hôtel le Galoubet. This 250-year-old, ivy-covered building is home to a spacious, airy hotel that's within a stone's throw of the sights. The hospitable, multilingual management operates a good restaurant on the ground floor. Newly renovated rooms run 280F–350F. *18 rue du Dr. Fanton, tel. 04–90–93–18–11. From train station, follow the Rhône, turn left on rue Dominique Maisto (which becomes rue Hôtel de Ville), right on rue du Dr. Fanton. 8 rooms, all with shower or bath. Restaurant.*

Hôtel du Musée. Surrounded by the elegance of a 16th-century private home, the spacious and air-conditioned quarters, private breakfast patio, and regal feel draw quite a crowd. Count on 230F–340F for a double. *11 rue du Grand Prieuré, tel. 04–90–93–88–88, fax 04–90–49–98–15. 20 rooms, all with shower or bath.*

HOSTEL

Auberge de Jeunesse. This hostel (a 5-minute walk from town and 30 minutes from the train station) is great, except when it's overrun by screaming children or when you have to deal with the unaccommo-

IN THE FOOTSTEPS
OF THE ARTIST

"The hills here are full of thyme . . . and thanks to the transparency of the air, we see so much further here than at home," van Gogh said of Arles. Though he lived in the town for only 15 months (1888–90), van Gogh's paintings of Arles and the surrounding countryside have come to define Provence has much as the herbs and the traditional costumes. Van Gogh was ill-received and ostracized during his time in Arles, but these days the town has no qualms about cashing in on his genius. The Fondation van Gogh renders homage to the painter, and signs throughout town mark the places where he painted. Even though most of the actual sites were destroyed during World War II, the vibrant swirls of yellow, orange, and blue in works like "Starry Night" and "Café de Nuit" still evoke these places. If you want to attempt to re-create the romantic "Café de Nuit" scene, the Café van Gogh on place du Forum willingly provides the setting, even if it isn't quite true to history. The Espace van Gogh, too, looks like it does in van Gogh's rendition of the Hôpital Hôtel-Dieu, especially in spring and summer, when blooming flowers decorate the live canvas.

dating staff. Facilities include a cafeteria, bar, bureau de change, and free private lockers. A bed costs 80F (with HI card, 19F extra without) the first night and 68F thereafter, breakfast included. Dinner is 48F. *20 av. Maréchal Foch, tel. 04–90–96–18–25. From train station, take the Starlette bus, transfer to Bus 3 on blvd. des Lices. 110 beds. Reception open daily 7–10 AM and 5–11 PM. Lockout 10–5. Curfew 11 PM, 1 AM during photography festival. Closed Jan.*

CAMPING

Camping Les Rosiers. Although it's 1 km (½ mi) farther from town than Camping City, this site at the end of the Bus 2 line is much nicer than the competition. Amenities include volleyball nets, a pool, and a washing machine. Even better, they won't accept super-big RVs. Sites are 16F plus 17F per person. *Pont du Crau, tel. 04–90–96–02–12, fax 04–90–93–36–72. Showers. Closed mid-Oct.–mid-Mar.*

FOOD

Stay away from the restaurants on the central boulevard des Lices, which charge high prices for mediocre food. Bustling cafés and restaurants enliven **place du Forum** and **place Voltaire,** where you can have coffee or eat a full three-course meal for under 100F. The narrow streets leading away from the squares are lined with more intimate restaurants with comparable prices. A good cluster is on **rue Porte de Laure,** just south of the Arènes. For a quick fix of crepes or pizzettas, go to **rue Hôtel de Ville.** A spectacular produce and clothing **market,** where traditional regional wares are sold, is held Wednesday mornings on boulevard Émile Combes. People come from all over to shop at the even bigger market on Saturday mornings on boulevard des Lices. For groceries, go to the **Monoprix** (pl. Lamartine, tel. 04–90–93–62–74) near the train station—it's open Monday–Saturday 8–8—or the **Casino** (rue du Président Wilson), not far from the tourist office. It's open Monday–Saturday 7:30–12:30 and 3:30–7:30, Sunday 8:30–12:30, all day July–August.

UNDER 75F • Restaurant d'Arlaten. At this rustic, homey restaurant you can get a three-course meal for 70F. Sit out on the terrace and enjoy the traditional Provençal cuisine and the regional specialties. *5 rue de la Cavalerie, near pl. Lamartine, tel. 04–90–96–24–85. Closed Wed.*

Bodega La Cueva. You have to search to get here, but the reward is worth the effort. The setting is authentic, the food good and cheap—tapas (13F), raciones (big tapas portions; 40F), gazpacho (65F), a main dish of fish or meat (65F). Come early, stay late; it's lively until 2 AM. *13 rue Tour du Fabre., tel. 04-90-93-91-11. Closed Mon.*

La Mule Blanche. Locals go to this busy restaurant near Espace van Gogh for real Provençal cooking. Sit out on the terrace and enjoy a Marrakech salad (grilled peppers and onions in cumin and olive oil; 50F), or go for the pastis-drenched shrimp flambé (55F). Menus start at 85F. *9 rue du Président Wilson, tel. 04-90-93-98-54. Closed Sun.*

Vitamine. Salads (20F–50F) and main dishes (50F–75F) at this vegetarian restaurant are made with every imaginable vegetable and are guaranteed to restore your health after weeks of nothing but baguettes. *16 rue du Dr. Fanton, tel. 04-90-93-77-36. Closed Sun. No dinner Sat.*

UNDER 100F • Le Constantin. For 92F you'll get three substantial courses at this tiny, cheerful restaurant. Your meal might include homemade terrines, grilled tuna, steaks with *pommes frites* (french fries), and dessert. *6 rue Dominique Maïsto, tel. 04-90-93-48-64. Closed Wed. Cash only.*

La Paillotte. Try the *aïoli Provençale* (a dish with a famous garlic-based mayonnaise; 78F) or the bouillabaisse (108F). *28 rue du Dr. Fanton, tel. 04-90-96-33-15. Closed Thurs.*

Le Poisson Banane. This Antillean restaurant is open for dinner only with menus starting at 79F. If you really want to splurge, try the house namesake, *poisson banane* (banana fish; 90F). *6 rue du Forum, off pl. du Forum, tel. 04-90-96-02-58. Closed Sun.*

WORTH SEEING

Arles's historic sites are first-rate. Ancient baths and a magnificent amphitheater provide ample evidence of Provence's Roman heritage. All sights are in the vieille ville, and a 60F ticket gets you into everything. Sold at all the attractions, the ticket is valid indefinitely, which is a good thing since it takes more than a day to do the full cultural circuit. Check with the tourist office for visiting hours, since they tend to change constantly.

In addition to covering the sights mentioned below, the pass is also valid for the **Cryptoporticus** (rue Balze, near Hôtel de Ville), an eerie maze of underground galleries that once formed the base of a Roman forum; enter through the 17th-century chapel on rue Balze. The galleries were discovered when the chapel was built, but they weren't excavated until the 20th century. The **Alyscamps** (av. des Alyscamps, south of blvd. des Lices) is a vast cemetery begun in Roman times, later to become the home to St-Honorat abbey in the 12th century. Van Gogh immortalized these in his paintings. Take the passage underneath the **Hôtel de Ville** and look at the beautiful archways built entirely out of stone. The church of **St-Trophime** (pl. de la République) displays both Roman and Gothic architecture, and has a beautifully sculpted facade. Walk through the cloister at sunset, when the building and garden are tinted a fading rose.

Unless otherwise indicated, these and the following monuments charge 15F admission and are open Oct.–Mar., daily 10–noon and 2–4:30; Apr.–mid-June and last 2 wks Sept., daily 9–12:30 and 2–7; mid-June–mid-Sept., daily 9–7.

ARENES

This 2nd-century Roman amphitheater is not as well preserved as the one in Nîmes, but it *is* wider, if only by 10 ft. Begun as a venue for gladiator duels, it was turned into a fortress (three watchtowers remain), a medieval housing development, and once again an amphitheater. In its earlier days, saffron and lavender were burned to hide the smell of rotting corpses. It holds up to 20,000 spectators during the bullfights, concerts, and performances that take place here in summer. Check the flyers around the amphitheater to find out about upcoming events. *Rond-Point des Arènes, tel. 04-90-49-36-86.*

MUSEE DE L'ARLES ANTIQUE

Get an insightful look into Arles's rich Roman past at this modern museum. The excellent collection includes ancient statues, tombs, floor mosaics, and sarcophagi. Especially interesting are displays on Roman daily life (including a good explanation of their running-water system). Although the exhibits are entirely in French, they are easy to appreciate. To get here, take the free **Starlette** shuttle from boulevard Clemenceau, which runs Monday–Saturday every half hour 7:30–7:30, or walk. *Presqu'île du Cirque Romain, on av. Jean Monnet, tel. 04-90-18-88-88. Admission 35F. Open Apr.–mid-Sept., daily 9–7; mid-Sept.–Mar., daily 9:30–noon and 1:30–6.*

MUSEE REATTU

Named after the 18th-century painter Jacques Réattu, this museum houses a collection of contemporary art, 57 prized sketches by Picasso, and one of the largest collections of contemporary photography in France. The exhibit is well presented in a beautiful house that once belonged to the Knights of Malta and later served as a Provençal art school. *10 rue du Grand Prieuré, tel. 04–90–49–37–68.*

MUSEON ARLATEN

Provençal poet Frédéric Mistral used the money he received for his 1904 Nobel Prize to buy a Renaissance hotel and found a museum to preserve the customs and traditions of Provence. On display are furniture, ceramics, 18th-century clothing, and life-size re-creations of Provençal families at home. *29 rue de la République, tel. 04–90–96–08–23. Admission 20F. Open Nov.–Mar., 9–noon and 2–5; Apr.–May and Sept., 9–noon and 2–6; June, 9–noon and 2–6:30; July and Aug. 9–noon and 2–7; Oct., 9–noon and 2–5:30. Closed Tues. except in July, Aug., and Sept.*

THEATRE ANTIQUE

On the quiet edge of town behind the amphitheater is the Roman theater built during Augustus's reign in the 1st century BC. The semicircular seating tiers still stand, but only two columns and a few stumps remain of the stage. On summer nights, the theater becomes the backdrop for everything from classical music to dance to fashion shows. Check at the tourist office for schedules and prices. *Rue du Cloître.*

THERMES DE CONSTANTIN

Edifices of stone and brick re-create the structures of these 4th-century Roman baths. The height and area of the structure are impressive, but it's difficult to tell which parts belong to the original and which parts have been reconfigured. The various bathing compartments—the cold frigidarium, the warmer tepidarium, and the hot caldarium—attest to the elaborate bathing practices of the Romans. The baths weren't just for bathing; they were the equivalent of the modern gym, lecture hall, and social club all in one. *Rue Dominique-Maïsto, near rue du 4-Septembre.*

FESTIVALS

The **Rencontres Internationales de la Photographie** (10 rond point des Arènes, tel. 04–90–96–76–06) is a world-class photography festival that takes place early July–mid-August. Each year, more than 50 displays from artists around the world are shown throughout Arles. For 20F–35F, you can visit one or more of the exhibits. Pick up a free brochure from the tourist office listing expo locations.

In summer, a festival of music, dance, and theater takes place in the Arènes and Théâtre Antique. The Arènes becomes the site of bullfights, both the Provençal and bloody kind, during the **Féria Pascale** on Easter, the **Fête des Gardians** on May 1, and the **Prémices du Riz,** the second week of September. During the last week of June and the first week of July, Arles gets into its Provençal spirit with **Fêtes d'Arles** (35 pl. de la République, tel. 04–90–96–81–18). Parades, regional music and dance, Provençal costumes, and torch-lit processions fill the streets. Although most events are free, special performances may have a 10F–150F admission fee.

AFTER DARK

Despite the fact that Arles spawned the Gypsy Kings, the music scene is sadly lacking—locals usually head to Avignon. In Arles, you'll have to make do with the bars and restaurants on place du Forum and place Voltaire and a few late-night options that are mildly entertaining. At **Le Tropical** (28 rue Porte de Laure, next to Arènes, tel. 04–90–96–94–16), Spanish-owner José will happily recommend one of his international beers or cocktails (22F–59F) while the Stones play in the background. Arles has three movie theaters; most interesting is **Cinéma le Méjan/Actes Sud** (quai M. Dormoy, tel. 04–90–93–33–56), a multimedia complex featuring avant-garde movies (often in the original-language version), a bookstore, an art gallery, and a restaurant.

NEAR ARLES

STES-MARIES-DE-LA-MER

Forty kilometers (25 mi) from Arles, Stes-Maries is a beach town par excellence, with miles of sandy beaches lapped by Mediterranean waves. Although the proximity of the beach has turned Stes-Maries-de-la-Mer into a summer resort town, locals attest to the fact that winter is the best time to see the nearby Camargue (*see below*), marshland with exceptional wildlife. Stes-Maries owes its name (and Gypsy contingency) to the legend that Mary Jacobe (the sister of the Virgin Mary), Mary Salome (the mother of the apostles John and James), Mary Magdalene, and their Egyptian servant Sarah all came here in AD 40 to escape persecution in the Holy Land.

The fortified medieval **church** in the middle of town has a chapel with relics of the first two martyrs and a crypt that contains relics of Sarah. It's open November—February, daily 8–6; March–April and mid-September—October, daily 8–7; May–mid-September, daily 8–noon and 2–7. Gypsies chose Sarah as a patron saint. Every May 24–26 and third or fourth Sunday in October the annual **Pèlerinage des Gitans** (Gypsy Pilgrimage) attracts Gypsies from all over the world for a huge celebration. The festival is essentially a religious event, marked by the Gypsies carrying a statue of St. Sarah to the water's edge in remembrance of the original pilgrimage. The town also explodes with music and dancing, and people camp in the streets and on the beach. The **Féria du Cheval,** held in the second week of July, features horse shows and horse-related exhibitions for a pricey 100F–350F per ticket. For more information about these and other events, stop by the **tourist office** (5 av. van Gogh, tel. 04–90–97–82–55, fax 04–90–97–71–15), open November—February, daily 9–5; March and October, daily 9–6; April–June, daily 9–7; and July–August, daily 9–8.

COMING AND GOING

Buses leave Arles every two hours (1 hr, 34F) for Stes-Maries-de-la-Mer. In summer, buses also make the trip from Nîmes (1¼ hrs, 52F) and Aigues-Mortes. Although it's easy to get around town on foot, you can rent a bike at **Le Vélociste** (7 rue de la République, tel. 04–90–97–83–26) for 80F a day. Ask for the free map of six proposed bike routes. There's also a bus from the hostel (11F).

WHERE TO SLEEP

Most hotels charge steep prices and fill up quickly on summer weekends. The cheapest are **Le Méditerranée** (4 rue F. Mistral, tel. 04–90–97–82–09, fax 04–90–97–76–37), with rooms starting at 180F in low season and 200F in high season, and **Hôtel les Vagues** (12 av. Th. Aubanel, tel. 04–90–97–84–40, fax 04–90–97–84–40), with 200F–300F doubles. Staying at the **Auberge de Jeunesse Hameau de Pioch-Badet** (rte. de Cocharelles, tel. 04–90–97–51–72) costs 130F (with a HI card, 19F more without), with breakfast and dinner included. It's a 15-minute ride from town on the bus to Arles (during the week the last bus leaves Stes-Maries at 7:30 PM). Otherwise, camp near the beach at Stes-Maries's **La Brise** (tel. 04–90–97–84–67, fax 04–90–97–72–01), a five-minute walk from the centre ville; sites are 86F–109F for two people.

FOOD

A number of cheap, good restaurants line rue Frédéric Mistral. For a traditional Camarguaise meal, head to **La Grange** (23 rue F. Mistral, tel. 04–90–97–98–05), where the 79F menu often includes *daube de Toros* (bull stewed in red wine). Another local favorite is **Le Provençal** (1 pl. Esprit Pioch, tel. 04–90–97–94–23), which has regional cuisine menus for 68F–99F. Gypsy bands liven up the atmosphere on some Friday and Saturday nights. For a quick, cheap meal, take your pick of the sandwich and crepe stands on avenue Victor Hugo. Buy groceries at **Casino** on the same street or at the Monday and Friday morning produce **markets** on place des Gitans.

OUTDOOR ACTIVITIES

It goes without saying that the stretch of beach is the biggest draw. You can rent pedal boats (50F per half hour) near the strip closest to the tourist office, or Windsurfers (75F per hour) farther east toward the campground. (A quick shower on the beach will cost you 4F per minute.) For a day of cruising downstream or moseying along on horseback, head to the Camargue (*see below*).

A KINDER, GENTLER MATADOR

Bullfights take place in Arles's and Nîmes's amphitheaters from Easter to September. The events usually resemble the "corrida," those bloody spectacles that end with a dead bull (or, more rarely, with a dead or mutilated matador). You will also see "Corrida portugese," in which the matador and his accomplices annoy the hell out of the bull but never administer the coup de grâce, as well as the "Course Camarguaise," in which the bull has a rose or ribbon tied between its horns that a "razateur" must clip off. The white-clad razateur chases the bull, jumping out of the arena before the bull gets too peeved.

THE CAMARGUE

Wedged between the Petit Rhône, the Grand Rhône, and the Mediterranean, the Camargue is the famed marshland of the Rhône delta, represented in tourist brochures with pictures of Gypsies and *gardians* (Provençal cowboys) roping in herds of sheep and horses. Exotic flora and fauna (especially bird life), not to mention ravenous mosquitoes, live in splendor in the lagoons and salt marshes. Much of the area has been cordoned off as a nature reserve, closed to visitors without a special permit. It can be a little tricky getting around this area, but the sight of white horses, pink flamingos, and bulls roaming through the swamps and lagoons is worth the logistical acrobatics. Try to avoid coming in July and August, when it's hot, crowded, and most difficult to view the wildlife. For more information on the Camargue and its protected environment, contact **Park Information** (pont de Gau, tel. 04–90–97–86–32, fax 04–90–97–70–82), 4 km (2½ mi) from Stes-Maries-de-la-Mer. It's open October–March, Saturday–Thursday 9:30–5, and April–September, daily 9–6.

COMING AND GOING

To visit the Camargue, you're best off staying in Stes-Maries-de-la-Mer (*see above*), especially if you are dependent on public transportation. It is possible, however, to take a bus tour of the Camargue leaving from Arles; contact **Cars de Camargue** (24 blvd. G. Clemenceau, tel. 04–90–96–94–78), which has a five-hour, 90F tour and a nine-hour, 145F tour. From Stes-Maries-de-la-Mer, there are basically five ways to explore the Camargue: on foot, bike, horse, Jeep, or boat. The last two, while requiring little physical effort, limit what you can see. Jeep rides with **Camargue Safaris** (tel. 04–90–97–86–93) leave from near the tourist office and cost around 90F for 1½ hours of bumpy going. Ask beforehand if the driver speaks English.

OUTDOOR ACTIVITIES

Boat rides, which float you down the Petit Rhône of the Camargue, cost around 60F for 1½ hours; check with **Quatre Maries** (36 rue Th. Aubanel, tel. 04–90–97–70–10) or **Tiki III** (Grau d'Orgen, tel. 04–90–97–81–68). If you're going by foot, get a free trail map from the tourist office in Stes-Maries-de-la-Mer. It's possible to bike on many of these trails, although heavy winds, slippery sand, and blood-sucking mosquitoes can make it tough going. The best way to view the area is on horseback; for a wild ride over hill and dale, try the **Mas du Grand Frigoulès Pioch-Badet** (rte. du Cacharel, tel. 06–12–44–64–74), where the bilingual guide leads horseback adventures. It costs 75F an hour or 200F for a half day (sometimes slightly less if you're staying at the hostel).

LES-BAUX-DE-PROVENCE

Wedged in the side of a calcareous rock rising up out of the valley, this tiny village just 18 km (11 mi) from Arles teems with tourists in summer, but is well worth the visit. Balanced on the windy plateau are medieval ruins from the days when the town crammed in 6,000 residents. Especially during the summer, there are many things happening in and around the village. Check at the **tourist office** (Ilot Post Tenebras Lux, tel. 04–90–54–34–39, fax 04–90–54–51–15) for the latest. It is open April–November 9–7 and December–March 9–5.

COMING AND GOING

The best way to get to Les-Baux (29 km/18 mi south of Avignon, 15 km/9 mi east of Arles) besides driving there is to take the bus from Avignon or Arles. Check at the bus station in Arles or Avignon for bus times, as they are quite erratic any time but July and August. Les-Baux is not the place for a cheap sleep. But if you are set on sleeping on the rock, try **Le Benvengudo** (on the main village road, tel. 04–90–54–32–54, fax 04–90–54–42–58), where doubles run (gulp) 630F.

WORTH SEEING

The **Tour du Brau** (rue du Trencart, tel. 04–90–54–55–56), the entrance to the fortress, is also a history and archaeology museum. Climb out to the farthest end of the rock, next to the monument to Provençal poet Charloun Rieu (1846–1924), for a spectacular view of the valley. In the little village down below you'll find medieval manuscripts and ancient relics in the **Fondation Louis-Jou** (Hôtel Brion, Grande-Rue, tel. 04–90–54–34–17), a 12th-century church. Shepherds still take their lambs to midnight mass here at Christmas. Close by is the 17th-century **Chapelle St-Blaise,** decorated with Yves Brayer's frescoes (1974). It also houses the **Musée de l'Olivier** (Olive Tree Museum), where you can learn how olive oil is made.

NIMES

With one of the best-preserved Roman amphitheaters in the world and a near-perfect Roman temple, Nîmes beats out Arles for the title of "French City Best Able to Cash In on the Roman Empire's Former Glory." The ruins in Nîmes are the main reason to come here, though more recent elements, like the city's modern architecture and refurbished medieval streets in the centre ville, add to Nîmes's appeal. Seasonal bullfights (which take place in the amphitheater), as well as theater and concert events—mostly in summer—also contribute to Nîmes's vitality. The city is a good departure point for visiting the Pont du Gard (*see below*), a magnificent Roman bridge and aqueduct spanning the Gordon Valley, and for exploring the surrounding limestone hills (*garrigues*). Just southwest of Nîmes in **Vergèze,** natural spring water is put into little green bottles and packaged and shipped to the world as Perrier.

BASICS

BUREAU DE CHANGE

Banque de France has good rates and charges no commission, but each transaction takes so long you'd think they were actually printing the money themselves. *2 sq. du 11 Novembre, tel. 04–66–76–82–00. Open weekdays 8:30–12:15 and 1:45–3:30.*

INTERNET ACCESS

Le Vauban (34 ter rue Clérisseau, parallel to blvd. Gambetta to the north, tel. 04–66–76–09–71) and **Le Plug'in** (17 rue Porte d'Alès, perpendicular to blvd. Gambetta off rue des Halles, tel. 04–66–21–49–51) are two cybercafés, somewhat inconveniently located north of the old town, that both charge 50F an hour for use of their computers.

LAUNDRY

Every day of the week between 7 AM and 8 PM, for about 40F, you can suds your T-shirts not far from the station at 5 rue Notre-Dame (off square de la Couronne), or in the north of the city at 14 rue Nationale.

MAIL

The main **post office** is in the vieille ville and provides fast, efficient service, including currency exchange. The postal code for poste restante is 30006. *1 blvd. de Bruxelles, at av. Feuchères, tel. 04–66–76–67–03. Open weekdays 8–7, Sat. 8–noon.*

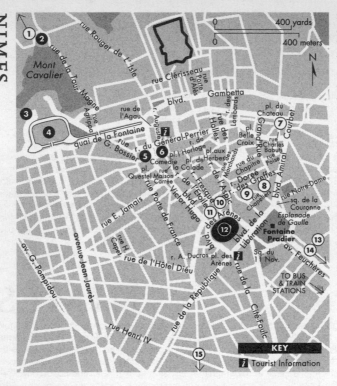

NIMES

Sights ●	
Arènes,	12
Carré d'Art,	5
Jardin de la Fontaine,	4
Maison Carrée,	6
Temple de Diane,	3
Tour Magne,	2

Lodging ○	
Auberge de Jeunesse,	1
Domaine de la Bastide,	15
Hôtel l'Amphithéâtre,	10
Hôtel Audrans Terminus,	13
Hôtel Concorde,	9
Hôtel Le France,	11
Hôtel de la Mairie,	8
Hôtel de Milan,	14
Hôtel du Temple,	7

KEY

i Tourist Information

VISITOR INFORMATION

There's a tourist office branch in the train station (tel. 04–66–84–18–13). Otherwise, head to the **main office** for all the maps and brochures you could ever want. You can also pick up a copy of *Rendez-vous,* a free monthly listing of cultural events, and *Nîmescope,* another free monthly with movie, restaurant, concert, and sports information. For a 1% commission, the staff changes money when the banks are closed. *6 rue Auguste, ½ block north of Maison Carrée, tel. 04–66–67–29–11, fax 04–66–21–81–04. Open Oct.–Feb., weekdays 8:30–7, Sat. 9–7, Sun. 10–6; Mar.–Sept., daily 8–7 (July–Aug. until 8).*

For regional information, consult the **Maison de Tourisme,** which has many of the same publications as the main tourist office. *3 pl. des Arènes, tel. 04–66–36–96–30. Open weekdays 8–7:30, Sat. 9:30–6; in off-season, weekdays 8:45–6, Sat. 9:30–noon.*

COMING AND GOING

BY TRAIN

Frequent daily trains run from Nîmes to Arles (20 mins, 41F), Avignon (30 mins, 46F), Montpellier (30 mins, 46F), Marseille (1¼ hrs, 95F), and Paris (4 hrs, 336F–431F by TGV). Services at the station include a tourist office, bureau de change, and cafeteria. To reach the old city, walk north on avenue Feuchères.

BY BUS

The **bus station** (rue Ste-Félicité, tel. 04–66–29–52–00), behind the train station, has service to Montpellier (54F), Alès (40F), Uzès (32F), and Pont du Gard (32F), each about 40 minutes away. Buy your ticket when you board the bus. If you plan on just a day trip, be sure to ask the driver for an *aller-retour* (round-trip) ticket and sometimes you'll get a slight discount.

GETTING AROUND

Restaurants, sights, and shops are concentrated in the vieille ville, where the narrow streets are generally limited to pedestrians. The vieille ville is encircled by wide, paved boulevards: boulevard Gambetta, boulevard Victor Hugo, and boulevard Amiral Courbet. The rest of Nîmes sprawls out into modern, primarily residential terrain.

If you want to go to the vieille ville, you're best off taking the bus; frequent **TCN** (tel. 04–66–38–15–40) buses charge 6F for an hour of transport. Bikes (85F a day plus a passport deposit) and scooters (165F a day plus deposit) can be rented from **Cruz Location** (23 blvd. Talabot, tel. 04–66–21–91–03). For bike tours and organized outdoor activities (like spelunking, rock climbing, canyoning, and hiking) in the surrounding region, contact **Soleil Sport Nature** (Les Hauts de Nîmes, tel. 04–66–23–78–23). If you want to get around in the comfort of a car, try a taxi tour organized through the tourist office. For 150F, **taxi T.R.A.N.** (tel. 04–66–29–40–11) will give up to four people a one-hour guided glance of must-see Nîmes.

WHERE TO SLEEP

Cheap hotels in Nîmes are old and invariably lacking in splendor. One cluster of hotels is by the train station. Directly across the street is **Hôtel Audrans Terminus** (23 av. Feuchères, tel. 04–66–29–20–14, fax 04–66–29–08–24), where comfortable rooms go for 159F–270F, all with private bath. **Hôtel de Milan** (17 av. Feuchères, tel. 04–66–29–29–90, fax 04–66–29–05–31) also has decent rooms (200F–235F) and is a short walk toward the centre ville.

UNDER 150F • Hôtel Le France. The arena view from the rooms offsets their slightly dingy air. Plus the price is right (100F–125F for a single and 125F–140F for a double). *4 blvd. des Arènes, tel. 04–66–67–23–05, fax 04–66–67–76–93. 15 rooms, 11 with shower or bath.*

UNDER 200F • Hôtel Concorde. You'll have to climb at least two narrow flights of stairs to reach your room, but it's worth the effort. Rooms are clean and quiet, and the proprietor is amiable. Singles are 110F; showerless doubles are 125F (showers cost 20F); rooms with shower are 160F–180F. Reserve ahead in summer. *3 rue des Chapeliers, tel./fax 04–66–67–91–03. From blvd. de la Libération, take rue Régale to rue Chapeliers. 10 rooms, 6 with shower. Reception closes 11 PM.*

Hôtel du Temple. Around the corner from lively place Gabriel Peri and place des Carmes (and its St-Baudile church) is an odd little side street with this treat of a hotel. Spotlessly clean and affectionately run, this family-run enterprise is an old-fashioned find. Rooms run 130F–190F. *1 rue Charles Babut, tel. 04–66–67–54–61, fax 04–66–36–04–36. 20 rooms, all with shower or bath.*

UNDER 250F • Hôtel l'Amphithéâtre. A stone staircase, elaborate iron railings, red carpeting, and heavy, engraved-wood doors make you feel like you're in the lap of luxury. The rooms are modern and have TVs. Singles cost 180F–230F, doubles 200F–280F. *4 rue des Arènes, tel. 04–66–67–28–51, fax 04–66–67–07–79. 17 rooms, all with bath. Closed Jan.*

Hôtel de la Mairie. This hotel has a huge, spiral staircase, with rooms haphazardly tacked on to each of its three floors. Singles and doubles with sinks are 120F–130F (the shower costs 20F), 160F–240F with shower. *11 rue des Greffes, tel. 04–66–67–65–91. From sq. de la Couronne, walk 2 blocks on blvd. Amiral Courbet to rue des Greffes. 13 rooms, 11 with bath.*

HOSTEL

Auberge de Jeunesse. A secluded garden provides the setting for this small and newly renovated hostel. The bar attracts a lively crowd. The drawback is that it's a 20-minute bus ride or at least a half-hour walk from town. Rooms have two, four, or six beds. The rate is 69F per night with breakfast (plus 19F if you don't have an HI card); sheets are 17F. There's no lockout or curfew. *Chemin de la Cigale, tel. 04–66–23–25–04, fax 04–66–23–84–27. From av. Feuchères in front of train station, take Bus 2 (last bus at 8 PM), get off at Stade stop, and follow signs uphill. Or walk west on quai de la Fontaine, turn right on rte. d'Arles, and follow signs. 80 beds. Reception open daily 7 AM–1 AM.*

CAMPING

Domaine de la Bastide. This peaceful campground has access to a snack bar, grocery store, phones, showers, and washing machines. The price per night is 65F for two people and a tent. Check in before 9:30 PM. *Rte. de Générac, tel./fax 04–66–38–09–21. From the train station, take Bus D all the way to the last stop, La Bastide. 240 sites.*

FROM NIMES, WITH LOVE

Blue jeans were first created in Nîmes: The word "denim" is derived from the phrase "de Nîmes" ("from Nîmes"). Originally used by local farmers to make wagon covers and work clothes, denim soon made its way to San Francisco thanks to Bavarian merchant Levi Strauss. Strauss's durable denim work pants, or jeans (which, incidentally, comes from the American mispronunciation of the Italian port Gènes, from which the fabric was originally shipped), became an instant success with gold miners.

FOOD

Restaurants of all varieties (even a San Francisco steak house at 33 rue Roussy) are concentrated in the vieille ville. Two good streets worth exploring are **rue Fresque** and **rue de l'Étoile.** Expect a decent lunch to cost 45F–70F and a hearty dinner to run 60F–100F. Nîmes is the place to try *tapenade,* a dip made with crushed olives and olive oil, and *brandade de morue,* dry cod crushed with olive oil and served in a pastry or soufflé. On the sweeter side, Nîmes's famous *croquants* are tasty biscuits named for the sound they make as you bite into them.

An exceptionally good sandwich stand, **Miam Miam** (41 rue Fresque, tel. 04–66–36–11–33) sells pizza and sandwiches for 10F–20F; it operates at noontime on the corner of rue Fresque and place du Marché in the old town. The 40F–65F salads at **O'Délices** (2 pl. aux Herbes, tel. 04–66–36–11–16) are another good bet. **Le Bistrot de l'Horloge** (2 pl. de l'Horloge, tel. 04–66–67–30–35) is a two-level café with a terrace next to the clock tower; go for 40F–50F salads or the frothy 15F *café crème* (coffee with hot milk). You can buy groceries at **Prisunic** (sq. de la Couronne) or produce at the daily morning **market** on rue des Halles.

UNDER 75F • Bistrot de Tatie Agnès. A wall of glass lets you admire the interior of this family-run bistrot on a side street behind the Maison Carrée. Try a enormous salad (40F–55F), daily specials (46F), or a healthy serving of meat (52F–65F). *16 rue Maison Carrée, tel. 04–66–21–00–81. Closed Sun.*

La Calèche. The food is copious and cheap: 49F will get you an all-you-can-eat appetizer buffet and a main dish. More (59F–119F) will get you . . . more. *6 rue Notre Dame, tel. 04–66–21–88–84.*

La Casa Don Miguel. This *bodega de tapas* has a wide selection from which to choose for 15F a plate (or 10F during happy hour—7:30–8:30 PM on Thursday, Friday, and Saturday). It's also got a lively and young atmosphere. *18 rue de l'Horloge, tel. 04–66–76–07–09.*

El Rinconcito. Although this Chilean restaurant is in the middle of the old city, it's hard to find because it's in a tiny courtyard. Keep looking—the search is worth it. Try the gazpacho for 22F, chile con carne for 48F, or *pastel de choclo* (beef, chicken, and corn casserole) for 57F. *7 rue des Marchands, off passage du Vieux Nîmes near pl. aux Herbes, tel. 04–66–76–17–30. Closed Sun. and Mon.*

La Truye Qui Filhe. Enjoy your self-serve lunch under 14th-century archways at this little spot near the Maison Carrée. Dishes reflect the products of the region: A main course and dessert are only 50F, a three-course meal only 5F more. *9 rue Fresque, tel. 04–66–21–76–33. Closed Sun. No dinner.*

UNDER 100F • Chez Jacotte. This quiet, colorful restaurant packs a plate with as much attention as it does the *salle.* The varied lunch menu (70F) is different every day, and main dinner dishes (no menu) are 65F–80F. *15 rue Fresque (Impasse), tel. 04–66–21–64–59.*

UNDER 125F • Les Alizés. The food is fine, the service electric, and the clients all smiles whether they go à la carte or with dinner prix fixe (100F–110F). *26 blvd. Victor Hugo, tel. 04–66–67–08–17.*

Les Quatre Saisons. Squeeze in with the locals at this fabulous crêperie, which features a three-course meal (including wine) for 55F at lunch, and 75F or 125F at dinner. *3 rue des Greffes, 3 blocks west of blvd. Amiral Courbet, tel. 04–66–67–21–70. Closed Sun.*

UNDER 150F • Nicolas. You'll hear the noise of this homey place before you open the door. A friendly, frazzled staff serves up delicious *bourride* (fish soup) and other local specialties on the 70F–140F menus. *1 rue Poise, tel. 04–66–67–50–47. Closed Mon., 1st 2 wks in July, and mid-Dec.–1st wk in Jan. No lunch Sat.*

Le Wine Bar. You might almost miss this traditional restaurant, tucked into a corner of square de la Couronne, in the glow of nearby neon. Both the lunch menu (77F) and seafood special dinner menu (130F) are excellent. *11 sq. de la Couronne, tel. 04–66–76–19–59. Closed Sun. No lunch Mon.*

WORTH SEEING

There's something surreal about the way Nîmois go about their daily lives, oblivious to the 2,000-year-old ruins surrounding them. The Arènes, Maison Carrée, Tour Magne, and Temple de Diane glorify Nîmes's Roman ancestry, while the Carré d'Art is a testament to Nîmes's modern aspirations. The Jardin de la Fontaine, the spot for picnicking, alleviates all that museum stress. You probably see everything in one day, but it would be a rush, especially if you try to tackle the panoply of city museums spread throughout the city. Opt for the three-day pass, which includes most of the monuments for 60F and can be purchased at the Arènes and Tour Magne.

ARENES

Built in the 1st century AD, this huge Roman amphitheater is the center of Nîmes's cultural life. Bullfights, theater, and musical performances continue to take place here before audiences as large as 24,000. In winter it is covered so events can take place. In Roman times, the amphitheater was the site of bloody animal and gladiator fights. It doubled as a fortress during the Middle Ages and as a housing complex for more than 800 people in the 18th century. For an extra 6F, your ticket buys admission to the Tour Magne (*see below*). *Blvd. Victor Hugo. Admission and guided tour 28F. Open June–Sept., daily 9–7; Oct.–May, daily 9–noon and 2–5:30.*

CARRE D'ART

Nîmes's answer to the Centre Pompidou, the Carré d'Art houses a modern art museum, library, bookstore, and terraced restaurant. The all-glass and Plexiglas building, designed by architect Norman Foster, is the modern answer to the Maison Carrée (*see below*). The museum features art from 1960 to the present. *Pl. de la Maison Carrée, tel. 04–66–76–35–35 general information, 04–66–76–35–70 museum. Admission 26F. Open Tues.–Sun. 11–6.*

JARDIN DE LA FONTAINE

Unlike measly city parks that call themselves "jardins," this "garden of the fountain" is the real thing. The central fountain is fed by the waters of the Nemausus spring, which is said to have attracted the Romans to Nîmes, and you can envision Romans (or yourself, perhaps) relaxing and socializing in the baths nearby. The garden slopes upward, and at the top stands the **Tour Magne,** almost 98 ft tall, one of the few remainders of the ramparts that surrounded Nîmes in Roman times; climb a tiny staircase to the top for a view of the city and the Cévennes in the distance. The **Temple de Diane,** built in AD 2, stands in ruins at the bottom of the gardens, near the fountain. *Quai de la Fontaine. Admission to Tour Magne 12F, or 34F for the Tower and the Arena. Open summer, daily 9–7; winter, daily 9–5.*

MAISON CARREE

Northwest of the Arènes, the Maison Carrée, built in the Augustan age, is one of the best-preserved Roman temples anywhere. Although its name means Square House, it is rectangular in shape, surrounded by columns with elaborate Corinthian capitals in excellent condition. Thomas Jefferson liked the temple so much that he had drawings of it sent to Virginia in 1787 as a model for the state capitol, and Napoléon used it for the model of the Église de la Madeleine in Paris. The Maison Carrée now houses a minishrine to itself detailing its history and construction (all in French). It also hosts exhibits of contemporary art exhibits, including works by American painter Julian Schnabel. *Blvd. Victor Hugo. Admission free. Open summer, daily 9–noon and 2:30–7; winter, daily 9–12:30 and 2–6.*

FESTIVALS

Big cultural events in Nîmes revolve around the Arènes (*see above*), where concerts, theater, and bullfights take place in summer and winter. Bullfighting has three seasons: **Féria Primavera** is during the last weekend of February; **Féria de Pentecôte** is at the end of May to early June; and **Féria de Vendanges** is in mid-September. Tickets for the corridas (*see below*) cost 90F–510F. Try to make reservations at least three weeks in advance. For more information or tickets, contact **Bureau de Locations des Arènes** (1 rue Alexandre Ducros, tel. 04–66–67–28–02). Ask at the tourist office for the guide *L'Été de Nîmes,* which lists concerts, photo exhibits, ballets, and whatnot, all held mid-June–early August. On Thursday nights (5 PM–10 PM) in July and August, musicians, artisans, and dancers congregate in the old city's squares to celebrate the **Marchés du Soir** (also known as Les Jeudis de Nîmes).

AFTER DARK

Bars are dispersed throughout the city. A younger crowd has been going to the cluster of bars on boulevard Victor Hugo (like **Le Napoléon** and **Le Parisian**) for years. But the bars of the moment are **Le Bureau** (blvd. Amiral Courbet, tel. 04–66–67–34–59) and the sprawling terrace of **Bar de la Bourse** (2 blvd. Victor Hugo, tel. 04–66–67–44–31), across from the Arènes. An artsy crowd hangs out at the cover-free **Haddock Café** (13 rue de l'Agau, tel. 04–66–67–86–57), which has live music Thursday nights and 20F–40F beers. **Le Diagonal** (41 bis rue Émile Jamais, tel. 04–66–21–70–01) has live jazz and blues bands with no cover. **Lulu** (10 impasse de la Curaterie, tel. 04–66–36–28–20), a good gay disco, blares dance tunes Tuesday–Saturday, starting at 11 PM.

Sémaphore (25 rue Porte de France, tel. 04–66–67–88–04) hosts foreign film festivals and often devotes several days a month to films of individual actors and actresses (always shown in the original language), all for prices lower than normal cinemas. **Théâtre de Nîmes** (1 pl. de la Calade, tel. 04–66–36–65–00) is home to major concerts and theatrical events. Smaller theaters include **La Movida** (7 rue Hugue Capet, tel. 04–66–67–80–90), a café-concert establishment, where for 40F you can enjoy Spanish music on weekend nights (September–June only).

NEAR NIMES

PONT DU GARD

It's not often that a bridge becomes a destination of its own, but the Pont du Gard is such a marvelous display of Roman technological and aesthetic capability that it merits a special visit. Built in 19 BC as part of a project to transfer water 50 km (30 mi) from the Eure spring east of Uzès to the people of Nîmes, the 161-ft-high bridge was necessary to carry the aqueduct over the deep Gordon Valley (now a river). The three-tier structure, with its magnificent arches and stones weighing up to 6 tons each, remains in excellent condition. You can still take a dizzying walk along the upper-level aqueduct. To cross the river, people now use the comparatively modern bridge (built in 1743) that runs alongside the Pont du Gard.

In addition to seeing the bridge, you can spend the day at the Pont du Gard lying out along the banks of the Gordon River, diving off its rocks, and swimming in its calm, warm waters. Pay a visit to the **tourist office** (tel. 04–66–37–00–02), and then rent kayaks from **Kayak Vert** (right uphill from the bridge, tel. 04–66–22–80–76), which organizes trips down the river. During the summer, you can have a two-person kayak all day for 180F, or a one-person for 100F. There are 6 km (4 mi) of river to paddle and you get a return trip by shuttle bus. There are a few cafés and ice cream stands that spring to life in summer, but other than that the area is pretty deserted.

COMING AND GOING

The Pont du Gard is a 40-minute bus ride from Nîmes (32F) and only 15 minutes by bus from Uzès (20F). The bus drops you off 1 km (½ mi) from the bridge at the **Auberge Blanche** (rte. du Pont du Gard, tel. 04–66–37–18–08, fax 04–66–37–22–25); if you get stuck here (the last bus to Nîmes during the week leaves at 4:55 PM, 6:20 on Saturday, and 7:10 on Sunday) or decide to stay, this hotel has not-too-fancy rooms for 180F–220F. There's a restaurant, too, but the cheapest menu is 85F. Otherwise, try camping at **La Sousta** (rte. du Pont du Gard, tel. 04–66–37–12–80, fax 04–66–37–23–69) for 66F–83F for two people.

Finally, a travel companion that doesn't snore on the plane or eat all your peanuts.

When traveling, your MCI WorldCom Card is the best way to keep in touch. Our operators speak your language, so they'll be able to connect you back home—no matter where your travels take you. Plus, your MCI WorldCom Card is easy to use, and even earns you frequent flyer miles every time you use it. When you add in our great rates, you get something even more valuable: peace-of-mind. So go ahead. Travel the world. MCI WorldCom just brought it a whole lot closer.

You can even sign up today at www.mci.com/worldphone or ask your operator to make a collect call to 1-410-314-2938.

EASY TO CALL WORLDWIDE

1 Just dial the WorldPhone access number of the country you're calling from.
2 Dial or give the operator your MCI WorldCom Card number.
3 Dial or give the number you're calling.

France ♦	0-800-99-0019
Germany	0800-888-8000
Ireland	1-800-55-1001
Italy ♦	172-1022
Spain	900-99-0014
Sweden ♦	020-795-922
Switzerland ♦	0800-89-0222
United Kingdom	
To call using BT	0800-89-0222
To call using CWC	0500-89-0222

For your complete WorldPhone calling guide, dial the WorldPhone access number for the country you're in and ask the operator for Customer Service. In the U.S. call 1-800-431-5402.

♦ Public phones may require deposit of coin or phone card for dial tone.

EARN FREQUENT FLYER MILES

Distinctive guides packed with up-to-date expert advice and smart choices for every type of traveler.

Fodor's. For the world of ways you travel.

MONTPELLIER

Montpellier, with its 25% student population, has a laid-back Provençal feel and a dynamic cultural identity. Since 1220, the city has been home to one of Europe's best medical schools (in addition to its fine law, literature, and science schools). June–September, when many students leave for the summer, Montpellier quiets down a bit. But a number of music, theater, and dance festivals keep it active.

The 1,000-year-old history of Montpellier is revealed through the hodgepodge of medieval, classical, and 19th-century architectural styles. The historic centre ville is the gem of Montpellier, characterized by *hôtels particuliers* (aristocratic town houses), shops, bookstores, and churches. At the center of it all is the classy **place de la Comédie,** known fondly as l'Oeuf (the Egg), bounded by the Opéra-Bastille to the south, the esplanade de Charles de Gaulle to the north, and le Triangle to the east. **Le Triangle** is a modern shopping area that culminates in le Polygone, an American-style shopping center. Behind le Polygone is **Antigone**—Montpellier's official nod to the future. A neoclassic symmetrical wonder, it was designed by Catalonian architect Ricardo Bofill to house low- to middle-income families. Compare this structure to the 13th-century Tour de la Babote, also in the centre ville, and you get a good sense of the range of historical influences in Montpellier. Yet the diversity here isn't limited to architecture; the many North African immigrants and foreign students give the city a cosmopolitan air.

BASICS

BUREAUX DE CHANGE

The exchange booth at the train station, open daily 8–8, has decent rates with no commission. **Banque Courtois** (pl. de la Comédie, tel. 04–67–06–26–16) charges a 1% commission on traveler's checks and has a 24-hour cash exchange machine; it's open weekdays 9–12:30 and 2–4:30.

DISCOUNT TRAVEL AGENCIES

Buy tickets at one of the two **Wasteels** offices. Though they specialize in discount student train fares (*see* Train Travel, *in* Chapter 1) and sell ISIC cards, they also are general travel agencies. *6 rue de la Saunerie, tel. 08–03–88–70—49; 1 rue Cambacérès, tel. 04–67–66–20–19. Open weekdays 9–12:30 and 2–6:30, Sat. 9:30–12:30 and 2–5:30.*

ENGLISH-LANGUAGE BOOKSTORES

For travel books and novels, head to the **Bookshop** (4 rue de l'Université, tel. 04–67–66–09–08). For a scone, some joe, and a few pages of Dickens, there's **Bill's Book Company and Coffee House** (44 rue de l'Université, tel. 04–67–66–37–11).

INTERNET ACCESS

Station Internet (6–8 pl. du Marché aux Fleurs, tel. 08–00–35–25–15) provides good connections for 30F a half hour, 50F an hour, and 110F for three hours, open Monday 2 PM–8 PM and Tuesday–Saturday 10 AM–8 PM. For the midnight cyber junkies, head out to Antigone for **Le Cyber Surf** (22–24 pl. du Millénaire, tel. 04–67–20–03–50), where you can surf the night away every day until midnight for 30F per half hour, 50F per hour.

LAUNDRY

There are do-it-yourself-o-mats at 11 rue Ste-Anne and on place de la Chapelle Neuve. A load of laundry is 20F and dryers are 4F for 15 minutes 7:30 AM–9 PM daily.

MAIL

Exchange money and make phone calls at the **main post office.** A smaller but more central post office is on place des Martyrs de la Résistance (tel. 04–67–60–67–95). Montpellier's postal code is 34000; send poste restante to the main office (code 34026). *15 rue Rondelet, tel. 04–67–34–50–00. Open weekdays 8–7, Sat. 8–6.*

MEDICAL AID

If you need a pharmacy after hours, call the **Commissariat** (tel. 04–67–22–78–22) to find out which pharmacy is open. You can get emergency care from **Hôpital Lapeyronie** (371 av. du Doyen G. Giraud, tel. 04–67–33–80–12).

VISITOR INFORMATION

The **tourist office** is off place de la Comédie in le Triangle and has an annex in the train station (tel. 04–67–92–90–03). In addition to making hotel reservations, the staff gives out maps and brochures galore and runs guided city tours, but only in French. To find out about weekly events, pick up a free copy of *Sortir*. Don't exchange money here because they charge a 3% commission. *Esplanade-Comédie–30 allée Jean de Lattre de Tassigny, tel. 04–67–60–60–60, fax 04–67–60–60–61. Open weekdays 9–1 and 2–6, Sat. 10–1 and 2–6, Sun. 10–1 and 2–5.*

COMING AND GOING

BY TRAIN

The **train station** (pl. Auguste Giberte) is a few minutes' walk from the city's central square, place de la Comédie. Upstairs, you'll find train information and ticket sales, money exchange, and a magazine shop. Downstairs is a tourist office, travel agency, restaurant, and access to rue Maguelone. Walk directly down this street to get to place de la Comédie. Destinations from here include Paris (8 daily, 4 hrs, 373F–439F), Nice (5 hrs, 229F), Avignon (1 hr, 79F), Perpignan (2 hrs, 113F), Toulouse (2¼ hrs, 158F), Marseille (1½ hours, 123F), and even Barcelona (4 hrs, 253F).

BY BUS

The **gare routière** (pl. du Bicentenaire, tel. 04–67–92–01–43) is next to the train station and can be reached from its second floor. Four buses a day go to Nîmes (30 mins, 54F), Sète (1 hr, 35F), Alès (1½ hrs, 69F), Béziers (1½ hrs, 70F), and to the beach at nearby Palavas (20 mins, 7F).

GETTING AROUND

The historic centre ville is a pedestrian's paradise, with a labyrinth of stone paths and alleys leading from courtyard to courtyard. Hotels, hostels, restaurants, and sights are all within walking distance of place de la Comédie, but Montpellier also has a comprehensive bus system. **SMTU** (23 rue Maguelone, tel. 04–67–22–87–87) has route maps and sells books of 10 one-way tickets for 53F. You can also buy individual tickets (7F) from the driver as you board.

But bikes are definitely a better bet if you are planning on covering a lot of ground. Take advantage of some of the 65 km (40 mi) of clearly marked bike paths and 1,200 bike parking spaces! Rent from **Vil-l'à Vélo** (Gare routière, pl. du Bicentenaire, tel. 04–67–92–92–67), open April–September, daily 9–7:30, and October–March, daily 9–6:30. Rates are 10F an hour, 20F for a half day, 40F a day. Helmets and pumps are provided. A deposit of 1,000F is required. For a **taxi** try calling 04–67–10–00–00.

WHERE TO SLEEP

Just about all the budget hotels and the hostel are at the southern end of the centre ville, a 5- to 10-minute walk from the train station, with doubles ranging from 140F to 280F. If the hotels below are filled, try **Touristes** (10 rue Baudin, tel. 04–67–58–42–37, fax 04–67–92–61–37), where 15 rooms run 150F–200F, or **Aficion** (8 pl. Laissac, tel. 04–67–92–13–62), where 10 rooms go for 160F–219F. You might also try the cluster on rue A. Ollivier. There are no campgrounds right in Montpellier, but there is one a 20-minute bus ride away: Take Bus 17 (direction: Lattes; 8.20F) to the **campground** (tel. 04–67–68–01–28) at Palavas beach. A tent for two people costs 76F–104F; it's closed October–April.

UNDER 150F • Hôtel Abysse. The name may not be encouraging, but the rates (139F singles, 159 doubles) certainly are. The hotel is also on a quiet side street 10 minutes from the center of town. *13 rue du Général Campredon, tel. 04–67–92–39–05. From train station, take rue de la République through Halles Laissac (when it becomes blvd. du Jeu de Paume) until left on rue A. Michel, then right on rue du Général Campredon. 9 rooms, 2 with shower. Cash only.*

UNDER 200F • Hôtel des Etuves. On a quiet street off the main square, this hotel has large rooms with immaculate bathrooms. Be sure to ask the accommodating staff for a room facing rue des Étuves (the rooms in the back are dark and have small windows). Singles with showers run 140F–160F; doubles are 150F–185F. *24 rue des Étuves, tel./fax 04–67–60–78–19. From train station, take rue Maguelone to pl. de la Comédie and turn left on rue des Étuves. 13 rooms, 12 with bath.*

Hôtel les Fauvettes. In a little house on a peaceful street, this hotel has small, old-fashioned rooms overlooking a courtyard. Doubles are 130F, 160F–180F with shower. *8 rue Bonnard, near the Jardin des Plantes, tel. 04–67–63–17–60. 19 rooms, 9 with shower or bath.*

Hôtel de Paradys. Within eyeshot of the main square, this little hotel is right in the thick of cafés and near a movie theater. Small, tidy singles start at 100F; doubles run 150F–200F. *14 rue Boussairolles, tel. 04–67–58–42–54, fax 04–67–92–72–34. From train station, take rue Maguelone to main square, turn right on rue Boussairolles. 15 rooms, 10 with bath.*

HOSTEL • Auberge de Jeunesse. With a bar that blasts music until 1 AM, this is not the greatest place to get a lot of sleep. But standard, single-sex dorm rooms sleeping 3–10 are 67F (plus 19F if you do not have a HI card); prices include breakfast. Take a bus from the train station or, if you're feeling energetic, walk for 15 minutes up to place de la Comédie, pass the second McDonald's, take a right on rue Jacques Coeur, and at place Notre Dame follow rue de l'Aiguillerie. *2 impasse de la Petite Corraterie, off rue des Écoles Laïques, tel. 04–67–60–32–22, fax 04–67–60–32–30. From train station, take Bus 3, 5, 6, or 7; from rue de la République, take Bus 2 or 9 to blvd. Louis Blanc. 89 beds. Reception open 8 AM– midnight. Lockout 10–1. Curfew 2 AM.*

FOOD

You'll actually get value for your money once you trek beyond the obvious rip-offs on place Jean Jaurès and the restaurants on place du Marché aux Fleurs and place de la Chapelle Neuve. Hit the side streets. One such street in the centre ville is **rue des Écoles Laïques,** where many ethnic restaurants have menus for 40F–70F. At **Pita Pain** (1 rue Pila St-Gély, at rue de l'Aiguillerie, tel. 04–67–60–81–30) you can have a good-size falafel and a glass of wine for less than 40F. Crepe stands abound, but none are better than **Acadie** (3 pl. Notre-Dame des Tables, tel. 04–67–52–84–02); try the 45F menu or the 43F *saramaka* (bananas, chocolate, vanilla ice cream, and whipped cream) for a sugar high. Two other good side streets are **rue de l'Université** and **rue de Candolle,** with student-frequented cafés and restaurants. Regional fruits are sold at the **market** on place de la Comédie and the neighboring Halles Castellane daily until noon. Or, hit the **Monoprix** on place de la Comédie for groceries.

UNDER 50F • Art et Buffet. This salon de thé–*saladerie* (salad shop)–art gallery–miniature library is trying to be a jacques-of-all-trades. Grab a book inside and read it out on the terrace while you sip your tea and nibble on a *Madame Butterfly* salad (47F) of chicken, cucumber, gouda, rice, soy, and curry. *Pl. St-Roch, tel. 04–67–60–87–87.*

Mie Gourmande. The food is surprisingly solid and very, very cheap: Daily specials are rarely more than 40F and sandwiches hover around 30F. There are salads, hot drinks, and a stone-arched décor. *24 rue de l'Aiguillerie, tel. 04–67–66–17–43. Closed Sun.*

UNDER 75F • Le Brasero–La Table d'Angèle. This first-rate pizzeria off place St-Roch has a three-course meal guaranteed to leave you happily stuffed for 40F–69F at lunch and 90F at dinner. *5 rue des Teissiers, tel. 04–67–60–48–76. Closed Mon. No lunch weekends.*

Restaurant l'Image. This little hole-in-the-wall serves copious portions of authentic French food, such as rabbit terrine with a muscadet sauce, with live music in the background. Come before 8 PM for the 75F–99F menu. *6 rue du Puits-des-Esquilles, tel. 04–67–60–47–79. Closed Sun.*

Restaurant le Petit Landais du Palais. Candlelight, excellent French cuisine, and an 18th-century chapel—the only thing missing here is a violinist and you and your *chéri.* Three-course menus start around 60F. *14 rue du Palais-des-Guilhem, tel. 04–67–60–69–93.*

Tripti Kulai. The name means "Nest of Satisfaction" in Bengali, and the chef claims that her cooking will satisfy the body and the soul. The 69F menu includes items like moussaka (Greek casserole), eggplant caviar, and Indian-style carrots. *20 rue Jacques Coeur, off rue de la Loge, tel. 04–67–66–30–51. Cash only under 100F. Closed Sun., and last 2 wks in Aug. No dinner Mon.*

UNDER 100F • Le César. This lunch spot in the heart of the Antigone district is especially ideal on a sunny day, when you can sit outside. The best bets are the 70F *menu rapide* (two courses) or the 100F, four-course menu. *17 pl. du Nombre d'Or, tel. 04–67–64–87–87.*

WORTH SEEING

The centre ville, known as *vieux Montpellier* (old Montpellier), is filled with picturesque winding streets. Many of the 17th- and 18th-century hôtels particuliers are along rue de la Loge, rue de l'Argenterie, rue St-Guilhem, and rue des Étuves. Rue de l'Ancien-Courrier, rue St-Fermin, rue de Cannau, and rue Emboque d'Or also give a good sense of Montpellier's history.

At the intersection of rue Foch and boulevard Professeur Louis Vialleton is Montpellier's version of the **Arc de Triomphe.** It isn't as grand as the one in Paris, but then there aren't 10 lanes of traffic circling it either. Built in 1689 to honor Louis "Sun King" XIV, it enhances the regal aura of this already posh part of town. Past the arch is the **promenade du Peyrou,** designed by d'Aviler in 1689 and finished up by Giral in 1776. Note the statue of Louis XIV in the center of this park—and notice that his royal stirrups are missing. No big deal? Well, when the sculptor realized his blunder, he committed suicide.

If you continue to the end of the park, you'll find the **Château d'Eau,** a Corinthian temple and the terminal for **Les Arceaux,** an 18th-century aqueduct made up of 53 arches. On a clear day, the view from here is spectacular: You can see the Cévennes mountains, the Mediterranean sea, and dozens of red-tiled roofs. Come back at night to see the entire promenade lit up.

Founded in the 13th century, Montpellier's university is still highly regarded, especially the **Faculté de Médecine** (School of Medicine) on rue de l'École-de-Médecine. Petrarch, the father of the Italian Renaissance, came to study law here in 1323; François Rabelais, humanist and author of *Gargantua and Pantagruel,* left Franciscan convent life to study medicine here, receiving his doctorate in 1537. The med school's **Musée Atger** (2 rue de l'École de Médecine, tel. 04–67–66–27–77) has a collection of regional drawings and Renaissance works; it's open Monday, Wednesday, and Friday 1:30–5 and admission is free. Across the street from the med school is the **Jardin des Plantes,** the first botanical garden in France. Henri IV commissioned it in 1593 so that students could study medicinal herbs.

The **Musée Fabre** houses one of France's best collections of 16th- to 18th-century European art, including works by French painters Ingres, Delacroix, and Courbet. You'll also find ceramics, sculpture, and contemporary paintings on the top floor. The plot of land where the museum was founded in 1825 harbors its own bit of history: Molière hung out here during the winter of 1654–55, a fact that is commemorated by a bronze placard on the side of the museum. Across the way is the **Pavillon du Musée Fabre** (tel. 04–67–66–13–46), which hosts temporary art exhibits focusing on a particular artist each summer. It has a separate 25F admission fee. *39 blvd. Bonne Nouvelle, on left side of esplanade from pl. de la Comédie, tel. 04–67–14–83–00. Admission 20F. Open Tues.–Fri. 9–5:30, weekends 9:30–5.*

CHEAP THRILLS

If you want to see the French go gaga over old clothes and trinkets, take Bus 1 (direction: La Paillade) to the **marché aux puces** (Flea Market), held every Sunday 6 AM–1:30 PM. You'll find books, music, used bikes, lots of junk, and an occasional antique. Get here early if you're a serious flea marketeer.

FESTIVALS

Montpellier has a tremendous summer-festival lineup. From mid-June to early July, **Printemps des Comédiens** (Château d'Ô, av. des Moulins, tel. 04–67–63–66–67) sponsors theatrical events throughout town; tickets cost 40F–140F. **Montpellier Danse** (Hôtel d'Assas, 6 rue Vieille Aiguillerie, tel. 04–67–60–83–60) holds all dance workshops and performances in late June and early July. Although you need tickets for many of the performances (50F–220F), there are several free shows on the esplanade.

Classical, opera, and jazz concerts are held mid-July–early August during the **Festival International de Radio France et de Montpellier** (tel. 04–67–02–02–01). In late October and early November, the **Festival International du Cinéma Méditerrané de Montpellier** (tel. 04–67–66–36–36), unlike the festival in Cannes, actually focuses on the films instead of the film stars.

AFTER DARK

Montpellier is as entertaining at night as it is during the day. If you want to hang with young folks and rabble-rousers, head to **place Jean-Jaurès:** What acts as a marketplace by day is a hopping cluster of bars and cafés by night. To get information about the many cultural events in town, pick up a free copy of *Sortir* or *Diagonal* for information on specials at the city's cinemas. Both are available in front of the Gaumont theater on place de la Comédie and at the tourist office.

Begin the night at **L'Ecusson** (Vieujot Franck, 18 rue de l'Aiguillerie, tel. 04–67–60–20–36), where you can indulge in big beers (14F, half price 7 PM–10 PM); be sure to check out the exotic sitting room downstairs, with its mirrored walls and multicolor throw pillows. Then dance the night away at the animated **Rockstore** (20 rue de Verdun, tel. 04–67–58–70–10), where a huge dance floor, live rock music on some nights, and three bars await you. There's no cover charge weekdays 11–11:30; otherwise, you may pay 50F to get in. Or, grab a seat in the white sands of **Via Brazil** (7 rue Verdun, off pl. de la Comédie, tel. 04–67–58–63–33)—but only long enough to down the national cocktail *caipirinha* (rum, lemon, and vodka; 49F)—and then make your way through the tropical jungle they've created to the dance floor. If you're looking for jazz, try **Jam–Jazz Action** (100 rue Ferdinand de Lesseps, tel. 04–67–58–30–30), which sells tickets for weekly concerts, or head to **Summertime Café** (98 av. Pont Juvénal, tel. 04–67–65–65–25), which features cocktails and live performances.

On Saturday nights promenade Peyrou becomes a meet-and-greet spot, but finding an exclusively gay bar or club is tough. **Café de la Mer** (5 pl. du Marché-aux-Fleurs, tel. 04–67–60–79–65) is a lively meeting place for gays and lesbians, with 15F beers and an outdoor terrace. Another cool and crowded gay disco, 3 km (2 mi) outside Montpellier, is **Villa Rouge** (rte. De Palavas, tel. 04–67–06–52–15), where the cover is 60F–70F, depending on the night.

NEAR MONTPELLIER

The tourist office in Montpellier can give you basic information on sights near the city. For specifics on transportation, call or visit **Courriers du Midi** (tel. 04–67–06–03–67) at the bus station. Prices and routes are seasonal.

SETE

Approximately one hour (35F) away from Montpellier by bus or 30 minutes (29F) by train is the working port town of Sète, the Mediterranean's biggest fishing port. Don't look for major cultural monuments or historical artifacts; Sète is a place where you can see what the glorified fisherman's life is like. The canals winding through town make it fun to stroll around, and there are a number of good walking paths leading to the beach (about 30 minutes to the west). Although it's small and unspectacular, Plage de la Corniche has calm, pristine waters that are perfect for swimming. Ask the **tourist service** (60 Grand' Rue Mario Roustan, near Vieux Port, tel. 04–67–74–71–71, fax 04–67–46–17–54) for a map and a list of campsites. It's open mid-September–mid-June, Monday–Saturday 9–noon and 2–6, and mid-June–mid-September, daily 9–8. For a panoramic view of the area, climb **Mont St-Clair** or **Les Pierres Blanches** and pick a beach to settle down on.

Sète is extremely lively during July and August, when tourists flock to it for the beaches and many free activities. One of the biggest draws is the **Tournois de Joutes,** when men in boats try to joust each other into the water. It's like watching a medieval version of *American Gladiators*. There are also weekly free fun-and-games in Les Quilles, the resort area to the west of the city: Tuesdays are "welcome" evenings with dancing and food 8–midnight; Wednesdays 6–9 are given over to jousting sports where you can give it a shot for 10F; Thursdays have a considerable crafts fair open 9–midnight; Fridays 6 PM–1 AM are the boules contests. These events and the jousting tournament all culminate in a **Festival St-Louis–Fête de la Ville,** August 20–25.

WHERE TO SLEEP

If you want to spend the night, there are a few budget options in town. **Le Valéry** (20 rue Denfert-Rochereau, tel. 04–67–74–77–51, fax 04–67–46–12–84) offers basic rooms for 110F–160F in the summer high season. **La Tramontane** (5 rue Frédéric Mistral, tel. 04–67–74–37–92) welcomes people from around the world to 130F–245F doubles. The **hostel** (tel. 04–67–53–46–68, fax 04–67–51–34–01) is a bit of a walk up rue Général-Revest. In summer, beds are 118F per night, including dinner and breakfast; in winter bed-and-breakfast runs 69F.

FOOD

Restaurants serving fresh fish line the Canal Royal; at **Chez François** (8 quai Général Durand, tel. 04–67–74–59–69) you can try a *violet* (5F) from the mollusk family, stronger and uglier than an oyster, or you can indulge yourself with escargots (45F). Slightly inland at **Au Feu de Bois** (8 bis rue Frédéric Mistral, tel. 06–67–74–77–56), menus run 55F–115F for good grilled meats.

GORGES ET VALLEE DE L'HERAULT

A half hour north of Montpellier, the spectacular Hérault Gorge stretches for 50 km (30 mi) along the Hérault River. The gorgeous 9th-century abbey of **St-Guilhem-le-Désert** is in this valley, and ancient, narrow houses built along a riverbed make this one of the most beautiful villages in France. In summer, take a bus from Montpellier and spend the day hiking in the lush countryside.

If you tire quickly of super-quaint towns, fill up your water bottle at the fountain in front of the abbey and hit the trail. You can pick up the GR653 or GR74 and climb to the château ruins on the hilltop for a great panoramic view. Just take a right when the path curls away from the ruins; the climb takes about 30 minutes. Or walk or bike 3 km (2 mi) toward Montpellier to the **Pont du Diable** (literally, the "Devil's bridge"). Here you can swim in the beautiful waters under a Roman bridge. Although not as impressive as the Pont du Gard (see *Near Nîmes,* above*), it makes for great swimming and rock diving. You can also take a canoe down the river if you're feeling adventurous. Canoe rentals from one of the many boat shops in St-Guilhem run about 250F per day.*

COMING AND GOING

Buses run mid-June to mid-September, and the hour-long trek costs 33F, including the bus change in Gignac. Once in St-Guilhem-le-Désert, stop at the **tourist office** (tel. 04–67–57–44–33), open daily 10:30–12:30 and 2–5, for a map of the town.

WHERE TO SLEEP AND EAT

To really take advantage of the area, stay in the **Club Alpin Français** refuge. These dorm-style accommodations have kitchen facilities, a fireplace, showers, and bathrooms for 51F (or 32F if you have proof of membership in another Alpine club). The refuge is in an old building near the abbey, a *boulangerie* (bakery), and a grocery store. For information and reservations, contact the extremely friendly M. Rocco (6 rue du Téron, tel. 04–67–73–12–78).

AIX-EN-PROVENCE

Come to Aix to see the city's impressive architecture and elegant fountains and to join all those fashionable folks for whom café sitting, people-watching, and boutique shopping are a way of life. On the other hand, if you're trying to avoid busloads of tourists and Parisian prices, Aix is probably not for you.

In recent years, Aix has become a bedroom community for those who couldn't stomach the harsh urban realities of Marseille and could afford to move away. Aix is only 25 km (16 mi) north of Marseille, but in terms of lifestyle, the two cities are worlds apart. Some of Marseille's spirit has spilled over, though, and the university is host to a number of study-abroad and language programs that make Aix an important college town for French and foreign students.

Throughout the centuries, Aix flourished as both a cultural and a political capital of Provence. Festivals help maintain the cultural traditions, and the city's elegant architectural layout attests to its prominent past. The leafy boulevard **cours Mirabeau** is lined with 17th- and 18th-century hôtels particuliers, which now house banks and private offices. Luxurious fountains grace every square; one of the most impressive is the **Fontaine de la Rotonde** on place du Général de Gaulle, at the west end of cours Mirabeau.

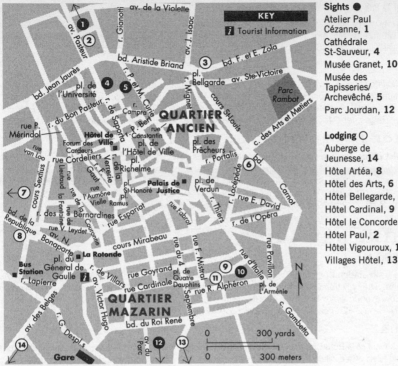

Sights ●

Atelier Paul
Cézanne, **1**

Cathédrale
St-Sauveur, **4**

Musée Granet, **10**

Musée des
Tapisseries/
Archevêché, **5**

Parc Jourdan, **12**

Lodging ○

Auberge de
Jeunesse, **14**

Hôtel Artéa, **8**

Hôtel des Arts, **6**

Hôtel Bellegarde, **3**

Hôtel Cardinal, **9**

Hôtel le Concorde, **7**

Hôtel Paul, **2**

Hôtel Vigouroux, **11**

Villages Hôtel, **13**

BASICS

AMERICAN EXPRESS

This AmEx office, actually called **L'Agence,** will hold mail and offers all the usual cardmember services except card replacement. If you're a student with ID, you can get a special exchange rate. *15 cours Mirabeau, tel. 04–42–26–84–77. Open weekdays 9–7, Sat. 9–5.*

BUREAU DE CHANGE

The best rates in town are at the **Banque de France** (18 rue du 4-Septembre, tel. 04–42–93–66–33), open weekdays 9–12:15 and 1:30–3:30.

DISCOUNT TRAVEL AGENCIES

In good **Council Travel** (12 rue Victor Leydet, near pl. des Augustins, tel. 04–42–38–58–82) tradition, the office here knows about all cheap deals and student fares. It's open weekdays 9:30–6:30, Saturday 9:30–12:30. **Nouvelles Frontières** (52 cours Sextius, tel. 04–42–26–47–22) is another source of discount train and plane tickets.

ENGLISH-LANGUAGE BOOKSTORE

Paradox Bookstore (15 pl. des Quatre Dauphins, tel. 04–42–26–47–99) has a large variety of literature, fiction, dictionaries, and travel books. Its hours are 9–12:30 and 2–6:30 daily.

INTERNET ACCESS

Hublot (17 rue Paul Bert, tel. 04–42–21—37–31) offers a bar and food with connections that run 30F for a half hour, 50F an hour. Closer to the tourist office and train station is **Net'Games** (52 rue de l'Aumône Vieille, off pl. des Tanneurs, tel. 04–43–36–60–41). It's open daily noon–1 AM; one hour costs 35F.

LAUNDRY

This is a city with a active student population, thus there are plenty of good laundromats around. There are four within easy reach of the tourist office. The closest is at 5 **rue de la Fontaine,** open daily 7 AM–8 PM. A wash costs 18F–36F, drying is 2F for 4 minutes, and a small box of soap is 2F.

MAIL

The inefficiency of government bureaucracy reaches new heights in the **main post office.** Luckily, automated stamping can be done without waiting in line. The bureau de change charges a whopping commission. The postal codes for the city are 13100 or 13090; use 13100 for poste restante. *2 rue Lapierre, at av. des Belges, tel. 04–42–16–01–50. Open weekdays 8:30–7, Sat. 8:30–noon.*

VISITOR INFORMATION

The **tourist office** has free copies of the monthly "Mois à Aix," which lists all cultural activities in town. The staff will also set you up with heaps of free maps and information on Aixois life past and present. Need an overview? Sign up for a 50F city tour in English, given July–September every Wednesday at 9:30 AM. *2 pl. du Général de Gaulle, tel. 04–42–16–11–61, fax 04–42–16–11–62. Open Sept.–June, Mon.–Sat. 8:30–7, Sun. 10–1 and 2–6; July–Aug., daily 8:30 AM–10 PM.*

COMING AND GOING

BY TRAIN

From the **train station** there are hourly trains to Marseille (30 mins, 37F); the first leaves at 6 AM, the last at 9 PM. The only trains that don't connect through Marseille go to Briançon (east of Aix). To get to town, follow avenue Victor Hugo five minutes until you hit place du Général de Gaulle. *Pl. Victor Hugo, tel. 04–91–62–12–80. Ticket office open daily 6 AM–9 PM.*

BY BUS

One block west of la Rotonde, the **bus station** (rue Lapierre, tel. 04–42–27–17–91) is dismal and confusing and filled with a zillion independent bus companies. The bulletin board inside should clear things up, listing departure times and platform numbers. The bus lines offer regional service only, the farthest destinations being Orange (2½ hrs, 91F) and Nice (2½ hrs, 124F). Buses run hourly to Marseille (30 mins, 27F), six times daily to Avignon (1¼ hrs, 88F), and twice daily to Arles (2 hrs, 68F).

GETTING AROUND

Aix's centre ville is a maze of narrow, commercial streets, and it's difficult to keep your sense of direction. The main drag is the tree-lined cours Mirabeau, which divides old Aix in half, with the **Quartier Ancien's** narrow medieval streets to the north and the hôtels particuliers and fancy restaurants of the **Quartier Mazarin** to the south. **Place Richelme** and **place de l'Hôtel de Ville,** the main squares (where people and café tables take up every square inch), are in the Quartier Ancien. Most museums, fountains, and hôtels particuliers are within central Aix, where walking is the best way to get around. The larger, newer Aix that sprawls around the centre ville is served by a municipal **bus system.** Tickets cost 7F, and you can pick up a map of routes at the tourist office. Most lines stop at la Rotonde, at the west end of cours Mirabeau. If you are gripped by the urge to be mobile on two wheels, call **Cycles Naddeo** (54 av. de Lattre de Tassigny, tel. 04–42–21–06–93). A day's rental will run you 100F. **Taxis** can be called 24 hours a day at 04–42–27–71–11.

WHERE TO SLEEP

Aix has lots of pricey hotels, though there are a few cheaper options. A notch above the places listed below are **Hôtel le Concorde** (68 blvd. du Roi René, tel. 04–42–26–03–95), with doubles for 225F–370F, and **Hôtel Artea** (4 blvd. de la République, tel. 04–42–27–36–00, fax 04–42–27–28–76), with doubles for 190F–380F.

UNDER 175F • Hôtel Bellegarde. On the edge of the old town due north of place des Prêcheurs, this local bar-hotel offers owners who are charming, good coffee, and decent rooms for 160F. *2 pl. Belle-garde, tel. 04–42–23–43–37. 10 rooms, half with bath.*

Villages Hôtel. This new and clean modern chain hotel is one of the cheapest around. Rooms for one, two, or three people go for 155F, and a family room (for two adults and two children) is only 195F. *Av. Arc de Meyran, tel. 04–42–93–56–16, fax 04–42–93–56–17. 80 rooms, all with bath.*

UNDER 250F • Hôtel des Arts. Although dimly lit and small, this place benefits from its location near the art school (hence the name). Lots of cheap restaurants, fun bars, and a laundromat are just around the corner. The rooms are clean but very small. Doubles run 180F–205F, singles 150F–205F. *69 blvd. Carnot, tel. 04–42–38–11–77. From cours Mirabeau, take rue Lacépède and turn right on blvd. Carnot. 16 rooms, all with bath.*

Hôtel Paul. What this hotel lacks in charm it makes up for in convenience. It's just outside the centre ville, and the rooms are well maintained. Doubles and singles with shower are 190F–250F (street-side versus park-side), and triples are 300F. *10 av. Pasteur, at north entrance of centre ville, tel. 04–42–23–23–89, fax 04–42–63–17–80. 24 rooms, 23 with bath.*

UNDER 275F • Hôtel Vigouroux. You can only stay here in summer, because it is a boardinghouse for university students October–June. Rooms have hardwood floors and antique furniture; singles without shower go for 160F, singles and doubles with shower are 270F, and rooms with a kitchen for two to three people are 300F. Rates are lower for guests staying three or more days. *27 rue Cardinale, near Musée Granet, tel. 04–42–38–26–42. 11 rooms, 6 with bath.*

UNDER 350F • Hôtel Cardinal. In the heart of the quartier Mazarin, this hotel is like a step back to the 18th century. Rooms have period furniture and intricate woodwork (one even has access to a patio and a fountain). Doubles start at 340F. *24 rue Cardinale, tel. 04–42–38–32–30, fax 04–42–26–39–05. 30 rooms, all with bath.*

HOSTEL

Auberge de Jeunesse. The staff at this hostel must have formerly run a prison, seeing how rigid and humorless they are. The hostel's worst sin, though, is its location: The last bus leaves the centre ville at 8 PM, and if you miss it, it's a half-hour walk. On the bright side, all this hassle gives you access to tennis and volleyball courts, laundry machines, a TV room, and a bar. Bed, breakfast, and sheets cost 79F for the first night and 68F thereafter (plus 19F a night if you do not already have an HI card). Half-board costs 127F the first night and 116F if you stick around. *3 av. Marcel Pagnol, tel. 04–42–20–15–99, fax 04–42–59–36–12. From la Rotonde, take Bus 12, or walk down av. de l'Europe and follow signs. 100 beds. Reception open daily 7–11 and 5–11. Lockout 11–5. Curfew 11 PM, midnight Sat.*

CAMPING

Avoid the campground **Arc en Ciel** (Pont des Trois-Sautets, rte. de Nice, tel. 04–42–26–14–28), 3 km (2 mi) outside town, unless you want to stay in a trailer park. **Camping Chanteclerc** (Val St-André, rte. de Nice, tel. 04–42–26–12–98), 2 km (1 mi) from town, is a zillion times better. It's not exactly a nature paradise (it has more amenities than most hotels), but it only charges 30F per person and 35F per site. Take Bus 3 from La Rotonde.

FOOD

Restaurants in Aix tend to be big-time operations that charge at least 60F–80F for a basic plate of food. Inexpensive holes-in-the-wall are hard to come by, except for the medium-priced ethnic restaurants of all stripes on rue Van Loo, place Ramus and the adjacent rues de la Verrerie, Aumône Vieille, and des Marseillais. If you are looking for a cluster of Provençal kitchens that might spark some interest, try those on rue Félibre Gaut or on forum des Cardeurs. A terrific slice goes for 12F at **Pizza Capri** (rue Farbot, just off cours Mirabeau, tel. 04–42–38–55–43). Other options include grocery stores such as **Monoprix** (cours Mirabeau) or the considerably cheaper **Ed** (next to the bus station). Fresh produce is available Tuesday, Thursday, and Saturday mornings at the open-air **markets** on place Richelme, place de Verdun, place des Prêcheurs, and by the Hôtel de Ville.

UNDER 50F • Le Steph and Co. Fresh salads (25F), hot and cold sandwiches (13F–25F), and daily meat platters (35F) explain why the line here is so long at lunch. *38 av. Victor Hugo, tel. 04–42–26–38–80.*

UNDER 100F • Les Agapes. Treat yourself to Provençal cuisine at this classy restaurant with a garden. The house special, fillet of sole with paprika (78F), is excellent. *11 rue des Bernardines, tel. 04–42–38–47–66. From la Rotonde, take rue Espariat to pl. des Augustins, turn left on rue de la Couronne, left on rue des Bernardines. No lunch.*

L'Arbre à Pain. Cheerful decor is the background to creative meals at the only vegetarian joint in town. The staff favorite is the 40F *salade campagnarde* (lettuce, chickpeas, carrots, potatoes, hard-boiled egg, and olives); the three-course menu is 78F at lunch and 98F at dinner. *12 rue Constantin, a few blocks east of Hôtel de Ville, tel. 04–42–96–99–95. Closed Sun. and Mon.*

La Crêpe d'Or. Candlelight flickers upon stone walls as the friendly staff prepares delectable crepes. A three-course crepe meal is available at lunch for 48F–55F, but count on 70F–80F for dinner if you want an entrée and dessert crepe. *8 rue Lieutaud, east of cours Sextius, tel. 04–42–27–50–99. Closed Sun. No lunch Sat.*

Zorba. You wouldn't know it from walking by, but this small restaurant near the eastern edge of the centre ville serves some of the best Greek food around. A meal will run you about 100F, including six appetizers, an entrée, and dessert. *1 rue Portalis, near pl. des Prêcheurs, tel. 04–42–38–02–89.*

UNDER 150F • Chez Maxime's. Aixois will steer you toward Chez Maxime's to sample southwestern French cuisine. Whether you're in the mood for cassoulet (a hearty stew with vegetables, lentils, and lamb or sausage), clams, or steak, you can't go wrong at this bastion of gastronomy. Come at lunch, when the 95F menu is considerably cheaper than its 130F dinner counterpart. *12 pl. Ramus, tel. 04–42–26–28–51. Closed Sun. No lunch Mon.*

CAFES

Aix has a vibrant café scene. The celebrated **Les Deux Garçons** (53 cours Mirabeau, tel. 04–42–26–00–51) opened in Louis-Phillipe's time and has entertained the likes of Cézanne, Zola, Camus, and Cocteau. Prices, however, reflect this claim to fame. A collegiate crowd frequents **Café de Paris** (41 cours Mirabeau, tel. 04–42–26–04–51), where there's often live music. Low-key cafés cluster around place des Prêcheurs and place de Verdun, in front of the colossal **Palais de Justice.** The ever-crowded **l'Unic Bar** (pl. Richelme, tel. 04–42–96–38–28) specializes in fruity concoctions (14F–18F) and generous lunch platters (45F).

WORTH SEEING

The museums and churches in Aix are overshadowed by the city itself, with its beautiful fountains and elegant hôtels particuliers. Get a detailed map from the tourist office, and be sure to check out the **fountain** on place des Quatre Dauphins.

ATELIER PAUL CEZANNE

Beyond the north end of the vieille ville is the house and studio where impressionist Paul Cézanne lived in the 1890s. The painter was born in Aix, and though he spent much time away, the city always lured him back. No major works are on display here, but the studio remains as he left it at the time of his death in 1906, with his cloak, hat, and cane awaiting his return. Check out the view of Mont Ste-Victoire from the first floor. *9 av. Paul Cézanne, tel. 04–42–21–06–53. Admission 25F. Open daily 10–noon and 2–5 (2:30–6 Apr.–Sept.).*

CATHEDRALE ST-SAUVEUR

A jumble of architectural styles dating from the 5th to 17th centuries gives this cathedral at the north end of the vieille ville a confused air, but the structure is still impressive. Next door you can admire the simple architecture of the Romanesque **Cloître St-Sauveur.** *34 pl. des Martyrs de la Résistance, tel. 04–42–23–45–65.*

MUSEE GRANET

Not surprisingly, the works of Aix painter François Granet (1775–1849) dominate the Granet Museum. Other works include paintings by members of the great European schools (David, Ingres, Rubens) and eight oil canvases by Cézanne. The exhibition space is crowded, and not everything is spectacular. In the basement, archaeological galleries display the Celtic-Ligurian remains of ancient Aix. *Pl. St-Jean de Malte, tel. 04–42–38–14–70. Admission 10F. Open Wed.–Mon. 10–noon and 2–6.*

MUSEE DES TAPISSERIES

The 17th-century Archbishop's Palace, the **Archevêché,** is home to the Tapestry Museum. The bishops collected 17th- and 18th-century tapestries to decorate their classy abode. Note that the striking series of 17 tapestries made in Beauvais illustrates the adventures of Don Quixote. *28 pl. des Martyrs de la Résistance, tel. 04–42–23–09–91. Admission 10F. Open Wed.–Mon. 10–noon and 2–6.*

PARC JOURDAN

Next to the university campus on avenue Jules Ferry, this beautiful park occupies a full city block and provides refuge from the hubbub of the centre ville. Students lounge in the sun and colonize its lawns, despite the signs warning them to stay off the grass. The park is also known as a popular gay hangout and meeting place. For all its daytime beauty, avoid it at night; the place is notorious for flashers and other exhibitionists.

PAUL CEZANNE TRAIL

It's amazing how much energy Aix puts into touting its affiliation with Cézanne, since he was virtually laughed out of town when he was alive. According to some, Cézanne was so put off by the way he was treated that he refused to show his artwork to interested Aixois. But this is all behind them, and now art enthusiasts can pick up a map of Cézanne's "footsteps" at the tourist office. Gold studs in the pavement chronicle where the painter worked, went to school, and got married. The walk begins at the tourist office and finishes on the cours Sextius. The written commentary is, unfortunately, devoid of the spice of life that brewed in this temperamental man. True fans can also venture to the sights of his famous landscapes outside Aix; see the tourist office for more information.

FESTIVALS

Aix's annual **Festival International d'Art Lyrique et de Musique** (tel. 04–42–17–34–34) takes place in July and is a momentous event in the music world. Cathédrale St-Saveur, its cloister, and the Théâtre de l'Archevêché tremble with the sounds of excellent operas and orchestras. Unfortunately, tickets cost 125F–1,200F. Luckily, free impromptu musical events pop up all over town.

An event more accessible to the masses is **Aix en Musique** (espace Forbin, 3 pl. John Rewald, tel. 04–42–21–69–69), which, throughout the year except in summer, brings musicians of all kinds to parks, churches, and hôtels particuliers. Admission to concerts is either free or well under 100F. The **Festival International de Danse** (espace Forbin, cours Gambetta, tel. 04–42–96–05–01), more commonly known as **Danse à Aix,** features modern ballet and jazz dance from July to August. Although there are a few free performances, most cost 100F–250F. Tickets go on sale two weeks before the shows and can be purchased at the tourist office.

AFTER DARK

When the sun goes down, Aixois spring to life. Many people start their night at one of the outdoor cafés along the cours Mirabeau (*see above*) before heading off to the bars. **Bistrot Aixois** (37 cours Sextius, tel. 04–42–27–50–10) is a very popular indoor-outdoor bar with a small dance floor and 25F beers. Close by and frequented by French locals is **L'I.P.N.** (23 cours Sextius, tel. 04–42–26–25–17), which has a 15F cover and 15F beers on tap. Scads of great bars with a hip twentysomething crowd line rue de la Verrerie. **Bugsy** (25 rue Verrerie, tel. 04–42–38–25–22) is a favorite place to down beers (15F), play pool (10F), and listen to music. The best jazz clubs are **Hot Brass** (chemin de la Plaine des Verguetiers, tel. 04–42–21–05–57) and **Le Scat Club** (rue de la Verrerie, tel. 04–42–23–00–23), each with a hefty 80F–100F cover on Friday and Saturday. Many people end their night dancing to techno at **Richelme** (24 rue de la Verrerie, tel. 04–42–23–49–29), which has an 80F–100F cover on weekends. **La Chimère** (rte. d'Avignon, tel. 04–42–23–36–28) is a popular gay dance club outside of town. There's no cover before midnight; afterward, the cover, including one drink, is 80F.

NEAR AIX-EN-PROVENCE

MONT STE-VICTOIRE

Aix has such a metropolitan air, it's hard to believe that the sparsely populated countryside is only 20 minutes away. Ocher soil and cypress trees back the striking Mont Ste-Victoire. Painted countless times by Cézanne, the mountain rears its chalky head over the flatlands, providing ample opportunity for day hikes or treks taking several days. In August 1989, a spark from a chain saw, combined with gusting winds, set 12,350 acres ablaze. The forest is still recuperating from the fire and major precautions are being taken to prevent another; for this reason you may not be able to hike here in July or August.

On the top of the mountain is the **Croix de Provence** (Cross of Provence), which a sailor saved from a shipwreck and put up here in 1871. On the south side of the mountain is an abyss, the *garagaïum*, which has been dubbed the "chimney of hell" (probably by hikers who attacked it in the blazing heat). You can reach the south side of the mountain by taking a bus from Aix to Puyloubier. To get to the north side of Mont Ste-Victoire, take a bus from Aix to Vauvenaugues (from both of these stops, you'll have to hike a while before you can climb). You can also reach the mountain by cycling; the Aix tourist office will set you up with pertinent maps. It'll also sell you information on hiking trails for 30F; ask for the *Sentiers Balisés* or contact the **Association des Excursionnistes Provençaux** (8 rue Littéra, tel. 04–42–21–03–53) directly. If you're hoping to stay near the mountain for a couple days, April–October you can camp in Puyloubier at **Le Cézanne** (chemin de la Pallière, tel. 04–42–66–34–45).

MARSEILLE

A huge city, Marseille occupies twice the amount of land as Paris and is Europe's second-largest port. Many cultures meet in Marseille—a defining characteristic of the city is its diverse immigrant population, including recent influxes of Italians, Greeks, Armenians, and North Africans. Its heterogeneous population keeps the city lively and interesting, but it also has made for racial tensions—the ultraright Front National wins many votes here. The racism stems in part from frustration at rising unemployment, for which the North African and Arab communities are often made a scapegoat.

After visiting the rest of France, you may be taken aback by Marseille's realness: There is a grittiness here that is not found in other places. Marseille has little regard for those in search of the picturesque and is plagued with social conflict, political corruption, drug dealing (mostly heroin), and crime. As in any big city, you should definitely look out for yourself here. But Marseille also distinguishes itself from other French cities through its colorful, almost defiant spirit.

The **Vieux Port** (Old Port), with its small boats, fish markets, port-side restaurants, and cafés, forms the heart of the city. Although the southern neighborhoods are more moneyed and chic, you would never mistake Marseille for a glamorous city. The neighborhoods toward the north are some of the poorest. But if you're tired of seeing busloads of tourists and are craving *real* nightlife, Marseille is still a thriving cosmopolitan center. An important transportation hub, Marseille is a convenient stopover before you make train and airplane connections to other exotic destinations. The nearby beaches of **Cassis** and the **Calanques** are most easily reached from here as well.

BASICS

AMERICAN EXPRESS

This office has all the usual ArnEx services. *39 la Canebière, tel. 04–91–13–71–21. Métro: Vieux-Port. Open weekdays 9–6 (Sat. 9–noon and 2–4 for money exchange only).*

BUREAUX DE CHANGE

The best place to change your money is at one of the banks lining la Canebière. Many have ATMs that accept credit cards and Cirrus cards; the BNP has ATMs that also accept Plus cards.

CONSULATES

United Kingdom: *24 av. du Prado, tel. 04–91–15–72–10. Open weekdays 9–noon and 2–5.*
United States: *12 blvd. Paul Peytral, tel. 04–91–54–92–00. Open weekdays 8:30–noon and 1:30–5.*

DISCOUNT TRAVEL AGENCY

Wasteels is an efficient discount travel agency with an English-speaking staff. *67 la Canebière, tel. 04–95–09–30–20, fax 04–91–90–36–81. Métro: Vieux-Port. Open weekdays 9–12:30 and 2–6:30, Sat. 9–12:30 and 2–5:30.*

EMERGENCY NUMBERS

If you find yourself in need of immediate assistance, dial 15 or 04–91–49–91–91 for an **ambulance.** For the **police,** dial 17. For the **rape crisis** center, call 04–91–56–04–10. Each district has its own hos-

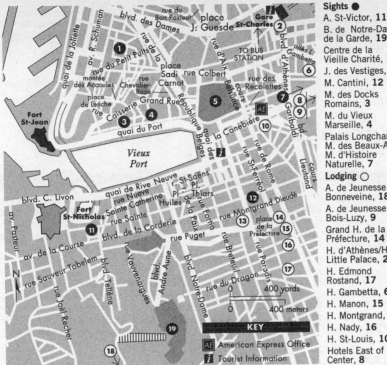

Sights ●
A. St-Victor, **11**
B. de Notre-Dame de la Garde, **19**
Centre de la Vieille Charité, **1**
J. des Vestiges, **5**
M. Cantini, **12**
M. des Docks Romains, **3**
M. du Vieux Marseille, **4**
Palais Longchamp/ M. des Beaux-Arts/ M. d'Histoire Naturelle, **7**

Lodging ○
A. de Jeunesse Bonneveine, **18**
A. de Jeunesse de Bois-Luzy, **9**
Grand H. de la Préfecture, **14**
H. d'Athènes/Hôtel Little Palace, **2**
H. Edmond Rostand, **17**
H. Gambetta, **6**
H. Manon, **15**
H. Montgrand, **13**
H. Nady, **16**
H. St-Louis, **10**
Hotels East of Center, **8**

KEY

AE American Express Office

i Tourist Information

pital, but the main one is **Hôpital de la Timone** (264 rue St-Pierre, tel. 04–91–38–60–00, métro La Timone).

INTERNET ACCESS

All of Marseille's cybercafés are in the southern part of the city. **Le Rezo** (68 cours Julien, tel. 04–91–42–70–02) is open Monday–Saturday 9:30 AM–10 PM, Sunday 10–10. Rates are 30F for 30 minutes and 50F an hour. The **Genius Café** (227 rue Paradis, tel. 04–91–57–07–34, open daily 7:30 AM–2 AM) and **Magic Café** (20 rue Docteur Escat, tel. 04–91–13–75–76), open Monday–Saturday 10 AM–2 AM and Sunday 2–8, both run 50F an hour with special deals for additional time.

LAUNDRY

Laverie des Allées (15 allées Léon Gambetta) lets you wash and dry smelly socks for about 40F and is open daily 9–8.

MAIL

The **main post office** occupies practically a whole city block. The postal code is 13001. *1 pl. Hôtel des Postes, corner rues Colbert and Henri-Barbusse, tel. 04–91–15–47–00. Métro: Vieux-Port. Open weekdays 8–7, Sat. 8–noon.*

VISITOR INFORMATION

You won't have to fight crowds to get your questions answered at the abundantly staffed **main tourist office**. It also has the booklet *Lieux Culturels de Marseille,* which lists hotels, restaurants, stores, clubs, and bars. Look for other offices in the train station and, in summer only, on the quai des Belges. *4 la Canebière, tel. 04–91–13–89–00, fax 04–91–13–89–20. Métro: Vieux-Port. Open summer daily 9–8; off-season, Mon.–Sat. 9–7, Sun. 10–5.*

The **departmental** and **regional tourist offices,** Comité Départemental de Tourisme and Comité Régional de Tourisme, both provide maps and brochures on Provence, the Alps, and the Côte d'Azur.

The former is south of the Palais de Justice and the latter west of the Jardin des Vestiges. *Departmental office: 13 rue Roux de Brignoles, tel. 04–91–13–84–13, fax 04–91–33–01–82. Regional office: 14 rue St-Barbe, tel. 04–91–39–38–00, fax 04–91–56–66–61. Both open weekdays 9–12:30 and 2–6.*

For hiking information in and around Marseille, contact **Club Alpin Français.** *12 rue Fort Notre-Dame, near pl. Huiles, tel. 04–91–54–36–94. Open Mon. 10–1 and 4–6, Thurs. 10–1 and 4–8.*

For general city information, pick up the free weekly **Taktik,** published every Wednesday. *Main office: 55 cours Julien, tel. 04–91–92–65–65, fax 04–91–92–77–77. Métro: Notre-Dame du Mont. Open weekdays 10–7.*

COMING AND GOING

BY TRAIN

Marseille's enormous and well-organized **train station** (esplanade St-Charles, 04–91–50–00–00) serves all regions of France. Trains run almost hourly to Arles (45 mins, 70F), Aix-en-Provence (30 mins, 37F), Nîmes (1¼ hrs, 95F), Avignon (1 hr, 91F), Toulon (1 hr, 58F), and Nice (2¼ hrs, 147F). There are also 12 daily superfast trains, TGVs (trains à grande vitesse*) to Paris (4½ hrs, 373F–439F). Services at the station include a snack bar, police station, and tourist office. There is no luggage storage. The station, at the northern end of the centre ville, is a 20-minute walk from the Vieux Port and a 10- to 30-minute walk from most budget hotels.*

BY BUS

Tons of companies run frequent buses to surrounding cities from the **gare routière** (3 pl. Victor Hugo, tel. 04–91–08–16–40, métro St-Charles) at the east end of the train station. **Ceyte Tourisme Méditerranée** (tel. 04–90–93–74–90) sends five buses a day to Arles (2 hrs, 85F); and several companies run buses about every half hour to Aix-en-Provence (30 mins, 26F), less often to Nice (3 hrs, 140F), Cassis (35 mins, 23F), and Avignon (2⅛ hrs, 91F). Call the bus station for information, and buy tickets on the bus.

BY FERRY

SNCM sends ferries to Corsica (12 hrs, 620F round-trip), Sardinia, and North Africa. Discounts are available to those under 25. *61 blvd. des Dames, tel. 08–36–67–95–00 for information and reservations. Métro: Joliette. Open weekdays 8–5:30, Sat. 8:30–11:30 and 2–5:30.*

BY PLANE

The **Aéroport Marseille-Provence** (tel. 04–42–14–14–14) is 25 km (16 mi) from Marseille. Twenty-six airlines (domestic and international) make daily flights to 81 different cities. The airport has a 24-hour **information desk** (tel. 04–42–14–21–14). Other services at the airport include a bureau de change (open daily 6 AM–8 PM) and car-rental agencies.

TO AND FROM THE AIRPORT • The cheapest way to get from the airport to Marseille is by bus with **Transports Routiers Passagers Aériens.** Buses depart every 20 minutes or so from the airport 6:15 AM–10:50 PM, and from Marseille's St-Charles train station 5:30 AM–9:50 PM. The 46F ride takes 25 minutes. Call 04–91–50–59–34 at the train station and 04–42–14–31–27 at the airport.

GETTING AROUND

Marseille is a huge city, subdivided into 16 *arrondissements* (districts). The Vieux Port, the surrounding centre ville, and the main street, **la Canebière,** make up the city's nerve center. The Vieux Port, too shallow to accommodate large ships, is packed with fishing boats and pleasure craft. On the north side near the train station is the **Quartier Belsunce,** a neighborhood that is home to Arab, Armenian, and Libyan immigrants. Here you'll find everything from saffron and cumin to three-piece suits being traded on the streets. The Quartier Belsunce is between rue d'Aix, cours Belsunce, and boulevard d'Athènes. North of the Vieux Port is another North African quarter, **le Panier,** the city's oldest, with narrow, winding streets and stairs. Only slightly east of the center at place Jean Jaurès, known locally as **la Plaine,** is the busy hoppingest after-hours area. The relatively new tourist-trap restaurant zone just to the south of the Vieux Port also sees a fair bit of bustle after the sun goes down. The farther distant southern neighborhoods are cleaner, more sedate, and have better beach access.

BY BUS AND METRO

Many points of interest are clustered around the Vieux Port, but you'll have to use public transportation to get from one end of town to the other. Fortunately, the bus system and the two métro lines are efficient. You can get a useful mass-transit map at the tourist office or at the **RTM (Réseau de Transport Marseillais) information desk** (6–8 rue des Fabres, tel. 04–91–91–92–10), open weekdays 8:30–6 and Saturday 9–5:30, near the intersection of la Canebière and cours Belsunce. Most buses stop around 8 or 9 PM and have limited service on Sunday. After this the night bus service, called the Fluobus, functions 9:15 PM–12:30 AM. Be sure to pick up a guide if you plan on staying out late. Locals warn that *contrôleurs* often check the last night bus, fining those who are using the same ticket over and over. Métro trains run 5 AM–9 PM. Tickets cost 9F and are valid for both the métro and bus; you can buy them at any RTM booth, at bus terminals in the centre ville, or at métro stations. The main tourist office also has special 25F day passes that are good for one day of unlimited métro and bus rides.

BY TAXI

It's a good idea to take a taxi if you have to travel at night alone. Make sure the driver turns on the meter so you don't get ripped off. Rates are usually around 7F a kilometer (½ mi) during the day, 9F–10F a kilometer at night. Rates are indicated on the door, and be sure the driver knows you're aware of that fact. To request a cab, call **Taxi Plus** (tel. 04–91–03–60–03) or **Taxi Radio** (tel. 04–91–05–80–80); the latter has better rates at night.

WHERE TO SLEEP

Stay away from the really seedy and dilapidated hotels on **rue du Théâtre Français** (off la Canebière, 1 block east of boulevard Garibaldi) and the intersecting **rue Mazagran**. If you arrive at night, it's probably a good idea to stay at one of the hotels near the stations, or to catch a cab directly to your hotel. North of La Canebière, you'll find a number of cheap hotels clustered around **allée Léon Gambetta**, off boulevard d'Athènes between the centre ville and train station. South of La Canebière, you'll find better-maintained hotels closer to the Vieux Port and around the Prefecture.

UNDER 150F • Hôtel Ozéa. This is by far a better, if not the best, bottom-of-the-barrel option in the neighborhood. Rooms cost 120F or 150F (with and without showers, respectively) and, while clean, are very simple. *12 rue Barbaroux, tel. 04–91–47–91–84. Métro: Réformés. 16 rooms, 7 with showers.*

Hôtel Pied-à-Terre. You won't be getting a lot with your room, but then again, at this price, you aren't asking for it. Nevertheless, the sheets are clean, the windows lock, the toilets flush, and the reception is always very friendly. Doubles are 120F–150F. *18 rue Barbaroux, tel. 04–91–92–00–95. Métro: Réformés. 17 rooms, 9 with shower.*

UNDER 200F • Hôtel du Coq. In the quiet side streets south of the train station but before the noise of la Canebière, there is hope for a comfortable night's sleep. An unsung bargain, this pleasant hotel offers clean doubles for 165F–195F, including breakfast. *26 rue du Coq, tel. 04–91–62–61–29. Métro: Réformés. 17 rooms, 7 with shower.*

Hôtel Little Palace. Go straight when you reach the bottom of the staircase of the train station and you'll find this hotel on the right. The carpeting is a little dingy, but the rooms are better, cleaner, and quieter than most in the area. Rooms are 160F–250F. *37–39 blvd. d'Athènes, tel. 04–91–90–03–83. Métro: St-Charles. 21 rooms, all with bath.*

Hôtel Nady. The management in this small, newly refitted hotel, within walking distance of cours Julien and the Prefecture, is eager and responsible. Rooms are 110F–240F. There are also six small showerless rooms in the annex built around a small courtyard; showers are 15F. *157 cours Lieutaud, tel. 04–91–48–70–21, fax 04–91–92–69–59. Métro: Castellane. 19 rooms, 9 with showers.*

UNDER 250F • Hôtel Gambetta. This place has simple rooms and tiled bathrooms that are well maintained by the friendly management. Doubles run 170F–235F, singles 105F–145F. Showers are 15F. *49 allée Léon Gambetta, tel. 04–91–62–07–88, fax 04–91–64–81–54. Métro: Réformés. 18 rooms, 15 with bath.*

Hôtel Manon. On a street that seems to have escaped city cartographers' notice (and is thus hard to locate), this "find" deserves to be found by everyone. Doubles cost 170F–210F. *36 blvd. Louis Salvator, tel. 04–91–48–67–01, fax 04–91–47–23–04. Head down cours Lieutaud or rue de Rome until even with front of Préfecture and at blvd. Salvator. Métro: Notre-Dame du Mont or Estrangin. 15 rooms, 11 with showers.*

Grand Hôtel de la Préfecture. In this bright, modern, two-star establishment, you will get all the comforts you want and more: an elevator, televisions, air-conditioning, soundproofing, bathrooms, and showers. Rooms run 160F–210F. *9 blvd. Louis Salvator, tel. 04–91–54–31–60, fax 04–91–54–24–95. Up the uphill street from front of Préfecture. Métro: Notre-Dame du Mont or Estrangin. 41 rooms, all with bath.*

Hôtel St-Louis. In a beautifully renovated building dating from Napoléon I's time, this hotel is right near the Vieux Port. For 220F you'll get a double and a balcony over the lively road below, as well as your own TV. Show your Fodor's book and you'll get a 5% reduction. *2 rue des Récolettes, tel. 04–91–54–02–74, fax 04–91–33–78–59. Off la Canebière; or take métro to Vieux Port. 22 rooms, all with bath.*

UNDER 300F • Hôtel d'Athènes. This hotel near the train station shares a lobby with the Little Palace (*see above*). It's a good bet if the Palace is full; the prices are a little steeper and the rooms a little nicer. Doubles and singles (with TV and shower) start at 225F. *37–39 blvd. d'Athènes, tel. 04–91–90–03–83. 20 rooms, all with bath.*

Hôtel Azur. The fine tree-lined boulevard that extends east from la Canebière is a leafy welcome to this classic hotel. If you can pay the price, this is great value for it. Doubles come in at 270F–310F. *24 cours Franklin-Roosevelt, tel. 04–91–42–74–38, fax 04–91–47–27–91. Métro: Réformés. 18 rooms, all with bath or shower.*

Hôtel Edmond Rostand. This hospitable haven is hidden in a placid part of the city south of the Préfecture. The large, airy lobby lets you know what you can expect from the rooms—elegance and charm. Double rooms run 250F–290F. *31 rue Dragon, tel. 04–91–37–74–95, fax 04–91–57–19–04. Métro: Estrangin. 16 rooms, all with bath.*

Hôtel Lutetia. Across the square from the Hôtel Azur (*see above*) is this less-expensive but also less-elegant affair (doubles are 240F–270F). *38 allée Léon Gambetta, tel. 04–91–50–81–78, fax 04–91–50–23–52. Métro: Réformés. 29 rooms, all with bath.*

Hôtel Montgrand. Clean, comfortable, and nicely decorated singles and doubles are 110F–300F. Hall showers are 15F. *50 rue Montgrand, tel. 04–91–00–35–20, fax 04–91–33–75–89. Take métro to Vieux Port and walk up rue Montgrand. 18 rooms, 11 with bath.*

HOSTEL • Auberge de Jeunesse Bonneveine. It's only a five-minute walk from the beach of La Pointe Rouge, and it definitely caters to an international sunning and sporting crowd. A bed with breakfast will cost you 83F–90F (with an HI card). Sheets are 17F. *47 av. Joseph-Vidal, tel. 04–91–73–21–81. From train station, take métro to Rond Point du Prado, then Bus 44 to pl. Bonnefoy; or take métro to Ste-Marguerite Dromel, then Bus 47. 150 beds. Reception open 24 hrs. Curfew 1 AM.*

Auberge de Jeunesse de Bois-Luzy. A 19th-century château has been converted into a beautiful and impeccably clean hostel overlooking the city. It has a communal kitchen and meal options (when groups are present), but unfortunately there's a 10:30 PM curfew. It's also a 15-minute bus ride from the centre ville, and buses stop running at 9 PM. A bed is 45F–50F a night with a hostel card, and sheets are 16F. *Allée des Primevères, tel. 04–91–49–06–18. From train station, take métro to Canebière-Réformés, then Bus 6 to Marius Richard. 90 beds. Reception open daily 7–noon and 5–11. Lockout noon–5. Kitchen.*

FOOD

Eats are cheap in Marseille, but the food-stand fare is greasier and staler than elsewhere in France, so take a good look before you buy. The largest concentration of restaurants and cafés surrounds the Vieux Port. Restaurants on **quai de Rive Neuve** have decent deals, and many feature the city's fish stew specialty—bouillabaisse. The parallel and somewhat pricey **rue St-Saëns, cours Honoré d'Estienne d'Orvès**, also known as place Thiars, and **rue Sainte** are other areas to explore, as is the other side of the port along the **quai du Port.**

For pizza, sandwich, and produce stands, go to **rue de Rome** and the side streets to the east. South of la Canebière and east of boulevard Garibaldi are **cours Julien, place Notre-Dame du Mont,** and **place Jean Jaurès,** lined with interesting restaurants and cafés. If it's couscous you want, try the **Quartier Belsunce** or **le Panier.** Do your grocery shopping at the morning **markets,** on central squares Monday–Saturday throughout town. Or stock up at **Baze** on la Canebière, a large supermarket owned by Monoprix. There's also a **Prisunic** supermarket next to the Castellane métro stop.

If you taste three new things while in Marseille, they might as well be what the city can offer like no other place in the world. First, **bouillabaisse:** Originally a peasant dish made from fish that went unsold at the market, today it is haute cuisine and composed only of the best of any catch. There are two parts to a true bouillabaisse: the broth, which is poured over and slurped with garlic- and rouille-rubbed toasted bits of bread; and the fish, de-boned before your eyes and eaten with the broth. Keep in mind that this is not the same as *soupe de poisson,* also eaten with the toast, garlic, and rouille, but made with different kinds of chopped fish and crab, cooked in a broth with leeks, onions, garlic, peeled tomatoes, and spices, and then pureed. Second, **rouille**: A sauce of crushed garlic, egg yolk, and spices, this flavorful concoction is indispensable with a true bouillabaisse. Finally, **pieds et paquets**: Made from sheep stomach stuffed with chopped intestines, salted meat, garlic, and parsley, all of which is then rolled into "paquets" and cooked in tomato-and-white-wine sauce for a minimum of seven hours, it tastes much better than it sounds.

UNDER 50F • Il Caftea. This brasserie oozes hospitality. Best bet is one of the excellent salads (40F–50F), served on an alluring terrace. *63 cours Julien, tel. 04–91–42–02–19, Métro: Notre-Dame du Mont.*

Hammeche. For the best couscous in town, plunge into what feels like it has been pulled straight out of a medina of the Maghreb. At lunch, 30F will get you a drink, a *salade méchouia* (a spicy vegetable puree of tomatoes, eggplant, roasted garlic, and olive oil) or other appetizer, and a main course (like a heaping bowl of couscous). *31 rue du Bon Pasteur. No phone. Métro: Jules Guesde.*

UNDER 75F • L'Art et les Thés. Within the walls of the Vieille Charité, this tearoom will allow you to take in the 17th-century surroundings at the speed of a sip. Lunch menus run 70F for a salad and a main course. Saturday nights, there is a dinner jazz spectacle for 115F. *Centre de la Vieille Charité–2 rue de la Vieille Charité, tel. 04–91–14–58–71. Closed Sun. and all evenings but Sat.*

Marseille has a high incidence of crime and violence, so be careful cruising the streets after dark, and don't forget that many bus lines stop running at 8 or 9 PM.

Auberge'In. This vegetarian hole-in-the-wall is a friendly spot where earthy types converge around polished picnic tables. A three-course meal with wine, which includes a braised vegetable dish on a corn crepe, goes for 65F. *25 rue Chevalier-Roze, tel. 04–91–90–51–59. Métro: Vieux-Port. Parallel to rue de la République off Grande Rue. Closed Sun.*

UNDER 100F • Le Caveau des Accoules. With low lights, blackboards boasting daily regional specials (60F–100F), and simple wood tables, this local dive is Marseille as it was. There's live music on Friday and Saturday, and cold beer every night. Follow the *cave à bières* sign up the steps from the Grand' Rue/rue Caisserie in the Panier. *8 montée des Accoules, tel. 04–91–56–02–52. Closed Sun.*

Chez Madie–les Galinettes. Every morning Madie Minassian, the colorful *patronne,* bustles along the quayside to trade insults with the fishwives and scour their catch for the freshest specimens. They swiftly end up in her bouillabaisse, fish soup, and *favouilles* (sauce of tiny local crabs). Go for the 85F or 100F menu, or splurge on the 150F menu or à la carte. *138 quai du Port, tel. 04–91–90–40–87. Métro: Vieux-Port. Closed Sun. and most of Aug.*

WORTH SEEING

Marseille's museums are numerous, but not all sparkle with brilliance. The **Palais Longchamp** (blvd. Philippon) is an imposing 19th-century building that used to be the end of an aqueduct. It now houses the **Musée des Beaux-Arts** (tel. 04–91–14–59–30), whose collection of paintings and sculptures includes works by 18th-century Italian artist Giovanni Battista Tiepolo, Peter Paul Rubens, and French caricaturist and painter Honoré Daumier. Also in the Palais Longchamp, the **Musée d'Histoire Naturelle** (tel. 04–91–14–59–50) has stuffed wildlife. North of the Vieux Port, the **Musée du Vieux Marseille** (in the 16th-century Maison Diamantée, rue de la Prison, tel. 04–91–55–10–19), which may still be closed for renovation, depicts daily life in Marseille during the 18th and 19th centuries. The museums are open Tuesday–Sunday 10–5 in winter and 11–6 in summer, and all charge a 12F admission.

ABBAYE ST-VICTOR

This abbey was built in the 5th century in honor of St. Victor, the patron saint of sailors and millers. The abbey was destroyed in the 10th century during the Saracen invasion and rebuilt in the 11th and 12th centuries with an emphasis on fortification. In the spooky underground **crypt** (admission 10F), you can see what's left of the 5th-century abbey, as well as pagan and Christian sarcophagi. *Rue Sainte. Admission free. Open daily 8:30 AM–9:15 PM.*

BASILIQUE DE NOTRE-DAME DE LA GARDE

The most imposing structure of Marseille's cityscape, this 19th-century basilica overlooks the city from a limestone cliff. The Virgin Mary guards Marseille from atop the tower. Inside, colorful murals and mosaics shroud the walls, and there is a vaulted crypt. *Blvd. A. Aune. Take Bus 60 from cours Jean Ballard, just south of quai des Belges, or walk 30 mins through Jardin de la Colonne above cours Pierre Puget. Open daily 7 AM–8 PM (until 7 off-season).*

CENTRE DE LA VIEILLE CHARITE

This restored 17th-century hospice and present-day cultural center is probably the sight most worth your time. Trek through the winding streets of le Panier to get here, and you'll be rewarded with excellent and diverse exhibits. The **Musée d'Archéologie Méditerranéenne** displays primarily Egyptian and Celto-Ligurian artifacts, and the **Musée des Arts Africains, Océaniens et Amerindiens** has traditional art from Africa, Oceania, and the Americas. *2 rue de la Charité, tel. 04–91–14–58–80. Admission is 12F for each museum or 25F–30F for a museum and its temporary exhibits. Open June–Sept., Tues.–Sun. 11–6; Oct.–May, Tues.–Sun. 10–5.*

JARDIN DES VESTIGES

One block north of la Canebière, the Jardin des Vestiges is a shady retreat from city mayhem. Plots of grass surround excavated ruins of the ancient Greek settlement and port. On the premises you'll find the **Musée d'Histoire de Marseille** (tel. 04–91–90–42–22), a simple museum that enlightens you about Marseille's ancient history (in French only) and displays the freeze-dried wooden remains of an ancient Roman ship. The museum is open Monday–Saturday noon–7; admission is 10F.

MUSEE CANTINI

The 17th-century Hôtel de Montgrand houses an excellent collection of modern art. The permanent display of fauvist, cubist, and surrealist works includes canvases by Dufy, Le Corbusier, Matisse, and Picasso. Also watch for impressive temporary exhibits of contemporary art. *19 rue Grignan, tel. 04–91–54–77–75. Admission 12F. Open Tues.–Sun. 11–6 (until 5 off-season).*

MUSEE DES DOCKS ROMAINS

Housing the remains of one of the rare existing Roman warehouses known in the world, this impressive space is also devoted to archaeological objects related to trade in ancient Marseille. *Pl. Vivaux on rue du Lacydon, parallel to rue du Port, tel. 04–91–91–24–62. Admission 12F. Open Oct.–May, Tues.–Sun. 10–5; June–Sept., Tues.–Sun. 11–6.*

CHEAP THRILLS

The most easily accessible thrill is the daily **morning fish market** on quai des Belges; it's open 8 AM–1 PM but is most active from 9 to 11. If fish don't thrill you, you might peruse the other markets: On Tuesday, Thursday, Friday, and Saturday mornings, everything from used clothing to tomatoes is on sale at place Jean Jaurès; a similar market at place Castellane is held Monday–Saturday mornings, the one on Friday being the biggest. Food is available daily except Sunday 8–7 on place des Capucins.

FESTIVALS

Marseille's biggest festivals take place in July. The **Festival de Marseille** (6 pl. Sadi Carnot, tel. 04–91–99–00–20, fax 04–91–99–00–22) celebrates the city's rich heritage with numerous concerts and exhibits. Tickets are 120F–400F. Thursday–Saturday in October, at the Docks des Suds, the **Fiesta des Suds** (12 rue Urbain V, tel. 04–91–99–00–00) has food, events, and ongoing music from artists celebrating what it means to be Mediterranean. Events/concerts cost 50F–100F. Film buffs will enjoy the **Vue sur les Docs** (3 sq. Stalingrad, tel. 04–95–04–44–90) in June. Devoted to documentary films, it sees 100 films from 20 countries projected, discussed, and rewarded. Inquire at the tourist office about other festivals and free concerts.

AFTER DARK

Partly due to its huge student population, Marseille is a city that gets going when the sun sets. The hottest glitzy bar and restaurant scenes are along **cours Honoré d'Estienne d'Orvès** and **place de**

Thiars, by the Vieux Port. In contrast, **cours Julien, place Jean Jaurès,** and the streets in between (**rue des Trois-Rois** and **rue des Trois-Mages**) attract a younger, cooler, funkier crowd. Pick up a free copy of *Taktik* at the tourist office or around town to find out about concerts and theater performances.

Near the Vieux Port, **Bistrot Thiars** (38 pl. Thiars, tel. 04–91–33–07–25) has music and a nice outdoor terrace. For a mellow night, go to the beautifully decorated **Café Parisian** (1 pl. Sadi Carnot, tel. 04–91–90–05–77), where you can study the art on the walls or play a game of chess until as late as 4 AM. An eclectic crowd goes to **La Maison Hantée** (10 rue Vian, tel. 04–91–92–09–40), where the cover is 30F–50F. The only two gay bars in Marseille, predominantly for men, are located next to each other: **Kempson** (22 rue Beauvau, tel. 04–91–33–79–20) and **MP Bar** (10 rue Beauvau, tel. 04–91–33–64–79).

May Be Blues (2 rue Poggioli, tel. 04–91–42–41–00) is a low-key jazz and blues club with no cover (but slightly expensive drinks). At **Garbo** (9 quai de Rive Neuve, tel. 04–91–33–34–20) you can rub elbows with hip, well-dressed locals for no cover. **New Can-Can** (3–7 rue Sénac de Meilhan, tel. 04–91–48–59–76) is a popular gay disco with a 60F–90F cover; it's closed Tuesday and Wednesday.

OUTDOOR ACTIVITIES

Considering Marseille's dirty, big-city reputation, the tranquil beaches stretching eastward come as a welcome surprise. Take Bus 19 (9F) from the Old Port to reach the **Prado bathing area,** which has pebbly shores; calm, light blue waters; and access to Windsurfer rentals. The best beaches and swim spots are farther along the coast at **Cassis** and **Les Calanques** (*see* Near Marseille, *below*). Les Calanques are also ideal for scuba diving, snorkeling, hiking, and climbing; the GR98 parallels the coastline from Callelongue to Cassis. Further information on these activities can be obtained from the Marseille tourist office. Ask for a free copy of *Marseille by the Sea.*

As long as the skies are clear (and they invariably are), head to the beach. If rain strikes, drown your sorrows in a glass of the famed white wine and try your luck at Cassis's Casino Municipal (av. du Prof. Leriche, tel. 04–42–01–78–32).

NEAR MARSEILLE

CHATEAU D'IF

Imagine an ancient Alcatraz off the coast of Marseille instead of San Francisco and there you have Château d'If—a 16th-century fortress turned prison surrounded by the sea, from which few inmates ever returned. During the 17th-century Religious Wars, more than 3,500 Protestants were imprisoned and killed here, and when you enter the castle, you'll find a note of apology for what happened. The château's most memorable prisoner was Alexander Dumas's Count of Monte Cristo, and you can still see the hole from which he is said to have made his escape.

As you wander about the castle, note the graffiti engraved by prisoners along the crumbling walls. There are also a number of temporary photographic exhibits in the cells. You can get to the roof of the castle via an old spiral staircase and from there enjoy a spectacular view of Marseille and the surrounding coastline. Once you leave the castle, it's possible to meander around the fortified walls of the perimeter. You can also swim off the island's rocky edges, but better swimming conditions are found next door at the Iles du Frioul. *Admission 25F. Open Apr.–Sept., daily 9–7; Oct.–Mar., Tues.–Sun. 9–5:30.*

COMING AND GOING

G.A.C.M. boats (tel. 04–91–55–50–09) leave nearly every hour between 7 AM and 6:30 PM from 1 quai des Belges at Marseille's Old Port. The 15-minute ride to the Ile d'If costs 50F round-trip; you can include the Iles du Frioul for 80F.

CASSIS

Cassis serves as a reminder of why so many artists have flocked to the Mediterranean. It's a beautiful merging of sea, sand, and sun. Originally a coral-fishing village, the tiny port is now an upscale beach town filled with restaurants, shops, and expensive villas.

Directly in front of the town is the beach, **plage de la Grande Mer.** In summer, it is equipped with lockers (10F), private showers (15F), and snack bars. You can rent a Windsurfer for 70F an hour on the beach (tel. 04–42–01–80–01). Ask at the **tourist office** (pl. Baragnon, tel. 04–42–01–71–17, fax 04–42–01–28–31) for free **hiking maps** to the Calanques (*see below*), a succession of breathtaking white cliffs and coves extending from Cassis to Marseille. It's open September–April, Monday–Saturday 9–1 and 2–6, Sunday 9–12:30; June, daily 9–6; and July–August, daily 9–7:30. The tourist office will also set you up with a list of vineyards in the area, where you can taste the city's famous white wines.

COMING AND GOING

The best way to reach Cassis is by bus, because the train station is 3 km (2 mi) from town. From Marseille, the **Cariane Provence** (tel. 04–91–79–81–82) bus takes 40 minutes and costs 22F, but the bus driver might make you shell out another 8F for luggage. The first bus to Cassis leaves at 7:40 AM and the last returns to Marseille at 6:30 PM.

WHERE TO SLEEP

If you plan to stay overnight, the cheapest hotels in town are 195F–290F for a double at **Hôtel le Laurence** (8 rte. de l'Arène, tel. 04–42–01–88–78) or 190F–250F at **Hôtel le Provençal** (7 av. Victor Hugo, tel. 04–42–01–72–13). The prices of the latter go up by 100F per room in July and August. A one-hour walk uphill from Cassis on a bluff overlooking the ocean is the **Auberge de Jeunesse** (tel. 04–42–01–02–72). Reception is open 8 AM–10 AM and 5 PM–11 PM). This compulsively eco-friendly hostel is perfectly positioned for a hike down to Les Calanques (*see below*). Beds cost 50F with HI card, 69F without; bring your own groceries to cook in the kitchen. Ten minutes by foot from town is **Camping Les Cigales** (rte. de Marseille, tel. 04–42–01–07–34), which charges 60F for a tent site. Some travelers try sleeping on the beach, though it does get pretty windy and lighting a fire is strictly forbidden—the area was badly burned in 1989.

FOOD

Le Chaudron (4 rue Adolphe Thier, tel. 04–42–01–74–18), which has a great outdoor terrace, serves fresh pastas (around 50F–65F) and good Provençal food (100F prix fixe). Stock up on groceries at one of the three **Casino** supermarkets (there's one next to the port at 2 av. Victor Hugo), or go to the **market** Wednesday and Friday mornings on place du Marché.

LES CALANQUES

The coastline between Marseille and Cassis is dominated by steep limestone cliffs protecting calm aquamarine water. Millions of years of shifts in the earth's crust have produced stratified white cliffs, from which species of fern stretch diagonally toward the sky. The picturesque *calanques* (coves), which stretch 20 km (12 mi), make you feel as if you've stumbled onto the set of *The Blue Lagoon*. Unfortunately, they're hardly a secret, and you'll find plenty of nude bathers, snorkelers, and swimmers. This is undeniably one of the best places to hike, mountain climb, bird-watch, and snorkel.

COMING AND GOING

GACM (1 quai des Belges, tel. 04–91–55–50–09) conducts 100F boat tours year-round on weekends and Wednesday (daily in July and August), leaving from Marseille's Vieux Port at 2 PM and returning at 6 PM. This tour does not, however, actually *stop* at Les Calanques.

Some people believe that a better way to explore is from Cassis (*see above*). Boats leave from the port of Cassis for various destinations in Les Calanques for 50F–90F. A basic 50F trip includes stops at the three closest calanques, **Port Miou, Port Pin,** and **En Vau,** and lasts about 55 minutes; for 90F you can see all eight. If you're feeling active, the tourist office in Cassis has maps that show how to get to Les Calanques on foot. From Cassis, it's a half-hour walk to Port Miou, the first calanque, which is packed with sailboats; in another half hour you'll reach Port Pin, where pine trees descend down to the water. Be sure to bring lots of water, as the sun and salt take their toll.

HYÈRES AND LES ÎLES D'HYÈRES

The aristocrats and the famous may have moved farther into the hills or to Cannes and Nice, but Hyères—a modern resort town and a traditional medieval village above the Mediterranean—is still a great vacation spot for those with leaner pocketbooks. Once luminaries such as Madame de Stael,

Queen Victoria, Tolstoy, and Robert Louis Stevenson all alighted on this breezy plateau, and the town has somehow conserved its allure and been spared the onslaught of tourists. Palm trees grace the boulevards leading up to the old town, and the medieval centre ville capped with castle ruins has a vil-lagelike feel. Just off the coast are the Iles d'Hyères, a set of small islands known as the *îles d'or* (golden islands) because of the sun glinting off the rocks. The islands seem to have escaped the worst of the tourist glitz that plagues other Riviera spots. Nevertheless, hotels and restaurants are still super-expen-sive; make a day of it and stay in Hyères or Toulon.

The largest of the three islands, **Porquerolles,** is 8 km (5 mi) long, 2 km (1 mi) wide, and popular for its white beaches and pristine, turquoise waters. Rent a bike in the little village and cruise around this most mountainous and densely forested of the three islands. You can rent Windsurfers on the biggest beach, **plage de Notre Dame.** For more information, contact the tourist office (tel. 04–94–58–33–76, fax 04–94–58–36–39). The entire island of **Port-Cros** is a national park, with exotic flora that you can see by hiking along one of the numerous trails. The **tourist office** there (tel. 04–94–12–82–30, fax 04–94–12–82–31) hands out brochures for the popular botanical walk; the island's greenery is particularly lush because of the natural springs on the island. Bring along your snorkeling gear: The underwater world is as scenic as the one above. If you visit **Ile du Levant,** you can leave your clothes behind—the island is home to France's first nudist colony, **Héliopolis.** Don't expect *Baywatch* when you go; the island is mainly fre-quented by families and naturalists. Ironically, the other 90% of the island is inaccessible military terrain. This is the only island you can camp on.

BASICS

The **tourist office** (av. de Belgique, tel. 04–94–65–18–55, fax 04–94–35–85–05) in Hyères is in the old, resort-style Rotonde Jean Salusse. Ask about information on hotels and the Iles d'Hyères. It's open April–September, weekdays 8:30–5:30, and Saturday 10–noon and 2–5; October–March, weekdays 8:30—6, and Saturday 10–noon and 2–5.

COMING AND GOING

You can get to Ile du Levant from Hyères (66F one-way or 115 round-trip) with **TLV** (tel. 04–94–58–21–81), or from le Lavandou (70F one-way or 124F round-trip) via **Vedettes des Iles d'Or** (tel. 04–94–71–01–02). From Toulon, it's easier to reach Porquerolles and Port Cros than Ile du Levant. **Le Batelier de la Rade** (tel. 04–94–46–24–65) makes two trips a day during July and August to Porquerolles and Port-Cros, and **Transmed 2000** (tel. 04–94–92–96–82) makes three. Trips are more infrequent outside of July and August, usually with just one departure at 10 AM and one return at 5 PM from Porquerolles. Check at the dock for exact times. The price with both companies is 100F round-trip. Hyères is an easy trip from Marseille on the **TER Metra-Côte d'Azur** line (1½ hrs, 70F); Toulon is halfway in between (45 min, 75F). The train station is a little less than 2 km (1 mi) from the centre ville; follow avenue Edith Cavell up the hill, cross the busy highway, and continue up to the old town.

WHERE TO SLEEP AND EAT

In Hyères, stay in the superfriendly **Hôtel du Portalet** (4 rue de Limans, tel. 04–94–65–39–40, fax 04–94–35–86–33) in the heart of the old town. Doubles run 195F–230F. Hyères has some good restaurants with outdoor terraces on **place Massillon,** or try the excellent and reasonable American-owned **La Coupole** (2 rue Léon Gautier, tel. 04–94–12–88–00).

THE RIVIERA

UPDATED BY SOPHIE MACKENZIE SMITH

The French Riviera, or the Côte d'Azur, is a stunning stretch of Mediterranean coastline that sweeps from St-Tropez to the Italian border. For decades the Riviera has been the playground of Europe, conjuring up images of beautiful beach resorts and the expensive, glamorous lifestyles of celebrities. Although these images belie reality—many beaches are pebbly and overcrowded, and the movie stars have fled to hidden estates in the hills—the sun, the sights, and the sparkling Mediterranean are still alluring. Furthermore, if you venture beyond Nice, Cannes, and Monaco, you will find small resort towns with their own distinctive character; hilltop medieval villages with narrow, winding streets; and olive trees anchored in the slopes above the sea.

Life along the coast revolves around the beach, although some places charge up to 150F for the right to a plot of sand, a foam pad, and an umbrella. More active sun worshipers take to beachside activities like snorkeling, diving, and windsurfing, as well as to the pick-up scene that rages throughout Cannes and Nice. Hiking on the trails that wind upward through coastal villages is an excellent way to avoid throngs of tourists in July and August and to wonder at the spectacular views commanding the coastline. If you prefer history and culture to the beach (or like them both), head to Vence, St-Paul-de-Vence, Antibes, Menton, and Cagnes, which attracted the likes of Picasso, Matisse, Miró, Renoir, and Cocteau, who left a trail of modest but impressive museums.

In addition to enjoying more than 300 days of sun per year, the Riviera is blessed with multiple mountain ranges that protect the coast from harsh northern winds. Running east to west, these include the snowcapped peaks of the Alpes Maritimes; the Massif des Maures, which stretches 64 km (40 mi) toward Fréjus; and the red volcanic rocks of the Massif de l'Esterel, which tumble their way toward Cannes. Fortunately, the lifestyle among these hills and mountains transcends the superficial quality of beach resorts.

If you can, come to the Riviera between April and early June or September, when prices are lower, the crowds aren't so dense, the weather is perfect, and there's plenty going on. May brings the manic **Cannes Film Festival.** The biggest party in Europe occurs during Nice's **Carnival,** two weeks before Lent. July and August bring what feels like all of Europe and half of the United States (including jazz greats at Juan-les-Pins's international jazz festival). Restaurant prices rise and hotel rates soar as much as 50%. Then again, many of the beach towns come out of hibernation *only* in summer, and most hostels and campgrounds are open June–September only. Most of the museums stay open year-round.

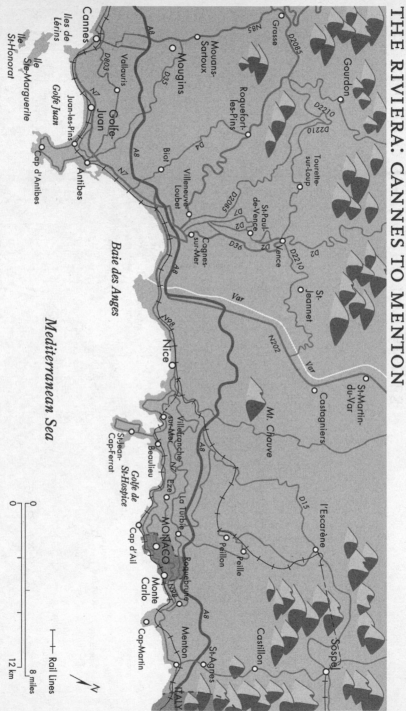

THE RIVIERA: CANNES TO MENTON

Cannes
Iles de Lérins
Golfe Juan
Ile Ste-Marguerite
Ile St-Honorat

Mediterranean Sea

Baie des Anges

Cap d'Antibes
Antibes
Juan-les-Pins
Golfe-Juan
Vallauris
Mougins
Mouans-Sartoux
Grasse
Gourdon

D803
N7
D35
A8
N85
D2085
D2210

Biot
Roquefort-les-Pins
Villeneuve-Loubet
Cagnes-sur-Mer
St-Paul-de-Vence
Vence
Tourette-sur-Loup
D4
D7
D2
D36
N2
D2085
D2210

Var
St-Jeannet
St-Jeannet

Nice
N98
Mt. Chauve
Castagniers
St-Martin-du-Var
N202
A8

Villefranche-sur-Mer
Beaulieu
St-Jean-Cap-Ferrat
Golfe de St-Hospice
Cap d'Ail
Eze
La Turbie
MONACO
Monte Carlo
Roquebrune
Peillon
Peille
l'Escarène
Sospel
Castillon
D15
A8
N7
N98

Cap-Martin
Menton
St-Agnès
ITALY

N
Rail Lines

0   8 miles
0   12 km

367

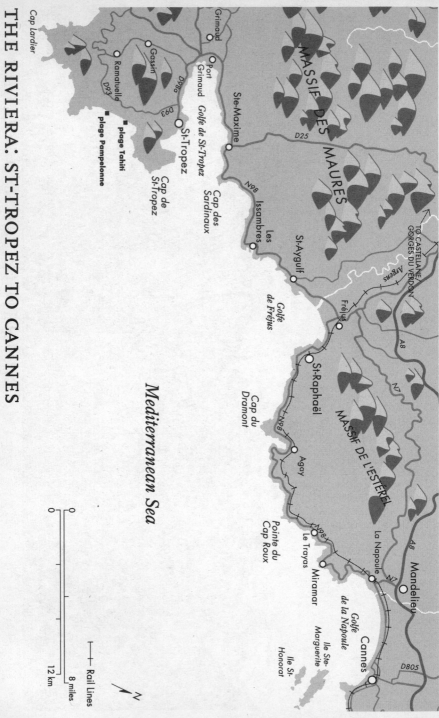

THE RIVIERA: ST-TROPEZ TO CANNES

Cap Lardier

Grimaud

Gassin

Ramatuelle

D93

plage Tahiti

plage Pampelonne

Port Grimaud

St-Tropez

Cap de St-Tropez

Golfe de St-Tropez

D98A

Ste-Maxime

Cap des Sardinaux

Les Issambres

N98

St-Aygulf

MASSIF DES MAURES

D25

Golfe de Fréjus

Fréjus

Argens

A8

N7

TO CASTELLANE, GORGES DU VERDON

St-Raphaël

Cap du Dramont

N98

Agay

MASSIF DE L'ESTEREL

Pointe du Cap Roux

Le Trayas

N98

Miramar

La Napoule

N7

A8

Mandelieu

Golfe de la Napoule

Cannes

Ile Ste-Marguerite

Ile St-Honorat

D805

Mediterranean Sea

N

12 km

8 miles

Rail Lines

BASICS

VISITOR INFORMATION

All tourist offices provide maps, hotel and camping lists, calendars of festivals and events, and museum info. Most keep longer hours in summer, and some even give up their precious midday lunch break. The regional tourist office, the **Comité Régional Riviera Côte d'Azur** (55 promenade des Anglais, tel. 04–93–37–78–78), is in Nice, as is the **Centre Régional Information Jeunesse Côte d'Azur** (19 rue Gioffredo, tel. 04–93–80–93–93), which distributes information on hostels, camping, sports, and special deals for people under 26.

The Blue Coast Journal and *The Riviera Reporter,* two monthly English-language magazines, are worth checking out for info on upcoming attractions, local history and current events and for snippets of useful local information for ex-pats; their classified sections also list short-term rentals. You can find them in some tourist offices, English-language bookstores, and *tabacs* (tobacco shops). **Riviera Radio,** 106.3 and 106.5 FM, is an English-speaking radio station that broadcasts up and down the coast.

GETTING AROUND

The **Métrazur** (TER) rail line runs along the coast from Fréjus in the west to Ventimiglia, Italy, in the east for 12F–80F one way, depending on the distance you go; trains come about every half hour. The journey provides fantastic views of the Riviera as the train dives into tunnels and then bursts into the sunlight above sparkling bays. To reach coastal towns farther west, such as St-Tropez, or to get to inland towns, you have to take a bus. The big train stations in St-Raphaël, Cannes, and Nice all have direct lines to Paris.

Biking is also an excellent way to explore the Riviera's mountains and beaches. Be careful on the roads that run parallel to the coast: Bike lanes have not yet caught on here. Quieter roads run inland, and many hiking trails are accessible by mountain bikes. You can take bikes on most trains for free, but try traveling in the morning or evening to avoid crowds. Bikes go for 50F–150F a day; the cheapest moped is 100F a day; for both, expect to leave a hefty deposit or a credit card. Rent a helmet, too, or you may end up paying a whopping 900F penalty. Bicycles and motorbikes are allowed on the N98, or Corniche, which runs parallel to the Riviera coast and has spectacular views. Just follow road signs that say BORD DU MER (along the water).

If you are sticking to the coast, public transportation is adequate; inland it is worth renting a **car,** although it can be expensive. Reserve well in advance as there is an overall shortage of car rentals on the Côte d'Azur and be sure to use the correct type of gas. To go any distance use the A8, but scenically it is worth taking the small coast roads. Be aware, however, that in the summer these roads back up for miles, especially in the evening when people are leaving the beaches.

WHERE TO SLEEP

The Riviera is one of the most expensive regions of Europe. Much to the chagrin of the jet-setters, however, more and more budget hotels have opened in recent years. Getting a room at one of these places is another matter entirely: In summer, reserving in advance is essential. Patrolling cops may thwart any intentions to crash on the beach; you're better off going to one of the Côte d'Azur's many campgrounds, for 50F–100F for two. Pick up the *Camping Caravaning* brochure in any tourist office.

NICE

If a quiet, beach-town escape is what you're looking for, then Nice is not the destination for you. But if you're after top-notch museums, a charming old quarter, scads of ethnic restaurants, and a raging nightlife (not to mention an overabundance of tourists), then you'll have a blast. With nearly 450,000 residents and more than 3 million visitors annually, Nice is the Riviera's largest, most dynamic city. In summer, the boulevards are jam-packed and the pebbly beaches along the Promenade des Anglais are swarming with scantily clad bodies; in winter, Nice remains active while other Riviera towns snooze. Because of the budget options available, Nice makes an excellent base from which to take day trips into the surrounding area. The most exciting time to visit Nice is during **Carnival,** a celebration with parades, music, dancing, and general debauchery two weeks before Lent.

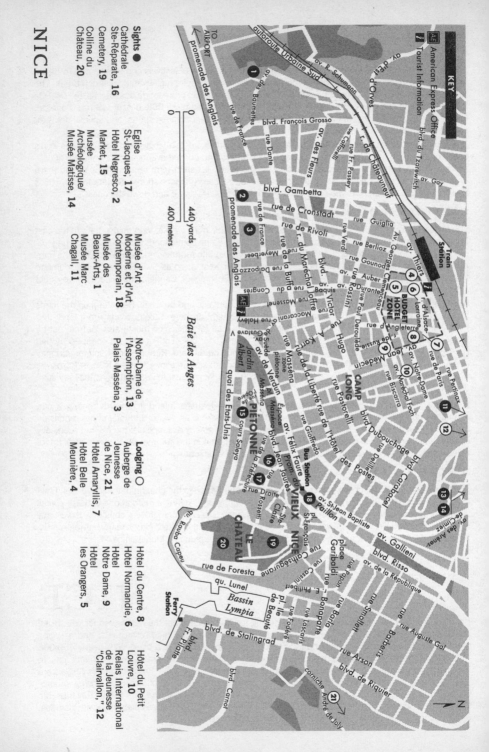

NICE

Sights ●

Cathédrale
Ste-Réparate, **16**
Cemetery, **19**
Colline du
Château, **20**

Eglise
St-Jacques, **17**
Hôtel Negresco, **2**
Market, **15**
Musée
Archéologique/
Musée Matisse, **14**

Musée d'Art
Moderne et d'Art
Contemporain, **18**
Musée des
Beaux-Arts, **1**
Musée Marc
Chagall, **11**

Notre-Dame de
l'Assomption, **13**
Palais Masséna, **3**

Lodging ○

Auberge de
Jeunesse
de Nice, **21**
Hôtel Amaryllis, **7**
Hôtel Belle
Meunière, **4**

Hôtel du Centre, **8**
Hôtel Normandie, **6**
Hôtel
Nôtre Dame, **9**
Hôtel
les Orangers, **5**

Hôtel du Petit
Louvre, **10**
Relais International
de la Jeunesse
"Clairvallon," **12**

BASICS

AMERICAN EXPRESS

The main AmEx office has the best exchange rates on itstraveler's checks. *11 promenade des Anglais, at rue du Congrès, tel. 04–93–16–53–53. Open daily 9–8 in winter,8–11 in summer.*

BUREAUX DE CHANGE

Thomas Cook offices, banks, and automated change machines are all over the city, especially near the train station and along avenue Jean Médecin. All offer comparable rates and charge no commission.

DISCOUNT TRAVEL AGENCIES

Wasteels (32 rue de l'Hôtel des Postes, tel. 08–03–88–70–54) is a place for discounts as well as ferry tickets to Corsica.

ENGLISH-LANGUAGE BOOKSTORE

The **Cat's Whiskers** (30 rue Lamartine, tel. 04–93–80–02–66) sells classics, best-sellers, travel books, and phrase books. It's closed daily for lunch.

LAUNDRY

Two Laundromats in the budget hotel area are **Le Salon Lavoir** (16 rue d'Angleterre), open daily 7 AM–9 PM; and **Laverie du Mono Laundry** (8 rue de Belgique), open daily 7 AM–11 PM. Figure about 30F–40F per load to wash and dry, and another 4F for soap from the dispenser.

MAIL

The main **post office** (23 av. Thiers, tel. 04–93–82–65–00) is directly across from the train station. Most branch offices are open weekdays 8–7 and Saturday 8–noon, although some close the first and third Tuesday and Wednesday of the month. Nice's postal code is 06000.

MEDICAL AID

Pharmacies abound, each one displaying on the door the closest late-night drugstore. There's a **24-hour pharmacy** (except Sunday) in the *zone piétonne* (pedestrian zone); look for it at 7 rue Masséna (tel. 04–93–87–78–94). In case of emergency, contact the **Hôpital St-Roch** (5 rue Pierre-Dévoluy, tel. 04–92–03–33–33).

VISITOR INFORMATION

The first **tourist office** (tel. 04–93–87–07–07) you encounter is to your left as you exit the train station. The staff reserves rooms, doles out maps, and can point you in the right direction. They also have brochures in English on lodging, transportation, and upcoming events. Other tourist office branches are near the **beach** (5 Promenade des Anglais, tel. 04–92–14–48–00); at **Nice-Ferber** (on Promenade des Anglais, near airport, tel. 04–93–83–32–64); and at the **airport** (Terminal 1, tel. 04–93–21–44–11). All four offices keep similar hours: open mid-September–June, daily 9–6; July–mid-September, daily 8–8.

COMING AND GOING

BY TRAIN

Nice has three train stations; be sure you have the right one. The main train station is **Thiers** (av. Thiers, tel. 08–36–35–35–35), on the north edge of town; it serves all lines along the Riviera and the main lines to Paris and other major cities. The other two, **Gare de Riquier** (east side of town) and **Gare St-Augustin** (west side of town), serve the local lines along the coast. There are no luggage carts and only one *baggagiste* (porter). Paris takes more than 10 hours overnight (430F; reserve a 90F overnight sleeping car, or *couchette*). Or zip to Nice via Marseille in about seven hours (430F) on the TGV. The luggage-service desk, open daily 7 AM–10 PM, stores bags in lockers for 30F per day; 35F for a bicycle.

BY BUS

RCA runs buses every half hour between Nice and Cannes 6 AM–9 PM Monday–Saturday and 8:30 AM–8 PM on Sunday. This bus stops at Cagnes-sur-Mer (35 mins, 16F), Antibes (1 hr 10 mins, 25F), and Juan-les-Pins (1 hr 15 mins, 27F). RCA also runs three buses per hour to Menton (1 hr 10 mins, 24F),

CUISINE PROVENCALE

Riviera cuisine is a blend of seafood, herbs, and fresh produce from the fields of Provence. Specialties include the following: aioli (a garlicky, mayonnaise-based sauce); bouillabaisse (a fish stew, served with rouille, a spicy hot-pepper and saffron sauce); pan-bagnat (sandwiches of anchovies, tomatoes, tuna, and olives); pissaladière (pizza with onions, olives, and anchovies); porchetta (roast pork with herbs and spices); ratatouille (zucchini, eggplant, onions, peppers, and tomatoes simmered in herbs); salade niçoise (greens with tomatoes, tuna, anchovies, and olives); socca (a chickpea crepe); and tapenade (an olive paste).

with stops in Villefranche-sur-Mer (20 mins, 9F), St-Jean-Cap-Ferrat (25 mins, 12F), Èze (30 mins, 14F), Cap d'Ail (35 mins, 20F), and Monaco (45 mins, 18F). **SAP** buses makes the one-hour, 24F trip to Vence Monday–Saturday, 22 times a day. **Phoceens-Cars** will take you farther to Aix-en-Provence, Marseille, and Avignon twice daily for 125F–150F. *Bus station: Promenade du Paillon, on edge of Vieux Nice, tel. 04–93–85–61–81. Open Mon.—Sat. 6:30 AM–8 PM.*

BY PLANE

More than 30 airlines serve the international Aéroport Nice–Côte d'Azur. **Air France** (tel. 08–02–80–28–02 toll free) flights leave for Paris more than 20 times a day and cost 345F–1,000F (depending on your age and the season). It also provides service to Corsica.

To get to the **airport,** take Bus 23 or 24 (direction: St-Laurent-du-Var) from the train station. One bus leaves every 30 minutes and costs 8F for the 45-minute trip. The Aèroport–Nice Direct bus takes less time but costs 21F; buses leave every 20 minutes.

BY FERRY

SNCM runs ferries to Corsica from the Old Port six–seven times per day in the summer. Sailing from Nice is cheaper and quicker than from anywhere else in France. Full-price tickets run around 282F. Buy tickets in advance, particularly in summer. *See* Chapter 13 for more information. *Quai du Commerce, tel. 04–93–13–66–99.*

GETTING AROUND

Nice extends southward from the train station toward the deep-blue waters of the **Baie des Anges** (Bay of Angels). Walking down avenue Jean Médicin from the train station takes you to the chic pedestrian zone of place Masséna. Not far to the east is **Vieux Nice** (Old Nice), a maze of quaint, commercial streets. The Promenade des Anglais, a crowded beachfront stretch in the newer part of town, is just a 10-minute walk from the train station; it becomes quai des Etats-Unis as you walk east into the Old Town. **Les Trains Touristiques de Nice** operates a miniature, open-air train that departs from Casino Ruhl on Promenade des Anglais and travels through Vieux Nice, giving you a good feel for the city. Trains run daily 10–6; the 40-minute round-trip costs 30F.

BY BUS

If you get tired of walking, **Service Urbain de Nice (SUN)** runs air-conditioned buses throughout the city. A ticket costs 8F if you buy it on the bus; a carnet (booklet) of five tickets costs 34F. Day passes are 22F. Carnets and passes can be purchased at the **central station** (10 av. Félix Faure, tel. 04–93–16–52–10) or in tabacs around town.

BY BIKE OR MOPED

A good place to rent bikes and mopeds is **Nicea Location Rent** (9 av. Thiers, tel. 04–93–82–42–71), across from the train station and open daily 9–6. Bicycles are 120F a day or 650F a week, plus a 1,500F deposit. Mopeds require a 4,000F deposit and cost 150F a day or 945F a week. Mandatory helmet rental is 15F. At least they take Visa and American Express.

WHERE TO SLEEP

A number of budget hotels, especially in the area just south of the train station, makes Nice a good base for exploring the pricey Riviera. Prices are considerably higher in July and August and drop 10% off-season.

UNDER 150F • Hôtel Belle Meunière. Americans swarm to this conveniently located, family-run hotel with spartan and cramped but clean rooms. Dorm spaces (in rooms with four beds) are 75F and 85F with shower; both include breakfast. Doubles are 145F–275F with shower and breakfast included. A room for two with kitchenette is 190F—a good bet if you want to take advantage of the local food markets. Hall showers are 10F for five minutes. *21 av. Durante, tel. 04–93–88–66–15. 17 rooms, 12 with bath. Laundry. Closed Dec. and Jan.*

UNDER 200F • Hôtel du Centre. Recently renovated rooms, under new management, are bright, as is the communal TV space. The international crowd that stays here further livens the scene. Single rooms start at 174F, doubles go for 207F, and those for up to four people are 100F per person. *2 rue de Suisse, tel. 04–93–88–83–85, fax 04–93–82–29–80. 28 rooms, 20 with shower.*

Hôtel les Orangers. Popular with Americans and Australians, this hotel has showers and refrigerators in every room and is surprisingly cheap: Dorm spaces go for 85F, singles for 90F, and doubles for 180F–200F. For 20F more, you even get breakfast in bed! The management works hard to guarantee the safety of its guests, making this a great place for women traveling alone. *10 bis av. Durante, tel. 04–93–87–51–41, fax 04–93–82–57–82. 12 rooms, all with bath. Refrigerators.*

> *If you get tired of the sun, sea, and sand, head for the hills. Biot, St-Paul-de-Vence, and Grasse all make great day trips. Ask at any regional tourist office for "Les Balades de Cimazur," booklets describing the best of back-road exploring in the area.*

UNDER 250F • Hôtel du Petit Louvre. This homey hotel is full of charm and character. Singles start at 165F with shower; 220F gets you a double with shower. Triples are 270F. *10 rue Emma Tiranty, tel. 04–93–80–15–54, fax 04–93–62–45–08. 34 rooms, all with bath. Closed Nov.–Jan.*

UNDER 350F • Hotel Amaryllis. This modern, welcoming hotel has doubles for 330F. It is on a street with other budget hotels near the station but is a cut above in standard and service. Mention Fodor's for a 6% discount. *5 rue Alsace Lorraine, tel. 04–93–88–20–24, fax 04–93–87–13–25. 34 rooms, all with bath. Closed mid-Nov.–last wk Dec.*

Hotel Normandie. The management here is so eager to please that there's a welcoming cocktail party and the owner personally brings guests breakfast in bed. Air-conditioned doubles with en-suite bathroom, satellite TV, and telephone run 295F–350F in peak season. *18 rue Paganini, tel. 04–93–88–48–83. 44 rooms, all with shower.*

Hotel Notre Dame. This clean and simple hotel above the restaurant Au Soleil is a five minute-walk from the station, 10 minutes from the sea. Double rooms are 240F, and rooms for four in bunks are 350F. *22 rue de Russie, tel. 04–93–88–70–44, fax 04–93–82–20–38. 17 rooms, all with shower.*

HOSTELS

Auberge de Jeunesse de Nice. Everyone takes the bus out to this small hostel overlooking Nice. It's often filled with Americans, so don't count on practicing your French. For 68F you get a bed, breakfast, and shower; sheets are 17F extra. Arrive early—the hostel opens at 6:30 AM—if you want a spot in the summer. If you arrive later, the staff posts the number of beds left at 5 PM. *Rte. Forestière du Mont-Alban, tel. 04–93– 89–23–64. Take Bus 14 from pl. Masséna. 56 beds. Check-in begins at 6:30 AM. Lockout 12:30 AM–5 PM. Curfew midnight. Kitchen.*

Relais International de la Jeunesse "Clairvallon." This clean, safe villa is huge, so there's usually room after the Auberge de Jeunesse has filled up. Although you have to trek 4 km (2½ mi) northeast of town, you'll be rewarded with tennis and basketball courts, a pool, garden, and cheap prices: 72F for bed and breakfast, 135F for half-board. A note of caution, however: The staff can be rude and are reluctant to speak English. *26 av. Scudéri, tel. 04–93–81–27–63. Take Bus 15 from in front of the station to stop Scudéri. 150 beds. Check-in 5 PM. Curfew 11 PM.*

CAMPING

There is no camping in Nice proper, but the tourist office will give you a list of plenty of other sites nearby. Some 15 km (9 mi) from the town center, **Terry Camping** is closest and has showers, an on-site restaurant and bar, a pool, and tennis courts. Depending on the season, tents run 50F–75F for one or two people. Reservations are advised July–August. *768 rte. de Grenoble-St-Isadore, tel. 04–93–08–11–58. Take Bus 700 from bus station. 14 sites.*

FOOD

There are temptations at nearly every corner of Nice, particularly in the streets around cours Saleya, with a huge range of styles and prices. There are sandwich stalls, bakeries, ice cream stalls, pavement cafés, and brasserie-style restaurants; colorful awnings and signs signal well-priced and authentic French cuisine. For lunch it is worth shopping in the famous **market** on cours Saleya, where stalls overflow with local produce. The Old Port restaurants are especially romantic in the evening, overlooking the yachts in the harbor. Generally, the farther you venture away from Promenade des Anglais, the better deals you'll find. You can find Middle Eastern, North African, and Asian food near the budget hotels; a delicious and relatively cheap deli serving Chinese, Vietnamese, and Thai specialties is **Asia Fast Food** (9 av. Thiers), across from the station.

UNDER 50F • Nissa Socca. With 40F niçoise specialties and swarms of locals crammed in eating them, this little dive can't be beat. Go for the zucchini beignets or pesto pasta. Everything is served with a huge basket of bread. *5 rue Ste-Réparate, tel. 04–93–80–18–35. Cash only. Closed Mon. and Jan.*

UNDER 75F • La Brasserie de l'Union. If you want to eat like the Niçois, in an atmosphere to match, then try this traditional brasserie. Dishes are made from family recipes and start at 55F. *1 rue Michelet, tel. 04–93–84–65–27.*

Le Toscan. Despite the trilingual menu, you'll find yourself jostling elbows with locals at this super-friendly joint around the corner from the train station. You can't go wrong with the 62F menu, which has generous portions of fresh seafood or steak prepared with Italian spices. The fillet of sole, fries, and Roquefort salad make a great combo. *1 rue Belgique, tel. 04–93–88–40–54. Closed Sun.*

UNDER 100F • Manoir Art Café. This restaurant doubles as a gallery for young local artists to display their work. The building is the same height as the Olympic pole vaulting record, which is held by the proprietor. A good choice is a fresh tomato and olive salad and herb-grilled fish followed by a dessert or a plate of cheese for 98F. *32 rue de France, tel. 04–93–16–36–16.*

UNDER 125F • L'Escalinada. Spring for the 100F menu or tease your palette with 40F deals like olive-oil-brushed gnocchis or spinach and pine-nut *tourtes* (tarts). Either way, we promise you'll come away begging for more cuisine niçoise. *22 rue Pairolière (in the Old Town), tel. 04–93–62–11–71.*

UNDER 200F • Les Dents de la Mer. This restaurant is at its best in the evening when you feel as if you are in a sunken galleon with fish tanks in the walls providing the effect. Menus at 146F and 199F have delicious recipes made with local produce and just-caught fresh fish. *2 rue St.François de Paule, tel. 04–93–80–99–16.*

WORTH SEEING

COLLINE DU CHATEAU

The château that used to top the hill has long since crumbled, but Castle Hill is well worth a climb for its stunning views of Nice and the azure waters below. Take the 400 stairs at the turning point of the quai des États-Unis or the elevator for 5F; it runs daily 10–6. At the north end of the hill is a huge cemetery with fantastically sculpted tombs.

VIEUX NICE

Also called the Vieille Ville (Old Town), Vieux Nice (Old Nice) is the oldest and most interesting part of town, bounded by the Colline du Château to the east, boulevard Jean-Jaurès to the north and west, and the cours Saleya to the south. The narrow, winding streets of the pedestrian zone are great places to mingle with locals and munch on regional specialties. **Cours Saleya** sets the stage for a colorful market that takes place daily until noon (except Monday, when food is replaced by antiques), overflowing with flowers, fresh fruit, seafood, vegetables, olives, honey, and herbs. If you are up early enough you can watch the chefs squabble over the best produce. Summer evenings, the restaurants' terraces are lively. **Place Rosetti** is home to the **Cathédrale Ste-Réparate,** a 17th-century church with an immense organ and ornate stained-glass windows. A few streets from place Rosetti, **Église St-Jacques** (rue du Jésus) holds a mass that sometimes features mandolin-playing priests.

CIMIEZ

Nice's smartest residential zone (Queen Victoria of England was a regular visitor), this hilly area 4 km (2½ mi) north of the town center has beautiful public gardens and the remains of a Roman arena, the **Arènes de Cimiez.** Amid the ruins, a 17th-century villa houses two museums: the **Musée Archéologique** (160 av. des Arènes-de-Cimiez, tel. 04–93–81–59–57), which displays the city's history from medieval times, open December–October, Tuesday–Sunday 10–noon and 2–6; and the **Musée Matisse** (164 av. des Arènes-de-Cimiez, tel. 04–93–81–08–08), open April–September, Tuesday–Sunday 10–6, and October–March, Tuesday–Sunday 10–5. Admission is 25F for each. The artist's personal collection, ranging from early still-life works to the more dynamic designs of later years, is on display. Matisse settled in this Genoan-style villa, set in an extensive olive grove, after World War I and remained until his death in 1954. Also, check out the medieval pictures at the nearby Franciscan monastery of **Notre-Dame-de-l'Assomption,** open weekdays 10–noon and 3–6.

MUSEUMS

Musée d'Art Moderne et d'Art Contemporain (MAMAC). The imposing Museum of Modern and Contemporary Art houses a wealth of European and American avant-garde treasures of the past 40 years. Don't miss the Warhol and Lichtenstein collections. Make sure you visit the roof terrace to see Yves Klein's *Wall of Fire. Promenade des Arts, tel. 04–93–62–61–62. Admission 25F July–Aug., free Sept.–June. Open Wed.–Mon. 11 AM–6 PM (Fri. until 10 PM).*

Musée des Beaux Arts. This fine-arts museum, in the 19th-century palace of Ukrainian princess Kotschoubey, has paintings and sculptures from the last three centuries on display. Included are works by Fragonard, Rodin, Monet, Vuillard, Bonnard, and Dufy. There is also a plaster cast of Rodin's world famous *The Kiss. 33 av. des Baumettes, tel. 04–93–44–50–72. Admission 25F. Open Wed.–Mon. 10–noon and 2–6.*

Musée Marc Chagall. Painter Marc Chagall (1887–1985), who drew many of his themes from Jewish-Russian folklore, spent his last years on the Riviera. This museum is dedicated to Chagall's monumental 17-canvas *Biblical Message,* with floating visions of biblical characters in swirls of greens and blues. The gardens and outdoor café, open April–October, are heaven in the middle of a hard day of traveling. *Av. Dr-Ménard, tel. 04–93–53–87–20. Admission 30F. Open Oct.–June, Wed.–Mon. 10–5; July–Sept., Wed.–Mon. 10–6.*

Palais Masséna. This gorgeous villa was built for the Massénas, one of Napoléon Bonaparte's pet families, and given to the town in 1919. Today it is a museum of regional culture and Niçois history. There's also a library with old maps, atlases, and books from the region. *65 rue de France, tel. 04–93–88–11–34. Admission 25F. Open Oct. and Dec.–Apr., Tues.–Sun. 10–noon and 2–5; May–Sept., Tues.–Sun. 10–noon and 2–6.*

AFTER DARK

Nice presents an enormous diversity of cafés, theaters, bars, and discos. Most of the city's after-dark scene is concentrated in Vieux Nice. Beers range from 13F for a piddling *pression* (half pint) to 50F for a mug, and cocktails hover around 40F, but many bars have happy hours with reduced evening prices. Pick up a free copy of **L'Exces,** readily available around town, for information on concerts, events, disco parties, theater performances, and film showings. English-language films are shown at the **Rialto** (4 pl. de Rivoli, tel. 04–93–88–08–41).

The gay scene is alive and well in Nice; check out the "Nuit Gay" section of *L'Exces* for a list of monthly events, or look for the journal *Lynx* at any of the places below. **Beach Coco** is a gay beach at the east end of the Old Port. A 30-minute walk from downtown, **Blue Boy** (9 rue Jean-Baptiste Spinetta, tel. 04–

93– 44–68–24) is a small club open every day, year-round. **L'Avantscène** (12 av. St-Jean Baptiste, tel. 04–93–62–64– 14), also open nightly, has various shows on weekends and no cover.

In Vieux Nice, consider starting your night along the **cours Saleya,** where dozens of bars, cafés, and restaurants compete for your attention. **Pub Oxford** (4 rue Mascoinat, tel. 04–93–92–24–54) charges no cover and has live guitar music nightly. The hip **Le Transformer** (18 rue François Guisol, tel. 04–93– 56–93–10) plays good music and serves drinks starting at 20F. **Le Van Gogh** (7 rue du Pont-Vieux, tel. 04–43–80–34–44) is a relatively quiet, comfortable bar with a pool table; try the expensive but delicious *framboise* (raspberry-flavored) beer (40F).

Most nightclubs stick you with a 50F–100F cover that includes a drink, but don't be surprised to see "regulars" ushered in for free. Different nights feature different music—techno, jungle, acid jazz, soul, hip-hop—so check flyers before forking over the cover charge. The club of the moment is **Le Studio Grand Escurial** (29 rue Alphonse Karr, tel. 04–93–82–37–66). **Le B-52** (8 Descente Crotti, tel. 04–93– 62–59–60) and **News** (passage Éile Négrin, tel. 04–93–87–76–30) are also very popular. **Le Salon** (2 rue Brea, tel. 04–9–92–92–91) is a velvety music bar behind the discreet but luxurious restaurant Le Comptoir. Clubs usually start heating up around midnight.

NEAR NICE

VENCE

Vence is 22 km (14 mi) northwest of Nice, a one-hour, 18F bus ride away; from here you can take the five-minute ride (7F) to St-Paul-de-Vence (*see below*). Built on a hill overlooking green countryside, the town of Vence manages to maintain its medieval charm despite large-scale commercialization. The heart of the town is the Cité Historique (Historical City). Wander through the tiny streets packed with artists' galleries, shops, terraced restaurants, and outdoor markets. Visit the Chapelle du Rosaire, now the **Chapelle du Matisse** (av. Henri Matisse), which Matisse designed and decorated to thank the Dominican nuns who nursed him back to health after he fell gravely ill in Vence during World War II. He illustrated the stations of the cross in the chapel with black line drawings, the color being provided by the light streaming in through small stained-glass windows. It's only open Tuesday and Thursday 10– 11:30 and 2:30–5:30 and costs 10F to see its simple interior. But you can also get a look at the windows from avenue de Provence.

WHERE TO SLEEP AND EAT • Perched on a hill overlooking the Old Town, **La Roserie** (av. Henri Giraud, tel. 04–93–58–02–20) is reason enough to come to Vence. Handmade tiles, antique furniture, Provençal decor, and homemade croissants in the morning make this French-style bed-and-breakfast well worth the 480F and 65F for breakfast. After a day of walking, choose from the many different piz-zas (around 40F each) at **Le Pêcheur du Soleil** (1 pl. Godeau, tel. 04–93–58–32–56). Or spend an evening enjoying excellent Provençal cuisine (menu 115F) on the garden patio of **Restaurant la Farigoule** (15 rue Henri-Isnard, 04–93–58–01–27). It's closed Tuesday and Wednesday.

ST-PAUL-DE-VENCE

Whether you're taking the bus 18 km (11 mi) from Nice (35 mins, 19F) or walking 4 km (2½ mi) from Vence, the sight of St-Paul-de-Vence's stone, red-roofed buildings and tiny, winding cobblestone streets is impressive. This little medieval town is devoted to art. The steep and winding streets throng with gal-leries and exhibitions. As young artists still do, Picasso, Bonnard, Modigliani, and their set hung out in St-Paul; they used to stay at Auberge de la Colombe d'Or and pay for their lodgings with paintings. As a result, the auberge's collection is as fabulous as the prices.

The **Fondation Maeght,** one of the world's most famous small museums of modern art, is a big reason to come to St-Paul. Just follow the signs leading to a hill northwest of the village. The gallery was designed to make the most out of natural light and includes an outdoor sculpture and fountain garden created for the museum by Joan Miró. There's also a courtyard full of Alberto Giacometti's elongated creations. The rooms inside display the works of nearly every famous artist of the past 50 years, includ-ing Miró, Georges Braque, Wassily Kandinsky, Pierre Bonnard, and Henri Matisse. Admission gives you free use of the museum's extensive modern art library (open all summer, by appointment only in winter) and cinema screenings. *Tel. 04–93–32–81–63. Admission July–Sept. 50F, Oct.–June 45F. Open July–Sept., daily 10–7; Oct.–June, daily 10–12:30 and 2:30–6.*

VILLEFRANCHE-SUR-MER

It would be easy to pass through Villefranche on the Basse Corniche heading for Monaco or Nice, but try not to. It has one of the deepest and most beautiful bays on the Riviera and the town has managed to preserve its charm in spite of its location (the Niçois make the short drive to lounge on the white-pebble beach during their midday break). Villefranche is also full of history and character. The defensive **Citadelle** was constructed in 1560 and houses the Hôtel de Ville, Musée Volti (sculpture), Collection Roux (ceramics), a museum of underwater archaeology, and an open-air theater. The frescoes inside **Chapelle St-Pierre** (Quai Courbet, admission 12F) were painted by the writer, surrealist film director, and visual artist Jean Cocteau, who lived in Villefranche between the two world wars. The shade and scent of the magnolia tree close by provides a perfect spot for a picnic such as one from **L'Express** (rue du Poilu, near pl. de la République), open mornings and 2–7 (closed Sunday). **La Caravelle** (3 rue de l'Église, tel. 04–93–01–81–10) serves three courses for 78F–100F. **L'Echalotte** (7 rue de l'Église, tel. 04–93–01–71–11), which specializes in Provençal food, offers three courses for 119F.

Hotels in Villefranche are expensive; one option is **Hôtel Provençal** (4 av. Marital Joffre, tel. 04–93–76–53–53), where a simple double with TV and shower starts at 300F. The **tourist office** (pl. Binon, tel. 04–93–01–73–68) is open Monday–Saturday 8:30–noon and 2–5, 8–8 in the summer.

BEAULIEU-SUR-MER

Beaulieu was at its most fashionable at the turn of the century, when it was a favored spot for European royalty to spend the winter. Beaulieu's sheltered position makes it the warmest town on the Riviera and accounts for the beach's nickname, **Petite Afrique.** The temperature may be hot but the nightlife is decidedly cool, so Beaulieu is best suited as a day trip. From Nice it is just 10 minutes and 10F by train. The **tourist office** (tel. 04–93–01–02–21) is just to the right as you exit the train station. If you are looking for a quiet escape, the **Hotel Riviera** (6 rue Paul Doumer, tel. 04–93–01–04–92) once provided accommodation to the traveling servants of the visiting aristocracy; a double room starts at 190F.

The **Villa Kérylos** is indisputable evidence of Beaulieu's former opulence. In 1908 the eccentric archaeologist and Hellanophile Théodore Reinach built this accurate reconstruction of an ancient Greek villa. *Rue Gustave Eiffel, tel. 04–93–01–01–44. Admission 40F. Open daily 10:30–12:30 and 2–6.*

From the villa, **promenade Maurice Rouvier,** a paved pedestrian path, will lead you to St-Jean-Cap-Ferrat (*see below*). The 30-minute walk winds seaside along the **Baie des Fourmis** (Bay of Ants), whose name alludes to the black rocks "crawling" up from the sea. The name doesn't quite fit, but the walk will give you great views of the sparkling Mediterranean and surrounding mountains.

ST-JEAN-CAP-FERRAT

A 20-minute drive east from Nice (10 km/6 mi), or a half-hour walk from Beaulieu (2 km/1 mi; *see above*), brings you to St-Jean, one of the most stunning and peaceful towns on the Riviera. St-Jean sits on Cap-Ferrat, a jagged peninsula whose mountains rise steeply from the sea. This has long been a favorite spot for movie scenes and stars.

The signs pointing to all the different walkways and sights in St-Jean are confusing; if you're really at a loss, visit the **tourist office** (59 av. Denis-Sémérria, tel. 04–93–76–08–90). Otherwise, just go south on the **Promenade Maurice Rouvier,** which runs along the eastern edge of the peninsula. You'll stumble upon reasonably priced cafés, pizzerias, and ice cream parlors on the promenade of the **Plage de St-Jean.** The best swimming is a bit farther south, past the port, at **Plage Paloma.** Keep trekking around the wooded area where a beautiful path (*sentier pédestre*) leads along the outermost edge of Cap-Ferrat. Other than the occasional yacht, all traces of civilization disappear, and the water is a dizzying blue. If you're feeling particularly sporty, follow the path along the coast all the way to Villefranche-sur-Mer (*see above*), a two-hour walk past another lighthouse and some incredible coastal scenery. You'll find a trail map posted near the entrance to the peninsula loop trail.

The views from the **Villa Ephrussi de Rothschild** are phenomenal. Built in 1912 for the Baroness Ephrussi de Rothschild, the villa's collection was donated to the Académie des Beaux-Arts in 1934. (The baron and his wife lived here only three years before deciding that they preferred their room at the Hôtel de Paris in Monte Carlo.) It'll cost you 40F to enter and either follow a one-hour tour (in French only) or wander at will. Admirers of beautiful furnishings, reams of antique rose chintz, and Spanish and Japanese gardens will find it's worth the money. *Av. Villa Ephrussi de Rothschild, tel. 04–93–01–33–09. Admission 40F. Open mid-Feb.–Oct., daily 10–6; Nov.–mid-Feb., weekdays 2–6, weekends 10–6.*

It is not recommended to stay on Cap Ferrat because of the prices, but **Hôtel Résidence Bagatelle** (av. Honoré-Sauvan, tel. 04–93–01–32–86) may be worth the splurge (though you will need to book months in advance as the same French families return year after year). Doubles start at 350F and go to 500F. The olive tree in the garden needs seven people holding hands to reach around the trunk!

MONACO

If much of the world lives in misery, neither Monaco nor its 30,000 seven-digit-income citizens know about it. Each of the 474 acres of this tiny principality is decked out in belle epoque grandeur with grandiose mansions and gorgeous beaches, all officially designated for Monaco's royal family's pleasure (which doesn't mind the millions the tourists bring in while romping on their grounds). Prince Rainier III's family has been ruling Europe's last constitutional autocracy since 1297. For your purposes, though, this might as well be France: The currency is the same, the language (excepting the few Monágasques who pay no taxes and speak their Italian-influenced dialect) is the same as are governmental policies, influence by French ministers. You do, however, have to dial 00–377 (plus the eight-digit number) when dialing from outside the principality, and just the eight-digit number within.

Monaco is famous for its **Monte-Carlo Casino, International Sporting Club,** and annual **Grand Prix** (*see box, below*). But you don't have to be a high roller or a Ferrari fanatic to enjoy coming here. At the base of the Alps-Maritimes and overlooking the Mediterranean, Monaco has an enchanting setting, the outstanding **Musée Océanographique** (Oceanographic Museum), and the **Jardin Exotique** (Exotic Garden). But Monaco is not a place to spend the night on a budget unless you can squeeze into the hostel or one of the few budget hotels; you're better off staying in Cap d'Ail, Menton, or Beausoleil.

BASICS

AMERICAN EXPRESS

The **AmEx Travel Office** (35 blvd. Princesse Charlotte, tel. 93–25–74–45) in Monte Carlo has mail-holding and 24-hour refund services. The **American Express Bank** (5 av. Princesse Alice, tel. 93–50–07–77), open weekly 9–noon and 2–4, is just south of the casino. From train or bus station, take Bus 1, 2 (from the port) or 4 (from the station) to Casino-Tourisme.

MAIL

Postage rates in Monaco are the same as in France. However, you can only use Monaco stamps in Monaco and French stamps in France. The postal code for Monte Carlo is 98000, for the rest of Monaco 98030. The main **post office** (Palais de la Scala, sq. Beaumarchais, tel. 97–97–25–00), near the casino in Monte Carlo, is one of eight branches.

VISITOR INFORMATION

Bienvenue! is a free monthly guide of events, tourist attractions, and nightlife. Ask for it at the tourist office, train or bus stations, or hotels. Maps posted all over let you know where you are. The main **tourist office** near the casino never seems to have enough visitors to keep its English-speaking staff busy. From mid-June to mid-September it opens additional offices around town. *Main office: 2a blvd. des Moulins, tel. 92–16–61–16. From train station, take Bus 1 or 2 from the port or 4 from the station to Casino-Tourisme stop. Open Mon.–Sat. 9–7, Sun. 10–noon.*

COMING AND GOING

Monaco is 25 minutes (20F) east of Nice (20 km/13 mi); trains run between the two every half hour. The **train station** (av. Prince Pierre, tel. 93–10–60–15) has a restaurant, phones, a summer tourist information desk, and money exchange with rates comparable to those in town. At press time, a new station underground station was expected to open in Vallon de St-Dévote after 10 years of rock blasting. Train times and phone numbers are expected to remain the same. **Buses** also connect Monaco to all points along the Riviera at prices comparable to trains, but they often take longer. The main pick-up point is on avenue Prince Pierre, right by the train station. Buy tickets from the driver.

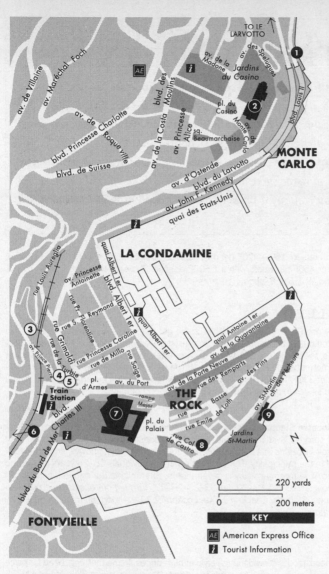

Sights ●

Casino de
Monte Carlo, **2**

Cathédrale, **8**

Jardin Exotique, **6**

Jardin Japonaise, **1**

Musée
Océanographique, **9**

Palais du Prince, **7**

Lodging ○

Centre de la
Jeunesse Princesse
Stephanie, **3**

Hôtel
Cosmopolite, **5**

Hôtel de France, **4**

**MONTE
CARLO**

LA CONDAMINE

**THE
ROCK**

FONTVIEILLE

0		220 yards
0		200 meters

KEY

AE American Express Office

i Tourist Information

GETTING AROUND

On a high rocky promontory that extends to the sea is the old town of **Monaco-Ville** (a.k.a. **The Rock**), one of five sections of Monaco. Most of the attractions worth seeing are in this area, an easy walk from the train station. North of the promontory is **La Condamine,** the commercial harbor area with expensive apartments and businesses. Farther north is **Monte Carlo,** the modern gambling town, and then Le Larvotto, a 15-minute walk north of Monte Carlo, which has an artificial beach with good swimming conditions. **Fontvieille** is the industrial district by the port.

Six bus lines travel to all the major points of interest in Monaco. The 9F fare includes a transfer good for 30 minutes. A card for four rides costs 19F; 30F gets you eight. You can buy cards and get a bus map from **Compagnie des Autobus de Monaco** (3 av. Président J. F. Kennedy, tel. 93–50–62–41).

CRASHING THE GRAND PRIX

In late May, the entire racing world speeds to Monaco to see the best Formula One drivers compete in the Grand Prix. Monaco on the day of the race is one big human sardine can, so buy your train ticket ahead of time. Though reserved bleacher seats start at 1,000F and are sold months in advance, tickets for the section along the cliffs under the palace, called "Secteur rocher," cost a mere 200F. Come before 10 AM to stake out a place where thousands of people won't block your view. You can buy a ticket at box offices all around town until the race starts at 3:30 PM.

Auto Moto Garage rents scooters for 150F–270F per day, plus a 2,500F deposit or a credit-card imprint. Ten-speeds are 80F a day or 450F per week, with a 1,500F deposit. *7 rue de Millo, tel. 93–50–10–80. Open weekdays 8–noon and 2–7, Sat. 8–noon.*

WHERE TO SLEEP

The hostel is the only truly good deal in Monaco. If you can't get in there, you're best off sleeping in nearby Nice, Cap d'Ail, Menton, or Beausoleil. But if you insist on playing Prince, try the **Hôtel Cosmopolite** (4 rue de la Turbie, tel. 93–30–16–95), where old, cramped, but clean doubles without shower go for 240F–265F. At the more upscale **Hôtel de France** (6 rue de la Turbie, tel. 93–30–24–64), spotless modern doubles start at 330F. In summer, Monaco is crowded, and don't even think of finding a room, much less a place to sit down, during the Grand Prix at the end of May.

HOSTEL

Centre de la Jeunesse Princesse Stephanie. Perched high above the city, this may be the nicest hostel on the Riviera and, not surprisingly, it's often full. In summer, people arrive by 9:30 AM to get their numbered tickets and check-in begins at 11 AM. At just 80F for a bed, sheets, shower, and breakfast, it's the only deal of its kind in the principality. The hostel is open to individuals 16–26 years of age and students up to 31 years old. The maximum stay is seven nights, three nights during peak periods. *24 av. Prince Pierre de Monaco, tel. 93–50–83–20, fax 93–25–29–82. Turn left out of station, cross overpass, and follow yellow arrows. 32 beds. Check-in 11 AM. Lockout 9:30 AM–noon. Midnight curfew, 1 AM curfew July–mid-Sept. Laundry.*

FOOD

Like everything else in Monaco, food is served in high style at high prices. In the morning, head for place d'Armes, near the train station, where there's an **outdoor market.** If you miss the market, **Marché U** (35 blvd. Princesse Charlotte) can set you up with all your picnicking needs, as can the supermarket **Casino** (17 blvd. Albert I, tel. 93–30–56–78), open Monday–Saturday 8:30–8. A lot of the cheaper restaurants and take-out stands are in the old section of Monaco, east of the palace. For a sit-down crepe or pizza for less than 50F, try **Crêperie-Pizzeria du Rocher** (12 rue C. Félix Gastaldi, tel. 93–30–09–64). At the convivial **Restaurant Le Bacchus** (13 rue de la Turbie, tel. 93–30–19–35), a generous 80F menu of traditional French cuisine will leave you happily stuffed. La Condamine section of town is good for crepe stands and cafés serving sandwiches at fair prices. **Calypso** (blvd. Louis II, Jetée du Port du Monaco, tel. 93–15–07–77) may be hard to find (on the far side of the port wall off av. J. F. Kennedy) but it is worth the hunt to munch on great pizzas loaded with anchovies and seafood.

WORTH SEEING

PALAIS DU PRINCE

The Prince's Palace is anchored on a rock in Monaco-Ville. A 40-minute guided tour takes you through lavish state rooms furnished with priceless antiques and paintings, including portraits of the royal family. The private apartments where the family actually lives are off-limits (so you'll never know for sure if they really do put on their pants one leg at a time like the rest of us). In front of the main entrance on **place du Palais** you can watch the daily changing of the humorless guards at 11:55 AM. One wing of the palace houses a **museum** with many Napoleonic souvenirs (you can ooh and over the general's sock) and documents related to Monaco's history. *Tel. 93–25–18–31. Admission to palace 30F. Open June–Sept., daily 9:30–6:30; Oct., daily 10–5. Admission to museum 20F. Open Dec.–May, Tues.–Sun. 10:30–12:30 and 2–5; June–Sept., daily 9:30–6:30; Oct., daily 10–5.*

CASINOS

Don't expect Vegas when you set out for the casinos in Monte Carlo: Free drinks, cheap grub, and late-night specials are not the scene. The high rollers who frequent these ritzy joints never ask prices before ordering, so slip into something sleek and be ready for the big time. In a carefully manicured sculpture garden, the **Casino de Monte Carlo** (pl. du Casino, tel. 92–16–21–21) is one of the most famous buildings on the Riviera. Sport your passport to prove you're over 21, and slide into the main gambling hall, the American Room. Adjoining the American Room is the Pink Salon, a bar where naked nymphs smoking cigarillos float on the ceiling. The *salons privées* (private rooms) require jacket and tie and lots of cash. If you would prefer to play roulette, craps, and blackjack elsewhere, head across the street to **Le Café de Paris** (pl. du Casino, tel. 92–16–23–00) or the nearby **Monte Carlo Grande Hotel's Casino** (12 av. des Spélugues, tel. 93–50–65–00), which also has slot machines and no admission charge.

CATHÉDRALE

The Cathédrale de Monaco-Ville, built between 1875 and 1903, contains the tombs of former princes of Monaco as well as an altarpiece by Louis Bréa. Grace Kelly is also buried here; pay homage to the great Hitchcockian heroine at the tomb inscribed "Gracia Patricia." *4 rue Colonel Bellando de Castro, near palace, tel. 93–30–88–13. Sun. mass at 10 AM.*

JARDIN EXOTIQUE

Thousands of cacti and all sorts of other desert and exotic plants grace the slopes of this fantastic (although pricey) garden. Admire the fabulous view and then descend into the cool caves of the **Musée d'Anthropologie Préhistorique** and the **Grottes de l'Observatoire,** where you can check out the rock formations (stalactites and stalagmites) that lie below Monaco. *Tel. 93–30–33–65. Walk uphill or take public elevator from vieille ville to rte. de la Moyenne Cornice, or take Bus 2 to Jardin Exotique stop. Admission 39F. Open May–Aug., daily 9–7; Sept.–Apr., daily 9–6.*

MUSEE OCEANOGRAPHIQUE

Forget the casino, forget the palace—this is the reason to come to Monaco. Prince Albert I founded the Musée Océanographique in 1910 to display objects he brought back from his deep-sea explorations. The museum has an amazing aquarium with nearly 3,000 fish and invertebrates, various halls of stuffed animals, exhibitions, and research laboratories. In the elegant conference hall you can watch a film by Jacques Cousteau, director of the museum from 1957 to 1988. Check out the view from the museum terrace and come early to avoid the crowds. *Av. St-Martin, tel. 93–15–36–00. Follow signs from vieille ville or palace. Admission 60F. Open Oct.–Mar., daily 9:30–7; Apr.–June and Sept., daily 9–7; Nov.–Feb., daily 10–6; July–Aug., daily 9–8.*

CHEAP THRILLS

If all the Rolls-Royces, Bentleys, BMWs, and Mercedes crowding the streets of Monaco make you long for some unpretentious air, take to the hills. Walking west along a very pretty costal path will lead you to Cap d'Ail (*see below*), or you can walk uphill (or take an elevator) from the vieille ville and the palace to the route de la Moyenne Corniche. Wander through the cactus collection at the Jardin Exotique (*see above*), and continue into Cap d'Ail. Wind down through some nice neighborhoods before reaching the beach. Escape the clamor in the casinos by ambling down avenue des Spélugues to the **Jardin Japonaise** (Japanese Garden), open daily 9–sunset, overlooking the Mediterranean.

AFTER DARK

Monaco's social scene is very snobby, so unless you know the value of your stocks and have a coat and tie handy, go elsewhere for a good time. The following are among the few joints that don't have so much attitude: The English-speaking barman at **Maky's Pub** (57 rue Grimaldi, tel. 92–16–12–40) can tell you all about the history of the area, and he'll even commiserate about how overdeveloped it is. The pub serves beers for 15F–20F, sandwiches for 20F–25F, and turns into a piano bar on weekends. **McArthy's Irish Pub** (7 rue Portier, tel. 93–25–87–67) is a great place to meet an English-speaking crowd. If you are missing home, pop into **Stars and Bars** on the port (tel. 93–50–95–95) for all-American food but packed with locals. To spot the sports cars and dance with the rich (but not necessarily famous) try **La Racasse** (rue Antoine, tel. 93–25–56–90). **Bombay Frigo** (3 av. Princesse Grace, tel. 93–25–57–00) is the chichi bar of the moment. **Jimmy's** (26 av. Princesse Grace, tel. 93–16–22–77), with its drag queens, beautiful people, and exotic cocktails, has more personality than other Monaco bars.

OUTDOOR ACTIVITIES

Ski Vol (tel. 93–50–86–45) on Larvotto Beach rents water-skiing, jet-skiing, and parasailing equipment from its beachside dock June–September. Pedal boats and canoes can be rented at the various private beach clubs for about 100F per hour. You can rent windsurfing equipment at the **Beach Plaza Sea Club** (22 av. Princesse Grace, tel. 93–30–98–80) May–September for 60F an hour. For a ride on the glass-bottom catamaran *Aqua Vision* (70F), contact the **Compagnie de Navigation et de Tourisme** (quai des États-Unis, tel. 92–16–15–15).

NEAR MONACO

CAP D'AIL

Cap d'Ail (Garlic Cape), just west of Monaco and east of Nice, is a great escape. The beaches, though small and rocky, are perfect for stretching out and forgetting civilization. For more social creatures, the sandy Plage Mala has chairs and umbrellas for rent, a bar, and two beachside restaurants. A cement walkway winds along the beachfront from Cap d'Ail to Monaco; it is a lovely walk but unlit at night. Cap d'Ail is also an easy train or bus ride from Nice (18 mins, 20F).

WHERE TO SLEEP AND EAT • Be aware that the town has few grocery stores (all clustered along the Moyenne Corniche), and the banks don't like to change money after noon—try the post office. Finding reasonably priced food and lodging is a challenge, but the prize of Cap d'Ail is the **Relais International de la Jeunesse Thalassa,** a secluded hostel right on the beach. Rooms sleep 8 to 12, and in summer they set up large tents, as well—come between 9 and 10 AM or at 5 PM to secure a spot. The hostel caters to groups and families as well as backpackers, so people of all ages socialize and bronze their bodies here. It's 70F the first night, 60F for the second and third; 125F for half-board. Prices include breakfast. *Rte. de la Mer, tel. 04–93–78–18–58. Follow signs from train station. 100 beds. Check-in 5 PM. Lockout 9–5. Curfew midnight. Closed Nov.–Apr.*

Another option is old-style **Hotel Miramar** (126 av. du Septembre, tel. 04–93–78–06–60), which offers rooms for 180F–350F, including a small terrace. Directly opposite, **Edmond's Bar Restaurant Hotel** (87 av. du Septembre, tel. 04–93–78–08–55) has rooms with TV and shower for 300F. Both hotels access the lovely Plage Mala (Princess Stephanie's favorite beach) via steep steps.

MENTON

Nestled in the center of an arc with Cap Martin on one side and Italy on the other, Menton (30 km/19 mi east of Nice, 40 mins, 27F by train; 9 km/5½ mi east of Monaco, 10 mins, 12F) is blessed with one of the warmest microclimates on the Riviera, as evidenced by the abundant gardens that spring forth flowers and citrus fruit all year long.

Menton has a reputation as an old folks' town, which it doesn't really deserve. The tourist board has done all it can to inject the city with some vitality, and all the festivals, cultural activities, and surrounding nature have attracted a younger and more energetic population. Menton is a good base for hikes into the high country and *villages perchés* (perched villages) or along the ocean to Cap St-Martin. Pay a visit to the infinitely knowledgeable staff at the **tourist office** (Palais de l'Europe, av. Boyer, tel. 04–93–57–57–00), which gives enlightening tours of the old town and the gardens. Try to come during Menton's homage to the lemon and all things citrus in February, the **Fête du Citron,** the largest festival on the Riviera after the Carnival in Nice. Menton has the only museum consecrated to painter-poet-filmmaker Jean Cocteau, the **Musée Jean Cocteau** (Bastion, Vieux Port, tel. 04–93–57–72–30), housed in a beautifully restored fortress overlooking the ocean. Admission is free; donations are requested. Cocteau also decorated the **Salle des Marriages** at the Hôtel de Ville, which has become the place for Japanese newlyweds to confirm their vows.

WHERE TO SLEEP AND EAT • A low-budget oceanfront view at the very friendly **Hôtel St-Michel** (1684 promenade du Soleil, tel. 04–93–57–46–33) starts around 320F and is a 10-minute walk from the station. Bus 6 will take you to the calm **Riviera Auberge de Jeunesse** (plateau St-Michel, tel. 04–93–35–93–14), where 70F (hostel card required) gets you bed and breakfast. **Crêperie de l'Atlantique** (16 av. Edouard VII, tel. 04–93–41–41–83) is a great dinner choice, with a 50F menu and some of the best crepes in the region.

ANTIBES

There isn't much to distinguish Antibes from other Riviera towns if you don't venture farther than the new town and the beach. But lose yourself in the maze of streets in the old town and you'll find that Antibes is overflowing with provençal culture and layered with history. Antibes's natural, protected port was used by the Greeks and then the Romans, and the town was destroyed and rebuilt countless times over the centuries, the same stones often being plopped into new buildings. Don't miss **Safranier,** a community where traditionalists preserve local culture among the tiny cobblestone streets and flower-boxed windowsills.

The Côte d'Azur landscape inspired many artists, hence the number of museums devoted to the artists who lived and worked in the area: Cocteau in Menton, Matisse in Vence, Chagall in Nice, and Picasso in Antibes, just to mention a few.

Antibes is first and foremost a summer resort: In July and August it explodes with festivals and huge crowds who drive prices through the roof. Street artists and musicians take over the public squares, and summer sports abound on the beautiful sandy beaches. For further escape, check out the spectacular views and million-dollar homes of the Cap d'Antibes, immortalized by F. Scott Fitzgerald in *Tender Is the Night.* You can see all the way to Italy from the lighthouse.

BASICS

ENGLISH-LANGUAGE BOOKSTORE

The **English Bookshop** (24 rue Aubernon, tel. 04–93–34–74–11) has well-priced reading material of all kinds and good local advice.

VISITOR INFORMATION

You'll see the signs for the **Maison de Tourisme** as soon as you exit the train station. The multilingual staff has numerous brochures on the area, as well as info on hiking and mountain biking in the Provence hills. *11 pl. du Général-de-Gaulle, tel. 04–92–90–53–00. Open Oct.–Apr., daily 9–12:30 and 2–7; May–Sept., daily 9–7:30.*

COMING AND GOING

Twenty minutes and 23F from Nice, Antibes's **train station** (av. Robert-Soleau, tel. 04–93–99–50–50) is at the far east end of town but still within walking distance of the vieille ville and only a block or so from the beach. For luggage storage, there's also a consignment desk that charges 30F for 24 hours.

Buses leave for interior villages from the **bus station** (1 pl. Guynemer, tel. 04–93–34–37–60). To get to Cannes (13F), Nice (25F), Cagnes-sur-Mer (12F), Juan-les-Pins (7F), or to catch local buses (7F), wait at the different posts on place du Général-de-Gaulle. Most lines run every 20 minutes.

WHERE TO SLEEP

Antibes has few budget hotels, and prices go up June–September. You aren't likely to find a room for less than 180F for a spartan double—you're better off crashing in Juan-les-Pins (*see below*). But, if you do want to stay in Antibes, the friendly but noisy and often full **Nouvel Hôtel** (1 av. du 24-Août, tel. 04–93–34–44–07), in the old part of town just steps from the bus station, has the cheapest rates: Doubles with a free communal hall shower run 200–330F. **Relais du Postillion** (18 rue de Championnet, tel. 04–93–34–20–77) is a good option with doubles at 255F and a private beach. For more upscale accommodations, go to the **Hôtel de l'Étoile** (2 av. Gambetta, tel. 04–93–34–26–30), where rooms with marine decor start at 320F. **Auberge Provençale** (61 pl. Nationale, tel. 04–93–34–89–88) is a gem of a hotel with just seven rooms (request one with a four-poster bed); doubles start at 450F. Antibes and Juan-les-Pins have many campgrounds that rent tents and caravans; most are open only April–September and charge 30F–60F for two people. Try **Le Rossignol** (2074 av. J-Michard Pelissier, tel. 04–93–33–56–98), just north of Antibes. Get a list of others from the tourist office.

HOSTEL • Relais International de la Jeunesse Caravelle 60. This hostel in Cap d'Antibes is a wonderful, cheap, out-of-the-way place to stay, but it fills up quickly in July and August. It's a long walk from anything but the beach (which is five minutes away), but beds and showers are only 70F, plus 10F for sheets. You can even rent pedal boats, Windsurfers, and canoes. Bus 2A makes the 30-minute, 7F trip from Antibes to Cap d'Antibes almost hourly 9 AM–7 PM. Get off at the Garoupe stop. *Rue de l'Antiquité, off rte. de la Garoupe, tel. 04–93–61–34–40. 100 beds. Reception open 10:30 AM–11 PM. Lockout 10–5. Curfew 11 PM. Closed Oct.–May.*

FOOD

Le Brûlot (3 rue Frédéric Isnard, tel. 04–93–34–17–76), in the old town, is a cozy, cavelike restaurant with a three-course, 69F menu that includes pastas and pizzas. For an authentic Provençal meal, seek out the sunny patio and 60F menu at the **Taverne le Safranier** (1 pl. du Safranier, tel. 04–93–34–80–50); it's closed Monday. Antibes has plenty of fruit stands, grocery stores, and sandwich shops. The lively **outdoor market** (cours Masséna), in the old section of town, is open daily 6 AM–1 PM, except Monday in winter.

WORTH SEEING

Inspired by Antibes and its origins, Picasso wed himself to the themes of mythology and sea during his six prolific months in the seaside Château Grimaldi in 1946. Now the **Musée Picasso**, the château houses all the works Picasso produced in this period and offers unrivaled views of the Cap d'Antibes. *Pl. Mariéjol, tel. 04–92–90–54–20. Admission 20F. Open Tues.–Sun. 10–noon and 2–6; summer, Tues.–Sun. 10–6).*

Be sure to take a walk along the city wall, which still keeps the sea out of the town. The route is marked from cours Masséna.

NEAR ANTIBES

JUAN-LES-PINS

Antibes and Juan-les-Pins (on the other side of Cap d'Antibes) officially form a single town. It takes 30 minutes to walk between the two, but buses run between them frequently, and Juan-les-Pins is on the coastal train line. Restaurants, cafés, budget hotels, and bars line the streets near the beach but only come alive in summer. In late July, Juan-les-Pins puts on the Riviera's top **jazz festival.** You can reserve the 150F–200F tickets through the **Maison de Tourisme** (51 blvd. Guillaumont, tel. 04–92–90–53–05). Other than that, the main reason to come to Juan-les-Pins is for its nightlife. During the day, this place has a plastic feel and you'll get more out of Antibes.

WHERE TO SLEEP • Hotels in Juan-les-Pins often charge 25% more in July and August (off-season prices are given below). One place that doesn't raise its prices is **Le Parisiana (16 av. de l'Estérel, tel. 04–93–61–27–03), between the train station and the beach. Singles start at 167F, doubles are 245F, and 328F gets you two adjoining rooms for up to four; all have TV and bath. **Hôtel de la Gare** (6 rue du Printemps, tel. 04–93–61–29–96) is 1½ blocks east (left) of the train station. As long as you don't mind the noise, the worn, cozy rooms are a deal at 180F for a double, 160F for a single. Near the Jardin de la Pinède, **Villa Christie** (11 rue de l'Oratoire, tel. 04–93–61–01–98) is a lovely English-style villa with doubles from 270F. Call ahead to reserve, or show up around 10 AM.

FOOD • You can snack at any time of the day on the crepes, sandwiches, ice cream, and kebabs at numerous stands and brasseries throughout Juan-les-Pins. Pick up all your beachside munchies at the **Casino** supermarket on rue Dautheville. When you're ready for a sit-down meal, head to the restaurant-lined rue Docteur Dautheville and scan the menus: **Le Romana** (tel. 04–93–61–05–66) at No. 21 has pastas for 50F–65F. At No. 12, **Le Pousse Pousse** (tel. 04–93–61–41–99) has a variety of Chinese, Viet-namese, and Thai dishes, including vegetarian plates for 50F–70F. At the beachside **La Petite Pinède** (5 blvd. de la Pinède, tel. 04–93–61–07–03), you can get fresh fish (around 85F) and salads and sand-wiches (25F–50F) into the wee hours.

AFTER DARK • In summer, this town has possibly the busiest nightlife outside Paris. If you're not dancing you can shop until midnight. It's everything you expect from a party à la *Baywatch*: tanned bod-ies milling around, loud music, neon lights, and lots of beer. Reggae dominates at two popular clubs, **Le Pam Pam** (rte. Wilson, tel. 04–93–61–11–05) and **Le Festival**, across the street. The former is sup-posed to have the better acts—people jam as if they were in Jamaica—but neither club is especially popular with locals. **Le Bureau** (av. G. Gallice, tel. 04–93–67–22–74) is a disco featuring lots of theme nights for a 100F cover (techno, retro, samba). **Le Joy's** (2 av. Guy de Maupassant, tel. 04–93–67–78–87) is a less pretentious *boîte* (club) with a view of the surrounding area. **Le Cambridge** (25 rue Docteur Hochet, tel. 04–93–67–49–89) is a relaxing pub and piano bar. In the second two weeks of August there are firework displays that light up the beaches to the sound of live music.

BIOT

Nestled in the hills 5 km (3 mi) from the sea, Biot is a charming, ancient village of 6,000 Provençals. Like St-Paul-de-Vence, Biot has a sizable artist community, but it tends to be less crowded. The town is also famous for its pottery and glasswork. Make the 2½-km (1½-mi) trek toward the beach (or take a short bus ride) to see **La Verrerie de Biot** (5 chemin des Combes, tel. 04–93–65–03–00), where you'll still see glassblowers hard at work. It's open Monday–Saturday 9–6:30 and Sunday 10:30–1 and 2:30–6:30. A little farther down the hill is the **Musée National Léger** (Chemin du Val de Pomme, tel. 04–92–91–51–30). Artist Fernand Léger (1881–1955) lived in Biot and hundreds of his paintings, ceramics, and tapestries are on display at the Léger Museum. It's open April—October, Wednesday–Monday 9–6, and November–March, Wednesday–Monday 10–12:30 and 2–5:30. Admission is 32F. Biot is only 7F by bus from Antibes, which takes you directly to the vieux village (the train drops you off 5 km/3 mi away, along the coast).

Most of the town's activity is concentrated along rue St-Sebastien, where you'll find the **tourist office** (pl. de la Chapelle, tel. 04–93–65–05–85). Stop in at one of the free art galleries; get lost among the narrow, cobblestone streets; and then retire to **Café Brun** (14 impasse St-Sébastien, tel. 04–93–65–04–83), a friendly Dutch pub with English owners, Indonesian food, European beers, and a predominantly French clientele. Several highlights to seek out include the sundials on several building facades, the cool inte-rior of the 15th-century church, and the view of the ocean from place Marius Auzias.

CAGNES

Twenty kilometers (12 mi) east of Antibes on the way to Nice, Cagnes is accessible both by train (14F from Antibes) and by bus. The train makes two stops: If you want to hit the beach, get off at **Cros de Cagnes,** and if you want to see the *centre ville* (town center) or Le Haut de Cagnes (the walled, medieval city), stop at **Cagnes-sur-Mer.** There's a bus that will take you to place Charles de Gaulle, in the unin-teresting city center, or you can make the 15-minute walk by turning right when you leave the **train sta-tion** (tel. 04–93–87–30–00), continuing under the highway, and turning left at boulevard du Maréchal-Juin. The staff at the **tourist office** (6 blvd. du Maréchal-Juin, tel. 04–93–20–61–64) will give you a map, city info, and a list of nearby campgrounds.

Just a short walk from place Charles de Gaulle is **Les Colettes,** Pierre-Auguste Renoir's (1841–1919) former home, now the **Musée Renoir** (av. des Colettes, tel. 04–93–20–61–07). One of the most famous—and some say happiest—of the Impressionist painters, Renoir spent the last 12 years of his life here after he fell in love with the colors of the region. His former home is open Wednesday–Monday 10–noon and 2–5 and closed mid-October–mid-November. It costs 20F to enter the museum, but you'll mostly see lithographs of Renoir's work and photos, although there are 10 original sensual canvases on the ground floor. Making the trek up to his house is worth a visit, if only to relax in the free gardens and groves of olive and orange trees.

In Le Haut de Cagnes, across the valley from Renoir's former abode, you'll find the impressive **Château Grimaldi** (pl. Grimaldi, tel. 04–93–20–85–57); to get here, take the free shuttle that leaves from place Charles de Gaulle in summer, or walk 1 km (½ mi). Once a 14th-century medieval fortress, the château now houses a permanent display explaining how olive oil is made, as well as temporary exhibits by artists who worked on the Côte d'Azur—including Chagall, Cocteau, and Dufy. Admission is 20F. It's open Easter–October, daily 10–noon and 2:30–6; and January–Easter, Wednesday–Monday 10–noon and 2–5.

CANNES

The sapphire-and-sunglasses set has been coming to the oceanfront sprawl of Cannes since the mid-1800s. The city is best known for the celluloid parade that flocks to the **Festival International du Film** (International Film Festival) every May and largely deserves its reputation as playground for the rich and famous.

Despite the immediate impression of a lack of culture, take the time to explore the vieille ville, known as **Le Suquet** for the hill on which it stands. It's a tangle of streets spiraling upward to a spectacular panorama and the medieval Saracen tower. The monks of Lérins used to live here, and you'll still find the **Chapelle Ste-Anne** as well as the **Musée de la Castre** (tel. 04–93–38–55–26). Here you can see exhibits on archaeology, primitive art, and paintings by regional artists. The old fishing town is also the best area to find good bars and cozy restaurants (*see below*).

If you decide to visit the beaches on La Croisette, expect to pay at least 70F to enter the territory of the neo-aristocrats. Better to go public on **Plages du Midi** and **Plages de la Bocca,** and then dip into the private sector for a comparably inexpensive 30F Coke. These beaches are lined with old aristocratic residences and attract a young, athletic group who play volleyball and swim to the docks moored just off the coast. The modern **Palais des Festivals,** a summer casino, and the **Vieux Port,** sit at the end of Plages de la Croisette nearest town; the winter casino and modern harbor occupy the other end. All along the promenade you'll find chichi cafés, expensive boutiques, and luxury hotels.

BASICS

AMERICAN EXPRESS

The **AmEx** office (8 rue des Belges, tel. 04–93–38–15–87), open weekdays 9–6, Saturday 9–1, offers the best rates on its traveler's checks and handles cardholder inquiries. The **American Express Bank** (1 bis rue Nótre Dame, tel. 04–93–99–05–45) can also cash your traveler's checks and is open weekdays 9–noon and 2–5.

BUREAUX DE CHANGE

You can change money across the street from the train station at **Office Provençal** (17 rue Maréchal-Foch, tel. 04–93–39–34–37), at the main post office (*see* Mail, *below*), and in banks all over the city. A 24-hour exchange machine at **Crédit Lyonnais** (corner rue Jean de Joffre and av. d'Antibes) converts crisp U.S. currency.

ENGLISH-LANGUAGE BOOKSTORE

Cannes is home to one of the best English-language bookstores in France, the **Cannes English Bookshop** (11 rue Bivouac-Napoléon, tel. 04–93–99–40–08).

LAUNDRY

Laverie Automatique (42 rue Jean Jaurès), close to the train station, is open daily 7 AM–9 PM. Expect to pay about 40F to wash and dry.

MAIL

The main **post office** is well marked. Services include telephones, telegram, poste restante, and money exchange at fair rates; the postal code is 06400. *22 rue Bivouac-Napoléon, tel. 04–93–39–14–11. Open weekdays 8–7, Sat. 8–noon.*

VISITOR INFORMATION

The free magazine *Cannes Communication,* published every two months, has sections on upcoming events, sports, and history in French. The biggest and best tourist office is in the **Palais des Festivals et des Congrès** (blvd. de la Croisette, tel. 04–93–39–24–53), the huge monolith by the water where they hold the film festival. The tourist office also has information about film festival events open to the public (with tickets, so call in advance).*Esplanade Georges Pompidou, tel. 04–93–99–8–27. Open Sept.–June, daily 9–6:30; July–Aug., daily 9–8.*

Forget the film festival: Cannes welcomes greats of another genre during summer's Nuits Musicals du Suquet. You can listen to soothing classical music above the old town in an atmosphere that is decidedly more low-key than that of its silver-screen sister.

COMING AND GOING

BY TRAIN

It's easiest to reach Cannes by **train.** The St-Raphaël–Ventimiglia train passes through Nice (25 mins, 31F) and Antibes (11 mins, 13F) and arrives here every half hour; you can take the TGV directly from Paris (6½ hrs, 430F) with a stop in Marseille. Don't get off at the "Cannes–La-Bocca" stop or you'll be stranded in a suburb of little interest. The **central station** (rue Jean Jaurès, tel. 04–93–99–50–50) is attached to one of the bus stations and is near cheap hotels, the two outdoor markets, and the bureaux de change. A luggage consignment desk will also store bags for 30F and bicycles for 35F per day.

BY BUS

Cannes has two **bus stations.** The one next to the train station (tel. 04–93–39–31–37) sends buses inland. The one on place de l'Hôtel-de-Ville (tel. 04–93–39–18–71) provides local service and access to coastal towns. The urban **Bus Azur** buses congregate near the Hôtel de Ville; Bus 8 runs out along the ritzy eastern beach and costs 7F. Maps at the bus stops around town explain the local lines in depth. **Rapides Côte d'Azur** (RCA; tel. 04–93–39–11–39) has an office right by the Hôtel de Ville and sends hourly buses to the airport in Nice for 70F 7 AM–7 PM. They also run a 27F bus to Nice; it stops in Juan-les-Pins, Antibes, and Cagnes (*see above*).

BY BIKE AND MOPED

You can rent 10-speeds and mountain bikes (80F for 24 hours with a 1,500F deposit) or 50cc scooters (250F for 24 hours with a 6,000F deposit) from **Holiday Bikes** (16 rue du 14-Juillet, tel. 04–93–94–61–00), open daily 8:30-7.

WHERE TO SLEEP

Cannes has a great selection of budget hotels within walking distance of the train station. Expect to pay 50F–100F more in July and August for hotels, and don't even consider staying here during the film festival in May—unless you have reserved months in advance. Cannes's tourist offices provide a full listing of hotels, as well as info on short-term apartment rentals. If you're planning on staying for five days or more, call the office in advance for the *forfait hôteliers* (hotel packages), which give you room, breakfast, museum passes, and visits to the islands for as little as 200F a day.

UNDER 150F • Hôtel Cybelle. One block from the train station, this worn but cheery hotel has singles and doubles for 120F and up. Cash in on the demi-pension, or half-board (breakfast for 25F and dinner for 95F), if you like to eat well; the proprietress also runs the popular Au Bec Fin restaurant downstairs. *12 rue de 24-Août, tel. 04–93–38–31–33, fax 04–93–38–43–47. 11 rooms, 7 with shower. Closed late Dec.–early Jan.*

UNDER 250F • Hôtel Atlantis. Modern singles and doubles start at 170F, and doubles with shower start at 230F. Some rooms come with a minibar or open onto the patio, and all have phones and cable TV. Get here early in high season; this hotel is very popular. Prices go up 20% in July and August. *4 rue du 24-Août, tel. 04–93–39–18–72. 38 rooms, 30 with bath.*

UNDER 300F • Le Florian. Monsieur Giordano welcomes you to his hotel in the golden core of Cannes with a hearty "Bonjour," "Hello," "Bongiorno," or whatever he thinks you might understand. He loves young people and families and is eager to offer you a *prix sympa*, or fair price—200F–300F—if you give him a good enough reason. Rooms have TV and are modern, spotless, and large for the price. *8 rue du Commandant André, tel. 04–93–39–24–82, fax 04–93–99–18–30. 20 rooms, all with bath.*

Hôtel Alnea. This hotel is an easy walk from the station and the port. The pink-and-white rooms are simple and clean and start at 300F for a double. *20 rue Jean de Riouffe, tel. 04–93–39–39–90. 14 rooms, 13 with bath.*

HOSTELS

Auberge de Jeunesse de Cannes. This hostel has spacious, apartment-like rooms containing six beds, laundry facilities, and communal kitchens. It's about a 15-minute hike uphill from the train station, but you're rewarded with modern and luxurious accommodations (by hostel standards, that is). It's 80F per night (no breakfast) with a hostel card. Blankets and sheets are free, and towels are 5F. *35 av. de Vallauris, tel./fax 04–93–99–26–79. From train station take underground passage and go right on blvd. d'Alsace, left on blvd. de la République, then right on av. de Vallauris. 64 beds. Midnight curfew, 1 AM on weekends.*

Le Châlit. Coed dorms with communal kitchen facilities at 80F a person (sheets 15F) make this a fun place to meet people and save money. Recently renovated (all the handiwork was done by the owners), this hostel aims for a homey, family atmosphere. There's no curfew. Reservations are advised. *27 av. Maréchal Galliéni, tel. 04–93–99–22–11, fax 04–93–39–00–28. From train station, take underground passage, turn left on blvd. d'Alsace, then right onto rue Maréchal Galliéni. 30 beds. Lockout 10:30–5.*

CAMPING

Although Cannes itself doesn't have any campgrounds, you'll find several nearby, open April–October. In Cannes's western suburb of La Bocca, accessible by train, is **Caravaning Bellevue** (67 av. Maurice Chevalier, tel. 04–93–47–28–97) with sites for 50F per person (90F in July and August). Bus 9 from Cannes to the Buissons Ardents stop will also get you there. Frequent buses go to two campgrounds 5 km (3 mi) northeast in the town of Le Cannet: **Le Grand Saule** (blvd. J. Moulin, at the end of av. M. Jourdan, tel. 04–93–90–55–10) has 55 partially shaded sites and a pool; take Bus 9 from the Hôtel de Ville. Bus 1 will get you to **Le Ranch Camping** (chemin St-Joseph, Rocheville, Quartier l'Aubarède, tel. 04–93–46–00–11), with 130 terraced sites. Both campgrounds charge 80F for one person and 120F for two; prices are 30F less off-season.

FOOD

Prices are never low in Cannes, but the cafés and restaurants farthest from the beach are usually the cheapest, and the ones in the vieille ville are the most fun. Outdoor fruit and vegetable markets are open Tuesday–Sunday; the morning market on rue Forville just north of Le Suquet is bigger than the one on place Marché Gambetta, three blocks east of the train station, but both have lots of colorful food, clothes, and characters. The supermarket **Monoprix** (2 rue Maréchal-Foch, tel. 04–93–39–35–01) is also near the station and is open 8:30–8 every day but Sunday. You can buy sandwiches and crepes along the beach, as well as on pedestrian rue Meynadier. The best pan-bagnats, though, are found in the **sandwich kiosk** at place Marché Gambetta (25F).

For restaurants at varying prices, walk along the packed row of restaurants, bistros, and trendy spots in Le Suquet. To enter into the spirit of Old Cannes without breaking the bank, try **La Crêperie** (66 rue Meynadier, tel. 04–93–99–00–00), where big salads and crepes from a true Breton stay in the 50F range. For some real Provençal cooking, go to **Le Papille** (38 rue Georges Clemenceau, tel. 04–93–39–27–28) and order the 92F menu. For great pizza, a free aperitif, and a fun and lively atmosphere, try popular **Papa Nino** (15 blvd. de la République, tel. 04–93–38–48–08). Its specialty, calzone (48F), makes a filling meal. A homey, country-house atmosphere can be found at **L'Épicerie** (4 rue de la Boucherie, tel. 04–93–39–84–73); the 95F menu might include a *tourte aux blettes* (spinach and pine-nut torte) and a sumptuous pear-and-almond tart.

AFTER DARK

The **Carlton Casino Club, Casino Croisette,** and **Hilton Casino** forbid shorts, sandals, and cameras, but if you want to dress up and try your luck, the *salons de jeux* (game rooms) roll 5 PM–4 AM. Tacky piano bars are also big in Cannes. No cover is charged but drinks start at 50F. Or stroll along La Croisette, the beachside promenade that often features performers and music. If you are heading east, walk out to Pointe de la Criosette for fabulous views of nature and money (catch those yachts). It will come as no surprise that movies are a specialty of Cannes. **Les Arcades** (77 rue Félix-Faure, tel. 04–93–39– 00–98), **Olympia** (16 rue de la Pompe, tel. 04–93–39–13–93), and **Star** (98 rue d'Antibes, tel. 04–93–68–18–08) collectively have 17 screens and show European and American films for about 50F, except Wednesday, when they're 32F.

For a night of jazz, go to **MJC Picaud** (23 av. du Dr-Picaud, tel. 04–93–06–29–90). You can dine and listen to jazz (about 200F) at **La Séguinière** (rte. de St-Laurent-du-Var, tel. 04–93–24–42–92), a villa with an immense garden terrace. Clubs in Cannes have mixed crowds, though there are a few predominantly gay hangouts, including **Disco 7** (7 rue Rouguière, off rue Félix-Faure, tel. 04–93–39–10–36), which features a transvestite show. Farther out of town, but popular with young hipsters, is the **Whisky à Gogo** (115 av. de Lérins, tel. 04–93–43–20–63).

OUTDOOR ACTIVITIES

The sandy beaches of Cannes (with the sand imported from North Africa) make excellent launching points for catamarans and Windsurfers. You can rent them off the beaches and take lessons on summer mornings. Walk west from the harbor area along boulevard du Midi to the **Plages du Midi** and **Plages de la Bocca,** where most sailing and windsurfing outfits set up: Check out **Station Voile** (tel. 04–93–18–88–88), which rents Windsurfers (85F per hour), Hobie Cats (200F per hour), and kayaks (60F per hour); call about private or group lessons.

The **Plongée Club de Cannes** (46 rue Georges Clemenceau, tel. 04–93–38–67–57) will take you on an introductory pool and ocean dive for 300F. France doesn't recognize international dive clubs like P.A.D.I. and N.A.U.I., so even certified divers must go this route. If they have room on the boat, they'll take nondivers and provide fins, a mask, and snorkel for only 60F. Look for their boat the *Plongée VIII* at the Vieux Port off quai St-Pierre.

NEAR CANNES

ILES DE LÉRINS

A pair of small islands that have been designated as national forests, the Iles de Lérins are a great escape just off the coast of Cannes. The bigger island, **Ile Ste-Marguerite,** is just over 3 km (2 mi) long and has nice beaches and places to swim, but the water around the port has become murky from all the boat traffic. Paths wind through the woods, and the **chemin de Ceinture** (Beltway) circles the entire island along the water's edge. According to legend, the 16th-century **Fort Vauban** (tel. 04–93–43–45–47) is one of the sites where the mysterious Man in the Iron Mask was imprisoned between 1689 and

1703 before being taken to the Bastille, where he died. Since you're not likely to stay as long as the masked guy did, eat elsewhere—the few restaurants and snack bars here are even more expensive than those in Cannes.

Ile St-Honorat is more peaceful and less traveled than Ile Ste-Marguerite. After wandering along its ocean paths and witnessing the views from the monastery, you'll be ready to make a vow of silence to stay here, too. Only Cistercian monks live on the island, cultivating lavender, grapes, and honey. Singing monks are the highlight of Sunday mass at **L'Abbaye de Lérins**; call 04–93–99–54–00 for more information. There's one overpriced café-bar on the island, **La Tonnelle des Iles** (tel. 04–93–99–18–07), but you're much better off bringing a picnic from the mainland.

BASICS • The **ferry** (tel. 04–93–38–66–33) leaves daily on the half hour (more often in summer) 7:30 AM–6:30 PM from Cannes's harbor near the Palais des Festivals; it takes 15 minutes to get to Ste-Marguerite (45F round-trip) and 30 minutes to St-Honorat (50F round-trip). To visit both islands costs 70F. Since the islands are considered national-forest property, smoking and camping are not allowed.

GRASSE

If you've got the latest French perfume gracing your wrist, chances are it came from Grasse. Sixteen kilometers (10 mi) inland from Cannes, Grasse is the perfume capital of the world, with 30 factories that peddle their essences to Estée Lauder, Christian Dior, and the queen of them all, Chanel (No. 5). An abundance of flowers gives the town its heavenly scent, and a medieval centre ville makes for a historically intriguing visit. The best factory to tour is **Fragonard** (blvd. Fragonard, tel. 04–93–36–44–65), which has been around since 1926 and has a museum detailing centuries of perfume making.

Go to the **tourist office** (pl. de la Foux, tel. 04–93–36–03–56) for more information on the town and its history, or check out the elegant **Musée d'Art et d'Histoire de Provence** (2 rue Mirabeau, tel. 04–93–36–01—61). It's open Wednesday–Sunday, June–September 10–7 and October–May 10–noon and 2–5. Admission is 25F. The cheapest hotel worth your money is the centrally located **Napoléon** (6 av. Thiers, tel. 04–93–36–05–87). The cozy rooms go for 130F–230F.

ST-RAPHAEL

Between the red cliffs of the Massif de l'Esterel and the high, rocky Massif des Maures, St-Raphaël is a quiet town with sandy beaches, marinas, and a casino. An important site during World War II, St-Raphaël served as a major landing base for American and French soldiers. Unfortunately, the town lost many of its beautiful belle epoque mansions during the war. Sunny days and a stunning coastline still remain, however. Though the beachfront can provide for all your needs, with supermarkets, cafés, bars, and cheap hotels, you can practice your French and escape the tourist throngs in the quiet bars and restaurants off **rue de la Liberté, avenue Général Leclerc,** and **rue Allonque,** all on the far side of the train tracks. This small commercial center where most locals live and work is almost entirely ignored by beach goers. Be careful of place Ortolan, though; not too pretty by day, it gets scuzzier by night. St-Raphaël has a good stretch of beach on which to while away your days in the sun, and it's a good base for exploring the surrounding area. It is worth a ride along the **Corniche d'Esterel** for some of the most stunning mountain and seascapes in Europe; if you can, make it a sunrise or sunset mission.

BASICS

The **Office de Tourisme** facing the train station will happily load you down with lots of free brochures on events, maps, bus and ferry schedules, and a list of area hotels and campgrounds. The friendly English-speaking staff can also sell you the National Forestry Service's map of all the footpaths and hiking routes in the Massif de l'Esterel. *Rue Waldeck-Rousseau, tel. 04–94–19–52–52. Open Mon.–Sat. 9–12:30 and 2–6:30.*

COMING AND GOING

BY TRAIN • St-Raphaël-Valescure is the name of St-Raphaël's **train station** (pl. de la Gare, tel. 04–94–91–50–50). St-Raphaël is the western terminus of the TER line that runs along the Riviera. To get to towns farther west on the Riviera, you have to go by bus. Trains from here go to Paris (430F) nine times a day and almost as often to Lyon (267F), Dijon (349F), and Marseille (111F). Even the bullet-fast TGV stops here.

BY BUS • The **bus station** is directly behind the train station. **Forum Cars** (tel. 04–94–95–16–71) go to Draguignan (30F), Cannes (35F), and Fréjus (8F) during the week. **SODETRAV** (tel. 04–94–95–24–82) takes you to St-Tropez (1½ hrs, 48F), with stops in Fréjus, St-Aygulf, and Ste-Maxime. **SNCF Excursions** runs 85F buses to the Gorges du Verdon (*see Near St-Raphaël, below*) every Thursday 7:30 AM–7 PM.

BY CAR • Rent a car in St-Raphaël if you want to get to some less-accessible areas near the town—the Gorges du Verdon, for example (*see below*). Major car rental agencies are on place de la Gare in front of the train station: **Hertz**(tel. 04–94–82–24–44).

BY FERRY • The ferries of **Les Bateaux de St-Raphaël** (tel. 04–94–95–17–46) leave from St-Raphaël's Vieux Port for St-Tropez (100F round-trip), the Iles-de-Lérins (150F round-trip), and the Calanques des Roches Rouges de l'Esterel (1½ hrs, 50F round-trip).

GETTING AROUND

Patrick Moto (260 av. Général Leclerc, tel. 04–94–53–65–99) rents bikes for 50F (800F deposit), mountain bikes for 90F (2,000F deposit), and scooters for 260F (6,000F deposit). It also takes MasterCard and Visa for the deposit.

WHERE TO SLEEP

St-Raphaël's budget hotels tend to be pretty dingy, but you can find a few nice, affordable places. **Hôtel des Pyramides** (77 av. Paul-Doumer, tel. 04–94–95–05–95), southeast of the train station and within view of the beach, has a garden patio; singles are 145F and doubles start at 200F. Almost directly opposite the station is **Hôtel de France** (25 pl. Galliéri, tel. 04–94–95–19–20), a simple, no-frills hotel; doubles are 299F in peak season. **Hôtel Europe** (358 pl. Pierre Coulet, tel. 04–94–95–42–91) is a grand old building with balustrade balconies; a double room with TV and shower is 260F–340F. If none of these pan out, take a bus or boat to St-Aygulf, a less-touristy beach town with cheaper accommodations and restaurants.

HOSTELS • **Auberge de Jeunesse.** Halfway between Cannes and St-Raphaël in Le Trayas, this isolated hostel has a wonderful view of both the water and mountains, but it's far out of town. A bus from the train station in Le Trayas takes you to the stop Trayas-Auberge, after which it's a 1½-km (1-mi) hike up the hill. It costs 66F for bed and breakfast (HI card required), plus 17F for sheets. Call ahead for availability. *9 av. de la Véronèse, tel. 04–93–75–40–23. 100 beds. Check-in 8–10 AM and 5:30–10 PM. Lockout 10:30–5. Closed Jan.*

Centre International du Manoir. This hostel is 5 km (3 mi) from St-Raphaël in the suburb of Boulouris. A clean, plain room with breakfast costs 115F (170F July–August) per person, and dorm rooms are 70F. Surrounded by a park and near the beach, the hostel offers activities like sailing, scuba diving, and tennis in summer. The staff is very helpful, the bar rocks into the wee hours, and there's no curfew. From July to mid-August, the hostel only accepts people between the ages of 18 and 35. Buses and trains go to Boulouris every 30 minutes from the St-Raphaël stations. Reservations are advised. *Chemin de l'Escale, tel. 04–94–95–20–58. 170 beds. Reception open 8–8. Laundry.*

CAMPING • **Parc de Camping de St-Aygulf.** A few steps from the beach and shaded by trees, the campground in St-Aygulf is one of the biggest (and most popular) in the region; call ahead. Showers, toilets, and big sinks for washing clothes are on-site, and grocery stores and restaurants are just a few paces away. You'll pay 25F per person plus 28F per site in summer. *270 av. Salvareli, tel. 04–94–17–62–49. Take bus from Fréjus or St-Raphaël and get off at 1st stop in St-Aygulf. 1,600 sites. Closed Oct.–Mar.*

FOOD

St-Raphaël has a range of snack stands, late-night pizza spots, and fine restaurants along its oceanfront. Open Tuesday–Sunday, a morning **outdoor market** (rue de la République, behind the bus station) sells nuts, olives, herbs, mustards, and nougat as well as the usual fruits and vegetables. Another daily **morning market** is on place Victor Hugo. There's a **Monoprix** (tel. 04–94–95–01–69) supermarket on boulevard Félix-Martin; it's closed Sunday.

Across from the train station, **Cristie's Pâtisserie** (40 rue Waldeck-Rousseau, tel. 04–94–40–55–30) has delicious sandwiches for 22F. For a cozy atmosphere and outstanding regional food, go to **La Grillade** (32 rue Boetman, tel. 04–94–95–15–16), where for 79F you can try the minestrone *au pistou* (French-style, with a garlic-basic sauce), homemade ravioli, and chocolate mousse. When you're ready to go out, the popular **Les Ambassadeurs** (171 quai Albert I, tel. 04–94–95–10–65) has live music on Friday and Saturday. Beers are 14F, cocktails 50F. Try homemade ice cream from **Le Poussin Bleu** (41 blvd. de la Libération, tel. 04–94–95–25–14).

NEAR ST-RAPHAEL

FREJUS

The old town of Fréjus, founded in 49 BC by Julius Caesar, has some ancient Roman monuments to prove its heritage. The town is about 1 km (½ mi) inland from Fréjus-Plage, which extends to St-Raphaël's beach (*see* St-Raphaël, *above*). Fréjus has more sights to see in its old town, but St-Raphaël has cheaper hotels and a long stretch of sandy beaches.

During the **Bravade de Fréjus,** held the third Sunday after Easter, artists and musicians fill the streets of Fréjus-Ville with the usual food, drink, and revelry to celebrate the town's history. All summer, Fréjus hosts the **Forum des Arts et de la Musique,** with classical and jazz music, ballet, and opera. Many of the events are free.

BASICS • Get a schedule of free events at the **tourist office** in town or on the beach. *325 rue Jean-Jaurès, Fréjus-Ville, tel. 04–94–51–83–83. Open July–Aug., Mon.–Sat. 9–7, Sun. 10–noon and 2:30–5:30; Sept.–June, daily 9–noon and 2–6:30. Other location: blvd. de la Libération, Fréjus-Plage, tel. 04–94–51–48–42; open similar hrs.*

COMING AND GOING • Fréjus-Ville has a small **train station** (rue Marin Bidouré), seconds away by rail from the larger one in St-Raphaël. If you are traveling from any of the towns on the St-Raphaël–Ventimiglia line, you have to get off in St-Raphaël and take a train going farther west toward Toulon or Marseille to reach Fréjus-Ville. Fréjus's **bus station** (corner blvd. Séverin Decuers and av. de Provence) is on the north side of the city center. **SODETRAV** (tel. 04–94–53–78–46) buses traveling between St-Tropez and St-Raphaël stop along the coast in Fréjus.

WHERE TO SLEEP • **Auberge de Jeunesse et Camping.** This hostel and campground is a good alternative to St-Raphaël hotels. For 65F, plus 16F for sheets, you can settle into this peaceful little lodging under the trees, far from the beach crowds. A bus leaves every morning in summer for St-Raphaël's beaches (8F). In July and August the place is constantly full (so arrive early); a hostel card is required, but you can buy one here. There are 10 rooms with five beds each (81F) that have full bathrooms. The hostel organizes day trips to St-Tropez (80F round-trip) and the Gorges du Verdon (85F round-trip). *Chemin du Counillier, tel. 04–94–53–18–75. From Fréjus, a 2-km (1-mi) walk from train station; follow signs. From St-Raphaël, take the 6 PM bus that leaves from platform 7; ask driver to stop at L'Auberge de Jeunesse, and walk up to hostel. 94 beds. Reception opens at 6 PM. Lockout 10 AM–6 PM. Curfew 11 PM. Kitchen.*

Le Pont d'Argens. This campground, about 4 km (2½ mi) south of Fréjus-Plage, is on the Corniche Inférieure (N98), the road running along the coast between Fréjus and St-Aygulf. For about 130F per night for two, you can get a campsite near the water and a pool. The campground's restaurant and bar attract hundreds looking to socialize. *Rte. N98, tel. 04–94–51–14–97. 500 sites. Closed mid-Oct.–Mar.*

FOOD • Fréjus has an **outdoor market** in the center of its vieille ville every Wednesday and Saturday morning. Should you miss it, you can pick up cheap sandwiches, socca, and other spicy Mediterranean specialties from delis or sidewalk cafés.

WORTH SEEING • The sights in Fréjus-Ville are scattered around town. The **Arènes,** at the west end, is a 2nd-century Roman amphitheater used today for summer festivals, bullfights, and other events. At the north end, the **Roman Théâtre** has lost much of its former glory thanks to modern bleachers. Northeast of town you'll find arches from the once 40-km (25-mi) **Roman aqueduct** that used to bring water from the Massif de l'Esterel. In the center of Fréjus's vieille ville, in an area known as La Cité Épiscopale (Episcopal City), is the splendid **cathédrale,** built from the 12th to 16th centuries. Next to the cathedral, the 5th-century octagonal **Baptistère** is the oldest one in France; the pool in the center was used to baptize worshipers before they attended mass.

GORGES DU VERDON

This 21-km (13-mi) stretch of rock and water is a dream come true if you love hiking, bicycling, or just enjoying the great outdoors. The fast-flowing Verdon River has carved this dramatic gorge out of the surrounding limestone, resulting in a canyon of stunning depth and beauty. The bad news is that the area is nearly impossible to explore via public transportation. One bus runs out here on Thursday (see Coming and Going in St-Raphaël, above), but it's a sightseeing excursion that doesn't actually let you walk around the gorges.

You can make it out here on your own, but it's a slow process—buses run from city to city only once a day or twice a week. From St-Raphaël you can take a bus to Draguignan. There the **tourist office** (9 blvd. Clemenceau, tel. 04–94–68–63–30) can load you down with information on the gorge, but to reach it you'll have to rent a car (see Coming and Going in St-Raphaël, above). Your other option is to catch another bus to **Castellane** from Draguignan. In July and August a free shuttle runs from Castellane to the trailheads. If you can get there by rented car, **La Palud sur Verdon** is a small town west of Castellane where you'll find a **hostel** (tel. 04–92–77–38–72) with 66F dorm rooms. For more info on hiking trails, bus routes, and lodging, call **Verdon Accueil** (tel. 04–94–70–21– 64). The friendly staff will try their hardest to figure out a way for you to reach the "Grand Canyon of Europe."

Le Touring Club de France created many of the *sentiers* (trails) that surround the canyon. The **Sentier du Couloir Sampson** is a two-hour hike to and from Point Sublime at the north end of the River Verdon, and it's one of the shorter and least strenuous trails. **Sentier Martel** is an eight-hour trail named after the explorer who discovered the canyon in 1905—bring a map; flashlight; warm, waterproof clothing; and a buddy. Be sure to cross the river only at the *passerelles* (footbridges)—the French government uses the Verdon to generate electricity, and the river rises considerably if the electric company decides it needs more juice.

Women travelers, especially those traveling alone, should know that Fréjus is home to the biggest naval air base in France. Beware of the young bald boys traveling in packs, more so around Fréjus-Plage than Fréjus-Ville.

If you decide to stay longer than a day near the Gorges, the village of **Castellane** has hotel-restaurants, campgrounds, and *gîtes d'étape* (rural hostels). The **tourist office** (rte. BP26, rue Nationale, tel. 04–92–83–61–14), closed for lunch, has information and advice on hiking, biking, and walking in the canyon, as well as on accommodations in the area.

ST-TROPEZ

On the east end of the Maures mountain range, St-Tropez is one of the ritziest French vacation spots. The town has become such a byword for wealth, sun, and glitter—the yachts are among the biggest in Europe and countless stars (like Brigitte Bardot) own homes here—that you might be surprised to find that it's so small and insulated. The lack of train service, casinos, chain hotels, and department stores keeps it that way. St-Tropez is a beautiful place to visit, but it is far from budget traveler–friendly. The restaurants and hotels are outrageously priced, it's hard to get to the beaches, and there's nowhere to store your bag even if you just want to come for the day to gawk at jet-setters. Come off-season to experience its real charm; the crowds of petulant glitterati are insupportable in July and August.

Place des Lices and **place du XVe Corps** connect to form the nucleus of the town. Here you'll find a market on Tuesday and Saturday and afternoon games of pétanque. If you wander down rue François Silibi or boutique-lined rue Gambetta, you will hit the harbor of the vieille ville, where the fashion-conscious stroll between crowded cafés, stopping to sip wine while the yacht-clubbers look on from their teak decks. On a small hill above the vieille ville, the **Citadelle,** a 16th-century fortress, is a perfect escape overlooking St-Tropez and the bay. Walking along its ramparts is the best way to experience the striking colors of the coast and town that have inspired so many painters.

BASICS

MAIL

The **post office** has phone booths and telegram, poste restante, and money-exchange services. The postal code is 83990. *Pl. Alphonse Celli, tel. 04–94–55–96–50. Open weekdays 9–noon and 2–5, Sat. 9–noon.*

VISITOR INFORMATION

The **tourist office,** which faces the port, has tons of brochures, maps of driving circuits for the surrounding area, and a hotel-reservation service. *Quai Jean Jaurès, tel. 04–94–97–45–21. Open weekdays 9–12:30 and 2–6; daily 9:30–1:30 and 2:30–11 in summer.*

COMING AND GOING

No matter how you do it, it's expensive to reach St-Tropez. The closest you can get by train is St-Raphaël (*see above*), about 25 km (16 mi) away; store your bags there since St-Tropez doesn't have any luggage-storage facilities. From St-Raphaël, you can either take a **SODETRAV** bus from the *gare routière* (bus station; tel. 04–94–97–88–51 in St-Tropez; sq. Régis, tel. 04–94–95–24–82 in St-Raphaël), or a boat with **Les Bateaux St-Raphaël** (Vieux Port de St-Raphaël, tel. 04–94–95–17–46). By bus from St-Raphaël it can be a gorgeous 1½-hour drive along the coast, with stops in St-Aygulf, Ste-Maxime, and Cogolin. But it can also be a traffic nightmare June–September, with buses being delayed 30–60 minutes. It's also a popular way to reach St-Tropez, so make sure you get to the bus station early or you'll be elbowed out of a seat by aggressive bronzed ladies and forced to stand the whole way. A one-way ticket is 48F. St-Tropez's **bus station** is on place Banqui, west of the center of town. The boat ride is shorter, less vulnerable to the whims of traffic, more reliable, and only 2F more; tickets cost 50F one-way.

GETTING AROUND

If you want to reach St-Tropez's main beaches, which are several miles from town, it's a good idea to rent a bike or scooter. Across from the bus station, you'll find **Espace 83 Yamaha** (2 av. Général Leclerc, tel. 04–94–55–80–00), where you can get a scooter for 220F plus a 8,000F (or credit-card) deposit. At **Location Vélos-Motos, Louis Mas** (5 rue Quaranta, tel. 04–94–97–00–60), near place des Lices, mountain bikes cost 80F a day with a 2,000F deposit; scooters are 210F with a 6,000F deposit. Both are open April–September. Credit-card imprints are accepted as deposits.

WHERE TO SLEEP

Finding a place to sleep in summer in St-Tropez is extremely difficult; you're better off staying in St-Raphaël, Fréjus, or Ste-Maxime and visiting St-Tropez for the day. Though prices usually drop in early spring and late fall, many of the lower-priced hotels also close then. Campgrounds are plentiful around St-Tropez and near the beaches of Ramatuelle, but they fill up quickly, charge at least 100F, and are not very accessible.

Near the center of St-Tropez (and the bus station), the **Hôtel les Chimères** (Port du Pilon, tel. 04–94–97–02–90) is a charmingly dilapidated option. Rooms start at 150F but escalate to 330F in July and August. Reserve far in advance in summer. You can also try **La Méditerranée** (21 blvd. Louis Blanc, tel. 04–94–97–00–44), but do not expect too much, considering a double in the high season starts at 250F. If you've got wheels and a tent, try driving around looking for CAMPING À LA FERME signs, where people charge a small fee (50F–100F) for you to pitch your tent in their yard.

FOOD

At the outdoor **market** on place des Lices every Tuesday and Saturday morning, you can buy fruits, vegetables, cheese, flowers, and *tarte tropeziennes* (cream-filled pastries named for St-Tropez). For fresh seafood, the **Marché aux Poissons** at place aux Herbes is open every morning, except Monday. **Prisunic** (pl. Blanqui, near the bus station), open Monday–Saturday 8–8, Sunday 8:30–12:30, is a good stop-off to load up on groceries.

Expensive ice-cream stands, cafés, and *crêperies* (crepe stands) line the port. The vieille ville is a good option for better prices. **Ghandi** (3 quai de l'Épi, tel. 04–94–97–71–71), on the vieux port, is a popular spot for a good Indian meal; the lunch menu is 58F and the dinner menus are 85F and 100F. At **L'Artichaut Barigoule** (pl. Grammont, tel. 04–94–97–02–73) you can get stuffed artichokes with tomatoes, salmon, and crab, for 20F–30F. **Le Café** (pl. des Lices, tel. 04–94–97–44–69), frequented by the St-Tropez elite over the years, has become a cultural cornerstone for the city and will sell a bottle of Bordeaux for as little as 190F (though you might instead opt for a coffee for 13F).

WORTH SEEING

The long beaches associated with St-Tropez are far from town and usually private. You'll find them around the cape from St-Tropez, along the coast of Ramatuelle (*see* Near St-Tropez, *below*). **Plage de la Bouillabaisse** is a nice sandy beach only 10 minutes by foot; just walk west from the port. In the other direction you'll reach **Plage des Cannebiers**. From here you can take a path that passes **Plage des Salins** (4 km/2½ mi from St-Tropez) and ends up at **Plage de Pampelonne** (8 km/5 mi from St-Tropez); these beaches are divided into alternating private and public plots of sand. Each beach club has its own clientele; **Plage de Tahiti**, at the north end of Pampelonne, is supposed to be a favorite of movie stars. The most convenient way to find the sand that's right for you is to rent a scooter (*see* Getting Around, *above*). **SODETRAV** buses bound for Plage de Pampelonne (15 mins, 15F) leave from the station three times daily, Monday–Saturday, in July and August.

The **Musée de l'Annonciade,** a church converted into a major art museum, is on the south corner of the port. The 19th- and 20th-century paintings and sculptures include works by Matisse, Braque, Dufy, and Paul Signac, the painter who turned sleepy St-Tropez into a renowned artists' haven in the late 19th century. *Pl. Grammont, tel. 04–94–97–04–01. Admission 30F. Open Oct. and Dec.–May, Wed.–Mon. 10–noon and 2–6; June–Sept., Wed.–Mon. 10–noon and 3–7.*

In the early evening take a walk to the hexagonal **Citadelle,** which gives views of the glowing old town of St-Tropez. Investigate the part of the town known as **La Ponche** (at the seaward end of quai Jean-Jaurès) and find tiny tidal beaches lapping right underneath the houses.

If you have time, other attractions worth visiting are **La Maison des Papillons** (9 rue Etienne Berny, tel. 04–94–97–63–45), the House of Butterflies, where you'll find a collection of 4,500 beautiful insects from all over France; and the **Coopérative Vinicole du Golfe de St-Tropez** (Wine Growers' Organization; av. Paul Roussel, tel. 04–94–97–01–60), where you can sample various wines of St-Tropez.

NEAR ST-TROPEZ

Near St-Tropez you'll find stunning, rugged coastline; the shady beach town of **Ste-Maxime**; and the old, hilltop village of **Ramatuelle**. From St-Tropez, SODETRAV buses (*see* Coming and Going, *above*) go inland to Ramatuelle and along the coast to St-Raphaël. The trip is 15F–35F, and the towns are 30–45 minutes apart).

RAMATUELLE

This small, medieval village is up in the hills, surrounded by miles of fields and vineyards. It's on the same small peninsula as St-Tropez, but inland and about 20 km (12 mi) southwest of the town center. It takes about an hour to walk from Ramatuelle to the popular **beaches** along the coast—Pampelonne, Tahiti, and Bora Bora are favorites among the rich and famous. Although officially in Ramatuelle, these beaches are often considered part of St-Tropez. July is a great time to visit Ramatuelle, when the town hosts its annual **wine festival** and summer **jazz festival.** Stop by the **Office de Tourisme** (pl. de l'Ormeau, tel. 04–94–79–26–04), closed winter, for a schedule of events.

WHERE TO SLEEP AND EAT • The village has almost everything you could need, but not a great choice of affordable hotels. **Chez Tony** (rue Clemenceau, tel. 04–94–79–20–46), run by Tony and his family, has eight small rooms with showers for 160F each. Camping near the beaches is big with the jet-setters, so it's expensive and often full. Open Easter–October, the campground **La Cigale** (cher Escalet, tel. 04–94–79–22–53) has a pizzeria and hot showers and is about 1 km (½ mi) from Plage de l'Escalet, southeast of Ramatuelle. Camping for two people with a tent is 109F; you can also rent bungalows here for 2,000F–3,800F per week. **Le Marché Provençal** is held Thursday and Sunday 8 AM–1 PM in place de l'Ormeau and has fresh produce and a particularly good assortment of clothes and handmade jewelry. For a good Provençal meal, go to **L'Écurie** (rte. des Moulins de Paillas, tel. 04–94–79–11–59) where a main dish is about 70F. The **Hôtel Lou Castellas** (rte. des Moulins de Paillas, tel. 04–94–77–20–67) has 15 simple rooms and is run by the same family as L'Écurie; doubles cost 280F.

STE-MAXIME

Surrounded by the high, red mountains of the Massif des Maures, Ste-Maxime has marvelous sandy beaches that face St-Tropez across the gulf. You can get here by bus or by boat from St-Tropez (64F); **Transports Maritimes MMG** (quai L. Condroyer, tel. 04–94–96–51–00) does by water what SODETRAV does by land. The well-stocked, beachside **Office de Tourisme** (promenade Simon Lorière, tel. 04–94–96–19–24) dispenses hiking and camping info and sells bus and boat tickets.

WHERE TO SLEEP AND EAT • Hotels in Ste-Maxime have a nasty habit of obliging you to pay for half-board during July and August and are often closed in winter. You'll find better deals during the shoulder season (May, June, and September). The best place to stay in Ste-Maxime is at the **Hôtel-Restaurant Castellamar** (8 av. Pompidou, tel. 04–94–96–19–97) at the southwest end of town, just over the yellow bridge (ask the driver to stop at the unmarked bus stop here). From there, walk three blocks inland to avenue Georges Pompidou, where the hotel sits tucked down a hedge-lined driveway to your left. Double rooms go for 175–225F off-season, and 250F–300F in July and August. The hotel is closed November–December.

Be sure to hit the **indoor market** (place du Marché) Tuesday–Sunday mornings for fruits and veggies. **May Ling** (1 bis Frédéric Mistral, tel. 04–94–96–28–24) serves great Chinese food Tuesday–Sunday and is one of the few restaurants in town with relatively reasonable prices (menus are 89F).

OUTDOOR ACTIVITIES • Many hiking trails stretch from Ste-Maxime along the coast or into the interior. At the tourist office, pick up the French-language "Promenez-vous dans Ste-Maxime et Sa Région" for descriptions of trails and "Excursions en Var" for a map. If you want to strike out on your own, the ancient **Sentier du Littoral,** designed to assure access to the sea at all points, winds picturesquely along the beach toward St-Tropez. To explore the neighboring countryside, rent a bike or moped from **Rent Bike** (13 rue Magali, tel. 04–94–43–98–07). Mountain bikes cost 80F a day with a 1,500F deposit; mopeds are 90F with a 2,500F deposit.

CORSICA

UPDATED BY CHRISTOPHER KNOWLES

O fficial borders aside, once you arrive in Corsica you're not in France anymore. The fourth-largest island in the Mediterranean, Corsica (La Corse in French) is both geographically and culturally closer to Italy and Sardinia than it is to France (though the locals see themselves purely as Corsican). The island has a laid-back tempo; your bus could be 20 minutes behind schedule, yet the driver will still stop midroute for coffee and a smoke. The heady scent of the maquis and the rugged granite peaks of this "mountain in the sea," along with the slow pace, make this wilderness island the perfect escape from the pressures of urban life.

For centuries, Corsica's strategic Mediterranean location and good harbors have made it a coveted spot for conquerors. The Greeks first colonized Corsica in 565 BC; in AD 1077, the Pisans took over in earnest—their churches still blanket the island. The Genoese arrived in the 13th and 14th centuries, building many of the citadels that still overlook every major Corsican town. These citadels, or giant stone forts, were designed to shelter the villages and provide resistance to hostile forces. The Italians controlled the island to a greater or lesser extent until the French assumed control in 1769. Over the next hundred years, Corsica became known for its banditry, with the fierce island spirit exploding in vendettas that make *Romeo and Juliet* look like child's play (*see* box An Eye for an Eye, *below*). By 1931, the French government had finally had enough: More than 600 soldiers invaded the island, seizing weapons, ransacking villages, making arrests, and ultimately banning the Corsican language. Though brutally repressive, the French did put an end to much of the bloodshed and so-called lawlessness.

For the 250,000 inhabitants of the island, France is only the most recent conqueror. In the early 1970s, nationalist groups began using strategically placed bombs and death threats to force the French out. These groups continue to target French cars, French-owned vacation homes, and buildings belonging to foreign and French companies. The Front de Libération Nationale de la Corse (FLNC) is the island's oldest and largest separatist group, responsible for most of the political graffiti you see. Nevertheless, most Corsicans do not support FLNC brutality and willingly accept their French citizenship. You may sense an initial distrust of tourists, but you'll also find that Corsicans, provided you treat them and their island respectfully, can be most hospitable.

Corsica is made up of Haute Corse (Upper Corsica) and Corse du Sud (Southern Corsica). The island's center and the west coast lay claim to the most dramatic scenery, complete with treacherous cliffs and mountains plunging into the sea; the east coast is much flatter. Inland, you'll find green mountains and

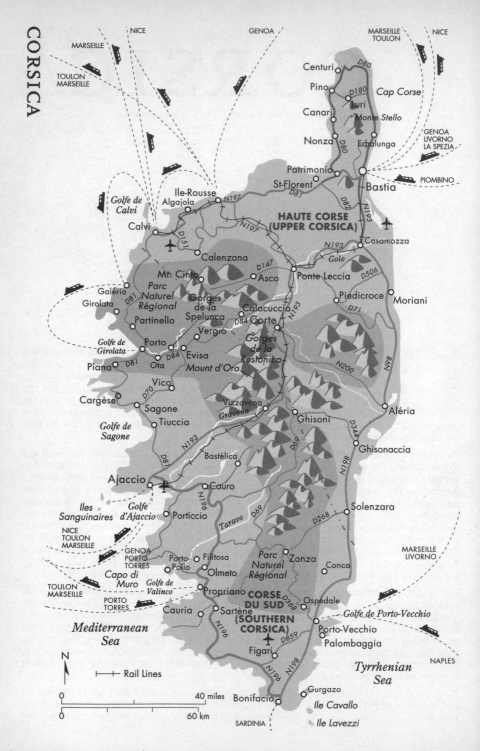

CORSICA

Centuri
Pino
Canari
Nonza
Luri
Monte Stello
Erbalunga
Cap Corse

D80
D180
D80
D82
D193

MARSEILLE
TOULON
MARSEILLE
NICE
GENOA
MARSEILLE
TOULON
NICE

GENOA
LIVORNO
LA SPEZIA

PIOMBINO

Patrimonio
St-Florent
Bastia

D81

Golfe de Calvi
Ile-Rousse
Algajola
Calvi

N197
N197

HAUTE CORSE
(UPPER CORSICA)

N193
Casamozza

D151
Calenzana

Mt. Cinto
Parc Naturel Régional
Partinello

D147
Asco
Ponte Leccia
Golo
D506

Piedicroce
Moriani

D71

Galéria
Girolata

D81

Gorges de la Spelunca
Calacuccia
Corte
D84

N193

Golfe de Girolata
Porto
Vergio
Evisa
Gorges de la Restonica

D84
Ota

N200

N198

Piana
Mount d'Oro
D81

Vico

D70

Cargèse
Sagone
Tiuccia
Golfe de Sagone

Vizzavona
Gravona

Ghisoni
Aléria

D69

Ghisonaccia

N193
Bastélica

D81

Ajaccio
Cauro

N196

Iles Sanguinaires
Golfe d'Ajaccio
Porticcio

Tavaro
D69

Solenzara

D344

D268

NICE
TOULON
MARSEILLE

GENOA
PORTO
TORRES
Porto-Pollo
Filitosa
Olmeto
Zonza
Conca

Parc Naturel Régional

Capo di Muro
Golfe de Valinco

TOULON
MARSEILLE

PORTO
TORRES
Propriano

CORSE DU SUD
(SOUTHERN CORSICA)

D268
Ospédale

MARSEILLE
LIVORNO

Golfe de Porto-Vecchio

Cauria
Sartène
Porto-Vecchio
Palombaggia

N196

Mediterranean Sea

Figari
D859

N198

NAPLES

N Rail Lines

Gurgazo
Tyrrhenian Sea

0   40 miles
0   60 km

Bonifacio
Ile Cavallo
Ile Lavezzi

SARDINIA

398

rural villages, as well as the Parc Naturel Régional de la Corse, which takes up almost a third of the island. A car is crucial if you want to visit the whole island, although an erratic transportation system inches its way to most of the popular spots (at least during July and August).

Museums aren't of much importance on the island, with the exception of Ajaccio's Musée Fesch, which has the best collection of Italian masters outside of Paris and Florence. Bonifacio is the most dramatic Corsican town in terms of its clifftop location, while Calvi has the best budget options and Riviera-like white-sand beaches. Bastia is the most industrial city, but it's also the best base for exploring Cap Corse, a peninsula whose topography replicates the whole island's—and arguably one of the best reasons to visit Corsica in the first place. Corte, which makes a good base for exploring the inland hiking trails, houses Corsica's only university—which means there's a hint of nightlife. Ajaccio has the most urban diversions, thanks to its size.

BASICS

WHEN TO GO

Visit Corsica in May or June, when the flowers are blooming and the tourist season is just getting under way, or in September or October, when tourism winds down but the weather and water are still warm. Avoid Corsica in July and don't even think about coming in August, when French, German, and Italian families invade the coastal towns. In late summer, prices soar, as does the temperature. Most of the island's hotels and campgrounds close November–March, when many smaller towns effectively shut down and high-altitude hiking trails get snowed in.

On August 15, Corsica goes berserk, melding "Fête de l'Assomption" (Assumption Day) with a birthday bash for the island's favorite son, Napoléon Bonaparte.

COMING AND GOING

Flights last under an hour from the Riviera, and the ferry takes 3–12 hours, depending on where and when you leave. In the high season, round-trip airfares (especially on charter flights) are often cheaper than the ferry. Eurail, InterRail, and the France Railpass do not get you any discounts for ferries to Corsica.

BY FERRY • SNCM (tel. 08–36–67–95–00 for 24-hour information and reservations) operates ferries from **Nice** (tel. 04–93–13–66–99) to Ajaccio, Bastia, Calvi, and Ile-Rousse; from **Marseille** (tel. 04–91–56–30–10) to Ajaccio, Bastia, Calvi, Ile-Rousse, Porto-Vecchio, and Propriano; and from **Toulon** (tel. 04–94–16–66–66) to Ajaccio, Bastia, and Propriano. Depending on the season, one-way fare from Nice is 282F–305F. Ferries from Marseille and Toulon are slightly more expensive: 285F–325F. The crossing lasts an entire day or night. If you don't need a 82F–97F *couchette* (sleeping compartment), reservations are not necessary (though they're not a bad idea, especially in late July and August)—just show up at the port at least a half hour before departure time. SNCM's speediest addition is the *navire rapide,* a lightning-fast boat that makes the crossing from Nice to Bastia or Calvi in under three hours. The navire rapide makes one or two trips per day in summer and is slightly less expensive than the regular ferry—make reservations early. Plan on infrequent service November–March, and don't be surprised by the fairly frequent strikes. There are also ferry services from the Italian ports of Genova and Livorno.

BY PLANE • Corsica has four airports. Your best option is to land in Ajaccio, Bastia, or Calvi; Corsica's fourth airport, at Figari, is in the middle of nowhere, north of Bonifacio. Fares to all four airports are identical. **Air Inter Europe** (part of Air France) and **Corse Méditerranée** work in tandem; contact either for flight information. The cheapest flights leave from Nice and take just under an hour; a one-way ticket to Bastia costs 410F–600F. A one-way flight from Paris costs 1,200F–1,500F. You can also fly directly to Corsica from Lyon, Marseille, Toulon, Geneva, and Amsterdam. Between April and October the small local airline **Corsicatours** (tel. 04–95–70–10–36) operates charter flights from Frankfurt, Geneva, London, and Zurich.

GETTING AROUND

BY TRAIN • SNCF trains travel from Ajaccio on the west coast, through the interior towns of Ponte Leccia and Corte, branching off northwest to Ile-Rousse and Calvi or northeast to Bastia. Corsican trains reveal the island's rural interior; your train might need to stop for goats and cows as they graze along the tracks. Compared to buses, the trains are remarkably punctual. Eurail and French rail passes are not valid here, but InterRailers get a 50% discount. The free booklet "Petit Guide Pratique du Train de

AN EYE FOR AN EYE

During the 17th and 18th centuries, more than 30,000 Corsicans fell victim to the blood feuds that pitted family against family in Corsica (even the Bonapartes were included). Rampant lawless vengeance was a result of intense frustration; locals were sick of Genoese rule and the lack of an impartial judiciary. Vendetta eventually died out under French government, but the old family feuds still surface in occasional bombings. Families that have bombed their enemies out of existence can join the separatist FLNC and continue the rebellion against foreign intervention in Corsican affairs.

Corse," available at the regional tourist office in Ajaccio, gives practical information about various stops along the route. You can also pick up *un horaire* (a schedule) of Corsican trains from tourist offices or train stations.

BY BUS • Where the train won't take you a bus will, but winding roads make for queasy bus rides. Ajaccio is the most comprehensive and efficient bus hub, home to **Eurocorse Voyages** (tel. 04–95–21–06–30), **SAIB** (tel. 04–95–22–41–99), and **Autocars Ricci** (tel. 04–95–51–08–19), as well as a handful of smaller, village-to-village companies. Check the cities reviewed below for specific times and prices. Bus travel is frustrating if you're on a tight schedule; buses often leave at odd hours (6 AM or 9 PM), leave only once a day, and are invariably late. Don't worry about missing your connection, since chances are it's late, too. Buses generally don't run on Sundays, though many companies add an extra bus or two to their daily routes July–mid-August. The off-season (October–June) brings even more sporadic service.

BY CAR • Renting a car makes a lot of sense if you want to go to smaller towns, do some camping, or visit the island in the off-season, when public transportation is at its sketchiest. If you're traveling in a group, a car can be cheaper (and safer) than scooters. If you're trying to cover a lot of ground, car rental is necessary, especially for Cap Corse. Rental rates drop by about 10% outside July and August, with smaller Corsican companies offering the cheapest rates. **Citer,** which has outlets in Ajaccio, Bastia, Calvi, and Porto-Vecchio, is by far the cheapest, going as low as 190F per day and 990F per week. **ADA** is your second-best bet; it has offices at all the airports and major cities. If you arrive by air and want to rent a car, try waiting until the airport has cleared out a bit and then bargain while business is slow. Big companies like **Hertz** and **Avis** won't bargain, don't rent to drivers under 26, and are expensive.

BY BIKE • Bike lanes are nonexistent, and Corsican drivers are all training for the Grand Prix, so a helmet is a necessary life-insurance plan. Still, Corsica provides some excellent mountain-biking terrain, especially in the mountainous interior. Daily bike rental usually runs 90F–125F. For 30F you can take your bike on the train and even on some buses. For information on long-term bike rentals and routes, contact Ajaccio's **Vivre la Corse en Vélo** (Résidence Napoléon, 23 av. du Général Leclerc, tel. 04–95–21–96–94 or 04–95–22–70–79). Note that renting a bike requires a hefty deposit as much as 1,500F.

BY MOPED • Stay off the dangerous national roads (the thick red lines on the Michelin map) in favor of smaller routes that often lead to remote villages and beaches. Rentals are expensive: about 225F per day or 1,250F per week and as much as 3,000F deposit. If you can only afford to rent a moped for a day or two, consider using it to get around Cap Corse (the peninsula near Bastia), or around the breathtakingly scenic coastal spots in the Bonifacio area.

WHERE TO SLEEP

Unless you're camping, finding a cheap place to stay will be your biggest obstacle: Corsica has no budget hotels and only a handful of hostels, and most hotels double or triple their rates July–early September. Rooms fill quickly in summer, so calling ahead is essential.

CAMPING AND RURAL HOSTELS • The Relais Régional des Gîtes Ruraux (contact Mme Chilotti, 1 rue Général Fiorella, Ajaccio, tel. 04–95–51–72–82, fax 04–95–51–72–89) has a combination of simple and often rustic accommodations at wallet-friendly farms. *Camping à la ferme,* or reasonably priced rooms in *ferme-auberges* (farms that double as inns), is the rule. Prices are 100F–150F per night; meals are 75F–100F. Campgrounds can stretch your budget in Corsica—ask at any tourist office for the booklet listing them. Most campgrounds also rent out bungalows with kitchens that cost 80F–400F for two or more people. Most campgrounds and gîtes close October–March.

GÎTES D'ÉTAPES AND REFUGES • If you're doing one of the hiking trails, a string of *gîtes d'étape* (way stations) will help you along the way, with a basic room going for 60F–90F per night and usually a hot meal costing another 45F–60F. *Refuges,* shelters with bunk beds and running water, cost 45F–60F a night; they dot the hiking trails and rarely need to turn guests away.

HOSTELS • Corsica has two good hostels in Calvi and one in Propriano. A few others lie in remote areas: one in **Galeria** (tel. 04–95–62–00–46), 30 minutes outside Calvi; another 10 km (6 mi) from Porto-Vecchio in **Sotta** (tel. 04–95–71–23–22); and finally the **Convent of Calacuccia** (tel. 04–95–48–00–11), 1½ hours from Bastia. Beds are 80F–100F per night, with meals for another 45F–80F. Pick up a complete list of hostels at the regional tourist office in Ajaccio or at the **Information Jeunesse** office in Bastia, Corte, Ajaccio, or Porto-Vecchio.

FOOD

Corsican food is simple and hearty. Corsican *charcuterie* (different varieties of sausage) has a unique flavor because the pigs live freely and feed naturally from the maquis, the thick brush covering much of Corsica; *sanglier* (wild boar) has a dark and aromatic aftertaste. *Brocciu,* a soft ricotta-like goat or sheep's whey product, is often used as a filling for omelets, trout, pasta, and pastries; *brebis* is a cheese made from ewe's milk and is commonly eaten as a dessert. Seafood is on most menus, though expensive (the fishermen of Cap Corse and Bonifacio are famous, so if you're going to splurge, do it here). The most popular dish is *l'aziminu,* Corsican bouillabaisse. *Canistrelli* are hard cookies much like Italian biscotti and are flavored with white wine, licorice, lemon, or orange. The island also has many vineyards that produce hearty reds, nutty whites, and refreshing rosés; bottles are clearly marked *Vins de Corse.* The maquis gives the local dark honey a rich flavor, and chefs make wise use of the island's abundant mint, rosemary, thyme, and myrtle. Chestnuts and chestnut flour are also used in everything from beer to bread to the famous *fritelli* (chestnut fritters).

OUTDOOR ACTIVITIES

Corsica is really just one big mountain, and if you come here without your hiking boots you'll feel sorely out of place. Covering more than a third of the island, the **Parc Naturel Régional de Corse** (tel. 04–95–21–56–54) has several hiking trails that run from one side of the island to the other. The most famous route is the **GR20,** which cuts a 160-km (100-mi) path from Calenzana (accessible by bus from Calvi) to Conca, near Porto-Vecchio. Reaching altitudes of more than 6,000 ft, the GR20 is one of the most difficult hiking trails in Europe: Open June–October only, it takes 15 days to complete (the rest of the year the weather is too stormy or snowy). Refuges dot the trail at roughly eight-hour intervals, providing dorm beds, stoves, and running water to weary hikers. While the GR20 sticks to the interior, there are also two **Mare e Monti** (sea-to-mountain) trails and three **Mare a Mare** (coast-to-coast) ones. Open all year, the first Mare e Monti goes from Calenzana to Cargese and takes 7–10 days; the southern Mare e Monti goes from Porticcio (near Ajaccio) to Propriano, takes 5–6 days, and is open all year. Only the southern Mare a Mare from Porto-Vecchio to Propriano is open all year; it takes five days. The northern coast-to-coast from Moriani to Cargese takes 8–12 days and is open only April–November. Also open April–November, the central Mare a Mare from Ghisonaccia to Ajaccio takes seven to eight days.

If you don't have the time or equipment to undertake a major trek, Corsica has plenty of day-tripping paths. Pick up area-specific leaflets called "Balades en Corse" at the park's **main office** (2 rue Sergent Casalonga, tel. 04–95–51–79–10) in Ajaccio; at one of the smaller outposts in Porto-Vecchio, Corte, or Calvi; or at most tourist offices. The English-language *Walks in Corsica* (100F), available at most bookstores and Parc Régional offices, outlines 600 km (373 mi) of footpaths (including the GR20). For organized hikes, contact Ajaccio's **Muntagne Corse in Libertà** (2 av. de la Grande Armée, tel. 04–95–20–53–14).

Water lovers have plenty of options throughout the island, from sailing and waterskiing in major resort towns or scuba diving off the dramatic west coast to white-water rafting and canoeing, or even fishing (if you buy a fishing license). You can also hang-glide, go horseback riding, and snow ski, provided you have the francs to burn.

HAUTE CORSE

The travel industry in Haute Corse (Upper Corsica) is slightly more developed than in the south and public transportation a bit less erratic. If you arrive in Bastia, stay just long enough to stock up on goods before going to Cap Corse, the peninsular "thumb" stretching north. Calvi, on the other hand, merits more time; there are tons of water activities and white-sand beaches that stretch to Ile-Rousse. Corte, smack in the center of the island, makes a great getaway from tourist crowds and should not be missed if you're seeking a more authentic Corsica and terrific hiking terrain.

BASTIA

The center of Corsica's one real industry—tobacco—and one of the island's two largest cities, Bastia is also the entry point for 50% of island visitors. With the sea forming its front lawn and lush, green mountains acting as a backyard, Bastia's crumbling facades have a certain charm. Bastia is also the departure point for Cap Corse (see Near Bastia, below), one of the island's most worthwhile, though frustratingly inconvenient, spots. Keep in mind that no regular buses or trains serve the peninsula (a rental car is a good option).

Bastia is divided into the port—train station, bus station, ferry terminal, and commercial center—and the *vieille ville* (old town). The narrow winding streets of the vieille ville, strewn with laundry lines and prowling cats, confirm Bastia's fame as Corsica's most Italian city. Lined with cafés and outdoor seating, **place St-Nicolas,** the official center of town, lies opposite the new port and is the heart of the city's action. On a clear day, head up to the 16th-century citadel for a terrific view of the islands of Capraja, Elba, Pianosa, and Monte-Cristo; if you're really lucky you might see all the way to Italy's Tuscan hills.

BASICS

BUREAUX DE CHANGE • Avoid the dreaded **Crédit Agricole** change booths at the *gare maritime* (port) and on avenue Maréchal Sébastiani. The **Banque de France** charges no commission and has excellent rates. *2 cours Henri Pierangeli, off pl. St-Nicolas, tel. 04–95–31–24–09. Open weekdays 8:45–noon and 1:30–3:30.*

MAIL • The **main post office** lies between the port and the train station. You'll find telephones, telegram service, poste restante, and Minitel access; you can even buy AmEx traveler's checks here. Bastia's postal code is 20200. *Av. Maréchal Sébastiani, tel. 04–95–32–80–70. Open weekdays 8–7, Sat. 8–noon.*

VISITOR INFORMATION • The **Office Municipal du Tourisme** has information on campgrounds, hotels, and the Cap Corse peninsula. *Pl. St-Nicolas, tel. 04–95–31–00–89 or 04–95–31–81–34. Open mid-Apr.–June and Sept.–Oct., daily 8–7; July–Aug., daily 8–8; Nov.–mid-Apr., Mon.–Sat. 8–6.*

COMING AND GOING

BY TRAIN • The **train station** (tel. 04–95–32–80–61) is several blocks from the port on square Leclerc. Trains leave twice daily for Calvi (3 hrs, 91F) and four times daily for Ajaccio (4 hrs, 119F). To reach Corte or Vizzavona, take the Ajaccio train; to reach Ile-Rousse, take the Calvi train.

BY BUS • The bus station is a parking lot next to place St-Nicolas. **Société des Autobus Bastiais** (tel. 04–95–31–06–65) runs the local bus system, and service to other towns is provided by companies such as **Rapides Bleus** (1 av. Maréchal Sébastiani, tel. 04–95–31–03–79), which sends two buses daily down the Côte Orientale to Porto-Vecchio (3 hrs, 110F). **Transports Micheli** (tel. 04–95–35–61–08) will get you to Erbalunga daily in summer, and **Transports Saoletti** (tel. 04–95–37–84–05) has a bus to Canari that stops in Nonza and Patrimonio. The tourist office has schedules.

BY FERRY • Bastia's **gare maritime** (tel. 04–95–31–02–04) has a miniature tourist office, a change booth, and luggage storage. The **SNCM office** (Nouveau Port, tel. 04–95–54–66–99), tucked under some trees, sends ferries to Nice (282F), Marseille (308F), and Toulon (308F). All fares are for the low season; expect to pay an extra 30F–40F in high season and 85F for the least expensive sleeping berth. **Corsica Ferries** (5 bis rue Chanoine Leschi, tel. 04–95–32–95–95) goes to the Italian cities of Genoa (195F) and Livorno (145F). Again, prices go up (about 25F–60F) in high season. You can also sail to the Italian island of Elba on **Moby Lines** (4 rue de Casabianca, tel. 04–95–31–46–29) for about 185F round-trip; inquire at their booth at the port for more information.

BY PLANE • The Aéroport Bastia-Poretta (tel. 04–95–54–54–54) is about 20 km (12 mi) south of the city. For information on **Air Inter Europe,** or **Air Corse Méditerranée** flights, call 04–95–31–79–79 or visit the airlines' office at 6 avenue Émile Sari. Société des Autobus Bastiais runs 42F buses out to the airport from the préfecture, opposite the train station.

GETTING AROUND

ADA has the cheapest car rentals, starting at 356F per day (249F with limited mileage), 560F per weekend, making it a feasible option for two or more people. You'll find ADA downtown (35 rue César-Campinchi, tel. 04–95–31–48–95) and at the airport (tel. 04–95–54–55–44). All you need is a driver's license and passport to rent. You'll also find **Hertz** downtown (sq. St-Victor, tel. 04–95–31–14–24) and at the airport (tel. 04–95–30–05–15), but it tends to have higher rates, as does **Europcar,** with offices at the port (1 rue de Nouveau-Port, tel. 04–95–31–59–29) and airport (tel. 04–95–36–03–55). You can rent scooters (200F a day) in Bastia at **Sarl Cinquini** (av. de la Libération, tel. 04–95–33–07–47), provided you've got a credit card for the 3,000F deposit.

WHERE TO SLEEP

UNDER 225F • Hôtel Central. This recently renovated hotel has small, clean rooms; a very kind owner; and, best of all, cheap prices. Singles start at 170F and doubles at 200F. *3 rue Miot, tel. 04–95–31–71–12, fax 04–95–31–82–40. 17 rooms, all with bath.*

UNDER 325F • Riviera-Hôtel. Recently remodeled and with a convenient location, this hotel wins the prize for being an all-around good deal. Most rooms have two twin beds, with singles and doubles from 250F (280F in July, 310F in August). Book months in advance for one of the 150F singles without bath. *1 rue du Nouveau-Port, tel. 04–95–31–07–16, fax 04–95–34–17–39. 20 rooms, 15 with bath.*

UNDER 375F • Hôtel Forum. You will find comfort in the rustic, Italian-style rooms that have TVs and phones. Singles are 250F, doubles 300F–350F. You might also try one of the six charming rooms at the Forum's sister **Hôtel Athena** (2 rue Miot, at blvd. Paoli, tel. 04–95–31–07–83). *20 blvd. Paoli, tel. 04–95–31–02–53, fax 04–95–31–26–41. 18 rooms, 16 with bath. Air-conditioning.*

Though the French government did not officially recognize "le Corse," the Corsican language, until 1974, it might actually be more like the original generic Romance language than either Italian or French; locals claim that le Corse is closest of all to Vulgar Latin.

UNDER 425 • Hôtel-Restaurant Les Voyageurs. Air-conditioned rooms, an excellent restaurant specializing in traditional Corsican fish dishes (75F–120F), and a central location only 100 yards from the train station make this a comfortable, well-priced deal. Double rooms range 200F–400F, depending on the season. *5 av. de Maréchal-Sébastian, tel. 04–95–31–29–31, fax 04–95–31–53–33. 20 rooms, all with bath.*

CAMPING • Camping les Orangers. You can get a comprehensive listing of nearby campgrounds at the tourist office, but this is the closest one, 4 km (2½ mi) from Bastia via Bus 7. The enthusiastic proprietors will usher you around their grassy, tent-friendly campground just across the road from a small beach. Sites are 24F per person, 12F per tent. *Tel. 04–95–33–24–09 or 04–95–33–23–65. 50 sites. Closed Oct.–Apr.*

Camping Merendella. A little farther away (40 km/25 mi) is this self-sufficient campground; besides an awesome beach location, it has a game room, pizzeria, washing machines, and a convenience store open seven days a week. Sites have electricity, drinking water, and hot showers. For an even cushier camping experience, try the cabins for four, with two bedrooms and a kitchen. Sites run about 44F–54F per person with tent; the cabins cost 1,400F–2,000F per week. *Moriani Plage, tel. 04–95–38–53–47, fax 04–95–38–44–01. 223 sites, 6 cabins. Closed mid-Oct.–Apr.*

FOOD

For a real meal, head to the old port, where you can try quality Corsican fare for under 90F. A colorful **outdoor market** fills place de l'Hôtel de Ville every morning except Monday. Anything else you could ever need awaits in the massive, impersonal aisles of **Toga Supermarché,** opposite the port at the roundabout connecting avenue Émile Sarl and route du Cap Corse.

UNDER 50F • Chief's Sandwiches. Despite the burning U.S. flag on the menu, this Indian-themed restaurant manages to do America right with "The Chief," a delicious cheeseburger variant (25F–28F) served with the fries stuffed inside. Other sandwiches include the vegetarian "Huron" (25F–28F), overflowing with avocado, tomatoes, and mozzarella. *Pl. St-Nicolas, tel. 04–95–31–21–81.*

UNDER 100F • L'Ambada. Watch local fishermen bring in their catch as you sit on the port side facing the citadel. L'Ambada serves a variety of Corsican specialties, including *beignets de calamars* (fried calamari), neatly packaged in 70F and 75F menus that include wine. À la carte pizzas start at 30F. *Vieux Port, tel. 04–95–31–00–90. No lunch weekends.*

Café Wha. Taking its name from the New York venue where Jimi Hendrix started out, this Mexican restaurant and cantina serves fajitas (75F) and chicken taco salads (45F) on an outdoor terrace. Live music plays on Thursday nights. *Vieux Port, tel. 04–95–34–25–79.*

NEAR BASTIA

CAP CORSE

The Cap Corse peninsula points northward from the island like a congratulatory thumb. If you only have one day to spend in Corsica, spend it here; Cap Corse mimics the geography of the rest of the island with its dramatic western coast, flattish eastern coast, and lush, mountainous interior. From Bastia, the D80 runs around almost the entire cape (40 km/25 mi) and through several villages—primo spots to visit with a car or scooter. If you feel compelled to stock up on tourist brochures before hitting the peninsula, you'll find the **Office du Tourisme du Cap Corse** (04–95–32–01–00) on the D80 (also known as the Route du Cap) in Ville-de-Pietrabugno, about 1 km (½ mi) out of Bastia.

Ten kilometers (6 mi) north of Bastia, **Erbalunga** gives you your first taste of the otherworldly Cap Corse. Built on cliffs, with waves lapping right up to the houses lining the tiny port, Erbalunga's *boulangeries* (bakeries) are great places to stock up on road snacks. Smack-dab in the middle of the peninsula, **Luri** is a group of remote villages lost in the overgrown mountains. It's a good place to stretch: Spend 30 minutes climbing the **tour de Sénèque,** an old tower that affords dazzling views. On the northwestern tip of the peninsula, **Centuri** is a picturesque fishing village; its small port, beach, and watchtower separate the mountains from the sea. From Centuri south to Patrimonio, the road twists and turns along the sheer coast. Halfway down the western coast, the medieval village of **Nonza** has a sweeping view of the sea from its rocky perch. Head for the Genoese tower for an incredible look at the black-sand beach sprawling below. The biggest and most civilized Cap Corse town you'll hit is **St-Florent**: The ritzy port, jammed with cafés, is a fun place to people-watch and nurse a coffee.

GETTING AROUND • From mid-June to mid-September, on Tuesday, Thursday, and Saturday, **Cars Micheli** (1 rue du Nouveau Port, Bastia, tel. 04–95–35–61–08) runs bus tours (90F) around the cape that stop in some villages, including Centuri. In the off-season you can catch a bus to Centuri, but you'll have to wait a full day to return. For more bus information, inquire at the tourist office in Bastia. Since hotels on the cape start at 300F a double, this is a good place to camp.

CALVI

Calvi, on Corsica's northwest coast, is one of the island's most popular resorts. In August, the number of Italian, French, and German visitors deepening their tans can be suffocating, but earlier in the summer you can enjoy the town's beaches and amenities without the crowds. A lively port and vieille ville cluster at the northwest end of the crescent-shape **Golfe de Calvi,** and mountains tower over the gulf and its narrow beach. The train station marks the border between the town's older and newer sections. The main drag running through the older Calvi is **boulevard Wilson**; as it hits the train station it becomes avenue de la République and heads toward Ile-Rousse. Water sports are big draws here, but they're fairly expensive—for rentals and instruction, just wander down to the port (*see* Outdoor Activities, *below*). For those stretching their travel francs, Calvi has two youth hostels, and the town's laid-back attitude is infectious; you'll probably plan on staying here two days but find yourself still hanging around a week later. If you decide to travel farther afield, Calvi is well connected to the rest of the island. In summer, special trains and buses make it a good base for exploring the Balagne, the coastal region between Calvi and Ile-Rousse. At the end of June, Calvi's hot and still nights are livened by a free **jazz festival,** and it's worth sleeping in the streets to witness the bacchanal event. For information on featured acts and reservations, call 04–95–65–16–67.

BASICS

MAIL • The **post office** handles telegrams and poste restante and has telephones. Calvi's postal code is 20260. *Blvd. Wilson at av. de la République, tel. 04–95–65–00–40. Open weekdays 8:30–5, Sat. 8:30–noon.*

VISITOR INFORMATION • The **tourist office** (where you can book rooms for a small fee) is next to the train station on quai Landry and up a flight of stairs from the port, off avenue de la République. You'll find information on nearby vineyards, restaurants, hotels, and campgrounds, and, in July and August, a staffed desk for the Parc Naturel Régional de la Corse. *Port de Plaisance, tel. 04–95–65–16–67. Open July–Aug., daily 8:30–8:30; Sept.–June, Mon.–Sat. 9–noon and 2–6.*

COMING AND GOING

BY TRAIN • Calvi's small **train station** (av. de la République, tel. 04–95–65–00–61) is next to the port in the center of town; it's open daily 6 AM–7 PM. A couple of trains travel daily through the mountains to Ajaccio (5 hrs, 140F), stopping on the way in Corte (2½ hrs, 75F). Trains also travel to Bastia (3 hrs, 95F) via Ile-Rousse (50 mins, 30F). Summer brings extra trains between Calvi and Ile-Rousse.

BY BUS • There's no bus station in Calvi; contact the private companies or go to the tourist office for information on schedules and routes. **Les Beaux Voyages** (pl. de la Porteuse d'Eau, tel. 04–95–65–11–35) sends a bus each morning to Bastia (2 hrs, 85F). If you're trying to reach Calenzana to start the GR20 (*see* Outdoor Activities *in* Chapter Basics, *above*), a bus (30 mins, 27F) runs twice daily July–September 10. From the end of March through October, Les Beaux Voyages has bus excursions to the Forêt de Bonifato (60F), Cap Corse (150F), and Porto (150F).

BY FERRY • Most ferries from France and Genoa (Italy) dock in nearby **Ile-Rousse** (*see* Near Calvi, *below*). **SNCM Ferryterranée** (tel. 04–95–65–17–77) runs a Nice–Calvi boat two to three times a week.

BY PLANE • **Corse Méditerranée** (tel. 04–95–65–20–09) has service to Marseille, Nice, and Geneva, Switzerland, and **Air Inter** (tel. 04–95–65–20–09) flies to Paris and Lyon. Calvi's airport (tel. 04–95–65–03–54) is 7 km (4½ mi) southwest of town; to get to town, you have to take a taxi for 75F–100F or rent a car.

In the citadel in Calvi, look for the plaque off rue Sperona marking Christophe Colomb's (a.k.a. Christopher Columbus's) alleged birthplace (his other, more likely birthplace being Genoa, Italy), hence the town's statues and street names commemorating the great navigator.

GETTING AROUND

Calvi is small enough to walk around, but you might consider renting a bike or scooter to visit the beaches between it and Ile-Rousse. **Calvi Moto Location** (behind port, tel. 04–95–65–16–78) rents mountain bikes for 100F per day (500F deposit) and scooters for 265F per day (1,000F deposit).

For car rentals, **Hertz** has an office in town (8 cours Grandval, tel. 04–95–21–70–94) and one at the airport (tel. 04–95–23–57–04). Summer prices start at 611F per day, 1,480F per week; subtract 10% off-season. **Budget** (tel. 04–95–23–57–21) also has an office at the airport, with rates starting at 565F per day, 1,500F per week in season. Some smaller companies at the airport, like **Citer** (tel. 04–95–65–16–06) and **ADA** (tel. 04–95–65–39–28), have substantially lower rates, especially if you keep the car for a week.

WHERE TO SLEEP

UNDER 325F • **Les Arbousiers.** Set 500 ft back from the beach on the newer side of town, this quality hotel offers a TV lounge, a flower garden, an English-speaking staff, and a mountain backdrop. In off-season, a double with bath and phone costs 200F–230F; mid-July–September that same room runs a whopping 300F. *Rte. de Pietra–Maggiore, toward Ile-Rousse and Bastia, tel. 04–95–65–04–47, fax 04–96–65–26–14. 40 rooms, all with bath. Closed Oct.–Apr.*

Hôtel Belvedere. The Belvedere has a worn entry but polished rooms, some overlooking the citadel. Doubles run 200F–230F off-season (it's one of the few hotels open in winter). The cheapest rooms cost 300F in July and August. *Av. de l'Uruguay, tel. 04–95–65–01–25, fax 04–95–65–43–51. 16 rooms, all with bath. Cash only.*

Résidence les Aloès. Located in the eastern part of the town and offering pleasant rooms, this spot has an eager staff and lovely views across the bay. Doubles are 250F–350F, depending on the season. *Av. Santa-Maria, quartier Donatéo, tel. 04–95–65–01–46. 26 rooms, all with bath. Closed Oct.–Apr.*

UNDER 400F • Hôtel Christophe Colomb. In the shadow of the citadel and a hop, skip, and a jump from the beach and bars, this hotel is so well situated the desk clerks don't need to be friendly . . . and they aren't. But the rooms are comfy and tasteful, and some even have ocean views. Doubles are 200F–250F; 250F–350F in July; and an ozone-busting 300F–450F in August and early September. *Pl. Christophe Colomb, tel. 04–95–65–06–04, fax 04–95–65–29–65. 22 rooms, all with bath. Cash only. Closed Oct.–Mar.*

HOSTELS • BVJ Corsotel. This pleasant hostel is big, spotless, and in the center of town. A bed in a two- to eight-person room costs 120F, including breakfast; some rooms even have a balcony and a sea view. A delicious Corsican dinner costs an extra 65F. Single-sex rooms (couples can ask for a double) come with sinks and portable showers. *Av. de la République, opposite train station, tel. 04–95–65–14–15, fax 04–95–65–33–72. 133 beds. Reception open 7–1:30 and 5–10, check-in 24 hrs, checkout 10 AM. Closed Nov.–Mar. 25.*

Relais International de la Jeunesse "U Carabellu." It's worth the 4-km (2½-mi) trip south of Calvi to stay in this hostel, filled with international backpackers, bicyclists, and motorbikers. As you struggle up the hill with your luggage, remind yourself that a gorgeous view of the Gulf of Calvi and the distant citadel awaits. Beds are 75F per night, including breakfast; 130F will get you dinner, as well. Call ahead to make sure there's room. *Rte. de Pietra-Maggiore, tel. 04–95–65–14–16, fax 04–93–80–65–33. 50 beds. Reception open 24 hrs, check-in 24 hrs, checkout 10 AM. Cash only. Closed Oct.–May.*

CAMPING • Les Castors. Roll out of your tent and onto the beach. Les Castors is a 10-minute walk east of Calvi or a 10F train trip to the Lido Plage stop. Sites are 75F for two people and a tent, 45F for one person. Two-person bungalows run 175F per day, with reduced weekly rates. The campgrounds have a money exchange, restaurant, and swimming pool. *Rte. de Pietra-Maggiore, tel. 04–95–65–13–30, fax 04–95–65–31–95. 80 sites. Closed Nov.–Mar.*

FOOD

For a resort atmosphere, dine along the port for 80F–150F or sit at one of its many cafés, which stay open almost all night in summer. Cheaper restaurants line boulevard Wilson and the small alleys in the vieille ville. Despite the touristy menu, **U San Carlu** (10 pl. St-Charles, tel. 04–95–65–21–93) is a true Corsican experience, with pleasant waiters and great food. For 80F–90F you'll get a traditional menu including salad, a meat dish, and Corsican cheese, or a vegetarian menu. **Le Chalet du Port** (Port Calvi, tel. 04–95–65–36–16) has wonderful pizzas and *brochettes d'agneau* (lamb brochettes). If you're in the mood for a crepe, try **U Caradellu** (13 rue Clemenceau, tel. 04–95–65–21–48), where "The Corsican," including ham, egg, and brocciu, is 38F. Fish lovers should not miss harborside **Le Calellu** (quai Landry, near the Citadel, tel. 04–95–65–22–18) for its fresh fish daily and a set menu at 95F. Reservations are essential. Serious grocery shoppers should head to **Super U** (tel. 04–95–65–04–32), past the train station on avenue Christophe Colomb, or hit the daily covered market near the church behind the citadel for fresh fruits and veggies.

AFTER DARK

Thanks to its beach, Calvi is a fairly festive, fun-in-the-sun kind of place. Lively bars line **quai Landry,** although drinks cost about as much as your ferry ticket. You'll often find loud live music at **Son des Guitares** (rue Clemenceau), with a happening dance floor on weekends. French speakers can check out the outdoor **Cinéma Pop Cyrnos** (near the Rallye Super on RN 197); sorry, no English subtitles.

OUTDOOR ACTIVITIES

Calvi's wonderful beaches extend east from its port, with an abundance of activities for water lovers. **Calvi Nautique** (Port de Plaisance, tel. 04–95–65–10–65), as you approach the beach from the port, rents sea kayaks (75F per hour), Windsurfers (75F per hour), and sailboats (125F per hour). If you're into scuba diving, Calvi, with its clear waters and abundant sea life, is perfect. The **École de Plongée Internationale de Calvi** (parking lot of port, tel. 04–95–65–42–22) has good deals: Introductory dives cost 240F, exploration dives 175F; both include equipment.

NEAR CALVI

ILE-ROUSSE

Taking the train to Ile-Rousse from Calvi is a great way to ease into Corsica. At Ile-Rousse you'll find one of the island's best white-sand beach strips, as well as a sunny, tree-lined main square, **place Paoli,** jammed with cafés and a farmers' market. Founded by Pasquale Paoli in 1758 as a Corsican competitor to the then-Genoese-controlled port of Calvi, Ile-Rousse is named for a red rock outcropping that is now used as the ferry landing. The road that links the landing to the mainland swings by a group of hostels and the railway station, then heads for place Paoli, where you'll find the **tourist office** (tel. 04–95–60–04–35), the outdoor market, and restaurants.

Between 8 AM and 7 PM, frequent trains travel from Calvi to Ile-Rousse (50 mins, 30F). Though Ile-Rousse makes a good day trip from Calvi, it's worth a night's stay if you can afford the luxurious singles (220F) and doubles (300F) with bath at **Hôtel Splendid** (Av. Comte–Valéry-François, tel. 04–95–60–00–24, fax 04–95–60–04–57); in July and August, prices soar to 400F.

CORTE

Although it's Corsica's largest inland city, Corte is no thriving metropolis. Rather, it's a small mountain town built around a 15th-century **citadel,** impressively perched on a cliff in the Tavignanu Valley. Visit Corte because it's the most authentic of Corsican towns and because the surrounding bare granite hills make for excellent hiking. This is also a perfect base for fueling up to hit the Vallée et Gorges de la Restonica. Corte was Corsica's official capital from 1755 to 1769, during the island's brief period of independence, and it continues to hold a special place in the minds of most Corsicans. (Corsican hero Pasquale Paoli led the independence movement and served as president here.) The town's **university** was founded in 1765 during the island's brief moment of self-government, only to be shut down in 1769 under French rule. Reestablished in 1981, the university (the only one on Corsica) is devoted to maintaining Corsican tradition, language, and culture. Corte's 3,000 students make for more bars, clubs, and budget action here than elsewhere, rendering Corte one of the few island towns with any life in the off-season. The young, friendly atmosphere makes Corte an easy place to meet locals and maybe even find a hiking companion.

BASICS

BUREAUX DE CHANGE • **Crédit Lyonnais, Société Generale,** and **Crédit Agricole** all change money and are on the cours Paoli, but only the last bank has an ATM with Cirrus access.

LAUNDRY • **Speed Laverie** (10 allée du 9-Septembre) is a five-minute walk from the train station along the N193 and is in the quartier Porette, next to supermarket **Casino.** Wash and dry costs about 40F.

MEDICAL AID • The **Hôpital Local de Corte** (av. Porette, tel. 04–95–45–05–00) is near the train station and has emergency and routine medical services.

VISITOR INFORMATION • The small **tourist office** will supply you with city and regional maps; information on hotels, camping, gîtes d'étape, and refuges; and advice on Corsican transportation. *Fontaine des Quatre Canons, tel. 04–95–46–26–70. Open Sept.–June, daily 9–noon and 2–5; July–Aug., daily 9–8.*

You can get regional hiking information, including maps, from the office of the **Parc Naturel Régional.** Just turn right out of the tourist office and head up the stairs. *15 rue Colonel Ferraci, tel. 04–95–46–00–97. Open Mon.–Sat. 9–noon and 2–6.*

COMING AND GOING

BY TRAIN • Four daily trains connect Corte with Ajaccio (2 hrs, 67F) and Bastia (1½ hrs, 55F). Two trains a day go to Calvi (3 hrs, 78F) with a connection in Ponte Leccia. To reach the center of town from the **train station,** make a right as you exit and follow the road uphill for about 15 minutes. *Rond Point de la Gare, tel. 04–95–46–00–97. Open weekdays 8–noon and 2–6:30, Sat. 8–11:30 and 3–6:30, Sun. 9–11 and 3:30–6.*

BY BUS • **Eurocourse Voyages** (tel. 04–95–21–06–30 in Ajaccio, 04–95–31–03–79 in Bastia) makes the scenic but sinuous bus journey twice a day Monday–Saturday between Ajaccio and Bastia, stopping in Corte. The 65F trip from Ajaccio to Corte takes 1¾ hours; from Bastia it takes 1¼ hours and costs 60F. Figuring out where the bus leaves can be challenging: Try outside the Hôtel-Bar Colonna on avenue Luciani or in the parking lot off avenue Jean Nicoli. Better yet, call the agency and ask them where buses stop.

WHERE TO SLEEP

The lodging scene in Corte is much more promising than in the coastal towns. If the hotels below are full, try **Hôtel Colonna** (3 av. Xavier Luciani, tel. 04–95–46–01–09); the reception desk is at **Bar Colonna.** Doubles run 190F–260F, with and without bath.

UNDER 175F • HR Hôtel. A stone's throw from the train station and 15 minutes from town, this sterile high-rise has clean, simple rooms starting at 140F for a single, 190F for a double with sink, 230F with shower. If you haven't worn yourself out hiking yet, take advantage of the fitness room and sauna. There's also a cozy restaurant downstairs that serves breakfast, lunch, and dinner at reasonable prices. *6 allée du 9-Septembre, tel. 04–95–45–11–11, fax 04–95–61–02–85. 135 rooms, 85 with shower. Restaurant.*

UNDER 250F • Hôtel de la Poste. This hotel is housed in one of Corte's vintage buildings, dating from the beginning of the century; it's on a quiet square in the middle of town. The simple, well-worn but perfectly adequate rooms include doubles from 245F and triples for 250F. *2 pl. du Duc-de- Padoue, off cours Paoli, tel. 04–95–46–01–37. 12 rooms, all with shower. Cash only. Closed 2 wks in Dec.*

SPLURGE • Hôtel le Refuge B Vallée de la Restonica. This place by the Restonica stream has clean, wood-trimmed rooms and a breezy dining terrace near the ice-cold water—perfect during the *canicule*, the dog days of summer. In summer you'll have to get a meal plan—a double with demi-pension (breakfast and dinner for two persons included) costs 600F; off-season it's 540F. This may seem expensive, but with the meals, it pays off. *Vallée de la Restonica, tel. 04–95–46–09–13, fax 0–95–46–22–38. 10 rooms with bath. Restaurant. Closed mid-Oct.–Mar.*

HOSTEL • U Tavignanu. Set behind a small stream and with a view of the citadel, this mom-and-pop operation is one of Corsica's best hostels, even if it's a 20-minute uphill hike. Dorm beds cost 60F, and the kind *patronne* serves delicious Corsican dinners (85F) nightly 8–9. Or bring your own food and enjoy it on the outdoor terrace. Bed, breakfast, and dinner are 165F per night. If all the beds are full, rent a tent and camp in back for 20F per person plus 10F per site. *Tel. 04–95–46–16–85, fax 04–95–61–14–01. From pl. Paoli in centre ville, take rue Prof. Santiaggi to chemin de Baliri and follow signs. From train station, turn left and follow signs to Bastia along the N193 to allée du 9-Septembre, cross pont Tavignano, turn left, and follow signs. Drivers leave vehicles at the bridge and walk 5 mins to hostel. 20 beds, 20 campsites. Reception open 24 hrs, check-in and checkout 24 hrs. Cash only.*

CAMPING • Restonica (rue du 9-Septembre, tel. 04–95–46–11-59) is one of the nicest campgrounds around Corte, close to civilization but tucked beside a rushing river. Its 60 shaded spots are open July–September, and each person pays 28F, plus 15F per tent. **Alivettu** (tel. 04–95–46–11–09) has 100 dusty but shaded spots nearby for similar prices.

FOOD

Cafés and restaurants serving island specialties pop up all over Corte's centre ville. Just follow cours Paoli to the car-packed **place Paoli.** For a more scenic meal, climb toward the citadel to **place Gaffory.** For the best value, consider making the trek to **U Tavignanu** (*see* Where to Sleep, *above*) for a homemade Corsican dinner. Be sure to call ahead, though. **U San Teofalu** (pl. Gaffory, tel. 04–95–46–05–39), on a small side street off rue Sculiscia, has a delicious 75F menu including Corsican staples such as soupe Corse and brocciu omelet; it also serves a decent pitcher of rosé for 20F. Locals say that **A Rusta** (19 cours Paoli, tel. 04–95–46–28–56) has the best Corsican meals outside their moms' kitchens. The 75F menu includes *sanglier* (wild boar) for those looking for a true taste of Corsica. Dishing up Italian and Corsican food, **A Sculiscia** (6 rue Sculiscia, tel. 04–95–61–08–15) has specialties like *frittata di ricotta* (a quiche with ricotta cheese) and fish soup. Enjoy the four-course, 62F menu on the outdoor terrace with a view of the mountains and the vieille ville. On the outskirts of town, and popular with the university students, is the **L'Oliveraie** (Lieu-dit Perru, tel. 04–95–46–06–32), which provides authentic Corsican dishes like *buglidicce* (a yogurtlike cheese fried in batter) and ground chestnut tart, with set meals for 65F–140F. **U Museu** (rampe Ribanelle, rue Colonel-Feracci) is beautifully located near the citadel and has a very good-value Corsican menu including herb tart and game stews for 80F–90F.

AFTER DARK

Unlike most cities, Corte is at its liveliest on weekdays during the off-season, when the students are still around. L'Aventure (rampe Pozza) is a popular dance club usually with an 80F cover that includes a drink. During summer, the swimming pool **La Piscine de Venaco** (tel. 04–95–46–11–99) hosts dance parties for the local disco contingent. If you're more interested in beer-swilling, **Le Trésor** (tel. 04–95–61–07–64) is a popular café on cours Paoli. The nearby **L'Arc en Ciel** (14 cours Paoli, no phone) is a small, dim pub frequented by an older crowd.

NEAR CORTE

VALLÉE ET GORGES DE LA RESTONICA

In the heart of Corsica, the Restonica glacial valley is a wilderness of mountains, canyons, lakes, and rivers. Although the entrance to the valley can be reached by foot from Corte (about a 30-minute walk), many of the most interesting hikes begin 16 km (10 mi) into the park. Ironically, this makes a vehicle a helpful hiking companion: Head southwest from Corte along the **D623**; after 5 km (3 mi) you'll reach an **information office** (open summer). Continue 11 km (7 mi) until the road ends and park. From there it's a good two-hour hike to **Lac du Melo,** 6,528 ft above sea level. Another, more challenging 90-minute climb takes you higher to **Lac de Capitello.** Swimming is possible, though—with plaques of snow usually present in mid-summer—chilly. Obtain hiking maps and further information from the **Park Naturel Régional** office in Corte (*see* Basics, *above*).

If you want to stay in the Restonica, **Le Refuge** (tel. 04–95–46–09–13), 2 km (1 mi) from Corte off the D623, is a beautiful hotel and restaurant overlooking the river. Each of the 10 comfortable rooms (260F–320F) has a great view and full bath, making this a worthwhile splurge. A cheaper and more rustic alternative is a couple of miles down the road: **Camping de Tuani** (tel. 04–95–46–11–65) charges 30F per person plus 14F for a tent and is also situated along the river. At Santo Pietro di Venaco, among the remote high peaks, the **Gîte-de St-Pierre-de-Venaco** (tel. 04–95–47–07–29) has small dormitories for 160F per person, including breakfast and dinner, and doubles for 250F with breakfast.

VIZZAVONA

Although Vizzavona lies on the Ajaccio–Ponte Leccia rail line and the GR20 hiking trail, you won't find this mountain village on most tourist itineraries. Surrounded by pine forests and massive granite outcroppings, Vizzavona is known for its hiking. Choose between an easy hour-long hike up to the **Cascade des Anglais** (English Waterfall) and a five-hour trek to **Mont d'Oro** (7,884 ft). From its summit you can see hundreds of miles of mountains, coastline, and, on a clear day, even Sardinia. Aside from a few hotels, Vizzavona's **train station** (tel. 04–95–47–21–02) composes the entire village. Three or four trains roll through daily, making it a reasonable day trip from Ajaccio (1 hr, 40F) or Corte (1 hr, 27F). Oddly enough, the train station does everything but take your vacation for you: It sells canned goods, chocolate, and bread; serves café-style meals; and acts as a tourist office.

If you decide to stay the night and tackle the forest and mountains, there are a couple of refuges—part rustic hotel and part gîte d'étape—opposite the train station. To the right of the station as you exit, **Hôtel I. Laricci** (La Gare, tel. 04–95–47–21–12) has a convenient location and a nice outdoor eating area facing the mountains. Gîte spaces go for 55F (including shower), and doubles here run 210F. The I. Laricci has 85F dinner menus and, considering there's not much else around, you'd better take your place at the table. The hotel is closed September–May.

CORSE DU SUD

Southern Corsica is tricky to explore without a vehicle, although buses do spring to life in summer and will help you get to most of the region's popular spots. Ajaccio, Corsica's largest city, is a bustling town of 60,000 inhabitants and, in addition to its Napoléon attractions and nearby beaches, makes a good base for day trips to Ota, Porto, and Piana. To the south, Bonifacio and Porto-Vecchio afford travelers picture-perfect impressions of Genoese life on the island. Descending from their citadels to remarkable coastlines, you will find beaches with turquoise seas and a wealth of water sports from which to choose.

AJACCIO

Closer to continental France and more visibly Gallic than any other Corsican town, Ajaccio is the capital of Corse du Sud. It stretches around a small bay on the island's west side and, though it's the island's largest town, Ajaccio feels more festive and less industrial than Bastia. No mention of Ajaccio can be made without adding that it's Napoléon Bonaparte's birthplace—reason enough to put it on the map. The little emperor is immortalized in statues, street names, postcards, and tacky souvenirs. You can see socioeconomic stratification in action as you travel Ajaccio's main drag, **cours Napoléon**—past the slums in the northern section to the luxury town houses, casinos, and villas west of **place Charles de Gaulle.** This square, together with the waterside **place Maréchal Foch** a few blocks away, makes up the heart of the city. Ajaccio has a lively vieille ville and port, a 15th-century **citadel** (blvd. Danielle Casanova), and an excellent collection of Italian paintings at the **Musée Fesch** (*see* Worth Seeing, *below*). However, as the hub of the island's marine and land transportation, Ajaccio suffers from industrialization, and you have to travel way out of town to hit decent beaches. That said, Ajaccio houses the best information clearinghouse for the Parc Naturel Régional and makes a good base for stocking up on maps, food, and gear.

BASICS

BUREAU DE CHANGE • Avoid the private change booths. Instead, head to **Banque de France,** which has the best rates and charges no commission. *8 rue Sergent-Casalonga, off cours Napoléon, tel. 04–95–51–72–40. Open weekdays 8:30–noon and 1:30–3:30.*

MAIL • The **main post office** has telephones and Minitel, handles telegrams and poste restante, and changes money. Ajaccio's postal code is 20000. *Hôtel des Postes, 13 cours Napoléon, near pl. du 24-Mai, tel. 04–95–51–84–65. Open weekdays 8–6:30, Sat. 8–noon.*

VISITOR INFORMATION • The **tourist office** is on the city's main square. Extracting information from the less-than-helpful staff can be frustrating. *Pl. Maréchal Foch, tel. 04–95–51–53–03. Open June–mid-Sept., daily 8:30–8; mid-Sept.–May, weekdays 8:30–6, Sat. 8:30–noon.*

The **Agence du Tourisme de la Corse** has a list of lodging throughout Corsica. When the main information desk is closed (October–April), go around the corner to the administrative office at 1 rue St-Roch. *17 blvd. du Roi Jérôme, tel. 04–95–51–77–77. Open weekdays 9–noon and 2–5.*

The well-informed folks at the **Bureau du Parc Régional** sell topographic maps (100F) and have a list of refuges and regional footpaths. *2 rue Sergent Casalonga, tel. 04–95–51–79–10. Open weekdays 8:30–noon and 2–6 (Fri. until 5).*

COMING AND GOING

BY TRAIN • The **train station** (av. Jean-Jérôme Levie, between cours Napoléon and blvd. Sampiero, tel. 04–95–23–11–03) is about a five-minute walk north of the town center. July–September four daily trains make the trip to Ponte Leccia (3 hrs, 85F), where you can catch a train to Bastia (1 hr, 37F), Ile-Rousse (1½ hrs, 41F), or Calvi (2 hrs, 85F). Corte (2 hrs, 65F) is on the route from Ajaccio to Ponte Leccia.

BY BUS • The **bus station** (tel. 04–95–21–28–01) is next to the gare maritime on quai l'Herminier. A half-dozen private bus companies have organized excursions and regular service. **Eurocorse Voyages** (tel. 04–95–21–06–30) runs three buses Monday–Saturday and two on Sunday to Bonifacio (4 hrs, 120F), stopping at Propriano (2 hrs, 65F), Sartène (2 hrs, 65F), and Porto-Vecchio (3½ hrs, 115F). Two buses head to Bastia (3 hrs, 110F), Corte (2 hrs, 60F), Ponte Leccia (3 hrs, 75F), and Calvi (5 hrs, 135F).

Autocars Ricci (tel. 04–95–51–08–19) heads into the Parc Régional at 3 and 4 PM daily, hitting Zonza (3 hrs, 90F) and Propriano (2 hrs, 60F). **Autocars SAIB** (tel. 04–95–22–41–99) runs two buses Monday–Saturday up to Ota (3 hrs, 75F), stopping near Piana (2 hrs, 65F) and Porto (2½ hrs, 68F).

BY FERRY • At the **gare maritime** (quai l'Herminier, tel. 04–95–29–66–99) you'll find booths for **SNCM** (tel. 04–95–29–66–88) ferries bound for Nice, Toulon, and Marseille. Nice is the least expensive ride, at 210F–308F one-way depending on the season. Bikes make the passage for 85F, and beds start at 82F. **Corsica Ferries** (tel. 04–95–32–95–95) will take you to Genoa (175F–225F) between May and September; night crossings and high-summer ferries are more expensive.

BY PLANE • Ajaccio's **Aéroport Campo del'Oro** (tel. 04–95–21–07–07) is several miles from the center of town. Between 7 AM and 10:15 PM, Bus 1 will take you into town or to the airport (both 20F) from one of the several bus stops along cours Napoléon. Buses leave about every 40 minutes; the trip takes about a half hour. **Air Inter Europe** and **Corse Méditerranée** share an office (3 blvd. Roi Jérôme, tel. 04–95–29–45–45) and have flights all over. Ticket prices to Paris vary according to the time of year, but they usually cost 750F–1,200F. Rates to Lyon also vary (500F–1,250F); fares to Marseille usually cost about 520F.

GETTING AROUND

BY BUS • Local **TCA** buses (tel. 04–95–51–43–23), which congregate around place de Gaulle, can take you to the airport and up the coast as far as Pointe de la Parata, near the Iles Sanguinaires. A single ticket (8F) gets you to the beach, two (15F) get you to Pointe de la Parata, and 20F gets you to the airport. Buy your tickets on the bus.

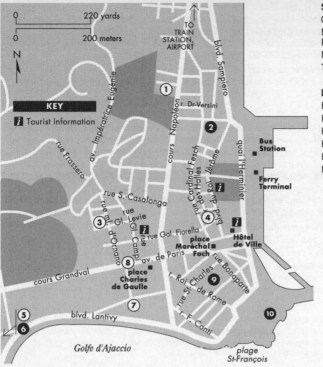

AJACCIO

0 — 220 yards
0 — 200 meters
N

TO TRAIN STATION, AIRPORT

KEY

i Tourist Information

Sights ●
Citadel, **10**
Maison Bonaparte, **9**
Musée Fesch, **2**
Tour de la Parata, **6**

Lodging ○
Barbicaja, **5**
Hôtel Bonaparte, **4**
Hôtel Colomba, **8**
Hôtel Kallysté, **1**
Hôtel Marengo, **7**
Meublé Forcioli, **3**

blvd. Sampiero
r. Dr-Versini
cours Napoléon
av. Impératrice Eugénie
rue Frassero
rue S.-Casalonga
rue Gl. Levie
rue Gl. Campi
rue d'Ornano
rue Gal. Fiorella
place Maréchal Foch
av. de Paris
cours Grandval
place Charles de Gaulle
blvd. Lantivy
Cardinal Fesch
rue des Halles
blvd. du Roi Jérôme
quai l'Herminier
Bus Station
Ferry Terminal
Hôtel de Ville
rue Bonaparte
r. Roi Charles
r. St-Charles
r. de Rome
r. F. Conti
Golfe d'Ajaccio
plage St-François

BY BIKE OR MOPED • Loca Corse, near the train station off cours Napoléon, rents mountain bikes (85F a day plus 2,000F deposit) and scooters (250F a day plus 5,000F deposit). It accepts credit cards. *10 Av. Beverini Vico, tel. 04–95–20–71–20. Open Mon.–Sat. 9–noon and 2–6:30.*

BY CAR • A car is a great idea if you want to see the magnificent coastline near Ajaccio, since the area isn't very well serviced by public transportation. Several rental agencies work out of shacks in the airport parking lot. For the cheapest rates, head to **Citer** (tel. 04–95–23–57–15), with rentals from 180F per day. Your next best choice is **Ada** (tel. 04–95–23–56–57), where cars go for 385F (280F with limited mileage) per day, 1,800F per week.

WHERE TO SLEEP

Renting a private room is probably your best option in Ajaccio: Try the clean rooms at **Meublé Forcioli** (9 rue Maréchal Ornano, tel. 04–95–21–71–54), just off place de Gaulle, where Madame Forcioli lets a pair of 150F doubles and two three-person studios (with kitchen and bath) for 180F.

UNDER 200F • Hôtel Colomba. This is Ajaccio's cheapest option, so reservations are crucial. On the third floor of a building overlooking place Charles de Gaulle, the hotel has clean and spacious rooms, some with ocean views, 185F for both singles and doubles with bath, 140F for rooms without bath. Madame Dazzi doesn't charge for the communal hall shower, but walking down the dark hallway means dodging her feisty kitty (actually, Madame's quite feisty herself). *8 av. de Paris, tel. 04–95–21–12–66 or 04–95–51–04–63. 10 rooms, 5 with bath. Cash only.*

UNDER 325F • Hôtel Bonaparte. In an alley behind the old market, this intimate little hideaway overlooks some of Ajaccio's coziest restaurants, which can be quite festive during summer evenings. Rooms are small and clean; some have views of the port. The nearby market bustles every morning from dawn to midday. Singles are 265F, doubles 300F. *Rue des Halles, between blvd. du Roi Jérôme and quai Napoléon, tel. 04–95–21–44–19. 16 rooms, all with shower. Closed mid-Oct.–mid-Mar.*

Hôtel Marengo. A warm welcome is guaranteed at this hotel, located near the beaches and in a quiet cul-de-sac overlooking a charming courtyard. It has double rooms with shower for 230F–250F (330F in peak season). *2 rue Marengo, tel. 04–95–21–43–66. 12 rooms, all with shower. Closed mid-Dec.–mid-Mar.*

SPLURGE • Hôtel Kallysté. This Spanish-style hotel on the main drag has attractive rooms with TVs, spotless new bathrooms, mini-refrigerators, and phones. This hotel is worth the extra francs—save money by staying in one of the studios with kitchenette and eating in. Doubles run 235F (300F–340F in July and August); studios are 260F–285F (335F in July, 380F in August). *51 cours Napoléon, tel. 04–95–51–34–45, fax 04–95–21–79–00. 32 rooms and studios, all with bath.*

CAMPING • The four-star **Barbicaja** has shady, dusty sites (40F per person, 14F per car, and 10F per tent) on a tree-covered hillside overlooking a beach. Take Bus 5 from place de Gaulle. *Rte. des Sanguinaires, tel. 04–95–52–01–17. 110 sites. Closed mid-Oct.–Apr.*

FOOD

Ajaccio has plenty of informal, inexpensive eateries, mostly outdoors in the narrow passageways of the vieille ville. Try almost any alley off **rue Cardinal Fesch** or **rue Bonaparte.** For a great selection of produce and Corsican wines and cheeses, stop by the outdoor morning **market** (every day but Monday) in the parking lot behind the tourist office. If you miss it, there's an afternoon market across the street on boulevard Roi Jérôme, and a **Monoprix** supermarket (39 cours Napoléon tel. 04–95–51–40–35). Rue des Halles is a mixed bag, with touristy but fun restaurants: **L'Aquarium** (2 rue des Halles, tel. 04–95–21–11–21), in the old town, is run by a former fisherman. It serves copious amounts of fresh fish and shellfish for 85F–95F with set meals from 70F. It's closed Mondays except July and August.

UNDER 50F • La Crêperie du Port. Watch old fishing boats snuggle up to sleek Italian yachts while you eat your *crêpe corse* (39F), filled with chèvre, tomatoes, and basil. Other crepes, salads, and sandwiches run 25F–45F. *4 quai Napoléon, in vieux port, tel. 04–95–21–58–01.*

UNDER 100F • A Casa. Aficionados of eccentricity, as well as good food, should enjoy this place, which serves wholesome food such as steaks, salads and pasta, all washed down with excellent wines. On Friday and Saturday evenings, the owner puts on his own magic show. *21 av. Noel-Franchini, tel. 04–95–22–34–78.*

Da Mamma. This little spot hidden away under a leafy rubber tree just up from 13 rue Fesch is a great find. Order simply and it can be very economical; try not to miss the *civet de sanglier* (wild boar stew) with wild mushrooms served in a bubbling earthenware casserole. Set menus start at 65F. *Passage Guingette, tel. 04–95–21–39–44.*

Restaurant Asia. The menu has Frenchified Thai and Chinese dishes à la carte, with some vegetarian selections; most are priced 40F–80F. The assorted Thai plate (80F) is delicious and can feed two. *7 rue des Halles, tel. 04–95–21–21–45. Closed Sun.*

UNDER 125F • U Borgu. In a stone passageway near the port, this tiny joint stays alive even in the off-season. Menus run 75F and 100F for a mix of Corsican cuisine and pizzas and pastas. For the ultimate Corsican seafood experience, try the local *bouillabaisse l'aziminu*, which is huge but expensive at 190F. *5 rue des Anciens Fossés, off pl. Maréchal Foch in the vieux port, tel. 04–95–21–17–47.*

WORTH SEEING

MAISON BONAPARTE • Wandering through the maze of streets in the vieille ville is the best way to find the Maison Bonaparte. The museum inside doesn't have much to do with Napoléon; it houses 18th-century Corsican furniture. Nevertheless, it is the house where the little giant spent his childhood. *Pl. Letizia, off rue St-Charles, tel. 04–95–21–43–89, fax 04–95–21–61–32. Admission 20F. Open Tues.–Sat. 9–noon and 2–6, Sun. 9–noon, Mon. 2–6.*

MUSÉE FESCH • The palatial Musée Fesch displays a collection of 14th- to 19th-century paintings miraculously acquired under controversial circumstances by Napoléon's uncle, Cardinal Fesch. Botticelli, Canaletto, De Tura, Titian, and a rendition of the swan raping Leda are among many great Italian masters the cardinal stashed in Corsica. *50 rue Cardinal Fesch, tel. 04–95–21–48–17. Admission 25F. Open Oct.–Apr., Tues.–Sat. 9:30–noon and 2:30–6; May and Sept., Mon.–Sat. 9:30–noon and 3–7; June, Tues.–Sat. 10–5:30; July–Aug., Tues.–Sat. 9 AM–midnight.*

AFTER DARK

It sure isn't Paris, except maybe in summer when the Café Fesch and others over the Plage St-François look like the Champs-Élysées, but even in winter you will find some fun bars and cafés clustered around the port and in the vieille ville. If you're desperate for flashing lights, loud pumping music, and sweaty bodies, head across the bay to **Porticcio,** 17 km (10 mi) south of Ajaccio. One of Corsica's glitzier, Club Med–like resorts, Porticcio features young bronzed bodies that flock to the dance club at the town's northern entrance. During summer, there's often a water taxi between Ajaccio and Porticcio. If not, you have to hitch or rent another means of transportation.

NEAR AJACCIO

The route north of Ajaccio to Calvi (184 km/115 mi) follows the island's most spectacular stretch of coastline, where the mountains of the interior meet the sea, creating a jagged shoreline that hides some spectacular beaches and gulfs. Public transportation is tricky here, since buses travel along the treacherous D81 coastal route mid-May–mid-October only. **Autocars SAIB** (tel. 04–95–22–41–99) runs between Calvi and Ota (3 hrs, 90F) mid-May–mid-October, with stops in Porto and Piana, and year-round between Porto and Ajaccio (2½ hrs, 65F). A combination boat-bus trip is a fun way to do the coast: You can travel between Ajaccio and Porto by bus and between Porto and Calvi by boat in summer. (For information on sights south of Ajaccio, *see* Near Bonifacio, *below.*) If you're considering cycling or driving, note that every one of those numerous roadside crosses posted along the way memorializes an accident victim.

OTA

Those who came to Corsica hankering for hikes shouldn't miss this tiny town with traditional stone houses, a gorgeous view of the surrounding mountains, and a mess of trailheads. Thanks to its primo location, Ota wins kudos as one of the island's few accessible *and* budget-friendly destinations. Five steep kilometers (3 mi) inland and uphill from Porto, Ota is packed with campers, hikers, cyclists, and little else. There are also two excellent gîtes d'étape open all year. **Les Chasseurs** (tel. 04–95–26–11–37), at Ota's entrance, has dorm-style rooms for 65F with shower as well as kitchen facilities and a full restaurant. Just up the road, **Chez Félix** (tel. 04–95–26–12–92) has 60F beds in two- to eight-person rooms with showers, balconies and a common kitchen area, as well as two-person studios (with kitchenette) for 220F. Chez Félix has both a restaurant and a good downstairs bar whose savvy, friendly barkeep will give you a free map detailing more than 20 day hikes in the area. Ota also has a small **grocery shop** that sells overpriced chocolate, soda, and crackers; it's open Monday–Saturday 8–noon and 3–7.

Colonial chic Ajaccio with its orderly French streets is the most Continental town on the island. When the late August boar-hunting season arrives, though, you'll know you're still in Corsica when you see many people toting firearms.

The village makes a great spot for hiking or for exploring the nearby coast. Although walking up the steep hill from Porto more than once can make even the heartiest outdoor enthusiast sweat and curse, there's an infrequent bus that makes the trip up to Chez Felix (10F). The most scenic route out of Ota (recommended by the barkeep at Chez Felix) is through the **Gorges de Spelunca** all the way to **Evisa** (about four hours), where you'll find more dorms. For about 200F, Chez Félix will supply you with a **taxi** in which to return to Ota. To stay in Evisa, contact Monsieur Ceccaldi (tel. 04–95–26–21–88), who charges 65F per person; there are communal showers.

PORTO

The massive pink granite mountains, red sunsets, and deep, dark-blue water make the Golfe de Porto one of Corsica's most amazing sights. The small town of Porto (population 150) has a tiny port and boardwalk with oceanfront restaurants and hotels. There you'll see the **tourist office** (tel. 04–95–26–10–55), open March–mid-October. A short hike from the boardwalk will bring you to a 16th-century Genoese tower overlooking the Porto bay. From the port you can also take a boat (April–October only, 175F) north to **Girolata** and the (largely underwater) **Réserve Naturelle de Scandola,** a gorgeous ensemble of jagged-red, volcanic formations.

The cheapest place to stay by the water is **Le Bon Accueil** (tel. 04–95–26–12–10), next to the port. Three thousand feet from the water, the 20 double rooms run 170F in the off-season and 200F with bath in summer. It's closed December–mid-March. On the hills of Porto is the **Hotel Bella Vista** (rte. de Calvi, tel. 04–95–26–11–08, fax 04–95–26–15–18), a charming place with views of the mountains run by a couple who also have a farm (it is their suckling pig that is served at dinner), where rooms with shower are 190F–270F in high season. For cheaper lodging options, *see* Ota, *above.* A 10-minute walk from the port are a bureau de change and a market. There are also a handful of campgrounds here, the best of which is **Sole e Vista** (tel. 04–95–26–15–71), open March 15–November, 1 km (½ mi) from the beach, with 200 sites for about 75F for two people and a tent. **Porto Locations** (tel. 04–95–26–10–13), across from the market, rents bikes for 90F per day, scooters for 320F per day, motorcycles for 400F per day, and cars for 390F per day.

BONIFACIO

On a small peninsula at Corsica's southernmost tip, Bonifacio's superb natural position is highlighted by white-chalk cliffs sculpted into fantastic curves by sea and wind. Naturally and architecturally beautiful, with 3 km (2 mi) of fortified ramparts, Bonifacio is one of the windiest cities on an already windy island, with gale winds blowing some 250 days a year. Rocky, shrubby land separates Bonifacio from the rest of the island, and the town feels strangely isolated. In fact, the nearest town is Santa Teresa di Gallura, 12 km (7 mi) across the water on the island of Sardinia. In this secluded environment, Bonifacians have developed a special Corsican dialect that even their fellow islanders can't understand. People have been living in this area on the tip of the island for a long time: The earliest human habitation dates from 6000 BC, and some historians hypothesize that Bonifacio is Lamos, home to the cannibalistic Laestrygons from whom Odysseus narrowly escaped in Homer's epic. The Genoese invaded the city in the 12th century and built the existing **citadel.** Bonifacio has since weathered many sieges, especially during the 12th to 16th centuries.

Today, Bonifacio is first and foremost a tourist town, which, despite the annoyance, also translates to fun restaurants and a friendly atmosphere. If you're ever going to take a hypertouristy boat ride, this is the place to do it. The citadel and *haute ville* (upper town) sit at the tip of a peninsula, and the Mediterranean thrusts a long, narrow finger inland, forming a harbor where pleasure boats anchor near a dizzying array of overpriced restaurants and hotels.

BASICS

BUREAU DE CHANGE • Bonifacio's one bank, **Société Générale,** has the best rates in town, even with the 25F commission. Try to change money before arriving in Bonifacio. *38 rue St-Erasme, tel. 04–95–73–02–49. Open weekdays 8–11:30 and 2–4:30.*

MAIL • The town's **post office** is above the tourist office and place Bonaparte. Bonifacio's postal code is 20169, and the office holds poste restante mail. *Pl. Carrega, tel. 04–95–73–01–55. Open July 4– Sept. 12, weekdays 8:30–8, Sat. 8:30–noon; Sept. 13–July 3, weekdays 9–noon and 2–5, Sat. 9–noon.*

MEDICAL AID • Bonifacio's **Hôpital Local** (tel. 04–95–73–95–73) sits off the southeastern corner of the port on the road toward Santa Manza.

VISITOR INFORMATION • By the time you reach the **tourist office,** you'll already know Bonifacio pretty well. To get here from the bus stop, cross the port, head to the haute ville, and walk through the citadel. Ask for the *Guide Officiel,* which includes a town map and a brief historical summary (in English). *Pl. de l'Europe, haute ville, tel. 04–95–73–11–88. Open July–Aug., daily 9–7; Sept.–June, weekdays 8:30–noon and 1:30–5.*

COMING AND GOING

BY BUS • **Eurocorse** (tel. 04–95–70–13–83) and **Corsicatours** (tel. 04–95–70–10–36) run three daily buses in summer from Bonifacio to Ajaccio (115F), two daily in winter. The bus stops in Porto-Vecchio (45F), Propriano (60F), and Sartène (170F) on the way, and no buses run on Sundays. You can also get to Bastia for 120F. There's also infrequent summer service to the neighboring beach stretches; inquire at the bus station near the tourist train.

BY FERRY • No ferries from France make the trip to Bonifacio; ferries only run to Santa Teresa on the island of Sardinia. **Moby Lines** (tel. 04–95–73–00–29) and **Saremar** (04–95–73–00–96) both make the one-hour trip (50F–70F) 14 times daily mid-July–early September, seven times daily in the off-season. The boats leave from the **Port de Commerce,** at the western tip of the southern side of the port, past the fishing boats.

BY TRAIN • Corsica's train lines don't make it to Bonifacio, but the **Petit Train de Bonifacio,** a rather tacky open-air train, will haul you and your backpack up to the citadel for 30F, historical commentary included (get the brochure to follow along in English). The train runs April–October, leaves from the bus station at the harbor, and takes 30 minutes.

WHERE TO SLEEP

It's impossible to find a hotel room here for under 200F in summer, and there's only one small campground nearby. If the "cheap" hotels are full, ask around at the shops near the port about *chambres à louer* (rooms for rent). You'll have to pay at least 200F for a double, but you may get lucky and come across a studio with a kitchen for the same price. Or consider staying in Porto-Vecchio (*see* Near Bonifacio, *below*).

UNDER 300F • **Hôtel des Étrangèers.** Not far from the port, this fairly large hotel on the main road outside town has doubles for 185F–265F, a great breakfast included. The rooms are tidy, with firm beds and modern amenities, but ask for one facing away from the road. The friendly management keeps a comfy, '70s-style lounge area with a TV and bar. *Av. Sylvère-Bohn, tel. 04–95–73–01–09, fax 04–95–73–16–97. 30 rooms, all with bath. Closed Nov.–Easter.*

Mme Bocognani. Across the street from the Hôtel des Étrangères, Madame Bocognani lets spotless, newly remodeled rooms with private baths on the ground floor of her red-shuttered house. From mid-July to the end of August, three bedrooms that sleep four start at 550F; at other times she'll take two people for 250F a night. *Av. Sylvère-Bohn, tel. 04–95–73–01–31. 3 rooms with bath. Cash only.*

SPLURGE • Le Royal. One of the few "affordable" hotels in the citadel area, Le Royal has small, air-conditioned doubles for 200F–250F (you pay more for a view) and climb steadily through the summer, hitting 450F in July and 600F in August. *8 rue Fred-Scamaroni, off pl. Bonaparte, tel. 04–95–73–00–51, fax 04–95–73–04–68. 14 rooms, all with bath. Air-conditioning.*

CAMPING • L'Araguina. On the main road into town and a few minutes' walk from the port, this site won't satisfy nature lovers (especially when they hear the traffic), but it's the only campground close to town (others are at least 5 km/3 mi away). Sandy, shady, slightly cramped spots await; bring a flashlight since the campground isn't lit at night. A site runs 29F per person, 14F per tent. Cute two- to five-person bungalows with kitchenettes go for 2,100F–4,200F per week in summer, 300F daily in the off-season. There's a laundry and a restaurant. *Av. Sylvère-Bohn, tel. 04–95–73–02–96, fax 04–95–73–01–92. 100 sites. Reception open daily 8–noon and 1:30–8. Closed Nov.–Easter.*

FOOD

Many restaurants close November–March, but markets and several places in the haute ville stay open all year. Small supermarkets, like **Simoni Supermarché,** on the south side of the port, have beach paraphernalia as well as picnic supplies.

UNDER 25F • Boulangerie-Pâtisserie Faby. Although it's not really a restaurant, this famed Corsican bakery makes specialties that could easily compose a meal. Don't go home without trying Faby's *faugazi* (a brioche made with white wine; 15F) or the intimidatingly named *pain des morts* (bread of the dead; 15F), hearty bread filled with nuts and raisins. *4 rue St-Jean Baptiste, tel. 04–95–73–14–73.*

UNDER 75F • Café de la Poste. Off place Bonaparte in the haute ville, this popular lunch and dinner spot serves a variety of pizzas and pastas, including cannelloni *au brocciu* (with brocciu, 50F). The best seats are out on the busy sidewalk. *6 rue Fred-Scamaroni, tel. 04–95–73–04–58.*

Clipper's. Tucked away in the heart of the citadel on an unmarked cobblestone alley, this restaurant is well worth the effort it takes to find it. In addition to a good 65F menu, there are specialties like bouillabaisse (150F), pizza (35F–50F), and a tasty *salade du pêcheur* (seafood salad; 45F). *10 rue Cardinal Zigliara, behind Ste-Marie church in haute ville, tel. 04–95–73–17–89.*

WORTH SEEING

Boat rides are tacky and touristy but still worthwhile: The cliffs are even more impressive when viewed from the sea. The portside companies hawk their offerings shamelessly, so haggle as vigorously as they do. A trip around the peninsula and into the magnificent grottoes is 35F–65F, and a jaunt to the **Iles Lavezzi** (Lavezzi Islands), a natural reserve where you can swim and picnic, is 75F–100F. Boats leave from the quai de la Marine at the head of Port de Plaisance. The citadel is worth an afternoon stroll, and be sure to make your way to the **Escalier du Roi d'Aragon** (King of Aragon's Staircase). According to legend, all 187 steps leading from the cliffs to the water's edge were built in one night by Aragonese soldiers in 1420. If you want to work up a sweat, fork over the 10F to climb them.

There's a small, very public beach, **Plage de Sotta Rocca,** just below the southeast corner of the citadel. To find more secluded sand, walk 40 minutes on the northern side of the port. Take the pathway by the gas station near Europcar to **Plage de la Catena** and **Plage de l'Arïnella.** Or consider a walk out to the **Phare de Pertusato** (lighthouse). The path begins at avenue Charles de Gaulle, and it's about a 45-minute cliff-side stroll. Fish fans might enjoy Bonifacio's small but impressive **aquarium.** *71 quai Comparetti, tel. 04–95–73–03–69. Admission 25F. Open 2nd wk of Apr.–Oct., daily 10–8.*

NEAR BONIFACIO

PORTO-VECCHIO

Temperate summer weather; a charming old town bursting with restaurants, bars, and cafés; two great beaches; a ferry terminal; and year-round bus service from Bastia and Ajaccio make Porto-Vecchio a great high-season stopover. Unfortunately, many other tourists think so, too. New ferry lines from Naples and Livorno have joined the existing line from Marseille to pave the way for an Italian invasion come July and August, which brings a steep rise in hotel rates. Hit Porto-Vecchio in June if you want to enjoy lower prices, and be warned that, between September and May, the place feels like a ghost town.

BASICS • The **tourist office** overlooks place de la République from its second-floor perch. *Pl. de l'Hôtel de Ville, tel. 04–95–70–09–58. Open mid-June–mid-Sept., daily 9–9; mid-Sept.–mid-June, weekdays 9–noon and 2–7.*

For more information regarding the Parc Naturel Régional de Corse, head to the **Parc Office** on one of the small streets of the centre ville's Citadella area. *Rue du Colonel Quenza, tel. 04–95–70–50–78. Open July–Sept., Mon.–Sat. 9–12:30 and 4:30–7:30.*

Point Information Jeunesse (6 rue Jean Nicoli, above Citadella, tel. 04–95–70–92–74) has a booklet, "Information Jeunesse Guide," which lists useful telephone numbers and reasonably priced excursions into the nearby mountains. The office can give you advice about scuba diving, sailing, and windsurfing opportunities in and around Porto-Vecchio.

Société Générale (5 rte. de Bastia, tel. 04–95–70–10–15) has the best exchange rates in town (even if they do charge a 25F commission), and the folks at the nearby **post office** (rte. de Bastia, tel. 04–95–70–18–77) are uncommonly friendly.

COMING AND GOING • Year-round buses make the trip from Bonifacio (30 mins, 35F), Ajaccio (5½ hrs, 115F), and Bastia (3 hrs, 110F). During summer, there are buses twice a day from Porto-Vecchio to **Palombaggia**, an unforgettable strip of sand 9 km (5½ mi) south of town. **Camping La Matonara,** 1 km (½ mi) from town down rue Général Leclerc, runs buses out to nearby beaches Monday–Saturday during summer. Hitching to the beaches or Bonifacio is relatively easy.

WHERE TO SLEEP • Porto-Vecchio is pricey. If you must have a bed, the one cheap option is **Hôtel Panorama** (12 rue Jean Nicoli, tel. 04–95–70–07–96), which charges 270F–310F for clean, bright doubles (11 rooms, 9 with shower), some with views of the gulf. The hotel is closed October–May.

An inexpensive option is camping. The sprawling **Camping La Matonara** (tel. 04–95–70–37–05) sits 1 km (½ mi) inland from Porto-Vecchio and charges roughly 75F for two people and a tent. From the tourist office, head down rue Général Leclerc; the campground office will be on your left at the traffic circle. The shady spots, friendly staff, nearby beaches, and clean bathrooms are definite pluses, as is the neighboring pizzeria, which hosts musicians during the high season. Minuses include hordes of mosquitoes and humans.

If you have a car, there's a memorable gîte d'étape called **Le Réfuge** (tel. 04–95–70–00–39) in the Ospédale forest. At 50F a night, this rustic resort is a hiker's paradise, with lakes and waterfalls within close proximity and the most authentic Corsican meal around: Corsican soup, *porc sauvage* (wild pig), dessert, and wine for 75F. If you want to try walking there, the tourist office will help you with routing. If you decide to drive, take the D368 to Ospédale and follow the signs for Cartalavonu. In summer, be sure to reserve in advance.

FOOD • As with lodging, low prices are hard to come by and most restaurants charge an arm and a leg for a tiny piece of meat or a pittance of leaves. **Chez Laurent** (rue Borgo, tel. 04–95–70–41–00) serves pasta for reasonable prices, but the real reason to come here is for the enchanted ocean-view terrace, sheltered by the ancient rocks of the citadel. **L'Antigu** at the top of the town (51 rue Borgo, tel. 04–95–70–39–33), also with a dining room and terrace overlooking the bay, serves up large, well-cooked portions of its specialty, roast suckling pig. Menus are 70F–136F. You'll find more genuine Corsican food at **Le Lucullus** (17 rue Général-de-Gaulle, tel. 04–95–70–10–17), where regional dishes stay in the 75F neighborhood.

AFTER DARK • If you choose to stay in Porto-Vecchio, by all means spend the rest of your francs listening to the blues at **Objéctif Lune** (rue Général-de-Gaulle, no phone), a fun, hip bar with more than 30 types of beer. **Pub le Bastion** (11 rue Citadella, tel. 04–95–70–69–70) has live music and has more than 300 beers (30F–40F).

OUTDOOR ACTIVITIES • For water sports, make your way to the blue-green sea off Palombaggia beach (*see* Coming and Going, *above*). Tons of seasonal stands rent Windsurfers and Wave Runners; ask about scuba diving options at the Point Information Jeunesse (*see* Basics, *above*). They'll also help you out with information on hikes to the Ospédale forest and nearby mountains. **Muntagna Nostra** (217 av. de la Marine-San-Ciprianu, tel. 04–95–70–03–90) arranges multiple-day hikes to surrounding areas.

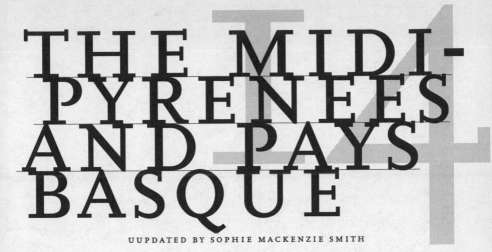

THE MIDI-PYRENEES AND PAYS BASQUE

UUPDATED BY SOPHIE MACKENZIE SMITH

From the Atlantic to the Mediterranean coast the Pyrénées span more than 400 km (250 mi). A voyage through these peaks, broad valleys, and the plains to the north is a journey through many climates, cultures, and worlds. This western half of southern France is less expensive, less pretentious, and less touristy than the Riviera and Provence; it also has more to offer adventurous travelers in the way of natural beauty and historical sites. Toulouse, capital and cultural center of the Midi-Pyrénées, is the fourth-largest city in France, but its narrow streets and candlelit cafés make it feel more like a town. To the southeast, among grapevines and dry, craggy peaks, Languedoc-Roussillon keeps secret the 12th-century châteaux of the Cathars (see box, below). Carcassonne's Cité, with the largest intact medieval edifice in Europe, draws people from throughout Europe to its Bastille Day (July 14) fireworks display. The warm, clean water of the Mediterranean is easily accessible from the long, sandy beaches that extend through Roussillon from Béziers to Collioure.

North of Toulouse are mostly quiet, medieval towns (surrounded by fields of sunflowers in July) and a few visitor hotbeds such as Albi. On the Atlantic coast Basque towns like St-Jean-de-Luz nestle among pine forests near sandy beaches, and idyllic bays and inlets. Surf conditions here are among the best in the world. *Ferias* (festivals), like those in Bayonne, include bullfights and weeks of song and dance. For a more intimate experience of Basque culture, inland towns like St-Jean-Pied-de-Port, have weekly pelota games and innumerable opportunities to try some of the best chèvre (goat cheese) in the world. The Pyrénées, which form a natural border with Spain, reach their peak in the Haute-Pyrénées south of Pau and Lourdes. For winter skiing or for summer hiking, the Pyrénées offer ample resources.

BASICS

WHEN TO GO

The weather turns pleasantly warm as early as April and can stay that way as late as October. However, be prepared for rainstorms, blizzards in the Hautes-Pyrénées, and/or heat waves at almost any time. The weather is especially unpredictable in the Pyrénées: A few passing clouds can rapidly turn into a full-blown storm. Ski season lasts December–early May, with the hiking season taking over May–early October. From mid-July to mid-August, Albi, Biarritz, Carcassonne, Cauterets, and all the towns on the Mediterranean coast get very crowded.

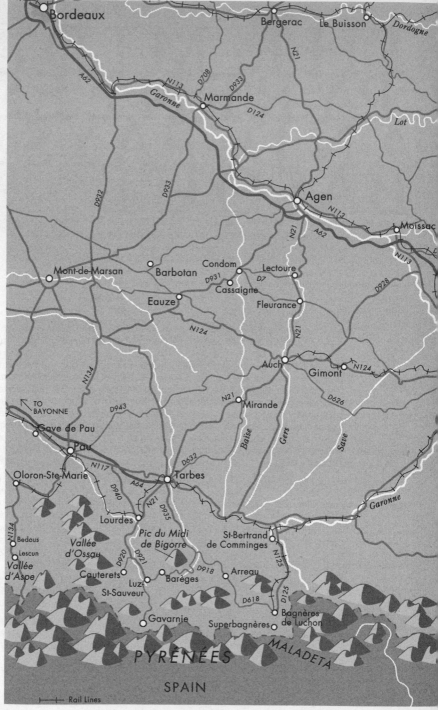

Bordeaux

Bergerac

Le Buisson

Dordogne

A62

N21

N113

D708

D933

Garonne

Marmande

D124

Lot

D932

D933

Agen

N113

A62

Moissac

N113

N21

Mont-de-Marsan

Barbotan

Condom

Lectoure

D931

D7

Cassaigne

Eauze

Fleurance

D928

N124

N21

N134

Auch

Gimont

N124

D626

Baïse

Gers

Save

N21

Mirande

D943

→ TO BAYONNE

Gave de Pau

Pau

D632

Tarbes

Garonne

Oloron-Ste-Marie

N117

A64

N21

D935

D940

Lourdes

St-Bertrand de Comminges

N134

Bedous

Lescun

Vallée d'Ossau

Pic du Midi de Bigorre

D620

D921

N125

Vallée d'Aspe

Cauterets

Luz-St-Sauveur

Barèges

D918

Arreau

D125

Gavarnie

Superbagnères

D618

Bagnères de Luchon

PYRÉNÉES

MALADETA

SPAIN

⊢———⊣ Rail Lines

418

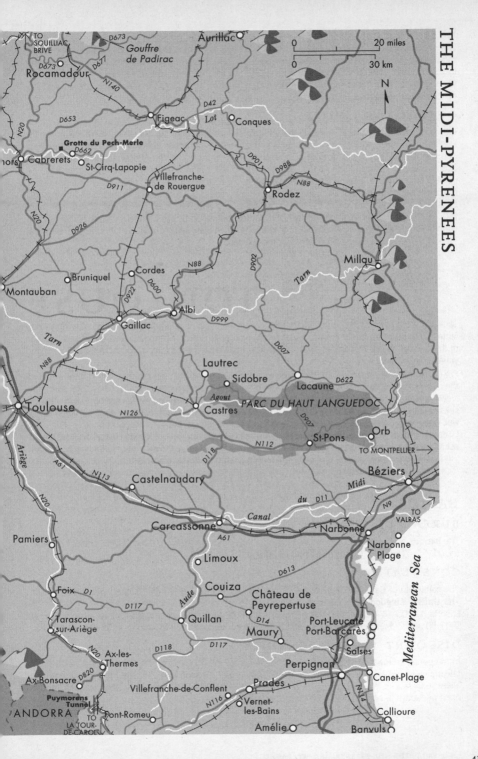

20 miles
30 km

N

TO
SOUILLAC
BRIVE
D673
Gouffre
de Padirac
Aurillac
Rocamadour
D673
D677
D673
N140
D653
D42
Figeac
Lot
Conques
Grotte du Pech-Merle
D662
D901
D988
Cabrerets
St-Cirq-Lapopie
N20
Villefranche-
de Rouergue
N88
D988
Rodez
N88
D911
D902
Millau
N20
D926
Tarn
Cordes
N88
Bruniquel
D922
D600
Montauban
Albi
D999
Gaillac
Tarn
D607
N88
Lautrec
D622
Sidobre
Lacaune
Agout
PARC DU HAUT LANGUEDOC
Toulouse
N126
Castres
D907
Ariège
St-Pons
Orb
A61
N112
TO MONTPELLIER →
D118
Béziers
N113
Castelnaudary
Midi
N20
du
D11
Canel
N9
Carcassonne
Narbonne
TO
VALRAS
A61
Pamiers
Narbonne
Plage
Limoux
D613
Foix
D1
Couiza
Château de
Peyrepertuse
Mediterranean Sea
Tarascon-
sur-Ariège
D117
Aude
Quillan
D14
Maury
Port-Leucate
Port-Barcarès
Ax-les-
Thermes
N20
D118
D117
Salses
Ax-Bonsacre
D820
Perpignan
Canet-Plage
Puymorens
Tunnel
Villefranche-de-Conflent
Prades
ANDORRA
TO
LA TOUR-
DE-CAROL
Font-Romeu
N116
Vernet-
les-Bains
Collioure
Amélie
Banyuls

419

COMING AND GOING

Train service in the Midi-Pyrénées is frequent, though few trains follow a north–south route (which means there aren't that many direct connections to Paris). Wherever you're going, you'll probably need to pass through Toulouse. On the Toulouse–Bordeaux and Toulouse–Bayonne lines, SNCF buses take you southward from the train stops. If your budget allows it, a car gives the freedom to explore and discover villages untouched by modern life.

OUTDOOR ACTIVITIES

Extensive hiking trails wind through the mountains and countryside. Whether you're hiking in the Pyrénées or walking in the hills of Gascony, you can follow a number of trails known as Grandes Randonnées (GRs). The GR10, for example, traverses the Pyrénées from the Atlantic to the Mediterranean. Even higher, cooler, and flatter is the HRP, the Haute Randonnée Pyrénéenne, which crosses the very crest of the cordillera. You can do the whole trail in six to seven weeks or choose a day hike from starting points like Cauterets or Kakouetta. Biking in the Pyrénées is spectacular; for hiking and biking contacts and itineraries, inquire at the tourist offices in Pau and Bayonne. The topographical IGN maps (50F–60F) and detailed explanations of GR10 routes, published by the Comité National des Sentiers de Grande Randonnée, are indispensable companions. They are available at Pau's Librairie du Palais (*see* Visitor Information *in* Pau, *below*), among other places.

TOULOUSE

Toulouse is the heart of the south, where high culture is an evening at an outdoor café, an art form perfected by the 80,000 students who make the city tick. In *la ville rose* (the pink city), so named because of the color of its brick buildings, you can absorb the Mediterranean pace, southern friendliness, and young spirit of the city.

For the Romans and the Visigoths, Toulouse was a major center, but after the medieval Cathar wars and the collapse of its prosperous pastel trade, the city lagged behind more industrial cities, like Bordeaux. Now the center of Europe's high-tech aviation industry (the Concorde and Airbus are built here), the city sees itself as the modern gateway to the south. Toulouse's new high-tech attitude hasn't infringed on the well-preserved *centre ville* (city center), the brick-paved streets between the Garonne River and the Canal du Midi. Here Toulouse still seems like a small town, where food, nouveau Beaujolais, and the latest rugby victory are the primary concerns. Except in July and August, when the students are gone and the town shuts down, Toulouse, the Pyrenean capital and historical cultural hub, makes an ideal base for exploring the entire region.

BASICS

BUREAU DE CHANGE

The **Banque de France** has excellent rates and charges no commission. *4 rue Deville, near pl. Capitole, tel. 05–61–61–35–35. Open weekdays 9–12:20 and 1:20–3:30.*

CONSULATES

The consulate of **Canada** (30 blvd. de Strasbourg, tel. 05–61–99–30–16) is open weekdays 9–noon. The **United Kingdom** (c/o Lucas Aerospace, Victoria Center Bât, Didier Daurat 20, 20 chemin de Laporte, tel. 05–61–15–02–02) has a branch office (of the Bordeaux consulate) here, open weekdays 9–12:30 and 2–5. It's closed Wednesday. If there is no response, call Bordeaux at 05–57–22–21–10.

DISCOUNT TRAVEL AGENCIES

In the center of town, **Usit Voyages** (5 rue des Lois, off pl. du Capitole, tel. 05–61–11–52–42) books cheap flights and is open weekdays 9:30–6:30, Saturday 10–noon and 2–5. Near the train station and allées Jean Jaurès, **Wasteels** (1 blvd. Bonrepos, tel. 08–03–88–70–63) also has cheap plane tickets. It's open weekdays 9–noon and 2–6:30, Saturday 9–12:30 and 2–5:30.

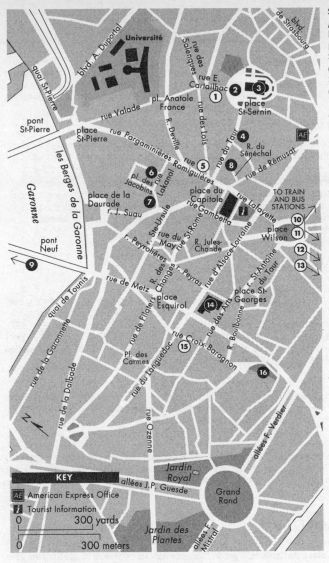

Sights ●

Ancien Collège de
Périgord, **4**

Basilique
St-Sernin, **3**

Cathédrale
St-Etienne, **16**

Château d'Eau, **9**

Eglise Notre-Dame-
du-Taur, **8**

Hôtel de Bernuy, **7**

Les Jacobins, **6**

Musée des
Augustins, **14**

Musée
St-Raymond, **2**

Lodging ○

Hôtel Beauséjour, **10**

Hôtel Croix-
Baragnon, **15**

Hôtel de
l'Université, **1**

Hôtel du
Grand Balcon, **5**

La Chartreuse, **11**

Hôtel Pays d'Oc, **12**

Hôtel Riquet, **13**

ENGLISH-LANGUAGE BOOKSTORE

The **Bookshop** (17 rue Lakanal, tel. 05–61–22–99–92) has a good range of modern classics.

LAUNDRY

Laverie Riquet (67 rue Riquet, tel. 05–61–63–95–52), between the train station and the centre ville, charges 20F per wash and 2F for six minutes of dryer time. Closer to the sights, **Laverie St-Sernin** (14 rue Emíle Cartailhac, tel. 05–61–74–75–08) is open daily 7 AM–10 PM.

MAIL

The mega **main post office,** opposite the tourist office, has poste restante, telegram, and currency-exchange services for a small commission. Both inside and outside the office there are ATM machines that take Cirrus, Plus, MasterCard, and Visa. The postal code is 31000. *9 rue Lafayette, tel. 05–62–15–30–00. Open weekdays 8–7, Sat. 8–noon.*

MEDICAL AID

Pharmacie de Nuit (13 rue du Sénéchal, tel. 05–61–21–81–20) is open nightly 8 PM–8 AM, but you have to ring the doorbell after midnight. In a medical emergency, call **Service Assistance Médicale Urgence** (tel. 05–61–49–33–33). **SOS Voyageurs** (gare Matabiau, tel. 05–61–62–27–30) can help you out in just about any crisis situation. Give them a call or visit the office in the train station weekdays 8–7, Saturday 8–2:30, and Sunday 4–9.

VISITOR INFORMATION

The **tourist office** has city maps, information on local events, and a special desk that handles flights. In summer art historians give guided tours in French through Toulouse's historical areas. *Donjon du Capitole, rue Lafayette, tel. 05–61–11–02–22. Open May–Sept., Mon.–Sat. 9–7, Sun. 9–1 and 2–6; Oct.–Apr., weekdays 9–6, Sat. 9–12:30 and 2–6, Sun. 10–12:30 and 2–5.*

The **Centre Régional Information Jeunesse** (17 rue de Metz, tel. 05–61–21–20–20), open Monday–Saturday 10–1 and 2–7, has tons of information on everything from rock concerts to rock climbing. For hiking and climbing information, equipment rental, and lists of expedition guides go to **Altitudes** (1 av. Maurice Hauriou, off rue de la Garonette, tel. 05–61–25–45–09).

COMING AND GOING

BY TRAIN

Toulouse is a major hub of the south. Trains travel to Paris (7 hrs, 351F; TGV 5 hrs 10 mins, 440F), Biarritz (4 hrs, 197F), Pau (2½ hrs, 143F), Perpignan (2½ hrs, 141F), Bordeaux (2¼ hrs, 163F), Montpellier (2 hrs, 158F), and Barcelona (6½ hrs, 174F). Trains also travel to regional destinations like Albi (1 hr, 63F), Castres (1 hr, 72F), Cordes-Vindrac (1 hr, 64F), Carcassonne (1 hr, 73F), Montauban (½ hr, 47F), Foix (1 hr, 68F), and Ax-les-Thermes (1¾ hrs, 93F). For reservations, call 08–36–35–35–35. At the **train station** (blvd. Pierre Sémard) you'll find luggage storage, an information booth, showers, and a restaurant.

BY BUS

Buses are slower and depart less frequently than trains but are normally 20%–30% cheaper. Buses travel daily to Castres (56F), Albi (60F), and Carcassonne (60F). The **gare routière** (bus station; 68–70 blvd. Pierre Sémard, tel. 05–61–61–67–67) is next to the train station.

BY PLANE

The **Aéroport de Toulouse-Blagnac** (tel. 05–61–42–44–00) is 10 km (6 mi) west of Toulouse. Every 20 minutes a bus (20 mins, 23F) travels from the airport to the gare routière. **Air France** (7 rue St-Jérome, tel. 08–02–80–28–02) has flights to Paris for 330F (with 14-day advance notice); ask about discounts if you're under 26.

GETTING AROUND

For the most part, hotels, restaurants, and sights are within walking distance of one another. The main square of the centre ville is **place du Capitole,** a good 15-minute walk (or two métro stops) from the train station but only a few blocks from the city's other focal points—place Wilson, place Esquirol, and Basilique St-Sernin.

The **métro** still has only one line, but you should try the high-tech driverless system at least once. It connects the Gare Matabiau with place du Capitole and place Esquirol. Machines at the entrances sell 8F tickets (10 for 60F), which are also good on the buses and valid for 45 minutes. The métro runs until midnight. The **Semvat bus** system (tel. 05–61–41–70–70) is efficient and comprehensive. A special night service kicks in 10 PM–midnight.

WHERE TO SLEEP

Most hotels in Toulouse are near the train station or in the centre ville near place du Capitole. The neighborhood near the train station is less animated and more run down than the center. Wherever you stay, you won't have to pay much; budget hotels are plentiful (thankfully, since there is no hostel in town).

UNDER 100F • Hôtel Beauséjour. On the north side of allées Jean Jaurès, the Beauséjour is near the red-light district but still reasonably safe. Clean but bare doubles start at 100F (150F with shower). Hall showers are 10F. *4 rue Cafarelli, tel. 05–61–62–77–59. From train station, turn left on blvd. de Bonrepos, right on allées Jean Jaurès, right on rue Cafarelli. 14 rooms, 4 with bath.*

Hôtel Pays d'Oc. This hotel on a quiet street is one of the cheapest in town: Singles start at 75F with shower, doubles at 95F. *53 rue Riquet, tel. 05–61–62–33–76. From train station, turn left on blvd. de Bonrepos across canal, right on allées Jean Jaurès, left on rue Riquet. 22.*

UNDER 125F • Hôtel de l'Université. It's in the center of town, near St-Sernin. Small, homey rooms are 110F per double without shower, 135F with. For an extra 35F, they'll add a bed, making a cheap three-person room. *26 rue Émile Cartailhac, tel. 05–61–21–35–69. 10 rooms, 6 with shower.*

UNDER 150F • Hôtel du Grand Balcon. This hotel is just off place du Capitole. Some of the large rooms are fully equipped with nonusable fireplace (unfortunately), phone, desk, gilded mirror, and huge windows that let in the breeze and, on the front side, the urban noise. Antoine de St-Exupéry, author of *The Little Prince,* stayed here in the 1920s and '30s; his old room is only 135F a night. Singles and doubles start at 125F. *8 rue Romiguières, tel. 05–61–21–48–08. 54 rooms, 30 with bath.*

It was from Toulouse that Antoine de St-Exupéry pioneered mail flights to Africa and over the Atlantic to South America.

UNDER 200F • La Chartreuse. Conveniently located near the station, these rooms are very quiet. Small doubles are 168F; breakfast costs 30F. *4 bis. blvd. Bonrepos, tel. 05–61–62–93–39. 28 rooms with bath.*

Hôtel Croix-Baragnon. On a narrow lane in the centre ville, this hotel is worth the extra francs. The modern rooms have views of the red rooftops of Toulouse and overlook a flower-filled courtyard. Singles are 175, doubles are 185 and up, and quads with television are 210F and up. *17 rue Croix-Baragnon, tel. 05–61–52–60–10. From train station, take Bus 2 to Esquirol-Rouex. 12 rooms, all with bath.*

Hôtel Riquet. This hotel has 70 rooms, so you should stand a chance of finding one even during peak periods. A double with shower is 210F. *92 rue Riquet, tel. 05–61–62–55–96. 70 rooms, 5 with bath.*

CAMPING

La Bouriette. About 5 km (3 mi) from Toulouse, this shaded campground costs 50F per day for the site for one person and 20F for each additional camper. Reception is open Monday–Saturday 10–noon and 4–7. *199 chemin de Tournefeuille, in St-Martin du Touch, tel. 05–61–49–64–46. From train station, take métro to Arènes, then Bus 64 to Bertier stop. 83 sites.*

Les Violettes. This rustic year-round site is close to the Canal du Midi but 15 km (9 mi) south of Toulouse. Sites cost 45F for one person, 65F for two. There's a restaurant (open in summer) and a bakery. Reception is open daily 8 AM–10:30 PM. *Deyme, tel. 05–61–81–72–07. From bus station, take a Courriers de la Garonne bus (direction: Carcassonne or Castelnaudary) to Deyme. 80 sites.*

FOOD

Avoid the pricey café-restaurants on place du Capitole—you'll do much better if you head down one of the many alleys and pedestrian streets that fan out from it. Rue des Lois has cheap ethnic eateries where touts invite you in by shouting at you across the street, including **Resto Cool** (6 rue des Lois, tel. 05–61–21–51–77), which has Lebanese falafel sandwiches (17F), tabbouleh (10F), and humus (22F). **La Trattoria** (2 rue Pargaminières, tel. 05–62–27–15–08) is a tiny dive with scrumptious food and a 28F menu.

Markets are a treat in Toulouse, not only for the heaps of fresh fruit, veggies, olives, antiques, books, and trinkets you can buy, but also for the fun of watching farmers yelling at each other in Occità, the all-but-lost language of France's southwestern Langue d'Oc region. **Boulevard de Strasbourg** is bustling Tuesday–Sunday mornings, as is the Sunday flea market around Basilique St-Sernin. Upstairs, over the indoor fish, cheese, and meat market, **Les Halles,** in place Victor Hugo (open Tuesday–Saturday mornings) is a very popular row of restaurants with top-value menus starting at 60F.

UNDER 25F • Arsenal. Okay, so it's one of the university cafeterias but the food is actually bearable. If you don't have an ISIC card or want a single meal, just buy a ticket from a student (13F) or go downstairs to the brasserie for an inexpensive tuna sandwich (10F), pizza (8F), or quiche (8F). If you do have an ISIC card, you can buy a pack of 10 meal tickets (123F) weekdays 11:30–1. *2 blvd. Armand Duportal, tel. 05–61–23–98–48. Cash only. Closed Sat. afternoon and Sun.*

UNDER 50F • La Cascade. The generous portions here match the genial attitude with which they are served. The couscous and *tagine* (Moroccan stew) for 55F is seriously filling. Sipping a post-dinner *thé à la menthe* (mint tea; 10F), a ceremony in itself, inspires longing for Morocco. *8 rue Maury, between rue Colombette and pl. de Danloup, tel. 05–61–99–30–33. Closed Sun. No lunch Sat.*

UNDER 75F • Bagamoyo. This happening place serves simple but delicious African fare. Opt for the 60F menu, which gives you an appetizer and lamb or chicken in spicy sauce with rice, plus dessert and a glass of wine. *27 rue des Couteliers, tel. 05–62–26–11–36. Cash only. No dinner weekends.*

UNDER 100F • Brasserie de l'Opera. This restaurant fulfills the requirements of the archetypal French brasserie without being a tourist trap. The food is traditional to the area: cassoulets, pig's trotters, and rabbit, as well as the more standard steak et frites. The menu du jour runs' about 100F. *Pl. du Capitole, tel. 05–61–21–37–03.*

Les Caves de la Maréchale. At this cavelike restaurant overlooking a courtyard, menus go for 65F and 85F. Both include a buffet of all-you-can-eat hors d'oeuvres. *3 rue Jules-Chalande, off rue St-Rome, tel. 05–61–23–89–88. Take a left into the small courtyard. Closed Sun. No lunch Mon.*

La Corde. It's worth seeking out this little spot dating from 1881 and built into a lovely corner tower hidden in the courtyard of the 16th-century Hôtel Bolé. À la carte items start at 80F; a good bet is the cassoulet. *4 rue Jules Chalande, tel. 05–61–29–09–43. Closed Sun. No lunch Mon.*

Le Ghandi. The area near the train station is packed with ethnic restaurants such as Le Ghandi, which is not afraid of seriously hot food. The 79F (85F for vegetarian) dinner menu includes samosas, tandoori chicken, and a mango dessert. There's a cheaper menu (35F) at lunch. *39 rue de l'Industrie, off rue G. Péri, tel. 05–61–99–21–03.*

CAFES

Start your day in the sun or pop in on a Sunday evening at **Café des Artistes** (pl. de la Daurade); then take one of the quayside walks at the top of the ramp down to the Garonne. With funky lace-covered hanging lamps and a wooden interior, **Le Sherpa** (46 rue du Taur, tel. 05–61–23–89–29) is packed at lunch and dinner; food is served until midnight. Across the street, pay the variable cover charge to get into **Cave Poésie** (71 rue du Taur, tel. 05–61–23–62–00) for readings and other cultural events. Whenever there's a full moon, Cave Poésie hosts *soirées portes ouvertes* (a free open mike).

Le Bol Bu. On a tiny street off rue St-Rome, this offbeat teahouse serves cheap crepes (15F–25F) and salads (14F–30F). *8 rue du Mai, tel. 05–61–21–11–31. Cash only. Closed Sun. and Aug.*

Le Bouchon. The *je m'en fiche* (I don't give a damn) attitude at this café goes well with the unpretentious, unlabeled Bordeaux red (20F). The restaurant in back serves a bittersweet *tarte aux pommes* (apple tart) and dishes like *confit de canard* (duck cooked in its own fat; 80F) at broad, candlelit wooden tables. *12 rue Ste-Ursule, near pl. du Capitole, tel. 05–61–62–97–43. Cash only.*

Père Louis. This old-fashioned wine bar has barrels for tables and vintage photographs around the walls. It hosts a fun Nouveau Beaujolais blowout on the third Thursday of November. *45 rue des Tourneurs, tel. 05–61–21–33–45. Cash only. Closed Sun.*

WORTH SEEING

Everything worth your time in Toulouse is conveniently concentrated in the centre ville, much of it accessible only to pedestrians and enclosed by the boulevards that marked the Roman ramparts. As you explore the small streets, particularly those around Cathédrale St-Étienne, venture into the passageways that lead to central courtyards of the *hôtels particuliers* (mansions). Built by Renaissance lords who cashed in on the pastel trade, many of these mansions have splendid towers with winding staircases. Take some time to wander down rue des Changes, which becomes rue St-Rome. It was once part of the Roman road that sliced through Toulouse from north to south; on and around it you'll find some of Toulouse's prettiest houses and finest shops.

BASILIQUE ST-SERNIN

Built in the 11th to 13th centuries, St-Sernin is the largest Romanesque church in the south of France and is renowned as a stop on the pilgrimage route to Santiago de Compostela. In 1860 some clumsy alterations ended up destroying much of the upper exterior, and it has only recently been restored it to its original state. The original church was built in the 4th century—before Charlemagne filled it with relics—to house the remains of the early Christian martyr and first bishop of Toulouse, St-Sernin (St. Saturnin). When Sernin refused in AD 250 to take part in a bull sacrifice, the Romans tied him to a bull's horns; the nearby 14th-century **Église Notre-Dame-du-Taur** (14 rue du Taur) was built on the spot where St. Saturnin was dragged to his death by said bull. *Pl. St-Sernin. Open July–Sept., daily 9–6:30; Oct.–June, daily 8–noon and 2–6.*

Opposite the basilica is the **Musée St-Raymond,** the city's archaeological museum. Long-term renovation now shows a fine collection of material tracing the progress of man to the year AD 1000. *Pl. St-Sernin, tel. 05–61–22–21–85. Admission 15F. Open daily 10–6.*

Follow rue du Taur to see the **Ancien Collège de Périgord** (Old Périgord College; 56–58 rue du Taur). The wooden structure on the street side of the courtyard is the oldest remnant of the 14th-century residential college.

CHATEAU D'EAU

The "Castle of Water" is the oldest and most popular photo gallery in France. It was built in 1823, the same year that Joseph Nicéphore Nièpce created the first permanent photographic images. The exhibits highlight photographic history as well as the works of contemporary photographers. *Pl. Laganne, across Pont Neuf, tel. 05–61–77–09–40. Admission 15F. Open Wed.–Mon. 1–7.*

"Le Petit Futé" is a guide to restaurants and bars in Toulouse (in French only). Flip through it at the tourist office or hostel, or buy one in a bookstore (40F).

LES JACOBINS

This 13th-century masterpiece of southern Gothic architecture usually plays second fiddle to the Basilique St-Sernin, but it is architecturally far more impressive. Above the column farthest from the entrance is said to be the world's finest example of palm-tree vaulting. It was here that St. Dominic founded the Dominican Order in 1215. The body of St. Thomas Aquinas was placed here in 1369. Under Napoléon I the buildings were used to barrack soldiers with horses temporarily stabled in the church itself. *Pl. des Jacobins, near rue Lakanal, tel. 05–61–22–21–92. Admission to cloisters 15F. Open Mon.–Sat. 10–noon and 2:30–6:30, Sun. 2:30–6.*

Around the corner from Les Jacobins, on rue Gambetta, is the 16th-century **Hôtel de Bernuy.** A palatial mansion built by the wealthy dye merchant Jean de Bernuy, it's now a private school. A monument to merchant wealth, the building is partially made of stone—a costly material in this region of brick—and has the highest stair tower in the city. It's open weekdays 8–5.

MUSEE DES AUGUSTINS

The collection of sculptures from the Roman era through the Renaissance is impressive, but the setting is even nicer than this museum's contents; the well-preserved medieval cloister almost makes you forget you're in the middle of the city. Upstairs are enormous tableaux, including works by Murillo and Rubens, depicting royalty, bloodshed, and glory. *21 rue de Metz, tel. 05–61–22–21–82. Admission 12F. Open Thurs.–Mon. 10–5 (June–Sept. until 6), Wed. until 9 (June–Sept. until 10).*

Off rue de Metz, on place St-Étienne, is the **Cathédrale St-Etienne.** No one could cough up enough money at one time, so construction lasted from the 11th to the 17th century, resulting in an amalgam of styles. Inside is a collection of 16th- and 17th-century tapestries tracing the life of St. Stephen. *Pl. St-Étienne. Open daily 7:30–7.*

CHEAP THRILLS

Toulouse gets humid and hot, and you may feel as if you're in a brick oven as you walk the streets in July and August. Consider going swimming at the immense **Piscine Municipale** (allée Gabriel-Biénès), out on the island by the stadium; admission is 15F. If it's sun you want, take a snooze on **les berges de la Garonne,** the grassy banks along the river. The **Espace Bazacle** (11 quai St-Pierre) is a converted mill with a clever (and free) *passe à poissons* (fish passage) that lets finny critters go upstream to their old breeding grounds.

FESTIVALS

In July and August, **Musique d'Été** (tel. 05–61–11–02–22) livens up the town with jazz concerts, piano and organ recitals, and dance performances in the city's churches and squares—take your pick. Tickets, which can be purchased at the tourist office, cost 50F–75F a show. On June 21, Toulouse honors the summer solstice with its own version of the nationwide **Fête de la Musique** (Music Festival). For concert information, call 05–61–44–83–05.

AFTER DARK

At night, the young and not-so-young congregate in bars and cafés in the centre ville. The most popular spots are around place Esquirol on both sides of rue de Metz, and place St-Pierre, especially **Bar Basque** at No. 7 and **Chez Tonton** at No. 16. Pick up a copy of *Flash* (6F) from any *tabac* (tobacco shop) for a complete list of what's going on each week. For a monthly account of cultural events, check out *Toulouse Culture,* free from the tourist office.

Movie theaters cluster around place Wilson. For quality European and international flicks, **Utopia** (24 rue Montardy, tel. 05–61–23–66–20) is the best and the cheapest at 35F. Mainstream French and American movies are about 40F at **Gaumont Wilson** (3 pl. Wilson, tel. 05–61–23–31–50) and **Gaumont Nouveautés** (56 blvd. Carnot). Call 08–36–68–76–55 for a recording of what's playing.

Major bar zones include place du Capitole, home to the popular **Le Florida** (12 pl. du Capitole, tel. 05–61–21–87–59) and tons of tourists. Mellow place St-Georges is home to **Le Van Gogh** (21 pl. St-Georges, tel. 05–61–21–03–15) and other pricey hangouts. On Thursday nights on place St-Pierre you can join rugby winners at **Chez Tonton** (16 pl. St-Pierre, tel. 05–61–21–89–54). Off rue St-Rome, try **Bar Champagne** (4 rue Peyras, tel. 05–61–21–24–67) or, by quai de Tounis, **La Tantina de Burgos** (27 rue de la Garonette, tel. 05–61–55–59–29), where the sangria flows and the guitarist plays all night.

Nightclubs (*boîtes de nuit*) take over after 2 AM when the bars quit. Most are cheap or free until Wednesday, and then have a 30F–50F cover through Saturday. For rock and a lively, young crowd, try **Le Bikini** (rte. de Lacroix-Falgarde, tel. 05–61–55–00–29). **Mandala** (23 rue des Amidonniers, tel. 05–61–21–10–05) has Latin jazz. The gay scene is alive and well at **Le Shanghai** (12 rue de la Pomme, tel. 05–61–23–37–80).

NEAR TOULOUSE

Albi, Montauban, Foix, and Ax-les-Thermes make fine day trips from Toulouse, but to really appreciate the Pyrénées you'll need to go farther afield and do some hiking. One of the best routes is eastward from Foix along the **Sentier Cathare** (Path of the Cathars). This tough, several-hundred-mile trail takes you through a chain of cliff-side châteaux all the way to the Mediterranean. Pick up maps in Toulouse.

FOIX

Eighty-three kilometers (52 mi) south of Toulouse, the green mountainside of the Pyrénées and the rushing waters of the Ariège River around Foix make city life seem farther away than it really is. The sleepy town of Foix makes a good starting point for biking in the hills and exploring nearby caves. It's also the ideal starting point for longer mountain hikes along the Sentier Cathare. Foix itself is a medieval city of about 10,000. The **Château des Comtes de Foix** (tel. 05–61–65–56–05) is a fairy-tale, 11th-century castle that dominates the town from its hilltop, providing panoramic views of the countryside. Admission is 25F and it's open May–September, Wednesday–Sunday 9:45–6; October–April, Wednesday–Sunday 10:30–noon and 2–5:30.

BASICS

The **tourist office** has information on camping and regional *gîtes d'étape* (way stations/rural hostels). To find out about hiking, pick up a copy of "Promenades et Randonnées" (Walks and Hikes) for the Ariège Pyrénées. *45 cours Gabriel Fauré, tel. 05–61–65–12–12. Open July–Aug., Mon.–Sat. 9–7, Sun. 10–12:30 and 3–6; June and Sept., Mon.–Sat. 9–noon and 2–7, Sun. 10–12:30; Oct.–May, weekdays 9–noon and 2–6, Sat. 9–12:30 and 2:30–6:30.*

If you are visiting any of the Cathar castles, pick up the English-language brochure "Cathar Castles" (35F) and IGN maps (Nos. 71 and 72; each 57F) from **Librairie Surre,** opposite the *VTT* (mountain bike) rental stand. *29 rue Delcassé, tel. 05-61-05-05-80.*

COMING AND GOING

Several trains a day travel the 84 km (52 mi) to Foix from Toulouse (1 hr, 71F). To reach the center of town from the **train station** (rue Pierre Sémard), make a right on cours Irénée Cros and then cross the first bridge on your right. A **Salt Autocars** bus (tel. 05-61-65-08-40) stops here on its way from Toulouse to Ax-les-Thermes (38F) and the Spanish border several times daily in summer. It departs from the train station and from behind the post office (rue du Sénateur Paul Laffont); check the schedule at the tourist office.

WHERE TO SLEEP

This is a good place to take advantage of campgrounds or rural gîtes; for information, contact the tourist office. Your hotel options include the **Hôtel Eychenne** (11 rue Peyrevidal, tel. 05-61-65-00-04), featuring caved-in mattresses in otherwise attractive rooms; doubles start at 160F. A more expensive option in the centre ville is **Hôtel Audoye-Lons** (4 pl. Georges-Duthil, tel. 05-61-65-52-44), a former post house with comfortable, modern rooms for 250F-320F and a restaurant. **Camping Municipal** (N20, tel. 05-61-65-11-58) is a 3-km (2-mi) walk from town, north along the road to Toulouse. The 300-odd sites are plain and a little cramped, but the location by the river more than makes up for it. It's open April–September and charges 10F per person, 9F per night, and 5F for showers.

At the intersection of rue des Changes and rue des Temponières in Toulouse, you'll find a building with trompe l'oeil windows. These bricked-in windows are a remnant of the window tax that all citizens of Toulouse once struggled so mightily to avoid.

FOOD

In addition to the small markets in town, you'll find lots of groceries at **Nouvelles Galeries** on rue Paul Laffont. **Self-service Gros** (allée de Villote, near Halle aux Grains, tel. 05-61-65-00-07) is a cafeteria with 30F-40F daily specials. For a proper meal, check the restaurants down rue de Lafaurie; **Le Jeu de L'Oie** (17 rue de Lafaurie, tel. 05-61-02-69-39), open for lunch and dinner, has an especially tasty 47F plat du jour. It's closed Sunday and for lunch Saturday.

OUTDOOR ACTIVITIES

The gorgeous countryside is what makes Foix worth visiting, and the best way to see it is by bike. **Intersport** (40 rue Delcassé, tel. 05-61-65-00-41) rents VTTs for 100F per day, 75F per half day with ID. It's an easy 6 km (4 mi) through flower-covered fields to the **Rivière Souterraine de Labouiche** (tel. 05-61-65-04-11), the closest of the region's caves. A small boat takes you through the caves 200 ft underground for more than an hour. Bring a jacket or sweater for the 13°C (55°F) chill. In July and August, come early to avoid the wait. Admission is 44F. It's open April–mid-November.

AX-LES-THERMES

A feasible day trip by train from Foix (40 mins, 38F) and Toulouse (1¾ hrs, 93F), Ax (42 km/26 mi southeast of both) is the perfect starting point for the hard-core 24-km (15-mi) bike ride up to the **Col de Chioula,** with stunning views of the surrounding mountains. **Telemark Pyrénées** (rue de l'Horloge, tel. 05-61-64-34-93) rents bikes for an ID and 110F per day. You can also camp at **Camping Rameil** on the road to the summit.

The town itself, full of folks soaking in the hot spring (open April–November), is unexciting at best. Though most people are there for medical reasons, you can use the spring for just one day (call 05-61-64-24-83 for information). The **tourist office** (pl. du Breilh, tel. 05-61-64-60-60) is about a five-minute walk to the left as you exit the **train station.** It has excellent information on hikes, camping, nearby hostels, and winter skiing. If you must spend the night in Ax, make a reservation. **Pension-Aliot** (6 pl. Roussel, tel. 05-61-64-22-01) retains some local flavor and has doubles for 150F-180F; for 200F meals are included. **Hôtel La Terrasse** (7 rue Marcailhou, tel. 05-61-64-20-33) also has reasonable doubles for 140F. Nearby on rue Rigal are a number of markets and restaurants. **Le Martudo** (6 rue de l'Horloge, tel. 05-61-64-60-25) has a 69F lunch menu of regional specialties. Try the fondue with meat or raclette cheese.

THE CATHARS AND THE CATHOLIC CHURCH

The dusty ruins high atop cliffs in southern Languedoc were once the refuges of the Cathars, an ascetic religious group persecuted out of existence by the Catholic Church. From the 12th to 14th century, the Cathars inhabited the area from present-day Germany all the way to the Atlantic Ocean. Adherents to this doctrine of material abnegation and spiritual revelation abstained from flesh in all forms—forgoing even procreation and the consumption of animal products.

Not thrilled by a religion that did not "go forth and multiply" (and that saw no need to pay taxes to the church), Pope Innocent III launched the Albigensian Crusade (Albi was one of the major Cathar centers), and Pope Gregory IX rounded up the stragglers during an inquisition started in 1233. In some cases, entire towns were judged guilty of heresy and inhabitants were thrown to their deaths from the high town walls. The persecuted "pure" took refuge in the Pyrénées, where they survived for 100 years. Now, you can visit the vacant stone staircases and roofless chapels of places like Peyrepertuse and Quéribus, but all that remains are stunning views from their former hideouts.

ALBI

Some 75 km (47 mi) northeast of Toulouse, along the Tarn River, Albi is choked with tourists and tacky shops but is still worth seeing. In its heyday during the Middle Ages, it was a major center for the Cathars, a.k.a. the Albigenses (*see box, below*). Albi's huge **Cathédrale Ste-Cécile,** with immense clif-flike brick walls, was a symbol of the church's victory over heretics. Beneath the organ is an impressive 15th-century mural depicting appropriate punishments for the seven deadly sins in the Last Judgment. The scenes of torture and hellfire give an indication of how the Vatican kept its Christian "subjects" in line during the crusade against the Cathars and the subsequent Inquisition trials.

Between the cathedral and the Pont Vieux (Old Bridge) is the Palais de la Berbie. Built between 1240 and 1245 as the Bishop's Palace, it was later transformed into a fortress, then into a museum honoring Albi's most famous son, belle epoque painter Henri de Toulouse-Lautrec (1864–1901). Inside, the **Musée de Toulouse-Lautrec** houses France's largest collection of his work. *Pl. Ste-Cécile, tel. 05–63–49–48–70. Admission 24F, gardens free. Open June–Sept., daily 9–noon and 2–6; Oct.–May, daily 10–noon and 2–5 (Apr.–May until 6).*

BASICS

At the **tourist office** next to Palais de la Berbie, you can change money, get hotel information, and buy tickets for events and performances. Ask about Albi's festivals, notably the Festival de la Musique (end of July) and Albi-Jazz (late May). Tickets to performances at either festival start at 100F. *Pl. Ste-Cécile, tel. 05–63–49–48–80. Open July–Aug., Mon.–Sat. 9–7:30, Sun. 10:30–1 and 3:30–6:30; Sept.–June, Mon.–Sat. 9–12:30 and 2–6, Sun. 10:30–12:30 and 3:30–5:30.*

COMING AND GOING

To reach Albi from the south, you have to go through Toulouse (1 hr, 63F). The center of town and most of the budget accommodations are about a 20-minute walk from the **train station** (pl. Stalingrad). To reach the center of town, take a left from the train station and then follow avenue Maréchal Joffre to avenue Général de Gaulle; at place Lapérouse, make a left on boulevard Général Sibille.

Buses to Castres (1 hr, 27F) leave year-round twice daily. Service to Cordes-sur-Ciel (1 hr, 22F) is infrequent and limited to the summer. For Montauban, take the SNCF regional bus (1½ hrs, 60F) from the train station or place Jean Jaurès—it's a bit more frequent than the Tarn Bus, which generally goes only twice a day. In all cases, check schedules at the tourist office and buy tickets as you board. At the driver's discretion, bikes are usually allowed in the luggage compartments under the bus at no extra charge. The **bus station** (pl. Jean Jaurès, tel. 05–63–54–58–61) is off Lices Jean Moulin, about a five-minute walk from the center of town.

WHERE TO SLEEP

Albi doesn't have many bargain hotels. Near the train station, the **Hôtel Le Terminus** (33 av. Maréchal Joffre, tel. 05–63–54–00–99) has basic rooms starting at 100F. A pricier option is the centrally located **Hôtel Chiffre** (50 rue Séré-de-Rivières, tel. 05–63–48–58–48), in a town house with impeccable rooms (300F with shower) overlooking a garden. The nearest **campground** (rte. de Millau, tel. 05–63–60–37–06), closed mid-October–March, is 2 km (1 mi) east of Albi. The 100 shady sites cost 65F for two. Mobile homes may also be rented here. Walk down rue de la République, or take Bus 5 to Les Trois Tarn stop.

HOSTEL • Maison des Jeunes et de la Culture. This dorm for French workers that doubles as a hostel is the best deal in town. The 16-bed dorms and shabby bathrooms are far from luxurious, but for 30F (HI members are preferred), plus 18F for sheets, you get a hot shower and a decent place to stay that's only 15 minutes by foot from the center. The kind staff prepares hearty meals for 42F, including wine; breakfast is 15F. Be prepared to pay a 20F *caution* (deposit), which is refunded when you leave. Be careful not to confuse this place (marked MDJ out front) with the Foyer des Jeunes Travailleurs around the corner, which has a minimum one-week stay. *13 rue de la République, tel. 05–63–54–53–65. From train station, Albibus Bus 1 (5F; direction: Cantepau) to République (last bus at 7 PM). Check-in weekdays 6 PM–9 PM, weekends 8 PM–9 PM.*

FOOD

The restaurants around place Ste-Cécile are pricey and filled with tourists. But it only takes five minutes to cross the center of town to **Le Tournesol** (rue de l'Ort en Salvy, tel. 05–63–38–38–14). This vegetarian restaurant with a terrace on a small pedestrian street behind place du Vigan serves up a 47F plat du jour. (Take the small street between Crédit Agricole Hotel de Vigan.) The restaurant is closed Sunday and Monday. The nearby **Casino Cafétéria** (39 lis Georges Pompidou, tel. 05–63–54–90–79) is a cheap eat, but avoid the cafés on expensive place du Vigan. Stock up on fruits and veggies at the **market** on place du Marché, above place Ste-Cécile; it's open Tuesday–Sunday until noonish.

CORDES-SUR-CIEL

Cordes-sur-Ciel is a steep medieval village overlooking a landscape of woods and meadows in the valley of the River Cerou. Established in 1222 by the Count of Toulouse, Cordes is still in a pristine state—it's the oldest and best preserved of the *bastides,* or planned towns (*see box, below*), in the southwest. At the top of town, along with great views of the valley, you'll find the beautiful wood-covered **Halle.** As in many bastide cities, this marketplace takes center stage, with the spireless **Église St-Michel,** near place St-Michel, pushed to the side. In the second week of July, Cordes celebrates the **Fête du Grand Fauconnier,** with everyone in medieval costume. Call the **tourist office** (Maison du Grand Fauconnier, tel. 05–63–56–00–52) for information and tickets. For long hikes in the region, pick up the list of gîtes and the suggested trails here. Across the street, the newspaper store stocks GR guides.

COMING AND GOING

In July and August, a bus runs the 25 km (16 mi) from place Jean-Jaurès in Albi to the bottom of Cordes (27F) twice daily. At other times of the year, you'll have to take the train to Cordes-Vindrac, which is frequently served from Toulouse (1¼ hrs, 65F) and Albi (via Gaillac; 1 hr, 44F). From here it's 5 km (3 mi) to Cordes-sur-Ciel, best accomplished by renting a bike for 55F at the station or calling 05–63–56–14–

80 to get a bus to come out for you (20F per person, 14F if there are three or more people). Note that traffic is banned in the upper town in the summer and parking nearby is virtually impossible.

WHERE TO SLEEP

The cheapest hotel around is **Chez Babar** (Les Cabannes, tel. 05–63–56–02–51), 1 km (½ mi) from Cordes-sur-Ciel toward Cordes-Vindrac; doubles with shower go for 200F. About 1½ km (1 mi) toward Gaillac is **Camping le Moulin de Julien** (tel. 05–63–56–01–42), a resort-type campground near a pool and lake. It's open April–September and costs 45F for one person, 70F for two.

MONTAUBAN

Montauban's past is more glorious than its somewhat dilapidated present. One of the original bastides (*see* box, *below*), Montauban, some 50 km (30 mi) north of Toulouse on the Tarn River, was created by the Count of Toulouse, Alphonse Jourdain, in the 12th century. During the 16th-century religious wars, it was the Protestant stronghold in France, protected by a wall of stones "borrowed" from Catholic churches and convents. Though Montauban shows off the region's distinctive architecture, it doesn't measure up to *la ville rouge* (Albi) or *la ville rose* (Toulouse). This town of faded brick and rubble has only two reminders of its heritage: the **Eglise St-Jacques** and the **Pont Vieux** (Old Bridge).

Today, most people come to Montauban to visit the **Musée Ingres.** The last of the great French classicists, Jean Auguste Dominique Ingres (1780–1867) was born in Montauban, and many of his most important works, including about 4,000 sketches and paintings, are here. You'll also find some sculptures by Bourdelle (1861–1929), student of Rodin, and another native son. *Pl. Bourdelle, tel. 05–63–22–12–92. Admission 20F. Open July–Aug., daily 9:30–noon and 1:30–6; Sept.–June, Tues.–Sun. 10–noon and 2–6.*

BASICS

The **tourist office** has decent city maps and information on the town's sights but doesn't have much on the surrounding region. Call here for information on the weeklong jazz festival (tickets 100F–190F) held in mid-July. *Pl. Prax-Paris, in Ancien Collège, tel. 05–63–63–60–60. Open July–Aug., Mon.–Sat. 9–7, Sun. 10–noon and 3–5.*

For information on gîtes in the area, ask for the list at the tourist office, or call the **Comité Départemental du Tourisme.** You're best off looking for gîtes near Moissac or Bruniquel—start with a phone call to their tourist offices (*see below*). *Hôtel des Intendants, pl. du Maréchal Foch, tel. 05–63–63–31–40.*

COMING AND GOING

Montauban is on the Paris–Toulouse rail line. Trains travel to Paris (6½ hrs, 330F), Toulouse (30 mins, 48F), Bordeaux (2 hrs, 135F), and Cahors (1¼ hrs, 55F). The center of town is a good 15-minute walk from the **train station** (av. Roger Salengro)—take avenue de Mayenne to place Alfred-Marty, cross the Vieux Pont (Old Bridge), and continue straight for four blocks to rue de la Comédie, where you turn right and continue four blocks to the tourist office. Bus 3 picks up at the train station and drops off on boulevard Midi-Pyrénées. Walk back one block for the tourist office.

The **bus station** (pl. Lalaque), two blocks from the train station, serves Cordes-sur-Ciel (1½ hrs, 49F) and Albi (2½ hrs, 54F) once a day Monday–Saturday. The Bruniquel bus leaves in the early afternoon Monday–Saturday and returns the next day. For schedules, check the boards in the train station, bus station, or call **Société Pascale** (tel. 05–63–31–13–30).

WHERE TO SLEEP

Avoid the sketchy neighborhood near the train station and head toward town. **Hôtel du Commerce** (9 pl. Franklin-D.-Roosevelt, tel. 05–63–66–31–32), directly across from the Cathédrale Notre-Dame, has simple singles for 110F, doubles for 140F; add 10F for a shower.

FOOD

Try the haute cuisine at **Le Contre Filet** (4–6 rue Princesse, tel. 05–63–20–19–75); the hearty menu of *grillades* (grilled meats) is 64F. **La Clef des Champs** (3 rue Armand Cambon, tel. 05–63–66–33–34) is an inexpensive vegetarian restaurant with daily specials for 45F; the must-try *tarte à la banane* (banana tart) is 18F. It's closed for dinner and Sunday. For market action, go to **place Lalaque** on Wednesday mornings and, on Saturday mornings, to **l'Halle Arnaud Ligou,** right next to the tourist office. The **place Nationale,** which hosts a daily market, is in the old center of town. The bars under its double arches are the coolest (literally) places in town—especially if you have a beer in hand.

ELSEWHERE NEAR TOULOUSE

LAUTREC

On a hill due south of Albi is the hilltop village of Lautrec, built in the 12th century by the Counts of Lautrec of whom the artist Toulouse-Lautrec was a direct descendent. The central square is surrounded by arcades and timber-framed houses. In the town hall is a museum of archaeology and local history. It is also worth visiting the 15th-century church of St-Rémy. The village is the center of pink garlic production, believed by experts to be the best; a garlic festival is held in August. There are no hotels in the village but there are three restaurants.

MOISSAC

The small town of Moissac, famous for the abbey church St-Pierre, is a 20-minute train ride (29F) from Montauban. A prime example of Romanesque art, the abbey's graceful 11th-century cloister and bell tower are worth seeing for their impressive carvings and marble-faced pillars. Equally striking, and perhaps more spiritually provocative, is the pedagogical portal of the church. There you'll see the Apocalypse according to St. John—very gory damnation stuff. To get to St-Pierre from the train station, walk down avenue Pierre Chabrié. Admission to the cloister is 22F, and it's open daily 9–noon and 2–6. Top off your day at a café on **place Roger Delthil,** next to the portal.

The **tourist office** (pl. Durand de Bredon, tel. 05–63–04–01–85), near the abbey, has information on gîtes in the area, including those on the pilgrimage route to Santiago de Compostela. The **campground** (Ile de Bidounet, tel. 05–63–32–52–52), open April–September, is on an island in the middle of the Tarn River; from town go south over Pont Napoléon. Each person pays 20F on top of an initial 15F for a private waterside site. The **gîte** at the camping entrance (same phone) has two dorms, each with 16 beds, for 45F a night, but this may only be used by pilgrims.

BRUNIQUEL

About 80 km (50 mi) north of Toulouse and a short bus ride (20F) east of Montauban is this cliff-side medieval town, overlooking the Gorges d'Aveyron. Bruniquel is named after Brunhilda, daughter of the King of the Visigoths, who invaded and inhabited the area in the 6th century. Legend holds that her enemies tied her to the tail of an unbroken horse that kicked her to death. Above Bruniquel's 14th- to 16th-century stone-and-wood houses and its 13th-century **Église St-Maffre** sits the forbidding **château** (tel. 05–63–67–27–67), admission 14F, divided into two parts. To give you an idea of Bruniquel's age, the *château jeune* (young castle) refers to the parts reconstructed between 1458 and 1510. The *château vieux* (old castle) comprises the 13th-century ramparts and the 12th-century dungeon. Bruniquel itself makes a good starting point for exploring the gorge on foot. The **tourist office** (av. du Ravulin, tel. 05–63–67–29–84) has lists of gîtes in the area.

LANGUEDOC-ROUSSILLON

Languedoc-Roussillon extends along the southern Mediterranean coast of France to the Pyrénées. City life is distinctly relaxed and friendly here. Spend a few days in **Béziers** or **Perpignan,** and you'll be taking afternoon *siestes* (naps) before you know it. **Carcassonne's** impressive medieval fortress is the region's most famous site, and probably the only place you'll run into many tourists.

Inland Languedoc-Roussillon, with its dry climate, is virtually one huge vineyard. The Canal du Midi flows through the region to **Le Littoral Languedocien** (the Languedoc Coast). Beaches stretch down the coast to Cerbère at the Spanish border. This strip is known as the **Côte Vermeille** (Vermilion Coast) and attracts droves of European tourists in summer despite the fact that the beaches are rocky. The farther south you go, the stronger the Spanish influence. Although the mix of Catalan and French identity is evident, you won't hear the cries for separatism in this region that you might in the Pays Basque (*see below*). The natives here are descended from the Occitan people. Though their ancestral language is all but extinct and struggling for survival, it is commemorated in the name of the region, *Languedoc,* meaning language of "oc" (the word for "yes" in Occità), the language of the Occitans.

COSMOPOLITAN
CARCASSONNE

Bastides are endemic to the southwest of France. Scattered throughout the Aude Valley to the south of Carcassonne, fortified towns like Limoux, Castelnaudary, and St-Louis (Carcassonne's lower town) were products of the massive shift from an agricultural to an urban economy. In the 13th century, feudal peasants felt, for the first time, the limitations of their natural resources, and many abandoned farming in favor of big-city life.

At the same time, counts in the north were also feeling the pinch and turned their roving eyes to the south, where land, they hoped, might be easily acquired. Capitalizing on the flight to the city, the counts built the bastides, all the better to entice peasants away from their lands.

With their mistrust of the Catholic Church, southern leaders were getting the evil eye from the Vatican, and northern counts were more than happy to oblige the pope with a little hounding, an inquisition or two, and some stake-burning—as long as asset-forfeiture laws worked in favor of the inquisitor, not the inquisitee. With southern religious and political leaders tortured and burned to death, it was easy as pie to govern the peasants, and the bastides' importance as an intimidating political presence diminished.

CASTRES

On the banks of the Agoût River, small and quiet Castres is of little intrinsic interest but is a good base from which to explore the Sidobre (*see below*) and the Parc Naturel Régional du Haut-Languedoc. The town's claims to fame include the **Musée Goya** (Hôtel de Ville, tel. 05–63–71–59–27), with its collection of Spanish paintings by 17th-century artists like Velázquez, Murillo, and Ribera. Admission is 20F and it's closed Monday. Goya fans can revel in the museum's much-acclaimed pieces.

Castres is also the birthplace of French politician and journalist Jean Jaurès, an active and controversial socialist assassinated in 1914 in a Paris café—there's a street named after him in almost every French town. The modern **Centre National et Musée Jean Jaurès** (2 pl. Pélisson, tel. 05–63–72–01–01) has an interesting collection of memorabilia of late-19th-century French political life. Admission is 10F and it's closed Monday.

BASICS

The **tourist office** for Castres and the Sidobre has a city map, a list of events and sights, bus schedules, and a list of gîtes d'étape and campsites. The helpful staff can also direct you to biking and hiking routes. Invest in a topo map (namely the IGN 2343 Est; 57F); get it at tabacs in town. *3 rue Milhau Ducommun, tel. 05–63–62–63–62. Open Sept.–June 8:30–12:30 and 1:30–6:30; July–Aug. 8:30–7.*

COMING AND GOING

By train (74F), Castres is one hour from Toulouse (71 km/44 mi), and about eight trains make the trip daily. To reach the main tourist office and the centre ville (a 15-minute walk) from the **train station** (av. Albert 1er), exit left, take avenue Albert 1er to the crossroads, veer right on boulevard Henri Sizaire, and then follow the signs; continue north along the river and cross Pont Vieux to reach the tourist office. From the **bus station** (pl. Soult, tel. 05–63–35–37–31), on the eastern side of the Agoût River, there's service to Albi (50 mins, 33F) several times daily and service to Carcassonne (2 hrs, 70F) once daily at 7 AM.

GETTING AROUND

To get anywhere outside the walkable centre ville, the municipal bus company **RMTU** (tel. 05–63–71–56–95) costs 6F per trip. Most lines run past the Hôtel de Ville; service ends around 7 PM. The **Coche d'Eau** (25F), a wooden boat, runs up and down the river, connecting the center of Castres to the Parc de Gourjade. The boat leaves from the quay next to the tourist office five times daily July–August but only on Wednesday, Saturday, and Sunday afternoon in May, June, September, and October. **Tabarly** (38 pl. Soult, tel. 05–63–35–38–09), open Tuesday–Saturday 9–noon and 2–7, rents VTTs for 80F a day or 125F for a weekend; leave your ID as a deposit.

WHERE TO SLEEP

One good thing about Castres is that you won't have to compete with other tourists to find a cheap place to stay. Near the bus station, **Hôtel Bar Le Goya** (16 pl. Soult, tel. 05–63–35–38–24) has basic doubles starting at 170F; the reception is closed Sunday. In the centre ville, **Hôtel Périgord** (22 rue Émile Zola, tel. 05–63–59–04–74) has large doubles with showers starting at 165F and one simple single for 130F. Its reception is closed Friday evening and Saturday, and the hotel is closed the first two weeks of August. Closer to the river, **Hôtel Rivière** (10 quai Tourcaudière, tel. 05–63–59–04–53) has rooms starting at 120F for a single and 140F for a double.

CAMPING • The **Camping Gourjade** is in the city park 2 km (1 mi) north of town. Sites are shady, near the river, and cost only 26F for two people and a tent. You can get here via the Coche d'Eau during the summer and by bus in the winter (*see* Getting Around, *above*). *Parc de Gourjade, rte. de Roquecourbe, tel. 05–63–59–72–30.*

A testimony to just how many other people you may run into in Carcassone if you come in summer: The town was featured on a "60 Minutes" segment a number of years ago about overtouristed sights.

FOOD

Place Jean Jaurès has an open-air **market** in the mornings on Tuesday and Thursday–Saturday; the covered marketplace on place de l'Albinique is open Tuesday–Sunday mornings. On Thursday afternoons there is an organic market (referred to as *biologique* in France). Next to the bus station on place Soult, **Cafétéria du Mail** (tel. 05–63–35–76–09) has filling dishes including lamb couscous (35F) and roasted chicken (28F). For authentic Italian food, try the fresh pasta (45F) or thin pizza (42F) at **Mario Traiteur** (22 blvd. Carnot, tel. 05–63–35–87–00), on the corner of rue Fuzies. If you've been roughing it for too long, treat yourself to a fabulous French meal in a sophisticated setting (75F–90F) at **La Mandragore** (1 rue Malpas, tel. 05–63–59–51–27).

OUTDOOR ACTIVITIES

Located in the Parc Naturel Régional du Haut-Languedoc, and about 30 km (19 mi) north of Castres, the **Sidobre** is a mysterious and funky phenomenon of nature. Altered by erosion, the granite rocks are found balanced in improbable positions. Of the more interesting formations is the **Peyro Clabado,** a 780-ton granite rock held perfectly in balance by a tiny boulder. To reach the Sidobre from Castres, you can either take the minibus tour (65F) organized by Castres's tourist office on Tuesday and Wednesday in July and August or make the longish trek by bike (in which case you should pick up information on gîtes d'étape from Castres's tourist office before setting out).

CARCASSONNE

Once upon a time a bold knight traveled the fields of France slaying dragons, but above all he sought the love of the most beautiful princess in the land. The name of the town where she was held in a turret was Carcassonne. The Cité (upper town) still appears as if it's drawn from the pages of a fairy tale. For this reason, Carcassonne lures hordes of tourists, but it's still worth a visit.

In July, the **Festival de Carcassonne** brings concerts, dance, opera, and theater. Tickets start at 100F. The Cité goes medieval in mid-August with **Les Médiévales,** a festival of troubadour song, rich costumes, and jousting performances. The Bastille Day fireworks over the Cité are spectacular.

The Romans built the earliest sections of the city wall in the 1st century BC; the Visigoths later enlarged the settlement into a true fortress. In the 13th century, after a fierce attack made by Trenéavel's son (the rightful heir to Carcassonne), French king Louis IX strengthened the fortification and gave the Cité its present look. Six centuries later, a medieval fetish inspired the architect Viollet-le-Duc to push for Carcassonne's much-needed restoration.

BASICS

There are 2 **tourist offices** in Carcassonne. The main office (15 blvd. Camille Pelletan, on pl. Gambetta, tel. 04–68–10–24–30) is open daily 9–12:30 and 2–6:30. The other office is inside the main entrance to the medieval city (tel. 04–68–10–24–36) and is open daily 9–6.

COMING AND GOING

Trains connect Carcassonne to Toulouse (50 mins, 85F), Narbonne (30 mins, 58F), Bordeaux (3 hrs, 220F), and Montpellier (2½ hrs, 120F). From Paris you can go via Toulouse (8½ hrs, 390F) or Montpellier (6½ hrs, 425F). The **train station** (port du Canal du Midi) is in the *ville basse* (lower town). To reach the centre ville, cross the canal and go down **rue Georges Clemenceau,** the main pedestrian thoroughfare. Bus service from Carcassonne is limited and impractical. The **Transnod bus station** (blvd. de Varsovie, tel. 04–68–25–12–74) is next to the train station.

GETTING AROUND

You can easily walk to the Cité in about half an hour, but if you're lugging a heavy pack, the last 15 minutes uphill are hellish. Follow rue Georges Clemenceau, which turns into rue Courtejaire; hang a left on rue Voltaire; cross boulevard Camille Pelletan; and then cross the Pont Vieux. Local **C.A.R.T.** (tel. 04–68–47–82–22) Bus 2 runs twice an hour from the train station to the Cité (6F) until a little before 7 PM, except on Sunday. If you are staying in one of the three hotels within the Cité, you have to leave your car outside the city walls.

WHERE TO SLEEP

If you have the supplies, camping is the way to go in Carcassonne; from the campground there is a great view of the Cité. The modern and immaculate hostel is also a good choice, especially if you want to stay within the medieval fortress. Otherwise, there are several decent hotels in the ville basse.

UNDER 150F • Hôtel le Cathare. On a quiet street parallel to the pedestrian path in the centre ville, this small hotel has clean doubles for 120F (160F with shower and TV); an extra bed costs 25F more. The hotel restaurant has a menu for 65F. *53 rue Jean Bringer, tel. 04–68–25–65–92. From train station, turn left on blvd. Omer Sarraut, right on rue Jean Bringer. 12 rooms, 6 with shower.*

Hôtel St-Joseph. The rooms are a bit haphazardly decorated but are generally bright and clean. A couple of singles go for 110F, and the spacious doubles are 130F (145F with shower). Ask for one of the quieter back rooms. Private parking is available for 20F per day. *81 rue de la Liberté, tel. 04–68–25–10–94. From train station, cross canal, turn right on blvd. Omer Sarraut, left on rue du Dr. A-Tomey, right on rue de la Liberté. 37 rooms, 4 with bath.*

HOSTEL • Auberge de Jeunesse. This cheap sleep has has beds in four- to six-person rooms for 74F (including breakfast) a night (plus 17F for sheets). You must have an HI card to stay (also sold at the front desk). *Rue de Vicomte Trencavel, tel. 04–68–25–23–16, fax 04–68–71–14–84. From train station, take Bus 2 and follow signs. 120 beds. Reception open weekdays 7 AM–1 AM, weekends 8–noon and 5–1 AM. Lockout 10 AM–2 PM. Curfew 1 AM. Kitchen, laundry. Closed mid-Dec.–Jan.*

CAMPING • Campéole la Cité. On the banks of the Aude River, this manicured 200-site campground feels like Club Med with its swimming pool and tennis courts. It's about 3 km (2 mi) south of the train station and 1 km (½ mi) from the Cité, a 15-minute walk along the river. Rates are 93F per day for two in high season. *Rte. de St-Hilaire, near D104, tel. 04–68–25–11–77. From train station, take Bus 5. Open Mar.–Oct. 8. Restaurant, laundry.*

FOOD

In the ville basse, there are cheap restaurants along rue Aimé-Ramond and rue Verdun. Inside the medieval walls, several outdoor restaurants fill **place Marcou,** inside the Porte Narbonnaise to the left. Farther into the Cité, try either **Le Vieux Four** (9 rue St-Louis) or **L'Hostal** (rue Viollet-le-Duc, tel. for both 04–68–47–88–80). **L'Auberge du Grand Puits** (pl. du Grand Puits, tel. 04–68–71–27–88) has good-value menus of regional specialties for 110F in a cozy atmosphere. There's a market on **Place Carnot** Tuesday, Thursday, and Saturday until noon. Cassoulet, the delicious southwest French staple of duck, sausage, and white beans, is on the menu at more than half of the restaurants in town; don't miss it. **Le Bar à Vins** (6 rue du Plô, tel. 04–68–47–38–38) serves cassoulet (55F) with a good, strong, local red wine called Fitou (15F per glass) on its shady patio at the base of the medieval ramparts.

WORTH SEEING

La Porte Narbonnaise is the main entrance to the Cité. Walking between the ramparts and around the inner city is free, but it costs 30F if you want a 50-minute guided tour that takes you along the top of the ramparts and towers as well as into the **Château Comtal** (tel. 04–68–25–01–66), the 12th-century inner bastion. There are two daily English-language tours June–September; otherwise, brush up on your French. Don't miss a cool respite in **Basilique St-Nazaire,** to the left of the château, featuring gargoyles on the outside, a Romanesque nave and Gothic altar inside, and a stunning display of 13th- and 14th-century stained glass. If you're lucky you may catch a free organ recital in summer.

PERPIGNAN

At the foot of the Pyrénées-Orientales, Perpignan, capital of Roussillon, is one of the sunniest places in France, both in terms of the weather and the social life. It gets so hot here in July and August that the 10-km (6-mi) bus ride to the beach is mandatory in the afternoon. Although it's a big city, the few squares of the centre ville, grouped together near the quays of the Basse River, are the place to be for evening concerts and casual tapas and beer sessions. When you're here, less than 50 km (30 mi) from the border, you can feel the strong Spanish influence in Perpignan's laid-back atmosphere and love of

Salvador Dalí once called Perpignan's train station "the center of the world," where he experienced a sort of "cosmological ecstasy."

festivals. In July, **Les Estivales** animates the city with a mixture of culturally diverse music, theater, and expositions. In the **Rivesaltes** region, which borders Perpignan to the north and west, vineyards begin harvesting grapes as early as September. Autumn, when temperatures are cooler and the tourist season has mellowed out a bit, is a good time to enjoy the countryside.

Established in the 10th century by the Counts of Roussillon, Perpignan's heyday was between 1276 and 1344, when it served as the capital of the kingdom of Roussillon and residence of the Kings of Majorca. The city's Catalan heritage was politically severed in 1659 when the region was annexed by France in the Treaty of the Pyrénées. Culturally, however, Perpignan is a Catalan city. There isn't much reason to stay in Perpignan once you've explored its handful of sights; consider coastal Collioure instead. If you're traveling alone, be wary of venturing outside the centre ville—Perpignan's suburbs are sketchy.

BASICS

The **Office Municipal de Tourisme** (Palais des Congrès, pl. Armand Lanoux, tel. 04–68–66–30–30) is a 10-minute walk from the centre ville. In the same building, you'll find a ticket booth for Perpignan's festivals. Next door is a bureau de change with average rates. The **Comité Départemental de Tourisme** (7 quai de Lattre de Tassigny, near pl. Arago, tel. 04–68–34–29–94) has information on the Conflent region and the Côte Vermeille. If you've just finished your book and need to restock, the **Maison de la Presse** (51 quai Vauban, tel. 04–68–35–23–44) has English-language books, from classics to the latest Stephen King, in its basement section.

Just down the street from the regional tourist office, the **main post office** (quai de Barcelone, tel. 04–68–51–99–12) holds poste restante (postal code 66000) and receives faxes. You can do laundry at **Lavomatic** (5 pl. Jean Paysa, tel. 04–68–34–75–89), five minutes from the youth hostel, and get a sprained ankle fixed at the **hospital** (20 av. du Languedoc, tel. 04–68–61–66–33).

COMING AND GOING

BY TRAIN • Trains travel to Collioure (20 mins, 28F), Narbonne (45 mins, 54F), Prades (45 mins, 39F), Toulouse (2 hrs, 140F), Montpellier (2 hrs, 110F), Barcelona (3½ hrs, 120–130F), and Paris (via Montpellier; 7 hrs, 460F). The colorful **train station** (av. du Général de Gaulle, tel. 04–68–35–50–50) has luggage storage and a restaurant. Cheap hotels and the hostel are all within a five-minute walk. To reach hotels and the center of town, walk up avenue du Général de Gaulle.

BY BUS • **Les Courriers Catalans** (tel. 04–68–55–68–00) sends buses down the Côte Vermeille; **Capeille** (tel. 04–68–05–80–31) buses cover the Conflent region. Buses travel from Perpignan to Col-

THE LITTLE YELLOW TRAIN THAT COULD

"Le petit train jaune" is a fun way to see some of the most spectacular countryside in the Pyrénées. This life-size toy train makes the 63-km (40-mi), 2½-hour trip from the village of Villefranche-de-Conflent to La Tour de Carol about five times a day. Take the regular train from Perpignan to Villefranche-de-Conflent (45 mins, 41F), where you change to the cute yellow caterpillar (100F; train passes valid). When the weather is nice, ride in one of the open-air cars. For information, call Villefranche's train station (tel. 04–68–96–56–62).

lioure (32F), Prades (42F), Salses (22F), Font-Romeu (75F), and La Tour de Carol (85F), where the noon bus from the station will get you into Andorra. **Eurolines** (tel. 04–68–34–11–46) has two daily buses to Barcelona (110F) that leave from the train station. For information, inquire at the **bus station** (tel. 04–68–35–29–02), at the intersection of avenue du Général Leclerc and rue Francisco Ferrer.

GETTING AROUND

Although Perpignan is a large city, the centre ville is very compact, and the train station and hotels are only a short walk away. Comprehensive local **CTP buses** (tel. 04–68–61–01–13) take you around town for 7F a ticket; tickets are available on board or at the CTP kiosk on place Gabriel Péri. From the train station, Bus 2 stops at Le Castillet, the large, fortlike structure in the center of town; Bus 1 goes to the beach Carnet-Plage (20 mins) and costs 15F (26F round-trip). It leaves about every 30 minutes from place Catalogne in summer. Rent VTTs at **Cycles Mercier** (1 rue du Prés Doumer, at av. Julien Panchot, tel. 04–68–85–02–71) for 85F a day. It's open Tuesday–Saturday 9–7:30.

WHERE TO SLEEP

UNDER 125F • Hôtel Avenir. On a quiet street off avenue du Général de Gaulle, this simple hotel has singles for 90F and doubles for 110F. Hall showers are 15F. The location, a few blocks from the train station toward the centre ville, is convenient. *11 rue de l'Avenir, tel. 04–68–34–20–30. 20 rooms, 11 with bath.*

Hôtel le Berry. Across the street from the train station, this hotel gives you the basics: a bed, a sink, and a bidet. If you can do without a private shower, the hotel has singles starting at 90F (hall showers are 12F). Doubles with shower are only 110F, and triples are 150F. This place is often full, so call ahead. *6 av. du Général de Gaulle, tel. 04–68–34–59–02. 14 rooms, 10 with bath.*

Hôtel le Métropole. Hidden in the middle of the vieille ville, the Métropole has a large, rustic lobby with floor tiles, ironwork, and a spiral staircase, giving it a Spanish flavor. The rooms themselves are bare but cheap: Doubles are 75F–135F a night. Add 12F for a shower down the hall. Weekly rates are even cheaper. Call ahead for a reservation (which usually requires a deposit). *3 rue des Cardeurs, off rue des Marchands by pl. de la Loge, near Castillet, tel. 04–68–34–43–34. From train station, take Bus 2 to Castillet. Or, walk 15 mins up av. du Général de Gaulle, cross pl. de Catalogne to rue de la République, then cross pl. Bardou veering right toward pl. Péri, which takes you to rue Alsace Lorraine. This becomes rue de la Barre; turn left on rue des Cardeurs. 20 rooms, some with bath.*

UNDER 200F • Hôtel de la Poste et de la Perdrix. This hotel with old French charm is in the centre ville next to Le Castillet, Perpigan's most emblematic structure. Doubles without shower are 170F; a room with shower will cost you 250F. *6 rue Fabriques Nabot, tel. 04–68–34–42–53. 38 rooms, 18 with shower or bath. Restaurant.*

HOSTEL • Auberge de Jeunesse. In a Spanish villa behind the Parc Pépinière, this hostel usually has space. Unfortunately, the 11 AM–4 PM lockout makes it hard to find refuge from summer heat (though luggage can be left at any time) and the highway behind the hostel makes the back rooms noisy. Beds are 70F a night (with HI card), including breakfast. Sheets are 18F. *Allée Pierre-Marc, tel. 04–68–34 63–32, fax 04–68–51–16–02. From train station, turn left on rue Valette, right on av. de Grande-Bre-*

tagne, left on path with AUBERGE DE JEUNESSE sign (a 10-to 15-min walk). 49 beds. Reception open daily 7:30–10:30 and 5–11. Closed mid-Dec.–mid-Jan.

CAMPING • Camping le Catalan (rte. de Bompas, tel. 04–68–63–16–92) has 94 sites, laundry facilities, a snack bar, and a swimming pool, but it's a 10-minute bus ride from Perpignan. Sites are 41F for one person, 55F for two (add 40% in July and August). It's closed November–March. Take the Bompas Bus 42 or 43 from the train station. **Camping la Garrigole** (2 rue M. Levy, tel. 04–68–54–66–10) won't satisfy nature lovers, but it's close to the centre ville. Starting in July, sites go for 37F for one person, 60F for two. Prices drop 5% off-season. It's closed in December.

FOOD

Most restaurants, cafés, and bars are clustered around the Castillet in the vieille ville. **Place de La Loge** has a bunch of brasseries, but the small lanes that fan away from it, such as rue Fabriques Couvertes, have cheaper deals. **Place Arago** is also cluttered with outdoor cafés. On a tight budget? Look for the huge palm trees surrounding the **Palmarium Cafétéria** (pl. Arago, tel. 04–68–34–51–31), which has great self-service food. There's also a **Supermarché Casino** (tel. 04–68–34–74–42) on boulevard Felix Mercader. Perpignan's food vendors congregate every day until noon at the **outdoor markets** on place Cassanyes and place de la République.

UNDER 25F • L'Espartinette. At this informal "crepe bar" you sit at the counter and watch your meal being made. Besides a large selection of dessert crepes (10F–18F), there are *espartinettes* (warm meat-filled sandwiches; 18F), other light meals, and fresh juices (14F). *3 rue Louis Blanc, off pl. de Verdun, tel. 04–68–34–91–03. Cash only. Closed Sun.*

UNDER 100F • Le Sud. Though the food is impressive, the best reason to come to the Mediterranean-influenced Le Sud, in the St-Jacques quarter, is the live music at night. Most of the grilled meat and fish dishes are 65F–90F; the chef makes vegetarian dishes upon request. *12 rue Louis Bausil, tel. 04–68–34–55–71. From Palais des Congrès, take rue Elie Delcros, left on rue François Rabelais (go past Chapelle St-Dominique). Closed Jan.–Mar.*

WORTH SEEING

The 14th-century redbrick fortress **Le Castillet** marks the center of the vieille ville. After serving as a defense for the city, it became a prison under Louis XIV. Inside, there's a small Catalan folklore museum, the **Casa Païral.** For a fine view of the surrounding region and the densely packed rooftops of Perpignan, climb the Castillet's tower. *Pl. du Verdun, tel. 04–68–35–42–05. Admission free. Open mid-June–mid-Sept., Wed.–Mon. 9:30–7; mid-Sept.–mid-June, Wed.–Mon. 9–6.*

Built within a massive citadel, the **Palais des Rois de Majorque,** a 13th-century palace, is the oldest royal palace in France. Perched atop **Puig del Rei** (King's Hill), one of the two hills in Perpignan, the mostly Romanesque structure includes a Gothic chapel. In 1493, after Isabella and Ferdinand spent a short time in the palace, it was declared to be in a "state of decay." Despite some improvements over the past 500 years, it still looks tired. Call for information about summer concerts at the palace; tickets cost 75F–100F. *2 rue des Archeurs, tel. 04–68–34–48–29. Admission 22F. Open June–Sept., daily 10–6; Oct.–May, daily 9–5.*

CHEAP THRILLS

To buy some of the region's wine at rock-bottom prices (5F–6F per liter), stop by **Estaminet** (10 rue Grande la Monnaie, tel. 04–68–34–36–79). On the second Saturday of each month, 7 AM–5 PM, there's an **antiques market** on the promenade des Platanes. A **flea market** is held in Parc d'Expositions on Sunday 8 AM–1 PM.

AFTER DARK

In keeping with this town's Spanish style, Perpignan is alive and kicking until the wee hours of the morning. The many bars in the centre ville have a young and energetic atmosphere and good music with no cover charge. **Répulic Café** (2 pl. de la République, tel. 04–68–51–11–64), open 3 PM–2 AM, is one of the most popular places in town. Down the quay is **Le Vauban** (29 quai Vauban, tel. 04–68–51–05–10), with a mellower crowd.

NEAR PERPIGNAN

PRADES

Just west of Perpignan, the vineyards of the Côtes du Roussillon rise gently into the lower slopes of the Pyrénées-Orientales. In the region of Le Conflent, small villages, abbeys, and numerous campsites are here for you if you're looking for beauty and tranquillity off the beaten track. Prades, the biggest town in the region, has a sleepy mountain pace but comes to life in summer for two important cultural events. The **Festival Pablo Casals** (tel. 04–68–96–33–07), started in the 1950s, is a world-renowned classical music festival held from the end of July to the middle of August. Ticket prices range 75F–125F. The **Rencontres Cinématographiques Internationales,** also in July, features a retrospective on a particular director (Louis Malle, for example) and shows dozens of films from around the world.

Unfortunately, the four hotels here are expensive. However, there are *chambres d'hôtes* (bed-and-breakfasts) in the villages near Prades; contact the tourist office for information. If you're a student or with a group, try the **Centre d'Accueil** (ask at the Cinéma Lido on the rte. Nationale across from the police station, tel. 04–68–05–31–80). There are 50 bunks in rooms for two, three, or four for 55F and breakfast for another 6F. For more information on lodging and festivals, contact the **town hall–tourist office** (4 rue Victor Hugo, tel. 04–68–05–41–02), which also has a free, permanent display of works by local Catalan painter Martin Vives. It's open weekdays 9–noon and 2–5 and weekends in July and August.

COLLIOURE

This seaside fishing village 27 km (17 mi) south of Perpignan is the jewel of the rocky Côte Vermeille coastline. The dramatic combination of sea, sun, and hills in Collioure inspired Matisse and Derain, and reproductions of many of their works are scattered around town. Collioure's magic has not gone unnoticed: Its population of 3,000 swells to 15,000 during July and August—try to come in June or September or, even better, in the dead of winter. If you can't avoid the crowds, get up before everyone does to admire the awe-inspiring view from the jetty near **Église Notre-Dame des Anges.** Just down the shore is the medieval **Château Royale** (pl. du 8-Mai-1945, tel. 04–68–82–06–43). If you're looking for refuge from sun and crowds, head into the **studios** scattered throughout the pedestrian streets near the tourist office where contemporary artists have free displays of their work. For 15F visit Collioure's **Musée de l'Art Moderne** (rte. de Port Vendres, 04–68–82–10–19), where the collection includes works by Picasso and Cocteau. It's open 10–noon and 2–7 (to 6 in winter). If you're around the first Sunday of September, the **Concours de Sardanes** is a festival of Catalan dance and music.

BASICS

The helpful staff at the **tourist office** (pl. du 18-Juin, tel. 04–68–82–15–47) has information about boat excursions and other outdoor activities, including hiking, waterskiing, and windsurfing.

COMING AND GOING

From Perpignan, take one of the dozen or so daily trains to Collioure (20 mins, 28F); the trains continue on to Port Bou, Spain. Collioure's **train station** is at the end of avenue Aristide Maillol, less than a five-minute walk from the center of town. To reach the tourist office, exit right from the station. From place Général Leclerc follow rue Camille Pelletan. One street before the beach, turn left onto place du 18 Juin. Otherwise, **Car Inter 66** (tel. 04–68–35–29–02) operates a bus between Perpignan and Collioure (1 hr, 26F).

WHERE TO SLEEP

Hotels in Collioure are expensive and often filled to the brim. Fortunately, **Hubert Peroneille** (20 rue Pasteur, tel. 04–68–82–15–31), a self-styled anarchist who does without the government's "hôtel" label, rents 15 lovely and immaculate rooms all year long. Singles are 185F, doubles 255F; quads with shower (380F) are the best deal. **Hôtel le Majorque** (16 av. du Général de Gaulle, tel. 04–68–82–29–22), open April–November, has doubles for 160F (180F with shower) and quads with shower for 250F. **Les Templiers** (quai de l'Amiranté, tel. 04–68–98–31–10) has double rooms overlooking the château ranging from 280F in winter to 325F in summer. It's closed January.

CAMPING • Decent campsites are just north of town. The best is **Les Calanques de l'Ouille** (tel. 04–68–81–12–49), which has a ton of tent sites on a hill overlooking the Mediterranean. Each site is 23F, plus an additional 24F per person (be careful to tie down your tent, because the wind here can blow it right out to sea). **Les Amandiers** (tel. 04–68–81–14–69) has shady sites for 20F, plus 25F a person. To reach the campgrounds, turn left onto the waterfront boulevard du Boramar from the tourist office. Pass the clock tower and church in order to take the path from the northernmost beach in Collioure and follow it along the cliff's edge for about 20 minutes. Both campgrounds are closed October–March.

FOOD

Collioure is the perfect place to have a picnic. Several local markets can help you out, including **Shopi** (off pl. du 8-Mai-1945), up the street from the post office. For the best deals on produce, local farmers sell fruit out of a garage on **rue du Docteur Coste**—look for the yellow and green PRODUITS DE LA FERME sign. On Tuesday and Sunday mornings, there's an outdoor **market** on place Maréchal Leclerc. Beachfront **rue de la Démocratie,** on the south side of the château from the tourist office, has a slew of sandwich stands. At **Cave Arago** (18 rue Arago, tel. 04–68–82–48–84), open evenings after 7 PM, try the regional aperitif *banyuls* (a naturally sweet wine), or have fresh salmon (35F) or a fancy vegetable concoction (20F). Try to catch Collioure's August Saturday *sardinades* (grilled sardine banquets), where for about 40F you can mingle on the waterfront with locals and eat a hearty meal of sardines.

BEZIERS

The ancient town of Béziers sits on a plateau on the banks of the Orb River and is encircled by vineyards. It makes a perfect base if you enjoy wine tasting, as this is the center of Languedoc's *capitale du vin* (wine capital). The town is dedicated to having a good time with lively bars, theaters, markets and festivals all year round. The town surpasses itself in August during **La Feria** (for information, call 04–67–36–73–73); hedonism reaches a peak with street dancing and bullfighting in the amphitheater. Béziers's most famous citizen was Pierre-Paul Riquet, who designed the Canal du Midi that brought such prosperity to the Languedoc region; his statue stands on the fine esplanade that bears his name.

If you're interested in grape stomping and other arduous vine-related tasks, pick up a list of vineyards from the tourist office in Béziers or from Béziers Oenopole. Most jobs are available in late August and September.

BASICS

The **tourist office** dispenses maps and lots of brochures. *27 rue du 4-Septembre, tel. 04–67–76–47–00. Open July–Aug., Mon.–Sat. 9–7, Sun. 10–noon; Sept.–June, weekdays 9–noon and 2–6:30 (Mon. until 6), Sat. 9–noon and 3–6.*

COMING AND GOING

The cheapest and easiest way into or out of Béziers is by train through Montpellier (45 mins, 60F), Narbonne (15 mins, 28F), Perpignan (1 hr, 72), Carcassonne (40 mins, 71F), or Toulouse (1½ hrs, 119F). The town is a 5- to 10-minute walk up the hill from the **train station** (av. Gambetta).

Several bus companies service regional cities and nearby villages from the **bus station** on place Jean-Jaurès. **Courriers du Midi** buses (3 pl. Jean Jaurès, tel. 04–67–28–23–85) go to Montpellier (1¾ hrs, 69F), Narbonne (45 mins, 27F), and Bédarieux (50 mins, 35F). To reach Murviel, a nearby wine village, take **Cars Theron** (2 rue Germain Galinié, tel. 04–67–36–00–50) Bus 391 (21F). Most of the buses leave fairly regularly throughout the week (except on Sunday).

GETTING AROUND

Béziers's vieille ville is bordered by the esplanade **allée Paul Riquet** to the northeast and the Orb River to the southwest. From the train station, it's a short walk up avenue Gambetta or through the graceful public garden, **Plateau des Poètes,** to the esplanade. The city bus company, **RMTB** (tel. 04–67–28–36–41), goes to the Valras beach (20 mins, 8F) from place du Général de Gaulle.

WHERE TO SLEEP

If you come to Béziers in summer, be sure to reserve ahead. The **Hôtel d'Angleterre** (22 pl. Jean-Jaurès, tel. 04–67–28–48–42) offers neat, clean rooms for great value: A double with sink is 140F; a room for four with shower is just 280F. The **Hôtel des Poetes** (80 allée Paul Riquet, tel. 04–67–76–38–66) overlooks the gardens of the Plateau des Poètes and offers double rooms for 180F. Lacking charm, but close to the railway station, the **Hôtel Terminus** (78 av. Gambetta, tel. 04–67–49–23–64) and **Hôtel de Paris** (70 av. Gambetta, tel. 04–67–28–43–80) have doubles for about 250F.

FOOD

On allée Paul Riquet, near the entrance of Plateau des Poètes, you'll find a fruit and vegetable **market** open daily until noon. Farther down, across from rue de la République, is a **Monoprix** grocery store. Cheap eats (crepes, couscous, pizza) fill **rue Viennet** near the cathedral. Splurge on a French meal at **La Clef de Voûte** (13 rue Général Miquel, tel. 04–67–28–46–57); the 70F menu includes a self-serve entrée bar, a plat du jour, and dessert.

WORTH SEEING

Béziers's most noteworthy sight is the **Cathédrale St-Nazaire** (pl. Monseigneur Blaquière), open daily 9–noon and 2:30–7. Largely destroyed in 1209 by crusaders who set fire to it (burning alive the Catholics and Cathars seeking refuge within), it was later rebuilt, its architecture spanning the 8th to the 18th centuries. The nearby **Jardin des Évêques** (Bishops' Garden) displays a superb and cost-free view of the Orb Valley. L'Hôtel Fayet and L'Hôtel Fabrégat make up the **Musée des Beaux-Arts** (6 rue August Fabrégat, off pl. de la Révolution), which houses collections of 15th- to 20th-century paintings and sculptures, including works by Delacroix, Géricault, and Soutine. This fine arts museum is open Tuesday–Saturday 9–noon and 2–6 and on Sunday afternoons; admission is 12F.

NEAR BEZIERS

As in most other wine-producing regions of France, visiting the wine cellars around Béziers is easiest with a car. Luckily, the villages are clustered relatively close together in this area, and buses are frequent enough that it *is* possible to do some serious wine sipping without a car. Before you head out, a stop at **Béziers Oenopole** (3 rue Paul Riquet, tel. 04–67–76–20–20), in the Maison des Arts on a tiny street behind the main post office, is a must. The busy staff will help you map out where to go and what to taste in this region best known for its Minervois and Fougères appellations.

NARBONNE

This town, 27 km (17 mi) south of Béziers, was the Romans' first colonial outpost in Gaul, established by the Senate of Rome in 118 BC. Today, it's overshadowed by its neighbor, festive Béziers, and too far from the sea to be a beach town. If you find yourself here, check out Narbonne's haunting Gothic ensemble, the **Cathédrale St-Just** and the **Palais des Archevêques** (Archbishops' Palace). The stone interior of the cathedral is marked by 135-ft vaults and beautiful stained-glass windows from the 14th century. Next door, through the **cour de la Madeleine** (Madeleine courtyard), is the archbishop's residence. The climb up the 162 steps of the palace's tower is worthwhile for the view from its upper terrace. The cathedral is just off place Salengro, near the **tourist office** (4 pl. Salengro, tel. 04–68–65–15–60).

COMING AND GOING • Narbonne is a 15-minute train hop from Béziers (28F) and 30 minutes from Carcassonne (55F). To reach place Salengro from the **train station** (av. Carnot, tel. 04–67–62–50–50), turn right onto avenue Carnot (which becomes boulevard Frédéric Mistral) and turn left onto rue Chennebier; it's a 10-minute walk.

WHERE TO SLEEP • **Le Novelty** (33 av. des Pyrénées, tel. 04–68–42–24–28), two blocks south of where the canal meets the train tracks, has doubles for 100F, as well as triples (130F) and quads (155F). **Languedoc** (22 blvd. Gambetta, tel. 04–68–65–14–74) has smallish doubles for 250F. The hotel's **La Petite Cour** restaurant has menus of regional dishes starting at 90F. The **Foyer Mixte des Jeunes Travailleurs "Le Capitole"** (45 av. de Provence, tel. 04–68–90–67–68) rents spacious singles with breakfast for 102F (doubles 170F) to people under 25 in summer.

FOOD • If you go behind the cathedral from place Salengro over to rue Droite, you'll find several cheap ethnic restaurants and snack bars. **Restaurant Littéraire** (75 rue Droite, tel. 04–68–32–47–22) is a dark, art-filled nook with long, conversation-inspiring tables. It serves salads (14F–50F) and a four-course menu including wine (55F lunch, 75F dinner). It's closed Tuesday.

VALRAS

The clean and expansive (though virtually waveless) beach at Valras is 13 km (8 mi) from Béziers. Hourly **RMTB** buses (tel. 04–67–36–73–36) make the trek in 20 minutes for 20F. The holiday season in this easygoing seaside town starts after Easter, but things don't really get going until June, when there are festivals, an active nightlife, and lots of tourists. The **tourist office** (pl. René Cassin, tel. 04–67–32–

36–04) has a list of more than 20 campgrounds lining the beaches. The cheaper and more remote ones start 2½ km (1½ mi) down the beach (some buses from Béziers continue there—check with the driver). **Le Marina** (chemin Montilles Vendres, tel. 04–67–37–33–80), one of the cheaper options, costs 44F a site plus 13F a person in late summer (30% cheaper in early summer). It's closed mid-September–April. If you're not into camping, **L'Auberge Provençale** (15 allée Charles de Gaulle, tel. 04–67–32–03–50) is a hotel in a well-aged, old house near the beach. Doubles run 160F–260F. Its restaurant serves seafood and regional specialties. **Rue Charles Thomas,** which later becomes allée Charles de Gaulle, is the main drag in town, lined with hotels, shops, snack bars, and expensive restaurants. If you keep walking toward the sea, you'll come across **Le Margency** (2 allée Charles de Gaulle, tel. 04–67–32–53–51), a snack bar that cooks up cheap plates of chicken and fries for 60F.

GASCONY

Tucked in the southwest corner of France, Gascony is bordered by the Bay of Biscay to the west, the Pyrénées to the south, and the Garonne River to the north and east. A sign on a wooden post just outside Auch, the capital of Gascony, proclaims PAS DE PAYS, SANS PAYSANS ("It's not country without country people")—a strong sentiment that sheds grim light on the state of the countryside in northern Gascony. As young villagers flee the region to find work in the cities, scattered old farmhouses are left deserted, decrepit, and for sale. Those

The basketball team in Pau is one of the best in France, and games get the university crowd in this town all riled up.

that remain are struggling to keep their agricultural traditions in the face of international competition.

Pretty **Pau** is the most culturally vibrant city in Gascony. In addition to its impressive château, Pau offers sweeping views of the magnificent Haute-Pyrénées. As you head south past **Lourdes** to **Cauterets,** the scenery becomes even more spectacular. Hiking possibilities are endless—just make sure you have the proper maps and gear. The Maison du Parc National tourist office (*see* Cauterets, *below*) gives invaluable advice and information on hiking, biking, and skiing.

BASICS

Trains only go as far south as Lourdes. Efficient SNCF buses can take you down to Cauterets, but to get to smaller villages and natural sites you'll have to hike, bike, or drive. There aren't any traditional HI hostels in the heart of Gascony, but you'll find many campsites and gîtes d'étape.

FOOD

Gascony is celebrated as France's largest producer of foie gras (goose-liver pâté). Other regional delicacies are *magret du canard* (duck breast) and confit de canard. For dessert or with tea, try *pastis gascon,* a layered fruit cake, usually with apple or plum. Armagnac is a world-famous, locally produced brandy, and Jurançon and Madiran are the regional wines.

PAU

The stunning views, mild climate, and the elegance of Pau make it a lovely place to visit and a convenient gateway to the Pyrénées. Now in the region of Pyrénées-Atlantique, Pau is the historic capital of Béarn (as in Béarnaise sauce) and has the honor of being the birthplace of Henri IV of France. The town was particularly prominent in the late 19th century when the English flocked here believing in the medicinal benefits of mountain air (later shifting their loyalties to Biarritz for the sea air). They left behind a golf course, horse racing, cricket, and the famous British tea shop where students now smoke strong cigarettes over black coffee.

BASICS

BUREAUX DE CHANGE • For the best rates and no commission, go to **Banque de France** (7 rue Louis Barthou, tel. 05–59–82–28–28), open weekdays 8:30–noon and 1:30–3:30. You can also change money at the post office on cours Bosquet for a 1.2% commission on traveler's checks.

VISITOR INFORMATION • The **tourist office** is next to the Hôtel de Ville, just up the hill from the train station. Besides maps and regional information (including lodging), don't forget to pick up "L'Été à Pau," a listing of the city's free (most of the time) summer events, and "Authentic Pau," an English summary of same. *Pl. Royale, tel. 05–59–27–27–08. Open July–Aug., Mon.–Sat. 9–6, Sun. 10–1 and 2–5; Sept.–June, Mon.–Sat. 9–noon and 2–6.*

The **Librairie du Palais** is a well-stocked outpost for maps, guides, and hiking information. *33 rue Cordeliers, tel. 05–59–27–33–19. Open Mon.–Sat. 10–12:30 and 2–6.*

COMING AND GOING

Trains connect Pau to Lourdes (30 mins, 42F), Bayonne (1¼ hrs, 85F), Biarritz (1½ hrs, 96F), and Toulouse (2¾ hrs, 150F). Pau is also on the Tarbes–Paris line; the TGV goes to Paris in just over five hours for 610F. To reach the center of town from the **train station** (av. Gaston-Lacoste), cross the street and take the free funicular up the hill to place Royale. **T.P.R. buses** (2 pl. Clemenceau, tel. 05–59–27–45–98) go to Lourdes (1 hr, 38F) about eight times a day. They also travel three or four times daily to Biarritz (85F), stopping in Bayonne (85F) and Anglet (87F). It costs 32F extra to take a bike on the bus.

WHERE TO SLEEP

Since winter sports and summer festivals are popular here, reservations are always a good idea. The cheap hotels are clustered around the center of town. The hostel is a 20-minute walk from the train station or 10–15 minutes from the bus station. The well-kept **Hôtel le Béarn** (5 rue Maréchal Joffre, tel. 05–59–27–52–50), five minutes from the train station and most of Pau's sights, has singles for 90F, doubles with shower for 135F, and quads for 150F (parking available). At the basic **Hôtel de Bayonne** (6 rue d'Étigny, tel. 05–59–27–01–06), near the château, the proprietors won't hesitate to lock you out after their midnight bedtime. Singles are 95F and doubles are 120F (155F with shower).

HOSTEL • **Foyer Mixte des Jeunes Travailleurs.** It usually has space in summer, even though it's more of a dorm than a traveler's hangout (there's normally a five-day minimum stay). Most of the modern singles have showers; but there are excellent hallway bathrooms and showers. There's also a cafeteria, bar, and washer and dryer. The building is open all day, and you can leave your bags if you arrive early. Beds are 70F if you're under 25 or have a youth hostel card; otherwise, they're 94F. Sheets are 18F. Breakfast is included, and dinner is 35F in the cafeteria. *30 rue Michel Honnau, tel. 05–59–72–61–00. From pl. Royale, take rue St-Louis to rue des Cordeliers, right on rue St-Jacques, continue up rue Carnot, right on rue Louis-Lacaze, cross intersection to rue Honnau. 80 rooms. Check-in 4 PM–9 PM.*

FOOD

To splurge on a traditional meal (dinner menus from 95F), indulge at one of the restaurants near the château. **Chez Olive** (9 rue du Château, tel. 05–59–27–81–19) fits the bill with tasty magret du canard followed by *poire Henri IV,* a pear covered with sauce and fresh whipped cream; it's closed in June. A slightly cheaper traditional restaurant is the popular **Le Berry** (4 rue Gachet, tel. 05–59–27–42–95), near place Clemenceau, where the portions are decidedly generous on the 45F lunch menu. For cheaper bites, or head down rue Émile Guichenné to **Le Chameleon** (No. 15, tel. 05–59–82–87–89) for tasty kabob-style sandwiches with fries (25F). For a tearoom with a twist, try **L'Isle au Jasmin** (28 blvd. des Pyrénées, tel. 05–59–27–34–82), where exotic teas are served outside so you can take in the view. For groceries, go to the **Champion** supermarket in the Centre Bosquet, on cours Bosquet at rue Jean Monnet. There's also a food **market** every morning on place Marguérite Laborde and a Saturday-morning market on place de la République.

WORTH SEEING

Pau's **château** is the former residence of the viscounts of Béarn and later the Kings of Navarre. It was also the birthplace of France's Henri IV, known as "The Good King" because he was so friendly with his subjects. The **Musée National du Château de Pau** has guided tours every 15 minutes (or when there are enough people) of the château's royal apartments. The tours are in French only, but don't let that stop you from seeing the well-preserved, ornate interior. *Rue du Château, tel. 05–59–82–38–00. Admission 30F. Open daily 9:30–11:45 and 2–5:15.*

To continue on your royal path, follow the **Sentiers du Roy** (King's Paths), a marked trail just below the boulevard des Pyrénées. When you reach the top, walk along until the sights line up with the mountain peaks you see. The **Musée des Beaux-Arts** (rue Mathieu-Lalanne, tel. 05–59–27–33–02) has a rich selection of Spanish sculptures and French paintings, including works by El Greco, Degas, and Rodin. It's open Wednesday–Monday 10–noon and 2–6. Admission is 12F.

AFTER DARK

Pau is generally mellow after dark and is known as a gay-friendly place. Despite a rude staff, **Le Caveau** (18 rue Castelnau, tel. 05–59–27–35–37) is a good bet and does not close until 2 AM.

NEAR PAU

VALLEE D'ASPE

The valley you see due south from Pau is the Vallée d'Ossau, crowned by the Pic du Midi d'Ossau (9,462 ft). The hiking, however, is better in the next valley to the west, the **Vallée d'Aspe.** The best base for treks into the magnificent peaks is the tiny, untouched village of **Lescun.** From the friendly **gîte d'étape** (opposite Hôtel Pic d'Anie, tel. 05–59–34–71–54), you can make some amazing day hikes up to the Pic d'Anie (8,215 ft), with a view all the way to the Atlantic Ocean, or to the needlelike rocks of the Aiguilles d'Ansabère. For longer hikes to the narrow Gorges de Kakouetta, take the GR10 westward. Pick up gîte information in Pau (*see* Visitor Information, *above*). The **Maison du Parc National** has hiking and weather information; call 05–59–05–32–13 for the Ossau Valley or 05–59–34–88–30 for the Aspe Valley. From Pau, take a train to Oloron-Ste-Marie (40 mins, 37F) and then hop on the SNCF bus that goes up the valley to Lescun (38F) and into Spain.

LOURDES

The mountain town of Lourdes is probably the most famous Catholic pilgrimage site (and sight) in the world. Some 5 million visitors come each year from every corner of the globe, many of whom are not Christians.

To say that Lourdes capitalizes on its holy status is an understatement. It may be the only place in the world where you can buy a translucent poster of a winking Jesus.

The origin of what is now a big business for some people lies in the humblest of origins: In 1858 a young miller's daughter named Bernadette Soubirous experienced apparitions of the Virgin Mary. During the ninth of her 18 visions, Bernadette fell to her knees near the river and, digging with her hands, released a gush of clear water where no spring had previously existed. This, not the river, is the source of the Healing Waters of Lourdes.

The grotto is like no other. Huge cement walkways lead up to the **Basilique Supérieure** and down to the massive **Basilique St-Pie X** (built in 1958), two edifices that complement the amusement-park atmosphere of Lourdes. Between the church and the river is the actual grotto where people with plastic bottles come to collect holy water from faucets alongside the church. The streets leading up to La Grotte are unbelievably jam-packed with hotels, restaurants, and kitsch shops. For the international Mass on Sunday, Lourdes is transformed by the prayers and singing of some 20,000 people. Official pilgrimage season is from Easter to mid-October; the largest swarms come on August 15 (Assumption Day).

In addition to a host of religious-relic museums, Lourdes has a large, 14th-century fortified **château** (25 rue du Fort, tel. 05–62–94–02–04) with great views of the Pyrénées from the ramparts. Here you'll also find a museum on local culture, the **Musée Pyrénéen.** Admission is 28F and the château is open Easter–mid-October, daily 9–noon and 2–7, and mid-October–Easter, Wednesday–Monday only. The **tourist office** (pl. Peyramale, tel. 05–62–42–77–40), in the town center, is well stocked with pamphlets on skiing near Lourdes and lodging and activities in the Pyrénées.

COMING AND GOING

Lourdes's **train station** (av. de la Gare, tel. 05–62–42–55–64) is one of the busiest in the country. So many pilgrim trains arrive between Easter and October that the station has a separate entrance to accommodate the masses. From the train station, local buses go to the grotto every 15 minutes (Easter–October) for 10F, but you probably need not bother; the walk is short, downhill, and quite an experience. Trains go directly to Pau (25 mins, 41F), Bayonne (1¾ hrs, 106F), Toulouse (2 hrs, 129F), and Cauterets (55 mins, 44F).

WHERE TO SLEEP

If you want to avoid the frenzied boulevard de la Grotte, consider staying on avenue de la Gare—try **Hôtel Marie-Amélie** (27 av. de la Gare, tel. 05–62–94–60–64), with 120F doubles, or **Hôtel d'Annecy** (13 av. de la Gare, tel. 05–62–94–13–75), where off-the-street rooms are 95F for one (135F with shower), 148F for two. Farther away, in between the tourist office and the train station, the quieter **Hôtel du Centre** (18 av. Marasin, tel. 05–62–94–79–74) has modest doubles for 165F. The tourist office can provide a list of hotels (there are approximately 350 from which to choose).

FOOD

One thing you'll get in Lourdes is cheap and unexciting food. Head down **boulevard de la Grotte** or any of the adjoining streets. The sheer number of generic cafés and restaurants (and snack bars, and ice cream stands . . .) is dizzying. An outdoor **market** fills place du Champ near Les Halles every morning. If a real meal is in order, **Le Magret** (10 rue des quatre Frères Soulas, tel. 05–62–94–20–55), just across from the tourist office, serves an 80F menu including salad, pâté, potatoes, and dessert.

CAUTERETS

Nestled high in the Pyrénées at 3,058 ft, Cauterets is basically a slick tourist village that makes a comfortable base from which to hike (June–September) or ski (mid-December–May). In the mid-19th century, Cauterets's thermal springs attracted the likes of Vicomte de Chateaubriand, Victor Hugo, and George Sand. Today, the mountains continue to inspire.

Though it takes an extra effort to reach Cauterets without a car, and the town is costly compared to other tourist spots, the scenery and outdoor activities here are outstanding. The immense **Parc National des Pyrénées** begins just south of Cauterets, so whether you're here for a few day hikes or want to fully explore this mountain range, you probably won't need to deal with the town itself. If you can, avoid August, when the most popular trails are packed; in October come with your own gear, because the town basically shuts down. Weather here is unpredictable, so bring rain gear.

BASICS

The **tourist office** has a list of the dozen campsites north of town on the road to Lourdes. *Pl. Foch, tel. 05–62–92–50–27. Open daily 9–12:30 and 2–6:30.*

For information on hikes, visit the **Maison du Parc National** next to the bus station. The staff will help you plan hikes, including five-day routes into Spain and half-day hikes in the vicinity of Cauterets. IGN Topo 25 maps (60F) are indispensable and available in most local tabacs. Mountain huts are plentiful in the area and often have supplies for sale. Call the **Park Main Office** in Tarbes to find out about reservations (59 rte. de Pau, tel. 05–62–44–36–60). Bikes and pets aren't allowed in the park. *Tel. 05–62–92–52–56. Open daily 9:30–noon and 3:30–7 (July–Aug. until 7:30). Closed 1st 2 wks in Nov.*

COMING AND GOING

Unless you hike into Cauterets, only one road leads into town, on which **SNCF buses** travel to and from Lourdes's train station several times a day (55 mins, 39F). Inside the bus station there's an SNCF ticket office (tel. 05–62–92–53–70), open June–September only, daily 8:30–noon and 3:30–6:30.

WHERE TO SLEEP

Hotels in Cauterets are expensive. In town, the cheapest sleep is at the gîte d'étape or at one of the campgrounds (ask at the tourist office), though if you're going to camp you might as well enter the park and do it for free (*see* Pont d'Espagne, *below*). Most budget hotels are on rue Rallière and avenue Leclerc. If the places below are filled, try **Hôtel Chantilly** (10 rue Rallière, tel. 05–62–92–52–77), with doubles from 120F, or **Hôtel Béarn** (4 av. Leclerc, tel. 05–62–92–53–54), with doubles from 140F.

UNDER 200F • Bigorre-Hôtel. Across the bridge from the bus station, this spacious hotel has a flower-filled courtyard, a comfortable TV room, scrumptious meals, and charming management. Doubles start at 160F, singles at 100F. Hall showers are 10F. In winter, this place swings with the ski scene, and in summer it's full of spa-going seniors. *15 rue de Belfort, tel. 05–62–92–52–81. 25 rooms, 13 with bath. Closed mid-Oct.–late Dec. and Easter–mid-May.*

Le Pas de l'Ours. A good place to rejuvenate after hiking or skiing, this gîte d'étape has two coed dorms, a kitchen, and hot showers. Beds go for 70F; with full board, rooms cost 170F per person. *21 rue de la Rallière, tel. 05–62–92–58–07. 20 beds. Closed mid-Oct.–mid-Dec. and mid-Apr.–mid-May.*

FOOD

Your best bet is the **Codec** market (av. Leclerc), open Monday–Saturday 8:30–12:30 and 2–7:30, Sunday 8:30–12:30. For a real meal, try **La Fondue** (7 av. de l'Esplanade, tel. 05–62–92–62–60), which serves salads (40F) and fondues (80F–110F). Up the street, the lively **La Bodega** (11 rue de la Raillière, tel. 05–62–92–60–21) has a 65F menu and filling paella à la carte for 65F per person (two-person minimum). Across from the tourist office on place de la Mairie, **Café le Paris** (tel. 05–62–92–52–98) dishes up some of the cheapest food in town—*galettes* (buckwheat pancakes), crepes (10F–25F), and lasagna (40F). **La Gourmandise** (1 rue Belfort, tel. 05–62–92–59–46) has ham and melted cheese sandwiches (18F), crepes (8F–32F), and pizzas (35F–50F) to go.

NEAR CAUTERETS

PONT D'ESPAGNE

It's an easy 2½-hour hike from the center of Cauterets to Pont d'Espagne (4,908 ft), a small bridge over an amazing waterfall. Getting to Pont d'Espagne is more than half the fun. The rocky and sometimes soggy trail takes you through colorful forest, past gushing waterfalls. From Pont d'Espagne you can hike for another hour or so to **Le Lac de Gaube** (Lake Gaube); or June–October you can take the *télésiège* (chairlift) straight up the mountain for 30F round-trip. From the lake you have a terrific view of Spain on the other side. Though Pont d'Espagne has a café-restaurant, it's overpriced; you're better off picnicking. You can camp anywhere here for free, though there's a five-day limit (in the rest of the park there's a one-day limit).

COMING AND GOING • To hike to Pont d'Espagne, follow the road behind the Casino-Piscine complex in Cauterets; once you cross the first bridge (there's a sign pointing to Pauze), leave the road and take the trail on your right. When you meet up with the road again, cross over and take the stairs up to La Raillière (an old building). From here, it's just a five-minute walk to the beginning of the GR10 (in the parking lot next to Café Avalanche), a trail that goes right past the bridge. If you don't want to walk, a *navette* (shuttle) makes the Cauterets–Pont d'Espagne run every two hours from the bus station (28F round-trip, 19F one-way) when there is enough demand.

> *InterSport (1 pl. Foch, tel. 05–62–92–51–26), in Cauterets, carries tents, sleeping bags, stoves, boots, hats, sunglasses . . . you name it. Now you have no excuse not to get out there and hike the Pyrénées.*

GAVARNIE

A ski station in winter and hiking base in summer, Gavarnie represents the Pyrénées at their most magnificent. About 40 km (25 mi) from Cauterets, the small village—make that small tourist center—faces the **Cirque de Gavarnie,** a stunning example of glacial erosion with waterfalls spilling over the top. Gavarnie makes an excellent two-day hike from Cauterets via the GR10, and you can camp at the base of the Cirque. Call the **Maison du Parc National** (tel. 05–62–92–38–38 or 05–62–92–83–61) for information on the Luz-Gavarnie Valley. The IGN Topo 25 Map 1748 Gavarnie, available in Pau and Cauterets bookstores (27F), will help you plan your trip.

If you're not into hiking, Gavarnie can be tough to reach. Besides renting a car, you could take the SNCF bus from Lourdes to Luz-St-Sauveur, from where you can grab one of two daily buses for the 20-km (12-mi), 40-minute ride up the valley. Check at Lourdes's tourist office. As a last resort, **Bordenave Excursions** (pl. de la Mairie, tel. 05–62–92–53–68) has afternoon trips to Gavarnie for 65F. They give you just enough time to hike to the center of the Cirque and back (about 2½ hrs). In Gavarnie, the **tourist office** (tel. 05–62–92–49–10) is at place de la Bergère.

PARC NATIONAL DES PYRENEES

One of France's seven national parks, the Parc National des Pyrénées encompasses six valleys along a 100-km (60-mi) strip on the edge of the French-Spanish border. This is the most spectacular section of the Pyrénées, with the steep, rocky peaks reaching their highest at **Mont Vignemale** (10,820 ft). You can explore the park best on foot in the spring, when the gorges, lakes, and waterfalls are alive from the snowmelt. The natural-preserve status prohibits biking and fires but tolerates *camping sauvage*, which means you can pitch a tent wherever, as long as you don't spend more than one night in the same spot. If you don't have a tent, you can sleep (and usually eat) in the many refuges along the trails for about 85F–125F per night. But stays are often limited and sometimes full board is included . . . whether you want it or not. The **GR10** and the HRP, which cross the Pyrénées coast to coast, are the main paths through the park. Higher up along the peaks are tougher unmarked trails; only attempt these with a topo map and some serious hiking know-how. A visit to Cauterets's Maison du Parc National (*see above*) is a must for help with planning. When you see birds circling low to the ground, expect a rainstorm. If you don't buy this piece of folk wisdom, call 08–36–65–02–65 for the Haute-Pyrénées weather forecast (in French).

THE PAYS BASQUE

From Atlantic beaches to the mountain passes, what you see when you travel in the Pays Basque is green, and lots of it. Though the Basque people speak French on this side of the border, they consider Euskera their first language and identify themselves as Basque, not French. There are seven Basque provinces, four of which are in Spain. The three French provinces, from west to east, are Labourd, Basse Navarre, and Soule. Labourd, on the Atlantic coast, includes **Bayonne,** whose languid pace and Spanish flair make it a great place to warm up to life south of the border. To the south, **St-Jean-de-Luz** is the only coastal town with any Basque character. Basse Navarre, with the exception of **St-Jean-Pied-de-Port,** contains endless miles of rolling hills and small farming communities. In the Soule province, high hills give way to the stark granite peaks of the central Pyrénées. Here hikers can explore gorges like those at **Kakouetta,** experiencing the waterfalls and magical landscapes that are at the heart of Basque folklore. (For a map of the region, *see* the map of Bordeaux and the Aquitaine *in* Chapter 15.) For goat cheese fanatics, it doesn't get any better than what the farmers sell from their doorsteps up here. The Pays Basque has a very moist climate, due in large part to the strong Atlantic winds from the west hitting the Pyrénées and then sinking into the valleys. As a result, traditional Basque houses—whitewashed buildings with red and green trim—have a protective outer wall on the west side to guard them against the fierce wind and rain by extra walls on the west side.

The coastal Basques were among the first whalers in Europe. In the 18th century, when the whale population declined, these fishermen turned privateers, or "corsairs," who raided Spanish and English ships for French kings. Since Basque culture has existed as a cohesive unit since pre-Celtic times—long before nations like France and Spain came into existence—Basque history is that of a minority people struggling to maintain cultural integrity. During Franco's dictatorial reign, the Basques in Spain were so persecuted that many emigrated to the French Basque provinces. Today, although some Basques support ETA, a terrorist band whose bombings and assassinations of innocent people purport to force Basque political autonomy, Basque militancy isn't as much of an issue in France as it is in Spain. The French Basques mainly set themselves apart by performing local dances, playing pelota or *cesta punta* (squashlike ball games played with bare hands, bats, or baskets), eating *piperades* (a mild chili sauce made with tomato and bell pepper), and drinking *izarra* (a bright green or yellow liqueur).

GETTING AROUND

Bayonne is the main hub for trains and buses and the only entry point from Bordeaux, Toulouse, and Pau. From Bayonne, trains travel down the coast to beach villages and the small inland town of St-Jean-Pied-de-Port. A few trains travel between Biarritz and Bayonne, but **STAB buses** serve the Bayonne-Anglet–Biarritz metropolitan area best. The **ATCRB bus** service takes you up and down the coast.

WHERE TO SLEEP

Anglet's hostel is the best base in the Biarritz area; gîtes d'étape are a good option in the mountains. Along the coast, campgrounds abound. No matter where you plan to stay, call ahead in July and August. Throughout the region, most hotels and campgrounds close October–April.

FOOD

In coastal towns you'll find beach food that is cheap and unexciting (steak and fries, waffles, omelets). Markets are a better and more economic option for fruit, vegetables, and breads as well as *brebis* (ewe's milk cheese) and chèvre. Bayonne ham, which is salt-cured for several days before being dry-aged for up to a year, is the subject of festivals and the pride of Basque *charcuteries* (meat shops). A taste of a small *gâteau basque* (Basque cake) filled with cream or cherry jam is an absolute must.

OUTDOOR ACTIVITIES

Hossegor, 20 km (12 mi) north of Bayonne, hosts the world surf championships every August because surf conditions between here and Spain are ideal. Since Biarritz is more sheltered, it's generally the hangout when waves thunder with too much force elsewhere. The GR10 and the HRP lead hikers through the heart of Basque valleys and pastures toward the dramatic heights of the Midi. If you continue the length of it, this footpath goes the length of the Pyrénées to Banyuls-sur-Mer on the Mediterranean. For information on cycling routes in the Pyrénées, contact **Cyclo Club Béarnais** in Pau (59 rue Louis Sallenave, tel. 05–59–84–32–64). Most tourist offices stock the pamphlet "Découvertes et Activités en Pays Basque," a comprehensive guide to activities and events in the region.

BAYONNE

A small port city at the confluence of the Adour and Nive rivers, Bayonne is the capital of the Pays Basque and a good base for exploring the rural Basque region that stretches south of town and across the Spanish border. Bayonne doesn't draw as many tourists as the coastal resorts (after all, it's a whole 6 km/4 mi from the Atlantic), but its languid pace and interesting cathedrals and museums make it a worthwhile stop.

The English held sway over the town from 1154 to 1451, building up Bayonne's fishing fleet and shipbuilding industry. When the Spanish decided it was their turn to profit from Bayonne's commercial success, they were greeted with the town's recent invention, the bayonet. Undaunted, the Spanish took over and got down to serious business: making chocolate (Bayonne was one of the first cities to import cocoa from the New World). Today, you can stop by **Chocolat Cazenave** (19 arceaux du Pont-Neuf, tel. 05–59–59–03–16), Bayonne's premier chocolate maker.

Basques call themselves the "Euskaldunak" (the "Basque speakers"), but the Basque language remains a mystery to linguists; it's unrelated to any other language.

In the 4th century, **Grand Bayonne**'s narrow, arched passages were waterways that served as extensions of the port. Later on, these canals made it easy for merchants to stock goods and keep up with the demands of a bustling medieval market economy. In **Petit Bayonne,** across the Nive River, half-timbered buildings housing residences, bars, and shops line the riverbanks. **St-Esprit,** the third of Bayonne's districts, contains the train station and a few cheap hotels.

BASICS

The helpful staff at the **tourist office** in Grand Bayonne has a list of campsites, bus schedules, and information on events in the Basque region. Guided tours of Grand Bayonne are given once daily Monday–Saturday, July–September. If you plan to bike down the coast, ask the tourist office about the "Liaison Cyclable Bayonne–Hendaye," a varied 40-km (31-mi) bike route. *Pl. des Basques, tel. 05–59–46–01–46. Open July–Aug., Mon.–Sat. 9–7, Sun. 10–1; Sept.–June, weekdays 9–6:30, Sat. 10–6.*

BUREAUX DE CHANGE • Comptoir Bayonnais d'Or et de Change (30 rue Lormand, tel. 05–59–25–58–59) and **Basco Landaise de Change** (17 rue Thiers, tel. 05–59–59–07–07) are both a short distance from the tourist office. The post office charges the least commission (about 1%–2%), but it only takes American Express traveler's checks.

MAIL • The post office on rue Labat, two blocks from the tourist office, is the only branch in Bayonne that changes money and holds poste restante. To recover mail or faxes (17F per page), a passport is required. Those sending mail should indicate rue Labat and postal code 64100 on the envelope. *11 rue Labat, tel. 05–59–46–33–60, fax 05–59–46–33–69. Open weekdays 8–6, Sat. 8–noon.*

COMING AND GOING

BY TRAIN • Most of the trains that travel down the Basque coastline stop at Bayonne's **train station** (quartier St-Esprit, tel. 08–36–35–35–35). From here there's service to St-Jean-de-Luz (25 mins, 28F), St-Jean-Pied-de-Port (1 hr, 49F), Toulouse (4 hrs, 215F), Bordeaux (1¾ hrs, 137F), Pau (1¼ hrs, 83F), and Paris (10 hrs, 372F). Trains make the short 12F jaunt from Biarritz frequently in summer; in winter, consider taking the bus instead. Luggage storage at the information desk starts at 34F a bag per day. Near the station, **Pascal Voyages** (8 allée Boufflers, tel. 05–59–25–48–48) can help with travel arrangements.

BY BUS • A comprehensive bus system operates between Bayonne, Anglet, and Biarritz. Tickets cost 8F, but you can buy a book of 5 (33F) or 10 (65F) from tabacs and from the **STAB bus information booth** (Hôtel de Ville, tel. 05–59–59–04–61) in Grand Bayonne at the foot of Pont St-Esprit (on your right if you're coming from the train station). Buses run about twice an hour until around 8 PM. **Transports**

Basques Associés (tel. 05–59–65–73–11) has an office directly across from Église St-André in Petit Bayonne. Weekday buses depart from the parking lot beside St-André on their way to Baigorry (3½ hrs, 72F). These buses stop in St-Jean-Pied-de-Port (3 hrs, 57F) on the way. At the discretion of the driver, bikes go in the luggage compartments at no extra charge.

WHERE TO SLEEP

Hotels in Grand Bayonne tend to be more expensive than those in Petit Bayonne.

UNDER 125F • Hôtel des Basques. In Petit Bayonne, this hotel has neat, orderly rooms with windows facing a small, animated square. If sleep is what you desire the most, ask for a room without a view. Doubles are 135F (170F with shower); simple triples and quads are 230F. Hall showers are 10F. *4 rue des Lisses, tel. 05–59–59–08–02. From train station, cross bridge, turn left on rue Bourgneuf, right on rue des Lisses to pl. Paul Bert. 16 rooms, 4 with shower. Cash only.*

Hôtel Paris-Madrid. Right near the train station, the Paris-Madrid is comfortable and spacious. Singles are 95F, doubles 125F (170F with shower), triples 205F, and quads 250F. Hall showers are 5F. *Pl. de la Gare, tel. 05–59–55–13–98. 24 rooms, 13 with bath. Closed late Dec.–early Jan.*

UNDER 150F • Hôtel des Arceaux. This hotel faces the main pedestrian street in Grand Bayonne; the rooms don't get much sun but are clean. Doubles start at 130F and there's no extra charge for showers. *26 rue Pont-Neuf, tel. 05–59–59–15–53. From train station, cross Pont St-Esprit to pl. du Réduit, then cross Pont Mayou to pl. de la Liberté, turn left on rue Pont-Neuf. 17 rooms, some with bath.*

Hôtel San Miguel. The owner of this tidy place near the train station will set you up in a showerless double for 160F or a quad with shower for 300F. These immaculate rooms on a quiet pedestrian street are definitely a great find for groups. *8 rue Ste-Catherine, tel. 05–59–55–17–82. From train station, head for rue Ste-Catherine off pl. de la République, the only pedestrian street. 18 rooms, 14 with bath.*

FOOD

You will find great places to eat in Petit Bayonne, particularly along the river and in the little side streets that run off the quay. **Le Petit Chahut** (quai Galuperie, tel. 05–59–25–54–60) has delicious seafood served in the Basque tradition.

UNDER 75F • Restaurant Irintzina. This Petit Bayonne Basque restaurant serves an excellent three-course menu for 60F. The narrow alley location foils tourists and makes this a casual hangout for locals and the military. Try the *poulet basquaise* (Basque chicken) or the traditional *piperade jambon* (a regional ham). *9 rue Marengo, tel. 05–59–59–02–51. Closed Sun. and Oct.*

Le Talo. This traditional Basque restaurant in Petit Bayonne has two-course (60F) menus, highlighting dishes like paella and *axoa* (ground veal served atop a thick wheat and corn crepe). *10 rue des Tonneliers, tel. 05–59–59–43–29. Closed Sun. and Mon.*

WORTH SEEING

The Gothic 13th-century **Cathédrale Ste-Marie,** in the center of town, is hard to miss; look for the stunning cloisters. The highly touted **Musée Basque** (quai des Corsaires) has been closed since 1989 for restoration but is due to reopen in 2001. Console yourself with the impressive **Musée Bonnat** (5 rue Jacques-Laffitte, tel. 05–59–59–08–52), which has a collection of 15th-century religious paintings and Belgian tapestries, including works by Rubens, El Greco, and Goya. Admission is 20F and it's open Wednesday–Monday.

The most renowned city in France when it comes to **bullfights** (100F–250F), Bayonne kicks off its festivities on August 1 and continues throughout the month. The **Bayonne Jazz Festival** means cheap tickets to great shows for five days, usually mid-July. During the three-day **Marché Médiéval** (Medieval Market), starting the second Friday of July, place Montant is flooded with troubadour song and medieval cuisine. For a free visit and tasting of Basque ham, stop by the **Conserverie Artisanale du Jambon** (41 rue des Cordeliers, in Petit Bayonne, tel. 05–59–25–65–30).

AFTER DARK

Most of Bayonne goes to sleep early; the sole exceptions are the following parallel streets off place Paul Bert in Petit Bayonne: **rue des Tonneliers, rue Pannecau,** and **rue Cordeliers.** The string of Spanish-style bodegas all host either an older local crowd or big boys doing military service. **Le P'tit Pub** (6 rue des Tonneliers, tel. 05–59–59–38–94) is welcoming, with a smoky pool-table area in the back and outdoor tables under the arches out front. It stays open until 2 AM. For a dose of Basque relaxation and a taste of izarra, **Euskalduna Ostatua** (61 Pannecau Karrika, tel. 05–59–59–28–02) is the place to be.

NEAR BAYONNE

HOSSEGOR

The **RipCurl Pro** and **International Surf Championships** held here every August, as well as the long stretches of white sandy beach, make this one of the most crowded summer spots in France. Pelote matches, played several times a week June–August, are a big draw as well. Twenty-five kilometers (15½ miles) from Bayonne, Hossegor is a 40-minute (30F) bus ride from the train station, and it's a perfect beachy, sandy, sun-drenched day trip. In summer, **RDTL buses** (tel. 05–59–55–17–59) depart hourly. The beaches, forests, and lakes surrounding Hossegor are full of hiking, biking, and surfing options. **Magic Glisse** (tel. 05–58–43–92–90), just south of **Le Point d'Or,** the central beach, gives one-hour surfing lessons (200F) and a week's worth for 880F, including equipment. Camping options are plentiful but demand is high in July and August—it's a good idea to call ahead. **Camping Municipal la Forêt** (4015 av. de Bourdeaux, tel. 05–58–43–75–92) has sites for 25F per person and is open April–October. **Hôtel Amigo** (blvd. de la Dune, tel. 05–58–43–54–38) is a stone's throw from the main beach, with doubles for 165F–200F (360F in July and August). **Avenue Lahary,** extending from the centre ville toward the beach, overflows with ice cream stands, boulangeries, and small markets providing all the essentials for a day at the beach. The **tourist office** (44 av. de Paris, tel. 05–58–41–79–00) is located between the post office and the town hall.

In early September, Biarritz is swamped with surfers and spectators here for the Biarritz Surf Masters, a pro surfing world championship.

BIARRITZ

This glitzy Atlantic resort of the southwest isn't quite what it used to be. During the belle epoque, Spanish and French nobility (including the future Emperor Napoléon III) graced its posh resort villas and palaces. Even after World War I, Biarritz continued to lure the likes of Charlie Chaplin and Coco Chanel. The stylish architecture and rocky coast remain, but its glitz is less noble: These days, Biarritz merely caters to wealthy international tourists. If you're simply looking for a patch of sand on which to bask you'll do better farther north. Yet for a glimpse of the high life, a day or two in Biarritz will do the trick.

BASICS

BUREAUX DE CHANGE • Though changing money isn't hard to do in Biarritz, most banks charge high commissions and give below-average rates. Be wary of street-corner exchange booths that advertise "*pas de commission*" (no commission) but don't tell you about their extortionate rates.

MAIL • The **main post office** holds poste restante and offers fax services. The postal code is 64200. *17 rue de la Poste, off pl. Clemenceau, tel. 05–59–22–41–10. Open weekdays 8:30–7, Sat. 8:30–noon.*

MEDICAL AID • **Polyclinique** (21 rue de l'Estagnas, tel. 05–59–22–46–22) is the main hospital. If you need medications after hours, the **police** (1 rue Louis-Barthou, tel.05–59—01–22–22) know which pharmacist is on late-night call.

VISITOR INFORMATION • The **information booth** at the train station will help you get oriented with a city map, but it has limited information on the region. *Open June–Sept. 15, daily 9–12:15, 3–6:30, and 8:10–8:50.*

The **main tourist office,** up the street from the Hôtel de Ville, has hotel listings and maps, as well as a booklet of monthly events, "Programmes des Fêtes." The eager staff have information on local surfing and outdoor activities in the Pays Basque, and they can also help you find a room. *1 square d'Ixelles, tel. 05–59–22–37–10. Open summer, daily 8–8; off-season, daily 9–6:45.*

COMING AND GOING

Trains travel to Bayonne (8 mins, 15F), Bordeaux (2 hrs, 149F), Toulouse (4 hrs, 205F), and St-Jean-de-Luz (15 mins, 20F). Biarritz's small **train station,** known as La Négresse (18 allée Moura, tel. 05–59–23–04–84), is 3 km (2 mi) southeast of the centre ville. Hop on Bus 2 to reach the centrally located Hôtel de Ville, a few blocks southeast of the main beach.

Most buses to Bayonne and the hostel in Anglet run from the **STAB bus booth** (rue Louis Barthou, tel. 05-59–24-26–53), near the main tourist office. Tickets cost 8F on board, 31F for a book of five bought at the booth. The **ATCRB bus** has regular service to other Basque towns, including Bidart (6F50), Guéthary (11F), St-Jean-de-Luz (15F), and Hendaye (28F).

WHERE TO SLEEP

In July and August, most rooms have been reserved weeks or months in advance. If you can't score a dorm bed at the Barnetche, try the **Hôtel de la Marine** (1 rue des Goëlands, tel. 05–59–24–34–09), which has doubles for 180F with shower and triples for 220F. **Hôtel du Rocher de la Vierge** (13 rue du Port Vieux, tel. 05–59–24–11–74) has singles from 150F and doubles for 170F–300F. Add 25F for a shower if you haven't taken advantage of the free ones on the beach.

Hôtel Barnetche. It's the only semicheap hotel in Biarritz that's likely to have space in summer (and it's in the center of town). Beds in a spick-and-span 12-person dorm are 180F each. Private doubles start at 250F per person, 30F for breakfast. In July and August, single rooms jump to 390F and private doubles peak at 620F; you're paying extra for mandatory half-board. But in the dorm you only pay 85F. *5 bis av. Charles Floquet, tel. 05–59–24–22–25, fax 05–59–24–98–71. 15 rooms, 11 with bath; 1 dorm with 12 beds. Cash only. Closed Oct.–Apr.*

CAMPING • Biarritz Camping has decent sites (105F) and is 3 km (2 mi) from town, but it is expensive. From the train station, take Bus 9. Be sure to make reservations in July and August. *28 rue d'Harcet, tel. 05–59–23–00–12. Closed Oct.–Apr.*

FOOD

Cheap snacks and fast food are near the beach on boulevard du Général de Gaulle. For fresh produce, baked goods, and cheese, go to the covered **Les Halles Centrales** on place V. Sobradiel; it's open daily 7–1. There's a **Codec** supermarket near the same square on rue des Halles.

UNDER 50F • Le Blé Noir. This casual, oceanfront *crêperie-saladerie* (crepe and salad restaurant) sits above the Grande Plage. The delicious salads (around 40F) make satisfying meals. Galettes are 15F–40F, scrumptious dessert crepes 12F–32F. *Blvd. du Général de Gaulle, below pl. Bellevue, tel. 05–59–24–31–77. Closed early Oct.–mid-June.*

UNDER 75F • Les Princes. When you burn out on French cuisine, try the filling pizzas (40F–60F) or pasta dishes at this festive pizzeria near Les Halles. You can eat in or get it *à emporter* (to go). *13 rue Gambetta, tel. 05–59–24–21–78. Closed Wed.–Thurs.*

SPLURGE • The Blue Cargo. This restaurant-bar is located at the base of a cliff in its own quiet, oceanside cove. The food upstairs is a splurge (about 120F), but the drinks at the bar downstairs are reasonably priced, at about 45F, and wow, what a view. *From Biarritz, take Bus 9 to the av. Ilbarritz/Marbella stop. Walk five minutes down the hill toward the beach, past the golf course. On a bike, from RN10 take rue Francis Jammes from the Biarritz train station to av. Ilbarritz. Tel. 05–59–23–54–87.*

WORTH SEEING

Biarritz's main beach, the **Grande Plage,** is the town's focal point, especially for those who don't have money to lose in the resort casinos. Before hitting any waves, though, read the signs posted to tell you when it's safe to swim. The big waves and treacherous undercurrent are no joke. Just above the beach, **Casino Bellevue** sits imposingly on the hillside.

After catching some rays on the beach, join the crowds on the **Rocher de la Vierge** (Rock of the Virgin), an impressive rock formation southwest of the Grande Plage. But this spot also has a quirky, practical side: The bridge connecting it to the mainland is made out of a piece of metal left over from the Eiffel Tower. Between the Grande Plage and the Rocher is the **Port des Pêcheurs,** a busy fishing port built in 1870. Note: This is also a famous male prostitution zone.

AFTER DARK

Bar Jean (5 rue des Halles, tel. 05–59–24–80–38), closed Tuesday and Wednesday, has tasty tapas (6F) and fresh oysters. When the rest of town is quiet, **Ventilo Caffee** (30 rue Mazagran, tel. 05–59–24–31–42) is packed with the glowing faces of the *après-plage* (after-beach) twentysomething crowd. Come early to get an outdoor spot. A slightly older (and louder) crowd packs the piano bar **Le Brasilia** (22 av. Edouard VII, tel. 05–59–24–65–39). Gay men dominate the all-night club **Le Caveau** (4 rue Gambetta, tel. 05–59–24–16–17). The mostly straight **Le Copacabana** (24 av. Edouard VII, tel. 05–59–24–65–39) is the classic *boîte*: super-crowded, loud, and expensive, but still fun. Arrive around midnight if you don't want to deal with obnoxious doormen. The 65F cover includes one drink.

OUTDOOR ACTIVITIES

Surf shops are scattered all over town, most renting boards for about 90F a day, wet suits for 50F, and Boogie boards for 80F. For bike and scooter rentals, **Sobilo** (24 rue Peyroloubilh, tel. 05–59–24–94–47) is near the intersection with rue Gambetta at carrefour d'Helianthe. The helpful English-speaking staff rents VTTs for 65F a day, 300F a week. Scooter rentals start at about 190F a day. It's a good idea to make a reservation, especially for scooter rentals, in July or August. Sobilo is open daily in summer 9–12:30 and 3–6:30, in winter 10–noon and 3–6. Before you sign up for *école de surf* (surf school) in Biarritz, make sure the shop or school has a visible *brève d'état* (state license). Remember that it's the surf here that's renowned, not the surf schools.

ANGLET

If you're into surfing, Anglet and Hossegor are the places to be in France. In fact, besides going to the beach, or getting into the bar scene at the crowded campground, the only thing to do in Anglet is take a walk in the pine-filled **Forêt du Chiberta** on the north side of town. A slice of suburbia wedged between Bayonne and Biarritz, Anglet is good for cheap lodging and easy access to the surf on any of its eight beaches. **La Barre** beach in the north is less crowded and doubles as the hangout for dedicated surfers who live out of their vans. On the southern end (by the Anglet-Biarritz border) are surf shops, snack bars, and one boulangerie. These give the main beach drag, **Chambre d'Amour,** a decidedly California flair. Check costs at surf shops: Price wars often mean good deals. **Line Up Surf Shop** (Plage des Sables d'Or, tel. 05–59–03–51–22) rents surfboards (90F a day), Boogie boards (70F), wet suits (50F), and long boards (130F). They hold a credit card and ID until they get their goods back in one piece. A half-day surfboard rental and a 1½-hour lesson are 210F.

BASICS

The **main tourist office** (1 av. de la Chambre d'Amour, tel. 05–59–03–77–01) is open Monday–Saturday 9–6. Off-season it closes for lunch and on Saturday afternoon. Next door is the tiny town center, known as **Cinq Cantons,** which has phone booths, a bank, a post office, a tabac, cafés, a boulangerie, and an overpriced indoor fruit market. In the block between the tourist office and the right turn up the hill to Fontaine Labourd camping is the one small **market** in this part of town. Buy your goods here to avoid the doubled prices at the campsite supply store. Call 08–36–68–13–60 for surf and weather reports, and pick up tide calendars at the tourist office.

COMING AND GOING

If you're coming by train, you have to get off in Bayonne or Biarritz and transfer to a bus to Anglet. **STAB buses** (tel. 05–59–52–59–52) conveniently pass through Anglet on Bayonne–Biarritz runs: Bus 2 takes you to place Leclerc in the center and Bus 4 or 9 goes to the northern beach and campground (in summer, Bus 9 continues down the coast past all the beaches, the youth hostel, and into Biarritz). Unfortunately, buses stop running around 8 PM, which is a problem if your train arrives late or you want to go carousing in Biarritz (it takes 30 minutes to walk from the center of Biarritz to Anglet).

WHERE TO SLEEP AND EAT

At **Hôtel le Parc** (57 av. de la Chambre d'Amour, tel. 05–59–03–82–61), a five-minute walk past the tourist office, large clean doubles start at about 160F. **Hôtel Arguia** (9 av. des Crêtes, tel. 05–59–63–83–82) has clean doubles in a garden setting for 120F (160F with shower); it's open mid-April–September. Of the dozen restaurants in the parking lot just off the Chambre d'Amour beach, **Pollos Asados** (tel. 05–59–03–56–31) is the most satisfying deal; the poulet basquaise (60F) includes chicken in a pepper and tomato sauce.

HOSTEL • Auberge de Jeunesse. Anglet's hostel is cheap at 73F per night including breakfast (plus a 20F deposit). It's also only five minutes from the beach. If you want to be outdoors, pitch your tent on the hostel grounds for 48F per person, including breakfast. There's no lockout or curfew. You can use the kitchen October–April; the rest of the year, you can eat cheap dishes (35F) in the cafeteria. Ask at the reception desk for information on VTT and surfboard rentals. *19 rte. des Vignes, tel. 05–59–58–70–00, fax 05–59–58–70–07. Bus 9 from Biarritz or Bayonne to pl. Leclerc and walk 10 mins following AUBERGE DE JEUNESSE signs. 96 beds. Reception 8:30 AM–10 PM. Kitchen.*

CAMPING • Camping Fontaine Laborde. This campground, with a young surfer spirit, is excellent and is in a prime location between the hostel and the beach. You can arrive here without supplies (baguette, water, toothpaste) thanks to the general store at this little surf village, but things are less expensive at **Alimentation des Fleurs** (tel. 05–59–03–19–70) down the street and to the left on boulevard de la

Plage. Sites are 20F plus 22F per person. *15 allée Fontaine Laborde, tel. 05–59–03–48–16. Bus 4 from Biarritz and Bayonne stops in front. Closed mid-Oct.–mid-Apr.*

ST-JEAN-PIED-DE-PORT

This typical Basque town sits in the foothills of the Pyrénées surrounded by peaceful hills and grazing sheep. It was once the spot where religious pilgrims converged before crossing the mountains into Spain and continuing on to Santiago de Compostela. From the 13th-century **citadelle** you can look south at the mountain pass where in AD 778 Roland, Charlemagne's legendary hero, was killed by Basques during an invasion of Moorish Spain.

Today, despite the colorful architecture and flower-filled balconies, it's not hard to tell that St-Jean-Pied-de-Port has sold itself to tourism. The men in black berets who joke at bars in Basque seem to ignore the hordes successfully, but the prices of everything from a slice of Bayonne ham to a pair of locally made espadrilles are depressing. The moral: Spend your days hiking in the hills, conferring with your handy topographical map, "IGN Carte des Randonnées Pays Basque Ouest" (62F), available in local tabacs and bookstores, or make the town a base from which you can get to nearby towns.

BASICS

The staff at the small **tourist office** have town maps, regional information, and schedules for Saturday cesta punta games. *14 pl. du Général de Gaulle, tel. 05–59–37–03–57. Open weekdays 9–noon and 2–7, Sat. 9–noon and 2–6.*

COMING AND GOING

The best way to reach St-Jean-Pied-de-Port is by train from Bayonne (1 hr, 47F). Veer left as you come out of the **train station** and take avenue Renaud into town. You can rent a VTT near the train station at **Cycles Garazi** (1 pl. St-Laurent, tel. 05–59–37–21–79). Rates are 80F a day, 50F a half day, and 450F a week. The helpful owner also gives tips about the best routes in the area.

WHERE TO SLEEP

The cheapest lodging in town is at the **gîte d'étape** (9 rte. d'Uhart, tel. 05–59–37–12–08), where you can crash on a bunk (46F) and fix your own meals in the little kitchenette. The same proprietress runs a chambre d'hôte next door with 120F doubles (150F with shower). Call ahead in July and August. Of them, **Hôtel des Remparts** (16 pl. Floquet, tel. 05–59–37–13–79), in a typical *maison basque* (Basque house), has 14 small but comfortable doubles starting at 210F. The aptly named **Central Hôtel** (1 pl. Charles-de-Gaulle, tel. 05–59–37–00–22) in the middle of town is a bit more expensive but an excellent value; doubles overlooking the Nive River start at 320F.

CAMPING • The **municipal campground** is in a convenient spot by the river next to the old town. Prices are reasonable at 10F per site and 13F per person. *Av. du Fronton, tel. 05–59–37–11–19. From pl. du Général de Gaulle, walk along river parallel to rue de l'Église and cross wooden bridge. Closed mid-Oct.–Easter.*

FOOD

If you happen to win big in Biarritz and have an extra 250F–300F to spend, consider the four-course meal-of-a-lifetime at the Arrambide's **Les Pyrénées** (19 pl. du Général de Gaulle, tel. 05–59–37–01–01), one of the premier restaurants in France. Otherwise, try the poulet basquaise on the 55F menu at **Chocolainia** (1 pl. de Trinquet, tel. 05–59–37–01–55). At the top of the hill on rue Zuharpeta, **Zuharpeta Bar/Restaurant** (tel. 05–59–37–35–88) caters to a young crowd. Ham sandwiches and salads are 35F–50F. Fruit stands line **rue d'Espagne** in the old part of town. There's also a covered **market** on place des Remparts across the Jardin d'Enfants from place Floquet.

OUTDOOR ACTIVITIES

From June through August there's action every evening at the *fronton municipal* (the wall in the geographical and social center of every Basque town), a five-minute walk from the tourist office following the signs. Dances, open markets, and pelote matches (80F) are everyday occurrences. Hiking options from here are unlimited; tons of small roads and trails head off into the hills. The GR10 comes through town, so you can head west on a day trip or follow it all the way to the coast. St-Jean-Pied-de-Port is also on the GR65, which can take you on an excellent six-hour passage over the **Col de Bentarte** (4,386 ft) to Roncevalles, Spain. The region is ideal for biking, too, with deserted roads and hard-packed trails for all levels. The steepest mountain-bike trails are just north of town on the **Pic d'Arradoy** (2,165 ft). It's a challenging climb to the top, but the steep descents are well worth it. Leaving town to the east, take the road to Jaxu for 2 km (1 mi), and then go left up the hill.

ST-JEAN-DE-LUZ

A colorful fishing port 15 km (9 mi) south of Biarritz, St-Jean-de-Luz is the only coastal town that has managed to retain its Basque character, thanks largely to the small harbor that it shares with its sister town Ciboure, on the other side of the Nivelle River. The glorious days of whaling and cod fishing are long gone, but the colorful houses around the docks and the sounds and smells of a port in action are reminders that this is still the center of town.

Much of St-Jean-de-Luz, however, is a pedestrian area designed for bored, sun-loving tourists. Don't let that deter you, though—the beach is calm, protected by the pier and fort of Socoa, and when it gets too packed, the parks on the cliffs at the north end of town are good escape options. Though St-Jean-de-Luz suffers from a lodging shortage, it possesses some of the best campsites along the coast. It's also a great breather from surf culture and a good starting point for hikes.

BASICS

The **tourist office** is near the port and a short walk from the train station. *Pl. Maréchal Foch, tel. 05–59–26–03–16. Open Mon.–Sat. 9–12:30 and 2–7; July–Aug., also Sun. 10–noon and 3–7.*

COMING AND GOING

The **train station** (av. de Verdun) has frequent service to Biarritz (15 mins, 19F), Bayonne (25 mins, 29F), and Hendaye (10 mins, 19F). Regional **ATCRB buses** (tel. 05–59–26–06–99) leave from place Maréchal Foch by the tourist office. They're slower but cheaper than the train and give you more beach-town options, including Bayonne (40 mins, 25F), Biarritz (35 mins, 19F), Bidart (15 mins, 15F), and Guéthary (10–15 mins, 9F). They also have service to San Sebastián in Spain (28F).

WHERE TO SLEEP

St-Jean-de-Luz is great for campers but tough on others. The **Centre Leo Lagrange** (8 rue Simone-Menez, tel. 05–59–47–04–79) normally houses groups of scuba divers but usually has some spare bunks that go for 70F, including breakfast. From the tourist office and train station, it's a 15-minute walk: Cross the bridge to Ciboure, turn right onto rue du Docteur Micé, then left onto the small rue Marion Garay. **Hôtel le Verdun** (13 av. de Verdun, tel. 05–59–26–02–55) is a sweet but somewhat ramshackle place right across from the train station. Doubles are 140F–250F. If you are prepared to pay a little extra, then **Hotel Ohartzia** (28 rue Garat, tel. 05–59–26–00–06) has immaculate doubles for 300F.

CAMPING • There are about 15 campgrounds north of town along the cliff, grouped in two coves; **Camping International Erromardie** (tel. 05–59–26–07–74), 2 km (1 mi) away, is closest. Erromardie is a huge camping city including a restaurant, arcade, general store, and bar. Sites are 66F most of the year, and 85F in July and August. At **Bord de Mer** (Erromardie Beach, tel. 05–59–26–24–61) you pay 75F for two people on a sloping beachfront site; it's closed November–February.

FOOD

Beach picnics are your best option. The daily **market** at Les Halles on boulevard Victor Hugo has all the goodies. If you're in the mood for local specialties like grilled sardines (35F) or fish soup (38F), **La Trinquette des Halles** serves them up hot from a small counter situated on the southernmost outside wall of Les Halles market. Otherwise, head near the port to **La Grillerie de Sardines** (quai Maréchal Leclerc, tel. 05–59–51–18–29) for sardines (35F a plateful) or grilled tuna (45F). At **Le Sud** (20 pl. de la Pergole, tel. 05–59–51–13–51), your choice of any of 11 salads is 40F, a steak and fries 35F. For fabulous oysters go to **La Kayola** (18 rue de la République, tel. 05–59–51–01–12) for 98F menus.

AFTER DARK

Head into town toward **place Louis XIV.** This is where, on the first Saturday in July, the town hosts its **Fête du Thon** (Tuna Festival), with music and tuna tasting. A good bet for late bars and a young crowd is to wander along rue de la République and take your pick.

NEAR ST-JEAN-DE-LUZ

Three of the prettiest villages that show off the colorful, asymmetric architecture of the Basque are **Ascain, Sare,** and **Ainhoa,** all best reached from St-Jean-de-Luz. Each is smaller, less touristy, and better preserved than the last, though you'll find charming white houses with red shutters, beams, and eaves in all. **Les Autocars Basques Bondissants** buses (tel. 05–59–26–25–87) leave from the train station in St-Jean-de-Luz and can drop you in Ascain (7F) or Sare (15F). To reach Ainhoa you'll need wheels. If you're coming from Bayonne, you can take the train to Cambo-les-Bains (on the way to St-Jean-Pied-de-Port) and then bike the remaining 13 km (8 mi) to Ainhoa. If you call in advance, **Breuille VTT** (tel. 05–59–24–73–10) will meet you at the station with a bike for 100F per day. In St-Jean-de-Luz, **Ado** (7 av. Labrouche, tel. 05–59–26–14–95) rents standard bikes for 60F a day, VTTs for 80F, and mopeds for 210F.

BIDART AND GUETHARY

Adjacent coastal villages between Biarritz and St-Jean-de-Luz, Bidart and Guéthary have long stretches of sand. Both villages are easy to reach along N10 if you're biking or traveling by ATCRB buses from Bayonne or Biarritz. Guéthary is a steep, cliff-side village with a modest port. To get on the scenic coastal path, get off the bus or turn off at the GUÉTHARY ÉGLISE sign. The **tourist offices** in Bidart (rue de la Plage, tel. 05–59–54–93–85) and Guéthary (in the train station, tel. 05–59–26–56–60) have lists of accommodations.

BORDEAUX AND THE AQUITAINE

UPDATED BY CHRISTOPHER KNOWLES

A fter its descent from the mountainous Massif Central, the Dordogne River sweeps westward, weaving through the patchwork of vineyards and forests that surround the wine capital of the world, Bordeaux. At Pech-Merle and Lascaux, remarkable 20,000-year-old wall paintings glow within dark caves. Astounding, too, are the medieval cliff-hewn villages of Rocamadour and St-Émilion—provided that you manage to peer through the crowds in high season. Smaller towns like riverside St-Cirq-Lapopie also have their undiscovered charms.

The region's rugged physiognomy and *nature sauvage* (wilderness) make it ideal for hiking and bicycling. Erratically strewn medieval towns, châteaux, and forests keep the countryside interesting, and the Gouffre du Padiracis is a marvel of stalagmites and geological formations. In summer the French tend to make a beeline for Les Landes, a vast expanse of pine forest, and for the fabulous Atlantic Coast beaches, only one hour southwest of Bordeaux.

The Aquitaine is best visited in spring, when there are flowers scattered across the lush, green countryside, or in autumn, when the hillsides are ablaze with the red and orange hues of grapevines ready for harvest. It's not as pleasant in July and August when you'll find hordes of tourists and stifling heat. Although bus and train service in the region is extensive, some out-of-the-way places, including several vineyards and prehistoric caves, are most easily accessed with organized tours or by car.

BORDEAUX

The history, economy, and culture of Bordeaux have always been linked to the production and marketing of the region's wine. The birth of the first Bordeaux winery is said to have occurred between AD 37 and 68, when the Romans called this land *Burdigala*. From then on the wine trade in Bordeaux has prospered, riding out market fluctuations, the Hundred Years' War, and English domination of the wine industry in the 19th century.

Although industry operates at full throttle here, Bordeaux tends to lack the vibrancy and variety of cities like Paris. An active student population, however, does manage to infuse some new and foreign char-

acter into the general atmosphere of political conservatism. Thirty thousand students attend Bordeaux's university, founded in 1441. As the capital of the Gironde *département* (province), Bordeaux is also an important transportation hub for all those heading to southern France or Spain. And if you're a wine connoisseur, it is still the doorway to paradise: Sauternes lies to the south, flat and dusty Médoc to the northwest, and Pomerol and St-Émilion to the east. Many of the vineyards surrounding Bordeaux are tough to reach without a car, but it is possible to get to some of them by bike. The countryside is mostly flat or mildly hilly, and there are many quaint, small roads that are ideal for biking from one château to the next. If you only want a fleeting glance of the vineyards and a brief explanation of the Bordeaux wine industry the Bordeaux tourist office (*see below*) offers excellent bus tours of the region.

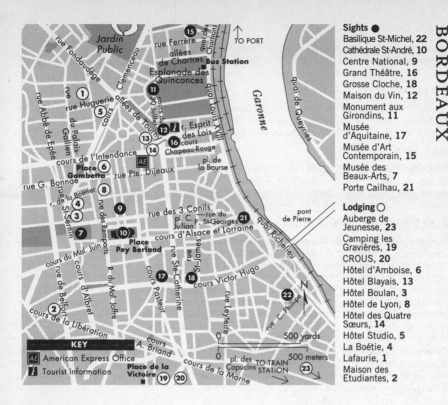

Sights ●
Basilique St-Michel, **22**
Cathédrale St-André, **10**
Centre National, **9**
Grand Théâtre, **16**
Grosse Cloche, **18**
Maison du Vin, **12**
Monument aux
Girondins, **11**
Musée
d'Aquitaine, **17**
Musée d'Art
Contemporain, **15**
Musée des
Beaux-Arts, **7**
Porte Cailhau, **21**

Lodging ○
Auberge de
Jeunesse, **23**
Camping les
Gravières, **19**
CROUS, **20**
Hôtel d'Amboise, **6**
Hôtel Blayais, **13**
Hôtel Boulan, **3**
Hôtel de Lyon, **8**
Hôtel des Quatre
Sœurs, **14**
Hôtel Studio, **5**
La Boétie, **4**
Lafaurie, **1**
Maison des
Etudiantes, **2**

BASICS

AMERICAN EXPRESS

The AmEx office cashes checks, replaces lost cards, holds mail for 30 days, and changes traveler's checks without commission. *14 cours de l'Intendance, tel. 05–56–00–63–33. Open weekdays 8:45–noon and 1:30–6.*

BUREAUX DE CHANGE

Thomas Cook (tel. 05–56–91–58–80), by the train station, has lousy rates and a hefty commission, but it's open Monday–Saturday 9–7. **Banque de France** (13 rue Esprit-des-Lois, tel. 05–56–00–14–14), which closes at 3 PM, has the best exchange deals.

CONSULATE

United Kingdom. *353 blvd. du Président Wilson, tel. 05–57–22–21–10. Open weekdays 9–12:30 and 2:30–5.*

DISCOUNT TRAVEL AGENCIES

Usit Voyages (284 rue Ste-Catherine, tel. 05–56–33–89–90), near the mobbed place de la Victoire, arranges cheap flights. **Wasteels** (13 pl. de Casablanca, tel. 05–56–48–29–39), across the street from the train station, sells BIJ tickets and discount airfares. A few doors down, **Eurolines** (32 rue Charles Domercq, tel. 05–56–92–50–42) has round-trip bus transport with particularly good rates for groups of more than 15 and for travelers under the age of 26.

ENGLISH-LANGUAGE BOOKSTORE

Bradley's Bookshop has novels and guidebooks in English, as well as translated French comic books. *32 pl. Gambetta, tel. 05–56–52–10–57. Open Mon. 2–7, Tues.–Sat. 9:30–12:30 and 2–7.*

LAUNDRY

Though there are a few scattered laundromats closer to the train station, **Laverie** (56 cours de la Marne) is worth the extra walk for its clean machines. **Espace Laverie** (6 rue Foundaudège) is a convenient walk from place Gambetta in the center of town.

MAIL

To reach the **main post office,** turn right on rue Georges-Bonnac from place Gambetta and continue for two blocks. Send your poste restante to postal code 33065; they'll hold it for 15 days. *52 Georges Bonnac, tel. 05–57–78–80–00. Open weekdays 8–7, Sat. 8–noon.*

MEDICAL AID

The **Centre Hospitalier** (tel. 05–56–79–56–79) can refer you to doctors 24 hours a day. The police station can also help in case of emergency (rue Abbé de l'Épée, tel. 05–56–99–77–77). For medical emergencies, call **SAMU** at 05–56–96–70–70. To reach the hospital, take Bus 12 from place de la Victoire, direction St-Augustin, and exit place Amèle Raba Léon.

VISITOR INFORMATION

There are two Bordeaux **city tourist offices**: The smaller office is just outside the train station, and the main office is at the Grand Théâtre stop on the 15-minute ride on Bus 7 from the train station. These offices provide tours (half day 150F, full day 290F) of nearby châteaux, vineyards, and wine cooperatives, and of the city itself (15F–50F). Both offices make hotel reservations year-round and rent bikes mid-June–mid-December. For the real lowdown on wines, cross the street from the main tourist office to the **Maison du Vin** (*see below*). For discounts on museums and tours ask about the Bordeaux Découverte card, which costs 100F and allows unlimited entry to a wide selection of Bordeaux's museums for one month. *12 cours du 30-Juillet, tel. 05–56–00–66–00, fax 05–56–00–66–01. Open June–Sept., Mon.–Sat. 9–8, Sun. 9–7; Oct.–May, daily 9–7.*

The **Maison du Tourisme de la Gironde** (21 cours de l'Intendance, tel. 05–56–52–61–40) has information on hotels, transportation, coastal activities, and wine regions near Bordeaux. Request a copy of their free Dordogne/Lot/Gironde or Landes accommodations booklet and outdoor itineraries (according to the region you plan to visit).

COMING AND GOING

BY TRAIN

Bordeaux is a major rail hub: Trains travel from its **Gare St-Jean** (tel. 05–56–35–35–35) to Paris (3 hrs, 345F by TGV), Périgueux (1¼ hrs, 105F), Bayonne (2¼ hrs, 140F), Carcassonne (3¼ hrs, 206F), Lyon (8 hrs, 313F) via Toulouse, Nice (8 hrs, 420F), St-Émilion (limited schedule, 42F), Pauillac (1 hr, 55F), and Bergerac (1¼ hrs, 80F). The beaches at Arcachon are a one-hour (55F) ride away. The station has 14F showers, car rental, a tourist office, and a bureau de change. You can store luggage at the baggage office for 35F per bag per day. The station is in an area full of sex shops and cheap hotels, about a 45-minute walk and 15-minute bus ride from the *centre ville* (town center).

BY BUS

Citram buses cover towns in the wine country and beach areas not well served by rail. One or two buses run daily to St-Émilion (1 hr), St-Macaire (1¼ hrs), and Lacanau (40 mins), each for about 40F. Round-trip to St-Émilion costs about 59F. To transport a bike, the train is a better option. Bike transport on buses costs an additional 20F. Buses leave from the station between the Esplanade des Quinconces and allée de Chartres, a five-minute walk from the tourist office. *8 rue Corneille, tel. 05–56–43–68–43. Information booth open weekdays 1 PM–8 PM, Sat. 9–noon.*

BY CAR

Since it is a long 579 km (360 mi) from Paris, it is cheaper to reach Bordeaux by train than by car. But once you are in Bordeaux, you might consider renting a car if you want to drive along the terrific, small country roads traversing the region (though you can get to most places by train). Biarritz is 190 km (118 mi) south, and Toulouse is 250 km (152 mi) west.

BY PLANE

Air France (29 rue Esprit-des-Lois, tel. 05–56–44–55–55) flies to Paris (510F–1,060F return, with discounts available depending on age and advance reservations) and Madrid (1250F–3,860F return). The **airport** (blvd. Kennedy, tel. 05–56–34–50–50) is in Mérignac, about 30 minutes outside Bordeaux. *Navettes* (shuttles) from the airport to the train station, the tourist office, and place Gambetta cost 33F and run every 40 minutes or so 5:30 AM–10 PM. Schedules are available at the tourist office.

GETTING AROUND

Bordeaux straddles a curve of the Garonne River. The centre ville, bounded roughly by cours Victor Hugo, place Gambetta, and cours Clemenceau, has most of the shops, sights, restaurants, and accommodations. Busy cours de l'Intendance and the pedestrian rue St-Catherine bisect the centre ville. The boardwalk along the Garonne provides daytime access to the centre ville from the train station on foot (30 mins) or by bike (10 mins). At night take Bus 7 or 8 to reach place de la Victoire, five minutes from the train station and the hostel.

BY BUS

City buses are efficient and frequent. A ticket costs 8F (36F for five) and is good for an hour of transport. The **CGFTE** office (4 rue Georges-Bonnac, near pl. Gambetta, tel. 05–57–57–88–88) has bus information. Bus maps are available at both tourist office locations; Buses 7 and 8 run between the station and the main tourist office, with stops at place Gambetta and place de la Victoire in between.

BY TAXI

Taxi stands are at the train station, on place de la Victoire, and next to the Grand Théâtre. You can also order a taxi from **Aquitaine Taxi Radio** (tel. 05–56–86–80–30); the pickup charge is 7F–9F. The ride from the train station to place de Victoire costs about 30F, 20F more to place Gambetta.

WHERE TO SLEEP

There are a few decent hotels and a hostel in the *quartier gare* (train-station district), but it's a long hike into town and the neighborhood is relatively unsafe after dark. The centre ville has better options. In July and August, reserve a day or two in advance.

UNDER 150F • Hôtel d'Amboise. The central location, off a pedestrian street near place Gambetta and Porte Dijeaux (the stone gate), is unbeatable. Rooms are clean and simply decorated with bright bedspreads. Many have only small windows so are dimly lit. Singles or doubles are 137F with shower and private toilet. The same proprietor also runs the more modern **Hôtel de Lyon** down the street, which has slightly larger rooms at similar prices. The reception desk for both is at the Hôtel de Lyon. *Amboise: 22 rue de la Vieille Tour, tel. 05–56–81–62–67, fax 05–56–52–92–82. 14 rooms, all with bath. Lyon: 31 rue des Remparts, tel. 05–56–81–34–38, same fax; 15 rooms, all with bath.*

Hôtel Boulan. This clean, family-run hotel on a quiet central street is cheap and easily accessible by bus. The automatic toilet-seat-cover changer is sure to excite the hygiene crowd. Doubles with basin cost 120F, with shower 140F. *28 rue Boulan, tel./fax 05–56–52–23–62. From train station, Bus 7 or 8 to Colonel Raynal stop, walk 1 block back to rue Boulan, and turn left. 16 rooms, 14 with bath.*

Hôtel Studio. Every room has a full bath, cable TV, phone, and refrigerator-bar and still only costs 120F–135F for a double. If the Studio is full, try the proprietor's other two hotels for the same rates: the **Lafaurie** (35 rue Lafaurie-de-Monbadon, tel. 05–56–48–16–33, fax 05–56–81–25–71), 9 rooms, all with bath, and **La Boétie** (4 rue de la Boétie, tel. 05–56–81–76–68, fax 05–56–81–24–72). *26 rue Huguerie, off pl. Tourny, tel. 05–56–48–00–14, fax 05–56–81–25–71. 15 rooms, all with bath.*

UNDER 200F • Hôtel Blayais. This small hotel on a quiet street in the city's center offers excellent value for money. Doubles with shower cost 170F. *17 rue Mautrec, tel. 05–56–48–17–87, fax 05–56–52–47–57. 12 rooms, all with shower.*

SPLURGE • Hôtel des Quatre Soeurs. In the center of town, between the Grand Théâtre and the city tourist office, this upscale hotel has well-kept singles (240F–430F) and doubles (350F–500F). Rooms are spacious and sunny and have modern decor and amenities like air-conditioning and TV with cable. The adjoining café is excellent for coffee and light meals. *6 cours du 30-Juillet, tel. 05–57–81–19–20, fax 05–56–01–04–28. 34 rooms, all with bath.*

HOSTELS

If you're under 26, single rooms are often available in summer outside town on the Campus de Talence (accessible by Bus F or U) for 50F–65F a night, including sheets. Stop by **CROUS** (18 rue du Hamel, tel. 05–56–33–92–17) for details. It's open weekdays 9:30–4.

Auberge de Jeunesse. Recently remodeled, this hostel's new and improved facilities complement the friendly and helpful staff. *22 cours Barbey, tel. 05–56–91–59–51, fax 05–56–92–59–39. From train station, go 5 blocks up cours de la Marne, left on cours Barbey. 250 beds. Reception 8–9:30 AM and 6–11 PM. Curfew 11 PM. Lockout 9:30 AM–6 PM. Kitchen, laundry.*

Maison des Étudiantes. This place is a better deal than the hostel if you're under 26. It's close to the centre ville, has no curfew, and houses lots of locals. Call several days ahead to reserve a room. A kitchen, dining area, and TV room are downstairs. Single rooms, sheets included, cost 48F (69F without ISIC card). The reception is open 24 hours. *50 rue Ligier, tel. 05–56–96–48–30. Take Bus 7 or 8 from the station to the Bourse du Travail stop, then walk to rue Ligier. 92 beds. Kitchen.*

CAMPING

Camping les Gravières. Just outside town in Villenave d'Ornon, this campground sits under the trees next to the Garonne River. Sites are 30F, plus 19F per tent. You can rent a tent for an additional 19F. There's a bar at the campground and laundry facilities. *Chemin de Macau, tel. 05–56–87–00–36. From train station, Bus 7 or 8 to pl. de la Victoire, then a 30-min ride on Bus B to Corréjean. 150 sites.*

FOOD

It's a cinch to eat cheaply in Bordeaux if you're not picky; sidewalk stands on **rue du Palais-Gallien,** near place Gambetta, sell kebab-stuffed baguettes, greasy fries, and a Coke for 25F. Along the quai near **Porte Cailhau,** near quai Richelieu and cours d'Alsace et Lorraine, are a bunch of cheap North African eateries. The **quartier St-Michel,** off cours Victor Hugo, has Turkish spice shops, restaurants serving couscous, and Asian markets and eateries. On Saturday mornings drop in at the open **market** on place Chanteloup in front of the Église St-Michel. For a wide array of traditional French cuisine and regional specialties, head for the cobblestone **rue du Pas St-Georges,** near place Camille Jullian in the oldest corner of town. The big **market** on place des Capucines is a daily affair (5 AM–1 PM). There is always the standby supermarket **Auchan** (rue Claude Bonnier, at rue du Château d'Eau) in the Centre Mériadeck.

UNDER 75F • Brasserie le Musée. Right next to St-André cathedral, this pub-style restaurant has a lunch menu (54F) that might include *salade aux noix* (salad with walnuts), *entrecôte grillée* (grilled rib steak), dessert, and wine. The view of flying buttresses is no extra charge. *37 pl. Pey-Berland, near rue du Maréchal Joffre, tel. 05–56–52–99–69.*

Francs Délices. At lunch, those in the know crowd this cheap restaurant. The 65F menu (served until 8 PM) includes foie gras (which usually costs about 70F on its own), plus a salad and dessert. It's open late—till 12:30 AM nightly. *54 rue de la Devise, off pl. St-Pierre near rue St-Catherine, tel. 05–56–52–28–22. No lunch Mon. Closed Sun., Sept.*

Maroc Inn. In the quiet shadows of the Église St-Pierre, Moroccan and Spanish music adds ambience to the air already scented with fresh calamari and steaming vegetable couscous (50F lunch, 70F dinner). Top your filling meal off with *tcharmila* (a spicy North African sauce) and mint tea. Kosher or vegetarian dishes are available a day in advance. *14 rue de la Cour des Aides, tel. 05–56–79–70–19.*

Restaurant L'Oiseau Bleu. Run by François Mitterrand's private chef at the Élysée, Vincent Poussard, set meals here start at 157F with the emphasis on traditional cuisine, such as fillets of mullet with tagliatelle in pesto. *65 cours de Verdun, tel. 05–56–81–09–39.*

Le Scaramucia. Just off place St-Pierre, this place consistently draws a lively crowd who come for the 50 varieties of pizza (35F–52F). Try the namesake, *scaramucia* (51F)—with tomatoes, garlic, onions, sausage, mushrooms, goat cheese, and olives—or the 50F multicourse lunch menu. *3 rue du Parlement Ste-Catherine, tel. 05–56–81–62–75. Closed Sun.*

UNDER 100F • Le Lautrec. This elegant restaurant serves a 50F dinner menu that might include artichokes *forestières* (buttered and garnished with mushrooms), veal *à la Viennoise* (breaded and served with a hard-boiled egg), and homemade apricot pie. The 80F menu comes with oysters, steak flambé, veggies, and dessert. *36 rue St-Sernin, at rue Georges Bonnac, tel. 05–56–81–59–08.*

Le Croc Loup. This friendly, unpretentious restaurant with set meals at 67F (lunch) and 115F (dinner) offers simple well-cooked dishes (cooked hams and salami are a specialty). *35 rue du Loup, tel. 05-56-44-21-19.*

SPLURGE • Vieux Bordeaux. This much-acclaimed haunt of nouvelle cuisine is on the fringe of the old town. Chef Michel Bordage concentrates on fresh produce and serves fish dishes. The dinner menu runs 155F-260F, but the lunch menu is only 100F. Dishes à la carte are 90F-160F. Reservations are essential. *27 rue Buhan, tel. 05-56-52-94-36. Closed Sun. and Aug. No lunch Sat.*

CAFES

Le Riche (1 rue Judaïque, tel. 05-56-44-52-84) draws a mellow crowd who come to sit on the terrace and watch people passing by. Occupying a small corner on the ancient stones of place St-Pierre—a part of town packed with anyone who knows where to enjoy a good drink on a warm evening—is **Le Cafecito** (7 rue Parlement St-Pierre). **Bar le Saint Georges** (33 rue Pas St-Georges, tel. 05-56-44-86-33) is a nice place to lounge on a sunny day, reading or writing.

WORTH SEEING

Although Bordeaux is hardly known for blockbuster attractions, it does have a few sights worth seeing. The **Musée des Beaux-Arts** (20 cours d'Albert, tel. 05-56-10-16-93) displays works of Toulouse-Lautrec, Delacroix, and Rubens. Admission is 20F, and free on Wednesday afternoons. The museum is open daily 10-12:30 and 1:30-6:00. In summer you can view rooftops and the Garonne from the top of **Porte Cailhau**, a 15th-century portal along the ramparts that once greeted the *noblesse du bouchon* (aristocratic wine merchants) on their way into town. Nearby is the 16th-century tower-gate **Grosse Cloche** (rue St-James, at cours Victor Hugo). The Gothic **Cathédrale St-André** (pl. Pey Berland, tel. 05-56-81-26-25) and **Basilique St-Michel** (pl. St-Michel, tel. 05-56-94-30-50) host summertime music concerts in the shadows of their bell towers. The **Conservatoire International de la Plaisance** (Dock 2, blvd. Alfred-Daney, tel. 05-56-76-83-63), tells all about yachts and other pleasure boats. It's open Wednesday-Friday 1-7, weekends 10-7. Admission is 45F.

CENTRE NATIONAL JEAN MOULIN

This museum is named for the legendary Resistance leader who worked with Charles de Gaulle, forming three separate resistance groups in Vichy-controlled France, before the infamous Klaus Barbie tortured Moulin to death in 1943. Next to the exhibits on the glory and heroism of the Resistance are souvenirs of collaborationist France, a subject many French are reluctant to discuss. *Pl. Jean Moulin, tel. 05-56-79-66-00. Admission free. Open weekdays 2-6.*

GRAND THEATRE

To grasp the scope of this 18th-century building, note that the staircase of Charles Garnier's opulent Opéra in Paris was inspired by the one here, in the Grand Théâtre's majestic foyer. Of course, the Parisians did it in glossy marble while the Bordeaux architect chose the plain white stone of local quarries. The idea was to create a simple frame to set off the sumptuous colors of the trompe l'oeil paintings. The tourist office's walking tour takes you up into the nosebleed seats for an eagle's-eye view of the magnificent ceiling. If you'd prefer the full effect, visit the box office daily 11-6:30 for opera, ballet, or symphony tickets (20F-150F). *Pl. de la Comédie, tel. 05-56-00-85-20.*

MAISON DU VIN

Along with Burgundy and Champagne, Bordeaux is one of the great wine regions of France and the world. Before you go exploring, stop by the stained-glass and bronze lobby of the Wine House, directly opposite the tourist office. The English-speaking staff give plenty of information, including the *Guide to Vineyards and Wine Cellars in the Bordeaux area,* an English-French guide to the vineyards and the art of tasting (*dégustation*). Tasting a red (like Pauillac or St-Émilion), a dry white (like an Entre-Deux-Mers or Côtes de Blaye), and a sweet white (like Sauternes or St-Macaire) will help you decide which of the seven wine regions to explore. Before visiting a château, call ahead to see if the tasting is free and whether you need to make a reservation. Bus tours led by the tourist office staff are the way to go if you want to see a lot in a short period of time. *1 cours du 30-Juillet, tel. 05-56-00-22-66, fax 05-56-00-22-77. Open weekdays 8:30-6 (also May-Oct., Sat. 9-12:30 and 1:30-5).*

MONUMENT AUX GIRONDINS

This massive statue near the tourist office at the esplanade des Quinconces was built at the turn of the century to commemorate the bravery of the Girondins, a local party that fought for the creation of a constitutional government and supported the French provinces over Paris in the later years of the French Revolution. Many were eventually arrested and executed. The statue here was meant to include some actual Girondins in its panoply of characters, but after chiseling all the horses, seashells, flying carp, laurels, and cherubs, the sculptors ran out of money (not to mention space). The symbolism is complex, but here's the *Reader's Digest* version: Liberty is on top; the Republic is tossing out the monarchy's vices on one side (the pig-eared figure represents excess and debauchery); on the other side, Bordeaux frolics in democratic harmony with the Garonne and Dordogne rivers.

MUSEE D'AQUITAINE

This excellent museum takes you on a trip through human history in Bordeaux, with an emphasis on Roman, medieval, Renaissance, colonial, and 20th-century daily life. The detailed prehistoric section saves you a trip to the Lascaux cave paintings, which are reproduced here in part. The exhibit also includes the 25,000-year-old statuette known as the *Vénus à la Corne,* which was found at Laussel. *20 cours Pasteur, tel. 05–56–01–51–00. Admission 18F, free Wed. Open Tues.–Sun. 10–6 (Wed. until 10).*

MUSEE D'ART CONTEMPORAIN

Bordeaux's modern art museum is on the wharf in an old 19th-century spice warehouse. Every year, the museum features four artists who use the huge expanse to do anything artistic. The space itself frequently becomes the art, with hanging ropes and ladders, large video screens, and human art forms lounging about (oh-so cutting edge). Since it's rarely overrun by tourists, take your time, enjoy the peace, and make it a day by visiting the unique **café** on the top floor or the art library. *7 rue Ferrère, tel. 05–56–00–81–50. Admission 30F, free noon–2. Open Tues.–Sun. noon–7 (Wed. until 10).*

CHEAP THRILLS

The best place to hang out or catch some rays is the 18th-century **Jardin Public** (tel. 05–56–52–18–77), open until 9 PM in summer, until 6 PM in winter. For 4F you can rent a little boat and cruise the park's lake. On summer weekends, check out the free 3 PM classic **puppet show,** the Guignol Guérin. For a dose of affordable international cinema (34F), the small and artsy **Trianon-J. Vigo** (6 rue Franklin, off cours de l'Intendance, tel. 05–56–44–35–17) screens works—all in the original version—by the likes of Fellini, Almodóvar, Fassbinder, and Woody Allen.

SHOPPING

Stylish shops abound in the commercial heart of Bordeaux, on the numerous pedestrian streets between the cathedral and the Grand Théâtre. **Vinothèque** (8 cours du 30-Juillet) has a wide selection of high-priced wines; if you are skipping out of the region without a tour of the vineyards, this is the place to buy a bottle. For a good look at a beautiful display of regional cheeses—and a taste, step into **Le Tranche-Caillé** (4 rue Montesquieu, tel. 05–56–44–29–66). Saturday mornings, when most of Bordeaux is a ghost town, a flea market animates place Chanteloup in front of the Basilique St-Michel.

AFTER DARK

Night owls start off around 9 PM in the cafés around **place St-Pierre** or **place de la Victoire. Chez Auguste** (3 pl. de Victoire, tel. 05–56–91–77–32) is a popular stop. After a few hours at discos and nightclubs along the river, diehards head back to the bars near **place des Capucins.** Pick up the bimonthly *Clubs et Concerts,* free at newsstands, for the scoop. *Bordeaux Plus* (2F) also has schedules for movies, theater, dance, and nightclubs.

Le Plana (22 pl. de la Victoire, tel. 05–56–91–73–23) is so trendy that people have been known to drive all the way from Pau, more than 200 km (124 mi) away, to quench their thirst at the crowded bar Tuesday nights. Anyone hankering for Irish hospitality should slip into **Connemara** (18 cours d'Albret, close to the Musée des Beaux-Arts, tel. 05–56–52–82–57). **La Palmeraie** (22 quai de la Monnaie, tel. 05–56–94–07–52) is a bar where Bordeaux's French-African population tosses beers back. A lesbian crowd congregates at **La Reine Carotte** (28 rue Chai des Farines, tel. 05–56–01–26–68). **L'Ane qui Tousse** (57 rue de Bègles, tel. 05–56–92–52–98) has exotic decor and clientele to match; the music alternates between reggae, salsa, zouk, and world beat. If you brought along your dancing shoes, **Sénéchal** (57 bis quai de Paludate) is the place to put them to use. Good jazz can be heard at **Les Argentiers** (7 quai Bacalan), a long-established Bordeaux haunt.

NEAR BORDEAUX

The Gironde département is divided into seven regions around Bordeaux, according to geography and the types of wine produced. These regions can be difficult to reach without a car. Public buses run frequently through the countryside, but stops often appear to be in the middle of nowhere and schedules are irregular. Get very specific information from the main tourist office and from the bus ticket office on the Esplanade des Quinconces, before boarding a bus. If you have access to a car, you'll find life much easier, particularly if you purchase a Michelin map (from the train-station tabac). Map number 234 covers a large portion of the southwest. Another option is go on a bus tour organized by the Bordeaux tourist office; trips go to various châteaux, usually with wine tasting included. Most of the more-famous vineyards like you to make an appointment, with the expectation that a purchase will be made.

MEDOC

The Médoc region spans the peninsula north of Bordeaux, extending from the Garonne River to the Atlantic coast. Dutch engineers drained this marshy landscape in the 18th century to expose the gravelly soil that is excellent for growing grapes. The Médoc is home to some of the most famous vineyards in the world, including Latour and Lafite-Rothschild.

MARGAUX

Thirty kilometers (19 mi) north of Bordeaux, on two-lane route D2, is the dusty town of **Margaux.** The well-informed, English-speaking staff at the **Margaux Maison du Vin** (tel. 05–57–88–70–82, fax 05–57–88–38–27) can direct you to châteaux such as **Lascombes** and **Palmer,** which have beautiful grounds and reasonably priced wines and are open without reservations. The less-accessible and more-expensive **Margaux** (tel. 05–57–88–83–83) château tour requires a reservation a month in advance; bottles go for $120 each.

PAUILLAC

Ninety kilometers (56 mi) north of Bordeaux on highway D2, Pauillac is a perfect waterfront base for visits to **Château Mouton-Rothschild** (entry 20F) and its wine museum (tel. 05–56–73–21–29). Renowned **Château Latour** (tel. 05–56–73–19–80) requires reservations a month in advance. These and the surrounding châteaux have been producing some of the best red wines in the world since 1855. If the posh prices of these two *grand crus* (world-famous wines) are not for you, rent a bike from the **tourist office** (La Verrerie, tel. 05–56–59–03–08) for 70F and visit any of the less-expensive surrounding wineries (ask at the tourist office). In July the lively **Jazz and Wine Festival** takes place.

BASICS • Trains from Bordeaux to Pauillac (1¼ hrs, 55F) run several times daily in summer, less frequently in winter. **Citram buses** (tel. 05–56–43–68–68) make the round-trip once daily for about the same price. The low-key **Hôtel Pauillac** (3 quai A. Pichon, tel. 05–56–59–01–20) has doubles for 250F–350F; ask for one overlooking the waterfront. Mid-October–mid April, the reception desk is closed Sunday evenings and Monday and the hotel as a whole is closed mid-December–mid-January. A less expensive option is **Camping Les Gabarreys** (tel. 05–56–59–10–03), 1 km (½ mi) south of the tourist office on the waterfront; it's closed October–May.

ENTRE-DEUX-MERS

The Entre-Deux-Mers, or "Between Two Seas," region actually lies between two rivers, the Garonne and the Dordogne. This area a couple of miles southeast of Bordeaux is dotted with tiny medieval towns and crumbling castles overlooking the rows of vines responsible for world-famous dry white wines. One of these is Sauvignon blanc—dry, aromatic, and oak-aged—which is often mixed with the sweeter Sémillon (produced in Sauternes 12 km/7½ mi southwest of St-Macaire) to create the renowned Graves wine.

ST-MACAIRE

Life is slow in this tiny hilltop town whose crumbling, ivy-swathed ramparts date from the 12th and 13th centuries. Check out the ramparts and the twisting cobbled streets, and then peek into the **Église St-Sauveur.** Nearby, housed in an old post office, the **Musée Régional des P.T.T. d'Aquitaine** (Regional Postal Museum; pl. du Mercadiou, tel. 05–56–63–08–81) displays tons of old stamps, postcards, franking machines, and the like. It's open Wednesday–Saturday 10–noon and 2–6:30; admission is 12F. For information on St-Macaire's main attractions—fishing spots and biking routes through the pleasant countryside—contact the tourist office, the **Maison du Pays** (8 rue du Canton, tel. 05–56–63–32–14). A couple of shops in neighboring Langon rent bikes.

BASICS • Two or three **Citram buses** make the Bordeaux–St-Macaire run daily, via Langon (1¼ hrs, 40F). **Camping les Remparts** (tel. 05–56–62–23–42), at the foot of the city walls, is a great place to wake up in the morning. Sites are 16F, plus 8F per person. It's open mid-June–mid-September only. The **Restaurant L'Abricotier** on the main road (2 rue Berzonj, tel. 05–56–76–83–63) offers set meals at 70F (lunch) and from 105F (dinner). Noteworthy dishes include a salad of duck's neck with artichokes and roast sea bass with asparagus accompanied by an excellent selection of Bordeaux wines. Alternatively consider treating yourself to a night in **Monsieur Ledru**'s 18th-century château (10 av. de la Porte-des-Tours, town of Monségur, tel. 05–56–61–80–22, fax 05–56–61–85–99), 40 km (25 mi) northwest of St-Macaire en route to Bergerac (via N113 and D668), to get a real notion of this region. Doubles are 280F and you can dine with your hosts (100F) with advance reservations.

ST-EMILION

Tourists jostle through the narrow streets of medieval St-Émilion, ravenous for the famous red wines and scrumptious macaroons that bear the town's name. Ignore the crowds, revel in the magnificent hillside views, and visit the sublime **Église Monolithe** on place du Marché. The church was built by monks faithful to the memory of St. Emilion (an 8th-century hermit who came to this spot to be alone but kept attracting followers as word of his miracles spread). An obligatory guided tour of the 9th- to 12th-century church—which is a marvel, painstakingly carved out of a cliff side—explores the saint's own *grotte* (cave) and some spooky catacombs. Its *clocher* (bell tower) affords a dizzying view (6F) of the vine-covered hills, best seen at sunset. The tourist office leads several church tours daily for 33F.

The patient English-speaking staff at the **tourist office** (pl. des Créneaux, tel. 05–57–24–72–03, fax 05–57–74–47–15) gives out a list of local châteaux offering wine tastings and tours; the office also leads its own tasting tours for 51F. It's open daily 9:30–12:30 and 1:45–6. Or stop by the town's **Maison du Vin** (pl. Pierre Meyrat, tel. 05–57–55–50–55, fax 05–57–24–65–57) to check out your options and then rent a bike (90F per day, with a credit card and passport deposit) from the tourist office. It's best to hit the road on a weekday, when more châteaux are open. You don't need to leave St-Émilion to taste wine, however; shops all over town vie for your attention and your francs. The best deal is in the cellars of the **Union des Producteurs,** a wine cooperative a 15-minute walk out of town.

COMING AND GOING

St-Émilion is most easily accessed by **car.** Bordeaux is 41 km (29 mi) to the west via Libourne on highway D664. Bergerac is 56 km (35 mi) east on highway D936. Four **trains** a day pass through from Bordeaux (40 mins, 44F), but the 2-km (1-mi) walk to town is long and the station building is closed, so you have to stand out on the platform to wait. Moreover, if you do not already have a ticket, you have to purchase one on the train, which can be expensive. The **Citram bus** (tel. 05–56–43–68–43) drops off in town and costs less than the train—67F round-trip from Bordeaux, 47F from Libourne. Unfortunately, service is infrequent. A better way to get around is by **bicycle**—this is a beautiful, relatively flat and dry region, which is good for biking. Consult Michelin map no. 75, and the biking guide no. 7, "St-Émilion," available from the Maison du Tourisme de la Gironde in Bordeaux (*see above*).

WHERE TO SLEEP

The two-story, 19th-century **Auberge de la Commanderie** (rue des Cordeliers, tel. 05–57–24–70–19, fax 05–57–74–44–53) is the cheapest hotel in town; it's closed mid-January–mid-February. The immaculate doubles (280F–550F) have views of the vineyards and the **Goullat** restaurant across the street has a good selection of local wines (it's closed Tuesday, except in July and August). **Madame Favard** (La Gomerie, tel. 05–57–24–68–85) runs a quaint and comfortable bed-and-breakfast 1½ km (1 mi) from town (via D243, direction Libourne). Doubles with shower are 200F. The cheapest place to sleep is

Camping la Barbanne (rte. de Montagne, tel. 05–57–24–75–80), 3 km (2 mi) northeast of town, where the proprietors levy 35F per site plus 21F per person, but the swimming pool is a relief in summer.

FOOD

Le Clocher (pl. du Clocher, tel. 05–57–74–43–04) serves a 70F menu including a small salad, steak, and ice cream, in addition to more expensive gourmet meals (95F). Laid-back Pizzeria de la Tour (19 rue de la Grande Fontaine, tel. 05–57–24–68–91) is a semiquiet place where you can have a ham and cheese *galette* (buckwheat pancake; 35F) on a small outdoor patio. Restaurant Francis Goullée (27 rue Guadet, tel. 05–57–24–70–49), considered among the best in town, is located in a narrow side street and serves traditional local recipes (try the breast of duck with roast potatoes) with weekday lunch starting at 90F. Family-run Chez Germaine (pl. du Clocher, tel. 05–57–24–70–88) has grilled meats and fish as house specialties (menus are 95F–120F). Don't leave town without treating yourself to macaroons; the 17th-century convent where the recipe was perfected is no longer around, but you can pig out at Mouliérac (rue du Clocher, tel. 05–57–74–41–84) on a box of 24 for 30F. The Sunday morning outdoor market at Porte Bouqueyre features locally produced goods.

LES LANDES DE GASCOGNE

In the Entre-Deux-Mers region, the Dordogne and Garonne rivers, the meeting of ocean and river produces an unusual phenomenon known as the "mascaret," a spectacular wave eagerly awaited by a small, extremely patient band of surfers.

Forming a triangle that stretches along the coast near Bordeaux to Bayonne and eastward along the Garonne River, the Landes region encompasses 2 million acres of flat, sandy pine forest. On the coast, the highest dune in Europe, the Dune du Pyla, piles up behind uninterrupted miles of sandy beach. More than a century ago the area was part desert, part marshy wilderness, with eccentric inhabitants who sported sheepskin jackets and stomped around the marshes on stilts. Some still do, but mainly for the benefit of tourists who come for the hiking, fishing, canoeing, and sand-skiing.

One of the most accessible and most touristed Les Landes towns, Arcachon has clean beaches, like the Plage Péreire, and fabulous eclectic villas among the pines. The town is a bustling boating center, but the ultimate sun-and-sand experience is actually about 6 km (4 mi) south of Arcachon at the end of a 14F bus ride that leaves every 45 minutes from the train station: the incredible Dune du Pyla, the highest mountain of sand—a phenomenal 384 ft—at the water's edge. Mounting the dune from the inland side is an easy climb up a wooden staircase. Bring plenty of water, food, and sunscreen. Sunsets up here are phenomenal, as are the generous scoops of ice cream at La Palombière (at the bottom of the only set of stairs that lead up the east side of the sand dune, tel. 05–56–22–78–54). A multitude of campsites make it easy to spontaneously decide to stay an extra day, but the hotels are all back in town. Cyclists should stick to the coast roads and pathways for easiest access to the dune, which is 8 km (5 mi) south of the train station. If you are around in mid-August don't miss the Fêtes de la Mer, Archachon's annual shindig.

Arcachon is at the southernmost tip of a chain of lakes connected by streams and canals. In the center of this chain is Lac de Lacanau, teeming with pike, perch, and eel, and linked by the Canal de Lège to the Bassin d'Arcachon. The bay is renowned both for its variety of migratory birds and for its excellent oyster beds, clustered around the Ile aux Oiseaux, a small island in the middle; inquire at the Archachon tourist office about getting to the island and guided nature tours of the reserve.

COMING AND GOING • Getting to Arcachon is a cinch, with about 20 trains daily from Bordeaux (40 mins, 53F); the beach is three blocks from the station. By car, Bordeaux is 64 km (40 mi) east via N250 or highway A63.

WHERE TO SLEEP AND EAT • The tourist office (esplanade Georges Pompidou, tel. 05–56–83–01–69, fax 05–57–52–22–10), just outside the train station, has listings of campgrounds, hotels, and beach houses; it's closed Sunday afternoon. If you want to stay the night, Le Bayonne (7 cours Lamarque, tel. 05–56–83–33–82, fax 05–56–83–73–06) has comfortable doubles for 450F–500F in July and August; prices are cheaper off-season. It's closed mid-October–mid-March. Five blocks to the west and one block from the beach on place Lucien de Gracia is a daily market, open 9–1. On the beach, Pizza Bolero (14 promenade Marcel Gounouilhou) serves up a tomato, onion, cheese, olive, and chorizo pizza for 50F. Local restaurants specialize in oysters; La Marée (21 rue du Lattre-de-Tassigny, tel. 05–56–83–24–05), a fish shop that dabbles in cooking, serves them for only 30F a dozen.

THE DORDOGNE

Cultivated by peasant farmers for centuries, the rolling countryside of the Dordogne—a term loosely referring not only to the Dordogne River valley but also to towns near the Vézère River to the north—is chock-full of riverside châteaux, medieval villages, and prehistoric sites. The département centers on **Sarlat,** whose impeccably restored medieval buildings make it a great place to use as a base for exploring the region. The surrounding countryside is honeycombed with dozens of caves filled with prehistoric drawings, etchings, and carvings. You can also see original works more than 20,000 years old at Font de Gaume in **Les Eyzies,** or visit a re-creation of France's most famous caves at **Lascaux,** just north of Sarlat.

The 10-km (6-mi) stretch of the Dordogne River from Montfort to Beynac is easily accessible by car, bike, canoe, or on foot and shouldn't be missed. Fields of sunflowers line the banks, and medieval châteaux perch high above the river. Another 30 km (19 mi) west, toward **Bergerac,** the land is dedicated to viticulture. All these attractions don't go unnoticed, of course; in July and August even the smallest village is often packed with tourists.

BERGERAC

Yes, this is the Bergerac of *Cyrano de Bergerac* fame—except that the real satirist and playwright Cyrano (1619–55), who inspired playwright Edmond Rostand's long-nosed swashbuckler, was born in Paris and never set foot anywhere near the town. This hasn't prevented the city fathers from adopting him as a native son and capitalizing on centuries' worth of good publicity. Bergerac's mellow streets, half-timbered houses, and verdant banks on the Dordogne make it a pleasant place to spend a quiet evening.

Eight or nine trains pass daily through Bergerac from Bordeaux (1¼ hrs, 78F) and Sarlat (1½ hrs, 59F); St-Émilion is also on this line (1 hr, 49F). A couple of **Citram buses** make the trip from Bordeaux (2½ hrs, 70F). Use your feet once you're here. Exiting right from the train station, take cours Alsace-Lorraine (continue as it turns into rue Ste-Catherine). Turn left on rue de la Résistance to reach place de la République and the **tourist office** (97 rue Neuve d'Argenson, tel. 05–53–57–03–11, fax 05–53–61–11–04) or continue straight from Alsace-Lorraine onto rue St-Esprit, where the pedestrian streets of the **vieille ville** (old town) begin.

WHERE TO SLEEP

Bergerac's reasonably priced hotels and ordinary campground usually don't fill up in summer. Just across from the station, **Le Moderne** (19 av. du 108ème R.I., tel. 05–53–57–19–62, fax 05–53–61–80–50) lives up to its name, with minimalist, modern decor; the clean doubles with TVs cost between 180F and 230F. The friendly patron of **Le Family** (pl. Cayla, tel. 05–53–57–80–90), in the centre ville, has comfortable rooms upstairs and a bar downstairs; doubles run 185F–250F with shower. **Camping Municipal la Pelouse** (8 rue Jean-Jacques Rousseau, tel. 05-53-57-06-67), a 25-minute walk from the station via the centre ville (turn right after crossing the Vieux Pont at the end of rue Neuve d'Argenson), is open all year and costs 14F per camper, 5F per site.

FOOD

Les Cricketeurs, next to the covered market on place Cayla, is a great spot for sandwiches (12F) and salads (10F). By night it's a mellow jazz bar with 10F tapas. At **Chez Jacques** (17 rue Colonel Chadois, tel. 05-53-57-59-84), rap with the friendly locals at the bar while Jacques fixes you a monstrous steak with fries (45F) or equally large mixed salad (35F). There's a **covered market** on the appropriately named place du Marché Couvert, a.k.a. place Cayla, before noon. The **outdoor market** near the Église Notre-Dame features everything from honey to espadrilles on Wednesday and Saturday mornings. Underrated local **wines** are available in shops all over the vieille ville for 25F–35F.

WORTH SEEING

The wine cellar in the **Cloître des Récollets,** built by 17th-century monks, now hosts the regional committee that doles out the *appellation d'origine contrôlée,* or the right to put "Bergerac" on a wine bottle. The tour of the cloisters takes you into the jury's tasting rooms and ends up in your own tasting room where you can try the region's sweet whites and fruity young reds. *2 pl. du Cayla, off pl. de la Myrpe, tel. 05-53-63-57-57. Guided tour 25F. July–Aug., daily tours every hr 10:30–11:30 and 1:30–5:30; mid-May–June and Sept.–mid-Oct., Tues.–Sat. at 3:30 and 4:30.*

The **Musée d'Intérêt National du Tabac** (*see* box, *above*), a museum dedicated to tobacco, will please both aficionados and enemies of the nicotine weed. *Pl. du Feu, tel. 05-53-63-04-13. Admission 15F. Open Tues.–Fri. 10–noon and 2–6, Sat. 10–noon and 2–5, Sun. 2:30–6:30.*

OUTDOOR ACTIVITIES

In Bergerac, rent bikes for 80F per day with an ID deposit at **Périgord Cycles** (11 pl. Gambetta, tel. 05-53-57-07-19), open Tuesday–Saturday 9–noon and 2–7. A good day- or weekend-long bicycling excursion through gently rolling wheat and poppy fields is along **route D32,** which begins at the east end of town and goes toward the minuscule town of **St-Alvère,** where the only thing that might wake you is the gurgle of a backyard creek or the crow of a feisty rooster. The round-trip between Bergerac and St-Alvère is 60 km (34 mi). Spend the night 1 km (½ mi) west of St-Alvère at the chambre d'hôte **Moulin-Latour** (off D32, tel. 05-53-57-80-90). Doubles are 180F–220F, including breakfast. After a night in St-Alvère, either return to Bergerac or head on to **Les Eyzies,** 23 km (14 mi) east. From St-Alvère take route D2 south 3 km (2 mi) until you reach route D703; take it east 13 km (8 mi) until you cross over the Vézère River. From here take D706 northeast 7 km (4½ mi) to Les Eyzies.

PERIGUEUX

A medium-size city, with a well-preserved centre ville, Périgueux is a good place to spend the night on your way to or from the quaint towns and prehistoric caves to the south. Gallo-Roman monuments sprout haphazardly on one end of town, surrounded by small city parks conducive to afternoon picnicking. But it is the echoing cobblestone alleys and the monumental cathedral, especially enchanting at twilight, that make Périgueux particularly worth visiting.

BASICS

The helpful and efficient **tourist office** gives out maps, information on Périgueux's monuments, and tours of the city. *26 pl. Francheville, tel. 05-53-53-10-63, fax 05-53-09-02-50. From train station, take rue des Mobiles-de-Coulmiers to rue du Président Wilson, right on cours Montaigne. Open mid-June–mid-Sept., daily 9–7; mid-Sept.–mid-June, Mon.–Sat. 9–noon and 2–6.*

COMING AND GOING

Several daily trains travel from Périgueux's **station** (rue Denis Papin, tel. 05-53-09-50-50) to Sarlat (1½ hrs, 73F, change at Le Buisson), Bergerac (1½ hrs, 75F), and Limoges (1 hr, 78F). Several bus companies, most reliably, **Trans-Périgord** (tel. 05-53-08-76-00) and **CFTA** (tel. 05-53-08-43-13), also cover the region. Sort out the bus schedules at the **bus station** on place Francheville. If you're a student, Trans-Périgord will give you a 30% discount; ask for it before they punch your ticket. **Cycles Cumenal**

(41 bis cours St-Georges, tel. 05–53–53–31–56) rents bikes (80F per day) that can be used for the 40-km (25-mi) ride to Brantôme.

GETTING AROUND

The infrequent **Péribuses** (pl. Montaigne, tel. 05–53–53–30–37) around town aren't much faster than your feet, but one ticket (7F) is good for an hour. The A and C lines stop at the train station on their way to the centre ville every half hour. The main part of town stretches east of cours Montaigne to the Isle River, bordered roughly by place Francheville on one side and cours Tourny on the other.

WHERE TO SLEEP

If you want to be by the train station, try the **Hôtel des Charentes** (16 rue Denis Papin, tel./fax 05–53–53–37–13), across the street. The classy doubles with shower go for 195F–250F. It's closed the last two weeks of December. On the border of the quaint and well-preserved center of town, the **Hôtel l'Univers** (18 cours Montaigne, tel. 05–53–53–34–79, fax 05–53–06–70–76) has modern, comfortable rooms (150F with sink, 250F with shower), a five-minute walk from the cafés and the picturesque cobblestone byways.

HOSTEL • The Foyer des Jeunes Travailleurs is a friendly place with bunk beds (four people per room) for 71F (per person) including breakfast and sheets. Mediocre cafeteria dinners are 30F. *Blvd. Lakanal, tel. 05–53–53–52–05, fax 05–53–54–37–46. From the tourist office on pl. Francheville it is a 10-min walk, 3 blocks to blvd. Lakanal, turn right. Follow blvd. Lakanal 5 blocks to the end, then enter the parking lot of Club Lakanal on the right and walk 50 yards to the little white gate in front of the residence. 180 beds. Reception 9 AM–noon and 4–8 PM.*

FOOD

In the train station area, go for the 50F menu at **Chez Pierrot** (78 rue Chanzy, tel. 05–53–53–43–22), where you'll get the works (soup, melon, a huge entrée, dessert, and all the wine you can drink) in the company of locals. In the vieille ville you won't be disappointed at cheery **Pain Malin** (10 rue St-Silain, tel. 05–53–09–87–18), where refreshing gourmet salads are 40F. The diverse three-course menu also highlights regional specialties such as foie gras and crème brûlée for 60F at lunch and 80F at dinner. It's closed Sunday night and Monday. More upscale, and a bit snooty, is **Restaurant le 8** (8 rue de la Clarté, tel. 05–53–35–15–15) near the cathedral. Reservations are essential if you want to partake of the fresh, four-course menus (160F–280F) featuring regional specialties like foie gras and duck. If you just want to pick up the makings for a picnic, place du Coderc is the scene of a daily outdoor **market,** and rue Wilson is where you'll find a **Monoprix** supermarket.

WORTH SEEING

The crumbling, ivy-covered, 1st-century **Arènes Romaines** (blvd. des Arènes) made it through 1,500 years of war but couldn't survive being used as a quarry—its small, brick-size stones were just right for building the houses you see in the city, and the ancient amphitheater is now a lovely shaded park. From here you can follow the well-marked tourist circuit past numerous ruins, including the medieval **Château Barrière** (rue Turenne) and the cracked **Tour de Vésone** (rue du Prof. Peyrot), part of a Gallo-Roman temple. Its missing side is reputed to have crumbled when St. Front cursed the last demons of paganism but is more likely the work of citizens who needed the stones to build a defensive wall.

Back in town, start your tour of the vieille ville near the tourist office at the **Tour Mataguerre,** the last of 28 towers that once encircled the city, and continue on the cobblestone streets to **Cathédrale St-Front** (open daily 8–12:30 and 2:30–7:30) with its unique pinecone-shape cupolas. If certain parts of the cathedral evoke Paris's Sacré-Coeur, it's because 19th-century French architect Paul Abadie restored the former before drawing plans for the latter. On your journey, traverse the centre ville's cobblestone pedestrian streets, lined with cafés and small shops. The overlap of diverse architectural styles and uses over the centuries has led to many creative adaptations. For a quiet stroll by the waterside on the outskirts of the city, follow boulevard Lakanal to the end and then cross under the train bridge.

The best way to spend your time indoors in Périgueux is in the **Musée du Périgord,** where there's a fascinating collection of indigenous materials from Europe, Oceania, Micronesia, Southeast Asia, and the Americas. The exhibits are well presented and mix in a healthy dose of Flemish paintings, Egyptology, and Limousin enamel. Ask for the English text to guide you around. *22 cours Tourny, tel. 05–53–53–16–42. Admission 20F. Open Wed.–Mon. 10–noon and 2–5.*

NEAR PERIGUEUX

BRANTOME

This tiny village—only 25 km (16 mi) north of Périgueux and accessible by Trans-Périgord bus (27F)—likes to think of itself as the "Venice of Périgord." Though it's built on an island in a bend of the Dronne River and has waterfront houses with colorful flowers and boats tooling around, you won't find it anything like its brooding big sister. It's just a beautiful, relaxed little village that makes a great day trip. While you're here, check out the **Abbaye Benedictine** (tel. 05–53–05–80–63) bell tower and caves, and a great view of the countryside, and then chill in the park.

WHERE TO SLEEP • The old-fashioned **Hôtel de la Poste** (33 rue Gambetta, tel. 05–53–05–78–55) has spacious singles and doubles for 120F–140F. Though the leaning staircase looks as if it has seen a lot of use, the rooms are spacious and comfortable enough. For a real splurge, head to the **Château de Vieux Mareuil** (rte. d'Angoulême, 15 km/9 mi north of town, tel. 05–53–60–77–15), where you can sleep in two types of rooms: spacious doubles for 550F furnished in contemporary style or breathtaking rooms in the tower for 700F with 18th- and 19th-century decor. It's closed January–mid-March. The expansive **camping municipal** (rte. de Thiviers, tel. 05–53–05–75–24), 2 km (½ mi) outside town, is open May–September and has peaceful riverside sites for 13F plus 13F per person.

FOOD • Start off the day with fresh-baked raisin-nut bread from the **boulangerie** (bakery) off place du Marché. For a snack in a cool cave, try **L'Arlequin** (18–20 blvd. Coligny, tel. 05–53–35–27–03), where 15F–40F crepes, salads, omelets, and ice cream are served until midnight in summer. Partake of regional specialties from the four-course menus starting at 85F at the **Relais du Périgord** (pl. du Marché, tel. 05–53–05–80–49).

LES EYZIES-DE-TAYAC

Between Périgueux and Sarlat, Les Eyzies sits comfortably under a limestone cliff. This 2-km (1-mi) strip of cafés, hotels, and tourist traps is the doorway to the prehistoric capital of France. A number of fascinating, excavated caves and grottoes, some with wall paintings, are open for public viewing. Before you go to the caves, check out the primitive sculptures, furniture, and tools in the **Musée National de Préhistoire** (tel. 05–53–06–45–45), on top of the cliffs. Admission is 25F, and it's open Tuesday–Sunday, mid-March–mid-November 9:30–nooon and 2–6 (July and August 9:30–7), and mid-November–mid-March, 9:30–noon and 2–5. Just 1 km (½ mi) from the town center is the region's most important cave, **Font de Gaume.** Forty-five-minute tours (in French) of a short stretch of the cave illustrate faint, but still recognizable, polychrome paintings. Reserve a couple of days in advance or sign up for a tour as early in the morning as possible. Near Font de Gaume are the impressive prehistoric carvings in the **Grotte des Combarelles.** Only six people can take the tour of the grotto at one time, so you'll get an intimate look at the carvings. A limited number of tickets are sold each day for the 45-minute tours; call in advance to reserve. *Tel. 05–53–06–90–80. Admission to each cave 35F. Open Apr.–Sept., Wed.–Mon. 9–noon and 2–6; Nov.–Feb., Wed.–Mon. 10–noon and 2–4; Mar. and Oct., Wed.–Mon. 9:30–noon and 2–5:30. Hours apply to both caves but Font de Gaume closed Tues., Combarelles Wed.*

BASICS

The **tourist office** has the lowdown on all the caves and museums in the area. If you were not able to call ahead for tickets, it is worth stopping by the cave of your choice even if the office says tickets are sold out—space often opens up. The office exchanges money with no commission and rent bikes for 40F per day and 240F per week at the tourist office. *Pl. Marie, tel. 05–53–06–97–05, fax 05–53–06–90–79. Open July–Aug., daily 9–7; mid-Mar.–June and Sept.–Oct., Mon.–Sat. 9–noon and 2–6; Nov.–mid-Mar., weekdays 10–noon and 2–5.*

COMING AND GOING

The **train station** is a few minutes' walk from the center of town and welcomes trains from Périgueux (30 mins, 41F), Sarlat (1 hr, 45F, change at Le Buisson), and Paris (6 hrs, 275F, via Limoges). By car, Périgueux is 45 km (25 mi) northwest via D47, D710, and N2089.

WHERE TO SLEEP

Le Centenaire (rocher de la Pennetel, tel. 05–53–06–68–68, fax 05–53–06–92–41) is a stylish, modern, and expensive (doubles 450F–900F) hotel that is known first and foremost for its restaurant, which is considered to be one of the best in the region. Gazpacho, risotto with truffles, and snails with ravioli are some noteworthy dishes. Four-course menus start at 295F. A jacket is required for this one. It's closed November–March and Tuesday lunch. A cheaper option is the **Hôtel de France** (rue du Moulin, tel. 05–53–06–97–23, fax 05–53–06–90–97), situated at the foot of the cliff, with doubles with shower from 205F to 330F. The inn also serves traditional meals starting at 70F; try the sliced duck with morels. Breakfast and dinner (required August 1–20) costs 320F. It's closed November to March.

There are tons of camping options in the area, from nicer sites to camping *à la ferme* (on a farm). The most convenient campground is **La Rivière** (rte. de Périgueux, tel. 05–53–06–97–14, fax 05–53–35–20–83), with sites for 31F plus 22F per person; it's closed October–March. Across the river from the train station, this campsite also has rooms for rent (doubles 180F), a laundromat, restaurant, pool, and bike and canoe rental. Another option is the marvelous cliff-carved *gîte d'étape* (rural hostel; rte. de St-Cirq, tel. 05–53–06–94–73) in **Les Eymaries,** 3 km (2 mi) out of town. It has hot showers and kitchen facilities, charges 40F per night, and is open April–October. To reach the gîte, follow the route de Périgueux out of Les Eyzies, cross the Vézère River, then look for the route de St-Cirq on your left.

FOOD

Les Eyzies lends itself to picnics. Otherwise, there are a handful of nothing-special restaurants lining the main drag that cater to those passing through. The exception is **Le Centenaire** (*see above*). If you miss the Monday market (held June–September), stop by the **Halle Paysanne des Eyzies** (rte. de Sarlat) for free tastes of regional specialties. Or pick up items at the small store just north of the tourist office on route D47, the only road through town.

OUTDOOR ACTIVITIES

One of the best ways to appreciate the area is from the Vézère River, which curves and winds down through the cliffs of the valley. Several companies, including **Jean Rivière Loisirs** (tel. 05–53–63–38–73), rent canoes (70F) and kayaks (100F) by the day and will take you upstream by car to let you off. They're all on the banks by the bridge on the Vézère. You can also rent canoes from **F.F.C.K.** on the route de Périgueux (tel. 05–53–29–64–44) for 70F a day (50F for 2½ hours); they'll come pick you up. Bikes, available at the tourist office (*see above*), are a fun way to get around, too.

SARLAT

Tucked among hills adorned in golden corn and wheat, Sarlat is a beautiful, well-preserved medieval city that attracts a lot of visitors but manages to retain something of its true character. Off the main pedestrian artery, **rue de la République** takes you through partially intact ramparts and narrow cobblestone alleys below golden brick houses with Renaissance-style, wood-beamed windows. Sarlat's most prominent sight is its 17th-century **Cathédrale St-Sacerdos,** but the more interesting sights lie around it. On the hill behind the cathedral, the 12th-century **Lanterne des Morts** served as a cemetery tower, then a chapel, a whorehouse, and finally a gunpowder reserve following the French Revolution. Michel de Montaigne's friend Étienne de La Boétie was once the proud owner of the **Maison de la Boétie** (on pl. de Peyrou), whose medieval facade is topped by more Renaissance windows and then 20th-century dormers. Opposite the central Hôtel Plamon, the **Ste-Marie Fountain** was the main water supply for the area from its initial origin. Sarlat began as a Benedictine abbey in the 9th century and endured the Black Plague (14th century), famine (15th century), and the whooping cough epidemic (16th century). While here, stop in at one of the thousand and one **foie gras** shops. Sarlat is a great base for excursions to the medieval remains of **Castelnaud,** the pretty countryside around **La Roque-Gageac,** and canoe trips along the Dordogne. Since sights are close together throughout this area and often inaccessible by public transportation, this is your chance to get on that bike and pedal up and down the hills rolling to the Dordogne 4 km (2½ mi) away. Rent one at **Cyclocuns** (8 av. Gambetta, 05–53–31–28–40).

BASICS

The **tourist office,** in the medieval Hôtel Maleville, is a paper-filled cubbyhole off place de la Liberté with a hurried but helpful staff. You can get a list of all the campsites along the river as well as information on canoeing and biking excursions, prehistoric caves, and the ruins and châteaux that dot the surrounding hillsides. *Pl. de la Liberté, tel. 05–53–59–27–67, fax 05–53–59–19–44. From rue de la République, turn right onto rue Victor Hugo to pl. de la Liberté. Open Mon.–Sat. 9–noon and 2–6; also open Sun. 10–noon and 4–6 July–Aug.*

COMING AND GOING

Direct trains from Bordeaux (2½ hrs, 115F) arrive five times a day at Sarlat's **station.** The train station (**SNCF,** tel. 05–53–59–00–21) is a 1½-km (1-mi) walk out of the centre ville and 2½ km (1½ mi) from the hostel. There is a free shuttle bus from the station to the town center. For trains to Les Eyzies (1 hr, 45F) and Périgueux (1½ hrs, 73F) you'll need to change at Le Buisson. **SNCF buses** also run to Sarlat about five times daily from the Souillac train station (40 mins, 31F); the last bus leaves around 10:30 PM and train passes are accepted. If you're taking the bus into Sarlat, *don't* get off at the Sarlat train station. Instead get off at place Pasteur, the next and final stop, and walk straight past the post office onto rue de la République. Pick up a copy of the *Guide Pratique* from the tourist office for the scoop on buses and trains to Souillac, Les Eyzies, Brive, Périgueux, and Bordeaux. The Sarlat–Périgueux bus line includes the stop at Montignac for the Lascaux II caves (*see* Near Sarlat, *below*). If you don't mind hills, biking to nearby destinations like the Dordogne (4 km/2½ mi) or Les Eyzies-de-Tayac (20 km/12 mi northwest via the picturesque and relatively quiet D6 and D47 roads) can be a blast. **Cycles Cumenal** (8 av. Gambetta, tel. 05–53–31–28–40) and **Sarlat Sport Gouloumes** (tel. 05–53–59–33–41) rent bikes for 90F a day or 50F per half day.

WHERE TO SLEEP

Be sure to reserve ahead in summer: Cheap hotels in Sarlat are nonexistent, and the hostel is often full, especially July–mid-August. The tourist office has a list of several chambres d'hôte in town with doubles for about 200F a night. The **Hôtel Marcel** (50 av. de Selves, tel. 05–53–59–21–98, fax 05–53–30–27–77) has 12 double rooms, all with bath, for 220F–290F and enough potted plants to start a nursery. It's closed mid-November–mid-February. The excellent restaurant downstairs has an 80F dinner menu. The **Hôtel des Récollets** (4 rue Jean-Jacques Rousseau, tel. 05–31–36–00, fax 05–53–30–32–62), superbly located on a narrow path on the quiet side of the vieille ville, has immaculate modern doubles are 200F–450F and a good 32F breakfast.

Come October, when cèpe (mushroom) harvesting begins, many restaurants will leave baskets of the fungi out front so that you can select the ones that will go with your meal.

HOSTEL • Auberge de Jeunesse. A well-equipped kitchen and outdoor patio make this rustic 40-bed hostel a congenial place to stay, once you've made the 2½-km (1½-mi) hike from the train station. Beds are 40F a night, and the hostel's small backyard fits about seven tents at 24F per person. It is essential to book in advance. One block away, the **Laverie de Selves** is a convenient place to do laundry (for about 24F) before line-drying it on the clothesline at the hostel. People traveling alone should be aware that this hostel is sometimes left unlocked throughout the night, which can be scary in the empty off-season. An HI card is required. *77 av. de Selves, tel. 05–53–59–47–59, fax 05–53–30–21–27. From rue de la République, walk 10 mins to av. Gambetta, then veer left onto av. de Selves. 30 beds. Reception open daily 6 PM–11 PM. Lockout 10 AM–6 PM. Kitchen. Closed Dec.–mid-Mar.*

FOOD

Despite Sarlat's abundance of restaurants and promises of authentic regional specialties, the budget dining scene is disappointing. That said, **Le Commerce** (4 rue Albéric Cahuet, tel. 05–53–59–04–26) has some of the cheapest menus in town (60F, 70F, and 80F) and dishes up a saucy cassoulet (a pork and bean stew) and other regional specialties in a large courtyard. On a sloping pedestrian alley in the medieval heart of Sarlat, **Restaurant Gueule et Gosier** (rue de la Salamandre, tel. 05–53–59–24–96) has three-course (70F) and four-course (80F) menus. Treat yourself to great atmosphere and specialties such as *pommes sarladaises* (a fabulous potato concoction) and the local favorite, walnut cake. A wonderful **outdoor market** fills the town center Wednesday and Saturday morning. **Intermarché,** 984 ft past the hostel on avenue de Selves, is open on Monday when everything else shuts down.

NEAR SARLAT

Pick up *Sarlat and the Black Périgord* from the Sarlat tourist office for more information on the caves, châteaux, and hiking routes of the region. One popular way to see the Dordogne's landscape is by canoe or kayak. Rental depots spring up frequently along the river, especially near campsites; one-person boats go for about 40F an hour or 80F per day, about twice that for two-person boats. Also inquire about longer trips. For more information, pick up a brochure at any tourist office in the region.

CHATEAUX AND MEDIEVAL VILLAGES

Unlike the Loire Valley, where attractions are far apart, the Dordogne offers a château practically every mile. From Sarlat, drive or bike 10 km (6 mi) south along D46 to the cliff-top *bastide* (fortified village) of **Domme.** The center of Domme is small and can become crowded, but if you climb up to the ramparts and along the cliff, you'll see a panoramic view of the valley that will remind you why you came. The **Nouvel Hotel** (pl. de la Halle, tel. 05–53–28–38–67, fax 05–53–28–27–13) has 17 rooms, all with shower 200F–290F. The hotel restaurant serves set meals for 70F–240F. It's closed November to mid-April. Since Domme *is,* after all, famous for its prehistoric caves, you may also want to visit the 500-yard-long illuminated galleries, lined with stalagmites and stalactites. *Pl. de la Halle. Admission 28F. Open Apr.–Sept., daily 9:30–noon and 2–6; Mar. and Oct., daily 2–6.*

Four-and-a-half kilometers (3 mi) farther west along the river, on D703, is **La Roque-Gageac,** a tiny, strikingly attractive village built into the side of a rocky mountain. Once you leave the main road and climb one of the steep cobblestone paths, you can check out the medieval houses on their natural perches and even hike up the mountain for a view down onto the village. Six kilometers (4 mi) farther west on D703 and D57 is the **Château de Castelnaud** (tel. 05–53–29–57–08), whose mountaintop setting is its most alluring feature, since the structure is hardly more than a facade: Only six rooms remain of this medieval castle, which constantly changed hands between the English and French during the Hundred Years' War. The 45-minute visit (in French) focuses on warfare in the Middle Ages. It's open July–August, 9 AM–8 PM, and September–June, 9 AM–7 PM. Admission is 30F.

To extend your exploration, continue 5 km (3 mi) past Castelnaud along D53; hikers take the 4-km (2½-mi) stretch along GR64. Both will take you to the small **Château des Milandes** (tel. 05–53–07–16–38), a break from the austere fortresslike style of its neighbors. Built around 1489 in Renaissance style, it has a lovely terrace and gardens and was the former home of the great Folies Bergères diva, Josephine Baker, who owned it between 1936 and 1969. It's open daily 9–7 June–August; and 10–6 September–October and March–May. Or, from Castelnaud, cross the river and continue westward 3 km (2 mi) to the wonderfully restored village of **Beynac,** crowned with its own massive **château** (tel. 05–53–29–50–40). The ascent to the château not only gives you a grand tour of the village but also superb views of the river. *Admission to each of the châteaux 30F–35F. Open daily 10–noon and 2–5:30.*

LASCAUX II

The undulating horses, cow, black bulls, and unicorn on the walls of the Lascaux caves are between 15,000 and 20,000 years old, making them some of the world's oldest known paintings. Unfortunately, the original Lascaux caves—accidentally discovered by some local kids in 1940—have been closed to the public since 1963 because carbon dioxide from myriad visitors' breath was damaging the paintings. Today, only five archaeologists per day are permitted to enter. In recompense, the French authorities have built Lascaux II, a formidable feat. They spent 12 years perfecting the facsimile, duplicating two of Lascaux's main caves so accurately that the copy is as awe-inspiring as the original. Unlike caves marked with authentic prehistoric art, Lascaux II is completely geared toward visitors: You can watch a fancy presentation detailing what cave art reveals about prehistoric life and culture, or take a 50-minute tour in the language of your choice.

Reaching Lascaux II is a major production without a car. If you're driving, from Sarlat, head to Montignac, 26 km (16 mi) north on route D704; Lascaux II is 1 km (½ mi) south of Montignac on route D704. If you're taking public transportation, get yourself to **Montignac** by bus from Sarlat or from Condat-le-Lardin (on the Bordeaux–Périgueux–Brive line), the nearest town with a train station. Sarlat has a 7 AM bus Monday–Saturday and another one at 9 AM on weekdays, both of which leave from place de la Petite Rigandie. In Montignac, buy tickets for Lascaux II next to the tourist office on place Bertran-de-Born. Be forewarned: You might get signed onto a tour that starts a couple hours hence, leaving you with time to kill. If so, have lunch, or (on the same ticket) visit **Le Thot,** an animal park 7 km (4½ mi) southwest that also shows a film on how Lascaux II was made. *Lascaux II: tel. 05–53–53–44–35. Admission 50F. Open Feb.–June and Sept.–Dec., Tues.–Sun. 10–noon and 2–5:30; July–Aug., Tues.–Sun. 9:30–7. Closed Jan.*

THE LOT

Less touristy and populated than the neighboring Dordogne, the Lot has a subtler charm. The cluster of towns along the Lot River and the smaller rivers that cut through the dry, vineyard-covered plateau have a magical, abandoned feel. Just an hour north of Toulouse by train is **Cahors,** the area's largest town and its information center. Cahors makes a fine base for exploring the Lot River valley, a 50-km (31-mi) gorge punctuated by barely inhabited medieval villages. The 24,000-year-old cave paintings at the **Grotte du Pech-Merle** are astounding, and the narrow **Célé valley,** with its flat roads, is great for cycling. North of Cahors, the dramatic medieval village of **Rocamadour** is a literal cliffhanger, and its famous Madonna is the region's main attraction. Nearby is the highly commercialized but stunning **Gouffre de Padirac** (Padirac Abyss). Just northwest is the small town of **Souillac,** a good starting point for trips into the lush neighboring Dordogne and worth visiting if only for its 12th-century church of Ste-Marie, which boasts a stupendous medieval carving of a writhing mass of creatures from Hell. The Lot's old windmills, farmhouses, and misty river gorges are best experienced on foot or by bike in spring or fall.

Frequent trains connect Souillac and Cahors; both of these towns are on the Paris–Toulouse line; for Rocamadour and Padirac you'll need to change at Brive farther north. Bus service is limited. Biking is one of the most popular ways to see the region, even though there are lots of steep hills, especially around Rocamadour and on the route south to Cahors. The excellent biking guide *Cyclotourisme dans Le Lot* (50F) is available in any local tourist office. The GR46 spans the interior of the Lot region, with breathtaking views of the limestone plateaus and quiet valleys between Rocamadour and St-Cirq-Lapopie.

One of the best reasons to visit Cahors is the annual Le Printemps de Cahors photo exhibition, usually held in mid-May. Past years have featured the work of Helmut Newton, Herb Ritts, and Joel Peter Witkin.

CAHORS

The largest city in the Lot River valley and midpoint on the Toulouse–Brive rail line, Cahors is the urban launching point for getaways to the countryside. The town is best known for its robust red wine, vin de Cahors—be sure to sample this deep, dark pleasure while you are here. Modern Cahors encircles its *ville antique* (old town), which dates from 1 BC. At the center of the old district, on the southeastern end of town, is the **Cathédrale St-Étienne** (pl. St-Étienne), built in the beginning of the 11th century and given a new facade in the 14th century. On the western side of town, the **Pont Valentré's** tall, elegant towers have spanned the Lot since 1360. The amazing Grotte du Pech-Merle and quaint town of St-Cirq-Lapopie (*see below*) are but a good biking day trip, short drive, or bus excursion away.

BASICS

The **tourist office** sells all kinds of booklets and maps and has plenty of free pamphlets on biking, hiking, and canoeing in the surrounding countryside. Pick up a copy of "Les Bus du Lot" for a complete rundown of regional bus service. *Pl. François Mitterrand, tel. 05–65–35–09–65, fax 05–65–53–20–74. Open Apr.–Sept., weekdays 10–noon and 2–7, Sat. 10–noon and 2–6, Sun. 10–noon and 3–5; Oct.–Mar., Mon.–Sat. 10–noon and 2–6.*

COMING AND GOING

Getting to Cahors is a snap—it's due north of Toulouse (1¼ hrs, 88F) and south of Souillac (50 mins, 58F) on the direct train line from Paris's Gare d'Austerlitz (6 hrs, 311F). It's also well connected by bus to Figeac, Rodez, Brive, and Bordeaux (3 hrs, 171F via Montauban). SNCF and privately operated buses leave from the **train station** (pl. Jouinot Gambetta, tel. 05–65–22–50–50). Boulevard Gambetta, the main commercial strip that leads to the tourist office and vieille ville, is a 10-minute walk from here: Walk up rue Joachim Murat (the street in front of the station) and turn right on boulevard Léon Gambetta. Rocamadour is 56 km (35 mi) north via N20. For fun exploration of the Lot Valley to the east, **Cycles 7** (417 quai de Regourd, tel. 05–65–22–66–60), by the river in the vieille ville, rents *VTTs* (mountain bikes) for 120F per day with a passport deposit.

WHERE TO SLEEP

Cahors has plenty of lodging options. **Hôtel de la Paix** (30 pl. St-Maurice, tel. 05–65–35–03–40), closed December–January, in the center of the vieille ville and market action, has basic doubles with bath for 170F. **Terminus** (5 av. Charles-de-Freycinet, tel. 05–65–35–24–50, fax 05–65–22–06–40), a more expensive option, is a quaint, ivy-covered hotel just a two-minute walk from the train station. Doubles start at 500F. The adjoining restaurant **La Balandre,** with Roaring '20s decor, is the spot's claim to high fame. Menus (125F–250F) showcase truffles in particular. It's closed Sunday and early June.

HOSTELS • **Foyer de Jeunes en Quercy.** Behind a bland facade is this charming hostel, which houses young workers throughout the year and travelers of all ages in summer. With a cozy living room, peaceful garden, and well-kept private rooms, it's the best place in town. For 58F you get a bed in a single, double, or triple, depending on availability. Breakfast (10F), lunch (35F), and dinner (31F) are all served. Call in advance and make reservations. *129 rue Fondue-Haute, tel. 05–65–35–29–32. From station, follow rue Joachim Murat into town, cross blvd. Gambetta, turn left on rue Fondue-Haute. 30 rooms. Reception open daily 8 AM–10:30 PM.*

Foyer des Jeunes Travailleurs. The bubbly atmosphere of this wood-and-iron complex near the town center makes up for the noisy rooms and the mushy beds. Year-round, you can stay in the 4- to 10-bed dorms; in summer, singles and doubles are often available. Beds are 47F with an HI card, 51F without. Sheets are 16F. Breakfast (18F) and dinner (45F) are served in the huge dining hall. There's no lockout. *20 rue Frédéric Suisse, tel. 05–65–35–64–71, fax 05–65–35–95–92. From train station, turn right onto rue Anatole France, left on rue Frédéric Suisse. 30 beds. Reception open weekdays 9–11:30 and 2–7, Sat. 10–11:30 and 6–10, Sun. 5–10.*

CAMPING • **Camping Municipal.** This place is just across the bridge at the south end of town on the extension of boulevard Gambetta. Sites running along the river's edge are assaulted with almost unbearable street noise and yet are still in great demand in July and August. You'll pay 14F plus 13F per camper for a site. *Chemin de la Chartreuse, tel. 05–65–35–04–64, fax 05–65–22–28–22. Closed Nov.–May.*

FOOD

Cahors is great for picnics, with lots of markets and riverside plateaus. The **covered market** near the cathedral on place Galdemar is open Tuesday–Saturday 7:30–12:30 and 3–7, Sunday 9–noon. Inside you can get great pizzas to go for 38F–50F. A lively **outdoor market** fills the space between the cathedral and the indoor market every Wednesday and Saturday until about noon. A **Prisunic** supermarket is next to the Théâtre Municipal, adjacent to place Aristide Briand.

Tucked in the alley next to Hôtel de France on place Maurice is **Le Troquet des Halles** (rue St-Maurice, tel. 05–65–22–15–81), where the 55F menu gives you a full home-cooked meal in a cheery setting. For good, affordable vegetarian food (lunch only), head over to **Restaurant Marie-Colline** (173 rue Clemenceau, tel. 05–65–35–59–96), where the plat du jour is 38F; it's closed in August. **Le Coq et la Pendule** (10 rue St-James) is a small, bustling café-restaurant on a pedestrian street near the cathedral, serving homey French cooking.

NEAR CAHORS

ST-CIRQ-LAPOPIE

Perched on the edge of a cliff, this well-preserved 13th-century village looks as though it could slide right into the Lot River. Traversing steep paths and alleyways among flower-filled balconies, you'll realize it deserves its popular description as one of the most beautiful villages in France. Residents actually outnumber tourists, and the view of the Lot Valley is sublime. Morning hikes in the misty gorges of the valley are beyond beautiful (pick up a guide from the tourist office in Cahors); and the Lot's faster-flowing tributary, the Célé, is perfect for kayaking past the countryside. Camping de la Plage (*see below*) leads 120F kayak day trips. In the center of the village, the **tourist office** (tel. 05–65–31–29–06) is open daily 10–7, with lunch break noon–2.

COMING AND GOING • The easiest way to reach St-Cirq-Lapopie from Cahors's train station is to take the **SNCF bus** bound for Figeac (40 mins, 28F); St-Cirq is a 25-minute walk from where the bus drops you off: From the bus stop Tour de Faure, go back to the D181 (sign says ST-CIRC-LAPOPIE 2 KM), cross the bridge, and walk uphill. The train tracks along the river unfortunately only carry the **Quercyrail** tourist train (tel. 05–65–35–09–56), a real gimmick that does full tours of the valley for 100F per person (rail passes are not accepted). By car or bike from Cahors, take D653, direction Figeac; after 8 km (5 mi) turn right on D662 and continue along the Lot River until a sign directs you over a narrow, one-lane bridge.

WHERE TO SLEEP AND EAT • For information on the half dozen hotels in town or the several quaint hotels a 10-minute drive away in the Célé Valley, inquire at the St-Cirq tourist office. The riverside **Camping de la Plage** (porte Roque, on the D42, tel. 05–65–30–29–51) is a steep, 10-minute descent from the center of town and has tent sites for 30F per person. **Camping La Truffière** (rte. de Concots, tel. 05–65–30–20–22) has sites for 28F per person and is 3 km (2 mi) up the hill away from the village. St-Cirq-Lapopie is a one-boulangerie town and the few restaurants are overpriced. **Bar Lapopie** (tel. 05–65–30–27–44), just off the main road, has decent sandwiches and salads (14F–20F) and overlooks the valley below from the outdoor terrace. Cozy restaurant **L'Atelier** (tel. 05–65–31–22–34), on your left as you are coming up the hill to town, serves a yummy salad with melted chèvre toasts (60F) and other typically French dishes, on a shady terrace.

GROTTE DU PECH-MERLE

Discovered in 1922, the Grotte du Pech-Merle displays 4,000 ft of prehistoric drawings and carvings. Particularly known for its peculiar polka-dot horses, impressions of the human hand, and footprints, this is the most impressive "real-thing" prehistoric cave that is open to the public in France. The admission charge includes a film, an hour-long tour, and a visit to the adjacent museum. Tel. 05–65–31–27–05. Admission 42F. Open daily 9:30–noon and 1:30–5:30. Closed Nov.–Mar. 24.

The hour-long bike ride between Rocamadour and the Gouffre de Padirac might just be one of your most memorable experiences in France.

COMING AND GOING • The Grotte du Pech-Merle is about 35 km (22 mi) from Cahors, and north of St-Cirq-Lapopie, 3 km (2 mi) from the town of **Cabrerets.** You could turn a visit here into a great biking day, or take the **SNCF bus** toward Figeac from Cahors, get off at Conduché (before St-Cirq-Lapopie), and walk the 7 km (4½ mi) along D41. Then again, you could always drive. From Cahors take D653 (7 km/4½ mi) to the left turn for the Celé Valley.

ROCAMADOUR

Billed as the "second most popular site in France" (Mont-St-Michel is the first), the medieval village of Rocamadour hangs dramatically on the edge of a cliff, 1,700 ft above the Alzou River gorge. The town became famous in 1166 when chroniclers recorded the miraculous discovery of the well-preserved body of St. Amadour under **Chapelle Notre-Dame**'s threshold; pilgrims have been coming ever since. A very small number of people actually live in Rocamadour; what they think about the yearly influx of 1½ million tourists and pilgrims can only be guessed at and, judging from the numbers of tacky souvenir shops in the village, not too poorly. Pilgrims (many of whom climb the 216 steps to the village on their knees) show up in droves around August 15 (Assumption Day) and during the week of September 8 (the Virgin Mary's birthday).

The town is split into three levels joined by steep stairs. On the uppermost plateau stands the **château.** It's silly that they charge 10F just to walk on the château's ramparts when you can see nearly the same thing from the free walkways leading up to the château. Either way, the view of the gorge is awesome. Next to the château are some expensive restaurants, a high-price market, and a few hotels, known collectively as **L'Hospitalet.** On the middle level, attached to the cliff's edge, is **place St-Amadour,** with seven small chapels around it, and the Chapelle Notre-Dame, featuring a famous black statue of the Virgin. On Rocamadour's lowest level you'll find a single pedestrian street—clogged by a crush of tourists—worth a visit only if you need cash (from the tourist office) or a bite to eat.

Five kilometers (3 mi) south of this densely touristed cliff side are serene limestone plateaus and awe-inspiring valleys. Consult IGN series *verte* (green) maps, available in local bookstores, for the GR46 hiking route, which descends through the pleasant Vers Valley before reaching the Lot River, 50 km (30 mi) away.

BASICS

From the train station it's a 40-minute hike to the closest **tourist office** (tel. 05–65–33–62–80, fax 05–65–33–74–14), open April–September only, in L'Hospitalet. Rocamadour's main tourist office is in the 15th-century Hôtel de Ville (Town Hall; rue Piétonne, tel. 05–65–33–62–59), on the pedestrian street in the medieval village below. You can change money here, though at a bad rate plus a 25F commission.

Both offices have great booklets (35F–65F) on biking and hiking, along with free lists of gîtes d'étape and a good map of town. Ask for the free *Practical Guide to Rocamadour*. Main office: July–Aug., Mon.–Sat. 10–8; Sept.–June, Mon.–Sat. 10–noon and 2–6.

COMING AND GOING

By car, Sarlat is 70 km (43 mi) northeast, via Souillac. The Rocamadour–Padirac **train station** is open daily 10–1 and 2–7:30; trains connect directly with Toulouse (1½ hrs, 134F) and Brive (45 mins, 43F). From the station you can rent a bike (55F per day, 46F per half day) for the 15-minute, 5-km (3-mi) ride along the plateau's winding road to Rocamadour. **JO Taxi** (tel. 05–65–33–72–27) will take you to Rocamadour for 50F–60F one-way from the train station or 220F for the round-trip to the Gouffre de Padirac. When you arrive at the uppermost level of Rocamadour, L'Hospitalet, go right along the cliff to the château and take the stairs down from there. An elevator awaits the weary (25F, 30F round-trip), but taking the steps isn't that painful. Bus excursions go from Rocamadour to the Gouffre de Padirac in July and August (*see* Near Rocamadour, *below*).

WHERE TO SLEEP

If you want to stay overnight, reserve well in advance. Not a bargain, but on the main pedestrian street, **Hôtel du Globe** (rue Piétonne, tel. 05–65–33–67–73, fax 05–65–33–17–10) has clean doubles with shower and phone for 170F for one and 190F for two. On the Hospitalet plateau, **Hôtel le Panorama** (tel. 05–65–33–62–13, fax 05–56–33–68–26) has five simply furnished doubles with shower for 175F, and triples for 195F; it's closed November–January. **Hôtel-Restaurant le Lion d'Or** (Cité Médiévale, tel. 05–65–33–62–04, fax 05–65–33–72–54), in the center of Rocamadour, has double rooms for 180F–250F, and a restaurant that serves set meals from 58F. Next to the train station, the small **Hôtel des Voyageurs** (pl. de la Gare, tel. 05–65–33–63–19) has very basic doubles for 125F.

CAMPING • If you're hiking from Souillac along the GR6, stay in one of the area's two gîtes d'étape: **Moulin de Caoulet** (Gorges de l'Ouysse, tel. 05–65–37–97–75) has 16 places in a large tent for 10F a night, including use of a kitchen. **La Grelottière** (Lafage, tel. 05–65–33–67–16) has 15 spaces at 45F a night, plus 65F for meals. Both are several miles from Rocamadour. **Camping Chez Branche** (tel. 05–65–33–63–37) is 1 km (½ mi) from L'Hospitalet on D247. Warm showers and a quiet place to put your tent cost only 16F per person; it's closed November–May.

FOOD

The only real commercial street is **rue Piétonne.** It has everything from crepe stands to restaurants with 180F menus, a couple of boulangeries, a fruit and vegetable stand, and two *salons de thé* (tea shops) serving salads (30F–40F) and crepes (20F–30F). At the far end of rue Piétonne, **Chez Anne-Marie** (tel. 05–65–71–80–91) has a colorful interior as well as a cliff-side terrace. The 65F lunch menu includes salad, a choice of simple main dishes, and dessert.

NEAR ROCAMADOUR

SOUILLAC

Officially part of the Lot département, but near the banks of the Dordogne River, the little town of Souillac is a convenient stop on the Paris–Toulouse rail line. The town's lone attraction is its massive, domed, 12th-century **Église Abbatiale Ste-Marie** and its fabulous medieval carvings on the west door. Souillac doesn't swarm with tourists like nearby Sarlat, but the town's proximity to Rocamadour and the Gouffre de Padirac still make it a bustling transit point in summer. Great canoeing and biking opportunities are also good reasons to come.

BASICS • The **tourist office** is on the town's main road, a 15-minute walk from the train station. *Blvd. Louis-Jean Malvy, tel. 05–65–37–81–56, fax 05–65–32–66–34. Open July–Aug., Mon.–Sat. 9:30–12:30 and 2–7, Sun. 9:30–12:30; Sept.–June, Mon.–Sat. 10–noon and 2–6.*

COMING AND GOING • Souillac is on the Paris–Toulouse rail line. Toulouse is two hours to the south (127F), Brive 25 minutes north (38F). By car or bike, Sarlat is 40 km (25 mi) west and Rocamadour is a rigorous 20 km (12 mi) southeast. From the **train station** (pl. de la Gare, tel. 05–65–32–78–21), four or five buses a day go to Sarlat (50 mins, 28F). Bikes can be rented at the station for 60F half day, 75F full day. The town center is a good 15- to 20-minute walk from the station along avenue Jean-Jaurès.

WHERE TO SLEEP AND EAT • Souillac has peaceful riverside camping and a couple of reasonable hotels in the town center. The **Auberge du Puits** (5 pl. du Puits, tel. 05–65–37–80–32) has four small but sunny doubles for 130F each. Larger rooms with showers start at about 210F. Beside the Dordogne River, **Camping les Ondines** (rte. de Sarlat, tel. 05–65–37–86–44) is a 10-minute walk from the center of town and shady sites cost 16F per person. From the train station, take avenue Jean-Jaurès to avenue Martin Malvy at the turnaround, and then go right on rue de la Frégière to route de Sarlat. It's closed mid-October–mid-April. **Le Beffroi** (pl. St-Martin, tel. 05–65–37–80–33), around the corner from the tourist office, serves great salads (36F) on a cool patio.

OUTDOOR ACTIVITIES • For canoe and kayak rentals, head to the Camping les Ondines (*see* Where to Sleep, *above*). **Copeyre Canoës** (Parc de Loisirs de Quercyland, tel. 05–65–37–33–51) will drop you off upstream for a mellow day floating down the Dordogne in a canoe (80F) or kayak (110F). If you want to stay out longer, they provide tents and waterproof casings. Their pickup/drop-off bus covers a total of some 45 km (28 mi) along the river. Mountain bikes are also available for 80F a day.

GOUFFRE DE PADIRAC

About 17 km (11 mi) northeast of Rocamadour in the middle of rolling countryside, this gigantic hole in the ground is one of the region's primary attractions. Once you descend into the *gouffre* (abyss) by way of stairs, elevators, and steep narrow paths, you'll think you're on a different planet, or at least on a sci-fi movie set. Notice the sheer size of the abyss and all the stalagmites, after you've blocked out the nauseating commercialism tacked on to this natural site. The view straight up is also indescribable. The visit takes about 1½ hours and includes a boat ride on a river 360 ft below ground. You're not allowed to take pictures, but tour operators take them while you're in the boat and try to sell you copies of them (long live highway robbery). Bring a raincoat—one of the chambers is very accurately named the **Lac de la Pluie** (Lake of Rain). *Tel. 05–65–33–64–56. Admission 43F. Open Apr.–June and Sept.–mid-Oct., daily 9–noon and 2–6; July, daily 8:30–noon and 2–6:30; Aug., daily 8–7.*

COMING AND GOING • If you are fortunate enough to have a car, the Gouffre de Padirac is a 16-km (10-mi) jaunt from Rocamadour along D673, with a left onto D90 for the last 3 km (2 mi). There is no public transportation to the Gouffre. Without four wheels the best route is from Rocamadour's train station (*see* Coming and Going, *above*) by two wheels (it's about an hour by bike). Get a full-day rental and don't worry—the incline is not excruciating. There is also the expensive taxi ride option. **Quercy Correze** (tel. 05–65–38–71–90) runs a Thursday-morning excursion (80F) from Rocamadour in July and August; call for reservations. If you are too tired to pedal back to the hotels in Rocamadour, **Camping Lechenne** (tel. 05–65–33–65–54) in the town of Padirac is open May–September, with sites for two at 60F; in July and August count on 80F.

THE ATLANTIC COAST

UPDATED BY SOPHIE MACKENZIE SMITH

The area that borders the Atlantic Ocean between Bordeaux and Brittany—here lumped under the title Atlantic Coast—has been tossed around like a chip in a historical poker game. The Visigoths invaded the region in the 5th century, but the Franks took it back in 507. The Muslims gambled for it, but Charles Martel drew a better hand and stopped them in Poitiers in 732. The Vikings plundered it in the 9th century, Eleanor of Aquitaine gave it to Henry II (King of England) with some furniture as part of her dowry (1152), and France got it back after the Hundred Years' War. Exasperated, cartographers just drew a line around the general area, called it Poitou-Charentes and Vendée, and forgot about it—oblivious to history and hopeful that those in power would take up knitting. Today, you'll find that inland and coastal towns, though very diverse, share a moderate climate with ample rain and glorious sunshine.

The Atlantic Coast has a little of everything—oyster beds, beaches, port towns, museums, and beautiful islands in the Bay of Biscay. There are miles of sun-drenched beaches along the western edge of Poitou-Charentes, often overlooked by American tourists on their way to the patches of pebbly sand on the Riviera. However, countless French and English families who appreciate a peaceful retreat from the madness of the Côte d'Azur have adopted Poitou-Charentes as a favorite vacation spot, making prices steep in the summer. Inland toward Poitiers is a biker's and rower's paradise—the Marais Poitevin, often called "Green Venice" because of the hundreds of canals that crisscross its lush fields and hedgerows. And even when it rains, you'll find plenty to do, whether you head for Saintes's traditional cathedrals, Cognac's aromatic distilleries, or La Rochelle's museums.

BASICS

The Atlantic Coast lacks the slick tourist packages that you'll find in other French regions, but the tourist office in La Rochelle (*see below*), as well as La Rochelle's **Comité Départemental du Tourisme** (11 bis rue des Augustins, tel. 05–46–41–43–33), has brochures on the region.

COMING AND GOING

The coast and its interior are primarily summer destinations, and the limited transportation schedules off-season reflect this. The islands are definitely the trickiest transportation challenge; boats, buses, and ferries can get you there, but they aren't very convenient and can be quite expensive. The **Inter-îles** (tel. 05–46–09–87–27) ferries have a monopoly on most transport to the islands, with a few smaller outfits squeezing in where they can, especially during peak season (June–October). The bus companies **Cit-**

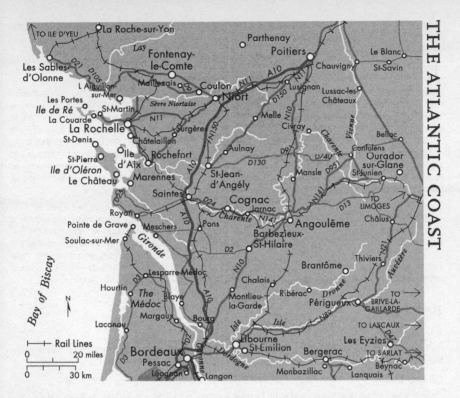

TO ILE D'YEU
La Roche-sur-Yon
Parthenay
Poitiers
Le Blanc
St-Savin
Chauvigny
Lay
Fontenay-le-Comte
Les Sables d'Olonne
L Aiguillon-sur-Mer
Maillezais
Coulon
Niort
Lusignan
Lussac-les-Châteaux
A10
N11
D150
Sèvre Niortaise
Les Portes
Ile de Ré
La Couarde
St-Martin
St-Denis
La Rochelle
Châtelaillon
Surgères
Melle
Civray
Bellac
St-Pierre
Ile d'Oléron
St-Denis
Ile d'Aix
Rochefort
Aulnay
Confolens
Ourador sur-Glane
St-Junien
Le Château
Marennes
St-Jean-d'Angély
Mansle
Saintes
Cognac
Jarnac
TO LIMOGES
Royan
Charente
Angoulême
Châlus
Pointe de Grave
Meschers
Pons
Barbezieux-St-Hilaire
Soulac-sur-Mer
Gironde
Brantôme
Thiviers
Lesparre-Médoc
Chalais
Ribérac
Dronne
TO BRIVE-LA-GAILLARDE
Hourtin
The Médoc
Blaye
Montlieu-la-Garde
Périgueux
Lacanau
Margaux
Bourg
Isle
Isle
TO LASCAUX
Libourne
St-Emilion
Les Eyzies
TO SARLAT
Bordeaux
Pessac
Bergerac
Beynac
Léognan
Langon
Monbazillac
Lanquais

Bay of Biscay

N

├─┼─ Rail Lines
0   20 miles
0   30 km

ram (tel. 05–46–50–53–57) and **Océcars** (tel. 05–46–99–23–65) do a good job serving coastal towns. Farther inland, Saintes, Cognac, Rochefort, and Angoulême are all frequently served by train.

POOR MAN'S RIVIERA

By some miracle of climate, the coastline stretch between Brittany and the Gironde estuary gets nearly as much sun as the Côte d'Azur. In fact, it's the poor traveler's Riviera: This is where you go if you're not chic enough, rich enough, or crazy enough to tackle the south in the middle of vacation season. Choose between the coastal resort towns, where the usual beach-and-boardwalk fare is spiced up with some ruins and museums, or several islands where facilities are a little more rustic. In high season, the area draws Germans and Brits but relatively few Americans.

Of the coastal towns, **La Rochelle** is the summer festival and cultural capital; snoozing **Rochefort** has little more than a handful of interesting museums; and **Les Sables d'Olonne** attracts a hard-partying, see-and-be-seen crowd to its boardwalk and windsurfing fans to its beach. Dotting the 100-km (62-mi) stretch of coast, the islands each have distinct personalities: **Aix** is cozy and rustic; **Ré** harbors fantastic beaches, salt marshes, and bird reserves; and **Oléron**'s sunseekers share the 70 km (43 mi) of sand with millions of oysters. Each island is accessible by ferry or bus from coastal ports that are, in turn, served by train or bus. Sounds simple enough, but just wait until you try to coordinate the two.

The islands can be quite breathtaking and serene in the rain, but if your idea of vacation necessarily includes sun, summer is the season to go. In the entire region, only La Rochelle has *anything* fun to do when the weather is bad, and in winter, tumultuous storms are not uncommon. A good time to visit is

June, before the crowds hit and prices go up. That said, a lot of places don't throw off their winter wraps before July. Reserve hotel rooms as far in advance as possible, especially in the summer.

LA ROCHELLE

During the Renaissance, La Rochelle was one of the best-fortified ports in France. The only entrance from the sea was between the heavily guarded towers, the Tour de la Chaîne and the Tour St-Nicolas; a chain was passed between them at night to bar enemy passage. When Cardinal Richelieu decided to attack the longtime Protestant stronghold in 1627, he devised a unique plan to destroy its defenses: He cut off all land routes to the city and built a massive jetty offshore to fend off the English, lest they try to come to La Rochelle's rescue. The town's inhabitants didn't pay much attention, thinking the jetty would surely break down under the waves. Sixteen months later, after 23,000 people had starved to death, the jetty did succumb to a storm, but the city had already capitulated a few weeks earlier. Richelieu had all the ramparts destroyed except for a small section that runs to the Tour de la Lanterne.

Today, La Rochelle is still one of the few Protestant towns in France; the **Musée** (2 rue St-Michel, tel. 05–46–50–88–03), next to a temple, provides a historical overview of French Protestantism; admission is 10F. Eighteenth-century stone houses line the **cours des Dames,** a spacious avenue that circles the historic harbor and its two 14th-century towers. Inland, a massive stone gate marks the entrance to the straight, narrow streets of the old town. The port's famous towers, historic houses, and museums draw visitors all year long, but summer is particularly crowded due to the city's proximity to the beaches of nearby **Ile de Ré** (*see below*) and the popular six-day **Francofolies** (*see* Festivals, *below*).

BASICS

BUREAUX DE CHANGE

Crédit Mutuel (2 rue Chaudrier, tel. 05–46–41–27–13) has an ATM machine that accepts Cirrus-system cards.

LAUNDRY

Cleanse your clothes of salt and sand at **Le Lavoire** for around 25F. *50 rue St-Jean de Pérot, tel. 05–46–41–27–17. Open daily 8 AM–8:30 PM.*

MAIL

The main **post office,** a block from the train station, holds poste restante for 15 days (postal code 17021) and changes U.S. dollars (av. de Mulhouse, tel. 05–46–51–25–00) The branch near the Hôtel de Ville (Town Hall), off rue Dupaty, has phone and fax services in addition to currency exchange. *Tel. 05–46–30–41–30. Open weekdays 8–7, Sat. 8–noon.*

MEDICAL AID

The **Centre Hospitalier** (rue du Docteur Schweitzer, tel. 05–46–45–50–50) takes care of emergencies day and night. For urgent pharmaceutical needs after 7:30 PM, call the **commissariat** (police station) at 05–46–51–36–36 for the names of pharmacists on call. Beware: Staffers rarely speak English.

VISITOR INFORMATION

The busy **tourist office** sells a comprehensive brochure (3F) about the town and makes hotel reservations for 10F. Pick up the free "Sortir à Tout Moment" for information on nightlife. The multilingual staff arranges tours of the city by foot (32F) or horse carriage (39F). *Pl. de la Petite-Sirène, tel. 05–46–41–14–68. Open June–Sept., Mon.–Sat. 9–7 (July and Aug. until 8), Sun. 10–5; Oct.–May, Mon.–Sat. 9–12:30 and 2–6, Sun. 10–noon.*

COMING AND GOING

BY TRAIN

La Rochelle is a major stop on the rail line between Nantes (2 hrs, 144F) and Bordeaux (2½ hrs, 132F); at least five trains pass through the station (pl. Pierre Semard, tel. 05–46–51–62–22, 08–36–35–35–35

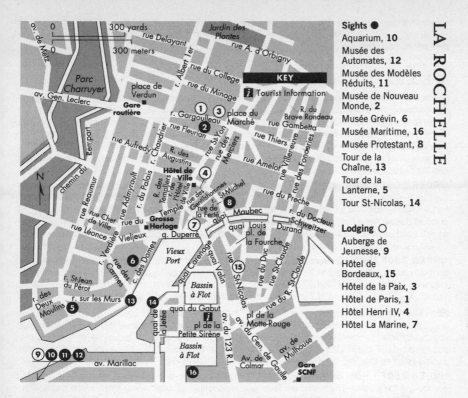

Sights ●

Aquarium, **10**

Musée des Automates, **12**

Musée des Modèles Réduits, **11**

Musée de Nouveau Monde, **2**

Musée Grévin, **6**

Musée Maritime, **16**

Musée Protestant, **8**

Tour de la Chaîne, **13**

Tour de la Lanterne, **5**

Tour St-Nicolas, **14**

Lodging ○

Auberge de Jeunesse, **9**

Hôtel de Bordeaux, **15**

Hôtel de la Paix, **3**

Hôtel de Paris, **1**

Hôtel Henri IV, **4**

Hôtel La Marine, **7**

reservations) each day. You can also come from Paris (5 hrs, 302F) via Poitiers (1½ hrs, 116F) three or four times daily, or from nearby Rochefort (25 mins, 30F) or Les Sables d'Olonne (3 hrs, 122F) via Roche-Sur-Yon. It's a five-minute walk to the center of town from the station: Follow avenue du Général de Gaulle past place de la Motte-Rouge to the harbor.

BY BUS

Océcars (pl. de Verdun, tel. 05–46–00–21–01) buses can whisk you to Rochefort (1¼ hr, 30F), the beach at Châtelaillon (25 mins, 8F), or Fouras (45 mins, 25F), the departure point for ferries to Ile d'Aix. The bus departs from the train station or the **bus station** (pl. de Verdun, tel. 05–46–34–02–22). Once in Rochefort, **Citram** (30 cours des Dames, tel. 05–46–50–53–57) buses continue to Ile d'Oléron (1 hr, 40F).

GETTING AROUND

To get to the hostel and campgrounds 20 minutes outside town in Les Minimes, take the green **Autoplus** bus (8F) from the place de Verdun. To get anywhere else you can pretty much walk. If you're lazy, the ecologically conscious Autoplus (tel. 05–46–34–02–22) buses, boats, bikes, scooters, and even electric cars are everywhere; the central point for rentals is the place de Verdun. You can go exploring on a yellow Autoplus electric scooter (40F half day, 70F all day) or in an electric car (60F half day, 100F all day)—both have 30 km to 50 km (20 to 30 mi) of quiet and effortless mobility. You must be 18, have a valid driver's license, have 2,500F free for a deposit on your credit card, and return the vehicles by 7 PM to get them juiced up for the next day. Bike rental is free for the first two hours; after that it's only 6F an hour if you leave an ID. If your exploring perimeter is outside of an electric plug—say l'Ile d'Oléron, l'Ile de Ré, Rochefort, or the Marais Poitevin—you can rent a small Fiat Punto at **ADA** (19 av. du Général de Gaulle, tel. 05–46–41–02–17) with 400 free km (248 mi) for 369F.

Press the button at the cours des Dames to call the **Passeur Autoplus** (4F), a boat service that will take you to the museums near La Ville en Bois (the section of town south of the historic port). Boats run daily 10–8 in June and until midnight in July and August. In addition, a **Bus de Mer** (10F) picks up passengers from the cours des Dames and drops them in Port des Minimes (the port south of La Ville en Bois). In July and August, the water bus runs every half hour until 11:30 PM; April–June and in September, it runs hourly until 7:30 PM.

WHERE TO SLEEP

La Rochelle is one of the most popular spots in France, and hotels jack up their prices during the summer (sometimes as high as an additional 100F during the Francofolies in the first half of July). The prices listed below start with the nonsummer prices followed by the higher summer prices. On the port, the very modern **Hôtel la Marine** (30 quai Duperré, tel. 05–46–50–51–63) has 13 rooms done up in navy colors, yellow and blue, with a few oak-color dressers to give it an older look. Some rooms have a port view along with its accompanying noise. Port-side doubles with shower cost 220F–400F in summer and 200F–220F in winter.

UNDER 200F • Hôtel de la Paix. This 18th-century bourgeois mansion has a sumptuous room for five (380F–450F) that may have been the former living room, with high ornate ceilings, a full-length mirror over a fireplace, and a large balcony. It's perfect for having breakfast in bed (for an extra 32F). The smallest double has a high skylight that keeps the room from getting gloomy. Doubles run 170F–280F; an extra bed costs 50F. *14 rue Gargoulleau, near pl. du Marché, tel. 05–46–41–33–44, fax 05–46–50–51–28. 19 rooms, 18 with shower.*

UNDER 250F • Hôtel de Bordeaux. The new wallpaper and the yellow and light blue decor brighten up this hotel. The beds are comfy, the rooms large, and the hall bathrooms are kept super-clean. Doubles with shower are 180F–220F (150F–180F without). *45 rue St-Nicolas, tel. 05–46–41–31–22, fax 05–46–41–24–43. 22 rooms, 12 with shower. Closed end of Dec.–1st 3 wks of Jan.*

Hôtel Henri IV. Smack-dab in the center of town, this hotel has winged gargoyles high up on the facade, a sign that it was once the mansion of a rich 16th-century Huguenot. The amenities, if not mansionlike, are comfortable. Two spiral staircases lead to rooms with predominantly brown decor. Doubles with shower are 185F–220F (165F–170F without). An extra bed costs 50F. *31 rue des Gentilshommes, behind Hôtel de Ville, tel. 05–46–41–25–79, fax 05–46–41–78–64. 24 rooms, 18 with shower.*

UNDER 300F • Hôtel de Paris. Eight of the rooms have their own balconies, perfect for a breakfast overlooking the garden. The rooms are large and welcoming, although some smell a little musty. Doubles are 180F–260F, quadruples 280F–360F; off-season, prices are negotiable (ask for a free breakfast). *18 rue Gargoulleau, off pl. de Verdun, tel. 05–46–41–03–59. 23 rooms, 20 with shower.*

HOSTEL

Auberge de Jeunesse. Two kilometers (1 mi) south of the train station, this modern building with enough space for 230 people looks and feels like a factory. Breakfast and sheets are included in the 72F price (75F in July and August, 107F for singles), but other meals cost 48F. An HI card is required and sold (70F) on the premises. *Av. des Minimes, tel. 05–46–44–43–11, fax 05–46–45–41–48. From av. de Colmar (1 block from train station), take Bus 10 to Lycée Hôtelier stop. 230 beds. Reception open 8–noon and 3–11, check-in after 2 PM, checkout 10 AM; midnight curfew in winter, 1:30 AM in summer; lockout 10 AM–12:30 PM. Cash only.*

FOOD

Avoid the crowded restaurants with expensive dockside views along cours des Dames—they're not worth the money. Instead, trek inland to the pedestrian part of rue du Temple and rue St-Nicolas, or walk up to the place de Verdun where you'll find the **Café de la Paix** (54 rue Chaudrier, tel. 05–46–41–39–79), the brasserie where George Simenon wrote his famous police novels. Classified a *monument historique,* it's a delightful place to drink a strong coffee (8F) or eat the plat du jour for around 50F; a house specialty is *gratin du lotte au poireau* (baked monkfish with leeks in a cheese crust). For unbeatable sandwiches, look no further than **L'Escapade** on rue Vieljeux. For 26F, a warm panini is served up with tasty slices of lamb, fresh off the *rôti,* and tomatoes. Finally, for groceries, head to **8 à Huit** (av. du Général de Gaulle), **Prisunic** (rue du Palais), or the **market** held every day on place du Marché.

UNDER 50F • Côté Sud. The friendliness and atmosphere are definitely southern, but the excellent *moulade Rochelaise* (curry mussels) for 49F are *très* local. Dutch sailors en route to India added spices to the old local recipe; the rest is gastronomic history. The house specialty is a *timbale de pecheur,* white fish cooked in an herb and mushroom sauce. *10 rue Chef de Ville, tel. 05–46–41–18–38.*

UNDER 75F • Galerie du Temple. This is an art gallery, an antiques shop, and a restaurant that serves Armenian–Iranian–Poitou-Charentes dishes. Their *caviar d'aubergine* (eggplant caviar; 38F) is delicious, and you can also split a bottle of wine between friends (60F). Thursday and Friday, there's music and poetry 8 PM–2 AM. *8 rue la Ferté, tel. 05–46–41–97–09.*

UNDER 150F • A Côté de Chez Fred. Fred—a guy who knows fish, sells fish, and serves fish— makes sure that his patrons get the catch of the day. Dishes of cheaper fish and sardines are 39F; Dover Sole and John Dory can run you up to 120F. The ambience is great, with nautical decor and outdoor tables. *30–32 rue St-Nicolas, off quai Louis Durand, tel. 05–46–41–65–76. Closed Sun.–Mon.*

WORTH SEEING

You could spend a whole day touring La Rochelle's quirky museums. In the not-too-important-but-still-interesting category are the **Musée des Automates** (tel. 05–46–41–68–08) and **Musée des Modèles Reduits** (tel. 05–46–41–64–51), which show off clever miniatures of everything from boats to race cars to acrobats. Both are on rue de la Désirée in La Ville en Bois and cost 40F each. If you want to see both, buy a joint ticket for 65F. There's also a creepy wax museum, the **Musée Grévin** (38 cours des Dames, tel. 05–46–41–08–71), which recounts La Rochelle's history, lingering on tales of torture and assassination, for 29F.

AQUARIUM

Unlike many aquariums in France, La Rochelle's displays its critters—eels, sea horses, tropical fish, turtles, sharks, and even piranhas—in large tanks that approximate their natural habitats. *Port des Minimes, tel. 05–46–34–00–00. Admission 42F. Open Sept.–Apr., daily 10–noon and 2–7; May–June, daily 9–7; July–Aug., daily 9–11.*

MUSEE MARITIME

The remote-control sailboats at the Maritime Museum are great fun. You can tack, jibe, and crash the miniature models in an indoor pool. Then follow the tide of visitors to the real boats docked in the port. *Pl. Moitessier, tel. 05–46–28–03–00. Admission 50F. Open daily 10–7.*

In the mid-17th century, La Rochelle was second after Nantes in trading through the slave triangle. More than 140,000 black slaves were transported from Senegal and Angola via La Rochelle to the plantations of the French-colonized West Indies.

MUSEE DU NOUVEAU MONDE

Inside the beautiful mansion of an 18th-century slave trader, the New World Museum exhibits maps, engravings, watercolors, and even wallpaper evoking the commercial links between La Rochelle and the New World. *10 rue Fleuriau, tel. 05–46–41–46–50. Admission 21F. Open Mon. and Wed.–Sat. 10:30–12:30 and 1:30–6, Sun. 3–6.*

VIEUX PORT

Tour St-Nicolas's labyrinthine passageways and multilayered fortifications open onto spectacular views of the port. Look for remnants of the huge chain dating from the Renaissance at the base of **Tour de la Chaîne,** but skip the *son et lumière* (sound and light) presentation inside. Continue along the ramparts to the **Tour de la Lanterne,** the oldest lighthouse in France, also used as a prison. It's known as La Tour des Quatres Sergents because four officers were jailed here for plotting to overthrow the Bourbon king and restore Bonaparte's government. In the stairs and cells, you'll find carvings embedded in the stone; the prisoners must have had time on their hands because some of them are detailed works of art. Check out the chiseled port of La Rochelle with its docked ships and the checkerboard carved into the floor. The top of the tower (reached by climbing a long, spiral staircase) has a magnificent panoramic view of the city. *Admission to Tour St-Nicolas and Tour de la Lanterne 22F. Open Apr.–Oct., daily 10–9; Nov.–Mar., daily 10:30–5:30. Admission to Tour de la Chaîne 20F. Open mid-Feb.–Nov. 11, daily 10–noon and 2–6; Nov. 12–Dec., daily 2–6.*

FESTIVALS

La Rochelle goes absolutely crazy for **Francofolies,** a music festival held for six days during the first two weeks of July, featuring dozens of jazz and pop groups of varying quality from French-speaking countries. Family vacationers are replaced by punks, skaters, and hippies, making the nightlife a little more interesting. Tickets are 50F–160F. Call 05–46–50–55–77 or write ahead to Francofolies (5 rue de l'Aimable Nanette, Le Gabut, 17000 La Rochelle) for detailed festival information.

SHOPPING

La Saponaire (33 rue du Temple, tel. 05–46–41–32–40) is a perfume shop where you can buy perfume miniatures for 79F–99F, and more expensive perfumes that are no longer easily available. Farther up the street, the shoe store **Chaussures Denis** (36 bis rue des Mercier, tel. 05–46–41–13–93) sells the famous Charentaise slippers for 38F–190F, depending on style and design. First custom-made for Louis XIV, it was rumored that the inner fur-lining cushions allowed the king to visit his mistresses without tell-tale squeaks. The late Diana, Princess of Wales, was a big fan of the slippers.

ILE DE RE

L'Ile de Ré used to be a cheap, hush-hush, keep-it-quiet alternative to the Riviera. The few in the know enjoyed more than 50 km (31 mi) of beaches with fine white sand, an ornithological reserve, a citadel, a lighthouse, and great seafood—as well as vineyards that sweep over the eastern part of the island and oyster beds that lie beneath the shallow waters to the west—all baked by a sun that seems brighter here than anywhere else in France. But the secret is out, and today the whole place smells more and more like burning money, with huge yachts in the old port towns, pompous intellectuals splitting hairs in cafés, and Rolex watches jingling on the dance floors. In the summer, it's best to make L'Ile de Ré a day trip; late September to early June, St-Martin, where you can rent a bike or scooter, makes the best hub to explore the island's 10 villages. For beaches, head to Les Portes, Couardes, or Le Bois; for oysters, go to Rivedoux; and to see a traditional fishing port, try Ars.

BASICS

Stop by the **tourist office** in St-Martin, open year-round, for a map of the island. The helpful staff has phone numbers of the local chambres d'hôtes (bed-and-breakfasts). *Av. Victor Bouthillier, tel. 05–46–09–20–06. Open Mon.–Sat. 10–noon and 3–5:30.*

COMING AND GOING

For the cheapest way to see the island, hop on the **Ré Bus** (tel. 05–46–09–20–15) at the train or bus stations in La Rochelle or any island town. The ride from La Rochelle to St-Martin takes about one hour and costs 28F. From there the fares are 16F–49F to get to any town on the island, and the longest ride to Les Portes takes around an hour. If you're planning to rent a car in La Rochelle to get here, keep in mind that it costs 110F in the summer to cross the bridge (60F off-season). Once in Ré, you can catch **Inter-îles** (tel. 05–46–09–87–27) ferries to Oléron or Aix from the beach at Sablanceaux. Renting a bike is de rigueur on Ré (*see* Worth Seeing, *below*), so ask at any tourist office for the *Guide des Itinéraires Cyclables*, which suggests five scenic bike routes.

WHERE TO SLEEP

Ré is a fairly convenient day trip from La Rochelle—a good thing, considering that hotel and camping prices are out of control. But if you're going to stay on the island, St-Martin makes a good hub, and **l'Hôtel Le Sully** (19 rue du Marché, tel. 05–46–09–26–94) is reasonable as far as island rates go; it's in an old house in the pedestrian quarter of St-Martin and has doubles with showers for 190F–240F in winter and 240F–290F in summer. Campgrounds are everywhere, and the farther you get from the bridge, the less likely they are to be full. In Les Bois, try camping at **Les Tamarins Plage** (rte. de la Couarde, tel. 05–46–09–42–67), where you'll pay 90F for a site; it's closed September–June.

FOOD

Though the pseudo-artist-owner can be snooty, **Kiss Me Not** (13 quai Clemenceau, tel. 05–46–09–02–77) is a great place to sip tea (16F) or swig the local pineau (a regional aperitif; 18F) while surrounded by pink sponged-painted walls where local artists hang their work. For a more raucous atmosphere, grab a seat at **Martin's Pub** (quai de la Poithevinière, tel. 05–46–09–15–87), and choose from more than 50 different beers. For food, either bring a picnic or try yet another **Café de la Paix** (11 quai de la Poithevinière, tel. 05–46–09–20–55)—they're everywhere on the island. This one has a terrace facing the port and serves good, quick meals at any time of the day. Salads are 25F–60F or there's a 69F, three-course menu. Each village has an **open-air market** every morning June–August.

WORTH SEEING

The town of **St-Martin**, the biggest on the island, is a good place to start a day trip. The town's only beach, **Plage de la Cible,** is just on the other side of the grass-covered citadel designed by Vauban. The citadel is still used as a prison, but ignore the NO ACCESS signs—they're just for cars. If you really want to find some great beaches, though, rent a scooter or a bike at **Cyclosurf** (av. V. Bouthillier, tel. 05–46–09–08–28). The day rates are 240F–260F for a scooter, 65F a day for a mountain bike, or 45F if you're happy with a "classic" bike. They require an 800F–1,500F deposit for bikes and 8,000–10,000F for a scooter on a Visa card before you can pedal or motor out of town. A couple of miles to the southwest, the town of **La Couarde** has great beaches and sailing spots. Right on the Plage du Peu Ragot, the **Club des Dauphins** (tel. 05–46–29–80–29) rents Windsurfers (170F–230F per day), dinghies (370F half day), and catamarans (590F half day). **Réserve de Lilleau des Niges** (tel. 05–46–29–50–74), a bird reserve toward the western tip of the island, charges 30F for a three-hour guided tour, but you can bike for free around the perimeter and see the nesting storks, herons, marsh hawks, oyster catchers, and other water birds. All the way out at the far end of Ré, the beaches in **Les Portes** are unappealing at low tide, but at least you'll have them all to yourself. **Plage de la Conche des Baleines** is a better beach, backed by dunes and pine trees. Climb the **Phare des Baleines** (a lighthouse west of the beach) for a great view.

ILE D'AIX

At low tide all the boats moored off Ile d'Aix become marooned in the mud, like something out of a Dalí painting.

Tiny, boomerang-shape Ile d'Aix sits off the Charentais coast, just out of reach of bridges from the mainland and tourist throngs. The island is virtually car-free; the silence is broken only by bicycle bells and squeaky wagon wheels. You can revel in the island's natural beauty, browse in the tourist shops, and relax on the beaches. Aix has not always lived off tourism. Fort Liédot hosted a number of prisoners—Russians, Prussians, and, in the 1960s, Algerians. Aix was also the last piece of French soil on which Napoléon set foot—after failing to escape to the United States, he surrendered here to the British. You can find out more about the Little Emperor's last stand at the **Musée Napoléonien** (30 rue Napoléon, tel. 05–46–84–66–40).

BASICS

There's no tourist office on the island, but the **mairie** (town hall, tel. 05–46–84–66–09) on the main street in Le Bourg can answer questions. It's only open weekdays 10–noon, but there are plenty of brochures outside the first-floor office door.

COMING AND GOING

Aix is an easy day trip from the coastal town of Fouras aboard a **Fouras Aix** ferry (tel. 05–46–84–60–50); the trip costs 55F round-trip. The ferry docks at Le Bourg, at the southern tip of the island, and makes the trip almost every half hour July–September, less frequently the rest of the year. **Citram** buses (tel. 05–46–82–31–30) from Rochefort (20 mins, 13F) and **Océcars** buses (tel. 05–46–99–23–65) from La Rochelle (45 mins, 25F) make trips to Fouras eight times daily; get off at the La Pointe de la Fumée stop if you're going to catch a ferry to Aix. Once on Aix, don't bother renting a bike; you can easily see everything in an afternoon on foot (it takes about two hours to walk the perimeter of the island).

WHERE TO SLEEP AND EAT

Camping Fort de la Rade (tel. 05–46–84–28–28), at the bottom tip of the island by Fort de La Rade, is the cheapest place to sleep. This is a gorgeous, uncrowded area sheltered from the wind. One person and a tent is 55F; add 25F for each additional person; it's closed October–March. Your only other option is **La Maison Familiale** (rue Marengo, in Le Bourg, tel. 05–46–84–62–08), where in July and August you can stay in a dormlike room and get three meals a day; rooms are only rented out on a weekly basis and cost 1,204F per person, meals included. The rest of the year, rooms are rented on a nightly basis (100F for two people), but there are no meals and you have to pay 70F extra for a membership card. It's closed November–March. The island has no cheap eats; do as the locals do and provision yourself on the mainland.

WORTH SEEING

Aix is great for sunbathing but lousy for swimming. At low tide the beaches turn to sticky, knee-deep mud, and if you try to hike out to the receding waves, you will cut your legs to shreds on submerged mollusks. At high tide, however, **Baby Plage,** on the far tip of the island, is gorgeous. **La Plage aux Coquillages,** in the boomerang's curve, has views of the French coast. At low tide the only swimming to be had is on **La Grande Plage** (though it can be pretty murky, too). When the tide is low, your best option is to head into the densely wooded section at the northeast end of the island to snooze until the tide rises.

LES SABLES D'OLONNE

Most of the year this coastal town is a dull fishing village with all its hatches safely battened down. But during the summer and at the start of the Vendée Globe circumnavigation race (early November), Les Sables is bursting with people looking for sea, sun, and the scarcest of commodities: a hotel room. Get ready for some nonstop action, as all types strut and stroll past the artists, bands, and jugglers on **promenade Clemenceau,** while horny teens look for a summer fling. If possible, time your visit to coincide with the folklore festival: a gathering of girls swirling in petticoats to the rhythmic beat of wooden dancing clogs (call the tourist office, *below,* as dates vary from year to year). Off-season, if the wind is up, get hold of a stunt kite and head for a stretch of sandy beach for some serious soaring.

BASICS

The helpful **tourist office** is located in the Palais de Congrais built in 1998. *1 Promenade Joffre, tel. 02–51–96–85–85. Open July–Aug., daily 9–7; Sept.–June daily 9–12:15 and 2–6:30.*

COMING AND GOING

Les Sables d'Olonne is accessible by train from Nantes (1½ hrs, 111F), La Rochelle (2 hrs, 146F), and Bordeaux (4 hrs, 238F). **Sovetours** buses (tel. 02–51–95–18–71) from Nantes (2 1/2 hrs, 75F) and La Rochelle (3 hrs, 90F) also serve Les Sables a few times a day. **CTA buses** (tel. 02–40–95–25–75) are usually reliable, but only run three times per day from Nantes (126F).

GETTING AROUND

The train and bus stations are next to each other, about a five-minute walk from place de la Liberté in the center of town. The place, however, is more commonly known as the **Jet d'Eau** because of its fountain. Blue and green **Tusco** buses (tel. 02–51–32–95–95) run from the Jet d'Eau to just about everywhere in town until 8 PM for 7F. In summer, a limited night service runs until 11 PM or so. To cross the harbor from Les Sables to neighboring La Chaume, take the **La Chaumoise** ferry (4F) from quai Guiné, which runs at least until 2 AM in summer, 9 PM otherwise.

WHERE TO SLEEP

There aren't many places to stay in Les Sables. Hotels seem to generate enough cash in one season to renovate and move up a star the next. The hostel is a gem but inconvenient once the buses and the ferry stop running; and you need a car or an exceptional talent for coordinating bus schedules if you want to camp at one of the scores of campgrounds on the coast north of Les Sables.

UNDER 150F • Hôtel les Sables d'Or. This simple restaurant-cum-hotel offers doubles in two flavors: port side (150F–170F) with a view, and starboard side with a courtyard (140F–160F). The shower in the hall is free, but during the summer the owner requires an extra 24F for breakfast and 60F for lunch or dinner. *2 quai Guiné, on the Port de Pêche, tel. 02–51–32–00–51. 12 rooms, 1 with shower.*

UNDER 250F • Hôtel du Pelican. This hotel is close to the train station and doesn't fill up as fast as beachside establishments. It's not luxurious, but it's decent. Noisy doubles are 179F with shower, rising to 220F–265F in July and August. *7 pl. du Général Collineau, near Jet d'Eau, tel. 02–51–32–06–16. 10 rooms, 7 with bath.*

Hôtel l'Étoile. A block from the boardwalk scam scene, this cheery hotel has clean, pretty rooms; the lack of an ocean view makes them affordable. Hip, young visitors often fill the large doubles (180F, 270F with shower) decorated with nautical mementos. *67 cours Blossac, tel. 02–51–32–02–05. 22 rooms, 17 with shower, 1 with bath.*

CAMPING • There are only two campsites in Sables d'Olonne, but there are an additional 10 sites in the nearby towns of Olonne sur Mer and Le Chateau d'Olonne. There is a list available at the tourist office. At **Camping des Dunes** the campground is indeed on a dune, a stone's throw from the water. It's clean, and there's a great pool. Arrive early; reservations aren't taken. Two people pay 80–128F; each additional person is 32F. *In La Chaume, tel. 02–51–32–31–21. From Jet d'Eau, Bus 2 to la Chauvetière. 350 sites. Closed Oct.–Mar.*

Camping Les Roses. This four-star campground is in town, near supermarkets and the beach. The facilities include washing machines and a heated pool. Two people and a car pay 80–128F; each extra person pays 30F. *Rue des Roses, tel. 02–51–95–10–42. From quai Clemenceau, turn left on rue des Deux Phares, right on blvd. Pasteur. 210 sites. Closed Oct.–Mar.*

FOOD

Scads of seafood restaurants line all the quays, and for a few hundred francs you can eat at one of them. Instead, visit the art deco **Les Halles Centrales,** next to the church, for fresh fish, bread, and produce; the market operates mornings Tuesday–Saturday. A **LARC** discount supermarket is a block from the tourist office on quai Franqueville. The restaurant **La Salsa** (20 quai Guiné, on the port, tel. 02–51–95–79–98) graces its walls with photos of movie stars (look for Gérard Départieu) and serves pizzas with salad (59F). Seafood goes Italian at the innovative **Le Grand Four** (69 rue du Palais, tel. 02–51–21–10–41), on a small street next to Les Halles. Try one of the exotic salad combinations. Another seafood option is **Le Port** (24 quai Georges V, tel. 02–51–32–07–52), next to the ferry stop in La Chaume. The 74F menu includes mussels or oysters, fish (try ray with capers), and dessert. *Moules marinières* (marinated mussels) are 40F. The dance club **Liberties** (Centre du Remblai, tel. 02–51–23–85–85) attracts a young, international crowd until 5 AM, and women get in free until midnight.

The Atlantic Coast islands are not the place to arrive without a reservation. Carry a tent and be willing to seek out remote campgrounds if you want to find a place at the last minute.

OUTDOOR ACTIVITIES

Besides swimming, sunbathing, and scamming on the boardwalk, the major sport in Les Sables is windsurfing. The **CREPS École de Voile** (1 av. Kennedy, tel. 02–51–95–15–66) gives lessons and rents equipment, including catamarans and kayaks, from the west end of the beach. You pay 200F for an hour-long private windsurfing lesson. At **Waimea Surf Shop** (68 promenade Clemenceau, tel. 02–51–95–23–10) surfboards are 90F a day. **Cyclotron** (66 promenade Clemenceau, tel. 02–51–32–64–15) rents mountain bikes (68F a day), beach bikes (49F a day), scooters (240F a day, 170F half day), and motorcycles (495F a day, 285F half day); these vehicles can carry two adults.

ROCHEFORT

The big town (or small city) of Rochefort was the result of Louis XIV's navy envy: He wanted to one-up the Brits by erecting huge frigates, and this city, protected from foreign invasion by tides and fortified islands off the coast, was ideal. So, to satisfy the king, architects leveled the randomly peppered fishermen's houses and rebuilt the city with the checkerboard blocks still visible today. The Charente River is at its worst here—polluted, brown, slow-moving, and ugly. Still, Rochefort's calm, flowered streets hide a handful of worthwhile museums, and accommodations and public transport are cheap and plentiful, which makes it a good place to drop your bags before heading off for relaxing day trips.

BASICS

The staff of the **tourist office** are extremely helpful and friendly; they have accurate maps and brochures. *Av. Sadi-Carnot, tel. 05–46–99–08–60. From pl. Colbert, walk west on rue Audry de Puyravault, turn right on rue du Docteur Peltier, immediate left on av. Sadi-Carnot. Open July–Aug., daily 9–8; June and Sept., daily 9–12:30 and 2–6:30; Oct.–May, Mon.–Sat. 9–12:30 and 2–6:30.*

COMING AND GOING

Your best bet is a train from Nantes (2 hrs, 161F) via La Rochelle (20 mins, 30F), or from Bordeaux (1¾ hr, 137F) via Saintes (30 mins, 63F). From the train station, take avenue Wilson until it meets rue Toufaire, and then go right on rue Audry de Puyravault; you'll wind up in place Colbert in the center of town. From the *gare routière,* or bus station (tel. 05–46–99–23–65), **Citram** buses run to Fouras (30 mins, 16F), the embarkation point to l'Ile d'Aix, and Oléron (1 hr, 40F); **Océcars** buses go to La Rochelle

FRUITS OF THE SEA

"Fruits de mer" (seafood) is a regional specialty, and "moules" (mussels)— often served "marinières" (marinated) with white wine and shallots—are a favorite. To look like an expert, eat the first mussel with a fork, then dig out the others with the empty shell. "Huîtres" (oysters) come on the half shell with a lemon wedge. "Soupe de poisson" (fish soup) arrives with sides of grated cheese, croutons, and sour cream. If you're a big eater, try the "plateau de mer"—a platter of whatever sea creatures came in that day.

(1 hr, 29F), Saintes (1 hr, 39F), or to the excellent beaches of Châtelaillon (45 mins, 18F). The bus station is on place de Verdun; to reach the tourist office, go two blocks north on rue du Docteur Peltier. Next to the tourist office, **Vélos Bleu** (call tourist office for more information) is a bike-rental tent that rents out clunkers for 12F a day with a 250F deposit, but they might take a passport if they like you.

WHERE TO SLEEP

If the hotels below are full, try the **Hôtel Lafayette** (10 av. Lafayette, tel. 05–46–99–03–31), where 150F gets you a double without shower. The **Camping du Rayonnement** (av. de la Fosse aux Mâts, tel. 05–46–99–14–33) is the closest campground to town but still a ¼-hour hike to the south. The two-star sites (12F per person for a tent site, 16F for a car site) are shady, the bathrooms clean, and the showers hot.

UNDER 200F • Les Messageries. This is the best deal in town, where 160F–180F in the summer gets you a double with a shower. The hotel, across the street from the train station, has been run by the same kind couple for the last decade. *Pl. F. Dorléac, tel. 05–46–99–00–90. 9 rooms, 5 with shower.*

UNDER 250F • Rocca Hotel. This hotel has huge but slightly run-down rooms with '70s decor resembling little apartments each with a separate shower room, toilet, and breakfast-table nook. Rooms face either the palm tree in the quiet courtyard or the garden. Doubles with shower and toilet are 245F (230F for shower and sink). There is also one room priced at 170F. *14 rue de la République, tel. 05–46–99–26–32, fax 05–46–87–49–48. 16 rooms, 12 with shower.*

HOSTEL • Auberge de Jeunesse, located in the *centre ville* (town center), is small, friendly, and off-limits to student groups. There is no curfew or lockout, and there's a nice garden in back. For 48F you get good kitchen facilities and spotless bathrooms with temperamental showers. Camping in the backyard is 26F. The hostel isn't well marked, but follow the signs from the train station to the Hôtel Roca Fortis (next door). If no one is at the desk, ring the bell, or go to the office at 97 rue de la République for check-in. Breakfast costs 19F, lunch 43F, picnic 27F. *20 rue de la République, tel. 05–46–99–74–62, fax 05–46–99–21–25. Reception open Sept.–June, daily 9–noon and 2–6:30; July–Aug., daily 8–10 and 5:30–8:30. Kitchen. Cash only.*

FOOD

On sunny days, **Café de la Paix** (tel. 05–46–99–00–89) spreads onto place Colbert. It's a good brasserie, with a 45F plat du jour. **Chez Nous** (72 rue Jean Jaurès, tel. 05–46–99–07–11) is the closest you can get to eating at home without having to wash the dishes. For 58F you get soup, salad, meat and potatoes, cheese, and dessert, plus all the bread and wine you can handle. In addition to the **covered market** (rue Jean Jaurès, at av. de Gaulle) every weekday morning, there's an **outdoor market** on avenue de Gaulle on Tuesday, Thursday, and Saturday mornings.

UNDER 100F • Le Cap Nell. The owner Nelly is charming, and her buddy in the kitchen whips up a great 40F *plat du bistrot* (house special) for lunch. For dinner, the fancy 84F *menu mer* (fish menu) or *menu terre* (meat menu) lets you select an appetizer and a dessert à la carte. *15 rue Lesson, tel. 05–46–87–31–77. Closed Sat. lunch and Sun.*

Le Jardin du Galion. Next to the Musée de la Marine, this stylish self-service restaurant has a 50F plat du jour and salads for under 48F. Cream and pineau mussels (43F) is a great local specialty. If you're feeling brave, try the eels. *38 rue Toufaire, tel. 05–46–87–03–77.*

WORTH SEEING

Rochefort was built in the 17th century to house workers and admirals from Louis XIV's new naval arsenal. Central to the arsenal was the **Corderie Royale,** or royal rope factory, which supplied ropes for French ships from 1670 to 1926. The 1,228-ft structure rests on a huge underground raft that prevents it from sinking into the Charente's muddy banks. Inside, the **Centre International de la Mer** (International Sea Center) explains the history of the Corderie, and of rope making in general, but it's not worth the admission. As with all of Rochefort's museums, your first visit at full price gets you a free *Carte Sésame,* which earns you a small discount at other museums. *Tel. 05–46–87–01–90. Admission 30F. Open Apr.–Aug., daily 9–7, Sept.–Apr., daily 9–6.*

Just south of the Corderie is the **Jardin des Retours,** a unique (and free) park with plants from exotic lands. Pass under the **Porte du Solcil,** a stone arch that bears more than a passing resemblance to the Arc de Triomphe. It earned its name, "Gateway of the Sun," because the sun rises and sets at its exact center each equinox. You can also get lost in the grass-hedge **labyrinth.**

The **Maison de Pierre Loti** was once home to the eccentric writer and traveler Pierre Loti (1850–1923), Rochefort's most famous son. A macabre fellow who liked to play dress-up (he powdered his face and put lifts in his shoes to make himself taller), Loti decorated each room of his house in a different theme and threw masked balls. Gothic, Renaissance, Turkish, and Moorish decor rub elbows here. The mandatory tours are in French, but you can purchase an English pamphlet for 15F. *141 rue Pierre-Loti, tel. 05–46–99–16–88. Admission 45F. Tours Oct.–June, Mon. and Wed.–Sat. at 10, 11, 2, 3, and 4, Sun. at 2, 3, and 4; July–Sept., Mon. and Wed.–Sat. every ½ hr 10–5:30, Sun. 2–5. Closed Jan. Note: Since these tours are so popular, make an advance reservation at the tourist office.*

To avoid catching hepatitis, the French shun oysters during months with no "R" in their spelling (mai, juin, juillet, août). And if your French isn't up to par, this rule conveniently works in English, too.

The **Ecomusée des Métiers de Mercure** is the product of a marriage between a girl who liked to collect aperitif bottles and a boy who was crazy for old bar glasses. They amassed such a heap of turn-of-the-century junk—bar napkins, fertilizer receipts, rusty tools—they had to open a museum. In the old warehouse, you stroll along the reconstructed old stores of the 1900s. *12 rue Lesson, 1 block east of pl. Colbert, tel. 05–46–83–91–50. Admission 30F. Open July–Aug., daily 10–8; Sept.–Dec. and Feb.–June, Mon. and Wed.–Sat. 10–noon and 2–7, Sun. 2–7.*

ILE D'OLERON

Combine easy accessibility (the island is anchored to the mainland by a bridge) with relatively warm water and you have a deluge of wimpy tourists who want all the "excitement" of an island without losing sight of terra firma. St-Denis, in the north, is the more savage and beautiful part of the island. With its high crags and desolate beaches, the town takes the brunt of the winter storms and has a more ravaged coast. The harsh sea conditions have turned the St-Denisais slightly aloof, in the summer, they never seem quite ready for the quadrupling of the tourist population. On the southern side of Oléron is the more touristy St-Trojan, famous for the fine-sand beaches west of town and the walking trails of the pine and oak forest you'll have to cross to get to them. St-Trojan also makes the best hub in summer or winter to explore the rest of the island. The village of **Le Château d'Oléron,** linked by bridge to what locals jokingly call "France," has a few Vauban fortifications (which are free to visit). Better yet, Le Château marks the beginning of *la routes des Huîtres* (the Oyster route), which includes a slew of *dégustations* (tastings) as it runs north along the coastal oyster beds to Boyardville.

BASICS

Le Château's **tourist office** (pl. de la République, tel. 05–46–47–60–51) has a good guide with a map and a list of the 60-odd campgrounds available on the whole island. In St-Trojan, the **tourist office** (carrefour de Port, tel. 05–46–76–00–86) has the same information, as well as a more detailed brochure of the town. During off-season, the staff at the **Hôtel de Ville** fills in.

COMING AND GOING

You'll probably start your visit at the bus station in the town of Le Château d'Oléron. From Rochefort, **Citram** (tel. 05–46–82–31–30) stops at Le Château (1 hr, 39F) only. From Saintes, the **Oléron Bus** (tel. 05–46–97–52–01) runs to Le Château (1 hr 10 mins, 61F) and to St-Trojan (1½ hrs, 63F), two good bases from which to explore the rest of the island. To get to St-Denis, it takes around 30 minutes from St-Trojan (31F) and Le Château (28F). Buses run more frequently in July and August, but a one-day excursion to the Ile is still possible during other months. Bike rentals are found in virtually every town; most of the southern beaches are within an hour's ride of Le Château. On the northern coast, St-Denis makes a good bike base.

WHERE TO SLEEP

It's the same old story—plenty of hotels, but few of them cheap and all of them booked solid in summer. Between the raucous, popular bar below and the early morning market next door, you won't get much peace and quiet at Le Château's **Hôtel Jean-Bart** (pl. de la République, tel. 05–46–47–60–04), but you can't beat 150F for clean, spacious doubles with showers (200F for quads with showers). Or try the family-run **Hôtel Le Mail** (blvd. Thiers, tel. 05–46–47–61–40), which has doubles with shower for 220F and 280F in summer. The nearest campground to the Le Château bus stop, **Camping les Remparts** (blvd. Daste, tel. 05–46–47–61–93) has clean, shady sites for 68F year-round.

In St-Trojan, the **Hôtel Le Coureau** (88 rue de la République, tel. 05–46–76–05–53), on a pedestrian street in the town center, has a few 160F doubles (free hall showers) with somewhat spongy mattresses. The reception is cheery, however, and three rooms have a view of the local bridge. Three campgrounds are at sites in the nearby forest on avenue des Bris; **Camping La Combinette** (36 av. des Bris, tel. 05–46–76–00–47) has woodsy sites for 64F; it's closed November–March. Reserve ahead for summer.

FOOD

Restaurants on the island are altogether uninspiring and you should avoid the expensive crêperies and pizzerias. If you're biking along *la route des Huîtres,* between le Château and Boyardville, keep a sharp eye out for the ramshackle **Chez Mamelou** (no address, no phone) for a taste of the islands' specialty: *l'églade* (mussels roasted with pine needles; 48F). You'll also find oysters in the 30F–50F range, as well as *palourdes* (small clams; 38F). For produce, take advantage of the open-air markets of the towns, open every morning during the summer. During the quiet off-season, buy your supplies in the **Super U** (tel. 05–46–47–70–22), a 10-minute walk from Le Château's bus stop along the RN 734. In St-Trojan, during the summer, églade and oysters are served all over town; the églade is famous at **La Cabane** (pl. de la Liberté, tel. 05–46–76–05–31), where dining takes place in the backyard of an Oléronais's house. In winter, ask the proprietress of l'Hôtel Le Coureau (*see* Where to Sleep, *above*) to fetch live oysters from her fishermen friends; a dozen will be opened and served in the hotel bar.

OUTDOOR ACTIVITIES

Cycle Demion (on the Port, tel. 05–46–76–02–63), in St-Trojan, rents a selection of bikes; VTTs run 70F to 90F, and classics are 45F to 60F. In Le Château, rent bikes at **Lacellerie Cycles** (5 rue Maréchal Foch, off pl. de la République, tel. 05–46–47–69–30) for around 47F a day for a regular bike, 65F a day for a VTT. If you're based on the northern side of the island, in St-Denis, head to **Loca Loisirs** (rue du Port, tel. 05–46–47–81–28) for a regular bike (50F a day) or a VTT (90F a day). All three operations require a passport deposit.

The best beaches for swimming and sunbathing are around **Domino,** on the northwest side of the island, and on the southern tip between **Le Grand Village** and **St-Trojan.** Otherwise, **Plage de Vert Bois** is a good place to watch mediocre surfers tackling mediocre waves. If you want to surf yourself, rent equipment at **W.O.C.** (tel. 05–46–75–44–16) above the beach in La Perroche. The 1½-hour rentals are 90F for Windsurfers, 190F–270F for different-size catamarans, and 80F for kayaks. On the northern end of the island, the beaches around **La Brée les Bains** are the best bet on windy days because they're protected from the elements. They're also the least popular with tourists and are rarely crowded. You can rent surf equipment at **La Manille** in St-Denis (av. des Pins, tel. 05–46–47–92–60) for 190F for a Windsurfer, 120F for a surfboard, and 550F for a catamaran. For something completely different, call Marc Texier (tel. 05–46–76–08–16) in St-Trojan to organize a tour of his **oyster park.** The tour times depend on the tides and cost 30F (37F if you need to borrow galoshes).

INLAND POITOU-CHARENTES

Heading inland along the Charente River, beaches and sand dunes give way to riverbanks and willow trees, and kids building sand castles are replaced by tourists with cognac snifters. The countryside begins to roll under the weight of sunflower and corn fields instead of beach resorts. This area doesn't have much for those seeking roaring nightlife or cultural enrichment, but it makes a relaxing detour.

SAINTES

Straddling the banks of the Charente River, Saintes likes to refer to its stores and shops as being either "Rive Gauche" or "Rive Droite," Parisian style, but the calm, quiet streets of Saintes are a far cry from the Champs-Élysées. Just the name, Saintes, describes the nightlife: By 11 PM it seems that everyone is in bed waiting for mass the next day—and there are plenty of choices because Saintes is packed with churches. There's enough here for an agreeable day's visit any time of year, but consider coming during the music festivals, when the crowds pump up Saintes's beatific nightlife and things become less than saintly. The **Jeux Santons** (second or third week of July) highlights world folk music, while the **Fête de Musique Ancienne** (first half of July) focuses on early music performed on period instruments. Call the tourist office for exact dates.

BASICS

The **tourist office** gives four interesting guided day (37F) and night (35F) tours of the abbey, the old town, the Église St-Eutrope, and the Roman amphitheater, and a nocturnal visit. Two visits cost 60F, three 80F. It also has festival information. *62 cours National, tel. 05–46–74–23–82. Take av. Gambetta (which becomes cours National) and follow signs. Open July–Aug., Mon.–Sat. 9–7, Sun. 10–1 and 2–6; June and Sept., Mon.–Sat. 9–1 and 2–6; Oct.–May 9:30–12:30 and 2–6.*

COMING AND GOING

You can get to Saintes by train from Cognac (20 mins, 27F), Rochefort (30 mins, 44F), Angoulême (1 hr, 64F), Niort (1 hr, 61F), La Rochelle (1 hr, 62F), or Bordeaux (1½ hr, 93F). The **train station** (pl. Pierre Semard) is two blocks north of Saintes's main artery, avenue Gambetta. Everything is within easy walking distance, but consider renting a bike (for rides along the river) at **Huriaud Cycles** (25 rue du Pérat, near av. Gambetta, tel. 05–46–92–13–45); it's open Tuesday–Saturday and charges 40F (60F for a VTT) per day plus a 1,000F deposit in traveler's checks or on a credit card.

WHERE TO SLEEP

You should have no problem finding a cheap hotel unless you come for the music festivals, in which case you should reserve a few weeks in advance. The convenient **Hôtel des Voyageurs** (131 av. Gambetta, tel. 05–46–95–09–69) has mediocre 120F doubles without shower (160F with), but some gorgeous four-person suites for 260F with full bath, living room, and terrace. The recently renovated **Hôtel St-Pallais** (1 pl. St-Pallais, tel. 05–46–92–51–03), with a view of the Abbaye-aux-Dames, has doubles for 220F, 250F with shower, and the added advantage of a good bar.

HOSTEL • By far the best and cleanest rooms are in the **Auberge de Jeunesse,** which has two-, four-, and six-bedrooms for 68F including breakfast. Hot meals (49F) and a common TV room are available, but a kitchen is not. You can sidestep the 11 PM curfew by asking for the code to the door. *2 pl. Geoffroy Martel, off rue Pont Amillon, tel. 05–46–92–14–92. Reception open daily 7–noon and 5–10 (11 in summer). Cash only. Closed mid-Dec.–mid-Jan.*

CAMPING • The excellent **Au Fil de l'Eau,** next to the Charente, has a heated pool, modern bathrooms, and laundry facilities, all for 70F for two people. *6 rue Courbiac, tel. 05–46–93–08–00. From train station, take av. Gambetta west, turn right on quai de L'Yser (which intersects rue de Courbiac). 214 sites. Closed mid-Sept.–mid-May.*

FOOD

The restaurants that fill the pedestrian streets between Cathédrale St-Pierre and the Palais de Justice serve a variety of cuisines and provide ample people-watching—but the bilingual menus are a good indication of high prices. At **Le Procopio** (5 rue de la Comédie, tel. 05–46–74–31–91), ask for the 56F four-pizza-in-one sampler. **Sarazine** (12 rue St-Michel, tel. 05–46–74–17–55) serves a 54F menu with two *galettes* (buckwheat crepes) and a dessert crepe. **Le Pistou** (3 pl. du Théâtre, tel. 05–46–74–47–53) has a 56F three-course fish menu. Wednesday and Saturday there's fresh produce outside the **Cathédrale St-Pierre** in the centre ville; Thursday and Sunday on avenue Gambetta near the train station at **Marché St-Pallais**; Tuesday and Friday at **place du 11-Novembre** on cours Reverseaux.

WORTH SEEING

The 1st-century **Arc de Germanicus** (pl. Bassompierre) pops up next to the river a few blocks from the train station amid a veritable forest of columns, capitals, and pedestals taken from other sites. This is the ultimate picnicking and people-watching spot in Saintes. The remains of the **Arènes Gallo-Romaines,** a 20,000-seat amphitheater that dates from the Roman Empire and is gradually succumbing to the forces of nature (it's also partially covered in grass), is worth the 15-minute walk west of the town center. To reach the Arènes, take cours Reverseaux from cours National; then take a right on rue St-Macoult and follow the signs.

Saintes's pride and joy is the **Abbaye-aux-Dames**. Founded in 1047, the abbey was headed by women for eight centuries without any major incidents until the 18th century, when the nuns were kicked out. The boys took over and the abbey got a dose of testosterone: It was a prison during the French Revolution and a military barrack under Napoléon, and it absorbed a nasty left hook from German bombs during World War II. It was rebuilt in 1988. Between July and September you can go on one of the daily 1½-hour guided tours at 10 and 2. *Pl. St-Palais, tel. 05–46–97–48–48. Admission 20F. Open mid-July–Sept. 10–12:30 and 2–7, Sept.–July 2–6.*

COGNAC

To the world, Cognac is not a place but a drink. That's fine with the locals, who are happy to take a backseat to the famous liquor that sweetens their air, blackens their houses, and pumps their economy. Cognac the drink is everywhere. You catch random whiffs of its powerful vapors as you walk around town. Look closer, and you see that the black marks on the walls aren't soot or grime but a microscopic mushroom that lives off the evaporated cognac. Locals like to say that you can't hide barrels of cognac because the mushrooms give you away. Despite the nearby countryside, which provides ample hiking, biking, and rowing opportunities, most people come to Cognac to do one thing and one thing only—taste cognac. The distilleries (*see* Worth Seeing, *below*) are happy to offer free samples accompanied by generous helpings of publicity for their brand. They also give warehouse tours and explanations of the cognac-making process, in English, lasting 45 minutes to an hour.

BASICS

The **tourist office** provides a map of the *chais* (cognac warehouses) and reserves rooms for the price of a phone call. In summer the staff conducts 20F guided tours of the historic parts of town. The office also sells bus tickets. *16 rue du 14-Juillet, 1 block west of pl. François 1er, tel. 05–45–82–10–71. Open July–Sept., Mon.–Sat. 9–6:30, Sun. 10:30–4; Oct.–June, Mon.–Sat. 9:30–12:30 and 1:30–6:30.*

You can change money Monday–Saturday at any of the various banks on and around place François 1er; **BNP** has good rates. **Banque Populaire,** next to the tourist office on rue du 14-Juillet, also gives good rates and has an ATM that accepts MasterCard and Visa. The **post office** (pl. Bayard, tel. 05–45–36–31–70) is a block from the tourist office. Send poste restante to postal code 16100.

COMING AND GOING

Cognac lies on the train line connecting Saintes (20 mins, 27F) and Angoulême (40 mins, 45F); about four trains run in each direction daily. You can catch connections to Poitiers (2 hrs, 137F) or Paris (5¼ hrs, 282F) in Angoulême, or a connection to Bordeaux (2 hrs, 123F) in Saintes. You can also get to La Rochelle in an hour (74F). The dinky **train station** (pl. de la Gare, off blvd. de Paris, tel. 08–36–35–35–35) is a 10-minute walk from the center of town; from the station take avenue du Général Leclerc, turn right on rue de Barbezieux, and right again on rue Bayard.

WHERE TO SLEEP

The lodging scene in Cognac is pitiful. The campground is great, but it's a 30-minute walk from the station, and the few cheap hotels in town aren't thrilling. If you're lucky, you'll get a clean 70F single or 120F double in the **Foyer des Jeunes Travailleurs** (12 rue Saulnier, tel. 05–45–82–04–90). The staff are extremely friendly and helpful, and they speak English—but in summer the office is usually full of French students who give guided tours of the chais. Another cheap option, across from the tourist office and a block from place François 1er, is the **Hôtel le Cheval Blanc** (4–6 pl. Bayard, tel. 05–45–82–09–55), but the rooms are a bit dingy and the reception is a tad cold. The bathrooms at least are in tip-top shape, and doubles with free showers down the hall are 150F.

UNDER 200F • Hôtel St-Martin. The atmosphere in this small hotel is warm and cheerful, and the cool English proprietor will make you feel right at home, and even throw in a few kooky jokes. The hotel is a 10-minute walk from the centre ville and close to the train station. Rooms are clean, well maintained, and pleasant. Singles are 135F–175F, doubles with showers 175F. *112 av. Paul Firino-Martell, tel. 05–45–35–01–29. 6 rooms. Closed 1 wk in Sept. and at Christmas.*

UNDER 300F • Hôtel la Résidence. The very bourgeois proprietress rents bright rooms, where the color of the comforters matches the curtains. The sponge-painted large bathrooms are immaculate, and there's even a minibar in most rooms (lacking cognac bottles). Doubles with shower start at 270F. *25 av. Victor Hugo, tel. 05–45–36–62–40, fax 05–45–36–62–49. 20 rooms, 17 with shower.*

The French, in case you didn't know, drink cognac after meals to ease digestion.

CAMPING • Camping Municipal. Near the banks of the Charente, this grassy, wooded campground is tough to find; from place François 1er take rue Henri Fichon; then stick to boulevard de Châtenay. Bus 5 (4F) runs daily at reasonable intervals from place François 1er to the camping stop. Sites cost 39F for one person, 67F for two. Perks include hot showers, phones, laundry facilities, and a minimarket. *Blvd. de Châtenay, tel. 05–45–32–13–32. Closed Nov.–Apr.*

FOOD

Radiating from place François 1er toward the river, Cognac's pedestrian streets are chock-full of chic little restaurants, none of them cheap. The small, cozy **La Sangria** (35 rue Grande, tel. 05–45–82–82–12) is tucked amid the distilleries and cobblestone streets and specializes in Spanish and Portuguese cuisine. Come slightly ravenous for the hefty paella (75F), a tasty rice and seafood dish, or the cod flambéed in cognac (70F). The daily **market** in Les Halles (blvd. Denfert Rochereau) has fresh seafood, cheese, and produce. For anything else, try **Prisunic** on place François 1er.

UNDER 75F • La Sarment Brûlant. The tables surround a large wood-burning stove that gives the meat dishes, such as *entrecôte* (rib steak; 70F) and *magret de canard* (duck cutlet; 72F), a delicious oaky flavor. The country-style dining room has unusual wood artwork—bouquets made from *sarment* (the bottom of local vines)—lining the walls. *42 rue Henri Fishons, tel. 05–45–32–35–39.*

UNDER 100F • Taverne du Coq d'Or. In the typical style of the real brasserie Parisienne, the Coq d'Or has impeccably dressed waiters, meals served from noon to midnight, and drinks poured in the appropriate glasses. For 50F you can have the plat du jour with cheese or dessert to follow. *33 pl. François 1er, tel. 05–45–82–02–56.*

WORTH SEEING

The cognac season runs approximately April–September, though the distilleries open their doors by appointment outside these months. In summer, the main houses are open daily 10 AM–5 PM, with the exception of Camus, which is closed weekends and two hours for lunch. Get a complete schedule from the tourist office.

The distillery **Otard** (127 blvd. Denfert-Rochereau, tel. 05–45–36–88–88) wins the history prize for being housed in the Château de Cognac, where future king and salamander freak François I was born in 1494. The tour (15F) is low key and the tasting is free, but the V.S.O.P. minibottles cost 20F. **Hennessy's** (quai Hennessy, next to Otard, tel. 05–45–35–72–68) has a torture barrel, where adulteresses had to poke their heads through a hole cut into the top of a large barrel. Unable to sit or stand, they ended up choking to death. You receive a little bottle of cognac at the end of the tour, which costs 30F. **Martell** (7 pl. Edouard Martell, tel. 05–45–36–33–33) has the most unabashed self-promotion of any tour, but it is free; the company is also generous with its samples and has a good bottling room. **Camus** (29 rue Marguérite de Navarre, tel. 05–45–32–28–28), a bit smaller than the other distilleries and with

MELLOW COGNAC

Cognac was supposedly developed by the knight of La Croix Maron, a fan of the local eau-de-vie (wine distilled to a high alcohol content). One night he had a dream about the devil and saving the "soul" of the eau-de-vie—which he interpreted as distilling it a second time to capture its essence. After his death, local monks inherited his twice-distilled concoction in oak casks but didn't bother to open them for 15 years. When they did, they found the liquid had turned a rich amber color. The modern recipe: Distill the region's white wine twice and put it in an oak barrel for years. Then hand over different batches to the Maître de Chais who, with his palate and million-dollar nose, mixes them to perfection.

a less elaborate free tour, has a cozy tasting room and gives samples of both its cognac and pineau wine. **Rémy-Martin** (Domaine de Merpins, rte. de Pons, D732, tel. 05–45–35–76–66) gives a first-rate train tour of its acreage, showing the whole operation from the vineyards to cognac in cobwebby warehouses. Too bad the tour starts 5 km (3 mi) southwest of town, costs 20F, and requires a reservation. Sadly, there's no public transport to the site.

FESTIVALS

Around the last week of March, first week of April, Cognac hosts the **Festival du Film Polar** (Police Thriller Film Festival), which attracts such celebrities as Alain Delon. Get ready for a *nuit blanche* (sleepless night) because the bars and cafés have live music until the wee hours. During the day, movie theaters project old classics and modern versions of the genre. Films cost 30F with some free showings at the Centre des Congrès. For information, contact the local tourist office (*see* Basics, *above*).

ANGOULEME

Divided into a sprawling new section and an old town hugging a hilltop, Angoulême managed to live its entire history without really being known for anything exciting—unless you consider 17th-century paper mills a cause for celebration. Winning the bid for France's national comic strip museum changed all that. The museum alone should convince you to detour for a day from Cognac, Saintes, or Poitiers. The town also has a 12th-century cathedral and a handful of museums.

BASICS

The main **tourist office** on place des Halles has maps and information about the town as well as schedules for the STGA city buses. *7 bis rue du Chat, tel. 05–45–95–16–84. Open July–Aug., Mon.–Sat. 9:30–7, Sun. 10–12 and 2–5; Sept.–June, weekdays 9:30–12:30 and 1–6, Sat. 10–noon and 2–5, Sun. 10–noon.*

COMING AND GOING

You can take the train to Angoulême from Cognac in under an hour for 45F, making this town good daytrip material. Trains also arrive here from Paris (2 hrs, 284F), Poitiers (1 hr, 98F), and Bordeaux (1¼ hrs, 109F). The **train station** is on avenue Gambetta (tel. 08–36–35–35–35). Buses from Cognac (1 hr, 44F) and La Rochelle (3 hrs, 103F) end up in Angoulême, too; call **Citram** (tel. 05–45–95–95–99) for details. To get around town, grab a map and timetables for the STGA city buses at the **tourist desk** right outside the train station, or at the main tourist office (*see* Basics, *above*). Buses cost 7F a ride and leave from place du Champ de Mars, a one-minute walk from the train station up avenue Gambetta.

WHERE TO SLEEP

Reasonable hotels line the streets from the station to place du Champ de Mars. Try **Hôtel le Crab** (27 rue Kleber, tel. 05–45–93–02–93); it's probably the cleanest, best deal in town, where doubles with free showers down the hall start at 150F and a croissant breakfast costs 24F. From the station, take avenue du Mar. de Lattre de Tassigny, turn right on rue Pierre Sémard, and left on rue Kleber. The well-situated **Hôtel de Palma** (4 rampe d'Aguesseau, tel. 05–45–95–22–89, fax 05–45–94–26–66), both a hotel and restaurant, has been in the same family for three generations. Doubles are 160F with shower (180F without). The two-star **Hôtel des Pyrénées** (80 rue St-Roch, tel. 05–45–95–20–45), just beyond the post office, has a few nice singles and doubles for 220F with shower (150F without). If you reserve a week in advance, you get two weekend nights for the price of one.

HOSTEL • Auberge de Jeunesse. On a lovely island in the Charente, the hostel is the best deal in town. A mere 70F per person plus an HI card gets you a two-bed in a spacious room and access to a clean kitchen; 51F in a six-bed dorm. Hot meals are an extra 48F; sheets are 17F for the week. There's no curfew. *Parc des Bourgines, tel. 05–45–92–45–80. From train station, walk northeast on av. du Mar. de Lattre de Tassigny, turn left on blvd. du 8-Mai-1945, left on blvd. Besson Bay, right on pedestrian overpass (hostel is on left); or take Bus 7 toward Grelet to Pont St-Antoine. 85 beds. Kitchen. Closed 2 wks in Dec.*

CAMPING • Camping Municipal. An excellent three-star wooded site on the same island as the youth hostel, the campground charges 56F per site for two persons and a car, 16F for each additional person. *Ile des Bourgines, tel. 05–45–92–83–22. 160 sites. Closed Oct.–Mar.*

FOOD

The pedestrian streets around the covered **market** at place des Halles and the Église St-André are packed with a diverse selection of restaurants. The chic **Le Shéhrazade** (6 rue Massillon, tel. 05–45–95–56–64) serves North African brochettes (68F); **Le Mektoub** (28 rue des Trois-Notre-Dame, tel. 05–45–92–60–96) has a copious 58F couscous; and **Indochine** (27 rue de Genève, tel. 05–45–94–82–30) has delicious 38F lunch plates such as black mushroom chicken served with a mountain of rice. For picnic items, stop at **Nouvelle Galerie** on place du Champ de Mars, or at the covered **Halles** (pl. des Halles), open every morning.

WORTH SEEING

Angoulême is to the *bande dessinée* or just BD (comic strip) what Cannes is to film; the **Centre National de la Bande Dessinée et l'Image (CNBDI),** housed in a gorgeous abbey-brewery-skyscraper, is the Louvre of comics. Most French citizens learned to read thanks to classic characters like Tintin, Astérix, and Lucky Luke, and they come here to contemplate—and get misty-eyed over—original drawings. Though most of the museum is dedicated to classic French cartoons and to internationally known favorites like Mickey Mouse and Peanuts, a whole floor is dedicated to other American strips, particularly the early Marvel comics. Another floor features the new generation of cartoonists like Robert Crumb, whose strips prove that BDs aren't just for kids. Upstairs, the CNBDI possesses the fabulous **médiathèque,** a cartoon library with more than 10,000 albums (some in English). The museum is near the CNBDI/Nile stop via Bus 3 or 5. *121 rue de Bordeaux, at av. de Cognac, tel. 05–45–38–65–65. From train station, go southwest on av. Gambetta, turn right on rue de la Corderie, bear left on rue Léonard Jarraud, continue to av. de Cognac. Admission 30F. Open Tues.–Fri. 10–7, weekends 2–7 (until 6 in winter).*

Across from the CNBDI is the **Atelier-Musée du Papier** (134 rue de Bordeaux, tel. 05–45–92–73–43), housed in the "Nil" factory, a former paper mill named after the cigarette paper produced there. Although the museum isn't terribly informative or exciting, it's completely free and worth a stop to see the building itself. The highlights of the museum are the temporary art exhibits, some very bizarre, by various local artists. The museum is open Tuesday–Sunday 2–6.

THE MARAIS POITEVIN

A vast network of little farming communities linked by tiny waterways, the Marais Poitevin stretches westward from Niort, a town about 72 km (45 mi) southwest of Poitiers. The Marais is not a monument that you go look at, photograph, and paste in your scrapbook. It's a living ecosystem and a way of life. Millennia ago the ocean reached all the way up to Coulon and Niort, but the gradual depositing of silt by the Lay and Sèvre Niortaise rivers turned the area into an impassable, sticky swamp. In the 11th century, after the dukes of Aquitaine freed the region from the Vikings, the monks moved in and tamed the swamp, creating a remarkable irrigation system that you still see today. They drained the bogs and dug up evacuation canals so that the rain would supply the earth with nutrients but then flow out into the sea. The monks also put locks at the ocean side of the canals that closed at rising tide to prevent the sea from flooding the inland Marais Mouillé (Wet Marsh). But they left the coastal Marais Desséché (Dry Marsh) around **L'Aiguillon-sur-Mer** untouched; these became inundated during the high equinox tides, thus saving the inhabitants of the Marais Mouillée from flooding. At times, however, these preventive measures failed and whole towns like Coulon (*see below*) were submerged in water.

The Marais poses a challenge for the visitor: To get to know it requires perseverance and strong rowing arms. Most travelers make it to Coulon (*see below*) and stop. **La Garette** (a Maraichin village similar to one in the period of Henry IV), **St-Hilaire la Palud** (the capital of the Marais sauvage), and **Arçais** (a little port town with double-entrance houses—for canal or road arrivals—and also the home of Camille Gougnard, the talented china-ink painter of the Marais) are less-touristed hamlets just big enough to support boat rentals. **Damvix** is one of the most typical Marais villages, with its houses strung out along the canals rather than clustered around a central square. **Maillezais** sits on the edge of the dry marsh, but you can get there by boat to check out its 10th-century Benedictine abbey. The problem, as always, is transportation. The best you can do without a car is to take a train to Niort, transfer to a bus or bike to Coulon, and row or bike from there to the more isolated towns. If you rent a car in Niort (*see* Coming and Going, *in* Niort, *below*), exploring the Marais becomes much easier.

NIORT

Niort is filled with insurance companies—there are more management schools than museums, more parking lots than parks, more businessfolk in power suits than tourists in T-shirts. As the major Marais Poitevin town on the train lines, however, it runs a little tourist trade on the side, and it's a cheap hub from which to explore this otherwise expensive region.

Otherwise, Niort is known for two things: its **donjon,** or dungeon (rue du Guesclin, tel. 05–49–28–14–28), built by Henry II in the 12th century, and the fact that Madame de Maintenon lived here. She was the governess of all of Louis XIV's bastard children and later became his morganatic wife.

BASICS

Before you venture into the Marais, visit the Niort **tourist office** and pick up its boat and bike rental brochures, as well as its camping guide (each town has a site). *Pl. de la Poste, tel. 05–49–24–18–79. Open weekdays 9:30—6, Sat. 9:30–1:20.*

COMING AND GOING

Trains take you directly to Niort from La Rochelle (1 hr, 76F) and Poitiers (45 mins, 76F) several times a day. To reach the center from the **train station** (pl. Pierre Sémard, tel. 05–49–24–50–50), walk down rue de la Gare, bear right on avenue de Verdun, then go past the tourist office to place de la Brèche. For local bus information, call **TAN** (tel. 05–49–24–50–56). All lines depart from place de la Brèche and cost 7F. To explore the Marais by car, **ADA** (97 av. de Paris, tel. 05–49–24–03–24) rents small Opel Corsas for 99F a day. They're fine for small trips, but the 1.45F you pay per kilometer starts adding up quickly.

WHERE TO SLEEP

Hotels are your best bet here. The well-kept **Hôtel La Marmotte** (106 rue de la Gare, tel. 05–49–24–11–47) couldn't be more convenient to the station. Doubles are 165F with shower and 185F with shower and toilet. Breakfast is 26F; for 30F you can have the luxury of breakfast in bed. **Hôtel St-Jean** (21 av. St-Jean d'Angély, tel. 05–49–79–20–76) has spacious, bright, and clean doubles for 165F–190F with shower. From the train station, take rue de la Gare, and turn left on avenue St-Jean d'Angély. You can also try either of the **Foyers des Jeunes Travailleurs** (Hôtel de la Roulière, 63 rue St-Gelais, tel. 05–49–24–50–68; 147 rue du Clou Bouchet, tel. 05–49–79–17–44). **Camping de Noron** (21 blvd. Salvador Allende, tel. 05–49–79–05–06) has shady sites near the mossy banks of the Sèvre Niortaise; it's closed mid-October–mid-April. One person can stay for 34F; each additional person costs 17F. Take Bus 2 to Chabot and walk down toward the river.

FOOD

Niort isn't known for its cuisine, and the best food in town isn't French. **La Case Créole** (54 rue du 24-Février, tel. 05–49–28–00–26) has spicy Antillais dinners (98F)—the exotic selection ranges from duckling in banana sauce to baby goat in curry—in a Caribbean setting. If you've wanted to try snail pizza (49F), **Le Sorrento** (7 av. de Paris, tel. 05–49–24–58–59) serves them up hot out of the oven; there's also a tasty pizza made with local cheeses and smoked Italian ham. For something more homey, the no-frills **Chez Marcel** (33 rue Berthet, tel. 05–49–79–20–52), near the Hôtel St-Jean, will stuff you with a delicious four-course meal and a glass of wine (54F); it's closed three weeks in August. For groceries, the pedestrian streets behind place de la Brèche harbor bakeries, butcher shops, and produce stores. Or you can bypass them all for the one-stop **Les Halles** next to the dungeon.

COULON

The inland Marais Mouillé of Coulon is still aquatic enough to have earned the title "Green Venice." The nickname is apt enough: With their slim *batai* (flat, narrow boats maneuvered with a long pole), the Maraichins do remind you of Venetian gondoliers, although "green" seems inadequate to describe the many brilliant colors that flicker above and beneath the water. Though it sees more visitors than any other Marais Poitevin town, Coulon, 11 km (7 mi) west of Niort, has not sold its soul to tourism. Small houses, each with its batai tied to the gate, line the main canal. In summer, Coulon's green banks swarm with tourists, but it's easy to leave them behind: Coulon is the perfect base from which to explore some of the region's hundreds of canals, lush fields, and hedgerows.

BASICS

Nathalie Thébault, the charming English- and Russian-speaking hostess of Coulon's **tourist office,** will find you the perfect hotel room or chambre d'hôte, as well as elucidate the mysteries of Coulon and the Marais Poitevin region. Ask for the free guide that covers hotels, camping, bed-and-breakfasts, and biking. *Pl. de l'Église, tel. 05–49–35–99–29. Open Mon.–Sat. 10–noon and 2–7.*

COMING AND GOING

Casa (tel. 05–49–24–93–47) buses go to Coulon from Niort around four times a day (25 mins, 16F) in the summer. Off-season, the service is limited to two buses daily during the week, two on Saturday afternoon, and one on Sunday afternoon. Coming and going in one day is realistic only during the week. School buses, which gladly take tourists, are also an option to Coulon and beyond on weekdays during the school year. Pick up schedules from the Niort tourist office (*see above*).

GETTING AROUND

La Garette is two hours by rowboat from Coulon. Renting a boat costs about 250F per day, which is worth it if you're two people. Otherwise, rent a bike (80F per day) at **La Libellule** (pl. de l'Église, across from church, tel. 05–49–35–83–42) to get to La Garette (2½ km/1½ mi), Arçais (10 km/6 mi), or St-Hilaire–la Palud (18 km/11 mi). Unless you have particularly strong biking legs or rowing arms, consider renting a car in Niort (*see* Coming and Going *in* Niort, *above*) to explore the Vendée side of the Marais (Damvix, Maillezais, Courdeau) or the Marais Mouillée (L'Aiguillon-sur-Mer).

WHERE TO SLEEP

Your best bet is to stay at a **chambre d'hôte** run by a local family. You can get a complete list from the tourist office in either Niort or Coulon—but you must reserve ahead in July and August. For the truly "à la campagne" experience, Monsieur et Madame Damour rent out two **chambres d'hôte** (Ste-Mégrine, tel. 05–49–35–98–25) that are as romantic as their name. Three kilometers (2 mi) from the center of Coulon, their rustic house has rooms (200F) with stone floors and beds with thick comforters. The birds will wake you up for the breakfast (price included) of brioche and homemade jams. At two-star **Camping de la Venise Verte** (tel. 05–49–35–90–36), a private spot by the water with your car may cost up to 100F per night in the high season. From the center of Coulon, follow the canal about 2 km (1 mi) in the direction of Irleau.

For lodgings more off the beaten track, Coulon is surrounded by several less-touristy villages. In La Garette, 3 km (2 mi) from Coulon, **La Vieille Auberge** (pl. du Port, tel. 05–49–35–92–62) has seven very plain doubles (140F) but a great view of the canal. Its downstairs restaurant serves local specialties, such as the *farci Poitevin* (34F), stuffed and baked vegetables, excellent snails, and an outstanding lamb dish cooked with white beans. In Courdault, next to Maillezais, you'll find a spartan *gîte d'étape* (hostel) at **Le Trou Vendéen** (tel. 02–51–52–41–51) with beds for 70F. You can eat elbow to elbow with other diners at one of the large tables in its restaurant. The three-course menu (100F) includes native entrées, such as frogs' legs and eel fricassee. In Arçais, Monsieur et Madame Deschamp rent out doubles (250F) in their pretty **chambres d'hôte** (10 chemin du Charret, tel. 05–49–35–43–34, fax 05–49–35–43–35) on the banks of a canal. It's a splurge, but they also let you borrow a rowboat, and though they don't have a restaurant, you can buy produce at the local market and cook it up in their kitchen. Bikes are also available for rent.

FOOD

The specialties of the region—escargots, eels, frogs, and *ragondin* (herbivorous rats)—are not for the faint of heart. You can sample the latter rodents at **La Passerelle** (86 quai L. Tardy, tel. 05–49–35–80–03). **La Loge du Picton** (4 rue du Couhé, tel. 05–49–35–85–85) serves a tasty 80F *poêlées d'anguilles persillées* (eel dish) and fresh fish caught daily; the patron is particularly proud of his snails. If you have a more conventional meal in mind, ignore the tourist-trap restaurants that line the main square, **place de l'Église,** and try the canal-side crêperies serving ice cream and cold drinks to weary rowers. An outdoor **market** sets up every Friday and Sunday morning next to the church; if you miss it, go to **Score** (tel. 05–49–35–91–64) on place de l'Église or, if its small selection doesn't satisfy your needs, head to **Super U** (rte. de Coulon à Majne, tel. 05–49–35–75–12) within a 15-minute walk from the centre ville.

WORTH SEEING

For about 150F an hour, a guide will take you through the green canals past willow, ash, and alder trees for a down-and-dirty tour of Coulon's **Venise Verte.** Some guides speak English, others don't, so shop around along Coulon's canals. The museum, **La Maison de Marais Mouillés** has "Maraiscope," a 20-minute sound-and-light show that probes the creation of the Marais. There is also an interesting re-creation of a late-19th-century Marais chambre, including an authentic bed *à quenouilles,* raised by high legs to stay dry during floods. *Pl. de la Coutume, tel. 05–49–35–81–04. Admission 28F. Open July–Aug., daily 10–8; Sept.–June, Tues.–Sun. 10–7, except at lunchtime.*

POITIERS

Poitiers became famous during one of the pivotal events of Western civilization. In AD 732 Charles Martel's army stopped the Saracen invasion from Spain and basically saved European Christianity. The fight was actually closer to Tours than Poitiers, but only people from Tours care about that. A few centuries later, Poitiers's university molded the minds of the raunchy Rabelais and the dualistic Descartes. But then, bang, nothing—a straight line on the electrocardiogram. It wasn't until the 20th century that Poitiers woke from its intellectual and economic coma with the birth of Michel Foucault (the philosopher whose convoluted writing escapes all classification) and the construction of the **Futuroscope** (*see* Near Poitiers, *below*), an architecturally futuristic cinema theme park. The student population of 26,000, a good chunk of which is international, has also livened up the old city, so you'll find a diverse selection of restaurants, hip cafés, and bars.

BASICS

MAIL • The main **post office** takes care of poste restante (not more than three months, postal code 86030) and has phones and a fax. You can change AmEx traveler's checks for a 1% commission. *16 rue Arthur Ranc, tel. 05–49–55–52–36. Open weekdays 8:30–7, Sat. 8:30–noon.*

MEDICAL AID • The **Hôpital Mileterie** (42 rue St-Simplicien, tel. 05–49–54–33–33) is next to the Baptistère St-Jean and has 24-hour emergency facilities.

VISITOR INFORMATION • The staff at the **tourist office** is friendly and efficient. Ask for bus schedules, maps, information on Futuroscope, and "Poitiers l'Été," the guide to free summer events. *8 rue des Grandes Écoles, tel. 05–49–41–21–24. Open July–Aug., weekdays 9–7, Sat. 10–7, Sun. 9:45–1 and 2:45–6; Sept.–June, weekdays 9–noon and 1:30–6, Sat. 9–noon and 2–6; also Sun. 9:45–1 and 2:45–6 mid-June–mid-Sept.*

At the **Centre d'Information Jeunesse,** pick up a copy of the monthly *Affiche,* with listings of live music, movies, exhibits, and special events. *64 rue Gambetta, tel. 05–49–60–68–68. Open weekdays 10–7, Sat. 10–noon and 2–6:30*

COMING AND GOING

Poitiers is a major train hub, with several TGV trains daily to Paris (1hrs, 230F), Niort (50 mins, 76F), Tours (1 hr, 91F), La Rochelle (1½ hrs, 116F), and Bordeaux (45 mins, 173F). The **train station** (blvd. du Grand Cerf) has a helpful information office. Buses 3, 6, 7, 9, 11, and 16 travel up the hill from the train station to place Leclerc/Hôtel de Ville in the centre ville. Bus tickets cost 8F for an hour's worth of transportation; a *carnet* (book) of five is a steal at 25F. Carnets and schedules are available at the **Espace Bus office** (6 rue du Chaudron d'Or, tel. 05–49–44–77–00), open weekdays 9:30–12:30 and 1:30–6:30.

WHERE TO SLEEP

Lots of cheap hotels line **boulevard du Grand Cerf** in front of the train station—but during summer, the Futuroscope crowds may have filled most of them. If so, look around the centre ville, where the quality is markedly better.

UNDER 200F • Hôtel Jules Ferry. Just a few blocks from the St-Hilaire church are small but well-kept (and recently redecorated) rooms with doubles starting at 140F, 210F with shower. Reserve ahead in July and August. Showers are 12F. *27 rue Jules Ferry, tel. 05–49–37–80–14, fax 05–49–53–15–02. From town center, head south on rue Carnot, turn right on rue Le Cesve, left on rue Jules Ferry. 25 rooms, 4 with bath, 8 with shower.*

Hôtel Victor Hugo. You're not getting any taller, the doors after the stone château steps are just really low. Doubles are 130F without shower and 160F for all the plumbing. The rooms under the eaves are tiny but very cute. An extra bed costs 55F. *5 ter rue Victor Hugo, tel. 05–49–41–12–16. 7 rooms, 4 with shower Cash only. Closed Sun.*

HOSTEL • Auberge de Jeunesse. Though a bit out of the way, this friendly hostel is clean and comfortable but crowded March–June, when the kiddies book it solid to see the Futuroscope. There is a kitchen, and the 39F meals served are delicious. Beds in huge, three-bed rooms with sinks cost 51F. The hostel has extensive grounds where you can swim and play volleyball and football. *1 allée Roget Tagault (formerly rue de la Jeunesse), tel. 05–49–30–09–75, fax 05–49–30–09–79. From station, Bus 3 (toward Pierre Loti) to Cap Sud stop. 131 beds. Reception open weekdays 7:30 AM–11 PM, weekends 7:30–1 and 7–11; checkout 10 AM. Closed end of Dec.–Jan. 2.*

CAMPING • Camping du Porteau. The closest campground to Poitiers is 3 km (1½ mi) north of town, along the Bus 7 route. Although it's popular with campers towing trailers, tents can squeeze in without any problem. A site for two people runs 48F. *117 rue du Porteau, tel. 05–49–41–44–88. 36 sites.*

FOOD

The eclectic selection of restaurants that pepper Poitiers streets makes up for the lack of budget dining. At **Le Poitevin** (76 rue Carnot, tel. 05–49–88–35–04) take a deep breath, hand over your 100F, and immerse yourself in four courses of gastronomic goodies. The Poitevin's specialties include vegetable terrines, smoked salmon and, if you are up to it, veal heads; you can stick to a goat's cheese and walnut salad if the thought of the above turns you into an instant vegetarian. **Les Bons Enfants** (11 rue Cloche-Perce, tel. 05–49–41–49–82) has a *salade folle* (crazy salad) for 65F with various duck parts like foie gras and giblets. You can stay within your budget by shopping at the **Monoprix** on rue des Cordeliers, or at the fresh outdoor **market** that sets up at place Charles de Gaulle on Tuesday, Thursday, and Saturday mornings.

UNDER 50F • La Bamba. It is a bit of a trot from the center of town, but the walk north of the Clain River is beautiful, and the restaurant's terrace on the banks of the water as well as 30 choices of 16F tapas are worth it. Sea snails in aioli sauce, paprika calamari, grilled frogs' legs in herbs and garlic, and potatoes with chorizo wash down well with the house sangria (30F for half liter). *122 rue des Quatre Roues, tel. 05–49–55–13–71. From Notre-Dame-La-Grande, take voie A. Malraux, cross the Clain River, then go right on rue des Quatre Roues. Closed Mon.*

UNDER 75F • La Fine Mouche. Bright Caribbean decor with Third World photos line the wall of this creative restaurant serving a combination of international cuisines. The 59F menu startles your taste buds with a Norwegian appetizer, followed by a Burmese entrée, and ending with a Lebanese dessert—or any other combination from the world over. *5 rue de la Chaîne, tel. 05–49–50–73–26. From Notre-Dame-La-Grande, take rue de la Régatterie, then right on rue Descartes. Closed Mon.*

WORTH SEEING

The 4th-century **Baptistère St-Jean** is France's oldest existing Christian edifice; all things considered, the building is in remarkably good shape. Inside is a 12th-century fresco of Emperor Constantine on horseback. *Rue Jean Jaurès. From pl. Leclerc, take rue des Grandes Écoles, turn right on rue Paul Guillon (which becomes rue Jean Jaurès). Admission 5F. Open Apr.–Oct., Wed.–Mon. 10:30–12:30 and 3–6 (July–Aug., also open Tues.); Nov.–Mar., Wed.–Mon. 2:30–5.*

The **Musée Ste-Croix** houses an interesting collection of modern paintings, most notably *Nuit d'Enfer d'Arthur Rimbaud*, in which the poet is all cubed up and convulsing. The star attractions are the three Camille Claudel sculptures that were stolen in 1993 and since recovered from Hungary. *61 rue St-Simplicien, tel. 05–49–41–07–53. Admission 15F. Open Tues.–Fri. 10–noon and 1–5, weekends 10–noon and 2–6.*

NEAR POITIERS

FUTUROSCOPE

Futuroscope is a cinema-going smorgasbord. Choose between half-dome screens (L'Omnimax), high-resolution screens (Cinéma haute résolution), a huge flat screen (Kinémax), and theaters with mechanical seat effects (Cinémas dynamiques). In the Cinema 360°, you stand in the middle of the theater as nine images shot in a circle re-create the sea experience of a trimaran race. The awesome Magic Carpet is an ingeniously designed theater that puts one huge screen in front of you and another below your feet. When the two images are synchronized it may seem like you're flying on a magic carpet. The newest attraction is the Solido, where they strap a pair of stereoscopic shades on your face and send you on a virtual swim. The last two screens have about an hour's line. *Tel. 05–49–37–04–18. Admission 195F per day includes a nocturnal laser show. Open daily 9–6 (until nightfall in summer).*

COMING AND GOING • STP Buses 16 and 17 make the 10-km (6-mi) trip from Poitiers (15F round-trip), leaving from both the train station and Hôtel de Ville. For exact times and pick-up points, call 05–49–44–77–00, or visit the Futuroscope information center inside Poitiers's train station. Service during school vacations is slightly reduced but adequate. Otherwise, a **taxi-shuttle** (45F round-trip) leaves from Poitiers's train station every half hour throughout the day. Poitiers is only 1½ hours from Paris and Montparnasse on the TGV; a day trip from the capital to Futuroscope is easily done.

INDEX

NOTES

NOTES

NOTES

NOTES

NOTES

IT'S YOUR TURN TO TALK BACK!

FILL OUT THIS QUICK SURVEY AND RECEIVE A FREE COPY OF FODOR'S *HOW TO PACK*.*

Which Fodor's upCLOSE guide did you buy?

_____

What was the duration of your trip?

_____

How much did you spend per day, not including airfare?

❑ $100 ❑ $300
❑ $150 ❑ Other_____
❑ $200

Why did you choose Fodor's upCLOSE?

❑ Budget focus
❑ Fodor's reputation
❑ Opinionated writing & comprehensive content
❑ Other_____

Would you use Fodor's upCLOSE again?

❑ Yes ❑ No

Which guides have you used in the past two years?

❑ Frommer's $-A-Day ❑ Let's Go
❑ Rough Guides ❑ Rick Steves'
❑ Lonely Planet ❑ None
❑ Other_____

Did you like Fodor's upCLOSE better?

❑ Yes ❑ No

Please rank the following features (1 = needs improvement / 2 = adequate / 3 = excellent).

Accommodations listings	1	2	3
Dining listings	1	2	3
Major sights	1	2	3
Off-the-beaten-path sights	1	2	3
Shopping listings	1	2	3
Nightlife listings	1	2	3
Public transportation	1	2	3

Please feel free to elaborate. _____

_____

_____

_____

Which of the following destinations would you like to see Fodor's upCLOSE cover?

❑ Alaska ❑ Pacific Northwest
❑ Australia ❑ South America
❑ Austria ❑ Southeast Asia
❑ Eastern Europe ❑ Switzerland
❑ Greece ❑ Turkey
❑ Israel ❑ More European cities
❑ New Zealand ❑ More U.S. cities
❑ Other_____

You are ❑ Male   ❑ Female

Your age is
❑ 18-24   ❑ 45-54
❑ 25-34   ❑ 55-64
❑ 35-44   ❑ 65+

You are ❑ Single   ❑ Married

Your occupation is
❑ Student (undergraduate)
❑ Student (graduate)
❑ Professional
❑ Executive/managerial/administrative
❑ Military
❑ Retired
❑ Other_____

Which choice best describes your household income?
❑ Under $10,000
❑ $10,000-$19,999
❑ $20,000-$29,999
❑ $30,000-$49,999
❑ $50,000-$74,999
❑ $75,000+

Your name and address are

_____
_____
_____

Your E-mail address is

_____

Would you like to receive informational E-mails from Fodor's?
❑ Yes   ❑ No

Please return this survey to Fodor's Travel Publications, Attn: Fodor's upCLOSE Survey, 1540 Broadway, New York, NY 10036, for a free copy of Fodor's *How to Pack* (while supplies last). You can also fill out this survey on the Web at www.fodors.com/upclose/upclosesurvey.html.

The information herein will be treated in confidence. Names and addresses will not be released to mailing-list houses or other organizations.

* While supplies last